W9-BVW-177

DHARMA LION
A Critical Biography of Allen Ginsberg

Photo by Miles Aronowitz

DHARMA LION

A Critical Biography of Allen Ginsberg

MICHAEL SCHUMACHER

St. Martin's Press

New York

The author is grateful to the following publishers, individuals, and literary agents for permission to reprint from previously copyrighted materials:

Selections from Allen Ginsberg's *Collected Poems 1947–1980* © 1984 by Allen Ginsberg. Reprinted by permission of the author.

Selections from Allen Ginsberg's *White Shroud* © 1986 by Allen Ginsberg. Reprinted by permission of the author.

Selections from Allen Ginsberg's unpublished poems, letters, and journal writings printed by permission of the author.

Selections from the letters of William S. Burroughs, Eugene Brooks, Lucien Carr, Lawrence Ferlinghetti, and Gary Snyder printed by permission of the authors.

Selections from the letters of Neal Cassady printed by permission of Carolyn Cassady.

Selections from the letters of Jack Kerouac reprinted by permission of Sterling Lord Literistic Inc. Copyright © 1992 by Jack Kerouac.

"The Red Wheelbarrow" by William Carlos Williams from *Collected Poems 1909–1939, Vol. I.* Copyright © 1938 by New Directions Publishing Corporation. Reprinted by permission of New Directions.

Selections from previously unpublished letters of William Carlos Williams © 1992 by William Eric Williams and Paul H. Williams. Reprinted by permission of New Directions.

Library of Congress Cataloging-in-Publication Data

Schumacher, Michael.
    Dharma Lion : a biography of Allen Ginsberg / Michael Schumacher.
       p.   cm.
    ISBN 0-312-08179-0
    1. Ginsberg, Allen, 1926–   —Biography.   2. Poets, American—20th century—Biography.   I. Title.
    PS3513.I74Z86   1992
    811'.54—dc20
    [B]   92-25224
                                                        CIP

First Edition: October 1992
10 9 8 7 6 5 4 3 2 1

To Susan

CONTENTS

BOOK THREE: TEACHER

ACKNOWLEDGMENTS

Over the course of the eight years that it took to research and write this book, I talked to scores of Allen Ginsberg's friends, family members, associates, editors, and, here and there, enemies. I found it noteworthy that, almost without exception, each person interviewed made a special point of mentioning Ginsberg's kindness and generosity. One could say that these remarks were obviously biased when coming from those who love Ginsberg personally or professionally, but even those who disagreed with Ginsberg's politics, lifestyle, poetics, or impact on society tempered their remarks by noting that, despite their differences, they found Allen's humanity to be exemplary. I was, quite literally, inundated with unsolicited anecdotes that underscored the point.

I first met Ginsberg in 1981, when I interviewed him about his musical recordings for a magazine article I was writing. Since then, I have talked to him formally and informally on numerous occasions, under all kinds of conditions, and judging from my own experiences, I can say that the accolades are anything but surprising. Even on those rare occasions when he was cranky or impatient, he always made an effort to supply me with whatever information I sought and, as any biographer can tell you, the demands for time and information can be endless. Many biographers will also tell you that they grew to dislike—or even hate—their subjects: in the process of research, reputations and images get tarnished, sometimes to the point of no return. Fortunately, I did not have this experience with Ginsberg. I found myself in disagreement with some of the courses he's taken in his life, and I was not always pleased with his poetry, but at no point did I lose respect for the man or his work. Despite what I perceived to be flaws—and it is, after all, easy to make such judgments when you're examining someone else's life in retrospect—I came away in admiration of Ginsberg's candor, generosity, and overall spirit of humanity.

I mention all this as a prerequisite to thanking, first and foremost, Allen Ginsberg for the invaluable contribution he provided in the making of this book. This is not an authorized biography in the sense that Ginsberg demanded to read and approve its contents prior to publication, although it should be noted that Ginsberg helped in every aspect of the research and did, in fact, look at the book before its publication. Nevertheless, he took an active role in aspects of this book's preparation. He sat for interviews; opened up his extensive archives at Columbia University for me; allowed me to read his private journals and letters; assisted me in securing of interviews; and provided many photographs and the generous permission to quote from his published and unpublished works. Furthermore, there were occasions when he offered a kind word to buoy my spirits when the going got tough. In short, he supplied me with a great deal, with no specific promises for returns, and while I am certain that he will take exception to some of the critical remarks in this book, I hope that, now that all is said and done, he will feel as if his trust was rewarded.

Bob Rosenthal, Ginsberg's secretary since 1977, was of tremendous assistance, and I thank him for his diligence and good cheer; anyone who has witnessed the controlled chaos that is the average workday at Ginsberg's office will tell you how amazing Bob Rosenthal is. My appreciation, also, to Jacqueline Gens, photo specialist at Ginsberg's office, who helped me on countless occasions when I called or dropped by, and who offered valuable suggestions about Allen, his work, and Buddhism. Juanita Lieberman Plimpton, a former office assistant now working in publishing, was of considerable assistance in the early goings.

Bill Morgan, Ginsberg's official bibliographer and archives specialist, was especially helpful when I needed information about Ginsberg's unpublished journals and manuscripts. Gordon Ball, scholar and editor of two of Ginsberg's books (*Journals Early Fifties Early Sixties*, *Allen Verbatim*), and presently at work in editing Ginsberg's journals from the 1950s, kindly supplied me with the transcripts of many unpublished journals. Jason Shinder provided me with many of the letters in the Ginsberg-Kerouac correspondence.

My gratitude to the many people who agreed to interviews, corresponded with me, supplied me with photographs or memorabilia, or otherwise assisted at one time or another, often in small but very helpful ways, in the researching of this book: Antler, Myles Aronowitz, Jerry Aronson, Eugene Brooks, William S. Burroughs, Reed Bye, Lucien Carr, Carolyn Cassady, Ann Charters, Andy Clausen, Elsa Dorfman, Susan Edwards, Larry Fagin, Frank Falduto, Shawn Falduto, Lawrence Ferlinghetti, Robert Frank, Edith Ginsberg, James Grauerholz, John Clellon Holmes, Shirley Holmes, Herbert Huncke, Larry Keenan, Arthur Winfield Knight, Kit Knight, Seymour Krim, Lisa Law, Seymour Lawrence, Robert LaVigne, Dr. Timothy Leary, Gordon Lish, Hannah Litzky, Leo Litzky, Paula Litzky, Michael McClure, Fred McDarrah, Gloria McDarrah, Dennis McNally, Barry Miles, Gerald Nicosia, Norman Podhoretz, Jeff Poniewaz, John Sampas, Richard Seaver, Harry Smith, Gary Snyder, Carl Solomon, Steven Taylor, John Tytell, Dan Wakefield, Anne Waldman, Philip Whalen, and Hal Willner.

The National Endowment for the Arts and the Wisconsin Arts Board supplied urgently needed money for the research of this book.

This book could not have been written without the assistance of people who offered me a place to stay when I traveled, rides to and from airports, encouragement, and other help in logistics. Thanks to Al and Diane Schumacher, Bill and Lorraine Landre, Karen Ade, Dawn Ade, Tom and June Landre, Jonathan Fox, Jim Van Metre, Jim Sieger, Glen Puterbaugh, Bill Robbins, Sue Rumachik, Anne and Ron Roscioli, Michael and Jill Fargo, Mark Gumbinger, and Roger Wyosnick.

In the course of writing this book, I was rewarded by the scholarship of others. The bibliography offers a selective list of useful works, but several books deserve special mention, lest they be lost in the list. Barry Miles's groundbreaking biography, *Ginsberg*, acted as a map on those occasions when

I was in danger of losing the road. Gerald Nicosia's *Memory Babe*, the most detailed biography of Jack Kerouac written to date, was very helpful, as were Ann Charters's *Kerouac*, Dennis McNally's *Desolate Angel*, and Barry Gifford and Lawrence Lee's *Jack's Book*. *Literary Outlaw*, the first biography of William S. Burroughs, written by Ted Morgan, offered numerous insights into a man who is still one of the most enigmatic figures in Ginsberg's circle of friends. I owe a debt to each of these books, both in terms of the information they provided and the pleasure I received in reading them.

The letters and manuscripts of many of the people mentioned in this book are stored at libraries throughout the United States, and I would like to take this opportunity to thank the following libraries and individuals for the use of their materials: Frank Walker and the Fales Library, New York University, for the manuscripts of "Kaddish"; the Harry Ransom Humanities Research Center at the University of Texas; and the Bancroft Library at the University of California, Berkeley. Of particular significance were the contributions of Kenneth A. Lohf, Bernard Crystal, Henry Rowan, and the rest of staff at the Special Collections Division of the Butler Library of Columbia University.

To special friends, special thanks: Peter Spielmann and Judy Hansen. You mean more to me than I can state here or elsewhere.

Extra gratitude to Bill Brohaugh, who knows why.

Kenny Ade, guru and friend—I would be lost without you.

Thanks to my patient agent, Connie Clausen, and her staff at Connie Clausen Associates. A tip of my cap to Guy Kettlehack, wherever he may be.

My appreciation to present and former staff at St. Martin's Press, including Linda O'Brien, Darlene Dobrin, Meg Drislane, and Paul Liepa, as well as all the others who took special care in helping make this book what I wanted it to be. Amelie Littell, managing editor at St. Martin's Press, deserves special note, both for her diligent work and for her cheer and companionship. Carol Edwards, an extraordinary copyeditor, worked overtime in helping check facts and providing valued friendship.

I cannot praise or thank enough Michael Denneny, my editor on this project. As anyone who has had the experience of working with Michael will attest, he has the skill of a Max Perkins, the wisdom and patience of a Zen saint, and the compassion of one's best friend, and I fear I tested all these traits in the writing of this book. His assistant, Keith Kahla, is another special person whom I am pleased to call a friend.

I save the most important for last. All my love and appreciation to my wife, Susan, to whom this book is rightfully dedicated, and to my children, Adam, Emily, and Jack Henry. They sacrificed and paid dearly during the creation of this book, and they deserve any of the good things that may result from it.

AUTHOR'S NOTE

As of this writing, Allen Ginsberg lives most of the year in New York and teaches at Brooklyn College. He is also active in the Jack Kerouac School of Disembodied Poetics at Naropa Institute in Boulder, Colorado, the poetics school he helped found and direct. His readings and lectures are in constant demand.

This biography covers the first twenty-five years of Ginsberg's public life, as well as the thirty years that led up to the writing of "Howl," his breakthrough work. My initial decision to conclude this book in 1981 was determined by a number of factors. First and perhaps most obvious is the convenience of ending on a high note—the twenty-fifth anniversary reading of the work that established Ginsberg's importance as a poet. Arguably, that work alone was enough to secure Ginsberg's permanent reputation in the literary pantheon, not just because it was a major poem that, like Eliot's "The Waste Land," broke through artistic barriers and influenced future generations of poets but also because "Howl" signified the arrival of an era during which literary and social standards would be challenged, debated, and reconstructed.

There were also pragmatic reasons for intending to stop this account at this point. With only a few exceptions, each of Ginsberg's published poems referred to in this book can be located in a single volume, *Collected Poems 1947–1980*. Any reader wishing to look up and read the poems mentioned can do so with very little effort. Furthermore, it seemed appropriate that this portion of Ginsberg's life be punctuated by his final works published by City Lights, included in *Plutonian Ode and Other Poems* (1981) and placed at the end of *Collected Poems*. The body of work published by Lawrence Ferlinghetti and City Lights Books, along with those occasional volumes issued by other small presses over the years, truly represents a lifetime's achievement.

Finally, there was the issue of one's writing a biography about a living subject. By nature, such a book is incomplete at the moment of publication, and because this is the case, it seemed sensible to stop at a significant point rather than continue forward, knowing full well that the biography would be incomplete regardless of its point of conclusion. However, a postscript, summarizing the years not covered previously in this book, has been included for those who wonder what Ginsberg has been doing in the ensuing years.

In researching this biography, I referred to the collected archives listed in the notes section of this book. Whenever possible, I used contemporaneous sources. Once collected and assembled in chronological order, Ginsberg's journals and letters make up a lengthy and extraordinarily detailed autobiography. I relied more heavily upon these documents, as well as the newspaper clippings, magazine articles, and transcripts of interviews, than on personal interviews, which could be tainted by failing memory or, at times, the need to revise history or mythologize. It should be noted here that Allen Ginsberg was generous about giving me access to these materials, and at no time did he attempt to interfere with the researching and writing of this book. One can only hope that he lives another twenty-five years, and that those years are as fulfilling and compelling as those presented herein.

—MICHAEL SCHUMACHER
May 22, 1992

PREFACE

On October 23, 1966, Allen Ginsberg took the short trip from New York City to Paterson, New Jersey, for a joint poetry reading with his father, Louis. It was Allen's first reading in his hometown since he had become one of the world's most visible and controversial poets. The younger Ginsberg's notoriety intensified the local interest in the father/son venture, with all of its obvious contrasts. Allen was volatile, a beatnik turned hippie whose literary works were laced with four-letter words and references to his homosexuality and drug use. His readings drew capacity crowds in college campus auditoriums across the country. In recent years, he had become almost as well known for his political stands as he was for his poetry, his cross-country jaunts finding him in the vortex of the growing protest movement against the Vietnam War and the expanding national interest in the use of recreational drugs. The year before, he had been expelled from both Cuba and Czechoslovakia when these countries' leaders rejected him as a bad influence on their youth. Bearded and beaded, wearing tennis shoes and clothes right out of the Goodwill store, Allen was the personification of Flower Power.

In contrast, Louis Ginsberg was an accomplished lyric poet who wrote the kind of poetry that had long been accepted by the academics. He was a dedicated family man who had traveled very little and, in fact, had spent virtually all of his life in New Jersey. An inveterate punster, he brought a warmth and wit to his readings that complemented the serious topics of his work. Neatly groomed and dressed, at ease in front of a group of people, he looked like a school-teacher—which, in fact, he was. In every respect, he was as Establishment as his son was counterculture.

Their reading was a rousing success. Allen read poems that combined his national political concerns ("America") with touches of local interest ("Paterson," "How Come He Got Canned at the Ribbon Factory"), while Louis read his more conventional verse to friends and colleagues who regarded him as a celebrity poet in his own right.

At one point during the reading, both poets spoke of their visiting Paterson's Passaic Falls together the preceding day.

"It was an intimate moment shared," Louis told his audience—and one can imagine that it was. Over the years, the relationship between father and son had been mercurial, marked by frequent, occasionally angry, arguments over their differing poetic, social, and political views. Louis disapproved of Allen's drug use, and he was strongly opposed to some of the public statements his son issued about his homosexuality. Louis was always urging Allen to tone down his poetry, to aim for a sensibility rooted firmly in the middle ground. Allen preferred to push the limits, break his own ground. Whenever they debated, concessions and compromises were begrudgingly offered, but no matter how bitterly they quarreled, they never broke off communication or failed to recognize the deep love they felt for each other.

After Louis spoke, Allen told the gathering in the serious, inimitable manner that had befuddled the media for nearly a decade, that he had smoked marijuana as he stood with his father and watched the falls, explaining that the drug helped him "bring back a full flavor of deeply moving episodes of my boyhood." If the remark shocked or angered anyone in attendance, neither Allen nor Louis heard about it that evening.

The following day, a bench warrant was issued for Allen Ginsberg's arrest, charging him with disorderly conduct in connection with his admitting in public that he had smoked marijuana. Paterson mayor Frank X. Graves, claiming his office had received numerous phone calls protesting Allen's public confession, said he would be held up to ridicule "if by silence we acquiesce and condone this action." A bearded, bespectacled Ginsberg look-alike was picked up by the police, briefly detained, and finally released when it was established that, indeed, he was not Allen Ginsberg, prompting bemused newspaper headlines such as COPS DO GINSBERG DOUBLE-TAKE and GINSBERG NOT ONLY BEARD WEARER, PATERSON DISCOVERS.

With business back in New York, Allen had left Paterson shortly after the reading and was surprised to hear of the uproar taking place in his absence. Contacted at his East Village apartment, Allen shrugged off the warrant with the wish that Paterson would go "back to sleep." Accustomed as he was to being near the center of controversy, Allen was growing weary of major battles being drawn around minor incidents—and this one in his hometown, of all places. This latest one was difficult to understand. "It seems like they're making a lot of excitement over nothing," he concluded.

Allen, at sixteen, from his East Side High School yearbook. *Courtesy Allen Ginsberg.*

Book One

POET

And I gave my heart to know wisdom, and to know
madness and folly: I perceived that this also is a vexation
of spirit. For in much wisdom is much grief: and he that
increaseth knowledge increaseth sorrow.

—Ecclesiastes 1:17—18

Below: Allen Ginsberg, 1926. *Courtesy Allen Ginsberg. Right:* Naomi Levy and Louis Ginsberg, Coney Island, New York, 1917. *Courtesy Allen Ginsberg.*

Allen and Eugene (second from right, and far right, respectively) with neighborhood friends. *Courtesy Allen Ginsberg.*

Allen visiting Naomi at Greystone,
ca. 1937. *Courtesy Allen Ginsberg.*

Allen Ginsberg, from a painting by
Naomi Ginsberg. *Courtesy Allen Ginsberg.*

Top: Wolfeans and non-Wolfeans: Hal Chase, Jack Kerouac, AG, and William Burroughs, Riverside Drive, New York City, 1945. *Courtesy Allen Ginsberg. Bottom left:* "Neal Cassady, old hero of travel lore alyosha idiot seek-train poems," in a 1946 photograph taken in a New York bus depot at a time when Ginsberg still harbored hopes for a great love affair. *Courtesy Allen Ginsberg. Bottom right:* New Visionaries: Lucien Carr and Allen Ginsberg, Columbia University, Easter Sunday, 1948. *Courtesy Allen Ginsberg.*

Left: In the Merchant Marines, 1947: "I, for the sake/of little but the causelessness of soul,/Am carried out of my chill hemisphere/To unfamiliar summer on the earth." *Courtesy Allen Ginsberg.* *Below*: Herbert Huncke, an early Beat model, "who walked all night with shoes full of blood on the snowbank docks waiting for a door in the East River to open to a room full of steamheat and opium." *Photo by Allen Ginsberg.*

Left: Neal Cassady and Jack Kerouac, 1952. *Photo by Carolyn Cassady.* *Below:* In Manhattan, 1953: "Five years unhappy labor/22 to 27 working/not a dime in the bank/to show for it anyway." *Courtesy Allen Ginsberg.*

Top: Jack Kerouac ("thru whose eyes I saw smog glory light gold over Mannahatta's spires"), New York, 1953. *Photo by Allen Ginsberg. Bottom left:* In Mexico, 1954, "where I come with my own mad mind to study alien hieroglyphs of Eternity." *Courtesy Allen Ginsberg. Bottom right:* Carl Solomon, one of AG's "best minds" and reluctant hero of "Howl." *Photo by Allen Ginsberg.*

Above: Peter Orlovsky in San Francisco, 1955: "my imagination of an eternal boy walks on the streets of San Francisco, handsome, and meets me in cafeteria and loves me." *Photo by Allen Ginsberg. Right:* Jack Kerouac, AG, Peter Orlovsky (standing), Gregory Corso, and Lafcadio Orlovsky (kneeling) in Mexico City, 1956. *Courtesy Allen Ginsberg.*

1
Garden State: Youth in New Jersey

The alleys, the dye works,
Mill Street in the smoke,
melancholy of the bars,
the sadness of long highways,
negroes climbing around
the rusted iron by the river,
the bathing pool hidden
behind the silk factory
fed by its drainage pipes;
all the pictures we carry in our mind. . . .

1

Irwin Allen Ginsberg was born in the early-morning hours of June 3, 1926, in Beth Israel Hospital in Newark, New Jersey, the second of Louis and Naomi Ginsberg's two sons. Named after his paternal great-grandfather, S'rul Avrum Ginsberg, Allen would always be referred to by his middle name, though Jack Kerouac, the novelist and Allen's closest friend as an adult, would borrow Allen's given first name and combine it with the nickname of Ginsberg's home state to create "Irwin Garden," the name he assigned to his Ginsberg character in four of his autobiographical novels. In retrospect, it seems fitting that one of the twentieth century's best-known and most influential poets would be born in a city so close to Camden, New Jersey, where Walt Whitman lived for much of his life and was finally put to rest, and to Rutherford, where William Carlos Williams spent his life as a doctor and poet. Both were of enormous influence to Ginsberg.

Louis Ginsberg, thirty-one years old at the time of Allen's birth, was a modestly successful lyric poet who published poems and puns in local newspapers, literary magazines of national repute, and, often enough to secure his reputation, such New York papers as *The New York Times* and *The New York Herald*. His work was also included in a number of poetry anthologies, including Louis Untermeyer's *Modern American and Modern British Poetry*, generally regarded at the time to be the most important poetry anthology in circulation. One could not easily raise a family on the meager payment given to poets, no matter what the poet's reputation, so to support his family, Louis worked as an

English teacher throughout his life. Photographs from the period show him to have been a slender man of medium height, well groomed, with clear, intelligent eyes and a broad, somewhat toothy smile—a handsome man who, one imagines, might have been quite a ladies' man, if that had been his inclination, in his youthful years. Eugene, the older of the two Ginsberg children, inherited his father's appearance.

Allen, on the other hand, took after his mother. A short woman with long black hair and large, expressive brown eyes, Naomi Ginsberg was slim and attractive in her younger days. Family members characterized her as a woman who smiled often, enjoyed her role as a mother, and loved to sing, often accompanying herself on the mandolin or piano. One of Allen's favorite childhood memories of his mother was of a young Naomi Ginsberg, a wreath of flowers encircling her head, sitting in a field dotted with wildflowers and playing the mandolin. She was a natural storyteller and, like Louis, a teacher for some time. She was also known to be strong-willed and, at times, combative, a woman who was not afraid to stand her ground in an era when women, although finally allowed the right to vote, were still expected to be silent and patronized. Fiercely political, with Communist roots dating back to her girlhood in Russia, Naomi would argue politics with any opposing view, peer or elder, man or woman.

Poetry and unconventional politics—passions for which Allen Ginsberg would become widely known—passed from parents to son like steely faiths, already forged, awaiting proper test.

2

By the time she immigrated to the United States in 1905, ten-year-old Naomi Livergant had been exposed to the consequences of political upheaval and rhetoric. She spent her early years in Nevel, a small village in western Russia not far from what is presently the Polish border. She had an older sister, Elanor, and two younger brothers, Max and Sam. Her parents, Mendel and Judith Livergant, opposed czarist rule and favored the revolutionary form of Marxism that was growing in popularity in Russia, and when, in 1904, it became apparent that Mendel might be drafted into the czar's army to serve in the Russo-Japanese War, Livergant, a sewing machine salesman, dispatched his wife and four children to live with his brother's family in Vitebsk while he and his brother Isser left for the United States. A year later, the first pogrom in the Northern Pale caused thousands of Jews, including the Livergants, to flee for their safety, traveling by boat to the United States. Naomi would later tell her sons of those last days in Vitebsk, when cossacks charged through the snow on horses; in her mind was a vivid picture of their leaving town in a carriage, barely escaping the brutality of the pogroms.

The family name was shortened to Levy at Ellis Island. Mendel Livergant, now Morris Levy, located his family in an established Jewish neighborhood in the Lower East Side of Manhattan, where he opened a candy store that specialized in hand-churned ice cream and homemade sodas. Day-to-day life was a challenge. There was never a lot of money around, and there was always the task of learning a new language and culture, all fitted within the framework of a government entirely different from the type of rule the Levys had fled in their homeland. There seemed to be something new to learn every day. As Allen Ginsberg noted in "Kaddish," his eulogy for his mother, Naomi was initially afraid to eat the tomatoes she saw for sale at the market; she had never seen tomatoes before she moved to the United States, and she had heard from other immigrants that they might be poisonous.

Naomi was exceptionally bright, and she was quickly educated into the American way of life. However, like most immigrants, she held fast to many of the beliefs and customs of the old country, the most significant being her support of communism. Vitebsk, one of the largest cities in its region of Russia, had been very receptive to the principles of communism drifting out of Germany at the turn of the century, and the Livergants had embraced communism to such an extent that both Elanor and Naomi would be active in the Party in America, Naomi eventually becoming the secretary of the Party's tiny branch in Paterson.

The Levys eventually moved from New York City to Newark, New Jersey. Naomi attended Barringer High School, considered then to be the best high school in the city. In 1912, she met a Barringer student named Louis Ginsberg, an aspiring poet with a good sense of humor whose Jewish ancestors had also come from Russia.

Louis Ginsberg's background, however, was dissimilar enough to ignite considerable family turmoil after he and Naomi married. Orphaned early in his life, Pinkus Ginsberg, Louis's father, had left Russia for the United States in the 1880s, settling with relatives in Newark. Pinkus was active in politics, but he favored socialism over communism, a preference he would pass on to his children. In Newark, he met Rebecca Schechtman, they married, and, in 1895, their first child, Louis, was born. In all, they would have five children: Louis, Abraham, Rose, Clara, and Hannah—all of whom would receive mention, at one time or another, in Allen Ginsberg's writings.

The Ginsberg family was a study of subtle contrasts, Pinkus being nonreligious and politically more progressive than Rebecca, who was very devoted to the religious, as well as the sociopolitical, elements of her Jewish heritage. Both belonged to the Yiddish Arbeiter Ring, known also as the Workman's Circle, and young Louis would often accompany his father to socialist meetings and lectures, where he was entranced by speeches by Eugene Debs, founder of the IWW. The Ginsbergs owned a laundry business. Louis, along with his brother, Abraham, helped Pinkus Ginsberg pick up and deliver laundry in a horse-drawn wagon. Louis did not have an interest in business, and it was soon apparent that he would not be involved in the family enterprise as an adult.

He did, however, possess a strong, creative mind, although his lifelong interest in writing poetry was, at the beginning, purely accidental. In high school, he was asked to write an imitation of Milton as an assignment for an English class, and when he turned in his paper, his efforts were so highly regarded and praised by his teacher that Louis decided to write poetry on his own. He was delighted when Barringer High School published one of his poems in its yearbook.

Neither of Louis's parents approved of his relationship with Naomi Levy, and both were unhappy when, in 1919, after a five-year courtship, Louis announced that he and Naomi were getting married. Louis's parents' opposition was both political and personal. During World War I (which Louis managed to avoid due to poor eyesight), there was great disagreement between the Communists and the socialists about American participation in the war in Europe, the Communists supporting U.S. involvement, while the socialists took an isolationist position. Never quiet about her political opinions, Naomi would argue the issue with Louis and his parents, her outspokenness doing little to endear her to Rebecca Ginsberg, who found Naomi too aggressive for her liking.

They were also concerned about Naomi's mental well-being, which was brought into question a short time after Louis announced his intentions of marrying her. After his graduation from high school in 1914, Louis had attended Rutgers University in New Brunswick. Going to an out-of-town college was unusual in those days, and Louis's enrollment at Rutgers put a strain on his family, who could have used his assistance in the laundry business and could ill afford to pay for his education. It was a proud day for the Ginsbergs when Louis earned his B.A., becoming the first person in the family to graduate from college.

Naomi had also attended school after graduation from high school. Wanting to teach grammar-school children, Naomi went to normal school for her training and, upon graduation, worked briefly at a public school in Newark before taking a job teaching at a school for educationally disadvantaged students in Woodbine, New Jersey. By all indications, she was an excellent teacher. Louis's sister Hannah, seventeen years younger than her brother, attended the Newark school where Naomi later taught, and she recalled Naomi as being good, though strict, with children. Hannah would always remember the day when she was in kindergarten and was singled out by her sister-in-law for chewing gum while she was standing in line on the playground.

During her teaching stretch at Woodbine, shortly before she and Louis were to marry, Naomi suffered a nervous breakdown, manifest by her hypersensitivity to light and sound. For several weeks, she stayed home from work, lying in a dark room and hoping that whatever afflicted her would pass. It did, but not before Louis's parents heard about her condition and tried to use it as another reason for their son to reconsider his plans to marry her.

Louis would hear none of their protests and, as soon as Naomi was healthy again, they were married in a small ceremony in a Woodbine mansion, Naomi looking splendid as she descended a staircase in her wedding dress. The newly-weds moved into an apartment not far from Louis's parents in Newark. For the young couple, their early years of marriage were a continual struggle to make ends meet. Louis took any teaching job that he could find, but the chance for tenure—and, therefore, financial security—was not immediately forthcoming. Louis and Naomi bickered about their financial woes and argued about politics, but, so far as the families could see, there was never any question about their devotion to each other.

Louis continued to develop as a poet, and by the time he and Naomi had married, his work was being published regularly in respected literary magazines. In addition, he was active in the poetry and intellectual circles gathering in Greenwich Village. He joined the Poetry Society of America, and he and

Naomi attended readings, lectures, and discussion groups, listening to the work and opinions voiced by such literary luminaries as Edwin Arlington Robinson, Marianne Moore, and John Dos Passos. These were heady times, with parlor rooms ringing with talk of literary and social change, excited speakers looking for new directions to pursue in the wake of a global war that seemed to demand a new approach to living.

On June 2, 1921, Naomi gave birth to Eugene Brooks Ginsberg. Named after Eugene Debs, Gene would become a respected poet in his own right, dropping the Ginsberg from his name and going by Eugene Brooks for most of his adult life; he would also become a successful attorney with an interest in space law.

Almost exactly five years later, at two in the morning, Allen was born.

3

One cannot form an accurate picture of Allen Ginsberg's childhood by reading the fragmentary accounts in his published poetry or unpublished journals. As an adult, Ginsberg would use the more dramatic episodes of his childhood as anecdotes necessary to create vivid pictures in his poetry, and from such poems as "Kaddish," " 'Drive All Blames into One,' " and "Garden State," one could easily conclude that Ginsberg's childhood had been an unhappy one, marked by Allen's confrontations with his mother's insanity, local anti-Semitism, his early awareness of his homosexuality, problems with his peers, and, to a lesser extent, poverty. In "Garden State," Ginsberg depicted his childhood years in Paterson as anything but pleasant:

> I was afraid to talk to anyone
> in Paterson, lest my sensitivity
> to sex, music, the universe, be discovered &
> I be laughed at, hit by colored boys.

In fact, by Ginsberg's own admission, as well as from the accounts provided by his family, Allen was a happy child, offered plenty of attention and physical affection by both of his parents. Average on the playground and superior in the classroom, Allen was known for his cheerful disposition and high energy.

Even as a toddler, he was exposed to poetry. Louis would move about their 163 Quitman Street apartment, reciting from memory the poetry of Dickinson, Poe, Shelley, Keats, and Milton as he did his daily chores. "It was part of the household," Allen commented decades later, comparing his father's poetry recitations to the way people sing while they work. Naomi loved to sing and play the mandolin, one of Allen's favorites being "Last Night the Nightingale Woke Me," which he would cite in "Kaddish." She also enjoyed telling Allen and Eugene stories she would make up on the spot, the archetypal one, Ginsberg remarked, being a tale in which "the king or prince went out and saw the condition of the workers and helped them out and everyone lived happily ever after." Allen and Eugene were often built-in characters in such thinly veiled political tales—especially later, when Naomi published some of her stories in a small local newspaper.

When Allen was three years old, Naomi had pancreatic surgery that nearly took her life and left her badly scarred, the "stitching of incisions . . . like hideous thick zippers," Allen would recall, shocked as a child at the sight. Naomi's sister, Elanor, offered to help take care of Naomi and watch her children during her recovery, and for half a year, the Ginsbergs lived with Elanor and her husband, Max, in the Bronx. During this period, Naomi had another nervous breakdown, this one more serious than her first, requiring her lengthy hospitalization in a sanatorium. Naomi's convalescence left Eugene and Allen with an unavoidable feeling of abandonment, despite Louis's efforts to take care of them and his dutiful visits with the boys to the sanatorium.

That fall, Louis secured a teaching job at Central High School in Paterson, and the family moved to an apartment at 83 Fair Street. The apartment was modest, located in a decaying Jewish neighborhood not far from the factory district and, from there, the slums of Paterson. The Ginsbergs lived in the constant din of a nearby silk-thread factory (which Allen would immortalize in his poem, "How Come He Got Canned at the Ribbon Factory"). Soon after they moved into the apartment, the telephone company erected an office building next door. Ironically, the Ginsbergs' five-year stay at this apartment had a positive effect on Allen: For the rest of his life, he would be comfortable living in any imaginable environment, and he would never be status-conscious. Long after he had achieved his international status as a poet and public figure, and was in the position to live wherever he wished, Ginsberg would continue to live in an apartment in a run-down neighborhood in New York's East Village, his friends and colleagues expressing amazement at his contentment in such an environment.

It also contributed to Allen's lifelong empathy with the underdog, an attitude reinforced by Naomi and Louis Ginsberg. Allen's earliest friends were from poor working-class neighborhoods; he grew up among blacks and fellow Jews, witnessing the vile effects of racial prejudice and anti-Semitism. Although he was too young to intellectualize what he saw, Allen remembered a number of incidents and wrote about them in his poetry and private journals throughout his life.

4

Allen's introduction to school was a disaster. With Louis working and Naomi still away at the Bloomingdale Sanitorium, the task of accompanying Allen to his first day of kindergarten at P.S. 1 fell upon a family friend. Allen was not about to be abandoned in a strange place, even if he was among his friends and only a short distance from home; he raised such a fuss that Louis was summoned to pick him up.

However, Allen soon discovered that he enjoyed school, and he established himself as one of the better students in his class. Throughout his school years, he would find that he possessed strong verbal and language skills, excelling in English and composition and foreign-language courses, while he would always have to work hard to achieve good reports in his science and math courses. He would never be much of an athlete, although he enjoyed swimming and running. As an adult, one of Allen's fondest childhood memories was of his racing with Louis, Eugene, and other young relatives when he was vacationing with his family.

Naomi was released from the sanatorium shortly after Allen began school, and she remained stable for nearly five years, taking care of the boys and growing active in local Communist party politics. In the summer months, she joined Louis and her sons on extended vacations in rural upstate New York. Louis, his sisters Rose and Clara, and their families would rent a small house and while away a summer sunning themselves on the beach, swimming and racing, talking, and exploring the wooded areas nearby. The families, Eugene later noted, were "very close," though he also pointed out that Naomi, never close to the Ginsberg side of the family, was not fond of these outings, and, as a compromise, she and Louis would alternate their summer vacations, one year going to Louis's family, the next to a place of Naomi's choosing, such as Indian Point, Woodstock, or, for two summers, a place called Camp Nicht-Gedeigat.

Camp Nicht-Gedeigat, a Yiddish term meaning "no worry," was a Communist-run summer camp located near Lake Monroe, and it was here that Naomi Ginsberg was truly happy. She loved sitting outdoors, enjoying the sun and listening to the birds chirping around her. In Paterson, she would take Gene and Allen to the park whenever she had the chance. Camp Nicht-Gedeigat, with its string of cabins set against the backdrop of dense green woods, represented the perfect conjunction of nature and ideals. The camp attracted ideologues passionately devoted to the principles of communism. While the children attended classes, picnicked in a nearby meadow, or swam in a swimming hole alive with salamanders, the adults debated ideology, pitting communism against the evils of capitalism or socialism. Pictures of the enemy—capitalists and socialists with exaggerated features, blood dripping from their hands—lined the walls of the mess halls. In the evenings, there were full-camp sing-alongs featuring songs in praise of the working masses. Both Allen and Eugene enjoyed the daily activities at the camp, although, as Eugene remarked, "the absolute dogmatism was a turnoff" to them.

"They lost all their reason when it came to talking about Russia," he said of the adults in attendance. "Remember the purge trials in Moscow? Well, one time they had a trial on the porch of the cafeteria. Some guy had half-propositioned the wife of another member, and they tried him on the porch, asking him questions and so forth. It was like Pucinski in the Catskills."

Fortunately for Louis, whose socialist sympathies would have made him an easy target at the camp, teaching summer school kept him away from Camp Nicht-Gedeigat except for weekends, when he was able to visit his wife and sons without incident. Things were not as easy for him at home. Naomi and her sister ridiculed Louis and his socialist ideals, calling him a "bourgeois poet." When Louis responded in anger, furious arguments would erupt, complete with childish name-calling and the inevitable pouting afterward. Naomi tried to raise her children to embrace Communist principles. She would take Allen to the Party cell meetings, held in a small room above a Paterson drugstore. For a nickel's admission fee, members would be given a snack of a handful of garbanzo beans, which they would munch on while listening to the likes of William Z. Foster, Israel Amter, and Scott Nearing give speeches about the need for a revolution of the working class.

In addition to their arguments about politics, Louis and Naomi fought about their lack of money. They had been plagued by money worries throughout their marriage, but Naomi's stay in the sanatorium had left Louis deeply in debt. Wanting the best for his wife, Louis had borrowed a large sum of money to enable her to stay in a private institution. Paying back the loan on a teacher's salary was difficult, and the family was always broke. In an early manifestation of the paranoia that would torment her in her later years, Naomi accused Louis of secretly turning his money over to his mother. Naomi had never forgiven Rebecca Ginsberg (known to the boys as "Buba") for her opposition to their marriage.

In spite of such family tension, Allen and Eugene were relatively carefree. Naomi worried that Eugene was too introverted, but that was never an issue with Allen, who always seemed to be playing in a circle of neighborhood friends. Gene enjoyed teasing Allen, as older brothers tend to do to their younger siblings, but the two were very close. When the family moved to 155 Haledon Avenue in 1934, Allen and Gene shared a bed, and the two would tickle each other. This kind of physicality was important to Allen, who had a great need for physical affection. To Gene's dismay, Allen liked to curl up next to him, Gene insisting that Allen stay on his side of the bed. Louis, often the recipient of Allen's physical affection, referred to Allen as his "little kissing bug."

By nature, Allen was openly affectionate, but in the period between 1934 to 1936, he seemed to require more assurance than usual that he was loved and accepted by his family and friends. The family moved twice during this period, and Allen experienced some difficulty in adjusting to new schools and new sets of friends. Furthermore, Naomi was starting to slip again. It was also during this period that Allen was beginning to realize his sexual nature. He was attracted to some of the boys at his school, and they found their way into his first erotic dreams.

By this time, it was apparent that Naomi Ginsberg's mental disorder was of a very serious—and possibly permanent—nature. For two months in 1935, she was again inflicted with the condition in which light and sound were intolerable to her, and, as she had done sixteen years earlier, she tried to fight off the symptoms by lying still in a darkened room. Doctors could not pin down the cause of this ailment, so all anyone could hope for was that she had recovered when the illness appeared to have run its course. Unfortunately, she had a serious relapse several months later, and this time the manifestations of her mental illness were much more disturbing. One minute, she would be function-ing normally; the next, she would be shouting at Louis, accusing him of entering into a conspiracy with his mother against her. She was convinced that Buba wanted to kill her. She heard voices, but she was uncertain how they were being transmitted into her head. At times, she would walk around naked in front of Allen and Eugene. Naomi was never threatening or dangerous to the family, but her disorder was frightening, nevertheless. Louis's sister Hannah was one of several family members enlisted on occasion to watch Naomi while

Louis worked and the boys attended school. "She imagined that my mother was trying to poison her," she recalled. "I remember her lying in bed, with pots over her ears to keep out the evil forces."

Louis tried to care for his wife at home for as long as possible, but her institutionalization was inevitable. Sending her back to Bloomingdale was out of the question, since Louis was still paying for her first stay at the private sanatorium, so he had little recourse but to place her in a state-run institution. For the next year, Naomi was a patient at Greystone, a large New Jersey facility. She was given forty insulin shock treatments, one of the standard treatments of the day for paranoid schizophrenics. She was also given Metrazol, which altered her metabolism and, combined with the sedate life on the ward, made her soft and flabby. The trim, youthful Naomi—the woman Allen would eulogize as the "beautiful Garbo of my Karma" in "Kaddish"—ceased to exist. She was replaced by a haunted, frightened woman lost in the maze of her own mind, her sharp intellect and happy disposition trapped and invisible in dark corridors of paranoia. She would return home to her husband and sons, but she would never be the same.

5

Allen was an excellent student, and his academic achievement, along with the look of intellectualism that accompanied the purchase of his first pair of eyeglasses, earned him the nickname of "The Professor"—a nomer that would stay with him through his high school years. As he grew a little older and began to feel the sting of anti-Semitic remarks, Allen learned that a quick mind could be as effective as physical force. In his short memoir, "My Son the Poet," Louis Ginsberg recalled an occasion in which Allen, harassed by an anti-Semitic playground bully, retaliated with a string of polysyllabic words that left the bully speechless. "He wondered what Allen meant, and in his wonderment the bully forgot his punitive intent and asked Allen what he had said. They began to talk and the threat was over. I believe that my son then felt the power of words."

For the Ginsbergs, their Jewish heritage was a clouded issue. As a Communist, Naomi had little use for any religion, but Louis was different. His father had been an atheist for much of his life, even though he could quote long passages from the Old Testament from memory, while Louis's mother had been semireligious, an occasional synagogue participant who adhered to many Jewish teachings but rejected others. It was important to her that Louis and Abe be bar-mitzvahed, but she showed little inclination to follow other traditional Jewish customs, such as cooking kosher. By all appearances, Louis shared this selective way of embracing his Jewish background. He did not attend the synagogue, but he clung to elements, cultural and religious, of his heritage. Whereas Naomi made a conscious choice between Judaism and Communist politics, Louis took a more pragmatic approach, siding always with the Russian Jews of his heritage and, later, the Israelis. Despite his claims to agnosticism, Louis observed the holy days and seasons of the Jewish faith.

Allen's faith was even more diluted. "Being communists and socialists, we were atheists and agnostics and I was not brought up in any kind of religious setting," Ginsberg said in 1982 in answer to a question about his Jewish upbringing. "I did go to a Hebrew school very briefly, but I got kicked out. I was not bar mitzvahed."

Like his father, Allen would develop an eclectic approach to his Jewish background. As an adult, he would describe himself as being nontheistic, yet at the same time he would admit that he identified with Judaism "because it's part of my background, particularly in America, the old Jewish socialist, anarchist scene." Critics would assail him for this stance, with little effect. He differed strongly with Louis on the idea of aligning himself at all times with Jewish political issues. He could accept the moral issues of Judaism, he claimed, but he felt no obligation to follow Jewish leaders blindly in political ones. "Once you get mixed up with politics you're just like any other politician and you have to suffer the consequences of manipulativeness," he said.

It was an issue that father and son would passionately debate and never quite resolve.

6

Naomi was released from Greystone after spending nearly a year in treatment. The Ginsbergs moved for a short time to an apartment at 72 Haledon Avenue, and then moved once again, this time to an apartment building at 288 Graham Avenue in downtown Paterson. The family would remain at this location until Allen was out of high school—a relief to Allen, who had lived in five different apartments and attended four schools in less than a decade. All the moving around, added to the problems the family was experiencing with Naomi, led to more than a few anxious moments for Allen.

He had little trouble keeping up with his schoolwork, which was fortunate, for they had no sooner moved to the Graham Street apartment when it became clear that Naomi had not recovered at Greystone and, in fact, was in as poor shape as she had ever been. From her treatments at Greystone, Naomi had come to believe that doctors had implanted wires in her head and sticks in her back. In her deluded state, she swore that she received signals from these implants, messages trying to corrupt her and turn her evil. By now, her complaints were all too familiar: Buba was trying to poison her; Louis had turned his money over to his mother. Louis tried to stay patient, even when Naomi ridiculed or badgered him, but the two often wound up quarreling bitterly. Naomi hinted that she might have had an affair with poet Maxwell Bodenheim during the time she and Louis had been members of the Poetry Society—a rumor, Allen said later, that was never substantiated and was probably devised as a means of tormenting Louis.

Eugene, a senior in high school, was able to avoid some of the turmoil by hanging out with friends, but eleven-year-old Allen was not so lucky. He entertained himself by reading, listening to the radio serials, and going to the movies, all of which offered temporary escape from the household problems. However, Naomi could not be left alone at home, and on those occasions when Louis could not find someone to stay with her while he was at work, the task fell to Allen or Gene. Oddly enough, when addressing as adults the fact that they had been kept out of school in order to watch their mother, neither Allen nor Eugene seemed to remember this sort of role reversal as being either traumatizing or particularly unusual; both approached it with remarkable maturity, as a necessary duty. Allen, who began keeping a diary a short time after the family moved into the apartment, would mention in his entries the times he stayed home with his mother—"My mother thinks she is going to die and is not so good"; "My mother is worse today"; "I stayed home to mind my mother"—but these entries were accorded no more significance than the other events of the day:

> June 24: I stayed home from school again only today I went to high school and saw my father teach. My mother locked herself in the bathroom early in the morning and my father had to break the glass to get in. She also went back to the sanitorium. I saw a newsreel of the Louis-Braddock fight, also "Dangerous Number" and another picture in the movies. I also developed a sty below my eye.

However, the occurrences of that June 24 were much more traumatic than one might conclude from the brief, if not casual, treatment they received in Ginsberg's diary, or from their mention in "Kaddish":

> Once locked herself in with razor or iodine—could hear
> her cough in tears at sink—Louis broke through glass green-
> painted door, we pulled her out to the bedroom.

For weeks, Naomi had been threatening to commit suicide, but Louis had tried to stall her actions by asking her to avoid doing anything until after Eugene had graduated from school; in making such a request, he hoped that time would calm her depression. It did not, however. Well before dawn on June 24, she locked herself in the bathroom. Louis attempted to talk her into coming out, his pleas waking up Allen and Eugene, who stood in the hallway, "shivering in their nightclothes, panic in their eyes," as Louis Ginsberg wrote in "My Son the Poet." Fearing the worst, Louis broke into the bathroom and found Naomi bleeding from cuts on her wrists. The injuries were not serious, but Louis could not help but wonder about how the boys, seeing their mother in a suicidal state, might be affected. He bandaged her wrists and saw her to bed. The next morning, he called an ambulance to take Naomi back to Greystone and, still concerned about Allen's state of mind, took him to work, where he could keep an eye on him. Naomi would remain in Greystone for more than two years.

7

By early 1938, war in Europe seemed inevitable, and Allen turned his attention to international politics. He collected news clippings from *The New York Times* and Paterson newspapers, and filled his diary with notations of the headlines and news stories of the day. "I expect to use this book for history," he wrote of the diary, noting that "the world is now in a turmoil." It was only a matter of time, Allen speculated, before another global war broke out, and he feared that the forces of Hitler and Mussolini might be too powerful for the rest of Europe. Hitler seized Austria, and reports of the Jewish purge made the daily papers. In addition, Japan and China were fighting, and a civil war had broken out in Spain. To Allen, there seemed to be no order anywhere. "The world is all agog," he wrote.

When he returned to P.S. 6 for his final year of grammar school, Allen found that he was still the smallest boy in his class. He was at that awkward age when one never feels settled with one's physical appearance, and with his slight build, glasses, and braces on his teeth, Allen was feeling gawky as he headed into puberty. He got along well with his classmates, but his greatest pleasures involved hobbies that he could do alone. In his diary, he listed as his hobbies collecting stamps, coins, rocks and minerals; on at least one occasion, he tried his hand at making puppets for his own show. His favorite pastime, however, was going to the movies, which he did once or twice a week, often sitting through a double feature more than once.

His life at home was stable. Louis had published *The Everlasting Minute*, his first volume of poetry, the previous year, and he had returned to writing a lot of poetry and attending meetings at local poetry clubs. Eugene was attending Montclair State Teachers College.

Allen continued to do quite well in school, especially in the language arts. A vocabulary test administered by his school revealed Allen to have the vocabulary of a high school graduate. He displayed strong writing skills, though his spelling was poor and his penmanship, at times, unreadable.

He graduated from grammar school on June 27, 1939, a few weeks after his thirteenth birthday. When asked in a school survey what he wanted to do with his life, Allen replied that he wanted to teach. He spent the summer with his family in Belmar, where he heard the news of the German invasion of Poland.

The new school year that fall found Allen attending Central High School. He liked the school and in no time became a member of the Literary and Debating Society, the Dramatic Club, and the Student Government Association's Board of Publications. Although he would later downplay his knowledge of current affairs as generalizations based upon received information, or "fourth-hand stereotypes," as he termed it, Allen knew much more about what was going on in the world than his classmates, and he used this knowledge to establish himself as a first-rate debater. He voiced strong opinions in favor of the United States entering the escalating war in Europe, decrying isolationist politics that seemed to encourage the country's standing idle while Hitler overran the Continent. Allen also became interested in writing. Central High had its own magazine, *The Spectator*, to which Allen hoped to contribute.

After a couple of false starts, Naomi Ginsberg was finally released from Greystone. She returned home shortly after the school year had begun. Allen and Gene were both very happy to see her again, but to Naomi, who had spent most of the last five years in a sanatorium, the apartment was at first a foreign place. She had hardly lived there before she had been readmitted to Greystone, and while she was gone, Louis had sold some of the furniture and rearranged the place. As Allen later recalled in "Kaddish," on the day of her return, Naomi retreated to her bedroom and spent the late afternoon in bed, with the shades drawn. When Allen joined her so she wouldn't be alone, Naomi expressed concern that she was alienated from her family. "Don't be afraid of me because I'm just coming back home from the mental hospital," she told Allen, "I'm your mother." Undaunted, Allen told her that he loved her and lay on the bed next to her for a while. "Was this the comfortless lone union?" he would wonder when he wrote "Kaddish."

Naomi adapted to the household soon enough, and for a time the Ginsbergs were a happy family. Naomi assumed the domestic chores while Louis taught school, Eugene commuted to college, and Allen attended his high school classes. Louis had befriended the editor of the *Paterson Press*, an alternative newspaper, and both he and Naomi became regular contributors, Louis submitting poems, Naomi writing her short parablelike stories. As always, Naomi and Louis bickered about politics, but for the most part, it was peaceful around the apartment.

By 1940, Allen was becoming increasingly aware of his homosexuality. He had been aware of his "baser emotions," as he termed his sexuality, since he was "about seven." His boyhood featured a number of incidents after which he must have realized that he was different from many of the boys with whom he was hanging out. As an adult, he was able to recount some of the more significant incidents. When he was around eight, he became infatuated with one of the boys in his class, culminating in a series of explicit sexual fantasies in which he was in control of his friends; shortly thereafter, in a scene fraught with Freudian underpinnings, Allen stood behind the porch rail of his home and exposed himself to passing cars and trucks, though no one took notice of the young boy who wanted both to bare and conceal his sexuality. On another occasion, Allen watched, silent but excited, as one of his classmates was ganged up on and had his pants pulled down. At the time, he had no way of knowing why he was excited by this incident, or by another, in which the same boy sat on a toilet seat while one of his friends kissed his penis. These memories remained with Allen for the rest of his life, however, just as he would always be intrigued, if not slightly troubled, by the fact that he had shared beds with his brother and father, a family setting that seemed innocent enough at the time. Allen's physicality represented little more than demands for affection, but later seemed more revealing of his developing sexuality. Throughout high school, he had adolescent crushes on classmates, but, the times being as they were, he had little recourse but to keep his feelings to himself.

For whatever reasons, Allen would always require more attention than the average person. He enjoyed being noticed and wanted to be popular. In his first year of high school, he discovered that his skills in debating and writing could garner him some of this attention. His first writings, "On Homework in General" and " 'Native Son' Makes Good," were published in the Easter 1941 issue of *The Spectator*. "On Homework in General," with its references to autocratic teachers and suffering students, was a brief satire in which Allen lampooned school life from a student's point of view, the piece being little more than safe, middle-of-the-road high school humor. " 'Native Son' Makes Good," the lead story in the publication, was much more sophisticated, an example of Allen's ability to fuse humor and poignant commentary. In the piece, a wealthy actor grants a young Paterson student an interview, which is actually more like an audience. After much verbal jockeying, during which the actor repeatedly displays his arrogance, the actor makes a pointed advertisement for his fried-chicken restaurants and tells his interviewer to see that all of his friends stop in. "And that's what the last five paragraphs are about," Allen concludes in disgust.

Allen also enjoyed his active membership in the Dramatic Club, becoming one of the featured players in "All Central Night," the high school's thirteenth annual variety show. The program from the two-evening production listed Allen as performing in two skits and being a member of the chorus; his big moment, however, was in Part III of the show, when he was premiere danseuse in "Ballet Loose," a humorous piece in which Allen and six other boys danced in tutus. It was a playful finale to a successful year.

8

After his sophomore year of high school, Allen was transferred to East Side High School, the school he was supposed to have been attending all along. Fortunately, switching schools was not as difficult now for Allen as his frequent change of grammar schools had been. At fifteen, he had much more self-confidence, which he duly noted in his diary, bordered at times on egocentricity. At his old school, he had been president of the Debating Society and had run for treasurer of the Student Government Association; he held the position of layout editor of *The Tattler*, the school paper, and he had been hired as high school columnist for the *Paterson Evening News*. With such success came adolescent egotism, present in many of his diary entries at the time. "I'll be a genius of some kind or other, probably in Literature," he boasted on one occasion, adding, "I have a fair degree of confidence in myself." Another puffy entry read: "Either I'm a genius, I'm egocentric, or I'm slightly schitsophrenic [sic] probably the first two."

Not surprisingly, Ginsberg cringed when he saw these jottings nearly a half century later, labeling the entries as "a kid writing egotistically," insisting that he "certainly wouldn't credit that intelligence for later literary things." In retrospect, however, these entries, along with others similar to it, are significant, for they reveal a substantial ego that Ginsberg subsequently spent much of his life trying to keep under control. He acknowledged this egotism in his later poetry ("I want people to bow as they see me and say he is gifted with poetry, he has seen the presence of the Creator," "I want to be known as the most brilliant man in America"), but he always viewed it as a personality trait that needed to be kept in check. Nevertheless, that self-assurance—the confidence that he had something important to say—was crucial to his development as an artist and, later, international figure. Ginsberg was never timid about expressing a strong opinion, regardless of its popularity, but without the formidable ego, he might have let fear of failure prohibit him from stepping forward.

An early writing model for Ginsberg was Walt Whitman, whom Allen learned about in the fall of 1941 from a teacher named Frances Durbin. In his

1979 reflection, "The School Day I Remember Most," Ginsberg recalled the afternoon during which his English teacher read aloud from Whitman's "Song of Myself" in a voice "so enthusiastic and joyous . . . so confident and lifted with laughter" that he immediately understood what Whitman was saying:

> [I] still remember her black-dressed bulk seated squat behind an English
> class desk, her embroidered collar, her voice powerful and high lilting
> Whitman's very words, and shafts of sunlight through school windows
> that looked down on green grass. . . .

9

Naomi Ginsberg's mental disorders, kept in control for the better part of two years, surfaced again in the winter of 1941. She resumed her paranoid accusations that Louis and Buba were conspiring against her, claiming now that such international figures as Hitler, Mussolini, and Roosevelt had in some vague way joined in the plot against her. She believed someone, probably Buba, was trying to poison her. To Louis Ginsberg's dismay, there was no reasoning with her, and he was forced to return to his policy of keeping someone with his wife at all times.

One evening, Naomi suffered what was, in all likelihood, an epileptic seizure. Allen and Louis found her in the bathroom, suffering her terrible indignation in a way that so traumatized Allen that he eventually included the frightening visual image in two of his poems. In "Kaddish," he characterized her suffering:

> like croaking up her soul—convulsions and red vomit coming
> out of her mouth—diarrhea water exploding from her behind
> —on all fours in front of the toilet—urine running between
> her legs—left retching on the tile floor smeared with her black
> feces—unfainted—

And, twenty-five years later, in "Black Shroud":

> Kunming Hotel, I vomited greasy chicken sandwiched
> in moldy bread, on my knees before a white toilet
> retching, a wave of nausea, bowels and bladder loose
> black on the bathroom floor like my mother groaning
> in Paterson. . . .

The seizure, with all its horrors, turned out to be a prelude to Allen's most harrowing childhood experience, which occurred one afternoon that same winter, on a day when Allen had been kept out of school to watch over his mother. Exasperated by Naomi's paranoid ramblings, Allen sat her on her bed and asked her to specify exactly what she was complaining about. She repeated what she had been saying all along. Using Louis's money, Buba had paid the Greystone doctors to torture her with shock treatments. They implanted sticks in her back so they could control her by sending signals through the wires.

Buba had hired spies to attack her in the hospital. Knowing that Allen would be no more inclined to believe these stories than Louis had been, Naomi dismissed Allen's objections before he stated them. "I've told you a hundred times and you'll never understand, you're too young to realize how cruel the world is," she told him.

Instead of arguing with her, Allen tried to prove her fears unfounded. When Naomi complained that the painful sticks were located near her shoulder blades, Allen rubbed her back, as if trying to find them; when she asserted that she could not specify the names of her would-be assassins for fear of being overheard, Allen handed her a pad and pencil and asked her to write down the names. As Naomi told him that the apartment had been bugged by the government, that wires in the ceiling were transmitting their conversation to her enemies, Allen stood on a chair and tapped the ceiling with a broom handle. "There's no place for wires," he suggested.

"They're smarter than you are," Naomi replied, rejecting all of Allen's attempts to reason with her. She told Allen that her enemies were calling her a whore because she had slept with Maxwell Bodenheim; they wanted her killed and had already dispatched an agent to accomplish the task. He and she were being watched, even as they spoke. To prove her point, Naomi walked to the window and peered out, standing to the side so she could not be seen by anyone outside. Allen followed her, and the two stared down at the church across the street on the corner of Broadway. Several people stood near the thick hedges in front of the church, waiting for a bus. Pointing to a well-dressed man wearing a hat, Naomi insisted, "That's the one, making believe he doesn't see us." Before Allen could restrain her, Naomi leaned out the window. "Go 'way, you rotten thing!" she shouted at the man, "the mystical assassin from Newark," as Allen referred to him in "Kaddish."

There was no calming her. If Allen loved her, he would help her escape, Naomi said. Certain that her therapist, Dr. Hans Wassing, would have her placed in a Lakewood, New Jersey, rest home, she instructed Allen to call the doctor. She was weak, she said, and needed a blood transfusion to regain her strength. Finally, to appease his mother, Allen called the doctor, who, for reasons no one was ever able to understand, agreed to recommend her admittance to a rest home in Lakewood. Still uncertain about the advisability of this action, Allen proposed that he call his father, but Naomi talked him out of it with her protests that Allen should not interrupt him at work.

They packed a suitcase and, in deference to Naomi's insistence that the apartment's elevator operator was part of the conspiracy, sneaked down the stairwell. As soon as they were outside, Naomi pulled the collar of her coat over her nose, a "gasmask against poison sneaked into downtown atmosphere, sprayed by Grandma." Allen hurried her down the street. At one point, they came upon a grammar school–aged boy. Seeing Naomi's suitcase and the fur collar drawn up to her face, the boy called out, "Where are you going, lady, to death?" He spirited away, laughing. Allen shuddered.

When they reached the bus terminal, Naomi noticed that their bus was empty and refused to board it, whispering to Allen that the driver intended to kidnap them. She proposed that they take a bus to New York and transfer from there to a bus to Lakewood. Reluctantly, Allen complied. The scene at Times

Square was a continuation of the nightmare, a two-hour wait during which Naomi went on about invisible bugs and poisoned air, Allen enduring it all, "hoping it would end in a quiet room in a victorian house by a lake."

There was no relief, even when Naomi was on the bus and presumably on her way to safety. For three hours, Allen sat beside his mother, listening to her rambling on about poison germs, the sticks in her back, Louis, and a recent day in which she claimed to have seen Buba, dressed like a man, climbing up the apartment building with a sack on her back. The couple sitting at the front of the bus drew Naomi's suspicions; to Allen's relief, they were sleeping and could not hear his mother's comments. The ride itself was a drive through beautiful countryside. Allen tried to distract himself by looking out the bus windows and admiring the view.

They arrived in Lakewood at dusk. Allen located the rest home and was negotiating Naomi's stay with the caretakers when Naomi began to rave about having her blood spoiled by electricity. Allen had advised his mother to stay out of sight while he was getting her admitted to the rest home—for good reason. The sight of Naomi, obviously in the midst of some type of psychotic episode, demanding a blood transfusion, was all the attendants needed to turn Allen and Naomi away. "This place is a rest home for elder people or people with mild nervous conditions," an attendant told Allen. "We haven't the facilities to handle your mother's case. This is not an insane asylum."

Allen tried several other rest homes in Lakewood—all with similar results—before he found one with an available room and the willingness to take in Naomi. After paying a week's rent, Allen accompanied his mother to a small room in the attic. His concerns, however, were far from over. Now that he had at last found her a room, he worried about how she would act when he left her alone:

> Would she hide in her room and come out cheerful for breakfast? Or lock her door and stare thru the window for side-street spies? Listen at keyholes for Hitlerian invisible gas?

The possibilities frightened him, especially since Naomi was already questioning whether the caretakers could be trusted. "Don't you *dare* say anything to them about your blood transfusion," Allen ordered, cautioning Naomi that she would be evicted from the rest home if she created a scene; she should rest while he went home and talked to Louis.

Naomi panicked when Allen mentioned Louis's name. He must not say a word to Louis about her whereabouts, she said; there was no telling what he might do if he knew where she was. Allen had heard enough. Angry with Naomi and fearful that their conversation might be overheard by the rest-home attendants, Allen pushed Naomi onto the bed. "For the love of God be quiet," he pleaded. They had taken the room by chance, Allen reassured her, and there was no way anyone could know she was there; she had to relax and get a good night's sleep.

The bus ride back to Paterson was fretful and depressing for Allen. He stared out the window into the dark night, his heart heavy and mind lost in the futility of his mother's plight. He wished she was dead, "safe in her coffin," rather than suffering in the senseless way she was. In an unpublished fragment of "Kaddish," written eighteen years later, Ginsberg described the gloom of his trip home:

> No greater depression since then—queer drugs jail
> suicide cocks—but this was the bottom—and what would
> become of her boarding house?

He knew, even if in his subconciousness, what would happen, as did Louis; it was unavoidable. When Allen returned home late that evening, he found Louis waiting in the living room. With no clue as to where Allen and Naomi had gone, Louis had spent hours worrying about them, and he was incredulous when he heard Allen's story of the day's events. How could Allen have taken her to the rest home? Didn't he realize that Naomi would go mad in Lakewood? Had he no idea of what would happen?

They received the inevitable phone call from the rest home at 2:00 A.M. Louis listened in horror as the attendant told him of Naomi's disruptive behavior after Allen's departure. She had removed her shoes and walked down the hallways of the rest home, knocking on doors and frightening the residents. When attendants had tried to calm her, she had crawled under her bed, fashioning her suitcase into a barricade. She had demanded a blood transfusion, shouting all the while about Louis and Buba and fascists and death. The attendants found Louis's number in Naomi's purse. They wanted him to take her home immediately. Louis explained that Naomi had been admitted without his knowledge or approval, even if her doctor had advised his son to take her there. He lived in Paterson, he said, and since he did not own a car, he would have to wait until morning to take an early bus or train to Lakewood. Throughout the conversation, Allen huddled on the couch, feeling guilty for having taken Naomi there in the first place.

The following morning, Louis went to Lakewood to retrieve his wife. Naomi was still barricaded under her bed when Louis arrived, and she became hysterical as soon as she saw him. One can imagine the scene: attendants and residents of the home watching in bewilderment as Louis patiently gathered Naomi's belongings and led her by the arm from the rest home, Naomi resisting, shouting for help, claiming that Louis was going to kill her. They walked up the sidewalk toward the bus stop two blocks away, Naomi carrying one of her shoes, insisting that a nail was poking up from it. She refused to walk any farther and sat down on the sidewalk, leaving Louis with no alternative but to hail a passing cab for the short trip to the bus stop.

Louis had to purchase a ticket at a pharmacy near the bus stop, and while he was doing so, Naomi carried on in a loud voice, demanding that the pharmacist give her a blood transfusion. Utterly defeated, Louis begged Naomi to be quiet. This only seemed to encourage her. She had an audience of Louis, the pharmacist, and a small group of Girl Scouts and commuters sitting at the soda fountain—all watching uncomfortably as Naomi, hair disheveled and dress unbuttoned, waved her shoe, raved about Louis, and sniffed the air for poisonous germs. When the bus pulled up outside, the driver noticed Naomi's condition and refused to take her as a passenger. At wit's end himself, Louis called

Greystone and was advised to bring Naomi in. He hired an ambulance for the trip, but instead of taking her to Greystone and into a depressing environment he hoped she could somehow avoid, Louis directed the driver to take them to a rest home in Passaic. They arrived by midafternoon, but she could not be admitted without the proper forms signed by a county physician. Getting that accomplished took hours. A doctor at the home administered Naomi a sedative while they waited.

It was late evening when a completely exhausted Louis Ginsberg arrived back at his home in Paterson. Allen was awake in the living room bed next to Louis's desk, dreading the news. Louis sat down next to Allen and tearfully recounted the day's events, father and son united in their trying experiences and, to a large degree, the despair they felt at the loss of Naomi. Within a week, she was back at Greystone.

10

The configuration of the Ginsberg family changed again in October 1942, when Eugene enlisted in the army and was posted to Great Britain. Allen, Louis, and Eugene had spent a final summer together at Belmar, although, as Allen remembered, it was not an especially happy time. When he returned to East Side High for his final year, Allen busied himself with his studies, taking courses in algebra, art, French, and English. He stayed active in extracurricular activities, and was elected president of the Debating Society and the Talent Club. In November, he took his first regular job, working for the next three months as a page at the Paterson Public Library.

With the United States now involved in World War II, Allen was as interested as ever in politics. His collection of press clippings grew thicker, and he wrote letters on a variety of topics to the editors of area newspapers. When the State Department decided to deport a labor activist for his Communist sympathies and isolationist beliefs, Allen fired off a three-page letter to *The New York Times*, arguing that a man's leftist sympathies or association with the Communist party did not necessarily make him a member of the Party, concluding that the United States, despite its differences with the Soviet Union, had to find a way to live peacefully with that country. "We are, or should be, building a world in which all nations will live together in amicable cooperation," he wrote. "If we are going to solve our problem with Russia and the Russian system by such negative actions . . . we are not beginning to practice the peace and harmony we preach."

It was an election year, and Allen tried to make himself useful by running errands for Irving Abramson, a popular labor leader who was again running for Congress against the incumbent, Gordon Canfield. In one of his speeches, Canfield made derogatory remarks about Abramson's liberal views, hinting that Abramson might be sympathetic to communism. Such a campaign ploy— linking union leadership with communism—was a standard practice of the day, but Allen was hearing none of it. In an angry letter to Canfield, he urged the politician to abandon the "smearing, red-baiting, political tomfoolery or name-calling, conscious or unconscious" and concentrate on an "honest discussion of principles involved . . . issues which you must face frankly if this election is not to be a farcical demonstration of the degradation of the Democratic philosophy of representative government."

As he would later admit, Allen was ambiguous about his political position. Like most Americans at the time, he was feeling patriotic, supportive of the war effort and disdainful of the isolationists, whose numbers were dwindling every day. He joined the Civilian Defense and spent an occasional evening patrolling his assigned neighborhoods. Despite this zeal, and an outspokenness that earned him the label of "philosopher of the class" in his high school yearbook, Allen was not enthusiastic about following his brother into the service, and he secretly hoped the war would end before he was faced with the prospect of enlistment.

On June 23, 1943, Allen graduated from high school, earning a diploma for General Course Study. At his graduation ceremony, he was given special honors certificates for holding at least a 90 percent average over a four-year period in both English and social studies; in addition, he was awarded a scholarship certificate for holding a minimum 80 percent average in all of his course studies over an eight-term period. In his yearbook, he was described as "a fiend of Beethoven and Charlie Chaplin," who "indulges in music, politics, history, [and] literature." Asked about his preferred peacetime occupation, Allen listed government or legal work as his first choice, and private law practice as his alternate. He was acknowledged by classmates as the "author" of the class, but curiously, although he did write a sentimental poem about his school that was included in the yearbook, he mentioned nothing in his yearbook—or, for that matter, in his diary—about his continuing to write poetry in the future.

As far as Allen could see, if he was going to make an impact on his world, it would be as a lawyer, not a writer.

2

Columbia and New York

**All ignus know each other in a moment's talk and measure
each other up at once. . . .**

1

Allen Ginsberg had just turned seventeen when he enrolled as a freshman at
Columbia University in 1943. Partially financed by a two-hundred-dollar scholarship from the New Jersey CIO and a one-hundred-dollar stipend from the university, Allen chose to attend Columbia partly because he had a secret crush on a
fellow Paterson high school student who was going to this New York school.
Although nothing ever resulted from his pursuit of the young man, Allen's selection
of Columbia proved to be one of the most important decisions of his life.

Located in the Morningside Heights section of Manhattan's Upper West
Side, not far from Harlem, Columbia University is one of the oldest and most
respected institutions in the country. The Ivy League school was chartered by
King George II in 1754 as King's College and renamed Columbia College after
the Revolutionary War. Nicholas Murray Butler, whose tenure was winding
down at the time Ginsberg enrolled at the college, had been the university's
president since 1902, and under his guidance Columbia had gained the reputation of being one of the finest urban colleges in the United States. Students
had both a distinguished faculty and America's largest city at their disposal, an
attraction that brought students from all over the country to New York.

Ginsberg originally intended to study law or labor economics at Columbia,
hoping to make a career as an attorney or labor organizer after he graduated.
On the ferry from New Jersey to Manhattan, Allen stood on the deck and made
a solemn, if somewhat romantic, vow to devote his life to the working oppressed. Given his background, as well as the fact that his brother had switched
from studying to be a teacher to studying law, it was not a particularly surprising
career choice.

Allen filled his class schedule with such courses as Intermediate French,

Trigonometry, English Composition, and History—the basic program for entry-level students of the day. Allen, however, was not the average student of the day. In his Paterson high schools, he had been able to distinguish himself in an environment of peers; he was a bright kid from the neighborhood, the Professor. At Columbia, he was in an entirely different environment. High scholarship among students was the rule rather than the exception. Further, most of Allen's classmates came from well-heeled families that not only could afford the school's stiff tuition but could also afford to keep their children well dressed and established in the social and political circles that would assure them of decent careers when they were through with their schooling. At seventeen, Allen was one of the youngest students at the school and, coming from a family of modest means, he seemed shabbily dressed in comparison to his classmates. With little chance—or, it should be noted, inclination—to become a part of that crowd, Ginsberg set out to distinguish himself in his own way.

In very little time, literature became Allen's main focus of interest. His favorite freshman course was a great-books seminar taught by renowned critic/essayist Lionel Trilling. Another Columbia professor, Pulitzer Prize–winning poet Mark Van Doren, was also very instrumental in interesting Allen in writing poetry, though both Trilling and Van Doren, Ginsberg later lamented, were far more concerned with teaching the classical Victorian forms of poetry than in studying more modern forms practiced by such poets as Walt Whitman, Ezra Pound, or William Carlos Williams.

"There was no genuine professional poetics taught at Columbia," Ginsberg said, pointing out that one young instructor informed him that "Whitman was not a serious writer because he had no discipline and William Carlos Williams was an awkward provincial [with] no craft, and Shelley was a sort of silly fool!"

In looking back at his college years, Ginsberg would cite Trilling, Van Doren, and Raymond Weaver, author of the first Melville biography and discoverer of Melville's *Billy Budd* manuscript, as being especially influential in his early development, even if he occasionally found himself in disagreement with them.

"In a way, I learned the most from Weaver," Ginsberg recalled, "because he already had some knowledge of Zen, and he used koans as part of his teaching method, which, at Columbia, was unknown. He was sort of like a Zen master with beetle brows and a frown, much liked and feared. He had a class called 'Communications 13,' a very famous class there at that time. He would hand out poems without giving them attribution—poems like Marvell's 'The Garden' or Wyatt's 'They Flee from Me'—and just examine them as texts. He was a tough teacher and his approval was very hard to get. I was really amazed and gratified when I showed him a poem I had written about Hart Crane and he liked it, saw something in it, and actually read it in class.

"He shared his office with Mark Van Doren, who was a real friend, actually. He was a poet who, like my father, was writing in more of an Edwin Arlington Robinson/Robert Frost vein. He wasn't as good at that as he was a good critic. He wrote a book of one-page commentaries on a hundred American poems, and they were quite bright. His sister, Irita Van Doren, was the editor of the Sunday *New York Herald Tribune* book section, and he got me some work reviewing books for the *Tribune*. I respected him and I liked him.

"In some ways, I was probably closest to Trilling because we were both Jewish and he sort of empathized with me. Also, I had him in class more than I had Van Doren or Weaver. He was always worried that I was getting in too deep. I was very frank with him, trying to explain about marijuana, or talking about Kerouac and Burroughs. But since they weren't in school and he didn't know them, he was unable to really accept them socially as interesting people. By this time, he was so academically oriented that he couldn't conceive of anybody outside of the academy as being distinguished."

All three professors took Allen seriously as a young, developing poet. Louis Ginsberg was a well-known figure in eastern poetry circles, and he had obviously passed on to Allen much of his knowledge of poetry and, in the judgment of his teachers, some of the talent. Allen was a raw, undeveloped poet well worth watching, and Trilling and Van Doren in particular went out of their way to advise and encourage him.

From the onset of his days at Columbia, Allen was eager to please yet insistent that he also be seen on his own terms. Throughout his years at Columbia, Allen would argue with his teachers, turn in papers on topics that were considered inappropriate even for a school with a relatively liberal reputation, associate with people whom faculty members disapproved of, and become involved in a series of events that would scandalize the school. In all of this, he was rarely apologetic. Diana Trilling, Professor Trilling's wife and an accomplished writer in her own right, once remarked that there seemed to be two motives driving Allen Ginsberg in his Columbia days, "the wish to shock his teacher, and the wish to meet the teacher on equal ground." When she asked her husband why he tolerated some of Allen's more rebellious behavior, why he didn't forbid him to act in such a manner, Lionel Trilling replied that he was in no position to make such demands; he wasn't Allen's father.

Perhaps not in a literal sense, or even in a figurative sense, in terms of the nature of teacher-student relationships at that time, but Trilling, along with Van Doren and Weaver, were authority figures to a greater degree than they might have cared to believe or take responsibility for—at least in Allen Ginsberg's case. Allen respected their knowledge and authority, as he respected those qualities in his own father; yet, at Columbia, he wanted to be afforded the same opportunities to think freely and speak his mind as he had had at home. The "shock" factor itself was consistent: Louis Ginsberg repeatedly accused Allen of trying to shock him (and readers), and those accusations would continue long after Allen had established his own name in the poetry community.

Despite his rebellious nature, Allen was looking for acceptance, if not outright approval. He was young, naïve, impressionable; still in need of shaping, still in need of finding his place in adult life and art. He would rebel, but only to a point. Even at a youthful age, Allen seemed to understand that he could not stand entirely outside of the system if he expected the system—be it academic, social, or political—to pay attention to him, other than to dismiss him as a troublemaker; instead, it was better to stay within the system, even if at the margins. In time, Ginsberg would become a master of maintaining a delicate, even if unlikely, balance of rebellion and conformity, of testing all limits but almost always stopping short of totally alienating the opposing viewpoint.

Columbia was his starting point.

2

As time would prove, Allen's first year at Columbia was more valuable for the friends he made than for the education he received there.

During his second freshman term, Allen moved to the seventh floor of the Union Theological Seminary on 122nd Street. The war had created a housing shortage for the many inductees into the navy, so Columbia was offering the V-12 cadets its dormitory space and relocating its students to nearby facilities. Allen roomed in a Morningside Drive apartment with two other students during his first semester, and they were all transferred to the Theological Seminary in early December.

One evening shortly after he moved, Allen heard the sounds of Brahms's Trio no. 1 coming from a room down the hall. He had never heard the music before, and he knocked on a door to inquire about it. To his surprise, the room was occupied by a fellow classmate in Lionel Trilling's course, a student named Lucien Carr. Allen asked about the music, telling Carr that it sounded like Brahms to him. Pleased to find what he called "a little oasis in this wasteland," Carr invited Ginsberg in.

Carr was a striking young man, and Allen was immediately attracted to him. Slender and compact, with unruly golden hair and almond-shaped eyes, Carr possessed a natural beauty and presence that turned heads wherever he went. Allen was impressed not only by Lucien's physical appearance but also by what he perceived to be the unusual combination of "youthful innocence" and "daemonic fury that seemed to dwell in his mind."

Two years older than Allen, Lucien was every bit as bright, yet far more sophisticated and experienced; he knew his way around the streets nearly as well as he knew his way around the textbooks. Self-confident to the point of arrogance, Lucien was known for his flashy dress, slicing wit, and impulsive behavior. He wouldn't hesitate to create a scene in a public place if he believed he could make a point in doing so. Gratuitous acts, such as chewing on slivers of glass, were commonplace. On occasion, he had to use his quick mind in order to avoid a nasty barroom altercation with someone he had offended.

Lucien was bold, whereas Allen was timid and insecure, and in the early days of their friendship, Lucien made a point of applying a liberal dose of youthful cynicism to Allen's naïveté. When Allen told Carr that he wanted to be a labor lawyer working on behalf of the masses, Lucien sneered at the ambition. "You've never worked a day in your life," Lucien told him. "You don't know what labor is."

Allen had to agree. "I was suddenly on the spot," he recalled years later. "I realized that I *didn't* know what I was talking about. I had never been a laborer and the idea was purely a stereotyped holdover from my childhood and my parents' ideals. I was embarrassed by the fact that I'd been living on secondhand opinion for so long—and had been very vehement about it—and I felt that what I should do was shut up and listen to people, learn what I could, and not assert my opinions."

The greatest difference between Allen and Lucien was in experience. The product of an established St. Louis family, Carr had been an excellent but hard-to-handle student. His educational background included a stint at Andover, where he had been expelled, as well as attendance at a school for difficult children and a summer school in Maine; he had also attended the University of Chicago for two semesters prior to leaving school and spending half a year knocking around the country. He had settled into the academic life at Columbia, where he hoped to receive training to become a writer.

Allen had been awed by some of the Ivy Leaguers he had seen around campus, but he had never met anyone quite like Carr. His intelligence and experience, coupled with the brand of cynicism, arrogance, and rebellion not at all uncommon to intelligent college students realizing their capacity to learn and grow, made Carr look light-years ahead of Ginsberg in terms of worldliness and maturity, at least as far as Allen was concerned. With the exception of his more harrowing experiences with his mother, Allen had lived a sheltered New Jersey life; next to Carr, he felt "jejune," little more than an intellectual impostor. In addition, with his bohemian affectations and volumes of poetry and prose unfamiliar to Ginsberg, Lucien had set himself apart from the students Allen was seeing at Columbia. "Know these words," Allen wrote in his journal, "and you speak the Carr language: fruit, phallus, clitoris, cacoethes, feces, foetus, womb, Rimbaud."

Lucien wasted no time in providing Allen with an informal education to go along with his formal one at Columbia. As Allen began a second-semester curriculum that included course studies in French literature and civilization, European literature and philosophy, and the development of Western institutions and social ideas, as well as a seminar in philosophy and the humanities, Lucien escorted Allen about the city, introducing him to some of his more noteworthy friends; as Allen poured over such classics as Cervantes's *Don Quixote*, James's *The American*, Wilde's *The Importance of Being Earnest*, Goethe's *Faust, Part I*, Spinoza's *Ethics*, Descartes's *Discourse on Method*, and selected plays by Molière, Lucien was engaging him in lengthy discussions about Rimbaud, Baudelaire, and French Impressionist painters. Lucien distrusted dualistic thinking, and he was constantly chiding Allen for taking naïve or party-line viewpoints to the arts and politics.

Allen and Lucien established a kind of banter typical, perhaps, of young men who view themselves and their lives as part of a larger drama. They even went so far as to assign themselves fictitious names. Lucien was Claude di Maubris, while Allen was known simply as Gillette. Their conversations and actions were hyperbolic. Each day was fraught with significance. They debated art and politics. They analyzed each other's character, actions, and motives. Allen had begun keeping a notebook journal in October 1943, into which he dutifully recorded what he believed to be the noteworthy conversations, events, and thoughts of his times. One of the preserved conversations between them exemplifies both the seriousness of their discussions and the exaggerated way in which they were carried out:

ALLEN: Well, really, art should communicate.
LUCIEN: Come now, Ginsberg, do you really think that art is communication?
ALLEN: (hesitatingly) No.
LUCIEN: But you just said that art is communication. Really, Ginsberg, you

ought to straighten these things out in your mind before you presume to
argue with me.

ALLEN: Abide with me. I'll get it out.

LUCIEN: Really, Ginsberg, you bore me.

ALLEN: Perhaps that shows a limitation on your part?

LUCIEN: (insultingly) Now, Ginsberg, don't take refuge in insult.

ALLEN: You're hypersensitive to insult.

LUCIEN: Oh, first you say I'm hypersensitive, then you tell me I'm limited.
Really, Ginsberg, you bore me.

ALLEN: (smiling shyly) I have a right to change my mind.

LUCIEN: Which just about shows how light your mind is.

ALLEN: (pensively, absently, as if he'd been thinking about it all along) But
has art no communicative faculty at all?

LUCIEN: (with assurance) If Michelangelo went over to the moon, would he
be appreciated? But it still would be art.

Lucien argued that art was "creative self-expression," that the artist's rewards
came in his feelings of self-satisfaction, while Allen insisted that art serve a
much higher purpose. By being humanitarian in its nature, Allen argued, art
was political. "The concomitant potential of all art is communication," he
wrote in his journal. "Art may communicate morality by open espousal of cause,
or by the enriching quality of expression, whatever the thought, which satisfies
the sensitive and happy few or the great masses."

It was an age-old debate, of course, and for Ginsberg, this early stance would
prove to be both enriching and limiting in later years—enriching when his
poetry served a higher purpose, limiting when his blind spots concerning the
value of pure self-expression caused him initially to miss the value of Jack
Kerouac's *Visions of Cody* and some of William S. Burroughs's experiments in
cut-up writing. He would be embarrassed by the blind spots, as well as by the
naïveté of these early discussions, but he would rarely stray far from these beliefs
in his own poetry practices.

Allen and Lucien saw each other almost every day. They would get together
in one of their rooms, or they would meet at a place such as the West End Bar,
a popular spot among college students, located at 113th Street and Broadway,
a short walk from Columbia. At the West End, the debates would rage long
into the night, the main topics of discussion being politics and literature, both
argued with almost equal passion. As one Columbia alumnus remembered:
"Everybody was very serious, and those of us interested in literature were deathly
serious about it. We had the kinds of fights about literature that later people
only had about politics. It was an unusual period, very serious intellectually."

On one occasion during the Christmas break, Lucien took Allen to Greenwich Village to meet an acquaintance named David Kammerer, a former St.
Louis physical education instructor and college English teacher who had known
Carr as a boy, become obsessed with his physical beauty, and followed him
across the country, from Missouri to Maine to Illinois to New York, supporting
himself by working odd jobs, all with the hope of making Lucien the object of
his love. To the people who knew Carr and Kammerer, the situation was sad,
pathetic: Lucien was decisively heterosexual, and the tall, red-headed and

bearded Kammerer, obsessed with Lucien to the point of forsaking his life and self-respect in his hopeless pursuit, became an inescapable shadow, following Carr from place to place, questioning his friends about his whereabouts, occasionally getting Lucien into trouble—even sneaking into his apartment to watch him sleep. Unable to escape Kammerer, Lucien had decided that his only workable alternative was to establish a rather uneasy friendship in which he dominated their relationship by calling all the shots. Lucien decided what they were doing, where they were going—and *if*, in fact, they were getting together in the first place. Although far from ideal, this type of association gave Lucien more control of his situation than he might otherwise have had.

The day he took Allen to meet Kammerer, Carr was pleased to find William Burroughs, another St. Louis friend, present in the apartment. Burroughs was a tall, thin, sandy-haired, impeccably dressed Harvard graduate who, at thirty, was far more advanced, in terms of world experience, than Carr. To Allen, Burroughs was an old man—a quiet, even stodgy presence—and their meeting was only memorable to Allen for one specific incident. When Lucien regaled Burroughs with a tale of how he had recently instigated a fight between Kammerer and a gay artist—an altercation that ultimately wound up with Lucien's biting both the painter and Kammerer—Burroughs dismissed the incident with a single line. "In the words of the immortal Bard," Burroughs said, pulling from memory a quotation from *Troilus and Cressida*, " 'tis too starved a subject for my sword.' " Burroughs's remark astonished Allen, who knew what it was like to respond to an uncomfortable situation by uttering a famous quotation. Allen had never heard someone put Shakespeare to such good use within the context of ordinary conversation.

As Allen would learn, Burroughs was anything but ordinary, and his remarks were only a sampling of an extraordinary mind that would be a lifelong influence on him.

3

William Seward Burroughs II was born in St. Louis on February 5, 1914, the younger of Mortimer and Laura Lee Burroughs's two sons. Bill's paternal grandfather and namesake was the inventer of the adding machine and founder of the Burroughs Corporation. He was not, however, much of a businessman, at one point resigning his position as head of his company and selling off most of his shares in the company stock, leaving some stock in trust funds that would find his family well set but nowhere near as wealthy as people at the time might have imagined. James Wideman Lee, Bill's maternal grandfather, was quite a contrast: A Methodist preacher from Georgia, Lee traveled throughout the state, preaching fire-and-brimstone sermons and eventually fathering twelve children, the eldest of whom wound up working as a media adviser for the Rockefellers.

By all indications, Bill's parents were much more sedentary than their respective fathers. An MIT graduate, Mortimer Burroughs worked for a time as a salesman for the Burroughs Company in Detroit, but he eventually sold off his shares of the company stock and, with the proceeds, moved his wife and son to St. Louis, where he founded a plate-glass company. A kind, intelligent man, Mortimer Burroughs was nevertheless somewhat formal around his two sons and was rarely physically affectionate with them. Of his children, he clearly preferred Mortimer, his older son and namesake, but on occasion he would take Bill duck hunting, and from this father-son pastime rose Bill's lifelong interest in guns. Burroughs's mother, Laura Lee, was a slender, attractive woman cast in the genteel mannerisms of the southern belle. Graceful yet cool toward her family and acquaintances, she loved arranging flowers, writing three books on the subject, but was thoroughly disgusted by so much as the mention of bodily functions. Bill, whom she adored, found this incongruous. Domestic chores were accomplished by a maid, cook, nanny, and gardener.

As a child, Bill was quiet and rather withdrawn, and bookish; although initially a poor reader, he loved to have stories read to him, especially tales of the sea such as *Moby-Dick* and *Treasure Island*. When he was eight, he read Ernest Thompson Seton's *The Biography of a Grizzly*, a sentimental tale of an old bear mourning the loss of his mate. Burroughs was so moved by the story that he wrote his own version of the account, a ten-page novel called *Autobiography of a Wolf*, in which the female wolf is shot by hunters and her grieving mate is eventually attacked and killed by a grizzly bear. Burroughs labeled his opus an "autobiography" because he identified so strongly with his story's main character.

On a personal level, it was an appropriate metaphor. As an adult, Burroughs would infuse the details of the horrors of his life into much of his fiction; in much of his childhood, he probably felt as if he were a lone wolf being victimized by forces much larger than he. In school, he was not fond of participating in group activities, nor did he care for the structured approach of day-to-day school life, in which finding a common denominator and fitting in—as opposed to standing out as an individual—were encouraged. Not so much a rebel as a loner, Bill preferred to go off on his own and explore whatever captured his fancy. On occasion, those explorations resulted in trouble. One time, while mixing chemicals in his chemistry set, Bill set off an explosion that nearly cost him his left hand; on another occasion, he built a homemade bomb and pitched it through the window of his principal's home, and while the bomb was harmless and did not explode, Bill found himself in trouble for the incident. The latter was a telling episode, illustrative of an inconsistency in Burroughs's personality that has never been explained: Although he always abhorred violence and was loath to get involved in so much as a playground fight, Burroughs also maintained a steadfast interest—some would say obsession—in guns and explosives.

Bill's inability to fit in, along with bad sinuses caused by asthma, convinced his mother that a change in environment might be in order, so in September 1929, when Bill was fifteen, he was shipped off to the Ranch School in Los Alamos, New Mexico, a high-priced institution run military-style by an administrator who referred to the students as "gibbons" and who had a definite misogynistic bent. Forced to wear a uniform and conform to a strict daily schedule, Burroughs was rarely happy. He was content when he was on the rifle range, working on his marksmanship, but these moments failed to offset his general feeling of uneasiness. He was involved in numerous scrapes with the school's authorities, gaining him the reputation of being a nonconformist. His homosexuality, now more obvious to others, set him apart from his schoolmates, who taunted him for his open interest in a particular boy at the school. His letters home detailed his depression, and finally, in April 1931, after he admitted his sexual preference to his terribly alarmed mother, he was withdrawn from the school, two months shy of his graduation. He would repeatedly refer to the school, in great sarcasm, as being significant to him because it was bought by the government, which, in turn, replaced young students with Manhattan Project scientists developing the atomic bomb.

Despite some of his run-ins with the educational system, there was never any doubt about Burroughs's intellectual capacity. It was quite apparent to his teachers and fellow students that he was brighter, even if in unconventional ways, than most of his peers, and with the help of a small private tutoring school that catered to a handful of gifted students, Bill completed his high school education in the spring of 1932. His next stop was Harvard.

In retrospect, Harvard, with its strong Ivy League tradition, would seem to be one of the least likely schools to leave a lasting positive impression on a person of Burroughs's disposition, and, with only a few exceptions, it did not. He hated the academic and social posturing, and he intentionally maintained a healthy distance from most of the students and teachers. He did not act up, however, and with the exception of his rather eccentric habit of keeping a pet ferret in his room, his behavior at the Cambridge school was not noteworthy in either a positive or negative sense. He didn't fit in, but he didn't stand out, either. He attended his classes, completed his assigned work, and moved on.

But for a few classes, his academic pursuits at Harvard were uneventful. He enjoyed classes on Chaucer and Shakespeare, the latter conducted by an eccentric professor who insisted that his students memorize numerous quotations from Shakespeare's works. Also fascinating to Burroughs was a class on Coleridge, taught by a scholar who lectured on the relationship between Coleridge's use of opium and his poetry. This issue—the link between creativity and a consciousness altered by drugs—would be meticulously explored by both Burroughs and Ginsberg in the decades to come.

Another foreshadowing, this one far more ominous, occurred during Bill's sophomore year. Although expressly forbidden by school rules, Bill kept a .32 caliber revolver in his room. One day, while engaging in some horseplay with a friend, believing the gun to be empty, he pointed it at his friend and pulled the trigger. Fortunately for Bill, his friend was athletic: Just as Bill was squeezing the trigger, his friend jumped at him and pushed the gun away. Instead of shooting the young man, Bill tore a hole in the wall. Two decades later, a similar prank with a handgun—finding Bill playing a drunken game of William Tell with his wife, who was balancing a glass on her head—would have fatal consequences.

Bill graduated from Harvard in June 1937 and immediately embarked on a tour of Europe. With a friend, he visited Paris, Vienna, Salzburg, Budapest, and Dubrovnik, Yugoslavia. Nazis were everywhere and tensions were running high, especially among Jews and homosexuals.

Shortly before they were scheduled to return to the United States, Bill decided to go back to Vienna and enroll in medical school, but his plans were cut short by an operation for appendicitis. Appalled by Nazi rhetoric and the violence in the streets, and needing time to recuperate from surgery, he traveled again to Dubrovnik, where he was reunited with a woman he had met several months before; the woman, a Jew, was desperate to leave the country, and marriage to an American was one way out. Against the wishes of his parents, Bill took the woman to Athens, married her, and then left alone for the United States.

For the next year, Bill lived in Cambridge, attending graduate school at Harvard, sharing a house with his friend Kells Elvins, and trying to determine what he should be doing with his life. Bill studied archaeology and was particularly fascinated by a course he took in Mayan civilization. He and Elvins collaborated on a routine, "Twilight's Last Gleaming," a savagely comic skit that today is regarded as an early Burroughs masterpiece, reflective of the sardonic declarative sentences characteristic of Burroughs's finest works. In the story, a *Titanic*-like ship is sinking, and the ensuing bedlam finds the captain, dressed in drag and smearing his face with cold cream, assisted by an Eagle Scout in boarding a raft filled with women and children, while in the background a recording of Fats Waller's version of the "Star-Spangled Banner" blares away. Not surprisingly, given the mood of the day, the piece was rejected when Burroughs submitted it to *Esquire*, and while in years to come the piece, like *Queer*, Burroughs's early novel, would achieve unpublished legend status among Burroughs's following, it would not be published until long after Burroughs had achieved a considerable literary reputation.

As with *Autobiography of a Wolf*, "Twilight's Last Gleaming" is indicative of a powerful imagination in collision with the artist's life and expanding intelligence. Considering the events leading to World War II, the image of a sinking ship was certainly not unique to Burroughs, but by the time he and Elvins collaborated on the story, Burroughs had studied English, medicine, and ethnology, and elements of all can be found in the skit. Burroughs was intrigued by the clash between the rational and the instinctive, the scientific and the primitive, an interest only fortified when he attended a series of lectures delivered by Count Alfred Korzybski in Chicago in 1939. In "Twilight's Last Gleaming," reason and decorum are replaced by the instinct to survive, and the routine's representative of science, the demented Dr. Benway (who would later appear as a major character in *Naked Lunch* and become one of Burroughs's most enduring characters), is the last person to trust. "This image—of conduct so outrageous it elicits laughter rather than censure—captured my imagination," Burroughs explained.

> I could see the heroic anti-hero often running more risk than Hercules or John Wayne. When the roll is called up yonder they'll be there. . . .
> There is, about all these anti-heroes, a purity of motive, a halo of dazzling shameless innocence. They are imbued with the primeval wisdom of children and animals. They know that the name of the game is SURVIVAL. . . .

On a personal level, Bill was experiencing his own clash between the rational and the instinctive. He had received an excellent education, in terms of formal, structured schooling, and he was inquisitive enough to deepen his knowledge through his own private investigations and experiences, but he had also come to believe, partially through cynicism and partially by examining the events taking place in the world around him, that intelligence could be a curse, that knowledge could cause you suffering. It was not unlike the ambivalence he felt about his sexuality, knowing full well that he was homosexual but at the same time realizing the turmoil that could cause. At one point, depressed and made desperate by an unsatisfactory love affair, he lopped off the end joint of the little finger of his left hand, an action that landed him in a psychiatric hospital for a month.

By the time he met Allen Ginsberg in early 1944, Burroughs had lived a short lifetime's worth of experiences to complement his formal education. He had been drafted into the army, only to be discharged when his psychiatric record was brought to the attention of the officials. He had worked for eight months as an exterminator in Chicago, a job that found him dealing with all kinds of people. While in Chicago, he ran into Lucien Carr and David Kammerer, old friends from his St. Louis days. When Carr moved to New York, with Kammerer in inevitable pursuit, Burroughs headed in the same direction, taking a job as a bartender in Greenwich Village and an apartment around the corner from Kammerer. He met Allen Ginsberg shortly after he moved.

4

For Ginsberg, it was a season of introductions. Although several months would pass before he would see Burroughs again, Allen was impressed enough with the man to make a mental note to look him up in the future. For the time being, there were other people occupying his time and attention. He saw Lucien Carr and David Kammerer on a regular basis, and through them he met a number of other people he found interesting. There was Celine Young, a Barnard student who had taken a strong liking to Lucien, much to David Kammerer's displeasure. To get away from Kammerer, Lucien and Celine would visit Edie Parker, a friend of Lucien's, and Edie's roommate, Joan Vollmer, a journalism student whose dark bohemian appearance seemed to complement her considerable intellect and wit perfectly. From Lucien, Allen heard a great deal about Edie's boyfriend, a former Columbia football player and aspiring writer named Jack Kerouac, whom, for one reason or another, Allen did not meet until later that spring.

Kerouac and Carr had met only a short time before, and they had engaged in all-night discussions about literature similar to the talks Allen was having with Lucien. Kerouac took his writing very seriously, the legend being that he had written a million words before he had entered Columbia in 1940. Like Lucien Carr, Jack Kerouac was looking for a new way to view the world and write about it, and together, Kerouac and Carr began to formulate what they called a "New Vision." As it was originally conceived, the New Vision underscored Carr's belief that self-expression was the highest purpose of art: Rather than be limited by the language and style and morality of established literature, the writer made literature out of his individual mind and experience. Rimbaud, whom Carr admired, had suggested that a supreme reality could be achieved only through a derangement of the senses in such a way that beauty *and* horror were defined by the individual through his experiences and senses. To Kerouac and Carr, this was the foundation of a new way of approaching art.

Lucien regaled Allen with talk of this New Vision and Kerouac. In his journal, Allen attempted to work out the differences between what he had been taught and what this new reality proposed. The previous semester, he had written a term paper on free will for Professor Weaver's class, and he expanded upon his thoughts in his journal, writing that "free will depends on free choice" and, since so many of a person's choices were determined by passion or emotion and not by the process of cool, conscious selection, there was a question as to whether free will existed at all. Allen made extensive notes addressing the topics of morality and ideals, citing Lucien's notion that "ideals are inextricably rooted in personality and character" as the basis for his conclusion that "ideals are an extension of the ego." Although these notions were not exactly indicative of a spirit of open rebellion on Ginsberg's part, they did reflect the seeds of a philosophy that would be connected to Ginsberg, Kerouac, Burroughs, and other principal members of the Beat Generation a decade later.

Not all of Ginsberg's hours were filled with esoteric ponderings and writings. Even as he was (as he later called it) "hung up on words," attempting to find language that defined and expressed a concept that, by its nature, could not be given universal application, Allen was also very busy with his life as a student. The war years, with their steady claim of student draftees, had necessitated a restructuring of the school year, with three semesters now compressed into a period that had once held two; for students, the work loads were fierce. Somehow, Allen managed to accommodate both active academic and social lives that found him reading books and writing term papers, participating in the Philolexian debating club, visiting with his professors, and keeping in constant contact with his growing number of friends. He was also writing poetry. The previous October, three of his poems—"Song for the Tender Hearted Liberal," "Pass the Biscuits Pappy O'Daniel," and "Rep Gordon Canfield (Mine Own Dear Congressman)"—all humorous rhymed lyrics, had appeared in the *Columbia Jester Review*, the campus literary magazine. In May 1944, "A Night in the Village," a fifty-four-line poem of rhymed couplets, modeled after Edgar Allan Poe and showing definite literary growth on the part of Ginsberg—who signed the poem "Edgar Allen Ginsberg"—was published in the same publication. All in all, it was a busy period.

In late spring, at Lucien Carr's suggestion, Allen decided to introduce himself to Jack Kerouac, who was staying with Edie Parker at her 421 West 118th Street apartment. Arriving at the apartment shortly after noon, Allen found Kerouac sitting in an armchair and eating a late breakfast. Allen was surprised: From his talks with Lucien, Allen had expected to encounter a kind of Melvillean figure, a writer/seaman both sensitive and rugged in a romanticized sense, more poet than brute. With his thick arms, powerfully built shoulders, and tough, brooding Breton looks, Kerouac did not exactly fit Allen's preconception. When Kerouac asked whether he wanted a beer, Allen nervously declined by dredging up the cliché "discretion is the better part of valor." Unimpressed and a little put off by Allen's remark, Kerouac responded by calling out to Edie and asking her to bring him more food.

Despite the inauspicious introduction, Ginsberg and Kerouac took little time in getting beyond the exteriors. Beneath Jack's gruff, macho exterior, Allen found an intellect of extraordinary sensitivity, a man who, as he later said, "was very handsome, very beautiful, and mellow—mellow in the sense of infinitely tolerant, like Shakespeare or Tolstoy or Dostoevsky, infinitely understanding." Almost as quickly, Jack determined that there was more to Allen than the "spindly Jewish kid with horn-rimmed glasses and tremendous ears sticking out, seventeen years old, burning black eyes, [and] a strangely deep voice" standing before him. Jack empathized with Allen's shyness and was impressed by his sincerity in the face of his nervousness; to Allen's surprise, he suggested that they take a walk.

As they walked around New York's Upper West Side, Allen opened up completely to Kerouac. He spoke of his childhood in Paterson, of how, when he was no more than ten or twelve, he would be walking home from the movies and, passing through the shadows of the tall hedges that grew along Graham Avenue, he would become aware of how small he was in the infinity of space. Allen had visualized himself as standing on a planet that was perched in the midst of something so vast that he could only wonder where—or if—the universe ended. At times, while on his walks or standing in his parents' backyard, he would sense a ghostly presence around him, a shadowy phantom that somehow encompassed the vast and timeless nature of the universe as he was coming to know it. This was heart talk as Allen had rarely experienced it: Rather than protect himself with a shield of clichés and received knowledge and transparent intellectualism, as he had done so often in his conversations at the West End or in Lucien's room, he was saying precisely what was on his mind; his thoughts were utterly naked. To Allen's amazement, Jack not only understood what he was saying but he also confessed to having similar thoughts himself.

Kerouac was unlike anyone Allen had met in recent months. Accustomed to being among people who talked nonstop, as if competing to have their ideas and opinions heard and accepted, Allen was pleased to find someone who would listen with patience and interest. Rather than look for a way to dismiss what others were saying, Jack seemed, by nature, to empathize. The fact that he was a dedicated writer with movie-star looks didn't hurt, either. Allen was in love with Jack before they had parted company that first day.

In the following weeks, Allen was a frequent visitor at Jack and Edie's apartment. He would hang around in the evenings, listening to Jack and Edie talk, becoming a nuisance when they wanted to be left alone, but on other occasions he and Jack would step out for walks around the Columbia area. If Edie and Jack were aware of Allen's sexual feelings toward Jack, they kept it to themselves, as did Allen.

There was one specific walk that Allen would never forget. He and Jack had walked to the Union Theological Seminary. Allen was moving again—this time to a small hotel that was housing students—and as he gathered up the last of his belongings, he explained to Jack how he had met Lucien Carr in this building only a few months before, and how he was feeling nostalgic about the place. He had grown a lot during the period in which he had stayed at the seminary. As he was leaving the building, he bade farewell to the familiar sights. He said good-bye to the closed door of the room once occupied by Lucien

Carr and, realizing that he would probably never step foot in the building again, he said good-bye to each stair and each landing in the seven-floor building. Once again, Jack identified with what Allen was doing. "I do that, too, when I say goodbye to a place," he told Allen.

Jack's remark sealed their friendship, bonding them in a way that would survive numerous disagreements, long periods of separation, political differences, and hard times in years to come.

"I suddenly realized that my own soul and his were akin," Ginsberg said, "and that if I actually confessed the secret tenderness of my soul he would understand nakedly who I was. And it was like I was already inside his body, we were identical in our most intimate feelings, so I came into an area of intimate feelings that I wanted to begin articulating outwardly to communicate with him, and join and be one with him."

5

Unlike the other principal figures in Allen Ginsberg's growing circle of friends, Jack Kerouac was from working-class stock. Born in Lowell, Massachusetts, on March 12, 1922, Jack was the youngest of his parents' three children, who included an older sister, Caroline, and the oldest, Gerard, who would die from rheumatic fever when Jack was four. Leo Kerouac, Jack's father, was a short, burly linotypist who, as often as not, bellowed when he talked. He also liked to bet on the horse races and stop at the corner tavern for a quick drink—two after work. Gabrielle Kerouac, called Mémère by the family, was a strict Roman Catholic and a dominating figure around the house, a good cook, possessive mother, and traditional French Canadian housewife who liked to play piano and sing. The Kerouacs could trace their ancestry to Brittany and, later, Quebec, and Leo and Gabrielle Kerouac were part of a French Canadian migration that settled in New England shortly after the turn of the century. Jack, nicknamed "Ti Jean" (Little Jack) by his family, spoke the Quebecois dialect of French until he was six, and for his entire life he spoke to his mother in her native tongue.

In a way, Jack was his brother's protégé, but following in Gerard's footsteps was a virtually impossible task. Gerard was gentle and uncommonly cheerful, considered a child saint by the neighborhood Catholics who watched him suffer in his final years. Jack would always remember Gerard's great love for animals and the way his brother nursed a trapped, injured mouse back to health, or the way he put out crumbs for the sparrows and cared for his pet rabbit. Their mother made no secret of her feeling that Gerard was goodness personified, an example she expected her youngest son to follow.

"For the first four years of my life," Kerouac wrote in *Visions of Gerard*, his fictionalized account of his early years,

> I was not Ti Jean Duluoz, I was Gerard, the world was his face, the flower of his face, the pale stooped disposition, the heartbreakingness and the holiness and his teachings of tenderness to me, and my

mother constantly reminding me to pay attention to his goodness and advice.

As Gerard's illness deepened, the Kerouac house took on chapel dimensions, frequented by priests and nuns, filled with holy cards and prayers. Jack listened in horror as his brother, barely able to breathe and racked with pain, wondered aloud why he was being punished by God.

Gerard's death left its scars on the Kerouac family. Leo, never very religious to begin with, quit going to church and seemed to delight in putting down religion whenever he had the opportunity. This shocked his wife, who wore a religious medal pinned to her dress and who lighted a candle in the church every day of the week; to Gabrielle, God had claimed Gerard as an early saint, and Leo's behavior was mortally sinful. They quarreled bitterly over religion and other issues, and in her frustration, Gabrielle grew all the more determined to see that her surviving son took on all the saintly qualities of her dead one. For Jack, the signals were continually mixed: One minute he would be virtually smothered by his mother, the next he was being told he was nowhere near as good as his brother; from the time of Gerard's death to the time of his own, Jack would struggle to win his mother's approval, never entirely convinced that he had gained it. Kerouac's belief in the beatitude in suffering would become the dominant theme of many of his books, and it would lead him to a lifetime's study of and devotion to Buddhism.

Jack's boyhood was filled with simple pleasures typical of New England life at the time. He loved listening to the radio, especially "The Shadow" serials. Through his father, who printed tickets for the local movie house, he attended movies in a soundless era, when one used one's mind to build upon what was showing on the screen. Also as a result of his father's connections, he was able to see a number of vaudeville performers, including W. C. Fields and the Marx Brothers, before they moved on to the movies.

Jack had a prodigious imagination, and he and his friends would stage their own adventures, with Jack often wearing the cape of the Shadow; snowball fights became wars that were resolved in the steamy, delicious smells of Mémère's kitchen, where Jack found warmth from the cold New England winters. He was a natural athlete who loved to play football, and a good student who was not afraid, as were many boys his age, to escape into the solitude of a good book. In fact, Jack found solitude appealing. Off on his own, he would play a horse-racing game he invented with marbles, writing short accounts of the results of the races in his own private newspaper. He created a baseball game, played with a deck of cards, for which he dutifully recorded the statistics of all his "players."

In high school, he became one of Lowell's star athletes, and since he wanted to attend college and knew that his father would not be able to afford to send him, he decided that an athletic scholarship was the only way he would get in. He did not stand out in track or basketball, and while he was a better than average baseball player, a fine fielder and feared power hitter, his main sport was football. In football, he was able to put his stocky frame and powerful legs to work for him. A perfectionist, Jack brooded when he failed to play up to his own expectations and seethed when, as an underclassman in high school, he didn't get as much playing time as he would have liked. When he had the opportunity, however, he usually made the most of it, and in one Thanksgiving game, played before fourteen thousand spectators, Jack scored his team's only touchdown in a victory between two of the area's rival schools.

Jack was awarded a football scholarship to Columbia, but the school insisted that he spend a year at Horace Mann, a New York prep school that groomed students for the rigors of an Ivy League education, before he attended Columbia; he was also expected to learn how to play football according to the standards set by Lou Little, Columbia's renowned coach. It was a tough year. Accustomed to being a star athlete and academically near the top of his class, Jack found himself to be just another face in New York. He struggled with his schoolwork and had to work hard to learn how to play football the way it was played in college. At Horace Mann, he did manage to write regular music critiques for the school paper, as well as two short stories.

He never had the opportunity to display his football skills fully at Columbia. In his first game, shortly after returning a kickoff for a touchdown, he suffered a hairline fracture of his right tibia while returning a punt, and his football-playing days were over for the year. The injury hurt Jack in more than one way, since Lou Little initially believed that Jack was faking his injury, and from that point on, the two never got along. Not that falling away from football bothered Jack. Time away from the practice field meant more time to explore New York City, catch up on his reading, and do some writing of his own. He returned to the football field the following year, but his heart wasn't in it. He fought with Little over his lack of playing time and walked out on the coach, effectively ending his association with Columbia. As Kerouac later saw it, "This was the most important decision of my life so far. What I was doing was telling everybody to go jump in the big fat ocean of their own folly. I was also telling myself to go jump in the big fat ocean of my own folly. What a bath!"

With the war escalating in Europe, Jack enlisted in the navy. To him, the sea represented romantic adventure. The previous year, not long after he had left the football team the first time, he had signed on as a crew member aboard a merchant marine ship on a run to Greenland; he had been shaken by two torpedo attacks on the ship and disillusioned by the whole idea of war, in which you were expected to kill or be killed by someone you didn't know, but he still found something appealing about the sea itself. He had also begun work on his first novel, *The Sea Is My Brother*, a work filled with sophomoric awe of the sea and rambling sentences imitative of Melville.

Jack's stint in the navy was a disaster. He hated military discipline and had little in common with his fellow recruits, most of whom were much younger than he. Furthermore, he was being trained to kill, and he found the idea intolerable. Since he was unable simply to walk away from the service, he decided to feign mental illness. One morning, he slugged his commanding officer for slapping an elicit cigarette from his mouth, and later in the day, he completed his mission by setting his rifle down on the drill field and walking to the library, where he was arrested. There was talk of a court-martial, but after undergoing a number of tests administered by navy psychiatrists, he was honorably discharged for "indifferent character." It was an appropriate label: "I was just about the least military guy you ever saw," Kerouac commented.

However, he was not away from the sea for long. Jack's parents had recently moved to Ozone Park, Queens, his father earning his wages as a linotypist in Manhattan, his mother working at a shoe factory in Brooklyn. Jack joined them for a few months, but he quickly developed the urge to move on. Once again, he looked to the merchant marine for the solution, signing on as an ordinary seaman on a ship taking bombs to Liverpool, and once again he found his ship under attack by German submarines, both when he was crossing the Atlantic and when he was returning. To make matters worse, the ship's first mate took a strong disliking to him and went out of his way to make his life miserable. During his quiet hours, Jack continued to work on *The Sea Is My Brother*, but it was his reading of Galsworthy's *The Forsyte Saga*, as well as the strength he saw in the citizens of war-torn Liverpool, that provided him with an idea he would pursue for most of his writing life: By writing a series of interlocking books, with common characters living ordinary lives, he could create his own legend of contemporary history, much the way Galsworthy had done in his books. His life would become his literature and, in turn, that literature would be a reflection of history itself:

> [I]t was that last morning before we got ready to sail to Brooklyn that I devised the idea of "The Duluoz Legend." . . . [I]t was a gray morning and I sat in the purser's office over his typewriter, he was having a last drunk I guess, and I saw it: a lifetime of writing about what I'd seen with my own eyes, told in my own words, according to the style I decided on at whether twenty-one years old or thirty or forty or what-ever later age, and put it all together as a contemporary history record for future times to see what really happened and what people really thought.

Back in New York, Jack was reunited with Edie Parker, a Columbia art student he had been seeing off and on since his football days at Columbia. Despite his mother's bitter protests, he moved into Edie's apartment, where he immediately began working on short stories and magazine pieces based on his adventures at sea. Edie and her roommate, Joan Vollmer, introduced him to a number of their friends, and it took very little time for Jack to become caught up in his New York life again, enjoying the sights and sounds of the city, reading and writing, visiting friends—all without the pressures of Columbia University closing in on him.

One of Edie's friends was a student named Lucien Carr, whom Jack initially sized up as being "a mischievous little prick," but that estimation was soon replaced by a spirit of camaraderie between the two. Lucien had a lust for life that Jack admired, a no-holds-barred attitude that differed immensely from that of the average Columbia student. According to Kerouac, Lucien's "sensibilities were affixed to his charm, and vice versa, and both had captivated me. He was unlike most people in that he never concealed the nature of his sensibilities." Before long, they were seeing each other regularly, arguing about literature, going out and getting drunk, singing songs at the top of their lungs; one night, Lucien persuaded Jack to climb into a barrel, and he rolled Jack down the sidewalks of Broadway.

Whether by incredible luck or by destiny, it was a true gathering of the forces. Allen Ginsberg, Jack Kerouac, William Burroughs, and Lucien Carr— all different ages and from different backgrounds, all meeting within a matter of months, all influential in their own ways in the development of a literary and social movement that would play a significant role in changing the world in the decades to come.

6

By early summer 1944, Allen and Jack decided that it might be a good idea to pay William Burroughs a formal visit, to "examine his soul and find out who he was and what he was," as Allen later remarked. Kerouac had met Burroughs informally shortly after he moved in with Edie, when Bill had dropped by to get information from Jack on how to join the merchant marine. Both Allen and Jack were intrigued by the man. Lucien Carr had spoken so often and highly of Burroughs that it seemed appropriate that they meet with him and have a serious conversation.

For Allen, it was time to separate myth from reality, secondhand information from the man himself. From what he had been told, as well as what he'd witnessed on his previous encounter with Burroughs, Allen perceived Burroughs to be a well-traveled, worldly scholar. He was especially impressed by what he called Burroughs's "contact with an older European tradition," by Bill's journeys to Vienna and Paris and Berlin, which, shortly before the war, were in a state of social and artistic flux, "a crucial time described by Isherwood in *Prater Violet* and *I Am a Camera*: the Berlin of Brecht and George Grosz, the glorious artistic time of the Weimar Republic in which, despite, or perhaps because of the obvious cruelty of the police state that was emerging, it was clear to more and more liberated minds how true, free, [and] tolerant a bohemian culture might be." Allen felt that Burroughs might be one of those liberated minds.

On the other hand, there was something vaguely sinister about Burroughs. His mannered formality, the trademark business suits and the snap-brim hat, his quiet behavior—all seemed out of place in the group of people with whom both Allen and Jack were associating. As Allen saw it, a formal visit would help Jack and him to determine "if he was really evil or like some sort of extraordinary melancholy blue child."

Neither Allen nor Jack was disappointed by the encounter. Bill's apartment was filled with books, many of the titles and authors unfamiliar to them. It was an eclectic collection, reflective of Bill's interests and continuing need for self-education. Allen recorded a list of the more prominent titles and decades later could still remember much of the list: Rimbaud's *A Season in Hell*, Kafka's *The Castle*, Melville's *Moby-Dick*, Cocteau's *Opium*, Céline's *Journey to the End of the Night*, Yeats's *A Vision*, Walter Van Tilburg Clark's *The Ox-Bow Incident*; there were volumes by Blake, Baudelaire, Gogol, Spengler, Raymond Chandler, and John O'Hara, as well as the Untermeyer poetry anthology, Wilhelm Reich's

The Cancer Biopathy, and Korzybski's *Science and Sanity*. To Allen, seeing the books and hearing Bill talk about them was like taking a tour of an utterly compelling intelligence: "Burroughs was primarily a master of gnostic curiosities and in his approach to the mind he had the same Yankee practicality and inquisitiveness as his grandfather who had invented an adding machine."

Allen was impressed. Bill's library was an introduction to a world of knowledge vastly different from what he was being exposed to at Columbia, and as he, Jack, and Bill talked, he concluded that what initially seemed like aloofness on Burroughs's part was actually a shyness. Burroughs, Allen believed, was both sensitive and generous. As their visit ended, Bill gave Allen a gift, Hart Crane's *Collected Poems*, and he gave Jack a copy of Spengler's *The Decline of the West*. The meeting signified a beginning, not only of lasting friendships but also of Burroughs's role as mentor to both Kerouac and Ginsberg. Both would create works greatly influenced by their association with him.

7

In *Vanity of Duluoz*, his novel based largely upon this period, Jack Kerouac characterized the summer of 1944 as an exciting, joyful season:

> There was the nostalgia of Johnnie and me in love, Claude and Cecily in love, Franz in love with Claude, Hubbard hovering like a shadow, Garden in love with Claude and Hubbard and me and Cecily and Johnnie and Franz, the war, the second front (which occured just before this time), the poetry, the soft city evenings, the cries of Rimbaud! "New Vision!", the great Götterdämmerung, the love song "You always Hurt the One You Love," the smell of beers and smoke in the West End Bar, the evenings we spent on the grass by the Hudson River on Riverside Drive at 116th Street watching the rose west, watching the freighters slide by. . . . *

However, not all of the times were so idyllic or romantic. Lucien Carr, for one, was experiencing myriad problems with David Kammerer. As Lucien began to spend more and more time with Celine Young, Kammerer found his and Lucien's friendship arrangement intolerable. He was hanging around the circle of friends as much as always, but he was feeling more like an intruder than a member of the group. Too often, Kammerer felt, Lucien was ignoring him or trying to avoid him. When he complained to Burroughs, Bill urged him to find someone else, even if that meant leaving town to do so, but Kammerer found this an unacceptable solution. He alternately loved and hated Lucien, and was tortured by jealousy on some occasions, while on others he swore he would

---

* The key for the fictional characters and their real-life counterparts in this passage from *Vanity of Duluoz* is:

Johnnie: Edie Parker	Franz: David Kammerer
Claude: Lucien Carr	Hubbard: William S. Burroughs
Cecily: Celine Young	Garden: Allen Ginsberg

never talk to him again. In desperation, he grew abusive toward Lucien and Celine. One night, when he and Bill Burroughs had stopped by to visit Lucien at Celine's apartment, only to find the two sleeping on the couch, Kammerer turned to Bill and said, "Doesn't he look pale, as though he were being sucked dry by a vampire." On another occasion, he climbed through the open window of Lucien's Warren Hall room, where he stood by Lucien's bed, watching him sleep, only to be nearly arrested when a guard caught him trying to sneak back out.

Lucien's dilemma was clear: The more Kammerer failed in his attempts to control Carr, the more determined he became. Kammerer was not going to leave or give up, and his recklessness had surpassed the stage of its being merely annoying or frustrating. It was one thing to endanger his own safety by scaling buildings and climbing into windows; there were other people to consider, as well. One time, in an act of vengeance, Kammerer had tried to hang Lucien's cat, and he might have succeeded if Bill Burroughs hadn't intervened. Three inches taller and forty-five pounds heavier than Carr, Kammerer posed a potential physical threat to Lucien. What would happen if Kammerer's obsession moved him to violence toward Lucien or Celine?

Looking for solutions, Lucien and Jack Kerouac finally concocted a plan that involved their signing on as seamen with a supply ship sailing to France, where they intended to jump ship and make their way across the countryside to Paris. According to the plan, Jack would speak the French dialect that he knew from his childhood days in Lowell, while Lucien pretended to be his deaf-mute brother. If all went well, they would be in Paris in time to witness the liberation of the city. Not only would they be seeing a great historical event but Lucien would be escaping his Kammerer dilemma and Jack would be finding a respite from his relationship with Edie, who was pushing him to marry her.

Once Lucien obtained the necessary papers qualifying him to work on a ship, he and Jack went to the National Maritime Union hall to inquire about a ship that was going to France and could take them both aboard. It took several trips, but finally, in late July, they found a supply vessel, the *Robert Hayes*, that fit their plans. They were told to report the next day, much to the disapproval of Edie and Celine.

Unfortunately for Jack and Lucien, their scheme dissolved almost as quickly as it had been devised that night a few weeks earlier at the West End Bar. When they arrived in Brooklyn, ready and enthusiastic about putting their plan in motion, they were warned by crewmen leaving the *Robert Hayes* that the ship's chief mate was brutally tough and demanding, a real hard-nosed case who would make their lives miserable. Despite this cautionary note, Jack and Lucien went aboard and proceeded to make themselves at home. They picked out bunks and dropped off their gear, and then Jack took Lucien on a tour of the ship. Belowdecks, they found the refrigeration storage and helped themselves to cold roast beef and milk. When they had finished eating, they went to the linen locker, grabbed a couple of towels, and took showers. They were back at their bunks, cozy in their new surroundings, when they were confronted by the chief mate, who shouted angrily at them for being aboard before they had formally signed on. When they suggested that they wanted to take a trial run to Albany, where the ship was taking on supplies, before they officially signed on for the trip to France, the chief mate threatened to remove them physically from the ship if they didn't leave immediately, thus ending any other thoughts they might have had of going off to Paris.

Allen Ginsberg had his own worries that summer, his moods shuffling between contentment and depression. His new circle of friends provided him with intellectual stimulation and many hours of pleasurable conversation, but much of the joy he might have derived from these occasions was tempered by the sexual desires he was struggling to keep hidden. At odds with his strong physical attraction to Jack Kerouac and Lucien Carr, Allen waged an inner war between his natural desires and the consequences he would suffer were he to make them known. "I want to unburden my soul to a loved one!" he wrote dramatically in his journal, "and yet, if people knew me, I should have to commit suicide!" Even his efforts with women, he noted, ended in frustration.

Still, there were moments when he felt strangely happy. In his August 3 journal entry, he described a walk on 115th Street, between Amsterdam and Morningside, in which he consciously recognized the importance of his being alive. He imagined that he had been elevated above the street and was watching himself as he took his walk, and he was filled with a feeling of wonder:

> Looking down on the street, I was struck by the fact that it was a stage—really, truly a stage. I played my part on it—I walked the street, lonely, in love, recovering from love. I had a tragic role. Yet I was conscious of my role, so conscious, in fact, that I almost treasured it for its nobility. Now I am acting this tragedy. In years to come I shall walk down this street, this stage, and look at it in retrospect. It shall not then be a part of the present, but a reminder of the past to me. I shall value it and love it for what it once meant.

In four years, Allen would experience similar feelings while he was lying in bed in his apartment, and he would refer to the experience as a "vision," but for the time being, he was too young, too unsure of himself, too caught up in the hyperbolic drama of the moment to do anything other than recognize his feelings.

Less than two weeks later, Allen was horrified to learn that David Kammerer, one of the major characters in the drama of his life, had been killed, and that Lucien Carr was being held by the police for stabbing him to death. Furthermore, Jack Kerouac was being detained as a material witness to the crime. To Allen, reality and his romanticized vision of reality—his play—had reached a climax that was too tragic, too abrupt: "And now, this curtain has been rung down!" he wrote. "Everything I have loved of the past year has fled into the past. . . ."

By talking to Bill Burroughs and others, as well as by thinking back on what he had seen, Allen was able to piece together the fateful hours of August 13.

It had begun innocently enough, with Allen meeting Kammerer in a chance encounter near Columbia. After a brief period of small talk, Kammerer told Allen that he intended to ship out soon, suggesting that Allen consider doing the same. Allen declined, saying that it would be "indiscreet," that "art waits on humanity for the moment." Kammerer said he was serious about leaving and mentioned that he might not see Allen again, but Allen didn't take the remark too seriously, figuring that he would probably see Kammerer later in the evening at the West End.

Shortly after he'd seen Kammerer, Allen ran into Lucien Carr. Lucien had stopped by Allen's room and, finding him gone, had read through his journal. Surprised and a little embarrassed when Carr told him this, Allen asked what he had seen. "Oh, a lot," Lucien replied. "I skipped most of the self-conscious sentimental stuff about yourself." "You missed the most charming part," Allen quipped. They discussed the journals for a while, particularly Allen's character sketch of Lucien, which Carr judged to be "competent."

That night, there was the usual meeting of friends, including Allen and Jack, at the West End. Lucien arrived later in the evening, already drunk; he'd had dinner with his mother and they'd had an argument. David Kammerer walked up to the booth as Lucien was describing the disagreement and made an offhand, yet insulting comment, prompting Lucien to pull him aside. The two sat at the bar, drinking and arguing, until the bar closed, and then they took a bottle to Riverside Park, near the banks of the Hudson River, where they continued to argue.

Given the circumstances—their evening of drinking and arguing, along with their long history of troubles, escalating in the recent months—it was probably unavoidable that their problems would come to a head that evening. Neither Carr nor Kammerer was noted for violent behavior, but both had reached a state of desperation. After a lengthy period of frustrating pursuit, resulting in Kammerer losing his livelihood and self-image, he was ready to leave the country, but not before he made one final attempt. Lucien, who had recently taken to chanting lines from Baudelaire, had reached a point where he could no longer run from Kammerer; instead, he felt he would have to confront the issue. As they sat in Riverside Park, Kammerer made drunken threats against Celine, and then jumped Lucien, telling him that he loved him, demanding sex, and threatening to kill him and take his own life. As they struggled, Lucien pulled out his Boy Scout knife and stabbed Kammerer twice in the heart. Terrified by the prospects of what might happen to him if his actions were discovered, Lucien tied Kammerer's hands and feet with shoelaces and tore Kammerer's shirt into strips, which he used to tie rocks to the body to weight it down. He labored to get it to the edge of the Hudson River, and, after removing his clothes, Lucien waded chin-deep into the water before he released Kammerer's body.

It was near dawn. His first stop was at Bill Burroughs's apartment. "I just killed the old man," he told Burroughs, making a grand gesture of offering him the last cigarette from a bloody package of Lucky Strikes. After hearing Lucien's story, Bill suggested that Lucien turn himself in, but Lucien rejected that solution. "I'll get the hot seat," he worried. Bill disagreed. He advised Carr to find a good lawyer and plead self-defense. *So this is how it all ends,* Burroughs thought. David Kammerer had been a longtime friend, dating back to their days in St. Louis, and Bill was saddened by his death, even if it seemed almost inevitable that he would meet a tragic end. Bill loaned Carr five dollars, and after Lucien left, Bill tore up the Lucky Strike pack and flushed it down the toilet.

Lucien went straight from Bill's apartment to Jack Kerouac's, awakening Jack as he had Burroughs only a short time before. Still badly shaken, Lucien related to Jack what had happened, showing him Kammerer's glasses. Lucien still had the bloody knife, and he wanted Jack to help him dispose of the evidence. Jack dressed and the two of them took a walk. With Jack watching for potential witnesses passing by, Lucien dropped the knife down a sewer grating; then, a short time later at Morningside Park, to distract passersby, Jack pretended to be urinating while Lucien buried David Kammerer's glasses. With the evidence gone, the two spent the rest of the day knocking around, trying to reestablish a sense of order. They drank a few beers, went to Times Square for hot dogs, watched Zoltan Korda's *The Four Feathers* at a movie house, and finished off the afternoon by walking through the Museum of Modern Art. Lucien remained undecided about a course of action to take, but he was now leaning toward turning himself in. He and Jack dropped by Lucien's psychiatrist's office to borrow some money, and then they split up, Jack returning to his apartment, Lucien leaving for his aunt's Manhattan home, where he planned to contact an attorney.

Two days later, in the company of his lawyer, Lucien turned himself in to the police, who were initially skeptical of his story but who booked him on murder charges when the Coast Guard located Kammerer's body floating in the Hudson River near 108th Street. Lucien took the police to the spot where he had buried the glasses.

Kerouac and Burroughs were arrested for their failure to report the crime. Mortimer Burroughs posted Bill's bail, but Leo Kerouac, blustery as ever, refused to help his son, calling him a family disgrace. Bill immediately departed for St. Louis, while Jack remained in jail. To make matters worse, Jack was taken to the morgue, where he was asked to identify Kammerer's remains.

David Kammerer's death was front-page news. *The New York Times* published its account under the headline COLUMBIA STUDENT KILLS FRIEND AND SINKS BODY IN HUDSON RIVER; the *New York Daily News* ran a photograph of Lucien pointing at the river, showing the police where he had left Kammerer's body. To the New York press, the story had elements setting it apart from any of the city's murder stories. It was a tragedy, an old-fashioned honor slaying, complete with a handsome, intelligent, boyish heterosexual and the tall, older, vaguely sinister homosexual who forced the issue to a violent conclusion. That two human souls had been reduced to being mere characters and that the tragic event had been boiled down to a radio-drama plot seemed to be recognized only by the *Columbia Spectator*, which noted that "[w]e only know that there is a complexity to the background of the case that will defy ordinary police and legal investigations. The search for motive will dig deep into the more hidden areas of the intellectual world."

Lucien Carr was indicted for second-degree murder. He was escorted to the Tombs, where he was held without bail. According to one published report, the two books he took with him were Yeats's *A Vision* and Rimbaud's *A Season in Hell*.

8

On September 7, Allen dreamed that a yellow-haired demon, "daring and miserable, haunted, hunted, fear ridden, [and] persecuted" for a crime he had committed, was being chased through a castle. As he was being pursued, the demon hid in the castle's closets and secret passageways, disguising himself in masks and costumes. He was eventually discovered by a guard, and in the ensuing struggle, the demon stabbed the guard with a silver clasp from a robe hanging in a closet. The demon was captured and just as he was about to be judged by a tribunal of nightmarish characters, including "a short man with an enormous green face, spotted with dripping birthmarks," the castle clocks struck twelve, ending the hour of retribution. The demon was judged guilty but set free because, as Ginsberg dreamed, "it was the beginning of the New Evil Years."

Troubled by the dream, Allen tried to find a way to interpret it. Some of the symbols, he realized, had been derived from recent events. The silver clasp could be interpreted as a symbol for the Boy Scout knife, while the changing of the clocks might be symbolic of the beginning of either the new season or the new school term. Allen had recently seen *Jane Eyre* at the movies, so the castle setting was not especially surprising. The general action—the pursuit, murder, and judgment—were symbols of Lucien's situation.

"The New Evil Years": It seemed that way to an eighteen-year-old student who had watched a year of memorable meetings and events change overnight into a time of very little promise. Lucien pleaded guilty to reduced charges of second-degree manslaughter and was sentenced to an indeterminable time in a reformatory. Although Bill and Jack escaped the more severe consequences of their knowledge of the events of Kammerer's death, both were out of town for an indefinite period of time. Bill was in St. Louis, while Jack, who hastily married Edie as a prerequisite to her family's bailing him out of jail, was living with Edie and her parents in Grosse Pointe, Michigan, and working in a ball-bearing factory.

Allen struggled with ambivalent feelings about the events of recent weeks, sympathizing with both Lucien and Kammerer: Lucien had his faults but was not by any stretch of the imagination a violent person or a cold-blooded killer; on the other hand, David Kammerer, with his maddening habit of following Lucien around or bothering his friends for information about his whereabouts, had been hard to put up with at times, but he was a tragic figure, not an evil one, and he should never have died the way he had, spiritually naked and ultimately scorned by those who read the lurid newspaper accounts. As a secret homosexual, Allen could empathize with the courage it took for a person to come out of the closet in those days, and with the terrible price one paid when one did. Shortly after Kammerer's death, Allen wrote in his journal a five-stanza lyric, a mournful, private epitaph, that lionized Kammerer's bravery:

> The credit's his—
> He was quite brave,

To shut his loving
In his grave.

For Allen, the New Evil Years of his dream had claimed their early victims, and while it was not difficult to identify the victims, it was virtually impossible to define the forces to blame. He had been brought up to see crime in very clear-cut terms, but this turn of events seemed to defy those terms. Depressed, Allen expressed his thoughts in his journal, but he could make no sense of what had happened or how he fit into it. He felt inadequate—"I have attempted little and been satisfied by nothing"—and the immediate prospects for improvement were grim. Kerouac may have put his finger on the main issue when, in a letter to Allen, he wrote, "You seek identity in the midst of indistinguishable chaos, in sprawling nameless reality."

As he would prove on numerous occasions in the future, Allen was a survivor in times of turmoil. He might stew or agonize over events, internalizing them or mulling over them in his journals, or he might lose his patience from time to time, but on the outside he was practical—a mind set to doing what had to be done, no matter how difficult. So it was during the period immediately following David Kammerer's death. Allen wrote letters of encouragement to Lucien and Jack, cooperated with those investigating the case and preparing Lucien's defense, even saw that Celine had comfort and support.

His prodigious energy carried him through.

3
Junkies and Geniuses

Intelligence of poets, saints and fair
Characters converse with me all night.
But all the streets are burning everywhere. . . .

1

By the end of his first year at Columbia, Allen Ginsberg had established himself
as a brilliant, if somewhat eccentric, figure about campus, the kind of student
who could pose serious problems with his less than conventional behavior—at
least as far as the authorities were concerned. His association with the figures
involved in David Kammerer's death did little to ingratiate him to university
officials. Kammerer's demise and the subsequent publicity had sent shock waves
through the Ivy League school—Seymour Lawrence, the respected publisher,
a Columbia student at the time, recalled his parents transferring him from
Columbia to Harvard because they had heard about the Kammerer story and
didn't want him associating with "bad influences."

As the new term began, Allen stayed as busy as ever while at the same time
maintaining a low profile and involving himself with what he called a "well-
rounded" circle of friends. In his typically exaggerated style, probably meant to
impress his older brother, Allen characterized his friends to Eugene as "some
neurotic, some insane, [and] some political," but the fact that he bothered to
list them at all was an indication that Allen had more than a casual interest in
the character of the people with whom he was associating.

He remained closest to Jack Kerouac, who was back in New York, having
skipped out on his marriage arrangement as soon as he had saved enough money
to repay his bail debt to Edie's father. After leaving Michigan, Jack had briefly
shipped out on a merchant marine vessel, but when he became convinced that
the ship's bos'n was a homosexual intent on raping him, he jumped ship in
Norfolk, Virginia, and caught a bus to New York, turning to Allen for a place
to stay until he could find a place of his own. Jack slept on Allen's bed, while
Allen slept on a mattress on the floor.

At first, these arrangements were not easy on Allen, who was still trying to keep his sexual attraction to Jack a secret, but after a series of very honest late-night conversations with Jack, Allen grew to believe that he was one of the most tolerant people he had ever known. As he later put it, "as a slightly older person and someone who I felt had more authority, his tolerance gave me *permission* to open up and to talk."

One evening, Allen did precisely that. "Jack, you know, I love you, and I want to sleep with you, and I really like men," Allen told a startled Kerouac, who groaned, "Oooooh no" in reply. Jack's response, however, was not meant as disapproval or rejection; if anything, it was the expression of surprise. Jack may well have suspected Allen's sexual inclination, but to hear him state it, at a time when homosexuals were still in the closet, probably caught him off guard. In any event, it had no effect on their friendship—if anything, it strengthened it. Over the years, Kerouac would praise Ginsberg for his courage, and this confession was surely a brave act on Allen's part.

That Jack was essentially heterosexual and refused to sleep with him immediately was not a major concern to Allen at the time; what mattered was the admission itself, the fact that he had finally found someone with whom he could confide his deepest secret. Jack was the first person he had told, and Allen was encouraged by Jack's tolerant response. Fear of rejection had kept him silent for all these years, but Kerouac's empathetic reaction was, to Allen, a sign that sexual preference would not be cause for his being rejected as a person. He could speak out with little fear—and did. "Very soon I was babbling at great length," Ginsberg recalled of that time.

Allen learned soon enough that Kerouac's tolerance was by no means a common trait, especially as far as the authorities were concerned. In November, for his creative writing class, Allen began working on a novel, based on the Carr-Kammerer episode and containing numerous references to homosexuality. He had no sooner turned in his first chapter when he heard from Nicholas McKnight, Columbia's associate dean, who cited "college policy" as a reason for his asking Allen to refrain from writing about the subject. When he visited McKnight to protest the decision and plead his case, he was informed that, in McKnight's opinion, Jack Kerouac was a "lout" and Allen's novel was "smutty." As far as Allen was concerned, McKnight's opinion was a reflection of the university's ridiculous concern about upholding its image. "The road to hell is paved with good intentions," he concluded.

The official Columbia reaction was disappointing, even if predictable. Allen had a wealth of material to write about. The Carr-Kammerer episode, he felt, possessed "much detail and significance that would make a brilliant, if pessimistic novel," but the university seemed to prefer that he continue to write in traditional style about safer subjects, such as his three poems published in the November *Columbia Jester Review*, typified by the following stanza:

> The rose that scents the summer air
> Grows from my beloved's hair
> For this, the rose's rooting spot
> Marks, as well, her coffin plot. . . .

Allen found the university's attitude unacceptable. He was as capable of imitating established poetry forms as anyone on campus, but he was looking for something new, a form that reflected the urgent concerns of his time, and if that could not be accomplished in verse, he could always turn to prose. Jack Kerouac was already working in this direction. He and Bill Burroughs had recently begun work on their own novel about the death of David Kammerer, Jack writing alternate chapters under the pen name of Mike Ryko, Bill writing as Will Dennison. Entitled *And the Hippos Were Boiled in Their Tanks* (the title coming from an item in a radio newscast Burroughs had heard a couple of years earlier), the novel was part hard-boiled detective story, part social satire, and though the book was never published, it was an important exercise for both men. Allen wanted to work on a similar project, but as a scholarship student, he had to be careful about the extent to which he challenged the university's established standards, at least as far as his on-campus activities were concerned.

The university officials weren't the only people with whom Allen found himself in disagreement. Louis Ginsberg was hearing nothing of Allen's defenses of homosexuality, Louis likening the homosexual to an insane person and calling him "a menace to society." Allen had yet to say anything to his father about his own homosexuality, but Louis even disapproved of his son's stated empathy, arguing that Allen was developed intellectually but, due to lack of experience, was lagging behind emotionally. "Your clever verbal solutions are incongruous with reality of life," he told Allen. As one who looked for a rational, ordered approach to life, Louis particularly distrusted Bill Burroughs, who had an obvious influence on Allen, and he discouraged Allen from continuing to see him. Burroughs's artistic values might be acceptable to people like Trilling, Van Doren, or Weaver, Louis said, but his social values would be rejected. "I tell you, Allen, you are living in an Ivory Tower," Louis concluded, suggesting that Allen consider consulting a psychiatrist.

Allen disagreed with his father, which in itself was anything but unusual, but he was now beyond the verbal stage of his rebellion against his father's ideals. He had only recently admitted to Louis that he was writing poetry—he had kept silent about it because he thought Louis would disapprove—and ignoring his father's objections, he continued to associate with people whom Louis found undesirable. The Carr-Kammerer tragedy had catalyzed his attitudes and actions, shaking him loose, as he later put it, "from the authoritarianism of the culture and from the authority of Columbia." He wanted to determine who—and what—was best for him.

Toward the end of the school term, Allen found himself again in trouble with the Columbia authorities. He and Jack had been going out drinking a couple of nights a week, and one evening they stayed at the West End beyond its 3:00 A.M. closing time. When the bartender reported the violation to Dean McKnight, Allen and Louis Ginsberg were summoned to his office for a conference. The tone of the conversation was grave. In terms of academics, Allen was an outstanding student, but, as the school official pointed out, decent grades were not the only standards by which the university judged its students. Hanging around with the likes of Jack Kerouac and drinking until all hours was definitely not the kind of behavior Columbia had in mind for students it was grooming for high positions in society. Allen had to conform to university standards or risk losing his scholarship, and since Louis could not afford to pay the costs of Allen's education, Allen's future was on the line. Utterly humiliated, Louis left the conference in tears.

This meeting, however, was only a prelude to difficulties to come.

2

According to his journal, Allen began writing what he called his first "real poems—first poems of genius?"—in January and February 1945, a short time after he had told his father that he wanted to write poetry. Allen had once heard Louis joke that by not writing poetry, Allen was probably the only "normal" member of the family. Eugene had been writing and publishing poetry for some time, and Louis had already established a strong reputation as a poet. The last thing Louis wanted for Allen was for him to be a reluctant follower, but once he had learned of Allen's aspirations, he went out of his way to encourage him.

Not that Allen needed it: By the time he made his formal notation about beginning his serious work as a poet, both he and Jack Kerouac had established dedicated writing schedules and were applying themselves to their writing with the most serious of intentions. Kerouac had gone to the dubious extreme of cutting his finger and squeezing his blood on a calling card, which he marked with the legend "The Blood of the Poet" and stuck to a wall, alongside a picture of Arthur Rimbaud. Kerouac was practicing art for art's sake, honing his writing skills the way jazz musicians would woodshed to practice their instruments, and after each workday, Jack would light a candle and ceremoniously burn his work. All this, he reasoned, would discourage anyone, including himself, from doubting his intentions as a serious artist.

Although he went to nowhere near these lengths, Allen showed surprising discipline for a young writer who was also trying to accommodate a busy academic and social life. While he maintained his full-time status as a student at Columbia, Allen also continued his private education, his prodigious list of outside reading sources including biographies of Baudelaire, Cocteau, Rimbaud, Shelley, and Verlaine. For classes, he wrote essays on Shelley, Baudelaire, and Rimbaud, as well as a lengthy piece on Coleridge's "Rime of the Ancient Mariner"; on his own, he structured notes for a long poem he was calling "The Last Voyage."

He was also concerned with his sense of self-definition, his musings ranging from the absurd, such as the time he decided that his new name as a poet should be Allen Raynard, to the significant, exemplified by his continuing discussion of the New Vision with Jack Kerouac. Allen agreed with Jack that the New Vision, and the expanded consciousness the term implied, should be approached "in terms of art," that it was the product of the writer's making use of "the humankind materials of art" as typified in Joyce's *Ulysses* and *Finnegans Wake* and Mann's *The Magic Mountain*.

In his journal, Allen wrote a second draft of the New Vision, as he and Jack had perceived it. "The new vision," Allen wrote, "is in a sense the product of a strictly rationalized system," a reaction against the established moral order that suggested that it was acceptable to step on an ant but not on a man. The ideal was to view the world, as Rimbaud had dictated, without ordered, rational preconception, and subsequently create a sense of order through the writing itself. "How shall I live?" Allen asked himself rhetorically, to which he answered, "as a dilletante [sic], not as an unconscious cog."

"The Last Voyage," Allen allowed, was an attempt to work these ideas into poetry, even if he did ultimately judge his own poem to be "somewhat bastardized by false sentiments." Modeled after Baudelaire's "Voyage" section of Les Fleurs du Mal, Rimbaud's "Drunken Boat," and Edgar Allan Poe's "Descent into the Maelstrom," the twelve-page poem, like Poe's story, was an account of a narrator's struggle with the world as he knows it and another form of consciousness. Death is the obvious alternative consciousness, as is the dream state, but in "The Last Voyage," Ginsberg was also considering other forms of consciousness, including the New Vision itself:

> Alas, there is no Mystery,
> But only highest consciousness;
> For our supreme reality
> Resides alone with nothingness . . .

and

> But, oh, my friend, you have no eye
> For symbols and you cannot see
> Disaster . . .

With its seemingly endless parade of rhymed couplets, "The Last Voyage" was an impressive technical achievement, but Ginsberg was ironically the victim of his own eye for symbolism, some symbols being naïve, others clichéd, while still others were either too obscure (such as his references to Rimbaud and Baudelaire) or too clever (as his reference to "a marijuana garden where/ Instantaneous visions bloom) to make the poem successful. Like the New Vision, the poem was composed of feelings and intentions that were virtually impossible to put into concrete images, and in trying to show the conflict between a consciousness formed by received ideas and another formed by a person's willingness to grasp reality without preconception, "The Last Voyage" was ultimately undermined by confusing lines ("We are blinded by our eyes"), resulting in a poem in which ideas were lost in language and form.

3

Allen's off-campus life picked up steadily with the return of his friends to New York. Bill Burroughs had returned shortly after Jack Kerouac, and just before Christmas, Jack had written Edie to ask whether she would join him in New York and help him make another trial run at their marriage. Joan Vollmer had also been away, and when she had returned in September, taking an apartment at 419 West 115th Street, she had an infant daughter with her, a reminder of a very brief marriage she'd had with a sailor now away at sea.

Joan needed assistance in paying the rent, and she was happy when Jack and Edie moved in with her. Also renting a room was Hal Chase, a young anthropology student from Denver. Blond and intelligent, Chase reminded Allen of Lucien Carr, though Chase was more reserved. Before long, the apartment was an unofficial meeting place, and Allen dropped by frequently.

He also kept in close touch with his family, taking the bus to Paterson to visit his father, or riding a subway to the Bronx, where his mother was now living. Louis and Naomi Ginsberg had split up permanently the year before, their many troubled years of marriage and Naomi's insanity finally splintering their relationship. Naomi had no sooner returned home from her most recent stay in the mental hospital when she began raging at Louis about their precarious financial situation. Raising a family on a teacher's salary was never the easiest of tasks, but in trying to provide Naomi with the best care he could find, Louis had depleted his finances. After twenty-two years, Louis's patience had finally been eroded by their nonstop fighting.

Naomi had initially moved in with her sister, Elanor, and had found a job at the Workman's Circle. She then met Dr. Leon Luria, a fellow Communist who worked as a physician for the National Maritime Union. They began seeing each other and, after a time, she moved in with him and worked as his secretary. Not surprisingly, the relationship fell apart. With Eugene now back from the war and studying law at NYU, Naomi suggested they take an apartment together, and they found a large furnished room in Manhattan. Living in such close quarters with Naomi while attending school and working was a strain on Eugene, however. Like Louis, Eugene was tolerant and sensitive, but he was bothered by Naomi's ravings about his father and Buba, as well as by her habit of walking naked around the apartment. During his visits to the apartment, Allen often acted as a calming influence, trying (though with little success) to convince Naomi that she was safe, that no plots were being hatched against her.

Jack Kerouac was also confronting a troublesome situation with his parents. Leo Kerouac had been diagnosed as having cancer of the spleen, and Jack spent as much time as he could at home, trying to make his father as comfortable as possible while offering reassurance to his mother. Neither of Jack's parents had any use for his friends, especially Allen and Bill Burroughs. Leo warned Jack to stay away from them, going so far as to hint that Allen, whom he once called a "cockroach," might steal Jack's ideas if he was to let Allen read his notebooks. Jack had always been greatly attached to his mother, and in these difficult times, when his father seemed to be either raging or suffering, he turned to her for solace as much as she did to him.

On the evening of March 16, Jack turned up at Allen's dormitory room to discuss a disturbing conversation he had just had with Burroughs. While they were talking, Bill had suggested that Jack's problem was that he was so attached to his mother that he would never break away from her influence and that this attachment would grow tighter and tighter over the years. Jack conceded that he had an especially close bond with his mother, but he was shaken by Bill's prediction. What if he couldn't break away from his mother's influence? Was his work a reflection of her attitudes rather than of his own ideas?

Allen and Jack talked for hours, long into the night. Allen, with mother troubles of his own, was a sympathetic listener. Burroughs showed a knack for seeing through to the heart of an issue, and although Allen himself had not taken notice of anything particularly unusual about Jack's frequent visits to his parents' home in Ozone Park, he felt that Bill's prophesy might be worth considering. In addition to this discussion, Jack also took the time to read through portions of "The Last Voyage" and offer Allen his insight and positive criticism about what he had read. By the time their conversation had wound down, it was late enough that Allen suggested Jack stay the night in his dorm room rather than go home. Jack was aware of Allen's sexual feelings toward him, but on that particular night, sex was not an issue for either of them. They stripped to their underwear and climbed into Allen's bed, leaving the door open between Allen's room and his roommate's, just in case there were any questions about improprieties taking place.

The next thing they knew, they were being confronted by Dean Ralph Furey of the university's student-faculty relationships department, who charged into the room under the auspices of answering a cleaning woman's complaint. Allen had been battling with the woman for some time, feeling that she was not only failing to do her job in her refusal to wash his dorm windows but also that there might have been an element of anti-Semitism in her treatment of him. To retaliate, and to force the woman to wash his windows, Allen had traced the words *Butler has no balls* into the grime, Butler being Nicholas Murray Butler, president of the university. He had also printed the legend "Fuck the Jews" into the dirt, and capped off the display with drawings of a skull and crossbones and male genitalia. Rather than clean the window and write off the incident as a college prank, the cleaning woman had registered a formal complaint with the university.

It was an awkward scene. Ever since the Carr-Kammerer episode, with its homosexual undercurrents and Kerouac's involvement as a material witness, Jack had been a persona non grata at Columbia. Besides that, Furey had been one of Lou Little's assistant coaches and he remembered Jack from his football days. As soon as Jack saw Furey, he jumped out of bed and ran into the next room, where he climbed into Allen's roommate's empty bed and pulled the covers up over his head, leaving Allen to answer Furey's questions. Allen initially believed that the big issue, as far as Furey was concerned, would be the fact that he had been caught sleeping with Kerouac, but that was not the case. Furey ordered Allen to clean off the windows and left.

An hour later, Allen received two communications from Dean Nicholas McKnight. The first was a bill, fining him $2.63 for having an unauthorized overnight guest. The second, a letter, was much more serious, informing Allen that he had been suspended from Columbia and could not attend classes or take part in any college activities. "I recommend that you arrange to spend the week-end with your father," wrote McKnight, "since the privilege of residence in Livingston has been withdrawn from you." He also sent a stern letter to Louis Ginsberg. The reasons for Allen's suspension, McKnight told Louis, were of such a nature that they "cannot be repeated in a letter," but he did say that they involved Allen's scribblings on the window and his entertaining a nonstudent guest "whose presence on the Campus is unwelcome." Fortunately for Allen, who had not yet spoken to his father about his sexual preference, there was not so much as a hint of any official suspicion of homosexual activity taking place in the room.

Nor would there be. To Allen's amazement, the university chose to focus on the window writings, as if Allen had committed a tremendous moral transgression in his prank. "Mr. Ginsberg, I hope you realize the *enormity* of what you've done," McKnight scolded when Allen visited his office the following Monday morning. Allen had arrived dressed up and prepared to deny any accusations of sexual wrongdoing, but the university seemed more focused on the words he had printed on the window than on any actions they might judge to be transgressions against the moral order. It was a lesson that would remain with Allen for the rest of his life, especially at times when his work was being attacked as obscene: In far too many instances, people would be blinded by words at the cost of missing the importance of an issue at hand; they were more concerned with images than reality.

Allen did his best to humor McKnight, to no avail. He had appealed to his roommate to testify on his behalf—Jack had fled to Ozone Park and was unavailable to corroborate Allen's insistence that nothing had happened that night—but the roommate's testimony, along with supportive words from Lionel Trilling and Mark Van Doren, did nothing to change McKnight's original decision. McKnight felt that Allen needed professional psychiatric counseling, along with a good dose of reality, and he told Allen that he could not reenroll at Columbia until he had seen a psychiatrist and worked at a job for a year.

A few months earlier, in journal notes for an essay on anarchism, Allen had written that "the argument of the idealist, the artist, [and] the anarchist is that he and others are oppressed and constricted by the injustice and mediocrity of the organized hypocrisy of law"; to be free to express himself, Allen claimed, the artist needed to break away from society's influence. At the time, Allen would not have chosen to have been expelled from Columbia as a means of fortifying his libertine thinking, nor did he have that in mind when he etched the offensive words on his dirty dorm window, but there is little doubt that he felt constricted and needed to break away. His expulsion from Columbia offered him that opportunity.

He immediately moved into Joan Vollmer's apartment, eager to begin an education that required firsthand knowledge acquired from experience, as opposed to the conventional wisdom that had been handed down, only to be moderately contested by academics, from century to century.

4

Allen was still a virgin when he moved into the 115th Street apartment in March 1945. He was highly ambivalent about how to satisfy his sexual longings, since the men he most wanted to sleep with were heterosexual and, since he kept his sexual preference a secret (except to Kerouac and Burroughs), he was not often in contact with potential gay partners. His love life, or lack of one, had become a major issue—a distraction even—and Allen was beginning to believe that his lack of physical love might be symptomatic of a larger problem, possibly of the feelings of rejection and abandonment that he'd had since the days of his mother's leaving for stays in mental hospitals.

Whenever he needed advice about matters of mind or heart, Allen tended to turn to Bill Burroughs, whom he regarded as a sort of elder, or to Jack Kerouac, who was generally a sympathetic figure. Allen and his father disagreed about the idea of Allen's seeing a psychiatrist, and in lieu of seeking professional counseling, Allen (and Jack) approached Burroughs for psychoanalysis. Every day for several months, Allen would lie on Burroughs's couch, talking about whatever came to mind, while Bill sat in a chair and listened, offering commentary whenever it seemed appropriate. Their hour-long sessions became increasingly disturbing to Allen as the weeks passed and he found himself digging deeper into his true feelings about himself, exploring the roots of his unhappiness and youthful confusion. Nobody loved him, Allen complained to Burroughs, who listened patiently but did not sympathize too much with Allen's self-pity. Lack of love, even if it was at the center of Allen's unhappiness, was something Allen would have to address on his own.

Convinced that any kind of sex was better than none, Allen looked for it wherever he could find it. He went to a gay bar and was picked up by a sailor much older than he, who demanded oral sex but refused to reciprocate; shortly thereafter, he met a student at the Museum of Modern Art and was finally able to engage in something representing tender sex.

His most memorable sexual encounter, such as it was, took place with Jack Kerouac. They had been out on one of their walks one evening when they found themselves in a parking lot in an industrial area near the waterfront. There, between two parked trucks, they engaged in mutual masturbation, and while it was far from the ideal sexual situation that Allen imagined for himself, he was again impressed by Jack's openheartedness. Throughout his life, Jack would feel guilty after his rare homosexual encounters, but he loved Allen in a Whitmanesque way and extended himself in a spirit of comradeship.

In general, it was a period of experimentation for Allen. To earn money and fulfill his employment requirement for reentry to Columbia, Allen worked a series of jobs, including employment as a spot welder at the Brooklyn Navy Yard, dishwasher at Bickford's cafeteria, and clerk at the Gotham Book Mart. He worked none of the jobs for any notable duration of time or to any great personal satisfaction. Most of Allen's friends, including everyone at the apartment, were leaving town for the summer, so he had to find his own ways to amuse himself.

Throughout the first half of the year, his writing remained one of the constants in his life. He had worked on "The Last Voyage" for most of the spring, finishing it in May. He wrote voluminously in his journal, recording dreams, thoughts, fragments of conversation, character sketches, lists of places to go or things to do, and lines of poetry. He began "Buba's Birthday," a short story about his paternal grandmother's seventy-fifth birthday. Regardless of the direction his day-to-day activities were pulling him in, Allen always maintained the discipline to read and write.

In late July, Allen decided to follow Jack Kerouac's example of shipping out to sea for some quick money and experience. Given the events of recent months, it was also logical that he get away and consider what had been going on around him. "I hope to tutor myself anew in all these strange realities I have learned from the purgatorial season," he told Jack, reassuring him that in entering the service he was by no means forsaking his Columbia education, even if his return to finish college turned out to be "only a pilgrimage of acceptance of former time." He enlisted in the U.S. Maritime Service, beginning his duty on August 1 at the training station in Sheepshead Bay.

Life in the service, although far from difficult, was anything but the romantic or adventuresome scenario that Allen had pictured it to be; in fact, he complained to Eugene, his daily life was as hermetic and unrealistic as the rarefied one he had left behind at Columbia. "By god those effete degenerates of Columbia were more disciplined and serious than this dreamworld," he groused. "I suspect that a modestly perspicacious poet from Bookworn Harvard has a better grasp on actuality than the higher officers of this place."

The routine, Allen pointed out, involved one's looking as busy as possible without getting anything accomplished. From the letters Gene had sent home while he was in the service, Allen had visualized the military life as one of teamwork, but from what he observed firsthand, there was a great deal of chaos and very little discipline—a deadly combination if one was hoping for any kind of efficiency. "The motivating sense is one of mass—things get done by sheer weight of numbers, and nothing more and nothing less," he wrote.

Part of Allen's sudden cynicism could be attributed to his unusual position of being older than most of the people around him. For the past two years, Allen had grown accustomed to being one of the youngest in the crowd, and all of a sudden the roles had been reversed. He was the elder, the one people approached for advice. Furthermore, the young men in the NMS had had far less education and experience than he'd had at Columbia. Allen found it difficult to identify with a group whose main preoccupations seemed to be learning how to swear and avoid work. Allen bided his time, fulfilling such menial duties as KP, buffing floors, washing dishes, and pulling occasional night watch. He read whenever he found the opportunity, wrote in his journal, and still managed to keep up a substantial volume of correspondence with his family and friends.

A good percentage of his letters was posted to Jack Kerouac. Allen was as enamored as ever with Jack, and Jack was more than a little uncomfortable with the tone of some of the letters. Troubled by feelings of guilt over the gay (or bisexual) aspects of his sexuality, Jack confronted his self-disgust by lashing out at Allen. He was repelled by homosexual behavior, he told him, and he was not happy about feeling as if he had to choose between two different worlds. Allen allowed that he had been the aggressor in pursuing sex with Jack, that Jack had "behaved like a gentleman" while Allen was being "rather crude" in trying to satisfy himself, but he was also hurt by the way Jack was pulling away from him. Jack, Allen believed, was forming the wrong impression about him. "I was surprised by your belief that whenever you show your affectionate nature to me I became condescending—I think it has been oppositely so," he wrote Jack, asking him whether he really believed some of the things he had written. On another occasion, Allen told Jack that rather than being "amused or wounded" by Kerouac's "unexpected attack on my 'stupidity and vanity,' " he was instead distressed by the tone of Jack's most recent letter. Jack responded by telling Allen that he had been "moved" by his honesty. "You shouldn't have been distressed by the tone of my last letter," he advised Allen. "It was only a mood."

The nature and tone of this kind of exchange was typical of their correspondence over the years. Jack used Allen as a sounding board, attacking him in some letters, praising him in others, all with the hope of better understanding himself as a result of Allen's responses. With Allen, more than with anyone else he knew, Kerouac felt he could be totally honest, as open in the bad times as in the good. Allen, who would become well known for his patience and tolerance—not only of Kerouac but of all kinds of people—put up with Jack's tirades on occasions when others would have written him off—and often did.

Allen's tour in the Maritime Service had taken a brief turn for the worse during this period in which he and Jack were exchanging their letters. Allen had caught a cold a few weeks after he had entered the service and it had developed into pneumonia. When he sought treatment in sick bay, Allen was scorned as a goldbricker, and he found himself in trouble when, later that same day, he vomited into a toilet that was off-limits to him. The day he was finally admitted to sick bay, he was so feverish that, as he told Jack, "I found myself worrying about the future of man's soul, my own in particular." The illness subsided quickly enough and Allen wound up with all kinds of recovery time on his hands, which he put to use by reading *The Way of All Flesh*, *The Bridge of San Luis Rey*, and *War and Peace*. "Even the militarists around here can't disturb my literary habits," he cracked to Eugene.

5

With the new school year came a new season, and although Hal Chase was the only one of the group attending school at the time, the end of the summer vacation found Allen's friends returning to Joan Vollmer's apartment. Allen completed his stint with the Maritime Service in November, and after using his seaman's card to help him get two brief jobs on ships immediately following his discharge, he rejoined his friends.

One new addition to the ménage was Bill Burroughs, who, with plenty of encouragement from Jack and Allen, had taken quite a liking to Joan Vollmer. With their similar intelligence and wit, spiced with sardonic commentary, Joan and Bill were a good match. Joan had a voracious appetite for sex, and though Bill was not by nature enthusiastic about engaging in sex with women, he complied with Joan's needs, as if it was part of their arrangement. Both— but especially Joan—had a taste for Benzedrine, which they would obtain by purchasing nasal inhalers, cracking them open, and consuming the small Benzedrine-saturated strips inside. For nights on end, they would prop them- selves up in Joan's bed, get high with anyone who happened to be around, and carry on intellectual discussions until the wee hours of the morning, the drug acting as a boosting agent to their conversations in much the same way alcohol had fueled their discussions a year earlier.

They had much to talk about. To Bill, the dropping of atomic bombs on Hiroshima and Nagasaki signified the destruction of civilization's most basic value system. President Harry Truman could attempt to rationalize his decision to deploy the bomb as a means of ending the global destruction—and thus, according to the standard line of thinking, *save* lives—but Bill felt that these actions were intolerable, symbolic of a spiritual and cultural degeneration that permitted any kind of mass behavior, including the annihilation of other cultures. The other reports that came out near the end of the war, from the genocide of the Jews in the Nazi death camps to the Allies' firebombing of Dresden, seemed to underscore the idea. What could be said about the state of a civilization in which armies could influence the cultural destinies of entire countries, where a country would attempt to demoralize another country, as Germany had attempted to do with its bombings of England? In such a world, survival of the individual was elemental.

For many months, Bill had been conducting his own private investigation into the ways that marginal individuals survived. Uninterested in the masses, whose behavior, Bill believed, was easily controlled, Burroughs directed his attention to the people living on the margins—to those who, by necessity and circumstance, lived by their wits at the fringes of society. These were people who skirted the control systems and in doing so developed their own sense of order. Petty criminals, small-time gangsters, drug addicts, hustlers, thieves, street people, pimps and prostitutes—all lived close enough to the edge to qualify themselves as worthy subjects for Bill's private study.

One of the more interesting characters was a Times Square hustler and junky named Herbert Huncke. Called "Creep" by the beat cops in the Times Square district, Huncke was a classic small-timer who, in 1928, at the age of twelve, had run away from his home in Chicago, hitchhiking cross-country to Geneva, New York. He had been picked up by the police and returned to Chicago, but from that point on, he had lived the life of a drifter. He smoked marijuana for the first time when he was fifteen and tried heroin a year later. He spent his teenage years on the road, drifting from job to job, working in such locations as Albuquerque and Miami, rustling up odd jobs to stay alive, his only baggage being a cigar box containing a handkerchief, toothbrush, razor, socks, and other toiletries.

He wound up in New York around 1940, where he quickly became part of the group of hustlers who worked the johns around Times Square. Small and thin, with heavy-lidded hazel-green eyes and sallow skin pit-marked from the days when he would ride on top of freight cars and get soot embedded in his skin, Huncke was anything but imposing, the type of person an antagonistic policeman could harass from time to time when the frustrations of his job sent him out looking for a victim to push around.

Bill Burroughs had met Huncke in January 1945, when he was looking for a buyer for a submachine gun and some morphine Syrettes. At the time, Burroughs had yet to try morphine, but he thought very little of obtaining drugs or stolen goods and marketing them on his own. Huncke and a roommate, Phil White, had recently returned to New York from a six-month stint at sea, having shipped out with the hopes of kicking their junk habits; instead, they had befriended the person in charge of the infirmary, who supplied them with enough morphine to put them in worse shape than they had been in when they left. They had an apartment on Henry Street, and on the night Burroughs met them, both were eager to buy any morphine that Bill might have to sell.

At first, Huncke was extremely suspicious of Burroughs. As he remembered.

> I took one look at him and said, "Jesus Christ, get him out of here, man. This guy is heat." He was standing there stiffly, with a chesterfield overcoat on, his snap brim hat sitting just so on the top of his head, wearing glasses, and obviously well groomed. Certainly his appearance was not indicative of anything suggesting nefarious activity.

To Huncke, who had a storehouse of bad prison memories, Burroughs was a threat. He did not know the underworld lingo; he was far too proper. The fact that he was wearing a suit and did not take off his coat made Huncke all the more anxious. All he wanted to do was get rid of Burroughs.

Phil White, however, had other plans. If Burroughs was carrying the morphine, he told Huncke, the least they could do was "get a little taste out of him." They sat and talked for a while at the living room table, Bill explaining that he had come into possession of the gun and Syrettes as the result of a drugstore burglary pulled off by an acquaintance. Burroughs told them that he had several gross of the morphine Syrettes and wanted to sell all but the few that he intended to save for personal use. Bill had brought along a pocketful of Syrettes, and when White suggested that he and Huncke shoot up, Bill mentioned that he'd always been interested in the drug and wanted to try it himself.

"I gave Burroughs his first shot," Huncke recalled in his autobiography, adding that he was amused by Bill's hygienic, scientific approach to receiving the shot. As they tied off his arm and prepared him for the injection, Bill mentioned that they might use alcohol to clean off the needle and his arm. Bill listened as Huncke described the immediate effects of morphine to a person's system, turning his head away for a moment when he was stuck.

"[H]e was so methodical about everything that I felt his approach came from a purely scientific standpoint," Huncke explained. "As I discovered later, it was. He became a drug addict principally as a result of research."

6

Allen Ginsberg had been intrigued by the prospects of experimenting with drugs almost from the time he'd met Bill Burroughs, yet he remained relatively inexperienced in their usage until he moved into Joan Vollmer's apartment. He had smoked marijuana in New Orleans while he was on one of his brief jaunts as a seaman shortly after his discharge from the Maritime Service, and he had tried Benzedrine, but he was nowhere near as experienced with drugs as Bill, Jack, or Joan—all of whom were especially involved in the use of Benzedrine. Kerouac occasionally used Benzedrine for additional stamina when he was writing, and his heavy recreational use of the drug resulted in his losing weight and hair. Joan also suffered from her use of Benzedrine; she became pale and gaunt, her attractive appearance declining as a result of her daily drug use, her sharp intelligence deteriorating, showing the initial signs of amphetamine psychosis.

Allen was interested in using drugs as a means of altering his consciousness and, like Bill Burroughs, he took a rather scientific approach to it. In his journal, he listed the various drugs he found interesting (including morphine, opium, marijuana, cocaine, codeine, and Benzedrine), along with detailed notes about the differing effects of the drugs. He tried writing poetry while he was under the influence of Benzedrine, but most of his efforts, as he later recounted in "Howl," were "stanzas of gibberish."

While Allen had been away in the service, Jack had become quite close to Hal Chase, who had a much more positive outlook toward America's future than either Allen or Bill. A voracious reader of considerable intelligence, Chase loved to talk about literature with Jack, who Hal thought had a remarkable facility for the *sound* of language. Jack saw America in panoramic and romantic terms, filled with epic-sized triumphs and tragedies; he was continually looking for a way to integrate the sound of American language into this vast novelistic landscape. Both Jack and Hal appreciated Joyce's use of language, with its wordplay and idiomatic quirks, but to Jack, Thomas Wolfe was a better model for the sweeping, rambling sentences he wanted to write, as well as for the American spirit he wished to portray in his fiction. Hal was very impressed with Jack's utter devotion to his craft, from the writing itself to the discipline he employed in his writing, and he became one of Jack's earliest supporters, promoting his talent to anyone who would listen.

Jack, on the other hand, was envious of Hal's sexual prowess. Hal was easygoing and smooth with women, whereas Jack was shy and awkward. Jack and Hal talked extensively about their attitudes about sex, including Jack's worries about his homosexual experiences and some of his more disturbing childhood memories of sexual awakening, but as far as Hal was concerned, there was altogether too much concern about sex among Jack and his friends. In Hal's opinion, the intellectualizing of sexuality, especially homosexuality, was not only irritating but also had a ring of falseness. In Denver, Hal had known a young hipster named Neal Cassady, whose prodigious sexual exploits and energy were matched, but not governed, by exceptional natural intelligence; Cassady, Hal told Jack, was essentially self-educated, the product of a street education, and used his sexuality and intellect instinctively rather than by design, which made his abilities all the more impressive. To Hal, this made more sense than a person's analyzing his sexuality to the point of sounding fatuous.

The divisions between the members of the group were brought into focus one evening in the fall of 1945. Allen, Jack, Hal, and Bill took Benzedrine and, in a strange design of fate, paired off in two beds, Allen and Bill lying on one, Jack and Hal sharing the other. The distinctions were clear and, to Allen, disturbing: Jack and Hal were "Wolfeans," heterosexual all-American boys with the sort of romantic, pioneering spirit reflective of America's always-searching, Western-tending spirit. Allen and Bill were "non-Wolfeans," homosexuals whose intellectual ancestry had definite ties to the East Coast and could ulti-mately be traced back to Europe. There was something sinister about the non-

Wolfeans, a sophistication (if not cynicism) that threatened to corrupt both the innocence of the Wolfeans' faith in America and their socially approved sexuality. Allen was very uncomfortable with this discussion, unhappy about its sexual divisions and, he thought, possible traces of anti-Semitism. Allen loved Jack, yet, by what Hal was implying and by the divisions that were being set up, he felt as if he was being rejected, his intellectual inclination, Jewishness, and homosexuality stacked up as negative qualities to be used against him. Allen craved physical and emotional love, someone to hold him and make him feel wanted, yet here he was being separated by what he called "transparent waterfalls of cellophane—pure synthetic abstraction" brought on, at least to a certain degree, by Benzedrine, fatigue, and household tensions. "So I talked all night," Allen remembered in a journal entry written years later, "explaining my delicate condition as hurt-voiced as I felt in my crying throat and sad warm 18 yr old breast."

The four quickly parlayed their Wolfean/non-Wolfean roles into exaggerated personas that became characters in improvisational skits that they acted out around the apartment. Allen played the Well-Groomed Hungarian, while Bill would don a wig and skirt for his role as the Lesbian Countess; Jack, complete with his father's straw hat and a hillbilly accent, was the American Bumpkin in Paris, and Hal rounded out the group as Child of the Rainbow, the somewhat naïve Denver mountaineer. In their routines, the non-Wolfean characters were constantly preying upon the Wolfeans, one of their favorite routines involving the Hungarian's trying to sell the American forged artworks supposedly smuggled out of Hungary at the time of Hitler's takeover. The Countess was the Hungarian's sinister sidekick, a shill who lured the innocent American into the Hungarian's lair. Bill was a natural at these types of routines, which ultimately served as models for the short fictional sketches that he included in such books as *Naked Lunch*, *Exterminator!* and *Interzone*.

7

By late fall, Jack Kerouac's father was in the last stages of his illness, and once again Jack began spending a lot of time in Ozone Park. On occasion, Allen would go out to visit, but at the very best he was tolerated by Jack's parents, who still distrusted him as a bad influence on their son. Allen and Leo Kerouac would argue about politics and religion, with Leo concluding that Allen, with his defense of communism and dismissal of the idea of a personal God, was little more than a crank. Neither of Jack's parents were sympathetic to Jack's ambitions to be a writer, so the fact that Allen wanted to write poetry did not endear him to them, either.

It was a critical time for Jack. On the outside, his father may have appeared to be blustery and rough around the edges, calling Jack no good and labeling his friends a bunch of dope fiends, but to Jack, his father provided a powerful male role model, a working stiff with permanently ink-stained hands who, in all manners of difficult times, had managed to endure and raise a good family. Jack and his father vehemently disagreed on all sorts of subjects, arguing bitterly until the very end, yet for Jack, watching his father suffer the painful effects of cancer, not unlike the way he had witnessed his brother Gerard's sufferings two decades earlier, was another brutal reminder of one's mortality. Depressed, Jack began to drink heavily and consume a large volume of Benzedrine, trying to offset the effects of the long hours he was spending in the care of his father. Just after Christmas, the physical exertion, exhaustion, and alcohol and drug abuse caught up with him in the form of a blood clot in his leg, putting him in the hospital, where doctors frightened him with horror stories of how his own life could be cut short if the clot was to break free and move up to his heart. In the hospital, Jack pondered his own mortality and, fearful that his father might have been prophetic in his claims that Jack would never amount to anything, vowed to work even harder to become a successful writer. From these thoughts sprang the initial plans for a book Jack called *Galloway*, a sprawling Wolfean novel that would encompass his feelings about himself, his family, his friends, and America.

Throughout this difficult period, Allen stayed close to Jack. They made plans for how they wanted to approach their writing, with Jack concluding that Allen was a good model for the way he should approach his own work. In the past, he had accused Allen of hiding behind a veil of masochism, as if being sad and tortured were necessary poses for a poet, but as an actual artist, Allen was sincere, and Jack admired him. Allen was interested in what united the members of the group rather than in what divided them, and by being less judgmental and more willing to listen to the others, he was, to Jack, less phony.

Both were writing continuously. While Jack was in the hospital, Allen sent him a tender prose poem that expressed his hopes for both the artist and man:

> I wish
> You, Jack, not well, because there always is
> A wound: and the most deeply cut of such
> Is this futility of consciousness,
> That hoping for your joy is vanity—
>
> I wish you nothing but necessity.

Like Jack, Allen had begun work on his own epic. Called "The Character of the Happy Warrior, or Death in Violence" (later shortened to "Death in Violence") and dedicated to Bill Burroughs, the work was, by Allen's description, "several satires, laments, celebrations, and an epitaph," including a thoughtful mixture of epigraphs by such artists as Rimbaud, Yeats, Mahler, Auden, Rilke, Kafka, St. John Perse, Eliot, and, of all people, Herbert Huncke, whose contribution was a short prison anecdote. In the poem, Ginsberg began with the Spenglerian assumption that civilization was disintegrating, and from there he applied himself to "considering the personality in a particularly unpleasant culture," the poem's goal being to determine whether a person could attain happiness in such an environment. Ginsberg's skeptical side argued that "it is difficult to conceive of any man escaping the evil effects of his culture by purely intellectual liberation, or by exile," but from his conversations with his group of friends, as well as from his budding friendship with Herbert Huncke, Ginsberg had come to believe that by nature the hipster or petty criminal was able to overcome the stifling restrictions placed on individualism in modern society. In his lengthy prose introduction to the poem, Ginsberg conceded that he was guilty of idealization, but he also argued that this kind of figure could be prominent in future literature as "a substitute for the sloppy improvisors of rebellion formerly known in literature variously as heroes, humanists, prome- theans, or decadents." To judge this type of person's actions, Ginsberg believed, was beside the point; he was more concerned about the relationship between individualism and happiness.

Ginsberg's technical virtuosity was again apparent in "Death in Violence," as it had been in "The Last Voyage," his other early epic. Even if "Death in Violence" was, as Allen lamented, "a literary white elephant," "a parade of sentimentalities" that, by its structure, failed to reach concrete conclusions, the poem was enormously important to Ginsberg for a number of reasons. First, it was by far his most ambitious work to date, a compression of virtually all of the major influences he had picked up since he had come to New York. The poem was filled with literary, philosophical, historical, and psychological references, and though most of these references were too obscure for anyone outside of Ginsberg's immediate circle of friends to recognize, "Death in Vio- lence" represented his first serious attempt to assert his own point of view in an extended work. Prior to "Death in Violence," Ginsberg had been caught in the trap of presenting a point of view that might be considered literarily or politically correct, as if he had to honor preconceived notions of what the poet's mind might be. In uniting his own feelings, even if with established (and, unfortunately, in this case, too many trite) images, Ginsberg produced his most honest work to date.

The poem also found Ginsberg experimenting with form, moving away from rhymed verse, incorporating modern language into his work, superimposing classic form onto the prose poetry that would become his main interest in several years. Ginsberg acknowledged the "faults in conception and difficiencies in execution" in the poem—apparent, for example, in its second section, in which Ginsberg employs overused crucifixion images to set up his hipster hero's sense of martyrdom, followed by an abrupt switch to modern voice and setting:

> You've nothing to say to court; thank God only in dreams
> does one beseech the judges for a better sentence.
> So as per schedule you fall in with the law;
> the plea is guilty and the judge suspends the sentence.
> Nothing would reach the papers.
> > The rap was indecent exposure.

For all its defects, "Death in Violence" was a significant work, a starting point, just as The Town and the City, which Jack Kerouac was writing at the time, would always be regarded as a derivative but important work for Kerouac. In both works, the clash between the traditional and the modern were signifi- cant themes, even if, in artistic terms, neither Ginsberg nor Kerouac was prepared to address them in his own original voice. Their group discussions and private studies were starting to pay off. With "Death in Violence," Ginsberg had begun an artistic exploration of theme that would become one of the focal points of the philosophy of the Beat Generation.

8

"There is something seductive about decadence," Ginsberg had written in his journal the year before. "Perhaps it is because it is accompanied by Bohemianism, in its turn, an outgrowth of Libertinism."

There was never a shortage of decadent behavior for Allen to explore. In recalling the period two decades later, Jack Kerouac referred to it as "a year of evil decadence," and while that might have been a hyperbolic assessment of the situation around Joan Vollmer's apartment, it was no doubt a period during which Allen, Jack, and others were testing the limits.

At the apartment, there was always an assortment of characters hanging around. Herbert Huncke was a regular visitor, as was a tall, pale, sunken-eyed junky named Bill Garver. A friend of Burroughs and Huncke, Garver was another example of the kind of nonthreatening social outcast that intrigued Allen and Bill. The son of a banker, Garver was sent a monthly stipend on the condition that he stay away from home. Now in his forties, Garver had a heroin habit that he managed to keep up by stealing overcoats and pawning them for ten or twenty dollars apiece. His method was simple: He would walk into a restaurant or cafeteria, buy a cup of coffee, and wait for a customer wearing an expensive overcoat to come in; as soon as the customer's back was turned, Garver would go to the coatrack, take the overcoat, and walk away as if he owned it. He seemed to know every restaurant and pawnshop in the city—a necessity lest he draw suspicion by frequenting one place too often—and by stealing a couple of coats per day, he was able to bankroll his junk habit.

Bill Burroughs also had a morphine habit, and there always seemed to be needles, drugs, and drug paraphernalia lying around the apartment, adding an element of danger to an atmosphere that was already brittle and starting to break apart. Bill was forging morphine prescriptions to maintain his supply. Huncke was breaking into cars and storing the stolen goods at the apartment. Phil White had brought over a gun to stash. Joan was now displaying signs of an advancing Benzedrine psychosis.

Joan's plight was especially disturbing to Allen. Her health was failing, and she had developed a limp from the damage the Benzedrine had done to her circulation. She also appeared to be losing her mind. She claimed to overhear conversations coming from other apartments in the building, in particular the one directly below them, which was occupied by an elderly couple. For five months, Joan regaled the group with stories of their conversations and exploits. According to Joan, the mean-spirited old couple had called her a whore and her friends dope fiends, hinting that they intended to call the police. The couple quarreled between themselves as well, usually about sex, and one night Joan told Allen and Jack that the old man was chasing his wife around the apartment and threatening to stab her. When Allen and Jack rushed downstairs to check on them, they found the apartment empty. As it turned out, Joan's overheard conversations were auditory hallucinations brought on by her excessive use of Benzedrine.

Hal Chase was the first to leave. By nature, he disliked large groups of people, and the comings and goings at the apartment, coupled with all the drug use, seemed to Hal to be a great waste of time. He could understand Allen's and Jack's fascination with the scene—they were, after all, writers gathering material for their work—but he had little use for it himself. He decided that he would be better off if he lived on campus.

Around the same time, April 1946, Bill Burroughs was arrested for obtaining drugs by means of fraud. Bill had written up some phony prescriptions on a pad that Herbert Huncke had stolen from a doctor's office in Brooklyn, and a pharmacist had grown suspicious when he noticed that Dilaudid had been misspelled on one of the bogus prescriptions. The police were called, the handwriting on Burroughs's prescription compared with the real doctor's handwriting, and a warrant issued for Bill's arrest. Since Bill had written his real name and address on the prescription, the police had no difficulty in locating him.

Huncke was the next to fall. A short time earlier, he had met a young junky on Forty-second Street and taken a liking to him. Huncke had been staying at Bill Burroughs's old Henry Street apartment in Greenwich Village and on occasion he would let the young man stay over, or he would supply him with drugs if the kid was running low. The police stopped the young man one evening and, frightened, he told them about Huncke, who was promptly arrested for drug possession and sent to the Bronx County Jail.

The scene was played out to its conclusion a few days later when Joan was admitted to Bellevue Hospital for acute amphetamine psychosis. Allen, who had watched the disintegration of his circle of friends with a mixture of dismay and interest, had little other choice than to shut down the apartment and move back to his father's house in Paterson. Another season had come to an end.

4
Book of Doldrums

we'd batter up the cloudy highway
where angels of anxiety
career through the trees
and scream out of the engine. . . .

1

Allen was back at Columbia in September. He had applied for readmission a few months earlier, and while Dean Nicholas McKnight was less than enthusiastic about allowing him to return, he relented when Allen presented him with a letter, signed by Dr. Hans Wassing, Naomi Ginsberg's former psychiatrist, informing McKnight that, in the doctor's opinion, Allen was "psychologically pretty much as sound as they come."

Not that Allen was ever very far removed from either the university or its academic environment. Throughout his year in exile, he had remained in contact with Lionel Trilling and Mark Van Doren, writing them letters and sending samples of his latest poetry. Trilling had sent back a detailed critique of "The Last Voyage" while Allen was in the Maritime Service, and throughout the following school year, Allen had maintained his dialogue about poetry with Trilling, through correspondence and personal visits. He had also held on to his position as assistant editor of the *Columbia Review*, despite the conditions of his suspension that prohibited it.

Even while he was away from the campus and classes, Allen kept a self-disciplined reading schedule that rivaled any reading requirements of university professors. During the summer months alone, while he was living at home and for the brief time that he was working on a ship, he had busied himself with works by Pound, William Carlos Williams, Flaubert, Yeats, Céline, and Thomas Wolfe. He had been especially impressed with Williams, and he was pleased when the *Passaic Valley Examiner* asked him to review Williams's book-length poem, *Paterson (Book One)*. He set about the task with vigor and, after several false starts, he turned in his review, only to be disappointed when he read the published version and determined it to be "juvenile and blatant" due to changes, deletions, and additions made by the newspaper's editors. "I should have known better," Allen concluded in disappointment, vowing to learn from the experience.

He had been struggling with his writing for most of the summer. His prose included a seven-page introduction to "Death in Violence," written under the influence of Benzedrine while the turmoil at the apartment was reaching its climax; numerous dream notations entered in his journal; and a review of a book about education at Columbia. He felt blocked, unable to accomplish creative work. "No new poems for months and months," he noted in his journal in early September.

No doubt the social distractions diminished some of his poetry writing, but the major factor was Allen's indecision about how to proceed with his future writings. He was growing increasingly dissatisfied with the traditional forms that he knew so well and was able to emulate in his own poetry, and his recent readings of Pound and Williams had greatly influenced him, showing him new directions in style and voice. He felt frozen by ineffectiveness—"I don't do anything with my life but romanticize and decay with indecision," he complained—and he was beginning to wonder whether he was capable of writing good poetry, "haunted by sterility" as he felt he was. He gave serious consideration to forsaking poetry in favor of writing prose, at least temporarily, but he rejected the notion. In summarizing his problems, Allen concluded, "I see my trouble comes from this confusion in the will: my difficulty in choosing an attitude and style is the difficulty in finding one."

In addition, he was troubled by his indecision in nonliterary matters. He wondered what he was going to do with his life, how he was going to earn a living. Clearly the product of both of his parents, Allen found himself influenced by both. Louis Ginsberg, always a proponent of reasoned behavior, encouraged him to earn his degree from Columbia and "find a job congenial to your nature." In the back of Louis's mind, there was concern that if Allen became entangled in serious trouble, he might wind up as his mother had. Allen understood this concern and, to an extent, he could envision the appeal of living the orderly academic life of his college professors.

Conversely, Louis Ginsberg, though pleased that Allen had chosen to write poetry, recognized the reality that the life of a poet, no matter how artistically rewarding, was not necessarily a rational one. There was very little money to be earned from such writing, and literary recognition was fleeting, as well. It was difficult to find any practical argument in favor of writing poetry, other than to recognize and honor the compelling drive of artistic expression, which, as both Allen and Louis knew, was the only important and true reason to write poetry in the first place.

Over the years, Allen had worked at a variety of jobs, and there was very little, in terms of "normal" employment, that appealed to him. He was intelligent enough to be successful in any number of professions, but he also understood that none of them would make him truly happy. His doubts about his literary abilities only clouded the issue. He questioned whether finding his path in poetry was actually a matter of time, maturity, and experience. "Until I am a man I shall never write good poetry," he wrote in his journal, "poetry which is tough in mind, poetry of which I approve: is spontaneous, rejoicing in beauty, sensuality, sensation."

To a large degree, these thoughts reflected Naomi Ginsberg's influence upon her son. Naomi's madness, for all the damage and sorrow that it inflicted upon the family, also contained, in its own strange way, many of the aesthetic qualities that Allen wanted to include in his poetry. Naomi was spontaneity personified; she had always possessed an enormous appetite for beauty, sensuality, and sensation. Allen's interest in New York's bohemian lifestyle, his friendships and conversations with Kerouac, Carr, and Burroughs, and his study of marginal characters had given him a greater sympathy for his mother.

This sympathy was further tempered by his recognition of his own differences from what was considered to be stable society. In the 1940s, homosexuality and madness were both regarded in the minds of the American public as aberrations, and homosexuality was actually considered to be a type of madness by a large portion of the public. As far as Allen could determine, he would never fit in, at least not totally, nor did he want to; he hoped to find a way of distinguishing himself while meeting his own needs. At twenty, he had no way of knowing for certain whether poetry was his answer.

2

Jack Kerouac may have suffered doubts of his own about how he wanted to write, but he never questioned his ability or his intention of making writing his vocation. His creative output in 1946 was prodigious. Earlier in the year, he had applied the finishing touches to *And the Hippos Were Boiled in Their Tanks*, the novel he had cowritten with Burroughs. To Lucien Carr's great disapproval, Jack was showing the novel to agents and publishers, though no one showed much interest in publishing it. Kerouac's main focus was *The Town and the City*, the *Galloway* novel that he was now expanding into a full-blown epic. Jack was convinced that this book, once completed and published, would put him on the literary map. As it was, he was gaining a modest literary reputation while the book was a work in progress, mainly because, in the eyes of his friends, it was one matter for aspiring writers to "talk" a good book, quite another for them actually to sit down and apply the time and discipline to writing one. After his father had died that spring, and throughout the tumultuous period of disintegration at Joan Vollmer's apartment, Jack had never strayed far from home, where he attended to his mother and applied himself to the writing of his novel. He had also stayed in touch with Hal Chase, who had returned to Denver for the summer. Hal's plan was to return to Columbia in the fall, settle on campus at Livingston Hall, and find a direction to his life. He remained steadfast in his belief that Jack was a talented writer destined to achieve a notable reputation in the literary world. He spoke often of Jack to his Denver friends, showing them Jack's letters and repeating stories about his and Jack's New York experiences.

Two of Hal's friends, Ed White and Neal Cassady, decided that they wanted to go to New York and enroll at Columbia. White, a future architect who loved literature, art, and jazz, attended Columbia that fall, and he and Jack took an instant liking to one another, spending many hours haunting jazz clubs and talking about literature. White was quiet and levelheaded, with a nature more like Jack's than most of the people Kerouac had been associating with in the past year or two, and though he was never a part of the inner circle of friends who would form the nucleus of the Beat Generation, White would eventually have a marked effect on both Kerouac's and Ginsberg's writing.

Neal Cassady, of whom Jack and Allen had heard plenty, did not turn up to enroll for the fall term at Columbia. Hal had gone out of his way to convince several Columbia professors, including Lionel Trilling, that Cassady should be admitted on the basis of his passing an oral examination, rather than the standard written examination, which Cassady had not taken, but when Cassady failed to arrive in New York for the appointed exam, he was quickly written off by university officials as an ingrate who was not serious about benefiting from the kind of education Columbia had to offer. It was a disappointing turn of events for Hal, who had gone to some lengths to secure Cassady the opportunity to attend the school and who correctly believed that Cassady was just the kind of character for Jack Kerouac to write about.

3

When Neal Cassady finally did arrive in New York City in December 1946, his sixteen-year-old wife, LuAnne, in tow, it was as a result of the type of cross-country journey that Kerouac would recount in *On the Road*, the book that made him (and Cassady) famous. Neal had left Denver in early December. He and LuAnne traveled to Nebraska, where they moved in with LuAnne's aunt and found jobs, Neal as a gas-station attendant, LuAnne as a maid. Neal, however, still wanted to go to New York, and before he and LuAnne had so much as the time to settle into their new environment, they were off to the big city, LuAnne stealing money from her aunt's strongbox to finance the trip, Neal "borrowing" her uncle's car to get them there. The car died out before they reached the Nebraska border, so they traveled the rest of the way by bus. They were tired and virtually out of money by the time they arrived in New York, but to Neal, who talked incessantly about his plans to study and write, the journey—the *motion*—was all that really mattered.

Neal Cassady's life itself was a study in motion, sped up and slowed down, never quite in sync with real time. Born on February 8, 1926, Cassady was a character not far removed from Dickens, the early victim of his father's broken dreams and alcoholism. He was born on the road, in a charity hospital in Salt Lake City, as his parents were making their way from Iowa to Hollywood, where Neal senior planned to open a barbershop. He did, but he had the tendency to drink for days on end, and his shop went under. The Cassadys moved to Denver in 1928, and four years later, Neal's parents broke up and Neal went off to live with his father in a series of skid-row flophouses. As an adult, Neal recalled being the only child among scores of losers, beggers, and drunks, "the sole replica of their own childhood to which their vision could daily turn." For a dollar a week, his father could share a room in a place like the Metropolitan, a condemned five-story building on the corner of Sixteenth and Market streets, his and his son's roommate being a double amputee named Shorty, who would go out begging by day and drink himself senseless at night. For a bed, the Cassadys shared a filthy mattress without sheets.

Neal was on his own almost from the beginning. In the morning, he would awaken to the pealings of a nearby bell tower and dress in old hand-me-downs from his half brothers, moving quietly in the cell so he would not awaken his father, who was usually in the process of sleeping off a drunk. He would eat breakfast at the Citizen's Mission, filling up on bread and oatmeal and sugary coffee before he walked to kindergarten, bouncing a tennis ball along the way. In no time, young Neal got to know the streets and alleys and shortcuts, as well as the unusual inhabitants along the mile-long stretch of deteriorating avenues between the Metropolitan and his school; and since it was the only life he knew, he enjoyed the company of the derelicts at the flophouse. He learned to improvise and make do with what little he had, his favorite toys being his tennis ball and a homemade dart constructed from a sewing needle stuck into a wooden match, complete with strips of newspaper for feathers.

On Saturdays, Neal accompanied his father to a nearby three-chair barbershop, where the elder Cassady would cut hair while Neal, taking in the sweet smell of talcum powder and hair pomades, read the newspapers and magazines lying around and waited for the movie house next door to open. Neal was revolted by the theater's pungent odor and clientele, but for a nickel he could sit by himself and escape into musicals or an endless number of Westerns, as well as occasional favorites such as *King Kong, The Invisible Man,* or *The Count of Monte Cristo.* By the time he was seven, Neal had learned to amuse himself for hours on end, whether he was alone in a movie house, sitting next to his father while Neal senior drank himself into a stupor, scouring the alleyways for trinkets that he would sell to bums or drug addicts, or skipping stones when he and his father took their Sunday forays to the South Platte River.

He further developed his mental resourcefulness when he was taken from his father by his older stepbrothers to live with his mother, the arrangement being that Neal would live with his mother during the school year and with his father during the summer months. If there was an element of Dickens to Neal's life with his father, the time he spent with his stepbrothers was a page right out of Poe, at least in terms of one frequently recurring event that took place over a stretch of a year's time. Neal's twelve-year-old half brother, Jimmy, a bully who took cruel pleasure in torturing cats or drowning them in toilets, would force seven-year-old Neal to lie on a wall bed, which he then pushed back into the wall. Entombed in the wall for hours, with less than a foot's clearance above him, Neal would lie in silence, afraid to call for help for fear of running out of air, or for fear of what he imagined might happen if Jimmy, rather than his mother, responded to his shouts. In his time alone in the darkness, Neal experienced a strange conjunction between his mental energy and his concept of time: In Cassady's mind, there was an incredible acceleration of image and thought, all rushing at him at alarming speed, overlapping with a dizzying effect. As Cassady described it in *The First Third,* his autobiography:

[I]t was simply an awareness that time, in my head, had gradually apexed to about triple its ordinary speed of passage, and while this thing was happening I thought of it as just a circular flying object twirling through my mind, for lack of a better way to think about this spinning sensation, but actually *felt* it (nervewise) for what it was— only a strangely pleasant, yet disturbing enough to frighten, quickening of my brain's action which resisted any rigorous attempt to throw it off and return to normal headedness. . . .

Cassady, who in years to come would be nicknamed "Speed Limit" and "Fastestmanalive," had somehow managed to experience a shifting in consciousness not unlike the hallucinatory shifts experienced by a person under the influence of LSD. Although it was not something he could control as a child— it happened, he recalled, "only while inside my mattressed jail, and then not every time"—as an adult he would be able to convert this into the incredibly quick mental loops and jumps for which he became known—the raps of free associations delivered at dazzling speed.

As he grew older, Neal became obsessed with two other preoccupations for which he would become well known: sex and driving. His first sexual experience occurred when he was nine, and from that point on there was no holding his libido in check. By the time he had reached his late teens, he had gained the reputation of being one of the greatest cocksmen in Denver. He could masturbate a half dozen times a day and still possess the will and drive to have sex with a woman on several other occasions on the same day.

He brought the same kind of energy to stealing cars, which he compared to an erotic experience. "The virgin emotion one builds when first stealing an auto—especially when one can hardly make it function properly, so takes full minutes to get away—is naturally strenuous on the nervous system, and I found it most exciting," he wrote, boasting that he stole his first car in 1940 and had stolen about five hundred cars by 1947. Like sex, which Cassady engaged in with no thought of commitment or morality, stealing cars was strictly for the adventure and sensual experience. Neal had no intention of keeping a stolen car or selling it whole or for parts; instead, he stole cars for joyrides, for their ability to keep him moving, even if aimlessly. More often than not, he would steal a car from a parking lot, drive it around for a few hours, and return it before its owner knew it was gone. He was not always so lucky, and by the time he traveled from Denver to New York in 1946, he had been arrested ten times, convicted six, and had served a little more than a year in jail.

Neal met Hal Chase through Justin Brierly, a civic leader, teacher, and Columbia alumnus who acted as mentor to a number of Denver students attending Columbia. Not surprisingly, the initial meeting between Brierly and Cassady was the result of one of Neal's sexual adventures. For some time, Neal had been having sex with an imbecile maid in exchange for meals, and one day Neal, stark naked, was confronted by the maid's employer, who was none other than Justin Brierly. The older man recognized in Neal a native intelligence and took him under his wing, trying to develop Neal's intellect further while he rehabilitated him. To Brierly, Cassady was a mass of contradictions, a fast-talking sexual psychopath/poolroom hustler/car thief/con man who, in contrast, had given himself an impressive self-education by sitting in the Denver library and reading through Schopenhauer, Nietzsche, Proust, Shakespeare, and Dostoyevski. Brierly felt that Neal could amount to something if supplied with some direction that would allow him to concentrate his physical and mental energy.

This, however, was not for Neal Cassady, who never could sit still for any notable period of time. In the summer of 1945, he walked into a drugstore, saw fifteen-year-old LuAnne Henderson sitting in a booth, and proceeded to sweep her off her feet.

"Neal was something to behold," LuAnne remarked. "I've never met anyone like him yet to this day. I doubt I ever will. Neal was a very, very unique individual. . . . Neal, when we first met, had a tremendous amount of ambition, which was why we went to New York."

4

Allen met Neal before Jack did, but for some reason, their initial encounter was far from memorable. Neal had heard about Allen from Hal Chase, who characterized Allen as "a terribly decadent intellectual," leaving Neal with the impression of Allen as "a young college Jew, whose amazing mind had the germ of decay in it and whose sterility had produced a blasé, yet fascinating mask," whose "soul had dried up into a mind which excreted verbalistic poetry, and his handmade sexlife had created a cynical, symbolic outlook toward all the confusion of life." Neal allowed that his impression, based only upon a twenty-minute conversation with Hal, was an abstraction, but he found himself thinking about Allen on and off in the months to come.

Shortly after Neal had arrived in New York, Hal began taking him on the rounds, introducing him to his friends. They ran into Allen at the West End. Allen was with friends and otherwise distracted, and he was stiffly formal when Hal introduced Neal and LuAnne, commenting only on LuAnne's unusual name and offering a suggestion as to where Neal might find a cheap place to live. Considering the impact that Neal would have on Allen's life, it was anything but a classic meeting.

With Jack Kerouac, it was an entirely different story. Kerouac was instantly drawn to Cassady. To Jack, Neal was like a long-lost brother. He was athletic, interested in many of the same books, even similar in appearance, though Neal was more wiry and had a fair complexion and lighter hair. In *On the Road*, Jack described him as "a young Gene Autry—trim, thin-hipped, blue-eyed, with a real Oklahoma accent—a sideburned hero of the snowy West." On the other hand, Neal possessed many qualities that Jack envied. He was not at all shy, constantly moving, bobbing up and down like a boxer when he talked or listened, interjecting "yass" and "that's right" into conversations until it became a personal trademark. He left the impression that he was totally at ease with who and what he was. On one occasion, he answered the door stark naked when Jack and Hal dropped by to visit. Neal was a con man, Jack felt, but in a sweetly innocent way. Unlike some of Jack's friends, who took an immediate disliking to the hustler qualities in Neal, Jack enjoyed the game, reveling in

Neal's enthusiasm rather than dismissing it as phony. "He was only conning because he wanted so much to live and to get involved with people who would otherwise pay no attention to him," Jack later remarked in Neal's defense. In almost every respect, Neal was the hero that Jack had been looking for, "a western kinsman of the sun."

On January 10, 1947, Allen again met Neal, but this time the encounter differed drastically from their meeting at the West End. Allen had stopped by the apartment of Vicki Russell, a friend he had met through Herbert Huncke and an occasional girlfriend of Kerouac's. While he was visiting her, Jack and Neal dropped by, Jack hoping to score some pot, which somehow, despite Cassady's worldly experiences, Neal had yet to try. On this occasion, Allen was not distracted and could devote all his attention to Neal, and Cassady, who enjoyed being the center of attention, could reciprocate. "Two keen minds that they are, they took to each other at the drop of a hat," Jack wrote of their meeting in On the Road. "Two piercing eyes glancing into two piercing eyes— the holy con-man with the shining mind, and the sorrowful poetic con-man with the dark mind. . . . Their energies met head-on."

Kerouac's account was not at all hyperbolic. Allen was physically and mentally attracted to Neal in a way that far surpassed mere infatuation. Allen sensed almost immediately that in Cassady there was the chance for a meaningful meeting of the minds. Allen also saw the similarities between Jack and Neal— both being, as he perceived them, "intelligent, sensitive jocks"—but unlike Kerouac, who was, by instinct and profession, an observer, Cassady was a man of action who appeared to be open to almost any experience. Allen was attracted to what he called the "pathos and fatality" in Neal. Like Allen, Neal had endured the troublesome aspects of his childhood and adolescence, but unlike Allen, who was given to extended periods of dark self-pity, Neal shrugged off the past and accepted it as so much history, even on those occasions when he felt twinges of guilt over his behavior. He preferred instead to live with enthusiasm in the present.

Although he was not as physically attracted to Allen as much as Ginsberg would have liked him to be, Cassady admired Allen's mind, finding him as much the somber intellectual as Hal Chase had made him out to be. Allen was barely more than a boy, yet he was already a strong mind among men, which Cassady envied. Despite all his reading and self-education, Neal felt intellectually inadequate among the Columbia intellectuals, and like a performer playing in front of a tough audience, Neal had to contend with his own self-doubts while at the same time trying to win over the skeptics. This was not the case with Allen. Intellectually the equal of those who were several years older than he and who, on occasion, would treat him like an annoying younger brother, Allen was prepared to accept Neal for the person he was, without judging his intelligence prejudiciously.

Allen remained discreet about his homosexuality. In Denver, Hal had told Neal about Allen's sexual preference, and though it did not seem to be an important issue to Neal, Allen didn't want to press it. Neal was a married man with a substantial heterosexual history, and despite being all but overwhelmed by Cassady's physical beauty, Allen could not harbor any realistic hopes of anything sexual developing out of their friendship.

However, later that same January evening, after hours of intimate conversation and a long walk with Jack and Neal, Allen found himself in bed with Cassady, under circumstances that had begun innocently enough. Neal was staying with a mutual friend of Allen's and Jack's, and by the time they had walked and talked their way back to the Spanish Harlem apartment where Neal was staying, it was late enough that neither Allen nor Jack wanted to venture back to their own respective places. After some discussion, they decided to stay overnight. There were only two beds in the apartment—a large double bed and a cot—and Jack shared the bed with their host, while Allen and Neal volunteered to sleep on the cot. Allen stripped to his shorts and lay in the darkness, frightened and ashamed, keeping his distance by huddling at the edge of the cot and hanging his arm and head over the edge. Sensing Allen's fear, Neal reached out to him and told him to draw near. As Allen recalled in "Many Loves," his 1956 poem detailing the evening:

> I began to tremble, he pulled me in closer with
>   his arm, and hugged me long and close
> my soul melted away, secrecy departed, I became
> Thenceforth open to his nature as a flower in
>   the shining sun.

For Allen, those moments in the darkness were too good to be true. With the exception of Jack, with whom his rare sexual experiences had been awkward and forced, with Jack acting more out of an extraordinarily tender friendship, Allen had not been able to enjoy his sexuality with any feeling of depth. He was, as he described himself years later, "a sensitive little kid, hiding, not able to touch anyone or speak my feelings out." Neal had accepted him with compassion, touching him not in disgust or out of any sense of obligation but because he had genuine feelings for Allen. In Allen's eyes, it was love accepted, love returned: "Thus I met Neal & thus we felt each other's flesh and owned each other bodies and soul."

As Allen noted years later, there was one negative element to the experience: By showing Neal how much he needed him sexually that first night, in showing his own uncertainty, weakness, and fear, Allen placed himself in a situation in which he could be easily dominated or manipulated. Neal had seen—*felt*—Allen's desperation, and given his marital status and heterosexual disposition, he was in the position to chart the course of their relationship in any fashion he chose.

Throughout his life, Allen would be sexually stimulated by scenarios in which he was either dominated or humiliated, many of those feelings finding their way into his poetry. An incident dating back to his childhood was recalled in " 'Drive All Blames into One' ":

> Last night I dreamt they blamed me again on the streetcorner
> They got me bent over with my pants down and
>   spanked my behind I was ashamed
> I was red faced my self was naked I got hot I had a hard on.

In another work written that same year (1976), actually no more than a pornographic recitation, he addressed the same theme of dominance:

> Spank me and Fuck me
> Got a hard on Spank me
> When you get a hard on Fuck me.

Both poems reflected the statements made in Ginsberg's controversial list poem, "Please Master" (1968), an elegy to Neal Cassady that detailed Ginsberg's feelings about their master/servant relationship:

> Please master call me a dog, an ass beast, a wet asshole,
> & fuck me more violent, my eyes hid with your palms
>   round my skull
> & plunge down in a brutal hard lash thru soft drip-flesh
> & throb thru five seconds to spurt out your semen heat
> over & over, bamming it in while I cry out your name I do
>   love you
> please Master.

The exhibitionistic qualities to these and other Ginsberg poems, shocking to many readers because of their graphic frankness and revolting to critics who ascribed to a mannered approach to poetry, held several important functions for Ginsberg. As a poet, Ginsberg remained consistent in his belief that erotic— or even pornographic—art was both valuable and liberating; by being willing to expose one's innermost secret longings, fantasies, and practices, the artist was opening an avenue in which others could feel comfortable with their own similar feelings. The artist was therefore extending an invitation for people to accept their own bodies and minds. Ginsberg was especially attuned to this idea in the 1960s and 1970s when, as one of the leaders in the gay liberation movement, he was confronted with the gamut of ideas of how sexual freedom might be politically achieved. The factions were widely divided, ranging from those who took a passive, tender approach to those who took a more militant stance. Ginsberg's poetry reflected the differences.

None of this occurred to Ginsberg at the time of his initial encounter with Neal, however. He had no choice but to accept Cassady's terms for the relationship. He was forced to conform to Neal's sexual approach or face the prospect of no sex at all. Cassady took an aggressive (and occasionally sadistic) approach to lovemaking, regardless of whether he was with a man or a woman.

Allen and Neal began to see a lot of each other, though, for Allen, their get-togethers were a mixed blessing. From the beginning, Allen had the feeling that his affair with Neal was doomed, but he was engaged in a mighty battle between mind and heart. No sooner would he conclude one of his romantic liaisons with Cassady than he started to express feelings of regret or self-pity about the hopelessness of their relationship. On January 21, less than two weeks after they had spent their first night together, Allen noted in his journal that he had "spent a wild weekend in sexual drama with Cassady," but rather than express exhilaration from the experience, Allen wrote that he felt "washed up on the shore of my 'despair' again," depressed to know that his pleasure with Neal only served as a reminder that, as a general rule, he was closed off from Cassady's world. Allen understood full well that if Neal was forced to choose between having sex with women or men, there was no question about which gender he preferred. Nevertheless, Allen was enjoying good sex for the first time in his life, and despite the complaints recorded in his journal, he had no intention of putting a stop to the season he was having with Neal.

If anyone had reason to complain, it was Cassady's wife. When they had first arrived in New York, Neal had given LuAnne quite a bit of attention, taking her around the city and showing her the sights. Shortly after their arrival, however, Neal had taken a cheap room in nearby Bayonne, New Jersey, and a job parking cars in Manhattan, and LuAnne saw less and less of him, even though they got along well when he was around. Now, with Allen in the picture, Neal's attention was even more divided.

Kerouac, too, was envious of the time Allen spent with Neal. Jack had just grown accustomed to seeing Neal on a regular basis when all of a sudden Allen was elbowing his way in on their time together. Allen's interference irritated him, as he wrote later in *On the Road*: "Wanting dearly to learn how to write like [Allen], the first thing you knew, [Neal] was attacking him with a great amorous soul such as only a con-man can have. . . . I didn't see them for about two weeks, during which time they cemented their relationship to fiendish allday-allnight-talk proportions."

With Neal scheduled to leave for Denver on March 4, Allen was, in essence, trying to compress an entire love affair into the span of a couple of months, and, in a way, he succeeded. There was an initial period during which everything was fresh, when they would literally spend hours staring into each other's eyes and share the secrets of their souls. Then there was a brief period during which they had grown used to each other and were looking for ways to maintain the initial spark of their relationship. In one journal entry from this time, Allen listed all the sexual positions he wanted to try with Neal. Finally, there was the period in which Allen questioned whether he wanted to continue the relationship at all. From their talks, their similarities were clear to Allen, but so, too, were their differences. Allen realized that he and Neal were worlds apart in many ways, and by the time Neal was preparing to return to Denver, Allen could only speculate about the durability of their affair:

> I think he *does* no longer excite me, I've almost used him up in a way, learned as much as I can, to no end, except final loss of feeling and love, and want no more of him. But of course I do want more of him . . . perhaps we will be most penetrated with grief for each other when we are apart.

Neal's departure date finally rolled around, and Allen and Jack accompanied him to the Thirty-fourth Street Greyhound station. The previous evening, Allen and Jack had resolved their differences and jealousies regarding their respective relationships with Neal, and at the bus station, the three were friendly and relaxed, although nostalgic and slightly sad. Allen and Neal had agreed to meet in Denver as soon as Allen had completed his term at Columbia, and Jack vowed that he would make a similar trip, possibly later in the spring. The three found a photo booth, where for a quarter they had their pictures taken, Allen removing his glasses for his, striking Jack as "the hornrimmed wild hip kid type you see everywhere," Neal looking dapper in his new western-cut suit. Jack joked that his own photo made him look "like a thirty-year-old Italian who'd kill anybody who said anything against his mother." Allen and Neal cut the group photo into pieces with a razor blade, Allen putting the picture of Neal in his wallet, Neal keeping the photo of Allen. When Neal's bus pulled in, with CHICAGO posted as its destination, Jack was hit by the reality of Neal's departure and the distance that would separate them, bemoaning the fact that he had "never been west of Jersey." They said their good-byes and the bus pulled away. "No tears, some melancholy," Allen wrote in his journal after he had walked back to his apartment, but his words were anything but convincing. He missed Neal almost as soon as he was out of sight.

5

For the next three months, Allen and Neal corresponded regularly, making plans for Allen's trip to Denver, gossiping, discussing in great detail the nature of their relationship, and considering the future. The tone of their correspondence was largely reliant upon Allen's moods. Once again, Allen felt abandoned by someone he loved, and, as in the case of his mother, the reasons for his being abandoned involved factors beyond his control. As a teenager, he had suffered the futility of trying to shout reason at his mother when there was no chance of her grasping it, and now, as a young adult, he was attempting to alter Neal Cassady's sexuality, a task destined to be similarly futile. In his letters to Cassady, Allen tried to convince Neal that there was a "sacramental" quality to their sexual relationship; sex was the sacrament that celebrated their kinship of mind and spirit. Neal, eager to please and still in awe of Allen's intellect, tried to play along by sending placating letters in which he claimed to understand and agree with Allen's position. Neal loved Allen, though not in the sexual way that Allen would have preferred, and the more aggressive Allen became in his letters, the more defensive Neal became in his replies. He wasn't homosexual, he told Ginsberg, and by pretending that he enjoyed this kind of sexual relationship, he was being dishonest with him:

> I *really don't* know how much I can be satisfied to love you, I mean bodily, you know I, somehow, disliked pricks & men & before you, had consciously forced myself to be homosexual, now, I'm not sure whether with you I was not just forceing [sic] myself unconsciously, that is to say, any falsity on my part was all physical, in fact, any disturbances in our affair was because of this. You meant so much to me, I now feel I [was] forcing a desire for you bodily as a compansation [sic] to you for all you were giving me. This is a sad state and upsets me for I want to become nearer to you than any one & still I don't

want to be unconsciously insincere by passing over my non-queerness
to please you.

Understandably enough, Allen found this statement unacceptable, just as
he could not agree with Neal's suggestion that in the fall they find a New York
apartment together and live with a woman. Neal and LuAnne had separated,
though Neal continued to see her (along with a number of other Denver
women), but Neal was convinced that it was impossible for him to live an
exclusively homosexual life. The way Neal saw it, he could live with Allen in
a scenario similar to the one Allen had witnessed with Bill and Joan, in which
sex might or might not be a factor but in which they could attain "psychological
oneness" and still pursue their individual lives. To this suggestion, Allen sent
back an angry reply, calling Neal a "dirty, double crossing, faithless bitch," yet
in the same letter, Allen urged Neal to be true to himself and not change his
emotions to accommodate him. Allen's sense of betrayal was heartfelt: In New
York, Neal had given him one impression of where their relationship stood,
but now that he was back in Denver, geographically removed from Allen and
resuming his active sex life with women, he was taking a slightly different
approach, leading Allen to believe that he was either teasing or conning him.
In one letter, Neal would tell Allen, "I need you now more than ever," giving
Allen a sense of security, and then, only a short time later, he would make
it very clear that he was put off by Allen's sexual overtures. Allen wanted
commitment, while Neal was looking for compromise. "I know I'm bisexual,
but prefer women," Neal wrote, trying to mollify Allen by adding that "there's
a slimmer line than you think between my attitude toward love and yours, don't
be concerned, it'll fall into line." Allen was indeed concerned, noting in his
journal that he was in a state of "sexual stasis again." That feeling could only
have been reinforced when Neal wrote just before Allen left for Denver, telling
him about "a wonderful girl" he was pursuing, a woman who left him with "a
sense of peace."

Nevertheless, Allen continued to plan his trip to Denver, his main concern
being a way to finance it. His money worries were partially resolved when
"Death in Violence" was awarded the George Edward Woodbury poetry prize
at Columbia, bringing him one hundred dollars for his journey. And when
Justin Brierly made one of his periodic trips to New York that spring, Allen
met with him and came away with a job offer at Denver's Central City Opera
festival. There were no guarantees that his trip would bring him satisfaction,
but Allen tried to stay optimistic as he made plans for it.

6

In June, Allen boarded a Greyhound bus and took the long trip to Denver.
True to his word, Neal met him at the station and drove him back to the
Colburn Hotel, where he introduced Allen to Carolyn Robinson, the latest
love in his life. A bright, attractive young woman who had been raised in a
wealthy Nashville family, Carolyn had studied at Bennington and was now

enrolled in the MFA program at the University of Denver, where she also earned some money by working as a teacher's assistant. Neal had described her to Allen as "a bit too straight for my temperament," meaning that she was, by his standards, too conventional in and out of bed, but he also praised her as someone who "knows all about the Theatre, draws a fine line, and is quite popular." With her cultured background, this blond and trim woman presented a challenge to both Neal and Allen.

Neal and Carolyn were staying together in one room in the hotel, and Neal had reserved another for Allen. He had told Carolyn very little about Allen, other then to mention that he was a Columbia student, poet, and quite brilliant; for obvious reasons, he had said nothing about his and Allen's sexual relationship. In fact, Neal had copied some of Allen's love poems and letters and presented them to Carolyn as if he had written them himself. As far as Carolyn knew, Allen was in Denver to visit and help Neal with his writing. "I was under the impression that he and Neal had known each other for years, not months, nor was I aware of the nature of their relationship or of Allen's love," Carolyn remembered.

At first, Carolyn had reservations about staying with a man who was still legally married, and she had put off Neal's initial sexual overtures, but she finally relented when she realized that she was falling in love with him, and when Neal managed to convince her that he was getting a divorce from Lu-Anne. This last bit of deception was pure Cassady. He and LuAnne were indeed getting divorced, but they had not ceased sleeping together, and Neal continued to see her on a regular basis.

Without immediate employment, Allen quickly ran out of money and soon had to give up his private room and move in with Neal and Carolyn, with disastrous results. With no knowledge of Neal and Allen's history, Carolyn could not understand the tension she felt with Allen; she had no way of knowing that he was lying on the couch in misery every night, listening, as he later described it, as Neal "climbed with Carolyn into her double bed and kissed and sucked and cocked and sweated and came to her sighing and crying all night— as I lay there jealous heart sick & crying trembling alone listening to loves' noises." He had arrived in Denver in a state of cautious optimism, yet his early experiences were, as he recorded in his journal, of "such terrible nights" that he began referring to his stay as his "Denver Doldrums."

Allen attempted to fit in and present himself in as cheerful an air as he could, given the circumstances. He helped Neal and Carolyn with some of the household chores, and when Carolyn was assigned an oral report for one of her classes, he assisted in organizing her notes and helping her prepare for her speech, resulting in Carolyn's delivering the best report of the class that term. Allen, Neal, and Carolyn frequented a nearby café, drinking coffee and talking for hours at a time, although Allen occasionally embarrassed Carolyn by his antics and by talking or laughing too loudly. One afternoon, Carolyn suggested that Allen read them his poetry while she drew a sketch of Neal. Both men liked the idea, though they countered that it should be a full-figure drawing of Neal in the nude. Although she was shocked by the idea, Carolyn spent hours on the drawing, Neal posing "much like a Greek statue, one knee flexed, the hip dropped, but with a twinkle in his eye" while Allen watched.

With Neal's help, Allen was able to secure a job with the May Company department store. Neal had a day job driving a station wagon for the company, shuttling its customers from the store to a nearby parking lot. Allen worked the third shift, earning twenty-eight dollars a week by vacuuming the store's second floor. As soon as he could afford it, he moved from the hotel to a damp basement apartment on Grant Street, which he rented for twenty dollars a month. To complete the lonely garret existence he felt as a poet and person, he furnished the apartment with a bed, table, chair, and candle. There, absorbed by self-pity to the point of despair, he wrote long journal passages analyzing himself and Neal, as if he might better understand the nature of their relationship by verbalizing it.

As an artist, he felt stifled. He complained, as he had in other journal entries, that his prose was no good and that his poems were as dreary and colorless as his life. He worked on the revisions of a sequence of poems entitled "Denver Doldrums," which were essentially written in one day after a particularly depressing, Benzedrine-fueled conversation with Neal. The "Denver Doldrums" were relentlessly depressing, bogged down by self-absorption and repressed images. As Ginsberg described the work, "the unity of the poem is intended to be the various metamorphoses of the single mood of doldrums, or irresolution & desperation," and in this regard, he succeeded. As poetry, the sequence was dismal, however, lacking even in the technical control he had displayed in earlier works. He was not entirely correct in his assessment of his writing abilities at the time. His formal attempts, such as "Denver Doldrums" and "Birthday Ode" (the latter a long poem written in commemoration of the birth of Bill and Joan's son), were well thought out but inadequately written, filled with the trite symbols that he had been using since he had begun writing poetry. However, as he would learn a few years later, he had a fine poet's eye and mind when he was not trying to force his poetry. His eye for detail, filtered through his poetic sensibilities, resulted in one early success, a journal notation written in Denver while he was waiting for Neal to come to his apartment, which later, under the encouragement and influence of William Carlos Williams, became "The Bricklayer's Lunch Hour," the first poem written in the objective style he would use for the rest of his life. It began with clear, vivid description:

> Two bricklayers are setting the walls
> of a cellar in a new dug out patch
> of dirt behind an old house of wood
> with brown gables grown over with ivy
> on a shady street in Denver. . . .

"The Bricklayer's Lunch Hour" was a happy accident, as Ginsberg had no intention of writing poetry when he jotted his descriptive passage into his notebook. By not being conscious of creating art, Ginsberg was not hindered by form: It was "just sort of like looking out of the window—sketching . . . actually, I got it off Kerouac, the idea of making a verbal picture. Like making a little pencil sketch. . . . A little shiver of eternal space, that's what I was looking for. Simply by looking outside of the window and seeing what was there. That is probably the earliest text I published which makes real sense."

Allen felt intense competition with Neal's women, and he was the only one who knew of Neal's method of trying to satisfy all of his lovers. Somehow, by working out an elaborate scheme, Neal was able to spend most of his available daytime and early-evening hours with Carolyn, his late-evening hours with LuAnne, and then return to Carolyn at the hotel, only to leave around six in the morning, when he would meet Allen, just out of work, and engage in long conversations and occasional sex at Allen's apartment. Unfortunately for Allen, Neal was being sexually satisfied by Carolyn and LuAnne, and he usually resisted Allen's advances. At times, he would avoid Allen completely, staying away for days on end, leaving Allen depressed and anxious.

Further cutting into Allen's time with Neal was the arrival of Jack Kerouac. Jack was on his first big road excursion, working his way cross-country from New York to San Francisco, where he intended to hook up with a friend and work for a while as an electrician on a ship before returning home. As soon as he arrived in Denver, Kerouac contacted Hal Chase, who had graduated from Columbia and was working at the Denver Art Museum. If Jack had hoped for a reunion of the New York–Denver connection, he was quickly enlightened on that score: Neither Hal, Ed White (who was also back in Denver), nor any of their friends wanted to have much to do with Neal Cassady or, for that matter, Allen Ginsberg. Their college days at Columbia were behind them and they were now busy trying to establish respectable adult lives. Only Hal had any understanding of what Jack found appealing about Neal, and virtually all of them regarded Neal as little more than a con artist. Throughout his life, Jack tried to find a balance between his love for "the mad ones, the ones who are mad to live, mad to talk, mad to be saved" and his other yearning to live a more conventional American life, such as the one exemplified by his parents. Early on in his ten-day stay in Denver, he found himself in the position of having to choose, at least temporarily, between friends. He chose Neal and Allen.

Carolyn was immediately impressed by Jack, finding his "good looks and shy, gentle nature . . . comforting and attractive," though she was troubled by his rootlessness, as she was by that same quality in Allen and Neal. Jack was warm, considerate, a great conversationalist, and, to Carolyn's delight, a good dancer. She, Jack, and Neal spent many hours together, Carolyn marveling at Jack's and Neal's animated discussions, feeling slightly guilty when she realized that she was attracted to Jack, and, for the first time since she had met Neal, feeling "the slightest doubt about [her] dedication to Neal." The attraction was mutual. Once, while they were dancing, Jack whispered to Carolyn, "It's too bad, but that's how it is—Neal saw you first."

Allen saw Kerouac a number of times, with or without Neal, while Jack was in Denver, but it was soon evident to everyone that another "season" was drawing to a close. Jack was due in San Francisco. Carolyn, whose job at the university had ended in early August, was planning to catch a ride with friends to Los Angeles, where she hoped to find a job designing costumes in Hollywood. Allen would soon be starting classes at Columbia. Neal had announced that he intended to marry Carolyn as soon as his divorce from LuAnne was final. Once again, individual plans were pulling the group apart.

Allen had hoped to visit Bill Burroughs in Texas on his way back to New

York, and in a last-ditch effort to get Neal alone, Allen suggested that Neal accompany him. Neal had wanted to meet Burroughs ever since he'd heard Allen and Jack talk about him, and he was excited about the prospect of seeing him, but Carolyn, who hoped that Neal would follow her west and marry her, was less than enthusiastic about the plan. In his usual persuasive manner, Neal explained to Carolyn that he felt guilty about ignoring Allen for so much of his visit to Denver. He told Carolyn that Allen was homosexual and in love with him, but he flatly denied ever having had sex with Allen.

Carolyn learned otherwise, in a shocking way, the day she was to leave for Los Angeles. She had been involved in a play at the university for the last week, and rather than return to the hotel room at the end of the day, she had been staying with a friend on campus. Shortly before she was to depart for California, she stopped by the hotel to surprise Neal and say her good-byes, but when she opened the door to their room, she was stunned by the sight of Neal lying in her bed, Allen and LuAnne on either side of him, all three naked. She didn't bother to wait for an explanation. She left for California, vowing that she would never see or sleep with him again.

7

Allen was in good spirits when he arrived at Bill Burroughs's farm on August 29, confident that he would enjoy "a happy holiday of God given sexuality" with Neal. Their hitchhiking journey from Denver to New Waverly, Texas, had been grueling. With rides coming few and far between, they had plenty of time to talk, and Allen believed that he and Neal had experienced a renewal in the seriousness of their relationship along the way. On one occasion, while they were in Oklahoma, literally caught at a desolate crossroads at sundown, Allen had convinced Neal to exchange vows with him. Kneeling in the center of the crossroads, Allen promised to teach Neal everything he knew; in exchange, Neal vowed to educate Allen in sexual and practical matters. Allen perceived their exchange of vows as a spiritual union. If they shared their strongest qualities, they would both be redeemed. Each needed what the other had to offer. "He accepted it all," Allen wrote of Neal. From Allen's standpoint, Neal was "just a poor lost soul, an orphan in fact, looking for a father seraph and I was looking for a seraphic boy." Allen explained to Neal that their union did not have to be physical, although he was certainly hoping for that by the time they made it to New Waverly.

He was therefore disappointed and angered to find that there was no bed awaiting them when they arrived at Burroughs's ranch. Not that Allen should have been surprised, given Bill's state at the time. For his misdemeanor drug conviction the previous year, Bill had been given a four-month suspended sentence and sent back to St. Louis, presumably to be under the supervision of his parents. He had hooked up with Kells Elvins, his Harvard friend and collaborator on "Twilight's Last Gleaming," and together they had decided to go into business. They had bought a ten-acre citrus grove in Pharr, Texas, located in western Texas's rich Rio Grande valley. Bill was also able to persuade his parents to loan him money for an additional fifty acres of cotton land. Since neither Elvins nor Burroughs knew anything about farming, they hired local laborers to do the work and were content to play the roles of land barons. However, Bill Burroughs found farming to be unstable, far too dependent upon such factors as consumer demand and the weather, and he soon grew bored with the business.

He was also concerned about Joan. Allen had written with the news of Joan's admission to the Bellevue psychiatric ward. Joan's father had custody of Joan's daughter, Julie, but Joan, with no money and a Benzedrine habit, was in a bad way. Bill traveled to New York to get her. Once back in Texas, Bill left his cotton fields to the care of Kells Elvins and bought a run-down farm in New Waverly, a tiny rural town about fifty miles north of Houston. The location was ideal, isolated from nosy neighbors yet near a large city and its drug supply. The farm itself was a ninety-seven-acre spread in bayou country, complete with groves of oak trees and Spanish moss. It was virtually useless for farming but fertile for growing marijuana, which Bill decided to plant as a cash crop. Not long after he moved in, Bill wrote Herbert Huncke and invited him to live with them. Huncke joined them in midwinter 1946 and made himself useful by helping with repairs, playing with Julie (whom Bill had picked up at Christmastime), and, perhaps most important of all as far as Bill and Joan were concerned, making occasional forays into Houston or other nearby cities for Benzedrine inhalers, morphine, and other drugs.

Life in New Waverly was sedate. Bill's property in Pharr provided him with a decent base income, and since he was not overly ambitious to begin with, he was able to sit back and enjoy life without the bother of burdening obligations. He would sit on the porch and read the newspapers he picked up in town, listening to Viennese waltzes playing on an old phonograph, or he might wander around his property, taking with him a gun for target practice. Other than correspondence, he was not writing. When Allen and Neal showed up, they were greeted by a rather unusual country family: Bill, Joan, Huncke, Julie, and William Burroughs, Jr., the latest edition, who had been born only a few months earlier.

Huncke, sensitive to Allen's needs and always helpful in small ways when he was someone's guest, was busy at work on a makeshift bed for Allen and Neal when they arrived. Huncke was going to let them use his room while they were visiting, but since his bed was too small for two people, he tried to construct a larger one from extra sideboards and two army cots. Allen tried to help, but neither Bill nor Neal would get involved. Neal felt that Huncke was being "very queer about the whole thing," and Huncke grew irritated by what he perceived to be "a lot of meanings read into my efforts that were simply not true." The bed was a miserable failure, sagging in the middle where the two sides met and ultimately collapsing when Allen and Neal tried to use it. Neal was able to find some humor in the situation, but Allen was crushed.

If anything, the incident was symbolic of the way Allen and Neal's relationship had deteriorated, Allen always trying to patch things up and keep them going, Neal a reluctant participant. In a sense, Allen's hopes fell apart with the bed, and two days after his arrival in Texas, he had written off his chances of sustaining any long-term affair with Cassady. "The sacramental honeymoon is over," he wrote in his journal on September 1, now resigned to the reality of Neal's claims that he was not sexually interested in him. "I had imagined myself in a sweet love relationship or the emergence of one—all by my faith and will. . . . He might have been more explicit but so what, what would I have done with such explicitness anyway. It's all now a drag to worry about."

For Allen, it was a very difficult conclusion to draw. To experience such rejection at a time when he was deeply exploring his love and sexuality for the first time was almost unbearably painful. Neal still felt that they should live together, but the thought of returning to New York with Neal was not especially appealing to Allen if there were to be no prospects of sexual fulfillment. What he needed was to get away, be off by himself, and work out of his doldrums, and he decided that the best way to accomplish that, as well as to earn some badly needed money, would be for him to find work on a ship that was going from Houston to New York. Feeling badly about the way things had turned out, Neal offered to accompany Allen to Houston, where they would spend one last night together.

Rather than being an evening of tender farewells, the night turned out to be a fiasco of almost surreal proportions. On September 3, Neal drove Allen and Huncke in Bill's jeep to the Brazos Hotel in Houston, which Huncke was familiar with from his previous trips to the city. After Allen went to the local Maritime Union Hall and secured a job as a messman on a ship going not to New York but to Marseilles, the three spent the early part of the evening in area jazz clubs. They then split up, Huncke hitting the streets in search of drug connections, Allen and Neal going back to their reserved hotel suite. As Neal later told Jack, he had reached the point where the thought of Allen's so much as touching him was more than he could tolerate, so they had no sooner returned to the hotel when Neal decided to go out again, leaving Allen waiting anxiously for him in the room. Driving around the area in search of a woman, Neal took some Nembutal, and by the time he found his date for the evening, a teenager just out of a mental institution, the drugs had taken effect and he was barely able to navigate the jeep back to the hotel. The young woman managed to get Neal to Allen's room, but it was apparent that Neal was in no condition to be of any use to either Allen or the girl. Infuriated, Allen protested that Neal was supposed to be spending the evening with him, that he had deceived him once again. Neal made separate, pitiful attempts to engage in sex with Allen and the girl, but he passed out before he was able to satisfy either. For Allen, it was another humiliating experience, further proof that it was time for him to forget Neal Cassady and move on with his life.

8

The next day, Allen found a ship embarking for Dakar. Due to his liaison with Cassady the night before, he missed the ship he originally had intended to sign up on, but the trip on the SS *John Blais* suited him well, even if working on it meant his missing the first term at Columbia. "My motives for shipping out are spiritual, to be sure (I'm tired of everybody) but are predominately practical, for financial reasons," he wrote his father, explaining that he needed more money to support himself than his allotted fifteen dollars' weekly allowance.

He also told Louis that he wanted to be psychoanalyzed before he returned to school, which would require additional money. He tried to reassure his father that he still intended to get his college degree and asked him not to worry about him. "I am aware of your consciousness & your anxieties about me, and have anxieties about myself equal & much greater," Allen told Louis, "so you must trust me to work things out."

The trip, his first outside of the United States, promised him precisely that opportunity. He would have time to consider and sort out his affairs, as well as to read and write. Although he complained about his writing in his journal, he had reason to be encouraged. Beside winning the Woodbury prize for "Death in Violence," Allen had also been awarded Columbia's Philolexian contest's second prize for "A Lover's Garden," which had been published in the *Columbia Review* in May.

His "onerous job," as he described his messman duties to Louis, might have been a less than ideal solution to his complex problems, but there is little question that his writing took an upward swing while he was gone. He struck a balance between prose and poetry, keeping his journal and writing "Dakar Doldrums," a sequence of poems similar in structure to his "Denver Doldrums." As Allen wrote in his notes, the "Dakar Doldrums" followed "the same process of continuous thought in development of 'decision' or the development & metamorphoses of mood . . . only here the time is twenty days that passed aboard a ship to Dakar."

The additional time that he devoted to the composition of the poem seemed to work better for Ginsberg in this latest series of "doldrums." Detailing mood in a lengthy sequence of poems compressed into a single day's composition ("Denver Doldrums") resulted not only in repetitious introspection, but in a cramped style, as well. In "Dakar Doldrums," one gets a stronger sense of the evolution of the poet's mood, with each poem in the sequence, obviously written in a separate sitting, displaying subtle shifts in movement. At the beginning of the poem, the poet's sense of loss is immediate, as fresh as Ginsberg's recent separation from Cassady; by the end of the sequence, Ginsberg is still grieving lost love, but his mood is tempered by a sense of resolve. He has crossed an ocean, moved from a familiar to an unfamiliar continent. His future is uncertain, but he is willing to face it with an open mind and heart, "with no promises and no prophecy"; he is ready to create his own destiny, even if, in his depressed state, his future looks unpromising.

"Dakar Doldrums" may have been more successful than "Denver Doldrums" because Allen was geographically removed from the source of his sorrow. The earlier poem lacks resolve, possibly because Cassady's presence still offered Ginsberg faint hope for renewal of his relationship; in the later poem, Ginsberg had to address the reality of his life.

By all indications, Allen's trip to Dakar was mostly a pleasant one. After their arrival in port, Allen was able to hire local laborers to do such duties as washing cookware and peeling potatoes, leaving him with an abundance of free time. He would lie on his bunk, reading Henry James (*Daisy Miller, The Wings of the Dove,* and *International Episodes*), or he would go sightseeing in Dakar. Much of what he saw, he wrote Herbert Huncke, reminded him of rural Texas. Market prices were low. To Allen's delight, marijuana could be purchased for a penny a joint, and it was never in short supply. Unfortunately, finding sexual gratification was an entirely different matter. For days, Allen tried to scout out local prospects, to no avail. "Sex is nowhere here," he complained to Huncke, but for the most part he was kept busy enough that it was not a major issue.

9

When he returned to New York, Allen was disappointed to learn that he had missed seeing Neal Cassady by only a couple of days. After Allen had left for Africa, Neal had hung around Texas, getting on both Burroughs's and Huncke's nerves. He was tolerated because Bill needed someone to help him transport his newly harvested marijuana crop to New York, and when it came to driving, Neal was as tireless as he was with sex. They made the trip to New York in three days, Huncke wedged in the backseat of the jeep between sacks of pot, Neal chattering nonstop behind the wheel, but when they arrived in the city, Neal had no place to stay for any extended period of time. He waited for word from Ginsberg, but when Allen failed to arrive, Neal left for California, leaving Allen a note saying that he was marrying Carolyn. When he read the note, Allen was again struck by the painful finality of his separation from Neal, and with this realization, Allen's already gloomy mood sunk into the bathetic. "Remember me well if you will remember me," he wrote Neal in melodramatic reply to his note.

At this point, Allen was a captive of his self, teetering at the edge of his own Baudelairean pit; he was as self-absorbed and self-pitying as he would ever be, and he seemed willing to risk everything, including any of his remaining self-respect, to continue his relationship with Cassady. When Neal sent him a patronizing response to his letter, Allen all but accused him of being cruel and insincere, yet instead of looking at Neal's letter for what it was—an attempt to reiterate his position without further hurting Allen's feelings—Allen used it as a springboard for two lengthy letters that found him groveling once again at Cassady's feet. "What must I do for you to get you back?" he asked Neal. "I will do anything. Any indecencies any revelations any creation, any miseries, will they please you. Or will they frighten you as this does?" Even as he wrote the letter, Allen recognized his pitiful tone, but he was compelled to send it, anyway. "There was something in the letter I wanted you to know, which perhaps you do know anyway," he wrote to Neal in his follow-up letter, "that I could not in part of mind, or on one complete level, accept the rupture." Rather than drag out the dialogue through the mails, Neal remained silent.

Allen was genuinely worried for his sanity. "I think my mind is crumbling, just like crackers," he confessed to Jack. He told Kerouac that he was having visions, but Jack was skeptical. Jack was also appalled by Allen's sexual obsessions, which he thought were "obnoxious." Allen had been frequenting the gay bars in Manhattan, and he seemed to delight in shocking Jack with accounts of his exploits or with explanations of the seedier aspects of his mind. "If you really want to know my true nature, I am at the moment one of those people who goes around showing his cock to juvenile delinquents," Allen told Jack.

From his life with his mother, Allen knew of the horror of insanity, and it was focused in his mind even more clearly when, on November 14, he received a letter from the director of Pilgrim State Hospital, where Naomi was now living. According to the doctor, Naomi's paranoia had reached such a state that she was now in danger of harming herself. Her blood pressure had risen to such a level that she was in danger of suffering a stroke, and she was so agitated that she would often bang her head against the wall. The doctor recommended that she receive a prefrontal lobotomy, and since Louis and Naomi Ginsberg were legally divorced, it was up to Allen or Eugene to sign the documents granting the hospital permission to perform the surgery. Although he had reservations that would haunt him for decades to come, Allen signed the papers.

10

Naomi Ginsberg's mental decline had been a painfully slow process, taking nearly thirty years, from her initial nervous breakdown to her recent admission to the mental hospital. There had been periods when she was relatively lucid and capable of working, taking care of her family, and otherwise functioning in society, but in recent years it had become apparent to her family that her condition was in a steady and irreversible decline. Her behavior was unruly, and there was no reasoning with her.

When Eugene had moved out of the apartment they were sharing, Naomi had moved to the Bronx to live with her sister, Elanor, and for a while, it looked as if the arrangement might work out. As Allen recalled in "Kaddish," Naomi attended painting classes at the adult high school, filling canvases with depictions of

> Humans sitting on the grass in some Camp No-Worry
> summers yore—saints with droopy faces and long-ill-fitting
> pants, from hospital—
> Brides in front of Lower East Side with short grooms—
> lost El trains running over the Babylonnian apartment rooftops
> in the Bronx. . . .

Before long, however, her paranoia began to surface again, with more violent consequences than in the past. She became convinced that Elanor was part of the conspiracy that already included Louis, his mother, Roosevelt, Hitler, Franco, and others—all trying to destroy her because she was a good woman, "a beautiful soul." She argued with Elanor, accusing her of trying to poison her. Believing Elanor was receiving her instructions from spies speaking to her from a radio, Naomi played the radio at six in the morning and listened for hidden messages. Elanor had a rheumatic heart and could ill afford the constant strain of Naomi's ravings, so after Naomi had kicked her during some of their arguments, it was decided that it would be better for everyone if Naomi stayed with her cousins Max and Edie Frohman, who lived in the same apartment building.

That arrangement also failed. Even though she had known Edie and Max when they were all living in the Soviet Union, Naomi was too lost in her paranoia to trust them; as far as she was concerned, everyone she knew was part of the conspiracy. Buba was "the head of a spider network," Edie was "a spy and Elanor a rat." Edie worked as a union organizer, and when she came home exhausted at the end of her workday, she would have to listen to Naomi go on about how the government had planted three wires in her back and was sending her horrible propagandistic messages through the wires. When Naomi became an impossible burden, Allen was asked to intervene.

At the time of the request, Allen was going through psychological turmoil of his own and was not inclined to confront the irrational. He had reached the conclusion that his "main psychic difficulty" was the result of what he called "the usual oedipal entanglement," his homosexuality at the root of his depression and feelings of guilt; his unhappy affair with Neal Cassady seemed to underscore the idea. Allen had spent months trying to sort out all the factors in his problem, looking for reasons or explanations, taking a rather scientific approach to his self-analysis. No matter how he summed up his psychological state, Naomi was part of the equation. She was his first model for unconventional behavior and "wild wisdom"; in her sad attempts to seduce him, and because of her nudism around the house, she had confused him sexually.

When he confronted her at Edie's apartment, it was with the same feelings of sorrow, rage, frustration, and despair that he felt for himself, as if by shouting reason at Naomi, he might instill it in himself. Backing her up against a door and shouting in her face, Allen tried desperately to bring Naomi back to reality, refuting her paranoid claims of conspiracies against her, demanding that she quit kicking Elanor and Edie. If she hoped to stay in the apartment and out of a mental institution, he warned her, she would have to be quiet and live by Edie and Max's rules. Even as he physically struggled with her, Allen repeatedly told Naomi that he loved her, begging her to see him for who he was, "your dear, your son, your second!" His pleading was futile. Naomi was caught in "the gamut of Hallucinations—for real—her own universe"; she stared at Allen in contempt, incredulous that he could be "so naïve, so dumb."

He was left with little recourse but to call the authorities—an irony that did not escape him in later years. Feeling betrayed, Naomi retreated to the bathroom and prepared herself for her fate, "looking in the mirror to see if the Insanity was Me or a carful of police," as Allen wrote of the episode in "Kaddish." Allen accompanied her to the station, holding her hand and trying to reassure her that he was acting in her best interests. Naomi was unimpressed. "Why did you do this?" she asked him.

The question haunted Allen for the better part of the following four decades. Allen, Louis, and Eugene had long been resigned to Naomi's madness and her eventual fate, but such acceptance did not make it any less painful to follow through with the inevitable course of action. This was especially true for Allen, who identified more closely with Naomi than anyone else in his family. He would always bear an uneasy guilt about his being the one who had had her committed to Pilgrim State and, ultimately, a lobotomy. It was a horror that invaded both his dreams and his poetry:

Some electric current flowing up her spine tortured her,
foot to scalp unbearable, some professional advice
required quick action, I took her wrists, and held her
bound to the sink, beheading her silently with swift
dispatch, one gesture, a stroke of the knife-like ax
that cut thru her neck like soft thick gum, dead quick.

What had I done, and why? . . .

11

Allen reenrolled at Columbia in February 1948, including in his class schedule
four English courses, a class in modern painting and sculpture, and one in
general psychology. His education, like much of the rest of his life at the time,
was in a holding pattern, a matter of his going through the motions with only
minimal interest. He attended classes and fulfilled his assignments, visited his
friends, worked on new poems—all with very little enthusiasm. He continued
to consult a Reichian analyst, hoping to work out his psychological and sexual
problems, but the sessions were provided him with no clear-cut directives. The
analyst disapproved of Allen's smoking marijuana and ordered him to stop.
When Allen refused, the analyst dismissed him.

Allen saw Kerouac only on rare occasions. Jack was still living with his
mother in Ozone Park, but now that he saw that he was nearing the end of his
writing *The Town and the City*, he was completely focused on the novel and
had little time for anything else. Allen had read selections from the book and
was eager to see the finished manuscript. Allen was a character in the book,
appearing as Leon Levinsky, the brooding, intellectual poet. Kerouac had also
worked "A Version of the Apocalypse," Allen's early prose sketch about Herbert
Huncke and Times Square, into the book's dialogue. The prospects of seeing
the book completed and eventually published were exciting to Allen, who
never flagged in his belief that Kerouac was an important writer. To see himself
and his friends immortalized in a serious work of fiction was indeed an honor,
an indication that his life, no matter how aimless or depressing it might have
seemed to him at the moment, had its own significance in the eyes of others
and in literature itself.

5
The Gates of Wrath

I came home and found a lion in my living room
Rushed out on the fire-escape screaming Lion! Lion!

1

For Allen Ginsberg, the summer of 1948 was stifling, and not only for its
weather. There was movement, though not always for the better, taking place
around him, but little from within. Jack Kerouac had completed *The Town and
the City* in the first week of May and had given Allen first reading of the
380,000-word, 1,000-page manuscript. Although Allen was awestruck by what
he read—"It is very great, beyond my wildest expectations," he wrote to Neal
Cassady—it also served to remind him about the distance he had to travel in
order to determine and express his own voice in permanent form. Neal Cassady had been heard from again, this time in a letter announcing that he
and Carolyn, who was now pregnant, had been married in San Francisco on
April 1. Allen posted a rather testy letter of congratulations, now aware that
the Cassady marriage and forthcoming child indicated Neal's commitment to
a life that excluded him. Bill Burroughs had moved to Algiers, a section of
New Orleans, where he had bought a one-hundred-acre tract of land and
continued to exercise his contempt for government regulations by surrounding
himself with drugs and guns. Then there was Naomi Ginsberg, isolated at the
Pilgrim State Hospital, prisoner of madness, fearful that hospital officials would
eventually act upon their belief that she would be better off if she was given a
prefrontal lobotomy. Her desperate letters to Allen, begging him to take her
home, were heartbreaking: "How I wish to be out walking the byways of a
country watching the crop extended: making friends with nature. I used to love
that as a child; the desire came back. . . ."

Allen initially attempted to work off his frustrations and uncertainties
through his poetry, but his rhymed verse, patterned after the poetry of Marvell,
Donne, and Blake, was not the proper vehicle to express what he had to say.

He had shown Lionel Trilling "Denver Doldrums" and a new sequence entitled "Later Dolours" but he lacked confidence in their value. "I don't know how good the poetry is, whether it will pass," he confessed to Trilling. "I feel for what I have done, but I know it is nowhere." Allen realized that the work lacked clarity, that the images, as his father had pointed out before, were not recognizable. In his journal, he noted as much:

> My mind travels a series of ways from the most general to the most abstract, this a cycle recurring at the moment. Not only reduplicated from time to time and then to season, each abstraction is an abstraction of an abstraction. And there we are again.

In "The Dark Corridor," a long poem recalling the time he spent in Denver, Ginsberg worked in familiar themes and images, his symbols far too weak for the powerful emotion charging them:

> This round world is a changeless passageway
> I never knew, in Denver, in the cellar
> at night, in the dark summer, I created
> an eternal prison in my prayer,
> In the dim basement of a summer day. . . .

Beside the frustration with his poetry, Allen was still at a sexual impasse. His sexual frustrations prompted him to frequent a number of gay bars in Greenwich Village and Times Square, and he even made a pass at Kerouac one evening in a subway station. ("Beat me up," he told Jack. "Do anything you like—anything!") Embarrassed, Kerouac declined as graciously as he could. Now aware of the intensity of Allen's feelings for Neal Cassady, Louis Ginsberg tried to discourage any further connection or contact Allen would have with Neal; in a two-word letter, written in early July, Louis urged Allen to "exorcise Neal."

As the summer moved along, Allen found himself in a lethargic rut, working two hours a day as a filing clerk at the American Academy of Political Science and spending his evening hours lying around, reading, sleeping, or visiting with Kerouac on those rare occasions when he happened to drop by. When he did go out to a party or host a gathering at his apartment, Allen's moods were volatile and unpredictable, ranging from angry, sullen silence to an almost giddy exuberance. As a person, he seemed to be as ill-defined as his poetry.

The Fourth of July weekend was sticky and hot. To escape his stuffy apartment on Saturday, July 3, Allen attended a party in Spanish Harlem thrown by Russell Durgin, one of his Columbia acquaintances. Kerouac also attended, as did Alan Harrington, a friend of Jack's. With Harrington was a man who had never met Kerouac or Ginsberg, although he had heard of Kerouac's novel, which was now being passed around in a black doctor's bag.

John Clellon Holmes was a tall, thin, angular man with sandy brown hair and black horn-rimmed glasses, a well-read intellectual who shared Kerouac's aspirations of becoming a novelist. Like Kerouac, Holmes was more of an observer than a participant, though Holmes tended to be more analytical or philosophical than Kerouac in his approach to capturing his observations on paper. Born in Holyoke, Massachusetts, on March 12, 1926—four years to the day after Kerouac was born, and twenty-nine years before jazz saxist Charlie Parker, a Beat Generation model, would die—Holmes spent a rootless childhood, moving twenty times in his first eighteen years. Holmes's parents' relationship was a rocky one (they divorced when John was seventeen), but both contributed significantly to his eventual interests. John McClellan Holmes, Sr., read aloud to his son, encouraging in him an almost obsessive interest in books. Elizabeth Holmes, a pianist, was responsible for introducing John to music, his other passion in the fine arts.

Although the frequent childhood moves eventually influenced Holmes's thematic interest in the rootlessness of modern Americans, World War II most profoundly affected his political and literary musings. In 1944, Holmes was drafted into the Navy Hospital Corps, where he spent his time taking care of Guadalcanal paraplegics. Faced with the horrors of the war, Holmes escaped into the world of fiction, his favorite authors being Tolstoy and Dostoyevski. The thought of a living purgatory, taking place in the navy hospital or presented on the printed page, forced on good people victimized by circumstance, contrasted sharply in Holmes's mind with the popular notions of blind pursuit of the American dream.

When he met Ginsberg and Kerouac at the party, Holmes was convinced that he had found two "brothers in spirit." He and Kerouac connected immediately, since both had many things in common, especially their desire to be fiction writers. In Ginsberg, Holmes saw a gentle, sometimes comic, sometimes tragic being whose spirit affected everyone around him. The Ginsberg Holmes met at the party was a fascinating character study, as Holmes later recalled:

> By all rights he should have been as painfully shy, myopic, scholarly and withdrawn as four or five other bespectacled, sallow young men who sulked in the corners of that party, looking like rabbinical students caught in a burlesque show. But instead he was excitable, infectious, direct. He said whatever came into his head, he brought himself frankly out before you. . . .

Allen's behavior at the July 3 party was revealing of his personality at the time. His internal pressures were forcing their way to the surface in a series of conflicting emotions. To liven up the party, Allen would set off firecrackers in ashtrays. He promoted Kerouac and his work to anyone who would listen— especially if the listener had so much as a remote connection to the publishing establishment. Yet darker, angry, more unstable spirits also surfaced. On another occasion, Herbert Gold—a Columbia classmate of Allen's, a man who would eventually become a successful novelist and essayist—had brought his wife to a party at Allen's apartment. Gold attempted to make conversation with Allen by asking him about his trip to Africa the previous summer, but the period was so depressing for Allen that he shrugged off the topic with little answer. When Gold's unsuspecting wife asked where he had been in Africa,

Ginsberg pointed out the location by throwing his wineglass at a large map that he had hanging on the wall, sending wine and shards of shattered glass throughout the room.

Four years earlier, Allen had characterized himself as a "lost child, a wandering child, in search of the womb of love." Now, a semester from his graduation from Columbia, caught at the doorway of the real world and having no visible future, Allen was tangled in his own uncertainty: "I wearied in an endless maze/ that men had walked for centuries."

However, his life was about to be changed by a series of visions that would alter, if not disintegrate, the walls of the maze.

2

Although Allen Ginsberg's name would eventually be associated with many types of political concerns and social activism over the decades to come, his mind was far removed from the 1948 presidential election. His interests were far more personal. Like driftwood bobbing on the ocean's surf, he stayed afloat, jouncing back and forth between land and the open sea, between the drudgery of his day-to-day existence and more mystical musings. Rather than concern himself with anti-Communist rhetoric espoused by Harry Truman on the presidential campaign trail, Allen wrestled with his own inner turmoil. He turned to mystical arts, submerging himself in the works of Blake, Yeats, and St. John of the Cross. Since he was subletting his Harlem apartment from a Columbia theology student, Allen found himself surrounded by egg-crate bookshelves crammed with books on theology and philosophy.

He continued to work on a book-length manuscript of poems he entitled *The Book of Doldrums*—poems reflecting a sense of isolation and bewilderment that led him to believe he was akin to Joseph K of Kafka's *The Trial*. In the Kafka novel, Joseph K awakens from a deep sleep, only to discover he is being tried for leading a worthless life. Like the Kafka character, Allen was bound by a state of what he characterized as "solitude and inattention and giving up."

In a letter to Neal Cassady, Allen complained that his life during the past five years had been one of "narrowing circles" involving his conceptualization of himself, sanity, and the universe in a manner that "had the ideas without the feelings." In looking for truth or wonder that he could apply to his life and poetry, Allen was searching for a crack in his consciousness, an elusive visionary experience similar to those experienced by the mystics he continued to study, which he could bring to his creative work:

> Oh pure idea! Imagination
> Is a grief gone mad, an ecstasy
> In the intelligence, and never real—
> Visions of the dark corridors of the sea.

Attempting to discover the catalyst to the marriage between mysticism and modern artistic expression, Allen studied the paintings of Paul Cézanne. The previous semester, following a suggestion of Lionel Trilling, Allen had taken an art course taught by Meyer Schapiro, one of the world's leading critics and scholars of modern art, and while Allen was intimidated by Schapiro's reputation and by a subject about which he admittedly knew nothing, he was overwhelmed by what he termed the "Cosmic Vibrations in Cezanne," of the way the painter used color—and the space between color—to create a dreamlike, eternal effect in his landscapes. Allen hoped to reproduce a similar effect in his poetry, using words and unspoken tensions between them to create universality in meaning and effect, but he had yet to determine the method by which to do so.

A combination of Allen's highly conceptual state of mind, his search for another level of consciousness, his reading of visionary theology texts, his intense study of the works of William Blake, and his loneliness led to a *satori* that would influence him for the next fifteen years of his life. It occurred one summer evening as dusk was beginning to settle over New York. Allen was lying in bed, his mind in a sort of dull postorgasmic blankness resulting from his having read Blake's poetry while he was idly masturbating. As he stared out his open window at the old cornices on the building tops of East Harlem, silhouetted against a cloudy sky, Allen heard a deep, rich voice reciting Blake's "Ah Sunflower":

> Ah Sunflower! weary of time
> Who counts the steps of the sun.
> Seeking after that sweet golden clime
> Where the traveller's journey is done. . . .

With his consciousness in a highly armored state from his recent readings, particularly of Blake's *Songs of Innocence* and *Songs of Experience*, Allen instinctively perceived the voice to be his own, projected throughout the room, but as it continued, reciting "The Sick Rose" and "The Little Girl Lost," he began to hear it as the voice of Blake, speaking to him through eternity. His perception shifted to a near-hallucinatory state in which, like Blake, he was capable of seeing eternity in a grain of sand, or the timelessness of the graying sky outside, without feeling foolish or untruthful. In one shudder of illumination, Allen reached the understanding that poetry was eternal: A poet's consciousness could travel timelessly, alter perception, and speak of universal vision to anyone attaining the same level of consciousness. Poetry, Allen understood, as did Blake, was a vehicle for visionary statement. It was suddenly very clear to him that he and Blake shared the same consciousness, though separated by centuries, exemplified by such lines as:

> Where the youth pined away with desire
> And the pale virgin shrouded in snow
> Arise from the graves, and aspire
> Where my Sun-flower wishes to go!

Looking out his window at the exquisite detail work in the cornices of the building tops around him, work that had been accomplished decades earlier, Allen felt as if he was receiving answers to some of the questions he had pondered as a youth in Paterson. He had once stared out at the stars and wondered where he stood in the universe, and now he knew. He was not only a part of a vast presence; he was also part of timeless eternity. Blake understood this, and now, so did he.

Stunned, Allen was at a loss as to what to do. His mind was in such a state that he could accept such a vision as a part of reality, but he was uncertain as to how he should respond to it. In the silence of his room, with sounds of the world outside filtering in through the open window, Allen concluded that whatever had happened would not be forgotten or denied, that this vision was what he had been born to witness; he would pursue it to its conclusion.

In many respects, this decision was at the same time both the easiest and the most difficult one he would make in reaction to the vision—easy because he must have known, even then, that he could never forget an apparition so mind-boggling; difficult because he then had to believe, in finality, that it actually *had* occurred. With all its implications and possible effects, the vision might have been easier for Ginsberg to deny, or at least rationalize as an especially powerful daydream or hallucination. Even accepting the vision as a form of madness—likening it to the voices heard by his mother—would have been the more "rational" conclusion, in terms of its being readily accepted by a world just growing accustomed to the fact that it had created, in the atomic bomb, its own suicide note.

Madness, the world would believe; visions, it would not. Immediately following his Blake vision, Ginsberg, in what he called "an exalted state of mind," climbed out on the fire escape and tapped on the window of the apartment next door. "I've seen God!" he told the two young women living there, prompting them to slam the window in his face. He then went to a public telephone to call his former analyst, but the psychiatrist refused to accept the charges or talk to him. With Kerouac and Burroughs out of town, Allen had no one to talk to in what he considered to be one of the most important moments of his life.

Returning to his room, Allen looked through other texts to see if it was possible to achieve this heightened awareness by reading other visionary writers. "I immediately rushed to Plato," he recalled, "and read some great image in the *Phaedrus* about horses flying through the sky, and rushed over to Saint John and started reading fragments of *con un no saber sabiendo . . . que me quede balbuciendo*, and rushed to the other part of the bookshelf and picked up Plotinus about The Alone—the Plotinus I found more difficult to interpret. But I immediately doubled my thinking process, quadrupled, and I was able to read almost any text and see all sorts of divine significance in it."

Over the next couple of days, he tried everything he could think of to bring on another visitation. In his kitchen, he danced like a shaman, hoping to conjure up a deeper spiritual awareness, quitting only when he had the eerie feeling that he was like a Faustian character trying to summon the devil. He reread passages in the metaphysical texts on his bookshelves. He began a series of poems that attempted to describe the sensations he felt at the moment of his vision.

Then, a few days after his initial vision, Allen had another mystical experience, this time in the Columbia bookstore. He was browsing in the poetry section, rereading a passage in Blake's "The Human Abstract," when he had the same shuddering sensation—a feeling that he was in an eternal place—that he'd had a few nights before. Looking around the bookstore, he was surprised to see that the people around him now had the faces of wild animals. The clerk, a man with a long face, had transmogrified into a giraffe. Looking at the man's face more closely, Allen sensed that he was "a great tormented soul" capable of the same elevated consciousness that he was experiencing in the store. Everybody in the bookstore knew these eternal truths, he felt, but they were so busy going about their daily lives that they did not dwell on their significance in the universe. Rather than face this cosmic consciousness, they hid their intelligence behind grotesque masks of self-deception. Perhaps this was for the best, he decided; if everyone faced this consciousness at the same moment, daily life should be terribly disrupted. People would be unable to accomplish even the most menial tasks.

Passing along this consciousness was the duty of the poet. It was the Supreme Reality—or New Vision—that Allen had been looking for over the last three years.

3

Ginsberg's visions elicited a mixed response from his friends. Kerouac worried that Allen was losing his mind, though he shared or sympathized with many of Allen's ideas about eternal truths projected in art. Burroughs was skeptical. Neal Cassady tried to understand the visions and apply Allen's breakthrough to his own life, but he was distracted by the more down-to-earth worries surrounding the pending birth of his and Carolyn's first child. Allen's analyst again rebuffed him, refusing to consider or discuss the matter. Of Ginsberg's academic acquaintances, only Mark Van Doren seemed interested enough to seriously question him about the visions. (Through some of Ginsberg's most troubled times, Van Doren would remain a sympathetic figure, helping Allen look for work, encouraging him in his attempts at his poetry, with such remarks as "you'll get there yet" and "you haven't written weak verse—except in spots, where I suppose you got tired and lost faith in the poem. . . .").

Not surprisingly, the strongest negative response came from Louis Ginsberg. Tormented by the difficult years he had endured with his wife, Louis reacted to his son's announcement with a mixture of sadness, fear, and pent-up fury. Louis tried to dismiss the visions, but when Allen insisted they were real, father and son quarreled bitterly, Louis wondering whether Allen had inherited his mother's mental disorders.

Allen desperately wanted to solicit a vision by means of his own willpower, by concentrating on the memorable aspects of the initial vision, but it proved to be futile. Focusing on "eternity" only clouded the mind's eye with ineffective words ("Language, language, Vision cries for language. . . ."); trying to sketch the visions into poetry was equally fruitless. The abstract qualities of the visions were impossible to put into concrete images that would evoke sympathy and understanding from readers. Ginsberg had yet to master Blake's method of including minute particulars into clear, concise poetry, nor was he familiar enough with the poetry of William Carlos Williams to apply Williams's "no ideas but in things" dictum to his work.

Instead, he worked with the models that he knew, fashioning his visionary poems after such poets as Wyatt or Marvell. The resulting works were, in turns, weighty with wooden images, egotistical, confusing, even coy. When placed next to Ginsberg's later, more successful efforts, the poems are interesting more as historical footnotes than for their literary value.

In "The Eye Altering Alters All," the first poem written after his visionary experiences, Ginsberg tries to explain his conclusion that the vast consciousness he sensed in his vision is something open to anyone willing to accept it. Most people, Ginsberg says, only experience that consciousness in their sleep, through their dreams, or in death. To those familiar with Ginsberg's visions, the poem, which borrows its title from William Blake, makes sense, but to those unaware of the poet's background, the poem's symbols are unclear. This problem bothers the entire sequence of poems written about the visions. Some of Ginsberg's symbols (hawk, dove, gull, and nightingale) seem vaguely familiar, perhaps even trite, while others (shadow, bone, darkness, light) are so vague that a reader cannot possibly understand what he means in the writing. In trying to find symbols with both universal and mystical meaning, Ginsberg is ultimately self-defeating.

No one needed to point out these weaknesses to him; he recognized them himself, and he would never present these poems as anything but early attempts. "I was just trying to arrange and rearrange sort of symbols of mystical experience, like the words 'light,' 'skull,' which were really very vague," he explained years later. "They referred to something Gnostic, but they didn't really describe anything seen. So it was the 'reference' rather than 'presentation.' I thought at the time that I would write a poem that was so dense and would have so much symbolic significance that it would be able to penetrate anybody else's consciousness."

Ginsberg also admitted that, in trying to create a "mystical riddle" of his visions, he failed to project his consciousness on his readers. Like many young poets, he was too focused on the idea that symbols made the poem. Ironically, a much more successful work, written in his 1947 journal and eventually published as "In Society" in Empty Mirror, was a direct transcription of a dream, with no effort on Ginsberg's part to create symbols or mask his consciousness in language. In not trying, he had succeeded, where in trying, he had failed.

Allen's efforts to recreate his visions brought about a frightening visitation that spelled an end to his pursuit. One evening, as he walked around the Columbia campus, he again focused his mind on Blake's "The Sick Rose." As had occurred in the initial vision, Allen deeply sensed the vastness of the sky, as if another being—a god figure, perhaps—was omnipresent. This time, however, the presence took on a terrifying dimension, as if a "giant octopus serpent-monster consciousness" was poised to devour him and destroy his consciousness. Horrified, Allen interpreted the vision as a sign from a greater power—a demand that he go no further. There were limits to human perception, and stepping beyond those limits was to dabble with something of enormous power, perhaps madness or death. Allen concluded that it was better "to shut up & live in the present temporary form" than to pass through what Blake—and, later, Aldous Huxley—labeled "the doors of perception."

Ginsberg eventually compared the visions to the types of insights he experienced under the suggestive influences of LSD, but in 1948, more than a decade before he would try the hallucinogenic drug, the visions were extremely unsettling. He had seen heaven and hell, and the sight was both a burden and a temptation to a young man about to enter his final semester at Columbia.

4

Autumn 1948 found Ginsberg suspended between a confused grasping for metaphysical understanding and the need to establish an orderly life. A dangling man, Allen was depressed by the notion that he was almost at the end of his formal schooling, with little to look forward to as a future. Most of the jobs for which he was qualified offered only minimum wage. "My time is worth more than that," he complained to his father. He explored the possibility of tutoring, but it offered little promise. He tried to find work with New York publishers, to no avail. He even considered working as a scriptwriter for television or radio shows, hoping to combine his visions into something on a large scale, convinced, as he explained to Cassady, that "steady creative labor will solve a lot of my problems."

On campus, he attempted to shed his eccentric image. He quit cutting classes and began wearing a black tie to school.

His letters home, however, were revealing of his inner turmoil. Allen had always tested his ideas on his father, and he now bantered with Louis through the mail, raging about the toll exacted from him for his internal battle between rational and irrational thought and behavior. The disputes intensified when Allen began portions of a never-completed "naturalistic-symbolistic novel" not unlike Kerouac's *The Town and the City* and sent them to his father. The novel, Ginsberg explained, attempted "to reproduce the actual life of a whole community—in its own terms." When Louis Ginsberg protested the terms, Allen defended the work's less savory details, claiming that performing cosmetic surgery on the text would damage its realism. "I won't rely on euphemism & presiosite or a censorship of crucial language and detail to make it palatable," he groused, stating an argument he would use repeatedly in years to come, whenever his father questioned his choice of language or symbol. On a different occasion, Allen touched upon another familiar theme of the future: "Very well, [I'd like] to be cheery, but in a situation like this, where it's a question of veritable survival, I can't feel very sanguine about pluck and life etc. Tell a man in a concentration camp to make the best of it. . . ."

Despite such protests, Allen displayed more conformity in his behavior than he had in previous semesters at Columbia. Some of this pursuit of an orderly life might be attributed to the endeavors of his friends. Jack Kerouac was holed up in Ozone Park, trying to put *The Town and the City* in marketable form. Kerouac had also begun working on a new novel, tentatively called *Dr. Sax: The Myth of the Rainy Night*, a supernatural novel combining Kerouac's childhood fantasies with the Shrouded Stranger/Shadow figure he had been developing with Allen for a couple of years. When at work, Kerouac was fiercely disciplined, an intense writer devoted to his art and little else.

Neal Cassady was also settling down, at least as far as Ginsberg could determine. On September 7, Carolyn had delivered a seven-pound, three-ounce girl, Cathleen JoAnne. With a new family to take care of, Neal had settled in San Francisco, as much as he was capable of "settling" anywhere, and it was clear to Allen that he had no plans to move as long as his railroad job continued to flourish. He was so confident of his security that he wrote Kerouac, seriously proposing that they buy a ranch together and move their friends west. Neal also wrote Allen a tender letter offering to finance his work for life if all worked out for him in San Francisco. Allen replied by thanking Neal for the offer but refusing assistance, claiming, "I must be my own angel if I am ever going to bring messages from heaven myself."

With his friends involved with their own lives and circumstances, Allen carried on alone, plodding on toward unknown destinations. He continued his in-depth study of Cézanne, writing a lengthy paper on the painter and his art. He labored on a series of disappointing rhymed poems, fretting again that he had no style or technique to call his own. "The clearest expression of what I have in mind is in Blake & Eliot," he wrote at the time.

Allen wasn't the only one experiencing difficulties with his writing. John Clellon Holmes was working on a novel that was going nowhere, and Kerouac was frustrated by the cutting required to make *The Town and the City* acceptable to a publisher, likening his compromising position to the shameful work of geeks in a circus. Holmes and Kerouac attended a few classes together at the New School, mostly so Jack could collect his GI benefits, which he spent on books, and Kerouac raged to Holmes about the price he had to pay to make his novel more marketable. He had plans for a long, rambling work, which he was calling *On the Road*, but the book had no chance if a traditionally structured novel like *The Town and the City* was having problems conforming to the standards of the day. Hammering his ideas on Holmes, Kerouac complained about the requirements publishers placed on those who wrote fiction, his mind filled, as Holmes recalled, with "vague, speculative doubts about his ability to do the book [*On the Road*] the way he felt it should be done." They spent many hours discussing the state of their lives and the future of their literature.

During one of their talks, Kerouac coined a term that would both propel him to the forefront of his literary generation and dog him through his eventual drunken, bitter decline. In trying to analyze the rather rootless direction taken by so many young men and women after the war, Holmes had asked Kerouac for his views on the "peculiar quality of mind" behind the young hipsters they saw on Times Square, people who seemed to Holmes to be "*in* the street but not *of* it."

Kerouac responded that the hipsters, like the members of his circle of friends, had an inner awareness of the futility of pursuing conventional ideas and mores. These people, whom Kerouac labeled "furtive," were weary of society's pressures to conform, and had thus formed another level of consciousness that allowed them to survive and accept their desperate existences.

"I guess you might say we're a *beat* generation," Kerouac concluded, creating a term that would become a common expression in a decade.

The remark, although spoken sincerely in the context of a passionate discussion, was hardly intended to be the definitive statement it wound up being, yet like so many of Kerouac's remarks, it was grounded in a deep-seated philosophy. Inherent in his observation was an idea that represented the motor drive behind the lives and literature of Ginsberg, Kerouac, Burroughs, Cassady, Holmes, and others who would later be identified as the nucleus of the new movement. The philosophy could be political as well as social and literary, its application depending upon the individual writing about it. The bombing of Hiroshima and Nagasaki, in the eyes of the Beat Generation, had changed the world forever. Mass death and destruction, sanctioned by a "sane" government, threw out of kilter all previous preconceptions about conventional mores. To drop a bomb—or kill millions, as was the case in the Nazi death camps—posed serious questions about human nature and the conventional idea of blindly trusting national leaders.

Thomas Merton, the Trappist monk noted for his humanistic writings and logic, focused the Beat Generation's philosophy in another context:

> We equate sanity with a sense of justice, with humaneness, with prudence, with the capacity to love and understand other people. We rely on the sane people of the world to preserve it from barbarism, madness, destruction. And now it begins to dawn on us that it is precisely the *sane* ones who are the most dangerous. . . .

This logic hit different members of the Beat Generation on varying levels and would come together only when the Cold War and McCarthyism brought it into deeper focus and to national attention. For Kerouac, who was never very political, and who tended to see the Beat Generation more in literary than social terms, *beat* would evolve into *beatific*, the idea stemming from the gentleness, grace, and inner wisdom found in the downtrodden and suffering. It was a notion that had haunted Kerouac since he was a child, formed as he watched his older brother, Gerard, quietly suffer and die at age nine from the painful effects of rheumatic fever. To devout Catholics in Lowell, Gerard was a saint; two decades later, it was almost natural for Kerouac to apply the standard to the beaten-down figures on Times Square. This quasireligious undertone would run through all of his writings.

Allen Ginsberg's confusion, anger, and depression in the fall of 1948 could also be applied to the new philosophy being formed by his circle of friends, but for Ginsberg, the application was much more direct. He had seen how nonconformity had claimed his mother's mind, while his father was constantly urging him to follow a normal path. That meant his graduating from school, finding a job and a girlfriend, and settling down. None of these appealed to a gay poet with Blake visions who was seeking to understand the place in eternity for beggars on the street. Nonconformity and its excesses were more appealing.

After all, it was William Blake who had claimed that "the road of excess leads to the palace of wisdom."

5

Neal Cassady blew into town at Christmastime 1948, and his arrival, as always, elicited powerful feelings from his New York acquaintances. For Allen Ginsberg, who had finally grown accustomed to Neal's existence being an occasional letter from the West Coast, Cassady's arrival was a mixed blessing, filled with elation of his physical presence yet doomed by the presence of his "road girlfriend," ex-wife LuAnne Henderson. Wherever Cassady was, the scene was so frantic that Allen often found himself just another figure vying for Neal's attention. For Jack Kerouac, Neal was badly needed inspiration for *On the Road*, his novel that was proceeding, as John Clellon Holmes recalled, in "fitful and abortive starts" but not going far beyond the planning stage.

Cassady's latest trip to New York, like his first, provided the material upon which episodes in a novel could be based. Shortly after the birth of his daughter, Neal had learned that he would be losing his railroad job due to a November 2 change in California's "full-crew" law. The new law stated that the railroad could cut back on its surplus help during the slow seasons, and because Neal had only brief tenure with the railroad, he would be one of the first to go. The termination of the railroad job caused him to forsake his plans to buy a ranch and move his friends west. Faced with the prospects of unemployment and a slow domestic life, Neal grew anxious to move. He found his escape when he saw a maroon and dark silver 1949 Hudson parked on a new car lot. He used virtually all of his family's savings to purchase the car.

A quarrel broke out between Neal and Carolyn over Neal's spending their savings on the car and abandoning her with a three-month-old baby at Christmastime, but Neal phoned Jack Kerouac on December 15 and announced that he was on his way to New York, anyway. From there, Neal told Jack, they would both hit the road and return to California. Jack promised to stake Neal some money for Carolyn's support while they were gone, and then he informed Neal that he would be at his sister's home in North Carolina, and not in New York, for Christmas. Neal insisted that he would find him, one way or another.

With his money nearly gone, Cassady needed help to finance his trip across the country. He turned to Al Hinkle, a fellow railroad employee and former Denver friend who, like Neal, was being laid off. Neal plied Hinkle with tales of the wild scene in the East, and Hinkle was enthusiastic. Unfortunately for Neal, Al was in no better financial condition than he was. However, Al's girlfriend, Helen, had a little money, though she refused to part with it unless she and Al were married. His mind working quickly, Neal suggested that the trip to New York could be the couple's honeymoon, and he scurried around San Francisco in an effort to obtain the necessary papers for the couple's wedding.

On December 16, Neal and Al and Helen Hinkle departed for the East. In Los Angeles, they visited the travel bureau and picked up a sailor bound for Indiana, who offered to pay fifteen dollars for gas and a ride. It wasn't long before Cassady's constant chatter, along with the music blaring from the car's radio and Neal's habit of smoking marijuana while he drove, started to get on Helen Hinkle's nerves. Helen, the product of an upbringing so strict that she had been forbidden by her parents to go to the movies or wear lipstick until she was an adult, had never seen marijuana smoked before, and she was appalled by the tales she had heard about drug users. She thought Neal was "the devil incarnate," and his behavior and apparent disregard for the necessities of life bothered her. Her complaints, however, went unanswered, and the men, depending on her money for their cross-country jaunt, were further frustrated when she insisted on spending her money on food and hotel accommodations. Their frayed spirits bottomed out in Tucson, where Helen announced she had run out of money. Still plotting, Neal handed Helen his railroad pass, which, he told her, would take her to New Orleans. She could get in touch with Bill Burroughs and stay with him. They promised to pick her up at Burroughs's home in a week.

If the honeymoon was ending for Helen Hinkle, Neal's trip for kicks was just beginning. After they had dispatched Helen to New Orleans, Neal and Al turned northward, speeding toward Denver. Away from Carolyn and a settled family life, Neal's considerable sexual impulses shifted into overdrive, and he suddenly *had* to talk LuAnne Henderson into joining them on their trip to New York. Neal was counting on his extraordinary powers of persuasion to overcome any of LuAnne's bad memories of their disastrous marriage and subsequent trip to New York in 1946.

When he found her in Denver, Neal wound up agreeing to LuAnne's terms about joining them on the trip. Currently engaged to a sailor who was at sea, LuAnne was bored with the role of fiancée-in-waiting, and a little spice in New York appealed to her. However, her experiences with Cassady warned her to establish ground rules before she agreed to accompany him. Her demands were basic: She was free and unattached, able to pursue her own desires, including sleeping with any man of her choice. Cassady had no problem with this, although he talked LuAnne into agreeing not to sleep with Al Hinkle, with whom Neal was in physical competition. By this time, the sailor they had picked up was distraught by the side trip and decided he had seen enough; he disappeared one evening while Neal, Al, and LuAnne were out on the town.

Their passage through the Plains states was grueling. They drove through a blizzard, and their car, lacking a heater, soon took on the dimensions of a runaway railroad refrigerator car rambling at breakneck speed through the flatlands. With an inch of ice frozen to the windshield and visibility near zero, Cassady donned a pair of goggles, wrapped a scarf around his head, and navigated by hanging his head out the window, making him look, as Kerouac later described him in *On the Road*, "like a monk peering into the manuscripts of the snow." Their luck ran out one morning when the Hudson skidded on an icy hill in Kansas and wound up in a ditch. A farmer came to their rescue, using two horses to pull the car from the ditch.

By this time, they were half-frozen, nearly broke, and only halfway to their destination. The car's bearings had been damaged by the run into the ditch, and without the wherewithal to fix the Hudson, Cassady had to drive it at a much more prudent speed, subjecting himself and his passengers to a longer period in the frigid car than he had planned. He thought he had found a lucky break when he picked up an old wino who promised to stake them gas money for the rest of their journey if they would drive him to Memphis, but he turned out to be as financially destitute as they were. Infuriated, Neal took out his frustrations on the wino, shocking Al and LuAnne, who had never seen Neal hit another man.

They arrived in Rocky Mount, North Carolina, on Christmas Eve. Jack Kerouac's sister and brother-in-law, Jack, his mother, and other relatives were just sitting down for their Christmas turkey when Cassady and company rolled in, looking like survivors of a great ordeal. All were tired and dirty, and Kerouac did not even recognize his friend at first, but, rather, "a stranger for all intents and purposes from California with corpses in a car outside." The trio in the car had eaten little more than candy and cheese crackers in thirty hours. Jack's relatives had no idea how to respond to the unshaven, red-eyed man in the doorway.

Jack knew what to do. He invited them in, told them to wash up, and prepared three more places at the dining room table.

It was only the beginning of a long and much-ballyhooed journey.

6

After overcoming the initial shock of realizing that Neal had indeed made the long cross-country haul after still another of his impulsive actions, Allen Ginsberg found himself at odds with some of Neal's decisions. Why had Neal abandoned his wife and infant daughter? What was he doing in town with LuAnne Henderson, of all people? Why had Al and Helen Hinkle married, and what was Al doing in New York while his new wife withered away in Louisiana? How did Allen fit into Cassady's plans? Ginsberg brooded over such questions, sulking in an armchair while Neal and Jack reveled. Allen recognized a different Jack Kerouac whenever Neal Cassady was around. Jack seemed to come alive in Neal's presence. He loved to engage in a comical game of one-upmanship in Neal's company, and it was amusing to watch the serious, quiet Canuck transformed into a joyful, fun-loving, kicks-seeking dynamo pounding rhythms on the dashboard of the car or on the bottoms of pots and pans, scat-singing with jazz records, looking for women—breaking away from the garret existence of the novelist at work. Without Neal, Jack was like a powerful engine without spark plugs. "Cody is the brother I lost," Kerouac later wrote of Cassady, referring to him by his fictional name. "He is the Arbiter of what I think. I'll follow, did I ever say I wouldn't follow? or did I ever ask to follow?"

Still, Allen was haunted by reservations. "What is the meaning of this voyage to New York?" he challenged Neal shortly after he arrived in New York. "What kind of sordid business are you on now? Whither goest thou, America, in thy shiny car in the night?"

The question shocked Cassady into silence, as if the sensibility of Allen's query, given poetically, froze his raw energy into a single frame. His only answer was to move on.

Allen's chidings, however, were only halfhearted, for he knew that emotionally Neal felt the burdens of his actions but by nature had little control over them; he was aware of his enigmatic nature. (Writing Carolyn from New York, Neal confessed, "I wound all the people I love—why?") Allen also realized that his impatience with Cassady, as well as his firm commitment to his job at the Associated Press and his lonely lifestyle, would dissipate as soon as he was swept into the vortex of Neal's quicktalk and frenetic pace. In no time, he had offered the use of his apartment to Neal, Al, and LuAnne for the duration of their visit.

New Year's Eve was the beginning of a three-day binge that found Ginsberg, Cassady, Kerouac, and the others rushing from one party to another, meeting old friends, drinking, hanging out, trying to score marijuana, crashing, smoking pot and opium, philosophizing, making love, feigning love, reaffirming love. Shielded from the blowing snow and winter chill by the blast-furnace heat supplied by hundreds of bodies packed into small buildings, their eyes stinging from a haze of smoke in the rooms, the group sweated and whooped through a huge party thrown in a friend's basement apartment. As Kerouac remembered, Neal Cassady "ran like Groucho Marx from group to group, digging everybody," his energy pouring out of him in nonstop activity.

Not everyone in the tightly knit group of friends was comfortable around Cassady. Lucien Carr, who had heard Kerouac talk about Cassady, felt competitive toward a man who so obviously captured Jack's total attention, if not devotion. John Clellon Holmes, who also had heard of Neal but had never met him before the binge, was somewhat intimidated by Neal's innocent ways of making people feel "inauthentic"; to Holmes, Neal was the personification of Dostoyevski's Kirilov in reverse, a man who seized joy in short, powerful bursts and seemed incapable of living outside of these moments. Bill Burroughs, who graciously fed and housed Helen Hinkle while her husband caroused in New York, sent several angry letters and telegrams damning Al Hinkle's behavior. "What kind of character is this Hinkle to leave his wife here with friends, then not even bother to let her know what his intentions are?" complained Burroughs. Jack Kerouac's current girlfriend, a married woman named Pauline, deplored Jack's behavior around Neal and used her disgust as a basis to terminate their relationship.

Kerouac summed up his group's attitude that weekend when he answered Pauline's objections to their behavior: "Ah, it's all right, it's just kicks. We only live once. We're having a good time."

The strongest bond continued to be that among Allen, Jack, and Neal. The intensity of their comradeship, heightened to the extent of their mythologizing each other in public, was the key element behind the lifestyle and formation of the group that would become known as the Beat Generation. Cassady even exerted a strong influence on Ginsberg's and Kerouac's writing, to different degrees. Without Cassady, Allen and Jack were confined to imitational literary forms, Ginsberg following Blake, Kerouac mimicking Thomas Wolfe; with Cassady around, they dabbled with his crazy, improvisational wordspeak, best exemplified in a fairly lengthy poem/jingle they composed together, a humorous lyric that Ginsberg half-seriously considered offering to Charlie Chaplin or Groucho Marx:

> Pull my daisy
> tip my cup
> all my doors are open
> Cut my thoughts

for coconuts
all my eggs are broken. . . .

Neal Cassady turned out to be a strengthening link in a chain of writers that would blow open the literary scene within a decade. If the Beat Generation was indeed "lifestyle as literature," as John Clellon Holmes later remarked, Cassady was the personification of the concept. For Kerouac, who admired the long, rambling lines of Thomas Wolfe and Herman Melville, Cassady—and later the improvisational jazz soloists such as Charlie Parker and Lester Young—supplied a bold new direction for using the long line in literature and music. For Ginsberg, Cassady formed a genesis for Allen's eventual use of transcribed oral poetry. Neal was *the* human example of poetry in motion, "the great experiencer & midwest driver and talker, gossiping of . . . eternities." Neal had neither the technical writing skills nor the self-discipline to put his life on paper, other than in his letters, but his lifestyle became his literature. Even Bill Burroughs, who tended to be critical of Cassady's aimlessness, especially on this most recent journey, had to admit that "Neal is, of course, the very soul of this voyage into pure, abstract, meaningless motion. He is the mover, compulsive, dedicated, ready to sacrifice family, friends, even his very car itself to the necessity of moving from one place to another. . . ." To Allen and Jack, Neal Cassady captured an American spirit and celebration of life similar, as they saw it, to Whitman's "Song of Myself."

The good times began to grind down as Neal's visit came to an end. The camaraderie between Allen and Neal deteriorated, no doubt because Neal was limiting himself to LuAnne and heterosexual encounters on this trip, though their sleeping arrangements at Ginsberg's apartment were unconventional, with Neal sleeping in the middle of Allen's cot, LuAnne's head propped on one of his shoulders, Allen's on the other, while Al Hinkle slept on the couch in another room. Allen had reluctantly settled into a "straight" life prior to Neal's arrival, and Cassady's appearance muddied things up, forcing him to consider again their improbable relationship. Carolyn was waiting for Neal in San Francisco, and Neal was getting the itch to move. There was also the matter of picking up Helen Hinkle, who was still the guest of an increasingly impatient Burroughs in Louisiana.

On January 19, 1949, Cassady, Kerouac, LuAnne Henderson, and Al Hinkle set out for the West. Their departure was traumatic for Allen: His three closest friends and mentors—Kerouac, Burroughs, and Cassady—had moved away from his life, toward destinations he could not share.

They were on the road—Kerouac's road, Cassady's road.

Allen remained at home, his mind in the doldrums, slouching toward a future dusted with holy visions and mad poetry.

7

In February 1949, Herbert Huncke arrived unexpectedly at Allen's 1401 York Avenue apartment. Allen had never seen him looking so "beat." Huncke had been released from prison a few weeks earlier, and he had spent much of his time out walking the streets in the bitter New York winter without food or sanctuary. Delirious and on the verge of suicide, Huncke was looking for a place to crash. Allen's heart immediately went out to the emaciated figure propped in his doorway, and he invited Herbert inside.

In many respects, Huncke was an apparition of Ginsberg's vision of a tragic Dostoyevskian figure. His torn, rumpled clothing hung on his wasted form. The sallow skin of his arms and legs was covered with scars from countless morphine injections. His socks were wet, and his cracked patent-leather shoes had savaged his feet into blistered, scabrous, bloody horrors. Yet somehow, Huncke viewed his condition as being inevitable; in his battered state, he was looking for a way to survive, not for pity.

"Don't bother with them," Huncke said when Ginsberg removed his shoes and saw his feet. "You'll only make yourself sick." Ignoring the comment, Allen prepared a boric-acid solution, and as he washed Huncke's feet with an old rag, he listened to the account of the hustler's latest misadventures.

After his release from Riker's Island, Huncke had connected with some of his underworld acquaintances. He gave them information in exchange for the money he needed for Benzedrine and the little food that he ate. As John Clellon Holmes recalled in a fictional account, much of Huncke's time was spent hanging out, finding out "who was in and who was out, who was hooked and who was off, what was available and what was going to be hard to get; all the rumors, speculations, gossip, warnings and messages that traveled from mouth to mouth and city to city among the restless, continually circulating fraternity to which he belonged."

Then the money ran out and his drug connections dried up. Starving, strung out from drug withdrawal, and half-frozen from exposure to the elements, Huncke wandered the city streets aimlessly, begging for food or coffee, sleeping in bus stations, looking for a way out. He found nothing. In desperation, he had gone to Ginsberg. In summing up his time on the street, Herbert told Allen that he was more concerned about his mental state than his physical health: "Sure, I'm old, and I'm evil, and I'm ugly, and I'm tired. But that isn't it. I've been this way for ten years, and I'm all down the main line now. And while I'm wandering around and waiting for something to come to my attention and interest me, I feel instead this dizziness, as if my mind were not in this room. . . . Something is happening to my mind, something happens when I am so dead."

Acting against the advice of his friends, Allen offered Herbert his apartment for as long as it took for his health to return. Burroughs in particular objected to Allen's decision. Bill warned Allen that Huncke was a parasite who would grow to resent and despise his host. Burroughs reminded Ginsberg that Huncke had lived with him in Algiers for a time; when Huncke had left, he offered his gratitude for Burroughs's hospitality by stealing an Oriental rug, the only possession of value in Bill's home. Every time he saw the bare wood of his floor, Burroughs wrote, he recalled Huncke's "vile act."

Allen had himself been victimized by Herbert less than a year earlier. In one of his brief stays at Allen's apartment, Huncke had stolen, by Ginsberg's estimation, "about $200 worth of goods," including rare books, silverware, clothing, and phonograph records, belonging to the man from whom Allen was subletting the apartment. The thefts had necessitated Allen's early departure from the apartment and subsequent move to the York Avenue apartment, and at the time Allen had angrily informed Huncke that he was no longer a welcome guest at his place. However, Allen relented shortly after Huncke had left, allowing that he was probably "now on Times Square. I'll take him in again perhaps when it gets good & cold & he comes crawling to my door."

Ginsberg recognized Huncke as a con man, but he also saw him in a more charitable light—certainly more so than his friends did. Like Neal Cassady, Herbert Huncke was a survivor, a man who used his wits and storytelling abilities to keep himself alive. Huncke *existed*, his life unaffected by any need for possessions or social standing. Allen was captivated by the man's transitory state and egoless existence. In "Howl," Ginsberg immortalized Huncke's appearance at the door by characterizing him as the man "who walked all night with shoes full of blood on the snow banks waiting for a door in the East River to open to a room full of steamheat and opium."

Allen also admired Huncke's early attempts at writing. Although Huncke didn't regard himself to be anywhere near the writer Jack Kerouac was, he was a natural storyteller who employed a style so simple and unassuming that it was almost childlike. His written vignettes, like his verbal takes, were nakedly honest and contained street language that captured the sense of the inevitable that Ginsberg wanted to integrate into his own poetry.

Bill Burroughs's warnings proved to be prophetic. Huncke collapsed on Ginsberg's couch, where he spent days on end sleeping off his illness and exhaustion while Allen attended to his needs, but once he had recovered, Herbert dominated the scene around the apartment, to the extent of rearranging the furniture and wearing Allen's clothing. Ginsberg was accustomed to a chaotic disarray in his apartment—from misplaced objects to the dust balls gathering in the corners of the rooms—and Huncke's tidiness bothered him. In the morning, Allen would return home from his midnight-to-eight shift as a copyboy for the Associated Press, only to find short messages, written on scraps of paper and deposited near an ashtray or on the kitchen table, directing him to "leave cigarettes" or "watch your ashes." It reached a point where Allen was almost afraid to climb the stairs to his apartment for fear of what he would find inside.

Despite the aggravation, Allen said little to Huncke, though he made his feelings known to his friends. "General intimidation" was the way he summarized the situation to Neal Cassady. "Herbert was beat, and now just begins to prosper, so I can't well put a stop to it all. Or not easily anyway. I guess this sounds cowardly; or maybe it's only a balloon I blow."

Quite simply, Allen was up against a series of conflicting interests and emotions. When Huncke had appeared at his door, Allen had feared for his friend's life; once Huncke was up and around, Allen viewed any actions as a positive sign, whether it involved Huncke's assuming control of his apartment or his stealing overcoats from parked cars.

"I was overjoyed!" Allen recalled years later. "He'd come back to life. He was back operating again, which meant he wasn't going to die. It was really a funny, paradoxical situation, because at the time there was all this talk at Columbia about what is right, what is wrong, what's ethics, what's morality, what's social good, what's social bad, what's utilitarianism, what's justifiable, what's unjustifiable—all of it from people who were fighting and scrambling to get ahead and making atom bombs. So I began to notice that Huncke was like a victim of a monstrosity of laws and attitudes."

Huncke's assessment of his situation was equally enigmatic: "For a time, I tried to justify my actions and my behavior and the things I did. Of course, it finally reached the place where I couldn't do that. I have done things that don't hew to the line by any means. I don't know whether I feel any shame about them or not. I don't think I really do."

The limits of such rationalizations were tested when Herbert introduced Allen to a paroled ex-convict named Little Jack Melody, who happened to be seeing Kerouac's old girlfriend Vicki Russell. Melody, whom Allen characterized as "a sort of subdivision cousin of the Mafia," was in many ways too gentle for his gangster reputation. He had helped Vicki through the rigors of heroin withdrawal, and when Allen fell ill with severe bronchitis, he and Huncke nursed him back to health, much the way Allen had helped Huncke. Vicki was "really a remarkable, beautiful, good-hearted, tender girl," in Allen's eyes, and she further endeared herself by supplying him with marijuana and a Victrola for his records. Though both lived outside the law, Allen never viewed them as dangerous; he accepted them as he did Herbert Huncke, as people forced to drop moral judgment in exchange for survival.

Herbert, Little Jack, and Vicki wasted little time in establishing Allen's apartment as a warehouse for stolen goods, and the place soon filled up with stolen furniture, clothing, silverware, and radios. For a brief period, a cigarette machine occupied a spot in the kitchen. Allen realized, too late, that he had become unwittingly involved in a burglary ring, and his uneasiness grew to near-terror when the trio broke into a detective's Harlem home and burglarized an estimated ten thousand dollars' worth of clothing and jewelry. Ever since Burroughs's apartment had been raided by the police the year before, Allen had worried that the police might have read his and Bill's correspondence, with their many references to drugs; he feared that they would burst in on him at any time. Now, with a member of the force victimized and an intensive investigation all but assured, Allen teetered on the brink of paranoia. Unable to confront the group, he hoped to escape the situation by visiting Bill and Joan in Louisiana, but these plans fell through when Joan wrote to inform him that Bill had been arrested on April 5 for drug and illegal firearms possession.

Allen's friends shared his concern. Jack Kerouac urged Allen to disassociate himself from the group, but he refused to become involved when Allen asked whether he could store his archives at Kerouac's home. "If you really wanted to get them out of the house, you would have done it already yourself," Kerouac claimed. Lucien Carr, recently paroled and now working as a wire-service editor, worried that the police would read the journals, with their references to Carr, and draw a connection between him and Ginsberg, should they ever discover the stolen property; the last thing he needed was even a far-reaching connection that might jeopardize the low profile he was trying to maintain. Allen felt he was on a fence, caught between the inspiration Huncke's activities might supply for his poetry and the consequence he would pay for sanctioning the burglaries.

One evening, Allen accompanied Huncke, Little Jack, and Vicki as they made their rounds. Although he rarely kept any of the stolen goods for himself, Allen admitted that he got a vicarious thrill when he saw some of the loot they had brought back to the apartment, and as a writer, he was interested in the details of their regular trips to the streets of New York. However, once he was in the car with them and saw them in action, Allen wanted no part of the stealing. When they asked him to stand guard as a lookout while they broke into a row of parked cars, Allen declined, with mixed feelings. "I had gone along with them on the ride, not knowing how I would react or what would happen," he wrote. "I thought, possibly, I might take part in a car haul. But I did not, when the opportunity arose, from a clammy feeling of fear and desire not to get involved in the actual operation."

Although they humored Allen when he was around, the group, particularly Little Jack and Vicki, preyed on Allen's naïveté and generosity. They had commandeered his apartment, and by storing stolen goods there, they had put him in a precarious position. Allen knew that he needed to take some kind of action.

Lucien finally persuaded Allen to move away from the apartment until things cooled down. Burroughs had posted bond in New Orleans and had fled the United States for Mexico, and Allen decided to visit him there, under the guise of helping Bill overcome his morphine addiction. When Vicki and Little Jack announced that they would occupy the apartment in his absence, Allen finally put his foot down and ordered them to remove their stolen property.

Too much was happening too quickly, and Allen, two months shy of his twenty-third birthday, was caught in the center of a storm raging out of his control. He was consorting with known criminals. Many of his acquaintances were hooked on drugs. His ambivalence about his homosexuality was further muddied by his association with Huncke, who had sexual hang-ups himself. His intellectual pursuits presented more questions than answers. He needed a starting point, a place to begin his pursuit of the possibilities offered in his Blake visions of the preceding summer.

Blake had believed that one had to confront terror, to pass through "the Gates of Wrath." Allen initially regarded Huncke as a modern-day model for Blake's observations, but after considering his visions and the events taking place around him, he concluded that Blake's instructions implied a death of ordinary consciousness, even if that meant embracing madness, to "die, go mad, drop dead":

> Zero is appealing
> Appearances are hazy.
> Smart went crazy,
> Smart went crazy.

8

Ginsberg's worst fears were finally realized on April 22, 1949—just over two months after he had taken Herbert Huncke into his apartment. Still hoping to visit Burroughs in Mexico, Allen had packed away many of his personal notes, journals, letters, and poetry, which he intended to store at his brother's house. Since these papers contained numerous references to his sexual behavior and drug use, Allen wisely wanted them removed from the apartment, in the event that the police raided it while he was away. Virtually penniless, Allen could not even afford subway fare across town, and he readily accepted when Little Jack and Vicki offered to drive him to Eugene's home.

For transportation, they were taking a car Little Jack had stolen a month earlier in Washington, D.C. When Allen climbed into the backseat of the car, he found himself surrounded by an array of stolen goods, including suits, coats, jewelry, and furs. Little Jack explained that he was taking the stolen items to his mother's house on Long Island for safekeeping.

It was nearing four o'clock in the afternoon when the car, driven by Little Jack, turned off a main thoroughfare in Bayside, Queens, and onto a one-way street. Unfortunately for Allen, they were traveling in the wrong direction, and a police patrol car was parked nearby. When a police officer tried to wave down the misdirected car, Little Jack panicked, hit the accelerator, and swerved around the squad car, nearly hitting a policeman standing in the street. A wild six-block chase ensued. With the police closing in, Little Jack tried to guide his car onto a side street at sixty-five miles per hour. He lost control of the car, jumped a curb, and hit a telephone pole. The force of the collision overturned the car several times. It came to rest upside down. Incredibly, no one was seriously injured.

With the sound of the sirens growing nearer, Allen realized that he had to act quickly, but he was frozen in panic. The incriminating papers were scattered throughout the overturned car. He couldn't find his glasses, which had been broken in the crash. He somehow had to get in touch with Herbert and tell him to remove the rest of the evidence from the apartment, but he had only seven cents in his pocket and couldn't afford so much as a phone call, let alone transportation home. Little Jack and Vicki were fleeing the car, each heading in different directions and leaving Allen to fend for himself.

The hopelessness of his plight hit him. He experienced a "very distinct sensation, slightly mystical, that all my mistakes of the past year—my moral indecision and my slight acquisitive nature in some of the loot that was coming into the house—had led in a chain to this one retribution moment where now I was going to have to pay for it." With his name and address written on his papers, his apprehension was inevitable. Still, Allen rationalized, he hadn't been seen driving the car and there was no way the police could connect the stolen goods in the car to him. If he somehow managed to get the remainder of the stolen property out of his apartment, he might have to answer only for the contents of his archives.

Without money, crazy with fear and remorse, and blurry-eyed from the loss of his glasses, Allen tried to make his way across the city to his apartment. With no idea where he was going, he wandered into a candy store, casually identified himself as a "naturalist" on a walk, and asked, "How do you get to New York?" After receiving directions and bumming enough money to phone Huncke with a warning to "clean up the place," Allen roamed and hitchhiked around until he found a familiar subway station. He managed to beg enough money for his fare, and when he finally arrived back at the apartment, he ran up the stairs and into his place, only to find Herbert stooped over a broom, calmly sweeping cigarette butts and bottle caps into a pile on the kitchen floor. Nothing had been moved or hidden.

"My God, Herbert, what are you doing?" Anger and disbelief overcame Allen. "You didn't have to *sweep* the place. The police will be here any minute now." He grabbed the drugs stashed in the apartment and flushed them down the toilet.

"Why get hung up?" Huncke asked, still sweeping. "It's hopeless now. I've been through this so many times. There's nothing you can do."

Huncke was correct in his assessment of their plight. Allen looked around the apartment at the furniture and clothing that would have taken hours to remove. All his friends' words of advice returned to him. It was over.

The police arrived a short time later.

9

The early editions of the April 23, 1949, *New York Times* ran a front-page story under the headline WRONG WAY TURN CLEARS UP ROBBERY. Allen Ginsberg's participation in the fiasco was naked to the world:

> One of the accused, Allen Ginsberg, 21 years old [sic], of 1401 York Avenue, told the police that he was a copy boy for a news service who had "tied-in" with the gang, all with police records, to obtain "realism" he needed to write a story.

A *World-Telegram* headline announced WRONG-WAY AUTO TIPS OFF POLICE TO NARCOTICS-RULED BURGLARY GANG, while the *Daily News* featured a front-page photograph of Ginsberg, Huncke, and Russell getting out of a police car. The reportage was predictably hyperbolic.

"I was advertised as the brilliant student genius who was plotting out big criminal scenes," Allen told *New Yorker* writer Jane Kramer years later. "Another newspaper had it that I was addicted to drugs, and this gang kept me supplied and forced me to mastermind robberies. It was all a bunch of awful misinterpretations."

His plight, however, was not exaggerated. Huncke and Melody had extensive criminal records, Huncke having served seven jail sentences (six for narcotics violations and one for burglary) and Melody with a record of eighteen arrests. Vicki Russell had on three occasions been arrested for narcotics addiction. Along with Ginsberg, all were charged with burglary, grand larceny, receiving stolen goods, and attempting to run over a policeman. Huncke and Melody were denied bail, while Allen and Vicki were held on $2,500 bond. A shamed, tearful Louis Ginsberg went to New York to pay Allen's bail.

Ironically, Columbia University supplied the key to Allen's defense. Although he was generally regarded as a troublemaker on campus, his professors believed that a prison sentence might be very damaging to his already-fragile state of mind. Mark Van Doren promised to put in a good word for him, but only after he lectured him on his behavior and advised him to abandon his current lifestyle. ("A lot of us around here have been thinking maybe you'd better hear the clank of iron, Ginsberg," Van Doren told Allen. "You don't seem to realize what you're doing. If you want my help, you've got to promise never to break the law again.") Lionel Trilling introduced Allen and Louis Ginsberg to Herbert Wechsler, a Columbia criminal law professor, who advised Allen to plead insanity. The Columbia dean, Harry Corman, called the district attorney, a Columbia alumnus, and arranged a plea of psychological disability, on condition that Ginsberg be placed in psychoanalytic therapy. Since he had, at best, a weak case against Allen, the district attorney agreed. Corman offered Allen the services of the Columbia Presbyterian Psychiatric Institute free of charge.

These arrangements had a mixed effect on Allen. He was relieved to have escaped a prison sentence, yet he felt guilty about retaining his freedom while the others suffered through five-year prison sentences. Moreover, he questioned his own assessment of Huncke's being a "saint of old in the making": If Herbert was indeed an innocent man suffering at the hands of, and responding to, his environment—a world of disassociation with humanity—shouldn't Allen be going to jail in order to go to heaven? Again, Allen found his singular philosophy grinding against gears of reality. Writing John Clellon Holmes shortly before he was committed, Allen mused that "it would be quite a miraculous and wonderful surprise if one day as the result of analysis I should have my eyes open and see that *I* am what is troubling me in the world at large, and in other people's conduct, ideas, etc. That, like Oedipus, I am the criminal that has been bringing on all the plague."

Allen stayed with Louis in Paterson while he waited for the legal issues of his case to be worked out. The tensions between father and son were excruciating, with Louis Ginsberg angry and incomprehensible about his son's talk of visions and dark saints. Both tried to maintain a civil environment, but strong arguments flared up frequently. The tensions and frustrations were manifest on one such occasion when Allen tried to type up a letter of application for a job, only to crumple it and pound at his head with his fists. Adding to the turmoil was the announcement that Naomi Ginsberg, about to be released from the mental hospital, wanted Allen to move into an apartment with her.

By the time he was admitted to the Psychiatric Institute in June, Allen was so overwrought that he wondered seriously whether he *was* indeed insane; nearly everyone representing "sane" society seemed to think so. He also wondered, as he stood in the corridors of the hospital, clutching a copy of the *Bhagavad-Gita* and waiting to be assigned his room, what it would be like living among the insane for months or maybe even years. The thought overwhelmed him. He was suddenly very angry with Huncke for getting him into this predicament; with the law for being so seemingly cruel and indifferent to the plight of people like him; with the mass media for its obsession with sensational cases like his; with the police for confiscating one of his books on mysticism, claiming, "We don't allow anything but religious books in the can." To Allen, everyone— including himself, his father, and his friends—were part of a cruel system that crushed the human spirit. He returned to the depression he'd felt nearly two years earlier, when he'd written in his journal:

I feel as if I am at a dead
end and so I am finished. . . .
Maybe if I continued things
would please me more but now
I have no hope and I am tired.

As he stood in the hall, pondering his bleak existence, Allen watched a man being wheeled into his ward. Clad in a bulky bathrobe and bloated from insulin shock treatments, the man got up and sauntered over to where Allen was standing. Thinking he was dealing with a lunatic, Allen began recalling aloud all of his visionary experiences. The man listened, unimpressed.

"Oh, well, you're new here," he told Allen, a trace of cynicism in his voice. "Wait awhile and you'll meet some of the other repentant mystics."

The comment stunned Ginsberg and, as was his habit when he was nervous or cornered, he let literature fire his next volley. When the man asked him who he was, Allen said, "I'm Myshkin," referring to the gentle but mentally disturbed prince in Dostoyevski's *The Idiot*.

"I'm Kirilov," the man shot back. In Dostoyevski's *The Possessed*, Kirilov was a cynical, suicidal character unable to tolerate joy or love.

The man's name was Carl Solomon, and the irony of a chance meeting of two highly intelligent men in a madhouse was not something that escaped Ginsberg. Their initial exchange was memorable not just because it was a witty or clever introduction between two men who would become in a few years well-known figures (though reluctantly, on Solomon's part) in a movement ill-defined by the news media and mythologized by its members; rather, the exchange symbolized a crucial element in the sanity/insanity question that would become a major theme in Beat Generation writings. The madhouse offered unique, startling, almost microscopic views of the mind turned away from the "norm." Both Solomon and Ginsberg were sensitive beings, cognizant of the potential for discovery—of self and others—in such an environment.

Ever since Allen and Lucien Carr had begun discussing their New Vision four years earlier at Columbia, Allen had been convinced that the post–World War II social and literary environment in the United States was destroying creativity and aesthetics. As far as Allen was concerned, Carl Solomon was living proof that the best minds of his generation were being destroyed by madness.

10

With his world split by a number of psychic fault lines, Allen needed a friend. Jack Kerouac had written sympathetic letters commending Allen's willingness to be committed to the Psychiatric Institute. "It shows your interest in things and people," he told Allen, though he also expressed fear that Allen might eventually go insane if he continued to believe or pretend he was. He also wondered whether Allen was "always trying to justify [his] ma's madness against the logical, sober but hateful society." In his letters, Jack tried to stay upbeat and encouraging. "Next year I'm getting a mountain ranch," he mentioned.

"Worry about green face, not laws. (I was once in a nuthouse, y'know.)" Now living in Denver, Jack was busy working on the proofs of *The Town and the City*, which, at Mark Van Doren's urging, had been accepted for publication by Harcourt, Brace. Jack missed Allen's companionship, and his letters to Allen were filled with encouragement aimed at helping Allen see himself in a better light. "I only want you to be happy and do your best toward that end . . . you are a great young poet and already a great man."

Bill Burroughs's assessment of Allen's situation was less kind. His letters to Jack and Allen expressed concern that Allen was not "rational." Burroughs questioned why Allen was allowing himself to be influenced by the authorities. "Imagine being herded around by a lot of old women like Louis Ginsberg and Van Doren," Burroughs wrote Kerouac. "Besides I don't see why Van Doren puts in his 2 cents worth. Sniveling old liberal fruit." Burroughs had had difficulties of his own with figures of authority. He'd been angry about his most recent drug bust, but even more so about the Border Patrol agents who were busy deporting many of the laborers on his cotton farm. He seethed when the bureaucrats from the Department of Agriculture gave him directives about what, where, and when to plant. He was fed up with what he felt was an oppressive situation, and he was all too glad to leave the country for Mexico. When Allen had written from the hospital with the news that he was reconsidering his career plans and thinking again of becoming a labor lawyer, Burroughs responded with a testy letter that not only put down Allen's aspirations but also rejected labor leaders, unions, and the general political climate in the United States itself. "I think the U.S. is heading in the direction of a Socialist police state similar to England, and not too different from Russia," Bill said. "I congratulate myself on my timely withdrawal."

As always, word from Neal Cassady was sporadic, further evidence of the gulf between Allen and Neal. The previous year, Allen had upset Neal with his response to Neal's announcement that he and Carolyn were getting married. "You and I are now further apart than ever," he had responded, telling Allen that he could remember him "only with effort" and suggesting that they quit communicating. Allen had refused the bait and their resulting correspondence had taken on friendlier tones, but it was obvious to Allen that Neal was otherwise preoccupied. Their letters were getting shallow: "Letters between you and me are like conversation between two equally beat bums, either we are garrulous and complaining or short-writ and enigmatic; but I don't think we make sense." Apparently in agreement, Neal wrote Allen very few letters.

One of the most empathetic responses came from Joan Vollmer, who in an October 31 letter told Allen that word of his hospitalization was no real surprise to her. She had been out of Bellevue for three years, yet she still felt, as she wrote Allen, "that anyone who doesn't blow his top once is no damn good." Joan knew what Allen meant when he spoke about visions, and she encouraged him not to reject them altogether.

Within the confines of the mental institution, Carl Solomon became Allen's closest confidant. A man of sharp contrasts, Solomon was a bright student of Surrealist writers, with a compelling interest in unconventional behavior, especially his own. Two years younger than Allen, Solomon boasted of experiences Ginsberg could only imagine. A brilliant student, Solomon had skipped four grades in public school and had attended a high school for the academically gifted. At fifteen, he had entered the City College of New York and joined a Marxist organization called the American Youth for Democracy. Two years later, in 1945, he joined the merchant marine, and he spent the next couple of years alternating his time between the merchant marine and school. In 1947, while stationed in France, he left his ship and attended a reading given by French Surrealist writer Antonin Artaud, gaining an appreciation for Artaud's literature as well as his distrust in any form of psychiatry. Upon returning to the States, he enrolled at Brooklyn College and moved to Greenwich Village, where he began associating with existentialist artists. Fascinated by the idea of gratuitous crime, and prompted by an almost suicidal nihilism, he stole a peanut-butter sandwich from Brooklyn College cafeteria and showed it to a policeman, hoping his actions would land him in a mental institution; he was ordered to consult a psychiatrist. On his twenty-first birthday, he arrived at the Psychiatric Institute asking for a lobotomy. The hospital refused. The day Allen met him, Solomon was emerging from a coma brought on by insulin shock treatment.

Solomon initially perceived Allen to be "literary, erudite, and puckish," judging him "insufficiently deranged by comparison with other patients to capture my attention." Intellectually, they were almost opposites, with Allen easily influenced and, Carl believed, "obviously the product of his own social circle." Solomon referred to Ginsberg as "the dopey daffodil" because Allen impressed him as being a naïve collegiate English major stuck on the ideas of poets as sensitive beings, while Solomon favored Artaud's concept of "the poet as brute." He appointed himself, somewhat arrogantly, as Allen's intellectual foil.

The two met daily on the ward, reading each other their work and arguing about everything from literature to politics to psychiatry. Carl recommended that Allen read books by Artaud, Genet, Isou, Michaux, and other French writers, and it wasn't long before Ginsberg was becoming as well schooled in these writings as Solomon. They bantered over the news of the day and its implications, discussing, in Solomon's words, "survival in a world containing much hostility as well as natural peril." Allen spoke to Solomon of his mother's illness, as well as mentioning, in his usual romanticized terms, his friendships with Kerouac and Burroughs.

In some ways, their relationship bore a strong resemblance to the ones Allen shared with Kerouac, Burroughs, and Lucien Carr. Solomon characterized his and Allen's association in the mental institution as a period of almost constant fighting, with each taking a watchdog approach to the other's "tendency toward intellectual laziness and opportunism." They wrote long letters to famous poets, such as T.S. Eliot and William Carlos Williams, but they never sent them. Solomon was not impressed with Allen's rhymed poetry, which he found to be "more concerned with technique than content." A student of Surrealism, Solomon had little interest in prosody.

Actually, Solomon taught Ginsberg much about unconventional behavior. Allen's remorse over "L'affaire auto," as he referred to his escapade with Little Jack Melody and Vicki Russell, had plunged him into self-loathing because of what his unconventional behavior had cost him, but by example, Carl Solomon showed him another side of the issue. Solomon may have been mad in the eyes of society, but he was also brilliant, attuned enough to himself to appreciate the improbability of society's acceptance of a person who was both ingenious and insane. "There are no intellectuals in madhouses," he wryly observed.

Allen saw much of himself, as well as his mother, in Solomon. Years later, when he wrote "Howl," he would not only dedicate the work to Solomon but would lionize him throughout the poem:

> I'm with you in Rockland
>> where fifty more shocks will never return your soul to its
>> body again from its pilgrimage to a cross in the void. . . .

Solomon's friendship helped Allen survive one of the most difficult periods of his life and, in all probability, he was largely responsible for helping Ginsberg retain his sanity. Columbia University officials might have felt that prison would have defeated Allen, but the mental hospital was not the answer, either. While he felt hopeful of reaching an understanding of himself through analysis, Allen also felt "empty and uninspired," as he wrote shortly before his admission to the Psychiatric Institute. The bureaucratic structure of the mental institution reminded him of the world outside—a world that demanded one obey rules, even at the cost of one's peace of mind.

Like Carl Solomon, Allen wanted to die but was afraid of suicide. Solomon believed that lobotomy was the most painless form of suicide; Allen argued otherwise. Believing, as he later said, that "my obligation was to annihilate my ordinary consciousness and expand my mystic consciousness through death," Allen turned to the one place he could shatter his present state without sacrificing his body: his poetry. Survival, if not outright sanity, depended upon his superimposing visionary consciousness onto everyday life:

> I am living in Eternity.
> The ways of the world
> Are the ways of Heaven.

6
Empty Mirror

All work has been an imitation of the literary cackle in my head. . . .

1

As his psychiatrists quickly determined, Allen was far from insane. His intelligence tests indicated him to be of superior, almost genius, intellect, and even if his behavior was regarded as unusual—to give him the benefit of the doubt—Ginsberg showed no signs of psychosis or dangerous mental disorder. The official opinion of Allen was that he was "an average neurotic." Still, in the judgment of the people at the Psychiatric Institute, Allen's behavior was of a disturbing nature, and the doctors felt that he had to learn to conform to society's standards if he ever expected to function normally in it. In essence, that meant finding a job, forsaking homosexuality in favor of a steady relationship with a woman, and following society's rules. After all he had been through in the past couple of years and the price it had exacted from his peace of mind, Allen tended to agree with the conclusion.

Allen spent more than eight months at the Psychiatric Institute, receiving his formal discharge on February 27, 1950. During his stay, he obeyed the hospital rules and was generally agreeable with the doctors he was consulting. No doubt part of this conformity could be attributed to his realization that he would not be released until his attendants believed he was adequately ready to function in society again, but another part reflected genuine effort on Allen's part to change his behavior. As a nonconformist, he had not been much better off than his mother, and he was weary from the long periods of depression. If playing by the rules held the promise of any kind of happiness, he was willing to try.

Allen declared to Jack Kerouac that his days of homosexuality were over. It was difficult enough to adopt an open gay lifestyle in that era, but Allen's tendency to fall for straight men seemed to magnify his frustration and unhappiness. He would try the heterosexual life, he told Kerouac, but it was not going to be easy. "I wish I could meet a really gone sweet girl who could love me," he wrote Jack shortly before he left the Psychiatric Institute, "[b]ut I guess a really gone sweet girl is too much to expect."

Back in Paterson, Allen kept up a good front in his father's house. Louis had remarried the previous year, and he and his new wife, Edith, had purchased a new house at 416 East Thirty-fourth Street. Since Edith had a son and daughter from a previous marriage, Allen found himself adapting to a new family, which turned out to be less trouble than he might have anticipated. Edith and Louis had met in 1947, and Allen had taken an immediate liking to Edith. She was bright and lively and, perhaps as important as anything to Allen at the time, tolerant of his homosexuality. As part of the Reichian therapy that he had undergone in 1948, Allen had told Louis of his sexual preference for men although, as he recalled in his poem " 'Don't Grow Old,' " he was not entirely honest with his father:

> A look startled his face. "You mean you like to take men's
> penises in your mouth?"
> Equally startled, "No, no," I lied, "that isn't what it means."

The way Allen had explained it to Louis, his homosexuality was a matter of his not being capable of being sexually stimulated by women. Even so, Louis had been deeply troubled by Allen's disclosure, and he was especially upset when he became aware of Allen's feelings toward Neal Cassady. In a 1948 letter, he had admonished Allen, "So, take my advice now, put a tourniquet knot around your affection for N.; tone your letters down properly." When Allen had been admitted to the Psychiatric Institute, Louis still harbored the hope that his son might be "cured" of his homosexuality, Louis believing, as did many people at the time, that homosexuality was a mental disorder.

Edith was an effective buffer between father and son, possessing an openminded sensibility throughout these impassioned times. She liked Allen's friends, particularly Jack. She had been through many trying experiences in her previous marriage, and she had learned the value of tolerance. Both she and Louis had been told by Allen's doctors that there was very little they could do about his homosexuality other than to accept it as part of his character— that is, if they intended to have any kind of close relationship with him.

Allen's outward pursuit of a "normal" existence kept affairs relatively peaceful around the Ginsberg household. However, as Allen had predicted, it was not easy. He had difficulty finding a job, even with his Columbia diploma. His search for reporting jobs with local papers, begun while he was still in the hospital, was frustrating. He was turned down by the *Paterson Morning Call* and the *Passaic Evening News* because there were no openings with those papers at the time. Perhaps most ironic of all, he was rejected by the conservative *Paterson Evening News* because of *Louis's* liberal political stances—or so Allen believed.

Trying to be responsible, Allen discovered, was problematic—more so than he had assumed it would be. People lived fearful lives, their thoughts and actions dictated by their beliefs that society rewarded only the conformists. "I am beginning to get a touch of just how strange and actually sordid the atmosphere here is among those who run the city officially," he complained to Kerouac. "Most people here who seem to be at all sensitive or powerful or rich seem to live lives and think thoughts dominated by the smallest sounding (to an outsider) fears for social security and business position. Friendship is actually political." Feeling as if he was being victimized by the machinery of the system, Allen wondered, in his self-pity, whether he would "actually be crucified after all." Fortunately, his Uncle Leo was able to help him secure a reporting job with the *Labor Herald*, a paper published by the New Jersey AFL.

For all his therapy at the Columbia Psychiatric Institute, Allen was still troubled and depressed. The real world, as it had been presented to him, seemed empty and meaningless. The ideals of youth were replaced soon enough by the cynical and sometimes destructive mechanizations of another life—one that left the individual feeling alone and lost. It was no wonder people disregarded or hid from the consciousness he had experienced in Harlem in the summer of 1948: Placed in the context of daily life, it could lead one to despair.

2

Although he was too occupied with other aspects of his life to realize it, Allen had made a major breakthrough in his writing, beginning at the time he had been admitted to the Psychiatric Institute. His main literary concern was the completion of his *Book of Doldrums*, which he still believed to be a significant work. That sequence of poems, in Allen's view, best represented the evolution of his present emotional state.

In reality, his best work was being recorded in his journal, not as formal poetry but as prose entries. His therapy had put him more in touch than ever with his inner feelings, and the notations in his journals were in effect a daily chart of his mental activity. As internal monologues, the entries contained the natural rhythms of speech, and since Ginsberg was writing for his own benefit and not with the idea of publishing the entries, he was unconcerned about the formal construction of proper image, meter, metaphor, rhyme, and other elements of poetry composition that had concerned him in the past.

"I was just writing prose and not thinking of it as poetry," Ginsberg said of the journal entries, many of which were later arranged as lines of poetry and included in *Empty Mirror*. "I didn't realize that it was that kind of succinct, objective notation that was the ideal way for me to go in terms of being real in the writing, which is to say to look outside yourself and write down some objective description of external or internal reality that other people could visualize or connect with. I didn't understand the literary value of the prose when I was writing it. It was accidental."

The difference between the formal poetry that Ginsberg was writing at the time (published in *The Gates of Wrath*) and the informal work eventually included in *Empty Mirror* is noteworthy, especially since both were written during the same time span. In terms of theme, Ginsberg is exploring the same territory in both; yet in the rhymed verse, his intent is buried in stilted imagery and metric schemes, the poet defeating himself by paying too much attention to structure at the cost of content, while in the prose entries, he is much more direct. This is especially apparent in a poem such as "The Trembling of the Veil," in which Ginsberg attempts to recreate, by using concrete detail, the sense of visionary experience that he had been unable to reproduce in his earlier vision-inspired poems of 1948:

> Today out of the window
> the trees looked like live
> organisms on the moon.
>
> Each bough extended upward
> covered at the north end
> with leaves, like a green
>
> hairy protuberance. . . .

This poem was buried in a lengthy journal entry. Shown in its context, "The Trembling of the Veil" is illustrative of Ginsberg's attempts to come to terms with the visionary elements of his life and work, and with the sense of realism that his analysts insisted he grasp:

> Trembling of veil today—out of window the trees seemed like live organisms on the moon. I got the idea originally from speculation on the look of the boughs—extending upward, covered at the north end with leaves like a green-hairy protuberance, with a scarlet-and-pink shot tip of budding leaves, waving delicately in the sunlight, being blown by the winds—all the arms of the trees bending & straining downward at once when the wind pushed them. I remember from my earlier visions that trees are live animals, but do not often think so. I know that everything is alive—but the precise vibrant quality of aliveness or life continually escapes my definition and understanding except for moments that are so far apart & so buried in the sands of thought that they are treasures I come upon only accidentally when I wander on the shore forgetful of my imagined purposes there.
>
> I was struck again today by the continuity of metaphysical illusion that occurs to me, and the depth of its deceptiveness, the length of its history (It goes back beyond memory. "Who am I?") am I face to face with the eternal, or am I the victim of fear and lethargy and all too human pride? Vanity? Am I becoming human or superhuman? The analysts say human. The poets say superhuman. What terms are there to get worried about?

The answer, of course, is that he was being *both* human and superhuman, but he had yet to realize it. As Ginsberg later noted, he wanted to gaze at the world as if he was having a vision, and by jotting down the minute particulars of what he was seeing, he might be able to create, through association in his readers, a feeling of shared vision: "I figured that if I was in Eternity, or if I was a poet, or if I was a spiritual angel, or if the mind was open, there wasn't anything I could do about it, except maybe look at something specific. And describe that. . . . In other words, the only way I could actually communicate the sense of eternity that I had, or might have, or wanted to have, was through concrete particular detail grounding my mind, like taking the opposite direction of the superhuman apocalyptic-light-hunger poetry that I'd been churning out before: taking exactly the opposite direction by turning around to face everyday universe, BE HUMAN!"

From the summer of 1949 to early 1952, Ginsberg wrote scores of prose passages from which he would glean the poems to appear in *Empty Mirror*. He remained interested in capturing the detail of all levels of consciousness, including the dream state ("The Blue Angel") and the mind altered by artificial means ("Marijuana Notation"). In the best entries, Ginsberg joined external and internal detail. "Marijuana Notation" finds the poet deploring the fact that he has always considered himself sick, then noting that Baudelaire, a poet known for his dark images, was able to convert his moments of solitude into flashes of epiphany. From this introspective mood, Ginsberg shifts abruptly and unexpectedly into a brief description of Christmas carolers standing outside a Paterson department store. The movement from internal to external is significant. The reader is given the rare opportunity to watch the shifting of thoughts, as one shifts from daydream consciousness to reality, much the way as happens to everyone every day, usually without one's taking notice.

During his treatment at the Psychiatric Institute, Ginsberg was encouraged to move away from his preoccupation with his visions and to return to terra firma. This led him not to reject his Blake visions but to use the objects of daily life as the focus of his concentration. Ginsberg recognized this when he noted that the ways of the earth were the ways of heaven—eternity was found in the here and now—but he was not totally ready to accept it as an artist. Even as he steadily wrote some of his best work in his journals, unaware that he was creating a form of literature, he continued to produce rhymed, Elizabethan-influenced works in his poetry.

3

On March 30, 1950, Allen wrote a letter that would dramatically alter the direction of both his poetry and his life. Two nights earlier, he had attended a poetry reading given by William Carlos Williams at the Guggenheim, but afterward, as eager as he was to meet the poet from nearby Rutherford, New Jersey, Allen was far too timid to approach Williams, so he waved at him and scurried off. He decided that a formal introduction, delivered by mail, would be easier for him and more respectful to Williams.

His letter began like almost any fan letter from one young poet to an elder, though Allen, in his own hyperbolic, almost comic style, made the introduction memorable:

Dear Doctor:

In spite of the grey secrecy of time and my own self-shuttering doubts in these youthful rainy days, I would like to make my presence in Paterson known to you, and I hope you will welcome this from me, an unknown young poet, to you, an unknown old poet, who live in the same rusty county of the world. Not only do I inscribe this missive somewhat in the style of those courteous sages of yore who recognized one another across the generations as brotherly children of the muses (which names they will know) but also as fellow citizenly Chinamen of the same province, whose gastanks, junkyards, fens of the alley, millways, funeral parlors, river-visions—aye! the falls itself—are images white-woven in their very beards. . . .

He may have been guilty of overstatement in his formal introduction, but Allen must have had Williams's full attention a few paragraphs into the letter, when he addressed his own goals as a poet:

I envision for myself some kind of new speech—different at least from what I have been writing down—in that it has to be clear statement of fact about misery (and not misery itself), and splendor if there is any out of the subjective wanderings through Paterson. This place is as I say my natural habitat by memory, and I am not following in your traces to be poetic: though I know you will be pleased to realize that at least one actual citizen of your community has inherited your experience in his struggle to love and know his own world-city, though your work, which is an accomplishment you almost cannot have hoped to achieve. . . . I may need a new measure myself, but though I have a flair for your style I seldom dig exactly what you are doing with cadences, line length, sometimes syntax, etc., and cannot handle your work as a solid object—which properties I assume you rightly claim. I don't understand the measure. I haven't worked with it much either, though, which must make the difference. But I would like to talk with you concretely on this. . . .

Allen enclosed nine poems—"samples of my best writing," as he called them—with the letter. All of the poems had been composed within the past three years and, as he noted in his letter, none so much as remotely resembled the type of poetry for which Williams was well known. Having read (and reviewed) Williams's *Paterson (Book One)*, Allen was familiar with the older poet's dictum—"no ideas but in things"—but there was nothing at all in Allen's poetry that suggested interest in objectivism or, as Ginsberg admitted himself, any understanding of it.

Williams, although happy to hear from a local poet who appreciated his work, was not excited about Allen's poetry. Allen had a better than average command of the rhymed, meticulously measured poetry written by nineteenth-century Englishmen, yet, as Williams pointed out to Allen, "In this mode, perfection is basic." Allen's poems, Williams hastened to mention, were not perfect. Nor was Williams particularly interested in contemporary poets who were following any of the traditional forms; instead, he was trying to move away from ponderous versifying, "[t]o make a start, out of particulars and make them general, rolling up the sum, by defective means. . . ." In his *Autobiography*, Williams expanded upon the idea, writing that "the poet's business" was "[n]ot to talk in vague categories but to write particularly, as a physician works, upon a patient, upon the thing before him, in the particular to discover the universal."

As a person, Williams was an interesting study. The son of an English father and Puerto Rican mother, William Carlos Williams was born on September 17, 1883. As a young man, he studied both poetry and painting, and along with his friends Ezra Pound, Louis Reznikoff, Louis Zukofsky, and others, he became one of the major influences in objectivist poetry. He was also a pediatrician who practiced mostly among the poor, resulting in his never making a lot of money but, in exchange, gaining a great wealth of experiences that he was able to infuse into his poetry, short stories, plays, and autobiographical writings. His demanding medical practice had the additional effect of influencing the actual form in which he wrote: Because he worked so many hours as a physician, he had to write whenever he could, often using the interim between patients to tap out a quick poem on his office typewriter. Consequently, his work, with its stark, vivid images and short lines, boasted an air of spontaneity that went against the grain of the highly polished and often overwrought poetry of his contemporaries. His best-known poem, "The Red Wheelbarrow," was as perfectly formed as a classic still-life painting, yet it carried the emotional impact of a poem many times its length:

> so much depends
> upon
>
> a red wheel
> barrow
> glazed with rain
> water
>
> beside the white
> chickens.

Williams further believed that the best way to present clarity of image involved the use of local idiom. In the past, poetry had been forced to conform with English manners, even in translation, which Williams found appalling. "Why bother with English when we have a language of our own?" he asked, more as a challenge than a rhetorical question. Contemporary language had its own built-in rhythms and meanings that could be put to use by the observant poet, and Williams staked his career and reputation, particularly in his later works, on his ability to align the images he was trying to present in his poetry with contemporary language.

Ginsberg was impressed by this approach. As he explained, "He was trying to adapt his poetry rhythms out of the actual talk rhythms he heard in the place that he was, rather than metronome or sing-song archaic literary rhythms he would hear in a place inside his head from having read other writings. I suddenly realized he was inventing out of the actual ground of Rutherford, New Jersey, a different body-speech and that anything he said was absolutely natural, and didn't violate human being talk, didn't come from another era but came directly from the ground that he stood on."

By the time Ginsberg met him in early 1950, Williams had a modest yet very loyal following that would continue to increase long after his death in 1963. As a poet who found himself at odds with so many of his contemporaries, Williams delighted in encouraging younger poets, especially if he sensed that their work might be a continuation of his own. He may not have cared for the first batch of poems submitted to him by Ginsberg, but he was both too wise and too generous to turn him away. He encouraged Allen to keep working at his poetry and to send him more.

4

For all his apparent attempts at living a more ordered, even if mundane, life, Allen never strayed far from the New York bohemian life that he found so compelling. On weekdays, he would get up early and take the bus to his job in Newark, put in his hours, and return home for a rather sedate life that found him spending time with his family, writing, wandering around the streets of Paterson, or even going on an occasional date. On weekends, he was off to New York, where he was able to satisfy that part of his spirit that could not be suppressed by psychoanalysis, ill luck, family, or the unbending restrictions of society.

It was an exciting time to be in New York. An entire culture of postwar avant-garde painters, musicians, writers, and performing artists had taken root in the city. On any given night, such Abstract Expressionist painters as Willem de Kooning, Jackson Pollock, or Franz Kline might be seen gathering with friends at the Cedar Tavern at Eighth Street and University Place. Musicians such as Charlie Parker, Miles Davis, Dizzy Gillespie, Coleman Hawkins, Gerry Mulligan, and George Shearing kept late hours at jazz clubs. Living Theatre founders Julian Beck and Judith Malina anchored a diverse group of artists that included dancer Merce Cunningham, avant-garde musician John Cage, and painter/musician Larry Rivers.

As always, Allen saw a lot of Jack Kerouac and Lucien Carr, and he continued to hang out with Carl Solomon. Through John Clellon Holmes, he met Jay Landesman, a St. Louis native who was launching a new magazine, *Neurotica*, and through Kerouac he met Bill Cannastra, a wild social dervish who seemed to know every literary figure in New York. Also included in Allen's immediate circle were John Kingsland, a friend from his Columbia days; Philip Lamantia, a young surrealist poet originally from San Francisco; and Alan Ansen, a wealthy acquaintance of Allen's and close friend of W. H. Auden. One of the group's favorite meeting places was the San Remo, a Greenwich Village bar whose clientele was largely a mixture of artists and Village bohemians. Allen later dubbed the ménage "the subterraneans"—a label that Jack Kerouac was to use as the title for a future novel.

Kerouac's *The Town and the City* had been published by Harcourt, Brace on March 2, and Jack filled his time by playing the role of recently published author, signing books and making promotional appearances, poring over reviews that compared him to Thomas Wolfe, savoring his first moments of attention from the literary community. He met Carl Sandburg, who offered words of encouragement. Jack had always dreamt of wealth and fame resulting from his writing, but the publication of *The Town and the City* provided him with an early lesson on the mechanizations of the publishing business. When the book was released, Jack's editor was out of the country, leaving Jack to shoulder a great amount of the book's promotion on his own. Jack enjoyed the attention to a certain extent but, being shy by nature, he also found it to be a burden. He was shocked to learn, in early April, that his publisher had ceased advertising the book. After a brief flurry of interest, the book's sales had dwindled, and without advertising support from the company, it was unlikely that the novel would earn back its advance, meaning that Jack would receive no royalties for his efforts. Under these circumstances, it was difficult for him to avoid bitterness.

As always, Allen was Jack's staunchest supporter. Not only was Allen pleased to be a featured character in Jack's book but he also got a vicarious thrill in knowing the author of such a large and generally well-received volume. The acceptance of Jack's book was the validation of their lives and beliefs. Allen had given *The Town and the City* a careful, thorough reading. He had offered Jack gentle criticism, expressing disappointment with some of the cuts made by Jack's editor and praising Jack's prose, much of which, in Allen's view, read like poetry. "It is a truly great book deserving of a great response and I am pretty sure that it will make a big stir and get singing reviews," he told Kerouac shortly before its publication. Knowing that Jack's sensitive nature could be easily bruised by harsh remarks directed toward him by friends and critics alike, Allen jumped quickly to Kerouac's defense. "[I]f anybody gets nasty call me in and I'll challenge him to a duel—you have nothing to be humiliated about in any way, it would be crass perversity to dislike your work (and you)."

Allen treated the book as if it was his own, talking up its merits to friends and professional acquaintances, lending his own copy to those who might not have read it due to lack of money. As he would prove to be throughout his life, Allen was a tireless promoter of his friends' works. When he learned that the advertising budget for the book had been dropped, he was nearly as angry as Jack, and he urged his friend to take immediate action. "This may sound like old wives gossip but my original optimistic prognosis, reinforced in my mind by reviews, is being rapidly undermined in my own mind by fears about some commercial slip up unforseen brought on by Harcourt. Do something. Man the lifeboats. . . . You have a duty to protect your investments. . . . Time is crucial."

Jack, who had planned to use his *The Town and the City* royalties to finance trips for his *On the Road* novel, was already plotting his next move. With the help of Justin Brierly, who offered to assist in a book-signing party in Denver, Jack was able to convince Harcourt, Brace to give him the money he needed to travel to Denver.

5

Allen enjoyed his own modest literary success in the spring of 1950 when Jay Landesman published an early, although abbreviated version of "Pull My Daisy," the poem written by Allen and Jack, in *Neurotica*. The magazine, known for its eccentric intellectualism, was a precursor to some of the successful underground magazines of the late fifties and sixties, a move away from the stuffy literary quarterlies. Allen was delighted to be a contributor, even if the circumstances leading to his publication—his first in a nationally distributed magazine—were less than ideal. Allen had to all but badger Landesman into publishing the poem, Landesman finally consenting on the condition that Allen trim the poem to four verses and retitle it. It was published as "Song: Fie My Fum." "It still looks good," Allen remarked, happy to see his work in print. Irrepressible as ever, he recommended that Landesman look at Carl Solomon's work, and then set Neal Cassady to work on a short memoir of his car-stealing days.

Neal had been in New York for months, but Allen rarely saw him. Neal's sexual philandering was finally catching up with him. A year earlier, he and LuAnne had split up, supposedly for good, though Neal always procrastinated in making permanent separations. He and Carolyn had attempted a reconciliation in San Francisco, but that, too, had faltered. Neal had left her a note promising not to bother her anymore. He then left with Jack, who was also in San Francisco at the time, for the East Coast. Once in New York, he had met still another woman, Diana Hansen, and began an affair with her. Diana learned that she was pregnant just about the time that Carolyn delivered Neal's second daughter, Jami, in January 1950. Neal wanted to legitimize his and Diana's child, but he was reluctant to divorce Carolyn formally. Caught up in a life of such soap-opera dimensions, Neal had little time to consider anything other than his own entangled affairs.

Not that it would have mattered much to Allen in any event, for Allen had begun, as he described it to Jack, "a new season, choosing women as my theme." As part of his therapy, Allen had been trying to approach women with heterosexual interest. It had been an awkward venture at first, but in late May, while taking a brief vacation near Cape Cod, he met a woman who absolutely enraptured him, physically and mentally. "I love Helen Parker and she loves me," Allen crooned, describing her to Jack as "a beautiful, intelligent woman who has been around and bears the scars of every type of knowledge and yet struggleth with the serpent knowing full well the loneliness of being left with the apple of knowledge and the snake only."

For three days, Allen reveled in Helen Parker's company. She was older than he, with two children and literary interests of her own. In a way, Allen told Jack, Helen reminded him of Joan Vollmer. (It was a comparison Ginsberg would make on a number of occasions over the years, whenever he met a woman of considerable intelligence and a bohemian inclination.) Once engaged to John Dos Passos, Helen Parker had met a number of well-known literary figures, including Ernest Hemingway, with whom she'd had lunch on one occasion. From these and other encounters, she had a sophistication that Allen admired. They talked about everything they could think of, from literature to metaphysics, and though Allen realized there was no way their relationship could become long-term or permanent, he approached his brief fling as if it was a wonderful gift. He had never had sex with a woman before, and now that he had, he was overjoyed by his belief that he was "a great lover," as he had predicted he might be, and he questioned the homosexuality in his past, wondering if it was "camp, unnecessary, [and] morbid, so lacking in completion and sharing of love as to be almost as bad as impotence and celibacy."

Helen Parker felt a mutual attraction to Allen and proposed that he move in with her on Cape Cod; she would work while he stayed at home and wrote and took care of her two sons. If the arrangement worked out, they could spend their winters in Key West. Allen pondered these suggestions but, with some unhappiness, turned them down, deciding that he wanted to keep his job in Paterson and continue seeing his therapist. He also questioned what kind of father figure he might be for her children. With such complications, the affair reached its conclusion, for all intents and purposes, as soon as Allen returned to Paterson. He continued to see her off and on for the next few months, but they were never again as close as they had been for that brief period on Cape Cod.

Throughout that summer, Allen developed plans for another epic poem, which he was calling "The Shroudy Stranger of the Night." He had long been fascinated with the idea of a mysterious, inexplicable ghost presence, his interests dating back to the days of his youth, when he walked past the shadowy hedges along Graham Avenue in Paterson. He had discussed these memories with Kerouac. Allen had been surprised to learn that Jack had similar fantasies of his own, rooted in his boyhood love of "The Shadow," which evolved into his own character, Doctor Sax, the ghostly presence in his novel of the same name. As an adult, Jack had a recurring nightmare of his being pursued by a hooded presence, which, he explained to Allen in 1949, he had come to believe was actually himself in disguise.

When Allen had begun planning his poem in March 1950, he intended it to be "a long poem about a man whose pride is swallowed by oblivion," though at the time he was uncertain as to what form and style to use. He initially considered writing it in terza rima or cantos form, but after contacting Williams and considering the older poet's use of objectivism in his poetry, Allen decided to write in a style that reflected the evolution of the Shroudy Stranger himself. As Allen conceived him, the Shroudy Stranger would start off as an ethereal presence, not quite human and veiled in mystery, only to evolve into a tragic yet decisively human figure—"an old beat out decayed Bum of America," as Ginsberg described his final form. To maintain his feeling of transitory existence, Allen wanted to set parts of the poem on a railroad bridge, under a river bridge, and in Times Square. As he noted in his journal, there would be shifting styles in the epic, drawing a parallel between the evolution of the Shroudy Stranger and the evolution of poetry itself, "a tour de force—from classic mystical shroudy psalmlike stanzas and rhymes, through the history of poetic language, to bare statement of fact objectivist speech. Begin with symbols and end with things."

As ambitious as these plans were, Allen was educated enough in the different poetic forms to be able at least to attempt the poem. In addition, he had experimented with the Shroudy Stranger figure in two earlier works ("Please Open the Window and Let Me In" and "The Shrouded Stranger," both published eventually in *The Gates of Wrath*), so the theme itself was not untested. Still, the poem turned out to be more difficult to write than he had anticipated. He struggled with the work, filling his notebook with fragments of poetry, revisions, meter schemes, notes, and numerous false starts.

Allen lost his reporting job near the end of September and, believing that he might fare better in a job demanding less mental attention, he took a job in a Paterson ribbon factory. Unfortunately, he was even less suited to this kind of work than he had been to his previous job at the *Labor Herald*. For a wage of $1.25 an hour, Allen was expected to pick up the broken threads and tie them back into the loom. The job itself was not difficult, but Allen would daydream or get lost in thought until he had fallen behind in his work, and he would then grow anxious as he hurried to catch up. His coworkers were little help, leaving him to fend for himself, and after two and a half weeks on the job, he was fired for incompetence. In a letter to Neal Cassady, a depressed Ginsberg worried that he might never be able to hold a decent job because he always found a way to mess up. "It's kind of a bug I have—that's why I never learned to drive," he wrote, ashamed by this sense of failure yet feeling powerless to change his fate. "Truly the real world is my downfall," he concluded.

The experience did provide him with the material for another poem, a humorous work that detailed his trials at the factory. In "How Come He Got Canned at the Ribbon Factory," a prose poem that is little more than a recitation of his failures on the job, Ginsberg made a crucial decision upon which the effectiveness of his poem is based: Rather than write in the introspective first-person voice typical of his writings of the period, Ginsberg elected to write the poem from the standpoint of his coworkers at the factory. The chorus of working girls, as Ginsberg called them, delight in watching Allen get his comeuppance. In their eyes, Allen acted as if the job was beneath him, the kind of employment given to people who are not intelligent enough to engage in more important work. He wanted to be "a god of all the knots," but instead he was a miserable failure. "Obviously he wasn't a real man anyway but a goop," they conclude.

In choosing this point of view, Ginsberg was able to poke fun at his own ego while at the same time commenting on his inability to fit into the real world— both of which were accomplished without his cluttering the poem with the self-pity typical of some of his other works of the time. The poem also found him moving closer to Williams in his use of active, concrete detail. Rather than search for a symbol for his message, Ginsberg let his anecdote tell the story.

6

On October 12, Allen was again badly shaken by the sudden death of one of his friends. This time, the victim was Bill Cannastra, a regular at the San Remo bar. Cannastra had been partying with three friends when, drunk and out of money, he decided to take the subway to Lucien Carr's apartment, where he hoped to borrow some money. The IRT train had just begun to pull away from the Bleecker Street subway platform when one of his companions mentioned the Bleecker Street Tavern and a barmaid they all knew. As a prank, Cannastra acted as if he intended to climb out of the train window, supposedly so he could jump back to the platform and return to the bar. He leaned out the window too far and was thrown hopelessly off-balance as the train lurched away from the platform. His friends, hearing his screams for help, tried to pull him back into the car by grabbing on to his coat, but the material tore away in their hands. The train, picking up speed, entered a tunnel and Cannastra hit his head against one of the tunnel pillars. He was pulled from the car and dragged along the tracks. He died in the ambulance on the way to the hospital.

The manner in which Cannastra died might have been horrifying to those who knew him, but few were surprised that his life ended as early and abruptly as it did. In fact, as Allen pointed out in a letter to Neal Cassady, there was some discussion about whether Cannastra's demise had been an accident at all. He had lived a life that tempted fate on many occasions. If anything, it seemed almost a miracle that he had survived for as long as he had.

Good-looking and exceptionally intelligent, Cannastra appeared to his friends to be the type of person who was either unwilling or unable to accept the gifts that life had given him. A Harvard Law School graduate, Cannastra had practiced law for a short time in New York, but he was eventually fired for tardiness and drunkenness. He had also worked briefly for Random House as a consultant in the compilation of their dictionary. He knew a number of well-known writers, including W. H. Auden and Tennessee Williams. With his intellect and gregarious nature, he seemed capable of succeeding in any career that he chose to pursue.

Instead, he turned his life into a test of limits, pushing himself and others to the brink, as if courage and character could be determined only by the way one reacted to (or, so often in his case, survived) the extremes. The more outrageous the behavior, the better. He danced barefoot on broken glass and lay down in the street in front of oncoming traffic; he was fond of getting drunk and frightening his friends by dancing on the ledges of tall buildings. The life of any party, he was expected to perform, and he rarely disappointed his audience. In "Howl," Ginsberg would characterize Cannastra as the one who "fell out of the subway window, jumped in the filthy Passaic, leaped on negroes, cried all over the street, danced on broken wine glasses barefoot, smashed phonograph records of nostalgic European 1930s jazz finished the whiskey and threw up groaning in the bloody toilet."

In time, however, Cannastra's actions began to look less like wild stunts and more like a death wish; people regarded him as a tragic figure headed directly to the doom of his own choosing. Unable to watch the inevitable, his closest friends abandoned him, leaving him mostly in the company of people who would encourage his death-defying behavior, only to judge him harshly for it afterward. As Ginsberg noted when word of Cannastra's death circulated among his friends and acquaintances, "[t]he great question on everybody's soul, was, was it an accident or did he do it on purpose?" Although he posed the question, he did not know the answer.

He was, however, very disturbed by Cannastra's death. Only a few nights before the accident, he and Cannastra had spent five hours discussing death, and now that it had occurred, Allen concluded that "every tragedy is preceded with intuitive warnings, where situation is [the] result of personal style and direction." The problem, Allen wrote, was that Cannastra did not truly consider the finality of death even as he was flirting with it, and because he did not realize the true consequences of his actions, he was destined to suffer them.

For Allen, these were sobering thoughts, a sort of image in negative of the price he paid for his Blake visions and obsession with unconventional behavior. In his case, Allen had acted in response to what he perceived to be an eternal message, while Cannastra had acted in defiance of eternity itself. Allen used the same phrase to describe the evolution of both his visions and Cannastra's actions: *shadow changes into bone.* There was a very real price that one paid for one's visions, and when all intellectualism was stripped away, the difference between insanity and death was almost indiscernible. Either way, one stared into oblivion.

7

One of the few bright spots in Bill Cannastra's final months had been his relationship with an attractive twenty-year-old woman named Joan Haverty. Raised by a strict mother in upstate New York, Joan had moved to the big city as an act of rebellion, and though she was out of her element in the Village bohemian crowd, she soon found herself under the guidance and protection of Cannastra, who engaged her in lively conversation and involved her in some of his less self-destructive pranks. Joan looked up to Cannastra, who, in turn, acted more in the role of a teacher than a lover in their relationship. That Bill was inclined to be more attracted to men than to women had little bearing on Joan's feelings for him. Crushed by his death, she moved into his loft, which she intended to preserve as a kind of shrine.

Allen knew Joan through his association with Cannastra. In addition, Lucien Carr's apartment was next door to Cannastra's, so Allen had been in the neighborhood, for one reason or another, on frequent occasions. Allen was fond of Joan Haverty, and he began paying her social calls shortly after Cannastra's death. By nature, Allen was supportive of those suffering from depression or anxiety, although his involvement with Joan went beyond his feelings of sympathy for her. Lucien had been encouraging Allen to see her in a more than casual way, but when Allen made his advances, he was rejected, Joan claiming that she was looking only for friendship from men and was not ready for any kind of romantic relationship.

Jack Kerouac was another story entirely. At one time, Kerouac had been much closer to Cannastra than Allen, and when Jack stopped by to visit Joan in early November, an immediate spark was struck between them. Maybe Jack was attracted to Joan's innocence, which would have made her more acceptable to his mother than some of the women he had taken home, or maybe he was looking for an anchor in his life; whatever the reason, the attraction was sudden and powerful, as it was for Joan. Jack proposed marriage the day after he visited Joan, and on November 17, barely a month after Cannastra's death, they were married before a judge, with Lucien and Allen acting as best men. There was a huge party afterward, with Seymour Krim, John Hollander, John Clellon Holmes, Alan Ansen, and Carl Solomon among the nearly two hundred people in attendance. In the wee hours of the morning, Jack, Allen, and Lucien broke out in a version of "Those Wedding Bells Are Breaking Apart That Old Gang of Mine," but, as Allen mentioned, their nostalgia was mostly superficial, "without real sadness, since we knew that anyway we could break into each others apartment still in the middle of the night."

Allen regarded the marriage with skepticism. Joan, he told Neal Cassady, could not compare with Kerouac's "largeness of spirit." As far as Allen could tell, it had been a marriage of convenience, and while he liked Joan and supported the marriage in public, he held private reservations about it. Jack, Allen felt, needed more than the domestic life, and he was not convinced that Joan, for all her attractive features, could provide them. "I don't know what she can give him except stability in sex life, housekeeping, and silent, probably sympathetic company while he's sitting around and children," he wrote Cassady. These observations turned out to be accurate, if not prophetic. As Allen anticipated, there was not enough holding Jack and Joan together to sustain a marriage. It lasted barely half a year.

8

Throughout that fall and early winter, Allen remained faithful to the guidelines of his therapy. He began to see a young aspiring painter from Wyoming named Dusty Moreland, and before too long he was spending a lot of time, including many of his nights, at her West Twelfth Street apartment. He looked around for a number of jobs, settling finally, in December, for a job with the National Opinion Research Center, for which he conducted public-opinion surveys. Apart from his work on his "Shrouded Stranger" poem, his writing was limited almost exclusively to jottings in his journal.

Then, as if in answer to a prayer, a massive letter to Jack Kerouac from Neal Cassady arrived, a twenty-thousand-word epic that sent both Allen and Jack reeling. The letter, dated December 17, was Neal personified, complete with rambling, lengthy passages of stream-of-consciousness prose that was raw but energetic, as fluid as if Cassady himself was in the room, moving about in his nonstop way and sputtering out his story as quickly as he could, lest he forget all the details needed to sustain his colorful monologue. Known today by Beat Generation scholars as the "Joan Anderson letter," it had captured, innocently enough and quite by accident, the spirit of spontaneous writing that both Allen and Jack had been seeking for their own work. Allen later referred to the letter as "a key moment and catalyst," a model for his and Kerouac's later spontaneous writing.

The letter was a mosaic of one man's consciousness, with woven narratives and asides, detailed descriptions of people and places, and heartfelt emotion applied convincingly to events, with little author concern for such formalities as punctuation or grammar. Since the text had been written as an exercise and not with publication in mind, Cassady could be as frank as he wanted to be, and this freedom afforded him the opportunity to write about such topics as suicide, homosexuality, and pregnancy with an honesty that would have been considered unacceptable by publishers at the time. As soon as Kerouac had finished reading the letter, he proclaimed Neal to be "a colossus risen to Destroy Denver!"

Allen, too, was astonished by Cassady's letter. Calling it "an almost pure masterpiece," Allen praised Neal for his "clarity and grace and vigor," adding that he now believed Neal's "salvation and joy lay in [his] recreating the universe in a novel" that had the qualities of his letter.

However, with his tendency to consider the marketability as well as the artistic value of a manuscript, Allen read the letter with a more critical eye than Jack, and where Jack had seen it as a perfect Dostoyevskian work, attractive for its flaws, Allen felt that it needed structuring and cleaning up before it could be sold as a work of fiction to a publisher. In his critique of the letter, Allen tried to nudge Neal into making what he considered to be necessary alterations.

"Mainly, since it was a rambling letter, the subplots and flashbacks were a little in the way but could be easily edited to fit right in, but since you stopped short of the ending, made more chaos. Finish the story then, either [send it] to me (I'd be flattered) or Jack (also I was hung up with personal interest while reading, not tutorial as now, I was humbler then) and I'm sure you can sell it for money with practically hardly any changes as it stands now."

Allen's and Jack's reactions to the letter were indicative of their respective opinions about literature and publishing at the time. Kerouac's publishing experiences, with the less than satisfactory editing and marketing of *The Town and the City*, had left him embittered about author concessions to the commercial aspects of art. Kerouac's next three book-length manuscripts (*On the Road*, *Visions of Cody*, and *The Subterraneans*) would reflect his growing appreciation for the spontaneity of Cassady's writing and disdain for long-accepted standards, and throughout the critical period during which these books were written, Kerouac would wage a stubborn war against the publishing world's insistence that he conform to their standards. Ginsberg, by contrast, was more willing to compromise. Even with his enormous admiration of originality and his desire to accomplish breakthrough works of his own, he still adhered to the ideal— as he once argued with Lucien Carr—that art had to communicate; to accomplish this, Allen argued, a work of art had to reach as many people as possible. Allen, like Jack, was drawn to the ideals of spontaneous writing, but Allen realized that publishing, like society itself, had standards to which one had to conform or else pay the price. Cassady's letter would have an enormous influence on Kerouac's and Ginsberg's works. Jack in particular would find Neal's spontaneous compositional style conducive to the freewheeling, conversational narrative structure he wanted for his novels.

Oddly enough, Allen's and Jack's response to the Joan Anderson letter had an adverse effect on Neal Cassady's writing, even as it was having a positive effect on their own. Neal wrote as he lived his life—in energetic bursts, almost void of self-discipline—and the response to his writing, while pleasing to him, made him self-conscious of what he was doing. "Can do same anytime," Neal boasted of the prose in his letter, which might have been true prior to his seeing the effect that his writing had on Allen and Jack, but now that he had been analyzed for doing something that came naturally to him, Neal found himself hung up on his own words, phrases, and meanings. In a sense, he no longer felt free to soar. He had been working on a novel at the time he'd sent the letter to Jack, and he felt himself blocked almost as soon as he heard from Allen and Jack.

"All the crazy fallderall [sic] you two boys make over my Big Letter just thrills the gurgles out of me, but we still know I'm a whiff and a dream," Neal wrote Allen. His novel in progress, he complained, was not good—it was "a horrible stinker, really a fart," he said—and he had no inclination to finish the story he was telling in the letter. He advised Allen to abandon any thoughts he had of trying to sell it to a magazine. Writing, whether letters or fiction, had become laborious: "The real reason I don't write is because there is so much to say and if I begin to get hung detailing everything . . . that's just too goddam much work." In subsequent letters, Neal expressed further doubt about his creativity and writing ability, and despite protests to the contrary from Allen and Jack, he virtually quit writing.

In April, inspired by Neal's letter, Jack Kerouac gathered together his journals and began the novel he had been wanting to write for nearly four years. Written over a frenetic twenty-one-day period and typed onto a single 120-yard roll of wallpaper Jack had found in Bill Cannastra's loft, the book was Kerouac's tribute to Neal Cassady—a mixture of biography, fiction, autobiography, and poetry, all skillfully blended into a new type of fiction that was as much an American original as Cassady himself. Jack gave the manuscript—a scroll, really—the title he had been carrying in his head for years and, on one occasion, had given to a novel that he had started and abandoned. He called his new book *On the Road*.

9

With Allen's encouragement, Bill Burroughs was doing some writing of his own, assembling his vignettes about drug addiction into the autobiographical novel *Junky*. Burroughs still did not consider himself to be much of a writer, but Allen had seen enough of Bill's work to conclude that Burroughs, with some encouragement and a third party who would assist him in the marketing of his work, might have some success in publishing. Bill knew the horrors of both drug addiction and withdrawal, and his writings contained the unlikely combination of a journalist's detachment and a novelist's sense of urgency. Burroughs had been working on *Junky* for months and in March he had written Allen with the news that he had kicked his heroin habit. Knowing that it would be difficult to sell *Junky* to New York publishers without at least a weak disclaimer, Allen suggested that *Junky* might be presented as the author's way of explaining his trials—an idea Burroughs quickly rejected. As he told Allen rather testily, he had not written *Junky* as a means of justifying his actions. "I don't justify nothing to nobody," he insisted. In writing the book, his goal had been simply to present a realistic portrayal. "I don't mean it as a justification or deterrent or anything but an accurate account of what I experienced during the time I was on the junk," he said.

At the time, Allen was becoming increasingly familiar with the realities and nuances of marketing, whether they involved selling book ideas to editors or hyping commercial products. In May, he had taken a job with Doherty, Clifford and Shenfield, a marketing company that had Ipana toothpaste as one of its clients. Allen was busy helping to plan the advertising strategy, trying to determine whether potential customers responded better to the slogan "Ipana makes your teeth glamorous" than to "Ipana makes your teeth sparkle." Between this job and his previous one of surveying public opinion, Allen was learning the skills needed for product marketing. These skills, combined with his natural abilities of persuasion and knowledge of books and publishing, gave him the confidence to act as an unofficial agent for Burroughs, Kerouac, and Cassady.

Since the beginning of the year, Allen had also devoted considerable time to reading books with an eye to both their artistic value and potential mass appeal. With the help of Mark Van Doren, whose sister Irita was the book editor of the *New York Herald Tribune*, Allen had written reviews of Nathaniel Burt's *Question on a Kite*, and Collister Hutchinson's *Toward Daybreak* for the New York paper. In July, he worked for a month as a book reviewer for *Newsweek*. He found the job somewhat appealing. Wearing a sport coat and tie and carrying a briefcase to work was not a bad life, Allen told Jack. "I sit at Cantwell's desk and get to know people, talk about books & events of world, gossip, begin office schemes to get permanent job," Ginsberg said. "I always longed to be a grown man in an office in the world, I am joyful to be received and my talents praised."

When Jack scoffed that in taking a job with *Newsweek*, Allen had "lost contact with the stars," Allen replied that "to have lost with the stars means for me to regain contact with man and earth—with society." Allen conceded that he wasn't as "socially useful" in this job as he would like to be, but he still preferred fitting into society to living alone and warring with it. He allowed that it was possible he was being insulated from the difficult life of an artist, as Jack had insinuated in his letter, but for the time being he needed comfort more than he needed a struggle.

Having finished *On the Road*, Jack Kerouac was feeling like an artist again. He had compromised nothing in the retelling of his and Neal's road adventures, and he was buoyed by some of the immediate response to his book. John Clellon Holmes had seen the manuscript first, reading the scroll in one marathon session, and, as he later recalled, his reaction had been supportive:

> I remember that eight-hour session as being on a rainy day, Lexington Avenue traffic roaring on outside, my response to the book intensifying even as I wearied. It left me with the feeling that straight-through readings of Jack's work always did: I was silent, admiring, depressed because of the glimpse into Jack's lonely soul, somehow altered. I remember that I met my wife, who worked during the day, at around five-thirty at the RKO Fifty-eighth Street Theater to see a movie, and that *On the Road* blurred the picture for me. I couldn't concentrate on it; I wanted to enthuse, and I felt both troubled and elated.

Allen, too, was impressed with *On the Road*, though he felt that it lacked the proper ending. He also believed that the book needed to be cut and revised, with the Cassady character (Dean Moriarty) developed even more than he was. Allen's reaction to the writing itself was another matter. Allen regarded Kerouac's prose as nothing less than an American original, and he felt that Jack had effectively captured the youthful spirit of their lives in the style in which the book had been written. "The writing is dewlike, everything happens as it really is, with the same juvenescent feel of spring," he told Neal Cassady.

Predictably, representatives of the publishing world were less enthusiastic. Robert Giroux, Kerouac's editor at Harcourt, Brace, watched Jack unroll the scroll on the floor of his office and commented that a manuscript in that form could not be revised. John Clellon Holmes's agent, who also spoke of its need for revision, thought it would be difficult to sell. Such remarks only infuriated Kerouac, who correctly believed that these readers had missed the point of his book. Neal Cassady was the personification of spontaneity, and to rework the story to accommodate the formalities of publishing would be to diminish the spirit and energy he had rushed to portray in the first place.

Jack was going through personal problems as well as literary ones. His marriage to Joan was all but finished, but their breakup was not going to be easy. Joan was now pregnant, and Jack, after initially reacting to this news with anger and worry, had taken to denying that she was pregnant. When that claim was obviously untrue, he insisted he was not the father of the child. In addition to this concern, Jack was also bothered by painful flare-ups of phlebitis in his leg. He spent most of August in a VA hospital bed, which meant postponing a planned trip to California. In his letters, Neal had been encouraging Jack to join him and Carolyn in San Francisco, where he would receive room and board in exchange for Jack's help with his writing. As an added incentive, Neal promised to help Jack find a job with the railroad. Kerouac accepted the invitation. According to Jack's plan, he would travel with Lucien Carr to Mexico City, where Lucien was headed for a wedding, get dropped off in Texas on the way back, and find a way to San Francisco. Unfortunately, his phlebitis canceled the trip to San Francisco indefinitely.

10

Allen wound up accompanying Lucien Carr on the trip to Mexico City. When they arrived, Burroughs was away, looking for land in Ecuador, and Allen found Joan in bad shape, her once-attractive features wasted from Benzedrine and alcohol abuse. She had her two children with her, and when Allen complimented eight-year-old Julie's good looks by saying that she would soon be giving Joan some competition, Joan shrugged it off by remarking that she was now out of the running. She seemed equally apathetic about Bill's whereabouts.

Both Lucien and Joan liked to drink, and for the next week they engaged in long drinking sessions, leaving Allen to watch the children or wander around the city on his own. One day, they decided to drive to Guadalajara. For Allen, the trip was such a nightmare that he wondered whether Joan didn't have a death wish that, in this instance, might include them all. While Allen and Joan's children cringed in the backseat of the car, Lucien and Joan shared a bottle of gin in the front, Lucien taking the tight mountain curves at imprudent speeds while Joan egged him on. When Lucien was too drunk to steer, he turned the wheel over to Joan and stretched out on the floor, pushing the accelerator while Joan steered and worked the brakes. Allen was furious that the two would frighten the children with such reckless behavior, but his anger had little effect on Lucien or Joan. "How fast can this heap go?" Joan shouted at Lucien, who seemed determined to find out.

Somehow, they escaped injury—or worse—and for the next two days the group went sight-seeing. They drove into Mazatlán, and then checked out the active volcano Parícutin. To approach the volcano, Lucien had to drive the car through fields of hardened lava. Every so often, the car would get stuck in the cracks in the lava field and the group would have to work to free it, but in reward for their efforts they were treated to the spectacular sight of the volcano shooting red lava into the evening sky. To Allen, it was a frightening yet exalting vision, not at all unlike the rush one received after surviving a terrifying experience.

The time passed quickly and soon enough it was time for Allen and Lucien to leave Mexico. It was a sad separation for all, but especially for Lucien and Joan, who had taken a great liking to each other. Lucien's car broke down just outside of Houston, and since he was due back at work in New York, he left Allen at an inexpensive hotel in Galveston. He would return to New York and within a week fly back and pick up Allen and the car. Alone, Allen whiled away his hours by touring the city or going to the beach.

On Friday, September 7, while he was still in Texas, Allen was stunned by a news item he came upon in a local newspaper: Joan Vollmer had been shot to death in Mexico City, apparently as she and Bill were playing a drunken game of William Tell. Reports of the shooting were confusing and sketchy, though the shooting was believed to have been an accident. Utterly shocked, Allen dashed off a quick note to Neal, filling him in on what few details he had gathered from what he read. "My imagination of the scene & psyches in Mexico is too limited to comprehend the vast misery & absurdity and sense of dream that must exist in Bill's mind now," he wrote. As for Joan, Allen could not help but privately wonder whether the William Tell incident had been the final scene played out in a death-wish drama he had witnessed in part while he visited her in Mexico. She had been so fatalistic about some of the dangerous stunts that she and Lucien had pulled off during their visit. Was it possible that she had challenged Bill the way she had goaded Lucien into taking reckless chances?

The written reports supplied very little in immediate answer to Allen's questions. In his initial statement, Burroughs said that he and Joan had been at a party, where, to show off his marksmanship, he had placed a glass of gin on Joan's head. Being drunk, he had misaimed his handgun and shot her in the forehead. However, after he had been arrested and had consulted with a local attorney, he changed his story and denied that he had been playing William Tell at all. Instead, he maintained he had shot her accidentally when he dropped his loaded gun. "I did not put any glass on her head," Burroughs said. "If she did, it was a joke. I certainly did not intend to shoot at it."

The latter account was consistent with the defense strategy proposed by Bill's attorney. The shooting had indeed been tragic and accidental, but Burroughs's lawyer believed that a totally truthful account might be badly received in the Mexican courts. Instead, the attorney suggested that Bill would be better off if he presented himself as a gun collector who, in the process of showing a new purchase to friends, had unwittingly discharged a loaded weapon. The lawyer was able to persuade three of the shooting's witnesses to corroborate this story when Burroughs presented it in front of a judge at a pretrial hearing. The judge accepted this explanation, and instead of charging Bill with homicide, he charged him with *imprudencia criminal*, an offense punishable by a maximum of five years' imprisonment. Bill pleaded guilty to the charges and was released on bail on September 21. He was to be sentenced within a year, but in the interim he could not leave the country.

Burroughs was badly shaken by Joan's death, and for many years he was unable to address publicly the events that took place on the night of September 6. Finally in 1985, in his introduction to *Queer*, Burroughs wrote of the significance the event had had on him as a writer:

> I am forced to the appalling conclusion that I would never have become a writer but for Joan's death, and to a realization of the extent to which this event has motivated and formulated my writing. I live with the constant threat of possession, and a constant need to escape from possession, from Control. So the death of Joan brought me in contact with the invader, the Ugly Spirit, and maneuvered me into a lifelong struggle, in which I had no choice except to write my way out.

11

At twenty-five, Allen Ginsberg had witnessed an unusual number of deaths among young friends or acquaintances. The deaths of David Kammerer, Bill Cannastra, and Joan Vollmer had left Allen stunned and depressed, even if in all these instances the people involved seemed fatally attracted to their own self-destruction. All had been exceptionally bright yet tormented by inner demons; all had paid the price. Fall 1951 gave Allen still another jolt—although not quite as painful—when he learned that Phil White, the junky friend of Burroughs and Huncke, had hanged himself in the Tombs. White had been arrested on three separate charges, two involving drugs, and he and the police had struck a deal in which charges against him would be dropped in return for information about a heroin dealer. White supplied the information, but the police backed out of the agreement, dropping only two of the charges and thus assuring White of inevitably meeting up with the dealer at Riker's Island in the future. Knowing what that would mean, White took his life while he was awaiting transfer to the prison.

Allen filled page after page in his notebook with attempts to work these deaths and his feelings about them into poetry:

> Joan, gone southward and from thy Albany;
> Under the boundaries of America,

                    to the balconies of Night in
                         Moorish lands
                    I loved you, Joan, for all your crazy moons. . . .

He sent one fragment of this new poem to Neal Cassady, with the notation,
"This is what I write like now":

                    Phil White hanging in the Tomb's
                         Labyrinth's last passage;
                    Passionate Kammerer, stabbed & aghast,
                         Fainting under Love's Nightmare—
                         Drunken gaze;
                    Cannastra's face in the windows underground,
                         Dragged yelling aginst the pillars of the
                              Subterranean world,
                    Skull broken under the Radiant Wheel
                         on the Iron Tracks—

   These fragments, more the exception than the rule of the type of poetry
Ginsberg was writing at the time, are early precursors of the style of writing he
would employ in "Howl" and other poems written in the next few years. Rather
than use the long Whitmanesque lines found in "Howl," Ginsberg was writing
in the shorter thought/breath break structure of Williams, who was a much
greater influence at this point in his life. However, in comparison, this poetry
itself is remarkably similar to his later efforts, from its rhythmic qualities,
influenced by the jazz and blues Ginsberg was listening to at the time, to
Ginsberg's early, yet not quite fully developed, use of ellipses ("crazy moons,"
"Radiant Wheel"). In "The Names," a poem written in 1958, Ginsberg wrote
again of Vollmer, Huncke, White, and Cannastra. As in "Howl," he used the
long line, but in some instances in "The Names," his phrasing was almost
identical to his notebook poems of early 1952:

                    Where he fell skull broken underground last, head
                         crushed by the radiant
                    wheel on iron track at Astor Place. . . .

   Ginsberg was at last developing his own style, taking what he considered to
be the best elements of Kerouac and Williams and combining them with his
own point of view. Ginsberg would never stake a claim to being an authentically
original American voice, at least in terms of creating a new style of influential
poetry in the manner of Pound or Eliot; instead, he worked with what he
considered to be the best aspects of existing forms, never settling on a single
style, always searching for the best form in which to present his message.
   His breakthrough was almost purely accidental. At the beginning of 1952,
he had sent William Carlos Williams a sheaf of ten poems that were really no
more than lines he had taken from his journals, broken down and rearranged
to look like poetry on the printed page. He had been wanting to send Williams

a batch of new poems for some time, but Williams had clearly disliked his derivative poems, and Ginsberg had nothing new from his notebooks that he could type up and send. In going through his journals, Allen found lines and thoughts and prose fragments that had strong individual impact. He devised his poems from these entries, though he had very little confidence in their value at the time he submitted them to Williams. In Allen's opinion, they were "weird poems," "a bunch of short crappy scraps I picked out of my journals and fixed up like poems, the like of which I could write 10 a day to order."

Allen could not have been more surprised, then, when he received Williams's enthusiastic response to his latest submission. "How many of such poems do you own?" Williams asked. "You *must* have a book. I shall see that you get it. Don't throw anything away. These are *it*." Williams was so impressed, he promised to use Allen's "Metaphysics" as an epigraph to *Paterson (Book Four)*, which he was then in the process of writing.

Overwhelmed by the letter, as well as by the unexpected ease with which he could write poetry that appealed to Williams, Allen dashed off a seven-page letter to Jack and Neal. In the letter, he included the poems that Williams had liked. Allen was positively giddy: "Now you realize you old bonepoles, the two of you, whuzzat means? I can get a book out if I want." Allen reasoned that Williams would show it to his publisher, New Directions, and since Williams was sympathetic to his mind, Allen further reasoned, the elder poet would no doubt be receptive to Jack's and Neal's work. To Ginsberg, this signaled the beginning of something big: "We'll have a huge collected anthology of American Kicks and Mental Muse-eries. The American Spiritual Museum. A gorgeous gallery of Hip American Devises."

Dating back to his days at Columbia, Allen had envisioned a grand plan for his circle of friends; they would, almost as a unit, assault the bland, conservative sensibilities of American literature, offering a bold new alternative in both poetry and prose. The New Vision had been the seed of this belief, and it had reached initial fruition with the publication of *The Town and the City*. Now, in early 1952, it seemed to Allen that a literary explosion was entirely possible. Under the sponsorship of William Carlos Williams, he would have a published book of poetry. Kerouac had finished *On the Road*, which Allen was calling "the first American Novel," and it was only a matter of time until that book would be published. Burroughs's *Junky* had been accepted for publication by Carl Solomon, who was now working for an uncle at Ace Books, and Bill was busy working on *Queer*, another autobiographical novel. John Clellon Holmes had sold *Go*, his roman à clef about the group in 1948 and 1949, to Scribner's. Neal Cassady was back at work on his novel. And this was only the beginning: There was a host of other writers, all friends of Allen's, who could jump on the bandwagon now that it was coming around.

One of Allen's more recent literary discoveries was a dark, handsome young poet named Gregory Corso. Born in 1930 above a funeral parlor in Little Italy, Corso had been abandoned by his mother and spent much of his childhood bouncing from one foster home to another. Intelligent and quick-witted, he learned how to survive on the streets, but not without running into his share of trouble. From the time he was twelve—when he broke into a restaurant for food because he was hungry—until he was twenty, he spent much of his time in prison, as well as a stretch in Bellevue following an altercation with a mental patient. As one of the youngest inmates in Clinton prison in upstate New York, Corso learned to use his sense of humor and intelligence to avoid being victimized by other prisoners. At Clinton, Corso was befriended by an older inmate, who gave him a dictionary and some novels, including *Les Misérables* and *The Brothers Karamazov*. Corso soon became a regular visitor at the prison library, where he checked out books on Greek and Roman history, as well as the literary classics. He loved poetry, particularly the works of Shelley, and he began writing his own.

Ginsberg met Corso a short time after Gregory was released from prison. Allen had stopped in for a drink at the Pony Stable, a Greenwich Village lesbian bar, and he saw Corso sitting at a table. Corso had a sheaf of neatly typed poems with him, and Allen introduced himself and asked whether he could read some of Corso's work. Ginsberg liked it, and he and Gregory spent much of the rest of the evening talking about poetry. As the night was drawing to a close, Corso astonished Allen with a story. For weeks, Gregory told Allen, he had been sitting at his apartment window and watching a girl in the apartment across the street get undressed, take a bath, and make love to her boyfriend. He had always fantasized about walking across the street and introducing himself to the girl. Allen thought it was an interesting idea. He asked Corso where he lived, and was stunned to learn that Gregory lived directly across the street from Dusty Moreland. For nearly a month, Gregory had been watching Allen and Dusty spend their evenings together. To seal their new friendship, Allen offered to introduce Gregory to Dusty.

In the weeks following the letter from Williams, Allen rushed around in a flurry of business activities, acting as an agent for both Burroughs and Kerouac, overseeing the editing and business dealings of *Junky*, and seeing that Solomon was paying appropriate attention to *On the Road*, which Jack had typed up and sent to Ace. Concerned that everyone receive proper credit for their original ideas, Allen worried about the cross-pollination of the group's creative ideas. "[M]y phantasies and phrases have gotten so lovingly mixed up in yours . . . I hardly knows whose is which and who's used what," he wrote Jack. "I'm not haggling I just want to know if it's OK to use anything I want that creeps in." Much of his "Shroudy Stranger" poem, he pointed out, could be attributed to his and Jack's conversations. Allen and John Clellon Holmes were also concerned about the title of John's book: Was *Go* the title of one of Jack's unpublished earlier works? In his excitement over the group's success, Jack was inclined to be generous. "Don't worry about that at all," he advised Allen, admitting that some of Allen's ideas could be found in his prose. As for the title of Holmes's book, Kerouac noted that " 'Go, Go, Go' was the title of a story I wrote about me n Neal in a jazzjoint, [but] it was Giroux [who] made up the title"; if *Go* worked as a title for Holmes's book, Jack said, then John should feel free to use it.

At times, Allen felt uneasy about his mother-hen approach to the business side of the group's writings, but he was experienced enough in both publishing and marketing to know that someone had to supply the organizational skills and impetus necessary to move the powers that be. As he complained to Jack, "You see I am hung up on commerce with publishers: if I don't do it I know nothing would ever happen here. As soon as I establish everybody's position and reputation, will get on better kick. But all would die in NY if I weren't around to clean up messes. They're all in another world."

Throughout the late winter and spring, Ginsberg, Kerouac, and Burroughs maintained frequent correspondence, the tone of their letters upbeat and congratulatory. They critiqued one another's works and, in their optimistic spirits, there were very few squabbles about a person's criticism or suggestions. "Little Allen," as Jack liked to playfully refer to Ginsberg, had come through for everyone; his youthful enthusiasm and energy—at times in the past annoying to the group—was now paying off.

Little did any of them realize how difficult the times ahead would be. Allen would not see a poetry book in publication for another four years, and On the Road would not be published for another five; Burroughs would go nearly a decade before his second book was printed in the United States. At a time when the country was reacting to the effects of McCarthyism and the Korean War, there would be very little interest in new literary visionaries.

12

The delay in the publication of a book of Allen's poems was not due to a lack of effort on the part of William Carlos Williams. He had no sooner finished reading Allen's poems than he began to promote their merits to his influential friends in the established poetry community. Young Ginsberg, Williams informed Robert Lowell, "is coming to personify the place the me," meaning that somehow, as a person and poet, Allen fulfilled Williams's desire to find and honor the personification of local grace and color in his work. Williams urged Marianne Moore to see Allen, describing him as "a clean, rigorously unrelenting mind that would do outstanding work if only the man can survive." He asked Random House to consider for publication a manuscript of Allen's poems.

Allen had been correct in his early assessment of Williams's eccentricity— "Williams is . . . nutty as a fruitcake," he'd told Jack and Neal—but he was mistaken in his judgment about how easy it would be to churn out poems that Williams would find acceptable. Immediately after receiving Williams's encouraging response to his new poems, Allen returned to his journals and searched for more material. Anything remotely interesting, including an occasional excerpt from his letters, was broken down and arranged into poetry lines. In no time, Allen had collected one hundred poems, most of them culled from his 1949 to 1951 journals, each poem short enough to fit on a single page. After cutting about twenty of the weaker poems, Allen assembled his manuscript and gave it to Williams. He toyed with the idea of titling the book Scratches in the Ledger, but he decided to go with Empty Mirror, a title descriptive of his feelings about himself at the time when most of the poems had been written.

Williams examined the manuscript with a critical eye. In his opinion, many of the poems, especially the earlier ones written while Allen had been in the Psychiatric Institute, were too passive and self-absorbed, lacking in concrete detail. He disliked all of Allen's rhymed poems and suggested that he cut them from the book. The best poems, as far as Williams was concerned, were the ones with active images ("In Society," "The Bricklayer's Lunch Hour," "Cézanne's Ports"). He suggested that Allen cut at least half of the poems in the manuscript. "The book would then emerge lean, trimmed for action, for it is action which is demanded at this date," he said.

The Williams-Ginsberg friendship was productive for both poets. Not only was Williams helping Allen in his efforts to be published and by his influence on Allen's writing but he was also establishing a teacher/student model that Ginsberg would use later, when he was a well-known poet being approached for advice by young unknown poets. Allen's contribution to the friendship was equally important. Williams had been struggling with the completion of *Paterson (Book Four)*, and Allen was surprised to learn that Williams had not been in Paterson since he was a young man and that his epic poem about the city had been constructed from memory or imagination. As their friendship developed, Allen acted as Williams's tour guide to the city, reinforcing Williams's belief in the importance of Paterson as the setting for his epic.

One time, in April, Allen and Williams spent an evening talking and riding around Paterson. Two months earlier, Allen had suggested that Williams visit a particular working-class bar on River Street, and after writing Louis Ginsberg to inform him of his intention of visiting the bar with Allen, Williams decided to go to Paterson for a closer look at the city. When he arrived, Allen took him up to his room and showed him some of his work, as well as writings and letters by Kerouac and Burroughs. They then retired to a downtown restaurant for dinner. Allen was delighted to show Williams some of the settings of his childhood, including his old swimming hole and the Paterson factory district. Allen had hoped to take Williams to some of the bars in the area, but after stopping in at one, Williams declined to visit any others, saying he was too old for it and wanted to go home.

Like many writers who become ruminative in their advancing years, Williams not only found himself contemplating his death but he was also concerned about the few works he had ahead of him. "What's it all for?" he asked Allen as they sat in the car, both of them slightly drunk. In two years, he would be seventy, he told Allen, and when Allen asked whether he was afraid of death, Williams replied, "Yes, I think that's it." On another occasion, when Allen was visiting him in Rutherford, Williams admitted that aging had benefits for the writer, the main one being that he could now be as honest in his poetry as he wanted to be. "My life is over, I've lived all now . . . why shouldn't I tell the truth?"

Williams saw Ginsberg as an upstart, a gifted young poet with the talent and spark necessary to continue the kind of work to which he had devoted his own career. He recognized Allen's fragile state of mind and was genuinely worried that if anything kept Ginsberg from succeeding, it might be depression. He encouraged Allen to be brash and forward and egotistical. Great artists, Williams believed, had to push themselves forward. "A young man can't think about anything but himself, that's how it has to be," he said.

Although he was showing more self-confidence in his work, Ginsberg was by no means over the hump in his ongoing confrontation with his self-image. He was still ambivalent about his sexuality and confused about what he was going to do with his life. In a journal entry written around the time of his birthday, Allen wrote an unusual synopsis of his life, notable both for its tone and its characteristic, if almost shocking, frankness:

A Novel

At 14 I was an introvert, an atheist, a Communist and a Jew, and I still wanted to be president of the United States.

At 19, being no longer a virgin, I was a cocksucker, and believed in a supreme reality, an anarchist, a hipster totally apolitical Reichian; I wanted to be a great poet instead.

At 22 I was a hallucinating mystic believing in the City of God and I wanted to be a saint.

At 23, a year later, I was already a criminal, a despairing sinner, a dope fiend; I wanted to get to reality.

At 24, after being a jailbird, a schizoid screwball in the bughouse, I got laid, girls, I was being psychoanalyzed.

At 26, I am shy, go out with girls, I write poetry, I am a freelance literary agent and a registered democrat [sic]; I want to find a job. Who cares?

Allen, of course, knew the answer to his two-word question, regardless of whether he chose to pose it cynically or with heartfelt emotion. However, he was also intelligent enough to know, even in moments of self-doubt or despair, that he could not rely on other caring beings to supply him with the answers to the other important questions of his life. Friends such as Kerouac, Burroughs, Carr, and Williams had expressed their concern for his sanity, but Allen knew that he himself was responsible for the direction his life would take in the future. He would have to take charge of the future himself.

In a second journal entry, written a few weeks after his "novel" entry, Allen, always an active compiler of lists, jotted down a sequence of thoughts regarding what he felt that entailed:

. . . I must abandon again this whole metaphysical urge that leads me further each month back to an uncreated world of bliss of my own making in my own head—bliss which I do not even remember any more, is just an idea—while the real world passes me by.

I must find a small cheap apartment of my own.

I must stop putting off looking for *any* kind of a job—and go out to get what I can. I think maybe a totally non-literary job.

What do I want to *do* in the world aside from "be a poet."

Must stop playing with my mind, with my life. . . .

What will I *make* happen to my life?

7
Reality Sandwiches

The problem is isolation
—there in the grave
or here in oblivion of light. . . .

1

Allen may have been suffering from feelings of inadequacy and uncertainty, but to his friends, Ginsberg's new style of poetry was an impressive success. Accustomed to the seemingly incompatible combination of Allen's bohemian personality and his conventional poetry, Allen's friends found his *Empty Mirror* cycle of poems nothing less than an astonishing breakthrough—and one that seemed more likely to be coming from the Allen Ginsberg they all knew.

"Blow, baby, blow!" Jack Kerouac exalted, using the slang they voiced when they were in a jazz club and urging a saxophonist to continue a particularly exhilarating solo. Jack told Allen, "When you 'open yr. mouth to sing,' you are the end . . . and the beginning . . . the greatest living poet in America & I guess the world." Jack agreed with Williams's devotion to working American idiom into poetry, and as an example of its effectiveness in Ginsberg's own poetry, he compared Allen's "Ode to the Setting Sun," written while Ginsberg was in the Psychiatric Institute, to "Sunset," a new poem dealing, in much sparser language, with the same theme. "The 'formal ode' is a dull suit covering the great exciting nude body of reality," Kerouac said, while, in his opinion, " 'Sunset' is greater . . . because steel is naked like naked thoughts unplanned but ored up from dark mind." Of Allen's recent poems, Jack was especially fond of the ones that appeared to have been spontaneously written, and he advised Allen to continue writing this way. "[T]he value of yr. mind is its spontaneity," he said.

In a letter responding to Jack's appraisals, Allen agreed with his comparison of his sunset poems, admitting that "informal might be better." He had labored meticulously, line by line, on "Ode to the Setting Sun," devoting almost all of his time in the Psychiatric Institute to that one poem and little else, whereas "Sunset," as Jack had pointed out, was indeed "naked thought," an almost verbatim transcription of his notebook musings. Although Allen valued Jack's comments—"your specific understanding of certain things is my salvation"— he was nevertheless reluctant to abandon totally the "mental work, time, patience, [and] craft" that went into a poem such as "Ode to the Setting Sun"; such hard work seemed to be the way true art was crafted. "Wish I could publish them side by side," Allen said of the two poems.

By this time, Jack was heavily committed to the method of spontaneous composition characteristic of virtually all of his future writing. A year earlier, after a conversation with Ed White, Jack had begun a daily practice of prose sketching, which he was now working into his revisions of On the Road. Jack and Ed had been discussing Jack's writing over dinner in a Chinese restaurant near Columbia, and White had suggested that Jack try putting word sketches into the pocket notebooks he carried with him wherever he went. An architect, White made a habit of carrying notebooks around New York and sketching interesting buildings. By employing a similar discipline, White proposed to Jack—"like a painter but with words"—a writer might be in better touch with his creative mind. Intrigued by the idea, Jack started sketching anything that caught his fancy. After a while, Kerouac discovered that such writing became unconscious, almost automatic, and the more one practiced it, the better one became. As he told Allen, "[Y]ou just have to purify your mind and let it pour . . . write with 100% personal honesty both psychic and social . . . and slap it all down shameless, nillywilly, rapidly." It might be embarrassing to stand out in the street and write in notebooks, Jack conceded, but it was a discipline that never let you down. "I read it and it seems like the confessions of an insane person . . . then the next day it reads like great prose."

Trying to integrate his sketching into the revisions of On the Road wound up in failure; Kerouac's new style differed greatly from the style of his Road manu- script, and with only a few exceptions, the new material was eventually with- drawn from the book. On the positive side, from the new sketches Jack now had almost enough new material for another novel about Neal Cassady, this one even more frenetic than On the Road. The new book was a nonlinear novel that bounced back and forth in time, covering much of Neal's Denver background and overlapping a lot of the material in On the Road. Its centerpiece was a series of transcribed, unedited conversations with Neal that Jack had taped in San Francisco while he and Neal were high on marijuana.

Allen regarded Jack's new material with mixed feelings. As an artist, he recognized the prose as some of the most beautiful writing he had ever read; it was nothing less than poetry. However, as the person representing Jack's busi- ness interests, Allen was disheartened, even a little angry, about Kerouac's latest work. For months, Allen had been trying to persuade Carl Solomon and his uncle to publish On the Road in its original form, which was much more traditional in plot structure and style than Jack's new book. As far as Allen could see, there was no way they would ever consider buying the new work, no matter how interesting the writing.

He tried to be gentle when he relayed this opinion to Jack, who had recently left the Cassadys and was now living with Bill Burroughs in Mexico City. Being as diplomatic as he could be, given the circumstances—Ace was proving to be problematic to Burroughs as well, with the editor's demands for changes in

Junky and the company's outright rejection of *Queer*—Allen tried to strike a balance between criticism and praise. "The language is great, the blowing is mostly great, [and] the inventions have full blown ecstatic style," Allen said in praise of the book, adding that "[w]hen you are writing steadily and well, the sketches, the exposition is the best that is written in America." That said, he switched into a frank discussion of what he considered to be the book's weaknesses. He worried about the narrative not being presented in chronological order, and of some of the book's more surrealistic passages; he felt that Kerouac's wordplay was compelling in a Joycean way, but he was convinced that it would never be accepted in New York. "I don't see how it will ever be published, it's so personal, it's so full of sex language, so full of our mythological references, I don't know if it would make sense to any publisher—any sense, I mean, if he could follow what happened to what characters where."

Allen was even more blunt when he offered his assessment of the novel to Neal. Calling the book "a holy mess," he complained that "it's great allright but he did everything he could to fuck it up with a lot of meaningless bullshit I think, page after page of surrealist free association that don't make sense to anybody except someone who has blown Jack. . . . Jack is an ignu and I all bow down to him, but he done fuck up his writing money-wise, and also writing wise. He was not experimenting and exploring in new deep form, he was purposely just screwing around as if anything he did no matter what he did was O.K. no bones attached."

Ginsberg was by no means unique in his reaction to the book. In years to come, the novel (eventually published posthumously in 1972 as *Visions of Cody*) would be scorned by editors and critics alike. However, Allen would later suffer deep regrets about his initial feelings. When, shortly after the publication of *Visions of Cody*, Ginsberg was reminded of what he had said in his letter to Neal, he cringed and admitted, with characteristic candor, "I changed my mind very soon after that. It was a sort of superficial egotism on my part not to understand what he was doing. I was just a stupid kid . . . very naïve, he taught me everything I knew about writing. It took a long time, a couple of years I think, for me to appreciate his ability there and even a longer time for me to begin practicing in spontaneous composition."

Allen would eventually adopt a combination of prose sketching and spontaneous composition in his own work. At its best, in such poems as "Wichita Vortex Sutra" and "Wales Visitation," as well as in many of the poems in his award-winning *The Fall of America* collection, the layering of detail, similar to Kerouac's in *Visions of Cody*, produced remarkably visual poetry. However, in 1952, Ginsberg still had room to grow.

2

In retrospect, it appears that the greatest obstacle to the publication of the early works of Allen Ginsberg, Jack Kerouac, and William S. Burroughs was a combination of the times in which the works were written and the trio's naïveté and inexperience with the publishing world. All of the books that Ginsberg was trying to market as a literary agent—his own *Empty Mirror*, Kerouac's *On the Road* and *Visions of Cody*, and Burroughs's *Junky* and *Queer*—were eventually published (although belatedly in the cases of *Cody* and *Queer*), but in 1952, with the middle-class and Cold War mentality taking root in the United States, the publishing establishment was as conservative as ever. "Certainly these indicated we were in the middle of an identity crisis prefiguring nervous breakdown for the whole United States," Ginsberg later wrote in his introduction to *Junky*; the challenge was getting the publishers to recognize the prophetic qualities of these books.

As an agent, Allen had an almost impossible task in front of him. Hardcover publishers dismissed the group's works with little consideration, and even getting a book accepted as a paperback original at Ace, where Allen had connections, was proving to be difficult. To further complicate matters, Allen was a close friend of his clients, and on too many occasions he was caught in the uncomfortable position between his personal and professional feelings for his clients.

At times, Allen's expansive tolerance was tested to its limits. Virtually every week, new letters with pressing new demands were arriving from Jack and Bill in Mexico City. Both were growing impatient with their personal and professional affairs. Both Bill and Jack were preparing to move on, Bill to South America, Jack to return to the Cassadys in San Jose. Bill was eager to venture to South America, where he hoped to find and try the hallucinogenic drug yage. Jack, having written most of still another novel (*Dr. Sax*) while he was staying with Burroughs, was going through a period of constant motion, partially due to his wanting to avoid his ex-wife, who was pressuring him for child support.

Compounding these distractions were the others that Allen was facing at home. He had moved back to New York, taking a small attic apartment. He and Dusty Moreland were living together, but their relationship was not going well, and the recent death of Dusty's cat had left her depressed and hard to get along with. Carl Solomon had suffered through a relapse and, as Allen reported to Jack and Bill, had gone on a two-week binge, during which he had attacked books with knives, thrown his briefcase and shoes at passing traffic, smeared his apartment walls with paint, and screamed in public; he had been in and out of Bellevue but, Allen added, he finally seemed to have settled down.

All of these distractions were hindering Allen in his efforts to get any work done. "This agenting is getting out of hand," he complained to Bill, "with your going off after your own kind of Mobydick, Carl crazy, Jack nutty as a fruitcake. Everybody seems off their heads, blowing tops around me. . . . I don't have a moment's peace from these people with their cats and yages and wives and voids and anger at the universe, why can't everybody calm down, I always say, like the nice people in the boobyhatch."

Allen's own poetry endeavors were equally stifled. At William Carlos Williams's suggestion, he had trimmed his *Empty Mirror* manuscript from eighty-nine to forty-seven poems, but to no avail. In early September, the book was rejected by Random House, the publisher's final decision based on the tough economic realities of publishing poetry: "In these days of exceedingly low sales of books of poetry we did not feel that publishing EMPTY MIRROR was a feasible venture for us," an editor informed Allen when rejecting the manuscript. Ginsberg's poetry submissions to magazines proved to be similarly futile.

With the high expectations of a few months earlier now brought back to reality, it was inevitable that the group's frustrations would boil over, and Jack Kerouac was the first to lose his composure. In a span of less than a year, Jack had written three novels, all of which, he felt, were worthy literature, but none had interested New York publishing houses. Ace had advanced him $250 for his original *On the Road* manuscript, but as time passed it had become clear to Jack that the publisher had little intention of publishing it. Adding to Jack's frustration was the success of *Go*, John Clellon Holmes's novel covering much of the same time period and using many of the same characters as *On the Road*. Jack could not conceal his envy when he heard that Holmes had received twenty thousand dollars for paperback rights. Driven to the edge by anger, jealousy, and depression, he lashed out in a venomous letter, listing every complaint that had been building up inside him over the past year. Not surprisingly, Allen was its recipient.

"This is to notify you and the rest of the whole lot what I think of you," Kerouac began, not even bothering to open his letter with a salutation. For three typed pages, he railed against the people who were in actuality his closest friends and greatest literary supporters. No one was exempt from the attack—not Allen, John Clellon Holmes, Gregory Corso, Hal Chase, Lucien Carr, Neal Cassady, or Carl Solomon. The assault was launched on both personal ("I realize that I am no longer attractive to you queers") and professional ("Is this the fate of an idiot who can't handle his own business or [is] it the general fartsmell of New York in general?") levels. Still angry about Allen's reaction to his *Visions of Cody* manuscript, Jack fired salvo after salvo at Allen: "And you who I thought was my friend—you sit there and look me in the eye and tell me On the Road I wrote at Neal's is 'imperfect' as though anything you ever did or anybody was so perfect? . . . don't lift a finger or say a word for it. . . . Do you think I don't realize how jealous you are. . . ." By the time he was finished with his tirade, Jack had all but accused Allen of trying to sabotage his career, closing off with a warning to leave him alone and never write or speak to him again.

Allen had endured Jack's tantrums before, and this one, like the others, was filed away, without response or comment. Allen had learned long ago that when Jack was being unreasonably hostile, he could be dealt with in one of two ways: You could ignore him and wait for him to cool down and come around to reason; or, if you felt that he was testing you with his anger, you could engage in a game of "dirty dozens," in which you would trade insults until one or the other gave in. In this instance, Allen wisely chose to let Jack vent his spleen without his returning with an angry or defensive reply.

The ploy worked. A couple of weeks later, Jack sent Allen the manuscript of *Dr. Sax*, which Allen read and appreciated. He sent Jack a letter critiquing the novel and, shortly thereafter, less than a month after he had sent his angry letter, Jack sent Allen a conciliatory letter, thanking him for trying to understand his writing and calling him "my little petushka . . . a little Russian brother." As was so often the case, Jack's anger had been a mask for the sorrow he felt when he placed his faith in a world that would snub him and break his heart.

3

On November 16, *The New York Times* published John Clellon Holmes's article, "This Is the Beat Generation," in its Sunday magazine section. Gilbert Millstein, an editor and book critic for the paper, had seen Holmes's reference to a "beat generation" in *Go* and he had asked Holmes to write an article explaining what the term meant. Giving Kerouac credit for coming up with the phrase, Holmes wrote eloquently, almost painstakingly, on both words in the phrase. "Any attempts to label an entire generation is unrewarding," he claimed, "and yet the generation which went through the last war, or at least could get a drink easily once it was over, seems to possess a uniform, general quality which demands an adjective." In defining *beat*, Holmes articulated his and Kerouac's discussion of 1948:

> More than weariness, it implies the feeling of having been used, of being raw. It involves a sort of nakedness of mind and, ultimately, of soul; a feeling of being reduced to the bedrock of consciousness. In short, it means being undramatically pushed up against the wall of oneself. A man is beat whenever he goes for broke and wages the sum of his resources on a single number. . . .

This description, of course, fit many of the characters in *Go* and in Kerouac's *The Town and the City*, which Holmes graciously mentioned in his article; it applied to the writers and their subjects alike. In his essay, Holmes, no doubt with an eye on the forthcoming publication of *Junky*, addressed the issue of alcohol and drug abuse among the youth of the day, arguing that this, as well as the sexual promiscuity among the Beat Generation, came "out of curiosity, not disillusionment."

It was an impressive essay, and both Allen and Jack were pleased with the way it turned out. In the past, both had been critical of Holmes for what they perceived as his tendency to be stiff and cerebral in his work, but in this essay, his formality worked to his advantage, since the *Times* readership was anything but ready for hiptalk. Ironically, the Beat Generation would not reach its peak as a cultural phenomenon for another half-dozen years, and by that time *Go* would be out of print and Holmes, the first formal spokesperson for the Beat Generation, had become a literary footnote, lost in the shadow of Kerouac and Ginsberg.

The new year found Allen living in a new apartment at 206 East Seventh Street on Manhattan's Lower East Side, an old section of New York known as the East Village. He continued to hang out at the San Remo and Cedar, associating with the subculture of avant-garde artists, jazz musicians, hipsters, bohemians, and literary dilettantes. This group of subterraneans, as Allen called them, was "hip without being slick, they are intelligent without being corny, they are intellectual as hell and know about Pound without being pretentious or talking too much about it, they are very quiet, they are very Christlike."

Jack Kerouac was back in New York, living with his mother in Richmond Hill, but Allen saw him only occasionally, Jack being involved in the writing of a book he was tentatively calling *Mary Cassady*, a short novel about a teenage love affair he'd had in Lowell. He and Allen had reconciled after his October letter, but there was still a trace of strain in their friendship. Although he saw Jack from time to time, Allen had the uneasy feeling that Jack was avoiding him.

One day in mid-January, after receiving a postcard from his mother begging him to come see her, Allen took the train to Long Island to visit Naomi at Pilgrim State Hospital. It had been nearly two years since he had seen her, and he was shocked by her deteriorated physical condition. Her hair had turned white, and her face, once full and enlivened by her winning smile, was gaunt and lined with age. Her head was scarred from her lobotomy. Partially paralyzed from a stroke, she was weak and had lost all of her excess weight, her clothes now hanging on a skeletal frame.

"Are you Allen," she asked, not recognizing him, "or are you a spy?" Weeping, Allen sat at a table and listened to Naomi's paranoid ramblings, as bad as they had been the last time he had seen her. He couldn't be Allen, she said; Allen would have rescued her from the hospital. He must be a spy, sent by Louis. She was receiving signals, transmitted by the radios in the ceiling to the wires in her back, warning her to beware of this visitor. After a short time, two nurses led her away, Naomi not so much as looking back at Allen. Rushing to a bathroom where he could be alone, Allen leaned against a wall and sobbed: "The horror, the horror." He had never imagined his mother as an old woman, let alone himself as an elderly man, and the sight of Naomi in this condition terrified him:

> Naomi! Naomi! is this what has come to you
> now—what I'll be when I'm mad as your hair in
> the 90's of the future! When I scream on roofs of
> synagogues bearded toward Heaven?

For Ginsberg, who from the beginning of his days as a poet had a notable preoccupation with the topics of aging and dying, the sight of his mother, "as if she were dead in her coffin thru funeral rot in the grave," was emotionally unbearable.

Although he had taken another job in market research, Allen continued to play an active role in Burroughs's and Kerouac's literary affairs. The trio's friendship was tested again in February when Jack refused Allen's request that he associate his name with the publicity for *Junky*, due to be published on April 15. Allen had been working closely with Carl Solomon and the Ace Books publicity department on the promotion of Bill's book, and one of their tactics involved supplying a brief news release to a *New York Times* literary gossip columnist. The release described Kerouac and John Clellon Holmes as "experts on the Beat Generation" who had included fictional portrayals of Burroughs in their respective novels. According to the release, the two authors believed Burroughs to be a key figure in the Beat Generation, and *Junky* was the first opportunity for the public to read the words of this literary mentor. In a letter to Kerouac, Allen asked that Jack grant permission for his name to be used in the release; Allen also requested Jack to write a two-sentence blurb that might be used in the promotion of the book. Holmes, Allen advised Jack, was doing the same.

To Allen's chagrin, Kerouac refused for what he called "strictly business" reasons, claiming that by using his real name, he could be prosecuted for his connection to a book about the use of illegal drugs, whereas Burroughs, who was being published under the pseudonym William Lee, would not be in any danger. It was, at best, a weak argument, made even more suspect when Jack insisted that neither his name nor the title of his book be mentioned in conjunction with John Clellon Holmes's name and book title. Virtually broke and living off his mother, Jack resented the money Holmes was earning from his writing, feeling that John was capitalizing on some of his literary turf—and with inferior writing to boot. In addition, he also detested Allen's earning a living in market research, hawking products such as deodorants and cosmetics, while he still pretended to be a serious artist.

This time, Allen could barely maintain his patience. Due to its subject matter, *Junky* promised to be a difficult book to sell to the public, even with its lurid cover, thirty-five-cent paperback price, and disclaimers from the publisher. By adding a glossary of drug-user slang and publishing the book as if it was a documentary, Ace was targeting *Junky* at the same readership that had purchased *Rebel Without a Cause* a few years earlier. With the uncertainties ahead, Allen had no use for Kerouac's petty bickering, and his and Jack's friendship might have been tested even more had Kerouac not sent a blurb for the book. Even so, Allen was upset enough to send Jack an overly formal letter that stewed in sarcasm. Allen thanked Kerouac for his blurb and then asked him to show discretion both in the way he conducted his literary business and in the way he treated John Holmes. Allen chose to ignore Jack's nasty remarks about his life as a businessman. Jack had novels to market, and Allen was confident that he would be hearing from him soon.

4

By late spring, Allen was immersed in two time-consuming projects: a study of Chinese painting and the composition of a lengthy poem about his and Neal's love affair. The previous months had been difficult, with Allen feeling, as he put it, "dissolute and beat" in his creative endeavors. He was exhausted from his business dealings with New York literary circles and, after his visit with his mother, he was worried that at twenty-seven he was getting older with little to show, in romance or career, for his years to date. "Amazing how truly aging is a process of horror and disillusioning to me," he wrote Neal Cassady. "However mad I was, I never dreamed it would be like this." Allen's ego took another bruising when, after he took a job with a literary agency, he was fired for being a sloppy typist. He secured part-time employment at his brother's law office, which turned out to be a blessing, for he now had time to pursue his own interests, his main one being a thorough study of Chinese painting.

His study had begun simply enough. After finishing work one afternoon in early May, Allen took the three-block walk from Eugene's office to the main branch of the New York Public Library on Forty-second Street. Sitting in the library's Fine Arts room, Allen examined a dozen volumes of reproductions of Chinese paintings and, totally absorbed by the quality of the older, pre–World War I hand-sewn books and the beautiful pictures therein, he initiated a study that in weeks to come found him spending most of his free time either at the public library or in the Columbia University library. As he told Neal Cassady, he had been fascinated by "the sublimity and sophistication (meaning learning and experience, not snideness) of the East" since his attendance of an exhibition of Japanese paintings at the Metropolitan Museum of Art, though he knew nothing about either Chinese paintings or the cultural background that influenced them. Allen was captivated by the deceptive simplicity of the paintings, and wanting to learn more about their history, he checked out dozens of volumes on Chinese history, religion, art, and philosophy. One of the books, *Introduction to Zen Buddhism* by D. T. Suzuki, was of special interest to him. From his classes with Raymond Weaver, Ginsberg had been exposed to Buddhism and Zen koans, but up until the point that he read Suzuki, Allen had found Buddhist texts to be "not interesting [and] vague," mainly because he had little understanding of what he called "the various dynasties and epochs of art and messianism and spiritual waves of hipness" latent in Buddhism and its background. From Suzuki, he learned some of the elemental thoughts behind the most basic Buddhist teachings. Allen concluded that when one was able to grasp the meaning of these teachings, "you begin to see the vastitude and intelligence of the yellow men, and you understand a lot of new mind and eyeball kicks."

It was only natural that he would try to write poetry about this latest preoccupation, and his subsequent poem, "Sakyamuni Coming Out from the Mountain," was a reasonably sound effort that combined elements of objectivism, verbal sketching, a new line arrangement, and aspects of what Ginsberg was learning in his early study of Buddhism. Written in one afternoon while Ginsberg was at the public library and looking at a twelfth-century painting by Liang Kai, the poem recounts the exhaustion that a holy man, possibly Buddha in one of his forms, feels after seeking enlightenment, only to experience a satori when "he realized/the land of blessedness exists/in the imagination." In its original composition, the poem looked similar on the printed page to the prose poems Ginsberg was writing during his *Empty Mirror* period:

> he knows nothing, like a god
> shaken:
>   meek wretch:
>   humility is beatness
> before the absolute World.

After studying some of William Carlos Williams's poems written in triadic form, however, Ginsberg decided to break his longer lines into three short lines, giving the poem a more pleasing visual effect on the page:

> he knows nothing
>   like a god:
>   shaken
>   meek wretch—
>   humility is beatness
>   before the absolute world.

Ginsberg was pleased with the poem, and many years later he would note how the three main themes of the poem—"collapse of the imagination, negation of aetherial vision, (and) acceptance of 'reality' world"—turned out to reflect the evolution of his own visionary quest from 1948 to 1961, traced in such poems as "Metaphysics," "Ode to My 24th Year," and "The Change."

Encouraged by the success of the poem, Allen immediately began to make plans for a longer, far more ambitious poem that addressed the history of his and Neal Cassady's love affair. From the beginning, he wanted to call the poem "The Green Automobile," green being the symbolic color of hope, as well as a reference to the green robes worn by the homosexual prostitutes in ancient Rome, the automobile symbolic not only of the transitory nature of their affair but also of Cassady's perpetual motion.

Allen intended the poem to be a personal step forward, a movement from the feeling of mental solitude, blankness, and inactivity expressed in *Empty Mirror* to his new belief, evident in "Sakyamuni Coming Out from the Mountain," that bliss exists in the imagination. At this point in his life, Allen was still focused on his lack of wish fulfillment, and his creativity was his way of combating depression. As he wrote Neal, "I discover life so unsatisfactory that I am beginning to use my imagination (as one uses it to make believe stories or heated dreams) to invent alternatives. . . . For that (imagination) seems to me in my state present to be my temporary only value salvation and Good."

"The Green Automobile," therefore, became Ginsberg's way of perfecting his past, of looking at his relationship with Neal Cassady and bringing it to the fulfillment he had imagined when he first met Neal. As he mentioned in his notes for the poem:

> The green auto is the occasion for the great return trip thru the west of youth-days doing things again greater than before with potential climaxes realized fulfilled. . . .

Instead of suffering doldrums in Denver and Texas, Allen, by using his imagination, could see his and Neal's love relationship fully realized. In the poem, Allen collects Neal from his wife and children and San Jose home, and subsequently the two of them travel back to their more carefree days, free of demanding jobs and commitments. There is no denial of reality in the poem: From the beginning, the actions are presented as fantasy, and at the end of the poem, Allen and Neal are back in their respective realities. The main body of the poem is the idealized daydream. Allen had recently read a ninth-century poem, written by Po-Chu-I, in which a man dreamt of meeting an old friend whom he had not seen for many years. The poem's main device is the narrator's description of the events that took place in his dream. Ginsberg used this poem as a model for "The Green Automobile."

In his notes for "Green Auto," Ginsberg expressed his wishes for a poem that alternated between the physical and metaphysical, with one stanza addressing reality, the next matters of the imagination, but as he began to work on the poem, he abandoned this structure. Instead, he superimposed imagination and reality, allowing his flights of fancy to perfect the actual occurrences of his and Cassady's affair:

> Denver! Denver! we'll return
>> roaring across the City and County Building lawn
>> which catches the pure emerald flame
>>> streaming in the wake of our auto.
>
> This time we'll buy up the city!
>> I cashed a great check in my skull bank
>> to found a miraculous college of body
>>> up on the bus terminal roof.

As he had done with "Sakyamuni," Allen broke his long line into shorter ones, this time using four-line stanzas. The result was a poem that was both visually pleasing and accommodating to the idea that line breaks be governed by breath measure. The exuberance and energy in the poem were pure Kerouac, an influence Ginsberg acknowledged when he was developing his early plans for the work: "I would like to build up a modern contemporary metaphorical yak-poem, using the kind of weaving original rhythms that Jack does in his prose, and the lush imagery."

The Kerouac influence was crucial—and ironic. Ginsberg may have had difficulty accepting Kerouac's early experimentations with spontaneous writing in prose, but he had no trouble adopting its spirit, if not its literal practice, in his poetry. At the time of Ginsberg's writing and revision of "The Green Automobile," Kerouac was compiling his thirty-point list, "Belief and Technique of Modern Prose," which, in essence, encouraged the writer to create art from "the unspeakable visions of the individual" without regard for the strictures and disciplines of commercial publishing. "Something that you feel will find its own form," Kerouac suggested, urging the writer to use that feeling, without shame or fear, as the grist for creative work.

Ginsberg had been moving, albeit slowly, in this direction over the past year or two. Kerouac was still ahead of him in terms of shaking loose the old traditions, but in "The Green Automobile," Ginsberg had taken a giant step in producing the "bookmovie" in his mind.

5

In September 1953, William Burroughs arrived in New York. It was the first time he had come to the city for any notable length of time since his departure for Texas in 1947. Allen was pleased to see his friend and former mentor, and he invited Burroughs to stay at his apartment for the duration of his visit.

For Burroughs, it had been an eventful year. Convinced that Mexican lawyers were trying to extort more money from him in exchange for keeping him out of jail on bail, Burroughs had left Mexico City and returned to the States. After a brief reunion with his parents and son in Palm Beach, Bill embarked on an extended journey to South America. He had concluded *Junky* with the statement, "Yage may be the final fix," and he was eager to determine for himself whether that was true. He had heard much about the hallucinogenic drug, also known in different regions as *ayahuasca* or *caapi*, which was made by pounding and boiling the bark stripped from banipsteriosis vines. The drug's effects were known to be extreme, complete with technicolor visionary hallucinations. The drug was used mainly by Amazon Indian doctors as a potion to help them locate lost souls. According to the myth, yage gave one telepathic powers, which Burroughs believed in and wanted to check out on his own.

Burroughs's journey had taken slightly more than six months, during which he kept Allen informed of his progress through a series of detailed letters. In Bogotá, he met a Harvard-educated botanist who had devoted his entire career to the study of narcotic and psychoactive plants. The botanist produced a dried specimen of the vine and then instructed Bill on the kind of gear necessary for his journey. As Burroughs soon determined, the search for yage could be time-consuming and frustrating. Finally, after spending nearly two and a half months in futile pursuit of the drug, Burroughs was able to locate an elderly medicine man willing to prepare and administer him a dose of it. The black oily liquid was bitter, and when he felt no immediate effects from the drug, Bill's impulse was to believe he had received a weak dose. This idea was momentary, for when the drug finally kicked in, Burroughs grew violently nauseous, dizzy, numb in the limbs, and chilled. The visual and auditory hallucinations were extraordinary. "Larval beings passed before my eyes in a blue haze, each one giving an obscene, mocking squawk," Burroughs wrote Allen, adding that he later reasoned that the croaking noises were coming from the nocturnal frogs in the area. For nearly four hours, Burroughs was gripped by delirium, the hallucinations as strong as anything he had ever experienced. He imagined himself to be alternately a man and a woman. He saw flashes of blue light. Characterizing the yage experience, Burroughs wrote:

> Yage is space time travel. The room seems to shake and vibrate with motion. The blood and substance of many races, Negro, Polynesian, Mountain Mongul, Desert Nomad, Polygot Near East, Indian—new races as yet unconceived and unborn, combinations not yet realized passes through your body. Migrations, incredible journeys through deserts. In jungles and mountains (stasis and death in closed mountain valleys where plants sprout out of the Rock and vast crustaceans hatch inside and break the shell of the body), across the Pacific in an outrigger canoe to Easter Island. The Composite City where all human potentials are spreadout in a vast silent market. . . .

The next morning, Bill was surprised to discover that there were few unpleasant after-effects from the drug. Hoping to try yage mixtures from other regions of South America, he spent the next three months in Ecuador, Colombia, and

Peru, and though he was able to obtain and take yage on several occasions, most of his time was spent exploring towns, learning local customs and attitudes, picking up boys, and hanging out. As the weeks passed, Burroughs grew increasingly impatient with the locals, some of whom had stolen some of his money and possessions, and he decided it was time to return to the United States. He paid his parents another visit but, feeling unwelcome, he started making plans for a trip to Tangier, Morocco. First, however, he would visit New York.

Bill's original intention was to stay in New York for a month. He figured on visiting Allen and other friends, conducting any business necessary in connection with his writing projects, and moving on; instead, he stayed for almost three months, during which he and Allen became as close as they had ever been. In the past, Burroughs, being older and more experienced in the world than Allen, had been more of a teacher and elder to him, but as a result of Allen's sympathy and tolerance throughout the difficult times in Bill's life in recent months, Burroughs respected Ginsberg as a peer and loved him as a dear friend. While he was Allen's guest, Bill initiated a sexual relationship that made Allen very uncomfortable.

At the time of Burroughs's arrival in New York, Allen was living a structured lifestyle, working the day shift as a copyboy at the *World-Telegram*, writing poetry, seeing a woman on a regular basis, and otherwise maintaining a rather active social life. Gregory Corso was staying at Allen's apartment, and the two had become close friends. When Burroughs arrived and met Corso, he did not take a liking to the younger poet, possibly because of Allen's obvious affection for him, and Corso quickly determined that he might be better off if he lived elsewhere.

Because of their age difference and the circumstances of their friendship, Allen had never given consideration to the possibility of having Bill as a sexual partner. He was consequently surprised—and, in a way, honored—when Bill made his advances. However, the situation was far from ideal. Allen was in no great way attracted to Bill in a physical sense, and his reciprocation was more out of friendship than the kind of involvement that Bill was seeking. For Allen, the partnership was more or less a reversal of the one he'd had with Neal Cassady a few years earlier. Allen recognized that as lovers, he and Bill were not compatible. Not only did Bill prefer a passive role in their sexual activities but during sex Bill also went through a personality change, shifting from the self-controlled, masculine figure that Allen knew to an effeminate one that Allen found less appealing. In addition, Burroughs was seeking a total and absolute union of an extraordinary nature. Bill wanted himself and Allen to merge—to possess and be possessed; in essence, to become one person, as if grafted physically and spiritually. "What I look for in any relationship is contact on the nonverbal level of intuition and feeling, that is, telepathic contact," Burroughs had written in *Junky*. That kind of commitment was the last thing Allen wanted at that point, but the more he resisted, the more Burroughs pressed. Allen had never admired Burroughs more, or felt closer to him—"he is very great, greater than I ever realized," he told Neal Cassady—but he was also troubled by the depth of Bill's feelings for him. Finally, in exasperation, he hurt Bill with an offhand remark. "I don't want your ugly old cock," he told Burroughs. The words cut deeper than Allen had intended, but they also achieved their purpose by effectively ending the physical aspects of their relationship.

Bill departed for Tangier in early December, which meant that Allen was free to do some traveling of his own. For over a year, Neal and Carolyn Cassady had been urging him to visit them in California, and Allen, weary of New York and seeking an extended travel period for what he called "my art and soul's sake," needed little persuasion to journey west. He was eager for a road adventure of his own, a lengthy trip similar to those taken by Jack and Neal. His itinerary included a swing down the eastern seaboard, with brief stops in Washington, D.C., Florida, and Cuba, followed by a tour of Mexico and a stay with the Cassadys in San Jose. In detailing his itinerary to the Cassadys, Allen stressed the importance of his going off on his own exploratory adventure:

> This is a rare & marvelous trip I need to feel (& free) my soul from 10 years of N.Y.C. which I can afford to make—and as you must agree should make so when I see you I'll be able to talk for hours about not only N.Y.C. intellectual beauties but also manly savage solitude of Jungles we've never seen—will add to our store of souls.

Allen needed world experience. He had yet to fly in an airplane, and with the exception of his 1947 trip to Denver and Texas, his brief trip to Mexico with Lucien Carr, and his short trips with the merchant marine, he had traveled very little. New York appeared to be an endless circle of repetitious activities leading him nowhere. His attempts to break into the closed environment of the publishing world had resulted in very few rewards, and he was now convinced that he might have to use his own money to publish himself, Kerouac, Burroughs, and Cassady. First, however, he needed to get away.

The trip promised to be a challenge. Outside of a few contacts, Allen would be completely on his own, reliant upon his wits and sensibilities for the duration of the journey. He had borrowed some money and sold a few possessions, and he added the sum of this money to the back pay he was expecting from the World-Telegram, giving him about three hundred dollars to live on in the months ahead. If all went according to his plan, he would be cut off, except by mail, from his friends and family.

Undaunted, he shipped some of his clothing and manuscripts to the Cassadys for safekeeping and, shortly before Christmas, he began his journey. Three years would pass before he would see New York again, and when that time came, he would be a nationally known poet.

6

The first planned stop on Allen's trip was in Washington, D.C. It was the holiday season, and on the bus from New York to the nation's capital, Allen stared out at the festive decorations that augmented the already-expansive network of lights illuminating the landscapes of such large cities as New York, Philadelphia, and Washington, D.C. In his journal, Allen scribbled in page after page of descriptive detail, beginning a practice of travel writing that he would continue for the rest of his life. These early jottings bore a remarkable resemblance, in their cadence and capturing of details, to the travel poems collected in *The Fall of America*, his lengthy travel sequence published two decades later:

> Square Cartaret with tanks that squat abulge with gas, and flames on tall pipes flueing out into the windy void. . . .

In Washington, D.C., Allen was disappointed when Ezra Pound, incarcerated in St. Elizabeth's Hospital, refused to see him. Visiting the aging poet had been Ginsberg's primary reason for stopping in the city. The father of imagist poetry in America, Pound was a longtime friend of William Carlos Williams, and Allen had hoped to connect with him, if not in the way he had connected with Williams a few years earlier, then at least in terms of their engaging in some kind of meaningful dialogue. At this stage of his life, Pound did not share Williams's spirit of poetic community, and he felt no obligation to meet with Allen, just as he felt no urge to comment on Allen's poetry when Williams had sent him a batch of poems a few years earlier. "Trip off to a bad start," a disappointed Ginsberg noted in his journal.

Allen made the most of his time in the city. He took a walking tour of the historical points of interest and visited the notable art galleries. He was impressed when he saw the Capitol at night, describing it as "dark like a film negative in the distance." Viewing the paintings and statuary in the National and Freer galleries, Allen was reminded of how a single moment, captured perfectly in art, could be passed on from century to century, leaving an immortal message with each person who paused to appreciate it. Now, instead of encountering Blake's sunflower, Allen was captivated by

> . . . the drum set in stone, stone music emerging out of silence of rock after a thousand years. . . .

His next stop was Florida, where he witnessed another element of the human drama. The *Brown* v. *the Board of Education, Topeka, Kansas* Supreme Court decision was still a few months away, as were the national manifestations of the civil rights movement, and the Florida Ginsberg encountered was still immersed in the old ways of the Deep South. While hitchhiking through the state, Allen was picked up by a truck driver who filled his ears with a lot of racist talk denouncing interracial marriage. The conversation touched off "immense preoccupied prophecies of final war between black and white" in Allen's mind. He couldn't help but take notice of the disparity in the lifestyles of the whites, who were thoroughly preoccupied with earning money and plugging into middle-class America, and the blacks, who continued to live in squalor predating the Civil War.

Allen spent Christmas with Bill Burroughs's parents, who, Allen reported in a letter to Kerouac and the Cassadys, seemed relieved when he told them that Bill was already a very good writer who might, in time, become "a very great writer." With all that Bill had been through in recent years, his parents were deeply concerned about their son's future, and Allen's praise for his writing abilities alleviated some of their fears, at least temporarily. They drove Allen around on a sight-seeing tour of Palm Beach, Allen taking a liking to Mortimer Burroughs and deciding that he was "a wise distinguished version of Bill tho not so fiery as his son."

After noneventful stops in Miami Beach and Key West—both impressing Ginsberg as being little more than tourist traps—he caught a plane to Havana. Allen was dazzled by his first flight, which featured a spectacular view of the Caribbean islands, but Cuba turned out to be a disappointment. He had heard rumors of a wild, permissive sexual climate in Havana, but this was not the case. Not only were there no sex orgies to be found but he also discovered he did not care much for the city or its people. Havana, as Ginsberg saw it, was a "kind of dreary rotting antiquity, rotting stone, *heaviness* all about." At one point, he found himself lost and without money in a small village twenty miles outside of Havana; he was rescued by a man who loaned him train fare and bought him drinks on his ride back to Havana. The environment was languid, and when the time came for his trip to Mexico, he was ready.

7

Allen celebrated New Year's Day in Mérida, the capital city of the Mexican state of Yucatán. The night before, he had attended a formal party at a country club, where, without a tuxedo, he felt out of place. Despite the size of the city, Allen had expected to encounter a modest citizenry living simple lives in keeping with the proximity of the ancient ruins, but he was surprised to find himself partying with wealthy, well-educated, cultured people dressed in formal wear and sipping champagne. It was more of the same on New Year's Day, when Allen attended a party at the city hall as a guest of the mayor's brother, whom he had met the night before. To Allen, the scene was amusing, not unlike a political celebration in the States: The mayor delivered an hour-long speech, his official photographer fell asleep, and the citizens filled up on free beer and sandwiches.

The next day, Allen journeyed to the Mayan ruins of Chichén Itzá, which proved to be more of what he had anticipated from the Yucatán region. Because of the holiday, the ruins were virtually abandoned, leaving Allen free reign to explore on his own. Through a connection at the Museum of Natural History in New York, he had been able to secure a pass that allowed him to stay without charge at the archaeological sites in the Yucatán Peninsula—a fortuitous circumstance, since he had only been in Mexico a few days and was already running low on money. Allen found a modest dirt-floor hut near the pyramid of El Castillo, and after nightfall, he climbed the stairs of the eleventh-century temple, where, as he would recall in "Siesta in Xbalba," he took some paracodin, hung his hammock in one of the chamber entrances, and spent an hour or two looking at the stars and listening to the sounds of tropical birds and insects filling the night. In the deserted ruins, every sound seemed to carry and echo:

the clap of hands reechoes from half dozen temples laid out at acoustical angles made for jazz and poetry and religion: the projection of a voice of stone, the echo of eternity. . . .

One could not help but think of past ages in such an environment, and in the ensuing days Allen made certain that he would hold it in his memory. He wrote impressions and details in his journal and he took dozens of photographs. He was awed by the sight of a death's-head, many centuries old, hewn into the stone by an unknown artist who, like the workers who had constructed the cornices on the building tops outside the Harlem apartment where he'd had his Blake visions, had no presumption of the effects that such work would have on a young poet in the future. Allen watched the light from his lantern play off the weathered surfaces of the ruins' huge stone portals, where moss covered carved rock structures nearly a thousand years old.

On January 6, Allen traveled to Tizimia to attend the Festival of the Three Kings, the oldest fiesta in Mexico. The trip was grueling, involving a ten-hour train ride that commenced at dawn and was marked by frequent stops for long intervals of time; crowded, standing-room-only conditions in a boxcar holding over one hundred people; and a train derailment. The ceremony, held in a four-hundred-year-old cathedral, was supervised by a Maryknoll priest who watched as hundreds of people from as far away as Chiapas formed a winding line and worked their way to the front of the church, where they presented hand-formed wax gifts to wooden statues of the magi. The priest beckoned Allen to the backstairs leading to the sacristy, where the two smoked cigarettes and the missionary complained about the ritual, which, although celebrating a Catholic feast day, seemed too paganistic to the reverend. The priest took Ginsberg home for dinner, and the next day, he drove Allen in his jeep to the forests of Quintana Roo. On the train trip back to Valladolid, Allen lost his seat and had to stand for the entire journey.

He returned to Mérida for a couple days, convening with local artists and seeking information on Mayan ruins from a visiting archaeologist. On January 12, he left for the Uxmal ruins, which proved to be a contrast to the ruins of Chichén Itzá, the latter being a small city set on a plain, whereas the former was a massive grouping of structures that seemed to rise out of the thick greenery of surrounding jungle. Much of Uxmal had been recently excavated and explored by archaeologists hoping to reconstruct the city and open it to tourists. In walking along the backwoods paths, Allen found beautiful shards of pottery littering the ground; there seemed to be artifacts strewn everywhere. Uxmal, with its many pyramids, plazas, and buildings, struck Allen as being "really quite beautiful in a classical Greek ruin way," with "more glory though less grandeur than Chichén Itzá."

Ginsberg's Mexico trip, for all the splendor it was providing him, began to wear on him. He was almost out of money. He had a mild case of dysentery, as well as a cold that he had been battling for more than a week. His financial and physical woes made him short-tempered with the locals, with whom he was having trouble communicating. He had not heard from his friends or family in the States and, after so much time by himself, he was lonely: "Worrying about my fate again—that small breeze of nostalgia fluttered in my heart, thinking a moment past, had someone in the room I loved with me—no ghosts—a man of flesh to talk to and hug."

By mid-January, Allen had worked his way across the Yucatán Peninsula, traveling southwest until he crossed into the state of Chiapas, the southern Mexican state on the Guatemalan border. The environment, with its tropical climate and jungle landscape, was as far removed from modern Western civilization as Allen had ever encountered, the Mayan ruins of Palenque the oldest of the ancient cities he had explored. "Landscape, mountains & jungle here the best of Mexico I've seen," he noted. "*Real* jungle, very hi trees, myriad butterflies, monkeys, dank floor."

It was also Allen's good fortune to meet Karena Shields, a middle-aged archaeologist called "White Goddess" by natives of the region. Raised on a rubber plantation near Palenque, Shields had spent her childhood exploring the ruins and neighboring jungles. She had studied Mayan history and culture with the Karivis Indians, the local natives who were descendants of the Mayans. She spoke knowledgeably about Mayan metaphysics and was well versed in their mythical lore and symbolism. She was familiar with all the ruins of southern Mexico and Guatamala and had herself discovered ancient cities in the region. Shields had also studied and worked in the United States, writing scholarly books and articles—her New York editor was Robert Giroux, Kerouac's editor—and, while working for a brief period as an actress, she had appeared as Jane in several early Tarzan movies. Tough and self-reliant, she now lived by herself and operated a cocoa *finca*.

Allen was delighted when she invited him for a visit. By Allen's estimation, she was "perhaps the person in the world most emotionally & knowledgeably tied to these ruins & this area," and he was eager to talk to her in detail. He could not have hired a better or more qualified tour guide—or, as it turned out, a better patron in his time of need.

To reach the Finca Tacalupan de San Leandro, Shields's cocoa plantation, one had to travel a large portion of the way by horseback—another new experience for Allen—moving through dense jungle, broken only by occasional settlements. It was a rigorous procedure, yet one that Allen enjoyed. Karena Shields lived in a region of Chiapas that the Karivis called Xibalba. * According to Mayan mythology, Xibalba was a region of purgatory or limbo, marked by a tall tree on the summit of nearby Mount Don Juan, in which the ghosts of Mayan craftsmen toiled, hoping to finish the work they had not completed at the time of their deaths. To Ginsberg, who had come to Mexico with his creative imagination still suspended between the mysticism of his Blake visions and the objective realities of his *Empty Mirror* poetics, the purgatory image was apt, compelling. He had ventured to what appeared to be one of the early points of civilized time, yet he was still only a good plane ride from the most modern manifestations of civilization. Having witnessed both, he was, in his own mind at least, suspended between them. Xibalba and the Mayan ruins of Mexico were places for contemplation:

---

* When writing his poem, "Siesta in Xbalba," Ginsberg misspelled the region's name. He elected to leave the misspelling intact in the published work.

Time's slow wall overtopping
                all that firmament of mind,
as if a shining waterfall of leaves and rain
were built down solid from the endless sky
                through which no thought can
        pass. . . .

   In his interlude from his daily troubles and responsibilities in the United
States, Allen found himself considering more expansive issues—questions posed
by a human ancestry that reached across time and the earth's continents. From
the beginning of civilization, people had been reaching for God, for spiritual
perfection and self-realization; their temples had reached for grandeur and had
been reduced to ruin. Now, with the invention and deployment of nuclear
weaponry, the end of civilization could arrive in a moment of earth-shattering
lightflash. As he sat with his journal near the base of Mount Don Juan, Allen
decided it was important that he make a similar pilgrimage to Europe:

                Yet these ruins so much
                        woke me to nostalgia
                for the classic stations
                        of the earth,
                the ancient continent
                        I have not seen
                and the few years
                        of memory left
                before the ultimate night
                        of war.

   As the weeks passed, Allen was less inclined to hurry back to the States. He
was still lonely and looking forward to seeing Jack and Neal in California, but
he had also become comfortable with his daily routine at the *finca*. He helped
with household chores and repairs. He built a hanging cage of baskets for
Karena Shields's pet pigeon, and on another occasion, he helped her build
shelves. He assisted in the care of the chickens that wandered around the yard
and laid their eggs under the floorboards of the porch, only a few feet from
where he hung his hammock. He also learned how to work on the cocoa
plantation and in the banana groves.
   The days he spent at the *finca* were among the most carefree times of his life
to that point. No longer concerned about looking like an East Coast marketing
agent, Allen let his hair grow longer, and he grew a goatee and mustache. He
ate frijoles and tortillas every meal, along with raw or fried bananas. As a child
and young man, he had developed a strong liking for Eastern European food,
and he was now pleasantly surprised by how much he enjoyed these Mexican
staples.
   He filled his leisure time with simple pleasures. In the mornings, he would
go horseback riding or hiking in the jungle. He studied the large broad-leafed
plants that flourished in the area. One day, he came upon a heart-shaped leaf

and mused "to whom shall I send this/anachronistic valentine?" composing a brief lyric poem on the spot:

> I walked in the forest to look for a sign
> Fortune to tell & thought to refine.
> My green Valentine, my green Valentine,
> What do I know of my green Valentine?

When temperatures heated up under the midday sun, Allen would remove his clothing and, wearing only hiking shoes, he would walk in solitude in the shallow waters of the rocky riverbed that wound through the jungle. In the evenings, he might amuse himself by accompanying the natives to nearby streams, where they would fish for lobster-sized crayfish, using flashlights and pronged spears.

Allen spent much of his time lounging around in his thatch-roof hut. "A great discovery I made here is the marvel of the hammock," he wrote Lucien Carr, launching into a long monologue of its virtues in comparison to those of a bed. Finding the hammock "a friendly womb for repose," Allen spent many hours reading the New Testament, Thomas Merton's *The Seven Storey Mountain*, Mexican guidebooks, *The Cloud of Unknowing*, and some of the texts of fourteenth-century Catholic mystics that Shields had at the *finca*. Every so often, when the mood struck him, he would go out in the yard and play a set of drums he had built out of logs and suspended on supports fashioned out of twigs and vines. The smallest drum was just over three feet and the largest was approximately seventeen feet; for drum sticks, Allen had tipped foot-long sticks with rubber that he tapped from a tree. "I break out in African reverberations which can be heard for miles around," Allen told Jack and Neal. "Am known as Señor Jalisco."

8

From early February into early April, the southern region of Mexico was hit by a series of earth tremors. The most powerful of the quakes, supposedly set off by a volcanic eruption of Acavalna, was said to have destroyed a four-century-old church in the nearby mountain village of Yajalón. According to the rumors Allen heard, eight people had died and the villagers were in a panic.

For the fearful or superstitious, there had been natural signs predicting the tremors. There had been a full lunar eclipse the night Allen had left for Palenque. A couple of weeks later, on February 5, Allen had seen a spectacular meteor that he described as being "so brilliant I thought it was the star of Bethlehem, burning blue & red, not white, lighting up half the whole sky." For weeks, Allen heard numerous rumors of destruction in the wake of the most serious tremor, and when none were substantiated, he decided to check them out on his own. He left the *finca* with nothing but one hundred pesos, a fountain pen and notebook, a sombrero, and the clothes on his back.

To reach Yajalón, one had to travel on mule for two days through mountainous terrain. Rather than take this long route, Allen hitched a perilous ride in a biplane—a fifteen-minute flight from Salto de Agua to Yajalón. The town, ten blocks long and four blocks wide, tucked in the mountains and surrounded by breathtaking scenery, had not been as damaged by the quake as Allen had heard. The church was still standing and the damage to Yajalón was minimal. There was even some question as to whether there had been a volcanic eruption at all. No reporters had visited the site, and the one geologist who had seen it reported a crack near the mouth of the volcano but was uncertain about actual volcanic activity. Curious as always, Allen chose to investigate the volcano himself. The town's *presidente* supplied him with a guide.

The next day, March 28, Allen and the guide set out on foot for Acavalna. On the way, they met a rancher en route to Yajalón. When Allen told him where he and the guide were traveling, the rancher loaned them his mule, insisting that he could easily walk to Yajalón. It was just one example of the generosity Allen encountered during his time in Mexico.

By noon, Allen and his guide had arrived at a coffee *finca* where, he later reported, he was treated like an "honored important guest." There was much evidence of minor structural damage in the *finca* from the tremors, and from the villagers Allen learned that for weeks the plantation had been rocked by several slight quakes each day. While he was visiting with the locals, two men from Yajalón joined them, saying that they had followed Allen and wanted to be a part of his expedition. Ginsberg, feeling confident in his role as an explorer, dismissed his guide and sent him back to Yajalón with the rancher's mule. At the *finca*, Allen was given blankets and a hammock for comfort on the cold mountain nights.

By late afternoon, Allen was in Zapata, another coffee-producing village. He spent the rest of the daylight hours talking with the men of the village. The town spokesman promised to provide him with men and supplies for the next day's journey. Just before dusk, as Allen was getting ready to eat, the ground began to rumble and the village dogs started barking. To Allen, who had never experienced anything like this, the sound was "like a colossal subway train suddenly passing under tons of concrete pavement." When the tremor had passed, he was told that Zapata had been getting about twenty such tremors a day since early February.

Allen attended a religious service that evening. The village women, holding taper candles and dressed in black dresses trimmed with brightly colored Mayan designs, sat in a circle on the dirt floor, while the men, dressed in white, sat on cedar logs lining the walls of the thatch-roof hut. On the glass-case altar were doll-like statues of Jesus, Mary, and various local saints, as well as halos of tulips, colorful bunting, reproductions of nineteenth-century religious paintings, medals, clay pots, and Mexican flags. After a recital of prayers, spoken in both Tzeltal (the local dialect) and Latin, a boy sitting next to Allen brought out a flute. He was joined by a drummer, and for a half hour they played what Ginsberg described as "repetitive melancholy variations on some atonal mountain thought." When they had finished, two men began to strum guitars.

At eight-thirty that evening, while the guitarists were still playing, the ground suddenly began to rumble and shake, the mountain roaring louder than it had earlier in the day. Screaming panic-stricken people ran for the door. The walls and beams of the church shook violently and hunks of adobe the size of tortillas broke away and fell, several grazing Allen's shoulders. The noise increased until it was deafening, "the whole mountain shaking and roaring, accumulating violence," as Allen remembered. And then, as suddenly as it had begun, it ceased and was quiet. Humbled by this terrifying display of nature's force, Allen stood in the room and trembled, wondering whether he should continue his explorations the next day.

After a restless night's sleep, interrupted by several minor aftershock tremors, Allen rose at dawn and, in the company of fifty-four men from Zapata and two neighboring villages, began his ascent of the mountain. The climb was slow but relatively easy, with rocks and fallen trees acting as a natural stairway up the mountain. Some of the natives claimed to have felt slight tremors while they were walking, but Allen felt no further rumblings. He was again confident in his ability to reach the summit, pleased that he was regarded as the group's leader and deferred to by those who knew the terrain and region much better than he. "Dozens of indians ready to run up and down mountains to get me horses or carry messages or perform any mysterious white man with beard wish," Allen wrote, confessing that he enjoyed the preferential treatment he was receiving.

When they reached the top of Acavalna, they found no hint of an active volcano, nor of the fissure reported by the geologist. Nor was there a secret mountain lake, as rumored to exist by the natives. Instead, they found rubble and boulders, shaken loose by the quakes, littering the ground. As a prank, some of the Indians set fire to a dead cedar tree, knowing that the sight of smoke coming from the mountaintop would frighten the people in the villages below.

They were back in Zapata by midafternoon. The purpose of their trek had been to separate fact from rumor—to find out whether indeed there had been any volcanic activity in the area—and now that he had explored the mountain on his own, Allen wrote an official report of his findings. Copies of the document, containing the official seals of three villages, the thumbprints of Zapata's spokesperson and *presidente*, and the names of all of the people who had accompanied Allen on the expedition, were dispatched to the Geological Institute, the Mexican government, and the neighboring towns. Allen was content, feeling that he had performed a valuable service while experiencing "a great trip into rarely seen parts more obscure than where I've been all along."

The following morning, Allen was greeted by forty Indians who had arisen before dawn and hiked five miles from La Ventana to see him. They inquired about what Allen had seen the day before, and then asked him to accompany them to the east side of the mountain, where there was supposed to be a giant cave, discovered years ago by two men from their village but unseen by anyone else. According to the Indians, a geologist had been informed of the discovery, but he had been skeptical and had not bothered to verify it. They would accompany Allen to the site of this legendary cave to confirm its existence and determine whether its entrance had been sealed by rock slides caused by the tremors.

The trip was through much more rugged terrain than Allen's excursion of the day before. This was land that had been left essentially to itself, untraveled and uncultivated for years, marked by maize patches gone wild, rotten logs, boulders, and very old lava formations. About twenty Indians moved ahead of the group, cutting through the milpa and overgrowth with machetes. After an hour or so of slow progress through the brush, the Indians preceding the expedition party gave out a collective shout. When Allen reached the others, he found them standing near a clearing, protected by a small ravine. As Ginsberg reported to Lucien Carr:

> I found the men lined up irregularly on stones and logs in front of a drop. A wide arch of roof overhead dwarfed the men. The mouth of an immense cavern, great as a cathedral, and in the light of the morning decorated like a wild cathedral full of colossal pulpits and arks and pilastors [sic], floor overgrown with green moss, lichen embroidering the giant sculptures, monumental arches and portals to interior darkness. Acavalna: House of Night.

"House of Night" or, in other words, dark cave: The reason for the mountain's name was suddenly clear to Allen. Ancient Mayans had seen the cave and had given the mountain its name in accordance with its main feature. They had no way of knowing that the cave would go unseen for centuries. "Indians have great poetic imagination for names," Allen wrote; "a mountain named house of night & forgotten why except for one or two who nobody believes centuries later." As far as he knew, he was the first white man to set eyes on the cave.

Reasoning that he needed to "do something brave to justify the honor," Allen led the group into the mouth of the cave, where they surveyed the damage done by the recent quakes. The edge of the overhang had fallen in, and boulders and trees, some with their leaves still green, were strewn about the opening. Allen moved in cautiously, alert for the sounds of rumblings. To his left was a huge pit, over which hung ten-foot stalactites; to his right was a small arch formed by adjoining stalactites. They heard the sound of stalactites falling to the floor deep within the cave just as a tremor shook the ground. Fortunately, it was only a slight quake and nothing else fell. Nevertheless, the party paused near the entrance, waiting for about fifteen minutes to make certain it was safe before they continued. Rather than venture too far into the cave, the group remained near its mouth, spending an hour exploring the limestone formations and gathering fragments as souvenirs and proof of their discovery. Allen had left his camera at Karena Shields's *finca*. He vowed to send for it as soon as he made it back to Yajalón. If he could find the time and means, he would return to the cave for pictures.

9

Allen was given a hero's welcome upon his return to Yajalón. He was offered a room in the vice president's house, and virtually all of his meals and expenses were paid for by the village. He was loaned a typewriter and informed that he would have guides and mules at his disposal if he chose to do more exploring.

This treatment could not have come at a more opportune time, for Allen was almost flat broke. Without money, he could do little further exploration in Mexico. Even more alarming, he was not certain he had the wherewithal to return to the United States. After he had returned to Yajalón, he had drawn up official documentation of his discovery for Mexican officials, and then he had written a report and sent it to Lucien Carr, with the hope that he might be able to earn a modest fee if UPI published his story in the American or Mexican wire services. To Allen's dismay, his timing was poor. Lucien had just departed for a brief vacation in Brazil, so Allen had not only wasted some of his badly needed money on postage and telegram fees but had also sent the only copy of his report to an empty office. Growing desperate, he wrote Neal and asked for a loan of twenty-five dollars.

Ironically, Allen's whereabouts and well-being were becoming of increasing concern to his friends—Bill Burroughs in particular. Throughout his stay in Mexico, Allen had maintained his correspondence with friends and family, but the further he moved away from the larger cities, the greater the delay in getting his letters out. Many of his letters had been lost.

Burroughs, now living in Tangier, had not heard from Allen in months. At first, he was peeved by Allen's lack of communication, reasoning that he was avoiding him in the aftermath of their breakup in New York. He had written Allen in care of the American Express office in Mexico City, as Allen had instructed him to do when they had discussed his tentative itinerary, but when his letters were returned unopened, Bill began to worry. For Allen to ignore his letters was out of character. Contacting Jack Kerouac, Burroughs asked Jack to intercede on his behalf. "You must remonstrate with him," Bill wrote, still thinking that Allen's silence might be deliberate. "No matter what Allen says I want to hear it understand? If he says something that you know would hurt me, please don't keep it from me. I want to know. Nothing is worse than waiting like this day after day for a letter that doesn't come."

Neal Cassady was also worried. When Allen had sent him an urgent request for money on April 6, Neal had immediately wired him twenty-five dollars; two weeks later, the money was returned unclaimed. The United States embassy had returned his last three letters to Allen, and this, along with the frantic letters Neal had been receiving from Burroughs on an almost daily basis, had Cassady fearing for the worst. "Naturally I'm very worried for your health and safety and wonder where the hell you are," Neal wrote Allen in a letter Ginsberg eventually received, weeks after it was posted; "here I was expecting you to show up hot on the heels of your last letter, but suddenly my money is returned and there's . . . no Allen, no news, nothing." He was going to wait for a couple more weeks, he advised Allen, and if he had not heard from him by then, he was going to consult an attorney about the best means of locating him.

Having lived in Mexico, Burroughs knew all too well how easily one could be lost or tangled up in the legal bureaucracy of the country. A man could disappear without a trace or, as Bill told Jack, he could rot in jail without hope of getting a word to the outside world. When he learned that Allen had not claimed Neal's money, Burroughs sent a letter to his parents in Florida, as well as one to Louis Ginsberg in New Jersey. Bill asked his parents to cable Allen some money and deduct it from his monthly allowance; he advised Louis

Ginsberg to consult with the U.S. embassy in Mexico City about Allen's whereabouts. To Kerouac, Burroughs mentioned that in one of Allen's earlier letters, "Allen said there was mounting tension and anti-American feeling in that area and he urgently wanted to leave as soon as he could get the money." Because the money had been returned, Bill suspected that Allen had encountered serious trouble. "It looks very bad indeed," he told Jack, "so for God's sake don't lose any time. . . . I don't know what I would do if anything happened to Allen."

For nearly six weeks, Ginsberg was unaware of these growing concerns. After leaving Yajalón, he had returned to Karena Shields's *finca*, where he had no choice but to stay put until he received the money he had requested from Neal. While he waited, he worked for five to ten hours each day on "Siesta in Xbalba," a lengthy poem recalling his earlier visits to the ruins in Chichén Itzá and Palenque. The early drafts were going well—the new poem, in Allen's judgment, being "better than Green Auto." The ruins, with their evidence of ancient Mayan art and craftsmanship, had inspired him, and by using his meditation at the death's-head at Chichén Itzá as the poem's central image, he was able to combine physical detail and metaphysical thought.

The ruins were an ideal setting for the poem. Ginsberg was still searching for a concrete object upon which he could build the sort of transcendental conclusions he had drawn from his Harlem visions. The silence of the ruins encouraged reflection and introspection. That the region was known to the natives as a limbo was an additional bonus: the reader, like Allen, was caught somewhere between the reality of ancient buildings and the sense of eternity that their deteriorating state inspired. Ginsberg wanted his poem to have the qualities of a siesta, that peaceful limbo between an awakened consciousness and death—a consciousness which, as Ginsberg noted in his poems of 1948, had a visionary quality of its own.

"Siesta in Xbalba" is packed with dreams, daydreams, remembrances, and drug-induced observations—all interspersed in some of Ginsberg's most descriptive writing to date. A party in New York is recalled, juxtaposed to a description of the Mexican mountains and jungles; a meditation in the Chichén Itzá ruins is preempted by the sounds of chirping crickets and birds. The Blake visions themselves are recalled:

> I thought, five years ago
> sitting in my apartment,
> my eyes were opened for an hour
> seeing in dreadful ecstasy
> the motionless buildings
> of New York rotting
> under the tides of Heaven.

The ruins, like the cornices in Harlem, represent a consciousness passed down through the ages. Ginsberg's intention in "Siesta in Xbalba" is to make that consciousness almost palpable to his readers, just as he is concerned with charting the immediate movement of the mind. In this sense, his meditation

at the death's-head, interrupted by the sounds of the night, is a continuation
of his "Marijuana Notation," in which his thoughts are interrupted by the
sounds of Christmas carolers. In fact, "Siesta in Xbalba" owes much to *Empty
Mirror*. If the stanzas of "Siesta in Xbalba" were to be isolated one to the page,
they would read much like the short individual poems of *Empty Mirror*, but in
"Siesta" Ginsberg is anchored to a sense of place, which gives his sequence a
sense of unity missing in the *Empty Mirror* poems. He recognized as much in
one of his journal entries:

> Empty Mirror poems now fallen together and synthesized in such man-
> ner that the casual fragments of thought utilized for short poems before
> are now linked together in a natural train of thought, or images, some
> very strong and powerful, very much paralleling the development of
> an intense meditation lying in a hammock just thinking along. . . .

The poem is also a precursor to such poems as "Angkor Wat" (1963) and
"Wales Visitation" (1967), long poems in which Ginsberg uses place as the
conduit between different types of consciousness. "Siesta in Xbalba" is less
than perfect, but it indicates the further evolution of the young poet, a matur-
ation that would be evident in less than a year, when Ginsberg would move
to San Francisco and begin one of the most important writing periods of his
life.

10

As soon as he became aware of his friends' concern about his safety and well-
being, Allen dispatched letters assuring everyone that he was all right. Bill
Burroughs had received one of his earlier letters, delayed on its way to Tangier,
and he had written Allen a letter citing all of his previous worries. Allen was
moved by Bill's concern, even though he was put off by the depth of Burroughs's
feelings for him. With Burroughs in northern Africa and he in Mexico, Allen
had figured that some of the emotional intensity would have dissipated. "He
sure is lonely or imagines himself such and I guess it drives him off the road at
times," Allen told Neal. Of his status in Mexico, Allen informed Neal that his
leaving the country was now a matter of coming up with the money to do so.
Both he and Karena Shields were virtually penniless. Shields was waiting for
royalty money to arrive from her publisher, while Ginsberg waited for a loan
from family or friends. In the meantime, Allen explored ruins neighboring the
finca and worked on "Siesta in Xbalba."

Shields's money finally arrived, and with the help of another loan from his
host, Allen was finally able to leave on May 13. His journey, recalled in Part
Two of "Siesta in Xbalba," commenced when he caught a train traveling from
Salto de Agua to Coatzcoalcos. As he traveled, Allen looked out his window
at the Mexican countryside that to him looked like "lunar landscape." In
Coatzcoalcos, he caught a bus that took him first to Veracruz, and then to
Mexico City. Just before dawn, while looking out the window into the mist,
Allen had a codeine-induced vision, in which he imagined:

> the far away likeness
> of a heavenly file
> of female saints
> stepping upward
> on miniature arches
> of a gold stairway
> into the starry sky,
> the thousands of little
> saintesses in blue hoods
> looking out at me
> and beckoning:
> SALVATION!

Allen scribbled this ethereal image in his journal. He would eventually include it as one of the central images in Part Two of "Siesta in Xbalba," which focused on his return to modern civilization after his dreamlike adventure with the past.

Allen spent four days in Mexico City, waiting for money to arrive. In contrast to the carefree time he had spent on a hammock in the southern Mexican air, Allen stayed in a cheap hotel room, where he spent solitary hours battling bedbugs, loneliness, and his anxiety over his financial plight. To pass time, he took long walks in the city, but he was haunted by his memories of Joan Vollmer and the time he, Joan, and Lucien Carr had visited the city. This time, the city had nowhere near the appeal it had offered Allen on his previous visit.

Despite his eagerness to return to the States, Allen took a methodical approach to his northward movement through Mexico. After leaving Mexico City, he stopped for three days in Pátzcuaro, followed by another three days in San Miguel de Allende, where he visited an artists' colony. One of the high points of his trip back—and a focal point in Part Two of "Siesta in Xbalba"— was his stop in Guanajuato. Once a mining town, it was now contemporary, with modern shops and fashionably dressed people. One of its tourist attractions was a hall of mummified corpses. Walking down the corridor and looking at the shriveled figures that stood in rows like ancient people waiting in a line, Allen was able to put his Mexico trip in perspective. A human being had a limited amount of time on earth, after which all that remained were artifacts and the empty shell of the once-living being. One had to make the most of a moment:

> of eternity we have
> a numbered score of years
> and fewer tender moments
> —one moment of tenderness
> and a year of intelligence
> and nerves: one moment of pure
> bodily tenderness—
> I could dismiss Allen with grim
> pleasure.

The nearer he got to California—and Neal Cassady—the more Allen pondered his lack-love state of existence. The months of solitude had left him yearning for physical tenderness, and he harbored the hope that he might be able to renew his affair with Neal in San Jose, even though Carolyn and their children would be there. In his journal, he noted that his "trip to Frisco [was] almost solely eternally for love."

Allen's entry proved to be prophetic. He would indeed find lasting love in California, though it would not be with Neal Cassady.

8
In Back of the Real

the weight,
the weight we carry
is love . . . .

1

Allen spent his last night in Mexico in the border town of Mexicali. He checked into an inexpensive hotel room and spent much of the evening wandering around town. He found the city to be dirty and noisy, its nighttime streets packed with concession stands selling cheap trinkets to tourists, drunken all-night revelers, street-corner mariachi bands, and tacky shops. It was a quick-sell culture, a direct contrast to the silence of the ancient ruins and the simplicity of the lives of the people Allen had lived among in southern Mexico. Allen wrote in his journal:

> I wound up spending last night in Mexico overlooking the poor barrio Casbah outside of my room on the garbage cliff of Mexicali, tin shacks down the cliff, white roofs and dirty little gardens with super highway and other cliff leading to uptown border hipsters streets. . . . I stood on a garbage cliff in darkness to see I was at the end of my Mexico trip.

Before continuing on to San Jose and his reunion with the Cassadys, Allen spent a week visiting his mother's relatives in Los Angeles. On the occasion of his twenty-eighth birthday, he was in a reflective mood. He had never envisioned himself reaching that age, and now that he had, he felt that some serious changes were called for. He did not question that he was different from the young man he had been when he entered Mexico on the first of the year. But he felt that he looked foolish with his beard, which he believed gave him the appearance of "a German geologist," and he was dissatisfied with what he termed "my character with its childish core." He needed to grow. He was eager to replace the Allen of his past with the character and artistry of his future adult life. "Must find energy & image & act on it," he advised himself in his journal.

2

Neal and Carolyn Cassady had undergone changes of their own since Allen had seen them last. In an effort to overcome some of their marital difficulties—Neal's sexual hang-ups in particular—the Cassadys had become avid followers of Edgar Cayce. Neal had found a copy of Gina Cerminara's *Many Mansions* on a car seat while he was working as a parking-lot attendant, and what began as casual interest evolved into a full-blown obsession. The Cassadys were intrigued by Cayce's talk of reincarnation and karma, and they were especially impressed with the positive, upbeat side of Cayce's philosophy. For years, Neal and Carolyn had struggled with feelings of inadequacy and guilt, and here was a man who preached that self-condemnation was a vice. They plunged into an all-out study of Cayce and his teachings, and before long they were utterly convinced that Cayce was the answer to their problems and domestic turmoil.

When he visited the Cassadys in February and March, Jack Kerouac had found Neal's blind allegiance to Cayce maddening. They argued constantly, Jack finding Neal to be cold, engrossed only in repeating the Cayce doctrine. In Jack's mind, Neal was presently little more than "Billy Graham in a suit," the antithesis of the Dean Moriarty he had celebrated in *On the Road*. Neal had not abandoned his old obsessions—cars, women, and marijuana—but his aggressive pursuit of these kicks, a personal trademark in the past, had since been replaced by a form of passive acceptance, as if he was resigned to his own obsessions. He was no longer driven, at least as far as Jack could tell. Neal would rather get high on marijuana and play chess for hours at a time with a neighbor than test his own personal limits.

Jack's stay, although generally trying and marked by angry disputes with Neal, resulted in one very important development for Kerouac: a deeper understanding of Buddhism. Kerouac had initiated his own study of Buddhism, and he had come to California prepared to extol its virtues to the Cassadys, but when Neal countered Jack's elementary Buddhist studies with the principles of Edgar Cayce, Jack realized that he needed further study if he intended to continue his debates with Neal. Edgar Cayce's philosophy was based to a great extent on Buddhist beliefs, so in an effort to better familiarize himself with Neal's latest passion, Jack visited the San Jose library and researched the basic Buddhist texts. Of particular interest to Kerouac was Dwight Goddard's *The Buddhist Bible*, an anthology of Buddhist and Taoist writings that included the "Surangama Sutra," the "Lankavatara Sutra," and Kerouac's favorite, the "Diamond Sutra"; he had also been impressed by Asvaghosha's *A Life of Buddha*.

Everywhere he turned in his sweeping study, Jack found statements that had a direct bearing on his own life. The first Noble Truth—"All Life Is Sorrowful"—helped him further define what he meant by *beat*: The beat characters he knew, rather then being beaten, were actually beatific in their nobility of suffering. To Kerouac's delight, he could accept this belief without compromising his

Catholic background, since Catholicism preached the ideal of the meek inheriting the earth and rewarded its suffering martyrs with sainthood. If one could accept the reality that life was sorrowful, it was not difficult to embrace Buddha's second Noble Truth, "The Cause of Suffering Is Ignorant Desire." This, too, fell in line with what Jack knew of the characters in his circle of friends and acquaintances. The people who suffered the most were the people who wanted the most.

In this light, it takes no stretch of the imagination to see why Jack became so frustrated with Neal. The old Neal—the Dean Moriarty/Cody Pomeroy hero figure of Kerouac's two novels based on Cassady—had accepted the suffering and hardship of his life and had lived nobly within that suffering; the Neal that Jack encountered in early 1954 was tied up by desire, absorbed by the need for possessions. The previous April, Neal had seriously injured his ankle and foot in an accident that occurred while he was working for the railroad, and throughout Jack's visit Neal talked incessantly about how the lawsuit he had filed against the railroad would net him seventeen thousand dollars, which he intended to apply to the purchase of his dream house. As far as Jack could see, Neal was being absorbed into middle-class America, and that would only cause him suffering. And it was inexcusable that he would simply rationalize or dismiss the troublesome aspects of his life by delving into one of his past lives.

Jack's arguments with Neal only reaffirmed his developing interests in Buddhism. At the library, he took copious notes on his readings, and for Allen he prepared a one-hundred-page document based on those notes, which he was calling *Some of the Dharma.* In his letters, Jack prodded Allen into a study of Buddhism. He drew up reading lists and included quotations from his readings. He conceded the esoteric nature of his latest obsession—"I know that now I am a dehumanized beast and maybe you don't understand me any more," he said to Allen—but he urged Ginsberg to read some of his recommended books, beginning with *A Life of Buddha.* If Allen gave these readings a chance, Jack said confidently, he would see that many of their past discussions, such as those about the Shroudy Stranger, were even more valid than they had suspected. "Don't you forget our liquid ghosts oogling behind buildings, and the eternity radar machines in the sky, and dead eyes see, because, boy, I've now found that it was all instinct pure and true, and I must say, we weren't so dumb," Jack wrote.

Unable to reconcile his philosophical differences with Neal, Jack left the Cassadys in March. He spent a month in San Francisco, staying in a skid-row flophouse and working on a sequence of spontaneously composed poems he called *San Francisco Blues.* He was back in New York living with his mother by the time Allen arrived in San Jose.

The Cassadys were happy to see Allen, although Carolyn later admitted that at first she felt very uneasy around him. She was afraid that he disliked her, despite their correspondence that indicated otherwise. As soon as he had stored his gear, Allen presented Neal and Carolyn with the souvenirs he had brought back from Mexico for them—carved wooden figurines, several masks, and two handwoven bags. That first evening, he insisted upon preparing dinner for the family, an act of friendship that impressed Carolyn.

Throughout his stay, Allen spent a great amount of time with Carolyn. An ideal houseguest, Allen helped with chores and errands; he enjoyed playing with the children. He accompanied Carolyn when she went out to inspect prospective lots for the house she and Neal hoped to build. Carolyn responded to Allen's warmth by sketching his portrait, the picture depicting a clean-shaven Ginsberg, with a slightly receding hairline but still boyish, peering pensively through his trademark black-rimmed glasses. Carolyn enjoyed Allen's company. As she later recalled, he was "more considerate, aware, patient and kind than anyone I'd ever known besides Neal":

> He filled each day with a variety of enthusiasms, always stimulating and amusing, and like me he enjoyed sharing; I was never bored or lonely. Once in awhile we'd go to a movie in the evening; it was almost like having a "date" again and afterward we'd sit at a café counter drinking cokes and bringing our superior critical intellects to bear on every facet of the film we'd seen.

The situation was different with Neal, who was working full-time and was gone much of the time. At home, he and Allen might smoke marijuana and record their conversations or Allen's drumming on Neal's wire recorder, or they would occasionally go to San Francisco for an evening, but more often than not—by Ginsberg's account, at least—Neal would come home, clean up, and spend the evening playing chess with his neighbor, leaving Allen to watch the three children if Carolyn happened to be out for the evening. In his letters to Jack, Allen complained repeatedly about how Neal's obsession with chess was robbing them of their time together. "The *chess*, maniacal—he won't talk to me, except in a sort of disassociated way," Allen wrote.

With high expectations of renewing his romantic involvement with Neal, Allen had set himself up for disappointment similar to the time he visited Cassady in Denver in 1947. Neal was no longer interested in a physical relationship with him—certainly not a lasting one—and the few times they did engage in sex were, as Allen reported to Kerouac, "cold and bitter." When he first arrived in San Jose, Allen was dizzied by the mere sight of Cassady, as if Neal, gone for so long, had returned "by resurrection from dead past, fresh and full of life." His "greatest pleasure," Allen told Jack, was simply "looking at him as in a great dream, the unreality of it, that we are in the same space-time room again." Allen initially judged Neal's quiet demeanor to be the result of unsolved problems of their past. However, in the following weeks, he wound up agreeing with Jack's earlier conclusion that Neal had grown indifferent and withdrawn. From the time he arrived at the Cassadys, Allen had been tape-recording all his poetry to date, but Neal was interested in neither the taped poetry (including "The Green Automobile," which Allen recorded several times) nor in any of Allen's new work. Persuaded by his Cayce study group that his writing, with all its explicit sexual content, was "sinful," Neal had quit writing and, to Allen's dismay, he had thrown out almost all of his work. His driving, once a great passion, had become frantic and far from enjoyable for him, as he was now hateful and impatient with other drivers on the road. Perhaps most shocking to Allen were Neal's sexual activities. He had quit sleeping with Carolyn and, in lieu of seeking satisfaction with his wife, he had taken on a variety of one-night sex partners, including a seventy-year-old spiritualist in San Jose. Much of Neal's sexual activity, Allen recounted, was masturbatory. One night, while he was on duty at the railroad, Neal had been caught masturbating by the conductor and had nearly lost his job. On other occasions, when he and Allen would rendezvous at a hotel in San Francisco, Neal would get in bed and proceed to masturbate rather than have sex with Allen. When Allen confronted him about this lack of warmth, Neal replied, "I have no feelings—never had."

Allen concluded Neal's problem was that he felt trapped in his household. In looking for an explanation for Neal's behavior, Allen turned unfairly on Carolyn. As he saw it, Neal had married a woman whose ideas came straight out of *House Beautiful*; she wanted a man, several children, a home in the suburbs, a television, and a new car parked in the driveway. Not only was Neal malcontent working at a job he hated in order to provide for her, but when he failed to make such provisions he lashed out with cold, cruel, or even violent behavior. Kerouac had reported one incident, occurring while he had visited the Cassadys, in which Neal had knocked his daughter Cathy across the room. Such violence was out of character for Cassady and Allen did not witness anything similar during his stay, though he did see Neal fly into rages of frustration at times. Almost as frightening were those occasions during which Neal would go blank, as if he had disconnected himself from those around him and could not relate to them. Allen was crushed. "Would be willing to take vows to leave him alone etc. if he would only be sweet & carefree again and open to gentle kicks & images & poetry & digging things of all nature," he wrote sadly.

Allen was more tolerant than Jack of the Cassadys' fixation on Edgar Cayce, but, like Kerouac, he wondered whether Neal and Carolyn had been brainwashed by some of Cayce's teachings. It seemed to be the one topic that Neal was enthusiastic about discussing. Neal espoused the Cayce philosophy "like some doctrine in an asylum," Allen observed. Out of curiosity, Allen read Gina Cerminara's *Cayce System Book*, as well as Cayce's *Extracts from Readings*, but he was not impressed. He accompanied Carolyn to an evening lecture on hypnotism and trance, where they met an investment broker who tried to convince Carolyn that a hypnotist could help Neal solve some of his problems, but Allen was skeptical, especially when he looked around and saw some of the fanatics in attendance at the lecture. As Carolyn recalled, when she and Allen visited the hypnotist's home to investigate the broker's story, they found that "everyone was more interested in such occult phenomenon as pendulums and ouija boards than a philosophy to live by." After witnessing the aspects of fanaticism enveloping Cayce's followers, Allen concluded that Cayce was a "crackpot," even if there was redeeming value to some of his philosophy.

If Neal was indeed feeling as if he had run out of options, he was not alone. Allen was feeling trapped himself. With no job or money, he was reliant upon the Cassadys' hospitality, and he believed that by placing further demands upon Neal, such as vying for attention or sexual favor, he was being impositional:

> I feel like a strange idiot, standing there among wife & children all to whom he gives needs of affection and attention, asking for some special side extra sacrifice of attention to me—as if like some nowhere evil

beast intruding I were competing for his care with his own children &
wife and job which seems to occupy energize bore & tire him.

3

To stave off his depression, Allen turned his attention to his poetry, as he had
under similar circumstances in the past. He worked on the revisions of "Siesta
in Xbalba" and continued to record his poetry. With two long poems ("Siesta
in Xbalba" and "The Green Automobile") already written, Allen felt that he
had the foundation for a new book, though both of these longer works still
required more attention; as Allen told his father, "it takes me half a year or so
to be finished with anything over 2 pages." During this period, he wrote other
new poems that he would eventually deem meritorious enough to include in
poetry collections: "Song," a poem reflecting Allen's urgent need for love;
"On Burroughs' Work," a three-stanza poem that explained the nature of the
"routines" Burroughs was sending him from Tangier; "In back of the real," a
short work describing Ginsberg's finding a sunflower in a railroad yard; and
"Love Poem on Theme by Whitman," a fantasy poem that updated the perfected
reality he had attempted to create in "The Green Automobile."

From its simple opening declaration—"The weight of the world is love"—
to its penultimate statement—"I always wanted to return to the body where I
was born"—"Song" would appear to be a logical depiction of yearning and
fulfillment. The need to love and be loved, Ginsberg says, is behind everything
we do, but that same love, or lack of it, can be a terrible burden. The poem's
central image is a brief sensual passage that stands in stark contrast to the
feelings of yearning expressed earlier in the poem:

> The warm bodies
>   shine together
> in the darkness,
>   the hand moves
> to the center
>   of the flesh,
> the skin trembles
>   in happiness
> and the soul comes
>   joyful to the eye. . . .

The poem, though hardly a breakthrough or major work, is noteworthy, a
representation of the poet's personal movement from lacklove to being loved.
A reader would have no way of knowing it, but the poem was composed in
three different sittings over the course of a year, at times crucial to Ginsberg's
personal life. The earliest writing took place in his journals, in April 1954,
when he was still in Mexico, a time when he was trying to mark a sense of
resolve over the direction his life was taking. The upbeat last two stanzas were
written during this period. The second writing (the early portion of the poem)
occurred while Ginsberg was staying with the Cassadys and despairing over his

failure to gain the love he sought. The third writing—a brief fragment making up the third stanza of the poem—was written in January 1955, during the early stages of Ginsberg's relationship with Peter Orlovsky, who would become his lifetime companion. The writing in "Song" is so convincing because Ginsberg was writing from immediate experience.

At the time he wrote "On Burroughs' Work," Allen had been receiving the routines Burroughs was writing in Tangier—the short fragmentary bits of fiction that would wind up in such books as *Interzone* or *Naked Lunch*. The routines, including "Dr. Benway in the Operating Room" and "The Talking Asshole," were written in stripped-down prose that hit readers like blunt objects. It was a style Ginsberg admired. As it was later expressed by Burroughs, a naked lunch was that moment in which someone saw something as it really was, when the metaphorical fork was frozen in midair and one saw exactly what one was about to eat. There was no "symbolic meat" involved. In "On Burroughs' Work," Ginsberg paid tribute to the idea:

> A naked lunch is natural to us,
>   we eat reality sandwiches.
> But allegories are so much lettuce.
> Don't hide the madness.

"In back of the real," one of Ginsberg's better early efforts, finds the poet in a reflective mood yet never too distant from Williams's "no ideas but in things" dictum. In the poem, a predecessor to Ginsberg's later "Sunflower Sutra," the narrator goes for a walk in a railroad yard and comes upon a grimy sunflower, prompting a short soliloquy about salvation for the meek. With its religious underpinnings ("corolla of yellowing dirty/spikes like Jesus' inchlong/crown") along with Ginsberg's tendency to sentimentalize and overstate his symbolism in his early poems, "In back of the real" could easily have fallen victim to hyperbole. Instead, Ginsberg eases the burden on his symbol (the sunflower as the common man) and message ("This is the flower of the world") with a striking portrait of the flower, arguably his best descriptive passage since "The Bricklayer's Lunch Hour":

> . . . and a soiled
> dry center cotton tuft
>   like a used shaving brush
> that's been lying under
>   the garage for a year.

Ginsberg would address the same theme in "Sunflower Sutra," using the same central symbol, with all its references to his 1948 Blake visions, but in the later poem he would use the long line, letting images rush past readers in long, jazzy stream-of-consciousness word blasts ("corolla of bleary spikes pushed down and broken like a battered crown, seeds fallen out of its face, soon-to-be toothless mouth of sunny air, sunrays obliterated on its hairy head like a dried wire spiderweb"); with its short, tightly written lines, "In back of the real" is as profound in its simplicity as the subject it celebrates.

The best of Ginsberg's San Jose poems, "Love Poem on Theme by Whitman" is the direct result of Ginsberg's unhappiness with his stay at the Cassadys. In his journal, he described the sexual tensions in the household, calling the situation "artificial," full of possibilities, none of them acceptable:

> I can sleep with Neal, sleep with Carolyn, sleep with no one, and stay.
> Or sleep with both and no one alternately amid confusions. Or I can
> end this mad triangle, all three of us blocked, by leaving.

This confused sexuality haunted Ginsberg throughout his San Jose visit. He had a number of dreams, several recorded in his journals, in which his homosexuality was contrasted to a heterosexual majority. In one dream, Cassady and Ginsberg were at Allen's family's house at dinnertime, and when Allen left the table and joined Neal in the bathroom, where he had been hiding, Allen was horrified to find that he was sexually constricted, his mouth and throat clogged with hair. In another dream, Allen and an unnamed boy were lying together on the ground next to Louis and Eugene, their tentative fumblings around tainted by Allen's fear that his father or brother would see them. In still another entry, Ginsberg recalled the way he slept with his father and brother until he was well into puberty.

Ginsberg's sexual confusion was compounded by his enormous need for love, tenderness, and acceptance. As he noted in his journal, he was willing to suffer humiliation or degradation in exchange for a moment's love, but he was also wise enough to realize that his willingness for such an exchange was exacting a high price on his own self-esteem. "Once again I've maneuvered myself into a frustrating idealistic situation where I am reduced to pathetic beggary," he wrote of his situation with Neal.

"Love Poem on Theme by Whitman" became his way of addressing his idealized life with the Cassadys. While staying with them, Ginsberg had concluded that Carolyn would accept his friendship with Neal as long as it did not become too intimate, and in her autobiography, Carolyn agreed with Allen's assessment, writing that when Allen had shown her "Green Auto" and other love poems written to her husband, she found them to be beautiful. She wrote later that she "felt no threat, trusting what he had written some years before about having overcome his sexual desire for Neal."

Allen, however, needed a physical manifestation of such acceptance. Borrowing a line from Whitman, Ginsberg explored the ideal in which both Neal and Carolyn could accept him with tenderness and love:

> I'll go into the bedroom silently and lie down between the
>   bridegroom and the bride,
> those bodies fallen from heaven stretched out waiting naked and
>   restless,
> arms resting over their eyes in the darkness,
> bury my face in their shoulders and breasts, breathing their
>   skin. . . .

In "The Green Automobile," Ginsberg attempted to perfect his past; in "Love Poem on Theme by Whitman," he was dealing with the present. Both works are fantasy poems, "Green Auto" concluding with Allen and Neal returning to their respective realities, "Love Poem" ending with Allen's recognition of his poem's aura of fantasy:

> all before the mind wakes, behind shades and closed doors
>   in a darkened house
> where the inhabitants roam unsatisfied in the night,
> nude ghosts seeking each other out in silence.

At the time when he was preparing notes for and writing "Love Poem," Ginsberg had accepted the reality of his place in Neal Cassady's life. Any sexual involvement with Neal would be purely physical. There would be no vows taken at an Oklahoma crossroads, no chance of their relationship's being anything more than physical. Ginsberg conceded this in a ten-page letter to Kerouac, in which he detailed the nature of his and Cassady's friendship. Neal, Allen wrote, had been "in a weird way very nice to me" during his stay in San Jose, but from the tone of the letter, one senses that Cassady's treatment of Ginsberg was a concession to their past friendship, or, even worse, patronage. His journal entries of the period confirm this:

> I feel myself sacrificing part of my being to him—and he has sacrificed money and some time & attention to me, given it, but no sacrifice of being or self, not much sign of interest except in offhand and patronizing ways, except for a few moments of tenderness that are hard fought for and accidental rare infusions of pleasure into my otherwise bad-feeling starved routine here. . . .

Therefore, "Love Poem on Theme by Whitman," even if in ways as whimsical as "The Green Automobile," is less hopeful. At its core is a sense of loss. Perhaps this is the reason that "Love Poem" is more sexually graphic than "Green Auto": The further he moved away from Cassady, the more explicit Ginsberg needed to be in his fantasy to keep Neal alive in memory. Not surprisingly, "Love Poem" is the more tender of the two.

In "Love Poem," for all its elements of fantasy, Ginsberg makes two important self-discoveries: He reaffirms his homosexuality with the hope that he will be loved and accepted by the heterosexual world, just as Whitman had been a century earlier, and he admits, by the nature of his poem, that his season with Neal Cassady has reached its final days.

4

Allen's six-week stay at the Cassadys', like his 1947 visit to Denver, came to an abrupt ending, under similar circumstances. One August morning, Carolyn went to Allen's room to consult with Neal on a family matter. She knew that

Neal was in the room at the time. Although the door was closed, Carolyn presumed that Neal and Allen were talking, so she thought nothing of knocking and entering without waiting for a response. When she saw Allen engaged in oral sex with Neal, she let out a scream. As she recalled, she was revolted and stunned:

> The force of the shock nearly knocked my head off, or so it felt. . . .
> In that brief instant the picture registered in toto. Allen had lifted his head quizzically, but I was gone—to tremble, pace, cry to heaven, wring my hands and fight down the revulsion that threatened to turn me inside out.

Allen was left with no alternative but to leave. Immediately following the incident, Neal went blank and refused to address the issue; he left for work almost as soon as he had dressed. Allen, on the other hand, took a seat in an armchair facing Carolyn and listened as she voiced her anger, fear, disgust, and shame. She apologized repeatedly, trying to convince Allen that she was not homophobic. Her reaction, she insisted, was the same as it would have been if she had caught Neal in bed with another woman. She was aware of Allen's love for Neal, she said, but she had been under the impression that the sexual longing had ceased years ago. In her anger, Carolyn accused Allen of trying to come between her and Neal. Allen listened without offering much of a response, saying only that he had not come to visit with the intention of hurting them or destroying their marriage. "I went cold with horror—felt steeped with evil," Allen recalled:

> I felt evil around me—her vehemence and the feeling of horror that I had reminded me of moments in the N.J. hospital when my mother was seized by a fit of frenzied insistent accusation and yelled at me that I was a spy . . . the sense of finality and absolute tired despair & hopeless futility I felt when at age 14 I took my mother on a mad horrible trip to Lakewood where I left her to fall apart in paranoic fear with shoe in hand surrounded by cops in a drugstore. . . .

Carolyn told Allen that he had to leave, insisting that he never see Neal again. For some time, Allen had been giving some thought to enrolling in the graduate-school program at the University of California at Berkeley, reasoning that he could live and work in San Francisco while he attended school across the Bay. The following week, after Allen had packed and made hasty arrangements to stay at an inexpensive hotel, Carolyn drove him to Berkeley. As he got out of the car, she loaned him twenty dollars and apologized one final time for the bad ending to what could have been a happy visit.

For the first time in months, Allen was faced with the prospects of finding an apartment and job. For the time being, he took up residence at the Hotel Marconi at 554 Broadway in San Francisco, where, for six dollars a week, he had a nicely carpeted midsized room and plenty of privacy. The hotel, Allen related to Jack, was managed by a couple of lesbians who told Allen they had no objection to his bringing guests to his room. Al Sublette, a seaman friend of Kerouac's, lived upstairs, and he and Allen spent a lot of time together. The first Friday he was in San Francisco, Allen, along with Sublette and a young poet nicknamed Cosmo, was arrested when police walked into a coffeehouse at 4:30 A.M., searched the three, and mistook a bag of foot powder on Cosmo for heroin. Allen and Sublette stayed in a holding cell overnight and were released the next morning, Cosmo a few days later, after the police had determined the actual contents of the bag.

Not long after he arrived in the city, Allen met an attractive twenty-two-year-old woman name Sheila Williams Boucher, a one-time roadhouse singer who knew some of the local jazz musicians and was familiar with the hipster culture in the Bay Area. They took an instant liking to each other, Allen finding her to possess "a wild mind—finer than *any* girl I met." He was pleased that she had a sincere appreciation of his poetry and could offer meaningful appraisals of his work, as opposed to the general or patronizing criticism he was accustomed to receiving from others. They saw each other daily, and within a few weeks Allen moved into her roomy Nob Hill apartment. Sheila had a job as a copywriter for the May Company and a four-year-old son from her first marriage, so once again Allen found himself living a rather domesticated life. He was prepared to live as a heterosexual, even if this sexuality was interrupted on occasion by visits from Neal Cassady, who would drop in from time to time, when his job brought him to town. Allen kept his past a secret from Sheila.

San Francisco had a widely varying cultural and artistic environment, with a reputation of being tolerant of all manner of alternative lifestyles. The city's North Beach section acted as a magnet for radicals, anarchists, populists, Communists, Wobblies, bohemians, Abstract Expressionist painters, performance artists, poets, jazz musicians, playwrights in experimental theater, atheists, Buddhists, and street musicians—all living in a free-spirited environment that seemed to defy the cautious national sociopolitical climate caused by McCarthyism. Painters like Mark Rothko or Clyfford Still might have showings of their work one week, and the next week Dylan Thomas or W. H. Auden might show up for poetry readings. The City Lights Bookstore, cofounded in June 1953 by poet Lawrence Ferlinghetti and publisher/editor Peter Martin, attracted a substantial number of customers who would browse through the store well into the late hours of the evening. In October 1954, six painters, intent on experimenting with combining art exhibits with poetry or music, converted an old automobile repair garage on Union and Fillmore into the Six Gallery. On the whole, San Francisco had almost as much to offer as New York, but with its smaller size and more agreeable attitude, there was a greater sense of artistic community open to those who chose to experience its bounties.

Where Allen judged New York to be rigid with what he termed "the coldest aspects of American frozen consciousness," he found San Francisco to be "perceptive" and open to experimentation in thought and form in all of the arts. As he remembered years later:

> It had a tradition of philosophical anarchism with the anarchist club that Rexroth belonged to, a tradition receptive to person rather than officialdom or officiousness. There already had been a sort of Berkeley Renaissance in 1948 with Jack Spicer poet, Robert Duncan poet, Robin

Blaser poet, Timothy Leary psychologist, [and] Harry Smith, great underground filmmaker, one of the people who originated the mixed media light shows. . . . And specifically there were little magazines like *Circle* magazine . . . that didn't exist in the more money-success-*Time*-magazine-oriented New York scene.

Allen wasted little time in asserting himself into this environment. Kenneth Rexroth, the acknowledged leader of the San Francisco literary scene, held weekly Friday-night meetings in his spacious, book-lined home, where an assortment of Bay Area social, literary, and religious figures gathered to debate the issues of the day and listen to Rexroth expound on any topics that struck his fancy. Allen regularly attended these sessions. Beside being a distinguished poet, essayist, book reviewer, and translator, Rexroth was a manuscript reader for New Directions, William Carlos Williams's publisher. Before Ginsberg had left New York for Mexico, Williams had given him a letter of introduction to present to Rexroth upon his arrival in San Francisco. Allen also brought his *Empty Mirror* manuscript, its introduction written by Williams, with the hope that Rexroth would read and recommend it to New Directions. That recommendation was not forthcoming, but Allen nevertheless benefited enormously from his early association with Rexroth.

Through Rexroth, Allen met many of the influential figures writing in the San Francisco area. He met Kenneth Patchen, whose poetry of social protest acted as a model for similar poetry published in the fifties and sixties. Ginsberg was also reunited with Philip Lamantia, a young surrealist poet he had met in New York a few years earlier. He was introduced to Thomas Parkinson, a poet and professor at the University of California at Berkeley; poets Chris MacClaine and Gerd Stein; and Jack Spicer, who, along with Robert Duncan, had formed a literary group similar to Rexroth's.

Allen visited Duncan and gave him his *Empty Mirror* manuscript to read. Duncan was less than overwhelmed by the collection, finding the poetry too self-absorbed for his taste. The two remained friendly, however, and on the day that Duncan returned Allen's manuscript, he noted a typed copy of Jack Kerouac's "The Essentials of Spontaneous Prose" on Ginsberg's wall. He admired what Kerouac had written about avoiding revision, as well as his overall concept of spontaneous writing, and he asked Allen whether he could borrow the copy and make one for himself.

5

During his first few months in San Francisco, Allen wrote very little other than occasional journal entries describing San Francisco landmarks, or character sketches of some of his new friends. He was too busy establishing himself in his new environment to take on new projects; he needed every bit of his seemingly boundless energy to maintain all his levels of activity. He had a girlfriend, a new job working in market research for Towne-Oller, and new friends, all of which he managed to accommodate without losing touch with Jack Kerouac, Bill Burroughs, and Neal Cassady.

Allen had given Kenneth Rexroth a copy of Burroughs's *Junky*, along with some of the routines from Burroughs's new work in progress, tentatively entitled *Naked Lunch*. He had also supplied Rexroth with excerpts of Kerouac's prose. Now that he was becoming comfortable with some of the literati in San Francisco, Allen was prepared to act again in his capacity as agent for his friends.

Allen wrote Kerouac numerous letters, keeping Jack up-to-date on his West Coast life and discussing Buddhism, Jack's latest obsession. He also kept abreast of Kerouac's literary activities in New York. Since his return to the city, Jack had been working closely with Malcolm Cowley, an editor at Viking Press, in preparing *On the Road* for publication. Cowley thought *On the Road* was a brilliant novel, but he was having trouble convincing fellow editors at the publishing house of the book's importance. Cowley had shown an excerpt of the novel, a story Jack called "Jazz of the Beat Generation," to a friend at *New World Writing*, a prestigious literary magazine that accepted the excerpt for publication. Kerouac also had another excerpt, entitled "The Mexican Girl," that he and Cowley were trying to place with another magazine.

Kerouac had sent Ginsberg selections from his "San Francisco Blues" sequence. Allen read them thoughtfully, jotting his favorite lines, along with his own commentary, into his journal. Allen was impressed. "They are nearer to center of poetry than elsewhere can be found," he wrote Kerouac. Of his own poetry, he was less certain, writing, "My effort in last 2 yrs. has been to find a Formal Look (as Cezanne says he wants to paint pictures that look like classics in museums, and did)." As always, Allen's correspondence was full of gossip, encouragement to Jack, details of his daily life, and philosophical meanderings.

Things were more complicated for Allen in his correspondence with Bill Burroughs. For months, Bill had been planning to return to the United States and join Allen in San Francisco. When Allen had been in Mexico and out of touch with him, Burroughs had learned the depth of his feelings for Allen. Bill confessed to Kerouac that he was "hooked" on Allen, "[unable to] make it without him." In reply, Jack had suggested that Bill return to the country and live with Allen in San Francisco, and while Burroughs had no desire to move to California—"the whole state is police ridden," he scoffed—he figured he would do so if that was what it took to be with Allen.

Ginsberg was caught in a dilemma. He had invited Burroughs to San Francisco before his relationship with Sheila had developed, and now that he was living a heterosexual lifestyle, Burroughs's pending arrival presented problems. Bill had made it clear that he could not live with Allen if sex was not part of the arrangement. Allen remembered all too well the effects of his previous rejection of Burroughs in New York, and he was still stinging from his own recent rejection by Neal Cassady. He had been forthright with Bill about his affair with Sheila, but Burroughs still continued to make plans to go to the West Coast.

Kerouac complicated the situation shortly after Bill arrived in New York. Hearing Burroughs complain about Allen's romantic involvement with a woman, Jack suggested that Allen might be acting coy, playing hard to get. This deception on Jack's part angered Allen, who insisted that his wanting to see Bill was not "a queer matter" but one of genuine friendship. "I dig Bill as much as ever," Allen insisted, but with his new life in San Francisco, coupled with his knowledge of the demands Burroughs placed on a relationship, Allen feared that Bill's visit "would end in some kind of absolute sad idiocy." Kerouac's interference, Allen felt, only added to the wrong impressions Burroughs was forming from Ginsberg's invitation.

As it was, Jack was unhappy with his role as intermediary between Allen and Bill. He was not an authority on "the cupidities and concupiscences of homosexuality," he told Allen; besides, Burroughs was aware of Allen's involvement with a woman. In Jack's opinion, it was time for all parties involved to be totally truthful with one another. "I am not going to deceive or conceal anything for anyone and I call now for all of us to return to Beat Generation 1947 confessions & honesties," he told Allen.

Allen agreed. In trying to avoid hurting Bill's feelings, he had perhaps been too vague and misleading in his letters, which only made his inevitable rejection more painful for both of them. To set the matter straight, Allen sent Bill a frank and pointed letter that explained the situation, effectively putting an end to Bill's plans to join him in California. Instead, Bill visited his parents in Florida and left shortly thereafter for Tangier.

To Allen, it must have seemed as if his past love interests were closing in and threatening to smother him. In addition to dealing with Burroughs, Allen had to contend with Neal Cassady, who had become a frequent visitor. Allen received him enthusiastically, although he worried about Neal's mental well-being. Neal had recently taken a Rorschach test, with sobering results. According to those interpreting the test, Neal showed signs of prepsychotic thinking and sexual sadism; he was anxiety-ridden and suffered from a delusive thought system. After living with Neal and observing his behavior in recent months, Allen was inclined to agree, at least to a certain extent. Neal's self-destructive tendencies were as apparent as ever. His marriage was a shambles and his womanizing and long absences from home were doing nothing to improve the situation. He was smoking a huge amount of marijuana, to the point of jeopardizing his job; his coworkers had complained about him and he had been written up several times. He had alienated friends, who found some of his behavior—especially his obsessions with pot, Edgar Cayce, and chess—intolerable. Allen had reservations of his own. In a letter to Kerouac, he complained that "everytime you talk to him as soon as it gets interesting he suddenly turns a switch in his head and the CAYCE Jones locomotive blackens the horizon—he begins repeating the same ideas, more simplified and unrelated (whirling around fragments of former perceptions and mad thoughts) in answer to anything that he thinks about for more than 37 seconds. . . . [He] can't listen to a paragraph of writing easily, nor read . . . can't concentrate enough to write you a letter. . . ."

By early November, Allen's affair with Sheila was beginning to disintegrate. From the beginning of their time together, Allen had noted the differences in their personalities—being younger, Sheila tended to be "more prey to girlish psychological self-dramatizations," Allen thought—and the strain of the past months had affected Allen, making him somber and irritable. On November 10, he began seeing a psychiatrist at the Langley Porter Clinic, where, for a dollar an hour, he could consult with a therapist about his problems, many of which, of course, were rooted in his sexual history and confusions. In an effort to be totally truthful about his past, Allen told Sheila about his love affair with Neal Cassady. Repulsed by Allen's confession, Sheila refused to sleep with him. She suggested that it might be better for both of them if he left, and while Allen did not move out of her apartment immediately, the following weeks were tense, characterized by constant bickering and destructive conjecture about the nature of their relationship. When Sheila wondered whether Allen still preferred men to women, he was left without a reply.

One evening in early December, Allen found himself wandering the streets of San Francisco. He had fought with Sheila earlier in the day and had spent the early part of the evening trying to drink off some of his depression and frustration. He stopped in Foster's Cafeteria, an artists' hangout, and seeing no one he knew, he approached a young bearded man seated at a table and inquired about the whereabouts of Peter DuPeru, a colorful local figure whom Allen had met shortly after his arrival in San Francisco. The young man, painter Robert LaVigne, had no idea where DuPeru was, but as he and Allen talked about art, LaVigne was impressed by Allen's stories about his New York artist acquaintances. LaVigne lived a few blocks away, and he asked Allen whether he would be interested in looking at his paintings.

At LaVigne's home, Allen viewed numerous paintings of a young and attractive yellow-haired boy. One particular painting, a seven-by-seven-foot canvas portraying the youth reclining naked on a couch, a bunch of onions gathered at his feet, was particularly striking to Allen. Wanting to meet the model, Ginsberg asked LaVigne who he was. "Oh, that's Peter," LaVigne replied, and to Allen's amazement, LaVigne told him that Peter lived with him. "He's here. He's home," LaVigne said and, as if on cue, the young man walked into the room.

In an instant, Allen fell in love with the tall, innocent-looking young man whose name was Peter Orlovsky.

9
Howl

I saw the best minds of my generation destroyed by madness,
  starving hysterical naked,
dragging themselves through the negro streets at dawn looking for
  an angry fix,
angelheaded hipsters burning for the ancient heavenly connection
  to the starry dynamo in the machinery of night. . . .

1

Peter Orlovsky, Allen discovered, had come from a background almost as bleak as Neal Cassady's. His father was an impoverished Russian immigrant, his mother a onetime aspiring writer who was plagued by depression and alcoholism. As a young man, Oleg Orlovsky, Peter's father, had served as a cadet in the czar's army in St. Petersburg, fighting with the White Army during the Russian Revolution. In 1917, while serving as a guard at the Winter Palace, he had barely avoided death during a battle by ducking into a doorway and witnessing the carnage taking place around him. He was captured by the Red Army but managed to escape, fleeing first to Istanbul and, in 1921, to the United States.

In 1926, Oleg Orlovsky married Katherine Schwarten, a seventeen-year-old from Yonkers who had left home and moved to Manhattan's Lower East Side to pursue a career as a writer. Dorothy Parker had seen Katherine's work and encouraged her to write, but the births of the Orlovsky children, along with a botched mastoid operation in 1927 that left her deaf and with partially paralyzed facial muscles, put an end to her artistic aspirations.

Born on July 8, 1933, Peter was the third of his parents' five children. Quiet and mild-mannered, he watched his father, an entrepreneur who painted silk neckties, suffer through a series of business failures that left the family in disarray and ultimately led to alcoholism. "He didn't have any friends and was always occupied in his business, making ties, silk-screening ties in New York," Peter said of his father. "One business went to another, one failure to another failure, and so he was spending all his time at work, hardly any time at home. My mother . . . stayed up all night and drank—they drank a lot in the daytime during the forties, when I was growing up. The house was very disorganized and messy, and it was just a bad situation."

The Orlovskys lived in a converted chicken coop in Northport. The children, occasional victims of their father's drunken rages, worked at Oleg's tie shop, devoting much of their youths to a business doomed to fail due to the influx of foreign imports. Katherine Orlovsky eventually left her husband and took her children to live in Queens. The effects of the family's difficult, impoverished years were manifest when Peter's older brother Julius was institutionalized for catatonic schizophrenia—the first of three Orlovsky children to spend time in institutions as a result of mental disorders. Unable to support her children, Katherine Orlovsky asked Peter to drop out of school and leave home in 1950, when he was a senior in high school. As Peter recalled, she walked around him several times and said, "You're a big, handsome boy with strong hands. You'll have no difficulty getting jobs in your life."

His early jobs involved his working many hours in menial labor for very little pay. In his first job, he worked twelve hours a day, six days a week for a hospital in Queens, earning seventy-five cents an hour. He quit this job to work at Creedmore State Mental Hospital, where his duties included taking care of senile patients, feeding them and changing their sheets, and mopping floors. The job depressed him. "After a year and a half working there I ended up crying in the wards myself and thinking, 'My God, this is the way the whole world is,' " Orlovsky remembered. In the evenings, he attended school to earn his high school diploma.

In 1953, Peter was drafted into the army to serve in the Korean War. He attended boot camp in West Virginia. When a lieutenant observed him reading a book by Erich Fromm and demanded to know whether Orlovsky was a Communist, Peter replied, "An army is an army against love." He was subsequently shipped to an army hospital in San Francisco, where he spent the rest of his military service working as a medic.

Orlovsky later admitted that by the time he arrived in San Francisco, his past employment, combined with the loneliness he felt living in a large city where he knew no one and was so far from home, had placed a substantial emotional and mental strain on him; he was sad, fragile. When he met Robert LaVigne, he was still a virgin, and while he was (and always would be) primarily heterosexual, Peter had a loving relationship with LaVigne, who took him into his home and looked after his needs. Because of his inexperience, Peter was frightened by sex, but he was even more terrified by the prospects of living alone for the rest of his life. He was comforted by LaVigne's friendship and impressed by his artistic ability.

Yet, as Allen Ginsberg would learn over the span of the next three decades, Peter could be difficult to live with, subject to severe bouts of depression that would find him locking himself in his room and weeping for days on end. With his almost childlike innocence came a dependence that could stifle a lover's freedom. Peter's vulnerability required a great deal from those who loved him. When Allen met Peter in December 1954, the relationship between Orlovsky and LaVigne was all but finished. For Allen, emerging from yet another disappointing love affair, the timing could not have been better.

2

Allen's initial encounter with Peter Orlovsky was little more than a formal introduction. On his next visit to LaVigne's apartment about a week later, Allen brought along Neal Cassady, who reacted to a LaVigne painting of a nude red-haired woman in virtually the same manner as Allen had reacted to LaVigne's study of Orlovsky. The woman, Natalie Jackson, lived in an apartment in the building, and Neal wasted no time in getting to know her. Soon, Allen and Neal became regular visitors at LaVigne's apartment.

Allen was scheduled to leave town to attend his brother's wedding in New York, but before he left, he spent a night with Peter. Aware of Peter's shyness, Allen was careful to avoid forcing himself on Orlovsky. Allen, like Peter, needed tenderness. As Ginsberg told an interviewer many years later, he felt like "a tired dog, in the sense of the defeats of love, not having made it, not having found a permanent life companion. . . . I was already 29. I wasn't a 20-year-old kid with romantic notions." On their first night together, Peter told Allen that he had dreamed about walking up to Allen and putting his arms around his waist, and that in the dream, Allen had been surprised by the gesture. This said, Peter drew Allen to him, and the two spent the night embracing each other, although no sex was involved. Overjoyed, Allen wrote Kerouac, "Real sweetness in my breast, too much, I'd almost cry, but it's such a poor pitiful fleeting human life, what do I want anyway? Nature boy—to be loved in return."

Aware of what was happening between Peter and Allen, LaVigne told Ginsberg that he would be leaving town to paint in San Diego as soon as his current art show ended in San Francisco. Peter would need a companion while he was gone, LaVigne suggested, and since Peter knew and liked Allen, would Ginsberg be willing to see Peter as often as possible while he was away? Allen was initially suspicious of LaVigne's proposal; he wondered whether LaVigne was mocking him. LaVigne assured Ginsberg that he was serious, that he and Peter were about to break up, and if Allen so desired, he would talk to Peter to ascertain that the arrangement was acceptable to him.

On December 14, Allen flew to New York to attend Eugene's wedding. It was the first time he had been home in nearly a year, but with all the festivities involved in his brother's nuptials, he had little time to visit with his New York friends. He and Jack met at the San Remo, where they engaged in a long conversation about Buddhism. Allen also took the time to visit his mother at Pilgrim State Hospital. It was a painful visit. Naomi was little more than a confused old woman, tearfully begging Allen to take her home and talking about the wires in her head. Allen was helpless to do anything but listen. Although he had no reason to suspect it at the time, it was the last time he would see his mother.

Shortly after Allen returned to San Francisco, he and Peter consummated their affair. Allen had never experienced homoeroticism to such an extent—both giving and receiving—in any of his past encounters. With Kerouac and Cassady, Allen felt as if he was forcing his sexuality on partners who obliged him more out of friendship or a sense of duty than out of mutual interest; with

Burroughs, the situation had been reversed. One-night stands had sprung out of desperation or boredom. With Peter, Allen sensed a person who accepted him as a friend and lover and who was willing to offer the same in return.

At Robert LaVigne's invitation, Allen moved into LaVigne's 1403 Gough Street apartment, and for a few weeks he lived in the sort of frenzied, yet curiously idyllic environment he had enjoyed for a brief period at Joan Vollmer's 115th Street apartment in New York. Neal Cassady had also moved into the apartment building, and was staying in Natalie Jackson's room, which was just down the hall from Peter's. With Neal nearby, there was bound to be a flurry of activity, which Allen described to Jack as "big messy rooms, tea in kitchen, just like youth, we gather, talk, Neal rushes in 9 AM WC Fields–Oliver Hardy pulling on or off his pants, makes it with girl, laughs again, puts on her clothes, she his vest, they blast—and he and I agree on nostalgia of the front door, we've both gained so much tender youth kicks in last 2 weeks. . . ." Allen was rereading Kerouac's *Visions of Cody*, which he was now calling *Visions of Neal*, and one of his pleasures was to read passages aloud to the group at the apartment. Allen had considerably altered his opinion of the novel. "Don't think I don't realize how great, sketch by sketch, *sentence by sentence*, Visions of Neal is," he told Jack. "It's late for me to say it but I see how much better you are than I."

Despite the outward appearance of happy surroundings and his belief that his life had "changed in California, like a dream," Allen was nevertheless troubled by the complexities of his new affair. In late December, he began a new journal in which he detailed some of his concerns. Peter had wept after their initial lovemaking—his reaction, Allen believed, the result of his awareness of "how much he was giving me and how much I was demanding, asking and taking." Allen had been moved by the knowledge that he could have such an effect on a lover, yet he was also concerned about his "domineering, sadism part" that was both "flattered and erotically aroused" by it. When he considered the ego gratification involved in his lovemaking with Peter, he was reminded of his non-Wolfean identity at the 115th Street apartment. As Hal Chase had once proposed it, non-Wolfean homosexuality was guilty of trying to seduce and corrupt heterosexual innocence, and Allen wondered whether this was the case with Peter. He hardly knew Peter, but what he did know was that Peter was basically heterosexual, inexperienced, and vulnerable. Was he guilty of preying on Peter's sexuality in order to gratify his own?

These confusions were exacerbated by the presence of Robert LaVigne, who was protective of Peter and perhaps a little envious of Allen and Peter's developing affair; he was second-guessing his decision to leave Peter and move out of the city. Although he continued to see Peter, Allen questioned his involvement's effect on LaVigne. His January 1, 1955, journal entry reflected his concern. "For the first time in life I feel evil: conscious loss of innocence, betrayal of Robert," he wrote. Ginsberg, LaVigne, and Orlovsky were all very frank with each other about their feelings, but this honesty led more to further tension than to solutions. Peter was caught in a classic love triangle, forced to make a choice between a past lover, who had been kind and decent to him, and a new one, who was bright, experienced in the world, and fresh. In no time, Peter grew exasperated with the competitive feeling between the two men. "You're both a pain in the ass," he declared during one of their group discussions.

After weeks of uneasy debate, the three concluded that it might be best if they all went their separate ways. While he waited for his next paycheck, Allen checked into a neighborhood hotel, where he had a room overlooking Foster's Cafeteria. He spent much of his free time brooding and writing. Peter moved into the Hotel Wentley, which was directly across the street from where Allen was staying. Wrapped in self-pity and battling a fever he had been fighting since the first of the year, Allen poured out his feelings in his journal, filling over fifty pages in a two-week span. One of his more interesting exercises was a poem directed to Jack Kerouac, which expressed his urgent need to be loved and his happiness now that he had found it:

> I'm happy, Kerouac, your madman Allen's
> finally made it: discovered a young new cat,
> and my imagination of an eternal boy
> walks on the streets of San Francisco. . . .

The poem, "Malest Cornifici Tuo Catullo," is an homage to Catullus— specifically to Catullus's "Poem XXXVIII"—and considering the brevity and relative minor literary importance of the Ginsberg poem, "Malest Cornifici" took up what would appear to be an inordinate amount of Ginsberg's time and energy. In his notebook, he worked and reworked the poem, checking its metric scheme against the Latin and then the English translation of the Catullus poem. It was important to Ginsberg that the adaptation be precise to the final beat. Furthermore, it was critical that it be written in modern, hipster idiom, as if to show the timelessness of the yearning for love and its fulfillment.

The poem also had therapeutic value to Ginsberg at the time of its composition. The original opening to the poem was "I'm sick, Kerouac . . ." and while Allen was indeed physically ill, suffering from a prolonged bout with the flu at the time of the poem's writing, he was also emotionally sick from his up-and-down relationship with Peter Orlovsky. In addition, he was still consulting a psychiatrist for guidance concerning his lingering depression about the direction his life was taking. In changing the opening of the poem, Ginsberg was in effect trying to *will* himself a happier state of mind.

The permanent solution to Allen's dilemma over how to spend his life came from an unexpected source. Despite his busy schedule of recent weeks, he had been faithful to his analysis at Langley Porter Clinic, and he had informed his psychiatrist, Dr. Philip Hicks, of his problems with Peter. One day in mid-January, Allen told Hicks that he was hesitant to become too involved with Peter, since it was possible that Peter would not love him when he grew old. He concluded that maybe it would be better if he tried to live as a heterosexual. When Hicks asked him what he really wanted to do, Allen replied that he would like to find an apartment, live with Peter, quit working, and write poems.

"So why don't you do that?" Hicks challenged. In response, Allen again mentioned that he was afraid of growing old. "Oh, you're a nice person," Hicks said; "there's always people who will like you."

"It was the last thing I expected him to say," Ginsberg told Jane Kramer in 1968:

I asked him what the American Psychoanalytic Association would say about *that*, and he said, "There's no party line, no red book on how people are supposed to live. If that is what you really feel would please you, what in the world is stopping you from doing it?"

On February 3, Allen moved out of the hotel and into an apartment at 1010 Montgomery Street; eight days later, Peter Orlovsky moved in with him. For over a month, Allen had been contemplating a way to seal the future of his and Peter's relationship. Allen favored a formal exchange of vows, not unlike the vows he and Neal had exchanged in 1947, wherein Allen would offer Peter his "two special talents—[his] creative sense of literary craft kicks, and [his] insight into mystical Sanctity union with God" in return for Peter's physical and emotional love. In a way, it was Ginsberg's attempt to realize his "Green Auto" fantasy, as well as a continuation of the teacher/pupil scenario he had set up with Cassady a decade earlier. By Allen's account, the vows amounted to "an exchange of souls & bodies—but a *serious* exchange of talents & purposes." Peter would be free to satisfy his heterosexual desires with women as long as he would be available to Allen, as well.

Allen regarded such vows seriously, in a spiritual as well as physical sense. As Allen saw it, at the center of the vows was a mutual promise "to stay with each other to whatever eternal consciousness." In the *Baghavad-Gita*, Allen had read a mythological tale in which Arjuna, upon reaching the gates of heaven with his dog, repeatedly refused to enter unless his dog was admitted with him; the dog turned out to be Krishna, ruler of heaven and the universe, in disguise, and Arjuna's loyalty and commitment were being tested. Allen believed his and Peter's vows were "a limited version" of that: "neither of us would go to heaven," he noted, "unless we could get the other one in—like a mutual Bodhisattva's vow."

Allen and Peter discussed these promises, and in mid-February at Foster's Cafeteria they made their formal commitment. Ginsberg described the exchange of vows:

> . . . We held hands, took a vow: I do, I do, you promise? yes, I do. At that instant we looked in each other's eyes and there was a kind of celestial cold fire that crept over us and blazed up and illuminated the entire cafeteria and made it an eternal place.
>
> I found somebody who'd accept my devotion, and he found somebody who'd accept his devotion and who was devoted to him. It was really a fulfillment of a fantasy, to a point where fantasy and reality finally merged. Desire illuminated the room, because it was a fulfillment of all my fantasies since I was nine, when I began to have erotic love fantasies. And that vow has stuck as the primary core of our relationship. . . . It's really the basic human relationship—you give yourself to each other, help each other and don't go to heaven without each other.

It was a vow that Allen would keep throughout his life, despite whatever turmoil their relationship would be in, despite Peter's eventual troubles with drugs and mental illness. For Allen, these vows were the equivalent of marriage vows, and he honored them with a sense of commitment rivaled only, perhaps, by his commitment to his work.

3

Throughout his early days with Peter, Allen kept Jack Kerouac informed of the progress and digressions of his developing relationship. Jack, genuinely happy for Allen, did his best to encourage him. Their friendship was in one of its peak periods, with Kerouac referring to Ginsberg as "my fine sweet Allen" and calling him "a real saint." He urged Allen not to be concerned about their past arguments, claiming that he would never get angry with him again. Of Peter Orlovsky, Jack wrote reassuringly, advising Allen to use kindness as a means of dealing with Peter's moodiness during their difficult period at the beginning of the year. "Peter O. sounds very great and I know that whatever happens you will know how to reassure the sad heart therein," he told Allen.

Jack was enduring another trying stretch in his life. He had produced a large body of work in recent years, but nearly five years had lapsed since the publication of *The Town and the City*. Kerouac was still looking for a publisher for *On the Road*, and to add to his frustration, Little, Brown had recently rejected *The Subterraneans*, his novel about his 1953 affair with Mardou Fox. Allen had given a manuscript of *Visions of Neal* to Kenneth Rexroth, who was unenthusiastic about the novel but nevertheless agreed to show it to James Laughlin, his New Directions publisher. Allen also had copies of *Dr. Sax* and *San Francisco Blues* and was showing them to anyone who might be a sympathetic reader. Robert Duncan liked some of Jack's work, particularly the spontaneous descriptive passages in *Visions of Neal*. Lawrence Ferlinghetti, though not impressed with Kerouac's poetry, appreciated selections of Jack's prose, but he was in no position to publish a novel through City Lights Books, his newly formed publishing company geared to printing slender, inexpensive volumes of poetry. Now fully devoted to his study of Buddhism, Jack tried to offset his frustrations with the rationalization that he could not be famous if he ever hoped to be a bodhisattva, but he conceded that toiling in anonymity had its drawbacks, as well. In *Some of the Dharma*, he wrote that the wise man is faced with two unattractive alternatives in life: "Being famous, he will be hounded to his death; being a nonentity, no one will want to use him."

For nearly a year, Allen's and Jack's correspondence had been filled with discussions of Buddhism. Jack offered Allen comprehensive reading lists, opinions, and text interpretations. With Allen's encouragement, Jack had designated himself as Allen's teacher. "For your beginning studies of Buddhism, you must listen to me carefully and implicitly as tho I was Einstein teaching you relativity or Eliot teaching the Formulas of Objective Correlation on a blackboard in Princeton," Jack stated, still feeling self-righteous in the aftermath of his arguments with Neal over the merits of Buddhism versus the teachings of Edgar Cayce. However, as time passed and Kerouac struggled with aligning Buddhism with his deep-seated Catholicism, he became less inclined to lecture as if he was an authority. Instead, he tried to offer guidance, such as his recommendations that Allen read the "Diamond Sutra," or practice *dhyana*, a meditation exercise where a person could achieve a blissful state of mind by sitting quietly and concentrating on his breathing. *Dhyana*, Kerouac suggested, afforded a person a new level of consciousness, in which one could accept reality without the mind's becoming entangled with images or the wordy concepts surrounding that reality.

This was the kind of thinking that Allen wanted to hear. For nearly seven years, he had been trying to find a practical way of advancing the altered level of consciousness he had experienced in 1948 in his Blake visions. *Dhyana*, with its promise of self-ultimacy through meditation, bore many similarities to the consciousness of his Blake visions, which had occurred only when Allen's mind was "totally empty," free from the clutter of preconception. "I am presuming your Buddha experience and my Blake ones are on the same level," Allen wrote Jack.

In the future, Ginsberg would take Buddhist vows, go on retreats, speak and write extensively on Buddhism, and meditate on a daily basis. His own practice would differ measurably from Kerouac's, but he would always credit Jack's enthusiasm, expressed in his letters of 1954 to 1955, as having an enormous influence upon his own pursuits. In this way, Jack became Allen's spiritual, as well as literary, guru.

4

Even as Jack continued to experience difficulty in his literary endeavors in New York, Allen was having no better success on the West Coast. He had attempted to place *Empty Mirror* with Lawrence Ferlinghetti's City Lights Books, but Ferlinghetti, with plans to publish Kenneth Rexroth and Kenneth Patchen, along with his own *Pictures of the Gone World*, as the inaugural editions of his "Pocket Poets" series, had neither the money nor enthusiasm to publish Ginsberg's collection. Allen considered using a mimeograph machine to self-publish a small volume of his poems in a limited edition of twenty-five copies for his friends, but he decided to wait until he had completed or revised his more recent poems.

For months, he had tried to develop plans for a movie featuring Bill Burroughs. While in Mexico, Allen had had a Kafkaesque dream in which Burroughs, traveling by bus from Italy to Spain, was being pursued by a spy, symbolic of either fate or the future. The spy was intent upon defeating Burroughs with what Ginsberg described as "rational inanity." Allen's planned movie, which he was calling *Bill in Europe*, was to be a series of Burroughs-like routines, culminating in Bill's being driven to insanity as a result of the spy's long pursuit. As Allen had told Kerouac, the movie could be "the last great European movie, the pictures of actuality of Burroughs in the continent, not a story but a fragmentary biography of the facts of him there. A movie, made like your prose, of the living history." Kerouac responded favorably, praising Allen's idea as being "so sublime, so accurate." Allen continued to work sporadically on the project's development, combining elements of the Wolfean/non-Wolfean skits of the past with the spirit of the routines that Bill was regularly dispatching from Tangiers. By late 1954, the idea had evolved into *Burroughs on Earth,* an even more ambitious project combining aspects of Kerouac's *Dr. Sax,* Burroughs's early *Naked Lunch* routines, cinema verité, and Buddhism, the film's plot focusing on Burroughs returning to earth in a future lifetime. Shortly after his move to San Francisco, Allen had met independent filmmaker Jordan Belson, who Ginsberg hoped would oversee and film the project. However, when Belson read Burroughs's letters about his yage expedition and did not care for them, Allen abandoned the project.

The idea, however, was still very much on Allen's mind as late as spring 1955. He was intrigued by the premise of a strong intellect being driven to the point of madness by an unfeeling society. It was an idea being explored by his friends, as well. Kerouac had broached a similar theme in a recently written short story, "cityCityCITY," a Burroughs-influenced futuristic tale in which power-hungry government agents destroy innocent citizens for their own personal gain. The themes of mind control and destruction were prevalent in many of Burroughs's routines. In his mind, intelligence was a curse that would necessarily pit the individual against those powers that sought control. Contrary to the beliefs of the day, Burroughs was not one to place intelligence and madness on opposite sides of the coin.

Madness was a topic never too far removed from Allen's mind. He still received an occasional letter from his mother, who was lost in a world of paranoid fears. Two of Peter's brothers, Nicholas and Julius, had been institutionalized in New York for mental disorders, and a third brother, Lafcadio, was reportedly having difficulties of his own. In April, Allen received word from Eugene that Carl Solomon, who had left his publishing job and was currently working as a Good Humor salesman in New York, had been hospitalized in Pilgrim State, the same hospital where Naomi was a patient. The news was disturbing. "What'll happen to Carl in time," a concerned Ginsberg wondered.

Acting upon his psychiatrist's suggestion, Allen began to plan a means by which he would be free of his job and able to pursue his poetry full-time. Rather than resign his position at Towne-Oller, he worked out an ingenious scheme. He proposed that he could be replaced by an IBM computer, and then, to the delight of his employers, he worked out the details to see that he was. His job ended on May 1. Able to live for six months on his unemployment benefits, Allen considered his options. He could go to graduate school in Berkeley or, almost as inviting, spend the summer in Los Angeles. His main objective was to complete a volume of poems, regardless of how or where he spent the next half year.

There was always something going on around his Montgomery Street apartment. Neal Cassady, now separated from Carolyn, was a frequent visitor, as were Al Hinkle and Allen's ex-girlfriend, Sheila. Al Sublette, back in San Francisco after another stint at sea, stopped by regularly. Neal often brought Natalie Jackson for weekends. For the normally gregarious Ginsberg, there were too many people, activities, and distractions for him to get any work done; he longed for peace and quiet. "Except for Neal who's always welcome and Peter I can talk to no one and wish to be alone to read and write," Allen told Kerouac.

Ginsberg's reading was as prodigious as ever. Along with his sampling of classic poetry by Greek and Roman poets, Allen read the Ezra Pound–translated and –edited anthology of Chinese odes, *The Classic Anthology, Defined by Confucius*; in addition, he reread all of Eliot's poetry aloud. For his study of Buddhism, he examined Herman Hesse's novel *Siddhartha*, which he judged to be "nowhere particular," and he struggled through the "Surangama Sutra," which he found "hard to follow [and] understand."

At this point, Allen's writing was virtually dormant. He had written only a few new poems since his arrival in San Francisco, and his revision of his older poems was going slowly. He had grown tired of writing in his journal, which he dismissed as "an egocentric method" that "promotes slop." However, his literary output aside, it was a crucial period for Ginsberg, who took copious notes in his journal about the books he was reading and how those readings could affect his own writing. He was specifically concerned with the way his poetry looked on the printed page: "Lately in revising I've noticed a tendency . . . to adjust the notes [in] to small groups of lines as in 3-line stanza," he wrote in his journal, noting that he based his divisions on "active words, number of active words in a phrase."

Ginsberg was interested in Williams's triadic structure, yet he was equally fascinated by Kerouac's long line, particularly in the rambling descriptive passages of *Visions of Neal*. The line, Ginsberg concluded, could be governed by breath measures, image, or thought. The poet's decision about where to break the line would have great bearing on his ability to coax the reader into the level of consciousness that he desired.

Allen had also resumed his study of Cézanne. He read two Cézanne biographies and studied color reproductions of his paintings, all in an effort to understand better the way the Post-Impressionist painter juxtaposed planes or made use of what he called *petite sensation* in such a way as to induce quick flashes of illumination in those looking at his works. In his Harlem visions, Allen had experienced such flashes as the result of the juxtaposition of his immediate foreground (his bedroom) against a background of the Harlem building tops in silhouette against the evening sky. Allen believed Cézanne to be a visionary, and he wondered whether the painter had had similar experiences. In a painting such as *The Great Bathers*, two unrelated images—the bathers in the foreground and the townscape in the background—were juxtaposed by Cézanne's use of color, the technique leaving Ginsberg with an illuminative flash not unlike the sensation he'd experienced in his Blake vision.

What Allen hoped to achieve was a similar sensation in his poetry. He realized readers were accustomed to focusing their attention on a single image, just as the eye was trained to focus on a "hot" or "cool" color, but painters, beginning with Cézanne, seemed to be surmounting that limitation. Dadaists and Surrealists had attempted to break down consciousness in their works, and over the centuries practitioners of haiku had juxtaposed disparate images in their brief poems. Allen wanted to take it a step further. Could one produce these flashes of recognition—or "eyeball kicks," as he and Kerouac liked to call them—in the juxtaposition of "hot" and "cool" images and words in poetry?

Allen attempted to insinuate *petite sensation* into a poem immediately following an arresting dream he had in early June. In his dream, Allen was back in Mexico City, where he ran into Joan Vollmer and had a brief conversation

with her. His account of their meeting, "Dream Record: June 8, 1955," is a
study of juxtaposition. In the early portion of the poem, Ginsberg uses concrete
detail ("leaning/forward in a garden-chair, arms/on her knees . . .") to give
Joan a realistic presence in his dream, and he closes out the poem with another
powerfully descriptive passage that leaves no uncertainty about the reality of
her death:

> I saw her rainstained tombstone
> rear an illegible epitaph
> under the gnarled branch of a small
> tree in the wild grass
> of an unvisited garden in Mexico.

A dream and death: two levels of consciousness that had been Ginsberg
obsessions from the days when he was seeking to find a way to apply Rimbaud's
derangement of the senses to poetry. By writing of a dream and death in such
a descriptive way, Ginsberg was trying to create a cosmic consciousness. The
"color" separating these fragments can be seen in the center of the poem, which
is void of such concrete images. Instead, Ginsberg uses ethereal expressions
("notebooks filled with Buddha," "golden in the East") to describe the current—and very real—state of affairs of his and Joan's mutual acquaintances.
The resulting effect is twofold. First, by staying vague in his description of the
real world, Ginsberg deepens the reader's sensation of the "unreal" world
(dream, death) and makes it even more vivid. Second, the contrast gives the
reader a greater connection to Ginsberg's rather uneasy vision of eternity: Who,
after all, is living in eternity, the departed or the person left behind?

Immediate response to the poem was mixed. Kenneth Rexroth, now occupying in Ginsberg's life the position of literary elder that Allen had once
accorded Lionel Trilling and Mark Van Doren, was not at all impressed with
the poem, which he found "stilted & somewhat academic." On the other hand,
William Burroughs, who for obvious reasons had a great personal interest in
the poem, praised it as being "completely successful." The poem was so precise,
Burroughs told Ginsberg, that he felt as if he was experiencing the poet's vision
as he was reading the work; he could see what Ginsberg saw in his dream. "In
a way, a poem is a means of evoking, conveying telepathic image from the
poet's mind to the mind of the reader," Burroughs wrote Ginsberg, adding that
"Baudelaire remarked on this when he spoke of poetry as a form of ritual or
incantation, magic words to evoke an image or series of images in the reader's
psyche." Allen could not have been more pleased by the response. This power
of poetic telepathy, which he had experienced during his Blake visions, was
precisely the effect that he was hoping to achieve in his work.

5

Following his heart's desire did not assure him happiness, Allen quickly determined. He had quit his job, moved into an apartment with his lover, and made
the conscious decision to spend the rest of his life writing poetry, but all of

these ideals were soon greeted by the harsh indifference of reality. In time, Ginsberg would romanticize this period as his dark night of the soul before his personal and poetic breakthrough, yet it is clear from his journal entries and letters from the period that the late spring and summer of 1955 offered a series of serious challenges to his endurance and commitment to his ideals.

With no more than his thirty dollars per week unemployment to rely upon for his support, Allen had to be frugal with his money. He could pay his rent and buy food, but he had little money for anything else. He still hoped to travel to Europe sometime in the next year or two, but with barely enough money to survive, saving money for travel was impossible. "Money problems of reality are not ghostly at all, they're solid as a rock I keep hitting my head on," he complained to Jack. "How the hell are we going to get up $$ to get to Europe, and when that $$'s gone what are we going to do? How can we live with no future abuilding?"

The problem, Allen conceded, was that there was no living to be earned from writing poetry. Most poetry magazines, especially those willing to look at work from newcomers, were modest enterprises that compensated their contributors with copies of the magazines rather than with money. And even those magazines that paid money offered minimal remuneration for a poem. To make matters worse, Allen's writer's block kept him from producing any new work, which only underscored his worry about the relationship between art and commerce. The whole concept of the starving artist had its romantic side, but in the real world, worries about finances could stifle creativity and, as Allen was learning, if the creative writer didn't work, he could not sell his art, which only reinforced the poverty. It was a cyclical situation. "I'm not writing so will never make it occupy my existence enough to obliterate external world & Time," he wrote in his journal.

Allen also attributed some of his inability to write to problematic relations with Peter Orlovsky. Their relationship would always be mercurial, and in late spring 1955 they were in the middle of one of their downswings, with Peter moody and refusing to sleep with Allen. Furthermore, Peter was making plans to travel to Long Island, New York, where he intended to spend several weeks visiting his family before retrieving his fifteen-year-old brother, Lafcadio, from his problems. Allen responded to Peter's impending absence with a prolonged, characteristic period of moody self-pity.

Ginsberg turned twenty-nine on June 3, and by his own account, he felt "harsh and bleak," as if time was passing him by without his achieving his dreams. "I am no closer to the end of the line except death than I was ten years ago and more removed from the innocence that then gave promise of sweetness thru experience," he wrote. To Kerouac, he was even more specific, describing his life as a "monstrous nightmare" that had him "on the verge of true despair." In his letter to Jack, Allen detailed his money woes and described his problems with Peter. As for his poetry, he complained that no one was interested in what he had to say, but even that might be justified, he allowed, since all he seemed to do was bemoan his fate and "trouble deaf heaven with my bootless cries."

At the end of June, Peter embarked on his hitchhiking journey to the East Coast. Allen joined him on the first leg of his trip, visiting Yosemite, Reno, Lake Tahoe, and Virginia City before returning to San Francisco. In Peter's absence, Allen resolved to put his life in order. Since it was likely that he would have to teach to support himself and his poetry, he decided that he should attend graduate school. In late July, he enrolled for the fall term at the University of California at Berkeley. He also inquired about the possibility of working as a teacher's aide when his unemployment benefits expired. To Jack Kerouac's horror, Allen considered a study of "Greek or prosody" at the Berkeley campus. As far as Jack was concerned, this was a step backward. "It's a Buddhist, AN EASTERN FUTURE ahead," Jack offered in reprimand, advising Allen that classic Greek poetry—or even the poetry of Ezra Pound, which Allen admired—was "child's play" in which poets were too absorbed in the precocity of their words for Kerouac's taste. "Please, Allen, wake up," Jack implored.

Allen finished his revisions of "Catullus Malest Cornifici" the first week of August, and he continued to polish "The Green Automobile" and "Dream Record." At this point, poetry was coming to him in flashes—in individual lines that Ginsberg would scribble into his journal: "Denver is lonesome for her heroes." "What consciousness in oblivion?" "How to say no in America of stone bombs and libraries full of tears?" These lines lay fallow, isolated, and unworked upon while Allen waited for the appropriate place to use them or the inspiration to build upon them.

Buried in the journal, tucked between two incomplete, never-to-be-published poems, was a variation of a line that would become one of the best-known and most frequently cited lines of a twentieth-century American poem. "*I saw the best mind angel-headed hipster damned*," Allen wrote, his mind on the plight of Carl Solomon. One early-August afternoon, a week or two after he had written the line, he sat down at his desk and began to expand upon it.

6

Allen Ginsberg wrote the first—and lengthiest—section of "Howl" in one sitting. In the past, his poems had been composed in handscript, almost always in notebooks or journals. It was a deliberate method of writing, friendly to instant revision or the poet's pause for reflection. With this new poem, he was working with a different method of composition. "Howl," written with Jack Kerouac's method of spontaneous composition very much on Ginsberg's mind, was written directly on a typewriter. As Allen remembered three decades later:

I sat idly at my desk by the first-floor window facing Montgomery Street's slope to gay Broadway—only a few blocks from City Lights literary paperback bookshop. I had a secondhand typewriter, some cheap scratch paper. I began typing, not with the idea of writing a formal poem, but stating my imaginative sympathies, whatever they were worth. As my loves were impractical and my thoughts relatively unworldly, I had nothing to gain, only the pleasure of enjoying on paper those sympathies most intimate to myself and most awkward in the great world of family, formal education, business and current literature.

For all the analysis the poem would receive in decades to come, along with the hundreds of hours Allen would spend in discussing the poem, "Howl" was relatively easy for him to write. After opening with a thematic statement ("I saw the best minds of my generation/generation destroyed by madness/starving mystical naked"), Allen followed with a seven-page single-spaced typed listing of all the spirits broken, impaired, or thoroughly destroyed by a force he would not name until a few weeks later when he wrote the second part of the poem. For continuity, he employed the cataloging style of Whitman's "Song of Myself," along with the fixed base system of Christopher Smart's "Jubilate Agno." Since he did not regard what he was writing as a work for future publication, he felt free to experiment. He discarded the short-line style he had been using in his recent poetry, electing instead to work with a long line, influenced in part by Kerouac and also by the long saxophone lines he had heard in jazz clubs. He broke his long lines into a triadic ladder structure he had learned from Williams, returning after each line to the "base" word—*who*—to begin again:

> who poverty and tatters and fantastic minds
>   sat up all night in lofts
>   contemplating jazz,
> who bared their brains to heaven under the El
> and saw Mohammedan angels staggering
>   on tenement roofs illuminated . . .

Each line had the spontaneous, barely-in-control feeling of a Neal Cassady wordrap—"a huge sad comedy of wild phrasing, meaningless images for the beauty of abstract poetry of mind running along making awkward combinations like Charlie Chaplin's walk, long saxophone-like chorus lines I knew Kerouac would hear the *sound* of," as Ginsberg described it.

For Ginsberg, the poem's format was nearly perfect: With a base to return to—and to unify the poem's contents with its opening line—he could continue indefinitely. Rhythm and style were not difficult to maintain. Consequently, he was able virtually to empty his mind without risking damage to the poem, and this realization served to inspire him all the more.

As he typed, he could feel his confidence growing, his voice assuming an authoritative, prophetic tone. It was his own private proclamation, sounded in a voice as frank as he had ever dared to be. All the mad episodes and anecdotes he had witnessed or heard of were included, from Carl Solomon's throwing potato salad at a Dadaist lecturer at City College of New York to poet Louis Simpson's throwing a watch from an apartment window and proclaiming, "We don't need time, we're already in eternity." Allen wrote in hyperbole, more concerned about the sound and rhythm of his writing than with accuracy of statement. The exaggeration gave the poem great energy and, to a large degree, humor. William Cannastra, whose outrageous behavior had amused and eventually horrified his friends in the late forties, became the character "who bit detectives in the neck and climbed green smokestacks," while Allen himself was the one "who passed through universities with radiant cool eyes hallucinating anarchy & Blake-light tragedy among the post-war cynical scholars."

The poem expanded into a long litany of sympathetic proclamations for

Allen's "mad" acquaintances, present or departed. Lines were devoted to Carl Solomon, Herbert Huncke, Neal Cassady, Bill Garver, Philip Lamantia, the Greenwich Village subterraneans, underground play producers Julian Beck and Judith Malina, David Kammerer, and William Cannastra, among others. Naomi Ginsberg, as responsible as Carl Solomon for Allen's reflections, was immortalized in a few lines. Kerouac and Burroughs were conspicuously absent in all but a few passing references in the poem because, as Allen later explained, he did not see them as having been destroyed by madness, literally or figuratively. Ginsberg did not exempt himself from scrutiny. Threaded in throughout the poem were references to his life at Columbia, his trip to Texas in 1947, his Blake visions, his stolen-goods fiasco with Herbert Huncke and Little Jack Melody and subsequent stay at the Psychiatric Institute, and his attempts to live a "normal" life in Paterson. In a departure from his earlier work, he made no effort to avoid or conceal references to his homosexuality.

Carl Solomon, however, was at the center of the poem, not only in terms of Allen's frequent recitation of the events of Solomon's life but also in terms of inspiration. Allen had been troubled for weeks by the news of Solomon's admittance to Pilgrim State Hospital, and Ginsberg's concern for his friend, along with his strong feelings of guilt over his signing the legal documents granting permission for his mother's lobotomy, catalyzed his compassion and sympathy for the lives he mythologized in "Howl." These feelings were also powerfully influential in the point of view and tone Ginsberg used in "Howl": Although he used only the first-person singular twice in the first draft of the eighty-seven-line poem ("*I* saw the best minds of *my* generation . . ."), Ginsberg's sympathetic treatment of the details of his friends' lives placed him squarely in their midst, rather than off to the side as an impartial observer. Given the literary traditions of the day, it was a courageous stance for him to take, especially when he made his eventual decision to publish the work. It was one matter for poets of the Academy to look upon their subjects with a lofty or detached sense of pity, quite another to identify openly with them. Edwin Arlington Robinson had looked upon one of his most famous subjects, Richard Corey, with a sense of wonder and confusion, the poet implying surprise by what appeared to be the inexplicable suicide of his character; in "Howl," by placing himself among his characters, Ginsberg did not afford himself convenient removal from the more troubling aspects of his characters.

As if this wasn't enough, Allen decided to state specifically his identification with Solomon and the others. He had no sooner finished his exhaustive writing session on the first part of "Howl" when, on that very same day, he inserted a new sheet of paper into his typewriter and began to write what was to become the third section of the poem:

> Carl Solomon!
> I am with you in Rockland
>> where the faculties of the skull no longer admit the worms
>> of the senses
> I am with you in Rockland
>> where you divide the tea of the breast of the spinsters
>> of Utica

I am with you in Rockland
    where you pun on the bodies of your nurses the harpies
    of the Bronx . . .

As he had done in the first section, Allen employed the Whitmanesque cataloging style, complete with a fixed base from which to begin each new line. Now comfortable with the long line, he had no difficulty writing two additional pages in which he stated his identification with his poem's central figure. The writing on this new section went well: In months to come, he would make substantial revisions on the first section of "Howl," but he would leave the third part virtually intact, with the exception of his fleshing out the poem and rearranging some of the lines; he would also make the important decision to change the words *I am* to *I'm* for the sake of better cadence.

By the time he had finished writing that day, Allen knew he had created something of importance, even if he did judge its contents to be too private for publication. The poem was a catharsis, spiritually and artistically. For the first time in months, he had risen above the self-pity that blocked his attempts to move forward in his life. Similarly, the writing of the poem sounded an ending to the writer's block that had plagued him since his move to San Francisco. He found working with the long line agreeable, and he would use it in almost all of his poetry of the next year.

7

Allen realized the new poem was far from perfect or complete, and he immediately began the task of reshaping its structure. He divided its contents into four basic units based loosely either on the themes of the individual lines or on the time frames in which the incidents depicted in the poem occurred. From this outline structure, he was able, as he described it years later, to "rearrange and rehook the verses into their appropriate groups" and "refine rhythm, syntax and diction to create an even and elastic flow verse to verse."

After completing his initial revisions, Allen retyped the poem, gave it its title, * and sent the first six pages of the original unaltered draft to Jack Kerouac, who was now staying temporarily in Mexico and writing a sequence of poems he was calling *Mexico City Blues*. "I enclose first draft scribblenotes of a poem

---

* In the years following the publication of "Howl," there was a degree of confusion (or mythologizing) connected to the means by which Ginsberg decided upon the poem's title. Ginsberg sent Jack Kerouac the original first draft typescript, with the legend "Howl for Carl Solomon" printed in pink pencil (the same pencil used for the poem's initial corrections), with his own handwriting across the top of the first page. He kept for himself a retyped copy, which he entitled "Strophes" (after the long-line style of the poem). When Kerouac commented on the poem in his August 19, 1955, letter, Allen had forgotten that he had given the poem its title and thus gave Kerouac credit for the title—a misunderstanding unresolved until 1980, when the original draft was returned to Ginsberg by John Clellon Holmes, who had received it from Kerouac. Nor was "Howl for Carl Solomon" a title selected on the spur of the moment, as Ginsberg's memory lapse might seem to indicate. In his 1954 journal, Ginsberg had written a poem to which he had affixed the same title, and while the journal poem was not about the same subject matter and was never published, the title obviously stayed in Ginsberg's mind, if not his thoughts, for some time prior to his August 1955 writing of "Howl."

I was writing, nearer to your style than anything," Allen told Jack, declining any further comment on the poem or its contents.

Kerouac responded with a ten-page letter which he printed hastily on pocket notebook pages. Jack lauded "Howl" as being "very powerful," although he mistook the overstrikes on Allen's manuscript for revisions and demanded that Allen send him the original unrevised manuscript. Kerouac told Allen that he wanted to see his "lingual spontaneity" or nothing at all. Obviously impressed with the daring of Ginsberg's unprecedented frankness in his poetry, Kerouac singled out such phrases as "with a vision of ultimate cunt or come," "waving genitals and manuscripts," "died in Denver again," and "self-delivered Truth's final lobotomy" as the expressions that he found especially effective.

Ginsberg was gratified by Kerouac's response. He assured Jack that he had sent him "the first pages put down, as is," that the overstrikes on his manuscript were the resulting sloppiness of his composing the poem directly on the typewriter, not indications of revision. He used the occasion to praise Kerouac on his method of spontaneous composition, admitting that it had been his model when he was writing "Howl." "I realize how right you are, that was the first time I sat down to blow, it came out in your method, sounding like you, an imitation practically. How far advanced you are on this. I don't know what I'm doing with poetry. I need years of isolation and constant everyday writing to attain your volume & freedom & knowledge of the form." A case in point, Allen noted in his letter, were the selections of *Mexico City Blues* that Kerouac had sent, which Allen thought were "lovely."

Allen had also shown "Howl" to Lawrence Ferlinghetti, who was as impressed with it as Kerouac. Ferlinghetti was planning to publish a series of fifty-page poetry pamphlets through his City Lights Bookstore, and he offered to publish "Howl" as part of the series. Allen was ecstatic. "One booklet for that poem," Allen wrote happily. "Nothing else—it will fill a booklet."

Ginsberg took a cautious approach in his selection of "Howl" 's early readers. He did not rush to show the poem to his father, who was certain to be offended by the poem's profanity and references to homosexuality, or to William Carlos Williams, who might have taken issue with Ginsberg's use of the long line. Nor did Allen immediately submit the poem for consideration to Mark Van Doren or Lionel Trilling. Instead, he gave copies of the poem to those most likely to be sympathetic to the work. Kerouac and Ferlinghetti did not disappoint him in their reactions to "Howl," and William Burroughs, though far less specific in his appraisal, followed suit. "To my mind [it is] the best thing you have done," Bill wrote of "Howl." "I do not single out lines, because it is all excellent."

8

Peter Orlovsky returned to San Francisco within a few days of Allen's initial work on "Howl." His trip to Long Island had been nightmarish. His two older brothers were catatonic, confined in a mental hospital. Peter wept when he saw them. Lafcadio, who would retreat to the bathroom for hours on end and talk incessantly about making millions of dollars, was not much better off. Peter had packed up Lafcadio and the two had hitchhiked back to San Francisco. Their cross-country trip had been long and exhaustive. As Allen recalled, Peter "walked in at 3AM & threw arms around me at door, New York hell over, scratching head over new responsibility for strange brother."

Lafcadio proved to be a challenge to the household. Allen and Peter were accustomed to coming and going as they pleased, eating whenever and wherever they chose, but with the demands of caring for this new houseguest, they were forced to keep a more disciplined daily schedule. To Allen, the scenario seemed too much "like being married & having [an] overgrown problem child" on hand. Allen had just grown comfortable with a solitary life, and having people around was as disruptive to his work schedule as it had been earlier in the year, when he had been living at Robert LaVigne's apartment. Allen still wanted to be with Peter, but he also needed time alone to think and work.

Fortunately, the beginning of the school year brought a solution to this problem. To be closer to the campus, Allen moved across the Bay to Berkeley. He found a tiny rose-covered one-room cottage set in back of a large house at 1624 Milvia Street, where, for thirty-five dollars a month, he could live in a pastoral setting, surrounded by flowers and with the sunlight flooding in through his kitchen window. The back porch, though decaying and slumping toward the ground, came complete with a rocking chair—an ideal place to read or think. There was a large garden brimming with tomato plants, as well as apricot and plum trees, in his backyard. The air was filled with the scent of the mint that grew wild in the yard. Blackberries grew along a battered brown fence, giving the yard a rustic appearance. The cottage was only six blocks from the Berkeley campus, and there was a trolley station nearby. All in all, it was an ideal setting, the "perfect place to retreat [and] be quiet," as Ginsberg described it. Content again, he wrote two new poems, "A Strange New Cottage in Berkeley," about his new home, and "A Supermarket in California," a dreamy poem about a chance encounter with Walt Whitman in a California grocery store. Both poems were quiet and reflective, indicative of Ginsberg's happier mood.

Allen continued to work on "Howl," which now had an additional section that acted as a bridge between the two earlier-written sections. Shortly after Peter Orlovsky's return from the East Coast, Allen and Peter had taken peyote and gone for a long evening walk on the streets of San Francisco, where Allen had a drug-enhanced vision. Prior to the walk, Allen had taken peyote on at least two previous occasions. In April 1952, while he was living at his father's house in Paterson, he had tried peyote for the first time, and the experience had been serene. He had also taken peyote a short time after he moved to San Francisco—this time with much different results. In the backyard of his father's house, Allen had noticed the peaceful activity of nature, as insects and birds moved around him; in San Francisco, sitting in his room and looking out his Nob Hill apartment window, he could see the Sir Francis Drake Hotel, which struck him as looking like a grim monster staring into the sky. The towering hotel, with its huge beam light at the top, reminded Allen of a cyclopslike presence; the lighted windows below, Allen remarked, looked like "the robot skullface of Moloch . . . glaring into my window." Ginsberg described it in greater detail in his journal:

> Uprising in the timeless city gloom, Dark Tower above ruddy build-ing, suddenly a vision the Death Head—The building an evil mon-ster—A tower in Hell—("Those poor souls making it up in the tower")—Two eyes blast light far apart brick glass illuminated from within—A painter might make it look like surrealistic reality, that would be too corny—this is deep gong religious.
>
> Impassive robot (antennalike structure) of Sir Francis Drake Hotel.
>
> And quite vegetable that monster too—it may be coming to eat me someday. . . .

Now, as he and Peter walked about the city, Allen arrived again at the Drake Hotel, with a similar vision of its demonic presence. Because he had been working so diligently on the revisions of the first part of "Howl," he was able to recognize the significance of a cityscape monster metaphor to his poem. By using it in the second part of "Howl," he was able to unite the two parts he had written so far. As he explained it a year later, the poem now had continuity to its theme:

> Part I deals sympathetically with individual cases. Part II describes and rejects the Moloch of society which confounds and suppresses individ-ual experience and forces the individual to consider himself mad if he does not reject his own deepest senses. Part III is an expression of sympathy and identification with C.S. [Carl Solomon] who is in the madhouse—saying that his madness basically is rebellion against Mo-loch and I am with him, and extending my hand in union.

Entranced by his Drake Hotel vision, Allen focused on using it as a modern symbol for Moloch, the Canaanite fire god who was worshiped in a rite in which parents burned their children in sacrifice. Inspired, he went right to work on inserting the image into his poem. "I wandered down Powell street muttering 'Moloch Moloch' all night and wrote 'Howl II' nearly intact in cafeteria at foot of Drake Hotel, deep in the hellish vale," Ginsberg wrote in remembrance of the occasion. In the cafeteria, Allen scribbled the notes that would be the basis for the second part of his poem. He included a striking reference to William Cannastra's death, as well as references to his mother and to Bill Keck, a New York friend who loved harpsichord music, and whose wife Allen had encoun-tered on his way to the cafeteria. The New York subways, Allen felt, were natu-ral symbols for his depiction of a spirit-consuming inferno, as were the stark images of concrete superstructures, and he included them in the new section. Although he did not initially use a base word for the beginning of each line, as he had in his earlier writings of "Howl," he had no trouble finding the impetus to outline the bridge between the first and third parts of his poem:

> Moloch! Molock! Whose hand ripped out their brains
> and scattered their minds on the wheels of subways?

Moloch! Filth! Ugliness! Ashcans and unobtainable dollars!
Beauties dying in lofts! Harpsichords unbuilt! Children
screaming under the stairways! old men weeping in the parks!
    Children! children! The very children breaking their
backs under the subways. Breaking their backs trying to lift the
Whole City on their backs—Pavements! Buildings! Trees
Rockefeller Center Tons—The whole damned lot of it—the
screaming radios—Hitler! Stalin! Christmas! Jesus!
The wires coming out of our ears—lifting the city on our backs!
To heaven—

In the weeks following this initial notation for the second part of "Howl,"
Allen expanded on his notes. He also assigned the word *Moloch* as the base for
the long lines that followed, giving a sense of structural continuity to the three
parts of the poem. Ginsberg's writing style in the second part of "Howl"—short
phrases punctuated by exclamation points, all within the framework of the long
line—gave it three distinct musical movements: the first part with its hot
saxophonic expressions, reminiscent of the jazz lines of Charlie Parker and
Lester Young; the second part, with short "squawks" or statements, not unlike
those played by Miles Davis; and the third part, with a cool bluesy and lyrical
feeling similar to the moody music played by John Coltrane. In every respect,
"Howl" was, as Ginsberg noted, "really a new poetry," a work that brought
together the influences of Whitman and Williams, the American idiom, elements of jazz, the philosophy of the Beat Generation, the spontaneous writing
style of Jack Kerouac, Ginsberg's homage to Cézanne, his sympathy for Carl
Solomon and other friends, and autobiographical detail.

9

In 1982, over twenty-five years after he had written "Howl," Allen Ginsberg
was asked about the mental and creative elements necessary for the spontaneous
composition of such a poem. In reply, Ginsberg said, "You have to be inspired
to write something like that. It's not something you can very easily do just by
pressing a button. You have to have the right historical situation, the right
physical combination, the right mental formation, the right courage, the right
sense of prophecy, and the right information." It was also important that the
poet possess the correct intentions and ambition, he added.

These remarks might appear to be a catalog of the general and the obvious,
as far as an explanation of creativity is concerned, but a close examination of
"Howl" reveals the poet to be more exact in his response than one might
suspect. In fact, it is possible to use all of Ginsberg's remarks as the criteria for
examining each of the poet's major works. Whenever Ginsberg was working
masterfully, he was making use of all the mental and creative factors listed in
his reply.

At the time of writing "Howl," Ginsberg's "historical situation," both immediate and long-term, had prepared him for the poem's composition. Most
apparent, of course, is the autobiographical background cited in the first part

of the poem. His early poems were displays of inexperience—of a young, albeit talented, voice limited in firsthand knowledge. Quite simply, Ginsberg did not actually know enough to write with the authority and cohesiveness he displayed in "Howl."

Not that he didn't try. Ginsberg's early journals contain numerous topic lists, some quite detailed, drawn up by a young poet eager to write about his life's experiences. However, he was wise enough to recognize that most of the listed items lacked the sense of drama necessary to create the urgency that propels good poetry, and on those occasions when his life provided him with the grist for writing such a powerful work—his Blake visions, for example—he was lacking other creative components.

Given the circumstances of his life, it was inevitable that he would write about madness, although the specific subject of his mother's insanity, even in 1955, was too painful for him to address directly in his poetry. He had witnessed the incomprehensible and the insane on numerous occasions in his youth, but so far those events, coupled with his sympathy toward society's truly "beat" individuals, were topics he had been unable to approach suitably in his poetry. He needed a historical catalyst, an event that would compel him to write in his own voice, and it presented itself when Ginsberg learned that Carl Solomon had been admitted to a mental hospital. Solomon was both a friend and one of the more intelligent people Ginsberg knew, and his 1955 incarceration prompted in Ginsberg a long contemplation of other "best minds . . . destroyed by madness"—a reflection that led him back to his mother, even as he was writing the poem that he dedicated to Carl Solomon:

> I realized after I wrote it that it was addressed to her. . . . *Howl* is actually to her rather than to Carl in a sense. Because the emotion that comes from it is built on my mother, not on anything as superficial as a later acquaintance, such as Carl.

In a sense, the writing of "Howl" was not unlike Ginsberg's Blake visions. Once again, he found himself alone, brooding over a lost love and struggling to find a direction for his life. The Blake vision had been the result of his reaching a state of what he called "ordinary mind," where conceptualization fell away and he was able to view the world without the interference of language. So it was with "Howl." No longer caring about the different concepts of poetry composition, he was able to write a major work that, even with some of its almost surreal aspects, was utterly clear.

On a different historical plane, contemporary world events were of enormous influence to the composition of "Howl," particularly in the poem's second part, in which Ginsberg names his villain. In the wake of the U.S. deployment of nuclear weaponry, the Korean War, and the escalation of the Cold War, the idea of America's feeding its children in sacrifice to a fire god was a frightening, realistic image to the poet—thus, Moloch, the destroyer of the human spirit, the black heart behind the collapse of civilization. In a 1954 letter to Jack Kerouac, Ginsberg expressed his concern over the historical situation of the day:

There's too many poems to finish and not one done, all these fragments small and large. And the possibility now after Indo China and Ike's admission that U.S. contingency policy would be replaced by a weaker more limited policy of cold war—are we losing? Is the Fall of America upon us? The Great Fall we once prophesied? . . . So the possibility of a prophetic poem, using ideas of politics and war and calling on love and reality for salvation. . . .

However, for all its tirades against the system, "Howl" is not a political poem in the sense that later poems, such as "Wichita Vortex Sutra," "Hūm Bom," "Pentagon Exorcism," and "Plutonium Ode," were political ones. In "Howl," Ginsberg focuses on individuals, the mass of which, he implies, constitute a repressed society. This, of course, is a political statement, but in his later poems, he is much more specific, integrating into his works news items and headlines, names and dates—the whole historical consequence. If "Howl" is significant to Ginsberg's future as a political gadfly, it would be as a result of the prophetic voice established in the poem's first line. This voice, influenced by the voices of biblical prophets, pushes Ginsberg to the forefront of his poem, giving everything that follows a prophetic aura. It is a voice that he would use in poems addressing specific political issues.

In years to come, Ginsberg would become more focused on the physiological—or "right physical combination"—in the composition of poetry, mostly as a result of his mantra chanting, Buddhist sitting practice, blues singing, and growing interest in spontaneous oral poetry. As he matured as a poet and gathered years of poetry reading experiences behind him, he would reach the conclusion that different forms of poetry merged from different parts of the body, and that to use all of one's self in a work of art, the poet had to align thought with physiology. Pitch and tone, suggested to a large degree by the poet's use of vowel sounds, governed the physiology when the poem was read aloud.

When he wrote "Howl," Ginsberg had never read his poetry aloud, except to a few friends, and from all indications, judging from his public statements over the years, he had no intention of reading "Howl" in public. Still, through his association with Jack Kerouac, Ginsberg was becoming more aware of the sound of written language, as well as the poet's physical involvement with breath-length lines. The length of a line not only dictated the physical act of drawing a breath but it also suggested the union of the physical and emotional states during the actual composition of the poem itself.

This is very apparent when one compares the line structure of the three distinct movements of "Howl." The long rhapsodic lines of the first part suggest an entirely different emotion from the shorter lines, broken even further by Ginsberg's use of dashes and exclamation points, in the second part; the third part begins with short lines ("Carl Solomon! I'm with you in Rockland/where you're madder than I am") and builds emotional momentum with each successive line, which tends to be longer than the preceding one, until the final line ("I'm with you in Rockland/in my dreams you walk dripping from a sea journey on the highway across America in tears to the door of my cottage in the Western night"), in which breath/thought line length is similar to the lines in the poem's first section. A physical and literary balance is achieved.

Ginsberg's "mental formation" at the time he was writing "Howl" is noteworthy for its ironic contribution to the poem's success. As already noted, he was steeped in self-pity during the summer of 1955, and no doubt this emotional status contributed to his sympathetic feelings toward suffering comrades. For most people, the search for the less fortunate is armor against self-pity—or at least temporary medicine for those suffering from it. However, as one of postmodern literature's great survivors, Ginsberg went beyond the temptation of temporary relief. The voice in "Howl" is not the sound of a man weakened from mental suffering; instead, it is a powerful outcry of rage and indignation, tempered by the sympathy Ginsberg felt for the afflictions heaped upon the named and unnamed souls in his poem.

For Ginsberg, this was an important breakthrough, a grasping of the correct mental formation that spelled the difference between the failings of his earlier works and the ultimate success of "Howl." Ginsberg had a history of falling victim to bouts of depression and self-pity, and far too often his poetry—especially the unpublished notebook poems, but even some of the poems in *The Gates of Wrath* and *Empty Mirror*—was undermined by his inability (or unwillingness) to unite his intelligence and artistic skill in such a way as to avoid self-defeating emotionalism. "Howl" finds Ginsberg counterpunching, angered into action by his mental state. Rather than assume the passive, defensive posture of many of his earlier efforts, he took a more confident stance in "Howl."

This position was misinterpreted by numerous critics as being a violent stance. In fact, "Howl" is a much more gentle poem than its title implies. Despite the critical outrage expressed over such phrases as "who let themselves be fucked in the ass by saintly motorcyclists, and screamed with joy" and "who howled on their knees in the subway and were dragged off the roof waving genitals and manuscripts," along with Ginsberg's repeated use of imagery implying violence to the spirit, if not the body, "Howl" is not an aggressive work. One of the poem's key phrases, "O starry spangled shock of mercy," placed in the context of Part III's cries of sympathy for Solomon, is a call for peace, not violence. The plea is underscored in "Footnote to Howl," the brief addendum written a short time after the composition of the main body of the poem, in which Ginsberg declares all things to be holy, concluding with "Holy the supernatural extra brilliant intelligent kindness of the soul."

To take the stance that all things were holy, including those thoughts and actions deemed in the 1950s to be inappropriate or "dirty," was a courageous position for Ginsberg to assume. Courage is an attribute that had been continually denied him over the years, usually by those who claim that he, like the child who curses loudly in the temple, is simply seeking attention or aiming to shock for the sake of shock. There is no question that Ginsberg sought attention throughout his life—possibly more than any other poet in history—just as it is true that he used shock as a tool in his writing, but to write off his intentions with such a simplistic explanation is to deny him the careful consideration he gave to each line in "Howl."

"Howl" was Ginsberg's "coming out" poem, a work in which he clearly, for the first time, identifies his spirit, sympathies, and sexuality to anyone reading it. Obviously, all of Ginsberg's friends were aware of these traits, but when he decided to publish "Howl," he was doing so at considerable risk. His friends, Kerouac in particular, had encouraged him to be totally frank in his work, which is fine when, to paraphrase Kerouac, one is scribbling in notebooks for one's own joy, but to put that voice, with all its intimations, forward in public, a poet is not just cursing in the temple; he is building an entirely different church.

10

If it could be said that the events of Allen Ginsberg's life had conditioned and prepared him to write "Howl," it could also be suggested that San Francisco, with its open artistic environment, was prepared to hear the poem. Poets thrived in the city, mingling well with its bohemian community and the intellectualism cultivated by the nearby university. The Kenneth Rexroth and Robert Duncan poetry groups attracted enthusiastic followings. Late in 1954, Ruth Witt-Diamant opened the San Francisco Poetry Center, which booked readings by nationally acclaimed poets.

For some time, Allen had been looking for a reading venue that featured himself, Jack Kerouac, and Neal Cassady. Jack intended to visit San Francisco in the near future, as soon as he left Mexico, and Allen, thoroughly impressed with Kerouac's new *Mexico City Blues* sequence, was eager to find a way to get Jack's poetry in front of the San Francisco literary community. He was also becoming interested in reading "Howl" in front of an audience.

A chance encounter with poet Michael McClure afforded him the opportunity to organize such a reading. Allen had met McClure, a young poet from Kansas, at the Auden reading at the Poetry Center the previous fall, and the two poets found that they shared a strong interest in William Blake. In addition to writing poetry, McClure was interested in painting, which he had studied, along with anthropology, at the University of Arizona. He had met his wife-to-be, Joanna, while he was attending the university, and he had followed her to San Francisco when she moved there in 1954. McClure had hoped to study under Mark Rothko and Clyfford Still, his interest being in the visual look of poetry on the page, but the two painters were no longer teaching in San Francisco by the time McClure arrived, so he enrolled in Robert Duncan's poetry workshop instead. He quickly became one of Duncan's favorite students and in no time a close friend. Through Duncan, McClure was introduced to other notable members of the city's poetry scene. He and Duncan attended Kenneth Rexroth's weekly soirees. One of McClure's early friends was Philip Lamantia, the surrealist poet who knew Ginsberg from New York.

As Allen learned, McClure had been invited to organize a poetry reading at the Six Gallery, but he had been too busy to put the reading together. Allen told McClure that he would be happy to organize the event, and in return McClure agreed to read some of his work. Inexperienced at organizing gatherings of this nature, Allen turned to Kenneth Rexroth for advice on whom to invite to read. Rexroth recommended Gary Snyder, a Berkeley poet who shared Rexroth's enthusiasm for Chinese and Japanese poetry.

Allen liked Snyder as soon as he met him, and the two became fast friends. A twenty-five-year-old graduate student, Snyder had been born in San Francisco but was raised in a rural area of Washington, near Seattle. As a youth, his greatest pleasures were derived from his natural environment. He loved to hike and climb mountains. By the time he had reached his teens and moved with his family to rural Oregon, Snyder had developed an array of woodsman skills that made him self-sufficient in even the most primitive surroundings, and these proved to be useful later in his life when he took jobs as a fire lookout in the Pacific Northwest. Many of Snyder's childhood neighbors were North American Indians, and from them Snyder learned a great deal about native skills, customs, rituals, and folklore—all of which made their way into his poetry. Snyder enjoyed reading, especially the works of naturalist Ernest Thompson Seton, whom Snyder would cite as being the greatest influence of his childhood.

Snyder attended Reed College in Portland, Oregon, where he took courses in anthropology and literature. He also began to write poetry, publishing his early works in the campus journal. While studying at Reed, Snyder met Philip Whalen and Lew Welch, two poets who became his roommates and steadfast friends. In 1950, William Carlos Williams visited the Reed campus—an event of enormous importance to the three poets. Lew Welch remembered the occasion:

> Whalen, Snyder and I were asked by the school, Reed was a really groovy place then, to go meet him at the airport. After all, we were the poets of Reed, and the faculty was sort of embarrassed about it all. So we got him into his hotel and rapped with him, it was like meeting a saint, a really important man, but he came on like a Middle Western hick, really, shy and everything. . . .
>
> He was so sweet and humble and we loved him so much. He had saved our lives. And when we told him how he had, truly, defeated T.S. Eliot, he was really touched. That young men, poets, would come to him and say he had won the battle of his life.
>
> We took him to our pad, where Whalen and Snyder and I lived, and we played poetry games and talked and we gave him our stuff. . . .

Ginsberg was quite naturally fascinated by Gary Snyder's connection with Williams, but what really sealed his friendship with the poet was Snyder's knowledge of Buddhism and Far Eastern cultures. Snyder was, in every way imaginable, a scholar, a man who integrated his acquired knowledge into his daily life and hungered for more. After his graduation from Reed, Snyder enrolled in a graduate program at the University of Indiana, where he studied linguistic anthropology for a semester before moving to the West Coast. At Berkeley, he was taking graduate courses in Japanese and Chinese, and he planned to study in Japan the following spring. Like Kerouac, Gary Snyder meditated, but his understanding of Buddhism went much deeper than Jack's. He lived a simple, rather austere life that immediately impressed Allen and, a short time later, Jack Kerouac. In *The Dharma Bums*, his fictional memoir of his 1955 to 1956 friendship with Snyder, Kerouac was reverential in his description of Snyder's cottage:

> Japhy [Snyder] lived in his own shack which was . . . about twelve by twelve, with nothing in it but typical Japhy appurtenances that showed his belief in the simple monastic life—no chairs at all, not even one sentimental rocking chair, but just straw mats. In the corner was his famous rucksack with cleaned-up pots and pans all fitting into one another in a compact unit and all tied and put away inside a knotted-up blue bandana. . . . He had a slew of orange crates all filled with beautiful scholarly books, some of them in Oriental languages, all the great sutras, comments on sutras, the complete works of D. T. Suzuki and a fine quadruple-volume edition of Japanese haikus. He also had an immense collection of valuable general poetry. In fact if a thief should have broken in there the only things of real value were the books. . . .

Allen and Gary spent much of their first day together talking, exchanging stories about their backgrounds, and discussing poetry. Gary told Allen about Philip Whalen, who was to arrive in Berkeley the next day, and Allen, in turn, told Snyder about Jack Kerouac, who was also due in town anytime. Gary was enthusiastic about participating in a reading at the Six Gallery, and having seen some of Snyder's poetry, Allen was all too happy to include him on his list of readers.

As fate had it, Jack Kerouac arrived in Berkeley on the afternoon that Ginsberg met Snyder. When Allen returned home that evening, he found Jack sitting in his cottage and playing music on his three-speed phonograph. Allen briefed Kerouac on the day's events, and Jack made plans to visit Snyder, who appeared to be as kindred a spirit as Neal Cassady had been a few years earlier. To Allen's disappointment, Jack adamantly refused to read at the Six Gallery. Kerouac was terrified by the prospects of reading his work in front of a large group of people, even though he read very well and was not bashful about reading his work to a small gathering of friends. He would attend the reading, Jack told Allen, but as a member of the audience rather than a participant onstage.

Allen filled out his roster of readers by adding Philip Lamantia and Philip Whalen. Like Gary Snyder, Whalen was a devoted student of Buddhism and a poet with a unique voice. Born in Portland in 1923, Whalen spent his youth in a small town on the Columbia River. A high school teacher recognized Whalen's creative talent and encouraged him to write, and while Whalen wrote poetry, he also wrote short stories and even attempted to write a novel while he was in the Army Air Corps. His interests in Buddhism came early, as well. He would visit the Portland Public Library and read such books as Lin Yutang's *Wisdom of China and India* and A. P. Sinnett's *Esoteric Buddhism*; by the time he met Gary Snyder at Reed in 1949, Whalen was studying Buddhism and other Oriental philosophies and religions with a fervor that would eventually lead him to become a Buddhist monk.

With five poets scheduled to read, the evening at the Six Gallery promised to be an eclectic event. Allen asked Kenneth Rexroth to act as the reading's master of ceremonies—a nod of respect to a literary elder and, in practical terms, a wise move, since the poets were unknown; Rexroth's participation would not only be viewed as an endorsement but would also help boost attendance. To publicize the event, Allen posted handbills in a number of North Beach bars. He also had a hundred postcards printed:

> Six poets at the Six Gallery. Kenneth Rexroth, M.C. Remarkable collection of angels all gathered at once in the same spot. Wine, music, dancing girls, serious poetry, free satori. Small collection for wine and postcards. Charming event.

Ginsberg later acknowledged his approach to organizing the Six Gallery reading to be "purely amateur and goofy," but it gained the desired results: When the poets took the stage on Thursday, October 13, 1955, they were greeted by a standing-room-only audience.

11

The Six Gallery was a modest enterprise creatively fashioned from what had once been the two repair bays of an auto repair shop. On a typical night, the adjoining rooms could easily accommodate the small groups that customarily attended poetry readings, but on the evening of October 13, with a crowd of over one hundred, the building was packed with people seated in chairs, standing along the walls, or taking places along the front of the small platform stage. Previous events at the Six Gallery, combining painting exhibitions with poetry readings, music, and film presentations, had been attended by small but enthusiastic groups, but a recent production of Robert Duncan's controversial play, *Faust Foutu*, had given the Six Gallery an aura of notoriety that helped attract larger crowds. Begun as an experiment, the Six Gallery was picking up a following.

On the night of its most historic reading, the Six Gallery seemed to have attracted every significant member of what would later be termed the San Francisco Poetry Renaissance. From the beginning, there was a festive atmosphere to the event. To assure a loose, free-spirited reading, Jack Kerouac scurried around the rooms, collecting donations for wine, the reading itself delayed while he ran out for gallon jugs, which were passed around throughout the reading.

Onstage, the poets were seated in a semicircle behind the podium. Kenneth Rexroth, dressed in a bow tie and a cutaway pinstripe suit, opened the evening with a few brief introductory remarks. Taking notice of the mixture of literary and political interests represented by those in attendance as well as by those onstage, Rexroth compared the climate of San Francisco to that of Barcelona at the time of the Spanish anarchists, where culture survived despite an oppressive national political environment.

He then turned the podium over to Philip Lamantia, whom Kerouac later characterized as looking like "a young priest." Rather than read his own poetry,

Lamantia decided to read work by John Hoffman, a young surrealist poet who had recently died in Mexico City, reportedly from a peyote overdose. The poems, which struck Michael McClure as being "beautiful prose poems that left orange stripes and colored visions in the air," set the tone for the evening.

McClure was next in line. He had participated in the earlier presentation of *Faust Foutu* and now read poems that stated his passionate concern for the relationship between the natural biological world and humankind's intervening spiritual world, the poems reflective of early environmentalist interests that would bloom into a nationwide ecology movement in decades to come. "Point Lobos Animism," a poem written in response to McClure's admiration of Artaud, was his attempt to enjoin himself viscerally with nature. In "For the Death of 100 Whales," a poem he had written a year earlier in reaction to a news item he had seen in *Time* magazine, McClure protested the slaughter of a pack of killer whales by bored NATO troops in Iceland.

Philip Whalen was the evening's third reader. A large, burly man, Whalen applied a gentle and humorous touch to the reading with his presentation of "Plus Ça Change . . ." and "the Martyrdom of Two Pagans," the former a wry dialogue poem in which the two conversers attempt to cope with the fact that they have changed into parakeets.

After a brief intermission, Allen Ginsberg moved to the podium for his first public reading of "Howl." A number of people in attendance—including Kerouac, Ferlinghetti, Snyder, and Whalen—had read "Howl" in manuscript, but no one was prepared for the impact of Allen's dramatic reading of the poem. Allen had been drinking wine throughout the evening and, by his own later admission, he was intoxicated by the time the lights dimmed and he began his reading. Somewhat nervous, he started in a calm, quiet tone, letting the poem's words achieve their own impact, but before long he gained confidence and began to sway rhythmically with the music of his poetry, responding to the enthusiasm of the audience, which was transfixed by "Howl" 's powerful imagery. Jack Kerouac, sitting at the edge of the platform, pounded in accompaniment on a wine jug, shouting "GO!" at the end of each long line. The crowd quickly joined him in punctuating Allen's lines with shouts of encouragement, and Allen, inspired by the intensity in the room, responded with an even greater flourish to his reading. By the time he had concluded, he was in tears, as was Kenneth Rexroth. The audience erupted in appreciation of the work, as if each person in attendance recognized that literary history had been made.

"In all our memories no one had been so outspoken in poetry before," Michael McClure remembered.

> We had gone beyond a point of no return—and we were ready for it, for a point of no return. None of us wanted to go back to the gray, chill, militaristic silence, to the intellective void—to the land without poetry—to the spiritual drabness. We wanted to make it new and we wanted to invent it and the process of it as we went into it. We wanted voice and we wanted vision.

Ginsberg's reading of "Howl"—as well as the overall success of the Six Gallery reading—provided the voice and vision necessary to nudge the varying

San Francisco poetry interests into a unified direction. Noting that the poets at the time "had no sense of community of poets and even less of an audience," Gary Snyder called the Six Gallery reading "a curious kind of turning point in American poetry," the beginning of a surge of poetry readings that brought poets into contact with their audiences and reestablished poetry as an oral form:

> It succeeded beyond our wildest thoughts. In fact, we weren't even thinking of success; we were just trying to invite some friends and potential friends. . . . Poetry suddenly seemed useful in 1955 San Francisco. From that day to this, there has never been a week without a reading in the Bay area. . . .

Snyder concluded the evening's events with a reading of "A Berry Feast," a poem celebrating the traditional and ritualistic communing with nature as symbolized in an Indian first-fruits festival, and with excerpts from *Myths and Texts*, a lengthy poetry sequence he had begun in the summer of 1952 and was still developing at the time of the reading. Snyder's selections were an appropriate conclusion to the evening, a call for the return to nature's open community. Reading in a voice that Kerouac later described as "deep and resonant and somehow brave, like the voice of oldtime American heroes and orators," Snyder effectively summarized the spirit of the evening, the feeling that the human race was losing sight of its own basic consciousness and spirituality, that its sense of growth and self-determination were being undermined by its self-destructive modern tendencies. Unlike Robinson Jeffers, whose poetry could be characterized as pessimistic in its outlook, Snyder delivered a hopeful yet urgent message: The world's people had to return to the consciousness of their forebears, who gratified their spiritual natures through simple work and ritual.

After the reading, the poets and a number of their friends repaired first to Sam Wo, a Chinese restaurant, and then to The Place, a popular tavern among poets. All agreed that the evening had been remarkable, magical; the poets were convinced that they had participated in an event of local, if not national, importance. When Kerouac had congratulated Allen after his reading of "Howl," he told him that his words would make him famous in San Francisco. Overhearing Jack's remark, Kenneth Rexroth disagreed with the assessment, finding it much too modest. "This poem will make you famous from bridge to bridge," an exuberant Rexroth informed Ginsberg.

Lawrence Ferlinghetti did not accompany the poets on their rounds that evening. He, too, had been overwhelmed by what he had seen and heard at the reading, and when it ended, he returned home, retired to the desk in his study, and typed out a telegram that borrowed from Ralph Waldo Emerson's famous response to Walt Whitman's *Leaves of Grass*.

Wrote Ferlinghetti: "I greet you at the beginning of a great career. When do I get the manuscript? . . ."

10

The San Francisco Poetry Renaissance

We are a legend, invisible but
legendary, as prophesied. . . .

1

Allen went immediately to work on putting "Howl" into publishable form. Based on the enthusiastic reaction the poem had received at Bay Area readings subsequent to the one at the Six Gallery, Allen no longer believed "Howl" to be too private for others to read, though he still had no inclination of the overwhelming response it would receive from a national audience. Even as he revised and shaped it into its final form, he perceived "Howl" to be a poem of local interest—fascinating, perhaps, to his circle of friends and to those who heard him perform it at local poetry readings—but of little interest elsewhere.

The "Moloch" section required the most attention. Believing them to be incomplete, Allen had not read the second or third parts of "Howl" at the Six Gallery, but he began reading these sections at readings shortly thereafter, testing the "Moloch" section for audience response and modifying it in a way that included the phrases that received the most favorable reaction. Audiences loved this section when it was performed: They booed, hissed, clapped, chanted, and snapped their fingers whenever Allen recited the word *Moloch*. Revisions for this section were problematic. In the early drafts, it lacked the patterned rhythms of the other two sections of "Howl," as well as the fixed base upon which each line could be built; the staccato rhythms of the second part were effective as shouts of ecstasy or rage whenever Allen read the poem, but they seemed to be lacking something on the printed page. He remained patient, rearranging lines on the page, reading them aloud for sound and rhythm, shortening some phrases and lengthening others. His revisions for this section alone involved more than twenty drafts, from his initial changes to the minor alterations submitted just before publication.

In Allen's opinion, "Howl" still needed a coda, a feeling of affirmation to give it a sense of balance. It came to him one afternoon while he was riding a bus in San Francisco:

> Holy Peter Holy Allen Holy Kerouac Holy Huncke
> Holy the numberless & the unknown beggars & bums
> Holy the hipsters Holy the Junkies & Criminals
> Holy the Damned Holy the Saved! Holy the Holy . . .

Allen worked as fast as he could, jotting his poem into the notebook he carried with him wherever he went. Caught up in the writing, he wept as he wrote, filling an entire page while he rode on the bus. *Holy* was the ideal word and idea to use in counterpoint to *Moloch* in the second section of "Howl," and Allen was convinced that he had found a fourth and final part for the poem. However, he met resistance when he showed the new section to Kenneth Rexroth, who disapproved of further additions to it. "No, no, that's enough," Rexroth said, advising Allen to leave the poem in its original three parts.

"Howl" was by no means the only object of Allen's attention that fall. Stimulated by his newfound acceptance in the poetry community, he enjoyed one of his most productive creative periods. On September 8, while listening to Bach's Organ Prelude and Fugue in A Minor, he had begun a poem that celebrated "the straining aching joy of knowledge"—the vision—he felt as he contemplated a tall long-stemmed flower he had placed in a peanut bottle: just as all things exist, all things were also created. Hearing the masterful work of Bach reminded Allen of the sensation he had felt in Harlem when he looked at the cornices of the building roofs and realized that the struggle to create was also the struggle to survive. Time passed, nature was cyclical, but in art, one could offer "the presence of the Creator" to the world. In his new poem, initially entitled "The Trembling of the Veil" but changed later to "Transcription of Organ Music," Ginsberg used his now-familiar flower symbol to demonstrate the natural yearning to grow and survive, even if nature demanded death at the end of a season.

Throughout this fertile writing period, Allen filled his journal pages with anything that crossed his mind—single lines of poetry for later use, longer fragments of poems, dream entries, notes for composition, lines of conversation, sketches, and improvisational haiku; he was coming up with more ideas than he had time to develop into poetry. In recent years, he had mulled over a way to write a long prophetic poem that addressed what he perceived to be the spiritual and cultural decline of America. In his journal, he began notes for such a poem, employing the fixed-base method that had been so useful in "Howl":

> America I've given you all and now I'm nothing—
> America when will we end the war?
> America when will you be angelic?
> America when will you take off your clothes and be human?
> America when will you give me back my mother?
> America when will you look at yourself through the grave?
> America when will you be worthy of your million Christs?
> America what's wrong? Why are your libraries full of tears?

America when will you send your eggs to India?
America when will you stop destroying human souls? You lost
    my soul?
America when will you send me a lover?
I Allen Ginsberg Bard out of New Jersey take up the laurel
    tree cudgel from Whitman.

Like "Howl," "America" was a poem that could be infinitely expanded, and
also like "Howl," it was a poem that demanded discipline and restraint on the
part of the poet. If the poem went on too long, it could lose its impact; if it
overextended its use of hyperbole, it would lose the seriousness of its intent.
For the next few months, Allen worked carefully on the poem, working with
its rhythms until he had built a poem with a series of emotional peaks and
valleys. A section would build momentum, reach a climax, and then Ginsberg
would repeat the process. The poem's parting shot—"America I'm putting my
queer shoulder to the wheel"—became one of Ginsberg's most famous lines,
one that managed to encompass both the humor and sense of determination
present throughout the work. The tone of the poem, like the tone present in
most of Ginsberg's Berkeley-period poems, was direct, confident. It was the
voice of the witness/prophet speaking to the masses, the song of a poet convinced that his voice represented the spirits, if not actual experiences, of his
readers: "It occurs to me that I am America." Echoing sentiments expressed a
century earlier by Walt Whitman, Ginsberg was proclaiming in public his
acceptance of his own body and spirit. As he later explained, "*America* is an
unsystematic and rather gay exposition of my own private feelings contrary to
the official dogmas, but really rather universal as far as private opinions about
what I mention. It says 'I am thus and so I have a right to do so, and I'm saying
it out loud for all to hear.' "

This attitude was expanded upon in "Sunflower Sutra," perhaps the most
remarkable of Ginsberg's Berkeley poems. He had been walking in a San
Francisco railroad yard with Jack Kerouac and Philip Whalen when they came
upon an old, battered sunflower, grimy from the dust and soot blown up by
passing trains, "a dead gray shadow against the sky, big as a man, sitting dry
on top of a pile of ancient sawdust," as Allen described it. This was the Blakean
sunflower, wearying of its climb, gone to seed and suffering the indignity of the
discarded refuse blowing about and collecting at its base. Allen was initially
struck by the visual image of the once-beautiful and majestic flower slowly
battered by time and the effects of industrialized civilization; the thought stayed
with him throughout the afternoon. That evening, as he and Kerouac were
starting out for a party, Allen decided to jot down his thoughts, and while Jack
stood waiting by the door, he grabbed a pencil and scribbled down the poem,
describing the scene at the railroad yard as he remembered it. He celebrated
the sunflower's life as he celebrated his own, concluding with a statement that
summarized, in one long line, the Whitmanesque celebration of self that became
the central theme of many of his Berkeley poems:

We're not our skin of grime, we're not a dread bleak dusty
imageless locomotive, we're all beautiful golden sunflowers

inside, we're blessed by our own seed & golden hairy naked
accomplishment bodies growing into mad black formal
sunflowers in the sunset, spied on by our eyes under the
shadow of the mad locomotive riverbank sunset Frisco hilly
tincan evening sitdown vision.

Composed in only twenty minutes, "Sunflower Sutra" is by far the most
successful of Ginsberg's spontaneously composed poems. With the exception of
only a few words, the published version is identical to the original draft, with
no rearrangement of lines or thoughts. In writing the poem, Ginsberg borrowed
heavily from "In back of the real," his earlier San Jose poem about finding a
flower in a railroad yard, but his use of the long line in the newer poem enabled
his thoughts to gain momentum and, ultimately, greater impact. Ginsberg's use
of physical detail heightens the visionary aspects of the poem while reducing
the sentimentality that might have lessened its artistic value:

leaves stuck out like arms out of the stem, gestures from the
    sawdust root, broke pieces of plaster fallen out of the black
    twigs, a dead fly in its ear
Unholy battered old thing you were, my sunflower O my soul
    I loved you then! . . .

In a five-month period, Allen had written or begun three major works
("Howl," "America," "Sunflower Sutra") and a handful of lesser, yet still-
effective poems (including "Transcription of Organ Music," "A Supermarket
in California," "A Strange New Cottage in Berkeley," and "Sather Gate Illumination"). In retrospect, it is not difficult to see why this happened. For Ginsberg,
the circumstances could not have been better. Throughout his life, Ginsberg
enjoyed his most productive periods when he could rely on friends—particularly
Kerouac and Burroughs—for artistic input. Unlike many writers and poets who
rely on solitude as a prerequisite for the creation of their work, Ginsberg thrived
in a community setting. In Berkeley, he had Kerouac, Cassady, and Orlovsky
nearby, and he was developing lasting friendships with Snyder, Whalen, Mc-
Clure, Ferlinghetti, and others; in Kenneth Rexroth, he had a literary elder.
These people, combined with the success of the Six Gallery, the added incentive
of the impending publication of his work, and the fact that he was working
full-time as a poet for the first time in his life, formed an ideal environment for
Ginsberg. In the span of a half year, he had grown and matured far beyond the
changes he had undergone in Mexico. He was no longer the uncertain, rather
directionless poet he had been, yearning for love and acceptance. He was self-
confident as a person and poet, ready to help launch, if not lead, a new literary
movement into public awareness.

2

The Six Gallery reading solidified the already-forming spirit of community
among the San Francisco poets. Poetry readings abounded, the artists sharing
a sense of camaraderie rather than competition, as a result of the attention they

were gaining. The East Coast faction—Kerouac and Ginsberg, particularly, and, to a lesser extent, Philip Lamantia, who had moved from New York to San Francisco years earlier—fit in well with the West Coast artists, though Allen missed Bill Burroughs and wished he was present to take part in the revelry. "Burroughs is in Tangiers I don't think he'll come back it's sinister," he wrote, all the while making a point of keeping Bill abreast of the goings-on in Berkeley and San Francisco.

At the center of the literary activity in the Bay Area was the City Lights Bookstore, which featured the best selection of small press and university publications, quality paperbacks, poetry broadsides, radical political texts, and pamphlets and papers available on the West Coast. Lawrence Ferlinghetti loved the eclectic nature of his bookstore's selections and was happy that his shop acted as a lightning rod for the poets, writers, and artists who gathered there and used it as much as a social club as a business enterprise. However, Ferlinghetti was suspicious of the talk he was hearing of a poetry movement or renaissance and, being a true individualist, he was reluctant to become too publicly connected to any group. In addition, as a publisher, he had to maintain a sense of objectivity, even if he was publishing works by people he knew.

Ferlinghetti was born on March 24, in either 1919 or 1920 (he was never absolutely certain) in Yonkers, New York, the youngest of his parents' five sons. His father, Charles Ferlinghetti, had come from northern Italy, changing his name to Ferling sometime after he arrived in the United States. An auctioneer turned real estate agent, Ferling died of a heart attack the October before Lawrence was born. Lawrence's mother, Clemence, never recovered from the loss of her husband and was admitted to a state mental hospital in Poughkeepsie, New York, before Lawrence had reached his first birthday. The family broke up, the four older boys going to live in an Ossining, New York, boarding house while Lawrence stayed in New York City with his mother's uncle, Ludovic Monsanto, and his French wife, Emily. The Monsanto marriage broke up shortly after Lawrence arrived. Emily took Lawrence to live in Strasbourg, a city in northern France near the German border. Lawrence's first language was French, and from his years in the country, he formed a lasting love of the culture.

Four years later, Lawrence returned to the States, due to a reconciliation between the Monsantos. The marriage failed again, and Emily Monsanto, unable to care for Lawrence, sent him to an orphanage in Chappaqua, New York. A half year later, Emily found employment as a governess for Presley and Anna Lawrence Bisland, a wealthy family living in a Bronxville mansion. The job provided room and board, as well as an environment in which Emily could keep an eye on a child, so as soon as she was established, Emily sent for Lawrence.

The arrangement did not last long. For a while, Emily continued to act as Ferlinghetti's mother, taking care of him and teaching him to read, but one Sunday, on her usual day off, she left the mansion and never came back. Rather than return Lawrence to an orphanage, the Bislands kept him with them. Anna Bisland's father, William Van Duzer Lawrence, had founded Sarah Lawrence College, and the Bislands, not surprisingly, placed great value on education and culture. Presley Bisland had a large library well stocked with Greek and Roman classics, which he encouraged Lawrence to read; he also did a little writing of his own and started a small newsletter that published poetry and short fiction. If the Bislands had a flaw, it was that they were not physically affectionate or demonstrative people. They took good care of Lawrence, providing him with every comfort except, perhaps, the feeling of love that a young child craves.

The Bislands lost a large amount of money when the stock market crashed in 1929, and though they were not financially ruined, they determined that they could no longer afford to provide Lawrence with the standard of education they felt he deserved. Once again, he was on the move, this time to live with Zolla Larned Wilson and her fifteen-year-old son, Bill. Lawrence adapted to his new home. He got along well with Bill, who taught him how to play basketball and assumed the role of an older brother. As an adolescent, Lawrence was part Tom Sawyer, part Huck Finn: He played on a basketball team, delivered newspapers, joined the Boy Scouts, and enjoyed working in his junior high school print shop; he also cut classes on occasion and ran around with a rowdy group of boys who called themselves the Parkway Road Pirates. He had no sooner earned his Eagle Scout ranking than he was picked up for shoplifting pencils at a dime store, hardly a capital offense, but enough to make his foster mother wonder whether he needed more discipline than she was giving him.

Mrs. Wilson enrolled Lawrence in Mount Hermon, a private boys school in Massachusetts known for its strict academic and behavior standards. Ferlinghetti resumed his reading of the classics, including *Don Quixote, Walden, Look Homeward, Angel,* and *The Scarlet Letter*—all books which, in one way or another, dealt with the loners of society. For his sixteenth birthday he was given a French-English volume of Baudelaire's poetry, which instilled in him the desire to write poetry. When he graduated from high school in 1937, he made a significant name change, going from the Lawrence Ferling Monsanto of his boyhood to Lawrence Monsanto Ferling, a name he would keep until 1955, when he discovered the surname Ferlinghetti on his birth certificate.

His appreciation of Thomas Wolfe led him to the University of North Carolina, the school that Wolfe had attended. By this time, he was writing a great deal. Beside the articles he wrote as a member of the sports staff at *Carolina Magazine,* he was writing poems and short stories and had attempted a novel. He enrolled in a creative writing class taught by Phillips Russell, whose literary tastes included such populist poets as Carl Sandburg, Edgar Lee Masters, and Vachel Lindsay. Ferlinghetti was a mediocre student, earning his B.S. in 1941. Carl Sandburg delivered his class's commencement address.

In June 1941, Ferlinghetti enlisted in the navy, setting into motion the events that would have tremendous impact on his life. Although the United States had yet to formally enter World War II, the navy had initiated a vigorous officer-training program in which qualified candidates were put through an intense three-month training regimen, emerging as commissioned officers upon completion of the program. Ferlinghetti was one of these "ninety-day wonders." He began his active duty as an ensign and was eventually promoted to the rank of lieutenant. For nearly two years, he performed his duties in relative safety, working first as part of a convoy protecting merchant ships traveling along the East Coast, and in the Murmansk run—a huge convoy across the Atlantic. He then moved across the ocean, where he received his first command, as skipper in charge of a subchaser protecting ships along the coast of England. In early June

1944, he was dispatched to France, where he became a part of the historic D-Day invasion and liberation of Paris. Looking out at the horizon and seeing the massive armada of ships advancing toward the beach in the early morning hours of June 6 was "a fantastic, dramatic sight"—one he would never forget. It would have been difficult for a young man not to be impressed by the sight of such power converging on its mission. Ferlinghetti, however, was not to be spared a glimpse of the awful effects of great military power put into motion. With the Allies assuming control of the European front, Ferlinghetti was eventually transferred to the Pacific front. He docked in Sasebo, Japan, on August 28, 1945, nineteen days after the bombing of Nagasaki and the first day of the American occupation. During his stay in Japan, Ferlinghetti took a train to Nagasaki, where he saw firsthand the decimation caused by the atom bomb. "You'd see hands sticking out of the mud," he told biographer Neeli Cherkovski, "all kinds of broken teacups . . . hair sticking out of the road—a quagmire— people didn't realize how total the destruction was." To that point, he had seen war from one perspective, but the horrors of Nagasaki changed him permanently.

After the war, Ferlinghetti used the GI Bill to enroll in graduate school at Columbia. He was impressed by Lionel Trilling, Mark Van Doren, and other members of the school's notable faculty. Allen Ginsberg and his friends were still around campus, but Ferlinghetti, as a graduate student, did not have occasion to meet them. He received his M.A. in 1947 and, with money still coming to him from the GI Bill, he returned to France, where he planned to pursue his doctorate degree and write. He worked on a novel, *The Way of Dispossession*, which he submitted unsuccessfully first to a contest sponsored by Doubleday, and then to Simon & Schuster. He began a series of cantos and took notes for a new novel, eventually published as *Her*.

Ferlinghetti immersed himself in the activities of Paris. He may not have been comfortable in New York, but he was enamored with the French capital, with its cafés, bookshops, museums, and theaters. His ambitious doctoral thesis, "The City as a Symbol: In Search of a Metropolitan Tradition," required voluminous reading, and he spent many hours studying the works of Eliot, Crane, Mayakovsky, García Lorca, Whitman, and others. Beside his own creative writing, which was still his major focus, Ferlinghetti renewed his long-standing interest in painting; he hung around two art schools and joined their life drawing and painting classes without formally enrolling.

He received his degree from the Sorbonne in 1949. A short time later, he began seeing a lot of Seldon Kirby-Smith. Kirby had attended Columbia at the same time as Ferlinghetti and had even attended some of the same classes; she had noticed him there and had wanted to meet him, but she never found the right opportunity. They spent many hours together in France and, upon returning to the States in December 1950, decided to get married. They moved to San Francisco shortly after their April 1951 wedding.

In Ferlinghetti's eyes, San Francisco had a cosmopolitan environment not unlike the one he had experienced in Paris. He found a job writing art criticism, covering the art exhibits in San Francisco for *Art Digest*. It was low-paying work, but a valuable experience that afforded him the chance to combine two of his great loves, writing and art. He wrote for other publications as well, including the *San Francisco Chronicle*, for which he reviewed books of poems. He met a number of local poets, including Kenneth Patchen, Kenneth Rexroth, and Robert Duncan, Ferlinghetti becoming a regular visitor to Rexroth's and Duncan's respective poetry meetings, where poetry and politics were discussed with the same passion as in Paris's café society.

One of the local publishing figures Ferlinghetti met was Peter Martin, editor of *City Lights*, a magazine devoted to early pop culture. Ferlinghetti submitted his translations of five poems by French poet Jacques Prévert for publication in the magazine, and Martin came to regard Ferlinghetti more as an authority on poetry and as a translator than as a poet himself. Martin discussed with Ferlinghetti the idea of opening a bookstore that dealt almost exclusively in paperbacks, which Martin felt were the publishing trend of the future. Ferlinghetti was enthusiastic about the plan. Each invested five hundred dollars for stock and in June 1953, the City Lights Bookstore was opened for business. The store was tiny, but once word about its unique nature spread around the Bay Area, it became one of the popular meeting spots in the area.

For Ferlinghetti, that was only the beginning. He had entertained publishing ambitions that dated back to his boyhood print-shop experiences, and he saw the bookstore enterprise as an ideal way to launch a series of inexpensive poetry pamphlets. The pamphlets could be published under the City Lights imprint and sold in the store. Running a bookstore was a huge challenge in itself. After Martin sold his share of the bookstore to Ferlinghetti and moved to New York in 1955, Ferlinghetti published *Pictures of the Gone World*, a sequence of untitled autobiographical poems that helped establish his reputation as a poet in San Francisco. With its small, square format, the book became the prototype for the City Lights "Pocket Poets" series to follow.

Ferlinghetti met Allen Ginsberg that same August. Ginsberg was searching for a publisher for *Empty Mirror*. He also brought word about two of his friends, Jack Kerouac and William Burroughs, neither of whom were in town. Both, Allen assured Ferlinghetti, were excellent writers. Although he rejected Ginsberg's volume of poems, Ferlinghetti liked Allen personally, and the two were sometimes seen together in the local nightspots and cafés. When Allen showed Lawrence a draft of his poem "Howl," Ferlinghetti was convinced that he had heard one of the voices of the future, and he was eager to publish Ginsberg's poem as an important part of his "Pocket Poets" series. He would be Ginsberg's main publisher for the next twenty-five years and, in return, Ginsberg would supply him with work that would help secure the success of his publishing adventure.

3

By late 1955, Allen Ginsberg had enough confidence in his work that he sent copies of a revised (yet still incomplete) version of "Howl," as well as a sheaf of his other Berkeley poems, to his father and William Carlos Williams. Allen had not been in contact with Williams since his departure from New York in late 1953, and the evolution of his poetry was nothing less than astonishing. "Look what I have done with the long line," he told Williams, suggesting that the poems were "best & clearest [when] read aloud." The long line, Allen wrote, encouraged the spontaneous notation of the "expressive human feeling" that he felt was generally missing in the works of academically accepted contemporary poets. "The release of emotion is one with the rhythmical buildup of the long line," he concluded.

Williams's response was favorable, though somewhat guarded. "You have something to say and say it supremely well," Williams replied, acknowledging "Howl" to be Ginsberg's most successful poem to date. Williams had suffered a stroke and had difficulty reading long poems, and as a result he was generally unenthusiastic about seeing poems of "Howl" 's length; further, he thought "Howl" was weak toward the end of its first part and he advised Allen to do "a little pruning at that point." Ferlinghetti had written Williams with the request that he introduce Allen's book of poems, and Williams had agreed. Despite all this, Williams was not as sold on the merits of the Bay Area poets as was Allen. Although he didn't say as much to Ginsberg, Williams had reservations about what he called the "nutty experimentation" in some of the new poetry being written by the San Francisco poets. Yet, as he allowed to fellow poet Louis Zukofsky, the poor poetry would be forgotten soon enough, along with the stodgy academic poetry that was preventing American literature from experiencing the "great dawn" it so deserved.

Louis Ginsberg's reactions to Allen's poems were equally mixed. From a personal standpoint, Louis wanted his son to succeed and he was gratified by Allen's early success on the West Coast. However, as a poet trying to access Allen's work with a critical eye, Louis was offended by Allen's use of profanity, which he strongly urged Allen to trim from the final versions of the poems. "There is no need for dirty, ugly words, as they will entangle you, unnecessarily, in trouble," Louis counseled his son. When Allen subsequently argued that as an artist he needed the freedom to express himself without such restraints, Louis disagreed. "Too many writers will not be able to distinguish between filth and zealism," he insisted. "To act out inner fantasy is a danger touched with psychopathology and lunacy. There must be a bar somewhere: I go for rivers, even strong ones, having *banks*." These misgivings stated, Louis praised "Howl" as "a wild, rhapsodic, explosive outpouring with good figures of speech flashing by on its volcanic rushing," "a hot geyser of emotion suddenly released in wild abandon from subterranean depths of your being." He wished both poet and poem well.

In January 1956, Allen and Gary Snyder set off on a hitchhiking journey to Seattle. Both were scheduled to read at Reed College, Snyder's alma mater, as well as at the University of Washington and the Community Theatre in Bellingham, and Allen used the occasion to clear his head of the San Francisco scene, which now, with all the work on his poetry and readings and socializing, seemed barely under control. He and his friends had been partying almost nightly, drinking too much and taking part in the late-night orgies that Kerouac would describe in great detail in *The Dharma Bums*, his novel about the period. On one occasion, Allen and Jack had been kicked out of Kenneth Rexroth's home for their drunken rowdyism; Allen had suggested that he was the better poet, which, to Rexroth, was about as great an insult as he intended to listen to from the young upstart poets.

If all this wasn't enough of a distraction, there had been a tragic occurrence

on November 30 when Natalie Jackson, Neal Cassady's lover since his separation from Carolyn, had fallen six stories from the top of a building to her death,
a victim of circumstances that stunned Allen, Neal, Jack, and their circle of
friends. After he moved to San Francisco, Neal had become obsessed with
horse racing and tried to devise a betting scheme to use at the racetrack.
Believing he had a foolproof system, he went to Cupertino to withdraw ten
thousand dollars he and Carolyn had accumulated from their investments, and
because he needed Carolyn's signature to withdraw the money, he took Natalie
Jackson along to pose as his wife and forge her signature on the papers. When
Carolyn found out about the withdrawal, she wrote Neal to inform him of her
knowledge of his deception. The bank official wanted to press charges against
Natalie, Carolyn wrote Neal, but she had talked him out of it, going so far as
to drive to Cupertino and give the papers a legitimate signature. "I tried to
explain that you thrive on punishment," Carolyn told Neal of her conversation
with the banker, concluding that there was now "nothing to do but try something different, and hope the horses come in."

The horses did not come in and, in fact, Neal lost all the money. Overwhelmed by guilt from her duplicity in Neal's crime, Natalie grew despondent,
taking amphetamines until, in a week's time, she was pale and gaunt. She was
convinced that the police were going to arrest her, despite Carolyn's letter and
Neal's claims to the contrary. One night, she tried to commit suicide by cutting
her wrists, but she used a dull knife and the cuts were superficial. Still, as Kerouac later remarked of Cassady and himself, "we should have known from her
arms how far she wanted to go." On November 30, Neal asked Jack to keep her
company while he went to work. Natalie was especially depressed, telling Jack
that "this is my last night on earth," and Kerouac could find no way to console
her. Later in the evening, after Neal had returned and gone to bed, Natalie
went up to the apartment building's roof. She broke the glass of the skylight and
used a sliver to cut her wrists. A neighbor, hearing the commotion and seeing
Natalie walking on the roof in nothing but a bathrobe and T-shirt, called the
police. When Natalie saw the police, she panicked, believing they had come to
arrest her, and she moved toward the edge of the building. A police officer
rushed toward her, grabbing her by the wrist, but Natalie slipped out of her
bathrobe and his grip. In trying to escape, she lost her balance and fell off the
roof.

Neal was horrified, "sobered with grief," as Carolyn wrote in her memoir *Off
the Road*; he immediately moved back in with Carolyn, who ignored the events
of recent months and did her best to comfort him. Kerouac was equally shocked.
He had been planning to move on, and within a week he determined that he
should "hit the road and get out of that city of ignorance which is the modern
city." He was at his sister's house in Rocky Mount, North Carolina, by Christmas. As for Allen, Natalie's death signified a time to take refuge. Like Jack and
Neal, he had seen warning signals of Natalie's death wish—"In the car over
for Thanksgiving/you gave me a look so tearful/I knew it was death," he wrote
in an elegiac poem in his journal—yet like his friends, he had not believed
what he saw. In this way, Natalie Jackson was as tragic a figure to Ginsberg as
William Cannastra and Joan Vollmer had been.

Ginsberg's and Snyder's trip to Seattle provided a respite from the events in

San Francisco. Allen walked around the city, filling his notebook with the details that he would work into the poem "Afternoon Seattle." Natalie Jackson's death, along with an altercation he'd had with Gary Snyder, had put Allen in a reflective state, and he would break into tears at the slightest provocation, such as when he listened to certain passages of Bach or visited Seattle's Wobbly Hall or wandered about the city's skid-row district. He went to Bellingham and, from there, took a bus to Vancouver, which impressed him as "a veritable London" with its damp, foggy weather and people garbed in wool sweaters, mackinaws, and thick plaid shirts. His long solitary walks rewarded him with sights that suggested the universality of the human experience:

> Walking down backstreet Dock area sundown back of broke city hall, Salvation Army, rummage sale, swap shops, waterfront cafe, the Shroudy Stranger's hairy boylike rendezvous, like Paterson when he runs down the tincan rubber embankment covered with hay & wilted horse grass to the tackle-field below, happily, a bodhisattva-angel— saint of yore, whirling his rags about him as he gazes at the stars (he knows their names) and runs on the planet from city to city contacting angels of all descriptions in all walks of life.

He returned to San Francisco on February 16, where he was reunited with Peter Orlovsky. During his separation from Peter, Allen had fretted about the nature of their relationship, and he was gratified by Peter's warm welcome. He spent a few days checking in with his friends, filling their ears with details of his trip and participating in the orgiastic scene that was now commonplace in his circle of friends. Then, the reality of daily life setting in once again, he set out to look for a job. Despite all the talk and ideals of living as a full-time poet, he needed money to get by, and since he still hoped to travel to Europe, he needed to save money, as well. He found a job working in the baggage room at the San Francisco Greyhound bus terminal, where he had worked as an extra during the holiday season, loading and unloading buses for fifty dollars a week. The job kept him away from his Berkeley cottage all but a few days a week. The rest of the time, he lived with friends, sleeping on their couches. In no time, he was complaining to friends and family about how his job was taking him away from his real work of writing poetry.

In addition to his job at Greyhound, Allen taught one night a week at San Francisco State, the college responsible for setting up many of the area's poetry readings and workshops. Robert Duncan, a regular teacher, had recently left for Europe, and Ruth Witt-Diamant, one of Ginsberg's biggest boosters, arranged to have him take over the class. Allen liked teaching but found it to be a lot of work. "The thing I do in class is get them personally involved in what they're writing and lambaste anything which sounds at all like they're writing 'literature,' " Allen wrote his father, saying that his goal was "to get them to actually express secret life in whatever form it comes out." Allen went to great extents to make his point. He would talk about Whitman, discuss the merits of smoking marijuana, bring in North Beach street people and poets, and goad his students into angry discussions about spontaneous behavior—anything to get the class to respond. "I practically take off my clothes in class . . . to do it," he quipped, conceding that Louis would probably be shocked if he was to see some of his techniques, noting that his antics would "certainly get me kicked out of anywhere else."

As Kenneth Rexroth noted, San Francisco was by this time the center of a major poetry renaissance, and the rest of the nation was beginning to take notice. A repeat performance of the Six Gallery reading, staged in a Berkeley theater and featuring the same poets who had read at the original gathering, was recorded for possible distribution as a record album. The reading, a huge success, was attended by journalists and photographers from all along the West Coast. *The New York Times* dispatched critic/poet Richard Eberhart to San Francisco to check out the poetry scene and file a report. Ever the promoter, Allen escorted Eberhart about the city and introduced him to some of the local poets, making certain that Eberhart knew about Kerouac, Burroughs, and Corso, among others. At a dinner at Ruth Witt-Diamant's, he read "Howl" in its entirety for Eberhart. In return, Eberhart took Allen to meet Karl Shapiro, whom Allen disliked almost immediately; in Ginsberg's opinion, Shapiro was too stodgy and academic, and he was dismayed by Shapiro's talk of his visit to India and by what he considered to be Shapiro's lack of compassion for the suffering masses in that country.

By the time he left San Francisco, Richard Eberhart was convinced that "the West Coast [was] the liveliest spot in the country in poetry." He liked Allen, finding him to possess a "spiritual quality," "a grasp of significance beyond real things" that he found admirable. He judged "Howl" to be an important work, though he was troubled that the poem did not suggest specifically a better life to replace the evils it depicted.

Allen would discuss the issue with Eberhart at another time. For the moment, he had a much larger debate to consider. When he learned that Ferlinghetti's British printers might experience difficulty getting his book past the customs censors, and that Ferlinghetti had consulted with the American Civil Liberties Union about representation in the event that "Howl" was derailed by the government, Allen prepared himself for battle. He was feeling confident and self-righteous. "I am almost ready to tackle the U.S. Govt out of sheer self delight," he told Louis. Even in his brash enthusiasm, he could not have known how prophetic those words would turn out to be.

4

In April William Carlos Williams delivered to Allen his introduction for *Howl*. Allen had sent Williams a revised version of "Howl" a month earlier, and the New Jersey poet had been excited by it. In his introduction, Williams wrote of the troubled young Ginsberg he had met in the late 1940s:

> [H]e disturbed me, I never thought he'd live to grow up and write a book of poems. His ability to survive, travel, and go on writing aston-ishes me. That he has gone on developing and perfecting his art is no less amazing to me.

Unlike those critics who would see only the violent language and imagery in "Howl" at the cost of missing the poem's sensitivity, humor, and sympathetic stance, Williams targeted the heart of the poem with a few well-aimed sentences. "Howl," he wrote, was indeed a trip through hell, but it was more than the story of one man's survival:

> The wonder of the thing is not that he has survived but that he, from the very depths, has found a fellow whom he can love, a love he celebrates without looking aside in these poems. Say what you will, he proves to us, in spite of the most debasing experiences that life can offer a man, the spirit of love survives to ennoble our lives if we have the wit and the courage and the faith—and the art! to persist.

Allen was pleased by Williams's introduction, and now that he had received it, he was compelled to finalize the book itself. Beside "Howl" and "Footnote to Howl," he wanted to include "Sunflower Sutra," "America," "A Supermarket in California," "Transcription of Organ Music," and "The Green Automobile" in the collection. His publisher had ideas of his own. Arguing that "Green Auto" might diminish the impact of some of the other poems in the book, Ferlinghetti discouraged Ginsberg from including it. This left the collection somewhere between pamphlet and booklet size, and since Ferlinghetti intended to add it to the "Pocket Poets" series, it needed a few more poems to round it out. Ferlinghetti suggested "In the Baggage Room at Greyhound," a recent poem that Allen had composed from notes taken while he was working at the bus depot, but Allen resisted the idea, feeling that the poem was too weak in comparison to the others. He looked through his manuscripts and notebooks for other poems to include, setting for himself a May 1 deadline for the completion of the manuscript.

5

Jack Kerouac was back on the West Coast. Over the holiday season, in the late-night solitude of his sister's kitchen in Rocky Mount, he had written in longhand another short novel. One of Kerouac's most beautiful novels, *Visions of Gerard* was a hymn of devotion for Jack's lost brother. The book covered Jack's early years in Lowell, focusing on Gerard's beatitude in suffering. In writing the book, Jack was able to align his inbred Catholicism with his newer passion for Buddhism, all within the context of his brother's final years. Kerouac would always be at his best when he explored his own spirit through the celebration of another, and *Visions of Gerard*, when placed in the chronology of Kerouac's "Duluoz Legend," becomes a crucial statement if one wishes to understand the man Duluoz (Kerouac) grew up to be.

After completing *Visions of Gerard*, Kerouac traveled to New York for a brief visit to Manhattan. He showed the manuscript of his latest novel to an approving Lucien Carr and haunted the neighborhood bars, feeling lonely and old in the presence of unfamiliar young faces. He then returned to North Carolina, where he originally planned to stay until he began his job as a forest lookout in Washington State that summer. Restless and out of place, Jack was happy to leave for the West Coast when Gary Snyder wrote with the news that he was presently staying with a friend in Mill Valley, and that Jack could stay with them if he wished to come out. While in New York, Jack had been disappointed to learn that his Viking Press editor, Malcolm Cowley, was at Stanford rather than his Manhattan office; Cowley and Kerouac had been working together in an effort to put On the Road in a form acceptable to the publisher, and Jack had hoped to see him while he was in New York. Now he had a new plan. He would visit Cowley at Stanford and, when their work was finished, drop by Synder's before he went to Washington and Gary departed for Japan.

The cross-country journey took longer than Jack had anticipated, and Cowley was no longer at Stanford when he arrived. The trip, however, was not a total loss. His reunion with Snyder was both joyful and productive. When Gary suggested that Jack write his own sutra, Jack responded with The Scripture of the Golden Eternity, a beautiful statement of philosophy based on his Catholic and Buddhist beliefs.

Mill Valley was a short ride from San Francisco, and to Allen Ginsberg's delight, Jack was a frequent visitor to the city. When the Six Gallery reading was re-created in Berkeley, Jack was in his familiar place, passing the hat and buying wine and acting as the reading's main cheerleader. As far as Allen was concerned, Kerouac was an essential component in the movement taking place in the Bay Area. Even if he chose not to read, he was an important presence, an inspirational force uniting the East and West coasts, prose and poetry.

Another influential figure from the East to visit California that spring was Robert Creeley, poet and teacher at Black Mountain College in North Carolina. Featuring such resident artists/teachers as dancer Merce Cunningham, painter Willem de Kooning, poet Charles Olson, and composer John Cage, Black Mountain College boasted one of the most innovative faculties in the country. Creeley edited the Black Mountain Review, the school's distinguished literary magazine. He knew of Jack Kerouac, having read "Jazz of the Beat Generation" and "The Mexican Girl," the latter an excerpt from On the Road that had recently been published in The Paris Review. Through Rexroth, a contributor to his magazine, Creeley had heard of the burgeoning poetry scene in San Francisco. He had come to the West Coast with the hope of meeting Kerouac and finding contributors to his magazine.

Not surprisingly, he ran into Allen before he met Jack. Allen was full of news about the West Coast poets and their individual abilities, so much so that Creeley eventually appointed Allen guest coeditor of the Spring 1957 issue— an important decision because, in selecting works by Kerouac, Burroughs, Snyder, Whalen, McClure, and himself for inclusion in the issue, Ginsberg was in effect bringing the West Coast poetry movement to the East. Allen arranged for Creeley to meet Kerouac at The Place, a North Beach tavern, and the two hit it off well. Creeley, a tall, dark New Englander with a quick temper, was not only enthusiastic about discussing poetry but he could match Jack drink for drink in a bar, as well. On occasion, Creeley's drinking got him in trouble. During his stay in San Francisco, he was involved in several drunken altercations. More harmful perhaps, Creeley, who had recently separated from his wife, met and fell in love with Martha Rexroth. When Kenneth Rexroth learned of their affair, he blamed Kerouac, now one of Creeley's constant companions, for somehow orchestrating their meeting.

In early May, Gary Snyder left for his two-year stay in Japan. Before he left, there was a wild three-day party in Mill Valley, an event that in some ways represented the last gasp of true unity among the San Francisco poets. There were already noticeable tensions setting in among the various members of the group, and these, combined with the poets' travelings, threatened to disrupt the camaraderie they had enjoyed for over six months. At Snyder's party, food and wine circulated freely, Rexroth expounded on poetry, and people took turns pounding bongo rhythms on overturned cans. Music blared into the night; people danced. John Montgomery, wearing a sharp new suit, sat by himself and read *Mad* magazine. A bonfire burned out in the yard. Allen, Gary, and Peter walked around naked, living symbols of the nakedness they wished to achieve in their poetry. At the end of one day, people slept in blankets and sleeping bags on the floor, only to rise and begin anew the next. On the last day of the party, Kerouac and Snyder snuck out for one final hike, Gary preparing a special meal to celebrate their last time together in nature. They discussed East and West, Buddhism and Christianity. After teasing Jack that he was, and always would be, Catholic—"I can just see you on your death bed kissing the cross like some old Karamozov or like our old friend Dwight Goddard who spent his life as a Buddhist and suddenly returned to Christianity in his last days"—Gary Snyder made a prediction that, in retrospect, was a remarkably accurate forecast of what would occur in the 1960s. Kerouac recorded the statement in *The Dharma Bums*:

> East'll meet West anyway. Think of what a great world revolution will take place when East meets West finally, and it'll be guys like us that can start the thing. Think of the millions of guys with rucksacks on their backs tramping around the back country and hitchhiking and bringing the word down to everybody.

6

Allen still had his mind set on visiting Europe, with maybe a stop in Tangier along the way. He heard from Bill Burroughs almost every week. Bill's letters were full of newsy items of his life in Morocco, but even more important, as far as Allen was concerned, were the short "routines" that Bill enclosed with his letters. Allen had been enjoying Burroughs's darkly comic sketches for years, and it was now obvious, from the enclosures in Burroughs's mailings, that he had developed into a first-rate craftsman. With his continuing on-again, off-again problems with drugs, Burroughs needed someone—friend or editor—to help him organize his literary output into a publishable form, and Allen believed he might be able to help.

To earn money for such a trip, he signed on as a yeoman storekeeper on the *Pvt. Joseph F. Merrill*, a ship presently docked in the Bay Area. The ship was scheduled to depart on June 8 for Honolulu, return on June 30 to Seattle, and proceed from there to the Arctic. Allen was less than thrilled about having to wear khakis to work, but it was a small inconvenience when pitted against his $5,040 annual salary. With any luck, he wrote his brother, he would be able to save at least one thousand dollars for his European visit.

Allen had received splendid news from Eugene: On May 19, his wife, Connie, had delivered a nine-pound boy to whom they had given the name Alan Eugene. Allen was greatly moved by the honor. "Thanks for naming the baby after me," he wrote. "It'll be an illustrious name (but perhaps in disrepute when my poems are published). I almost cried thinking that you cared that much to name it Alan."

A few weeks later, Allen heard from Eugene again, but this time the news was not joyful. On June 9, Naomi Ginsberg had died unexpectedly of a cerebral hemorrhage in Greystone. Thinking that Allen might have left for Hawaii, Eugene sent a telegram to Peter Orlovsky in San Francisco, requesting that he forward the news to Allen. As it was, Allen was not at sea as planned but had been dividing his time between Peter's San Francisco apartment and the Milvia Street cottage, which, in his absence, he was leaving to Philip Whalen. He was not in San Francisco the evening the news arrived. Peter went to Berkeley and gently broke the news to Allen. Allen stepped outside the cottage and, as he wrote in "Kaddish," "bent my head to the ground under the bushes near the garage—knew she was better—at last—not left to look on Earth alone."

For years, Allen had felt helpless in watching his mother's losing battle against madness. As recently as May 18, he had tried to devise a way to free Naomi from the wards of Greystone. His latest plan, detailed in a letter to Eugene, involved his moving her in with Peter Orlovsky's mother on Long Island. "The main problem with Naomi is that nobody wants or can keep her," Allen said, offering to contribute to the cost of her stay with Katherine Orlovsky. "It's not necessary that she be sane to live outside, just peaceable, and the new pacifying drugs seem to do that from what I read in the papers."

Naomi's letters never failed to touch Allen's heart. Even as her mind betrayed her, she was capable of lovely maternal feelings. She would worry that Allen wasn't getting enough to eat, or about his general health; she advised him on his schooling and social life. "How is my young one?" she wrote as an opening to one letter, only to follow with messages that made clear the fact she was still mentally unbalanced, all of which left Allen in painful ambivalence. Soon after he sent his suggestion that Naomi move in with Peter's mother, Eugene and Connie Brooks visited Greystone to see whether Naomi was capable of handling such a move. Louis, too, had considered Allen's proposal. However, Naomi was in no shape to leave the sanatorium.

Naomi's death left Allen feeling empty. "My childhood is gone with my mother," he wrote in his journal. "My memory becomes less clear. My body will go. There is no me left. Naomi is a memory. My 30 years is a memory to me." He wrote Louis a loving letter, calling for the family to stay as close as they had all felt in remembering Naomi.

Allen did not make the cross-country trip to attend his mother's funeral and burial on June 11. Louis wanted a small service and, in fact, did not inform his side of the family of the services until after they had occurred, an unfortunate decision, because at the gravesite there were not enough men present to have a Kaddish read. With only seven mourners in the cortege, Eugene noted, "it was the smallest funeral on record." After viewing the body and saying a few prayers at a funeral parlor in Hempstead, Long Island, the group drove to Beth Moses Cemetery in Farmington—the same place where Naomi's sister, Elanor, was buried. A sexton read a few more prayers as the casket was lowered into the earth. She was finally at rest, thought Louis. "The pathos and tragedy of her well-meaning life, the constant struggles within her, the flashes of our happy early moments together—all blinded me," Louis said in a letter to Allen. "Though Fate had removed her physically from me the last few years, I confess she was in my heart always. There was no day during which I was in a crowd or happy that thoughts of Naomi, torn within herself and cooped up in a desolate room, did not invade my mind." He would sleep better in knowing that she was at peace.

In this family of poets, proper and heartfelt memorials followed. Eugene composed "To My Mother," an excellent poem that was published in *The New York Times*; two lines from the poem were placed on Naomi's headstone. Louis also wrote a poem, "Burial," a lyric piece about Naomi's funeral; it, too, appeared in the *Times*. Concerned that the Kaddish had not been read for his mother, Allen wrote his father and asked him to send a copy of this formal prayer. If it was impossible to have the Kaddish read, Allen thought, he would have to write one for her himself.

7

At the beginning of July, Allen was at sea, aboard the USNS *Sgt. Jack J. Pendleton*, a ship bound for the Arctic Circle. Allen figured the journey would be a long one. The ship was delivering supplies to the Distant Early Warning radar system and had to stop in Portland, Seattle, and Tacoma to pick up cargo. Allen estimated that he would be fortunate to be back in San Francisco by October. As he stood on the ship's deck in the late-afternoon light, watching San Francisco grow smaller until it appeared to be "a long green earthen isle set in the bay eroded & left there unused," he wondered what it would be like to stand on the ship's fantail deck and lean on an iron rail, "shouting my poetry to the pure roaring sea."

He took with him his journal, a satchel of poems, and the proofs for *Howl and Other Poems*. The proofs were a mess, requiring a lot of work. When they had submitted the manuscript to their printer, neither Ginsberg nor Ferlinghetti had sent the typesetter specific instructions regarding the line breaks on the printed page, an oversight that became problematic due to the unique smaller-page structure of "Pocket Poets" books. This left Ferlinghetti's English typesetter with the task of trying to judge where to break the long lines in "Howl," and when Allen saw the results, he was not at all pleased. "The writing is sloppy enough as it is without it being fouled up typographically too," he complained to Eugene. Still, he did not want to saddle Ferlinghetti with the burden of paying for corrections, so he wrote his publisher and offered to pay for them himself. *

Allen also learned from the proofs that he had misjudged how much space his poetry would take up in the book. He had come up short, and to fill out

---

* Ginsberg would always have a certain amount of difficulty with the typesetting of his poetry's long lines. Whitman, he explained, wanted his long lines to run entirely to the right margin of the published page—a format that Ginsberg himself preferred to follow and which, he said in 1922, he intended to apply eventually to all of his published long-line poetry.

the proposed fifty-page booklet, he would have to choose several more poems for inclusion. He was still reluctant to include "In the Baggage Room at Greyhound," which, he told Ferlinghetti somewhat hyperbolically, "stinks on ice." As an "appendix" to the book, he and Ferlinghetti considered some of Allen's early poems, settling on "An Asphodel," "Song," "Wild Orphan," and "In back of the real" as poems to be placed at the end of the book.

Allen was quite naturally concerned that his first book of poems turn out exactly the way he intended, even at the additional cost and delay of publication, but he was given added incentive when he arrived in Tacoma and received the mail that had been forwarded there by Philip Whalen. Among the correspondence was a letter from his mother, postmarked, oddly enough, two days after her death. It was one of the most lucid communications Allen had ever received from her. Naomi began by extending her best wishes on Allen's birthday, and from there she proceeded to offer maternal advice. She worried about his job and marital prospects, and she advised him to take plenty of warm clothing to the North Pole; she cautioned him against drinking too much. Allen had sent her a mimeographed copy of "Howl," which she had read. "It seemed to me your wording was a little hard. Do tell me what father thinks of it," Naomi wrote, adding that she was happy that Allen was getting his poetry published. The wires were still in her head, she informed Allen, but her doctors knew about it and were trying to correct it.

> I wish I were out of here and home at the time you were young; then
> I would be young. I'm in the prime of life now—
> Did you read about the two men who died at 139 and 149 yrs of age?
> I wonder how they lived.
> I'm looking for a good time.
> I hope you are not taking any drugs as suggested by your poetry.
> That would hurt me. Don't go in for ridiculous things.
>
> With love &
> good news,
> (mother) Naomi.

Deeply moved, Allen sent the letter to Eugene, with instructions that he read it and send it on to Naomi's brother in California. No doubt, Louis would see the letter as well. "I have been thinking a lot," Allen wrote to Eugene. "We all die, life's a short flash. Standing on the prow of the ship with roaring ocean and stars and force of wind in sleeves, great majesty and tenderness to life, at its heart, a kind of instantaneous universal joy at creation, and everything in the ocean moves."

The letter only strengthened Allen's resolve about seeing *Howl* into print the way he intended it. There was a spirit, not only in the title poem but in others ("we're all beautiful golden sunflowers inside," "I had a moment of clarity, saw the feeling in the heart of things, walked out to the garden crying"), that reflected Naomi's struggle to "think nothing but beautiful thoughts" in a world otherwise filled with madness. *Howl and Other Poems*, then, could stand as a memorial to his mother.

For his book's epigraph, Allen wanted a quote from Whitman. Looking through *Leaves of Grass*, he drew up a list of six quotations, each indicative of a different element of the book:

> I will therefore let flame from me the burning fires
>   that were threatening to consume me . . .
> I will give them complete abandonment
> I will write the evangel-poem of comrades and of love.
>   *
> Shall I postpone my acceptation and realization
>   and scream at my own eyes?
>   *
> This is the meal equally set, this is the meat for
>   natural hunger.
>   *
> My final merit I refuse you, I refuse putting from me
>   what I really am
> I know perfectly well my own egotism.
>   *
> America isolated yet embodying all, what is it finally
>   but myself.

And the quotation he eventually chose:

> Unscrew the locks from the doors!
> Unscrew the doors themselves from their jambs!

Given the nature of *Howl and Other Poems*, with its celebration of self, Ginsberg's selection was a natural one. In addition, he was reading *The Solitary Singer*, Gay Wilson Allen's critical biography of Whitman, a book that led Allen to conclude that Whitman was a saintlike figure whose repressed homosexuality was a tragic flaw. "His feelings were very real and there seemed no possibility of expression," Ginsberg wrote of Whitman in his journal. "Howl" was an extension of the Whitmanesque expression, without repression.

Allen's trip to the Arctic Circle constituted a time of meditation. Besides the Whitman biography, he read biographies of St. Francis of Assisi and St. Teresa of Avila, as well as a volume of the *Lives of the Saints*. He began the Old Testament and was determined to read it in its entirety before he returned to San Francisco. His mother's death reminded him more than ever of the transitory nature of human existence, and he was suddenly compelled to determine for himself how exemplary lives fit into history.

When his ship reached the Bering Strait on July 27, Allen strained for a view of Russia, his mother's homeland, but fog prevented him from seeing anything but birds flying between the two continents:

> Funny gaiety of Joke
> To cross the Bering Straits

and not see nothing but
the same old grey sea.

Allen stood on the deck, watching the birds fly over the whitecaps. After recording his impressions in his journal, he dug into his pockets and tossed seven cents into the sea, "in remembrance of Naomi, so near her Russia." He resolved to write a Kaddish for his mother while he was still at sea.

8

He did not write the Kaddish—not then, not for another two years. He was not yet ready.

As the *Pendleton* worked its way up the coast of Alaska, Allen turned his attention to other works. In his solitude, without other poets around to bolster his self-confidence, he was going through another period of self-doubt. "Earlier years had brought on wave after wave of major poems," he lamented in his journal, citing "Death in Violence," "Denver Doldrums," "The Green Automobile," "Siesta in Xbalba," and "Howl" as examples. Of these poems, only "Howl" had seen its way to publication. Literary magazines were clamoring for Ginsberg's shorter works, which Allen was all too happy to provide, but he could not help but wonder whether publishing his work in this manner was a case of taking the easy way out. Jack Kerouac, whom Allen considered to be a much better writer, had a trunkful of unpublished manuscripts, and Allen was envious of "Jack's holiness and devotion to singleminded expression in his writing," even if that meant struggling to be published. "I myself write nothing and am sick of fragment sketching," he wrote in his journal. "The poems I build are too fragmentary slight."

In the sheaf of poems he took on board, Allen had a revised version of "Siesta in Xbalba." On July 28, he typed up the twenty-two mimeograph sheets necessary to publish the poem himself. The title page read:

Siesta in Xbalba
Published by the Author
July 1956
Near
ICY CAPE, ALASKA
At the Sign of the Midnight Sun

Allen mimeographed fifty-two copies of the poem on the ship's machine and side-stapled them into booklets. He dedicated the poem to Karena Shields, his hostess at the Mexican *finca* where much of the poem had been written. In his journal, Allen was highly critical of the poem. He judged it to be "unbalanced and egotistic," although upon further reflection, he decided that he was being so negative because it seemed "shallow when reading the Life of St. Francis." Whatever his feelings, they did not prevent him from sending copies to his father, publisher, and friends.

In time, Allen would include "Siesta in Xbalba" whenever he listed what he considered to be his better early poems—and for good reason. After years of trying to write an epic-scale poem, only to be thwarted by his own limitations and inexperience, Ginsberg finally wrote a lengthy work that seemed to be freely written, loose from the restrictions of his father's influence, formal education, and youthful struggles to find a voice. In all likelihood, the poem's success can be traced to its prose origins: "Siesta" began as a series of journal entries, written in Ginsberg's shorthand prose, and when the time came for structuring his notes into poetry, the details in the poem were coming from his eyes rather than his mind. In later years, Ginsberg would point out that this is where true "vision" originated in the first place, but this had been a new lesson for him in 1954, when "Siesta" was written. The physical description of the ruins, written by a young poet obviously in awe of them, carries a much greater impact than Ginsberg's earlier word-cluttered works. Further, his own "Xbalba," perhaps best described as that place between the heart (heaven) and mind (earth), is openly evident in his poem. If one is to take at all seriously Ginsberg's prophetic role, one has to become comfortable with this place, for prophets are not mere soothsayers, as the word *prophet* seems to imply today; instead, they are explorers of a region caught between the past and the future, mapmakers using their vision of both to create signposts in the present.

In "Siesta in Xbalba," Ginsberg is clearly at work in this region, whether he is clapping his hands to hear the echoes in the ruins or describing a drug-induced vision of heaven. He is still too young and inexperienced to know what these signs mean either to himself or his readers—at least in terms of his putting his interpretation in clear language in a poem—but his shortcomings do not suffer from the poet's lack of resolve or effort. In "Siesta," Ginsberg continues to focus on place—a lesson he learned from Williams and that he attempted to work into his *Empty Mirror* poems, with varying success—and by using place as an anchor for his thoughts and emotions, he moved closer to presenting the visionary sensation he sought to create in his poems of the late 1940s.

9

Allen returned to San Francisco in September, about a month earlier than he had originally anticipated. With the money he earned from his work on the ship, combined with the thousand dollars he inherited from Naomi, Allen had enough money for a European trip. He had no sooner arrived in San Francisco than he began to make his initial plans for his overseas adventure.

He had seen a finished copy of *Howl and Other Poems* in August, when he received his mail at one of the ports his ship visited. The booklet pleased him. Number Four in the "Pocket Poets" series, *Howl* followed Ferlinghetti, Kenneth Rexroth, and Kenneth Patchen into publication—all very good company for him to keep. The printer had done a creditable job with the restorations of the long lines in the book, which, to Allen's delight, cost only twenty dollars. In a humble mood, he reread the book, "embarrassed by half of it," as he wrote Ferlinghetti. Now that his words were locked into print, he saw the flaws in his poetry, as well as some of the egotism present in the writing. "I'm not sure it deserves all the care you've put into it and the encouragement you've given me," Allen modestly told his publisher.

In the months prior to the publication of Howl, he had given careful consideration to the people to whom he wanted to send complimentary or review copies. There were the obvious choices of family and friends, but Allen, with his marketing experiences, knew the value of strategic product marketing. A few months earlier, he had sent the unpublished mimeographed copies of "Howl," as well as other selected poems, to Mark Van Doren, who was now retired from Columbia University. Allen hoped that Van Doren would comment favorably on the work and, with any luck, pass the poems on to a sympathetic potential reviewer. "If you like the poems please try to get them reviewed in the Tribune if you have any say at all—by someone like [Charles] Olson, someone at least eager & hip," he asked his former teacher. Allen was less certain about how the poems would be received by Lionel Trilling, though he sent him a sheaf of the mimeographed poems, as well. Allen felt the same way about showing his work to such contemporaries as John Hollander and Richard Howard—poets who, by his estimation, were too steeped in traditional, academically accepted forms to appreciate what he was trying to do in "Howl."

Still, there was more to be gained than lost by sending the book to the right people. With this in mind, Allen instructed Ferlinghetti to ship review copies to e. e. cummings, W. H. Auden, Louis Zukofsky, Marianne Moore, T. S. Eliot, Robinson Jeffers, Randall Jarrell, and Ezra Pound, as well as to those established poets he was certain he could count on, people such as Kenneth Rexroth, William Carlos Williams, Richard Eberhart, and Kenneth Patchen. He also had copies sent to Charlie Chaplin and Marlon Brando.

Exactly how Chaplin and Brando reacted to receiving the small square booklet with its stark black and white cover will never be known, but it did not take long for Allen to hear from some of the book's other recipients. Louis Ginsberg, who had seen the poems earlier in the year and remarked favorably on "Sunflower Sutra" and "Howl," used this most recent occasion to praise the shorter poems in the book; in particular, he liked "Song" and "In the Baggage Room at Greyhound," singling out the latter for its "imaginative and concrete details." William Carlos Williams sent Ferlinghetti a brief note, calling Howl "terrific" and saying that he was "flattered to find [himself] in such company." Mark Van Doren liked the poems' long lines. "It lets you say what you want, and furthermore I agree that you have said it," he wrote Allen.

Ginsberg's friends were equally impressed. Gary Snyder, writing from Kyoto, told Allen that he could not read the book without hearing the sound of Allen's voice "ringing in my ears"; "I am carefully figgering where to place these bombs," he said of the four additional copies he had ordered from City Lights. John Clellon Holmes commented on "the beautiful gentleness" of the poems, of their "real tenderness . . . the sweet humors, the wise giggles. . . . You make me love a world whose punished children still can love it so." Lucien Carr, like Holmes, remarked on the humor in "America," and he found the book "very impressive." Although "touched" by Allen's including him on the dedication page, Lucien requested that he omit his name from future editions. He prized "a certain anonymity in life," he said, and he could not maintain any kind of privacy if writers like Ginsberg and Kerouac kept bringing him up in their work.

"I hope you bear that idiosyncrasy in mind in your next book—'Moan,' " Lucien wrote in his trademark sarcasm.

Despite the generally favorable reception of *Howl*, there were two noteworthy voices of dissent. Ezra Pound refused to write Allen about the mimeographed poems he had sent him in early June, electing instead to send Ginsberg's letter to William Carlos Williams with a typed poem of admonishment. "You got more room in yr/house than I hv/in my cubicle," Pound wrote from Saint Elizabeth's mental hospital in Washington, D.C., where he was being held in lieu of being tried for treason for his radio messages during World War II. "If he's yours why dont you teach him the valu of time to those who want to/read something that wil tell 'em wot they dont know." He offered no comment, positive or negative, about Allen's poems.

This was not the case with Lionel Trilling, who was very explicit in his reaction to the poems Allen had sent prior to the publication of *Howl*. "I'm afraid I have to tell you that I don't like the poems at all," Professor Trilling wrote. The poems, in Trilling's view, were "dull," even with their violent or shocking language. "They are not like Whitman—they are all prose, all rhetoric, without any music. . . . There is no real voice here." At one time, Trilling said, he had admired Ginsberg's voice, regardless of his approval or disapproval of the individual poems, but Ginsberg's more recent writing lacked the natural quality that Trilling liked. He rejected the "doctrinal element" in the poems, maintaining that it seemed to be a rehash of a philosophy he had heard before.

Formal reviews of *Howl* were not immediately forthcoming. In the illustrious history of American literary criticism, poetry volumes are by tradition given short shrift in newspaper and magazine book-review sections, the bulk of such reviewing falling in the hands of the literary and university quarterlies. *Howl and Other Poems* was no exception. However, Ginsberg received a huge boost, as did the other poets in the Bay Area, when Richard Eberhart's eagerly awaited article "West Coast Rhythms" appeared in *The New York Times Book Review* on Sunday, September 2, 1956. After framing his article with a brief discussion of the poetry climate in San Francisco and Seattle, citing specifically the influences of Ruth Witt-Diamant and Kenneth Rexroth in the creation of the present poetry environment in San Francisco, Eberhart turned his attention to the individual poets, of whom Ginsberg was, by Eberhart's estimation, clearly the star. "The most remarkable poem of the young group, written during the past year, is *Howl*, by Allen Ginsberg," Eberhart wrote:

> My first reaction was that it is based on destructive violence. It is profoundly Jewish in temper. It is Biblical in its repetitive grammatical build-up. It is a howl against everything in our mechanistic civilization which kills the spirit, assuming that the louder you shout the more likely you are to be heard. It lays bare the nerves of suffering and spiritual struggle. Its positive force and energy come from a redemptive quality of love, although it destructively catalogues evils of our time from physical deprivation to madness.

Eberhart also noted the humor in "America" and "Supermarket in California," and he cited "Sunflower Sutra" as "a lyric poem marked by pathos." He then went on to list Lawrence Ferlinghetti, Philip Whalen, Gary Snyder, and Michael McClure, among others, as significant contributors to the San Francisco poetry movement. Although he took pains to point out that each poet possessed his own individual voice, and warned that one had to approach the concept of a group identity with caution, Eberhart also noted that there was a "new, vital group consciousness now among young poets in the Bay region. . . . They have exuberence and a young will to kick down the doors of older consciousness and established practice in favor of what they think is vital and new."

A widely respected poet's endorsement in the country's most influential book-review section was the greatest bit of publicity Ginsberg could have hoped to receive for his book; Eberhart's article was nothing less than a signal that the established literary community was at least willing to consider the merits of the new voices of the San Francisco poets. Allen made a commendable effort to stay levelheaded in the aftermath of this publicity—"Agh! I'm sick of the whole thing, that's all I think about, famous authorhood, like a happy dream," he wrote Kerouac—but he was nevertheless thrilled by all the attention. In its own way, Eberhart's article justified the past decade of Allen's work.

Louis Ginsberg was ecstatic. Despite his differences of literary opinion with Allen, Louis, ever the proud father, was gracious in extending his congratulations to his son. "Edith keeps a copy [of Eberhart's article] in her purse and shows it to all and sundry. I have passed it around the Newark folks. I rejoice that your book is coming out. I predict it will make a name for you. You may wake up some morning and find yourself famous. I do hope so."

Louis Ginsberg need not have wondered about his son's pending fame. By the time he had received Louis's congratulatory letter, Allen was all but assured of receiving all the attention he could handle. National magazines such as *Mademoiselle* and *Life* wanted to do photo essays on the San Francisco poets. Literary magazines, once unresponsive to Allen's poetry, were now quick to accept his work. Where he had once relied on small publications such as *The Berkeley Review* to print his poems, he now submitted work to such high-visibility periodicals as *Esquire* and *Mademoiselle*, and saw it accepted. New Directions, the distinguished New York publisher of such writers as Federico García Lorca, Ezra Pound, William Carlos Williams, and others, was beginning its own literary magazine, and it snapped up "Sunflower Sutra" and "The Bricklayer's Lunch Hour," among other Ginsberg poems. Barney Rosset and Donald Allen, editors at Grove Press, were also starting a magazine, *Evergreen Review*, the second issue of which was to excerpt Kerouac's *The Subterraneans*, and would eventually be devoted entirely to the San Francisco poets. In his capacity as guest coeditor of *Black Mountain Review*, Allen decided to publish "America," a portion of Kerouac's "October in the Railroad Earth," selections of Burroughs's *Naked Lunch*, and poetry by Gary Snyder, Philip Whalen, and Michael McClure. In historical terms, perhaps the biggest development of all was Viking Press's decision, after two years of discussion, to publish Jack Kerouac's *On the Road*.

Ironically, all the sudden attention paid the San Francisco poets eroded their sense of camaraderie. As unknowns, the poets had relied on each other for mutual support and encouragement; as budding celebrities, they started to feel resentment, competition, and outright hostility toward one another. Some of the older, established poets, such as Kenneth Rexroth and Robert Duncan, resented a bunch of New Yorkers like Ginsberg, Kerouac, and, most recently, Gregory Corso invading their territory and gaining the kind of attention the older poets had sought after years of working in relative anonymity, with only regional or hard-core followings. Rexroth, still blaming Kerouac for being a party in his losing his wife to Robert Creeley, distanced himself from the group. In the short time he had been in San Francisco, Gregory Corso had managed to anger both Neal Cassady and Michael McClure. Some of the younger poets, such as McClure and Philip Whalen, felt that Allen was being too pushy in his self-appointed role as the group's unofficial leader. Despite his good intentions, Allen had alienated some of his friends in his efforts to unite a disparate group of poets into a poetry movement strong enough to take on the literary establishment. Arguments and shouting matches erupted on the street and in corner taverns. Too often, Allen wound up an intermediary trying to soothe hurt feelings.

The widening split between poets was no more apparent than when *Mademoiselle* dispatched a photographer to the West Coast to take pictures of the central characters of what was now being publicly described as the San Francisco Poetry Renaissance. It was to be a group photo to accompany a magazine article about the group—a team picture, so to speak—but it wound up being a symbol of festering resentment. Robert Duncan and Michael McClure demanded separate photo sessions, while Kenneth Rexroth failed to show up at all. In the published photo, only Jack Kerouac, Allen Ginsberg, Gregory Corso, and Philip Whalen appeared in the picture, the photograph depicting four figures posing uncomfortably—a far cry from the free-spirited poets who only a year earlier had taken the city by storm.

10

It was time to move. Jack Kerouac left for Mexico City, where he hoped to finish the novel he had begun about a local prostitute and junky he'd fallen in love with the year before. Allen concocted a plan in which he, Corso, and Peter and Lafcadio Orlovsky would join Jack for a two- or three-week vacation before they headed back to New York. He had not seen his family in almost two years, and he wanted to visit them before he departed for Europe. Eventually, Allen figured, he, Peter, and Lafcadio would all visit Bill Burroughs in Tangier and then proceed to Europe from there.

On October 29, Allen and Gregory began their hitchhiking journey to Southern California. They stopped for a night's visit with the Cassadys in Los Gatos before continuing on to Los Angeles, where Allen had succeeded in getting a poetry reading scheduled for October 30.

The reading, sponsored by *Coastline*, a Los Angeles literary magazine, and emceed by writer/poet Lawrence Lipton, turned out to be almost as legendary as the Six Gallery reading. Although Anaïs Nin was in attendance with a group of Venice West bohemian intellectuals, the audience was largely comprised of the stuffy literary types Allen and Gregory had grown to dislike. As he had done in the past, Allen prefaced his reading with some heavy drinking, and he delivered "Howl" with his customary zest. However, the audience response in Los Angeles was less enthusiastic than it had been in the Bay Area. In San Francisco, Allen was accustomed to hearing drunken yelps of encouragement from his audiences; in Los Angeles, the vocalization from the drunks took the form of heckling.

One particular heckler harassed Ginsberg throughout his reading and was quieted only when Allen promised to give him the chance to express his opinions after the reading. However, he continued to disrupt the reading after Allen had turned it over to Corso. At one point, Gregory proposed a verbal duel with the heckler, the winner being the one with the best "images, metaphors, [and] magic." The heckler was more interested in engaging Corso in a fistfight. He taunted the poets, calling them cowards, insisting they explain what they were trying to prove onstage.

"Nakedness," Ginsberg replied. When the heckler demanded further explanation, Allen left the stage and approached him. He accused the man of wanting to do something brave in front of the audience and then challenged him to take off his clothes. As he walked toward the drunk, Allen stripped off all of his own clothing, hurling his pants and shirt at the now-retreating heckler. "Stand naked before the people," Allen said. "The poet always stands naked before the world." Defeated, the man backed into another room.

The sponsors of the reading were outraged by Ginsberg's conduct, but Lawrence Lipton interceded and was able to convince them to allow Allen and Gregory to finish. Three years later, in his account of the incident, Lipton noted that the heckler approached Allen after the reading, apologized for his behavior, and asked where he might purchase a copy of *Howl and Other Poems*.

Word of Allen's performance spread quickly, and though it would be associated with him—usually in negative terms—in decades to come, he showed no sign of remorse. "Reading we gave in L.A. was the most wild ever," he told Ferlinghetti. "I disrobed finally. Been wanting to onstage for years." When they heard of the incident, Kerouac and Burroughs were amused. "What's with you? You wig already and remove your dry goods inna public hall?" Bill wrote Allen. Jack later wrote a fictional account of the reading in his novel *Desolation Angels*.

On November 7, Allen, Gregory, Peter, and Lafcadio arrived in Mexico City at the 212 Orizaba apartment that Jack Kerouac shared with Burroughs's friend Bill Garver. After staying for a short time in San Francisco to close down Peter's Turner Terrace apartment, the Orlovskys had joined Allen and Gregory in Los Angeles, and from there the four had made their way slowly to Mexico City. They stopped in Tijuana for some sight-seeing, and then went on to Guadalajara, where they met Denise Levertov, a young English poet Allen had heard about. Buoyed by what they believed to be inevitably approaching fame, the group hoped to make their trip to Mexico a final fling before they were confined by the responsibilities of public life. They also hoped that Kerouac, a catalyst in the San Francisco poetry scene, would celebrate with them.

What the group found was an entirely different Kerouac. Wasted and sunken-eyed, Jack seemed content to skulk in the semidarkness of his slum apartment and watch the locals get high on marijuana or Benzedrine. On occasion, he would get high himself or wander the streets in search of a young prostitute. While the others spoke of breakthroughs in their careers—*Howl* was selling well in San Francisco, and Corso's *The Vestile Lady on Brattle* had so impressed Randall Jarrell that the Poetry Consultant to the Library of Congress had asked Gregory to visit him in Washington, D.C.—Jack could only see wheels spinning. He had ended his affair with Esperanza, the fifteen-year-old prostitute and subject of *Tristessa*—his most recently completed novel—on a negative note. He had begun a new novel about his stint as a fire lookout on Desolation Mountain, but he viewed work on the book, which he was calling *The Angels of the World*, as another long-term project that promised no certain returns. Even a five-hundred-dollar offer from Grove Press for the serialization of *The Subterraneans* in Grove's new literary magazine, *Evergreen Review*, failed to lift his spirits. *On the Road* was being prepared for publication, but as far as Jack could determine, it was more out of his threat of withdrawing it from Viking Press than from the publisher's interest in the book. Discouraged by the writing life and unimpressed with Allen's talk of celebrity, Jack considered a change in careers. Perhaps, he told Allen, he would be happier as a jazz singer, drummer, or painter.

Allen listened patiently to Jack's complaints, but he eventually chided his longtime friend for sounding "whiney," like an old junky wasting away to oblivion. They planned out their trip to Tangier, and Allen pepped Kerouac up by taking him on a Mexican sight-seeing tour. They surveyed the Teotihuacán pyramids, visited the Floating Gardens of Lake Xochimilco, and toured Mexico City College, where they met some old Mexican painters. They picked up male and female prostitutes, ate cheap steak dinners, and discussed the direction their lives were taking, the concensus being that they all could benefit by living out of the United States for a time. Agreeing that they were still a force as a group, they hired a sidewalk photographer to take their picture at the Alameda park in Mexico City. The photograph, showing the five men in a relaxed, unified pose, was a stark contrast to the one taken a month earlier by *Mademoiselle*.

Tired of the poor living conditions in Mexico City and around Kerouac's apartment, Gregory Corso moved into a posh hotel. In a few days, he caught a plane to Washington, D.C., where he hoped to hook up with Randall Jarrell. Allen, Jack, Peter, and Lafcadio pooled their money and answered a newspaper ad soliciting people willing to share expenses with an advertising agent bound for New York. With six men in the car, the three-thousand-mile trip was cramped and boring, but the men passed the time singing and telling stories. Even Kerouac's spirits had lifted noticeably by the time they were dropped off in New York.

It was late November—almost ten months before *On the Road* would be published and over a half year before Allen's name would be nationally known in connection with the *Howl* obscenity trial. Still, New York offered a number of indications that the rumpled, unshaven group of men would be media stars within a year.

11

Largely as a result of the Eberhart piece in the *Times*, New York's avant-garde community greeted Allen as an important new literary figure. However, *Howl* was available in only one of the city's bookstores, and it was selling so poorly that Allen wrote Ferlinghetti and asked his City Lights publisher whether the planned second printing of *Howl* was warranted by its sales figures.

Allen and Peter moved into an apartment shared by Elise Cowen, a New York friend of Allen's, and her friend, a woman named Sheila. Elise, a short dark-haired woman with black horn-rimmed glasses that made her look a little like Allen, had been enraptured by Ginsberg since she met him a few years earlier, and she was pleased to take care of all his domestic needs while he was on the East Coast. Allen had been away for almost three years, and he kept a very active schedule, touching base with all the people, friends and family alike, that he had not seen in that time. There was a joyful reunion with Louis and Edith Ginsberg, a somber visit to Naomi's grave site, and countless reunions with old friends.

In addition, there were numerous professional contacts to establish and maintain. Once again, Allen assumed his role as group leader. He had brought back manuscripts and books by Philip Whalen, Robert Duncan, Robert Creeley, Philip Lamantia, Michael McClure, Gary Snyder, Ed Dorn, and Denise Levertov, and he showed these texts, along with those by himself, Kerouac, and Corso, to anyone willing to take a look at them.

One interested party was Donald Allen, editor of *Evergreen Review*. Allen originally intended to publish only Kerouac in his magazine's first issue, but after looking over Ginsberg's huge sheaf of work by the other San Francisco poets, he decided to devote the entire second number of *Evergreen Review* to the San Francisco Poetry Renaissance. Ginsberg would be represented by "Howl," and instead of printing the planned installment of Kerouac's *The Subterraneans*, Donald Allen convinced Grove Press owner Barney Rosset to publish the entire book as a trade paperback original. Allen chose Kerouac's "October in the Railroad Earth" for the San Francisco poets issue.

Viewing this as a positive sign, Ginsberg stepped up his activities. He hit the literary party scene, pushing his poetry and the work of his friends on agents and editors. He attended a party thrown by Richard Eberhart and spent much of the evening trying to impress Arabelle Porter, editor of *New World Writing*, the magazine that had published an excerpt of *On the Road* in 1955. Known around the New York publishing establishment for his enormous energy, Allen seemed more determined than ever to thrust his group into the limelight. He and Kerouac met painter Salvador Dalí at the Russian Tea Room for dinner. He gave interviews to *The New York Times*, *World Telegram*, and *The Village Voice*, and he dropped off copies of *Howl and Other Poems* to such literary bastions as *Partisan Review*, *The New Yorker*, and *Hudson Review*. The ploy worked, at least to a small degree: *Howl* sold out in New York, and a second shipment to two bookstores sold at a brisk pace; poetry editors for influential magazines promised to review the book.

On January 11, 1957, Jack Kerouac formally signed his *On the Road* contract with Viking Press. In recent months, Allen had envisioned the Kerouac, Ginsberg, Corso trio as the nucleus of what he termed "the apocalypse," and now each had a major work in the offing. Allen talked his father into driving him, Jack, Gregory, and Peter to the Rutherford, New Jersey, home of William Carlos Williams, where the four spent the better part of a day reading their work to the aging poet. Williams was impressed by their poetry, and when

Kerouac asked him for advice, the older poet pointed out the window and warned them that there were "lotsa bastards out there," meaning the literary and publishing communities. He promised to help them by seeing if he could review Gregory's new collection, *Gasoline*, for *The New York Times*. The group, minus Gregory, then journeyed to Old Saybrook, Connecticut, where they spent a weekend drinking, reading poetry, and frolicking like kids in the snow at the home of John Clellon Holmes. As Holmes recalled, "The music was never off, the glasses were rarely empty, we played football in the snow, and Peter did perfect figure-eights on the ice-covered North Cove. . . . We all parted, quenched and affectionate."

Jack left for Tangier on February 15, with Gregory following two weeks later. Allen and Peter were delayed by their legal efforts to free Peter's brother, Julius, from an asylum, but the two sailed on March 8. Ironically, Allen would gain his greatest national notoriety while he was out of the country.

Photo by Larry Keenan

Book Two
PROPHET

What is now proved was once only imagin'd.
—William Blake
The Marriage of Heaven and Hell

Top: Gregory Corso, in his attic room at 9 rue Git-le-Coeur, Paris, 1957. *Photo by Allen Ginsberg.* *Middle:* "Seeking the Great Spirit of the Universe in Terrible Godly form," Ginsberg traveled to India and the Orient in 1962–63—this photo taken with the Himalayas as a backdrop. *Courtesy Allen Ginsberg. Bottom:* In New Delhi, Allen and Peter had a chance encounter with Chögyam Trungpa, who, a decade later, would become AG's Tibetan Buddhist teacher. *Courtesy Allen Ginsberg.*

Above: Miguel Grinberg, editor of *Eco Contemporaneo*, with AG in Havana, Cuba, January 1965. *Courtesy Allen Ginsberg.* *Right:* "And I am the King of May": Elected "Kral Majales" by Czechoslovakian students, Ginsberg was paraded through the streets of Prague on the back of a flatbed truck, May Day, 1965. *Courtesy Allen Ginsberg.* *Below:* Michael McClure, Bob Dylan, and AG, City Lights Bookstore, 1965. *Photo by Larry Keenan.*

Last gathering of the Beat Generation, City Lights Bookstore, 1965. Front row, left to right: Robert LaVigne, Shig Murao, Larry Fagin, Leland Meyezove (lying down), Lew Welch, Peter Orlovsky. Second row, left to right: David Meltzer, Michael McClure, Allen Ginsberg, Daniel Langton, a friend of AG's, Richard Brautigan, Gary Goodrow, Nemi Frost. Back row: Stella Levy, Lawrence Ferlinghetti. *Photo by Larry Keenan.*

Left: "The message is: Widen the area of consciousness": AG testifying on the topic of LSD before a Senate subcommittee, 1966. *Courtesy Allen Ginsberg. Below*: Jack Kerouac, Hyannis, Massachusetts, June 1966. *Photo by Ann Charters*.

Left: Dancing to the music of the Grateful Dead at the Human Be-In, San Francisco, 1967: "O go way man I can/ hypnotize this nation/I can shake the earth's foundation/with the Maple Leaf Rag." © *Lisa Law*.

Right: Gary Snyder (left) blows a note on a conch shell to signify the opening of the Human Be-In, Golden Gate Park, January 1967, as Michael McClure, AG, and Maretta Greer look on. © *Lisa Law*.

Above: Ezra Pound, AG, and Fernanda Pivano in Portofino, Italy, 1967. © *Ettore Sottsass*. *Left*: William Burroughs, with Jean Genet and AG, meets Abbie Hoffman in Lincoln Park during the week of the 1968 Democratic National Convention in Chicago. *Courtesy Allen Ginsberg*. *Below*: At the Democratic National Convention, Chicago, August 1968: "Miserable picnic, Police State or Garden of Eden?" *Courtesy Allen Ginsberg*.

11
Europe! Europe!

Now is the time for prophecy without death as a consequence. . . .

1

Over three years had passed since Bill Burroughs had seen Allen Ginsberg. Adding the time he had lived in Mexico, South America, and Tangier, Bill had spent nearly all of the past eight years out of the United States, and he generally found the life of the expatriate suitable to his temperament. In a foreign city such as Tangier, one could live inexpensively, with far less government interference in matters of drugs and sexual practices. For months, Bill had been sending a stream of letters to Allen and Jack, urging them to visit and filling them in with details of local customs and practices. In his letters to Allen, Bill portrayed Tangier as a sexual paradise where open homosexuality was tolerated by the residents. "The sexual mores here [are] unlike anything you can imagine," he told Allen. "So long as I go with Spanish boys, it is like having a girl in the U.S. I mean you feel yourself at one with society. No one disapproves or says anything."

Nor was there a shortage of available young men. Bill described with obvious relish his sexual exploits with any number of young men in Tangier. "I get an average of ten very attractive propositions a day," Bill wrote, claiming that he was so popular because he was highly regarded for his generosity and had the reputation of being "a perfect gentleman in every sense of the word." In fact, Bill quipped in an October 1956 letter, his sex life had been so active that he was "declaring a two-day sex Lent." Allen should come to Tangier before he spent the money he had earned that summer, Burroughs insisted, promising Allen that he would feel no pressure or jealousy from him after he arrived.

"There is something special about Tanger [*sic*]," Bill observed. "When I am there I don't want to be anyplace else. No stasis horrors here. And the beauty of this town that consists in changing combinations. Venice is beautiful, but it never changes. It is a dream congealed in stone. And it is someone else's dream."

Although he missed Allen much more than he allowed in his correspondence, and was probably building up Tangier as a means of enticing his friends to the faraway locale, Burroughs loved the city. He lived an orderly, if not charmed, life. He was writing on a regular schedule. He had kicked his morphine habit after a brief journey to London to see a specialist, who had treated him with apomorphine, a mixture of morphine and hydrochloric acid. He was taking care of himself, exercising every day to stay trim. Every morning before he sat down to write, he would go rowing in a nearby harbor. He had met and become a friend of Paul Bowles, the expatriate American writer living in Tangier. When Jack Kerouac stepped off the Yugoslavian freighter he had taken on his trip to northern Africa, he was greeted by a "tanned, muscular, and vigorous" Burroughs, who seemed to Jack to be an entirely different person from the Old Bill Lee character he had depicted in his novels. He had a bounce in his gait and Jack had to hurry to keep up with him when they went for their walks.

For all the appearances of the sedate life, complete with his late-afternoon snifters of cognac, there was plenty of the old Bill Burroughs for Jack to contend with. Bill still maintained a private arsenal of weapons, including a rifle, a switchblade and other assorted knives, and a machete; one of his walls was scarred with bullet holes. He might have been off morphine for the time being, but there was a variety of hashish, opium, and majoun—a candy made of chopped kef, cinnamon, and honey—to keep him happy. Burroughs could still amuse Kerouac by slipping into the persona of one of the characters in his routines, although on occasion these disappearances into character frightened Jack, giving him a Jekyll and Hyde vision of Bill that made him very uneasy.

Burroughs was parlaying these different characters into a series of roughly unified routines he was calling Word Horde. For Bill, the routines represented the exorcism of his worst junk nightmares, a horrific superimposition of futuristic images and the cold-sweat presence of chemical dependency. Burroughs's characters were slaves to their habits, prisoners of their sexual needs. His method of writing was unusual, if not unique: Every day, Burroughs would sit at his portable typewriter and work out whatever vision he had at the moment; when he completed a page, he would toss it over his shoulder and begin another, leaving the finished pages scattered and unorganized on the floor.

Kerouac, with his highly self-disciplined work habits, was appalled by the mess he found in Burroughs's workroom. It was one thing to follow stream of consciousness to unforeseen destinations, entirely another matter to allow that creativity to flutter into a carpet of pages that would blow into the courtyard outside whenever the wind shifted direction. Jack read some of the loose pages and was gripped by the writing. Burroughs, he felt, had finally found a way to align his singular mind with true creative talent. Jack gathered the loose pages and began to help Burroughs organize and type the mass of papers into a professionally prepared manuscript. In no time, Burroughs would change his novel's title back to the one Jack had suggested—and that he had considered—in the past: Naked Lunch.

The work on Burroughs's book distracted Jack from his own publishing woes. Viking Press had recently rejected Desolation Angels and Dr. Sax. Worse yet,

Jack was shocked and angered when he received the proofs of *The Subterraneans* from Donald Allen at Grove Press. The editor had taken a workmanlike ap-proach to converti˙ ˜ Jack's style to the recognizable, accepted style of the times. He had removed Kerouac's dashes—the unorthodox splits that Jack used to indicate breath changes, giving the book a jazzy flavor—and replaced them with standard punctuation. Long sentences had been broken down into shorter ones. Much of the novel had been cut. Incredulous, Jack ordered his agent to stop publication of the book. It would be published his way or not at all. Because of the autobiographical nature of the writing, Jack took Donald Allen's changes personally, as if his editor was cheapening the value of Kerouac's life by tampering with the way he presented it artistically.

Depressed, Jack applied himself to assisting Bill with his novel, but not without paying a price for his involvement. The hellish vignettes, combined with the large amount of kef that Kerouac was smoking every day, led to a series of nightmares, including one in which Jack dreamed of pulling an endless string of bolognas, like grotesque intestines, from his mouth. For Burroughs, writing the novel might have been a catharsis, a matter of his "shitting out my educated Middlewest background once and for all," as he told Jack, but to Kerouac, even the funny images were unnerving. Further, he wondered about the dark connection between the writer and some of his images.

As February passed into March, Bill grew apprehensive about Allen's and Peter's delayed arrival in Tangier. Alan Ansen had shown the prologue of *Word Horde* to an editor at the Olympia Press in Paris, and the editor expressed interest in seeing a completed manuscript. Bill used this bit of information to prod Ginsberg into moving more quickly. "I am badly in need of advice, editing, collaboration. . . . It is hard for me to evaluate this material," he wrote Allen, asking him to hurry to Tangier. More to the point, however, was Bill's need for Allen's physical presence. If nothing else, Ginsberg would be a welcome contrast to the moody Kerouac, who had already tired of Tangier with its slums, poor food, and, to the parsimonious Kerouac, high prices. He was already talking of moving on.

One evening, after a lavish meal at the Pename, Bill and Jack went to Kerouac's rooftop room in the Villa Muniriya. From the patio, they could see out over the rooftops to the bay. Using his binoculars, Bill stared out into the night at the twinkling lights of the ships and boats arriving in the harbor. "When will Allen get here?" he wondered. He began to cry. As Jack tried to comfort Bill, he was reminded of a time when Allen had drawn two hearts representing him and Bill, but when he drew the arrow, it had only pierced one heart. Bill later told Jack this oversight was symbolic of Allen's "autocratic" nature: He could "only fall in love with the image of himself." For all his talk of his sexual liberation in Tangier, Bill was still entangled in his past, tied to a longing that three years and thousands of miles' separation could not abolish.

2

Allen's and Peter's ship pulled into the Tangier harbor in late March. Jack and Bill, waving cheerfully, were at the dock to greet them.

Allen had left Paterson on March 7. At the bus stop outside a candy store, he and Louis had said tearful good-byes, Louis uncertain as to how long it would be before he saw his son again. Allen joined Peter in Brooklyn, and on March 8, with Elise and Sheila at the dock to see them off, they set sail on a freighter bound for Casablanca. Their ocean passage took eleven days, Allen spending much of his time on the ship's deck, watching the cloud formations over the ocean or writing in his journal. They spent three days in Casablanca, wandering around the Medina, the old Arab quarter, where emaciated or crippled beggars lined the doorways and narrow alleys and reached out for offerings from passersby. They visited a cemetery and looked at headstones weathered nameless by time and the elements. They met an Arab businessman who took them to a nearby café, where they were served a hot sweet mint tea and, to Allen's surprise, a hit off a long-stemmed brown kef pipe. Casablanca, Allen told Lucien Carr, was "much like Mexico . . . except Arab quarter very clean, streets and alleys spotless in the sun. Veiled women, Arabs in long white or black hooded shroudy stranger robes, adobe walled tenements, crisscross of crooked alleys, arches, roofs, rembrandt-interior cafes & shops, streetpeddlers selling delicious 2 cent napoleons & french pastries. . . ."

In his enthusiasm at seeing Allen, Burroughs got very drunk the first night Allen and Peter were in Tangier; he frightened everyone by waving his machete around until Allen asked him to stop. Bill's daily routine was disrupted by their arrival. As Kerouac recalled, "[Allen] wanted to do everything right. Dinners, walks around the Medina, a proposed railroad trip to Fez, circuses, cafes, swims in the ocean, hikes, I could see [Bill] grabbing his head in dismay."

Allen had been in Tangier only a few days when he learned that *Howl* had run into trouble back in the States. On March 25, the San Francisco office of U.S. customs, led by Chester McPhee, a known advocate of book censorship, seized 520 copies of the 3,000-copy shipment of the second printing of *Howl*. Lawrence Ferlinghetti had seen the potential for trouble and had taken measures to protect himself.

City Lights Books were typeset and printed by the Villiers press in England, and while the company specialized in small-press publications and was accustomed to dealing with controversial materials, it was very concerned about some of the contents of *Howl*. Earlier in the year, *Miscellaneous Man*, another publication typeset by Villiers, had been involved in a censorship action in San Francisco. Villiers agreed to print *Howl* on the condition that certain words be replaced with asterisks in the text. Ferlinghetti reluctantly agreed. For further protection, he submitted a typescript of *Howl and Other Poems* to the American Civil Liberties Union before the book was printed in England. The ACLU agreed to represent Ferlinghetti should the occasion present itself. The first printing of *Howl* arrived in San Francisco in October 1956 without incident. The second printing was not as fortunate.

The ACLU acted swiftly in retaliation to the confiscation. On April 3, it informed customs it intended to challenge the legality of the seizure in court. Ferlinghetti printed an offset edition of *Howl* to assure the book's publication outside the federal jurisdiction of customs. William Hogan, book review editor of the *San Francisco Chronicle*, allotted Ferlinghetti his May 19 column space for a commentary on the issue.

Ferlinghetti's argument was convincing. Skillfully combining a sense of humor with his feelings of outrage, the City Lights publisher argued that "Howl" was the most important poem to be published in America since World War II—possibly since T.S. Eliot's "Four Quartets." In presenting a poem detailing the ugliness and impersonality of American life, Ferlinghetti noted, Ginsberg had proven his point that spiritual values were slipping away from American grasp. Ginsberg wasn't obscene; he had simply chosen to align himself with those who refused to accept the philosophy of the times.

With outrage mounting against the seizure, a Washington, D.C., customs official advised the San Francisco U.S. Attorney not to take action against the book, and on May 29, customs released the confiscated copies of *Howl*.

As it turned out, this was only the beginning of the battle.

3

Jack Kerouac caught a train for Marseilles on April 5, less than two weeks after Allen's arrival in Tangier, but before he left, the four Americans spent a lot of time together, whiling away the hours on the beach and swimming in the surf, walking through the city, getting high, and engaging in provocative conversations. Allen in particular enjoyed his verbal sparring sessions with Burroughs. Bolstered by *majoun*, or by the marijuana they could legally purchase on the street at the rate of twenty joints for a nickel, Allen and Bill would stay up long into the night, arguing literature and philosophy, Bill assuming his familiar role as cynical devil's advocate. One evening, a group of French hipsters visited Bill's apartment; Allen found their jazzy conversation to be great fun, but Jack griped that they were "unable to convey anything of force or interest." On another occasion, while roaming around the city, Allen and Jack witnessed a small riot between Moroccan soldiers and the Spanish police.

Allen was bothered by the squalor of Arab life, and he was deeply troubled by the political tensions among Arabs and Jews, the Spanish, Moroccan, and French groups in Morocco, and the French and Arabs in Algeria. One night, as he and Peter were leaving a movie theater, Allen watched the Spanish police break up an innocent gathering of young people by waving guns and screaming at the crowd to disperse. Shaken by the event, as well as by Arab poverty, Allen admitted to Kerouac that "Howl" seemed to be an inadequate statement in comparison to the worldwide plight of the masses, and he vowed to write an epic poem that addressed the issue.

With a two-hundred-dollar grant from the National Academy of Arts and Sciences, arranged by William Carlos Williams, along with Peter's fifty-dollar monthly disability check from the government, Allen was able to assume Jack's rooftop apartment after Kerouac left for France. Allen would rise early and work on his own writing, and then he would go to Burroughs's place, where he and Bill and Alan Ansen, a recent arrival from Venice, would work on typing, cataloging, and arranging Burroughs's novel. It was hard work, made even more formidable when they reached the point where Allen had to go through Bill's old letters and extract material suitable for the book. From his experiences as Auden's secretary, Ansen was well versed in the tedious chore of sorting and cataloging scholarly material, and from his experiences in the New York publishing world, Ginsberg was equally knowledgeable about the mechanics of manuscript preparation. The work went slowly, but by the end of May, they had assembled more than two hundred pages of usable manuscript. According to the plan, Allen would remain in Tangier until most of the work on the manuscript had been completed; he would then travel to Europe, to be joined by Burroughs in Venice for a final run at finishing the book, and from there they would spirit off to Paris, where Allen hoped to sell the book to the Olympia Press. In the interim, Allen would search for magazines that might publish excerpts.

In applying his prodigious energy to the task, Ginsberg was in effect collaborating on the book that would thrust Burroughs into the spotlight and establish his literary reputation. Richard Seaver, Burroughs's American editor for nearly twenty-five years, would later recognize Ginsberg's contribution to the creation of *Naked Lunch*. "It was really Allen who put *Naked Lunch* together," Seaver said. "It was a massive manuscript, and Allen did a brilliant job of editing it into, I think, Burroughs' best book."

Even with all this work, Allen must have had his own misgivings about the possibility of the book's ever being published in the United States, for it now looked as if *Howl* was going to become involved in an all-out battle with censorship advocates in America. The showdown commenced on May 21, 1957—two days after Lawrence Ferlinghetti's defense of "Howl" had appeared in the *San Francisco Chronicle*—when two plainclothes police officers entered the City Lights Bookstore and purchased a copy of *Howl and Other Poems* for seventy-five cents. A short time later, the police arrested Shigeyoshi Murao, the bookstore clerk, and served a warrant for the arrest of Ferlinghetti, who was not in the store at the time. According to the warrant, Ferlinghetti did "willfully and lewdly print, publish, and sell obscene and indecent writings, papers, and books, to wit: 'Howl and Other Poems.' " Murao was taken to the police station, booked and fingerprinted, and placed in a holding cell until the ACLU arrived with his five-hundred-dollar bail money. Ferlinghetti was charged a short time later.

These legal actions confused, angered, and surprised the San Francisco literary community. Since "Howl" was largely considered to be not only a legitimate work of art but possibly a masterwork, there was a lot of speculation about why the police had become involved in the first place. One theory was that the police were trying to save face for Chester McPhee, the customs officer who failed in his attempt to block the poem's entry into the country. A standing joke was that the police department was being paid as a promotional agent for the book; the legal action certainly bolstered its sales figures. Even Ferlinghetti wryly noted that the prosecution's heart and mind seemed somewhere other than on the case at hand. Whatever the reasons, the penalties were considerable: If convicted, Ferlinghetti and Murao faced a sentence of up to six months in jail and a five-hundred-dollar fine.

The characters in the drama well represented the forces in conflict. Captain William Hanrahan, the Juvenile Bureau officer who had ordered the arrest, was a longtime proponent of book censorship and an outspoken critic of "Howl."

In a public statement issued a short time after Ferlinghetti's arrest, Hanrahan promised that a successful prosecution of *Howl and Other Poems* would open the door for similar obscenity trials in the future. Prosecuting the case was Ralph McIntosh, an assistant district attorney with his own reputation as a hard-line censorship advocate. Seeing the trial as a potential watershed test of the First Amendment, the Northern California Chapter of the American Civil Liberties Union assembled a formidable group itself. The ACLU retained the services, free of charge, of veteran criminal trial lawyer J. W. "Jake" Ehrlich, a flamboyant attorney nationally known for his defense of murderer Caryl Chessman. The trial, scheduled for August, promised to be a nationally covered event.

These most recent legal developments bothered Ginsberg much more than the customs actions, which Allen regarded as little more than a nuisance. "I guess this is more serious than the customs seizure since you can lose real money on this deal if they find you guilty," Allen wrote Ferlinghetti. Still, with such outraged literati as Kenneth Rexroth, William Carlos Williams, and Ruth Witt-Diamant throwing their support behind his work, Allen was confident that Ferlinghetti and Murao would be exonerated. The only real problem, Allen told Ferlinghetti, would occur if it was somehow ruled that the police could determine what was and what was not obscene. "I guess [an] open showdown is inevitable," he concluded.

Allen regretted that he was out of the country for the confrontation. With its new notoriety, *Howl* was selling better than ever and the Ginsberg name was being bandied about in literary conversations. Allen relished the thought of a battle. As he told Eugene, it would have been great if he was in San Francisco and was "to give a big reading now under official State College auspices at the City Museum—and invite the police. I'd probably wind up in jail for a few hours . . . but ACLU on hand to bail me out. Strange situation."

Allen felt the events in San Francisco could set important precedents. The *Howl* trial would act as a litmus test for *Naked Lunch*'s chances for publication and distribution in the United States. Allen carefully read the news clippings that Ferlinghetti sent him. Since he himself was not on trial, and since there was little he could do in the upcoming legal battle in San Francisco, Allen decided to continue with his European trip as planned.

In May, he finally got the opportunity to meet Paul Bowles, who had been away, traveling in Ceylon, when Ginsberg arrived in Tangier. Allen had heard much about Bowles from Burroughs, who considered him a kindred spirit. Their minds were so similar, Bill told Allen, that their thoughts were almost telepathic. "Don't recall I ever meet anyone I dug so quick as Bowles," Bill said. When Ginsberg was introduced to Bowles, Allen found him to be "very courteous and lively, also a little mechanical or remote," an observation not unlike Burroughs's first impression of the author. Allen found Bowles's wife, Jane, to be charming and witty in a way that reminded him of Joan Vollmer. Bowles proposed that everyone go to an expensive local restaurant for dinner and more conversation; when Allen said he was nearly broke and could not afford to eat at the restaurant, the English painter Francis Bacon, part of the Bowles entourage, offered to pay for Allen's meal. Allen liked Bacon and his daring style. "He's like Burroughs a little—painting a sideline, gambles at

Monte Carlo and wins and loses all his paint money, says he can always be a cook or trade if he fucks painting—most interesting person here," Allen wrote Kerouac.

By early June, Allen was ready to move on. There had been tension between Bill and Peter from the time they had arrived in Tangier, despite Bill's earlier proclamations that he would not be jealous of Allen's lover. Bill thought Peter was naïve, and he could not understand what Allen saw in him. Bill's snide, ridiculing remarks hurt Peter and offended Allen. Allen asked Bill to try to get along with Peter, to no avail. The issue came to a head one evening when, high on *majoun*, Bill mocked Allen for tolerating Peter's insensibility. Allen lost his temper and, grabbing a nearby hunting knife, cut Burroughs's khaki shirt. It was obvious to all that it was about time to leave.

4

Allen was eager to get to Europe. He needed a change of scenery, new inspiration for his writing. During his stay in Tangier, he had done very little writing either in his journal or of new poetry. The work on Burroughs's novel gratified him, and he had enjoyed his leisure time in Tangier, but he had reached the point where he was becoming alarmed at his own lack of new creative work. In addition, he wanted to see some of Spain before he and Peter traveled to Venice, where they were to summer with Alan Ansen.

On June 10, Allen said good-bye to Bill Burroughs and he and Peter departed for Spain. Their first stop was Granada, where they enjoyed sitting at outdoor cafés and watching evening strollers out on the town. Looming over the city was the Alhambra, the fourteenth-century castle made up of a vast series of Spanish and Arab battlements, all set on a hill that gave it an even greater majestic presence. The Alhambra, with its huge palace halls and seemingly numberless arches and patios, impressed Allen. The walls were covered with some of the most intricate and exquisite designs that he had ever seen, leading him to conclude that "only a people inspired by hashish would have taken the trouble with such detail—you can sit in a room and get high by osmosis contemplating the infinite structures of the human imagination."

Allen's insatiable curiosity made him a natural tourist. From studying maps and guidebooks, he was aware of the historical points of interest that each city had to offer, but he was by no means interested only in the sights that one could find pictured on the front of a postcard; he was equally compelled to see how people lived. When he visited Seville, one of the most beautiful cities in Spain and the setting for both *Don Quixote* and *Carmen*, Allen spent two days touring the city's many churches, including the Cathedral, the third-largest church in the world, but he also spent a great deal of time walking around the streets and alleyways, intrigued by such commonplace objects as the huge canvas awnings suspended over every street, protecting people from the hot afternoon sun. In Córdoba, the capital of Spain under both the Romans and Moors, he explored the Mezquite, the Moorish mosque erected in the eighth century, marveling at its hundreds of pillars and red and white arches, yet he was almost as fascinated by his walk to the Guadalquivir River, where he spent a lazy hour watching a group of local women washing clothes beneath the city's historic Roman bridge. By now, it was almost instinctive for him to place scenes of local color within the framework of a grander historical setting.

After touring Córdoba, Allen and Peter caught an overnight train to Madrid, a city Allen found so appealing that he considered abandoning his planned summer stay in Venice in favor of finding a job and staying longer in the modern Spanish capital. Housing was more expensive than in Tangier, he discovered, but otherwise the prices were right. For eight cents, you could buy a tiny but delicious steak, or for thirty cents you could purchase an entire meal of soup, meat, and dessert. Allen was immediately caught up in the spirit of the city. He and Peter walked the maze of downtown streets, stopping occasionally in small bars where, like the locals, they would purchase a small plate of shellfish, which they would eat while standing in booths.

The highlight of Allen's stay was the time he spent visiting the Prado, with its rooms of El Grecos, Brueghels, Goyas, Rubens, Titians, and Velazquezes. Allen had been looking forward to visiting the museum for a long time, but he was nevertheless unprepared for its effect on him. As he told Eugene, he had seen prints of the works of Hieronymus Bosch in art books, but the reproductions were so small that he couldn't begin to appreciate the wonder of the detail and brushwork in a painting such as *The Garden of Earthly Delights*. In the Prado, he devoted an hour to this painting alone. Each painting was a delight, and Allen regretted not having the time to give each work the viewing he felt it deserved. "It's a place you could get endless kicks from if there were world enough and time," he told Eugene.

His favorite painting was a Fra Angelico, which Allen proclaimed to be "the greatest painting I ever saw first hand." He was entranced by the brilliant golden rays of light, so remarkably preserved for five hundred years. Hard-pressed to find the words to describe it, he sent his brother a sketch to accompany his remarks. "I'd vaguely remembered it from *Life*, or art books—but wasn't aware of its perfection—delicacy and solid bright centuries of color," he wrote.

Allen's final stop in Spain was Barcelona, the coastal city that had given the world Picasso, Miró, and Gaudí. He visited the church of the Sagrada Familia, Gaudí's lifelong passion, a monumental achievement that managed to escape the church burnings during the Spanish Civil War. He climbed some of its many towers, from which he was rewarded with spectacular views of the Mediterranean. From there, he went to the Parc Güell, one of Gaudí's tributes to his financier, Count Eusebio Güell. As always, Allen took in plenty of local color, as apparent on Barcelona's narrow side streets as on the famous Ramblas, where throngs of people strolled down a long, wide strip of walkway positioned between rushing traffic traveling in either direction. In the poorer sections of town, there was still evidence of the bombing during the Spanish Civil War.

Despite the wonderful time he was having as a tourist, Allen was growing weary. He had traveled hundreds of miles by train, and he felt as if he had traveled nearly as many on foot. He was out of touch with his family and friends, his mail being forwarded to Alan Ansen in Venice. He was curious about the activities taking place in the States, now so far removed from him.

Allen left Spain in late June, traveling through southern France to reach Venice. He and Peter hitchhiked for the first part of their journey, stopping in every town they could along the way. In Montpellier, they happened upon a book fair sponsored by the Communist party, and Allen was reminded of the cell meetings he and his mother had attended on River Street in Paterson, except there was less ideological tension in France; rather than selling leaflets by Israel Amter and William Z. Foster, the French were selling books by Cocteau, Picasso, and Mayakovsky. They spent a morning in Marseilles and an afternoon on the French Riviera near Nice. France was in the midst of a heat wave, and Allen, tired and faint from his walking with a backpack, was grateful for the opportunity to take a dip in the cool waters of the Mediterranean. Their final stop was Milan, where they stayed an evening and the following day, walking the streets and exploring churches. At one point, a woman approached them and pointed to the spot in an empty square where Mussolini had been killed.

Allen had wanted to see as many historic sights as he could, and he had been enriched by his travels through Spain and southern France. These travels, however, were only a prelude to what he would experience in the year to come.

5

While Allen was busy sightseeing in Tangier and Spain, his reputation was growing in the United States. The first reviews of *Howl* were coming in, and, as Allen might have guessed, a number of critics took exception to the tone and language of the book's title poem. John Hollander, one of Allen's Columbia classmates and now a recognized poet/critic himself, condemned *Howl* as "a very short and very tiresome book," though he acknowledged Ginsberg as having "a real talent and a marvelous ear." Poet James Dickey, writing for *Sewanee Review*, called *Howl* "the skin of Rimbaud's *Une Saison en Enfer* thrown over the conventional maunderings of one American adolescent, who has discovered that machine civilization has no interest in his having read Blake." In his review for *Poetry* magazine, a long-standing bastion of serious literary and poetry criticism in the United States, Frederick Eckman proclaimed *Howl* to be "a very shaggy book, the shaggiest I've ever seen."

Not all reviews, of course, were negative. Two influential reviewers not only praised *Howl* but predicted that Ginsberg would be one of the poetry forces of the future. "He has brought a terrible psychological reality to the surface with enough originality to blast American verse a hairsbreadth forward in the process," wrote M. L. Rosenthal, who called *Howl* "poetry of genuine suffering." In "San Francisco Letter," published in the San Francisco poets issue of *Evergreen Review*, Kenneth Rexroth predicted, "if he keeps going, Ginsberg will be the first genuinely popular, genuine poet in over a generation—and he is already considerably the superior of predecessors like Lindsay and Sandburg."

Howl presented a unique challenge to its reviewers. For traditionalist critics, it was an easy target to attack on any number of fronts. However, as Rexroth pointed out somewhat glibly in his account, Ginsberg's poetry was also difficult to praise if a critic applied the standard criterion of judgment. "Nothing goes to show how square the squares are so much as the *favorable* reviews they've given it," Rexroth wrote of *Howl*. Like "The Waste Land," which attempted to redefine the boundaries of poetry, "Howl" occupied its own unique place in literature: It could not be defined, let alone judged, by the usual standards of criticism.

Nowhere was this as apparent as during the summer of 1957, when Lawrence Ferlinghetti and Shig Murao were tried in San Francisco for publishing and selling obscene material. The trial was a case of legal and literary forces colliding head-on in a clash that would determine the standards by which works of art, once deemed obscene by public standards, would be judged in the future. In retrospect, given today's standards, the trial appears to be almost fatuous, but in 1957, many precedents were yet to be set. *Playboy* magazine was only a few years old, and Hugh Hefner was still battling obscenity charges for publishing photographs that, by today's standards, were tame. Lenny Bruce was just beginning his controversial career as a stand-up comic and social commentator. Elvis Presley, with his gyrating hips, was both the rage and the scandal. Books by D. H. Lawrence and Henry Miller were still being published in foreign countries and smuggled into the States.

Ginsberg and Ferlinghetti may have been confident that poem and publisher would prevail in the courtroom, but the American Civil Liberties Union left nothing to chance in assembling its defense. Jake Ehrlich was joined by Lawrence Speiser, the ACLU's top trial lawyer, and Albert Bendich, an ACLU staff counsel who prepared the briefs for the *Howl* trial. A national audience watched as the trial began. Representatives from major newspapers and magazines attended and reported to readerships representing the spectrum of social and literary ideologies. The trial promised to be a war of words over words, with the burden of proof resting on the shoulders of attorneys armed with only the sketchiest of definitions of *obscene* and *indecent*. Hearing the case was Judge Clayton W. Horn, a Sunday school Bible teacher who had recently attracted national publicity by sentencing five women shoplifters to a screening of *The Ten Commandments* and the writing of essays on the moral lessons of the film.

In the early proceedings, both sides jockeyed for Judge Horn's favor. Ehrlich's strategy was to challenge the wording of the law. He hoped Horn would throw the case out of court on the merits of the judge's personal interpretations of the book. "I assume Your Honor has now read the book," Ehrlich stated after the trial had been adjourned to allow Horn the opportunity to read *Howl*. "The question then arises whether as the result of your reading you have been able to form judgment as to whether this book is or is not obscene. . . . If Your Honor determines that the book is not obscene under the law, then, of course, that's the end of the issue."

Judge Horn refused the gambit. With Ehrlich and McIntosh debating the letter of the law and citing its application in other court cases, Horn declared that it was the job of the defense to show the book's merits, while, by law, the prosecution had to prove Ferlinghetti's intent in publishing the work. Ehrlich attempted to enter into the record a number of testimonials to *Howl* submitted by various literary experts and publishers, but McIntosh objected. Horn agreed with McIntosh that "letters solicited specifically for the purpose of introducing self-serving declarations, or for the specific purpose of exonerating the defendant, would not be admissible." Only reviews written before Ferlinghetti's arrest would be allowed.

The ruling all but guaranteed a long trial. Ehrlich had hoped that written expert testimonials might eliminate much of the tedious courtroom testimony. After Ferlinghetti's arrest, a barrage of letters supporting Ginsberg and *Howl* had arrived in San Francisco. Among the favorable comments:

- *Howl* is one of the most important books of poetry published in the last ten years. Its power and eloquence are obvious, and the talent of Mr. Ginsberg is of the highest order. Even people who do not like the book are compelled to testify to its force and brilliance.
  —Thomas Parkinson, University of California

- Our final considered opinion was that Allen Ginsberg's *Howl* is an achieved poem and that it deserves to be considered as such.
  —Barney Rosset and Donald Allen,
  editors of *Evergreen Review*

- *Howl and Other Poems*, according to accepted, serious contemporary American literary standards, is a dignified, sincere, and admirable work of art.
  —William Hogan, *San Francisco Chronicle*

- I have read the book carefully and do not myself consider it offensive to good taste, likely to lead youth astray, or be injurious to public morals. I feel, furthermore, that the book has considerable distinction as literature, being a powerful and artistic expression of a meaningful philosophical attitude.
  —James Laughlin, New Directions

The discussion about the use of such written testimonials in court produced little agreement, other than Horn's observation that both sides were capable of producing witnesses in support of their individual arguments. Horn further forbade the attorneys to ask the specific question "Do you consider this book obscene?" of the trial's witnesses. "That is something the Court has to determine," he ruled. By making such a ruling, Horn was in essence setting up a debate on the book's literary merits. Could individual words, expressions, or ideas, placed within the context of the whole, negate the literary value of an entire work? Did those individual words, expressions, or ideas in themselves transmute a work of literature into mere pornography?

For all its publicity, the trial was a dreadful mismatch—a case of the defense overwhelming the prosecution's weak moralistic argument with an impressive battery of expert witnesses. A week into the trial, the charges against Shig Murao were dismissed because both sides agreed that, as an employee, he might not have read the book or had knowledge of its contents prior to his selling it to the undercover police officers. The case against Ferlinghetti was almost as weak.

The tone for the defense was established when Mark Schorer, professor of English at the University of California and a widely published book critic, took the stand as the first witness for the defense. In his early testimony, Schorer analyzed each of the title poem's three sections. As expected, he supported

"Howl" as a serious work of literature, asserting that the "language of the street" used in the poem, although not by tradition the language of poetry, was essential to the purposes of the work. "Each person had to determine his or her own language—from the level of their own body," Schorer maintained.

In his cross-examination, McIntosh held up a copy of *Howl*, with individual words and phrases underscored, and proceeded to ask Schorer to interpret what Ginsberg meant by an expression such as "angel headed hipsters." What, precisely, did that mean? Schorer countered that individual words, taken out of context, might seem incomprehensible, especially in poetry, which Schorer defined as "a heightened form of language through the use of figurative language." McIntosh then asked Schorer to translate the poetic language of "Howl" into prose that might be easier for the Court to understand, but Schorer insisted that this could not be done. "You can no more translate this book into logical prose English than you can say what a surrealist painting means in words," he said. What was important, Schorer testified, was the overall impression that the words made on the reader.

This line of cross-examination all but lost, McIntosh switched to a discussion of Ginsberg's use of such words as *fuck*, *cock*, and *balls*, as well as the meaning of the words struck from print as the result of Ferlinghetti's agreement with Villiers. Schorer testified that individual words and phrases could not be isolated in poetry; furthermore, Schorer continued, Ginsberg's use of sexual expressions—especially his references to homosexuality—only underscored the poet's contention that in the world depicted in "Howl," sexuality was confused and corrupt. "These words indicate a corrupt sexual act. Therefore, they are part of the essence of this picture which the author is trying to give us of modern life as a state of hell." Ginsberg might have disagreed with this assessment, especially in Schorer's misinterpretation of the homosexuality in *Howl*, but the testimony was nevertheless very effective.

Both sides grew frustrated, Ehrlich by the prosecution's line of questioning, McIntoch by Schorer's refusal or inability to translate the expressions into prose. According to the law, works had to be judged in their entirety, not by individual words or expressions, unless certain passages, considered obscene, were included only to appeal to salacious interests of the reader and had no bearing on the overall work. All of Ehrlich's witnesses were prepared to defend the poem's worth as a whole, so McIntosh was left with the unenviable task of attacking the individual words and passages.

The attending press recognized the folly of this position and hammered home the point in its coverage of the trial. "It is a case of provincial stupidity on the part of a customs inspector, a rectangular mayor, and a prosecuting attorney who should know better," John G. Fuller wrote in *The Saturday Review*; "[Howl] is obviously a very serious effort and must be judged, according to Federal law, as a whole—not censored on the grounds of individual words in it." Of the subject matter of "Howl," *The Nation* noted that " 'good taste' and conventional mores are not binding on a writer who wishes to comment persuasively on sections of society where such restraints are not recognized." Instead of presenting the details of the trial, *Life* ran a series of photographs—of Ehrlich and Ferlinghetti, as well as other San Francisco poets—and excerpts of poems, including "Howl."

It is possible that Ralph McIntosh realized his line of questioning was futile. Although he went into court well prepared and armed with past court cases to use as examples in his debate with Ehrlich, he was virtually limited to answering one particular question: If a poem contained certain words or ideas found offensive in the general vocabulary, could the poem have lasting literary value? Despite the objections by Ehrlich and admonitions of Judge Horn, McIntosh continued to question the defense witnesses in this area.

Unfortunately for McIntosh, the witnesses for the defense were a distinguished group, well prepared to argue what was and what was not of literary value. All nine witnesses had powerful credentials and some, like Mark Schorer, Kenneth Rexroth, and Leo Lowenthal, were nationally recognized as literary authorities. Each testified in favor of the literary value of *Howl*, though few were willing to stake their reputations on the issue of its lasting value in literature.

Ironically, the strongest support came from Kenneth Rexroth, who would spend the next few years demeaning the works of many of the Beat Generation writers, including Allen Ginsberg. In court, however, his feelings were still supportive. "I would say that a work like this . . . is probably the most remarkable single poem published by a young man since the second war," Rexroth stated. He labeled the poem prophetic, comparing points in the poem to biblical writings. It was an interesting and effective stance, especially since the book's opponents were attacking its moral value.

As the weeks passed, it became obvious to observers that Ehrlich had assembled, as Ferlinghetti wryly put it, "eloquent witnesses, together furnishing as good a one-sided critical survey of *Howl* as could possibly be got up in any literary magazine." Leo Lowenthal, also a professor at the University of California, tried to place "Howl" in a historical perspective, calling it a product of a period of tension and unrest. Said Lowenthal: "I was reminded by reading 'Howl' of many other literary works as they have been written after times of great upheavals, particularly after World War I, and I found this work very much in line with similar literary works." Herbert Blau, faculty member at San Francisco State College, also mentioned the art after World War I, particularly Dadaist art and literature, labeling it as "art of furious negation," a tradition that "Howl" followed. Describing "Howl" as "a vision of a modern hell," Vincent McHugh, a poet and novelist, testified that the poem had some of the works of Ezra Pound, Dante, and even Homer as its literary ancestors.

And so it went. Two other members of the San Francisco State College faculty—Arthur Foff and Mark Linenthal—testified on the poem's behalf. Walter Van Tilburg Clark, author of *The Ox-Bow Incident*, said that all the works in the volume appeared to him to be "the work of a thoroughly honest poet, who is also a highly competent technician." Of the nine defense witnesses, Luther Nichols, book critic for the *San Francisco Examiner*, may have summed up most succinctly the defense argument when he told the court that "Ginsberg's life is a vagabond one; it's colored by exposure to jazz, to Columbia University, to a liberal and Bohemian education, to a certain amount of bumming around. The words he has used are valid and necessary if he's to be honest with his purpose. I think to use euphemisms in describing this would be considered dishonest by Mr. Ginsberg."

In comparison to the defense witnesses, the two rebuttal witnesses called by McIntosh were very weak. David Kirk, assistant professor of English at the University of San Francisco, testified that he found "Howl" to be of negligible literary value because the poem, in his opinion, was a "weak imitation" of Whitman, with a statement of little validity. Furthermore, Kirk claimed, "Howl" was dedicated to Dadaism, a long-dead literary movement once committed to the destruction of the past.

In his cross-examination, Jake Ehrlich contested Kirk's assessment point by point. Kirk was unable to say whether Whitman had any influences of his own, thus damaging his testimony concerning imitation, since Kirk admitted that *Leaves of Grass* was great literature. In questioning Kirk's observations about the validity of Ginsberg's statements in "Howl," Ehrlich succeeded in showing that Kirk was uncertain as to what statements were and were not valid as literature. Some parts of "Howl," Kirk said, were valid, while others, in his opinion, were not. Finally, Ehrlich was able to funnel Kirk's statements about Dadaism into a muddy, esoteric discussion about the way literature appeals to its time. By the time he was finished testifying, Kirk had all but underscored a point made repeatedly throughout the trial: There was no definitive way of telling whether "Howl" had lasting value.

This was an important victory for the defense, mainly because nothing was said or hinted about the poem's being obscene or indecent. The prosecution was counting on Kirk's testifying that "Howl" was worthless in its literary merit, hoping that his credentials as a college professor would offset the positive criticism offered by Ehrlich's witnesses. At best, Kirk succeeded in showing only that there was an opposing position to that of *Howl*'s proponents.

The other rebuttal witness, Gail Potter, was a teacher at Catholic University of San Francisco. She, too, was to testify on the poem's lack of merit, but she jeopardized her credibility early in her testimony when, in citing her qualifications as a witness, she announced that she had rewritten *Faust* and *Everyman*. The courtroom burst into laughter, and Judge Horn had to remind the spectators that the trial was a serious matter. Unfortunately for the prosecution, Potter's tone was so high-minded that it bordered on parody. "He fails in rhetoric," she said, "because his figures of speech are crude and you feel like you are going through the gutter when you have to read that stuff. I didn't linger on it too long, I assure you." Ehrlich let her testimony hang on that note; he declined to cross-examine.

In his closing statement, McIntosh stayed with his strategy of attacking the language, rather than ideas, of "Howl." He asked Judge Horn whether this was the kind of material he wanted to see printed in the local newspaper or heard over the radio. "In other words, Your Honor, how far are we going to license the use of filthy, vulgar, obscene, and disgusting language? How far can we go?" In contrast, Ehrlich was skeptical of the effect that reading such poetry would have on a person's thoughts and actions. "You can't think common, rotten things just because you read something in a book," said Ehrlich, "unless it is your purpose to read common, rotten things and apply a common, rotten purpose to what you read."

On October 3, Judge Horn delivered his decision. Although it was apparent early in his opinion that he was going to find Ferlinghetti not guilty ("I do not believe that *Howl* is without redeeming social importance"), Horn used the occasion to outline the existing obscenity law and its interpretations. Anticipating future obscenity cases, Horn offered a twelve-point guideline for the prosecution in future trials. Among those points:

- If the material has the slightest redeeming social importance it is not obscene because it is protected by the First and Fourteenth Amendments of the United States Constitution.

- If the material is objectionable only because of coarse or vulgar language which is not erotic or aphrodisiac in character it is not obscene.

- In considering material claimed to be obscene it is well to remember the motto: "*Honi soit qui mal y pense.*" (Evil to him who evil thinks.)

In his decision, Horn detailed a logic that the prosecution apparently failed to see: If considering a work obscene was a matter of showing how it created lustful thoughts in its readers, or if words or phrases had to be proven to lead to corruption or depravity in the reader, the words had to be of an erotic nature. "If the material is disgusting, revolting, or filthy, to use just a few adjectives," Horn noted, "the antithesis of pleasurable sexual desires is born, and it cannot be obscene."

The ruling turned out to be a landmark decision for Ginsberg and the San Francisco poets. As predicted, the trial created a national awareness of *Howl*, its author, and his friends. *Howl* was in its fourth printing by the end of the trial, and countless mimeographed versions were being circulated throughout the United States.

A few years earlier, Ginsberg had walked into San Francisco and knocked on doors, hoping someone would listen to his poetry. With the court victory of *Howl*, Ginsberg had unscrewed the doors from their jambs, to paraphrase Whitman—not only to a city but to a nation interested in his singular voice.

6

Ginsberg arrived in Venice on July 1 and spent most of the next three months in the city. He would hear from time to time about the *Howl* trial, but most of the reports were sketchy, and Allen never did have an accurate picture of the proceedings in San Francisco until the trial had concluded. He had seen a copy of the San Francisco poets issue of *Evergreen Review*, and from letters from Jack Kerouac and Philip Whalen, he was aware of the stir the San Francisco poets, and "Howl" specifically, had created in the United States, but he was so involved in his travels that he had little time to appreciate fully what was happening back home.

Allen loved Venice and its museums, cafés, waterways, and old-world flavor. "Everywhere you walk it looks like a mad postcard view I saw as a child," he wrote Louis. Alan Ansen's residence was half a block from the Grand Canal, and Allen wasted no time in familiarizing himself with the city. Within a week of his arrival, he had ridden gondolas, rowboats, motorboats, and vaporettos all over Venice, yet, as was to be expected, most of his time exploring the city was spent on foot. He had never thought of Venice in terms of being a real place, he told Louis, but now that he was there, he intended to experience the city to the fullest extent that his time and limited budget would allow. He never wearied of visiting St. Mark's Square and its mammoth Byzantine basilica, resting place of the author of one of the four Gospels of the New Testament. He toured the church on numerous occasions, awed by its five onion-shaped domes, hundreds of columns, statuary of marble and alabaster figures, and enormous mosaic floor. In a letter to his brother, Allen described the sights: "From the front it looks like a vast circus calliope, full of gold statues and cupolas and marble and porphyry and basalt pillars and ancient bas-reliefs from Byzantium that have been built into the walls, pre-christian ornaments and statues of kings and horses cemented into the corners and sides, a whole museum made up of art booty from days of Venetian imperialism and conquest of the east and near east. Inside, there's 40,000 square feet of delicate mosaic in the 'golden gloom,' work of 9th and 10th century Yeats Byzantium and later additions and reconstructions, and a huge mosaic floor full of eye tricks and complex solar designs and arabesques laid down in different sized larger stones, warped by age and uneven settling on the piles over the marshes of Venice." Allen wrote no poetry about this and other Venetian experiences, however, despite the inspired descriptions that they elicited in his letters.

In late July, Allen and Peter took the three-hour train ride to Florence, where they spent three days touring the city's art galleries, including the Uffizi. Allen somehow managed to obtain a student's identification card, which gained him free admission to the galleries. He was taken by the paintings and statues, especially Michelangelo's *David*. In a letter to his father, he described Florence as "a very striking place," "the spot where all the medieval stiffness and religious fear gave way and Renaissance burst through with huge naked idealized human bodies—David's nakedness being Michelangelo's great historical statement."

Rome—Allen's next stop—was a contrast. In the Vatican, Allen was horrified to find Michelangelo's *Last Judgment* desecrated by moralists who had painted drapery over the naked bodies; similarly, fig leafs had been placed on the statues. "I never saw the church in such vulgar and ugly relief," Allen complained. "After Florence and its classical openness, and after seeing the statuary in the forum and state museums, to go in the Vatican and see them desecrating the very significance and point of ancient sculpture . . . it stands out like the piece of dirtymindedness that it is."

Although the Vatican soured him for much of the rest of his trip, Allen's journey to Rome was not a total loss. On the night he and Peter arrived, they took a mile-long moonlit walk to the Colosseum, where the moon shone through the huge arches of the ancient ruin, creating a spectacular effect while at the same time reminding Allen of the history of death that had taken place within the walls of the structure. There were tours of the ruins of the Forum and Capitoline and Palatine hills. He visited the graves of Keats and Shelley, picking clover from Shelley's grave for his father and Gregory Corso. In all, his four days in the Italian capital was a mixed experience.

His vexation with the Catholic Church did not improve when, a few days after visiting the Vatican, he took a train to Assisi, the beautiful mountain town and birthplace of St. Francis. A year earlier, while at sea, Allen had read a great volume of work by and about St. Francis, and he had admired him immensely. To Ginsberg, St. Francis's saintly, gentle behavior in the throes of poverty made him a "beat" figure in the classic way Kerouac had meant it. In Assisi, however, Allen found very little to like in the monks living in the order that St. Francis had founded. By the time he and Peter arrived, they were road-weary and unshaven and in need of a warm bath; they had eaten fruit and salami for their meals along the way, and they could have used something more substantial. Allen, always generous with his own apartment when people needed a place to stay, hoped that he might be able to sleep for a night or two in a room at the monastery, but he was turned away by the monks, who, to Allen's disbelief, had the audacity to request a donation while they were in the process of refusing him a room. Fortunately for Allen and Peter, the two nights they spent in Assisi were warm, and they were able to retire on the monastery lawn in their sleeping bags without discomfort. The monks were not amused. "I got the impression they'd be bugged by St. Francis himself if he reappeared on the streets of Assisi in his tattered cloak, begging and singing in the streets like he used to," Allen wrote in disgust.

He had come to Assisi with angry feelings toward the Catholic Church in Rome, and his experiences at the monastery left him just as disillusioned. After talking to several of the monks who knew English, Allen concluded that they were little more than "zombies" who had inherited none of the warmth and humanity of St. Francis. They were deluded by some kind of mind control, seeing what they were told to see and believing what they were told to believe. The monks had taken him to a historic bed of roses where, they told him, a miracle had occurred. According to the legend, St. Francis had thrown himself into the roses, and from that moment on, no thorns had grown on the rose stems. When he looked closely at the bushes, Allen could see thorns growing everywhere, but when he pointed this out to the monks, they looked at him as if he was "a poor hellbent atheist." "All in all the Catholics got on my nerves, more so in Vatican City than anywhere before," Allen wrote Eugene. "I'd always sort of admired them for having a great mystical organization over the thousands of years, but close up, in Rome and in the great Franciscan center of Assisi, they're nothing but a bunch of hard-up, fig-leaving politicians."

Allen was not about to have a group of contemporary monks tarnish his admiration for St. Francis, and he explored Assisi with his eyes more on the past than the present. He toured the tomb of St. Francis and saw the artifacts, relics, and robes he had left behind. He and Peter climbed the hills to reach the secret caves where St. Francis had spent his winters. They rose at dawn to see the daybreak sunlight flooding into Giotto's frescoes in the monastery church. Despite his misunderstandings with the monks, Allen told his father, his time in Assisi was as rewarding as any of the time he had spent in Europe.

When they were ready to leave Assisi, Allen and Peter were running out of money and could not afford train fare back to Venice. To make matters worse, they had poor luck with their hitchhiking, and before too long, Allen's feet were sore. They had enough money between them for inexpensive meals of fruit, cheese, bread, and ham, and in the evenings, they slept in fields, gazing up at a full moon and awakening to the splendid sight of the rural Italian landscape. Finally, after several days of slow traveling, they made it back to Florence, where they hooked up with someone who offered them a ride most of the way to Venice. Even then, they could afford train tickets that would take them only partway, so when the time came for them to get off the train, Allen and Peter hid in the rest room for the rest of the trip to Venice. "Arrived in Venice tired and without a cent but had a great perfect tour of Italy," Allen concluded.

7

By the time he returned to Venice, the *Howl* trial in San Francisco was in full swing, review copies of Jack Kerouac's *On the Road* were being distributed to potential reviewers, and the term *Beat Generation* was beginning to circulate around the United States. *Time* magazine, wishing to cover what looked like a developing trend, contacted Allen in Venice and asked whether he would be willing to travel to its bureau in Rome for an interview. Short-staffed due to summer schedules and vacations, the magazine was in no position to dispatch a reporter to Venice. Allen agreed to the interview on the condition that the magazine send him a round-trip air ticket and two days' expense money.

From his recent travels in Italy, he was developing into an expert on the art of traveling cheaply, and with the thirty-five dollars he received from *Time* for expenses, he was able to take a twelve-day side trip to Naples and the island of Ischia. After checking into a youth hostel in Naples, Allen spent a day going through the local museums, including one featuring a roomful of pornography from the ancient city of Pompeii. Mount Vesuvius loomed over the city in the near distance, and Allen spent the next day climbing the slope of the mountain and exploring the ruins of Pompeii. Although not active, Vesuvius, Allen discovered, was still a sight to behold, and he spent an hour watching the hot steam slip from the fissures in the rock around the great crater at the top of the mountain. Pompeii was deserted when he arrived at the ruins in the late afternoon. Allen walked alone among statuary featuring naked Venuses, satyrs, drunken Bacchuses, and mythological figures mounted on the walls of the ancient city.

Allen was able to catch a ride to the isle of Ischia on a local fishing boat. After spending a day exploring the island off the western coast of Italy, he set off to find W. H. Auden, who had spent his last ten summers on the island. Their meeting turned out to be a disappointment. Every evening, Auden and a small group of literary cronies would gather at a local bar where, as Allen put it, they would "vie with each other in making depreciating homemade sophisticated small talk." Auden seemed tired, old, and conservative, his political opinions on such topics as capital punishment and literary censorship so orthodox that they sounded to Allen as if they were coming straight from the pages of *Time*. When the discussion turned to poetry, the older poet seemed to delight in tweaking the younger poet's nose, which irritated Allen, who had been drinking enough to angrily challenge Auden's statements. Auden hated

Shelley, and the two quarreled bitterly over Whitman. Auden had read *Howl*, which he had dismissed as being too self-pitying. Frustrated, Allen wound up calling the poet and his friends "a bunch of shits" as he was leaving.

The encounter inspired still another angry long letter to Louis. "All this gives me the conviction, or strengthens the conviction I have had, that the republic of poetry needs a full scale revolution and upsetting of 'values' (and a return to a kind of imagination for life—in Whitman's 'Democratic Vistas' that I have been reading in Venice). . . . With great names like Auden and Marianne Moore trying to be conservative, and Eliot ambiguous and Pound partly nuts, Williams stands out as the only beautiful soul among the great poets who has tearfully clung to his humanity and has survived as a man to bequeath in America some semblance of the heritage of spiritual democracy in indestructable [*sic*] individuality."

Even as Allen was writing these words, a New York critic named Gilbert Millstein was applying similar sentiments to his review of Jack Kerouac's *On the Road*. Published in *The New York Times* on September 5, Millstein's review praised *On the Road* as "a major novel," "the clearest and most important utterance yet made by the generation Kerouac himself named years ago as 'beat.' " Kerouac's generation, Millstein wrote, was searching, physically and spiritually, for a refuge or affirmation it could not name. Further, this search was not limited to a group of San Francisco poets and artists; it spanned a nation. In this way, *On the Road* was a generational novel in the same sense that Hemingway's *The Sun Also Rises* was representative of the group known as the Lost Generation.

Millstein's review, the first published criticism of *On the Road*, was nothing less than the heralding of a new style in American literature. As Millstein pointed out in his review, the idea of a "beat generation" was not new; John Clellon Holmes's *Times* essay had appeared five years earlier. However, in *On the Road*, the Beat Generation had its own testament and literature.

8

Allen was thrilled when he saw the *Times* review. "I almost cried," he wrote Jack. "[The review was] so fine and true. Well, now you don't have to worry about existing only in my dedication and I will have to weep in your great shadow."

It was a modest, although inaccurate, assessment. Ginsberg would never again stand in anyone's shadow. His work was in great demand. *Howl* was City Lights's best-selling book. *Evergreen Review* accepted "Siesta in Xbalba" for publication in its next issue. Lawrence Ferlinghetti wrote and asked Allen to write an introduction to *Gasoline*, a collection of Gregory Corso's poems to be published in the "Pocket Poets" series. Grove Press released a recording of Ginsberg and other contemporary poets reading their work. The photo feature in *Life*, along with the publicity from the *Howl* trial, had given Allen more attention than he could have hoped for.

Early in September, Allen left Venice for Paris. As usual, he took his time getting there. He and Peter stopped briefly in Vienna, where they toured museums and were thrown out of the opera house for not wearing ties to the performance. After Vienna, they went to Munich, where they saw the grim remains of the Dachau crematorium. When they finally arrived in Paris, Allen was unable to find a room with cooking provisions that would be available prior to October 15. He stayed in Paris for a week, doing some preliminary sightseeing and dropping off Burroughs's almost complete manuscript of *Naked Lunch* at the Olympia Press. He then departed for Amsterdam, where he and Peter could stay for a few weeks with Gregory Corso. Allen was pleased to find Amsterdam enjoying a poetry movement of its own. The city had an impressive literary magazine, as well as art and poetry bars—all to complement the museums brimming with Van Goghs, Rembrandts, and the Dutch Masters.

Back in Paris, Allen moved into a room at 9 rue Git-le-Coeur, a run-down, unnamed residential hotel that in time would be referred to as the "Beat Hotel." For thirty dollars a month, a person traded physical comfort for some of the most unusual local color in the city. The forty-two-room hotel was over three hundred years old, and at times, the residents—many of whom were writers, painters, or musicians—must have felt as if it had not been remodeled or modernized during that three-century period. The walls were peeling and the ceilings leaked; the bare floors slanted from the building's settling over the ages. Each room was lighted by a bare forty-watt bulb, and the electrical system in the building was so rickety that circuits could be blown by a resident's plugging in a small appliance such as a radio or hot plate. There were no telephones. The tenants on each floor shared a French-style hole-in-the-floor toilet located at the landing, and if one wished to take a bath, one had to inform the caretaker to heat the water in the first-floor bathroom, a service for which there was an additional charge. Cracked or broken windows went unrepaired for indefinite periods of time.

Despite such ramshackle conditions, the hotel had its charms, not the least of which was its tiny, eccentric caretaker, a woman known only as Madame Rachou. A stern-looking but ultimately gentle woman, Madame Rachou was arbitrarily selective about whom she would take on as a tenant, but once accepted, a person would be treated like a family member. She looked out for her tenants' best interests and protected their privacy from unwanted intruders. She had an uncanny knack for knowing what was going on in each room of the building, yet at the same time, she was very permissive about what her tenants did and whom they brought to their rooms. She also ran a small bar and kitchen, which attracted residents to long discussions over coffee, beer, or wine and inexpensive home-cooked meals.

Allen's room, located on the third floor, was one of the better rooms in the hotel. It was well heated and had hot water three days a week. It also had a small gas stove, which pleased Allen, who loved to cook stews and soups. Gregory Corso had returned with them from Amsterdam, and he shared the room's large bed with Allen and Peter. To Allen, living in cramped, impoverished conditions was a reasonable exchange for the excitement provided by a city such as Paris.

Paris was a wonder—more than Allen had ever expected in all his fantasies of visiting the city. "Paris is beautiful, the only city I've seen so far that would tempt me to expatriate and settle down," he wrote. "The rest of Europe has been interesting, and each city has its one, two or three marvels or charms, but Paris has universal interest and permanent charm as a living place. . . . The very faces on the street look like they've stepped out of paintings by Lautrec and Van Gogh, the streets look like impressionist streets, the cars and faces look like Gershwin and Gertrude Stein and all the millions of Hemingway and legendary cafe and boulevard and movie recollections of Paris I've stored up since I got to college. Best place in Europe so far."

Allen toured the city with vigor. He rode the elevator up the Eiffel Tower and spent time in Notre Dame. He devoted several afternoons wandering through the Louvre. He visited Baudelaire's grave in the Montparnasse cemetery. Every day, he would get up around noon and spend the afternoon, alone or with Peter, on the streets of Paris, attending museum exhibits or window-shopping or simply taking in the city. In the evening, he would occasionally go to the movies or ballets, but more often than not he stayed home and read or wrote until late in the evening. "The days never seem long enough for what I have to do," he told Lucien Carr, "so I just loaf and take my time."

The city's illustrious literary tradition was alive and well, with a strong accent on the avant-garde as practiced by the editors of *Merlin* magazine and Olympia Press. Financed by a wealthy American, *Merlin* was edited and circulated by a small group of Americans, English, and Scots who believed that in postwar literature important writing needed a strong political slant. Although the magazine published works by American and British writers, it had a Continental flavor that distinguished it from *The Paris Review*, another quarterly founded by expatriates living in Paris. The *Merlin* editors prided themselves in publishing the works of such then-unknown writers as Genet and Ionesco and, perhaps most noteworthy, Samuel Beckett.

To publish legally in France, a newspaper, magazine, or publishing house had to hire a French citizen as its general manager, and acting in this capacity for *Merlin* was Maurice Giordias, publisher of Olympia Press. Giordias's father, Jack Kahane, had founded the Obelisk Press in the 1930s and was Henry Miller's first publisher. Giordias would publish books by Miller, D. H. Lawrence, Nabokov and, eventually, William Burroughs, but his main interest and biggest money-maker was his series of green-jacketed pornographic books that he sold to tourists, sailors, and mail-order customers. By acting as general manager of *Merlin*, Giordias was able to prove to the French authorities that he had higher interests than simply publishing dirty books—or db's, as he called them; by having Giordias on their staff, the expatriate editors of *Merlin* were able to publish legitimately in France. "We thought we were using him, and he thought he was using us," quipped Richard Seaver, an American editor at *Merlin* who eventually moved back to the United States to work for Grove Press.

Even though he published such controversial yet undeniably literary writers as Miller, Genet, J. P. Donleavy, and Apollinaire, Giordias was continually operating one step ahead of the law, his books regular items on the government's list of banned books. To stay in business, he had to publish and distribute his books quickly. Further complicating matters was his habit of accepting mail orders for books that had not yet been written. Subscribers to his newsletter would order books solely on the basis of the titles that Giordias had dreamed up; subsequently, once he had accepted and spent the subscribers' money, he had no alternative but to produce the books they ordered. This practice turned out to be a windfall for a number of serious writers living in Paris. Using such pseudonyms as Count Palmiro Vicarion and Carmencita de las Lunas, Christopher Logue and Alexander Trocchi would turn out quickie novels for the Olympia Press list. The five-hundred-dollar payment for one of the books, at the time a generous payment for relatively little work, financed the writers' more serious endeavors.

By merits of its title alone, *Naked Lunch* would seem to have fit in well with a publisher who was issuing such titles as *With Open Mouth*, *White Thighs*, and *Sin for Breakfast*, but Olympia Press rejected Burroughs's novel when Allen Ginsberg submitted it in an early draft to Maurice Giordias. Though displeased by the rejection, Allen was not about to give up on Burroughs's novel. He vowed to contact Samuel Beckett and see whether he would speak to Giordias on the book's behalf, and he showed the manuscript to Mason Hoffenberg, one of Olympia's main writers, who, in Allen's words, declared it to be "the greatest greatest book he read of all time."

Allen's move to Paris, like his move to San Francisco, ushered in the beginning of a significant period of creativity. Once again, the conditions were ideal. Paris represented not only a needed change of scenery; Allen's moving there on the heels of his explorations in Spain and Italy was as important to his creativity as his taking up residence in San Francisco after his explorations in Mexico. Seeing the relics and artifacts of past civilizations renewed his Blakean vow of 1948, and that, in addition to the stimulation provided by a change of environment, seemed to jog his creativity. Furthermore, he was again removed from his traditional sources of support and living in poverty. His nest egg from the summer of 1956 was spent, and while he was receiving periodic royalty checks and payments from magazines publishing his poetry, he was not earning enough money to live comfortably. Traveling and living abroad was expensive, Allen determined shortly after he journeyed to Europe, and he was experiencing difficulty paying his bills and buying food. Paris had its café society but, as Allen told his father, his shrinking funds prohibited him from participating to any notable extent in any of these activities. When he quit his job in San Francisco, he had been forced to examine his goals and determination to be a poet; in Paris, living in poverty, he found his commitment tested anew. It was as if now, more than usual, poetry had to justify the hardship of his life.

9

A year and a half had passed since the death of Naomi Ginsberg, and Allen was still determined to write an elegy to his mother. There had been several false starts. He believed that the poem, if he was to write it, had to be totally honest, and that required his delving into the sad, frustrating, maddening, and inexplicable sides of Naomi's personality and existence, which, understandably enough, he found difficult to address.

One day in early November, while sitting alone at a café, Le Select, he began to write his farewell to his mother. The composition moved him to tears:

Farewell
with long black shoe
Farewell
smoking corsets & ribs of steel
Farewell
communist party & broken stocking
Farewell
O mother
Farewell . . .

It was a beautiful, unsettling work—a crucial part of the poem that Robert Lowell would someday honor as "a terrible masterpiece." As he wrote, Allen was unsparing in his portrait. He listed, in startling detail, the wonder and horror: Naomi's love for the movies, her lovers, her radical politics, her paranoia, even the physical scars that ravaged her body—every image he could think of was included. He tried to see the world through her eyes, and what he saw was a lost, lonely place:

with your eyes of women's operations
with your eyes of shock
with your eyes of lobotomy
with your eyes of stroke
with your eyes of divorce
with your eyes alone
with your eyes
with your eyes
with your death full of flowers
with your death of the golden windows of sunlight . . .

Allen wept throughout the writing, the welling of emotion acting as a catalyst to the poem's composition, just as it had spurred him on when he was writing the "Footnote to Howl" on the bus in San Francisco. As he reported to Kerouac, "I write best when I weep. I wrote a lot of that ["Kaddish"] weeping anyway, and got idea for huge expandable form of such a poem, will finish later and make big elegy, perhaps less repetition in parts, but I gotta get a rhythm up to cry." Throughout the late fall and early winter, Allen worked in his notebooks, writing poem fragments to add to the elegy. He envisioned the finished work to be in different, distinct movements, similar to the structure of "Howl." However, he was unable to arrive at a style and content to run counterpoint to the work he had done at the café, and a year would pass before he would be able to finish it.

He was also at work on another epic poem, inspired by an unusual source. On October 4, while he was still in Amsterdam, the Russians had launched *Sputnik I*, the first orbital satellite in space, followed by *Sputnik II* on November 3. While contemporary historians and newspaper editorialists went on at length about the competitive aspects of a space race between the United States and the Soviet Union, threatening still another time to stir up the ill will generated between the two nations during the Cold War, Allen perceived the *Sputnik* launches as a momentous occasion for humankind. *Sputnik Zemli*, the full Soviet name given the satellites, meant "traveling companion of the world"; in scientific terms, this referred to the satellite's movement with the earth around the sun, but in poetic language, it had a different inference. Further, *Sputnik II* was launched with a living creature, a dog named Laika, aboard. That the satellites had been launched by the country of Allen's ancestry and the current enemy of the United States only made the event more intriguing to him.

"I am impressed by how far the Russians and Chinese have come," Allen commented to Louis, no doubt aware that his father would bristle at his praise of anything connected to the Soviet Union. "People starve there but communism has tried and succeeded in improving material living conditions. The present governments of Russia and China will undoubtedly change in the next hundred years. And with their populations they'll run the world."

To Jack Kerouac, he took a decisively less political tone. "I'm writing big poem to rest of Universe, now that we are out of Earth—biggest news event . . . since invention of Fire. Do you realize we'll (10 years) be on the moon, and in our lifetime get high with brother Martians? There [will] be others out there, and we'll reach them, I'm certain—and our poems too—I [am going to] rewrite Whitman for the entire universe—have big poem started. Other night in Amsterdam I looked at moon with new eyes."

Time would separate the prophecy and hyperbole in Ginsberg's remarks. In Allen's opinion, the *Sputnik* explorations symbolized the possibility of a change in the world order. Whitman had predicted that America would fall by the wayside, victim of its own lack of spiritual freedom and generosity. Allen felt his country was no longer the hope of humankind. It was too busy persecuting its minorities, hoarding its food while the people of other nations starved; it was so focused on its paranoia about the Soviet Union and communism that it refused to so much as publish Russian poetry or allow Charlie Chaplin to work in Hollywood. "If America is not America, what is she?" Allen wondered.

More than ever, he was convinced that he, Kerouac, Burroughs, and the other members of what the media was calling the Beat Generation were correct in their call for a change. Reviewers were criticizing *On the Road* and "Howl" as being documents of rebellion, but, as Allen pointed out, this was not their only function. "People keep seeing destruction or rebellion . . . but that is [a] very minor element, actually; it only seems to be so to people who have accepted standard American values as permanent. What we are saying is that these values are not really standard or permanent, and we are in a sense I think ahead of the times—though not too far ahead—Sputnik has already changed the content of the editorial pages I read. . . . Whitman long ago complained that unless the material power of America were leavened by some kind of spiritual infusion we would wind up among the 'fabled damned.' It seems we're approaching that state as far as I can see. Only way out is individuals taking responsibility and saying what they actually feel—which is an enormous human achievement in any society. That's just what we as a 'group' have been trying to do."

Now that he was in Europe and fulfilling his dream of seeing firsthand "the classic stations of the earth," Allen began to develop a new fantasy—a visit to the Soviet Union. He had heard that despite the political tensions between the United States and the Soviet Union, there was sincere interest in American literature in the Soviet Union. Allen wanted to see "Howl" published there, and he was interested in seeing whether the homeland of Dostoyevski would be willing to publish such books as On the Road and The Subterraneans. Ginsberg was under the impression that the Soviet government might sponsor visitations by American authors, and he dropped by the Russian embassy in Paris to see whether this was possible. However, nothing came of these inquiries, and it would be almost eight years before he stepped foot on Russian soil.

10

With the new year came another flurry of activities. Peter was needed by his family in New York, and he and Allen began making sad preparations for his imminent return to the States. At the same time, Gregory Corso, who had been away from 9 rue Git-le-Coeur, trying to earn money by selling encyclopedias in Germany, returned to the hotel. The big news, however, was Bill Burroughs's arrival from Tangier. He turned up on January 16, the day before Peter's departure.

Allen had conflicting emotions about Burroughs's arrival. He had been eager to see Bill and complete the work on Naked Lunch, but he also worried about their unresolved intimacy. With Peter leaving and Bill moving in, there were too many uncertainties to contend with. He loved Peter deeply, but in a different way from the love he felt for Bill, and Peter had no sooner left for the States than Allen grew depressed, almost despondent. Without Peter, he felt empty, confused about his future. "I cried the other night realizing you'd gone, thinking that love would go away with you and I'd be alone without connection," he wrote Peter. However, to Allen's surprise, Bill turned out to be more of a remedy than he had anticipated. Rather than complicate Allen's life, Burroughs provided him with a sense of stability.

Bill had changed since Allen had left him in Tangier. In his letters to Ginsberg, Burroughs had written about some of the changes, explaining that he had grown weary of the homosexual life and was thinking of forsaking men in favor of women. His life had been traumatic, he told Allen, and he needed to address the conflicts he felt taking place within himself. He put aside his writing and quit drinking; he even turned to meditation and prayer. Every day, in the afternoon, he would sit on his bed and try to sort out his fantasies and the events of his life, and instead of feeling the self-loathing or insecurity he had experienced in the past, he had learned to accept his personality, as if a sentient being had answered his prayers and given him permission to accept his life. "Rather than trying to combat and still and shut up his fantasies which fill his mind and shut out Bliss, he plunges into his fantasies, fills them out and feels them as much as he can," Allen told Peter. "All our fantasies . . . are really parts of us which are TRUE. Rather than shut them out suppress them let them come on in all force no matter how painful they are, accepting their reality."

This realization had a liberating effect upon Allen as well as Bill. For some time, Allen had been troubled by the dark fantasies and nightmares he, Bill, and Peter had experienced. Bill had imagined his murdering Allen or Peter, while Peter dreamed that he had been drowned by Allen, or that Allen had left him alone. Ginsberg's masochistic fantasies centered on his being screwed by Bill, Eugene, or Louis. There were a lot of obvious Freudian interpretations that could have been attached to each fantasy, and though Allen resisted the easy or obvious interpretations, he was nevertheless bothered by these subconscious revelations. His discussions with Bill eased much of his anxiety.

Bill had not come to Paris to rekindle his affair with Allen, and he told Ginsberg as much the night after he arrived. He sat opposite Allen at the kitchen table and for hours detailed the changes he had undergone in recent months. He realized that in the past he had placed Allen in an uncomfortable situation with his demands for intimacy, and he told Allen that he would no longer pressure him into seeing sex as an obligatory element to their friendship. He had come to Paris as a friend, not a lover, and he planned to see a psychiatrist to help him further the inroads he had made in his own self-analysis.

Allen was both relieved and elated by Bill's disclosures. In Peter's absence, he had found the "connection" he needed. If he was going to have sex with Bill—and he did—it would be as part of a new, more stable relationship. Allen was further pleased by the news that *Junky* had been purchased by an English publisher and by the arrival of an advance reading copy of Kerouac's *The Subterraneans*, which Ginsberg judged to be "very intimate and funny," even if the book did reveal Kerouac's women problems to be rooted in his attachment to his mother. When Louis wrote with a negative reaction to the unusual language and syntax in the novel, Allen jumped to Jack's defense. In *The Town and the City* and *On the Road*, Allen said, Kerouac had proven that he could master standard prose; in *The Subterraneans* Jack was narrating his story in the style of his own speech. He had given readers the sound of the American idiom. "Normal conversation does not necessarily follow formal syntax, nor need it as long as it's communicative," Allen argued on behalf of the novel. "Perhaps you find it uncommunicated or uncommunicating because you expect to see a different *written* order of syntax. But it actually gets across very well, what he's describing, faithful to his own way of talk."

Allen had enormous respect for Jack's writing style, even if he found it difficult to use in his own work. He was finally seeing Jack's writing for what it was—pure spontaneous expression, with little regard for the syntactical and grammatical formalities that slowed down the thought process. He had long ago abandoned the idea of advising Jack to clean up his prose. If anything, their roles had been reversed, and it was now Kerouac the novelist offering counsel to Ginsberg the poet (and former agent). Allen bristled when Kerouac became too lofty in his criticism, but he acknowledged that Kerouac, along with Gregory Corso, were ahead of him in their development of spontaneous writing. He vowed to try it more on his own, though he knew it would not be easy. "No more poesy for poesy sake," Allen declared to Jack, "though I have not yet as you and Greg gone through a purely manic unrevised phase of writing and still have to loosen up. . . . I write so little painfully and revise and I can't get settled down to free expression and have nightmares about ever holding my piece. It's not that I don't really agree with you about method of writing—I don't have your football energy for scrawling endlessly on pages—I am nervous and fretful and have to force myself to sit down—at least lately—other seasons it's been more natural—I guess all this publicity is bad."

Kerouac agreed that the sudden media attention being paid On the Road and Howl was a distraction. The temptation, he told Allen, was for the writer to become so involved in the pursuit of fame that the writing would suffer or, worse yet, cease entirely. "Beware of fame, poems will be nonsequitur," he warned Ginsberg.

Jack spoke from experience. Now living with his mother in Orlando, Florida, Jack was spending an inordinate amount of time taking calls from or writing letters to publishers. With the success of On the Road came the demand for more of his work, especially in the same vein. He obliged by working on The Dharma Bums, his fictional account of his friendship with Gary Snyder and the San Francisco poets. Ironically, the book maintained a much more standard, conservative style—closer, in fact, to Kerouac's writing in The Town and the City and On the Road than to his more recent work. Money was coming in, Jack was finally able to repay a long-standing debt to Allen, and with the prospects of enjoying an easier life than he had been living, he was ready to cash in on the fame, at least to a point.

Jack continued to be complimentary of Allen's poetry. He praised Allen's technical virtuosity, telling him that from a technical standpoint he was probably "the best writer in the world." Jack was also concerned about the depressing tone of Allen's poems, however. In his study of Buddhism, Kerouac had already learned to accept the belief that life was sorrowful, and it seemed to him that Ginsberg was too focused on the depressing aspects of life at the cost of devoting his art to something more spiritually uplifting. "You ARE a black blob of sorrow," he told Allen, trying to goad him into accepting Buddhism's first Noble Truth. Further, Kerouac, who was essentially nonpolitical, did not care for Allen's concentration on social and political issues, nor was he impressed with Ginsberg's goal of writing prophetic poems. In Kerouac's view, this only led to more depression. "Why don't you ignore war, ignore politics, ignore samsara unjust fuckups, they're endless. . . . Rid thee of thy wrath, go lamby, isn't it a better thing to do in eternity to leave everybody alone good and evil alike and just pile along glad?"

Allen was open and frank about his intention of writing a prophetic poem that followed in the tradition of Blake and Whitman. As an expatriate, he was able to judge the United States with even more detachment than he had felt when he was living there and feeling alienated from it. He was still obsessed with Whitman's prophecy about the fall of America, and he wanted to continue the development of the idea. "I'd like to write a monstrous and golden political or historical poem about the fall of America," he said. "If poetry can be made of ashcans why not newspaper headlines and politics? Talk about Dulles the way Blake talks about the kings of France shuddering icy chill runs down the arms to their sweating sceptres."

This grand-scale ambition, a line of thinking that would reach fruition in Ginsberg's mid-1960s poems, is evident in his journal poems from this Paris period. In terms of the sheer volume of his writing, he was definitely back on track. He was composing both in his journal and directly on the typewriter, his output once again prodigious. He continued to write in the long-line structure of his Berkeley days, but his writing was moving further away from Williams and closer to his own voice. The poems, as he expressed in his letters to Kerouac, reflected the headlines and issues of the day, and most, including the ones that were eventually shortened and published in *Kaddish and Other Poems*, were lengthy entries, as if Ginsberg hoped to write an epic every time he sat down to write.

Ginsberg's new poems from this period—in particular "Death to Van Gogh's Ear!" "Poem Rocket," "Europe! Europe!" and "At Apollinaire's Grave" (originally entitled "Now Time for Prophecy")—find the poet extending a confident, prophetic voice. "Poet is priest," Ginsberg declares at the beginning of "Death to Van Gogh's Ear!" According to Ginsberg, history and politics have destroyed the world, threatening its future, and some of the world's great poets (García Lorca, Mayakovsky, Crane, etc.) were martyred for being priests in a secular, money-conscious world. The poem calls for the world's assumption of Shelley's idea of poet as unacknowledged legislator, with Ginsberg proposing Vachel Lindsay's appointment to the position of secretary of the interior, with Edgar Allan Poe as secretary of the imagination, and Ezra Pound as secretary of economics.

> Man cannot long endure the hunger of the cannibal abstract
> War is abstract
> the world will be destroyed
> but I will die only for poetry, that will save the world.

At the conclusion of the poem, Ginsberg continues in the prophetic voice of the "Moloch" section of "Howl":

> Money! Money! Money! shrieking mad celestial money of
>   illusion! Money made of nothing, starvation, suicide!
>   Money of failure! Money of death!
> Money against Eternity! and eternity's strong mills grind
>   out vast paper of illusion!

"Poem Rocket," inspired by the *Sputnik* launchings and Gregory Corso's "Be a star-screwer" slogan, is a poem addressed to the future. Now that the human race had made its presence known in the heavens, what would happen to the universe? Would humans corrupt space the way they had corrupted earth? Once again, Ginsberg has occasion to address the familiar theme of his smallness in the universe, but even so, in the poem that acts as his rocket to another consciousness, Ginsberg calls for peace and gentility:

> Now at last I can speak to you beloved brothers of an unknown
>   moon
> real Yous squatting in whatever form amidst Platonic Vapors of
>   Eternity
> I am another Star.

Still very much preoccupied with his Blake visions, Ginsberg effectively addresses the past ("At Apollinaire's Grave") and the future ("Europe! Europe!") in his attempts to understand his present. Apollinaire had walked on these very streets of Paris five decades earlier, Ginsberg muses, and now, as Allen sits in his room and ponders the future, he wonders what will become of that very same city—of Europe itself—in the future. In "Europe! Europe!" Ginsberg abandons the long line and returns to the short lines of his *Empty Mirror* period. He fears for the future of the planet. With all the war and uneasy international politics around him, he questions whether Europe will survive the century.

In a sense, this sequence of poems unites the themes of "Siesta in Xbalba" and "Howl," two of Ginsberg's earlier epics. The sense of the vast and eternal, present in "Xbalba," and the threat of the machinery of destruction, depicted in "Howl," are brought together in Ginsberg's Parisian poems. He had found Europe to be everything he had imagined it to be, and he was angered and saddened to think that humankind's self-destructive impulses could end its great cultural and historical heritage. In his poems, he is a witness to a planet being edged toward its doom.

11

On February 1, Allen left Paris for a reading in England and brief tour of London. Thomas Parkinson, an English professor Ginsberg had known in Berkeley, had moved to London and, after visiting Allen in Paris during the holiday season, had invited him to London for a BBC-sponsored recording of his poetry. Allen, still stinging from the "Howl" obscenity trial, was cautious, if not skeptical, about the recording, saying that he would not censor his work to fit mannered British standards. Still, he could hardly pass up the opportunity to see William Blake's homeland. As he stood on the deck of the ferry crossing the English Channel, watching the white cliffs of Dover rising out of the mist before him, he was overcome by the thought of finally seeing England. "I cried on boat coming across Channel, thinking I would see the sad fogs of the land of Blake," he wrote Peter. He took out a pen and notebook and began a poem commemorating the occasion:

O Blake! Blake! Blake! The yellow sun spanning the green blind Channel.
How sad you'd be to see the dense human fog over London now.
     Green water, Dover's cliffs, silence, squeal of gulls afar
          as if the cliffs squeaked—
     The long green dusty 2'nd class Train at Dover—
I am not these properties: Howling Allen Ginsberg arriving enchanted
     in England.
Weeping at the Foggy earth of England's Blake. . . .

On his first trip to England, as with his initial visits to other countries, Allen sought out the sites and landmarks he had heard of or read about in his youth. He spent his first night in London taking a walking tour of the city. He hiked from Victoria Station to Trafalgar Square, and then walked on to Piccadilly Circus, which, on that Saturday night, was crowded and festive in a way that reminded him of Times Square. Big Ben and the Tower of London were bathed in a mist that was beautiful in the moonlight. Allen's first impression of London was of a city as splendid as some of the other European cities he had visited, but to him it lacked the sense of antiquity he felt in Paris. London had been renovated more recently than the French capital, and in the aftermath of the bombings of World War II, it had been rebuilt and modernized even more.

As he continued his tour, visiting the National Gallery, traveling with Parkinson to see Stonehenge and Salisbury Cathedral, and taking in such sights as the Houses of Parliament, Westminster Abbey, and the Thames, Allen grew even more reflective about the history of Europe and what was then that continent's largest city. Inspired, he continued his work on the long poem he had begun at the start of his trip, and he began notes for another work, tentatively entitled "World! World!" (which eventually evolved into "Europe! Europe!"); he wrote long, descriptive letters to his father, brother, and Peter. Allen was developing a global consciousness, abandoning his American ethnocentricity for a worldview he would maintain for the rest of his life. He would always be an American, he acknowledged, but he also recognized that too great an identification with nationality, race, or religion would only hinder one's ability to see the larger, global perspective. This ethnocentricity, Allen believed, was at the root of war, poverty, and human misery. Great writers such as Blake and Shakespeare had recognized this—and long before the world had been greeted by technology and mass communications and the ultimate weapons of destruction—and Ginsberg was greatly moved by their sense of prophecy.

He tested some of these thoughts on his father, who, not surprisingly, was not about to abandon his own views, developed over a lifetime, in favor of what he perceived to be a lot of political posturing uttered by a young upstart. Allen's letters, dispatched from London and Paris over the course of the next couple of months, were received with varying degrees of exasperation, outrage, amusement, anger, frustration, and patronage, but rarely with any agreement. Louis bristled when Allen defended Soviet foreign policy, and he was insulted by some of his son's pointed criticism of the United States. Allen maintained his belief that the Western countries, particularly the United States and those in Western Europe, were so paranoid about Soviet expansionism that they were willing to trade future world stability (or survival) for a reassurance brought on by a huge arms buildup. When Louis conceded that changes were necessary, but that inner changes in the individual countries took time, perhaps centuries, Allen disagreed. "We haven't got centuries to wait," he countered. "We have to understand that we are capable of awful deeds (blind like any neurotic is blind to his own aggression and can only see someone else's hostility, not his own), have done some really horrible things and *have* to be responsible for our own salvation's sake—and there isn't much time. I mean the world is bigger than we are finally, and is changing so rapidly, the changes of history are accelerating as rapidly as the changes in science." In Allen's opinion, the only way to turn the course of modern history around was for the United States to share its science, technology, and wealth with the rest of the world; it had to abolish its need to feel superior.

Louis was not prepared for such wholesale change. By early 1958, the Beat Generation was receiving its initial onslaught of publicity in the United States, and Louis could not agree with many of the statements he was reading in the newspapers and magazines, ideas issued by Allen and some of his friends, which Louis interpreted to be too general and negative. "Where I disagree with the Beat Generation," he wrote Allen, "is that it sees no good and no positive values at all. As I wrote, the Beat Generation throws out the baby with the dirty bath water. The Beat Generation sees no leavening influences, no positive values in our modern times. It disengages itself from all action, yielding only to its own undisciplined series of blind "kicks"—bright colored beads without a string of purpose."

Louis was especially angered by Allen's opinions regarding the Soviet Union. As far as he was concerned, Allen was exhibiting his naïvité when he defended communism and criticized socialism. For Louis, this was an old story, dating back to his arguments with Naomi and her sister. And Louis was infuriated when Allen suggested that as a poet he had to take a larger view than the one that was perhaps dictated by his Jewish heritage. "You *are* both a *Jew and a poet*," he told Allen. "You cannot escape your own self: your own biological inheritance flowing from untold generations of race. . . . Be your essential self and you'll escape the fiction you confuse with Allen Ginsberg."

In reality, Allen was not trying to create a deceptive or fictitious public persona; if anything, he was continuing his longtime pursuit to determine who he was as both a person and poet. He was confident in his political views, convinced that his role as a poet was a prophetic one, but he needed response to his new ideals. Burroughs was too alienated from the system to provide a clear, objective view, and Kerouac hated politics as a general rule. Louis became Allen's sounding board, just as Europe was the catalyst in the evolution of Allen's worldview.

Allen's BBC recording went better than he had anticipated. When he arrived at the recording studio, he was prepared to read for five minutes, his recitation to be just a modest contribution to Thomas Parkinson's series on American poets. However, he had no sooner begun his reading when the program director halted the recording and asked Allen whether he would read "A Supermarket in California" and "Howl" in its entirety. Allen obliged with one of his most dramatic readings of "Howl" to date. Believing that he was "speaking to England," as he told Peter Orlovsky, Allen put everything he had into the reading. "I started and gave slow sorrowful reading, built up, almost broke down in tears again, dreaming I was talking through microphone to the Soul in the Fog . . . to Blake himself," Allen said. Aside from the pure joy of giving a powerful reading of the poem, he had an additional reason for being pleased with his BBC reading. His earlier recording for Grove Records had gone poorly, leaving him dissatisfied with the results, so now he had put his most important work on tape the way he wanted it. He repeated his performance for a small gathering in Oxford, and he used the occasion to read works by Philip Whalen, Denise Levertov, and Robert Creeley, as well as his own.

With his three-week stay in London coming to an end, Allen took time to climb to the top of St. Paul's Cathedral, to the Whispering Gallery that overlooked London. He was thrilled by the panoramic view and immediately sat down and recorded his impressions in the notebook he had brought with him, much of the material finding its way into "Europe! Europe!"

Allen returned to France on a clear, chilly day. As was his habit, he spent a substantial amount of time on the deck of the ship, gazing out at the sea. The sun cut through "a great dreamcloud floating over the sky," sending down rays of light that refracted off the water. The sight prompted another meditation on the vastness of creation and time. Suddenly, as if it had been orchestrated by deity, Allen saw "a winged live seagull flying out of the cloudy glory and imagined all the dolphins streaming through the sea, creation streaming all over the universe." Such ponderings were suitable closure to a brief, though very influential journey that saw Allen renewing his sense of purpose. He was a small creature in an infinite universe, yet as a poet, he was in the position to sound his voice to speak to the ages.

12

Back in Paris, Allen resumed his hectic schedule. In his absence, Burroughs had fallen into a gloomy state and had begun taking paregoric, a legal and inexpensive elixir of opium that could be purchased in drugstores everywhere. One of Allen's first orders of business was to take Bill to a doctor, who helped him withdraw from his light habit by prescribing apomorphine. In his pile of unopened correspondence, Allen found letters from Jack Kerouac, Denise Levertov, and Robert Creeley, as well as clippings of John Clellon Holmes's "The Philosophy of the Beat Generation" (which had appeared in the February 1958 issue of *Esquire*), a *Time* magazine piece about Kerouac, and *New York Post* interviews, conducted by Mike Wallace, of Kerouac and Philip Lamantia. The Beat Generation was gaining impetus in the United States, even as Ginsberg, Burroughs, and Corso—three of its central figures—were living overseas.

Money was beginning to come in, and Allen was able to pay his outstanding debts and live a little more easily than before. *Evergreen Review* purchased "Siesta in Xbalba" for sixty-four dollars, and the Canadian Broadcasting Company sent a thirty-five-dollar payment for a seven-minute recording of Allen's poetry. Fantasy Records was offering $150 in advance for the recorded poetry Allen had given them. He was happy to receive the money, but the barrage of contracts, with all their legalities, left him feeling as if he was losing control of his poetry. He wanted to retain the right to send his poetry to whomever he preferred, without the headache or worry about what publishing rights had been assigned to whom.

As winter melted away into the first warm breezes of spring, Allen found himself missing Peter, and he began to think about returning to the States. Burroughs, too, was considering a trip back home, and he and Allen made tentative plans to leave in July. In the meantime, they ran with their respective groups. Allen was surprised by Burroughs's new assertiveness, which found Bill associating with a young group of expatriate hipsters who had formed their own

version of café society. Allen saw a lot of a young woman named Joy, and, for
a brief time, considered marrying her so she could move to the United States,
where she wanted to live. He spent a week with Larry Rivers, the painter who
would be featured in the film *Pull My Daisy*, and he had chance encounters
with folksinger Ramblin' Jack Elliott and Mason Hoffenberg, Terry Southern's
collaborator on *Candy*.

During the last week in March, Allen wrote a poem that finally addressed
his Blake visions in detail. He called the poem "The Lion for Real," the lion
being the presence of William Blake, the poem recalling, in almost literal
detail, the various responses to Ginsberg's talk of his visions:

> I came home & found a beautiful lion in my room
> Rushed on the Fire Escape screaming Lion! Lion!
> Two stenographers pulled their golden hair & banged the window shut
> I hurried home to milly Paterson & stayed two days
>
> Called up my old Reichian Analyst
> who'd kicked me out of therapy for smoking african marijuana
> "It happened" I panted "there's a lion in my apartment"
> "I'm afraid any discussion would have no value" he hung up.
>
> My father & I shrank from each other tearful & shaking
> He blamed it on my mother's nervous breakdown
> I tried to insist I never actually saw a Lion
> He didnt believe me & went to his job in the Zoo. . . .

Narrated in the form of a fable, "The Lion for Real" continues with the
story of the lion's vigil in Ginsberg's apartment. It refuses to leave or accept
nourishment, deaf to Ginsberg's suggestion that it eat him or face its own
destruction. Finally, it gets up one day and leaves, promising that it would
return. Ginsberg concludes:

> Lion I have remembered now for a whole decade knowing
>   only your time-rending hunger
> Not the bliss of your final satisfaction O roar of the
>   Universe How am I chosen
> In this life I have heard your direct and deafening
>   promise and seen
> Your starved and most pious ancient presence O Lord
>   I wait in your room at your mercy.

As specific as it was in its reference to Ginsberg's Blake visions and his
decade-long attempts to come to terms with them, the "lion" in the poem was
a powerful symbol open to the interpretation of individual readers. When
Burroughs heard Ginsberg read the poem, he interpreted the lion to be Allen's
heterosexual personality; when Allen read the poem at Columbia University a
few years later, Diana Trilling thought the lion was her husband. Even after he
had completed the first draft of the poem, Ginsberg worried that readers might

criticize him for seeming too self-pitying. As he wrote Peter, "I was ashamed of it too because it really tips my mit, I mean shows the fact that I am now *here* but pining for the world to come, and maybe damned for now, not really Zen or enlightened, but just still lovelorn for future Blue Balloons, but on the other hand at least the poem reveals that . . . the poem's true, I'd rather pray than make believe I'm God."

In addition to working on "The Lion for Real," "Europe! Europe!" and other poems in revision, Allen began a new extension of "Howl," a fragmentary poem he called "The Names." Much of the material in the poem, such as his dream conversation with Joan Vollmer, had been used in other poems, and without a "base word" structure, "The Names" did not fit into "Howl." Mixing eulogies for the dead (Bill Cannastra, Joan Vollmer, Phil White) with sympathy for the living (Herbert Huncke, Neal Cassady), Ginsberg tried to maintain the thematic unity he had established in "Howl," as if one day he, like Whitman, would be able to piece together a life's work in a sequence of poems with overlapping themes and messages. The characters, particularly Cassady, were more vivid in "The Names" than in "Howl," but the poem ultimately lacked a sense of completeness and would not be published for twenty years—and even then only as a fragment rather than a fully realized poem.

In April, Allen traveled again to England, accompanied by Gregory Corso. The two poets had been invited to give a reading at Oxford and, still relishing the success of his previous trip to London, Allen was happy to make the journey. This time, however, the reading did not go as well. In attendance were a number of students active in the campaign for nuclear disarmament, and when Gregory began to read "Bomb," his darkly humorous new poem about the hydrogen bomb, he was greeted by angry hecklers who disrupted his reading and threw shoes at him. "Do you know what it's like to die by an H-bomb?" they shouted at him. Gregory, a provocateur under normal circumstances, increased the tension by calling the students creeps. Assuming the role of peacemaker, Allen tried to explain Corso's poem, but the students were hearing none of it. Allen argued politics with them for a brief time and finally, in frustration, he wound up calling them "a bunch of assholes." Facing a near-riot, Allen and Gregory were escorted from the stage. They joined a number of sympathetic students and spent the rest of the evening partying and reading their poems.

Having Corso in tow seemed to bring out Allen's playful, irreverent side. When they were introduced to Dame Edith Sitwell, Allen mentioned that he was putting together a poetry anthology that was featuring photographs of its contributors in the nude. Perhaps, Allen suggested, she would like to contribute. If she was insulted by the suggestion, she did not indicate as much. In fact, she invited the two poets to have lunch with her in London's Sesame Club. Allen and Gregory turned up at the posh establishment in the Beat "uniform" of sandals, jeans, and turtleneck sweaters. Over a fancy luncheon of smoked salmon and lobster thermidor, the three carried on a long discussion about poetry. Dame Edith admired Ginsberg's and Corso's work, and she wished them success. However, she was less agreeable when the discussion turned to Aldous Huxley and the use of drugs as a means of expanding consciousness and heightening creativity. Dame Edith argued that an artist should not need artificial means to stimulate creativity, while Allen and Gregory supported the use of drugs in the name of art.

Allen also had occasion to meet again with W. H. Auden, who, Allen learned, felt badly about the way their earlier meeting in Ischia had gone. This time, Auden was warm and responsive to Allen and Gregory, and he invited them to tea and took them on a tour of Christ Church Cathedral. At one point during their conversation, Gregory playfully queried of his host, "Are birds spies?" to which Auden replied, "No, I don't think so. Who would they report to?" "The trees," Allen shot back, completing the exchange. Overall, their get-together was friendly, much better than their stormy encounter in Italy.

13

Ginsberg was back in Paris by late May. On his last day in England, he and Gregory visited Blake's grave in a London cemetery, Allen pausing by a large sandstone marker that said that Blake and his wife were buried somewhere near that spot, though it was not specific as to where. Allen had been reading a volume of Vachel Lindsay's collected poems, a gift from Gregory, and as soon as he returned to Paris, he wrote a poem addressing the dead American poet. He also returned to the Père Lachaise Cemetery and sat for a half hour at Apollinaire's resting place, sketching his tomb and taking notes for additions to the poem he had already begun in commemoration of the poet.

There were other projects, as well. Robert LaVigne had written with the news that he had an upcoming show in San Francisco, and he requested that Allen write some brief introductory remarks to accompany the exhibit. Allen responded with a five-hundred-word recollection of their initial meeting at Foster's Cafeteria. He topped off this fertile writing period with a love poem to Peter Orlovsky ("Message") and a poem about the Eiffel Tower.

In addition to his creative work, Allen maintained his extensive correspondence, much of it focusing on French politics. While he had been away in England, Charles de Gaulle had assumed control of the French government, and France was troubled by civil unrest, most of it aimed at the Algerian War. There had been some disturbances, but most of the demonstrating had been quelled by the time Allen returned to Paris. Still, he was as fascinated as ever by the political scene, which he followed closely and commented upon in his lengthy, ongoing correspondence with his father. He did witness one impressive display of the populist movement against de Gaulle, a huge demonstration watched over by hundreds of mounted police wearing silver helmets. To get a better view, Allen climbed first onto a statue and then onto the ledge of a bank. He was entranced by what he saw, which he described in a letter to Lucien Carr: "First great mob scene I witness since the old days in Journal Square passing out leaflets against Mayor Hague—same types of people, almost cried saw my mother and Aunt Elanor in the marchers with 'Vive La Republique!' and 'Front Populaire' slogans on lips and upraised comrade-salutes." Fortunately, the police kept their distance and there was no violence.

With his July departure date approaching more rapidly than he would have liked, Allen began to scurry to find a way to earn money for his trip home. He had originally hoped to finance the trip with money from a Guggenheim Fellowship, but when that fell through, Allen found himself virtually broke and with no substantial money expected in the near future. He was earning money in small parcels—enough to live on but nowhere near the sum needed to get back to New York. He missed his family, Peter, and his friends, but a part of him was reluctant to leave Paris. The Beat Generation had become a major cultural and literary phenomenon in the United States, and from what he had read in the papers and the clippings forwarded to him by Louis, Peter, and others, he could see the markings of an ugly backlash against the so-called movement. At first, he had been willing to accept any publicity, positive or negative, that came his way, but the mass-media coverage was now becoming tedious.

To Allen's horror, Neal Cassady had become the first well-known victim of the backlash. With all the attendant hubbub about the Beat Generation, the San Francisco police had decided to crack down on the city's bohemian culture. Herb Caen, San Francisco's popular newspaper columnist, had fanned the flames by labeling the group of poets, artists, and bohemians "beatniks," a snide reference playing off America's collective paranoia about the launching of *Sputnik* and the country's ensuing space race with the hated Russians. Caen had suggested that the smell of marijuana was stronger than the smell of garlic in the North Beach area, and the police made their presence known wherever the "beatniks" assembled—on the street, around the City Lights Bookstore, at jazz clubs, poetry readings, and art exhibits. Robert LaVigne's art showing was disrupted by police who claimed that there were too many people in attendance in the building. Allen received word that acquaintances had been harassed or arrested, Neal Cassady among them.

On April 8, Neal had been arrested for offering two undercover police three joints in exchange for a ride to work. Neal spent a week in the city jail, awaiting the convening of a grand jury, and when it finally met, charges were dropped due to insufficient evidence and Neal was released. The police, however, were not about to let the infamous "Dean Moriarty" slip away so easily, and the morning after he had been released, Neal was arrested again and charged with being a part of a marijuana smuggling ring. With bail set at twelve thousand dollars and Carolyn unwilling to put their house on the line to free him, Neal had no choice but to sit in the San Bruno County jail and wait for his upcoming trial.

When Allen heard the news, he was both worried and incensed. He knew that Neal would have a difficult time in confinement, and he had a brief but terrible premonition of Cassady's committing suicide in jail. "Is there anything we can do about Neal?" he wrote Jack Kerouac, who had been uncharacteristically silent in recent months. Allen proposed the gathering of character witnesses, people such as himself, Kerouac, Ruth Witt-Diamant, and Kenneth Rexroth, who could testify that Cassady was a writer and valuable contributor to society, not the drug dealer the police seemed to think he was. Allen saw Neal as a martyr who was being "crucified" by police who were so wrapped up in enforcing "evil laws" concerning marijuana that they would use any method, including entrapment, to make their arrests. It was a complaint that Ginsberg would voice often and publicly in the years to come.

Allen was prepared as much as ever for legal, social, or literary battles. He was fed up with American laws, particularly those restricting individual freedom of expression. Lawrence Ferlinghetti had recently written with the news that, given the current climate in San Francisco, and after consulting with his attorneys, there was no way that he could publish even so much as reasonable excerpts of the *Naked Lunch* and *Interzone* manuscripts that Allen had sent him; Burroughs would be better off, Ferlinghetti said, if, like Henry Miller, he was to publish his books in Paris. To Allen, this was unacceptable. Burroughs should be published in his native country, and Allen labored to see that it would happen. Editors of the *Chicago Review* had seen a portion of *Naked Lunch*, published under Burroughs's William Lee pseudonym, in the Fall 1957 issue of *Black Mountain Review*, and they had contacted Allen with the request that he send them work by himself, Burroughs, and Kerouac. Allen responded by typing selections of *Naked Lunch* and mailing them to the literary quarterly. He submitted additional excerpts, along with his "The Lion for Real," to *The Paris Review*.

In his final weeks in Paris, Allen had a number of meetings with well-known figures in the international arts community. Through newspaper columnist Art Buchwald, who had stopped by to interview Ginsberg and Corso, Allen met film director John Huston. Over coffee at the Bonaparte, Allen and Gregory suggested that *Naked Lunch* would make an excellent film, but Huston gracefully declined. He did, however, invite them to a cast party on a houseboat, which turned into a fiasco when a drunken actor friend of Gregory's, Bill's, and Allen's poured champagne over Errol Flynn's head and was subsequently thrown into the Seine by Flynn's bodyguards. Allen was mortified by the incident.

In recent weeks, Allen had been reading a thick anthology about Dadaist painters and poets, as well as seeing Surrealist films, so he was very pleased when, on successive nights during the second week of June, he was able first to meet Dadaist poet Tristan Tzara and then painter Marcel Duchamp, photographer Man Ray, and poet Benjamin Péret. Allen ran into Tzara at the Deux Magots café, and they had an interesting conversation. Allen believed Tzara to be "in a way the best writer" of the Dadaists because Tzara saw a similarity between Dadaist art and Zen koans. Both, Tzara believed, were riddles aimed at freeing the human mind. Allen met the other three when he, Burroughs, and Corso attended a party on Avenue Président Wilson. There was a lot of heavy drinking at the party, and Allen, who felt that Duchamp and Burroughs were kindred spirits, persuaded Duchamp to kiss Burroughs on the forehead. They got drunker as the night progressed, and Allen wound up crawling on the floor on all fours, clutching at Duchamp's pant legs and begging for his blessing. Amused, Duchamp laughed and said that he was only human, not some kind of deity.

There were two other notable meetings. In early July, Allen and Bill paid a visit to Louis-Ferdinand Céline, who was living with his wife in a large house in nearby Meudon. Céline's works, particularly *Journey to the End of the Night* and *Death on the Installment Plan*, had been enormously influential to Allen and Bill in the middle 1940s, when they were forming their own ideas about how literature should address society. Despite Céline's reputation for being an outspoken anti-Semite, they were eager to meet him. They greeted him with a letter of introduction written by his French publisher. Céline, who said he was still practicing medicine, looked like one of the characters out of his novels. He was tall and almost sickly thin, with long, unruly gray hair, and his clothing—including several sweaters that he wore at once—was ragged. He had a number of fierce-sounding dogs that barked at Allen and Bill as they were waiting to be admitted to the house, and when Céline saw that his guests were nervous around the dogs, he reassured them that they were not as dangerous as they seemed, that he kept them to protect himself from Jews and to ward off intruders. Although Allen cringed at such open anti-Semitism—he and his father had argued vehemently in the past about how Allen could accept the poetry of Ezra Pound, knowing as he did of the poet's anti-Semitic past—he decided to stay. Céline directed them to a wrought-iron table in a small unkempt courtyard near the house, and for the next few hours the three talked about whatever came to mind, including the French prison system, drug addiction, and Céline's medical practice, while Céline's wife, Lucette, served them wine and tea. Allen and Bill left copies of *Junky*, *Howl*, and *Gasoline* with the man they still considered to be France's greatest writer.

Allen's final meeting with a notable literary figure occurred just before he left for the United States. Years earlier, while he had been in the Psychiatric Institute, Allen had been encouraged by Carl Solomon to read the works of Surrealist poet Henri Michaux. Allen had been impressed, and he now hoped to see him while he was in Paris. He had sent him a postcard requesting a meeting, and Michaux had simply turned up, unannounced, one day. Their conversation was a delight. Michaux had written a number of poems under the influence of mescaline, and Allen and Bill were interested in how the drug had affected his writing. Gregory caused a slight stir when he urinated in the kitchen sink, which Michaux interpreted as a rebel's attempt to impress him, but the meeting was otherwise a good one. Michaux returned the following evening, and the group had dinner together and spent the rest of the evening talking about poetry.

For Allen, leaving Paris was a bittersweet experience. Neither Burroughs nor Corso was returning with him to the States, and Allen was saddened by the prospects of leaving them behind. His time in Paris had been productive, but he was anxious to get back to the United States and assemble a new book of poems.

12
Kaddish

Death which is the mother of the universe!—Now wear your nakedness forever, white flowers in your hair....

1

Allen was no sooner back in New York than he found himself in the center of the storm of activities whirling around the Beat Generation. For Allen and the others, the term had grown tiresome, so overworked that it seemed almost a mockery of the charming phrase Kerouac had uttered a decade earlier. The way the press presented it, the Beat Generation was a rebellious youth movement staged by those who refused to grow up. The behavior of the Beats was reckless and irresponsible and, at least according to some critics, criminal. Their jazz-influenced language was the subject of endless parody, their literature beside the point, and even on those rare occasions when their works were regarded by the press, they were usually dismissed as so much juvenilia, the writings of immature, uneducated, talent-free upstarts. Writing for *Partisan Review*, Norman Podhoretz, an underclassman at Columbia when Ginsberg was attending classes there, probably summed up the popular critical notion of the Beat Generation when he dismissed Kerouac and Ginsberg and other writers as antisocial, anti-intellectual "know-nothing bohemians." And this was only the beginning. The media attention would continue to grow until it reached its peak and fell off at the end of 1959.

With Ginsberg out of the country, the weight of the attention fell on the reluctant shoulders of Jack Kerouac. At one time, Jack had craved the riches and fame that befell a best-selling author, but now, in the wake of the success of *On the Road* and, more recently, *The Subterraneans*, Kerouac was learning that fame could be a terribly heavy burden to bear. He had recently purchased a home in Northport and moved his mother up from Florida, and both of their lives were continually interrupted by admirers dropping by at any time of the day or night, expecting an audience or night on the town with the "King of the Beats." Whenever he went out, Jack was applauded or baited—at times, it was difficult to determine which was worse—by people who recognized him from his television appearances or from his photographs in newspapers and magazines. On one occasion, he was badly beaten by a gay boxer who took exception to Kerouac's fictional portrayal of him in *The Subterraneans*.

Kerouac reacted with bitterness. By nature, he was neither a shill nor an apologist. He had not aspired to be anyone's leader, and he resented having his actions judged as if he was. He felt badly that his *On the Road* portrayal of Neal Cassady had been at least indirectly responsible for Neal's harassment in San Francisco, yet he was also angry with Cassady for being so reckless with his drug use in light of all the attention he was receiving. Depressed, Kerouac drank ferociously and fought off his demons by making a public spectacle of himself, only to retreat to his mother whenever he needed privacy and home-grown comfort.

Gabrielle Kerouac had always felt that Allen was a bad influence upon her son, and she had little trouble seeing him as the kind of disruptive force responsible for some of Jack's troubles. She had intercepted and read one of Allen's Paris letters to Jack, sent to Florida while Jack was in New York and looking for his new home. She was shocked by the letter and Allen's casual references to homosexuality and drug use, and she immediately responded with angry, hateful letters to Allen that, in this comedy of errors, were sent to Paris after Ginsberg had already returned to the States. Bill Burroughs, instructed by Allen to open all mail delivered to his Paris address, read Mrs. Kerouac's letters and forwarded one, along with his own commentary, to Allen in New York. Calling Jack's mother a "stupid, small minded vindictive peasant incapable of a generous thought or feeling," Bill advised Allen to show Mrs. Kerouac's letter to Jack for his reaction. If he chose to let his mother read his mail and order him around like a child, he was, in Bill's opinion, "a lost cause."

In reality, the letter was not unlike a couple of the nastier letters Allen had received from Jack in the past. After calling Allen "an immoral lout," Gabrielle Kerouac told him that she had raised her son to be a good Christian, and that she had promised her husband on his deathbed that she would keep Allen away from Jack. Her letter, then, was a warning. Allen was not to call or write or attempt to see Jack, nor was he to mention him in his books, as he had on the dedication page of *Howl*. She further mentioned that she had contacted the FBI to see that her wishes were met. If Allen wanted to pursue his "dirty actions," Mrs. Kerouac said, he had better find men of his "own kind." "I warn you again," she railed, "don't you dare write Jack again, and leave us alone and that goes for Bill too. We don't want sex fiends or dope fiends around us. We've had enough trouble with bums like you so [you'd] better watch your step."

When Jack learned of his mother's letters and the nature of their contents, he wrote a hasty letter, also mailed to Paris and read by an incredulous Bill Burroughs. In his letter, Jack tried to explain his position in a way that would appease Allen without Jack's having to condemn his mother. He had to consider his mother's feelings, he said, and, as if sensing Allen's disapproval of his not lifting a finger to help Neal, he reiterated his stance that Neal had been warned to behave himself. Bill seethed as he read the letter. Jack owed much of his fame and fortune to his friends—to Neal especially—Bill pointed out, and for

Kerouac to abandon them at his mother's request was, by Burroughs's estimation, a "weak and cowardly" act that was totally indefensible. No one could stand behind letters such as Mrs. Kerouac's and yet pretend to be the friend of the person she attacked. And for Jack to stand by and watch his mother attack Allen, of all people, was absurd, the act of an ingrate: "He seems to forget all your hours of work getting his manuscripts before publishers, agents, etc.," Bill wrote Allen.

Allen could understand Burroughs's wrath and indignation. There was truth to everything he wrote. However, Allen had had his tolerance tested before, especially by Jack, and his sense of loyalty overrode anything that Jack or his mother could put forth in an angry letter. He would wait out this latest tirade, as he had endured Jack's tantrums in the past. To Allen, this was another test of friendship.

2

In Allen's first month or two back in New York, he spent most of his time getting settled and trying to catch up on a year and a half's news. With all the visits to his family in New Jersey and friends in New York, there was very little time for writing, and he yearned for a quiet, private place where, unlike the last weeks in Paris and now in New York, he was not receiving so many visitors and overnight guests. He and Peter found an inexpensive four-room apartment at 170 East Second Street in the East Village, which Allen intended to use as a refuge from his busy activities, but his no-visitors policy did not last long. When his old San Francisco girlfriend, Sheila, showed up with a young painter she had met while fleeing her marriage and making her way cross-country, Allen generously offered them his spare bedroom until they found a place of their own. In addition, he heard from Robert LaVigne, who needed a place to stay while he visited New York, and from Carl Solomon, who was about to be released from Pilgrim State and would need an apartment. The scene threatened to become overwhelming.

As if this was not enough, Allen was busy trying to help the Orlovsky family, which, as always, was caught up in myriad problems. When Peter had returned to the United States earlier in the year, he met with his father, whom he had not seen in years, and the two rented a room together. Peter found a third-shift job at the Psychiatric Institute. Given the state of his family, it must have been a burden. Julius remained in a mental hospital, and Lafcadio seemed a likely candidate for admission in the near future. Julius had improved to the point where he now recognized Peter when he made his weekly visits to the institution, and to the surprise of his attending physicians, the usually catatonic Julius carried on brief conversations with his brother. There was faint hope for his release, but Peter was reluctant to move too quickly on the matter. He was happy to see his brother show signs of life, but he saw something in Julius's eyes, as well. "There's so much pain in his face, it's always there," he told Allen.

Because he was not in an institution, Lafcadio was even more of a challenge. At best, his behavior was calm but erratic. Lafcadio had recently come up with the idea that all of the best things on earth should be shipped into space on a rocket and, using the art supplies that Peter bought him with his VA checks, he spent hours drawing pictures of spaceships. Peter's mother felt that Lafcadio should have a lobotomy, but Peter resisted the idea, believing that he and Allen could take care of Lafcadio if his mother could no longer keep him with her in Northport. Lafcadio would occasionally do something inexplicable, such as the time he began to burn Peter's books, but with company and supervision, he was generally harmless to himself and others.

Allen accepted the problems in Peter's family the way he had accepted his own mother's mental illness. To Allen, they were family. "Lafcadio & Julius/ are my own brothers in Law/I accept their drunk cases," he had written in his first draft of "Message" while he was in Paris, and he had no intention of abandoning them now that he was back in the States. Allen went to Northport to visit the Orlovskys, and he was quickly taken into Lafcadio's confidence. Lafcadio told Allen that he was going to be saved by Martians who had visited the planet and saw him as one of earth's perfect men, and Allen, perhaps hearing strains of Naomi in Lafcadio's talk, went along with him on the topic. He told Peter's brother that there was room for him at his and Peter's apartment, but Lafcadio declined the invitation, fearing the dirtiness of the city and the chance that it would be bombed if there was a nuclear war. He told Allen he would stay in Northport, find a job, and take care of himself, though Allen doubted it would work.

Although Allen had no way of realizing it at the time, these events and conversations were acting as creative catalysts, much the way Carl Solomon's 1955 admittance to the mental institution had been a catalyst to the composition of "Howl." Allen had yet to find a way to complete the eulogy to his mother that he had begun in Paris, but now that he was back in the States, in touch with clinical insanity in a intimate way that he had not seen since Naomi's death, he was being prepared for a time when he would sit down and face an aspect of his past that had haunted him since his childhood.

3

Now back in the publishing capital of the world, Allen beefed up his literary activities, promoting his own work and championing the work of his friends. From Lawrence Ferlinghetti, Allen learned that the latest printing of *Howl*, now with twenty thousand copies in print, had sold out, and that City Lights planned to print another five thousand copies in October. For a poetry book, these were impressive numbers, even if Allen's 10 percent earnings on the book's seventy-five-cent cover price were not about to make him wealthy. However, Ferlinghetti seemed to possess a natural business acumen that enabled him to earn for his authors as much money as could be garnered from the market. He sold reprint rights to *Howl* at a brisk pace, helping Allen realize at least a reasonable remuneration for his decision to publish with a small press.

Allen tried to use all of his influence to get his friends published. He tried again to talk Ferlinghetti into publishing Burroughs, telling him it would be a mistake to pass him up. Ferlinghetti stood by his earlier decision, as he did with his decision not to publish Kerouac's *Mexico City Blues*. Ferlinghetti issued a broadside edition of Corso's "Bomb," but he was in no hurry to print a new collection of Gregory's poems. Nor was he interested in publishing Ginsberg-recommended collections by Gary Snyder and Philip Whalen. Undeterred, even if a little frustrated, Allen turned to other publishing houses. William Carlos Williams's latest *Paterson* volume, containing one of Allen's earlier letters to Williams, had just been published, and when Allen dropped by the New Directions office to pick up a copy, he met briefly with James Laughlin and tried to convince him to publish new works by Snyder and Whalen. "I explained how poetry appearances were getting fucked up by the absence of their highclass work and Ferlinghetti's blindness," Allen told Kerouac of the conversation. Laughlin, already in the process of preparing excerpts of *Visions of Neal* for publication, agreed to look at *Mexico City Blues*.

For all his problems with Kerouac, Allen continued to promote his work with the same vigor as he promoted his own. Jack had sent Allen an advance reading copy of *The Dharma Bums*, which Ginsberg read carefully, taking notes as he went along, and while Allen secretly believed the novel to be less successful than such spontaneous works as *Dr. Sax, Visions of Neal*, and *Mexico City Blues*, he responded enthusiastically to the book, calling it "a big teaching book which is rare and spooky," with "great funny sustained serious Final testament prose." He liked Kerouac's portrayals of Gary Snyder and John Montgomery but was less than thrilled with the way he himself turned out. He thought that Alvah Goldbrook (the Ginsberg character) was too inconsistent and, as he later admitted, he was put off by Kerouac's making him a heterosexual character in his novel. It was obvious to Allen that Jack was making concessions to commerce, which in itself was no sin, given Jack's financial struggles in the past, but he could not help but question whether some of Kerouac's career moves would have an effect on his writing. *On the Road* and *The Subterraneans* had been optioned by the movies, and Allen worried that Jack might be influenced by the money Hollywood had to offer. His publishers liked the "road" books (*On the Road* and *The Dharma Bums*) and it was apparent to Allen that they wanted Jack to continue to write that kind of book. Doing so, Allen told Jack, would be a mistake. "Don't let Madison Avenue . . . water you down and make you palatable to Reviewers Mentality," he advised Kerouac. "*Sax* is logical next book and you're in a position to do what you want now. Aesthetically *Sax* and *Visions of Neal* and poems. After *Sax*, they'd have to see prose beauty of *Neal* and also Hero's real beauty—they [have] been shitting on that pore boy and comparing him unfavorably with nice Japhy." Allen's instincts, as time would prove, were remarkably accurate: Kerouac's most enduring books were the ones written before he gained his fame.

Despite his mixed feelings about *The Dharma Bums*, Allen praised it heavily in a review he wrote for *The Village Voice*, in which he lauded the novel as "a record of various inner sign posts on the road to understanding the Illusion of Being." Overall, the reviews were a grab bag of opinions, some focusing on Kerouac, others using the occasion to comment on *On the Road* and the phenomenon of the Beat Generation, and a few going so far as to accuse Kerouac of attempting to capitalize on a growing national interest in Eastern religion and art. Many reviewers reverted to sloppy name-calling, referring to

Kerouac and his novel as juvenile or adolescent, as if true adults would not lower themselves to express the enthusiasm that Kerouac displayed in his latest novel.

One new—and valid—focus of criticism, mentioned in several reviews, concerned the presence and treatment of women in Kerouac's novels, as well as the way they were treated by the male members of the Beat Generation. Although there were always women characters in Jack's book, they were by and large window dressing or, in some of the worst scenes, mere sex objects, and this did not escape the attention of reviewers who called Kerouac to task for it. Writing for the *New York Post*, David Boroff may have summed up this line of criticism best, although rather sarcastically, when he wrote, "The role of women in the Beat eschatology is interesting. Clearly subordinate, they are relegated to a kind of quasi-concubine role. Since the real Buddhist revelations are not open to them, poor things, the best they can do is participate in pseudo-spiritual sex orgies."*

Critical response bore little relation to the public acceptance of the book, however. As they had done with *On the Road* and *Howl*, readers cast their votes of support by buying *The Dharma Bums*. Allen and Jack hit the literary-party and book-promotion scenes, taking on Beat Generation critics to the best of their respective abilities. Allen gave *The Village Voice* one of his best interviews to date, during which he was able to plug the works of Kerouac, Corso, Snyder, Whalen, McClure, and others. He also used the occasion to send out a volley in response to Norman Podhoretz, who, in "The Know-Nothing Bohemians," had assailed Ginsberg and Kerouac as anti-intellectuals who were "hostile to civilization." In his *Voice* interview, Allen countered that Podhoretz, "out of touch with twentieth century mind," was "writing for eighteenth century mind." He and Kerouac had attended the same school and received the same education as Podhoretz, Allen said, and to charge them with violent anti-intellectualism was "a piece of vanity" indicating that he had no idea about what they were trying to accomplish with their writing.

Allen was an excellent spokesman, eloquent and well prepared and analytical in his approach to interviews. From the time he had spent in market research, he knew what people expected to hear, and he knew how to bring the points across most effectively. Kerouac, on the other hand, was victim of his own shyness and naïveté; he answered from his heart, and on too many occasions his simple but truthful responses to interviewers' questions were misinterpreted by readers who did not (or could not) understand the workings of his mind. When Mike Wallace, then writing a daily newspaper column for the *New York Post*, interviewed Kerouac, whom he characterized as "a new kind of mystic,"

---

* These remarks about women and Buddhism were ludicrous—poets and Kerouac/Ginsberg friends such as Diane Di Prima, Joanne Kyger, and Anne Waldman became well known for their Buddhist practices— but the reviewer's point about the Beat Generation men and women is well worth noting, for the male writers' treatment of women is probably one of the true blind spots in the fiction and poetry of that group of writers. That a number of its writers had unusual relationships with their mothers, or that a number were raised in families without sister siblings, or that a number were homosexual are issues best left to Freudians, but from a literary standpoint, it is regrettable that the writers could not find a way to create realistic female characters who addressed the late 1950s sexism with the same earnest intent that those same writers took on other issues.

the exchange captured Kerouac's shyness and reluctance to be a spokesman, yet it also made Jack look evasive and, perhaps, lofty:

Q. What is the Beat Generation?
A. Well, actually it's just an old phrase. I knocked it off one day and they made a big fuss about it. It's not really a generation at all.
Q. It's a type of person?
A. Yeah. It starts with rock 'n' roll teenagers and runs up to 60-year-old junkies, old characters in the street. . . . It really began in 1910.
Q. Well, what links the junkie and the 14-year-old and Jack Kerouac? What *is* it to be Beat?
A. Well, it's a hipness. It's 20th Century hipness.
Q. Hip to what?
A. To life.
Q. What kind of life are they hip to?
A. . . . and religion.
Q. You mean Beat people are mystics?

And so it continued. In the hands of a skillful interviewer such as Wallace, Kerouac was out of his league. Jack was a writer, not a public figure, and at no time was this as apparent as when, on November 8, he and Allen went to a Brandeis University–sponsored forum, held at the Hunter College Playhouse, addressing the question, "Is there a Beat Generation?" Kerouac was to speak as part of a four-member panel, and Allen went along as moral support. Jack had originally turned down the engagement, as he regularly turned down requests for readings and speeches and other public appearances, but he finally relented and, misunderstanding the format for the evening, he had arrived with a written essay that he intended to read to those in attendance. To make matters worse, the other three panel members—James Wechsler, editor of the *New York Post*; Kingsley Amis, author of *Lucky Jim* and one of England's "Angry Young Men"; and Ashley Montagu, an anthropologist from Princeton—were prepared to take Kerouac on in debate.

Jack was the first to speak. Standing at the podium, his black and red checkered shirt and black jeans a vivid contrast to the three suited gentlemen seated at his side, he began his address by tracing the origins of *Beat* to down-and-out yet angelic figures exemplified by Harpo Marx. Interrupting his own discourse, Jack read his recently composed poem, "To Harpo," before he continued. Although he was serious about his speech, he was also very nervous and, unfortunately, rather drunk. He was barely into the twenty-minute speech he had been asked to deliver when he was informed by the moderator that his *five* minutes were up, and instead of leaving his talk in midair, Kerouac plowed on through, stalking about the stage, clowning one minute, deriding photographers the next. He denounced the elements of fadism that had corrupted the idea of *beat*; he outlined the idea of *beat* originating from *beatitude*, reverentially noting that Jesus Christ, the son of God, who was Love, was a kind of beat figure. The performance was pure Kerouac: well conceived but spontaneous, gentle, rude, as free as poetry spoken in solitude to the wind; it made no sense at all and it made perfect sense; it rambled but it reached its destination, soiled from the journey but somehow fresh upon arrival. From a promotional or public-relations standpoint, the speech was a disaster; from the standpoint of Jack's answering the question at hand, it was a success.

4

Allen enjoyed the advantages accorded him as a public figure. In the fall of 1958, he met D. T. Suzuki and jazz pianist Thelonius Monk, to whom he gave a copy of *Howl*. He got together with Norman Mailer, whose 1957 essay, "The White Negro," had been a controversial, thoughtful (if flawed, in the eyes of the Beats) study of hipsterism. At this point, Allen was received and seriously regarded by virtually every publisher in New York, including those who disagreed with his literary preferences or disliked his poetry. He was too important a figure to be ignored.

His poetry was in another period of transition. From his talks with Kerouac and readings of such books as *The Dharma Bums* and *Some of the Dharma*, Allen was once again steeped in Buddhism and the idea, voiced repeatedly by Kerouac, that life was illusory, open to the interpretation of the consciousness that was perceiving it; only death was capable of destroying the illusion. In new poems such as "Funny Death" and "Ignu," Allen wrote of ending the illusory life on earth by escaping into eternity through death. In a way, this was both an extension *and* a contradiction of Ginsberg's earlier Blake visions and subsequent attempts to recreate visionary experience. He had come to believe that the expansion of consciousness was limited by one's senses, and through his experimentation with different drugs, including marijuana, peyote, and morphine, he was trying to create a new consciousness by altering his senses. In artistic terms, this led to mixed results. Some of his poems, such as "Marijuana Notation" from his *Empty Mirror* period and, more recently, "Death to Van Gogh's Ear!" written while Ginsberg was on morphine, were moderately successful transcriptions of drug-altered thoughts into poetry; other works, such as those unpublished notebook poems from his Paris period, were little more than self-conscious doodlings.

One of the more interesting experiments was "Laughing Gas," a long poem sequence Ginsberg worked on throughout the fall of 1958. As soon as he had returned from Europe, Allen saw a dentist for some work on his teeth, and the nitrous oxide he received at the dentist's office was one of the most potent drugs he had experienced to that point. Laughing gas, Allen learned, slowly stripped down the senses as it led to unconsciousness. To Allen, this was as close a brush with death as he had ever been aware of, and in subsequent visits to the dentist, he sat in the chair with his notebook, taking notes until he went under. His sense of hearing, he determined, was the last sense to go, so even when he was unable to write, he tried to concentrate on what he heard and jot that down when he was brought back to consciousness, similar to the way he kept his journal next to his bed and tried to record his dreams as soon as he awoke. As Allen later reported, his dentist shared his fascination with the effects of laughing gas on his consciousness, and with Allen's approval, he experimented with putting him out and bringing him back. Said Ginsberg of the experience: "It gives the appearance of enlarging perception to a point where the totality of the universe invades the individual entity and dissolves the individual entity into the blackness of space. But the moment you grasp it, you go out. So, the only thing you can appreciate is coming back and realizing that you've grasped it—and that what you've grasped is something ungraspable by the human form and consciousness."

As far as Allen was concerned, this meant the Buddhists were on target with their beliefs about the illusory, transitory state of existence. Characteristically, Allen could barely wait to share the discovery with others. "I discovered for the first time at this late and draggy age that the universe is an illusion," he wrote Mark Van Doren, who had been sympathetic to Ginsberg's Blake visions and who, Allen believed, would want to hear of the evolution of his pursuit of their message. "I was all this time since 1948 coming to your desk to talk about LIGHT, hung on a golden I AM, but (for the first time in an obsessed decade for me) this seems to undercut that possibility." He was reading Buddhist texts and they were finally starting to make sense to him.

To Kerouac, he expanded upon the theme: "Nothing to fear in existence— death destroys the illusion. . . . I got the call ten years ago—little flickers of eternity in the mind—finally the void eating existence—frightened me then— I couldn't stand it." Jack had been addressing this issue in *Mexico City Blues*, but Allen had been unprepared to see or understand it, and he admitted as much to Kerouac. "I have always felt about your verse a greatness that ached by a tiny emptiness," Allen told Jack. "Poetry is not just Jack at a desk with machine typewriter, poetry is begging, a plea to dream, an addict to the strange, a power that can allow a crooked fish to re-discover its crooked sea."

"Laughing Gas" was as much an experiment for Ginsberg the poet as nitrous oxide was a new experience for him personally. For over a decade, he had been struggling with the restrictions of conventional poetic form, finding it, as he wrote in his journal, to be "too symmetrical, geometrical, numbered and pre-fixed." Nitrous oxide had led Ginsberg into unexplored regions of his consciousness, and he used the occasion to expand the actual form of his poetry. On the printed page, "Laughing Gas" is a radical departure from the neat, structured look of virtually all of his poems in the past, these newer stanzas arranged in the willy-nilly forms that thoughts take as one goes under and comes out from the influence of laughing gas, some stanzas stretched out to represent the slow, lethargic thoughts that come just before one loses consciousness or just after one returns to it, other stanzas written in prosaic wordbursts that indicate a different level of consciousness. The concrete details noticed in ordinary consciousness give way to the dreamy, esoteric state one feels when the drug is taking effect. The poem is a graph of a mind out of the individual's control, and as such, it has moments of utter clarity as well as moments of disjointed thought that at times approaches the absurd. In this way, Ginsberg was pursuing his new belief about poetic form: "Mind is shapely, Art is shapely." After his initial visit to the dentist's office, Ginsberg wrote two lines, eventually the poem's epigraph, that bring together the laughing gas experience and Buddhist thought:

> The red tin begging cup you gave me,
> I lost it but its contents are undisturbed.

This koanlike statement is fleshed out early in the poem when, sitting in the dentist's chair and listening to the contrasting sounds of the irritating dentist's drill grating against the Muzak playing from a speaker on the wall, Ginsberg states the theme of his poem:

> The universe is a void
> in which there is a dreamhole
> The dream disappears
>   the hole closes
>
> It's the instant of going
> into or coming out of
> existence that is
> important—to catch on
> to the secret of the magic
>   box. . . .

Birth and death: the two experiences in life in which consciousness confronts the void. Poets had mused over it for centuries, but rarely to the extent of simulating the experience through artificial means. Ginsberg was thrilled by the idea, and in the months to come, he would continue the experiment, using other types of drugs, including mescaline, lysergic acid, psilocybin, ether, and *ayahuasca.*

5

In his early efforts to market William Burroughs's *Naked Lunch* to publishers and literary magazines, Allen had found a strong source of support in the *Chicago Review*. The magazine's editors, particularly Irving Rosenthal, a graduate student at the University of Chicago, appreciated the work of the San Francisco writers, with Ginsberg and Kerouac being favorites. When he was in Paris, Allen had sent Rosenthal what he considered to be some of the more mainstream (that is, less offensive to the academics) passages from *Naked Lunch*, and the university-sponsored journal had published them without incident. Both Ginsberg and Burroughs had been pleased that Bill's work had been accepted by a well-respected literary magazine in the United States, and in his subsequent submissions, Burroughs sent Rosenthal any of his work that he felt the editor might appreciate, including passages that Rosenthal knew would be difficult to publish. The Fall 1958 issue of *Chicago Review* featured another sizable excerpt of *Naked Lunch*, complete with Burroughs's wickedly funny yet graphically depicted routines about homosexuality, and before long there was a major flap raised in the Windy City.

It began when Jack Mabley, a gossip columnist for the *Chicago Daily News*, launched an all-out assault in his October 25 column. Entitled "Filthy Writing on the Midway," the column attacked first Burroughs's writing and then the University of Chicago for allowing the editors of its literary magazine to publish it. Anything but a literary critic, Mabley focused his attack not on the value of the literature in the magazine but rather on Burroughs's use of four-letter words, which Mabley compared to "kids chalking a four-letter verb on the Oak Street underpass." By allowing its students to publish such filth, Mabley intimated, the university was responsible not only for the distribution of obscene material but also for the corruption of its students' minds. "The trustees should take a hard look at what is being circulated under their sponsorship," he advised.

Which is precisely what university officials did, although they publicly denied a connection between Mabley's column and their investigation. Their main concern, they said rather self-righteously, was that Rosenthal and other editors were so enamored with Burroughs and Kerouac and writers of their ilk that they were ignoring other schools of writing, and this was not acceptable in a literary magazine. From a public-relations standpoint, it was an effective position for the university to take, since it allowed university officials to suppress future publication of Burroughs without being accused of censorship. As it so happened, the Winter 1958 issue of *Chicago Review* was to be devoted entirely to the publication of a work by Edward Dahlberg, Jack Kerouac's Joycean poem, "Old Angel Midnight," and more excerpts of *Naked Lunch*. Dean of Humanities Napier Wilt, under pressure from the Chancellor Lawrence A. Kimpton and fellow faculty members, informed Irving Rosenthal that these writings could not be published. Rosenthal, along with poetry editor Paul Carroll and four others—in all, six of the review's seven acting editors—resigned in protest.

Allen was incensed when Rosenthal wired him the news. Ginsberg had been scheduled to give a reading at the university on December 5, and now that appeared to be out of the question, along with the hope of any further support that his, Burroughs's, or Kerouac's writing would receive from the *Chicago Review* in the future. Allen was in favor of a confrontation, of traveling to Chicago and giving a free reading at a location away from the university. The reading, Allen reasoned, would draw even more attention to the writings while making a statement about the university censorship of them. "Want to come to Chicago and be communist hassle martyr with me?" he asked Kerouac. Jack declined to have any part of it.

The reading was rescheduled for January. In the meantime, Allen devoted a lot of time and energy to getting the suppressed issue of the magazine published by someone else. He talked to editors at New Directions, and suggested to Rosenthal that he contact Ferlinghetti at City Lights. Ginsberg, however, might have been naïve in his assumption that other publishers would jump at the opportunity to publish the controversial material. The risks of publishing the issue were high. With all the publicity generated by the Rosenthal-university confrontation, there would almost certainly be legal action filed against anyone publishing the works, probably in the form of an obscenity trial. The costs of such a trial would be high, even if it was as successfully carried out as the "Howl" trial of the year before. Further, there was the question of the work itself. Even if Rosenthal and his friends wanted to publish the works, it did not necessarily mean that other editors would agree with their judgment of literary quality—a point that Ferlinghetti made to Allen after Rosenthal sent him a manuscript of the banned issue. Ferlinghetti liked "Old Angel Midnight," calling it "the best Kerouac I've read yet," but he had little use for the Burroughs and Dahlberg selections. He saw no reason to publish work he did not care for simply because it had been banned.

Rosenthal and Carroll decided to publish the issue themselves and, in a move that served as an example to scores of "underground" publications brought to life over the next two decades, they formed a nonprofit organization to back the issue. They called their magazine *Big Table*, a title suggested by Kerouac. The January Ginsberg reading would be a benefit reading, the proceeds going to the publication of future issues of the magazine. For his part, Allen was delighted to be involved in what was shaping up to be another battle over First Amendment rights.

6

Howl and Other Poems continued to be the best-selling book on the City Lights list, and Ferlinghetti wrote Allen to inform him that the book would go into another printing before Christmas. Interest in the Beat Generation was reaching its crest, and Ferlinghetti, perhaps acceding to Ginsberg's constant pressure to publish Snyder and Whalen, as well as Olson, Levertov, and Creeley, agreed to put out a Ginsberg-edited anthology of these and other poets. He also agreed to give Kerouac's *Visions of Neal*, now called *Visions of Cody*, another look and requested that Allen forward a manuscript as soon as he could. However, Ferlinghetti's main interest was a new collection of Ginsberg's poems. When, he asked, might that be forthcoming?

Allen could make no promises or even project a tentative date. He was writing as much as ever, but he was not satisfied with many of his new notebook poems, and the ones that he did like, such as "Ignu" and "My Sad Self," needed additional work before they would be ready for publication. In fact, his growing sheaf of unpublished poetry was full of such poems. "Laughing Gas," which Allen considered to be his latest major work, was nowhere near completion. Ginsberg informed Ferlinghetti that it would be a while before he would have a completed collection. As a sample of his latest style of writing, he sent his publisher "At Apollinaire's Grave," one of the few poems he considered to be in finished form.

One Friday evening in mid-November, Allen visited his friend Zev Putterman. The two sat up all night, talking and listening to Ray Charles records. At Gregory Corso's urging, Ginsberg had been reading through the works of Shelley, whom Allen found to be very moving and prophetic. In Putterman's apartment, Allen chanted excerpts of Shelley's "Adonais." He had chippied some morphine and methamphetamine, the latter a new experience for him, and he was feeling both energetic and nostalgic as the night edged toward the early hours of the morning. He told Putterman about his mother's insanity and of her time in the sanatorium, and of how the Kaddish had not been read for her at her burial. He had hoped to write a Kaddish in the form of a poem since that time, he said. Putterman still had his old bar-mitzvah copy of Jewish rituals, and from it he read to Allen the central passages of the Kaddish.

Inspired, Allen knew he had to write *something* but, as he later said, he had "no idea what Prophecy was at hand," though he figured it would be in the form of poetry. It was almost dawn by the time he left for his apartment, and as he walked in solitude through lower Manhattan, the rhythms of the Kaddish still playing in his head, he tried to imagine his mother living in Greenwich Village not long after the turn of the century. He glanced up at the battlements of the towering office buildings around him and wondered what the city must have looked like to a young, frightened Naomi seeing America for the first time. She was gone now, but the city remained.

When he reached his apartment, Allen sat down at his desk, took up a ballpoint pen, and began writing on onionskin typing paper. He opened with a recollection of his last few hours. He wrote of his visit to Putterman's apartment, of listening to Ray Charles and reciting Shelley and hearing the Kaddish read; he recalled his walk around Manhattan. Weeping as he wrote, he let the poem take him wherever it would. He moved quickly through the details of Naomi's life, the initial writing capturing her like fading snapshots in a photo album: The essential events were there, but he had by no means written a thorough account. In the composition, Allen used the long line structure, but instead of letting each line build up momentum, as he had with the biblical oratorical structure of "Howl," he broke many of the lines with dashes, so that thoughts (or long lines) would be broken by a series of "sobs."

He wrote continuously, filling page after page of the unlined paper in longhand, running out of ink and switching pens, moving from blue to red ink. The hours passed. He rose from his desk only for occasional trips to the bathroom. From time to time, Peter looked in on him and brought him a cup of coffee or a hard-boiled egg, and when he felt his energy flagging, Allen took Dexedrine tablets to keep going. When he had completed the opening section of his poem, he knew he had to go back and write the particulars of his mother's life; he had to be more specific. As he later wrote, "I realized that I hadn't gone back and told the whole secret family-self tale—my own one-and-only eternal child-youth memories which no one else could know—in all its eccentric detail. I realized that it would seem odd to others, but *family* odd, that is to say familiar—everybody had crazy cousins and aunts and brothers."

Memory brought Naomi back to life. In doubling back and remembering the pivotal events of Naomi's life and his own childhood, Allen was, in effect, writing a Kaddish for his youth. He included all the major events, no matter how painful to confront. In vivid detail, he recalled the day he had taken his mother to Lakewood; he superimposed the details of her youth upon his mournful reflections of the bus trip to and from the New Jersey rest home. He wrote of his family's attempts to keep her at home, of her paranoid ravings and seizures and attempted suicide, of her nudism and attempts to seduce him, of her brief stay with Eugene and longer stay with Elanor. He recalled her violent, irrational mood swings, as well as the days when she was sweet, loving, and maternal. He wrote about their final confrontation and his signing her over to a mental institution and of her subsequent years of wasting away in Greystone. Images flashed on the page: Naomi as a young woman, beautiful and smiling, a halo of flowers in her hair; Naomi scarred from her operations, overweight from shock treatment, frightened by sounds only she could hear; Naomi as an old woman, partially paralyzed by a stroke, her hair gone white and her skin hanging off her bones. He sketched his brother's "face of pain" when Eugene returned from college and learned that Naomi had been taken back to the sanatorium; he etched a portrait of his father seated at his desk and tearfully telling the sad story of his and Naomi's life together.

"Kaddish," however, became much more than the telling of one woman's— or one family's—story. Indeed, Naomi's story was archetypal, but not just in the terms of the way it addressed family eccentricity but also in the way it detailed the experience of being a woman in modern society. Although he could stake no claim to sitting down and writing a feminist poem—the word was not even being bandied around at that time—Allen, in giving the details of his mother's indignities, sufferings, frustrations, and struggles, had described in compelling metaphorical terms a woman's mad battle for personal and spiritual realization. Few poems written by a man would ever approach "Kaddish" for its understanding of all things *vital* to the contemporary woman. One can empathize with Naomi's need to have her own opinions heard, and of her feelings that she was being overwhelmed and shouted down by those who wanted to keep her in her "place," from loved ones (Louis, Buba) to international leaders and society (Roosevelt, Stalin, et cetera), the battle pulling at the seams of her individuality and spirituality until all reason and hope were lost, bursting out into darkness until the only relief could be found in the numbing conformity of lobotomy. In the end, youthful beauty, innocence, aspiration, passion, sensuality, and intelligence were literally and figuratively scarred by the incessant impositions of Man's world, the domination exacting its price by moment and incident until the damage was irreparable. In this way, Naomi Ginsberg became a heroic symbol, not of a generation but of an entire *gender* destroyed by madness.

Allen wrote "Kaddish" in a single marathon session lasting from 6:00 A.M. Saturday until 10:00 P.M. Sunday. In the early writing, he was conscious of writing poetry, but after about twenty hours, when he was physically, mentally, and emotionally exhausted, he concentrated solely on getting everything down on paper while he still had the will to do so, reasoning that he could always return to the work and clean it up later. In all, he filled fifty-eight pages, many marked by tears that fell onto the paper as he wrote.

Allen wanted the poem to work, like "Howl," in separate, distinct movements, and as soon as he had completed its long narrative section, which stood in contrast to the lament he had written a year earlier in Paris, he began a new section, which he entitled "Hymmnn," a movement similar in tone and structure to both his "Footnote to Howl" and to the Kaddish itself:

> Now, Naomi, Time, Time, Time.
>   To magnify thee, sanctify thy name.
> In the world which He has created according to
>   His will
>   Yis-gad-dal-n'yis-kad-ash
> Naomi Blessed, praised and glorified, exhaulted
>   extolled and honored, magnified and lauded
>   be the name of the Holy one . . .

This section, amended and shortened considerably between its initial writing and publication, was as tender a passage as Allen had written up to that point. In "Footnote to Howl," he had declared everything—the beautiful and the ugly—to be "holy"; in "Hymmnn," he similarly declared everything to be "blessed." At times, the section became repetitive or hyperbolic, but he kept writing, holding back nothing, figuring, as he had with the narrative section of the poem, that he could revise the work later. His final lines connected the two already-written sections of the poem:

> Blessed be Heaven Blessed be Heaven
> Blessed be He who builds heaven in Darkness
> Blessed be he! Blessed be he!
> Blessed be death for Naomi! Blessed be Naomi
>   in Death
> Blessed, Farewell, O death! O Naomi!
>   Blessed by He! Blessed be He!
> Blessed be Death on us all!

When he had finished, Allen did not know what to make of what he had written. When he had completed the long writing session on "Howl," he knew he had written something that was important, even if it was so personal that it might be unpublishable; if nothing else, the composition of "Howl" represented a personal breakthrough in the way he wrote poetry. He was more ambivalent about "Kaddish." Not only was it as personal a work as he had ever written but he was uncertain it was even poetry—at least in the terms he was using to define poetry at the time. As he later recalled, "I didn't look at the handwritten pages for a week . . . and when I reread the mass I was defeated, it seemed impossible to clean up and revise, the continuous impulse was there messy as it was, it was a patient scholar's task to figure how it could be made more shapely."

This time, there were no joyous manuscript mailings to Kerouac and others, as there had been with "Howl." Allen was either vague or tight-lipped about "Kaddish" in the months immediately following the poem's composition. He told others, including Kerouac and Ferlinghetti, that he had written an epic poem to his mother, but he offered very little specific information about the poem's content. On occasion, he would boast about the poem's merits, such as the time he described it as "higher and wilder than Howl," but there were an equal number of occasions when he wondered whether he would be able to work the poem into something publishable.

Then there was the issue of his family's reaction to the work. In writing the narrative, Allen included a number of scenes and descriptions that he knew would cause concern, if not anxiety or distress, in his family. Aside from Carl Solomon, he had not used names in "Howl," and his characters were identifiable only to the people who knew them; in "Kaddish," there was no mistaking whom he was writing about, and since his father and brother were not only living figures but also well respected in their professions, there was the danger of his hurting them or causing them great embarrassment if he published the poem. A few years earlier, Ferlinghetti had been concerned about Allen's obtaining signed release forms from the people depicted in "Howl," and it was a sure bet that "Kaddish" would pose a similar legal situation.

Allen was in no hurry to push these and other issues. He had a completed first draft and that, more than anything else, was what mattered. He put the pages aside. He would work on the poem off and on in the months to come and would read passages from it at his readings, but it would be almost a year before he revised it into its final published shape.

7

The new year brought an onslaught of new projects demanding Allen's attention. There were friends who needed assistance, travel plans to be made, works to be completed. Allen handled the demands on his time as he always did, using bursts of energy that accomplished the tasks but that also left him irritable and exhausted.

Shortly after the first of the year, Carolyn Cassady sent Allen a letter that brought him up to date on Neal's prison status. At his San Francisco trial the previous summer, Neal had run into a judge who seemed determined to make an example of him, and despite the fact that Neal's offense had been relatively minor and that he had a wife and three children who depended upon him for support, the judge sentenced Cassady on July 3 to five years to life in San Quentin for the possession and sale of several joints of marijuana. Once he was admitted to San Quentin, Carolyn reported to Allen, Neal had been placed in maximum security, where he was regarded as "one of the most desperate criminals and treated accordingly because of the California hysteria about narcotics." Carolyn visited whenever she could—usually every other week—but with the exception of his wife, Neal was not allowed to see visitors unless standard forms were filled out and submitted well in advance; nor could he receive mail or packages from the outside. Isolated in prison, he was "consumed with remorse, bitterness and guilt" and he simply wanted to fade into anonymity rather than be the celebrated Dean Moriarty hero of the Beat Generation. Neal had heard about Allen's hope to publish excerpts of *The First Third*, his uncompleted autobiography, and Carolyn was writing to forward Neal's request that Allen drop all literary efforts on his behalf.

In reality, the letter was a plea for help. Carolyn, already dependent upon the state for welfare and child-care benefits, was at a loss as to how to take on the iniquities and injustices of the penal system, and she hoped Allen might be able to use his intelligence and influence to assist her. Although he and Neal had been in contact only sporadically over the past year or two, Allen still regarded Neal as a dear friend, and he felt enormous sympathy for Carolyn, despite their problems over the years. In response to Carolyn's letter, Allen wrote that he would be in the Bay Area for a few weeks, beginning on May 1, for readings at the University of California at Berkeley and the San Francisco Poetry Center, and said he would do whatever he could to help while he was there. He asked her to send him the forms that needed to be completed in order to write or visit Neal. Finally, he told Carolyn about a reporter from the *New York Post* who was writing a multipart feature about the Beat Generation.

The reporter, Allen said, was visiting California to interview Lawrence Ferlinghetti, Gary Snyder, and other area poets, and Allen believed he might be useful to Carolyn. "I assume anyway he's sympathetic within the limitations of journalism," wrote Allen. "See him if you wish, or not. He might eventually if his story is sincere enough be able to help—he sees Neal as sort of a martyr, given [a] bad deal by Wicked Opinion, Law. Reporter's name is Al Aronowitz."

Aronowitz had already interviewed Ginsberg, Kerouac, Corso (who was now back in the States), John Clellon Holmes, William Carlos Williams, and others for his series, which promised to be the first serious, extended study of the Beat Generation writers. He was aware of their works—an unusual occurrence among the press, which continued to insist upon covering the Beats only as a social, rather than literary, phenomenon—and he appeared to be earnest about writing a fair, well-rounded analysis about the writers. Allen was more than willing to help the reporter and promote the works of his friends at the same time, and he worked closely with Aronowitz, just as he had worked with Richard Eberhart a few years earlier.

Throughout the month of January, Allen was kept busy on the first of his underground film projects, a small-budget movie being put together by Swiss photographer/filmmaker Robert Frank and painter Alfred Leslie. Frank had wanted to film *On the Road*, but with only fifteen thousand dollars to work with, he and Leslie were forced to narrow their focus considerably. They approached Kerouac for ideas. In late 1957, Kerouac had written a three-act play, *The Beat Generation*, which in its respective acts focused on a get-together with Neal at Al Sublette's apartment, a day at the horse races, and an evening during which a bishop visits the Cassady household. Neither Frank nor Leslie was impressed with the play until Leslie heard a tape of Jack's improvising the play's dialog to a jazz background. All the characters, Leslie decided, possessed elements of Jack's personality, and only when *he* read the play, taking on all the parts himself, did it come to life. The decision was made: The film would be a silent movie with a voice-over, Jack narrating the movie and speaking the dialogue of all its characters, as if he was reading from one of his own novels. The film would be based on the third act of the Kerouac play. Ironically, MGM had copyrighted Kerouac's title, *The Beat Generation*, and it could not be used on the Frank/Leslie film. The issue of the movie's title was resolved one day when Allen brought in some poems that he thought could be set to music for the film's sound track. The movie would be called *Pull My Daisy*, named after the funny jazzy lyrics Ginsberg and Kerouac had cowritten in the late 1940s.

The filming took place in Al Leslie's Lower East Side loft and, by all indications, it was a miracle that a finished movie was ever produced. Frank and Leslie were not interested in, nor could they afford, professional players for each of the roles, so they decided that for verisimilitude it would be best if Beat figures played the characters. Allen and Peter played themselves, while Gregory Corso took the Kerouac role. Larry Rivers played Neal (renamed Milo in the film), and musician David Amram played a hipster friend. Richard Bellamy portrayed the bishop. The sole professional in the cast was Delphine Seyrig, who took the Carolyn Cassady part. Predictably, the filming was chaotic and undisciplined, causing some tension on the set.

It could not have been any other way. Frank and Leslie wanted to capture the spontaneity associated with the Beat Generation, and that was not a sensation that could be easily written into a screenplay. In addition, the "actors" were not accustomed to the rigors of filmmaking, and Frank—at the time, at least—was more a still photographer than a cinematographer. As a result, the filming itself was filled with uncertainty, much to Seyrig's displeasure. There was friction between Kerouac and Leslie, who finally tossed Jack permanently from the set after he brought a Bowery bum to the filming and caused a disruption. Allen, Peter, and Gregory were involved in their own brand of high jinks, acting wise, pulling practical jokes, smoking marijuana, and, on occasion, taking off their clothes. Allen enjoyed the experience and the eighteen dollars per day it paid him although, he confessed to Carolyn, it was "harder to act than I thought, more wearying."

The finished twenty-eight-minute film was a pleasant surprise, a sort of cross between a scripted movie and cinema verité. Following the loosest of plots, *Pull My Daisy* managed to capture the Kerouackian wordflow of novels such as *Visions of Cody* and *Dr. Sax* while staying visually stimulating, thanks to a great extent to Robert Frank's unconventional camerawork. Kerouac's narration, recorded after the filming had been completed, carried the air of enthusiastic spontaneity that Leslie and Frank had been seeking when they were conceptualizing the film. When *Pull My Daisy* was eventually released, it was greeted by mixed reviews. Dwight Macdonald praised it for its humor and spontaneity. Peter Bogdanovich, writing for *The Village Voice*, judged it to be "brilliant." Taking a patronizing attitude, *Time* paid Kerouac a backhand compliment by calling him "the least dreary of the Beat writers," and while the magazine might not have intended as much, it may have given the film its highest praise when the reviewer wrote that *Pull My Daisy* was "the first pure-Beat film [that] gives an authentic impression of beatnik habits and tastes." To say that a diverse group's tastes and attitudes could be boiled down and represented in a half-hour film was the type of fatuous statement Ginsberg and Kerouac had come to expect from the mass media, but even if the statement itself was erroneous, it hinted at something that was spiritually correct. *Pull My Daisy* caught, for at least a few moments, the arc of the flight.

8

Ginsberg was always interested in the experimental, if not the confrontational, and throughout his life he would devote a lot of energy both to exploring and patronizing avant-garde theater, film, and music. When, in mid-January 1959, he learned that the Living Theatre needed financing to produce William Carlos Williams's experimental play, *Many Loves*, Allen held a benefit poetry reading to help raise funds. As he was quickly learning, there was more than just literary power in being a celebrity poet.

In Chicago, at the *Big Table* benefit reading, Allen had the chance to convene again with a mixture of a hostile press and respectful fans. The *Chicago Review* controversy had generated a heated debate over the last two months, and the Chicago media—already inclined to dislike the Beat Generation poets even as the newspapers rushed about to see that every angle on the Beats was covered—resented intruders from the East invading their city and becoming involved in their literary politics. Already a veteran of encounters with a negative press, Allen had learned how to deal with confrontational newsmen: Rather than waste his time by supplying serious interview answers that the media would either disregard or twist against him, Allen let his poetry do most of his talking for him, his interviews becoming playful jousting sessions in which he used glib or humorous answers to parry with the journalistic sword. It was an approach that would be used by Bob Dylan and the Beatles in the coming decade, and one that was proven to work. If you were going to be carved up in a mean-spirited critical account, regardless of what you said, why not have fun before the slaughter?

Perhaps because they were still in the process of filming *Pull My Daisy* and still in the spirit of performing, Allen and Gregory Corso were in top form when they met with the critics, journalists, and poetry enthusiasts in Chicago. The night before their *Big Table* benefit, they were guests at a fancy North Shore reception, where they were well treated by all but a Northwestern University English professor who took exception to Gregory's use of slang. The two exchanged words, but Corso dismissed the man as a bloodless "creep" and there was no further incident. When the poets were asked to introduce themselves, Peter began by saying, "I'm Peter Orlovsky. I'm very fine and happy and crazy as a wild flower." Allen followed: "I'm Allen Ginsberg and I'm crazy like a daisy." Gregory concluded: "I'm Gregory Corso, and I'm not crazy at all." It was not exactly the kind of formal introduction Chicago's upper-crust patrons of the arts might have expected but, as they discovered the following evening, these were not the types of poets, somber and academic and clad in tweeds, whom they were accustomed to seeing at their poetry readings.

The January 29 reading was a huge success. Over seven hundred people turned out, paying admission of a dollar and a half a head and braving a strong midwinter rainstorm. The reading, held in the Sherman Hotel, was sponsored by the Chicago Shaw Society. Allen gave an especially strong reading that featured such poems as "America," "Sunflower Sutra," and a particularly moving delivery of "Howl," but what made the reading noteworthy was Ginsberg's reading of selections from "Kaddish," which were very well received. Peter contributed to the reading with two of his poems, and Corso read a number of his works, including "Hair," "Bomb," "Marriage," and "Italian Extravaganza." After the reading, there was a panel discussion about poetry and the Beat Generation, followed by a champagne party.

One week later, on February 5, Allen, Peter, and Gregory repeated their performance, this time at Columbia University's McMillin Theatre. For Allen, the reading was a victorious homecoming, proof positive that he had succeeded on his own terms and not by the standards set forth by the university's English department. Fourteen hundred people attended, including Louis Ginsberg and other family members, and hundreds of others were turned away at the door. As in Chicago, the highlight of the evening was Allen's performance of "Kaddish," which left both father and son in tears. It was the first time Louis had heard the poem, and Allen was greatly moved by his response to it. He also read "The Lion for Real," which he dedicated, somewhat tongue-in-cheek, to Lionel Trilling. Allen's old college professor was not in attendance at the reading, but his wife, Diana, was, and she recorded her impressions in a lengthy essay for *Partisan Review*, in which she treated Ginsberg like a disobedient but lovable child. She seemed surprised that she had enjoyed the reading as much as she had, and while she obviously disapproved of Allen's criticizing the Columbia English department as being "stuck in the nineteenth century," she patronizingly allowed that this was Allen's way of being "drawn toward 'respectability.' "

The least of Allen's concerns was being considered respectable by the literati. If anything, the prospects made him nervous, for if he had ever been admitted to their inner circles, his work getting an approving nod from academics who considered it to be like their own work, he would have considered himself a failure. "Kaddish" may have moved Mrs. Trilling and others in the Columbia audience, but not because it bore any similarity to the works of T. S. Eliot, who the year before had been the last poet to read at the McMillin Theatre.

Al Aronowitz's series, simply entitled "The Beat Generation," appeared in twelve installments in the *New York Post*, beginning on Monday, March 9. As Allen had figured, it was very sympathetic, though he never could have predicted the extent to which Aronowitz labored to create as complete a picture as possible. The *Post* reporter had worked for three months on the series, and the result was a thorough, intelligent look at the literary and social elements attributed, rightfully or erroneously, to the Beat Generation. The series began with an article devoted to definition and overview, and from there Aronowitz alloted three individual installments to profiles of Kerouac, Cassady, and Ginsberg. One article examined Buddhism and its influence on the Beat Generation writers, while another dealt with the San Francisco Poetry Renaissance. The issues of violence and criminality were explored. All the major figures—and, in some cases, their influences—were interviewed. Aronowitz even managed to include a lengthy quote from Ernest Hemingway, who, at the beginning of his career, had been identified with the Lost Generation, the most recent generational movement of literary significance. Hemingway was not fond of any group's labeling itself and he was turned off by some of the self-promotional aspects of the Beat writers, but he praised them for having a lot of talent and wished them luck. "Is there a chance they'll be the voice of the 1950s?" he posed rhetorically. "I hope so. If the books are good enough, then they're read. If they're not, no amount of publicity will help."

As time would show, Hemingway's comments were astute, yet in making his remarks about their self-promotion, he was overlooking the fact that with only a few exceptions the writers immediately associated with the Beat Generation were poets. Fiction writers—and, to a degree, nonfiction writers—could count on reviews to help sell books and place their works before the public. For poets, the story was different. Well-known poets were accustomed to finding their books reviewed in large newspapers and magazines, but newcomers were virtually ignored except for mention or reviews in literary quarterlies. Further, the poets of the Beat Generation were seeking to break away from the hermetic existence long associated with poets of the past. By nature, many of the Beat poets were populist, and one of their main goals was to make their work accessible to as many people as possible. As a result, poetry readings—at one time occasional events confined to literary parlors, bookstores, and small university auditoriums in the large cities on the East and West coasts—were now becoming nightly occurrences that could spring up at any time, anywhere, for any reason.

In 1959, Allen did his best to enlarge upon this new turn of events. He gave formal readings at universities that were attended by masses of people interested in this controversial author of "Howl" and leading figure in the Beat Generation, and he gave small informal readings in coffeehouses and jazz clubs. Regardless of the location or the number of people in attendance, the message remained the same, and the message, first and foremost, was the poetry.

9

Allen decided that it was time to start gathering works for a new collection. He had kicked around the idea of grouping his longer poems, including the older "Siesta in Xbalba" and "The Green Automobile" and the newer "Kaddish" and "The Fall of America," into one collection, but Lawrence Ferlinghetti still preferred the idea of using the longer works as showcase—perhaps even title—poems in individual collections. "Kaddish" and "The Fall of America," he told Allen—prophetically as it turned out—were for separate books in the future. Ferlinghetti had been "thunderstruck" by "At Apollinaire's Grave," and after reading the poem he wired Allen to tell him that despite all the media attention, he was still the "hugest dark genius voice alive." Encouraged by the responses his poetry was receiving from his publisher and at readings, Allen put fresh effort into the revisions of such poems as "Ignu," "Poem Rocket," and, of course, "Kaddish."

He had just recently come up with a formal ending for "Kaddish." A couple of years earlier, when he had visited Naomi's grave for the first time, Allen had taken notice of the crows circling over it. In Poe, one of Allen's favorite poets as a youth, the raven is a powerful symbol of loss, and in the cemetery, the shrill caws of the crows seemed to indicate not only the finality and pain of the loss of Naomi but they also stood in stark contrast to the otherworldly silence of the grave. Allen carried the image in the back of his mind until, standing on the street corner one evening in early winter, he came up with the idea for the coda to his poem. He knew what he had to write:

> Caw caw caw shriek the crows in the white sun over
>   the grave in Long Island
> Lord Lord Lord time breaks me down to this my
>   mother's tomb & piece of grass . . .

He wrote the ending in one sitting. Now that he had a completed poem and his father had heard him read parts of it, Allen decided it was time for Louis to see the work in printed form. He typed a fresh copy of the manuscript and sent it to Louis, and in no time he received a response. Louis wrote, "I like it very much; it is nostalgic and poignant; some lines are heartwrenching, what with not only you but me being at that time in the middle of anguish. Some of the lines are poetically magnificent and imaginatively vivid. I do object to one line: about the 'beard about the vagina.' It's bad taste and offends my sensibilities. Also, to a lesser degree, I have reservations about all those 'caw caws' though you might have something there."

Allen knew even as he was writing the poem that some of the more graphic physical descriptions of his mother were toeing the edges of personal and poetic sensibility. In writing the narrative section of "Kaddish," he had forced himself to confront recollections and images, aspects of his childhood that he had thought about only once or twice since his youth—"embarrassing scenes I'd half amnesiaized," as he later wrote. He remembered the unpleasant moments when he had been unsettled by Naomi's nudism, by the flashes of surgical scars and pale flesh and pubic hair. He did not include these images in "Kaddish" without giving the matter serious consideration. His final decision was based upon his belief that he was not alone in such experiences and memories.

"The line about the 'beard around the vagina' is probably a sort of very common experience and image that children have who see their parents naked and it is an archtypical experience and nothing to be ashamed of," he wrote Louis in defense of using the expression. "It looks from the outside, objectively, probably much less shocking than it appears to you, I think—it's a universal experience which almost everyone has had though not many poets have referred to it but it can do no harm to be brought to consciousness."

Of Louis's reservations about the crow sounds in the final section of the poem, Allen wrote that he still preferred to leave them in. "It's the climax of a sort of musical form, a fugue—two themes (caw caw and Lord Lord—representing realistic bleakness-pain-materialistic versus Lord Lord, which is mystical aspiration) that alternate and in the last line merge into one cry." He had read this section at his recent poetry readings, he told Louis, and it had sounded all right.

Louis showed the poem to Eugene, who thought it was very powerful and moving. "I'm wondering if it would be possible to add a footstone to Naomi's grave with several lines of yours inscribed on it," Gene wrote Allen. Gene was especially impressed with the last two sections—the litany and fugue—and upon reconsideration, Louis decided that he may have been premature in his objection to the crow sounds. " 'Caw caw and Lord Lord' are good," he wrote Allen. "The unity of the assonance and the contrasting implications of the two names do hover about the grave." However, he remained firm in his other objection but seemed resigned to Allen's using the expressions he found offensive. "The decision is yours," he deferred to Allen, adding pointedly that "in words begin responsibilities."

13
Magic Psalm

**I am Thy prophet come home this world to scream an
unbearable Name thru my 5 senses hideous sixth . . .**

1

In April, Allen and Peter flew out to San Francisco to begin a few months' stay
on the West Coast. Despite official efforts to contain, if not eliminate, the
"beatnik" brand of bohemianism that was rapidly becoming part of the city's
identity, San Francisco continued to be a haven for experimental poetry,
theater, art, and music. Interest in the Beat generation was reaching its peak.
Establishments such as the Co-existence Bagel Shop, the Hungry i, and the
Gas Haven did a booming business, catering to clientele who dropped by to
hang out, discuss art and politics over mugs of steaming coffee, play chess, or,
in the case of tourists, gawk at the other customers. The City Lights Bookstore
was as busy as ever. Poetry readings and art exhibits thrived.

Allen and Peter stayed with Philip Whalen. Allen had a number of formal
poetry readings scheduled, including dates at the University of California at
Berkeley and San Francisco State, and in no time he was caught in the flow of
literary and social activities. The demands on his time were almost endless.
Beside catching up with friends he had not seen since he left the city in 1956,
Allen was constantly being introduced to new poets and artists. Fantasy Records
wanted him to complete his recording of poetry. The news media clamored for
interviews; new poetry publications solicited his work. Allen was pleased by the
attention, but there were times when the literary politics and media coverage got
the best of him. After his *Big Table* reading in Chicago, he had written in his
journal: "We came to present a Rose and save a historic magazine from destruction by the university. . . . We sang and prophesied as Heaven told us to. We
were insulted by a vulgar mob of newspapermen, we were called Beatniks, our
clothes and hair were mocked, [and] only those who heard us read knew we

were blowing the saxophone of Truth." Those sentiments could have been applied to his stay in San Francisco, as well.

However, such moments of impatience or self-pity were rare. Ironically, whenever Allen felt irritable or depressed as a result of his being overburdened or underappreciated, his solution was to dive into more work: No matter how misunderstood Ginsberg felt the Beat Generation writers were, he never tired of promoting their work. Two specific publications captured his immediate attention. The first, a literary magazine called *Beatitude*, featured the poetry of Ginsberg, Kerouac, Corso, Ferlinghetti, Whalen, and others. Allen was listed on the magazine's "bored of directors." He was also interested in the preservation of *Measure*, a literary magazine that due to a lack of funds was in danger of going under. Allen, along with Philip Whalen, Michael McClure, and other Bay Area poets, gave a benefit reading to help raise money for the magazine's next issue.

Another important item on Ginsberg's agenda was a visit to San Quentin. Before Allen had left for the West Coast, Jack Kerouac had sent him a check to be used to buy Neal Cassady a typewriter for use in his prison creative-writing class. Allen saw that the typewriter was purchased and delivered, and through Neal's writing teacher, he was able to visit the prison and give a reading. The reading took place on Mother's Day, and Allen, wearing baggy pants he borrowed from a prison chaplain, read "Kaddish" to a cheering group of prisoners.

2

In late spring, Allen became involved in the experimentation of lysergic acid (LSD–25), a drug that would have a profound effect on him over the next decade. Research on LSD was being conducted at the Mental Research Institute at Stanford University in Palo Alto, and Allen, aware of the effects of hallucinogens since his readings of Huxley's *The Doors of Perception*, was eager to try it. He received an invitation from researcher Gregory Bateson to take part in the experiment, and he drove down to Stanford one day in mid-May.

"It was astonishing," Allen wrote of the experience to Louis. "I lay back, listening to music, and went into a sort of trance state (somewhat similar to the high state of Laughing Gas) and in a fantasy much like a Coleridge world of Kubla Khan, [I] saw a vision of that part of my consciousness which deemed to be permanent and transcendent and identical with the origin of the universe—a sort of identity common with everything—but a clear and coherent sight of it."

The hallucinogenic drug, Allen discovered, could produce a sense of mystical experience in anyone using it; its visual images could be wonderfully detailed and beautiful. In his enthusiasm over this latest experience, he encouraged his father to locate someone at Rutgers who was conducting similar experiments and try it himself. "It's a very safe drug," Allen assured Louis, saying that the acid-trip experience was "like a cosmic movie."

Naturally, Allen wanted to know how the drug would affect the creative process, but he was disappointed to determine that when trying to write a poem that detailed the LSD experience, he became so self-conscious, so hung up on trying to relate what was going on in his mind, he could not describe the particulars of the experience. In a way, the conflict was similar to the one he had experienced when he tried to write poetry about his Blake visions: The mind became so clouded with words and concepts that it obscured the vision itself; he was too concerned with what he felt, at the cost of giving a precise description of what he saw.

He explained the problem to scholar Paul Portugés in 1976: "*Observation impeded function*—in the sense that the desire to write a tremendous visionary poem on acid always plunged me into a self-conscious hell. I felt that because I had a fixed idea, perhaps a totally passive, inert state of consciousness while in a state of acid vision, that it seemed contradictory to write. Or, that writing seemed to interrupt the compendium of multitudinous detail noticed in the acid visionary state. . . . In other words, I was still looking for a vision, trying to superimpose the acid vision on the old memory of a cosmic-consciousness, or to superimpose the old memory on the acid vision—so that I was not living in the present time, not noticing so much of what was in front of me."

These problems are apparent in "Lysergic Acid," a poem written on June 2, 1959. In the poem, Ginsberg describes the sense of despair he feels when, under the suggestive vision of LSD, he realizes that in his search for God he could be facing his own doom. During his acid trip, Ginsberg had received visual stimulation from an elephant mandala that he had borrowed from one of the university professors. He saw a series of vivid images in the patterns on the mandala, but rather than write concrete descriptions of what those images were, he tried to interpret what they meant. The result was some interesting, though confusing, writing:

> This image or energy which reproduces itself at the depths of
>   space from the very Beginning
> in what might be an O or an Aum
> and trailing variations made of the same Word circles round
>   itself in the same pattern as its original Appearance
> creating a larger lineage of itself throughout depths of Time
> outward circling thru bands of faroff Nebulae & vast Astrologies
> contained, to be true to itself, in a Mandala painted on an
>   Elephant's hide,
> or in a photograph of a painting on the side of an imaginary
>   Elephant which smiles, tho how the Elephant looks is an
>   irrelevant joke—
> it might be a Sign held by a Flaming Demon, or Ogre of
>   Transcience,
> or in a photograph of my own belly in the void. . . .

Ginsberg had yet to learn that the visionary consciousness produced from hallucinogenic drugs, like the consciousness he experienced in his Blake visions or, later, in meditation, could not be effectively *explained* in poetry. It could be shown but not dynamically interpreted. The flashes of physical description in "Lysergic Acid" are the most significant moments of the poem, but even these details are belabored when Ginsberg makes a conscious effort to create poetry from vision. In a letter to his father, Allen described a vision in a recent

LSD trip as "Hindu-type gods dancing on themselves"; in "Lysergic Acid," he writes of how "Gods danced on their own bodies," a reference to the same vision. The images may be similar, but in the prose passage of the letter, in which Ginsberg is simply stating a momentary flash of description, the detail is effective, whereas in the poem, where the moment is lost in a catalog of esoteric reaction, the detail is confusing, if not pointless, to the reader.

Ginsberg was aware of these problems and he worked to overcome them. In his notebooks, he sorted through his feelings, trying to find a concrete way of putting them on the page. In his opinion, understanding the vast consciousness affecting every human being was the key to solving the puzzling riddle of everyday problems on earth:

> America is schizophrenic
> Schizophrenic malady sweeping the worlds of
>   consciousness
> Nations armed with bombs dividing the continents
> the subconscience of US filled with poison gas,
>   secret bombs, nerve electricity, angeless
>   noises, buzzing of death
> The populace afraid to know afraid to find out
>   the secret
> and the monster is always silent . . . .

Science, Allen believed, had not only given the world the atomic bomb—and, therefore, the means to destroy human consciousness—but, in such drugs as LSD, it had also provided the human race with the means to confront a higher consciousness and save itself:

> Scientists open the door to God
> Mankind opens the door to Eternity
> God sits waiting for mankind to open the door to
>   Eternity. . . .

As far as Allen could tell, LSD was a link between Blake's "gates of wrath," Rimbaud's "derangement of the senses," and Huxley's "doors of perception." If there was such a thing as a Supreme Reality, maybe LSD was a tool one used to find it. God was "up there in the mind, alive, outside the chaos of Creation," and Ginsberg's goal was to "somehow slide under God's eyelid and peek into his mind," the vision of which he would then offer to the world—before it was too late.

3

Throughout his stay in San Francisco, Allen received testy letters from Jack Kerouac, who was having a much more difficult time handling the Beat Generation publicity in New York than Allen was having on the West Coast. *Dr. Sax* had been published to mixed reviews, Jack complaining that his reputation,

along with the public's obsession with the Beats, was obscuring interest in his
literary achievements. Things were getting so bad, Jack wrote, that he and
Gregory Corso could no longer take their walks through Washington Square
Park without running into the throngs of weekend beatniks decked out in full
regalia and talking the hip language of the day. "It's all too much and I'm afraid
now, we gotta get out of NY," Jack wrote, mentioning that he was considering
another retreat to Florida. Kerouac was trapped and he knew it. To make the
public aware of his writing, he had to engage in book signings and readings and
other public appearances, most of which he found to be distasteful dog-and-
pony shows that, ironically, attracted people who were anything but interested
in literature. "I am mentally exhausted and spiritually discouraged by this shit
of having to do what everybody wants me to do instead of just my old private
life of poesies & novelies as of yore," he told Allen. The money was rolling in,
but the literature was being lost: "What's going on, Allen? It's not money I'm
worried about any more, but the perversion of our teaching which began under
the Brooklyn Bridge long ago."

Allen was sympathetic. He, too, was growing weary of the literary wran-
gling, local politicking, and work on other's behalf—all of which seemed to
bring only minimal results. His efforts to help free Neal Cassady on parole,
he told Jack, had been a matter of "endless complications, newspapermen
with wisecracks and connections, lawyers, etc." In addition, he complained
to Kerouac, the young San Francisco poets, eager for literary connections and
exposure, were "tearing me apart psychically with their joyless ambitions."
The work on the recorded poetry was tedious, though it was nearly finished.
Jack was right to disappear to Florida, said Allen, admitting that he was
looking forward to leaving San Francisco and taking a "slow trip home"—if,
that is, he could find a driver who would be willing to take him and Peter
east via Death Valley and the Grand Canyon. He needed a break from the
action.

Although they both groused about the demands placed upon their time,
Allen and Jack could not have been more different in the way they handled
them. Despite his occasional protests to the contrary, Allen thrived on being
at the center of the storm; Jack truly wanted to be left alone. Allen was adept
and generous in applying his energy to the causes of his friends' literature,
whereas Jack was more concerned with his own life and work. Unlike Kerouac,
who let himself be too heavily influenced by his mother, friends, and agent,
and who made questionable decisions as a result, Allen maintained control of
his own affairs. He had an almost uncanny knack for knowing when to put
himself forward and when to hold back. When *Partisan Review* wrote with the
request that he write a response to Diana Trilling's "The Other Night at
Columbia," a smug, inaccurate essay that Ginsberg found embarrassing, "bitchy
and all balled up psychologically," Allen was wise enough to decline. However,
he did not hesitate to address some of the fallacies present in the reviews of
Kerouac's latest novel, and he sent *The New York Times* a two-page letter
pointing out the merits of *Dr. Sax*.

One significant answer to his critics was "Poetry, Violence, and The
Trembling Lambs," an essay published on July 26 in the *San Francisco Chronicle*.

Using all his skills of persuasion, Allen wrote an essay that was both an attack on the establishment and a gentle plea for sanity. It was forceful writing, as direct as Allen could make it:

> Recent history is the record of a vast conspiracy to impose one level of mechanical consciousness on mankind and exterminate all manifestations of that unique part of human sentience, identical in all men, which the individual shares with his Creator. The suppression of contemplative individuality is nearly complete.

With this opening statement acting as a warning, Ginsberg launched into an attack of the news media that attempted to lump the world into a common denominator and scorned all who failed to accept this categorization; of the government, which spent countless millions of dollars physically and mentally preparing its citizens for war; of the police, who seemed hell-bent on making life miserable for those who were involved in the use of such harmless drugs as marijuana and peyote; of the television and motion-picture industries that capitalized on the national interest in the Beat Generation while at the same time stereotyping and scorning the Beats. Allen employed every tool he could think of in the construction of his argument, from indignation ("Who shall prohibit an art from being published to the world?") to hyperbole ("To be a junky in America is like having been a Jew in Nazi Germany") to self-righteous wrath ("Who takes up arms, money, police and a million hands to murder the consciousness of God?"). The poets of San Francisco, Ginsberg wrote, "have had the luck and courage and fate to glimpse something new through the crack in mass consciousness," but through public misunderstanding and a concerted effort to vilify them, their message was not being heard. It was time for America to put aside its aggression and paranoia, and listen to its poets.

In retrospect, "Poetry, Violence, and The Trembling Lambs" stands as an important position paper. Using the prophetic voice that would become a trademark in following decades, Ginsberg stated—for the first time in public—his theories about a police-state bureaucracy, government abuse of drug users, and the U.S. military industrial complex. In referring to Whitman, Blake, and Thoreau in his essay, Ginsberg was making clear—if it had ever been doubted since the publication of "Howl"—the connection between literature and society and world affairs. In the two years that the Beats had been prominent media figures, they had been judged as rebels against fixed society. They were depicted as misanthropes, outcasts, pariahs, sociopaths, rebels, losers, and gadflies; they were the voices of the disaffiliated, and as such, they stood outside formal politics and posed no serious threat to those making the rules against which they so vocally rebelled. "Poetry, Violence, and The Trembling Lambs" represented a shift, not in Ginsberg's position, for he had always been interested in politics, but in the way he used his public standing to impact political events and change. In the past, Ginsberg and the Beats had been portrayed by a smirking press as frustrated children throwing temper tantrums and displaying outrageous behavior to irk their ever-patient parents. Ginsberg's pointed, intelligent essay served notice that the children had grown up and were ready to confront the authorities on their own turf. At this point, he had no intention of backing down to anyone.

4

As a result of his excursions to Palo Alto, Allen became more convinced than ever that the secrets to subconscious feelings and desires could be discovered through the use of different types of drugs. Each drug offered varying sensations and produced different results; each opened a different door. Before he had tried such drugs as marijuana, Benzedrine, morphine, peyote, mescaline, laughing gas, and LSD, Allen's subconscious had been revealed essentially through dreams over which he had no control; now, with the use of certain chemical substances, he could enter otherwise-hidden regions of the mind and will.

The importance of the exploration of different levels of consciousness was underscored in a dream Allen had shortly before he left San Francisco. In the dream, Allen had just finished dining with Peter at an elegant San Francisco restaurant when he saw Naomi stepping out of a sports car outside. She was as frail and old as she had been when he had seen her last. Utterly surprised, he greeted her happily, but she reacted to him with disdain.

"You've already forgotten me," she accused him. "You never cared to remember your mother."

"No! No!" Allen protested. "I thought of you all the time. I wrote huge sections of poetry to you."

Naomi didn't believe him. "You never gave a thought to your mother," she said, staring at him as if he had betrayed her.

Anguished, Allen fell to the pavement, "convulsed by love-pain and hurt," incredulous that his "Kaddish" had not reached Naomi in the afterlife. His entire life, he felt, was knotted in frustration. At that instant, he woke from the dream. In his journal, he tried to interpret what it meant. He thought that perhaps it symbolized his emotional ambivalence toward women; certainly it addressed the long-submerged guilt he felt about committing Naomi to an asylum and signing the papers authorizing her lobotomy. Whatever the reason, the dream was important: "Realized from that how solid and potent and present the emotion of buried life is," he wrote.

5

Allen and Peter returned to New York in August, and almost immediately Allen went to work on a new project—overseeing the U.S. publication of *Naked Lunch*.

William Burroughs's novel had been published in July in Paris. A month earlier, after seeing the excerpts of *Naked Lunch* in *Big Table*, Maurice Giordias had asked Burroughs whether he would reconsider publishing the book with Olympia Press. In no time, a contract had been drawn up, Burroughs was paid an eight-hundred-dollar advance, and the book was prepared for publication. Bill sent a copy to Allen, which Ginsberg read with great enthusiasm. "I shivered in my room on E. 2 St. seeing suddenly a flash out of 9 years work with Burroughs on the *Naked Lunch*," he wrote in his journal:

> He delivered
> I grasped
> What was beyond (us)
> in the living grave.

Difficult times were ahead; of that, Allen could be certain. Grove Press, the underwriter of *Evergreen Review*, had purchased the novel for U.S. publication, but as it was, Grove Press had already been in legal hot water for its publication of D. H. Lawrence's *Lady Chatterley's Lover* and was certain to face more of the same with its forthcoming publication of Henry Miller's *Tropic of Cancer*. Despite the controversy surrounding their respective books, Lawrence and Miller had established literary reputations in the United States—a claim Burroughs could not make. Allen was all but certain that the publication of *Naked Lunch* in the United States would be greeted by legal action against it.

If anything, Burroughs was caught in an air of notoriety. In March, the Chicago post office had barred the shipment of hundreds of copies of *Big Table* #1 (the issue with Kerouac's "Old Angel Midnight" and Burroughs's excerpts of *Naked Lunch*) through the mail. According to the post office, the magazine violated statutes prohibiting the distribution of obscene materials through the mails. The American Civil Liberties Union agreed to represent the magazine's editors in court, and the fight was on.

Outraged by the action, Ginsberg had written the court a four-page single-spaced typewritten defense of Burroughs and Kerouac. After stating his qualifications to give such testimony, he moved quickly to the point: "In my opinion the writers Jack Kerouac and William S. Burroughs are the most important prose geniuses to have emerged in America since the last war." Kerouac, Allen argued, was already an author of international repute, and while Burroughs was less known, there was no doubt that *Naked Lunch* was a serious literary effort following in the tradition of Swift's *Gulliver's Travels* and *A Modest Proposal*. Both authors, Ginsberg pointed out, were "concerned with an illumination of consciousness wherein the Divinity of the soul is revealed. The method of composition of both works is similar: a transcription of the inmost and deepest fantasies and insights of the authors, without care for anything but the truth of reporting." Such writing, Ginsberg went on, followed the examples set by Whitman and Thoreau and was reflective of the spirit of individualism upon which the country had been founded: "If the actual truthful mind of a man cannot be printed in America, as set forth after years of competent craftsmanship and practiced art, then it speaks less well for the official laws of the land than for the natural laws of the mind. If a man cannot communicate his mind through the mail, then perhaps it ought to be the mail that is to be stopped, rather than the mind."

Ginsberg's impassioned defense of Burroughs and Kerouac, it should be noted, was written in the same time frame as "Poetry, Violence, and The Trembling Lambs," and in all likelihood, the latter essay was heavily influenced by the proceedings against Kerouac and Burroughs. In Chicago, Judge Julius

Hoffman was not inclined to be persuaded to agree with Allen's idea of littera-teurs as saviors of the world, but he nevertheless ruled in June 1959 that Burroughs's work, while probably offensive to the average reader, was not obscene. *Big Table* won its battle and the magazine was allowed to be circulated through the mails.

The victory in Chicago offered no promise of easy sailing for the future publication of *Naked Lunch* in the United States, where First Amendment skirmishes were becoming commonplace. In addition, Burroughs had run into trouble with the French government, which, in a bizarre turn of affairs, had mistakenly linked him to a Tangier-Paris opium-trafficking ring. Although Burroughs had nothing to do with the drug trafficking, the government was basing its case against him on a letter he had written a known Tangier dealer, and Burroughs's involvement seemed even more credible in light of his being the author of a document such as *Naked Lunch*, which used drugs as its primary inspiration, and which so viciously satirized government regulations and law enforcement.

Faced with the prospects of losing his passport, being deported, or, in the worst-case scenario, landing in prison, Burroughs wrote Allen for help. His defense attorney was preparing to argue that he was a serious literary writer whose past had been troubled by drug addiction and bad associations, but that while guilty of making poor decisions, he was by no means a menacing international drug trafficker. For the preparation of his defense, Burroughs needed letters—preferably from non-French writers—that testified to the liter-ary value of his work. Besides helping with his own court case, such testimonials could prove useful in keeping French officials from acting against Maurice Giordias and Olympia Press in future obscenity actions. "Please do your best on this deal," Burroughs asked Allen, "if only your signature and Jack's. Those are the signatures in which he is the most interested."

Burroughs's fears proved to be larger than the case against him. When his case was finally heard, he was given a suspended sentence and fined eighty dollars.

6

Allen heard from other friends in need, as well. Gregory Corso had left for Greece a short time before Allen returned to New York, and he was struggling to get by. Herbert Huncke had been released from prison and he initially had no money or place to stay. He took a room at the YMCA, found a job, and asked Jack Kerouac for a twenty-five-dollar loan as start-up money. Kerouac, who had recently spent $2,500 remodeling his attic, ignored Huncke's request until Allen interceded on Herbert's behalf. Jack sent a check, which was quickly followed by another angry letter from his mother, who repeated her demand that Allen stay away from Jack. "Don't you ever dare again to ask for money for bums," she warned Allen, adding that her name was on the check as well as Jack's and that she expected Huncke to repay the loan. By now, Allen was as accustomed to her outbursts as he was to Jack's. He shrugged off the note. Eventually, he found Huncke an apartment in his own building.

Allen's apartment building, not unlike Joan Vollmer's old apartment or the hotel in Paris, became a kind of launching or crash pad for Allen's extended family of friends and acquaintances. It seemed as if half the people he knew either lived there or dropped by regularly. Elise Cowen, Allen's friend from the early 1950s, had an apartment upstairs and she and Allen saw a lot of each other. Ray Bremser, an ex-con whose poetry Allen liked, was an occasional visitor, as were Irving Rosenthal, Jack Kerouac, Carl Solomon, and Lucien Carr. Out-of-town poets headed straight for Allen's apartment when they arrived in New York. Alex Trocchi, whom Allen had known from his Paris days, lived nearby, and his apartment, too, turned into a gathering place. At times, it must have seemed as if the whole of Greenwich Village was a hangout. Poetry readings were staged before packed coffeehouses on any given night of the week, with such new names as LeRoi Jones, Diane Di Prima, and Ted Joans gaining reputations for their poetry.

As usual, there was no shortage of media attention. Searching for new angles for their stories, reporters interviewed psychologists for insight on Beat psyches and clergymen for opinions about the states of their souls. Two particularly obnoxious reports were published that fall. The first, "Good-By to the Beatniks!" was published in the Sunday magazine section of the *New York Herald Tribune*. The piece's author, writing that he felt he should explain the Beat Generation before it became extinct, regaled readers with one of the most sarcastic, fatuous articles written to date. Filled with errors, the article attempted to be both glib and informative, and it failed on both counts. Referring to the Beat Generation as a "cult of nothing new" and a "cult of uselessness," the author proceeded to label Dean Moriarty "one of the most unwholesome characters in literature," implying that he might be an apt symbol for the group of hedonists he portrayed the Beats to be: "Experiment is the order of the day for the true Beatnik. Experiments with every social taboo, including narcotics, crime and perversion, are conducted in the poorest and least sanitary conditions imaginable. Exotic religions and literature appeal to the Beatnik."

The second article, "The Only Rebellion Around," appeared in the November 30 issue of *Life*. Its author boasted a similar contempt for the Beat Generation writers and, true to Luce publications' form, approached them from the perspective of the disgusted conservative: "The bulk of Beat writers are undisciplined and slovenly amateurs who have deluded themselves into believing their lugubrious absurdities are art simply because they have rejected the form, style, and attitudes of previous generations and have seized upon obscenity as an expression of 'total personality.' " To illustrate its article, *Life* ran a photo of what it believed the "typical Beatnik pad" would look like, complete with a "beat chick" dressed in black, bongos, books in orange crates, and a winebottle candle holder.

Allen read these articles and other negative publicity with interest and mixed reactions. One day, he might be angry; the next, depressed. He would ignore or dismiss the criticism or, on bad days, he would sink into self-pity, wondering why people couldn't understand him. He especially hated to see the toll it was taking on Kerouac, who was drinking as heavily as ever. When the criticism reached the point of being mockingly spiteful, such as the time Kerouac was characterized as a "deadbeat," Allen rallied to his friend's defense, trying to mollify Jack by saying that it was impossible for the philistines to understand what he was trying to do with his literature. "How can a whole nation perceive the Illusion of life in one year?" Allen asked Kerouac, assuring him that "mockery is [an] inevitable compliment."

One young entepreneur found a unique way to capitalize on the public stereotype of the Beats while at the same time he found ways for the poets to earn money by reading their work. Fred McDarrah, a photographer for *The Village Voice*, began his "Rent a Beatnik" business in December, and it turned out to be successful. The enterprise started as a joke, when an acquaintance asked McDarrah where she could hire a Beat poet to read at a party. McDarrah found her a reader and it sparked an idea: For fees ranging from fifteen to two hundred dollars, McDarrah would arrange to have a poet (or poets) read poetry, play music, or lecture and answer questions about the Beat Generation. It was self-parody elevated to an art form: "Rent a Genuine Beatnik. Fully Equipped. Eye-Shades, Beard, Dirty Shirt. With or Without Sandals. Special Discounts for No Beard or No Bath." Funny ads notwithstanding, McDarrah was discriminating about to whom he would "rent" his poets. Customers had to understand that he was running a serious literary enterprise, as well as a gimmick, and through McDarrah, such poets as Ted Joans and Jack Micheline were able to earn badly needed money from their poetry.

Ginsberg saw a reprieve from the hoopla when Lawrence Ferlinghetti wrote to say that he and Allen had been invited to take part in a writers conference in Chile in January. A Chilean professor at Berkeley had published a pirated edition of "Howl" and, feeling guilty about not informing or paying Allen, had decided to even the score by inviting poet and publisher to the conference. Allen was delighted. He had wanted to travel to South America since Burroughs's yage expedition in 1953, and as long as he was going to be in Chile, he could travel to Peru and Bolivia, as well.

He immediately began to prepare for the conference and what he hoped would ultimately be a visionary experience on yage. Since he still needed to have work done on his teeth, he visited the dentist and used the occasion to complete "Laughing Gas," which had been lying around, unworked on, for months. The turning of a new decade, with all the uncertainty Allen felt about the future, seemed to fuel his sense of being in transition, moving from one level of consciousness to another, and he was able to give the poem a strong ending.

Allen rang in the 1960s with a New Year's Eve party that was attended by Jack Kerouac, Lucien and Francessa Carr, and Peter and Lafcadio Orlovsky, among others. Allen stayed up all night, and at dawn the next day, he commemorated the new decade with a long poem in his journal, the work reflecting his ambivalent feelings about the future:

> And tho we've been illuminated
> > for one decade of scribbling
> > > and publicity—
> The gooney bird arrives
> > Empire State looks cold
> > > as the eastern sky reddens.

7

When Allen arrived in Chile in mid-January, he was surprised to learn that the writers conference, held at the University of Concepción, was sponsored by the Communist party. Neither Allen nor Ferlinghetti had been advised of this prior to the conference—not that it would have made much difference, given the politics of the two poets or the fact that in Central and South America, where so many people were poor and illiterate and living in squalid conditions, the Communist party was favored by intellectuals who dreamed of the overthrow of the existing order. At the worst, Ginsberg's and Ferlinghetti's participation in the conference would add fuel to the rhetoric of the more paranoid Beat bashers in the States, who saw the Beat Generation as a menacing group poised to overturn the concepts of truth, justice, and the American way. One such person was J. Edgar Hoover, director of the FBI, who was already monitoring the actions of Allen and his friends, and who, a year later, would publicly declare the Beat Generation to be one of the three most threatening groups in the United States.

Besides Allen and Ferlinghetti, twenty-five writers from the Central and South American states attended the conference, which was as political as it was literary in tone. In Cuba, on New Year's Day, Fidel Castro had led a band of guerrilla soldiers in the overthrow of dictator Fulgencio Batista, and by the time the conference opened in Chile, Castro was in Havana and in control of Cuba. The new government, Castro promised the United States, would be a socialist rather than Communist one, and the United States supported his overthrow of Batista, who had proven himself to be corrupt and out of touch with his people.

The Central and South American countries had taken notice, and at the literary conference there was much debate about the events in Cuba, with talk of revolution hanging in the air like smoke. In principle, Ginsberg and Ferlinghetti tended to support a revolution that would put power back in the hands of the people, but both had reservations, as well. As always, Allen absorbed as much information as he could take in and he filled his journal with political reflections. It was difficult for him to figure exactly where he stood. From the other poets and writers at the conference, he was getting a different perspective of how the United States dealt with the countries in Central and South America. Too often, Latin delegates pointed out to Allen, the United States was guilty of supporting the policies of wealthy leaders, with little regard for the suffering masses. To emphasize the point, the Communist party took conference attendees on a tour of the coal mines in Lota. Allen was shaken by what he saw. For $1.20 a day, miners toiled for eleven hours in unspeakable conditions. The workers, looking like "dirty animals," moved in and out of black iron platform cages, and from their labor Allen could see little more than a continuation of such human suffering that all his idealistic political utterings of the past seemed like so much spent air. It was one thing for well-fed Americans to debate communism versus socialism, as his parents had done, or to make romantic vows about helping the masses, as he had done upon entering Columbia so many years ago, or even to talk about U.S. unresponsiveness to the people of the world; in the dim light of what he witnessed in the coal mines, the rhetoric seemed meaningless.

In addition, Allen was seeing firsthand the way poets really could be unacknowledged legislators. In Central and South America, poets strived for more than the creation of art for its own sake; they were active, well-respected political figures capable of moving the people to action. When it was his turn to address the conference, Allen gave an inspired lecture on prosody, jazz, drugs, and the soul, into which he worked passages from John Wieners's *Hotel Wentley Poems*, Gregory Corso's "Bomb," and selections from Philip Lamantia's *Narcotica*. A few days later, he and Ferlinghetti gave a poetry reading, and while Allen was disappointed that his reading was delivered "without real feeling," as he judged it, he was pleased that he had been able to acquaint those attending the conference with the works of some of the Beat poets. "We were a big hit," he wrote Peter, "and now Beat Generation is considered great American poetry and all the professors will bring it back to Uruguay and Argentina and perhaps Colombia."

The week-long conference ended and the poets returned to their respective countries, but Allen remained in Chile, ready to embark on explorations of his own. Characteristically, he was traveling on the cheap, but he was still unable to go anywhere until he received his royalty money from City Lights or payment from Fantasy Records for his poetry album. In the meantime, he stayed with Nicanor Parra, a forty-five-year-old poet and professor of mathematics and Newtonian physics. Having studied in the United States and England, Parra was fluent in English; not only did he act as an interpreter for Ginsberg, who spoke only passable Spanish, but he also served as a translator at a reading Allen gave at the University of Chile. Fortunately for Allen, life in Santiago was inexpensive, and he was generally content to wander around the city or spend his afternoon hours in cafés, where he would while away his time by discussing poetry with local students and poets. With his beard and coveralls, he stood out among the natives, but otherwise he fit in well. "Have run into a whole group of people at the University who are very sympathetic, and have been taking rides in the country and leading pleasant town social life," he wrote Lucien Carr; to Peter Orlovsky, he mentioned that he was "getting familiar with this whole world down here, more than I thought I would be."

Allen spent the first week of February in the small fishing village of Calbuco. It was a lazy, peaceful time that found him walking along beaches littered with seashells and gazing out at the sailboats and fishing boats that wound their way among the archipelago of offshore islands. The scenic landscape and villages reminded him of the paintings by Brueghel that he had seen in Europe. It was Allen's good fortune to find still another friendly sponsor willing to put him up for his stay—this time, an Italian poet who had left his homeland, settled in Chile, and opened a fish-canning factory. Allen enjoyed the solitude, which gave him pause to think about the frenzy of activities surrounding the Beat Generation in recent months. All the national attention, he realized with some displeasure, was feeding his ego in a way that was not entirely healthy. "The whole beat scene now seems very involved and mad," he wrote Peter. "We gotta get away." One such escape, which Allen had talked about off and on for over a year, was a trip to India, and when Gregory Corso wrote with the news that he had received a grant and was willing to finance Allen's and Peter's stay in India, Allen gave the proposal serious consideration. He rejected the offer, though, because he still wanted to see parts of South America and try the yage that Burroughs had told him about.

Allen explored the mountainous northern region of Argentina before returning to Santiago. His checks still hadn't arrived, and by early March his financial situation was getting grim. His plane ticket had expired and he needed to come up with the money for a new one. After many hours of arguing politics, he and Parra had grown tired of each other, and Allen hoped to find a new place to stay, preferably at a hotel. To add to his discomfort, he had developed a cluster of painful anal warts from his time in relatively primitive conditions without toilet facilities; from local doctors he learned that he would have to get them removed before the condition worsened. He wrote a prodigious amount in his journal, keeping detailed notes of his time in South America, but he wrote very little new poetry. He tried to revise "Kaddish" (which was now being translated into Spanish) and work on a new collection of poems, but he was too distracted to accomplish these tasks. Much of his time was spent in Santiago cafés, where he met with elderly Chilean poets and discussed literature and politics.

The anticipated money arrived the last week of March, along with some unexpected money from poetry sales that Peter forwarded from New York, and on April 1, Allen flew to La Paz, Bolivia, ready to take up the next leg of his journey. According to his plan, he would stay in La Paz for two or three weeks, sightseeing and waiting for his mail to arrive, and from there he would proceed to Peru, where he would hook up with people who could direct him to sources of yage.

La Paz was set in a canyon surrounded by mountains and jungle, its people dirt-poor and uneducated. He took an instant dislike to its government, which seemed corrupt and exploitative of the largely Indian population. There was a lot of talk about politics and reform but, as Allen noted, with people struggling to survive, it was unlikely that anything significant would occur in the near future. Coal miners labored under conditions similar to those he had observed in Chile, and from their small wages they were barely able to afford food and housing. "Anybody who can, leaves Bolivia," Allen wrote when he described the conditions to Peter. He had witnessed a large political rally, with "big hypocritical speeches" launched from a balcony near his hotel, and the experience left him cold. If anything, Allen's travels were fortifying beliefs he had held for a long time: Politics—regardless of country or party or ideology—were oppressive, rewarding to the few and disregarding of the masses.

Disgust over politics did not prohibit Ginsberg from making the most of his stay in La Paz. The marketplace, he wrote, was "the most fantastic I've seen from Tangier to Mexico." Indian women wearing brown bowlers and brilliantly colored scarves, shawls, and skirts lined the streets and sold foodstuffs and crafts. For thirty cents, Allen could buy a meal of soup, tasty pork or beef stew, and tea, and rather than pay the higher prices for meals at his hotel, he ate at the market every day. With money in his pockets, he went on a small spending spree, buying clothing and souvenirs that included small silver pins, scarves, masks, shawls, and a large multicolored rope woven from llama wool. To his amazement, he found an antique shop that offered authentic Oriental scrolls for thirty dollars. Many of the women sold coca leaves, which could be chewed or made into tea. Allen purchased some but was disappointed to discover that they had only "a mildly stimulating effect," not unlike the buzz he caught from Benzedrine.

He had hoped to see parts of the Amazon while he was in Bolivia, but time and a lack of funds were working against him. To reach the tropics, one had to descend the mountains slowly, taking narrow dirt roads that wound their way down the mountainside. Allen was able to find cheap transportation on an open truck loaded with bananas and Indians, and from this vantage point he was able to catch occasional glimpses of the cloudlike mists rising from the valley below. Small villages were built right into the sides of the mountains, and the truck seemed to stop in every one. Allen enjoyed these excursions, but he conceded that he would have to save serious exploration of the jungle for another time.

The mail kept him abreast of everything going on in the States. Peter wrote to say that Herbert Huncke had moved in with him, a situation that caused Allen some concern. As far as Allen was concerned, Peter already had his hands full in taking care of Lafcadio, and he advised Peter to see that Huncke did not grow too dependent on him. Activities around the apartment and Greenwich Village were as hectic as always, with Jack Kerouac stopping by to look in on Peter, other poets checking in from time to time, and Allen's mail piling up until it looked as if it would take him months to answer. Ferlinghetti wrote to inform Allen that he, too, had been in New York but was now back in San Francisco and hard at work on the publication of Kerouac's *Book of Dreams*, Frank O'Hara's *Lunch Poems*, and an anthology of the best writing from *Beatitude* magazine. *Howl* had just gone back to press for another ten-thousand-copy printing, and Ginsberg's poetry was appearing in more anthologies, domestic and foreign, than Ferlinghetti could keep track of. City Lights had projected a July publication date for *Kaddish*, Ginsberg's next volume of poetry, and Ferlinghetti had already taken advance orders for two thousand copies. In his letter to Allen, Ferlinghetti asked whether he might be able to get a finished manuscript—enough to fill a seventy-two-to-ninety-four-page volume—by the first of June. With "Kaddish" yet to be revised and no time to work on it in South America, Allen doubted it was possible.

By this time, he realized that his trip to South America was going to take much longer than he had anticipated. Allen had been there for three months and had yet to see Peru or locate yage; he had no intention of leaving South America until he had accomplished those goals.

8

Allen left La Paz for Peru in mid-April. The journey was not a comfortable one. For twelve hours, he shared the back of an overcrowded truck with a group of Indians, all suffering from the cramped conditions and the rain that pelted them for much of the journey. When he arrived in Puno, he was able to catch a train to Cuzco, where he took a whitewashed cell at a local hotel and relaxed.

The antiquity of Cuzco impressed him, the old decaying buildings striking him as "very picturesque." Having seen the Mayan ruins in Mexico, Allen was eager to explore the Incan ruins of nearby Machu Picchu, and he set off almost immediately for them.

The ruined Inca city was set on a cliff ledge overlooking the more modern city. Every day, early in the morning, Allen left his modestly priced hotel for a two-mile walk to a more expensive one that provided bus service to the ruins. Once there, he spent the day wandering among the ruins, his face shaded by a black hat sporting a bright yellow daisy. He would take a walking stick on those occasions when he followed the dirt paths to higher elevations, where the now-decaying forts and gates had once protected the Incas from attack from above.

Allen marveled at the sights. The thick, humid air had encouraged the accumulation of moss growing on the massive, irregularly shaped stones fit together to form the walls. The Incas, Allen determined, were utilitarian people. If they were building in an area that had a huge unmovable boulder, they would simply use it as part of a wall or structure. Along these lines, they constructed a city that was still dazzling to the eye five hundred years later. The lush green scenery around the city, as Allen reported to Peter, was equally breathtaking: "The view all around is universal canyons and cliffs and even snowpeaks above the near green peaktops—and white mist flows in below and obscures the river way down the size of a river."

He spent a week walking about the ruins. A caretaker offered him a bed in his house, and Allen accepted the invitation, moving in with his clothes and some supplies and canned goods. He was happy. At night, he wrote by candlelight, the light flickering off the newspaper covering the walls to keep the cold from entering the cracks in the building; he hung his hat from a nail. After nightfall, the ruins were an eerie presence, "fearful . . . in moonlight, all the possible ghosts." Allen tried to imagine what it would be like in a millennium if someone was to stand in this very spot and think about days a thousand years past:

> The half-mad scholar bending over his notebook in the darkness 1000 years hence—questioning the inhabitants—This I did with my beard, resting book on the balcony and peering at it to write, then looking sideways into the fields below.
>
> If I had summoned a ghost to talk to me, which I did not because of fear—in that vast obscurity . . .
>
> What language would we have spoken?
>
> The ghostly solitude—I am the king of the dead, on their ancient throne—sitting 1000 years later lording over their ghosts, questioning in the later moonlight, from the height of the sacrificial stone.
>
> And the stars over the dead city, so far away—suddenly in the presence of the Universe itself.

On May 4, Allen took the two-day, two-night bus ride from Cuzco to Lima. The city, much more modern and heavily populated than anyplace he had seen in recent weeks, reminded him of Mexico City. Knowing that Burroughs had been there almost exactly seven years ago to the day, Allen tried to see Lima as Bill had seen it. Despite its size and prominence, it was very inexpensive and Allen found that he could live like a millionaire for only a few dollars a day. He toured the local museums and art galleries, ate and scribbled in his journal in the city's large Chinatown section, touched base with as many of the city's literati as he could encounter, and met a doctor who offered to help him obtain *ayahuasca*.

The closer he came to realizing his original purpose of traveling to Peru, the more he prepared himself mentally for the experience. The recent execution of Caryl Chessman had angered Ginsberg, who, years earlier, had sent a telegram to the White House in protest of the execution of the Rosenbergs. He now saw the execution of Chessman as still another signal of the spiritual decline of America. That, coupled with his exploration of the ruins, left him pessimistic about the planet's future. Perfection was out there somewhere, but not on the usual level of consciousness that had been conditioned by society, government, education, religion, and day-to-day experience. In his experiments with various drugs, Allen had tried to find the level of consciousness that would lead him to God, to perfection, to ultimate self-realization, but, as he readily recognized, he was limited by his own conceptions, begun with his Blake visions and continued through his experiences with drugs, as to what that perfection was. He was in a maze that defied logic, especially when he tried to verbalize his feelings:

> . . . God is so beautiful it doesn't make any difference whether we see him or not.
> Or, there is an X resolution of the paradox of existence that is so perfectly sublime that it makes no difference whether we know it or not.
> Which seems to leave us out, as human level from importance, but as I warned you the resolution is so sublime it makes no difference that it includes us in an inconceivably beautiful way. . . .
> This is the Understanding perfected in nearly mathematical form in words. Now to the next stage which is to incorporate it in my body so that it makes no difference whether I live or not to the Consciousness which is called Allen Ginsberg & clings to that energetically, afraid of blood.
> Beauty or truth is so perfect it makes no difference whether the Universe exists or not.
> This reconciled the Void of Laughing Gas with the Transcendental Dancing Spirit of Lysergic Acid.
> Tomorrow to take Ayahuasca. . . .

9

Not long before he set off on his search for yage, Allen heard from Bill Burroughs in Europe. Disturbed by the political tone of Allen's recent letters and poems, Burroughs warned him to stay away from politics, calling them a "trap" for writers. The writer's role, Burroughs suggested, was that of the outsider, the observer. Burroughs was enthusiastic about Allen's search for yage and in his letter he gave Allen specific instructions as to how and where to obtain it and whom to see. "Make it, man," Burroughs wrote in encouragement.

Allen tried yage for the first time in his Lima hotel room on May 23. He had received a jar of an already-prepared solution that was nowhere near as potent as the mixture made by the Amazonians Burroughs had written about, but the experience was memorable nevertheless—rather similar, Allen noted, to the sensations he had experienced with LSD and mescaline: "I drifted away in bed in darkened hotel room and came to the gate of heaven and yelled in my mind, 'I am back home in the house of the splendid ancient Lord, and I am the son of the Lord, in fact I am the lord himself come back home and I want the gates open.' [I] got a minute of feeling near Union, but the dose was too small & I was too amazed to get completely lost."

A week later, he was on his way to Pucallpa, the town on the edge of the Ucayali River that Burroughs had recommended as a source of yage. By now, Allen was growing accustomed to the painfully slow travel conditions in Peru, and his trip northeast from Lima to Pucallpa was no exception. The farther he moved inland from the Pacific toward the Amazon, the slower the travel became. The solitude of travel, Ginsberg admitted to his father, was good for him; it afforded him the time to reflect on his life and future. "Being 'world-famous' is a minor childplay compared to the beauty and terror of what I can guess of the nature of the universe," he wrote. "That is to say, most of my consciousness activity is concerned with that obscure part of the mind which connects with the creator. I am more and more convinced I'll wind up studying mind-control in India for a few years, later."

Allen's journey, taking nearly a week in all, passed through such cities as Cerro de Pasco, Huanuco, and Tingo María. He spent his thirty-fourth birthday in Huanuco, where, befitting his being alone for the occasion, he felt nostalgic and slightly sad. The next day, he buoyed his spirits by hitchhiking beyond the outskirts of town and exploring a large jungle cave filled with owls. The last portion of the trip, from Tingo María to Pucallpa, found him stretched out on sacks of sugar in the back of a truck, the rickety vehicle negotiating the jungle terrain at seven miles per hour, the two-hundred-mile trip taking twenty-eight hours to accomplish. Lying on his back and watching the stars and moonlight filtering in through breaks in the trees, he thought back to the times he had spent with Neal Cassady, Jack Kerouac, and Peter Orlovsky—the great loves of his life—and from there his thoughts turned to the poet Catullus and "the sense of old reality of Catullus dead so long but his worries are still sad and true, and [I] can hear his voice in poems."

The journey was worth the inconvenience. As soon as he had settled into Pucallpa, Allen looked up a local authority on yage who, coincidentally, had known Robert Frank when the filmmaker was in South America. The man put him in touch with a *curandero* willing to administer him a dose of *ayahuasca*. Known as Maestro, the *curandero* had studied under a witch doctor and grew his own *Banisteriopsis caape* plants to use in his yage brew.

The ritual was held in the evening, and on a typical night there would be a group of five to thirty people taking the drug. On his first night, Allen was given a dose of older and slightly fermented yage that, though still more powerful than the earlier dose he had taken in Lima, did not produce the violent nausea and powerful visions that Burroughs had written about from his experiences. About forty-five minutes after drinking the liquid, Allen had a sense of being in the presence of "the Great Being," which was manifest in the form of an eye staring from a great black hole surrounded by hallucinatory apparitions of snakes, fish, butterflies, birds, and other creatures symbolizing, as far as he could tell, the entirety of creation. The feeling was pleasant, not unlike the sensation he had experienced during his first Blake vision, when he felt as if he was in the presence of an eternal being. The effects of the drug lasted about three hours. Allen had no sooner returned to his normal state when he began to look forward to his next experience.

However, it was different the next night, when he took a fresh and therefore much stronger dose. Maestro served the yage ceremoniously, blowing smoke over the enamel cup and humming a melancholy song before he handed it to Allen. As he felt himself getting high, Allen lay down on the ground and waited, expecting the same kind of pleasant visions as he had experienced the night before. Instead, as he reported to Burroughs, "the whole fucking Cosmos broke loose around me":

> I felt faced by Death, my skull in my beard on pallet on porch rolling back and forth and settling finally as if in reproduction of the last physical move I make before settling into real death—got nauseous, rushed out and began vomiting, all covered with snakes, like the Snake Seraph, colored serpents in aureole all around my body, I felt like a snake vomiting out the universe—or a Jivaro in head-dress with fangs vomiting up in realization of the Murder of the Universe—my death to come—everyone's death to come—all unready—I unready. . . .

The vision was similar in effect to Allen's third Blake vision, when the monster presence threatened to devour him. Terrified, Allen lay still and let the hallucinations roll over him. He felt as if he was in the presence of death and the sensation was oddly realistic and familiar to him. Despite Maestro's reassuring presence—the *curandero* checked on him from time to time, offering encouragement and counsel—Allen was not entirely convinced that he was *not* going to die and the thought made him sad. If he died, he would be leaving Peter and his father alone, perhaps in need. He thought of his mother, alone and insane in the asylum, confronting death, leaving behind a son who, in her place, might be confronting madness of his own. He realized that he had spent most of his life obsessed with death, unable to come to terms with its finality and meaning. The only way to encounter (or defeat) death, he speculated, was to continue life, to reproduce—a proposal he had not seriously considered before. As a homosexual, his attention had been on men, even though he had known and had relationships with women who would have been willing to have children with him. These women, Allen noted dolefully, had looked up to him as a superior intellect, when, in fact, they were capable of saving him from total obliteration. He began to see women from a new perspective:

I saw them as seraphs, ministering to my queer isolation—my lack of knowledge, contact with birth—my fear to be and die—to bear life— They resolved their death by giving birth first and continuing the race of time—God in this sphere—in this world—How deep do they know?—or perhaps it is I who am not deep and know nothing of the Great Radio Truth they all receive and send—to me, to contact me in time—to help my helpless soul—lost, I am the lost soul not those I curse and envy and love from afar in my own lonely way, exiled from Heaven and on Earth.

Allen was both elated and depressed by these flashes of insight. He was elated because the solution to his confronting death seemed so obvious and simple: He resolved to try to understand women better and, ultimately, have children. He was depressed because such changes would have a profound effect on his relationship with Peter. When he and Peter had exchanged their vows in San Francisco in 1955, Allen had promised that he would stay with Peter and help him reach heaven. Now, he realized, that might not be possible; he might have promised Peter more than he could deliver.

Unlike his Blake vision, which had shaken him so badly that he vowed to pursue the vison no further, the yage experience filled him with determination. As horrific as the vision had been, he would face it again—and again, if necessary. "I was all wrong—I am not ready to die," he wrote in his journal the next day. "No, I resign myself to thee, Mystery."

10

Ginsberg's decision to confront the horrors of death—and, subsequently, the mysteries of life in the universe—was important. A dozen years earlier, he had vowed to *remember* his Blake visions, but his memory only led to confusion and misguided notions about how to pursue the consciousness he had experienced. Even as he was experimenting with drugs, he knew they were not the answer. He wanted something pure, a higher consciousness attained without the use of artificial means.

Still, as long as he had reached the level of consciousness he had under the influence of yage, he would not abandon the drug. Since his childhood days and his Shroudy Stranger fantasies, he had been terrified of facing death, God, or whatever supreme consciousness was out there. Although, as he told Burroughs, he was not certain of the price he would pay for staring into the void, he would continue his quest until he had answers for some of his questions.

Night after night, he returned to Maestro for more yage, and each day following, he would write about the experience in his journals. Where these writings would take him, he had no way of knowing. "I wrote a great deal this month, huge ranting wild poems, psalms, notes, sketches, drawings, a whole book actually," he told Louis. "I'll have to reread it in a year and see if it's still hot. But poetry doesn't seem enough."

This objective opinion turned out to be correct: Of the many notebooks filled by Ginsberg during his South American journey, very little was ever published, mostly because the yage experience, like the LSD one, lost its magic in the process of translation. In Lima, he had sniffed ether and while high had written "Aether," a poem that accurately depicted the experience but that was weak as poetry. As a study of the mind under the influence of ether, the work displays the sometimes wonderful, sometimes disturbing mental loops and acrobatics of imagination that might have seemed compelling to Ginsberg, but that lacked the continuity or familiarity to be significant to most readers.

"Magic Psalm" and "The Reply," Ginsberg's two published poems written directly about the yage experience, are much more successful—for good reason. Both are disciplined and organized; one sees their purpose immediately. In "Magic Psalm," Ginsberg addresses the Great Being of his visions, imploring it to enter his spirit and devour him—if this would lead to his understanding of it. The plea is similar to the one expressed at the end of "The Lion for Real," except in "Magic Psalm" Ginsberg is more specific about why he wants to confront the vision:

> born in Newark come into Eternity in New York crying again
>   in Peru for human Tongue to psalm the Unspeakable,
> that I surpass desire for transcendency and enter the calm water
>   of the universe
> that I ride out this wave, not drown forever in the flood of my
>   imagination
> that I not be slain thru my own insane magic, this crime be
>   punishment in merciful jails of Death,
> men understand my speech out of their own Turkish heart,
>   the prophets aid me with Proclamation,
> the Saraphim acclaim Thy Name, Thyself at one in one huge
>   Mouth of Universe make meat reply.

Yage had led Ginsberg to believe he had lived a relatively empty life and that his failure to recognize the inevitability of death was a vanity that prohibited self-realization. "The Reply," the companion poem to "Magic Psalm," is Ginsberg's attempt to come to terms with this. In the poem, he notes that he can run from the reality of death, he can pretend that it does not exist, but he will not escape it:

> Escape, but not forever—the Presence will come, the hour
>   will come, a strange truth enter the universe, death
>   show its Being as before. . . .

Better, Ginsberg concludes, to recognize death's inevitability and be prepared for what is beyond. He does not speculate as to what follows death, but he hints that it is perfection, a point he elaborated on in a letter to his father, in which he detailed the yage experience: "It seemed that until I were *able* to freely give myself up, entrance into some great Joy (in life or beyond life) would not be seen—but that there is some kind of Inhuman Harmony yet to come. But this is speculation."

Neither "Magic Psalm" nor "The Reply" followed the path of the drug-inspired poems Ginsberg had written in recent months. In "Laughing Gas" and "Aether," he had tried to replicate his transcendental consciousness to such a degree that the actual structure of the poems themselves defied the standards of what the poem looked like on the printed page; the totally unconventional structure was intended to reflect the break with conventional, or normal, consciousness. Ginsberg was inviting his readers to touch the bare wires of his mind. In "Magic Psalm" and "The Reply," he returned to the long line structure that had worked so well for him in the past. The message, he seemed to be saying, was too important to be jeopardized by the kind of structural experimentation found in his other drug poems. Further, the poems represent the condensing of numerous yage trips and scores of pages of notebook notations. The other elements—the description of physical sensation and hallucination—are present but in a more pared-down way.

Ginsberg recognized that his drug poems were venturing into unexplored territory, and while his yage experiments often led him to hours of great suffering, he believed it was his obligation as a poet to bring that consciousness to his readers: "My poetry is now approaching the place where it is dangerous, when what I say may represent a real spirit talking to Universe in Universe thru Universe," he wrote in his journal, acknowledging that this was "Burroughs' frontier."

11

Ironically, the vision of death led Allen to grave doubts about his poetry. For fifteen years, he had labored to find a supreme reality to present to his readers; during this time, he had used death as one of the main subjects of his poetry. In Europe, he had assumed a prophetic voice, which he embraced even further in "Magic Psalm," when he told the Great Being "I am Thy prophet come home this world to scream an unbearable Name thru my 5 senses hideous sixth." In his journals, however, Allen expressed his self-doubts. His ambitions, he feared, were too lofty for his abilities. Worse yet, his poetry might not serve its purpose:

> . . . And the braggart and loudmouth boast of God in my poetry—
> Magic Psalm is rubbish—though on a human level it does point the
> way toward an area of consciousness—though not the thing itself—
> that's too real—so the poem "misses" and is a mess of lies and exaggera-
> tions—a deceit in fact—and what's all this external poetry anyway
> when the real drama's inside, in death where there's no poetry—Who
> am I trying to kid—myself?—that I am an important God representa-
> tive sent here to tell people something.
> Tell them what—to die? They will.
> Write a poem [to] tell them how to live?
> Why write poems when the Subject is gone, the Subject is unap-
> proachable in poetry—at least you haven't found the way to approach
> it with complete experience of the Subject. . . .

Allen hoped that subsequent doses of yage would provide him with answers. Instead, they presented him with more questions and worries. He was convinced that what he encountered on yage was what he would encounter one day at the moment of his death, the difference being, of course, that in death he would have no life to return to. His great fear was to find himself on his deathbed with the realization that he had wasted his life. What, he wondered, was the purpose of his life? At one time, when he saw himself as one of Blake's sunflowers, he had envisioned himself on a quest for eternity, but now that he had looked into the face of that eternity, what was left for him? He implored the master himself:

> O Blake Come help me now
> The tears run down the Cheek
>   That hides my skull.
> "Where the youth pined away with desire"
> as I have pined away,
>   and am no youth anymore. . . .

The answer, though not specified in his journal as coming from Blake, was:

> Widen the area of consciousness till it becomes so wide it includes its own death. This is the purpose of life.

Wanting to try mixtures of *ayahuasca* from other regions of Peru, Allen boarded a steamboat bound for Iquitos, a river port on the western end of the Amazon. The six-day journey commenced on June 16, with Allen rushing to board at the last minute, arriving "barefooted and hairy and [in] dirty dungarees and sweatstained khaki workshirt," the vision of a man who had just spent five months in and out of the jungle. The ship worked its way up the Ucayali River, stopping from time to time at the small shore towns and villages along the way. Allen set up a hammock on deck and lounged there during the daylight hours, reading or writing in his journal. At night, he would stare up at the stars and try to sort through the ideas he had formed in Pucallpa. He worked on the early revisions of "The Reply" and drew up a complete list of his visions, large and small, natural or drug-induced, since 1944. For his reading, he had volumes by William James, Kant, Wolfe, and H. G. Wells; in addition, he spent considerable time reading passages in the *Tibetan Book of the Dead* and the Bible, especially Revelation.

Allen's writing proved to be therapy for a tortured mind. He had never written as much in so short a period of time, though most of the writing found him working on variations of the same theme: If his yage visions had indeed been a gift, what was he to do with it? Burroughs had written about a great invader that had driven him to write, and Allen seemed to be facing one of his own, from which there was no escape: "Some joke metaphysical being, eyeless, taken to invading my life, all the dead details come alive with secret significance that awaits me—sneaking into popular songs, frog croaks, my cough, my stray thoughts, my very death to come." There *was* a connection between his experience and that of the Beat Generation writers—of that he was certain:

The Beat Generation, a decisive moment in American consciousness—henceforth the horses' heads are headed toward eternity. No
group as weird before. . . . The elements were present before in Poe,
Dickinson, Melville—Whitman—then Crane—An evolution of human consciousness—"Widen the area of consciousness."

How far back did this evolution go? Shakespeare's famous "To Be or Not to
Be" line from *Hamlet* had haunted Allen from his earliest experiences with
ayahuasca. It seemed to be the riddle to all thoughts about eternity.

As he suspected, the yage brewed in the Amazonian region of Peru differed
from that which he had taken in Pucallpa. The *mescla* used as a catalyst in the
mixture was different. Allen was eager to try it, as well as bring home a sample
for later consumption. After a week in Iquitos, he located a man living at the
outskirts of the city who was willing to give him a dose. On June 24, he took
three swallows of *ayahuasca* from a small gourd cup and, while the *brujo* sat
nearby, tapping his foot and whistling a tune, Allen was delivered to a multidi-
mentional universe watched over by a serpent so huge that the middle of its
body and tail disappeared into the void. The whistling sound became a part of
the vision—the sound the serpent made to signal "its Eternal presence at all
times and places." The serpent, for all its gigantic and powerful presence, was
not entirely frightening. It promised a resolution to death, the entrance into
its spirit and the understanding of this consciousness. The vision seemed to
imply that death, although unavoidable, was not as terrifying as Allen had
imagined it. Death, he reasoned, was the breakdown of a familiar dimension.

The next day, he was on a plane heading back to Lima. He was ready to
return to the United States. During his last week in Lima, he met with government officials, from whom he gained the permission to take yage out of the
country. Now that he and Burroughs had tried the drug, Allen was especially
interested in seeing how Jack Kerouac would react to it. Allen looked forward
to his return to the States. His new plan was to return to New York, assemble
a book of poems and take care of other business and literary concerns, and, as
soon as he could afford to make another trip, depart for India.

14
TV Baby

Speak up and tell yr secret, is it a
living animal out there you're
afraid of still—?

1

Poetry, politics, and drugs: In the fall of 1960, all three took up a great deal of
Allen Ginsberg's time and attention.

His first order of business was putting together a volume of poems. Four years
had passed since the publication of *Howl and Other Poems*, and while the book
continued to enjoy the largest sales on the City Lights list, it was time for a
new Ginsberg work to be issued to the public. Allen had a wealth of material
to choose from, his main task being the completion of "Kaddish."

He had yet to finish the poem's opening section to his satisfaction, and the
long narrative passages needed work. Some of the poem's transitions were rough
and its wording had to be tightened to give it consistent rhythm. Using a razor
blade, Allen cut portions of the narrative into strips and tried to piece the
poem into a more logical and unified—and less repetitive—work. Bothered by
self-doubt about its value as a poem, Allen wondered whether it would be of
interest to anyone other than him and his family. These struggles, he wrote in
retrospect, were ultimately beneficial: "Defeat like that is good for poetry—you
go so far out you don't know what you're doing, you lose touch with what's
been done before by anyone, you wind up creating a new poetry-universe."

On the afternoon of September 13, Allen went about the task of finishing
"Kaddish" in a fashion similar to the way he had begun it. Boosted by occasional
doses of Benzedrine and Dexedrine, he revised, edited, and added to "Kaddish"
in a marathon work session that found him working straight through to the
following evening. "I sat down at desk 3 pm last Wednesday and did not rise
except to pee till 9 pm Thursday nite, having typed up complete Kaddish mss.
adding in various Shelleyan Hymns written in sobwracked exhausted trances,"
Allen wrote Kerouac. He was still second-guessing the work, but rather than

stew over it until he reached a state that prohibited him from ever submitting it for publication, he packaged the manuscript and shipped it special delivery to Ferlinghetti. "Let me know what it looks like to you," Allen instructed his publisher, expressing his worries that the poem might be a "huge white-elephant."

Allen should have known better. Ferlinghetti had seen and praised earlier drafts of "Kaddish" and he was enthusiastic about the new version. There were repetitions in the narrative that could be trimmed, he told Allen, but otherwise it was ready to go to press. Ferlinghetti further advised Ginsberg that, due to the nature of the poem, he would need signed release forms from Louis and Eugene, but he doubted that would be any problem, since both were aware of the poem's content and neither had raised serious objections in the past, and because Eugene, as an attorney, was aware of the kind of legal wording needed for the release forms and could draw up the papers according to his specifications.

Louis was steadfast in his reservations about certain lines and phrases in "Kaddish," and he mentioned them again when he saw this latest version of the poem. After telling Allen that he had "read your Kaddish with tears," calling it "a magnificent, heart-wrenching poem," Louis stated his specific objections. He was still greatly offended by the phrase "long black beard around vagina," which he told Allen was "too obscene for reference to mother." He also advised him to delete his references to homosexuality. "You'll invite slander, irrelevant to literary merits," he cautioned. Finally, he was embarrassed by Allen's passing reference to an affair Louis had had years ago, while he was still married but during a time when Naomi was institutionalized. He requested that this, too, be stricken from the final draft of the poem.

These suggestions bothered Allen. "God, I'm having trouble with Poppa over Kaddish," he complained to Kerouac after he had seen the list of his father's objections. "He wants me to excise inneresting parts about his own private life, about an affair he had . . . 20 years ago. Doesn't even want to appear human. Well, I'll excise."

The rest of Louis's objections were overruled, and on October 12, Louis signed the release form absolving City Lights from any claims of libel or slander in the publication of "Kaddish." Eugene signed a similar statement, as well. These bits of legality out of the way, Ginsberg and Ferlinghetti were free to compile the rest of the collection. Due to the length of "Kaddish," there was little room for many more poems in the new volume, which was to be titled *Kaddish and Other Poems*. It would have the square black and white cover format of *Howl*, and it, too, would be part of the "Pocket Poets" series. Ferlinghetti liked the poems that Allen had written in Europe ("To Aunt Rose," "At Apollinaire's Grave," "Poem Rocket," "The Lion for Real," and "Europe! Europe!") and he suggested that Ginsberg include those, along with "Mescaline" and "Laughing Gas" and any other drug poems that he might have completed.

Allen was in agreement with Ferlinghetti about the selections, and he spent the last two weeks of September and the first ten days of October working on putting the book in order. He sent Ferlinghetti copies of "Magic Psalm" and "The Reply," along with another revised version of "Kaddish," for his publisher's commentary. Although he wanted to see parts of the "Kaddish" narrative compressed even further, Ferlinghetti offered a favorable response. "It's right, will be great huge book," he said.

Even with a new book going to press, Allen had a large supply of leftover poems on his hands. He had yet to include "Siesta in Xbalba" or "The Green Automobile" in a poetry collection, and he still had poems dating back to his San Francisco/Berkeley days, as well as works from his post-*Howl*, pre-Europe period, that he wanted to collect. "Aether" still required work, plus it was too long for inclusion in *Kaddish*. In short, he had enough poetry for another volume at least as long as the one about to be published. That, Allen decided, would be his next City Lights collection.

In addition, his friend Ted Wilentz was interested in publishing *Empty Mirror* as a part of his Corinth Press. Wilentz had recently published *The Beat Scene*, an anthology of Beat writings accompanied by the photographs of Fred McDarrah, and in the near future his list of authors would expand to include Jack Kerouac, Diane Di Prima, LeRoi Jones, and others. Allen, who had wanted to publish *Empty Mirror* for the better part of a decade, and who already had an introduction for the volume written by William Carlos Williams, could not have been happier with this turn of events and he went right to work on assembling the collection.

Thus went one of the most active periods in Ginsberg's publishing history, finding him putting the finishing touches on two volumes of poetry (*Kaddish* and *Empty Mirror*) and beginning the assembly of a third (*Reality Sandwiches*). These works, along with the recordings of his poetry and a movie, assured him of a name and reputation that superseded anything the critics could say about the Beat Generation's being a temporary fad or social movement making a few poets rich. Allen's star continued to rise.

2

Jack Kerouac, however, was in a period of personal and professional decline, stemming more from the toll public life had exacted upon him than from his own creative inability.

Kerouac was a mess, a punch-drunk fighter who had spent the best of his healthy years in training, only to suffer later by taking on too many opponents in too few years. His lifestyle had been knocked about in public, his literary ideals punished. By nature, he was more inclined to internalize his problems than to counterpunch, and by late 1960, it was obvious to those who knew him that Jack was in serious trouble.

From an artistic perspective, it should not have been a bad year. *Tristessa*, Kerouac's novel about his love affair with a Mexican prostitute, had been published as a paperback original, and LeRoi Jones had published *The Scripture of the Golden Eternity* at his Totem Press; *Lonesome Traveler*, a collection of Kerouac's travel essays, was scheduled to be published in late fall, and Ferlinghetti had purchased *Book of Dreams* for City Lights. Most writers would have been thrilled to see four books in publication within a year's time, but Kerouac, who could be as tough on himself as his harshest critic, was not about to gauge his literary success solely by the number of volumes published or money earned. None of these books was as good as—or offered the exuberance and impact of—an *On the Road* or *Dr. Sax* or *Visions of Cody*, and Kerouac knew it. He was looking to publish another *big* book—one that would be properly published and distributed, extensively reviewed, and widely accepted by readers.

He could no longer anticipate the response to his books. Two of his finest works, *Dr. Sax* and *Mexico City Blues*, had been published a year earlier, in 1959, as was *Maggie Cassidy*, his novel about his great teenage love affair. To Jack's horror, the books had been largely panned (or ignored) by critics, as if in backlash to his "sudden" success. To make matters worse, a Hollywood film version of *The Subterraneans*, starring George Peppard and Leslie Caron, had been released; the film was a slick, embarrassing contrast to the free-spirited *Pull My Daisy* and threatened to immortalize Kerouac as a caricature of himself.

Depressed, Jack drank until he became bloated and red-faced. His health began to fail. In an effort to get him away from his problems and back to creative work, Lawrence Ferlinghetti offered Jack the use of his Bixby Canyon cabin. With Ginsberg, Burroughs, and Corso all out of the country, Jack was feeling isolated anyway, so some time alone in Ferlinghetti's Big Sur cabin could not hurt.

Or so he thought. Jack arrived in California in late July, but with the exception of the composition of a Joycean poem written about the sounds of the ocean, his trip was a disaster. Never one to sit by himself for too great a period of time, he was driven to the brink of a nervous breakdown during his stay in Bixby Canyon. The first few weeks went well, with Jack reading and writing and communing with nature on his long walks through the rough, wooded terrain. After a while, however, onsetting boredom and his need for a drink drove him back to the city, and by the time he made his way back to San Francisco, walking a good percentage of the way because he, the author of *On the Road*, could no longer get drivers to pick him up, Jack was ready for a full-scale bender. Although he had such friends as Lawrence Ferlinghetti, Michael McClure, Philip Whalen, and Lew Welch to look after him, he was too far gone to do anything but sink into alcoholic depression. Even a brief reunion with Neal and Carolyn Cassady failed to bolster his spirits. His return to the cabin was followed by bouts of the d.t.'s, loneliness, and more drunken sessions with whoever stopped by to visit. His depression disarmed his sensibility, leading him to paranoid distrust of his friends. He had a brief fling with a girlfriend of Neal Cassady's, but he was in no condition to pursue it. By the time Jack's stay was winding down in early September, Ferlinghetti was so concerned about Kerouac's mental well-being that he suggested he consider checking into a sanatorium.

It was Jack's last big road trip. Still, for all his problems, Kerouac was far too gifted to let the experience lie fallow. He would turn it into *Big Sur*, the stunning book about mental decline that became one of his finest—and most underrated—novels. *Big Sur* would be compared to F. Scott Fitzgerald's *The Crack-Up*, and while Kerouac would have shuddered at the thought, he and Fitzgerald had more in common than anyone might have predicted. Both were romantics whose most enduring novels were about controversial, if not antiheroic, characters; both were depicted by the media as spokespersons for

their respective generations. Both were tormented about the relationship between money and art, and both suffered through severe bouts of alcoholism and
depression.

There was another similarity that Kerouac's friends probably suspected,
though they were helpless to do anything about it and would never have dared
to mention it out loud: Like Fitzgerald, Kerouac was pushing himself headlong
toward an early death. His star was burning out.

3

Hearing of Kerouac's problems, Allen sent Jack a flip, newsy letter intended
both to cheer him up and goad him into some kind of action. The three-page
letter was a masterwork of its kind, a nonstop stream-of-consciousness rap in
which Allen gave the details of the composition of "Kaddish" and included a
sizable excerpt; spoke of his conclusions from his yage experiments ("realized I
AM the emptiness that's movie-projecting Kali monster on my mindscreen,
projecting mindscreen even. So not scared anymore. But I still can't *stop* the
appearance of the fucking mindscreen, I mean I can't quiet my organism to
total silence. I'll have to study yoga or something, finally . . ."); reported the
comings and goings and mental conditions of mutual friends; and hinted at
plans for the future. He was still interested in Cuba in the aftermath of its
revolution, he told Jack, and if he could make the arrangements, he hoped to
travel there to see firsthand what was going on in that country.

Jack replied with a sober letter that announced he was living a quieter life
now; he was back in Northport, staying away from liquor, losing weight, and
spending his hours reading a recently purchased vintage twenty-nine-volume
edition of the *Encyclopaedia Britannica*. He downplayed his problems at Big Sur,
preferring instead to remember the good times and his composition of "Sea."
He had begun a new novel, he mentioned to Allen, but it had been a false
start. As for Ginsberg's talk about Cuban politics, Kerouac was hearing not one
thing: "What Logia Jesus said about astonishment of paradise seems to me much
more on the right tracks of world peace and joy than all the recent communist
and general political hysteria rioting and false screamings."

It was a presidential election year, and Allen was as interested in politics as
ever. In his opinion, the position of the United States as a major player in
international politics was absolutely critical to any hope of world peace, and
he was particularly interested in the country's relationship with Cuba. Castro's
takeover had rekindled U.S. preoccupation with communism as the destroyer
of freedom, but Allen continued to believe that Castro, even if a dictator, was
far less involved in "hysterical mind control" than the United States. As if to
prove his point, he made an effort to meet Castro when the Cuban leader
visited the United Nations in September, and at a press conference afterward,
Allen caused a stir when he asked Cuban delegates about their country's attitudes about marijuana. Neither Cuba nor the United States was prepared to
accept Allen's theory that marijuana was prohibited because national leaders
believed it invited its users to think clearly and rebel against oppression.

As impertinent as Ginsberg's question might have seemed, it represented his strong belief that the world—and the United States in particular—needed a radical change of consciousness to avoid self-destruction. Throughout that fall, Allen raged about politics in his journal, filling its pages with manifestos condemning the United States, the FBI, the CIA, academic institutions, international politics, middle-class life, critics, and the news media:

> What good are all our washmachines if our hair's dirty
>   with Algiers blood?
> If the Vice President sits around telling lies about
>   Guatemala what good television except get mad?
> What good being reasonable talking public if movie
>   stars're afraid they're queer?
> What good being Senator you can't confess your inmost
>   thought?
> What good utmost thought if murder gets away with the
>   newspaper?
> I got no mama, I got no Government, I got nobody but me
>   and my friends
> my friends all believe in different Unicorns. . . .

Although he conceded that most of his political poems were angry ravings unworthy of publication—and, in fact, none of the poems from this period was ever pulled from his journals and published separately, though some were presented at readings—Allen fully intended to write a grand-scale political poem. He had seen enough of the world to feel that he could hold the United States publicly accountable, directly or indirectly, for many of its miseries:

> What's happening who's starving where who's got the
>   gelt . . .
> Who's got the guilt?
> We have, America . . .
> So happens we missed the boat to the New World.
> And now ships are leaving for the moon,
> Have we anything to export to the Universe
> but a few dead prophets and a basketful of cranky
>   Formulae for Electricity? . . .

Allen had little reason to be optimistic. He liked neither of the presidential candidates. He saw Kennedy as just another pretty face and Nixon as a continuation of the odious practices instituted during the Eisenhower administration. For all her paranoid ravings about the government, Naomi Ginsberg had been judged to be insane, but now, in light of what he was witnessing, Allen wondered whether she might have been more prophetic than she was given credit for. What was he to think when he saw J. Edgar Hoover get up at the Republican National Convention and proclaim that "communists, beatniks, and eggheads" were America's greatest enemies; or when he read that Eisenhower had been given a copy of *Lady Chatterley's Lover*, with dirty passages underlined, only to agree with the postmaster general that something had to be done about such smut? Were these indicators of the "fall" Whitman had prophesied?

Ginsberg seethed while he watched the Nixon-Kennedy debates—the first time in history that U.S. presidential candidates had debated on television. As far as Allen could tell, Nixon was playing up to the national paranoia about communism, but both Kennedy and Nixon seemed ready to take action against Cuba. "Both are phony and both outright warmongers," Allen told Kerouac, chiding him for supporting Nixon. "You don't think anybody's starving in the world. Nobody in America thinks so. This country is Evil and Whitman and I now spit on it and tell it to be nice or die, because that's what's coming. I HATE AMERICA! Ugh. And Nixon and Kennedy combine all that's most obnoxious, but Nixon does take the cake. I suppose all this hate is unpatriotic to eternity but fuckit I'm going to die anyway."

For all his anger and hyperbolic invective against political leaders and their practices, Allen was remarkably astute in his assessments of his times. He had been collecting news clippings and magazine articles of interest since his childhood, and he was gifted in his ability to read between the lines of such clippings and piece together the larger picture. His understanding of human nature enabled him to predict motives and results. In a November dream about Richard Nixon, Allen envisioned Nixon at home with his wife and daughter, but rather than see him as the evil person he characterized him to be in his letter to Kerouac, he saw him as a sympathetic loner, "an abused prisoner alone in his breakfast nook nervously being self-contained reading the papers." In time, in the aftermath of Nixon's Watergate disgrace and resignation, he would be just such a figure.

His vision of Kennedy was even more eerie. On October 31, 1959—over a year before Kennedy would be elected President, Allen scribbled these two prophetic lines about Kennedy in his journal: "He has a hole in his back. Thru which Death will enter."

4

Ginsberg was by no means the only visible member of the literary community to become active in politics at the time. For liberals tired of sterile Eisenhower politics and the hangover of McCarthyism and the Cold War, the 1960 elections represented a potential turning point, and John Kennedy was the hero of the hour. Kennedy, a master of media manipulation, managed to unite and gather behind him a phalanx of writers who, on a good day, could barely bring themselves to agreement on the construction of a sentence, let alone the formulation of political ideology.

One Kennedy admirer was Norman Mailer, the controversial novelist and essayist whose book *Advertisements for Myself* had caused a literary furor when it was published in 1959, and whose essay "The White Negro" was still the subject of debate among those trying to align hipsters and Beats. Mailer's recent *Esquire* profile of Kennedy, "Superman Goes to the Supermart," had favorably depicted Kennedy as a sort of existential hero, the piece establishing a new Kennedy image among the cognoscenti.

Ginsberg had known Mailer for several years, and while he disagreed with Mailer's assessment of the psychopathic makeup of hipsters and Beats, judging "The White Negro" to be "well intentioned but poisonous," he did respect Mailer's intelligence and understanding of political theater. Like Ginsberg, Mailer was concerned about the individual's feeling of powerlessness in a government that seemed to be progressively more control-oriented. Mailer also shared Ginsberg's concern about the relationship between the United States and Cuba, Mailer believing that U.S. government officials feared that Castro's rebellion would incite to action those Americans who had been "fighting with sick dead hearts against the cold insidious cancer of the power that governs us . . . giving us hope they would not always win." Mailer, who had once written that "like many another vain, empty, and bullying body of our time, I have been running for President these last ten years in the privacy of my mind," decided in November that he was going to run for mayor of New York City. His campaign, organized under the Existential party banner, promised to be exciting political theater, even if it was inevitable that it would be unsuccessful. One of Mailer's first actions was to ask Allen Ginsberg, Seymour Krim, and Noel Permental, Jr., to act as his press secretaries.

According to the plan, Mailer was formally to announce his candidacy, as well as read his new essay, "Open Letter to Fidel Castro," at a combination birthday party/political rally at his Manhattan apartment on November 19. For Mailer, the evening turned out to be a personal and political disaster. Believing that he could win the election if he could unite a constituency of New York's disenfranchised citizens, Mailer had invited an unlikely combination of outcasts to mingle with his well-known guests. He added to the evening's tension by turning up drunk and combative for his own party.

For Allen, the occasion was memorable because of a fight he got into with Norman Podhoretz. Earlier in the year, Allen, Peter, and Jack had called Podhoretz on a whim and invited him to their apartment to try to iron out their disagreements stemming from Podhoretz's *Partisan Review* essay "The Know-Nothing Bohemians." Podhoretz, for reasons he was never able to recall, accepted their invitation. At best, the encounter was civil, with neither Allen, Jack, nor Podhoretz backing down on their positions. As far as Podhoretz was concerned, the Beat Generation was anti-intellectual and anti-authoritarian, "a conspiracy to overthrow civilization (which is created by men, not boys) and replace it *not* by the State of Nature where we can all romp around in a free-and-easy nakedness, but by a world of the adolescent street gang." He was hearing nothing of Kerouac's and Ginsberg's harangues against middle-class living and values, and he was not about to accept their invitation to smoke marijuana with them, as if doing so were tantamount to a passing of the peace pipe between factions of warring tribes.

Podhoretz was a friend of Norman Mailer's, despite his disapproval of Mailer's interest in the Beats and hipsters. If Mailer was one of literature's most visible "bad boys," Podhoretz was, by contrast, a subdued but influential member of the new critical establishment, and while neither Mailer nor Ginsberg aspired to win Podhoretz's approval of their literature or lifestyle, it would have been, in terms of literary politics, a coup if they had been able at least to gain a measure of respect from the camp he represented.

The confrontational atmosphere of Mailer's party was not the place for mending fences—or even for peaceful coexistence. As Ginsberg would later recall, Podhoretz approached him and told him that he was an intelligent, gifted writer who could be a valued member of the New York literary scene if he would only dump such friends as Kerouac and Burroughs, who would never fit in. For Allen, who had been working so hard to promote not only Jack's and Bill's work but also that of Gary Snyder, Philip Whalen, Michael McClure, and others, Podhoretz's suggestion was the proverbial last straw. Allen told Mailer biographer Peter Manso:

> To my eternal shame, I lost my temper. I suddenly saw myself in a B movie out of Balzac, with me as the distinguished provincial being tempted by the idiot worldly banker—"We'll give you a career if you renounce your mother and father and your background." It was so corny, like being propositioned by the devil or something, Blake's devil who is ignorance, so I started screaming at him, "You big dumb fuckhead! You idiot! You don't know anything about anything!"

Ironically, it was Mailer who acted the role of peacemaker in the confrontation. Frightened by Ginsberg's rage, Podhoretz had shouted out that Allen was going to get violent, and Mailer rushed over to break up any potential fisticuffs. Allen, who admitted that he was on his "high horse" and probably added to the already-existing tension, told Mailer that he had no intention of hitting Podhoretz. Shortly thereafter, he left the party with economist C. Wright Mills. The altercation, although harmless in itself, had long-lasting effects: If there ever was any hope of smoothing over the differences among Podhoretz and the writers of the Beat Generation, it disappeared the night of the Mailer party.

As did Mailer's hopes of running a successful campaign for mayor. In the early-morning hours, long after Allen had left the party, a hopelessly drunk and out-of-control Norman Mailer argued with his wife and in a fit of passion stabbed her with a penknife. Although Adele Mailer refused to press charges, Mailer's career as a politician was over. The campaign ended before it began.

5

Allen stepped up his experimentation with mind-expanding drugs throughout the fall and winter months. Where he had begun with the hope that such drugs would have a profound effect on the individual and his creativity, he now believed that the widespread use of hallucinogens could lead to the alteration of the public consciousness and a subsequent political change for the better. He made formal public calls for a change in marijuana laws and began to compile what would become, in time, one of the largest drug files on record. He, Peter, and Jack experimented with the gallon of yage Allen had brought back from Peru, and Allen added to his firsthand knowledge by reading extensively on the topic of the relationship between hallucinogenic drugs and the mind.

Allen's campaign for the legalization of marijuana caught the attention of an organization known as the Group for the Advancement of Psychiatry. Every year, the psychiatrists in the organization gathered to study the behavioral patterns of a particular group, and at their 1960 convention, they decided to focus on the Beat Generation. Allen and Peter were asked to address the convention.

The members of GAP could hardly have been prepared for what they heard. By 1960, the Beats had been analyzed and psychoanalyzed in public to such an extent that their public profile had become a cliché. Such television programs as "The Adventures of Dobie Gillis," "77 Sunset Strip," and "Route 66" had presented their own specific versions of the beatnik, ranging from the spaced-out but harmless Maynard G. Krebbs to the cool James Deanish Cookie Burns; even *Mad* magazine had taken a satirical run at the Beats. When Allen and Peter showed up at the GAP convention, they were probably expected to fit the profile of the angry, nihilistic, antisocial, pot-smoking hipster/beatnik that had been force-fed to the public for the past three years.

Instead, GAP members were treated to a poet who was still fresh from his South American journey and who was intelligent, eloquent, and as concerned with the state of the contemporary mind as they were. The poet read in a prophetic, rather than disaffiliated, voice from such works as "Laughing Gas," "Mescaline," "Lysergic Acid," "Magic Psalm," and "The Reply"; he spoke authoritatively on the effects of hallucinogenic drugs on his mind and what he had concluded from his experiments.

Typically, Allen elicited a mixed response from his audience, although in this case, oddly enough, he was rejected by the younger doctors just out of medical school who thought he was crazy and was listened to by the older psychiatrists whose experiences had left them open-minded to the potential for new discoveries in the field of psychiatry. One Canadian psychiatrist, Sir Humphrey Osmond, was especially interested in Allen's presentation. Osmond had been researching LSD for some time at Saskatchewan Hospital, and he had been the doctor responsible for helping Aldous Huxley with the peyote experiments that led to his book *The Doors of Perception*. Osmond, along with New York psychiatrist Edward Hornick, whom Allen knew, proposed that Allen meet a forty-year-old Harvard psychologist who was not in attendance at the conference but who, under the sponsorship of the university, was conducting his own research on mushrooms containing psilocybin. This doctor, they said, might be able to help further Ginsberg's experiments with hallucinogens.

The doctor's name was Timothy Leary.

6

Allen contacted Leary immediately, and within a week he turned up at Ginsberg's Lower East Side apartment. Allen was impressed that someone of Leary's stature would go to the bother of coming to New York for a meeting and that Leary was sincerely interested in his experiences with drugs. As they talked, Allen was surprised to hear that Leary had never smoked marijuana and knew very little about the drug use among the West Coast poets and underground.

Allen offered Leary some marijuana. After a long conversation, Leary extended the invitation for Allen to visit him in Boston.

Leary had been at Harvard since the beginning of the year. As a member of the university's Department of Social Relations, he taught a graduate course entitled Existential Transactional Behavior Change, and his drug experiments had been endorsed by the university. Leary was very serious in his approach to his research but, as Allen noted first in New York and later in Boston, he had been somewhat insulated by the university environment. He fully expected that his experiments would be embraced by the academics as "a polite, scholarly, socially acceptable, perfectly reasonable pursuit [that] would spread through the university and be automatically taken on as part of the curriculum." Ginsberg, already aware of the kind of opposition that drug experimentation could meet, advised Leary to take a subtle approach, to try the drug on artists and poets who were already respected and could articulate their experiences to the academics.

As Leary recalled, Allen sampled his first "magic mushrooms" on the evening of November 26, 1960. Leary was interested in the ritualistic aspects behind the drugs Allen had tried in South America, particularly the notion of having a *curandero* present to oversee the drug use and help the user along, and Allen outlined the procedure before he took the psilocybin. He spoke of his experiences in Peru, and it was apparent to Leary that Ginsberg was anything but casual about his approach to taking drugs. Leary liked the practice of having an elder helping with the experience. Leary later recounted that as he listened to Ginsberg talk, he realized Ginsberg was "shaping me up to help him. Allen was weaving a word spell, dark eyes gleaming through the glasses, chain-smoking, moving his hands, intense, chanting trance poetry."

After he had finished talking, Allen went upstairs in the Leary residence and began to prepare his environment for the experience. He borrowed albums of Beethoven and Wagner from Leary's study, and Leary brought him his teenaged daughter's record player to use. Allen removed his clothes, took off his glasses, and lay down on the bed, not bothering to pull back the covers. Peter, also naked, lay down next to him. Leary gave Allen 36 milligrams of psilocybin and, making sure that he was comfortable, assured him that he would check in on them every fifteen minutes.

When the drug began to take effect, Allen grew frightened and nauseous— a common reaction to psilocybin among novice users. Allen wondered whether he should vomit, as he had done with yage, or whether he should hold it back. It seemed to be an important decision: If he threw up, he reasoned, he would be conceding his spirit to whatever force or demon was rebelling within him, whereas by not vomiting, he would remain in the present universe. When Leary checked in on Allen, he found a man he described as being "shamelessly weak and shamelessly human and greatly classic," "patiently searching, pushing himself into panics and fears, into nausea, trying to learn something, trying to find meaning." Leary was moved by the fragility and strength he saw in Ginsberg's eyes, by the vulnerability that enabled him to see beyond the surface into the depths of what Leary believed to be a truly great man. For Allen, it was an electric moment, a turning point: "Professor Leary came into my room, looked in my eyes, and said that I was a great man. That determined me to make an effort to live here and now. . . . [I] swallowed down the vomit that beseiged from my stomach as if an independent being down there was rebelling at being dragged into existence."

Listening to Wagner's *Götterdämmerung*, Allen had a flash of insight different from the horrifying visions he had suffered through under *ayahuasca*. Rather than perceive a Great Being poised to devour human consciousness, Allen sensed a need for someone to "take on the responsibility of being the creative God and seize power over the universe." The world, he determined, was waiting for action—for revolution—and he decided he might as well be the person to begin it. He got out of bed and prepared to leave the room. "[I] pronounced my nakedness as the first act of revolution against the destroyers of the human image," he wrote later, remembering the experience.

Timothy Leary was in his daughter Susan's room when he heard the sound of bare footsteps on the carpeting outside. He looked out the door just in time to see Peter's naked form descending the stairwell. He ushered Susan to the third floor and then went downstairs to check on Allen and Peter. He found them in his study, talking to Frank Barron, a coworker who shared the house with him. Allen, completely naked except for his glasses, waved a finger in the air. "I'm the Messiah," he proclaimed. "I've come down to preach love to the world. We're going to walk through the streets and teach people to stop hating."

Barron told Allen it sounded like a good idea.

"Do you believe I'm the Messiah?" Allen asked Leary. "Look, I can prove it. I'm going to cure your hearing. Take off your hearing machine. Your ears are cured. Come on, take it off. You don't need it."

Leary removed his hearing aid and put it on his desk.

"And now your glasses," Allen said. "I'll heal your vision too."

As Leary took off his glasses and placed them beside his hearing aid on the desk, Allen grinned from ear to ear, convinced that he had healed the psychologist.

"But Allen, one thing," Leary said. "Your glasses. You're still wearing them. Why don't you cure your own vision?"

"Yes, you're right," Allen replied, surprised that he had not thought of that himself. He removed his glasses and laid them on the desk. Inspired, he urged Leary to follow him outside. "We're going down to the city streets to tell the people about peace and love. And we'll get lots of important people on a big telephone network to settle all this warfare bit."

Leary, too, had wondered what would happen if world leaders were to try psilocybin. Would there be politics of ecstasy, worldwide legislation born of the joy Ginsberg was now experiencing? At the moment, however, it was anything but practical for a naked Ginsberg to run down the street and spread the word.

Frank Barron felt the same way and suggested that Allen get the word out by telephone first.

"Who we gonna call?" Peter asked.

"Well, we'll call Kerouac on Long Island, and Kennedy and Khrushchev and Bill Burroughs in Paris and Norman Mailer. . . . We'll get them all hooked up in a big cosmic electronic love talk. War is just a hang-up. We'll get the love-thing flowing on the electric Bell Telephone network."

Allen wanted to begin with a call to Khrushchev, but Barron persuaded him to call Kerouac instead. Allen dialed the operator and waited. "Hello, operator, this is God, I want to talk to Kerouac. . . . To whom do I want to talk? Kerouac. . . . What's my name? This is God. G-O-D. . . . Okay. We'll try Capital 7-0563. . . . Where? Northport, Long Island. . . . Oh. Yes. That's right. That's the number of the house where I was born. Look, operator, I'll have to go upstairs to get the number. Then I'll call back."

Allen went upstairs to retrieve his address book and in a short time he had Kerouac on the line. The revolution had begun, he told Jack, and it was essential that he get on the next plane to Boston. Jack asked Allen whether he was stoned, then told him he could not come to Boston because he had his mother to take care of. "Bring your mother!" Allen ordered, refusing to take no for an answer. This was one time that Jack's mother was not going to get in the way. Jack, however, was too emotionally exhausted from the fallout of the Beat Generation movement to be much interested in participating in the beginning of a new one; he knew the price you paid for giving your heart and soul in an effort to change the world. When Allen asked him what he wanted to do, he said, "Lay down and die." Allen roared back his disapproval, accusing Jack of being afraid. Well, Allen said, *he* had been afraid of God, he had been afraid of death—until he realized that, as a life force, he *was* God. *He* was the Messiah and he was going to start his own peace and love movement; he would help settle the differences between Kennedy and Khrushchev; he would save the world! If Kerouac did not come to Boston that night, then he would have to do it sometime in the near future.

Allen talked to Kerouac for quite a while, and Leary finally stepped in and told him that for the price of the phone call, he could fly Kerouac to Boston. Embarrassed, Allen cut off the call, but he was far from finished. There were other people to call. He wanted to call William Carlos Williams, who was old and dying in New Jersey. He wanted to call Norman Mailer. Leary gently guided Allen away from the telephone and had him lie down on the couch. In a quiet tone, Allen described what he had seen, how he had felt. He was grateful to Leary for telling him he was a great man. He told Leary that the psilocybin, like yage, made him realize that he had to open the door to women and heterosexuality. Leary offered Allen a robe and asked him whether he wanted something to eat or drink. Allen refused any food, believing that "if I ate or shit again I would turn back to a mere non-messiah human," but he accepted a cup of warm milk. He spoke further of his visions and as the effects of the drug began to wear off, he talked passionately about the lost souls of New York, of the junkies and homeless and helpless and hopeless, of the powerful and the powerless. A new consciousness, aided by the use of this hallucinogenic drug, could bring people together:

> All these who are dancers in the memory of creation
> All these Eternal Spirits to be wakened in stores &
>   alleyways
> All these bodies to be touched and healed in their
>   windows
> All these Lacklove, all these suffering the Hate along
>   the avenues of rusty bedsprings

All couch'd with Evil, dreaming of the Void,
All dumbed under the rainbow snowstorm streets created
in the Great City of Eternity the Heaven of
Consciousness . . .

The way Allen saw it, by using every available means—"radio, newspapers, television, lottery banks & gossip"—the world could be connected to one consciousness, to a blissful state that would eliminate suffering, despair, cruelty, and anger: "Everyone plugged in at once announce the Coming Union of All consciousness. . . ."

Leary, too, was buoyed by the conversation: "It seemed to us that wars, class conflicts, racial tensions, economic exploitation, religious strife, ignorance, and prejudice were all caused by narrow social conditioning. Political problems were manifestations of psychological problems, which at bottom seemed to be neurological-hormonal-chemical. If we could help people plug into the empathy circuits of the brain, then positive social change could occur."

To implement these changes, Allen favored an egalitarian approach in which the drugs would be available to anyone who wished to take them. He believed this was everybody's right. However, that was the ideal—a far cry from the pragmatic. One had to consider research and licensing, as well as a way to educate the public on how to use psilocybin. Allen and Leary agreed that this would involve a lot of thought and debate, but at that moment, as they sat at Leary's kitchen table, everything seemed possible and both were ready to face the challenge.

"And then," Timothy Leary wrote later in his memoir of the evening, "we started planning the psychedelic revolution."

7

Allen planned the revolution with the fervor of a zealot. Since psilocybin was still an unknown drug being examined in an experimental manner, he realized he would have to take a cautious approach in spreading the word about its benefits. He had witnessed the way the police and government officials attacked the use of other drugs, particularly marijuana, and he did not want to see the authorities act against psilocybin before it had the chance to take root. The best idea, Allen told Leary, was to compile a list of respectable, articulate figures willing to try the drug, then use their positive testimonials to offset the inevitable negative reactions by the authorities. Since Leary was authorized to conduct these experiments, the process would be legal. He could come to New York on weekends, distribute the drug to selected individuals, record their reactions, and put together a file of notables who had used and approved of it. Allen offered to act as the go-between, connecting people to Leary, though he felt that he should keep a relatively low profile, reasoning that his high visibility as a "beatnik" could work against them if he spoke out too loudly and too soon. Besides, Allen told Leary, the doctor's credentials would inspire more confidence than he ever could.

Allen lined up participants, the first four being jazz musicians Thelonius

Monk and Dizzy Gillespie and painters Willem de Kooning and Franz Kline.
Kerouac agreed to try the drug, as did poet Robert Lowell. However, the effects
of psilocybin were not quite as universal as Allen had hoped they would be.
Monk was unimpressed, asking Allen whether he had anything stronger. Publisher Barney Rosset had a bad, anxiety-ridden trip. Lowell was awed by the
experience, telling Allen that he finally understood what Blake and St. John
of the Cross were talking about in their mystic writings. Kerouac's experience
was diminished by his drunken, aggressive state at the time of his taking the
pills, and he remained skeptical of the transcendental powers of psilocybin,
proclaiming that "walking on water wasn't made in a day."

Despite the mixed reactions, Allen's enthusiasm never dimmed. *"The Revolution Has Begun,"* he wrote in a Christmas message to Neal Cassady. "Stop giving
your authority to Christ and the Void and the Imagination—*you are it*, now,
the God—I will have babies instead of jacking off into Limbo—all's well—
we're starting a plot to get everyone in Power in America high." He wrote of
his experiences to Burroughs and even sent a letter to Aldous Huxley, asking
him how Bill might obtain psilocybin in Paris. In his journal, he wrote numerous
entries about his feelings, characterized best by a short poem entitled "Hurrah
for the American Revolution!"

> Light dies! all light is the same
> Light rays on over the coffin of the Seen
> The million stars conspire the Universe
> I am the Son of Man, I am the Sun of the Cosmos,
> I am the Father of the American Revolution.

Totally obsessed, Allen tried to write under the influence of any drug—or,
in some cases, combination of drugs—that he could obtain. He tried more
laughing gas, marijuana, cocaine, heroin, *ayahuasca*, and, of course, more
psilocybin. He knew from his experiences with Burroughs, Huncke, and others
which drugs had the highest potential for addiction, and he was cautious about
their use. However, for all his efforts and good intentions, very little of his
poetry from this period was publishable. Like his other drug-influenced poems,
they were fascinating depictions of his state of mind but as poems they fell short
of Ginsberg's literary standards.

One exception was a lengthy poem entitled "Television Was a Baby Crawling
Toward That Deathchamber." At the time of its February composition, Allen
had yet to try Methedrine, the new drug of choice around the East Village.
The amphetamine, which was taken by injection, produced hallucinations of
its own, and on the evening that he wrote "TV Baby" (Ginsberg's shortened
title for the poem), he mixed a concoction of Methedrine, heroin, and psilocybin that enabled him to write in another of his all-night sessions, the composition of "TV Baby" lasting from eight in the evening to the following noon.
The frenzied writing went on for ten typed pages, the poem an unchecked glut
of long-lined free associations, much of it written in shotgun rhythm, words
struck onto the page with the same sense of random placement as color on a
Jackson Pollock drip painting:

Here I am—old Betty Boop whoopsing behind the skull microphone
    wondering what Idiot soap opera horror show we broadcast by
    Mistake—full of communists and frankenstein cops and
mature capitalists running the State Department and the Daily
    News Editorial hynotizing millions of legion-eyed detectives
    to commit mass murder on the Invisible
which is only a bunch of women weeping hidden behind the newspapers
    in the Andes, conspired against by Standard Oil,
which is a big fat fairy monopolizing all Being that has form'd
    it self to Oil,
and nothing gets in its way so it grabs different oils in all poor
    mystic aboriginal Principalities too weak to
Screech out over the radio that Standard Oil is a bunch of spying
    Businessmen intent on building one Standard Oil in the whole
    universe like an egotistical cancer. . . .

In its attempt to combine personal and planetary consciousness, "TV Baby"
was a drug-laced progression of the elliptical elements of "Howl." It was Blake's
prophetic voice superimposed on radio/television consciousness. By early 1961,
William Burroughs was working on his "cut-up" method of writing—a method
by which two pages of prose were cut in half, with the half of one page joined
to a half of the second page and retyped, creating a different level of thought,
or consciousness—and Allen had tried this method on some of his poetry to
see how it worked. In "TV Baby," the "cut-up" was drug-induced, as if Ginsberg's thought process had been rent and reassembled to represent a line of
thought that was neither lucid prose nor gibberish. He included news items, bits
of his own (and, by extension, his mother's) political ravings, autobiographical
fragments, and hallucinogenic glimpses into another level of consciousness.
The long lines, like those in the first part of "Howl," signified the long cries of
a person shouting or chanting his words until he ran out of breath and had to
start again.

    For Ginsberg, the poem was as problematic as "Kaddish" had been. When
he looked at it with an objective, critical eye, he was not immediately convinced
that it was good poetry. He *was* certain that it needed a lot of work, and since
he was not at that time mentally prepared to take on what promised to be an
immense task of restructuring and/or revising, he placed it aside for a later date.
It would not be published for a half-dozen years.

8

Allen's scientific and systematic use of drugs was not a practice shared by most
of his friends and acquaintances, and as early as 1961 there were indications
that the extensive drug use in and around his apartment could be harmful to
the users. Peter had picked up a heroin habit to go along with the Methedrine
he was taking. Herbert Huncke and Peter's girlfriend, Janine, were mainlining
Methedrine. Alexander Trocchi, the Scottish writer Allen had met in Paris,

was living nearby, and his apartment, known as "Methedrine University," was a hangout for speed-freak artists who would shoot "meth" and spend hours under bare light bulbs, fashioning art from bits of wood or pieces of refuse they found in the street. Allen's own apartment was not much better, with people dropping in at all hours. It was soon apparent that he was in danger of losing control of his environment in much the same way as he had in 1949, when Herbert Huncke and Little Jack Melody had moved in and taken over the place.

This time, Allen found a way out. He had been wanting to visit India for some time, and this seemed as good a time to go as he could foresee. He would travel to Paris to visit Burroughs, Gregory Corso would come up from Athens to join them, and after their reunion, it would be on to India, where Allen hoped to live for about a year.

Before he left, he helped plan a fund-raiser for the Living Theatre. The avant-garde theater group hoped to take its show to Europe but, as always, was lacking funds. Someone decided it might be a good idea to hold a champagne party and auction, with writers and painters donating manuscripts and works to be sold off to raise money. De Kooning and Kline donated paintings and John Cage and Paul Goodman offered manuscripts. Even though he would be out of the country at the time of the party/auction, Allen, who was always close to Julian Beck and Judith Malina and who was a strong supporter of the Living Theatre, decided to donate a manuscript of his own. He wrote Lawrence Ferlinghetti and asked him to send the original handwritten manuscript of "Kaddish" to present to the auction. The manuscript, Allen figured, would probably raise enough money to give the Living Theatre quite a boost. Ferlinghetti could not have agreed more, but he felt that Allen could still make a generous donation without sacrificing what was certain to be a valuable first draft of a masterwork; perhaps another poem manuscript or a later draft of "Kaddish" would suffice, Ferlinghetti suggested. "PLEASE DO NOT THROW AWAY YOUR SHOES IN ORDER TO WALK BAREFOOT THRU INDIA, BECUZ WHEN YOU GIT BACK TO U.S. you will need dem shoes again," Ferlinghetti wrote, making a pointed reference to Allen's habit of being generous to the point of self-denial. In ten years, Ferlinghetti said, Allen could sell the manuscript for enough money to stay alive through the turn of the century.

Despite his publisher's pleas, Allen turned the manuscript over to the Living Theatre. As time would show, the gesture was vintage Ginsberg, just as it was typical of him to be extraordinarily patient with friends and acquaintances who tested his limits. Rather than object to those who invaded his apartment and stayed well beyond what would be considered their normal welcome, Allen remained patient. When he accepted a person as a friend, he did so with a sense of loyalty and commitment, even if that meant forgiving someone who had stolen from him, as Huncke had done in the past to support his drug habits, or tolerating outrageous behavior, as he would with Gregory Corso for over four decades. Nowhere was this more apparent than in the way he dealt with Jack Kerouac, who was again using Allen as a whipping boy for his own frustrations over his literary career. Drunk and abusive, Kerouac would offend Allen with his anti-Semitic remarks, which Jack directed at the publishing world in general. The New York publishers and intellectuals—all Jews, according to Kerouac—

were out to ruin him because he was Catholic, Jack said, adding that if that was the case, if the Jews were out to get the Christians, maybe Hitler had the right idea, after all. Allen hated to hear this kind of talk, even if Kerouac was drunk and trying to test him by saying things he did not really mean. "Don't be paranoiac about imaginary Jews," Allen wrote after one of Jack's particularly nasty outbursts. "The lineups are too mixed to categorize your 'enemies' as Jewish. You could make similar lineups of Catholics, Protestants." He drew up a list to prove his point. While Kerouac did indeed have Jewish enemies, he had a number of Jewish supporters, including Gilbert Millstein, Seymour Wyse, and Allen himself; the same could be said about his mixture of Christian supporters and enemies. As a writer, Kerouac should have known better than to stereotype people according to their creeds, Allen said. "You are talking Jewish to annoy me, and it does because you think I am a *Jewish* Truth Cloud. Are you a *Gentile* Truth Cloud?" At this point, when Allen was trying to find ways to create a universal consciousness free of hatred and aggression, the last thing he needed to hear was ranting from someone trying to divide people.

As the time for his departure drew near, Allen hurried to get his apartment matters in order. He paid the entire month's rent for March, assuring Huncke, Janine, and Lafcadio the time needed to move to new quarters. He left money for bills and utilities. He moved his letters, manuscripts, and important papers to his father's house in Paterson. Since his trip overseas was indefinite, he worked to see that there were no loose ends left anywhere.

9

On March 23, Allen and Peter departed for Paris on a ship named, aptly enough, the SS *America*. It was a cold, rainy day, and from the deck of the ship, Allen could see the mist enveloping much of the Empire State Building. On the dock, a small group of friends and family gathered in the sleet to see them off. Eugene, LeRoi Jones, and Carl Solomon were there, as was Louis Ginsberg, tearful and nostalgic as he always was when his son left for an extended trip. Elise Cowen, who had typed the final manuscript of "Kaddish" for Allen, declaring that he had not yet written the last word on his mother, peered over her black eyeglasses at Allen, not knowing she would never see him again. Blond-haired Janine, looking pale in her black jacket, waved a scarf at Peter and Allen, while Lafcadio Orlovsky, tipping his straw hat at the departing ship, stood nearby, a half smile on his face. Allen and Peter stood at the bow of the ship, waving their farewells, Allen writing later that "when I called their names I saw them, drifting away with their skulls." He had no way of knowing what lay ahead or when he would return.

A week earlier, Allen had tried to put his feelings about his pending journey into a poem. He was disappointed with his country. In his poetry, he had tried to speak to it, but it seemed wrapped up in furthering its own self-destruction. Depressed, Ginsberg could envision only his own death, not a happy future. Leaving the country, he realized, promised no relief, especially when it involved his traveling to the impoverished, heavily overpopulated country of India:

Who knows the terror of
    the wrath to come?
Who knows the Joys of
    waiting sages and
    sufferers
Who knows the banquet
    billions hungrily
    await in their dark
    beds in India—?
One Eye Sees All—the Hate
    and thwarted Joy.

In India, he would seek out holy men for answers. For all his visions, he had very few of his own.

15
Mediterranean Planet Waves

I have no name I wander in a nameless countryside. . . .

1

When Allen arrived in Paris, he was shocked to learn that Bill Burroughs had checked out of the Beat Hotel, leaving no forwarding address. Bill was well aware of Allen and Peter's pending arrival, and he had given Allen no reason to suspect that he would not be in Paris to greet them upon their arrival. This was mysterious behavior, even by Burroughs's standards. It was as if he was deliberately trying to avoid them.

As it turned out, that was precisely the case. In the three years since Allen had seen him last, Burroughs had undergone significant personal and professional changes, some for the better, some downright sinister or difficult to understand. Gregory Corso and Sinclair Beiles, a young South African poet, were living at the hotel, as was Burroughs's recent collaborator, Brion Gysin, and by talking to them Allen was able to piece together a profile of Burroughs and his recent activities.

Over the past year, Bill had been obsessed with the "cut-up" method of writing which, as he would explain, was as close as he could get to creating a dream consciousness, or "a certain juxtaposition of word and image." This method of writing was discovered by accident. One day in October 1959, while Burroughs was out to lunch, Gysin had sliced through some newspapers with a Stanley blade while he was making a mount for a drawing. On a lark, he began fitting the strips of cut newspaper together, and he discovered that funny, almost surreal sentences could be made from the pieced-together strips. By the time Bill had returned from lunch, Gysin had assembled an amusing collage of newspaper strips.

To Burroughs, this was an enormously important discovery, a natural progression of his work in *Naked Lunch*. The junkie dealt with the hazy juxtaposition of word and image, and to achieve this effect in *Naked Lunch*, Burroughs had broken down the traditional plot and thought structure of the novel by random sequencing of the book's episodes, which gave the book its dreamy quality. Cut-ups were a breakdown of the traditional fictional controls, the looping and joining of two thought processes to create a third. As radical as the process seemed, to Burroughs it was not much different from the visual effect of looking at any given page of a newspaper, with its unrelated columns of print and photographs. While reading a newspaper, a reader might catch a word, phrase, or bit of a photograph out of the corner of an eye, and that slight interruption or intrusion could change entirely the meaning of what was being read. How different was this from other normal, everyday occurrences, when a person's thoughts could be altered by something seen on the spur of the moment, or by a bit of overheard conversation on the street?

In no time, cut-ups were the main literary activity at the Beat Hotel, with Gregory Corso and Sinclair Beiles joining Burroughs and Gysin in cutting up every newspaper, magazine, and book in sight. Shakespeare, Rimbaud, Kafka, Eliot, Conrad, Kerouac—even *Naked Lunch* itself: pages from these authors' books were cut up and juxtaposed to others. As Burroughs explained, the fact that the reconstructions failed to follow the logic and structure of the traditional declarative sentence had very little to do with the effectiveness of this new form. Besides trying to do away with linear thinking, Burroughs was also attempting to eliminate dualism, as well:

It is unfortunately one of the great errors of Western thought, the whole either-or proposition. You remember Korzybski and his idea of non-Aristotelian logic. Either-or thinking just is not accurate thinking. That's not the way things occur, and I feel the Aristotelian construct is one of the great shackles of Western civilization. Cutups are a movement toward breaking this down. I should imagine it would be much easier to find acceptance of the cutups from, possibly, the Chinese, because you see already there are many ways that they can read any given ideograph. It's already cut up.

By doing away with linear thought and plot, the cut-up was breaking down the element of control that the writer had over the reader. It was a much more active exercise for the reader, whose own experiences, thoughts, and interpretations would affect the words in the cut-ups. All that was required of the reader was trust. "Don't think about it. Don't theorize. Try it," Burroughs had written Ginsberg in June 1960. "Always remember, 'Nothing is True. Everything is permitted.' Last words of Hassan Sabbah The Old Man Of The Mountain."

Minutes to Go, published in March 1960, was a cut-up collaboration of Burroughs, Gysin, Corso, and Beiles. For Corso and Beiles, it was an interesting exercise, although neither saw it as the kind of new-wave writing that Burroughs and Gysin perceived it to be. Corso had too much respect for the creative process to see his thoughts chopped up and rearranged with someone else's, and he did not like the notion, expressed by Gysin, who was not even a writer, that poetry should be rubbed out and recreated by anyone with a written text and a pair of scissors.

There is no question that Brion Gysin was an enormous influence on Burroughs—and not always for the best. Gysin had no use for women and he would go out of his way to denigrate them at any available opportunity. As far as Gysin was concerned, women were the ruination of the human race; they were vampires who used their sexuality to control men. Burroughs, who had never had much use for women in the first place, needed little encouragement to fall into step with this line of thinking, and before long his own misogynist inclinations were revealed in his thinking and writing. Some of his statements, such as those focusing on his theory that women were basically mistakes that should be eliminated from the population, or that women were evil agents from another planet, were both shocking and ludicrous, and would have been easily ignored or discarded if Burroughs and his work had not begun to build a following.

In the months just prior to Ginsberg's arrival in Paris, Burroughs had extended his cut-ups to include photography and tape recording. The more he studied cut-up options, the more he became convinced that sound and image were part of a network designed to control people's thoughts and actions. Gysin had addressed this issue when he suggested that all children should be paid to attend school, the children earning the most being the students who actually learned the most. Knowledge and free thinking broke down the controls. Burroughs found the idea fascinating, but he was less than convinced that it would work. With such government agencies as the CIA and the FBI controlling people's behavior and magazines such as *Time* dictating cultural values, free thinking was virtually impossible. In fact, Burroughs came to believe, in such a society as the one he was seeing, the ability to think freely was in itself a curse.

As he continued to explore the implications and options of cut-up composition, Burroughs concluded that one could determine motives and secret meanings in the juxtaposed lines and images of the cut-up. Further, if one were to examine the juxtaposition of events in one's own life, one could find the truth hidden therein. One simply had to peel back the fabric of the designed (or desired) image and look at the network of events and influences inside; one had to move beyond preconception and societal conditioning and cut the nerves of the ego.

2

At first, Allen was no more eager to embrace Burroughs's new method of composition than he had been to adopt Jack Kerouac's style of spontaneous prose. By Ginsberg's estimation, Burroughs's cut-ups, although amusing and fascinating, were so far off the beaten path that they had no chance of breaking through the already-rigid publishing venues. Further, Ginsberg was not entirely certain that they should. Poetry, with its sense of heightened language and image, was more accommodating to the kind of mental loops present in Burroughs's cut-ups; in prose, the breakdown of structure and order was more problematic, especially if the reader had to labor to understand what the writing was trying to say. This, of course, was precisely Burroughs's point: Readers had been conditioned to read and interpret in a given way, and his new writing was going to challenge those traditions. Allen was less than sold on the idea but, as an admirer of Dadaist and Surrealist writings, he kept his mind open and eventually came around to praising Burroughs's writing as a breakthrough in abstract writing, "a non-commital [sic] transcription into words of a succession of visual images passing in front of his mental eye."

Allen made the best of his time in Paris. Deducing that in all likelihood Burroughs had gone back to Tangier, Allen wrote him a series of letters and waited for Bill's response. In the meantime, he had projects of his own to keep him occupied. On April 17, Cuban exiles, acting under advisement of the United States and promised U.S. military support, invaded the southern section of Cuba known as the Bay of Pigs. President Kennedy, who had endorsed the rebellion, refused to authorize the military support, and the rebels were easily defeated. Infuriated by this turn of events, Allen wrote a long poem that expressed his disillusionment with the aggressive foreign policies of the United States. He had hoped that the Kennedy administration would be an improvement over the politics of suspicion of the 1950s, but it was now quite clear to him that, regardless of the national leader, there was little hope of reversing the trend:

> No I don't know what to do
> the riot squad is running America
> the liberals are bankrupt,
> > Kennedy the boy-man advertising
> > > fruit caught starting a war,
> > Denying his responsibility in
> > > crazy headlines. . . .

He raged on for pages and pages, citing every detail and the name of every politician involved. What was worse, the effort was endorsed by tax dollars—including his own—and the approval of all those celebrities who backed Kennedy, all duped by their hopes for liberal change. Ginsberg was unsparing in his damnation of the affair, ready to throw up his hands in despair. "WE ARE ALL DAMNED TO HELL," he wrote as the conclusion to the poem.

All of a sudden, saving the world seemed like a Sisyphean task, and a discouraged Ginsberg wondered about his role as a poet. Fortuitously, an answer—or at least urgently needed encouragement—arrived from the States in the form of a letter from Jack Kerouac. *Kaddish and Other Poems* had just been issued in the United States, and Jack was writing in response to his first reading of Allen's collection. This was the "old Jack" speaking, the Kerouac of Allen's youth, not the hard-drinking, bitter right-winger Allen had encountered in New York. Jack liked *Kaddish*, which he divined to be "explosive" with its title poem, works written in Paris, and visionary drug poems; the narrative section of "Kaddish," Jack wrote, had the "impact of [a] Dostoevskyan novel." Jack went on to tell Allen that he was laying off the bottle and reading volumes of Kant, Schopenhauer, and Spinoza, all of whom had philosophies in accordance with Buddhism. Even a paternity suit filed by Jack's former wife, Joan (who had delivered his only child, Janet Michelle, in 1952), failed to dampen Kerouac's spirits. He would be free of all that soon enough and therefore free to move on with his life.

Allen finally heard from Bill Burroughs, who had returned to Tangier as Ginsberg suspected. Bill invited Allen, Peter, and Gregory to visit him. They took a train from Paris to Cannes, where they all attended the annual film festival. From there it was on to St. Tropez for a brief stop, and then on to Marseilles, where they caught a ship bound for Tangier. Throughout the journey, Allen battled the gloomy mood that had plagued him off and on for months. He was about to turn thirty-five, and for all his fame as a poet, he was still uncertain as to whether his life's work was adding up to anything substantial:

> I graduated college and began counting
> up all the machinery to make a living,
> and being a failure at that, accepted the
> Cross of Poetry, thinking that
> was the sum total of Ambition—
> only to find myself 21 years later
> in the same ill-fitting clothes
> a famous personal American in the Port
> of St. Tropez among the rich
> eating lobster & scotch and worried about
> my figure in a cute blue bikini. . . .

Self-doubting prophet: It was a role Ginsberg wore as smartly as a tailor-cut suit, the belief in his significance spurring him on, the self-doubts keeping his substantial ego in check. It kept him on the level.

3

Allen's hopes for a great reunion with Burroughs were greeted by apathetic reality as soon as his ship docked in the Tangier harbor. Not only had Bill not bothered to come out to meet them upon their arrival but he was aloof and suspicious when Allen, Peter, and Gregory greeted him at his home. "Who are you an agent for?" he asked Allen when they were finally face-to-face.

The question was indicative of the recent changes in Burroughs. As a result of his personality cut-ups, Burroughs was now regarding people as a composite of all their influences and experiences, believing that it was only by "cutting up" a personality that one could see who a person really was. Allen, for instance, was his father and mother and Ivy League education; if Allen were cut up, Burroughs told him, they would probably find Lionel Trilling inside.

Bill's observation made Allen very uncomfortable. At a time when he was confronting his own identity and value as a poet, he did not need someone— especially a friend—telling him that, in essence, he had no identity of his own. In addition, Burroughs had with him two young confidants, both English, who egged him on at every turn. Allen took an immediate disliking to the two, whom he characterized to Jack Kerouac as "scampering and skipping behind [Burroughs's] elbows like demons, simpering at us all."

Ian Sommerville was Burroughs's current lover. Bill had met him in a Paris bookstore in 1959, when Burroughs was looking for a male nurse to administer his apomorphine and help him kick his heroin habit. Sommerville, a brilliant mathematics student at Cambridge and the secretary of an intellectual organization known as the Cantab Heretics Society, was as complex an individual as Burroughs, and a far cry from the boys Burroughs usually sought out for sexual gratification. Tall and thin, Sommerville even looked like Bill; he could have been a younger version of him.

Michael ("Mikey") Portman, by contrast, *wanted* to be Bill Burroughs—to such an extent that he dressed like Bill, mimicked his speech, and imitated his every move. Not yet eighteen, Portman had read *Naked Lunch* and decided that he had to meet the book's author, which he did when Burroughs was in London in October 1960. Portman was from a wealthy London family and he possessed the arrogance that all too often is a by-product of inherited wealth. At first, Bill was turned off by Portman's crude behavior, but after a time, undeniably attracted to Portman's physical beauty, he accepted him into his confidence. As Ginsberg quickly determined, you couldn't have Bill Burroughs without Mikey Portman, who was a constant, annoying presence. Allen described him as a "spoiled brat English Lord who looks like a pale faced Rimbaud but is a smart creep."

Much of Allen's dislike of the two young men could no doubt be traced to the envy he felt for the way they monopolized Bill's time and attention. From the day of Allen's arrival in Tangier, Bill had made it very clear that these two men, rather than Allen, Peter, and Gregory, were part of his inner circle. It was probably inevitable that the two factions would start sniping at one another, and as usual, it was Peter who took the brunt of the abuse. Knowing that Peter was essentially heterosexual and that Allen, as a result of his yage experiments, had decided that he should be kinder to women, Burroughs would go off on long, wicked antiwomen routines, repeating his theory that women were extraterrestrial agents sent by enemies to weaken the male species. They had "poison juices dripping all over 'em," Burroughs said, and if Allen and Peter knew what was good for them, they would stay away from women. Allen and Gregory had dealt with Burroughs and his routines long enough to know how to handle them, but Peter was deeply troubled by Burroughs's remarks and was not about to let him go on without an argument. To Peter, it did not matter whether Burroughs was speaking truthfully or acting out satirical fantasy.

The scene deteriorated into a rerun of Allen's earlier visit to Tangier, with Allen caught between Burroughs and Orlovsky in their arguments. Peter had never been an intellectual match for Burroughs in their disputes, but now, with Portman and Sommerville, both misogynists themselves, taking Bill's side and parroting his every view, Peter was overwhelmed. Once again, Allen tried to persuade Peter to ignore Burroughs's remarks, and once again he failed to do so. Intervening on Peter's behalf was pointless: Burroughs was as cold to Allen as he was to Peter.

By early July, Peter decided he had taken enough abuse and, deaf to Allen's tearful pleas that they try to work out a peaceful solution to the bickering, decided to set out on his own for Istanbul. He was interested not only in getting away from Burroughs and his friends; he had grown tired of Allen, as well. He and Allen had been quarreling throughout their stay in Tangier, often about Peter's fights with the others, and Peter wanted time alone. Furthermore, the separation was not necessarily going to be short-term; it might be years before he wanted to see Allen again, Peter said. There was no changing his mind and he made his plans to leave in late July. Allen, watching one of his life's stabilizing influences slip away, was beside himself as to what to do. "I wept, thinking of all the happy and past years we had lived together," Allen wrote in his journal on July 9, "how with this departure the sense of assurance and unity I enjoyed would be gone—and the sense of purpose to seek love—for what to seek now? As I am 35 and half my life [is] now past, I have no sure road ahead, but many to choose from, and none seem inevitable."

Allen had reached the point where he was literally getting sick because of the tension. He wanted to take a tolerant view and work out his difficulties with Burroughs, but, as he wrote Ferlinghetti, "Burroughs seems to have killed 'Hope' in any known form." He was "cold," impossible to reach. Alan Ansen arrived for a short vacation from Venice, and he, along with Paul Bowles, whom Allen saw a lot of, made the arguments with Burroughs a little more tolerable. Neither Ansen nor Bowles was very enthusiastic about Burroughs's cut-ups, and neither was shy about disagreeing with Bill's current philosophy. Then, as if there wasn't enough tension already, Gregory Corso got in a fight with Burroughs when, after growing ill from a bad batch of *majoun* prepared by Mikey Portman, Corso blamed Burroughs and confronted him in his hotel room.

It was into this scene, skidding recklessly out of control, that Timothy Leary arrived at the end of July. By coincidence, he saw Peter in the airport, heading through customs in the opposite direction. Earlier in the year, Leary had extended an invitation to Burroughs to participate in the American Psychological Association's symposium on psychedelic drugs in September, and Burroughs had agreed, inviting Leary to visit him in Morocco and work out the arrangements.

Burroughs had tried psilocybin on one previous occasion and found that the drug made him ill. On the night of Leary's arrival, he took it a second time, along with Ginsberg, Corso, and Ansen. Wanting to be left alone, Burroughs lay down on the bed in his darkened room while Leary and the others stepped out into the garden that overlooked the Tangier harbor. Allen was too depressed about Peter's departure to enjoy the drug, but Ansen and Corso were amazed at its effects. The Royal Fair was in Tangier, and they could see its well-lighted fairground in the distance and hear the sounds of music played on pipes and drums. Ansen was overwhelmed. "This can't be true," he said, shaking his head and laughing. "So beautiful. Heaven. But where is the devil's price? Anything this great must have a terrible flaw in it. It can't be this good. Will we ever come down?"

For Burroughs, the trip was another nightmare. When the group returned to his room, they found him sweating profusely and nearly passed out, leaning against the doorjamb to his room. "I'm not feeling too well," he informed them. "I was struck by the juxtaposition of purple fire mushrooms from the Pain Banks. Urgent warning. There are many hostile territories in the cerebral hemispheres. I think I'll stay here in this shriveling envelope of larval flesh. I'm going to take some apomorphine."

Psilocybin, he decided, was not for him.

4

Although, in Allen's words, there was "still a sort of cold war" being played out among the various factions in Tangier, Timothy Leary's visit had a calming effect on the open hostilities. Burroughs and Leary were in agreement that a psychedelic revolution would go beyond the idea of words and images, and if that was the case, poetry was moot. Leary was skeptical of poetry's ability to unite the world into a single consciousness—a stance that bothered Allen, whose identity and sense of security were rooted in seeing himself as a poet. Feeling as if he had been stripped of his two main anchors—his lover and his poetry—he reached a state of suicidal depression—"I didn't want to go through with it anymore," he wrote Peter, remembering the occasion—but he fought back, telling himself that maybe he had to be open to more options than he had given himself in the past. "During the day something slowly happened, ideas changed a little," he wrote, "and I realized that I was not tied down to being Allen Ginsberg—nor being a poet—so [I] decided to let my identity drop and my awareness grew and went through a day of bliss as I found I was free—lots happened, I saw Bill and since my eyes had changed, he changed too and I saw that his cut-up meant also this cut up of identity, nothing worse really."

Allen decided that it was time to reach an understanding with Bill, and he told Burroughs that he wanted to see him alone. Bill agreed, but the two found it a difficult task. Mikey Portman hung around the door to Bill's room like a bodyguard, and when Allen and Bill tried to escape him by going to lunch together, Portman tagged along. At one point during their lunch, when Portman had stepped away from the table, Burroughs admitted that Portman was too dependent on him, and Allen, impressed by the concession, realized that rather than being cold to him, Burroughs was trying to be accommodating to everyone in Tangier. To do so, however, meant not playing the old favorites against the new ones, even at the risk of seeming as if he was doing the opposite. People had to drop their identities, which in Allen's case meant shedding his identity as a poet and Peter's lover.

This was where their arguments about sex had originated, Bill said. For too many people, sex was an extension of ego, a form of possessiveness; a person's lover became part of his identity. Since he was interested in who a person really was, apart from all the baggage taken on over the course of a lifetime, Burroughs rejected sex if it was anything other than the "merger of souls on an ego-less basis." In their disputes, Bill was challenging Allen and Peter to come clean, to show the pure hearts beating beneath the visible armor of their relationship.

Allen, who tended to be possessive in his love relationships, agreed with Bill's assessment. Perhaps he *had* been too possessive of Peter and had driven him away in the process. As Allen explained it to Peter, "I was confused and since I was clinging to my identity with you I could not see through your identity to your heart, and I think you wound up over-affirming your identity and pressing down harder on it while it was under attack, instead of just giving it up and coming out free."

Allen's and Bill's conversation was a critical, vital statement of position, reminiscent of the Wolfean/non-Wolfean heart talks of their youth. As always,

Burroughs played the role of agitator, cutting through to the essence of some-thing very important, and Allen, for all his frustrations with Bill, was grateful for Burroughs's insights. Poet and literary anthropologist—old friends, both exploring new regions of consciousness—had returned to familiar territory, and while both had been changed by the years and their journeys, they found that they were still able to share their souls.

5

For all the mental stimulation that life in Tangier provided, Allen was finding it difficult to write. He worked on a prose account of the Cannes Film Festival, commissioned by *Show Business Illustrated*, but apart from that and his journal entries and correspondence, there was very little writing being accomplished—certainly nothing of significance in poetry. *Empty Mirror* was being prepared for publication and he worked on the book's galleys. In addition, Ferlinghetti had written with the request that Allen begin compiling a new volume of poetry for a possible January or February release. Initial sales of *Kaddish*, Ferlinghetti reported, had been disappointing, with *Howl* still outselling the newer volume, but there was no call for alarm. There had been only scattered reviews of the book, and with Allen out of country and therefore unavailable to help promote the book through poetry readings, word on its existence was slow in getting out.

The early reviews were the predictable mixture, the favorable and unfavor-able opinions divided into the open-form and academic camps. Furthermore—and perhaps even more significant—many reviews spent almost as much time addressing Ginsberg as a public figure as they devoted to his poetry. A. Alvarez, writing for the London *Observer*, allowed that "Kaddish" was "by far the most impressive poem Ginsberg has yet produced," yet he seemed reluctant to offer such praise, also calling it "psychotherapy" (a label that would often be applied to Ginsberg's poetry in the future) and suggesting that it was the exception rather than the rule of the poet's writing skills. Ginsberg and his cronies, Alvarez wrote, grouped together as a defensive measure, forcing poems such as those in *Kaddish* on a public that would not accept them if they stood alone. "True to form," he wrote, "Allen Ginsberg's *Kaddish and Other Poems* is dedi-cated to Orlovsky, quotes Corso, mentions other pals and includes a series of pieces on a Beat's best friend, his drugs."

Harvey Shapiro, in a sympathetic review that examined "Kaddish" in great detail, also wrote of Ginsberg's public image and the way it was getting in the way of a thoughtful reading of his poetry. "Ginsberg had become such a public issue that it's difficult now to read him naturally," Shapiro wrote. "You ask yourself after every line, am I for him or against him. And by and large that's the kind of criticism he has gotten—votes on a public issue."

Ironically, these and similar reviews were coming in at a time when Allen, as a result of his talk with Burroughs, was in the process of rejecting both his self-conceived and public images. He wanted to escape "this Allen Ginsberg trap," retreat from a constructed identity into something more natural. Bur-roughs had suggested that doing so meant moving away from words, language, and image—the essence of Ginsberg's identity as a poet and public figure—

and Allen had set out on that path. "Lately words and language itself seem to be a kind of mistake," he wrote Louis. "I would like to try to reach some level of consciousness involving another part of my brain . . . which reduces all experiences to 'structure,' 'meaning,' and words, language, logos. I get there with some drugs often, and it was a different universe—much richer and more 'real' though extremely painful as it involves the death of Self, etc."

Although these feelings contained an admirable spiritual ideal, Allen would learn that they posed new and difficult-to-overcome obstacles. Without words and images, he could not write, and he would go through a lengthy period of writer's block before he was again able to write what he considered to be satisfactory poetry. It also added to his already-confused sense of identity. Indeed, without words and images, the ego was successfully broken down, but it also left Ginsberg in a psychological limbo. Without a sense of self, he was losing his sense of mission.

6

Allen left Morocco on August 24. On the deck of the SS *Vulcania* bound for Greece, Allen stood alone with his ever-present journal, drawing sketches and recording his impressions of the slowly disappearing city of Tangier: "Church spire, apartments, hillside covered with Arab houses, white blocks, disappearing behind me in the blue mist—Alone, solitary, hopeless, tranquil, still with knapsack. . . ." He looked forward to seeing the pillars of the Acropolis.

His last weeks in Tangier had seen the different members of the group pulling up stakes and moving on. Timothy Leary left for Denmark; Alan Ansen returned to Venice. Bill Burroughs, due in the United States in September, decided to go to London first, and he, Mikey Portman, and Ian Sommerville left together, while Gregory Corso flew to Cambridge, ready to see England on his own.

The trip to Greece got off to a bad start. Not only was Allen in a melancholy frame of mind but he was also almost out of money. In Tangier, he had lent Gregory Corso a good sum of money, which Corso proceeded to lose at the casino, and despite Corso's promise to repay the loan when he got to England, Allen found when he checked the local American Express office upon his arrival in Greece that Corso had not fulfilled his promise. Infuriated, Allen sent Gregory a pointed letter demanding repayment of the debt.

It was Allen's good fortune that he had money coming in from other sources. Ferlinghetti was sending a royalty check from City Lights and he still had his fee coming from *Show Business Illustrated*. A $450 check from the latter arrived the next day, albeit with a rejoinder saying that the magazine's editor objected to Allen's use of the word *shit* at one point in the article. Ginsberg, already weary from censorship battles, replied that the magazine could not excise the word; he would pay back the money if they insisted on this bit of censorship. He was explicit in his objections to the censoring of so much as one of his words: "Censorship of language is direct censorship of consciousness; and if I don't fit in I can't change the shape of my mind. No. No revolution can succeed if it continues the puritanical censorship of consciousness imposed on the world by Russia and America. Succeed at what? Succeed at liberating the masses from domination by secret monopolists of communication."

Also greeting him upon his arrival in Greece was a letter from his friend Howard Schulman, now an editor of the Cuban magazine *Arriba*. Schulman requested that Allen send a poem addressing the Cuban revolution. With his latest obsession with rejecting his identity as a person and poet, Allen was not inclined to write a poem on the subject, nor was he particularly open to writing a formal essay addressing the issue. He put Schulman's letter aside, but a month later, while sitting at a Greek café on two successive days, he responded with a massive letter that was eventually edited and published as "Prose Contribution to Cuban Revolution."

The essay is interesting for the way it describes the evolution of Ginsberg's consciousness, from his Blake visions to his yage excursions to his recent discussions about cut-ups with Burroughs. In fact, for Ginsberg scholars of the future, this essay would be a kind of Rosetta stone in the delineation of Burroughs's influence on Ginsberg. In the past, Allen was quick to cite Jack Kerouac's influence on his poetry style, but he had never noted in quite the same detail Burroughs's considerable influence on his way of thinking. Burroughs, Ginsberg wrote, had been responsible for his "sense of Spenglerian history & respect for the 'irrational' or unconscious properties of the soul & disrespect for all Law"; under Burroughs's tutelage, Ginsberg had developed "a distrust of mental decisions, generalizations, sociology, a hip sense; plus the experience with love & with drugs actually causing telepathic & what were to me 'mystic' experiences."

After college, Ginsberg wrote, he, Burroughs, and Kerouac had gone their separate ways, Allen following what he considered to be guidelines posted by his Blake visions, life experiences, and, most recently, experiments with drugs. He fancied himself to be "Poet-prophet friend on the side of love and Wild Good"; he thought he had a good idea of who he was. Then he traveled to Tangier, where, he reported, "I met *someone I didn't know*; who rejected me, as far as Allen & Bill were concerned and all previous relationships they built up. And if I didn't know Bill I sure don't know myself, because he was my rock of Tolerance & Friendship & true Art." Burroughs, he discovered, was cutting up his own consciousness, escaping from his previous identity.

What did any of this have to do with the Cuban revolution—or with any kind of world politics, for that matter? In the latter part of his essay, Ginsberg tied together the development of his personal consciousness with the development of a global political consciousness. In his opinion, the problems of the world had nothing to do with capitalism or socialism or communism per se. The problems were conceptual, the result of the powers attempting to force a single consciousness on the masses. This was two-dimensional politics, an anti-evolutionary attitude that had brought the world to the edge of annihilation:

> All governments including the Cuban are still operating within the rules of identity forced on them by already outmoded modes of consciousness. I say outmoded since it has brought all Govts. to edge of world destruction. No govt., not even the most Marxist revolutionary & well-intentioned like Cuba presumably, is guiltless in the general

world mess, no one can afford to be righteous any more. Righteous &
right & wrong are still fakes of the old suicidal identity.

Ginsberg concluded his essay by saying that while he was against neither
Cuba nor its revolution, he was against the brand of nationalism, complete
with slogans and political rhetoric and logos, that led to a continuation of a
single consciousness forced upon the majority. By breaking down (or cutting up)
that kind of consciousness, countries would be losing their focus on individual
identity and gaining a sense of the planetary consciousness needed for the
continued survival of the world.

7

Allen's tour of Greece was a mixed success—a constant battle between his interest
in what he was seeing and the doldrums he could not seem to overcome. For all
his talk about setting Peter free in order to help them both hold on to their own
identities, Allen missed Peter terribly, and he began plotting a way to connect
with him in Israel, where Peter was now staying. He attempted to quit smoking,
but the nicotine withdrawal left him feeling light-headed. With all his preoccupations, Allen saw Greece with a rather jaundiced eye. "I am getting plenty of
Greek 'glory,' " he wrote his father, "but it doesn't seem to stand up against
the inhuman sense of things that is making my skin crawl lately."

He was not disappointed by the ancient Greek architecture, such as the ruins
of the Acropolis, whose "marble skeleton" impressed him as being the remains
of a once-glorious beast reduced by time to marble bones. "The light thru
Pantheon columns is a great white-blue solid color—like looking thru eye-
sockets of a skull," he wrote. He found someone to snap his picture as he sat
on a broken slab of marble in the foreground of the Acropolis, the photograph
depicting a still-youthful, clean-shaven Ginsberg staring grimly at the camera.

Allen spent the ensuing weeks wandering around Greece, knapsack on his
back, following the instructions of his guidebook leading to points of interest.
He took a bus to Delphi, where he climbed a small mountain for a look at the
Cave of the Muses and the patchwork valley below, the pastoral setting reminding him of the pictures he had seen of the Chinese Painted Valley. To get
a feeling for the ancient history and mythology of Greece, he read the *Iliad* and
the *Odyssey*. For all the wonder about him and with all the historical implications that Greece held as the cradle of democracy, Allen could not shake the
disturbing notion that all of this history was under attack. As far as he could
tell, from what he had seen and from his discussions with the locals, Greece
was as politically corrupt and oppressive as any other government, the general
populace resigned to their government and uninformed about world events.
This, he told Louis, was the problem everywhere he went, from North Africa
to South America, from France to Greece—it made no difference: "The whole
human race [is] at an impasse and everybody [is] willing to pour out their filth
and frustration on someone like Bertrand Russell, who at least makes sense and
takes individual action. Whole idea of individuality has become a disgusting

joke in U.S.A., and that's the only place there is hope—or was hope—for a humane alternative to mass mechanization under communism."

At the time of Allen's visit, Greece was preparing for a general election and political rhetoric was in the air. The Center Union, a party of moderates, stood in vocal opposition to Constantine Karamanlis and his right-wing rule. Allen was disturbed by reports of shootings at left-wing rallies, the imprisonment of intellectuals in opposition to the current regime, and government censorship of the arts. Ever inquisitive, he spent many hours at cafés and restaurants, talking to the locals about life in their country, unhappy with much of what he heard.

He continued his journey with a visit to Olympia, where he saw Praxiteles' statue *Hermes with the Infant Dionysus*, and then he moved off the mainland for a three-day stay on the island of Hydra, which with its colony of artists and writers was a pleasant respite from his solitary travel. From there, it was on to Argos, where he spotted both Gregory Corso's and General Erwin Rommel's names in a hotel guest book. In Mycenae, he repeated his practice of visiting ruins at nighttime, this time at the tomb of Agamemnon; as he lay on the steps near the bottom of the stairwell, enveloped in total darkness, he was again chilled by the prospects of being so near to an ancient ghostly presence. Later, he visited the Gate of Lions, built about 1400 B.C., where he sat beneath the two giant stone lions guarding the archway and wrote in his journal. On one of his walks in the country, he broke a sandal on the rocky roadway, but he "prodded on through the solitude bordered by olive groves and hills with the elevation of Hera's ruins on the right hand distance, singing to myself and the sky till tears came to my eyes while I lifted my voice, desolate in all that history, without any name for what I was."

8

By mid-October, Allen was back in Athens and prepared to move on to Israel. It had been months since he had seen Peter, and he reasoned if he arrived in Haifa shortly after the first of the month, he might be able to connect with Peter when he went to the American Express office to collect his VA check from the States. He took care of his remaining business in Athens and by late October was on a ship moving along the coast of Asia Minor, bound for the Middle East.

When Allen had written his father about the possibility of traveling to Israel, Louis was enthusiastic about the prospects of Allen seeing the nation of his cultural heritage. "Perhaps in Israel you might feel some emotional reverberations from the creation of that state," he suggested to his son. "We respond to some affinity with ancestral memories carried along in the blood stream and cached from ancient historical times in the genes. . . . Something in the psyche of the Jew was healed in the creation of the state of Israel."

These sentiments, however, were too nationalistic for Allen's feelings at the time. Interviewed in Israel by the *Jewish Post and Opinion*, he refused to look at the world's problems from the perspective of his heritage. "Yes, I am a Jew," he declared, "but at the same time you see I am not a Jew. I am not Allen

Ginsberg." He tried to explain the problems with identity by pointing out that Jews and Arabs, by his way of thinking, were not living harmoniously because they treated each other as objects rather than as people; this, Allen claimed, was the problem everywhere. "Jews and Arabs, Russians and Americans, all of them have preconceived notions about each other, not as people, but as objects of policy and prejudice."

Israel, Allen found, was still deeply involved in establishing its identity as an independent state; a pride in being Jewish, by nature and necessity, was everywhere he went. The country, a haven for the persecuted, was busy establishing a powerful sense of national identity just as Allen was involved in trying to find a way to abolish that line of thinking on a global scale. To him, Israel was just another interesting country. He explained his feelings to his father: "All I'm saying is that unless you have a pronounced single-minded dedication to an *exclusively* Jewish frame of mind in life, this place is not so exciting. Granted, it's fine as a refuge for the persecuted, and granted also that the persecuted themselves are not so kindly to their own Arab minority. But it's like being in a Chinese place where all the Chinamen are hung up on being Chinese and that's *all* they talk about—can be maddening too. It demands an *exclusively* Jewish mentality, whatever that is (everybody here's always arguing that) and I found that a definite limitation on my own mentality which is Jewish enough but a lot more than that. This is XX Century and I still say the old order of Identity is a big nationalistic hang up on every side."

Allen was now fully involved in exploring Burroughs's theories. He read Platanov's *The Word as Physiological and Therapeutic Factor,* and in his journal he jotted down a Pavlovian quote that he felt was especially apropos: "Owing to the entire preceding life of the human adult, a word is connected with all the external and internal stimuli coming to the cerebral hemispheres, signals all of them, replaces all of them and can, therefore, evoke all the actions and reactions of the organism which these stimuli produce." There it was, an idea that supported Burroughs's ideas about preconditioning! Burroughs had broken through to something vital.

Still, Allen could not help but be moved when he traveled through the Galilee region of northern Israel, including a visit to Nazareth, the hometown of Jesus. He even began a poem as he stood on the shores of the Sea of Galilee— one of the few poems he had attempted since his visit to Tangier:

> Fishermen-nets over wood walls, light wind in dead willow branch
> on a grassy bank—the saxophone relaxed and brutal, silver horns
>   echo—
> Was there a man named Solomon? Peter walked here? Christ on this
>   sweet water?
> Blessings on thee Peacemaker!

To Allen's disappointment, Peter was not in Haifa when he arrived in the city. Haifa was big and dirty and modern, "like a ratty looking Bronx," as Allen described it. A few days later, he was in Tel Aviv, where he met a second cousin on the paternal side of the family. Israel Vekselman told Allen that he had descended from a Russian writer named Achad Aham Ahad 'Haam. Allen spent several days with his second cousin's family, trading stories and visiting the Roman ruins of Caesarea.

Just when Allen was beginning to wonder whether he was going to hook up with Peter in Israel, he ran into him by chance on a street corner in Tel Aviv. Peter had just arrived from a trip to Jerusalem and, as Allen learned, he had done a great deal of traveling of his own, his journeys including time in Greece, Turkey, Syria, and Egypt. Allen, who only a few nights earlier had lain in bed, lonely and thinking about Peter, "reading books and remembering our old nights together naked," was overjoyed by the reunion. They would be traveling together to India, after all.

Travel plans proved to be complicated. Hostile relations between Israel and the Arab states made securing passports, visas, and other necessary papers difficult. Allen adjusted his plans. If he had to, he would fly to North Africa, spend the New Year with Paul Bowles, who was in Ceylon, link up with Gary Snyder (who was also due in Ceylon at the same time), and work his way east to India.

Allen and Peter traveled to Jerusalem, where they visited a Hasidic synagogue and witnessed a service where men and boys sang wonderful traditional songs on the Sabbath. After all the talk about the new state and its politics, Allen was awed by this dedication to a practice so ancient, and he judged it to be "the greatest thing in Israel." Allen took a bus through the desert where Moses had wandered thousands of years earlier; he stopped briefly at the Red Sea, where he donned a snorkel and mask and marveled at the purple and green fish swimming through the coral in the clear blue water.

While they were in Jerusalem, Allen and Peter met Martin Buber and cabala scholar Gershom Sholem. Allen was interested in Buber's visionary experiences and was eager to talk to him about magic mushrooms and Burroughs's cut-up method, but Buber, the apparition of an ancient rabbi, with his quiet demeanor and flowing long, white beard, advised Allen to avoid placing too much hope or significance on the mystical; the future, he claimed, was in the human universe, not the cosmos. Allen was not so certain. Everywhere he looked, he saw "too much American money, too many cars, the 'old spirit' giving way to television . . . same confusions as the rest of the world, except teetering on Arab brink but no worse than U.S. and Russia." How was he to live in the present, human-made universe when all the talk was about building bomb shelters?

"I been talking Transcendency to everyone from Morocco to Palestine," he wrote in his journal, still uncertain whether he was onto something important or whether in all his "endless jabber about drugs," he was "like the Ancient Mariner with his albatross." Science and technology had advanced the human race and now it threatened to destroy it; questions begat questions:

> The atombomb will solve one aspect of the population explosion caused by Science. Are the Scientists in charge here? LSD-25—another Atom Bomb. Inside & outside—an expanding universe. There are 10,000,000 possible inhabited planets? Plenty of room to spread. Sooner or later life will consume life. The secret of the universe is that it has no reason. No human comparison? Long ago and far away. Closing the eyes in question. Facing India.

16
The Change: India and the Orient

Hail to your fierce desire, your
Godly pride, my Heaven's gate
will not be closed until
we enter all—

1

Allen took a long route to India. After weeks of trying to find a way out of
Israel—time that found him and Peter running very low on money—he was
able to book passage on a ship bound for Mombasa, Kenya. The voyage was
slow, the ship inching its way down the length of the Red Sea, but Allen passed
his time by reading Arthur C. Clarke's *Childhood's End* and finishing Martin
Bormann's *Hitler's Table Talk*, the latter prompting a series of dreams and
meditations about the Nazis and death camps that led Allen to a better understanding of, if not agreement with, some of the nationalism he had witnessed
in Israel. As if to serve as personal reminders, he recorded a list of some of the
ghastliest examples of Nazi torture and degradation of Jews in his journal. "Yet
like a dream he could have existed, as if Ubu Roi became real and were in
charge of History," Ginsberg wrote of Hitler.

Allen and Peter spent a month in Africa. While they waited for an inexpensive fare to India, they explored as much of the eastern part of the continent
as their resources would allow. There were bus trips to Nairobi and Tanganyika;
from their windows they saw giraffes and zebras wandering along the savanna,
and Mount Kilimanjaro rising from the mist. On January 21, they attended a
huge political rally staged at Nairobi Stadium—an event that left a strong
impression on Allen. "Jomo Kenyatta main speaker, vast thousands of Negro
audience, Peter Orlovsky and I were literally the only white people in the
crowds—a weird dreamlike experience," Allen told his father.

In early February, they were aboard the SS *Amra*, bound for India. Allen
and Peter, along with hundreds of Indians traveling from East Africa to India,
had bunks in the ship's hold. Despite the crowded living quarters, the journey
was pleasant. A cool sea breeze blew in the portholes, and Allen was content

to spend most of his time lounging in his bunk. He tried to prepare himself mentally for the upcoming months in India by reading Rudyard Kipling's *Kim*, Mahatma Gandhi's autobiography, and assorted books about Indian history and culture. For all his efforts, however, he could not shake his feelings of doubt and apprehension, the familiar yet nevertheless disarming feeling of having no direction: "So cold not to know my way anymore, and nothing to say."

2

Allen arrived in Bombay on February 15, 1962. He had exactly one dollar in his pocket. His first order of business was a trip to the American Express office, a large gingerbread structure set in the middle of what looked to Allen like a scene out of Victorian England. A City Lights royalty check awaited him there. To his delight, the exchange rate on the black market was excellent. An American dollar was worth seven Indian rupees. Two rupees would buy an excellent meal and for a single rupee, he could purchase a tray of vegetables. Since he and Peter had no set plan for the length of their stay in India, such an exchange rate assured them of getting the most for their limited funds. By staying in dharmashalas (lodgings similar to American YMCAs), ashrams (religious retreats), hostels, or cheap hotels, they could make their money last even longer. "I never saw a place more convenient for wandering and travelling," Allen wrote Jack Kerouac, adding that neither he nor Peter had any difficulty with the country's food or water—something they had been warned about.

They spent two days in Bombay, walking about the city with the hope of finding Gary Snyder. They had planned to meet Snyder in Bombay on New Year's Day, but their travels to Africa changed that, and it was now obvious, with no sign of Snyder and no message left behind, that he had moved on when they failed to arrive on or around the agreed-upon date. Rather than wait to hear from Gary, they caught a train to Delhi. Allen was again amazed by how much one could get for so little money. For two rupees, he could purchase a third-class ticket that included a large bunk rack with a terrific view. The trip to Delhi was an all-day, all-night adventure, but Allen was content to lie back on an air mattress in his bunk rack and watch the scenery of India go by. There were vast plains with mountains in the distance. Men wearing only loincloths bathed in muddy rivers. Cows and water buffalo were in abundance. Allen was pleased by his first glimpse of India. "India is really great—don't know where to begin, there's so much to see and do," he wrote home.

The country was steeped in religion, mainly Hinduism, and Allen set out to learn as much as he could. On the train, he met a jeweler from Jaipur who was on a business trip to Delhi. The businessman, who introduced himself as Mr. Jain, was going to be staying at a dharmashala while he was in Delhi, and he suggested that Allen and Peter do the same. Mr. Jain was a member of the Jain religious sect, and from him, Allen received his initial briefing on just one of the many illustrious religious groups inhabiting India, each with its own colorful history and mythology. He was immediately impressed by the religious tolerance in the country. He conveyed this in a letter to Kerouac:

Everybody in India is religious. It's weird, everybody ON to some saddhana (method), and has family guru or Brahmin priest and knows all about how the universe is a big illusion; it's totally unlike the West—it really is another dimension of time-history here—in fact every middle class householder is expected at age 45 or 50, after he's founded family and business, to retire from [the] world, take brahma-cheri vows and orange robe and wander on the road in India with no possessions, living free in Ashrams (that's why there are ashrams all over, and Dharmashalas) and singing hymns and meditating on Shiva or Vishnu or whoever he chooses to represent the void. It's assumed that all gods are unreal so one should respect all gods as purely subjective forms of meditation to fix the mind on one image and still it down and be peaceful—the gods are all interchangeable and friendly—Saraswati for people hung on music and learning; Lakshmi for people hung on moviestars beauties and loot; Rhada for young lover devotees; Krishna for cocksmen-coyote types; Ganesha the elephant-headed god of pros-perity and slyness for the Jerry Newmans and Peter Orlovskys of the universe, Buddhas for the Jacks, Kalis and Durgas for Bill and ilk, anything you want—a huge cartoon religion with Disney gods with their heads and six arms killing buffalo demons—everyone so gentle about it all it's unbelievable—except the Moslems swept down in the 12th century with their One Allah like a bunch of hysterical Jews and smashed all the pretty Walt Disney statues before they calmed down and got happy like the Hindus.

Allen tried to imagine his father, recently retired from his full-time teaching duties, wandering around New Jersey in an orange robe, a serious but serene expression on his face. Life in India was indeed different from anything he had seen in the West.

3

William Burroughs's grand experiment with Timothy Leary, Allen learned from Bill, was a failure back in the States. Bill had flown to Boston late the previous August, and he was still complaining about it the following February. "I was under the mistaken impression he had some serious scientific project going," Bill wrote Allen; "I should have known better."

After his arrival in Boston, Burroughs had worked on his presentation for the American Psychological Association conference. Entitled "Points of Dis-tinction Among Psychoactive Drugs," Burroughs's paper was to be a scholarly comparison between psychedelic and narcotic drugs. With such presentations as "Set-and-Setting," "Unusual Realization and Alterations in Consciousness," and "Ecstatogenic Comments" being offered by Timothy Leary, Frank Barron, and Gerald Heard respectively, the conference promised to be esoteric. In fact, Burroughs had little problem with the conference itself; it was Leary, psilocybin, and Leary's research methods that Burroughs rejected.

Burroughs figured that a man of Leary's credentials and Harvard backing would be running a futuristic and revolutionary program. He expected the research to be well funded and scientifically conducted. As Leary later noted, Burroughs was far ahead of the Harvard researchers in his lifelong study of drugs and their effects. He had seen their use on the city streets of America; he had traveled to Mexico and South America and northern Africa in his quest for knowledge. He had written extensively about addiction and he had heard of all the "miracle cures." He himself had tried almost every drug imaginable. As Leary succinctly put it, "Don't talk to Burroughs about the cub scout god you just found in your hallucinatory baby carriage, man. He had seen them all."

What Burroughs saw at Leary's house seemed to be, in his words, "completely ill intentioned," with "utterly no interest in any serious scientific work, no equipment other than a faulty tape recorder, and no intention of acquiring any or making any equipment available to me." Leary's connection to Harvard was vague, and some of his funding, to Bill's disgust, might have been coming from the Luce family. Burroughs wanted to talk about computers, biofeedback, neurological implants, and other highly advanced nonchemical methods of understanding the mind, but Leary was more involved in the sociopolitical aspects of hallucinogens. Leary was interested in advancing his and Ginsberg's program of cosmic awareness and universal love. Burroughs was cynical. "He saw me as a Notre Dame coach of consciousness, giving my players locker-room pep talks about internal freedom," Leary remembered. In a letter to Ginsberg in which he angrily denounced Leary as being interested in him only as a means of persuading the Beat Generation to try mushrooms, Burroughs wrote off Leary as "a real wrong number."

Allen also heard from Lawrence Ferlinghetti, who continued to be quite successful in marketing Allen's work to anthologies and foreign publishers. The latest interest, Penguin Books in England, wanted to include eight of Allen's poems in one of its anthologies. Also in the works was an Italian translation of Ginsberg poetry, due to be published in January 1963; a German translation of *Kaddish*, also due in 1963; and a volume of selected poems to be published in Israel within a year. The clamor for Ginsberg poetry, new or reprinted, showed no sign of abating, and Ferlinghetti was eager to issue a new City Lights collection of his work. Allen had sent him a manuscript of older poems, including "The Green Automobile," "Siesta in Xbalba," "Love Poem on Theme by Whitman," and "A Strange New Cottage in Berkeley"; Allen's working title for the volume was *Hiccup*. Ferlinghetti hoped to go to press in April, but Allen, with *Empty Mirror* still fresh on the bookstore shelves and *Kaddish* just over a year old, decided to wait. Ferlinghetti agreed. Both had seen how flooding the market with books had hurt Jack Kerouac's sales over the past few years, and neither was in a hurry to risk that kind of performance with Ginsberg's work.

Allen had heard very little from Jack in recent months and what he heard about Kerouac from others was not encouraging. Jack was still very unhappy, ignoring his friends on one night and outraging them with his drunken behavior on another. His books, which he had always considered to be the validation of his life, were selling poorly. He fought with his friends about politics, primarily those issues pertaining to U.S. relations with Cuba. Fed up with the literary and political world in New York, he removed himself from the scene. He and his mother moved back to Florida.

4

Gary Snyder and his wife, poet Joanne Kyger, arrived in Delhi a short time after Allen and Peter. After living in Japan for nearly six years, Gary and Joanne had embarked on a long journey of their own, traveling throughout India, Ceylon, Nepal, and other points of interest. Allen was happy to see his old friend, and for the next week the group toured Delhi, seeing the sights and visiting temples and mosques. One day, they had a literary tea with Kushwant Singh, author of *The Voice of God*, a collection of short stories, and *Train to Pakistan*, a novel. Noting Singh's huge turban and native garb, Allen asked the author what it was like to be a Sikh. "Great," Singh replied, "because sikhs are famous warriors and I'm a coward, but people think I'm a famous warrior so nobody hits me." Allen found the comment charming and somehow poignant in its simple, direct way, much the way he had been amused several weeks earlier when Mr. Jain had told him that as a brahmachari, he had sworn himself to celibacy. "You must not give away your jew-els, you must retain your jew-els," Mr. Jain had said.

Allen, Peter, Gary, and Joanne left for the Himalayas, their first stop being the town of Rishikesh, located in the Himalayan foothills, where the Ganges River enters the Gangetic Plain. Their goal was a meeting with Swami Shivananda, the famous, aging holy man who had founded an ashram there. Shivananda, whose name meant "Shiva Lovebliss," had led a fruitful life in his four-score years. He claimed to have written 386 books—"I write with electric speed," he told Allen—and had founded hospitals and led what could only be described as an exemplary life. In India, he was a larger-than-life figure whose reputation was almost as significant as any of his messages.

When Allen and the rest of the group met him, Shivananda was in ill health, but even as he received them, lying on a couch, his shaved head propped up on pillows, he was a presence. As a gift, he gave each of the four an envelope containing five rupees, and he offered Allen a pamphlet entitled *Raja Yoga for Americans*. Allen had mixed emotions about the swami. Surrounded by a small group of American women who asked him nonstop questions about dualism, to which he invariably answered with an "Om," and sitting in the midst of boxes containing cardboard cutout images of himself, Shivananda seemed to be a "charlatan of mass-production international nirvana racket" to Ginsberg, but Allen also found that he liked the man, who struck him as being calm and holy.

His ashram reflected his peaceful simplicity. People took meditative walks in the nearby wooded foothills or bathed in a section of the Ganges that was filled with fish so friendly that they accepted bread crumbs, rice, or pieces of tomatoes from the hands of people who would never have considered eating them. The day after they arrived at the ashram, Allen asked Shivananda where he could find a guru. The swami smiled, touched his heart, and told Allen that "The only guru is your own heart. . . . You'll know your guru when you see him because you'll love him; otherwise don't bother." For Allen, still trying to get over some of the problems he'd had with Bill, Peter, and the others in Tangier, the swami's message was a boost to his spirits.

The following day, the group moved to an ashram across the Ganges. The building's conditions were austere, but Allen was content to drop his knapsack and stretch out his air mattress and white sheet in the large empty room they had been provided. In his travels in India, he was taking on the physical appearance of the Allen Ginsberg who would be familiar worldwide in the sixties. He had grown a full beard, and his hair, though thinning on the top of his head, was getting long, nearly shoulder-length on the sides and in back. In India, these characteristics, complemented by Allen's loose-fitting cotton Indian garb, were anything but unusual. "The way I look, nobody notices me, whereas if I dressed U.S. style everybody would stare and ask questions," Allen told Louis, joking that his "long-hairomania has finally found a practical use."

Allen and his friends stayed at the ashram for about a week, Allen remaining enthusiastic about virtually everything he saw. On one occasion, while walking along a path near the river, they came upon three bearded, half-naked sadhus sitting cross-legged on a deerskin mat under a tree. In the ground around them, they had stuck small Shiva tridents. A cow with a deformed jaw—a pet—stood nearby. The three sat motionless for hours, their eyes bloodshot from fixing their gazes. Allen was amazed that they could sit still for so long. The next day, they met a long-haired teenage boy just back from an excursion to the Himalayas. The English-speaking youth, clad in the orange robes of the bramacharia, invited them to lunch, and when Allen inquired about the three sadhus they had seen on the path, the youth laughed. "They're just advertisement posters for the real yogis whom you can't see, way back in the mountains," he said.

In Hardwar, a town a few miles from Rishikesh, Allen witnessed the opening festivities of Kumbh Mela, a gathering of holy men that occurred every twelve years. The two-month event attracted people from all parts of India. On the opening day, there was a huge procession through the city to the Ganges. Hundreds of naked sadhus with long, matted hair and beards, their bodies smeared with ash, some carrying tridents or swords, followed their leader, a heavy-set old man walking an elephant in front of the procession. Behind the men walked a large band of holy women with shaved heads. They wore orange robes and wailed and sang Sanskrit hymns to Nirvana. As the huge procession made its way through the city, the townspeople threw flowers in their path. One local *naga* (snake) sadhu who lived under a tree in Hardwar blew a conch horn to greet his fellow sadhus as they passed.

At the river, the leader stepped into the water and washed the ashes from his body. The other sadhus followed, the ritual symbolizing the purification of the Ganges after twelve years of laymen using it to wash away their sins. After the ceremony by the river, the crowd returned to the city. At the temple, they rang bells and smeared their bodies with fresh white ash.

Allen gave some thought to staying in Hardwar for the duration of Kumbh Mela, but he and the rest decided that it would be best if they stuck to their original travel plans. He enjoyed touring India with Gary, who seemed wiser and gentler for his stay in Japan, with a greater sense of play; Snyder knew a great deal about Zen meditation, which he patiently tried to teach Allen as they made their way around the country. Snyder had a way of explaining Buddhism in terms that Allen found easier to understand than the way it had been depicted in the books he'd read. Gary and Joanne would argue from time to time, and Joanne, not knowing Allen and Peter as well as Gary did, would occasionally find their antics irritating, but all in all they were a compatible foursome.

The group traveled to Almora, the Punjab, and Pathankot, where they stayed in bungalows at night and spent their days climbing around the higher elevations for panoramic views of the Himalayas. They took a train to Dharamsala, the town in which the exiled Dalai Lama had set up his Tibetan government. The Dalai Lama granted the Americans an hour's audience. Allen wanted to talk to the twenty-seven-year-old Dalai Lama about his experiences with drugs, particularly LSD and psilocybin. While the Dalai Lama was interested in Allen's stories, he cautioned him about relying too greatly upon drugs for insights into his unconscious. It was useful to glimpse into one's unconscious mind only if one could adjust the ego—preferably by a natural means—in accordance with what one learned, the Dalai Lama told his guests. The Dalai Lama was not interested in trying LSD, but he said he might be willing to try psilocybin. Allen promised to put him in touch with Timothy Leary. Gary was interested in talking to the Dalai Lama about meditation and sitting technique, and they spent the remainder of their time discussing those topics.

When they had completed their visit, the group boarded a train bound for Jaipur. Allen had heard about the city from Mr. Jain in Delhi. Jacqueline Kennedy had visited Jaipur the week before, and Allen was eager to see its famous maharajas' palaces. He came away disappointed by the city, which he thought was boring, but he was uncertain about how much of this dissatisfaction was his own doing. For all his talks with holy men in India, Allen was still restless, worried that he might wander and search throughout his life, never to find his purpose:

> Self Conscious, I have nowhere to go. Maybe might
>   as well leave it at that, continue to travel
>   and die as I am when I die.
> Avaloketesvara, Kuan Yin, Jaweh, Saints, Saddhus,
>   Rishis, benevolent ones, Compassionate
>   Superconscious ones, etc, what can you do for me
>   now? What's to be done with my life which has
>   lost its idea?

Allen enjoyed their next stops much more. First, they visited the stupas in Sanchi, where all were impressed by the enormous stone domes and ancient Buddhist carvings hewn into the rock. From there, they went on to Faridpur, where they explored the ancient temples built into the Caves of Ajanta. Allen examined the fading colors painted on the walls and ceilings of what had once been monastery caves and was again struck by the enormity of the age and ritual of non-Western religions.

Of all the places he visited on this leg of his Indian visit, he was most impressed with the cave temples of Ellora, a series of more than thirty caves designed by Buddhist, Hindu, and Jain worshipers. Like the Ajanta caves, the Ellora ones featured painted walls and ceilings, the intricacy and dedication of this work overwhelming Allen as he gazed upon them. To him, it was far greater than anything he had seen in Greece. One cave, built by Buddhists, was an enormous temple carved into rock. More than a month after he had visited the temple, he was still in awe of what he had seen, and he tried to describe its impact in a letter to Jack Kerouac: "The great rock cut cave temples of Ellora, where the Great GLORY of Indian art really is, makes Michelangelo's Renaissance look Western little," he said. "I mean, they got great dancing shivas balanced with ten arms doing cosmic dances of creation 20 feet tall, and fantastic skully Kalis invoking nightmare murders in another yuga, thousands of statues dancing all over huge temple built like Mt. Kailash the Himalayan abode of Shiva—And Genesha with fat belly and elephant head and snakehead belt and trunk in a bowlful of sweets riding on his vehicle, a mouse—How can Da Vinci beat an elephant on a mouse?—anyway all that statuary's endless and there are 30 caves full of it at Ellora."

Ironically, for all the lasting impressions these travels made on Allen, he did very little writing about them, even in his journals or letters. He was still struggling to get anything on paper and he had been far too active to sit still and catch up on his correspondence. He continued to record his dreams in his journal and occasionally made notations of his more interesting drug experiences—to the displeasure of Joanne Kyger, he and Peter used morphine or other drugs from time to time—but the long descriptive passages of prose, present in his journals from South America, Mexico, Europe, and other travels, were virtually nonexistent. In the past, such periods of nonproductivity represented the proverbial lull before the storm, the mental gathering of materials needed for the production of a major work. In India, however, Allen was anything but concerned about gathering literary material. He was doing no less than reconstructing his mind, looking to the East for ideas, comfort, inspiration, and answers. In so many ways, the West had already failed him.

5

After nearly two months of nonstop travel, Allen and company returned to Bombay. The warm season was about to begin and Allen wanted to settle down, catch up on his correspondence, and regain his bearings before he moved on to his planned visits to Calcutta and Benares. He was in no hurry. In Bombay, he, Peter, Gary, and Joanne stayed at the home of Radhika Jayakar, a wealthy twenty-two-year-old translator Allen had met in New York. After weeks of third-class travel in trains and sleeping on the floors in ashrams, Allen was grateful for the chance to collapse in the large house, where he was cooled by electric fans and served tea three times a day by the family's barefoot servant.

Their awaiting mail contained disturbing news. In February, Elise Cowen had taken her life by jumping from her parents' apartment window. Not long after Allen and Peter had departed for India, Elise had suffered a breakdown from her excessive amphetamine use. She had been taken to the Hillside mental hospital, where she had been diagnosed as being acutely schizophrenic. After her release, she lived with her parents, but she never recovered from her depression. At the time of her death, her parents had hoped to take her to Miami for a new start.

Ginsberg was badly shaken by the news. Elise had been a bright, sensitive, loving woman, willing to do anything for him, and he felt that he had somehow failed her by not reciprocating. As Joyce Johnson, author of *Minor Characters* and Jack Kerouac's girlfriend for a time, wrote in her memoir, Elise had seen Allen as her "intercessor," but he had been so preoccupied in New York that he had never been able or willing to give her the time she needed. "Elise," wrote Johnson, "was a moment in Allen's life," while "in Elise's life, Allen was an eternity." Allen had realized that Elise had been a troubled young woman, and he had seen her taking an excess of methamphetamine at the apartment in New York, but he had always maintained a distance from her. He admitted to others that he was sometimes repulsed by her gloominess, and now, upon reading about her suicide, he wished he had known in New York what he was now learning in India:

> All worlds, Cuban and Elise—voices etc. all seem illusions of a movie screen of consciousness, which alone is constant. So the local sages here in India preach attention to the neutral OM-Self, which like moviescreen is unchanged by the conspiracies of shadows flitting on it. Some such reference point might have given Elise something to grasp onto since she thought the passing phenomena (voices etc) were real. When they aren't any more real than automobiles, which are completely unreal shadows flitting across the screen. That's about as far as I've got, but meant quite literally. I was too trapped in my own death movie in NY last to be any help.

Elise's death would bother Allen for a long, long time.

Allen settled into routine living. Fully immersed in his study of Indian culture, he read voluminously on Hinduism, Buddhism, Tibetan yoga, Indian literature, and Eastern philosophy; he familiarized himself with classic Indian poetry, music, and mythology. He had been impressed by his meeting with the Dalai Lama, and he studied Tibetan Buddhist texts, concluding that the Tibetans "came up with as far as I can see the greatest culture on earth, bar none, something unique that could never flower elsewhere." He was as generous in his use of superlatives in praise of India, which he called "the greatest nation on earth" that he had seen thus far.

Gary and Joanne were due to leave the country, but before they went, Allen, Gary, and Peter gave a poetry reading that was attended by over a hundred people, including the American consul. Now that he had seen some of the tourist attractions the nation had to offer, Allen focused his attention on local day-to-day life in India. He walked around the streets of Bombay; he met with local intellectuals and discussed poetry and politics, and was interviewed for a profile in *Illustrated Weekly of India*. He visited the Chinese-run opium dens located in the city's slums. Since most people spoke English, Allen found it easier to navigate his way around the city and talk with the natives than it had been in Mexico, South America, and France.

One evening, he met a tabla player who advised him on the best Indian musicians to hear in concert, and Allen and Peter made a regular practice of attending inexpensive concerts featuring such musicians as Ravi Shankar, Ali Akbar Khan, and Chattur Lal. The sessions, often lasting through the night until dawn, were improvisational affairs, with musicians playing a seemingly endless number of choruses for hours at a time, which Allen described as "chasing each other a la purest improvised jazz with all the spontaneous comedy of that until they are in telepathic trance and leading each other back and forth across the floors of flowers of non-music, and they go *on*. . . ."

The music (as well as Indian dance, which Allen came to appreciate with equal enthusiasm), the scenes on the street, the meetings with local intellectuals and holy men—all seemed to unlock psychological and creative doors that had been closed to Allen for many months. He realized that he had locked those doors with his drug experiments and obsession with breaking through to new levels of consciousness. In his attempts to free his mind, he was forcing issues that had to come of their own volition or not at all. India, Allen wrote Jack Kerouac, was loosening him up:

> The subjective result on me of India has been to start dropping all spiritual activity initiated since Blake voice days and all mental activities I can discard, and stop straining at heaven's door and all that mysticism and drugs and cut-ups and gurus and fears of hell and desire for God and as such, as result, in sum, I feel better and more relaxed and don't give a shit and sometimes sit in cafe downtown Bombay . . . and my brain does get empty and filled with big thrilling cosmic Indic Persian Gulf sunset XX Century.

Although he was not conscious of it at the time, he was taking measures to heed the advice he had been given by Martin Buber and a number of Indian holy men: Rather than concentrate on escaping the human form by aspiring to reach a cosmic or mystical consciousness, he should be content to live in his normal consciousness. "A whole series of India holy men pointed back to the body—getting *in* the body rather than getting out of the human form," Allen told *Paris Review* interviewer Tom Clark a few years later. "The psychic problem I found myself in was that for various reasons it had seemed to me at one time or another that the best thing to do was to drop dead. Or not be afraid of death but go into death. Go into the nonhuman, go into the cosmic, so to speak; that God was death, and if I wanted to attain God I had to die. . . . So I thought that what I was put up to was to therefore break out of my body, if I wanted to attain complete consciousness." His experimentation with hallucinogenic drugs, he admitted, had helped him paint himself into this corner.

For the first time in months, Allen started writing on a self-disciplined basis. He began a long poem tentatively entitled "Stotras to Kali as Statue of Liberty," an ode to Kali in which he superimposed the ten arms of a Durgi-Kali onto the Statue of Liberty. Lady Liberty, like Kali, would possess an insatiable bloodthirst caused by her eating too many armies, and in each of her ten hands would be symbols of her destructiveness: "Air Raid siren howling into the ocean," "Electric chair lifted above Wall Street," "the H Bomb like a roary golden Flower"; high over her head, as a torch, she would be holding the theory of relativity, Einstein's equation being symbolic of the scientific and technological advancement that was leading the human race into the void. In Kali, Ginsberg had found another symbol, not unlike the Moloch of "Howl," from which to extend his prophetic voice. Rather than model the poem after a biblical form, as he had to a large extent with "Howl," Ginsberg used as his model for the new poem a classic hymn to Kali that he had recently read in translation from Sanskrit.

Allen worked on the poem, eventually published as "Stotras to Kali Destroyer of Illusions," for weeks. He also began making detailed plans for how he would spend the rest of the year in India. As long as he had the opportunity, he wanted to see as much of the country as possible. He had long ago concluded that all the negative talk he had heard about India had been exaggerated. Knowing of Kerouac's problems in the States, Allen wrote Jack and urged him to come to India, where prohibition laws would help him overcome his alcoholism and where the air of tolerance would afford him the opportunity to reclaim some of his youthful, pre–Beat Generation enthusiasm.

"We'll go naked or walking in white pajamas unbeknowable up and down the foothills of Sikkim and talk to refugee Tibetan lamas about balloons," Allen told Jack. "I do wish you were here, only calm and peaceful and not yelling at me much, and we could take long 3rd class comfy traintrips to the Himalayas and read Mahabharatas and spend a few months goofing in the Inde, and listen to music concerts. Even the journalists are gentle and would accept you as a saint-saddhu, not a mean beatnik—you'll see how much gentleness you're missing in Machineryland."

What Kerouac really thought of Allen's suggestion is unknown. He was busy with his own work, seeing *Big Sur* into publication and trying to complete the second part of *Desolation Angels*. He did not reply to Allen's letter and he did not go to India.

6

Peter and Allen caught a train for Calcutta in mid-May and arrived in the city in time for the beginning of the hot tropical season. Allen immediately set off for the north, stopping first in Darjeeling, where he visited a couple of monasteries and sat for an hour listening to sutra chanting, before moving on to Kalimpong, where he spent his thirty-sixth birthday meeting with Dudjom Rinpoche, the head of the N-'yingma sect of Tibetan Buddhism—the oldest school of Tibetan Buddhism. For Ginsberg, the meeting was memorable. In recent days, Allen had suffered through a series of bad dreams in which he was murdering someone or being murdered himself, and he was troubled by these dreams, as well as by some of the frightening hallucinations he had experienced under the influence of LSD and yage. Dudjom, whom Allen described as "looking like a woman—like an American Indian with hair done up in bun back of his head, and Tibetan skirt," listened as Ginsberg told him of his dreams and hallucinations. The holy man then gave Allen advice he would never forget. "Don't get attached to anything you see," he said. "If you see anything horrible, don't cling to it. If you see anything beautiful, don't cling to it." The advice, Allen later recalled, enabled him to escape the traps of his Blake visions, as well as the nightmarish visions he had under the influence of drugs.

Allen obtained a three-day pass to visit Sikkim, the small Himalayan state that is today sandwiched between Nepal and Bangladesh. He went directly to the capital city of Gangtok, where he took a room in a flophouse and busied himself making arrangements to meet with Gyalwa Karmapa, considered by his followers to be a direct descendant of—if not the reincarnation of—Milarepa, the Buddhist poet who had founded the sect nine centuries earlier. The meeting, Allen reported to Kerouac, went well. "He offered to teach me tantra and I offered to teach him pills," wrote Allen, noting that the Karmapa had called him a *Manjusri*—a bodhisattva of learning and wisdom. Unfortunately for Allen, three days in Sikkim did not afford him the time to take advantage of the Karmapa's wisdom. He decided to return to the Himalayan state if his schedule permitted.

He returned to Calcutta in early July. Lawrence Ferlinghetti had written to announce that Allen's new collection of poems was being typeset and that the book was essentially ready for publication. However, there were two matters that needed immediate attention. First, there were questions about some of the terms and spellings in "Aether" that Ferlinghetti needed to have answered before the poem was set in type. Second, Ferlinghetti was not fond of either of Allen's suggested titles for the book (*Bunch of Poems, Hiccup*), and he suggested a title of his own (*Alba*). Allen was not satisfied with Ferlinghetti's proposed title, either. The book's publication would be stalled for several months by the indecision, with Allen finally coming up with a title that Ferlinghetti deemed to be "perfect": *Reality Sandwiches*. The title came from a line in Allen's poem, "On Burroughs' Work," and the volume would include Ginsberg's uncollected poetry written between 1953 and 1960, the works presented in chronological order. Allen now had three books in the "Pocket Poets" series—more than any author on the list.

The summer season was beginning to take its toll on the travelers, and Allen in particular felt lethargic from the heat. He and Peter took malaria pills, and fortunately neither was affected by a mild outbreak of cholera in Calcutta. Allen, however, was beseiged by a series of less serious ailments, including a chronic case of bronchitis, a minor kidney infection, influenza, dysentery, and pinworms. He consulted an Indian physician and obtained medication for these afflictions, but the medicine, along with the oppressive heat, left him in a state of torpor, unable to do much of anything but lie under the ceiling fans and read. One evening, he wrote a new will in his journal, leaving all his literary properties to Peter.

In late July, he received a letter from his father informing him that Buba—Louis's mother—had passed away at the age of ninety-two. At her grave, Louis wrote, he was struck by a series of flashing images—"like a rapidly running movie"—of the scenes of her life; of her coming to the United States and getting married; of Louis's childhood in Newark and his mother defending him when he wrote instead of helping his father with the laundry business; of

Buba's efforts to console Allen and Eugene at Belmar when Naomi was in the sanatorium. Allen regretted not being with his father at this time. "I'm sorry I was not there to comfort you if there is any comfort or if any is needed," Allen wrote, "but I guess the whole family must have had a mass vision of Time, all gathered together at once to see the last word spoken on all our childhoods. . . . What kind of mind was grandma in the last weeks? Did she have anything special coming through? Or was she too weak to remember much? And what do you feel like now orphaned so old—I guess you were used to your mother as a permanent fixture of life. . . . Are you OK?"

Buba's death came at a time when Allen was fretting about his own. By coincidence, he had written a long, brooding poem about the deaths of his family members and friends only a few days before Louis's letter arrived. "I am amazed by the dead population that must grow to include me with the rest," he wrote. "This is all I'm afraid of I guess."

He spent the early weeks of the fall working on revisions of "The Names," the addendum to "Howl" that he had begun in Paris in 1957. Although he judged the poem to be "very romantic [and] idealistic," perhaps even immature in comparison to his more recent works, Allen hoped to include it as a last-minute addition to *Reality Sandwiches*. The poem was an historically important link between "The Green Automobile," to be published in the forthcoming collection, and "Howl." With Burroughs's cut-up method still very much on his mind, Allen went over the old manuscript, taking out articles and punctuation marks, all with the hope of juxtaposing thoughts and creating "deeper images":

> Time comes spirit weakens and goes blank apartment
>   shuffled through and forgotten
> The dead in their cenotaphs locomotive high schools
>   & African cities small town motorcycle graves
> O America what saints given vision are shrouded in
>   junk their elegy nameless hoodlum elegance
>   leaning against truths military garage . . .

Ironically, Ginsberg changed most of the names in the poem, due mostly to his desire to protect the privacy of both the living and the dead. Ginsberg's friends would have little difficulty recognizing such characters as Bill Cannastra, Joan Vollmer, and Phil White in the poem, as well as the living characters who had been assigned new names, but Allen was concerned about offending certain parties or facing legal reprisal by exposing the characters to the general public, now much more familiar with the members of his circle of friends than it had been several years earlier, at the time of the publication of "Howl." Only Herbert Huncke and Neal Cassady were mentioned by their real names, and since Allen was aware that Cassady was sensitive about being further connected to the Beat Generation, he wrote Neal a letter that included the poem and a request that he send him written permission to use his name.

Neal could not bring himself to reply, so the unpleasant task of rejecting Allen was left to Carolyn, who tried to be as diplomatic as possible. Her children, she began, were reaching the age where they could be hurt by any publicity resulting from the poem, and since they had already been through a lot resulting from Neal's notoriety as Dean Moriarty and subsequent imprisonment for drug-law violations, both she and Neal were worried about how further publicity or recriminations could affect their children. "We both think your poem is beautiful and are perfectly happy to be (and to have him be) a part of it," Carolyn wrote, asking that Allen find a compromise between full disclosure and eliminating the name; perhaps he could use initials or a first name only— anything that left room for doubt. Things were just too sensitive for the poem to be published the way it had been written.

Carolyn's letter put an end to "The Names"—at least for the time being— as well as to a new fragment that Allen had been working on, a poem that made reference to Bill Burroughs, Natalie Jackson, Elise Cowen, Ray Bremser, and Jack Kerouac, among others. Allen may not have agreed with Carolyn about the poem's potential for further damage to the Cassady household, but he honored her request. "The Names" would not be published until nearly a decade after Neal's death.

7

On October 8, Calcutta began its three-day weekend Durga Puja holiday to honor Kali, the Hindu goddess of destruction and namesake of the city. Throughout Calcutta, people hung papier-mâché statues of the multi-armed Kali in tents, and throngs of citizens celebrated in the streets, a large percentage high on *ganja* (marijuana) or *bhang*, a legal concoction made of marijuana and almond milk. A few days earlier, Allen had befriended a handsome thirty-seven-year-old fakir named Asoke. At one time, the fakir had been a professional magician and actor, but after having a mystical experience in which he claimed to have seen the feet of Kali, the fakir had abandoned the worldly life and now spent all his time smoking *ganja* and wandering around the streets in a saffron-colored robe, begging for money and food. He reminded Allen of his mother and some of the street people he had seen in New York.

Asoke became Allen's guide to the Durga Puja festivities. "We went around city smoking pot and sitting with halfnaked ashsmeared holymen under the great Howrah road Bridge over Ganges," Allen wrote Kerouac in his abbreviated style, "in tents passing pipe around and the sadhus singing mystic songs to Krishna and Shiva and lifting special ganja pipes to sky shouting BOOM BOOM MAHADEVA before blasting—it's a whole classic ritual [with] little flowers and incenses and special mantras for pot communions." He noted that all around them were the sounds of people singing, beating drums, and banging gongs.

That weekend, Allen made a point of visiting the Nimtallah Ghats, which, he intimated to Kerouac, might have been terrifying had he not been smoking marijuana. To Allen, it was "a strange visionary experience," almost surreal in its ritual. Used in Hindu funeral rites, the burning ghats were located near the river and attended to by fakirs and sadhus who sat in small groups and passed around a red clay *ganja* pipe. White-robed mourners, smoking *ganja* and singing hymns, stood nearby, while a group of blind beggars provided a drumbeat. Some of the sadhus, covered with ash, danced in a vaguely sensual way to the beat. In all, there were about a half-dozen funeral pyres burning on the night of Ginsberg's initial visit to the ghats. Allen walked about, transfixed by the sights. He witnessed the body of a three-year-old boy being oiled and placed on a pile of wood. On another pyre, a lawyer, his torso already burned away, was watched over by youthful attendants who turned him into the flames with long bamboo poles. The smoke from the pyres swirled around Allen's head before rising and disappearing into the trees. "There's nobody inside his head anymore," he thought as he watched the lawyer's head catch fire and burn until his skull was exposed. "It shows death [is] nothing," he remarked to Kerouac, "but how beautiful a movie to see when high." When he learned that these rituals were conducted twice a week, Allen became a regular visitor.

The longer he stayed in India, the more he loved the country. Unlike other American tourists, put off by the poverty, disease, and squalid living conditions in Calcutta, Allen viewed the street life, with its beggars, lepers, and homeless, as a panorama of one level of human existence. Nearly two decades earlier, over bottles of Pernod, he had spoken about the faceless, voiceless masses in such romanticized terms that Lucien Carr had silenced him with well-aimed rebuttals; now, living on the third floor of a slum hotel and looking down at all the unfortunates lining the streets and doorways, he was getting a firsthand lesson on who those masses of people really were.

Allen continued to seek out respected religious figures for advice. On one occasion, he met with a swami who had two thumbs on his right hand. Allen read him some of his poetry and talked about politics. Wasn't the swami worried about the conditions of the world, living in times when nuclear bombs could end the human race? Allen wondered. The swami replied that he was indeed concerned about these matters but that his mind was on God and he therefore did not care whether his body was blown away. "My message is: we should all be like flowers," he told Allen, "be flowers on the altar of the Lord." To the amazement of his disciples, the swami gave Allen a two-hour audience. As Ginsberg was leaving, the swami called him a pure soul and encouraged him to remain a sweet poet of the Lord. He could not tell Allen where he could find God, he said, but he wished him well in his search.

Allen's fears about a nuclear conflagration were well founded. At the very time the Indians were worshiping the goddess of absolute destruction, the Soviet Union was shipping nuclear warheads to Cuba. On October 22, President John Kennedy retaliated by establishing a naval blockade of the island, and for a time it seemed as if war was inevitable. In the United States, people hastily built bomb shelters and stocked their basements with emergency supplies, while news reports instructed people as to what they should do in the event of a nuclear attack.

Fearful and angry, Allen reacted to the Cuban missile crisis by taking an assortment of news clippings and performing Burroughs-like cut-ups on the stories about the crisis. As he noted in an October 24 journal entry, the politicians' words, cut up and juxtaposed, illustrated the inhumane folly of international politics of the time:

Revolt of machines—weapons systems enforce attitudes, Radio TV
teleprint enforce style of speech & statements, economy enforce living
habits etc—Cut up Kennedy and Tass statements on Cuba Crisis Blockade & the impersonal chatter of diplomatic newspaperese sounded like
metallo-mechano-averages computer of marketable ideas proceeding
from Nowhere, like a space ship telepathy station hovering over earth,
invisible, manned by science fiction aluminum-diamond attendants,
remote control a la Burroughs "Trust of giant insects from another
galaxy."

Allen didn't need an international event to precipitate a thundering of
political opinion. In his view, the peaceful spirituality of India clashed with
the strong-arm politics of the United States and the Soviet Union, and he used
his letters to his father, Jack Kerouac, and others as occasions to sound off with
his opinions on global politics or to solicit the opinions of others. In September,
he had received a letter from Nobel laureate Bertrand Russell, who offered a
very disturbing prophecy: "The nuclear technology is faulty. . . . It is a problem
in elementary mathematical statistics: nuclear war is a matter of statistical near
certainty unless we prevent it." Russell was writing as a mathematician of
statistical probability, not as a social commentator expressing pessimism. In
fact, Allen wrote Kerouac, Russell was taking strong positive measures—
through his opposition to the bomb—to refute his own claim. "Bertrand Russell
makes sense, more than anyone, on straightforward What To Do," Allen told
Jack.

"What do you think?" Allen asked Louis with regard to Russell's statement.
"If I thought his figures and reasoning were really correct, I would be inclined
to set out to do something. I'm not sure he's exaggerating or not. Yet on
thinking it does seem to make sense, that with all the hysteria and hairtrigger
network there will be bad trouble unexpectedly. . . . What do you think? I am
not sure whether to *do* something seriously, or not."

Allen was at a loss for answers. In his journal, he drew up a list of global
hostilities, ranging from border disputes (India and China) to general international disagreement (United States and Soviet Union); the list went on and
on. He knew the problem boiled down to the courses of action (or inaction)
to take—a problem that he likened to Hamlet's famous "To Be or Not to Be"
speech: If a nation took action, it could be destroyed by it; if the country
declined to take action, it could be destroyed, nonetheless. The Cuban missile
crisis seemed to prove Allen's theory that, armed with the physical power to
decimate the planet, a change in thinking was not only desirable, it was
necessary.

"If we're going to live together—I mean US and Russia—and China—if
we're *not* going to blow up the world—and we're not—that means we got to
make up our mind to really live together," Allen wrote. "That means the US
has got to stop hating communism and the communists stop hating us. . . .
The communists got to relax and gentle up, and the US got to relax and
get gentle to them—and no more paranoias. . . . We got to realize that the
Russians have as good or almost as good a case against 'capitalist warmongers'

as we got against communist slave state aggression. Both sides *are* right *and* wrong."

There was an even more basic—and more alarming—interpretation of the Hamlet phrase: What if the human race *chose* its own extinction? That was certainly a possibility at this juncture in history. In going over his notes for "Aether" for Ferlinghetti, Allen found himself pondering again his desire to confront oblivion, the death of consciousness. The experience had been both horrific and vaguely comforting. If Bertrand Russell was correct in his statement about the mathematical probability of nuclear extermination, perhaps "Not to Be" was an inevitability that had to be faced. "Is it worth doing anything about?" Allen asked Louis rhetorically. "Not that I don't like life and the human race but I wonder—*if* the race is threatened—if it is so important that the human experiment continues. I guess I would want it to be, yes."

Allen wrestled with these ideas throughout the late months of 1962. From his trips to Mexico, Europe, and Peru, he had formed a deep respect for what seemed to be the timelessness of the human aspiration to survive and leave behind artifacts that pointed to its existence. It was hard to believe the human race had reached such a point that it would leave as its final artifact a burned-out shell of a planet, little more than the charred bones on a funeral pyre—all for the sake of misguided ideals.

Even as these ponderings weighed him down, he found solace in one piece of news. Gregory Corso had completed his new collection of poems, which he was entitling *Long Live Man*. To Allen, the title was like another ballot being cast: Gregory said "To Be."

8

As 1962 drew to a close, Allen stepped up his travels in India. He visited Tarapith, a small village of thatch-roof huts, the nineteenth-century hometown of Hindu saint Bama Kape, now a gathering place for sadhus on their way from village to village. He stayed there for four days, taken by the sight of the many holy men smoking *ganja* in the temple or singing Baul songs in tiny cell-like dwellings under trees. It was like being in a combination religious retreat and hobo jungle. One evening, Allen visited a local swami who taught him a basic breathing exercise in which one inhaled through the mouth for four seconds, retained the breath for sixteen seconds, and then exhaled slowly through a single nostril for eight seconds. Allen, who had already practiced a similar method of breathing when he was smoking marijuana, found the exercise refreshing, and he made a practice of doing this exercise when he rose in the morning and before going to bed in the evening.

There were other stops: Puri, Navadip, Bubaneswar, Cuttack. Allen was now keeping extensive notes on his travels, which were eventually published in *Indian Journals*. He also jotted down the words to Indian songs and lists of terms and Indian myths, his education in the country rivaling any formal schooling he had received in the States. He bought souvenirs and books, most of which he sent home for safekeeping. Everywhere he went, there seemed to be another eye-opening experience.

Allen and Peter left for Benares on December 10, traveling third class on the Doon Express. As the train sped toward the ancient capital of Hinduism, Allen sat in his bunk, writing in his journal, reading Céline, and brooding, mostly about international politics. Disaster had been averted in the Cuban missile crisis when the Soviet Union agreed to withdraw its missiles from Cuba in exchange for a promise that the United States would not invade the island country, but with all the tension between various nations, the crisis seemed to be merely a prelude to a larger, more destructive confrontation. By Allen's thinking, there had to be a new world order, perhaps governed by an organization similar to the United Nations. In his journal, he drew up lists and recorded his thoughts on this issue, as if by putting the ideas on paper they would become clearer and, with luck, more pragmatic.

In Benares, they found a third-floor room near the Dasaswamedh Ghat. Their room led to a large stone balcony overlooking the Ganges, and among Allen's pleasures were the mornings he sat in the open air, meditating and feeding bananas to the monkeys that scurried about the city in great abundance. He settled in and during his early days there, he acclimated himself to the sights and sounds of the city; he visited some of the few miles of burning ghats, tried to learn the city's bus system, and in general attempted to get a feeling for his new environment.

For Christmas, Allen and Peter traveled to Agra to see the Taj Mahal. It was a special time for the seventeenth-century monument, since Shah Jehan's wife, for whom the tomb had been built, had died on Christmas in 1629, and the annual two-day festivities commemorating her death were spectacular. For forty-eight hours, the monument was kept open to the public, which celebrated by singing in Urdu and reciting poetry. In the building, Allen and Peter found an alcove and moved into what Allen called the "most stupendous motel in [the] Universe," the two sleeping on a marble window ledge. He was awed by the Taj Mahal's huge central dome, flanked by four individual towers. This alone was worth the price and hardship of a trip to India, as far as he was concerned.

Allen spent New Year's Eve in Mathura. As always at the beginning of a new year, he was reflective about the past year. He wrote that he had "survived, triumphed, flourished, sat with the burning dead and slept on the warm marble of Taj Mahal in misty nights with blankets." Sitting on the Ganges riverbank, he wrote a long poem that recollected some of the occurrences of the eventful year. He longed for his friends and family, wondered what they were doing as midnight approached.

Allen never wavered in his quest for spiritual enlightment. He convened with as many holy men as he could locate, and in his journal he kept a comprehensive list of others to contact. In the early part of 1963, he met two who offered him especially useful advice. Bankey Behari, whom Allen met in Brindiban not long after Christmas, urged him to "take Blake for your guru" when Allen told him of his visions and his quest for a spiritual teacher. Then, shortly after he returned to Benares in mid-January, he met Kali Pada Gaha Roy, a local wise man who told him that poetry was a form of yoga. Allen took both offerings of advice to heart.

Back in Benares, he and Peter became involved in a misadventure that was part misunderstanding, part government harassment, and part international intrigue. It began innocently enough when Allen gave a free poetry reading at Benares Hindu University. After the reading, the head of the English department confronted him and called his poetry vulgar. Allen retorted by saying that his poetry was not nearly as vulgar as the speech the English professor was presently making. Allen's statement served only to anger the teacher's acolytes, fringe members of the Communist party, who accused Allen of being racist. "You wouldn't have talked to him that way if his skin was white," they charged. "You Americans with your airplanes and rotten wheat, now you come here with your filthy 'fucks' to corrupt our pure Hindu poetry." It was an ugly scene in which neither side backed down. In retaliation to Allen's insult, the students gave copies of Allen's books, with their offensive words underscored, to India's Criminal Investigation Department. Ginsberg and Orlovsky, they told the CID, ought to be expelled from the country.

The CID needed little cause to investigate the two bearded, long-haired Americans who seemed to have no major means of income and who, for reasons the CID could not determine, didn't seem to mind living among the poor. Perhaps they were beatnik operatives working for the Central Intelligence Agency. Their suspicions heightened when a photographer from *Esquire* arrived to take photographs of Allen and Peter for a travel feature the magazine was doing on India. The ensuing CID harassment, complete with a constant stream of agents interrogating them, the dissemination of misinformation about them to people living in the neighborhood, and threats of expulsion, lasted for nearly two months. Agents would burst into Ginsberg's room without knocking or arrive unannounced and stay for hours, all in an effort to arouse suspicion about Ginsberg among the local people or to force Allen and Peter into leaving the country. Allen's appeals to the tourist bureau and the Foreigners' Registration Office fell on unsympathetic ears. Finally, in late February, Allen and Peter were informed that their visas had been revoked and that they were to leave the country immediately or risk a large fine and jail term.

Allen and Peter traveled to Delhi to see whether they could find someone there who would listen to their case. After a series of initial failures, with Allen growing increasingly impatient, they found a Home Ministry official who understood that they were visiting India for intellectual, rather than political, reasons. He validated their visas for another six months, ending the threat of expulsion. They then returned to Benares and resumed their normal activities. The government harassment ceased. When the Communist party determined which of its members had turned over the marked-up poetry to the CID, it ordered them to apologize to Allen.

The episode taught Ginsberg a valuable lesson he would utilize in years to come. In confronting the university professor, Allen had challenged his authority and left him with no way to save face in front of his students. Allen always had a formidable temper, but after his troubles in India, he concluded that he might have been able to defuse the original hostility if he had remained calm and recognized the professor's opinion, even if he did not agree with it.

"One conclusion I came to, [that] I already had [an] inkling of, is that I really should treat people gentler and not insult and drive them into corner so they claw out in self defense," Allen told Kerouac. "I have a tendency to flip into heroic outrages, Jeremiah-like, but aside from letting off my steam, that generally complicates [the] situation rather than resolves it in understanding. And I lose sight of variables, which, if I kept my nature more tranquil, instead of [in a] state of resentment, I would be able to conciliate. So my Peace Program is to pacify myself to begin with, i.e. not 'control' my anger but be aware of it as anger, and the pragmatic futility of that tends to quieten."

He was even more specific in a letter to his father:

> Biggest thing that is happening to me here in last year is slow attempt to keep my temper and not flip out with hostility and hatred and disgust every time I get crossed, but [to] cool it and try to pacify the scene. It began with letters to you and [the] insulting scene with head of English Department at BHU [Benares Hindu University], continued with trying not to scream at local FBI [CID] creeps that were harassing us, not scream at local communist apologists for Khrushchev speech, not scream at USIS people in Delhi when [they] wouldn't lift a finger to help us out of CID mess, not react *back* every time I get frustrated. I think it's the massive accumulation of *individual* frustration, angers amplified back and forth from person to person, that has built up into war psychosis. There seems no way out but individuals becoming more aware of the irrational/un-functional nature of their *resentments*. . . . Or at least no way out for me. Like living in madhouse, getting angry at patients, hopeless. . . . I wonder to what extent it is possible to totally neutralize emotional violence in environment by total impassivity/neutrality/indifference/unmoved awareness of self, i.e. not trying to *force* change on anybody.

The answers to this speculation would vary, but Allen would see them firsthand in years to come, such as when he confronted resentful Hell's Angels prepared to intimidate peace demonstrators in California, or when he witnessed the police riot at the Democratic National Convention in Chicago in 1968. He would practice this method of self-containment and self-control, to differing degrees of success and failure, for the rest of his life.

9

At times, Allen's compassion for the suffering made living in Benares very difficult. There seemed to be no limit to the lepers and homeless and emaciated, disease-ridden beggars on the streets and on the stairways to the ghats. It was virtually impossible for him to roam the streets of any city in India without feeling as if his heart were being broken. Sorrow, he determined quickly enough, was not sufficient to change anything. "It isn't enough for your heart to break because everybody's heart is broken now," he wrote.

In his own way, he tried to do his part artistically and personally to honor the suffering masses. His poem "Describe: The Rain on Dasawamedh" was a stark, disturbing homage to the street people he saw around his apartment:

Today on balcony in shorts leaning on iron rail I watched the
    leper who sat hidden behind a bicycle
emerge dragging his buttocks on the grey rainy ground by the
    glove-bandaged stumps of hands,
one foot chopped off below knee, round stump-knob wrapped with
    black rubber
pushing a tin can shiny size of his head with left hand (from
    which only a thumb emerged from leprous swathings)
beside him, lifting it with both ragbound palms down the curb
    into the puddled road. . . .

It was some of the most affecting poetry written by Ginsberg during his visit
to India, the inspiration, he explained later, coming from his reading of William
Carlos Williams's *Kora in Hell*. On the burning ghats, he had witnessed once-
living human beings burned away for eternity; on the streets he saw living
beings eaten away in the present eternity. No doubt the unpleasant visual
aspects of the ghat burnings steeled Allen for his physical depiction of the
horrors on the street, the objective description of "Describe" rivaled in its gut-
wrenching detail only by his journal entries about the funeral rites at the ghats.

Whenever he could, Allen tried to ease the misery of the people he saw. He
could not bear to see the wasted bodies, covered with feces and flies, the rheumy
yellow eyes gazing out to oblivion, of people left to die in the streets, passed
by citizens and tourists who preferred to think that such people did not exist.
One day, Allen stopped by a naked man who lay motionless, curled in the fetal
position, alive but obviously dying. He was nothing but bones, and flies lighted
on open, festering wounds. There was a red teacup nearby, and Allen washed
it out and offered the man a drink of fresh water. Then he brought him a plate
of curry potatoes, which, as it turned out, the man was too weak to eat. Later,
after washing his clothes in the Ganges, Allen returned to the scene, where he
saw the man lying in the same place, now exposed to the full sun. A young
man sat nearby.

Allen asked him what the older man needed or wanted, and was told that
he wanted to be taken to the water, where it was cooler. Then, with the help
of the young man, Allen and Peter carried the suffering man down to the river.
They washed him, and afterward Allen went for a doctor.

In subsequent weeks, Allen labored to help the man. He saw that he had
food, milk, and medicine; he and Peter hired the young man they had met to
wash him and see that he ate. They brought him a mattress. He grew stronger.
Allen eventually learned that the beggar had been tortured and had his tongue
cut out by Muslims, and that he had a brother who lived halfway across the
subcontinent. Allen saw that the brother was contacted. It happened that
the beggar was missed by his family and had been given up for dead, and as the
brother made his way across India to Benares, Allen approached hospital officials and, after some argument, managed to get the beggar admitted. By the
time the brother arrived, the man's health had improved to such an extent that
Allen was able to see them both leaving Benares by train.

He helped other people, as well. As an advocate, he was effective, never
settling for simplistic bureaucratic explanations, never letting up until he had

achieved his goals; he had a knack for finding the right officials needed to help him accomplish a task. It had been almost exactly twenty years since he had made his vow to help the masses, and while he was neither a lawyer nor capable of easing human suffering on a mass scale, he was doing his own part in fulfilling a longtime ambition.

10

Due in Canada in late July to participate in a poetry conference at the University of British Columbia in Vancouver, Allen prepared to leave India.

On March 20, 1963, he learned of William Carlos Williams's death and he wrote a poem to mark the occasion. Williams was gone, Allen wrote; he was now as physically unreachable as the stars in the Big Dipper, but his work lived on. It was being read aloud in rooms across the world, from college campuses in the United States to Benares University in India. Williams had always stressed the importance of celebrating your own place, no matter where you were, and his celebration of New Jersey had reached people who had never heard of the state but who were familiar with the humanity and spirit that was universal, regardless of location:

> . . . He isn't dead
> as the many pages of words arranged thrill
> with his intonations the mouths of meek kids
> becoming subtle even in Bengal. Thus
> there's a life moving out of his pages; Blake
> also "alive" thru his experienced machines. . . .

Allen's plans for the next few months included a trip through Southeast Asia, to be followed by a journey to Japan, where he hoped to spend a few weeks with Gary Snyder and Joanne Kyger in Kyoto before returning to North America. Fortuitously, Allen's payment for his participation in the Vancouver poetry conference was round-the-world airfare, so he could afford his travel itinerary. Unfortunately, Peter was not prepared to accompany him. Allen and Peter were reaching another point in their relationship where it was apparent that they would be better off going their separate ways, at least for a time. Peter was using morphine again and that, coupled with his resentment over Allen's going to teach in Vancouver, created a scenario that led Allen to write in his journal that "all personal relations [were] cold, exhausted":

> All month . . . Peter unwelcoming and silent and determined on his separate music and untouchable energies—slow drift to we silent and curt answers, neither raising voice in my sadness or he in his irritation and no long talk except one night on Morphine he telling me I'm washed up and sold out to go teach in Vancouver broken poetry Vow he judged—I had nothing to say, being washed up desolate on the Ganges bank, vegetarian and silent hardly writing and smoking no pot except many letters and kidney attacks don't care. Still this melancholy aloneness is like returning home.

Before leaving India, Allen and Peter took one final journey together, this time to small villages in the foothills of the Himalayas. Allen was still enormously interested in learning more about Tibetan Buddhism and he wanted to learn more about the history of the Dalai Lama's exile to India. On their trip, Allen and Peter stayed in small hill stations that at one time had been used by the British to escape the summer heat. In Bodh Gaya, Allen spent a couple of nights sleeping under a Bo tree near a temple; he plucked a leaf from the tree and sent it to Kerouac. In Rajagriha, he climbed Vulture Peak, where Buddha had once lived and where, according to legend, Bimbisara had climbed off his elephant, leaving his armies for a consultation with Buddha. Allen explored the ruins in the valley below, including an ancient temple predating Buddha, in which humans and goats had once been sacrificed to the gods.

There were more consultations with holy men, all of whom advised Ginsberg to follow his own heart. Throughout his long stay in India, he had been impressed by the tolerance of its people, with its holy men urging people to live the lives of their choosing. "All the holymen have a kind of quiet reassurance gesture . . . and curious shake of the head [that] everything's kindly OK," Allen wrote Kerouac. "I notice the same manner of tranquil hand gestures and head shakes and un-inflamed voice, voices always natural and calm, rather tender in fact, eccentric little voices with grandfatherly quavers."

Allen found their urging for self-acceptance comforting. As he later recalled, "The gesture or feeling I got from them was always this kindly *abhya mudra:* 'Don't worry, you're acceptable,' 'We love you,' 'Stop tormenting yourself.' . . . They just laid their hands on my body and said, 'Get back in your skin,' 'Get back in your body,' or 'accept your body'—which means 'accept your sexuality, accept your love, your loves; believe your own loves.' "

This message, of course, would be the central one of the countercultural movement of the 1960s. John Lennon and the Beatles would sing "All You Need Is Love." Haight-Ashbury hippies would wear flowers in their hair and talk of universal love. Ultimately, antiwar demonstrators would place flowers in the barrels of soldiers' guns. At this point, however, Ginsberg was a distance from the day when he would coin the term *Flower Power;* he had heard the message but still needed further convincing that it was possible.

11

Allen flew from Calcutta to Bangkok in late May. Since he had to follow a tighter schedule than he had in India, he did not have the time to travel to inland Thailand as he had originally hoped. Instead, he elected to try to get a feeling for the capital city. He liked Bangkok, which was much different from the cities he had seen in India. There was nowhere near the poverty, and the city was more classically Oriental. The people were friendly and polite. After having spent a year eating almost entirely vegetarian meals, Allen gorged himself on pork, Peking duck, shrimp, and pork wonton soup, the meals being inexpensive but delicious. A canal running through the heart of the city reminded him of Venice, whereas the friendly male prostitutes who hung around King Rama's statue in Lumbini Park reminded him of Tangier. Allen went through the museum and marveled at the twelfth-century Sukothai statuary, and he attended a little theater featuring Siamese dancers and kick boxers. One day, he met a twenty-five-year-old poet who showed Allen his work and took him on a tour of the banana and palm tree–lined suburbs. Allen was impressed. "This is a place [where I] could spend some time," he wrote Peter.

On June 1, he flew to Saigon. The United States was increasing its military presence in Vietnam, and Allen was eager to learn as much as he could about U.S. support of the corrupt Diem government. He spent five days—including his thirty-seventh birthday—in the country. He met with Buddhist priests protesting Diem's persecution of Vietnamese Buddhists; he talked with State Department and army officials. Most of his time, however, was spent with reporters and newsmen who, despite the anti-Communist, domino-theory American positions cited in their respective publications, spoke truthfully about the goings-on in Vietnam. Allen was offered the opportunity to see the inland hamlets and perhaps even witness a battle firsthand, but the thought frightened him and he declined. The country, Allen told Louis, was the "horrible mess as you can read in the papers," but he was glad to have seen what little of it that he did in the limited time he had in the country, even if it did give him "a nervous stomach after a week."

His next stop was Cambodia. Allen's hectic travel schedule, a great contrast to his type of slow-paced travel in the recent past, left him with a numb feeling of culture shock: "Travelling by jetplane kind of a gas, you do get in and out of centuries from airport hangers and glassy modern downtowns to jungle floating markets and 900-year-old stone cities in a matter of minutes and hours instead of weeks and months. Like space cut-ups or collages, one minute paranoiac spyridden Vietnam streets, the same afternoon Cambodian riversides." This kind of breakneck travel would be common for Ginsberg within a few years, and he would parlay the feeling of cut-up or collage into the series of poems that comprised *The Fall of America*, his award-winning and most ambitious collection of poetry.

His main purpose for traveling to Cambodia was his desire to see the ruins of Angkor Wat, a temple complex built under the guidance of King Suryavarman II in the twelfth century. Angkor had been the capital of Cambodia and center of Hinduism for nearly six centuries, and Angkor Wat was the dynasty's crowning jewel, an enormous complex erected in honor of the king, who was supposedly the reincarnation of Vishnu. Like some of the ruins Allen had seen in Mexico and South America, Angkor Wat was surrounded by dense jungle, the foliage and giant root system of neighboring trees invading the ruins like "serpent arms." In the jungle, parrots squawked, "wire singings of telegraph signaling thru the clearing from the singing trees like a Mars," while in the complex itself, an abundance of insects and tropical snakes maintained a long-held dominion. Moss covered the faces carved into stone. For five days, Allen toured the massive ruins, awed at the crumbling statuary devoted to the telling of Vishnu's story. In his journal, he wrote "Angkor Wat," a long poem that combined impressionistic sketches of the ruins, travel notes, and political musings.

On June 11, he caught an evening flight bound for Tokyo. Fighting off sleep, he gazed out the window, saluting China as the plane passed over the country's

coastline and regretting not having the proper papers or the time for a stop in
Hong Kong. A short time later, they were over Japan. Allen pulled out his
journal and noted the moment: "Tint blue lights like fireflies along coast being
first thing I saw of Japan." Tokyo, he discovered from his short walk in the
city, was very modern, with "huge dark misty newyorklike streets—viaducts
and railroad overpasses and wet streets cabs and yowling ambulances in the
midnight silence." With no place to stay overnight, and wanting to save money,
he walked to the train station and slept there.

The next morning, he was on a train to Kyoto. In the distance, he could see
snow-covered Mount Fuji, a looming presence partially obscured by morning
mists. Ten years earlier, awed by the beauty of the mountain, he had bought a
series of Hiroshige matchbox prints of Fuji in San Francisco; now the presence
of the real thing was so overwhelming that Allen wept at the sight.

Allen was happy to see Gary and Joanne again. They had a lovely Japanese
house with mats on the floor and sliding screen and glass doors leading out into
a rock garden. Allen could barely get over the difference between Japanese
living and the lifestyle of the other countries he had seen in the last year and
a half. There was no political tension that he could determine, no feeling of
Cold War, Eastern versus Western politics; the people seemed to be devoted
to self-improvement. Young style-conscious Japanese looked as if they had just
stepped off the pages of Italian fashion magazines, the women wearing Jackie
Kennedy hairstyles, the men wearing styles that reminded him of Marlon
Brando as Marc Antony. Japanese technology—transistor radios and cameras—
could be seen everywhere. "Japan amazing after all the other Asian and Arab
countries," Allen wrote Louis. "Nobody starving in his shit in the street like
India and everywhere else practically."

Japan had a calming effect on him. India, with its constant reminders of
suffering and death, had been much more psychologically traumatic than he
had realized while living there. In Kyoto, Allen had a dream that brought this
into focus. In the dream, he was taking a physical exam for a job. He had been
feeling poorly and when he went to the hospital for his examination, he noticed
the doctors talking among themselves as if there was something wrong with
him. Finally, the doctors asked what he had been doing lately and whether he
had been depressed.

"Well, young man," one of the doctors began, "it seems to me you have all
the symptoms, particularly around the face, of a long, sustained state of
SHOCK. What have you been doing lately, and where have you been eating
and living?"

"Travelling—writing, I suppose," Ginsberg replied. "Airplanes, Japan, bad
food in India." He said nothing about his experimentations with yage and
psilocybin, convinced that the doctors would attribute his condition to his use
of drugs.

"Quit it," the doctor advised Allen. "Go into lovemaking or politics or
something that builds up the 'human' reassuring ego."

The dream was a confirmation of the advice Allen had received from the
holy men in India. It was also a subconscious manifestation of the shock he
had endured during his stay in the country. In Japan, where he could see that
life was not always miserable, he was able to clear his head and look objectively

at the last year of his life. He had learned many lessons, but he still had to sort out which ones to heed.

Meditation helped him a great deal. At the time of his arrival in Japan, Gary Snyder was participating in a Zen meditation week, and Allen accompanied him to some of his evening sittings. Allen was not accustomed to sitting perfectly still, cross-legged and back straight, for two-and-a-half-hour sessions, concentrating on inhaling slowly into the stomach and focusing on that area of the body before exhaling. His ankles bothered him after his first couple sessions but, as he told his father, the meditation led to "interesting subjective effects." The discipline kept his mind focused, his body balanced and relaxed.

Allen's time in Kyoto passed quickly. In the mornings, he would sit at a floor desk and write letters or work on his poetry; in the afternoons and evenings, he would explore the city. Ferlinghetti had written about his interest in publishing William Burroughs's yage letters to Allen and he wanted permission to include Ginsberg's long letter to Burroughs from Peru as a coda to the book, as "a kind of 7-year delayed answer to *his* yage letters." Allen was delighted to be included in the book, to be a part of a new work by his old mentor. He was less pleased, however, by Ferlinghetti calling him the "greatest living American poet," which was a label that Allen felt was both embarrassing and egotistic to assume, especially at a time when he was staying as a guest in the home of two excellent poets and was about to leave for a poetry conference featuring Charles Olson, Robert Duncan, Robert Creeley, and Denise Levertov, all of whom he admired and respected as peers and fellow pioneers in the establishment of a new type of American poetry.

12

Allen stayed in Kyoto for five weeks. On July 17, he said good-bye to Gary and Joanne and climbed aboard the Kyoto-Tokyo Express. As he settled in for the seven-hour journey, he began to summarize the discoveries he had made during his trip to India and the Orient. For fifteen years—from 1948 to 1963—he had been shackled to his Blake visions. His search for illumination had been constant. He had tried various drugs to alter his consciousness, as if it was his duty as a poet to do so; he had consulted Indian holy men for advice. He had confronted the void through drugs and he had witnessed death on the streets of Calcutta and Benares. The best and most consistent advice that he had been given dealt with forsaking the metaphysical for the physical: *Live in your own body*, he had been told repeatedly.

A combination of self-absorption and day-to-day preoccupations kept Allen from seeing the truth in this advice. He had seen flashes of it in the past—in Paris, when Burroughs told him that he had learned to accept himself, and in Snyder and Kerouac's studies of Buddhism—but he had never consciously given his own self-acceptance a fair shot. Now, as the train sped toward Kyoto, he was overwhelmed by the wisdom that had been handed to him; it made perfect sense. It did not matter what happened after death, or in one's unconsciousness, if one could not accept and make the best use of the here and now.

"I suddenly didn't want to be *dominated* by that nonhuman any more, or even be dominated by the moral obligation to enlarge my consciousness any more," Ginsberg said later about his thoughts on the train. "Or do anything any more except *be* my heart—which just desired to be and be alive now. I had a very strange ecstatic experience then and there, once I had gotten that burden off my back, because I was suddenly free to love myself again, and therefore love the people around me, in the form that they already were. And love myself in my own form as I am."

His experience on the train was similar to his second Blake vision—the one he had experienced in the Columbia bookstore. "I started weeping and sobbing that I was still alive in a body that was going to die. Then I began looking around on the train and seeing all the other mortal faces, 'with their noses of weakness and woe,' and I saw how exquisitely dear they all were—we all were—so I pulled out my notebook, while the illumination was still glowing in my body, and, while my breath was still fitted to weeping, scribbled everything that came into my thought-stream—all the immediate perceptions of the moment in the order in which I could record them fastest."

Ginsberg's poem "The Change" expresses his vow to live in his own form and accept his death when the time arrived. The poem opens with a graphic description of the burning ghats in India, combined with the hallucinatory qualities of Ginsberg's nightmarish experiences with lysergic acid and *ayahuasca*:

> Shit! Intestines boiling in sand fire
> creep yellow brain cold sweat
> earth unbalanced vomit thru
> tears, snot ganglia buzzing
> the Electric Snake rising hypnotic
> shuffling metal-eyed coils
> whirling rings within wheels
> from asshole up the spine
> Acid in the throat the chest
> a knot trembling Swallow back
> the black furry ball of the great
> Fear—

The poem becomes a catalog of human misery: the man in India, suffering from starvation and dysentery, his head in a urinal; the frightened shopkeeper in Vietnam, about to see his country rent by foreign soldiers; the Southern black in the United States, persecuted by Ku Klux Klansmen. In the history of humankind, all people were "seeking the Great Spirit of the Universe in Terrible Godly form," regardless of their suffering. Ginsberg was a part of this.

In "confronting the horrific," as critic Ekbart Fass called it, Ginsberg is able to neutralize the domination his mind and ego claimed over his body. "I am a mass of sores and worms & baldness & belly & smell," Ginsberg declared; he is the worm of Blake's "The Sick Rose." These, however, are not claims of masochistic self-loathing or defeat, for Ginsberg's "change" is a proclamation that, in his humility, he is one of Whitman's "Children of Adam," prepared to celebrate his *self*, regardless of his lot in life. For fifteen years, Ginsberg had been trying to find God—in death, in poetry, in other forms of consciousness; now he is prepared to find God in the self and accept what he discovers:

> I am that I am I am the
> man & the Adam of hair in
> my loins. This is my spirit and
> physical shape I inhabit
> this Universe Oh weeping
> against what is my
> own nature for now . . .

Reaching this moment of self-acceptance was, for Ginsberg, a moment of sublime ecstasy. His life had been a mighty struggle with this issue. There had been moments of personal breakthrough in which he had been able to address the issues of his mother's madness ("Kaddish"), his homosexuality ("Love Poem on Theme by Whitman"), his sympathy and identification with "beat" souls ("Howl"); in such poems as "In back of the real" and "Sunflower Sutra," he had proclaimed the beauty of the individual. The key, no matter how subtle, to his failure to accept himself had been in focus: More often than not, he saw the beauty in *others*; he looked to *others* for answers. Despite a substantial ego that led him to make prophetic statements in his poetry and led him to believe that he possessed a voice worth hearing, Ginsberg had never accepted himself— not entirely, at least, not in a way that ended his quest.

In "The Change," he summons his yearning back to his body—and urges others to do the same:

> Come, sweet lonely Spirit, back
> to your bodies, come great God
> back to your only image, come
> to your many eyes & breasts,
> come thru thought and
> motion up all your
> arms the great gesture of
> Peace and acceptance. . . .

To reach this state, Allen had to "renounce my power, so that I do live I will die"; he was compelled to renounce his metaphysical quest—including his Blake visions—and live in the present. As he explained, "The change for me was finally a precipitation of my awareness back into my body from wandering in various alternative possible metaphysical universes, experienced in visions or experienced under drugs, as the mind can imagine any universe. But there is only one universe where we can all be together, and *that* universe is the universe where we do exist *here* in our bodies and accept each other's bodies in tenderness. Because that's the only common place where everybody can meet— where everybody is invited to the festival."

As a poet, Ginsberg was not prepared to reject vision entirely. That would have been too damaging to the creative process. What he hoped to do as a poet and as a person was to follow Dudjom Rinpoche's advice ("If you see anything horrible, don't cling to it. If you see anything beautiful, don't cling to it."). By doing this, he would be able to accept the metaphysical without becoming enslaved by it.

Returning to the body meant being aware of it, and in India and the Orient Allen had found two practical ways of accomplishing this: mantra chanting and meditation. Both required concentration on one's breath and, as a result, awareness of the body and self. Both required self-discipline. Allen decided to pursue these disciplines. Swami Shivananda had taught him the Hare Krishna mantra (a chant in which the different names of Vishnu are recited and repeated), and he had written the words to the mantra in his journal; in addition, when he had gone with Gary Snyder to the Ajanta caves in Faridpur, Allen had listened to Gary chanting the Prajnaparamita Sutra to a wonderful effect. Allen decided to chant mantras at his readings in the future, reasoning that if he could persuade his audiences to chant along with him, he might be able to achieve the oneness in mind and body that struck him as being so important as he rode the train to Tokyo. He would also try the breathing exercises he had learned from a swami in Tarapith and from Snyder in Japan. This form of meditation had been useful, leading to a calming of the mind and body.

With this new sense of resolve, Allen prepared to take his message to the United States.

17
Planet News

What does this mean? Don't ask me today, I'm still thinking,
Trying to remember what happened while it's still happening—
I wrote a "poem," I scribbled quotation marks everywhere
over Fate passing by. . . .

1

A formal announcement was not needed when Allen returned to North America for the Vancouver poetry conference: To the people in attendance who knew him, it was obvious that he had undergone tremendous personal change during his time overseas. He was still the same talkative, energetic Ginsberg whom they had known over the years, but his actions and ideas were governed by his experiences out of the country, particularly the "change."

Before leaving Japan, Allen had spent a week in Tokyo. Like Scrooge on Christmas morning, ecstatic to be alive and living in the present after being haunted by his visions, he roamed the streets of Tokyo in a state of ecstasy, his thoughts turned from sorrowful suffering to the joys of being alive. In his journal, he recorded a number of poems reflective of his personal metamorphosis. In "Grand Chorale in Honor of Human Being," he proclaimed:

> Listen to Everybody and hear a truth
> Thru their anger & wrath,
>   what they had to say
> reflecting on your smile.
> What is there to prophesy but
>   Happiness, dearies?

And, in an untitled poem:

> I worship Man
> that his generations become
> more beautiful and tender

Blue boys walking on the moon
As Christ's blessing falls on
all generations—
that Man's heart be peaceful
and he accept the Joy of his lot,
to trust him Self on his day
of Death
And not regret the begotten of
Body. . . .

This was the spirit Allen brought to the University of British Columbia in late July 1963. With his "long Naomi hair and Abraham beard and cracked eyeglasses," he was a different-looking Ginsberg, as well. At times, he could be overbearing because of his crying jags, joyful exclamations, and mantra singing, but he was generally accepted as a changed man. Robert Creeley, who had organized the conference, was especially sympathetic to Allen's conversion. In the past, Creeley had referred to "the *place* we are" in his poetry discussions— meaning, Allen thought, that the poet's place was the divine place, if he could make that place known to readers. At the conference, Charles Olson told Allen, "I am one with my skin," which Allen interpreted to be a statement that he, too, had returned to his body. To Allen, the poets were reaching the same point at the same time—a kind of kismet that was too good to ignore. "It *seemed* to me at the time when I got back to Vancouver that everybody had been precipitated back into their bodies at the same time," he explained later.

The conference was a success, a sort of prelude to the "be-ins" of the late sixties. Between the discussions about poetry and the group seminars, the poets and students interacted on a physical basis. Allen's vision of universal love and acceptance seemed possible. *Anything* seemed possible, if one can judge from Allen's letter to his father on the last day of the conference: "Wrapped up teaching great spirit poetry course all last 3 weeks—lovely union of souls—I seem to be back on girls again after all!—maybe I'll bring you back some baby Ginsbergs after all. . . . Because of Fate, poesy, Drugs, Loves, etc. I seem finally to be returned back into my body after many years absence. . . . I'm actually happy!"

After the conference, Allen made a grand return visit to San Francisco. He lived with Lawrence and Kirby Ferlinghetti for the early portion of his stay in the city. He renewed old acquaintances, seeing Michael and Joanna McClure, Philip Whalen, Charles Plymell, Larry Fagin, and others. To Allen's surprise, Lucien Carr was in town, having traveled cross-country on the spur of the moment, not even aware that Ginsberg was going to be in San Francisco. As usual, Allen was a lightning rod for Bay Area activities, introducing poets and organizing readings and keeping a busy social calendar. He brought the Vancouver spirit of love and sexual freedom with him, and the San Francisco orgy scene picked up where it had left off in the mid-fifties, "like huge nine year cycle come full around," as he explained it to Peter Orlovsky.

One of Allen's pet projects was a film adaptation of "Kaddish." Robert Frank, who had filmed *Pull My Daisy* a few years earlier, was in town, and he and Allen worked out a treatment for a script, Allen writing the dialogue himself.

Ironically, he found it very difficult to adapt the extremely personal aspects of his youth to the screen. Putting down the words—where the reader would have to visualize the events, the picture left in the reader's mind—was one matter; it was entirely different to place the visuals directly in front of a theatergoer. The prospects made him uncomfortable. He worked on the script but ultimately found it an impossible task. "Cannot write Kaddish movie," he noted in his journal. "The effort of becoming more autobiographically detailed and transcribing the real scenes as of conversations with Louis is too difficult—whole areas of embarrassment and invasion of privacy."

In early October, he completed his full-circle swing in San Francisco by moving into his old 1403 Gough Street apartment and, incredibly enough, having Neal Cassady and his new girlfriend, Anne Murphy, move in with him. Since his release from San Quentin on Independence Day of 1960, Neal, too, had retraced some of his steps. He had returned to Carolyn and found a job, but he was not long either for marriage or employment. He had met one of Timothy Leary's protégés, a writer named Ken Kesey, and he became a part of the West Coast LSD scene and Kesey's Merry Pranksters. He also started seeing other women and going to the racetrack again. Carolyn's patience for Neal's antics long gone, she filed for divorce shortly before Allen arrived in San Francisco.

The routine at the Gough Street apartment was not unlike that in 1956. Allen worked on his poetry, Neal arrived and left at all hours of the day and night, and there seemed to be a constant influx of visitors. Allen was happy. The drug use in Greenwich Village had made life around the apartment there tense; it was easier in San Francisco. "General feel of things is New Hope, the 30's are back, life begins again, young folks having babies, no more deaths, just the old methedrine horrors on a few people still hung up in crystalline nonhuman universe," Allen wrote Peter, counseling him to stay away from damaging drugs, especially heroin.

After all he had seen in India and Southeast Asia, Allen was greatly interested in politics in that part of the world, and when he learned that Madame Nhu, wife of Vietnam's chief of secret police and sister-in-law of President Diem, was going to be in San Francisco, he decided to join the large number of protesters picketing her appearance. Madame Nhu's tour of the United States was a public-relations maneuver. Diem had been persecuting Vietnamese Buddhist monks, and in recent months in the United States, a number of Buddhist monks had set fire to themselves as a way of raising American awareness of Diem's brutal tactics. Madame Nhu was in the country to deny charges against her brother-in-law.

Allen composed a special poem for the demonstration, calling for an end to war, which he labeled "black magic":

> Name hypnosis and fear is the
> Enemy—Satan go home!
> I accept America and Red China
> To the human race.
> Madame Nhu and Mao-Tse Tung
> Are in the same boat of meat.

He printed the poem on a large sign, onto which he also drew the symbol of Buddha's footprint—three fish bodies joined at one head. On October 28, Allen joined over five hundred people in a demonstration at San Francisco's Sheraton Palace Hotel, where Madame Nhu was giving her address. Not only was he one of the best-known of the demonstrators; with his long hair and trademark black hornrimmed glasses, he was also one of the most visible. (By chance, on the day of the picketing, Al Capp's syndicated satirical cartoon strip, "Li'l Abner," lampooned a creature known as the "Hairy-Breasted Gins- bird.") It was Allen's first demonstration, but he handled it like an old-timer, singing mantras and displaying his sign for hours.

A few weeks later, he was at it again, this time at a literary gathering honoring Tamara Motoyleva, a Russian specialist in American literature. Allen had read the reports about battles for freedom of expression in Soviet-dominated Czechoslovakia and of a possible loosening of censorship in that Iron Curtain country. He had always hoped to see his and Kerouac's work published in the Soviet Union, so he used the occasion of the literary gathering to inquire about the prospects. With the news media looking on, Allen asked Motoyleva whether Kerouac would be translated into Russian. Motoyleva replied that if it was up to her, he wouldn't be, and that it was unlikely in any event, since there was no demand for his literature in her country. "I heard otherwise," Allen replied, leaning in closer to her and tapping her on the arm. "I say, I heard otherwise."

2

The sad fact is, there was little demand for Kerouac in his own country. The Beat Generation was no longer a media pastime, Kerouac's new books were selling poorly, and Kerouac himself seemed tired of writing and living. The narrators of On the Road and The Dharma Bums, Kerouac's two most popular books, had been youthful, energetic figures singing the praises of heroes of the American West; the pioneering spirit, whether in search of kicks or mysticism, permeated these novels like the hint of old cigar smoke in courthouse wood. Big Sur, published in 1962, was also set in the West, but it was far from a celebration. In Big Sur, there were no "Paradise" characters extolling the virtues of western kinsmen of the sun. This time, the Pacific Ocean represented the end of the road, a place where the lonesome traveler wrestled with his own tired, aging spirit. At stake was not the dawning of a new day or new adventure, but a hold on sanity itself.

"It seems very late in the day to try to say anything useful about Jack Kerouac," one critic wrote as an opening to a review of Kerouac's most recently published work, Visions of Gerard—and he was probably correct. It mattered not that Visions of Gerard was one of Kerouac's most deeply personal and tender books, or that this book, along with Big Sur, represented some of Kerouac's best writing in a long time. All that mattered was that the sun had set on the Beat Generation—and none too soon, according to its most vocal critics—and it was time to write the literary obituary for the King of the Beats. Kerouac had published twelve novels—enough for a career perspective—and critics, squinting hard to see beyond the length of their own noses, took aim, one going so far as to call Kerouac "the most lazy man of any temperament, class or nationality ever to publish (as distinct from write, merely *write*) books." Indeed, *Big Sur* had received a number of favorable reviews, but these notices were not enough to offset the damage caused by the negative reviews and poor sales in the mind of a writer obsessed with death and slowly committing suicide in public.

William Burroughs was also the target of hostile criticism, but unlike Kerouac, who wanted critical acceptance (despite some of his public statements to the contrary), Burroughs was fully prepared for rejection. If Kerouac's *Big Sur* was an excursion into mental purgatory, *Naked Lunch*, published at almost the same time, was a descent into hell. If, as Burroughs described it in his introduction to the novel, a naked lunch was "the frozen moment when everyone sees what is on the end of every fork," *Naked Lunch* represented the creation of a new form of literature—surreal journalism. Described as a "shapeless panorama of perversity" and called "disgusting and sometimes tiresome"—and these comments from *favorable* reviews—*Naked Lunch* was a sort of surreal freak show, a compilation of drug-induced routines, sometimes humorous and sometimes frightening, that the reader was compelled to look at, no matter how displeasing the sight might be. Burroughs's laconic style gave the book the feeling of journalism, yet it was a difficult book to label easily. One reviewer called it "a meeting ground for the insufferable sinner and the insufferable prig."

That such a book was not embraced by the general public was no surprise to Burroughs. He had no intention of writing mainstream fiction or of becoming the darling of the critics. At the time, James Bond novels were the most popular books on the market, and Burroughs was about as far removed from Ian Fleming as Doctor Benway was from Agent 007. Still, *Naked Lunch* was a book that could not be ignored, and it was the subject of fierce literary debates and essays many months after its publication date—a sure sign that Burroughs was being regarded seriously as a writer, even if his work repelled readers.

Allen Ginsberg read the reviews of his friends' works, adding them to ever-expanding clipping files that included reviews of his own work. *Reality Sandwiches* had received a mixed response, though Ginsberg had attained a status that set him apart from Kerouac and Burroughs. No one was about to label him a flash in the pan or washed up—labels now being attached to Kerouac by those who continued to insist that he was a cultural rather than a literary figure—nor was Ginsberg to be too severely criticized for the nightmarish visions in some of his poems. Ironically, Allen was praised for his spontaneity by the same mind-set that condemned the spontaneous writing of Kerouac, and reviewers were finally starting to acknowledge his education and influences. " 'Reality Sandwiches' is a sharp reminder . . . that Ginsberg knows, has assimilated, and writes in the general tradition of English poetry," one reviewer wrote, a remark that no doubt had a mixed effect on Ginsberg when he read the review. Another review, published in *Poetry*, devoted all of its time to examining the line structure of the poems in the collection, the critic concluding that "Ginsberg's music"—his line structure and meter—was "instinctive," an "inexplicable gift."

Ginsberg himself was ambivalent about the literary value of *Reality Sandwiches*, especially in comparison to the new Kerouac and Burroughs books, which he considered to be major works. The poems in *Reality Sandwiches* were older works—many quite different from what he was working on now—and while he was fond of "The Green Automobile," "Siesta in Xbalba," and some of the shorter poems that he referred to as "tasty scribbles," he also confided to Kerouac that the book contained "no big pronouncements," that it was "just a wind up book of uncollected poems."

As he also told Jack, he had much more ambitious projects in mind for the future.

3

On November 22, President John Kennedy was shot to death while traveling in a motorcade in Dallas. Allen was sitting at his kitchen table, eating a midmorning breakfast, when Neal Cassady burst into the room with the news.

"What do you think will happen?" Neal asked Allen.

Ginsberg, who had just been musing about the way the mass media's version of the truth did not address the sufferings he had seen, was pessimistic. "The country will go into a tailspin," he said.

Like most Americans, Allen spent much of the day watching the news coverage on television. The drama unfolded. Lee Harvey Oswald, a former marine with Cuban sympathies, was arrested and charged with murder, setting off angry rhetoric against the Fair Play for Cuba Committee. Lyndon Johnson was sworn into office as President. To clear his head, Allen went for a walk in North Beach, but even then he could not escape the public feeling of anger and depression. On a street corner, an overweight drunk, taking notice of Allen's appearance and judging him to be a left-wing radical, snarled to Allen that he should go to hell. Allen continued to walk, feeling "fear in my intestines," "singing Hare Krishna to the television still blue in the window, speeches against the Left wing." He stayed up all night, greatly upset and "feeling alone."

Allen had good reason for his initial pessimism. The Cuban missile crisis was still fresh in people's minds, and the hint of a possible Cuban connection to Kennedy's death, fueled by media speculation, threatened to fuel another round of angry anti-Communist rhetoric. Sympathy for Oswald, gunned down by Jack Ruby two days after Kennedy's death, was hard to find.

Four days after the Kennedy assassination, Allen was interviewed by Leland S. Meyerzova of *The Burning Bush*, a nationally distributed Jewish periodical. Kennedy had been a strong supporter of the civil rights movement, and the magazine was interested in Allen's views on the relationship between Jews and blacks, as well as the relationship between American and Israeli Jews. Allen, still agitated by Kennedy's death and the possibility of an anti-Communist backlash that would undermine his hopes for world brotherhood, issued a pointed, strongly worded statement that was brutal in its honesty. His own family, which considered itself liberal, did not have any Negro friends and would have been upset if any of their daughters married a Negro or non-Jew, Allen said, noting that when Eugene had married the daughter of a Southern Baptist minister, Buba, his grandmother, had pulled him aside and pinched him in anger. "In other words, Jewish race consciousness is built upon the same stuff that killed President Kennedy, to the extent that it excludes other human images as clan to its family consciousness."

One can imagine Louis Ginsberg's reaction when he read these words. Not only had Allen singled out his own family as an example in his statement but he had also implied that its attitudes were reflective of the mind-set responsible for the death of a beloved national figure. As imflammatory as that statement seemed, however, it paled in comparison to Allen's statement about the Israelis.

"The trouble with the Israelis is that they are *Jewish,* they were hypnotized by the Nazis and all other racist magic hypnotists of previous eras. Astonishing mirror image resemblance between Nazi theory of racial superiority and Jewish hang-up as chosen race. They didn't desire it—any of them. Any fixed static categorized image of the Self is a big goof."

The statement was Ginsberg at his best and worst. Allen knew his history and knew what happened when people took a mannered approach to addressing social change; further, he had witnessed the way countless thousands suffered in the streets of India while well-fed bureaucrats shrugged and suggested that little could be done to comfort or help these people. Incendiary remarks spurred people to action. Still, in making these statements, Ginsberg alienated a huge number of people who might have been sympathetic to his general message.

Allen's main message was clearly stated, sandwiched between his remarks about Jews and blacks, and Israel: "It's time for everybody's image to be bankrupt so we can all enter the New Jerusalem, which has already arrived on earth. . . . Everybody should stop worrying about being Jewish or being Negro and live in that one place where we have *common* suffering identity which is this nameless planet we are on."

For Ginsberg, this was only the beginning of the battle. In years to come, he would see—repeatedly—that ethnocentricity and patriotism and racial identity were so deeply ingrained in most people that it was virtually impossible to get them to forsake these preconditions for something new. The message of universal love was not difficult to hear, but it was almost impossible to embrace on a pragmatic scale.

4

It was time to return to the East Coast. Allen had not seen his family in nearly three years. Peter had arrived in New York in November, and from the tender tone of his and Allen's correspondence in recent months, Allen believed that he and Peter should be together again. Allen caught a flight for New York on November 30. For all his travel experience, he was still slightly nervous about flying, so to occupy his time on the cross-country trip, he took out a notebook and composed a long poem that described what he saw when he looked out the plane's window, along with his anticipation about returning home:

> O New York O bright winter sunlight & happy thanks
>   to be returned home round the planet
> to Times Square & skyscraper business elevator shafts &
>   5th Avenue Christmas shops be crowded

with patrons of the Museum of Modern Art cocktail parties
Whoops what beds what bodies what sweet legs & eyes &
    kisses—
what long walks in the Lower East Side snow. . . .

Allen stayed with Eugene and his family on Long Island for a while, and
from there it was back to Paterson, where he spent some time with Louis and
Edith. There was a lot of catching up to do. While away, Allen had been
dutiful about writing his family and he had shipped home numerous parcels of
books and souvenirs, but as Edith Ginsberg recalled, it was not difficult to lose
track of where Allen had been and what he had seen. "He was gone for so long
that we had a hard time keeping up with him," she said.

One reunion that did not immediately transpire, despite Allen's repeated
efforts, was a meeting with Jack Kerouac. Jack's move to Orlando had been an
unhappy one and he had moved back to Northport in 1962. Allen tried to visit
him there, hiding in the bushes while Peter stood alone at the door, but Jack's
mother refused to let Peter in. When Allen tried to call, Jack was not at home
and Mrs. Kerouac refused to take a number or message. The only way he could
reach Jack was by letter and even then there was no guarantee of a response.

Gabrielle Kerouac's intrusions upon her son's life threatened to have an
adverse effect on Jack's career as well as on his social life. When Fernanda
Pivano, the Italian translator for many Beat writers, including Allen and Jack,
tried to put together a biographical précis about the authors, she received an
angry letter from Mrs. Kerouac, demanding that she not connect Jack with
Allen or Gregory Corso in any way; in addition, she had taken Pivano's
biography, already corrected by Jack, and marked it with additions and deletions
of her own. Pivano contacted Allen, telling him of her difficulties and asking
him to intercede on her behalf. "This problem with Jack is really overwhelming
me," she wrote. "I told you the story because I know that you are a friend of
his and the only one who can suggest to me what to do."

Perplexed, Allen asked Jack about what was going on. All of Pivano's other
biographies, he noted, were consistent in their mention of dates, historical
meetings, and general chronology. Was Jack trying to rewrite history, which
was ridiculous, or were the revisions his mother's idea? "You can't have her
EDITING your literary traces, it's idiotic," Allen wrote, adding as an after-
thought that Jack might consider placing his manuscripts in a safe place lest
they be burned if he was to die before his mother. Allen could not figure out
what was occurring in the Kerouac household, but he had grown weary of Jack's
mother and wanted no part of any future bickering or hostility. "DON'T show
my letters to your mother any more," he instructed Kerouac. "She's gone too
far. Give her my love and tell her the nice dream I had about her, but *keep me
out* of any further aggravating scenes."

During this difficult period that found him putting one friendship on temporary hold, Allen was introduced to another person who would become a lasting
friend and strong influence. After leaving his father's house, he and Peter
moved back to New York, staying at Ted Wilentz's apartment while they
searched for a place of their own. Wilentz and his Corinth Press were becoming
well known for the publication of breakthrough literature, and his apartment

was a meeting place for a number of interesting people. One day in early 1964, Al Aronowitz, the journalist who had written the series about the Beat Generation for the *New York Post*, stopped by Wilentz's apartment for a visit. He brought a friend with him—poet/songwriter Bob Dylan.

Allen had never spoken to Dylan before, but he, like much of the rest of the music-listening public, was familiar with his music. His lyrics were not only exquisite poetry but on his two albums (*Bob Dylan* and *Freewheelin' Bob Dylan*), featuring such compositions as "Blowin' in the Wind," "A Hard Rain's A-Gonna Fall," and "Masters of War," Dylan displayed a sense of social consciousness that Allen found admirable. Ginsberg and Dylan seemed to be traveling on the same path—to the extent that Dylan was now playing his folk and blues-flavored music in some of the same venues that Allen had used for his poetry readings only a few years before. And Ginsberg was delighted to be introduced to the musician.

As it turned out, Dylan was equally interested in meeting Allen. He had read Allen's poetry—as well as work by Kerouac, Corso, and Ferlinghetti—while he was attending high school in Minnesota, and aside from Woody Guthrie, the Dust Bowl balladeer who was presently living his final years in New York, the Beat Generation writers had the most profound influence on the way Dylan wrote his lyrics.

The early basis for the Ginsberg/Dylan friendship was mutual admiration. Dylan was an elusive personality, sometimes withdrawn and sometimes egotistical, always changing, as hard to grasp as mercury; he was not quick to warm up to new acquaintances, and while he was in no way a hermit or misanthrope, he preferred to distance himself from all but a very tight circle of friends. Gregarious and inquisitive, Allen could have been the flip side to Dylan's personality. Still, the two shared a common interest in poetry and music, and their initial encounter was a positive one. In years to come, Allen would find himself connected to a number of Dylan projects. He would be pictured, clean-shaven and wearing a top hat, on Dylan's 1965 album, *Bringing It All Back Home*. He would have a featured role in Dylan's "Rolling Thunder Revue" tour in the mid-seventies. He would write the liner notes to Dylan's *Desire* recording. Dylan, in return, would counsel and encourage Allen in the creation of his own music, a major Ginsberg preoccupation in the seventies and eighties.

5

Although he occasionally accompanied himself on a harmonium when he sang mantras, Allen was not prepared to go into music—not yet, in any event. He was, however, eager to expand his artistic horizons, and if his life in 1964 could be characterized in a simple statement, it would be that the year found him experimenting in film and theater—that and politics. In 1964, Allen made the transition from interested party and occasional public commentator to fully involved participant. He also became a fixture in New York's East Village scene.

Allen and Peter found a three-room apartment on the sixth floor at 704 East Fifth Street in the East Village. The apartment building was dingy, located near Avenue C—a high crime area—but for thirty-five dollars a month, they had a sunny apartment that looked out over the rooftops to the towers of Wall Street. They furnished it with a new rug and some discarded furniture they found on the street and Allen built himself a desk out of sawhorses. On the walls, they hung their Chinese scrolls and Indian prints, giving the rooms plenty of color.

The East Village was again becoming one of New York's hot spots for the arts. Tired of the increasing rents in some of the city's other neighborhoods, poets, painters, writers, actors, filmmakers, musicians, and dancers were relocating to the Tompkins Square area of the Lower East Side, where old rundown apartments could be rented for a fraction of what it cost to live elsewhere. The area was a true melting pot: Ukranians, Russians, Germans, Poles, Czechs, and Italians lived side by side in neighborhoods with an old-world flavor. It seemed to be an ideal location for an artistic, bohemian-flavored community. In characterizing the neighborhood for a newspaper feature, one writer quipped that "there are more beards and black sunglasses per square foot of the East Village than fish in a dimestore aquarium. Bluejeans, sweaters, leather jackets and beat-up raincoats are the accepted mode of dress for both males and females. Hair grows long for both sexes." The New Bohemians, the writer continued, differed from those in Kerouac's *On the Road* in the sense that their "highway leads not so much through the Whitmanian wonderment of these United States as through the more currently relevant Whitmanian social awareness of 'the development of comradship [*sic*], the beautiful and sane affection of man for man.' "

In retrospect, the East Village scene can be looked upon as one of the seeds of the hippie/Flower Power movement of the sixties. In a commune such as the Kerista collective, you had group cohabitation similar to the hippie communes that sprang up across the country a few years later. People lived together, shared expenses (and partners), and divided household labors in a kibbutzlike environment. Ginsberg was an occasional visitor and vocal supporter of Kerista. "It represents the slow dismantling of the superstructure of sexual oppression that has burdened everybody since childhood," Allen said. "New forms of physical tenderness are springing up everywhere—dancing at The Dom—dancing for joy, and, yes The Beatles—what pent-up joys they've released!"

To Allen's delight, people *were* returning to their bodies, even if in a small geographical area. Allen was confident that the concept of free love was contagious and that with proper care it could become a national phenomenon.

6

Allen still hoped to finish a screenplay based on "Kaddish" and he spent much of the early part of the year huddled with Robert Frank, going back over the work he had done in San Francisco and trying to expand the scenes. The major events in the poem were present in the screenplay: young Allen sitting his mother on a bed and questioning her about the voices she claimed to be hearing; his taking Naomi to the rest home in Lakewood and Louis going to bring her home; Allen and Eugene visiting her in Greystone; Naomi's homecoming; Naomi living in the Bronx; Allen turning her over to the police; a final visit to the hospital; and Peter telling Allen that his mother had died. Woven into the screenplay were flashback scenes of Naomi's (and Allen's and Eugene's) youth. To give the film a sense of disjointedness parallel to Naomi's fragile mind, Ginsberg and Frank wrote quick cuts into the script, shots of Eugene Debs and the *Hindenburg* explosion and the Sacco and Vanzetti trial newsreels and other important fragments. There was even a humorous, ironic moment in which Allen and Eugene, as boys, stop to watch a bearded, long-haired evangelist raving on a soapbox in front of City Hall, the evangelist reading a selection from the Moloch section of "Howl."

As he had in San Francisco, Allen struggled with certain scenes in the screenplay, particularly those involving moments that might have been embarrassing to his father or brother. In addition, he was finding it difficult to pace himself for the writing of a screenplay. He had been able to sustain the consistent emotional level of the poem by writing its narrative in one continuous writing session; writing for the screen was different, involving numerous writing sessions and interruptions, and he struggled with this method of writing, judging his work to be "piecemeal and weak." This time, however, he managed to get the events on paper and was finally able to complete a working script for the film. Unfortunately, Robert Frank had difficulty securing the funding for the project and it had to be set aside.

About the time he was completing his work on the screenplay, Allen met Andy Warhol. Like Robert Frank, Warhol was an underground filmmaker who had gained his fame in another medium. Warhol's iconoclastic approach to popular art made him one of the world's most intriguing and controversial artists. Outraged critics could not accept or understand the value of silk-screen paintings or posters of Marilyn Monroe, Elvis Presley, automobile accidents, and Campbell's soup cans. Serious art was supposed to be created for the ages, and here was a man creating it for the moment. To Warhol, art was sensory— an assault on the consciousness through the senses—and since most sensory gratification occurred in quick, fleeting moments, art to the individual could be disposable; it could arrive and disappear in a flash. On a mass scale, the lasting value of a piece of art—as well as its durability—depended upon how many people could experience similar flashes of appreciation over the months or years.

Warhol brought the same attitude to his underground films, whether he was filming someone getting a haircut, the sun rising and setting on the Empire State Building, or people sitting around in the mundane setting of a kitchen. At the end of 1963, Warhol moved into a loft in an old factory building on East Forty-seventh Street and the Factory was born. With its concrete floors, aluminum foil–covered walls, pay telephone, and secondhand furniture, the place was unique, even by New York avant-garde standards. It was both a place to work and a place to play. Warhol and his assistant, poet Gerard Malanga, worked on Warhol's silk screens, spreading the materials on the floor of the loft. The Factory was inundated with friends and guests, many of whom came by to party, others to crash; drug use was open and free. Warhol even had a house band, the Velvet Underground, whose lead singer/songwriter, Lou Reed, would become one of the most influential figures in the underground (and, later, punk) music scene.

Ginsberg was more fascinated by the activities around the Factory than a part of them, and it is not difficult to see why. It offered the same air of spontaneity that he had enjoyed in some of his apartments on both coasts— but on a much larger scale. Allen had been introduced to Warhol by Barbara Rubin, another underground filmmaker whose work Allen found interesting, and while he would watch Warhol's films with the same fascination that he had for Rubin's films, Allen maintained a distance from the Factory group. He did not approve of the extensive use of amphetamines in Warhol's crowd. He had to deal with more than his fair share of that with the guests at his own apartment and he knew what kind of damage excessive drug use could cause.

Still, it was an exciting time, and before long, Allen began to fill pages of his journal with notes for experimental theater and film projects of his own, including an ambitious "Vietnam Morality Play" that included as characters Diem, Madame Nhu, Cardinal Spellman, and the ghosts of John Foster Dulles, Stalin, Hitler, and Roosevelt. The play would never grow beyond the initial planning stage, but it serves as an example of Allen's expanding artistic horizons, as well as his continuing interest in combining politics and planet news with art.

7

There was resistance to the radical changes taking place in New York's bohemian community, and soon enough Allen found himself battling the political forces that advocated censorship in opposition to such wholesale freedom of expression.

The opportunity for a confrontation arose when the city government tried to restrict Village gatherings by enforcing a number of strict building-code and cabaret-permit laws that were virtually impossible for small coffeehouses, clubs, and cafés to comply with. On March 29, 1962, supposedly in response to complaints filed by cabaret owners, entertainment unions, and people living in neighborhoods with popular coffeehouses, the New York Coffee House Law had been passed. According to the law, any restaurant without a liquor license was required to purchase a coffeehouse license if it intended to present any form of live entertainment other than background music. To obtain such a permit, a coffeehouse owner had to comply with such building and safety codes as the submission of blueprints, installation of fire sprinklers, multiple fire exits, and kitchen flues—the codes to be enforced by the building and fire departments. Until February 1964, the law had not been enforced, due mostly to loopholes in it (it was amended) and the fact that poetry readings were no longer attracting the large crowds that had gathered during the heyday of the Beat Generation.

However, with the new community spirit in the Village came a renewal of well-attended readings and performances. One Wednesday night in February 1964, a license inspector entered the Café Le Metro during a Jackson MacLow reading and issued the establishment's owner a court summons. The city regarded the action as enforcement of the law; the arts community saw it as censorship and harassment.

Allen and friends went immediately to work, petitioning the help of any city official who might be able to nudge their case forward. Allen met with the Village Independent Democrats, a powerful reformist organization that put him in touch with the assistant borough president and the East Village councilman. Allen pleaded his case and won them over. He and Henry Stern, the assistant borough president, then met with members of the Department of Licensing, who wanted to know why the poets did not simply go to larger, already-licensed coffeehouses. Allen patiently explained that the poets were uninterested in the commerce of poetry readings, that the smaller venues provided the intimate atmosphere conducive to a good poetry reading. The director was not only sympathetic to the poets' cause but helped them enlist the American Civil Liberties Union for their defense. The court case, like the "Howl" obscenity trial in San Francisco nearly seven years earlier, was one-sided, with the defense ready to present an overwhelming battery of testimony and legal precedents in its favor. To prohibit such readings, the defense argued, was not an entertainment issue; it was a matter of free speech being violated in a nonprofit scenario. The judge agreed and ruled in favor of the defense.

This was only the beginning of the battle. With one judgment in their favor, Allen and company turned their attention to other examples of what they considered to be violations of the First Amendment. There were a number of them in New York alone. Jonas Mekas, a filmmaker friend of Allen's and director of the Film-Maker's Cooperative, had been charged with obscenity for showing Jack Smith's *Flaming Creatures* and Jean Genet's *Un Chant d'Amour*. The Living Theatre's directors, Julian Beck and Judith Malina, had been harassed by the federal government in a series of confrontations. There had been numerous licensing problems connected to small Off-Broadway theaters, movie houses, and coffeehouses. Books such as *Fanny Hill* and *Tropic of Cancer* were still suppressed. Allen, already known for his ever-increasing network of contacts, took to the telephone. He called civic leaders and attorneys, badgered media figures for news coverage, and connected interested parties—all the while seeing that they understood that the legal roadblocks were poorly disguised efforts to crack down on the avant-garde. Through *The Village Voice*, he solicited detailed information about any cases involving harassment of the arts.

In time, the groups became very knowledgeable about how to organize and demonstrate. Formal committees, sporting such names as Committee for Freedom of the Arts and Committee on Poetry, were formed; rallies were planned. On April 22, Julian Beck and Diane Di Prima led a march through a steady drizzle from Bryant Park to Lincoln Center "to protest governmental limitations on freedom of the arts." Ginsberg, now famous enough to be included in the latest edition of *Who's Who in America*, quickly learned that an event was taken seriously or covered simply because his name was identified with or connected to it.

The war on censorship continued and Allen remained in the center of it. When he learned that the police in Wichita, Kansas, were taking measures to block the sale of his and other poets' work, he dispatched a strongly worded letter of protest to the *Wichita Beacon*. His work, he noted, had already been judged not to be obscene in a San Francisco court and, further, it was being translated into a number of foreign languages. He had lectured at prestigious universities in the United States and abroad and was included in *Who's Who*. What, he wondered, was going on in Wichita?

> Is the mayor's office so provincial that it has no control over local police officers and cannot better advise its captains? Are the citizens of Wichita so apathetic they have no control over their bureaucracies in matters like this? Is the faculty of the local colleges so indifferent to the community that it cannot intervene and straighten this hassle out? Are the local patrons of the arts and local lawyers so buried in their TV sets that they can't bring moral suasions to bear on city officialdom to be more reasonable when such a crucial constitutional matter as freedom of expression is concerned? Is anybody home in Wichita?

From all his recent encounters with censorship, Allen could have been addressing these questions to his own city of New York—or, for that matter, with a few word changes, to the nation itself. The forces of censorship were everywhere. The Olympia Press had gone under in Paris. Allen's friend Barney Rosset, publisher of Grove Press, was so embattled that he had to sell off property in order to afford the legal fees in defense of such books as *Lady Chatterley's Lover, Tropic of Cancer,* and *Tropic of Capricorn*; Burroughs's *Naked Lunch* would be next.

In New York, Allen's next cause was the defense of controversial comic and social commentator Lenny Bruce. On April 3, Bruce had been pulled from the stage of a New York dinner club and booked on charges of indecent performance; for good measure, the police repeated the process on April 7. Bruce, the thirty-eight-year-old creator of such satirical sketches as "How to Relax Your Colored Friends at Parties," "Religions, Incorporated," and "Christ Meets Moses," was a veteran of obscenity trials in cities across the United States. At the time of his New York arrest, he had cases pending in Los Angeles and Chicago. In recent months, Bruce had turned his excoriating humor on the justice system itself, using his nightclub performances as occasions to comment on his own legal tribulations.

Allen was incensed by Bruce's New York arrests. Since no one had filed a complaint with the police department, he concluded that the actions were the brainchild of an assistant district attorney who had acted unilaterally in ordering Bruce's arrest. Using his Committee on Poetry letterhead, he typed out a news release that summarized Bruce's legal problems and quoted the favorable criticism the humorist had received in the past from critics in the United States and England. From there, he went on to write a brief petition protesting Bruce's arrest:

> We the undersigned are agreed that the recent arrests of nightclub entertainer Lenny Bruce by the New York police department on charges of indecent performance constitute a violation of civil liberties as guaranteed by the first and fourteenth amendments of the United States Constitution.
>
> Lenny Bruce is a popular and controversial performer in the field of

social satire in the tradition of Swift, Rabelais and Twain. Although Bruce makes use of the vernacular in his night club performances, he does so within the context of his satirical intent and not to arouse the prurient interests of his listeners. It is up to the audience to determine what is offensive to them; it is not a function of the police department of New York or any other city to decide what adult private citizens may or may not hear.

Whether we regard Bruce as a moral spokesperson or simply as an entertainer, we believe he should be allowed to perform free from censorship or harrassment.

The list of people signing the petition was impressive, including Woody Allen, James Baldwin, Bob Dylan, Joseph Heller, Lillian Hellman, Robert Lowell, Norman Mailer, Henry Miller, Paul Newman, Susan Sontag, John Updike, Rudy Vallee, and Gore Vidal. Theologian Reinhold Niebuhr signed the document, as did notable psychoanalyst Theodor Reik. Such publishers, editors, and critics as Lawrence Ferlinghetti, Robert Gottlieb, Irving Howe, William Phillips, George Plimpton, Norman Podhoretz, and Barney Rosset added their signatures.

One person whose name was absent from the list—to Allen's great displeasure—was Jack Kerouac. Jack did not care for Lenny Bruce, whose assaults on religious hypocrisy offended his sensibilities. Allen argued that this was beside the point, that one had to set aside personal approval or disapproval for the welfare of the larger issue. "Bruce [is] only part of a larger Catholic-WASP backlash which will ultimately affect your poesie [sic] and mine," Allen told Jack. "If this trend continues, *Grove* [will] be out of business, as Olympia is now. *Visions of Cody* [will] again become 'dangerous' to publish."

These appeals failed to change Jack's mind and he refused to sign the petition. For his part, Allen concluded his involvement in the Bruce affair by shaving off his beard and sending the clippings to the assistant district attorney—a bit of political theatricality that no doubt amused those who felt that he was in need of a good shave in any event, regardless of his politics.

8

If anything suffered as a result of Allen's intense political involvement, it was his poetry. Unacknowledged legislator or not, this was one poet who was getting very little new verse written.

This did not concern Ginsberg too much, even if he did complain about it from time to time. He was happy to be able to use his name and influence to see other tasks accomplished—and this included literary as well as social interests. When he heard that Hubert Selby, Jr.'s first book, *Last Exit to Brooklyn*, was about to be published by Grove Press, he graciously wrote a cover blurb saying that the collection of controversial interconnected stories about urban America "should explode like a rusty hellish bombshell over America and still be eagerly read in a hundred years." He wrote an introduction to Philip Lamantia's new collection of poems. He published, at his own expense, *Roosevelt After*

Inauguration, a William Burroughs routine left out of *The Yage Letters*. For Lawrence Ferlinghetti's annual magazine, *City Lights Journal*, Allen wrote a brief introduction to the works of the Indian poets to be published in that issue.

Ferlinghetti had long ago abandoned the idea of issuing a new Ginsberg collection in the near future. In January, he had written Allen to inquire whether he had a manuscript in the works. In recognition of Allen's current interests, Ferlinghetti suggested *Politics* as the title of what he hoped would be the twentieth volume in the "Pocket Poets" series, the title poem to be a long one that Allen was trying to revise (most likely "TV Baby"). Allen was too busy to complete a new book of poems, which suited Ferlinghetti fine, although he did use the occasion to joke that Allen was "so gregarious" in all of his various interests that he had little time to sit down and get his work accomplished. "Be a nice boy & stop running around," Ferlinghetti quipped.

Allen, of course, was not about to do that. If anything, he was just finding his wind, gathering his energy for the long-distance run. When citizens of Greenwich Village held a town meeting to decry the bohemianism that was becoming such a focal point in the Village's identity, Allen met with them and tried to assuage their fears. When his translators wrote with questions about the meanings of expressions in his poetry, he wrote them lengthy letters explaining everything from the important biographical events in his life, as they were cited in his works, to his selection of epigraphs for his books.

Since it was an election year, Allen kept close watch on the rhetoric spoken by the presidential candidates. He was dissatisfied with both. Lyndon Johnson seemed committed to an escalation of the war in Vietnam, while Barry Goldwater, also in support of the war, seemed to represent a conservative backlash that would return the country to the Eisenhower days. Both men, Allen felt, were a threat to his vision of a world brotherhood/sisterhood of individuals, and from his recent skirmishes with censors on local levels, he feared what might happen on a national level if either of the two was elected.

He decided to put some of these feelings in writing. Over the July 4 weekend, Allen wrote "Back to the Wall," a manifesto expressing his concern. "The individual soul is under attack," he began, and from there he went on to argue how the suppression of individual feelings led to larger, organized planetary evils. For its presidential election, the United States had chosen candidates that were somewhere "between middle and right" (as opposed to being between middle and left), Johnson being "an oldfashioned politician . . . which is to say conservative and an outright Authoritarian rightwinger," Goldwater being "an Android" leftover from Eisenhower. American voters appeared to be content with these choices, and Allen was both frightened and outraged by it: "To live in a country which supposedly dominates the entire planet and to be responsible for the outrages of one's own country! Woe to the Germans silent under Hitler, woe to the Americans silent now."

The avant-garde, Ginsberg continued, was one of the few places where the individual voice rang out against the mass media and political blather, and for this reason the forces that be were attacking it constantly. To prove his point, Ginsberg cited the recent coffeehouse, Lenny Bruce, and Wichita cases, as well as an instance in Oregon in which a university magazine editor had been fired for printing Artaud's "To Be Done with the Judgment of Good." All this suppression might be temporary, Ginsberg allowed, but as a result of all his "legal calculations" and "screaming at newspapermen and college professors [that] IT'S HAPPENING HERE," he had been unable to do his own work; he was "artistically sterilized."

The essay, another of Allen's position papers, was a mixed bag, at times rambling and in danger of losing its focus, at other times direct and convincing. One passage addressed Ginsberg's latest interest in filmmaking:

> What's happening now in the U.S.? Amazingly enough, MOVIES. After having been absent from the land for three years, I found on my return an excitement, a group, an art-gang, a society of friendly individuals who were running all around the streets with home movie cameras taking each other's pictures, just as—a decade ago—poets were running around the streets of NY and San Francisco recording each other's visions in spontaneous language. So now the present moment is being captured on film. This is nothing like the commercial film of Banks distributors money-stars etc. This is the film of cranks, eccentrics, sensitives, individuals one man one camera one movie—that is to say the work of individual persons, not corporations.

These filmmakers, like other avant-garde artists, were under attack, and while Ginsberg was unable to provide a specific plan of action against those who suppressed the individual, his essay made one thing clear: If, in fact, the United States was the world leader, its recent actions, steeped in aggression rather than tenderness, spelled a dim future for the planet.

9

In early September, Allen took the stage in New York's Judson Hall as part of Karlheinz Stockhausen's *Originale*. More performance art than a structured play, *Originale* featured, in the words of a *Newsweek* writer, a "queer assortment of sights and sounds"—birdcalls, ringing telephone bells, saxophone, music, and human voice. Allen's role was to recite a poem, accompanying himself on the harmonium. It was the kind of performance—an audiovisual cut-up—that Burroughs might have appreciated.

For Allen, one of the highlights of the fall season was the arrival of Ken Kesey and his Merry Pranksters, their wildly painted psychedelic bus driven by none other than Neal Cassady. If Timothy Leary was the high priest of the acid revolution, Kesey was one of his original apostles. A graduate of the University of Oregon, he had been attending graduate school at Stanford in 1960 when the early LSD experiments were being conducted on the West Coast. He volunteered to take acid and other drugs as part of the experiment. It so happened that he was working in the psychiatric ward at a nearby veterans hospital at the same time. From the insights into his own mind, obtained from the use of LSD, Kesey, a putative writer, found the empathy needed to write about the patients he saw on the wards.

One Flew Over the Cuckoo's Nest earned him enough money to buy a six-acre farm near La Honda, California. Kesey and his friends, who called themselves the Merry Pranksters, began conducting acid tests of their own—at the time, LSD was not an illegal substance and could be obtained relatively easily—and their experiments, involving the use of lights, sound, and vocal raps, many of which were filmed, were not unlike some of the experimental movies being made on the East Coast in Andy Warhol's Factory. They decided to take their show on the road. They bought a 1939 International Harvester bus, painted it in psychedelic Day-Glo colors, installed the word *Further* in its destination window, and set off on a series of adventures, first up and down the California coastline, then across the country. Neal Cassady, whom Kesey had met earlier, was the driver, the man known as "Speed Limit." Kesey had admired *On the Road*, and having the original Dean Moriarty as a friend and symbolic figurehead was the crowning touch to his literal and figurative journey. For Cassady, divorced and out of work but as energetic as ever, the trip was one final grasp for his youth.

Neal called Allen as soon as he reached New York City. Kesey and the Pranksters were staying in an elegant Park Avenue apartment on the Upper East Side, and Allen and Peter set out immediately to meet them. Neal was thinner than he had been when Allen had seen him last and looked a little older, his strong chin and jawline, as Allen noted, looking "eaten away by talk and amphetamine driving down future boulevards." Neal suggested that they drive out to Northport to pick up Jack Kerouac, even though it was past midnight and Neal was exhausted from the day's drive.

One can only imagine what Kerouac thought when he caught sight of the bus, A VOTE FOR GOLDWATER IS A VOTE FOR FUN emblazoned on its side, his old pals Neal and Allen stopping by in the wee hours to play. At this point, Jack was ensconced in middle-class living, with his ranch home, well-tended lawn, and corner-bar drinking buddies. Neal was like a ghost from his past, while Allen, with his wild hair and politics, was a part of a future he had no desire to see. Jack initially rejected Neal's pleas to go to the city to meet Kesey and his friends, but he finally relented.

Kesey had been looking forward to meeting Kerouac, but their encounter wound up being a disappointment. With rock 'n' roll music blaring throughout the apartment and the Pranksters scampering around, smoking pot and taking movies of each other, it was far too noisy and hectic for any kind of conversation. Kerouac refused all offers of drugs, and while he did take an occasional pull from a wine bottle, it was clear that he wanted nothing to do with the activities taking place in the apartment. The Pranksters had placed an American flag along the back of the couch to honor Jack, author of the great postmodern American novel, but as soon as he saw it, an offended Kerouac folded it carefully and put it aside. Allen later made note of the occasion:

> Kesey respectful welcoming & silent, fatherly timid host, myself marvelling and sad, it was all out of my hands now, History was even out of Jack's hands now, he'd already written it 15 years before, he could only watch hopelessly one of his more magically colored prophecy shows, the Hope Show of Ghost Wisdoms made Modern Chemical

and Mechanic, in this Kali Yuga, he knew the worser death gloom to come, already on him in his alcohol ridden trembling no longer sexually tender looking corpus.

On the afternoon of November 11, Allen flew to Boston to begin a three-week stay that included readings with Peter Orlovsky and John Wieners at Harvard, as well as a reading at Brandeis. Still trying to break out of a dry period of poetry writing, Allen made numerous attempts to write new poetry in his journal, keeping detailed notes of his brief journey, but he was not satisfied with the results. "I should write poems of situations varied as the places I've been, making a spectrum to cover my traces, footprints," he wrote in his journal, "but I'm not patiently observant enough that I can remember the epiphanous relationships."

These observations were true enough, at least to a degree. At his best, Allen acted as a kind of filter for the detail he observed, his sensibility as a poet dictating the inclusion or exclusion of detail. In recent months, he had written extensively in his journal, but most of his efforts were false starts, many dealing with politics. Despite his claims to the contrary, Ginsberg's powers of observation were not hindered or lacking in any way; if anything, he was so preoccupied with other matters that he did not have the time to sit down and mine his work, as he had done in the past, for the best lines and fragments to include in his poetry.

Allen enjoyed his stay in Boston. Numerous young men and women made themselves available—so much so that when word got out about the orgy scenes being played out on campus, Allen and Peter were asked to stay elsewhere. The readings were a success, especially at Brandeis, where Allen gave a complete and moving reading of "Kaddish," which was taped and eventually made into a recording. The trip ended on a negative note, however, when Allen returned to New York and discovered that people had broken into his apartment and stolen his mementos from India and the Far East.

10

Allen was invited by Cuba's minister of culture to participate in an all-expenses-paid writer's conference in Havana in January. He accepted, setting off a series of legal maneuvers that proved to be both frustrating and, in the long run, rewarding. At first, the State Department refused to issue Allen a travel permit, but it backed off when he threatened legal action. The United States had broken off relations with Cuba, so to reach the country, Allen had to fly to Havana from Mexico City. This, too, proved to be problematic: He could fly out of Mexico to Cuba but, due to diplomatic pressure from the United States, Mexico would not permit him to fly back in. Instead, he would have to fly to Prague and return to the United States from there. Allen accepted these arrangements. His poetry was popular among the students in Czechoslovakia, even if it was suffering from government oppression; a trip to Prague would afford him the opportunity to see the drama firsthand. In addition, as long as he was being accepted into one Iron Curtain state, he might be able to take a side trip to the Soviet Union, which he had been wanting to see for years. He began planning the trip with great anticipation.

In December, proponents for the legalization of marijuana, led by Allen and poet/musician Ed Sanders, banded together to form LeMar, an organization slated to lobby federal officials and raise public consciousness about pot laws. (In 1964, a person convicted of armed robbery or manslaughter could conceivably draw a lighter sentence than a person convicted of marijuana possession.) They held their first demonstration in front of the Department of Welfare building on December 27. Carrying placards with such slogans as POT IS A REALITY KICK and SMOKE POT: IT'S CHEAPER AND HEALTHIER THAN LIQUOR, the small group trudged through the snow and sludge, to the general apathy of the public. Allen chanted a mantra that he described to reporters as "a magical invocation to Shiva, the god of yoga and marijuana."

Allen closed out a year's censorship battles with two final parries. The first was a written defense of painter Wyn Chamberlain's collection of nude portraits. The brief statement was Whitmanesque in tone, a celebration of the individual body despite its flaws: "I'm interested in nakedness, I love my old love's nakedness, I love anyone's nakedness that expresses their acceptance of being born in this body in this flesh on this planet that will die. This flesh is only an episode, what will we do, reject it because of liver complaints?"

Ginsberg's second challenge was far more foreboding. In January 1963, a Boston bookstore owner had been arrested for selling *Naked Lunch*, which the city's district attorney deemed to be obscene material. After some legal maneuvering by Edward de Grazia, Grove Press's attorney, the Massachusetts attorney general's office agreed to forego a criminal trial in favor of a trial against the book itself. The hearing would be in front of a lone judge rather than a jury. Allen was asked to testify on behalf of the book, as were Norman Mailer and John Ciardi and a small group of academics. Ginsberg flew to Boston on January 11.

At the trial, Ciardi compared Burroughs to Hieronymus Bosch; *Naked Lunch* depicted a nightmare world that by nature had to be ugly, Ciardi claimed. Mailer, confessing that as a professional writer he was not in the habit of praising other writers, called *Naked Lunch* the work of an "extraordinary talent" and said that Burroughs was "possibly . . . the most talented writer in America." Mailer, too, compared *Naked Lunch* to Bosch's paintings:

> Just as Hieronymus Bosch set down the most diabolical and blood-curdling details with a delicacy of line and a Puckish humor which left one with a sense of the mansions of horror attendant upon Hell, so, too, does Burroughs leave you with an intimate, detailed vision of what Hell might be like, a Hell which may be waiting as the culmination, the final product, of the scientific revolution. At the end of medication is dope; at the end of life is death; at the end of man may be the Hell which arrives from the vanities of the mind.

Not surprisingly, considering his friendship with Burroughs and his history of working on *Naked Lunch*, Allen Ginsberg was the best prepared to refer to specific phrases and passages in his defense of the book. Conservatively attired in a jacket and tie, he presented himself not as the wild-eyed beatnik portrayed so often by the media but as a calm, respectful, knowledgeable source ready to testify not in hyperbolic language but in chapter and verse.

Judge Eugene A. Hudson interrupted Allen's testimony on numerous occasions with questions of his own, but Allen remained patient. He explained what Burroughs meant by his phrase "The Algebra of Need," pointing out that *Naked Lunch* was not simply a book about drug addiction but of many types of addiction and the controls employed to keep people in line. When the judge asked Allen whether he thought the book was obscene, he replied that he did not—nor did Burroughs. The judge appeared to be more concerned about Burroughs's satire of American politics than anything else, and he led Allen through a series of questions in this area: Nonplussed, Allen answered that Burroughs favored neither liberalism nor conservatism, that passages that could be misconstrued as racist or anti-Semitic were, in fact, lampoons of people who held such beliefs. Burroughs, Allen said, had "enormous courage" in practicing the kind of literary art found in *Naked Lunch* and he had the writing skills to match:

> That kind of courage and that kind of impulse as a kind of idealism on the part of the author, I feel is an integral part of literary art. On a more superficial level there is the question of style of composition, like mosaic, I was saying. The passages have been put in place like a mosaic, dealt out with great finesse and great beauty in this book. . . . There is a great deal of very pure language and pure poetry in the book that is as great as any poetry being written in America.

Allen could just as easily have been speaking about "Howl," which he had not had the opportunity to defend when it was on trial in San Francisco. De Grazia probably recognized as much, but he avoided discussion or mention of the controversial poem, despite its court victory, electing instead to ask Allen to read his poem "On Burroughs' Work" into the court record.

"Don't hide the madness": Apparently the judge felt otherwise, for he ruled *Naked Lunch* to be obscene. The decision would be overturned by the Massachusetts Supreme Court on July 7, 1966, but for the time being, the book was one of a growing list that could boast of having been "banned in Boston."

18
Kral Majales

**I am the King of May, tho' paranoid, for the Kingdom of
May is too beautiful to last for more than a month. . . .**

1

I was at last stepping on the
giant bird to fly to the
Island of Cuba and premonitions
of Marxist Historical Revolutionary
futurity with Wagnerian overtones
lifted my heart. . . .

Thus began another trip abroad, Allen sitting in the window seat of another
airplane, looking out at the field of blue lights lining the tarmac of Kennedy
Airport as the plane lifted off into the twilight.

Eugene had dropped him off at the airport, putting an end to a flurry of last-
minute activities and preparations. Two days earlier, Allen had been on the
witness stand at the *Naked Lunch* hearing; three days before that, he and LeMar
members had picketed the Women's House of Detention in Greenwich Village,
demanding the release of those incarcerated there for using marijuana. There
had been the usual rush of taking care of last-minute details, the sadness of
again saying good-bye to Peter. Allen left on Friday, January 15. He would
spend the weekend in Mexico City before venturing on to Havana.

He was in good spirits, ready for whatever adventures lay ahead in Cuba and
Czechoslovakia and beyond. As he stepped off the plane in Mexico City, he
took in the dank, tropical-smelling air, happy to be in what seemed like another
season, half a world away from the cold and snow of New York. Once in the
city, he strolled into a park and walked along a red tiled path under brightly
colored lamps. Around him, he could hear the sounds of young men playing

guitars and transistor radios. He put down his shoulder bag and rested for a while on an iron park bench. Large-leafed plants grew in great abundance around the park, making everything seem green, the traditional color of hope. "I forgot how beautiful and relaxed Mexico City is," he wrote, showing once again how selective memory can be.

The weekend was a happy reverie. Allen played the tourist, visiting museums during the day and wandering about the streets at night. To his surprise, some of the familiar nightclubs were closed, and while there was never a shortage of mariachi street bands, there was very little to do in the evenings for entertainment. Many of the regular musicians, he learned, were in the army.

On Monday morning, he had to hurry to the embassy to get a visa before departing for Cuba. There was some confusion, but he managed to secure the proper papers just before his flight was scheduled to leave. On the plane, he was able to relax again. Singing a mantra under his breath, he pulled out his notebook and recorded a poem:

> I come flying so solidly myself singing
>   Gopola Gopola Devaki Nandina Gopola
>   and what thinketh Blake—the plane wing
>   dips in the long yellow sunlight
>   over Eternal beds of Cloud to the Horizon. . . .

2

In Cuba, Allen was given a room in the Havana Riviera, a luxurious structure with spacious rooms and an elegant dining room. From the huge window in his room, he could see out over the tops of balconied apartments to the Caribbean. The accommodations were wonderful, but he could not help but think that "being treated as a guest is a subtle form of brainwash": He would be expected to be on his best behavior in exchange for the hospitality.

Allen's stay in Havana got off to an auspicious start. On his first night in town, donning a serape and black and red scarf to keep himself from catching a chill (he arrived in Cuba with the flu), he took a bus to La Rampa, a strip of the city known for its nightlife. There he was approached by three young men. They asked whether he was Allen Ginsberg and told him they had been trying to contact him all day. They asked him to come with them. Allen followed them to a street corner several blocks away, where five other youths and a young woman were gathered, talking and passing around a bottle of rum. After introductions, the group took a bus to an obscure, nearly empty nightclub where they felt free to talk without danger of being overheard.

The youths published a magazine called *El Puente* (*The Bridge*) and occasional volumes of poetry. They were funded, they said, by a group of right-wingers who gave them very little money. In Cuba, the arts were supported by groups of aficionados, and without the support of these groups, poets and artists were left out in the cold. Allen, who knew firsthand about the problems of arts funding, was sympathetic.

They passed around the rum bottle until all were getting drunk. Feeling safe with Allen in this out-of-the-way location, the youths began to tell him about the oppression in Cuba. A special police group known as Lacra Social was cracking down on homosexuals and the Cuban version of beatniks, known as *los infermos* ("the sick"). People in the arts—particularly members of a local theater group—were harassed, intimidated, and called fairies; people could be arrested for having beards and long hair, even though that was the style of Castro and his revolutionaries. "They've forgotten the revolutionary beards already," one of the youths said sadly. *They* supported the revolution, the youths said, yet they felt threatened by the people they supported. Allen grew angry as he listened. He told the group that in his opinion, capital punishment should be abolished in Cuba. "Tell Castro," they replied. Allen doubted that he would have the opportunity to meet Castro, but the members of the group assured him he would.

On January 20, his second full day in Cuba, Allen spent his afternoon with an assistant editor of *Cuba* magazine. Still outraged by what he had been told by the *El Puente* writers, Allen complained about Lacra Social. Speaking like an authority on the topic, he said that for two years Lacra Social had been setting their own policies toward homosexuals, marijuana smoking, and *los infermos* on La Rampa. A lot of young people had been wrongfully arrested or accused of being homosexual, often with no evidence other than the fact they wore tight pants or beards.

Allen was informed that two prominent Cuban poets had secretly met with the minister of the interior to express similar concerns, and that the Lacra Social had been dissolved, even though nothing of the controversy had been published in the newspapers. Allen, who had seen the political latitude given the CID in India and who was well versed on the FBI abuses of power in the United States, was skeptical. *Somebody* was persecuting these young people.

After dinner that same day, Allen was visited by a reporter from *Hoy*. He noted that the reporter wore a beard, even if in his suit and tie he was not about to be mistaken for a hipster, beatnik, or member of *los infermos*. Allen and the reporter had just begun their interview when Allen's phone rang. Two young men from *El Puente* were down in the lobby. They had brought Allen their translation of "Kaddish," but hotel management would not permit them to go up to his room. This seemed to Allen like another case of harassment of the youths. Infuriated, he rushed down to the lobby, taking the *Hoy* reporter along as a witness.

In the lobby, a government guide tried to explain to Ginsberg that the hotel's strict no-visitors policy had been instituted to keep away the large number of prostitutes that hung around hotel lobbies; in addition, he said, visiting farmers were known to try to move their livestock in with them, using the elevator to transport cows to their rooms. The young poets had been refused admission because only one of them had identification papers, but now that Allen had identified them, they were free to go to his room. Still trembling with anger, Allen seized the "Kaddish" manuscript from one of the youths and thrust it in the guide's face. "That's his identification," Allen remarked; "he translates some texts of mine." It was a clumsy, embarrassing moment—it was already clear that the youths were going to be admitted and that the guide was simply trying to explain the hotel policy to Allen—so Ginsberg tried to alleviate the tension by adding, somewhat sheepishly, that he had the flu and his doctor had told him to stay in. "Obviously I have to receive people upstairs—journalists, poets, etcetera," he said.

They all went back to Allen's room, where they sat and talked until midnight. The hotel policy, the youths told Allen, was based on puritanism and nothing more. If anything, it was symbolic of Cuba's sexual oppression. The Lacra Social had arrested and held a fourteen-year-old boy for three days merely because a passerby had heard him in a men's room and told the police he suspected something was going on there. A friend had been denied admission to the university because he was suspected of being homosexual. Allen listened to these stories with great interest. Less than two months earlier, he and Peter had been thrown off the Harvard campus for being too open about their sexual freedom; in Cuba, things were much worse, even if, as his visitors pointed out, the oppression was not expected to last.

Allen worked with the young poet on his translation of "Kaddish." He then dictated a one-page statement to the *Hoy* reporter. In his statement, he offered an appreciation of the revolution, but his sympathy with the Cuban cause was tempered by his concerns about the Lacra Social's harassment of homosexuals and *los infermos*. Whitman had called for tenderness between men, Allen pointed out, and that acted as an adhesive element in both democracy and communism. He finished his statement by quoting Russian poet Andrei Voznesensky: "Communism comes from the heart."

The *Hoy* reporter, genuinely interested in what Ginsberg had to say, asked what he would propose to Castro if he was to meet him. Allen said he would be interested in discussing three issues. First, he would ask why the government permitted Lacra Social's abusive treatment of *los infermos* and homosexuals. Next, he would ask Castro why marijuana was not legal in Cuba. Finally, he would propose that rather than executing opponents of the revolution and political terrorists, Cuba give these people magic mushrooms and innocuous jobs such as positions as elevator operators at the Havana Riviera Hotel.

One can only imagine the reporter's thoughts in response to these suggestions. His country had been through a difficult revolution and transition period afterward. The United States had organized an economic blockade, leaving Castro dependent upon the Soviet Union and other Communist countries for assistance—a situation that only aggravated United States suspicions about Cuba. In pressing for reforms within his own nation, Castro had taken measures that left him unpopular both with his own comrades and foreigners. Now here was a poet—a visitor to the country—suggesting that drugs might have a calming effect on the people.

After dictating his statement, Allen asked the reporter whether there was any chance of his words being published in *Hoy*. If not, he said, he would see that the statement was printed in the *Evergreen Review*, which would be widely circulated. That way, sympathizers of the revolution—people like Jean-Paul Sartre—would get a clearer picture of what was actually happening in Cuba.

3

Cuba is a small country, and in several days' time, Allen had made his presence well known. "I just shot my mouth off," he remembered later. "I just continued talking there as I would talk here [in the United States] in terms of being anti-authoritarian. But my basic feeling there was sympathetic to the revolution."

In retrospect, he might have fared better in the country had he known more about it before he began issuing statements and proposing changes. In some ways, the citizens were in better touch with their leaders than the people of the United States were with theirs. Indeed, there was no free press as there was in the United States but, as Allen learned from María Rosa Almendres—head of Casa de las Americas, Ginsberg's sponsor in Cuba—and her husband—the country was small enough that everyone knew what was going on in any event. "We all know each other," they told Allen. "You can always complain to Fidel or take up a grievance personally with someone in power."

Allen was not so certain. He was still obsessed with the reports he'd heard about Lacra Social. From what he had seen of Castro on television, he was impressed with the Cuban leader, who with his khaki shirt open at the neck and tousled hair and beard seemed "ten times more natural than Johnson, in fact human" to Ginsberg. His rapid-fire speech reminded Allen of Neal Cassady. Nevertheless, he was a man facing many national problems, and who was to say what measures he might take in trying to solve them?

Allen was determined to learn as much as he could about the country; he was equally determined to speak out if the occasion arose. He was impatient with people who parroted the party line. When a reporter from *Revolución* came to his hotel to interview him, Allen grew impatient when she repeated the now-familiar story about prostitutes, thieves, and farmers with their livestock as reasons for the denial of visitors to the hotel; a new wrinkle to this rationale was a purported fear for Allen's safety, with the possibility of counterrevolutionaries stealing into the hotel and assassinating the famous American poet. The interview, which was supposed to be on literary topics, went well. Allen talked about William Carlos Williams's influence on American poetry, the arts community of New York's Lower East Side, Indian mantras, and the relationship between breathing exercises and the expression of feeling in poetry. Still, he could not pass up the opportunity to repeat the gossip he had heard about the Lacra Social and he went on for nearly an hour on the topic, only to become irritated when his interviewer mentioned that she could not publish his remarks on nonliterary matters. Besides, she said, Lacra Social had been dissolved. Allen disagreed, telling her that a boy on La Rampa had been arrested just the previous week, at a time when the special police organization was supposedly disbanded.

Whatever his reasons, Allen tended to believe the reports issued by dissenting voices. In his journal, he kept detailed notes on everything he saw or heard. There were good and bad elements to the country, he decided, but there was no doubt in his mind that it was better off now that it had been when he visited the island in 1953, and compared to the other Latin American countries he had visited, the people in Cuba were much better off economically. Cubans had food and clothes, jobs, and a decent education. Castro was a national hero, very much loved by Cubans who believed he would lead them out of their internal and external turmoils. In a letter to his father, Allen tried to describe the national mood: "A quasi police state with no constitutional protection, and on the other hand a fantastic optimistic unanimity of agreement to go ahead with the 'revolution' which is spoken of everywhere and which has changed everybody's life—so it's a weird scene—all in all rather hopeful than not, despite my own direct experiences with limitations on freedom of expression." To Peter, Allen characterized Cuba as being "both great and horrible, half police state half summer camp—mixed."

Allen, of course, was quite accustomed to speaking his mind—of challenging the people he loved, of criticizing institutions he otherwise respected, of squaring off against or playing devil's advocate with figures of authority, of protesting whatever aspects of government and society he found undesirable. In the United States, doing so was simply an exercise in free speech. In Cuba, however, he was more than just a rabble-rouser; he was seen as an embarrassment to his hosts and a possible threat to the government. And at the time, Cuba needed little reason to be suspicious of anything or anyone American.

For all his preoccupation with Cuban politics, Allen devoted plenty of time to visiting the country's historical sites and points of interest. He particularly enjoyed his tour of Hemingway's old house, which had been preserved intact by Cubans who still considered him a sort of folk hero. The house was filled with bookshelves, hunting trophies, weapons, and favorite bits of memorabilia; the furniture remained exactly where it had been on the day the Hemingways had to leave the island during the revolution. His typewriter sat on a bookshelf, propped on a volume of Who's Who in America. Walking about the house with a small group of tourists, listening to a young guide speak of how Hemingway had occasionally spent entire days fishing with Castro or how he had once kissed the Cuban flag upon his return to the country after an absence, Allen felt a trace of sorrow, as if the man they were talking about had died yesterday, not four years before. "Really sad, the skeleton remains of his grand domesticity with the Person gone," he noted in his journal. After seeing the house, he was taken to the small bay that Hemingway used as a model in The Old Man and the Sea and to Hemingway's favorite restaurant.

Other delegates began to arrive for the convention. Allen was reunited with Nicanor Parra, the Chilean poet he had met and stayed with in Santiago in 1960, and Miguel Grinberg, editor of Eco Contemporaneo, an Argentinean avant-garde magazine. Allen noticed that Parra was no longer the angry ideologue he had been when Allen had seen him at the writer's conference in Chile. He seemed more relaxed, as Allen noted in his journal: "The politics metaphysic arguments we had four years ago all vanished like mist, both of us later sitting by Cienfuego Hotel swim pool exchanging gossip and amazed to be in the same amiable place in our bodies in Cuba."

4

The conference began. Allen was one of the judges of the event's poetry competition, and at a meeting at Casa de las Americas, director Haydée Santamaría instructed the judges to give the prize to the best work outside of politics, adding that they should feel free to talk to anyone they wanted.

Judging the competition proved to be a daunting task. There were ninety-one entries, all carbon manuscripts typed in Spanish. Fortunately for Allen, Manuel Ballagas, the seventeen-year-old poet who had translated "Kaddish," volunteered to translate the entries into English for him. Unfortunately for Ballagas, the Cuban authorities took notice of the great amount of time he was spending with the increasingly unwelcome American. One evening after Allen dropped him off at his home following a day's work, Ballagas was taken to the police station and questioned about his involvement with Ginsberg. He was detained overnight and then taken the next morning to his mother, who was asked to sign "probation" papers agreeing to take him to the station whenever the police called. In Cuba, it was a minor incident, but to Allen, who was absolutely obsessed with hotel regulations, harassment of youths, and government attitudes toward homosexuals, the incident was just another example of the police-state mentality that seemed to fly in the face of Castro's proclaimed humanist revolution.

Allen repeated his feelings about all this when he was visited by two more reporters from *Hoy*, a husband-and-wife journalistic team that was far less interested in Allen's political opinions than in his views on poetry. Allen, who admitted that he was growing paranoid about the way he was being perceived in Cuba, offered up the usual mixture of conversation—a discussion about Williams and objectivist writing, followed by more talk about marijuana and his homosexuality. He was determined to get his message across. If people were allowed to live within their own bodies and consciousness, free from social or political interference and judgment, the world would be a much calmer place and literature itself would be more natural and expressive. His interviewers took a more pragmatic—and, to Allen, stereotypical—stance. "You must understand," they told him, "the Revolution is more concerned with basic issues like raising production, feeding and educating people, and defending ourselves from U.S. pressure. Later on these aesthetic issues can be discussed." It was a familiar theme throughout Allen's stay in Cuba.

That evening, he met with a group of young poets at the Writer's Union headquarters. He brought along a few records by Bob Dylan and Ray Charles, which they listened to while spending hours talking about poetry and politics. The Cubans were very interested in this American music, and later in the evening, they returned the cultural favor by taking Allen, Nicanor Parra, and other convention delegates to a theater to listen to the new "feeling" music that was popular in their country. Allen enjoyed the music, which he described as "little sketch-dramas fit for a Supper Club." The otherwise-pleasant evening was marred later when, back in his hotel, Allen received a call informing him that Manuel Ballagas and another youth had been arrested as they were leaving the theater.

Allen appealed to María Rosa Almendres for an explanation, but he found that she had grown impatient with his interference in Cuban affairs. "Perhaps you don't understand how hard we have to struggle to keep the Revolution clean," she said. "You have to understand that the stupid ones—the squares here—think it's bad for us to have the young ones washing our dirty linen in public, discussing problems with foreigners. After all, *we* have to struggle with threats from the outside, not you." As for the two arrested young men, Almendres told Allen that Haydée Santamaría would address the problem.

A revered figure in Cuba, Santamaría had been a hero during the revolution, and for her valor she had been given the office of minister of culture. She, too, was irritated by some of Allen's pronouncements, especially since most of his opinions were based on gossip he had picked up from the *El Puente* poets. Cuba had to address the issue of homosexuality, she told Allen, because too many gays were making public spectacles of themselves and seducing impressionable young boys. Allen was not interested in more official-sounding rationalizations, so he interrupted her explanation, saying that it was too theoretical for the issue at hand. He was more concerned about the arrested youths. Allen explained what he knew of the situation, and Santamaría promised to look into it and see to their release. They talked for a while about the Revolutionary Council. Allen did not care for her too much; he felt that she talked "like a woman making a speech to high school girls, too rapidly and with too much authority, as if her word were some kind of government policy"—which, he conceded, it was. Despite his misgivings, he heard her out and tried to stay friendly, going so far as to create a minor stir when he reached out and slapped her on the behind as she was leaving the room.

It was now becoming clear to Allen that he was considered a persona non grata by Cuban officials. A scheduled reading at the university was suddenly canceled and students warned not to visit Allen. Another *El Puente* poet was taken in for questioning. Gossip about Allen and his group was in the air, some of it overheard by an astonished Ginsberg himself. Allen felt as if he were caught up in some kind of "Orwellian dreamworld," isolated in his own paranoia and fear, the feeling "like having a nervous breakdown." He had not come to Cuba to cause trouble or instigate further tension between Americans and Cubans, but that seemed to be the result of his visit. He had hoped to challenge the artists and political thinkers—the kind of people who could handle such provocation in the United States and other countries—but his intentions were being misinterpreted.

This became obvious when he was asked not to accompany the convention delegates to a meeting with Prime Minister Dorticos. Instead, Allen met with María Rosa Almendres, who again tried to explain to him the furor he was creating in her country. Haydée Santamaría, Almendres reported, was quite angry with Allen for making certain remarks. According to the gossip circulating around Havana, Allen was supposed to have said that Raul Castro was gay and that Ché Guevara was cute. Allen admitted to making these comments, but he could not remember when he had made them or to whom.

Haydée Santamaría voiced her own concerns a few days later at a conference luncheon at a country club. As soon as she saw Allen, she formally shook hands with him and then began talking in her rapid-fire Spanish about the Cuban revolution. Allen had been drinking iced rum drinks, and that, coupled with his marginal understanding of Spanish, made her monologue difficult to follow. Rather than get angry, he silently repeated a mantra to himself. At the first opportunity, he changed subjects, addressing their earlier meeting, when he had slapped her backside. "I hope you didn't misunderstand," he said, explaining that he meant no disrespect but that he had become caught up in the sense of rapport he felt from their conversation. The slap had been a friendly gesture, he said.

That kind of behavior might be acceptable in the United States, she replied, but Allen's brand of bohemianism was not welcome in Cuba, where it could not be applied. She was especially concerned about his talk about marijuana. In Cuba, she said, smoking pot was a crime, and that's how it had to be. Allen pointed out that he meant no harm, that he was simply attempting to bring real information into the debate about marijuana as a social problem, as opposed to listening to the old rumors that marijuana had been banned because Batista's soldiers had a habit of getting high and shooting at civilians—a rumor that Allen doubted. If marijuana was going to be a topic of discussion, Allen asserted, then scientific data ought to be used.

"Yes," Santamaría said, "but we have work to do and cannot afford these extra luxuries which impede the senses. . . . Though you may discuss such matters with people on a high level or mature officials, you understand we cannot have you spreading such ideas which are against the laws of our country and our policy among young people." She pointedly reminded Allen that, famous poet or not, he was a guest of Cuba and that they could not support his speaking out against official policy.

The gulf between Allen's position and the official state position could not have been more evident. He still insisted that to break down the Cold War and achieve world unity, a mass change of consciousness was required; faced with the task of feeding, educating, and providing adequate medical services and facilities to their citizens, Cuban leaders were not interested in such esoterica—and certainly not the kind that would promote individualism at a time when they were seeking national unity.

Allen tried another approach. While he and Santamaría were talking, Tom Maschler, an English editor and conference attendee, walked by, and Allen drew him into the conversation. Maschler had recently published John Lennon's A Spaniard in the Works, and he and Allen agreed that it might be a meaningful international gesture if Cuba invited the Beatles—then the most popular band in the world—to give a concert there.

"They have no ideology," Haydée Santamaría answered. "We are trying to build a revolution with an ideology."

That might be true, Maschler conceded, but there was no denying their appeal among the young. If Cuba wanted to bring the revolution to its young people, it might begin by appeasing them with an appearance by the Beatles.

The discussion had reached an impasse. Santamaría pointed out that the revolution was striving to reach something of permanence and that could be achieved only through a strong ideology, not something as contrived and temporary as a rock concert. "The Beatles will come and it will be like our Fiesta. Everybody will be excited for a few days and then that will be the end of it. We want to give our people something more. Some truth and work and food."

For all his disagreement with the country's policies, Allen admired the revolution and Cuba's efforts to build a new government. "All told, Cuba is pretty good," he wrote Peter Orlovsky. "I mean, people working and building, like they say, a new society—which is remarkable for any South American country." In his journal, he noted his sympathy for the task ahead: "They obviously do have a tough struggle to survive, [and] their defiance and resentment of U.S. obnoxious intrusion and blockade is understandable completely, and even their blank dumb miscomprehension of my own queer rare literary extravaganza, and they do suffer too much to take it easy."

5

Allen's days in Cuba were numbered, even if he had no hint of it. In fact, he was hoping to stay on in the country longer than he had originally intended. He continued his work at the conference, giving lectures consciously designed to avoid topics that might embarrass his hosts. Things quieted down and he was convinced that as long as he could hold his temper, he would have no further trouble in Cuba. The controversy seemed to have dissipated. None of his interviews for *Hoy* had been published and the *El Puente* poets were left alone by the police. Allen religiously maintained his journals, filling them with his impressions of Cuba, political gossip, diary entries, and occasional poetry; by mid-February, he had written over two hundred pages.

One day, Allen and other delegates were flown to Santiago de Cuba, a city at the base of the Sierra Maestra range. The delegates piled into trucks and slowly wound their way up a dusty road until they reached a large school set in the mountains. Thousands of teenagers were training to be teachers here, in a setting that was part classroom, part campground. They followed a disciplined daily schedule that included classes in reading, writing, biology, and Marxism; when the day was done, they sang songs in homage to Castro and the revolution. Allen learned that upon their graduation, the young teachers were expected to go off to small mountain villages, where they would build thatch-roof schoolhouses and teach the natives. It was a side of Cuba Allen had not imagined.

Back in Havana, he set up a meeting with Yves Espin, an architect who was a fan of his poetry; he also happened to be Raul Castro's brother-in-law. Espin brought Allen to his apartment in Vedado, where an audience of well-dressed friends awaited their arrival. Allen was served rum and ice water and treated like a celebrity. Espin's guests asked him numerous questions, including his opinions about the revolution. Allen replied that there was still too much suppression of unconscious personal feelings, that there was too much fear in Cuba. Artists were not truly free to express themselves—not if they had to fear being branded anti-Castro or antirevolution. "If a big Dostoevsky, with no sense of guilt and a huge brown humor, wrote a novel here about Lacra Social and a terrible in-group club and art school and everybody's sex lives and Marxist dogma and gossip, could it be published here?" Allen wondered aloud. He then answered his own question. "Nobody here wants that kind of genius art." Laughing, Espin agreed this was true.

The party went on for hours, Allen entertaining the guests with stories about Timothy Leary and psilocybin; he sang an Indian mantra, accompanying himself with finger cymbals. He enjoyed himself immensely and it was nearly two o'clock in the morning when Espin delivered him back to his hotel.

The night, however, was far from over. Allen had no sooner returned to his room and prepared himself for bed when he received a telephone call. There was a party going on in one of the delegate's rooms. He put on his white linen Indian pajamas and two sets of beads and set off barefoot for the party. All the conference speakers were there, drinking heartily and singing songs. Allen's outfit was a hit. He celebrated with them for nearly three hours, leaving at about 5:00 A.M.

At eight, he was awakened from a deep sleep by a sharp knock on his door. A government official, accompanied by three soldiers in olive green uniforms, told Allen to dress and pack. The head of the immigration department wanted to see him. Still groggy from sleep but feeling a cold chill of fear, Allen cleaned up and dressed. He packed his knapsack to the bursting point, making sure that he kept all of his papers with him; his journals, with their analyses of Cuban politics and descriptions of his sexual activities, were stowed at the bottom of the bag, away from immediate scrutiny. Allen asked whether they had called Haydée Santamaría; then he demanded to be allowed to call Casa de las Americas. He was told that he was not permitted to make any calls. In the hotel lobby, Allen saw Nicanor Parra and shouted that he was being deported and that Parra should call the Casa and warn them.

At the immigration building, he was taken to a small cell, where he was given a chair, newspaper, and cigarettes. To calm his fears, he quietly chanted a mantra. After a short time, a uniformed man—the head of immigration—joined Allen and informed him that he was being deported; a flight had been booked for Prague. Allen asked whether a mistake had been made, whether the immigration people had consulted with his hosts, but he was ordered into a car waiting to drive them to the airport. As they sped along the Cuban coastline, Allen asked again why he was being deported.

"For breaking the laws of Cuba," the immigration chief replied.

"What laws?"

"You'll have to ask yourself that."

The response reminded Allen of an occasion when, two decades earlier, he had stood before Dean Nicholas McKnight at Columbia and was told that he was being dismissed from the university. When Allen had asked why he was being expelled, he had received the same kind of answer.

He made a final attempt to convince the immigration officer to call Haydée Santamaría on his behalf, but to no avail. A jet with CESKOSLOVENSKE painted on its side was waiting on one of the runways.

6

Looking back on his expulsion from Cuba, Ginsberg insisted that he had merely been a component in a much larger game, and for that reason he did not protest his deportation too greatly.

"I didn't go round screaming to *Time* magazine that I'd been unjustly kicked out of Cuba," he said. "I just gave them the benefit of the doubt, understanding that I was like a pawn. It was a fight between the liberal groups and the military bureaucracy groups. I realized also that the more the United States put pressure on Cuba, the more power the right wing military, police bureaucracy and Party hacks would get. The real problem was to relieve the pressure in America, to end the blockade rather than to 'blame' the Cuban Revolution, Castro, or Marxism."

Describing his dismissal from Cuba as "half Kafkian and half funny," Allen tried to explain the situation to his father. "The interesting thing about the communist countries is the interior balance of forces working one way or the other. One group humane, other group sectarian police state oriented. Same *types* of people you find in U.S. proposing *soft* and *hard* lines. The essential thing to do is to help out the liberal types here (and in U.S.)—the heavier the Cold War attack, the more the liberals suffer. Like, in Cuba, the more *pressure* the U.S. puts against Castro, the more difficult it is for liberals to fight police state tendencies."

Allen did not hold himself completely guiltless in his assessment of his expulsion. Although he was steadfast in maintaining that he had done nothing so grave as to warrant the action, he admitted that he was not entirely innocent, either: "In Cuba I committed about every 'infraction of totalitarian laws' I could think of, verbally, and they finally flipped out and gave me the bum's rush," he told Louis.

Ironically, Allen was sent to a country that was not only aware of him and his work but that had also experienced a small degree of internal strife as an indirect result of the Beat Generation's influence. In 1963, Czechoslovakian leaders, encouraged by Premier Nikita Khrushchev's proposal for a thaw behind the Iron Curtain, loosened the tight government regulations on art and literature in effect since 1956. Freedom of expression, at least to a much greater extent, was again possible. Youthful writers and artists looked to the West, calling for the importation of books and art from the United States. The Viola café, a poetry and jazz nightclub similar to the clubs in Greenwich Village, did a thriving business, especially among the Czechoslovakian bohemians, who sat among enlarged photographs of Ginsberg, Corso, and Kerouac. Literary journals published work that a few years earlier might have landed their authors in prison.

However, these changes were not wholesale, nor were the results always government-approved. The state intervened if the works became too critical of the Communist party. On one occasion, President Anton Novotny summoned a group of the country's most critical writers to Prague and warned them they could be expelled from the Communist party if they continued their criticism of the government. Of the groups scrutinized by the government, the Czech beatniks, who proclaimed Ginsberg and Corso to be their favorite American poets, were considered to be the most rebellious and, hence, potentially harmful to government order.

Since Allen had had no way to contact anyone in Czechoslovakia about his expulsion from Cuba, his arrival in the country was unexpected. Fortunately, he was able to contact a poet friend who helped put him in touch with the Writer's Union. Allen learned that he had royalties coming from a book of his poems that had been translated into Czech two years earlier, and there was additional money coming in performance royalties from the Ginsberg poetry read by others at the Viola. To complete his windfall, as a guest of the state and Writer's Union, Allen was given a large suite at the Hotel Ambassador and seventy-five dollars spending money. His mind went to work immediately. If he lived modestly, he had enough money for a month's stay in Prague and could probably afford his anticipated trip to the Soviet Union. "I have enough money for four days in Moscow," Allen wrote Louis. "I hear also that the Russians will invite me to stay at least a week at their expense, and I'll see how long I can stretch that out." With any luck, he continued, he might be able to add Warsaw to his itinerary.

Prague was a delight. Its people seemed relaxed, much more so than in Havana. The 1950s had been a nightmare, people told Allen, and they were just now reaching a point where they were emerging from the oppression. After years of government censorship, Kafka's *The Trial* was being published in his native land again. To Allen, this was one way by which he could measure political change. The city itself was more than he had expected, both in beauty and charm. With its old stone buildings, bridges, snow-covered rooftops, and, as Allen described it, "19th century nostalgia all over the streets," Prague had a medieval feeling. He took in the sights, visiting cathedrals, synagogues, and Kafka's house. He toured the city's historic Jewish section, which once boasted a population of 77,000 people that fell to only several thousand after Hitler's purge.

Allen could not help but be flattered by all the attention he was given in Prague. He received carte-blanche treatment wherever he went, especially at the Viola, where he was revered as a folk hero. Writers from local literary magazines and newspapers lined up for interviews. The youthful population, to Allen's delight, was more sexually liberated than in Cuba—homosexuality was not illegal in Czechoslovakia—and he was never lacking for a partner. The general scene, he reported to Louis, was rather frenetic: "I run around with teenage gangs and have orgies and then rush up to the Writer's Union and give lectures on the glories of U.S. pornography, Henry Miller, etc. All very happy."

From his experiences in Havana, Allen knew better than to come to Czechoslovakia and immediately start speaking about whatever topic struck his fancy. After a few weeks, though, he determined that he could discuss some of the topics that had gotten him in trouble in Cuba, as long as he remained discreet in the way he chose to talk about them. People did not frown upon his discussing LSD and marijuana and poetic consciousness, and they were respectful when he talked about Indian mantras. And, despite warnings from his Czech translator, the homosexual references in his poetry did not solicit official government warnings or rebuttals. This he discovered when he read "Howl" and "Message II," his newest love poem to Peter Orlovsky, at Charles University, the oldest university in Europe, located on the banks of the Moldau River. Five hundred students attended the reading, which was followed by a question-and-answer session that addressed such topics as homosexuality and government brainwashing.

"Message II" was very similar in both style and content to "Message," which Allen had written in Paris in 1958. It had the same sense of tenderness, the same yearning brought on by separation, even a similar sense of detail. In the earlier poem, Ginsberg seemed to despair at his loneliness ("It is too long that

I'm here alone/It is too long that I've sat up in bed/without anyone to touch on the knee"), whereas in the new work, he seemed more resigned to it ("I'm still alone with long black beard and shining eyes/walking down black smokey tramcar streets at night"). Perhaps the acceptance of the latter poem is due to Ginsberg's being resigned to the mercurial nature of his and Peter's relationship, or to his seeing other men while he was in Prague, but there is no denying the deep love expressed in the final lines of the two poems. In "Message," he concludes with "I will be home in 2 months and look in your eyes," while in "Message II," he finishes with "Salute beloved comrade I'll send you my tears from Moscow." The poems rank as two of Ginsberg's most beautiful love poems, even if one concludes with a promise to return, the other with the two moving farther apart.

7

Late in the afternoon of March 18, Allen boarded the red Moscoka-Prague train bound for the homeland of his forebears. It was a warm, sunny day, and from his vantage point in the compartment he shared with several Czech military attachés, he could see green and brown fields, often broken by stands of tall trees. By now, his travel pattern had been long established. He would experience strong feelings about his own transitory existence, which, coupled with the expectations he felt toward his destination, almost invariably led to poetry:

> My Slavic Soul, we are coming home again—
> once more on Red Square by Kremlin wall
>   in the snow to sit and write Prophecy—
> Prince-Comrades of Russia, I have
>   come from America to lay my beard
>   at your beautiful feet!

Allen stepped on Russian soil for the first time when the train stopped briefly at the station in the border town of Chop. "First smell of Russia at Chop was surprisingly the same musty-shit-earth smell as Mexico tropic," he wrote in his journal. Chickens moved about the wet roads in a village scene that seemed to spring from a Chagall painting.

The train continued its eastward journey through the Ukraine, home of Allen's maternal ancestors. "Elanor and Max, thou shouldst be living at this hour!" Allen thought as he scribbled photographic impressions into his journal:

Mud roads. Black fields. Landscape rolling small flat hills between Lvov and Kiev. Horses in distance drawing sleighs thru mud. Isolated houses, figures in black clothes walking up snowy roads thru fields. Women shovelling dirt, in black boots. Police with long 19th century coats and epaulets. Lvov cathedral in the distance from the R.R. station. A country church, bulb-topped and brown shingled. Dark falling over the trees and snow, in mist.

By the time he reached the outskirts of Moscow two days after leaving Czechoslovakia, Allen had many journal pages with such detail.

At the Moscow station, he was greeted by Ylena Romanova, who chaired the Western Literature department at Moscow University. They took a taxi to the Minsk Hotel, where Allen checked in and dropped off his bags, then they were off to the Writer's Union for lunch. At one time Tolstoy's mansion, the Writer's Union was a testament to Soviet elegance—and a great contrast to the peasant countryside Allen had witnessed over the last forty-eight hours. The restaurant featured mahogany balconies and alcoves, and from its high ceiling hung great chandeliers. Ginsberg and Romanova were met by Frieda Lurie, Allen's escort in the Soviet Union, and over a dinner of borscht, smoked salmon, caviar, steak, and vodka, they held a discussion about Soviet etiquette. Allen was not anxious to repeat the events of Cuba, which he explained with some hesitation and uneasiness to the women.

"Let me advise you that we have an experience—a war—and a different life," Frieda Lurie said, "so certain things are best not spoken about, especially to journalists. People don't—won't—understand. We hope you'll come to see our point of view." With regard to Ginsberg's interest in talking about homosexuality, Lurie advised him to be cautious. "We all have a . . . normal . . . love life here," she said diplomatically. "Russians may not appreciate your interests, though possibly you may have some truth or some valuable opinion. Still, your proposal to be silent and watch is best."

Ylena Romanova agreed. Russians, she pointed out, were more private about sex, in both their daily lives and in their literature. "We have a long history of happy love, or of deep private affairs," she said. "We are all people of some experience. But we don't talk about it in public. We find those who talk most are the people least sexually satisfied. There's no reason to write about such things."

Allen, of course, disagreed. Sex was a serious part of the life of the dramatic literary novel, he argued; Henry Miller had proven as much. Frieda Lurie surprised him by saying that she had started but could not finish one of Miller's books because she found it uninteresting. "The Russian people would not have interest in such a thing," she told him, noting that there were so many other books to read that she would not be inclined to read something like *Tropic of Cancer*. Since he hoped to stay in the country for a while, Allen decided not to press the issue any further and held his temper.

After lunch, he set off to explore the Kremlin. It was much more spacious than he had imagined, "as if all the steppes and 'Asiatic vague immensities' were on display in the Central Powerhouse Castle," as he put it. He was impressed by the variety of structures within the Kremlin walls. There were cathedrals and palaces from centuries long gone, architectural contrasts to the often-seen onion-domed buildings from another period. It was as if he had walked through a gate and encountered a vast museum devoted to the buildings of the past four of five centuries. "I felt like a provincial from Pinsk or Magnito-gorsk, seeing the World's Fair Ancient Center," he wrote in his journal.

In the early evening, he attended the circus, which he found too orchestrated and unexpressive for his taste, the performers skillful but seemingly disinter-ested, the audience impressing him as being a collective of pharmacists clapping in rigid unison. After a late dinner of smoked salmon, sturgeon, and milk, he went back to Red Square, armed with his journal for a midnight writing session. Lenin's black and white marble mausoleum, set in the center of the Kremlin wall and watched over by two guards, reminded him of St. Mark's Square in Venice. He judged St. Basil's Cathedral, with its many onion-shaped domes and cones, to be almost as beautiful as the Taj Mahal. Allen found a plank to sit on and concluded his busy day by writing descriptive passages of everything he had seen and heard:

> After midnight,
>   the red brick Kremlin wall, old bells,
>   deep red electric stars atop
>   Ruby gate peaks,
>   the golden clock moves slowly,
> bootsteps echo on the vast black
>   lawn of cobblestone. . . .

8

Allen's second day in Moscow was as eventful as his first. He spent the day touring the Kremlin with a rabbi from the Bronx, a tea merchant from Hong Kong, and their wives, taking extensive notes along the way. Then he returned to the hotel, where he was to meet his mother's cousin Joe Levy.

The meeting turned out to be one of the high points of Allen's visit to the Soviet Union. Joe was seventy-two, and he and Allen had not seen each other since Allen was five. After a rather tentative meeting in the hotel lobby, they sat down for a long talk, Joe giving Allen the history of the Livergant immigration to the United States. Allen, hearing the complete story for the first time, was deeply moved.

Naomi's father, Mendel, and Joe's father, Isser, were brothers. Mendel had made it to the United States without a problem, but Isser, who had a bald spot on his head that immigration officials judged to be the manifestation of a disease, was turned away at Ellis Island. He went to London and through the help of friends secured passage to Canada one year later. For Allen, this was an important revelation, for he had never understood why his mother's family had immigrated to the United States, while his cousin's family had entered North America through Canada. The entire family was eventually reunited in New York and New Jersey. In 1931, a group of Newark relatives had returned to the Soviet Union for a visit, and Joe and his wife, Anne, had decided to stay.

Joe and Anne had no children, and as he sat and listened to the story, Allen had the eerie feeling that he would be the last person to hear the entire history of their family. He had come to the Soviet Union to get a sense of his ancestry, and here he was, recipient of an extensive oral history from perhaps the only person who could tell the tale. Joe invited Allen to his home and they arrived just as Anne Levy was putting dinner on the table.

That evening, they looked tearfully through the family photograph album. There were pictures of Allen as a thin four-year-old wearing shorts, and Eugene as a ten-year-old, squinting painfully through his glasses at the bright New Jersey sky; photos of Louis the schoolteacher, looking dapper in his trimmed mustache, and of a young Naomi wearing tennis clothes; portraits of cousins, aunts, and uncles, many still alive, some living in the Soviet Union. There were photographs of American ancestors Joe and Anne had never met. Although in many respects he was claiming a family history that had eluded him or that he had forgotten over the decades, Allen noted that "the expression, the sad tragic aloneness never changes in half a century. . . . Anne and I were sad, and tears rolled down our cheeks as we came to the end, the last pictures of the unknown newly grown children in America."

They told Allen about their lives in the Soviet Union. It had been difficult. Joe had found a good job working as an electrician for the Moscow subway, but he had lost it when Stalin began his campaign against the Jews. Joe and Anne disagreed on their interpretation of Stalin's treatment of Russian Jews and why it had happened, but Joe made it clear that he still supported the Communist government. The masses had to stay together, Joe said; the infighting and disagreement among members had ruined the party in the United States. "The collective heart is the most important thing about communism," he said, echoing sentiments Allen had heard in his youth. Allen spoke of his travels and offered his opinions. He sang the Hare Krishna mantra, which Anne liked but Joe felt would have no effect in his country. Allen could not help but wonder to himself what these aging relatives really thought of him and his ideas, their lives and beliefs being so different from his own.

9

A longtime devotee of Russian literature, Allen wanted to meet some of the prominent Soviet poets. He was interested not only in trading notes on poetry composition but in hearing of how poetry was written in a country known for its restrictions on free speech. At the time, Joseph Brodsky's poetry was being suppressed and he was due to go on trial for some of his statements against the state. When Allen made inquiries about the case at the Writer's Union, however, Frieda Lurie warned him about asking too many questions or making too big an issue of Brodsky, citing again the differences between the Soviet Union and the United States as a reason for Allen's not understanding the story. She told him his interest would be understood but not his opinions. Allen resented being treated as a foreigner rather than as a poet in a world literary community, but there was little that he could do.

His hope to meet Yevgeny Yevtushenko, Russia's best-known poet, was realized by chance encounter. On March 22, Allen met an interpreter and two members of the Writer's Union for dinner. They talked for a long time and were drinking heavily, and Allen was quite drunk when he got up to leave. On the steps outside the restaurant, Yevtushenko approached Allen and identified himself. As a sign of respect, Allen dropped to his knees and tried to tell the Russian poet how much he admired him, but he was too far gone to engage in any kind of meaningful conversation. Yevtushenko suggested they meet at his home the next evening.

Yevtushenko was not at home when Allen arrived, so Allen and Yevtushenko's wife Genia sat on the front steps and talked until he returned. The
Yevtushenkos lived in an old section of the city that was presently undergoing
renovation. The streets were not yet finished and several old wooden buildings
stood in contrast to the more modern apartment buildings, such as Yevtushenko's. The poet finally arrived, wearing a beautiful fur coat and apologizing
for his tardiness, explaining that he had just come from a dinner with a number
of theater people at a Georgian restaurant. He led Allen into his apartment,
helped him with his coat, and offered him some soup. When Yevtushenko
mentioned their meeting of the night before, Allen was forced to admit that
he remembered very little of their conversation.

"I saw that you were a good man," Yevtushenko said hospitably. "Here, we
hear many bad things about you, that you are a pederast, scandals, but I know
it is not true."

"It's all true," Allen admitted. He then tried to detail the evolution of his
own consciousness, from his Blake visions to the "change." He had only recently
come to accept his own body as the place where he had to live. "As for
homosexuality," he said, "that's my experience and that's the situation I'm in,
so the scandal comes from my talking openly about it."

"I know nothing of such matters," Yevtushenko replied, clearly uncomfortable with the discussion. Allen changed subjects and began to tell Yevtushenko
about his experiences with different drugs. This did not interest the Russian
poet, either. "Why are you interested in such matters?" he asked. Allen replied
that drugs were an integral part of religious rites all over the world. *Ganja* was
used in Shivaite ceremonies in India, *ayahuasca* in South America. Peyote was
a part of rituals in Mexico and North America and LSD was being experimented
with in the United States. Yevtushenko seemed bored by the discussion. Allen
had just launched into a monologue about how the unconscious felt when the
Russian poet stopped him.

"Please, Allen," he said, "I like you. I like you as a poet, but these are your
personal problems. Please don't speak to me about them. They are not interesting to me. I respect you as a great man and a great poet, but these two subjects—
homosexuality and narcotics—are not known to me and I feel they are juvenile
preoccupations. They have no importance here in Russia to us. It only disturbs
my impression of you. Please don't talk to me about these two matters."

"I feel rejected," Allen said when the interpreter had finished translating
Yevtushenko's words. He had expected more from a fellow poet and a man
known for his literary activism.

"I have problems more important than these," Yevtushenko explained.

"Okay," Allen said, "tell me all your problems and all the problems of
Russia."

Yevtushenko began with an anecdote about John Steinbeck's visit to the
country. The Nobel laureate had challenged his audience of Russian youths to
speak out, to tell him of the problems there. He had spoken for an hour about
the problems in the United States and about his disagreement with certain
policies. Then he had asked his audience to show their "wolves teeth" by telling
him what they thought was bad about their country. No one said a word.

"Not that they were lying or stupid," Yevtushenko said, "but this was not the place. It was a provocation. Many people there were not our friends or personal familiars. They were waiting for us to say something." Steinbeck, Yevtushenko continued, finally addressed a beautiful young poet in the audience. Why did she look so forlorn? he asked. Because, she replied, she had lost her driver's license yesterday.

In his anecdote, Yevtushenko was trying to illustrate a fact that seemed to elude people from the Western world. They took many freedoms and conveniences in their daily lives for granted to such an extent that they felt free to attack their leaders on an ideological plane; they had free speech and freedom of movement, but they wanted more. In the Soviet Union, daily life could be a struggle; the simplest conveniences could be withdrawn in a moment. Under Stalin's rule, 20 million people had been arrested and as many as 15 million may have died in prison or been executed. Every family in Russia knew someone who had fallen under Stalin. Yevtushenko's grandparents had disappeared. It had stopped under Khrushchev, but change was slow in coming. It could not happen overnight.

"We believe in Russia and our system," said Yevtushenko. "What would it mean to be anti-communist? To go back to monarchy or capitalism? Nobody—very few people—want that in this country. So we have to work our problems out. It's slow, it's terribly slow, but we think we'll win. You can't expect to get to the bottom of our situation on a visit here. No American could."

He went on to tell Allen about censorship in the Soviet Union. Public readings had been halted, perhaps temporarily, maybe permanently; he did not know. To publish so much as a single poem, a person had to submit the work to a censor. One of his long poems had been in proof for a year, unpublished, awaiting government-approved changes. He said he had made 450 changes thus far because so many passages had been questioned, but it would eventually be published in a magazine with a circulation of over a million. "So, you see, it is worth it. You have to pay for it, but it is worth it all."

"Do you have many unpublishable poems?" Allen wondered.

"Oh, yes." Yevtushenko sighed and then laughed.

"Your best?"

"Probably."

He recited a recently published poem for Allen. He was sorry that there would be no readings for him to attend. He remembered reading in front of fourteen thousand Russians in Moscow, and even though his wife accused him of being a narcissist, he enjoyed reading his work to other people. He played a recording of a poem he had once read in Paris. As he listened, his lips moved silently with the voice on the record; his face softened. "This is a part of my early days—another Yevtushenko," he said, deeply moved. He stood up and hugged and kissed Allen.

They concluded their evening in a Georgian restaurant. By this time, Yevtushenko's guard was up again. They talked more about poetry composition, but Yevtushenko could not accept Kerouac's theories about spontaneous composition. Allen asked about Brodsky, but Yevtushenko was unwilling to talk about him. Like Frieda Lurie, he suggested that Allen avoid mentioning him in public.

"If you talk, it'll only make things worse," he said. "It would be like my coming to the United States and giving speeches about Negroes in Alabama."

"That would be the best thing you could do," Allen quipped, and Yevtushenko laughed and shook his head.

Allen was troubled by their conversation. The evening had gone well and he was grateful for the chance to talk to Yevtushenko, but from what he had heard, he was again reminded of the tremendous gulf between the American and Russian cultures. He woke the next morning depressed, wondering whether he and Yevtushenko had communicated at all.

10

Allen's week in Moscow passed faster than he would have liked. Fortunately, Ylena Romanova was able to arrange through the Writer's Union another all-expenses-paid week. Allen visited the Pushkin Museum, where he was awed by paintings by Cézanne, Gauguin, Picasso, Goya, Matisse, and Rembrandt. He toured the Mayakovski Museum, where he saw the poet's suicide bed and grew frustrated by his guide's passive acceptance of Mayakovski's death.

He used some of his money for a three-day trip to Leningrad. He made the rounds, checking out the historical sites he had heard about since his youth. He visited the huge cemetery where eighty thousand Russians who starved during the war blockade were buried. He attended the ballet. For the better part of two days, he toured the Hermitage, writing in his journal about the paintings he saw there. By now, after a seemingly endless number of tours in art museums in cities throughout the world, Allen was starting to feel like "an old veteran" of the famous art gallery circuit, but he was always amazed by what he discovered in each museum. At the Hermitage, there were entire rooms given over to Cézanne and Gauguin alone, and in one room hung Rembrandt's *The Return of the Prodigal Son*, which so impressed Allen that he paused before the painting for a long time, moving closer and closer until his nose was virtually pressed against the glass in his effort to see Rembrandt's detail work.

Allen returned to Moscow and checked into the Hotel Bucharest, an elegant establishment that offered him a large room with a view of St. Basil's Cathedral and the Kremlin clock tower. With his visa about to expire and little hope of its being renewed, he filled his daily schedule with as many activities as he could manage. He attended the Moscow Symphony, where he heard Tchaikovsky's First Symphony performed; he spent an evening at the Moscow Ballet. At the Writer's Union, he met with twenty professors, translators, and students, reading them "Sunflower Sutra," "Transcription of Organ Music," and a selection from "Kaddish." Now that his time was running out, he grew bolder, less concerned about offending Russian officials and being expelled from the country. At a meeting for an amateur drama group at the university, he read "Magic Psalm" and "The Reply" and then talked and answered questions for several hours about Kerouac and spontaneous composition, avant-garde movies, and drugs and consciousness alteration. Despite all he had heard to the contrary, there seemed to be a large number of Russians eager to discuss these topics.

Ginsberg had one more significant meeting before he left Moscow. For some time, he had been trying to contact Andrei Voznesensky, a young Russian poet whose work he admired. Voznesensky had been away throughout Allen's stay, but they were finally able to get together on one of Allen's last days in the country. Voznesensky spoke English and their meeting at the poet's house, without the usual presence of a translator or guide, was informal. They talked for a long time about poetry and determined they had much in common in their compositional style, especially in the way they thought in rhythms. At last, Allen had found someone in the Soviet Union who appreciated the method of spontaneous composition, even if Voznesensky did not share his enthusiasm for writing under the influence of drugs. Allen read him selections from "Howl," and Voznesensky said that he liked the poem's rhythmic quality, although he did not understand all the words.

It was time to leave. Allen wanted to be back in Czechoslovakia in time for the country's May Day celebration, but with several weeks on his hands before then, he decided to take a short side trip to Poland. He could stay in Warsaw as a guest of the Writer's Union, and since he was owed a modest sum from the Polish translation of "Howl," he would have enough money to get by. He caught a train for Warsaw on April 7.

In the two decades since the end of the war, Warsaw had been slowly rebuilding. To Allen's dismay, the Warsaw ghetto was being completely re-worked into a complex of modern apartment buildings, and other than the large commemorative monument erected in the city after the war, there was no sign of the historical section of Warsaw where brave Jews had confronted the forces of Nazism; it was as if a significant piece of history had been wiped out and replaced by an entirely different universe. Allen wept at the sight. Later, in a Warsaw café, he began a poem:

> O Polish spectres what've you suffered since Chopin wept into
>   his romantic piano
> old buildings rubbed down, gaiety of all night parties under the
>   air bombs
> first screams of the vanishing ghetto—Workmen step thru
>   prewar pink-blue bedroom walls demolishing sunny ruins—

Allen took a train to Krakow, the old Polish city near the Czech border, where he spent a week walking about the city's main square, hanging out in cafés, meeting with poets, and unwinding from his last six weeks' travels. He was growing weary from all his wandering about, but he still wondered whether he should try to visit Berlin before returning to the United States. Seeing the divided city seemed significant, given his worldview and what he had seen of the free and Iron Country countries during his recent travels. As it turned out, he would have little say in the matter. His travel plans would be made for him.

11

He concluded his trip to Poland by driving to Auschwitz and touring the remains of the infamous concentration camp. He spent a final day in Wraclow, where he caught a midnight train to Prague.

Majales, the traditional Czechoslovakian festival honoring May Day, dated back to medieval times. As part of the festivities, students voted for a May king and held a beauty pageant to select the queen. They were then ceremoniously paraded through the streets of Prague in a celebration that ended with a symbolic wedding.

The Communists had abolished the festival when they assumed power after World War II. In recent years, instead of celebrating Majales, Czech youths had been rioting against police in a nearby park. This year, 1965, would be different: For the first time in two decades, the Majales festival would be permitted. The different schools at the university would elect a candidate for king and queen and each school would have its own procession through the streets, culminating in a general election held at the Park of Culture and Rest.

Allen Ginsberg became "Kral Majales," the King of May, partly by default, partly as a gesture of respect, and partly as an act of defiance. The university's technical school had originally selected poet Josef Skvorecky as its King of May, but Skvorecky was ill and could not participate. When he learned that Ginsberg had returned to Prague, Skvorecky called him and asked whether he would like the honor. Allen was hesitant. "Is it all right?" he asked Skvorecky. "What does it mean?" The last thing Allen wanted at that point was to become involved in a political incident. He was assured that it was all in good humor, that politics was no part of it. He would ride on the back of a truck to the fairground where the election would be held. It would be humorous—that an American would be Prague's May king—and Allen was informed that he stood a good chance of winning. He finally agreed.

Unbeknownst to Allen, recent translations and readings of his poetry, with their references to drugs and homosexuality, had caused some concern among Czech officials, who, like officials in Cuba, worried about the American poet's influence over their country's young people. His rebellious nature had also raised some questions. Still, as a guest of the country and the Writer's Union, he presented a diplomatic dilemma. Even if his presence was considered to be a bad influence on the youths of Prague, there was little the officials could do, as long as he complied with Czech laws. Homosexuality was not illegal and up to this point Allen had been a model visitor.

On the morning of May 1, Allen was awakened at 7:30 and escorted by two friends to the May Day parade. They walked in the throngs of people along the parade route, past the bandstand seating President Novotny and his entourage. Afterward, they retired to an outdoor café for hot dogs and lemonade. Then Allen headed back to his hotel room, where he hoped to rest before the Kral Majales festivities. At one o'clock, there was a knock on the door and Allen was greeted by a large group of students, some dressed formally in suits and bowlers, others in attire from the 1890s, the men wearing top hats and waist-coats and carrying canes, the women in hoopskirts and carrying parasols. A few were dressed as court jesters. After a ceremonial trumpet flourish, the master of ceremonies approached Allen and made his official proclamation: "Mr. Ginsberg, we have the honor to beg your presence in procession to the crowning of King of May, and to accept our support for your candidacy of Kral Majales, and we humbly offer you crown and throne." Five beautiful young women approached Allen, bearing a cardboard crown that had been painted gold.

Before he was seated on his throne—a chair draped in thick crimson cloth—Allen grabbed his coat, finger cymbals, and Indian statue of Ganesh.

Allen was not prepared for the scene that followed. He was driven on the back of a flatbed truck to the technical school at the university. He sipped beer and chanted mantras while students crowded around the truck, singing songs and marching in the parade. At the polytechnic, there was a crowd of several thousand jubilant students waiting. Allen was transferred to a larger truck, this one equipped with a loudspeaker, a sign reading GINSBERGUM KRAL MAJALES, cases of beer, and, amazingly, a small Dixieland band. The crowd called out for a speech. Allen stood and offered two lines: "I'll be the first kind king and bow down before my subjects. I'll be the first naked king."

This said, the procession began. It worked its way along the streets of Prague, weaving in and out of traffic, picking up more people as it went along. Allen played his finger cymbals and sang mantras—"Hare Om Namo Shiva" and "Om Sri Maitreya." He described the parade in a letter to Peter: "Nobody expected . . . what happened . . . everybody who could walk in Prague came out and lined the streets—almost bigger than the regular May Day Parade—and we rolled around the old town streets and under Kafka's house, gathering thousands and thousands more. I kept getting up and making drunken speeches, dedicating my crown to Kafka, and stopped this huge parade under the house where he wrote The Trial—and made a big announcement for that and sang Mantra Hare Om Namo Shiva there—Meanwhile the streets were getting lined with people, it was a huge happy crowd come out for a non-political good time party for the first time in 20 years—Everybody good mood and all the police off the streets."

To reach the park, they had to cross a bridge over the river. Allen looked around and saw masses of people sitting on the riverbanks and crowds sitting on rooftops. He waved to everyone "like a big idiot politician," as he later wrote, amazed like everyone else by the enormous turnout in the Park of Culture and Rest—a hundred thousand in all. Several rock 'n' roll bands played in different sections of the park and there was dancing everywhere.

Allen was led to a huge hall, where he and four other candidates were hoisted onto a platform, signifying the official beginning of the election. The other candidates, dressed as kings or clowns, gave short speeches. Allen, dressed in an old work shirt and blue jeans, sang the "Om Sri Maitreya" and sat down without saying anything else. The votes were cast and Allen was elected Kral Majales by a landslide.

The revelry continued long into the night. At midnight, the students held the election for queen. Allen had been looking forward to this moment, since he had every intention of sleeping with his "wife," but it was not to be. Infuriated by an American's being elected Kral Majales, the party secretary for cultural affairs, in attendance in the park, ordered him deposed. A formal announcement was made and Allen's short reign came to an end.

12

His problems, however, were only beginning. For the next few days, Allen had the feeling that he was being watched—which, in fact, he was. Despite his fears, he made no effort to curtail his activities or maintain a low profile. He met with reporters, sang the Hare Krishna mantra for a local filmmaker, and wined, dined, and slept with students; he spoke out on whatever topics he chose. Allen determined that the Czechs, like the students he had met in Moscow, were eager to discuss social reform. "The one thing that I found particularly significant," Allen later recalled, "was that the young people seemed particularly eager to discuss academic freedom. I did not have to coax them, or draw them into it, but once I started talking about it, they quickly joined the conversation and made what I considered many significant contributions to the philosophies of this pursuit of reform."

On May 3, upon returning to his hotel after an afternoon out, Allen discovered one of his notebooks was missing. Fortunately, it was the journal he had begun on his return to Prague and so not too much had been lost. Still, there were entries describing his sexual activities, as well as the continuation of his running commentary about Czech society and government. The only poem of historical significance in the journal was a poem he had written while he was seated on his May Day throne.

That evening, at the Viola café, two men in business suits approached him and bought him drinks until he became very drunk. Allen was singing a mantra as he left at midnight. The police happened by at that moment; since he did not have his passport or other suitable identification with him, they took him to the station, where he was questioned and released. Although it was possible that he had been picked up for a legitimate reason, Allen had his doubts. After the events of May Day, he was a highly visible figure and it seemed unlikely that in a single day's time both a journal would disappear and he would be taken in for questioning because he failed to have proper identification papers. Allen suspected official involvement in both affairs.

Two nights later as he and a young couple were leaving the Viola and walking down the street, a man rushed at Allen, hesitated for a moment, and suddenly began shouting, "Bouzerant! Bouzerant!" ("Fairy! Fairy!") He punched Allen in the face, knocking him down. Allen tried to flee, but his attacker chased him, caught up with him, and knocked him to the pavement again. Police, with clubs drawn, arrived almost instantly. Fearful that they were going to strike him, Allen hummed "Om" in an effort to calm himself. The police took Allen, his assailant, and the young couple to the station for questioning, the man who attacked Allen insisting to the police that Allen had exposed himself and that the three had attacked him. When Allen became angry and demanded to see an attorney or an official from the American embassy, everyone, including the assailant, was released. "I couldn't figure it out, except I think he was a police agent—'provocateur,' as they say," Allen recalled.

The next day, he made hasty plans to leave the country. The previous evening's attack, along with the fact that he was now constantly followed by agents who made no attempt to disguise or hide themselves, convinced him that he was in serious trouble. Allen accomplished his last scheduled bit of business, a radio interview, and left the station with friends. They were sitting in a restaurant near the outskirts of town when he was approached by plainclothes police. "We found your notebook," they told him. "Come with us a half an hour and you'll get it back." Allen went with them to the police station.

He identified the missing journal. As soon as he had signed for it, they took it back, saying, "We must inform you that we are turning your notebook over to the public prosecutor for closer examination, because rapid survey of its contents indicates illegal writings." Allen was then released.

The following morning, he was again approached by plainclothesmen, this time while he was eating breakfast at a downtown café. They ordered him to go with them and when Allen asked whether he could make a phone call, they told him that he could—at the police station. When he arrived at the station, he was denied his telephone call. Instead, he was ushered to a room and seated at a table with the head of immigration and four other bureaucrats. "Due to many complaints about your presence in Prague from parents and scientists and educators who disapprove of your sexual theories, we are shortening your visa and you will leave Czechoslovakia today," they told him. Allen replied that he already had a ticket to London for the next day and that it might be more diplomatic and less embarrassing if they simply let him leave of his own accord. The officials were adamant about his departing that day, however. He was driven back to his hotel room and held incommunicado, watched over by a detective until the next scheduled flight from Prague to London. Although the officials promised to return Allen's journal, it never materialized—an effective form of blackmail, Ginsberg reasoned, because if he dared to complain in public about his treatment by the authorities, Czech officials would be able to harass or arrest the people named in his journal. He never saw it again.

13

Fortunately, none of Allen's other possessions—including his early Czechoslovakia, Moscow, and Poland journals—were confiscated. On his flight from Prague to London, he took out a new journal and began a poem recounting his experiences in Prague. It began with an angry indictment of the Communists ("have nothing to offer but fat cheeks and eyeglasses and policemen that tell lies") and capitalists ("proffer napalm to Vietnam and money in green suitcases to the Naked in Dominican Republic") alike. He wrote of the three times he had been taken to the police station in Prague and of his expulsion from Cuba. Then, assuming his prophetic, oratorical voice, he wrote:

> And I am the King of May, which is power of
>   sexual youth,
> and I am the King of May, which is industry
>   in eloquence and action in amour
> and I am the King of May, which is long hair,
>   Adam and the Beard of my own body
> and I am the King of May, which is Kral Majales
>   in the Czechoslovakian tongue,
> and I am the King of May, which is old Human
>   poesy, and 100,000 people chose my name. . . .

Like "Sunflower Sutra," "Kral Majales" stands as one of Ginsberg's best spontaneous poems. With the exception of minor adjustments ("policemen who tell lies" being altered to "lying policemen," "Human poesy" to "Human poetry," etc.) and a few deletions, the poem was eventually published as written. The superimposition of the details of his oppression and the freedom of the human spirit, given impact by Ginsberg's use of Whitmanesque long lines and tone, is as effective as any Ginsberg poem since his Paris poems. "Kral Majales" is simply stated yet eloquently argued. In its repetition, the phrase "I am the King of May" has the sound of a mantra that is surprisingly ironic.

And what of Ginsberg's expulsion from Czechoslovakia?

The incident was widely reported and commented on for years and was not without immediate repercussions. Predictably, the Czech government blamed Ginsberg for bringing his expulsion upon himself, even if he did not break any Czech laws while he was in the country. (He refrained from using drugs while in Czechoslovakia.) Upon expelling him from the country, a statement was issued by Czech officials:

> On May 7th, 1965, Irwin Allen Ginsberg, American poet, born on June 3, 1926, in New Jersey in the U.S.A., was summoned before the passport and visa section of the local administrative branch of the Ministry of the Interior in Prague where he was told that his presence was no longer considered desirable and that he was required to leave Czechoslovakia immediately. Allen Ginsberg accepted this pronouncement without protest, and on May 7th at 17.30 hours flew from Prague Airport to London.

The Czech government felt justified in expelling him on grounds of what it considered to be his dubious moral character and officials went out of their way to see the citizens of the country—particularly the youths—were well informed on the official position for throwing the poet out. In a radio address, President Novotny condemned Ginsberg as a bad influence who was deliberately trying to corrupt the country's youth. *Mlanda fronta* (*Youth Front*), the official Czech newspaper for youths, went to great lengths to portray Ginsberg as a pervert and drug addict, publishing unauthorized excerpts of the confiscated journal as proof. Letters supposedly written by irate parents were prominently displayed in the Czech papers. It didn't seem to matter that the "evidence" against Ginsberg was based on hearsay information or on entries in a diary obtained by questionable means at best, nor was there great attention or concern paid to the factual content of the reports. The campaign against Ginsberg was typical of all propaganda: Truth is immaterial.

Ginsberg was strong enough to withstand the attacks, whether they took the form of government pronouncements or media sneering. (One of the more ridiculous headlines came from a paper in his own country, when the *New York Herald Tribune*, probably imagining itself to be quite clever, offered a short explanation of Ginsberg's expulsion under the headline LIKE SPLIT, DIG?) What was harmful was the ammunition that Ginsberg gave Stalinists in Czechoslovakia, who were seeking ways to denigrate the more liberal political atmosphere of recent years. Igor Hajek, who had written a favorable essay about Ginsberg for the literary magazine *Literarni novini*, came under attack, as did the Writer's Union that sponsored Ginsberg. The Czech literary scene survived the right-wing offensive, but the Ginsberg incident was disruptive enough to make editors cautious about offending government officials for some time to come. It also spelled an ending, at least for the time being, of the Majales festival.

For his part, however, Ginsberg was hardly an innocent martyr in these affairs, no matter how hard he tried to convince the world of it. Indeed, he was frightened and concerned about the direction of postwar international politics, and his outspoken, prophetic voice, if one can judge by his public statements and private journal entries, was the product of genuine humanistic concern rather than a need for ego gratification. He felt compelled to use whatever power he possessed to alter the course of history as it was being currently written, no matter how modest the results. Still, as admirable as this vision may have been, Ginsberg could be accused—and was—of being unreasonable or naïve in expecting that he would be able to enter a country with a totalitarian government, speak his mind and challenge the system, and then spirit away uncontested. If anything, he had too much faith the human spirit could escape the cages built by those leaders who would confine it. This was certainly the case in Cuba. In Czechoslovakia and the Soviet Union, he had been much more cautious, yet he had still been more provocative than the citizens of those countries would have ever dared to be. Just because he was a guest of these countries did not mean that he was immune from their laws or customs. Eugene Brooks may have offered a valid perspective when he wrote, shortly after his brother's Czech expulsion, "Aren't you sacrificing political and moral leverage by not confining yourself to advocating your ideas, rather than by practicing them and no doubt violating all the penal laws?"

Not surprisingly, Ginsberg rejected the notion that he had acted out of place. Rather, he said he had been acting in the interests of global brotherhood, advocating change by example. Although his demeanor was generally gentle and always nonviolent, Ginsberg preferred to take a confrontational approach to change. He considered himself an activist and on occasion expressed dissatisfaction with the passive resistance practiced by a figure such as Martin Luther King. "Pacifism is a trap because 'powerstructure' status quo is violent," he wrote in 1966. "Pacifism is negative defense rather than active manifestation of political vision."

In the case of his actions in Cuba and Czechoslovakia, Ginsberg was taking an activist position simply by speaking out. In a 1969 letter to Gregory Corso, he presented his interpretation of his expulsion from Czechoslovakia: "What had happened to me was I behaved well in public, and by freak chance got elected May King, and that was the beginning of Democratization because it was a giant friendly public be-in. . . . The Commissioner of Ideology objected, had me followed, stole my notebook and bounced me secretly and even suppressed news of my being May King and expulsion for several weeks. 'Complaints' by parents were manipulated and phoney like Kafka. . . . It just looked from Prague official version (and inept Western reports) that I might have misbehaved or acted crass, but that (as Bill B points out) is exactly the police bureaucracy brainwash tactic—feeling exactly like Time-Mag-type putdowns—to make people feel that, because you're vaguely shameful, they have the right to SMASH YOUR TEETH OUT."

Regardless of how the events in Cuba and Czechoslovakia are interpreted, the expulsions encouraged—rather than discouraged or silenced—him to continue to challenge authorities. If there is such a thing as a turning point in Ginsberg's shift from literary to public prophet, it occurred when the King of May was exiled to the inevitable kingdom of his own making.

14

If Allen needed somewhere to recover after the events of Czechoslovakia, England was not a bad place to be. For the past two years, the homeland of Shakespeare and Blake had been the center of a maelstrom of entertainment and social activities, due mostly to the efforts of a rock 'n' roll foursome that exerted unfathomable influence not only upon its own country but on the world. The Beatles had become the first global rock band. Their music, with its multicultural roots, had galvanized the interests of the baby-boom generation in the United States, who suddenly could not get enough of anything British.

Allen, of course, was interested in any phenomenon capable of capturing such widespread appeal. He had seen it once before, with Elvis Presley, and in Bob Dylan he had seen the potential for serious poetry being embraced by a mass audience. In some ways, Dylan and the Beatles were accomplishing what Allen himself dreamed of accomplishing.

As fate had it, Dylan happened to be performing in London at the prestigious Royal Albert Hall for two nights, beginning the evening after Allen's arrival in the city. As soon as he arrived in London, Allen looked him up and was invited to Dylan's hotel suite. By this time, Dylan had fully realized the enigmatic persona, part myth and part reality, that would be connected to him for the rest of his life. In many respects, he was the flip side of the Beatles. Dylan was reclusive, where the Beatles were accessible. Dylan's music was darkly intellectual, where the Beatles were pop. Dylan moved about the edges of society and challenged it, where the Beatles were in the process of helping to re-create aspects of society—or so it seemed. Even their respective movies about public life bespoke their differences. The Beatles starred in *A Hard Day's Night*; Dylan was in the process of making *Don't Look Back*.

Dylan invited Allen to his Albert Hall concerts. After the first one, Allen returned with the Dylan entourage for a party thrown by Albert Grossman, Dylan's manager, at the hotel. Dylan did not attend; instead, he received the Beatles in his own private suite. The meeting went poorly and after a while, Dylan sent for Ginsberg. When Allen arrived, he found the Beatles, their wives and girlfriends, and their road managers sitting silently in the room with Dylan. A year before, a similar meeting between Dylan and the Beatles had been successful, but this time the atmosphere was tense. Perhaps there was a pervasive feeling of professional jealousy or even a clash of egos between the two factions, but whatever the reasons, the room was totally silent.

Allen walked in and sat down on the armrest of Dylan's chair, eliciting a scornful response from John Lennon. "Why don't you sit a little closer?" he said sarcastically. Not about to be defeated by the remark, Allen fell forward into Lennon's lap. "Have you ever read William Blake?" he asked a startled Lennon. His antics relieved some of the tension, although neither Dylan nor the Beatles let down their guards that evening.

In the weeks that followed, Allen reacquainted himself with London and visited other cities in England. The spring weather was wonderful. "Travelling around countryside," he wrote Louis, "England very beautiful, May sunshine." Allen spent a weekend in Newcastle, where he gave a reading and had occasion to meet aging poet Basil Bunting. He then moved on to the port city of Liverpool, hometown of the Beatles and one of Allen's favorite stops on his trip. "Liverpool," he told British interviewer Edward Lucie-Smith, "is at the present moment the center of the consciousness of the human universe. They're resurrecting the human form divine there—and those beautiful youths with long, golden archangelic hair." Allen gave a reading in the city, but otherwise he was on a holiday, walking about Liverpool by day and spending his evenings in the city's many rock 'n' roll clubs.

He was back in London in time for his thirty-ninth birthday, much of which he spent with writers for *The New York Times* and London *Times* and with George Dowden, a scholar who would eventually compile Ginsberg's first bibliography for City Lights. The demands on his time were enormous, especially now that the details of his Czech expulsion were beginning to make the rounds in the international newspapers. The British liked their literature and their gossip, and Allen provided them with both.

Allen was delighted by the arrival of some of his friends in London. Lawrence Ferlinghetti turned up, as did filmmaker and sometime Ginsberg girlfriend Barbara Rubin; Andrei Voznesensky, who had seen Allen briefly in Warsaw and who was on a tour of his own, was the next to arrive. Allen had hoped to conclude his six months outside the United States with a brief jaunt to Paris, where he planned to visit Gregory Corso for a week, but now that he had a circle of poets gathered about him, he started to think in terms of staging a large poetry reading in England. London, like San Francisco a decade earlier, seemed to be primed for a poetry breakthrough. This time, however, the anticipated breakthrough reading would have an international flavor, with participating poets from the United States, Great Britain, Russia, Finland, Scotland, and Austria.

Allen had just the poem for the occasion, a new work that called for universal love and tenderness. Entitled "Who Be Kind To," the poem was a Ginsbergian sermon that opened with a call for self-love and acceptance ("Be kind to your self, it is the only one and perishable/of many on the planet . . ."), which could then be extended to all creatures of the world:

> Be kind to your neighbor who weeps solid tears on the
>   television sofa—
> He has no other home, and hears nothing but the hard
>   voice of telephones—
> Click, buzz, switch channel and the inspired melodrama
>   disappears
> and he's left alone for the night, he disappears in bed. . . .

Anger, loneliness, despair, hatred, aggression, distrust—all, Allen felt, sprang from the lack of self-love and the inability to love others as one loved oneself. It was a message that had been passed down through the ages but had never been taken to heart universally. If "The Change" had spelled an ending to the visionary quest that had begun for Allen in Harlem in 1948, "Who Be Kind To" was a sort of postscript, a shift from the personal to the universal, as if he could not totally accept what he had learned on the Kyoto-Tokyo Express if he could not see it extended to the world:

> Tonite let's all make love in London as if it were 2001
>   the years of thrilling god—
> and be kind to the poor soul that cries in a crack in
>   the pavement because he has no body—
> our prayers to the ghosts and demons, the lackloves in
>   the UN and frightened congresses, who make sadistic
>   noises on the radio—
> Statue destroyers and tank captains, unhappy murderers
>   in Meking and Congo—
> That a new kind of man has come to his bliss to end a
>   cold war he has borne against his own kind flesh
>   since the days of the snake.

"Who Be Kind To," written in one sitting between two and four in the morning on June 8, was consciously designed for the International Poetry Reading three days later. Allen had not been speaking hyperbolically when he called Liverpool the center of consciousness in the human universe; he held the strong belief that the Beatles, as much as any political leaders of the time, had found a way to speak to all nations and cultures. As long as he was in England—the focus of world attention and a city in the process of undergoing a huge youth movement itself—Allen wished to contribute his own treatise to what he hoped would be the beginning of a serious turn in history.

The International Poetry Reading, held on June 11 at the Royal Albert Hall, was a mixed success but hardly the breakthrough the Six Gallery reading had been in 1955. Nineteen poets read from their works. Under the best circumstances, that number of poets would have been too large to sustain the kind of attention needed at a poetry reading, and at the Albert Hall reading, the circumstances were far from optimum. Too many of the poets offered weak selections, which, in turn, detracted from the stronger works read by other poets. In addition, Pablo Neruda, the Chilean poet who was expected to be one of the headliners, had other commitments and could not attend, while Andrei Voznesensky, although in attendance, turned his poetry over to Allen to read rather than performing it himself. However, the reading, attended by seven thousand people, including Indira Gandhi, was not without its high points. Ernst Jandl read sound poems that received enthusiastic response. The disembodied voice of William Burroughs, broadcast over the hall's sound system, added an eerie shading to the event. Harry Fainlight read psychedelic poetry, while Lawrence Ferlinghetti offered a political manifesto, "To Fuck Is to Love Again," that was in keeping with the evening's spirit of international brotherhood. Gregory Corso, in from Paris, read "Mutation of the Spirit," a provocative new work. Allen, the evening's final reader, presented spirited readings of "Who Be Kind To" and "The Change" before leading the audience in a session of mantra singing.

Despite the uneven quality of the works and poor performances by some of the poets, Allen was happy with the overall effect of the event, which he described as "a 'happening' . . . a manifestation of some kind of faith in poetry and the human voice." With only a few exceptions, the London press, using such headlines as MAN, JUST DIG THESE CRAZY COUPLETS and POETS, BUT YOU WOULDN'T KNOW IT, held a different opinion of the reading, many reporters objecting to the four-letter words used in some of the poems. Ironically, a streamlined version of the reading, featuring Ginsberg, Corso, Ferlinghetti, and Voznesensky (who read his own poetry this time), fared much better a few days later at a smaller and less hyped reading at the Architectural Institute.

As planned, Allen spent a final week in Paris before returning to the United States. Exhausted from his travels, he spent much of his time in cafés, writing descriptive doodles of passersby. After weeks of nonstop activity and celebrity limelight, he was on his own again, feeling lonely, his ego a bit bruised because he was not as recognized on the avenues of Paris as he had been in England:

> I'm tired, and the sun warms the page, and the pen's
>   blue as my heart
> and was alone, and unrecognized in my garish black hair
>   circling the streets looking redsweatered
>   boulevardiers in the eye,
> and casting my eye down for shame—Who am I? looked in
>   a big cafe mirror. . . .

19
Wichita Vortex Sutra

I search for the language
that is also yours—
almost all our language has been taxed by war. . . .

1

When Allen arrived in New York on June 29, 1965, he probably wished he was as unrecognizable as he had been in Paris. At the airport, he was pulled aside by customs officials and strip-searched, the agents emptying his pockets and combing through the lint and tobacco granules they found. While he waited, Allen stole a peek at some documents on a table, which noted that his "files" had been reactivated and Peter Orlovsky's were still active. "These persons are reported to be engaged in smuggling narcotics," one of the documents read.

For Allen, this was the first indication of the kind of harassment that lay ahead. FBI director J. Edgar Hoover, engineer of what would later prove to be an incredibly intricate civilian spy network, had already assembled an extensive file on Ginsberg and was seeing that certain incriminating documents were landing in the possession of such organizations as the Federal Bureau of Narcotics and the Secret Service. In an April 26, 1965, document signed by Hoover, Ginsberg was portrayed as being potentially dangerous—certainly disruptive and possibly violent—because of his antiestablishment statements; he was believed to be emotionally unstable and irrational, and Hoover considered him a security risk, especially in the light of his recent journey to Cuba. The New York Bureau of Narcotics, no doubt inspired by Ginsberg's statements about legalizing marijuana and his open admittance of drug use, decided that he was a drug dealer and would launch its own campaign of harassment in months to come.

Allen was in New York less than two weeks—just long enough to drop off his gear, visit with his family, and prepare for another cross-country jaunt. In early July, he and Peter were off to California, Allen to participate in the Berkeley Poetry Conference, which, like the Vancouver conference in 1963, brought together poets from Black Mountain (Charles Olson, Robert Creeley), the Bay Area (Robert Duncan, Jack Spicer), the East Coast (LeRoi Jones, John Wieners, Ginsberg), and elsewhere. Allen was reunited with Gary Snyder, who was back from Japan, and Neal Cassady. In the aftermath of the Berkeley Free Speech protests, the Bay Area was again a center for radical politics, poetry readings and art shows, and bohemian lifestyle, and Allen wasted no time familiarizing himself with what had been going on during his absence.

There was good news from other fronts. In England, Peter Whitehead was editing a film of the Albert Hall reading, and "Angkor Wat," Allen's long poem about his visit to the ruins in Cambodia, was being prepared for publication. Best of all, he had been awarded a Guggenheim Foundation grant, which gave him the funds to finance a new poetry project—a 1960s poetry version of *On the Road*. Allen would travel cross-country and rediscover America on his own, describing what he saw in a series of related poems. With the Guggenheim money, he purchased a Volkswagen camper, which he stocked with a bed, desk, and refrigerator.

After the poetry conference, Allen and Gary journeyed up the coast for a month of camping, backpacking, and hiking in Oregon and Washington. Allen had recently read *Desolation Angels*, Jack Kerouac's most recently published novel, a book largely devoted to the time he had spent as a fire lookout in the Pacific Northwest wilderness, and Ginsberg was eager to see some of this wilderness himself. He got what he bargained for. Snyder, an expert woodsman and climber, took him on expeditions in Crater Lake National Park and Mount Ranier National Park and Glacier Peak, where they camped in the open air, feasted on wild berries, climbed and hiked until they were exhausted, and marveled at some of the most spectacular sights that nature had to offer. There were side trips to Portland, where Allen saw the Beatles perform at the Portland Coliseum, and Seattle, where he was disappointed to find the old Wobbly Hall closed down. Allen and Gary spent a great deal of time talking about Buddhism and reading each other passages from *100,000 Songs of Milarepa*, and that, along with the usual feelings of transitory existence that Allen experienced whenever he traveled, put him in another of his reflective moods. Once again, he questioned his role and value as a poet:

> I have nothing to say to anyone
> I have written Green Automotive Siesta
>   in Xbalba, Howl, Kaddish, the
>   Change and now Kral Majales is enough.
> I am where everyone else is. . . .

Ginsberg, like Kerouac a decade earlier, found Gary Snyder to be a great inspiration, an exemplar of intellect, individualism, and artistry—all grounded in his devotion to Buddhism. Allen was impressed by Gary's meditation practice, which seemed to Ginsberg to be a direction he ought to be taking. Being the public figure he was, Allen thought, was not necessarily the best path for his life: "I am wrong to make a public image of myself and be identifiable at all instead of slipping silently into my enlightenment and calmer peaceful obscurity traveling beardless in Volkswagen or hiding out on a farm because when the war hysteria hits a peak and chaos police emerge victorious I'll get my neck cut off for bragging and screaming in public with my picture in the paper and a sign hanging round my neck 'Smoke Marijuana.' " Allen would realize some of these more serene ambitions with his cross-country travels in his camper and, a few years later, when he purchased a secluded farm in upstate New York, but for the time being, he could not avoid active involvement in the growing protest movement against the Vietnam War. No matter how much he admired Gary Snyder's sense of peace and focus, he was not by nature one to sit quietly in one place for very long.

He had just returned to San Francisco when he was off again, on the road with Peter and Julius Orlovsky, Neal Cassady, Anne Murphy, and Steven Bornstein, a New York friend now on the West Coast. The group made the rounds, stopping in Los Gatos to visit Carolyn Cassady and in La Honda to see Ken Kesey, after which they spent ten days in Lawrence Ferlinghetti's Big Sur cabin. Allen's stay at the cabin was restful, finding him chanting mantras and practicing his meditation. One afternoon, he took some LSD—the first he had taken in several years—and rather than experiencing some of the horrific visions typical of his earlier acid trips, he had beautiful ones. Sitting on the banks of a stream that emptied into the ocean, gigantic cliffs looming behind him, Allen was inspired by the sheer beauty of the nature surrounding him: "Very beautiful afternoon on magic earth, the ancient ocean and titanic cliffs and old sun solid in the atmosphere, great masses of kelp life-forms washed up on the beach, and the tiniest flower on the path a violet jewel."

"The day I took the LSD was the same day that President Johnson went into the operating room for his gall bladder illness," Ginsberg later recalled.

As I walked in the forest, wondering what my feelings toward him were . . . the awesome place I was in impressed me with its old tree and ocean cliff majesty. Many tiny jewelled violet flowers along the path of a living brook that looked like Blake's illustration for a canal in grassy Eden: huge Pacific watery shore. I saw a friend [Peter Orlovsky] dancing long haired before giant green waves, under cliffs of titantic nature that Wordsworth described in his poetry, and a great yellow sun veiled with mist hanging over the planet's ocean horizon. Armies at war on the other side of the planet. Berkeley's Vietnam protestors sadly preparing manifestos for our march toward Oakland police and Hell's Angels, and the President in the valley of the shadow—himself experiencing what fear or grief? I realized that more vile words from me would send out negative vibrations into the atmosphere—more hatred amassed against his poor flesh and soul on trial. So I knelt on the sand surrounded by masses of green kelp washed up by a storm, and prayed for President Johnson's tranquil health. Certainly more public hostility would not help him or me or anyone come through to some less rigid and more flexible awareness of ourselves as Victim.

2

In the fall of 1965, President Lyndon Johnson still had a majority backing the war in Vietnam, but the numbers opposing him were increasing. Demonstrations against the war were neither uncommon nor limited to small radical splinter groups. Escalation of American involvement in the war was the subject of fierce debate on college campuses across the United States. Furthermore, the war was impacting on the economically disadvantaged, who, due to limited options, either enlisted or were drafted into the service—a scenario that did not sit well with the civil rights movement. Although Martin Luther King would not oppose the war publicly for another two years, he and other black leaders were aware of the inequity of a draft system that conscripted those unable to find school deferments or use their connections to avoid the service.

In the Bay Area, a number of marches and demonstrations were planned by the Vietnam Day Committee, led by Berkeley activist Jerry Rubin. According to the plan, the initial march would begin at the University of California at Berkeley, proceed through Oakland's black district, and wind up in downtown Oakland. That way, the group would be protesting not only the war itself but the draft system that claimed the underprivileged and economically disadvantaged.

Allen and Gary Snyder took part in the first October demonstration. Riding in a sound truck, Allen and Gary chanted mantras to calm the demonstrators, who feared a violent confrontation with the Oakland police. At the Oakland city limits, police dressed in riot gear told the protesters they could not enter the city, and the demonstration broke up. The next day, another march was held, with a similar confrontation at the city limits. This time, however, the demonstrators did not disperse. Upon being informed that they could not enter Oakland, thousands of marchers sat down in the street and speeches were broadcast over the sound truck's loudspeakers. They had barely begun when, from the police side of the line, a Hell's Angel nicknamed Tiny, accompanied by seven other members of the motorcycle club, rushed the demonstrators and tore down the PEACE IN VIETNAM sign that was being held up at the front of the march. He then ran to the sound truck and cut the speaker wires, effectively ending the demonstration. The police did nothing to stop their actions.

En masse, with their outlaw reputations and instantly identifiable "colors" of leather and denim, the Hell's Angels were a fearsome group, and the Oakland chapter, led by Ralph "Sonny" Barger, was generally acknowledged as the toughest gang in the area. Although they were despised by the authorities and shunned and feared by a public that regarded them as misfits and outcasts, the Hell's Angels considered themselves to be patriotic. Their right-wing politics, backed by their collective muscle, were just the antidote needed by a reactionary vigilante group such as the Oakland Citizens Aroused, as well as by a faction of the Oakland Police Department—all content to stand by and let the Angels do their dirty work.

An ugly, violent altercation seemed inevitable when the Vietnam Day Committee announced its intention of staging another march and mass rally in November, and Hell's Angels countered with threats of bodily harm to anyone who participated in the march or got in their way. The VDC called a mass meeting to discuss strategy. Some members, feeling that a fight was unavoidable, called for marchers to prepare themselves for a confrontation. One member, comparing Hell's Angels to the Nazi brownshirts under Hitler, suggested that the marchers wear black and white armbands and arm themselves with long sticks and batons for self-defense.

Allen felt otherwise. After the incident with the college professor in India, he had seen what could happen if you challenged someone and then did not give him a reasonable way out of the confrontation. As Kral Majales in Czechoslovakia, he had witnessed the gigantic but peaceful spectacle that broke through two decades of oppression in that country. In Ginsberg's opinion, there had to be a way to stage a similar demonstration that was nonthreatening to its opponents—one that made its point while giving Hell's Angels the opportunity to back away without losing face. After all, Allen pointed out to VDC members, the rally was supposed to be a march *for* peace, not the staging for additional violence.

"It wasn't just a political march where people were supposed to run and march angry, shouting slogans," Ginsberg remembered. "It could be seen as theater, as almost all political activity was. And given the situation, the best kind of theater would manifest the Peace that we were protesting. Pro-test being 'pro-attestation,' testimony *in favor* of something. So if we were going to be a peace-protest march, then we should have to be peaceful, and being peaceful took skillful means under such anxious circumstances."

Allen came to the meeting prepared with a plan of his own. He distributed a handbill he had drawn up and printed—"How to Make a March/Spectacle"—that outlined an imaginative way in which "a spectacle can be made, an unmistakable statement OUTSIDE the war psychology which is leading nowhere"—which, Allen assured the group, "would be heard around the world with relief." Fear, anger, anxiety, and violence were precisely the elements that opponents of the march thrived on, he said, proposing that the march be designed to move away from those elements. It should be perceived as a *parade*, a positive aggregation, rather than a *demonstration*, which had myriad built-in negative connotations. To achieve and maintain this effect, Allen offered a twenty-one-point plan that suggested the use of old-fashioned floats, masses of flowers, music, flags and pennants, costumes, mimes, and signs. The march, Ginsberg went on, should be publicized as a safe, nonviolent affair, suitable for all ages and all people. "The parade can embody an example of peaceable health which is the reverse of fighting back blindly," he said, adding that his suggestions "manifest or embody what I believe to be the conscious psychology of latent understanding of the majority of the youth and many elders who come out to march."

The people at the meeting agreed. They decided the march would be open to the community and held in an air of festivity. Flower Power—the affirmation of group opposition, stated gently and peacefully—was born.

Despite Allen's good intentions, Hell's Angels were not ready to back down on their position. They believed the demonstrators were led by a bunch of Communists; as far as the bikers were concerned, the Vietnam War was a fight for freedom, or democracy, against oppression, or communism. They stood by their pledge to disrupt the march, now scheduled for November 20. Foreseeing this possibility, Allen had built provisions into his program, a behavioral code to adopt in the event of a confrontation. The provisions included offering the Angels flowers and candy, sitting peacefully and singing or praying, and offering no resistance.

Still, Allen believed that much of the problem was a lack of communication between the two factions, that the Angels would leave the marchers alone if they could be convinced that the two sides were not enemies—even if they did disagree about the war. In an attempt to open the lines of communication, Allen and others arranged for an open forum—an informal debate between the VDC and the Hell's Angels—to be held on November 12 at San Jose State College. The forum, widely reported in the Bay Area, confirmed the impasse between the two sides. Allen opened the proceedings by singing a mantra and accompanying himself on finger cymbals. He began the debate by stating that the marchers were afraid they were going to be attacked and beaten by the bikers, and they wondered why. "We wonder whether they're doing it for kicks, publicity, to take the heat off themselves, to win the goodwill of the Oakland police and the press, or for right-wing money," Allen said. A lone representative of Hell's Angels, flanked by members of the Nightriders and the Gypsy Jokers— two San Jose biker clubs offering support to the Angels—replied that they had no intention of stepping outside of the law in their disruption of the march. They said they would become violent only in self-defense. As for the reasons for disrupting the march, the bikers claimed they would be staging a patriotic counterdisplay against the Communist-led war protesters.

The two-hour forum offered no solution to the dilemma. The people who turned out for the debate, basically conservative middle-class students who shared their parents' fears based on the domino theory, jeered Ginsberg and other VDC members and egged on the motorcycle gang members, applauding wildly when Allen asked whether they wanted to see blood spilled during the march. Allen was shocked by the reaction, but neither he nor other VDC members swayed from their solid insistence that they intended to be peaceful. Later, when asked what would happen if violence broke out during the demonstration, Jerry Rubin responded, "If there is any attack on us, our only defense will be to bleed."

With time running out, the march organizers feared for the worst. Acting as a mediator between the two sides, Ken Kesey proposed an eleventh-hour meeting with Sonny Barger—a combination of business and pleasure that would find the two groups trying to iron out their differences and partying together afterward. The Angels agreed to the meeting. Allen and Kesey arrived at Barger's house with Neal Cassady and a small group of Merry Pranksters, the latter dressed in costumes. Barger had with him about twenty Hell's Angels, all dressed in their colors. To Allen, the spectacle seemed "like some strange giant puppet theater, the Pranksters in the strange Prankster costumes and Angels in their Angel costumes," as if both sides were using the garb both to identify themselves and disguise who they really were. Allen had brought along some LSD and everyone in the house immediately dropped acid—except Allen, who, by his own account, was afraid of having a bad trip in already-tense circumstances. The conversation went poorly at first, with neither Ginsberg nor Kesey able to convince the Hell's Angels that antiwar activists were not part of a Communist plot designed to overthrow the United States. The Angels' motto was "We gotta fight 'em here or there." Allen and Kesey contended that there was no reason to fight at all, that it was the United States that had invaded Vietnam, not the other way around.

Seeing the conversation turning hostile, Allen took out his harmonium and began to chant the Prajnaparamita ("Highest Perfect Wisdom") Sutra. His chanting, as he described it later, was neither argumentative nor threatening but "simply a tone of voice from the abdomen," a "monosyllabic deep-voiced monochordal chant." After several minutes, Tiny—the Angel who had disrupted the earlier march—joined in, making up his own words ("Om, om, zoom, zoom, zoom, om!") as he went along. Before long, everyone in the room, Hell's Angels, Kesey, Cassady, and Ginsberg, was chanting together, the potentially nasty situation turned mellow. Allen was astonished, realizing that it was an historic moment: For the first time, he had been able to use mantra chanting to settle not only his own fear and anxiety but that of others, as well.

"It brought the whole scene down from the argument to some kind of common tone—because they were desperate too," Allen recalled. "They were just arguing because they were desperate; they didn't know what else to do except argue and maintain their righteous wrath. It settled everybody's breath there in a neutral territory where there was neither attack nor defense."

The meeting ended peacefully and reached its desired resolution: A few days later, the Hell's Angels issued a newspaper declaration stating that they would be demeaning themselves by attacking a bunch of dirty Communists—that they wouldn't touch the filthy marchers with ten-foot poles—and that they had sent President Johnson a telegram offering their services as "gorilla" soldiers in Vietnam. The march commenced as planned, without incident or violence, and Hell's Angels were able to walk away from a volatile and potentially violent scenario with their images intact.

3

There were other meetings with Hell's Angels, all on a social level. Not long after the peace march, Ken Kesey invited them to his La Honda home, an encounter that Ginsberg recalled in his poem "First Party at Ken Kesey's with Hell's Angels." On another occasion, when Bob Dylan arrived in town to play a series of concerts in the Bay Area and offered Allen several dozen tickets to his show at the Berkeley Community Theatre, Allen handed out the tickets to his friends, a number of VDC activists, and a group of Hell's Angels. The unusual mixture of people attended the concert and a party afterward.

Allen saw a lot of Bob Dylan while he was on the West Coast. The two were comfortable together, and they discussed the idea of working on a project—most likely a film. Allen made notes in his journal for such a project, but nothing came of it. Now obsessed with the Vietnam War, Allen hoped to persuade Dylan to take a more active stance in opposing it, but Dylan was reluctant. Indeed, he had helped spearhead the protest movement with such songs as "Masters of War" and "A Hard Rain's A-Gonna Fall," but in recent months, coinciding with his decision to use electric instruments in his performances, he was changing his stance and moving away from political commentary in his songwriting. The sense of rebellion could still be heard in such songs as "Maggie's Farm" and "Gates of Eden," but Dylan was not inclined to join a movement of any sort, no matter how well-intentioned. He saw himself primarily as an artist and he was moving on to another artistic phase. At one point,

Allen had Dylan interested in participating in a festive kind of demonstration, but that, like the film project, never reached fruition.

Allen was less tolerant of his father's opinions about the Vietnam War, and throughout the autumn they traded excoriating letters arguing their respective positions. Louis, who tended to be against U.S. military involvement when the United States was officially acting only in an advisory capacity, now supported Johnson's policies. The war, he argued, was not the civil war Allen and other protesters claimed it to be; instead, it was a matter of the United States fighting Communist aggression against the peaceful people of South Vietnam. Louis was still not entirely convinced that war was the answer, but he felt it necessary for the United States to honor its commitment to South Vietnam. Allen vehemently disagreed. Louis's opinions, he charged, were based on "a continuous barrage of overheated imagery in the papers and a lot of pictures and soft soap on television"; Louis was the victim of "mass hypnosis." Allen resented his father calling him a Communist; he complained that this was the same kind of name-calling he heard from Hell's Angels and other war supporters on the West Coast. Yes, he admitted to Louis, he had been more tolerant of the bikers than he had been with his own father, but that was because he expected so much more from a man of Louis's intelligence and education.

The correspondence was important for both men. Louis was struggling to find his position on the war, distrustful as he was of communism but equally confused about the role of the United States in the configuration of politics in Southeast Asia. A gentle man, Louis was by nature repulsed by warfare and fighting, but the events in Eastern Europe over the past two decades had led him to believe that the Communists were not only aggressive but expansionist, unwilling to stop with the conquest of South Vietnam. Allen, for his part, was again using Louis as a sounding board, as a means of identifying and sharpening his opinions about the war. Allen hated dealing with generalities and slogans, but he also recognized as the war heated up in Vietnam that he would be facing a barrage of both as U.S. government officials sought to find a common denominator to unite the people behind them. Louis's arguments were a mixture of specifics and generalizations reflective of a complex (no matter how simply stated) set of opinions, and in his arguments with his father, Allen was effectively honing the statements he would put forth in public. He was also able to unload a lot of hostility and frustration that, if stated publicly, might have damaged his credibility or alienated the people he hoped to win over to his way of thinking.

Not all of Allen's time, of course, was spent arguing politics or participating in demonstrations and marches—even if it might have seemed that way to him. He saw a lot of Lawrence Ferlinghetti, Michael McClure, Gary Snyder, Robert Duncan, and other poets while he was in California, and many hours were devoted to reading and discussing poetry. On December 5, Ferlinghetti gathered a large group of the poets, writers, artists, and actors outside his City Lights Bookstore for a photo session that would capture, if just for an instant, the spirit of artistic camaraderie so prevalent in the Bay Area. "I was looking at those great photographs of the Paris surrealists in the 20's, and I thought it'd be a good thing to get one like that before the whole scene disappears in a cloud," Ferlinghetti explained. In the photograph, published on the cover of

City Lights Journal Number 3, Ginsberg is standing in the center of the group, surrounded by Peter Orlovsky, Michael McClure, Richard Brautigan, Robert LaVigne, Shig Murao, David Meltzer, and a host of others. Ferlinghetti, opening his umbrella as if to signify the group's gathering under the sponsorship of City Lights, stands behind the assembly. Conspicuously absent from the photograph are Jack Kerouac, a major influence on many of those present, who was not in San Francisco at the time, and Bob Dylan, representative of one aspect of the evolution of the Beats, who was at City Lights at the time of the shooting but who preferred not to be in the picture. As it turned out, Ferlinghetti was justified in his concern about documenting the moment: The scene was never quite the same again, and while the people pictured would go on to produce numerous major works, they were never again gathered in one group and photographed in such a manner.

4

The history of Allen's desire to write good spontaneous poetry went back a long way—to Neal Cassady's "Joan Anderson" letter, to Ed White's discussions about verbal sketching with Jack Kerouac, to Kerouac's own theories about spontaneous composition. Allen had spent nearly a decade and a half trying to find his own method, but with the notable exceptions of such poems as "Sunflower Sutra," "The Bricklayer's Lunch Hour," "Kral Majales," and a few others, he had yet to produce pure spontaneous work that met his own standards. He could catch the *spirit* of such writing, and did so in "Howl," "Kaddish," and numerous other poems, including his drug-induced ones, but he always found himself returning to the poems, restructuring and tightening them, cleaning up syntax and shaping internal rhythms. Although he would have been loath to admit it, he was still too tightly bound to his academic background and his own father's influences, too regulated by the format of the printed page, to make the leap with his poetry that Kerouac had made with his prose. Despite all his talk about consciousness and his experimentation with form, he was still directed by his artistic sensibilities, as if in the process of transferring thought to the printed page and then in the reworking itself, some of the spark was lost.

In December 1965, Bob Dylan gave Allen a gift that would have an enormous impact on his movement toward more spontaneous expression over the next few years. In a moment of generosity, Dylan gave Ginsberg six hundred dollars, which Allen then used to purchase a state-of-the-art reel-to-reel Uher tape recorder. The machine not only afforded him the opportunity to record his thoughts instantly without even the slight intrusion of having to put them on paper but it also had the effect of providing him with an instant cut-up when the machine picked up all the sounds around him. Delighted, Allen immediately went to work to learn how to make the best use of the recorder. He took the portable machine with him everywhere, recording his impressions of what he saw on his walks in the woods or drives along the highway. When he, Peter, Julius, and Steven Bornstein stayed for a week with Ferlinghetti at his cabin, Allen spent a lot of time at the ocean, recording his mantra chanting with the sounds of the sea as a backdrop. He improvised poetry. In essence, he was carrying the concept of verbal sketching a step beyond Kerouac.

In September, Allen had begun what he was tentatively calling "Poem of These States," an ambitious project designed to update and rethink Whitman's celebration of America. The country was at an historic crossroads, Allen believed, and he wanted to determine from his travels throughout the United States what its spirit really was. Although the idea was far from original, it offered great promise. A few years earlier, Robert Frank had published a collection of photographs entitled *The Americans*, with an introductory text written by Jack Kerouac. It explored aspects of the country often overlooked by those seeking to chronicle the spirit of the nation; arguably, it was the most important book of its kind since James Agee and Walker Evans teamed up on *Let Us Now Praise Famous Men*. Ginsberg, an excellent photographer himself, sought to use his eye for detail and ear for poetic sound in a multitextured series of poems that blended poetry, travel writing, personal experience, snippets of conversation, fragments of news broadcasts and newspaper headlines, songs heard on the radio, and other elements into a unified work. Williams had advised poets to celebrate place, and *Paterson*, his long poem sequence published in five volumes, had included many of the elements Allen hoped to include in his. As for place, Ginsberg was in *America*, and beginning with a poem written in the Pacific Northwest, using Whitman's long line and Williams's objective writing, he had begun his own celebration:

> Under the bluffs of Oroville, blue cloud September
> skies, entering U.S. border, red red apples bend their tree
> boughs propt with sticks—
> At Omak a fat girl in dungarees leads her big brown
> horse by asphalt highway. . . .

The initial poem, composed from notes taken while Allen and Gary Snyder traveled up the highway in Allen's Volkswagen camper, set the tone for all the poems to follow. The fragments of conversation and song lyrics, integrated with exquisitely written detail, gave the poem a sense of immediacy that Ginsberg had admired in Kerouac's *Visions of Cody*. "Moon like a Coleman lantern dimming icicle-point stars" was an expression that could have been right out of Kerouac; it was as vivid as Jack's classic description of sunlight playing off a car's fender. Now, by using a tape recorder, Allen would be able to record even more detail, and much more quickly.

They spent the holiday season in Los Angeles, where Allen got caught up in the frenetic activities of the different entertainment industries. He gave a long interview to a local underground newspaper and engaged in several debates on narcotics laws on television. He met members of the Byrds—a folk-rock band that had played Dylan's music on electric instruments before Dylan himself—and record producer Phil Spector, who offered to help Allen with a recording of his mantra chanting. When he learned that the most recent issue of Ed Sanders's literary magazine, *Fuck You/A Magazine of the Arts*, had been confiscated by New York police, Allen put together a benefit reading to help with Sanders's legal expenses. Much of his three weeks' time in Southern

California, Allen admitted in a letter to Lucien Carr, was spent simply hanging around Hollywood's Sunset Strip.

Allen continued to work on what he was now calling his "auto poesy"—the spontaneous poetry dictated into his tape recorder. With readings scheduled in Kansas the first week of February, and his trip there involving a swing through Arizona, New Mexico, and Texas, he had plenty of opportunity to hone his craft. The first night on the road, they camped in the snow in the Arizona desert, and from there it was on to Albuquerque for a brief visit with Robert Creeley, who was now teaching at the nearby University of New Mexico. While Peter drove, Allen looked out the passenger window and recorded his vision of America:

> Spectacle of Afternoon,
> > giant pipes glistening in the universe
> Magic that weighs tons and tons,
> > Old bum with his rough
> > > tattered pack hunched
> walking up the hill hanging
> > to Ukipah
> cloth cap pulled over his head
> > > black fingernails. . . .

Allen could not help but notice such contrasts, the signs of scientific and technological advances, visible everywhere, standing in contrast to some of the country's constants, from its ageless physical beauty to its many underprivileged citizens. The radio itself provided cut-ups of such contrasts: Nelson Eddy singing "Oh, What a Beautiful Morning" followed immediately by a news report on the Vietnam War.

In Allen's mind, Kansas bore special significance. Set in the Great Plains, and the setting for Frank Baum's great fable, *The Wizard of Oz*, Kansas was symbolic of what Allen considered to be a spiritually barren citizenship that blindly accepted the war edicts from Washington, D.C., its people as silent as its seemingly endless flatlands of wheat and corn. Although he had never stepped foot in the state, it had, at least in a small way, passed judgment on him when his books had been subjected to a police hassle in Wichita. Ironically, Allen knew a number of poets, including Michael McClure and Charles Plymell, who had roots in the state—artists who managed to succeed despite what Allen felt was a stifling environment:

> Onward to Wichita!
> > Onward to the Vortex!
> > To the Birchite Hate Riddles,
> cock-detesting, pussy-smearing
> > dry ladies and evil Police
> > > of Central Plains' State
> where boredom & fury
> > magick bars and sirens around
> > > the innocent citykid eye

& Vampire stake of politics Patriotism's driven
        into the white breast of Teenage
                joyful murmurers
                in carpet livingrooms
                    on sidestreets—
Beautiful children've been driven from Wichita. . . .

Ginsberg's wrath was directed at the incongruity and hypocrisy of a state that, while considering itself to be patriotic, refused to tolerate freedom of speech; it regarded itself as a religious state, yet it tolerated John Birch Society politics. This was the heartland of America and Ginsberg was entering it with his own brand of wooden stakes—poetry, mantras, and open discussion of forbidden topics.

It is not difficult to see why his emotions ran so high. The radio was full of news about the escalated U.S. involvement in Vietnam—a stark contrast to the glut of religious programs offered on the Bible Belt stations heard throughout the region. Sergeant Barry Sadler's "Ballad of the Green Beret" was the most popular new recording in the music industry. Newspaper editorials supported Operation Rolling Thunder, the relentless bombing in North Vietnam. Everywhere he turned, Allen was confronted by the language of war. The turning spool of his tape recorder picked up the language as the microbus moved across the snow-covered expanses of highway leading to Wichita.

The readings in Wichita, Kansas City, Topeka, and Lawrence were very successful, with sold-out crowds and a large contingent of the press. By now, Allen had given enough readings that he was becoming a master at it. He delivered his poetry like rock musicians working off a set playlist. With the exceptions of "Howl" and "Kaddish"—both of which took a long time to read and were generally not included—Allen offered a generous sampling of his "greatest hits," worked into a program of recently composed poetry, sometimes read directly from the pages of his journal. He would offer explanations about the origins of some of the poems, while other works gave him the opportunity to climb on his soapbox and expound on drugs, politics, and homosexuality. He was now opening each reading with a brief period of mantra chanting. No matter where he read, from a packed house at the University of Kansas, to a group of psychologists and psychiatrists at the Menninger Clinic, to poetry enthusiasts in clubs such as the Showboat and the CAC Gallery, Allen delivered the same essential message: "Kansas must love its own body before it is to be reborn. People must be free to embrace each other to break the spell that hangs over the vortex. In other words, physical affection—what Walt Whitman called adhesiveness—is a necessary food to the human mammal. It is no luxury. It is absolutely necessary for survival of the species."

How the conservative Midwesterners reacted to this message is anyone's guess. Newspaper accounts of the readings suggest a mixture of responses. The hippie garb, accented by Allen's long hair and beard, was greeted by a certain amount of amusement—a reaction not by any means limited to the Midwest. Nor was the Midwest alone in its initial confusion greeting Allen's frenetic mantra chanting. The four-letter words in his poems received plenty of mention in the press accounts, as did his references to homosexuality and drugs. (Ironically, on February 16 at a reading in Wichita, Allen had to intercede on another poet's behalf when the Wichita police deemed the young poet's work to be offensive.) For his part, Allen, who likened himself to "O. Wilde bringin' the Gospel of Beauty to the Midwest," was pleased with his reception, happy that he was getting what he considered to be "more accurate pro reporting" in Kansas than he was accustomed to receiving in supposedly more sophisticated areas of the country.

Allen stayed in eastern Kansas for several weeks, taking a side trip to give a reading in Lincoln, Nebraska. Throughout his stay, he was obsessed with the notion that language was magic. It could be manipulated, like a sleight-of-hand trick used to make people believe in the impossible. Cleverly manipulated language created the black magic of war, so it only stood to reason that the thoughtful arrangement of language could create the magic of peace. As obedient servants of the government, manipulated by the language of patriotism, the people of Kansas—symbolic of Middle America and middle-class values—had been sold a bill of goods, a war that would claim its tender young sons. Although it would send thousands of youthful men to their deaths, the government itself had failed to find an official language for its actual involvement in Southeast Asia: The war in Vietnam was an undeclared one.

Allen mulled over the concept of the magic of language as his Volkswagen circled about the midwestern vortex. The reports on the radio or in newspapers only confirmed his theories about the power of language. A newspaper headline in Lincoln proclaimed VIETNAM WAR BRINGS PROSPERITY, while one in Omaha read RUSK SAYS TOUGHNESS ESSENTIAL FOR PEACE. Language: People were being tricked into basing their faith on magic; if something was said, it became real. The war was real because our leaders said it was, just as in India, when mantras were chanted, the gods became real simply through the process of reciting their names.

On his side trip to and from Nebraska, Allen worked on a segment of highway poesy that would become "Wichita Vortex Sutra," his most renowned poem of the 1960s. The first part of the poem, dictated into the Uher while he was traveling from Wichita to Lincoln, was originally entitled "To Nebraska" and slotted to be a part of his long "Poem of These States." The poem contains the same objective detail ("orange gas flares/beneath pillows of smoke, flames in machinery—/transparent towers at dusk"), and it carries a similar sense of cut-up thoughts, but the poem's tone is a departure of sorts from the earlier written works in the sequence. The poet's voice is stronger, messianic ("Thy sins are forgiven, Wichita!/Thy lonesomeness annulled, O Kansas dear!"), the message consistent with Ginsberg's fixation on Whitman's call for tenderness among men.

> No more fear of tenderness, much delight in weeping, ecstasy
> in singing, laughter rises that confounds
> staring Idiot mayors
> and stony politicians eyeing
> Thy breast,
> O Man of America, be born!

Ginsberg's voice gains additional strength from its depiction of the flat landscape around him; it rises triumphant in the silence of the wasteland. Ginsberg is making a mantra from the American language, more authentic and easier to identify with than the language of those making war. He expresses a message of universal tenderness and love that ironically stands in stark contrast to the language of President Johnson, J. Edgar Hoover, and Cardinal Spellman—all of whom are cited in the poem.

The second part of "Wichita Vortex Sutra," composed during Ginsberg's return journey to Wichita from Nebraska and given the title of "Vortex Sutra" in his journal transcription of the tape, continues his citations of the language of war, offering numerous examples of the folly of such language. Most noteworthy is the example that opens this section of the poem. While riding through Hickman, Nebraska, heading south toward Wichita, Allen listened to a broadcast of the popular program "Face the Nation." That particular Sunday's guest was Republican Senator Aiken and the topic was the Vietnam War. According to Aiken's badly worded statement, Robert McNamara, secretary of defense under Kennedy, had made a "bad guess" in 1962 when he estimated that it would take only eight thousand American troops to handle the "situation" in Vietnam. Bad guess? Situation? Thousands of human beings were losing their lives in the fighting and bombing, and the language of war trivialized the horror as if the decision makers had blown their pick for the sixth race at Belmont. In "Wichita Vortex Sutra," Ginsberg calls the authorities to task for their language:

> Put it this way on the radio
> Put it this way in television language
> Use the words
> language, language:
> "A bad guess" . . .

If, as Ginsberg defined it to poet/critic Paul Carroll, a mantra is "a short magic formula usually invoking an aspect of the Divine, usually given as meditation exercise by guru to student . . . considered to be identical with the god named, and have inevitable power attached to its pronunciation," the language of war, although containing many of the same powers, was its antithesis:

> Black Magic language,
> formulas for reality—
> Communism is a 9 letter word
> used by inferior magicians with
> the wrong alchemical formula for transforming earth into gold
> —funky warlocks operating on guesswork . . .

The listing continues, Ginsberg offering example after example of how the language of war is defeating the language of love. He finds it no less maddening and depressing than the unheard voices that claimed the mind of his mother, but rather than fall victim to its power, he uses language to mount his own counteroffensive. "I call all Powers of imagination/to my side in this auto to make Prophecy," he writes, summoning all spiritual leaders, including Jesus

Christ, Allah, Jaweh, Krishna, and the Indian holy men who advised him—
"all ancient Seraphim of heavenly Desire, Devas, yogi & holymen I chant
to"—to give him guidance in what he must do next:

> I lift my voice aloud,
>> make Mantra of American language now,
>>> I here declare the end of the War!
>>>> Ancient days' Illusion!—
>> and pronounce words beginning my own millennium. . . .

This may be the first time in recorded history that a private citizen "undeclared" a war, but Ginsberg was absolutely earnest in doing so. In a statement
written in the form of a poem, issued to the press shortly after the composition
of "Wichita Vortex Sutra," Ginsberg explained his position. The statement,
in part:

> As U.S. language chief I hereby use language to make a unilateral
>> declaration of the end of the Vietnam War,
> The poet says the whole war's nothing but black magic caused by
>> the wrong language
> & authoritatively cancels all previous magic formulas & wipes
>> out the whole war scene without further delay.

"Authoritatively cancels" is a bold proclamation, based on the belief that in
a democracy a single citizen has a voice that will be heard and, in this instance,
the confidence that there were enough individual (although silent) citizens
behind him to comprise the majority—or at least the potential for a future
majority. Whether this was true as early as February 1966 is a subject of
debate. Americans, especially those ineligible for conscription, have a history of
supporting United States military involvement in almost any war. But Ginsberg's point is well made: If the government can use black magic to secure a
majority supporting the war, he could use his own form of magic to sway a
majority to oppose it. Once again, the key was *language*: Someone had to step
forward and declare an end to the war.

In a 1968 interview with Michael Aldrich, published three years later as
the booklet *Improvised Poetics*, Ginsberg offered a detailed description of his
intent:

> So I wanted to—in the English language—make a series of syllables
> that would be identical with a historical event. I wanted the historical
> event to be the end of the war, and so I prepared the declaration of
> the historical event. *I here declare the end of the war!*—and set up a
> force field of language which is so solid and absolute as a statement and
> a realization of an assertion by my will, conscious will power, that it
> will contradict—counteract and ultimately overwhelm the force field of
> language pronounced out of the State Department and out of Johnson's
> mouth. When they say, "I declare—We declare war," they can say "I

declare war"—their mantras are black mantras, so to speak. They pronounce their words, and then they sign a piece of paper, of other words, and a hundred thousand soldiers go across the ocean. So I pronounce *my* word, and so the point is, how strong is my word?

Well, since Shelley says that the poet's word is the strongest, the unacknowledged legislator's, the next thing is: let the president execute his desire, and the Congress do what *they* want to do, but I'm going to do what *I* want to do. . . . If *one* single person *wakes up* out of the mass hallucination and pronounces a contrary order, a declaration, contrary state, instruction to the state, to the Government, if *one* person wakes up out of the Vast Dream of America and says I declare the end of the war, well, what'll happen? It was an interesting experiment, to see if that *one* assertion of language will precipitate other consciousnesses to make the same assertion, until it spreads and finally until there's a majority of the consciousnesses making the same assertion, until that assertion contradicts the other assertion, because the whole War is WILL-FULL-NESS, and the War is a Poetry, in the sense that the War is the *Happening*, the *Poem* invented and imagined by Johnson and Rusk and Dulles, Luce, and Spellman and all those people; so the *end* of the War is the *Happening*, the Poem invented by Spock, or myself, or Phil Ochs, or Dylan, or Sanders, or A. J. Muste's ghost, or Dorothy Day, or David McReynolds, or Dave Dellinger, or anybody who wishes to make a contrary statement of pronouncement.

Ginsberg's pronouncement made, the remainder of the poem becomes anti-climactic, with Ginsberg now trying to apply the language of love to the same terrain he had described in the first part of the poem. Indeed, it is the same Kansas—the state that had given America prohibitionist Carry Nation—and the radio stations still blared out commercial jingles and wartime news reports, but Ginsberg was accepting none of it.

> Some of the
> > Language language
> > > Communist
> > > > Language language soldiers
> charged so desperately
> > they were struck with six or seven bullets before they fell
> > Language Language M 60 Machine Guns
> > > Language language in La Drang Valley
> the terrain is rougher infested with leeches and scorpions
> > The war was over several hours ago!

Maybe so, but it is here that Ginsberg hits his snag: He can *declare* the war has ended all he wishes—he can scorn its language in powerful eloquence—but the war is still going on. By itself, language cannot defeat the actions of men. Nowhere is this as apparent as in Ginsberg's memorable closing lines:

The war is over now—
    Except for the souls
        held prisoner in Niggertown
Still pining for love of your tender white bodies O children of Wichita!

As a closeout to the poem, the lines have the rhythm and momentum of a runaway freight train, implying that what the poet has begun will gain strength and momentum until it is picked up by a nation—yes, even by the people of the midwestern vortex. Time, of course, would prove this to be true. Nevertheless, Ginsberg's blunt reference to the section of Wichita known as Niggertown is evidence of both the power and weakness of language. Few words in the American idiom are as obscene and forceful as *nigger*, and while "Niggertown" in the poem is a direct reference to that section of Wichita from Hydraulic to Seventeenth streets, it could be pointed out that every metropolitan area in the United States has its own "niggertown" in which blacks, certainly useful as military fodder in Vietnam and other wars, are imprisoned by social and economic conditions defying the language of civil rights legislation, the Amendments to the United States Constitution, and the Emancipation Proclamation. That "niggertowns" continue to exist is testament to the weakness of language, and for all of Ginsberg's mention of love, his words were not necessarily going to change the course of history—not as long as racists had hateful mantras of their own.

5

Allen was very excited about this latest poem. Not only did it represent his best effort to date in spontaneous, vocalized poetry but its theme seemed to be the central issue of his sequence of poems about the United States. He went immediately to work at transcribing the tapes and working his words into a pleasing visual form.

    The method of the arrangement of the words on the page was determined in the transcription. The On/Off switch on Allen's microphone produced a distinct clicking sound when it was being used, and the clicks on the tape, marking the beginning or end of a moment of thought, were useful in indicating potential line breaks:

    That the rest of the earth is unseen, [click]
                            an outer universe invisible, [click]
        Unknown [click] except thru
             [click] language
                [click] airprint
                    [click] magic images
      or prophecy of the secret [click]
            heart of the same [click]
            in Waterville as Saigon one human form [click]. . . .

Ginsberg explained the process to Michael Aldrich:

It's not the clicks that I use, it's simply the use of pauses—exactly the same as writing on a page: where you stop, you write; in the little notebook, you write that one line or one phrase on one line, and then you have to wait for another phrase to come, so you go on then to another line, represented by another click. . . .

Of course, this could be put on one line: "Unknown except thru language airprint magic images or prophecy of the secret heart." . . . Then you could have another line—"the same in Waterville as Saigon one human form." These could be rearranged. But these lines in "Wichita" are arranged according to their organic time-spacing as per the mind's coming up with the phrases and the mouth pronouncing them. With pauses maybe of a minute or two minutes between each line as I'm formulating it in my mind and the recording.

Ginsberg would use this method for all of the auto poesy composed on his travels throughout the United States and eventually included—with the notable exception of "Wichita Vortex Sutra"—in *The Fall of America*. He would continue to use notebooks when he traveled by plane, although for sake of continuity, he would maintain the same kind of line structure. He was very interested in the concept of making his poetry "a graph of the mind," as Philip Whalen called it, and the auto poesy—at its best in a poem like "Wichita Vortex Sutra"—represented some of his earliest conscious efforts to create this kind of poetry.

The Kansas readings completed, the group headed east. On March 1, Allen and Peter gave a reading at the University of Indiana and, as long as they were in the state, Allen decided to visit the Kinsey Sex Institute. By March 11, they were back in New York State, with Allen reading at the University of Buffalo. Speaking out against the war remained a major objective, as was the continuation of his auto poesy. On their return trip to New York, the group had had minor run-ins with the authorities. The police in Kansas and Nebraska had kept an eye on them and they had been stopped in both states. In Indiana, the state legislature, outraged by Peter's reading of one of his "Sex Experiments" transcripts, hinted at an investigation. None of these incidents, however, fully prepared Allen for the political and legal snafus that lay ahead in New York.

6

"Shit's hit the fan on Leary and LSD in New York and phone's ringing in every direction." This is how Ginsberg described to Ferlinghetti the mess that awaited him upon his return to New York after a nine-month absence. The day of retribution seemed to be on the figures supporting the LSD revolution, and when that day arrived, it displayed the great lengths to which the authorities would go to silence or thwart the likes of Timothy Leary and Allen Ginsberg.

Leary's problems began on December 23, 1965, in Laredo, Texas. Three days earlier, Leary, his son, Jack, his daughter, Susan, and two members of his Castalia Foundation staff had left New York for the Yucatán, where Leary hoped to complete the autobiography he was writing for a New York publisher.

The group crossed the International Bridge at Laredo, but their car was stopped before they entered Mexico. A Secret Service agent from Mexico—one of the agents who had closed down Leary's psychedelic training center in Mexico City three years earlier—greeted Leary in the station's waiting room and told him that he could not enter the country until certain legalities had been worked out. Leary turned his car around and headed back across the bridge.

In Laredo, customs officials ordered Leary and the group out of the car and then searched it and its occupanats. The officials found slightly less than half an ounce of marijuana on Susan Leary, which her father quickly admitted was his own. Leary and his daughter were arrested and charged with smuggling, transporting, and failing to pay taxes on marijuana. Both pled not guilty to the charges.

Their trial began on March 9. Since the car had not been admitted to Mexico, the smuggling charges were dropped. The defense argued that the current marijuana laws were unconstitutional and Timothy Leary argued that he should be allowed to live his private life and conduct his research as he saw fit, as long as he did not present a clear and present danger to society. Leary had written fifty-two books and articles on consciousness and spirituality, but despite such credentials, presented in conjunction with the testimony of experts who claimed that marijuana was not only not dangerous but also less harmful than alcohol, the judge was interested in only one issue: Did Leary possess marijuana in violation of the law? The jury had no difficulty with this question, and when it found Leary and his daughter guilty, Leary was given the maximum sentence for both counts against him: thirty years in prison, a thirty-thousand-dollar fine and commitment to a psychiatric hospital for observation. Susan was handed a five-year sentence. The defense immediately filed an appeal, keeping Timothy and Susan Leary out of confinement for the time being.

The efforts to trap Ginsberg were even more insidious and involved. For all his talk about changing marijuana laws and about his own drug use, he had never been found to be in possession of controlled or illegal substances—not that this was a concern to the Bureau of Narcotics, which had decided, despite the lack of evidence, that he had to be involved in drug sales. If they couldn't catch Ginsberg red-handed, officials decided, they might be able to find another way to trap him.

They had implemented their plan a year earlier, a short time after Allen had returned to the United States, when a young jazz musician, Jack Martin, and a friend, George Wilbourne, were arrested for marijuana possession in New York. Narcotics agent Bruce Jensen and several others met with Martin and told him he was not the man they wanted but that they wanted him to help them set up Allen Ginsberg. If he cooperated, Martin was told, he would get off with a light sentence; if not, his bail would be doubled, additional charges would be added, and his wife might even be arrested. The fact that Martin had never met Ginsberg didn't seem to matter to the agents.

On August 11, 1965, there had been a benefit at the Broadway Central Hotel in Greenwich Village to help raise funds for Wilbourne's bail. Martin, who had posted his own bail, stood before the gathering and began to recite the details of the proposed conspiracy against Ginsberg. During Martin's speech, three men approached the stage and engaged in a shouting match with him.

Filmmakers Jack Smith and Piero Heliczer, believing Martin was about to be attacked, came to his assistance. After some pushing and shoving, Martin, Smith, and Heliczer were taken into custody by the three men, who turned out to be undercover narcotics agents. The three were charged with assault and resisting arrest, even though the agents had offered neither identification nor warrants when they approached Martin and disrupted the benefit.

Allen had been in San Francisco at the time, oblivious to the plot against him, but he was a very visible figure in the courtroom in New York when the legal proceedings against the three commenced in April 1966. During the trial, Martin spoke of the agents' attempts to coerce him into helping them set up Ginsberg, and Agent Jensen admitted that he had once asked Martin to assist the bureau as an informant. Interviewed after one of the court sessions, Allen told reporters that he felt as if "the noose of the police state" was closing around his neck, and he compared the official attitude to that in Czechoslovakia. Furthermore, he said, there were others, including William Burroughs, who were on a list of people marked for harassment. On April 15, the three defendants were found guilty of the charges against them, prompting an angry and lengthy Ginsberg editorial—"Who Are We?"—an indictment against the measures taken by authorities against private citizens. It ended with an ominous prediction:

> Such crudity of judgment and public cruelty has come to dominate much of our public life at the expense of the common humanity of our nation. If we suffer now our greatest suffering has been the authoritarian hypnosis under which we have come to accept such assaults on person and sensibility as if it were characteristic of humankind-ness. We are assaulted on every side by rancor and hostility multiplied billionfold megaphoned into our senses by electronic media, till the populace has lost contact with its own meaty Self. We are not born for this, and we will destroy ourselves if it continues.

Two days after the trial of Martin and the others ended, Timothy Leary was in the news again—this time as the result of a raid by Dutchess County police in Millbrook, New York. Around 1:30 A.M., enforcement officials, led by G. Gordon Liddy—later famous for his involvement in the Watergate fiasco—stormed into the mansion of Leary's 2,500-acre complex, searching each of its sixty-four rooms and its twenty-nine guests for drugs. No drugs were found, although Liddy ordered Leary arrested for possession of what he called "obviously a high-grade brand of marijuana"—which turned out to be peat moss. Charges were eventually dropped for lack of evidence, but not before Leary and a number of others endured still another series of indignities in what amounted to no less than sustained police harassment.

Allen used all possible venues to battle back and raise public awareness of what was going on. He gave interviews and made public appearances. He continued to compile what is now regarded to be one of the largest and most authoritative files on drug laws and cases in the United States. He worked on the Timothy Leary Defense Fund, helping assemble a full-page ad and petition in *The New York Times*, entitled "The Responsible Community Shocked at the

Harsh Sentencing of Psychologist Dr. Timothy Leary," signed by such notables as Alan Watts, Susan Sontag, Norman Mailer, Albert Grossman, Diane Di Prima, and Jason Epstein. However, for all his efforts, results were slow in coming.

7

By this time, Allen was again wrapped up in social and political causes at the expense of writing new poetry. His skills at organization and debate made him a natural candidate for this kind of activity, and by mid-1967, his public reputation had undergone a significant shift: Although he was an open critic of the media, he was also adept at using television, radio, and newspapers to his benefit, and from his media exposure he was becoming as well known for his political stances as he was for his poetry. People who had never read or heard a line of his work were aware of the name Allen Ginsberg.

"Wichita Vortex Sutra" was published to great fanfare in *The Village Voice* on April 28, further establishing Allen's reputaton as one of the country's most vocal opponents of the Vietnam War. He formed the Committee on Poetry, a nonprofit organization designed to assist "poets and philosophers who lacked personal finance and wherewithal to accomplish small material projects in the society at large," funded largely by payments he received for poetry readings. Money was no longer an issue in Allen's daily life. He had never demanded much—he still lived in a run-down section of the East Village and bought much of his clothing from secondhand stores—and from the sales of his work and his busy reading schedule, he was earning by his own admission amounts of money in excess of his actual needs. He was distressed that money earned from his art, collected by the Internal Revenue Service, was being applied to the Vietnam War, and the Committee on Poetry became a way of helping starving artists while keeping as much money as possible from the war effort.

On the local level, Allen became involved with an organization known as the New York Eternal Committee for Freedom of the Arts, a group battling what it considered to be still another crackdown on the avant-garde in the East Village. As before, the focus of the complaint was on licensing procedures. On April 11, the License Department, upon hearing that a flag had been burned at a performance at the Bridge Theater, called the establishment's operators and demanded that they show cause for not having its license revoked. The next day, the 41st Street Theater was given a similar directive, based on the License Department's feeling that the films shown at the Film Maker's Cinematheque, housed by the theater, were sexually immoral. Finally, the Astor Place Playhouse, which had been staging performances by Ed Sanders and Tuli Kupferberg's band, the Fugs, was warned that its license would be revoked unless the band "toned down" its show. Ginsberg, on the committee with Andy Warhol, Jonas Mekas, Shirley Clark, and four others, called for a meeting with city officials to iron out the problems. Although there was much discussion about free speech and censorship, Allen tried to keep the tone of the group's actions positive. "We want to meet with more responsible officials, perhaps even show them what we're doing," he stated. "We feel they are capable of greater artistic appreciation of our work, and that by talking to them we can create a situation where the possible violations are discussed before the summons are issued." The approach worked. Mayor John Lindsay met with the group in a closed meeting and assured the members that he was not directing an effort to crack down on the avant-garde. He promised to look into the licensing practices, and the threats against the theaters ceased.

Allen's reading schedule had been busy almost from the day he returned to New York. He read for the first time with his father, drawing a packed house at the reading sponsored by the Poetry Society of America. He appeared with Timothy Leary at American University on May 5, and three days later he participated in a Read-In for Peace at the University of Pennsylvania, where he read "Wichita Vortex Sutra" to a crowd of eight hundred cheering people.

Ironically, for all the controversy he generated virtually everywhere he went, Allen was reaching the status of literary elder. Jonathan Cape, his British publishing house, consulted with him about issuing his collected poems—an honor usually bestowed upon poets of considerable stature. The paperback would be published by Penguin, a large English house. Naturally, Allen began thinking about having a similar collection available in the United States. The problem, he realized, was in distribution: City Lights, to whom he felt very loyal, was not equipped to distribute the book the way such presses as Grove or New Directions could. Allen wrote Ferlinghetti and asked what he thought of the possibility of a joint imprint, with City Lights sharing the publishing credit with a publisher such as Grove or Doubleday. Ferlinghetti, trying to be as diplomatic as possible given the fact that Ginsberg was his best-selling author, conceded that "we can't compete with big commercial scenes like Grove" and encouraged Allen to work out whatever arrangements he could, as long as City Lights would maintain the right to publish and distribute its own "Pocket Poets" editions of his work. Ferlinghetti suggested that Allen publish his collected poems through New Directions, pointing out that the company had treated him and Gregory Corso very well and that it had produced a beautiful volume of Ezra Pound's collected *Cantos*. Allen's loyalty to Ferlinghetti prevailed: His volume of collected poems would not be issued in the United States until the mid-1980s, despite lucrative offers from large publishers.

Another indication of Allen's literary status was his interview in *The Paris Review*. The literary quarterly had the long-held reputation of publishing interviews with the most significant names in literature, and to be included as an interview subject was a form of recognition that meant you were considered an important, enduring writer or poet. Allen's interview, appearing in the Spring 1966 issue, was conducted by poet/critic Tom Clark and was especially notable because Allen gave an in-depth description of his Blake visions and the events leading up to the "change" for the first time in a large publication. The interview captured the complexity of Allen's personality; he was in turns modest and egotistical, understated and hyberbolic. He gave a brilliant dissertation of Cézanne's influence on his poetry and offered key insights into the way his use of drugs influenced his poetic consciousness. Needless to say, Louis Ginsberg was thrilled by the interview, congratulating Allen on his "stimulating and inspiring" discourses on poetry, his disagreements with Allen on poetry composition overcome by an understandable sense of paternal pride. Allen had achieved a reputation Louis would never have dreamed possible for himself.

8

On June 14, Allen was in Washington, D.C., testifying before the Judiciary Subcommittee on Juvenile Delinquency, which was investigating the use of LSD in the United States. At the time, it was not illegal to possess or use LSD, although it was unlawful to manufacture, sell, or purchase without the approval of the Food and Drug Administration. The Senate, considering a change in LSD laws, was gathering information from authorities on LSD experimentation and research, although it was clear from the line of questions asked by the subcommittee that government officials believed LSD to be dangerous—especially to young people—and would eventually act against its use by private citizens. Timothy Leary had testified prior to Ginsberg, and Leary and Senator Edward Kennedy had engaged in an exchange that left no doubt that even the liberal factions in Washington frowned upon the drug's use.

Allen's statement was a work of art, a tightly constructed summary of his personal history of drug use, his own scholarship on LSD, and his recommendations for its future in the country. Dressed sharply in a suit and tie, and speaking in a low, respectful tone, he began his address by admitting that he was uneasy about appearing before the subcommittee, worried as he was that its members might have prejudged him by his public "bearded image."

"I am a little frightened to present myself—the fear of your rejection of me, the fear of not being tranquil enough to reassure you that we can talk together, make sense, and perhaps even like each other—enough to want not to offend, or speak in a way which is abrupt or hard to understand," Ginsberg declared. This said, he went on to speak of the importance of individualism in the United States—a tradition, he pointed out, that dated back to the country's founding fathers and such revered thinkers and philosophers as Thoreau, Emerson, and Whitman. The complexities of modern civilization—"a sort of science fiction Space Age," as he called the times—were changing the way people lived, perhaps to the detriment of individual vision.

Knowing that diplomacy was necessary in discussing what might be considered libertine ideas with politicians whose success depended upon their appealing to the masses, Allen moved ahead cautiously, seeing that he stayed in the first-person plural in his analysis of life in modern America. "We all know and complain about the drawbacks: a feeling of being caught in a bureaucratic machine which is not built to serve some of our deepest feelings. A machine which closes down on our senses, reduces our language and thoughts to uniformity, reduces our sources of inspiration and fact to fewer and fewer channels—as TV does—and monopolizes our attention with second-hand imagery—packaged news and entertainment hours a day—and doesn't really satisfy our deeper needs—healthy personal adventure in environment where we have living contact with each other in the flesh, the human universe we are built to enjoy and grow in."

Allen's humanist message had a familiar ring: If the human race expected to survive the dangers it had placed upon itself with its scientific and technological advances, people were obliged to interact in a loving way. It was Whitman's message in the nineteenth century, and now in the twentieth, it was Ginsberg who was compelled to deliver it with urgency before government officials. "We can't treat each other only as objects, categories of citizens, role players, big names, small names, objects of research or legislation," Allen told the subcommittee. "We can't treat each other as Things lacking sympathy. Our humanity would atrophy crippled and die—*want* to die—because life without feeling is just more 'Thing,' more inhuman universe."

Now that he had set the table, so to speak, Allen was free to move on to the point of his testimony—the idea that psychedelic drugs offered the potential for personal discovery that could lead to a better society. He spoke of his experiences with peyote, of how that particular drug had helped him get in touch with feelings that had been buried in his subconscious and held there by societal conditioning. He detailed his yage experiences in Peru, noting that they had opened his mind and heart to women, making possible the kind of relationships that had been previously impossible, due in part to the frightening experiences he had gone through with his mother. He talked about his experiences with LSD and described his and Ken Kesey's encounter with the Hell's Angels, stating that "LSD helped break down the fear barrier" in defusing a potential confrontation between peace marchers and the motorcycle club. "With psychedelics as catalysts, I have seen the world more deeply at specific times," Allen said, concluding the anecdotal portion of his presentation, "and that has made me more peaceable."

He hoped to make three main points about LSD to the subcommittee. First, much of the panic or disapproval over psychedelic drugs was the result of exaggeration or inaccuracy in reporting by the media. To illustrate his point, Allen referred to an item that had run in the New York newspapers the previous week. According to the reports, a five-year-old girl had accidentally swallowed an LSD-laced sugar cube that she found in the refrigerator at her home. The initial account, filed in the *New York Post* on April 6, reported that the child had gone "wild"—the reporter writing that it was not uncommon for people under the influence of LSD to go berserk or, in extraordinary cases, murder someone or commit suicide. The next day's report in the same paper had the girl in "very critical condition," "clinging to life" while doctors worked frantically to save her. As it turned out, the reports had been less than truthful. In reality, Allen testified, providing an April 14 copy of the *New York Telegram and Sun* as evidence, the girl had been taken to the hospital for observation, and within hours of her admittance, the effects of the drug began to wear off; she started to behave normally again and was released. Quoting noteworthy doctors, Allen pointed out that at that time there had been no deaths reported anywhere that could be directly attributed to the drug. In its never-ending search for hot copy, the media had greatly exaggerated the truth.

Allen's second point also dealt with the difference between perception and reality: Statistics did not bear out the growing public fear of LSD-induced psychoses in either healthy or mentally ill people. Once again, he offered clippings from his files—scholarly studies indicating that the number of reported instances of psychotic behavior in relation to the number of people estimated to be using LSD was very low. "The incidence of semipermanent breakdown [from LSD]," Allen testified, "may be lower than [in] liquor drinking, auto driving, and marriage—much less war making, or any business activity where a healthy amount of stress is encountered."

His last point had much greater political implications, hinting of the separation between church and state. Not only had psychedelic drugs such as peyote and *ayahuasca* been used in religious ceremony for hundreds of years but even in modern times, when such drugs and LSD were taken by individuals for nonreligious reasons, people were known to have "religious or transcendental or serious blissful experiences through psychedelics." Government officials ought to take this into account and "treat LSD use with proper humanity and respect," Allen suggested, leaving unstated the fact that freedom to pursue spirituality is a constitutionally guaranteed right, as long as that pursuit is conducted within the framework of the law.

In addressing questions from the senators on the subcommittee, Allen was not subjected to the kind of hectoring that had marked Timothy Leary's appearance only a couple of weeks earlier, but the line of questioning was sharp nonetheless. When asked by North Dakota's Senator Quentin Burdick whether he would recommend LSD to college students, Allen took a cautious approach in responding. To recommend drugs to youths of any age was not useful, he replied, because doing so only frightened people who were unfamiliar with the drugs; the key, he said, was to demystify LSD, to study it and give a clear picture of what it really was. "The first recommendation I would make," he offered, "is a recommendation for massive institutional research into it, a broad enough research so that any younger person, student, who wished to avail himself of the LSD experiences might have an opportunity to do so under safe circumstances."

Burdick moved on to a discussion about marijuana, giving Allen the opportunity to enter into the *Congressional Record* a statement that made his position on the topic absolutely clear then and in years to come:

> I think there is no danger at all with marijuana. In fact, there is much more danger in keeping the laws against marijuana than there is in liberalizing them because, as it is, so many people smoke marijuana everywhere that it is like the old prohibition problem we had before I was conscious. The danger in illegalizing marijuana now is that you make criminals out of the most intelligent and sensitive people in the country. You create a climate of fear. You create police state conditions in that area with policy spying, with attempts to set people up. You send young kids to jail and ruin their careers. There is the real danger. You get real breakdown and madness and often, I suppose, the possibility of suicide through that kind of social pressure.
>
> I think this country would be a much healthier place if we got rid of the marijuana laws, or else made some amelioration which made it sensible to a point where what we all know unofficially becomes officially accepted.

Senator Jacob Javits took exception to Allen's speaking as if he was an authority and making recommendations to the subcommittee—even if, in fact,

Allen would not have been invited to testify had it not been believed that he
was capable of doing both. On several occasions, Javits made a point of reminding Allen that he was not a doctor, scientist, or researcher—that he
was a poet—and while their exchange may not have been hostile, it could
nevertheless be characterized as brusque, less than friendly:

Q. Do you agree that research has not yet demonstrated the fact that [LSD]
   is or is not a dangerous drug, or what dosages should or should not be taken
   without great harm, what frequency and so on?
A. Yes, I think there is already sufficient research to show what dosages are
   dangerous and whether or not there is immediate danger. For instance, we
   have the experience of the American Indians for the last 70 years who
   have used peyote, which is a psychedelic drug.
Q. That is not LSD.
A. They are very, very similar in effect.
Q. That is your opinion. Are you a doctor? Do you have any credentials to
   make scientific evaluations of this drug, its dosage, its effect and so on, on
   anyone but yourself?
A. Except for the reading or the fact that I might cite the *Pharmacology of
   Therapeutics*, which puts peyote and LSD together in the same class and
   says their effects are similar.
Q. Do you consider yourself qualified to give a medical opinion which will
   determine the fate of my 16½-year-old-son?
A. No, I am not pharmacologically qualified to give a judgment like that.
A. Of course you are not, and that is the important point that must be made
   to those who will listen to you.

Despite this kind of exchange, Allen held his temper and remained respectful. He maintained his recommendation that more research be conducted before
the laws were changed, and he offered a detailed plan, drawn up in consultation
with doctors, of how that research might be conducted. He supplied the senators
with copies of clippings and research from his files.

For all his efforts, his testimony had little impact on the subcommittee's
decisions. Chairman Thomas Dodd might have tipped off the group's predisposition when he referred to psychedelic drugs as a "menace"; the subcommittee
recommended legislating against LSD. Allen's testimony, *The Village Voice*
reported, was in essence a curiosity, "Archy the Cockroach come to life, telling
the depression-ridden America of the '30s to be gentle and look at themselves.
But America still stomped on roaches and Ginsberg's testimony may have been
equally futile against the 'just the facts, ma'am' scrutiny of the Subcommittee. . . . He was not rebuked. More likely, he received the much-tauted, 'white
liberal' treatment. He was smiled at and ignored."

9

Allen may have been ignored by government officials but, as Senator Javits not
so delicately brought forward, he did have a large influence on the country's

youth. He was enthusiastically received at his poetry readings and on those occasions when he was asked to sit on discussion panels. Although he was rapidly approaching the age of forty, he was perceived to be more in touch with the younger generation than most people his age. When Princeton University hosted a panel discussion of the arts, Allen joined journalist Tom Wolfe, German author Günter Grass, editor Paul Krassner, and filmmaker Gregory Markapoulos in a spirited debate. Typically, Allen was open to any new form of expression, from underground films to Andy Warhol's Pop Art. The growing use of LSD was creating a market for a new kind of art, Allen told the capacity audience, predicting that one future trend in the arts might stem from "some kind of psychedelic-colored expressionism"—a statement realized over the next several years in the poster art of Peter Max and others, as well as in the continuing output of Warhol.

The day after giving his testimony in Washington, D.C., Allen was back on the West Coast, participating in a flurry of activities that included a benefit reading for the Artists Liberation Front, readings in smaller venues, and a panel discussion on narcotics sponsored by *Playboy* magazine. San Francisco was on the verge of birthing the hippie culture that would be so nationally prominent within a year, during the "Summer of Love," and Allen easily fit into the milieu of mid-sixties bohemianism that now had rock 'n' roll rather than jazz as its sound track. Ralph J. Gleason, covering a multimedia show that featured Ginsberg, the rock 'n' roll band Sopwith Camel, a mime troupe, and a dance company—Allen appearing onstage in an Uncle Sam top hat, reading "Wichita Vortex Sutra"—may have caught the flavor of the West Coast in his descriptive account of the evening: "It was a mardi gras, a masked ball with people in costumes, painted with designs, carrying plasticine banners through the audi-ence while multi-colored liquid light projections played around them." Gins-berg, Gleason noted, had reached such a stage as an artist that he was "on the edge of doing, from another direction, what Dylan has done—speak through mass media."

The demands on Ginsberg's time were equalled only, perhaps, by the de-mands for his work. Small press and alternative newspapers and magazines constantly solicited it. There were the collected poems volume for England, a proposed anthology of interviews and essays for a publisher in the United States, the possibility of two volumes of journals—all clamoring for Allen's attention at a time when he was trying to assemble a new "Pockets Poets" volume that he was calling *Planet News*. The taped auto poesy still awaited transcription. At times, the work load was suffocating: "Yes, I write, that's the easy part," Allen wrote Philip Whalen. "The hard thing is letters, editing, phone calls, people busted, time demands—keeping organized and transcribing and editing, I've fallen behind."

On July 22, Allen boarded a train bound for Chicago. From there, he caught a bus to New York. He had his Uher with him and as he made his way cross-country, he dictated another long poem onto tape. "Iron Horse," though lacking the impact of "Wichita Vortex Sutra," became an important part of the Ginsberg sequence of poems about America. For one thing, he now had four of the major forms of transportation—air, rail, bus, and automobile—represented in his sequence, and with a decreasing number of passenger trains running long-distance routes in the United States, Allen was again reminded of the enormous progress that had taken place over the past four decades, as well as of how some things never seemed to change, especially humankind's tendency to wage war:

> Who's the enemy, year after year?
> War after war, who's the enemy?
> What's the weapon, battle after battle?
> What's the news, defeat after defeat?
> What's the picture, decade after decade?
> Television shows blood,
> print broken arms burning skin photographs,
> wounded bodies revealed on the screen
> Cut sound out of television you won't tell who's Victim
> Cut language off the Visual you'll never know
> Who's Aggressor—
> cut commentary from Newscast
> you'll see a mass of madmen at murder. . . .

In this account of his journey, Ginsberg grows nostalgic for better times. He remembers the time he spent with Kerouac in Mexico, as well as his own private exploration of the ruins in the Yucatán. Traveling on the train with a group of young soldiers, he is disturbed by their kill-or-be-killed mentality, which, after all, is merely a reflection of the official attitude. Only a few months earlier, he had declared an end to the war, lifting his voice in confidence, a prophet speaking for the people's secret desires; now he is depressed, feeling like a pariah:

> Too late, too late
> the Iron Horse hurrying to war,
> too late for laments
> too late for warning—
> I'm a stranger alone in my country again. . . .

Discouraged, he wonders whether he would be better off if he moved out of the public light and retreated to a quiet house on the banks of the Mississippi, a cabin in Big Sur, a farmhouse in Oregon, or some other out-of-the-way place. Maybe, he thinks, he might be better off if he was to withdraw from the madness and find an isolated spot for the solitary life, where he could exist like Thoreau:

> Better to meditate under a tree
> Better become a nun in the forest
> Better turn flapjacks in Omaha
> than be a prophet on the electric Networks—
> There's nothing left for this country but doom
> There's nothing left for this country but death. . . .

"Iron Horse," published as a booklet by City Lights in 1974, is a strange poem inasmuch as by itself it is not the major work that Ginsberg probably hoped it would be. Yet, placed in its proper context, following "Wichita Vortex Sutra" and preceding many of Ginsberg's *Fall of America* poems, it adds a crucial dimension to the sequence. A careful reading of this sequence finds Ginsberg exploring the same themes, using many of the same devices and expressions, his moods fluctuating like the moods of the country itself. In "Wichita Vortex Sutra," he attempts to will a democratic victory over the mechanizations of war; in "Iron Horse," the masses seem to be lost, blurred by the rush of the train and bus (or passing time), doomed figures in America's inevitable fall.

10

Allen, of course, did not retreat from the public eye. In all probability, it would have been impossible. His work was reaching its peak in popularity. In June, City Lights had published another nine-thousand-copy run of *Howl and Other Poems*, and by the end of the summer, Ferlinghetti wrote to say that this latest printing was almost sold out and that City Lights would be running another edition of each of his books.

In addition, he was reaching his peak in exposure as a public figure. If this bothered him—and he would complain about it to his friends or make occasional reference to it in his poetry and journals—he certainly did very little to divert or discourage the attention. He maintained his schedule of readings, appeared in a forum with Dr. James Fox, a researcher for the Drug Control Abuse Bureau of the Food and Drug Administration, and read at a marathon poetry reading in Washington Square Park to reaffirm poets' rights to read in public parks without permits.

One offshoot of Allen's involvement in various literary, social, and political arenas was his development as an essayist. In the past, he had written and published an assortment of prose, from formal essays to book introductions, but the mid-sixties were by far his most productive years. Two essays from late 1966 typify his range. "Some Metamorphoses of Personal Prosody" is an abbreviated delineation of personal influences, beginning with Wyatt and running through the Beatles. Ginsberg had reached the point where his poetry was now the subject of scholarly papers and was being taught on college campuses across the country—Monarch Notes, one of the leading publishers of literary study guides, had even issued a pamphlet on Beat literature—and Allen was determined to set the record straight. He had evolved greatly as a poet in his decade in the public eye, and more often than not this development was misunderstood or misinterpreted. Concerned that the fallacies would "set another whole generation of unspecialized innocent students off on the wrong track again," Allen felt an obligation to keep an accurate record, particularly in the case of his major works. Interviews were disposable—lost, cast aside, or forgotten as soon as a reader or viewer put aside a newspaper or magazine or shut off the television or radio—so Allen used his essays, which he intended to gather eventually into one volume, to address the background relevant to his major works. He had already done so with "Howl" and "Kaddish" in earlier essays. "Some Metamorphoses of Personal Prosody" dealt with "Wichita Vortex Sutra" in specific and his auto poesy in general, with Allen citing his interests in music and mantras as a direct influence on his new vocalized poetry. " 'Wichita Vortex Sutra,' a short fragment of longer trans-america poetries, is . . . composed directly on tape by voice, and then transcribed to page: page arrangement notates the thought-stops, breath-stops, runs of inspiration, changes of mind, startings and stoppings of car," Allen wrote, providing an addition to his canon of statements about spontaneous poetry composition.

The November 1966 edition of *Atlantic Monthly* published a lengthy essay on another topic of concern to Ginsberg. "The Great Marijuana Hoax: First Manifesto to End the Bringdown" was Allen's contribution to the demystification of public perception regarding marijuana laws and use. Heavily annotated from sources in the Ginsberg files, the essay, like Allen's testimony before the Senate subcommittee, was a formal attempt to separate the myth from reality, and the message was similar: Marijuana laws had been built on misinformation designed and circulated by the United States Treasury Department's Narcotics Bureau and such deceit needed to be brought into the open. Contrary to popular belief, Allen wrote, smoking marijuana did not make one a dope fiend; in fact, it was part of religious and cultural ceremony throughout the world. Nor did using marijuana lead one down the road to heroin abuse, as the government would have people believe. In fact, studies dating back to the 1890s indicated that marijuana was harmless. As for the connection between pot and criminality, Allen argued that the laws were such that the industry, by nature, was criminal, users and sellers alike. Some of the country's great minds were occasional marijuana users and these otherwise law-abiding citizens risked their futures every time they dared to light a joint. Ginsberg's essay was well conceived, argued, and documented, and its appearance in one of the country's most highly respected magazines gave it a further sense of credibility among the "squares" who might have waved it off as so much radical babbling had it been published in one of the many underground publications springing up across the country.

As it was, the authorities were doing their level best to squash any kind of different or radical thinking. When Allen spoke of smoking marijuana at a reading with his father in Paterson, his hometown's mayor ordered a warrant for his arrest. When Swami Bhaktivedanta located his International Society of Krishna Consciousness organization in a Second Avenue storefront, the Department of Immigration informed him that his visa had expired and would not be renewed, setting off a demonstration and chanting session in a Lower East Side park that Allen supported with his attendance.

If the opposition, harassment, or general apathy bothered Ginsberg—and it did—it failed to deter him from pursuing his own vision for America and the planet itself. He forged ahead, stating his message in his poetry and essays and to sold-out audiences attending his readings. If the message was not accepted, it would not be for his lack of effort.

20
The Fall of America

I will haunt these States
   with beard bald head
   eyes staring out plane window,
   hair hanging in Greyhound bus midnight
leaning over taxicab seat to admonish
      an angry cursing driver
      hand lifted to calm
      his outraged vehicle
that I pass with the Green Light of common law. . . .

1

"Turn on, tune in, drop out."

By the beginning of 1967, Timothy Leary's catchphrase was becoming the slogan of the hippie culture in the Haight-Ashbury area of San Francisco, where thousands of young people were casting aside the values of their parents and forming a society of their own. Their alternative lifestyle, contrary to the popular notion, involved much more than free sex and free use of drugs and freedom from work. Rebelling against the mind-set that propagated the Vietnam War, racial prejudice, the destruction of the natural environment, and excessive materialism, the hippies pressed for a more blissful, communal spirit between people. With their unique jargon, macrobiotic diets, secondhand clothing, love beads, and uncut hair, the hippies were as subject to scorn and parody as their predecessors, the beatniks, had been in the late 1950s. Their message of universal peace, love, and harmony seemed hopelessly idealistic to their counterparts, but in the early months of 1967, when the Vietnam War was claiming more lives than anyone would have predicted a few years earlier, Haight-Ashbury made more sense than Washington, D.C., to the growing ranks of youths dropping out of society.

To Allen, this was a dream come true, and he, along with Peter Orlovsky and Maretta Greer, flew out to San Francisco to check it out firsthand. A festival—known officially as the Gathering of the Tribes for a Human Be-In—was being organized for San Francisco's Golden Gate Park and Allen was serving on its planning committee. Since he had already scheduled readings for Pennsylvania, Illinois, and Missouri, commencing on January 21, he realized that his stay in San Francisco would by necessity be shorter than he would have liked it to be. As soon as he arrived on the West Coast, he was reunited with Gary Snyder, Michael McClure, and Jerry Rubin—all on the planning committee—and he was told that Timothy Leary was flying in for the occasion.

The festival was not without precedent in the San Francisco area. In 1966, there had been several notable events, beginning with the Trips Festival, held on January 21 to 23, and including a gathering for the summer solstice, a Love Pagent Rally, and, most recently on December 17, a celebration of Now Day. The festivals were multimedia events featuring music, poetry readings, performance art, political speeches, and, whenever possible, spectacular light and sound shows. The Human Be-In was planned to follow in this tradition. Posters advertising the event announced appearances by Ginsberg, Leary, McClure, Snyder, Rubin, poet Lenore Kandel, comic/activist Dick Gregory, Lawrence Ferlinghetti, and former Leary colleague Richard Alpert; an official press release encouraged attendants to bring costumes, blankets, bells, flags, symbols, cymbals, drums, beads, feathers, and flowers. The Human Be-In, said the organizers, was to be "the joyful, face-to-face beginning of a new epoch." By Ginsberg's description, the event was designed to be a "gathering together of younger people aware of the planetary fate that we are all sitting in the middle of, embued with a new consciousness and desiring of a new kind of society involving prayer, music and spiritual life together rather than competition, acquisition and war."

January 14, the day of the be-in, was warm and sunny and an estimated twenty to thirty thousand people gathered on the polo field of Golden Gate Park for the four-hour festival that, in retrospect, acted as a prefatory event to the Summer of Love. The Grateful Dead, Jefferson Airplane, and Quicksilver Messenger Service provided the music, and Ginsberg and Snyder read their poetry. Jerry Rubin and Timothy Leary gave speeches, Leary exhorting the gathering to "turn onto the scene, tune into what is happening, and drop out—of high school, college, grad school, junior executive, senior executive—and follow me." The Diggers, the area's best-known alternative community, distributed free sandwiches laced with LSD, while Hell's Angels acted as the event's security force. At one point, a man parachuted into the crowd, leading some of the tripping observers to believe that God or Buddha had joined them for the event. Allen had mixed feelings about the festival, no doubt tempered by an argument he'd had earlier in the day with Peter, who, high on speed, refused to attend. On the one hand, the incredible assembly, staged without a serious problem, appeared to be the manifestation of the "politics of ecstasy," a national evolution of the vision Allen and his friends had conceived two decades earlier; on the other hand, his experiences in Czechoslovakia on May Day 1965 had shown how a police state could still thwart the wills and efforts of the masses. Open displays of love and community goodwill, held under the auspices of a large day-long gathering, might not be strong enough to overcome the mentality that was still waging war overseas.

"What if we're all wrong?" Allen whispered onstage to Ferlinghetti at one point, posing a question that had passed through the minds of others, as well. Despite his doubts, Allen urged the crowd to continue its communal spirit. As the day drew to an end, he led the crowd in a mantra-chanting session and asked that they help clean the park as they were leaving. Gary Snyder signaled the conclusion of the be-in, as he had signaled its beginning, by blowing a sustained note on a conch shell.

The be-in passed without incident, without a confrontation with the police or civic authorities. As intended, it was both a big party and an important signal that the alternative lifestyle of these rebellious youths was not simply a fad. For Allen, it bordered on being a religious experience. In fact, it had been consciously organized that way. "We went to considerable lengths to follow the way a Hindu *mela*, or gathering of holy men and seekers, is conducted," he explained later. "We began by chanting a special mantra for removing disasters. There was a purifactory circumambulation of the polo field to drive away demons and bad influences."

Jane Kramer was in San Francisco at the time of the be-in, at work on a lengthy profile of Ginsberg for *The New Yorker* (eventually published in book form as *Allen Ginsberg in America*). Kramer used the be-in as the opening of her profile. Describing Allen as "a combination guru and paterfamilias" and "a kind of ultimate faculty advisor," Kramer attributed to Ginsberg the status of unofficial father of the Flower Power movement: "Preaching and colonizing a brave new never-never world of bearded, beaded, marijuana-smoking, mantra-chanting euphoria, Ginsberg set the style for the Be-Ins, Love-Ins, Kiss-Ins, Chant-Ins, sacred orgies, and demon dispelling circumambulations of local draft boards, all of which began with the San Francisco Gathering of the Tribes."

Allen's schedule was astonishing and it took someone of his energy to accommodate it. Not only was he making numerous appearances at universities and public events but he was zigzagging across the country at breakneck pace. Nevertheless, he managed to satisfy both his artistic and political interests. On February 12, he appeared with the Fugs at the University of Toronto, sharing the Perception '67 billing with Paul Krassner and Marshall McLuhan. On April 7 he was in Nashville, taking part in IMPACT '67, a series of lectures and symposiums that featured such noteworthy speakers as Martin Luther King, Jr., Senator Strom Thurmond, and journalist Rowland Evans. A few days later, he was in Cleveland, where he created a stir by defending controversial, often-arrested poet and publisher D. A. Levy, who was again being hounded for printing obscene materials, although it was likely that the main objection to Levy was his antiestablishment attitudes. Allen promised to help raise funds for his financial and moral support. "Social and political criticism is protected by the Constitution," Allen stated in Levy's defense, adding that "instead of persecuting him, he should be given a prize by the city for his poems about Cleveland. He stands alone in his effort to lift Cleveland . . . and he is being made to suffer in the classic American way."

Although he knew of Levy and his work—the surname alone must have captured his attention—Allen's involvement in Cleveland was representative of his interest and involvement in the cities he visited. He had long ago grown accustomed to the seemingly endless calls and letters requesting his assistance, and he was tireless in his efforts to give assistance whenever he could or, if that was impossible, put people in contact with others who could. His address book was legendary among those who knew him, its contents a veritable clearing-house of poets, writers, lawyers, politicians, media figures, bureaucrats, and countercultural figures. Whenever he visited a city, he read its newspapers and asked countless questions about its people and politics. Part of what he learned found its way into his poems about America, while part, if the occasion warranted, resulted in direct action.

His winter/spring tour continued. In the week's time between April 11 and April 18, Allen appeared at John Hopkins University in Baltimore, Oberlin College in Ohio, the University of Southern California, the University of Colorado, and the University of Texas. Despite such respect accorded by highly regarded academic institutions, the controversy associated with his name spawned many an argument at other colleges. In Oregon, for instance, Portland State College students and faculty debated whether to allow Ginsberg to appear at a scheduled May 22 reading. The president of the college worried that Allen's reading might result in a dropped enrollment of five hundred students and tarnish the college's image with the Oregon legislature.

School officials decided to permit the Ginsberg reading, but the controversy did not abate. A newspaper report mentioned that Ginsberg was "famous for taking off his clothes at climactic points in his readings," adding that he had agreed to behave himself and comply with university-imposed "propriety demands" as a condition for his reading at Portland State. Neither statement, as Allen later pointed out, was true. Then, a few days before his reading, The Vanguard, Portland State's student newspaper, published a Richard Avedon photograph of Allen posing naked, his left hand discreetly covering his genitals, his right hand raised, palm out. The photograph, widely circulated in newspapers and published in Avedon's book Nothing Personal, angered school officials, particularly President Branford P. Miller, who suspended publication of the school paper and issued a statement calling the photo a vulgar misrepresentation of Ginsberg and what he had to say.

Allen could not have disagreed more. "I am not one to be insulted by my own physical image, especially photo'd in the act of making religious hand signs," he wrote, explaining that his gestures were Buddhist mudras signifying contemplation and assurance. Furthermore, he had not taken off his clothes at a reading in a decade, and that occasion was in a private residence, not a university hall. From all he had read and heard, he concluded:

> All gossip I have heard to date emphasizes the fact that all this great flapping and fantasy are traceable back to groups of ladies and gentlemen over college age who neither attended the poetry reading nor understood the significance of the photograph, and who assume that I am some sort of obscene quack ripping off my clothes in public, mouthing four-letter words exclusively and mouthing them exclusively at Portland State, all this supposedly done for private financial gain or in an unAmerican attempt to subvert our tender youth who should be in training to die in Vietnam rather than listening to filthy poetry readings. This mentality had invaded the editorial columns of local and supposedly serious Portland newspapers, and, in fact, one hears, it is a similar opinionation held by various State Legislators that has caused President Miller to take rash action, issue [a] statement about my nudity

in newspapers, suspend and burn the Portland State student newspaper, etc.

The reading itself was a success, free of controversy or incident. Allen hung around Oregon for a week. Ken Kesey had recently purchased a farm near Eugene and Allen stopped by to visit him, Neal Cassady, and the other Merry Pranksters. Allen noticed the years of hard living were catching up with Cassady, who had grown gaunt and pale. Allen no longer found Neal sexually attractive, although he conceded, as he headed into middle age himself, that he was in all likelihood similarly unattractive to others. Cassady, however, had lost none of his sharp mind, and he entertained Allen and the others with his stream-of-consciousness raps. On May 25, Allen boarded the psychedelic bus with Kesey, Cassady, and the others and they all made a grand entrance at Western State College, where Allen and Neal appeared with the Jefferson Airplane.

It was time to start moving eastward again. Allen had July commitments in Italy and England and had offered to accompany Louis and Edith on their tour of Europe in August. Before he left the country, he hoped to catch up on his correspondence and set his affairs in order in New York. There was also a full slate of readings scheduled for the Midwest. Allen said good-bye to Kesey and Cassady, never suspecting that it would be the last time he would see Neal.

2

By the summer of 1967, the concept of Flower Power had blossomed into a nationwide movement, with the Haight-Ashbury section of San Francisco still acting as its unofficial headquarters. In virtually every large American city, throngs of long-haired hippies gathered to celebrate their alternative society and—if only for a short time—it looked as if the alternative could peacefully coexist with the society being rebelled against. The youths had their own news sources and publications, their own stores, their own social events. The Beatles' song "All You Need Is Love" became an anthem exhorting the young masses to abandon the aggressive society of their elders. The mainstream culture, initially amused by the movement's idealistic position, had no choice but to take notice, even if it still did not approve.

Ironically, Allen was out of the country for most of the Summer of Love. On July 5, he arrived in Italy, ready to participate in the annual Spoleto Festival. Ezra Pound, who had been honored at the preceding year's festival, was present and Allen finally had the opportunity to meet him, though Pound maintained the silence he had been holding in public for years and merely shook Ginsberg's hand. When it was his turn to read at the festival, Allen tried to further the spirit of international brotherhood and sisterhood by reading "Who Be Kind To"—a selection that ultimately caused him some inconvenience. That night, after the readings, Allen visited a small café with poets Octavio Paz and Desmond O'Grady. Their pleasant evening of talking and beer drinking was interrupted when Allen was approached by a man in a business suit who announced that he was with the police and that Allen had to come with him. Allen instantly thought of his troubles in Czechoslovakia and, frightened by what he described as the "sudden recall of the old police sensation, isolation trap," he tried to make certain that his journal and manuscripts were in safe hands. As he went to retrieve his shoulder bag, he told O'Grady that he was being arrested and asked him to call a translator and legal counsel. In his haste to secure his writings, Allen accidentally turned his bag upside down, sending its contents all over the café's marble floor. "Don't panic," O'Grady advised Allen, trying to calm him.

Allen was held at the police station for three hours. In Italy, Allen learned, the mere use of certain words in public could get one arrested—even if the words were used in artistic context. He was prepared to debate the issue, and when Fernanda Pivano, his Italian translator, arrived with a legal representative at the station, Allen engaged in a lengthy philosophical discussion with the police about obscenity and the law. When the officials asked him to sign a statement, he refused, claiming that the language in the statement was theirs, not his. They then worked on a new statement, Allen admitting that he had used some of the prohibited words in his poem but confessing to no wrongdoing. "Such lines taken out of context might be misunderstood," he wrote, making a point to note that the actual message of "Who Be Kind To" was "goodwill to peaceful men." Allen signed the statement and was allowed to leave.

Word of his arrest spread quickly and the paparazzi were waiting for him as he left the station to be escorted to the opera. Later that evening, Allen was informed that the charges had been dropped, but the damage was done. The next day's papers were full of accounts of the arrest, even if, as Louis Ginsberg remarked in a letter to Allen, the whole affair was little more than a "tempest in a teapot."

After the festival, Allen flew to London, where he had a number of engagements lined up. He had loved England from the first time he visited the country in 1958, and "Swinging London" in 1967 was an exciting addition to what he had witnessed in San Francisco. The psychedelic revolution, ushered in by the Beatles' masterwork album *Sgt. Pepper's Lonely Hearts Club Band,* was in evidence everywhere, London's avenues and shops alive with bright colors and swirling paisley designs. Allen took it all in, filling the pages of his journal with some of his most descriptive writing in months, as if after a long period of submersion in American political concerns, he had finally come to a calm surface where he was able to enjoy the exhilaration of art for its own sake. He met and partied with Mick Jagger of the Rolling Stones and on another occasion he visited Paul McCartney of the Beatles. Jagger and Stones songwriter/guitarist Keith Richards had been recently sentenced to jail terms for minor drug offenses, and the two had written "We Love You," a psychedelic account of their night in jail. Jagger invited Allen to the song's recording session.

Although the press had created a great sense of competition between the Rolling Stones and Beatles over the years, the members of the two bands were, in fact, friendly, and when Allen arrived at the recording studio, he was pleased to find John Lennon and Paul McCartney in attendance. The Beatles had paid good-humored tribute to the Stones on the cover of *Sgt. Pepper,* and the Stones would return the favor by hiding the Beatles' faces in the flowers pictured on the cover of *Their Satanic Majesty's Request*. Allen was delighted to be involved in a historic recording session involving members of the two most successful rock bands in the world. Beside "We Love You," the Stones were working on "Dandelion," their tribute to the flower children. When it came time to work on "We Love You," the two Beatles, sitting on high stools, joined the Stones for the recording of the vocals. Allen sat in the control room, entranced, conducting the singers with his Shiva beads and Tibetan oracle ring. "I stared and made mudras of Rakshan prayer," Allen wrote in his journal, describing the scene as "the flower moment of rue, richness as amethyst and pearl, diamond noise for the mind, majesty of the most delightful labor of the Universe, chanting music to the world, angels of the summit of meat." Allen envied them. They had musical talent and an incredibly large following. The session lasted all night, the musicians joining Allen in the control room to listen to the playback when they had finished recording.

While in England, Allen participated in several events of strong political purpose. On July 16, he attended a rally for the legalization of marijuana held in Hyde Park. Compared to the be-in in San Francisco, the assembly was small and far less organized. The British press estimated the crowd at five thousand, but it had dwindled considerably by the time Allen arrived. He had brought along his harmonium to use as accompaniment when he chanted his mantras, but he had no sooner begun when a policeman told him that music was not allowed in the park. Allen chanted the Hare Krishna mantra with a small group sitting in the grass near him. The afternoon was pleasant, but the rally as a whole was somewhat of a disappointment.

The other event, the Dialectics of Liberation conference, was much more significant to him. The conference, organized by radical psychologist R. D. Laing and held at London's Round House, was designed "to demystify human violence in all its forms, the social systems from which it emanates, and to explore new forms of action." Lecture and panel-discussion topics were widely varying, with Stokely Carmichael's lecture of black separatism drawing the most attention and controversy. Allen participated in several panel discussions and, on July 20, gave his address, "Consciousness and Practical Action." For Allen, the high point of the conference was Gregory Bateson's seminar, "Ecological Destruction by Technology." Allen had been interested in ecological issues from the time of his early meetings with Gary Snyder and Michael McClure in San Francisco, but he had not realized the enormity of the issues involved until he heard Bateson give an exposition about his then-radical theories concerning the greenhouse effect. Bateson, Allen noted later, gave him an "ecological perspective":

> Bateson gave a great lecture on ecological mind and perspectives, and just presented the information that Gary and McClure were talking about with our discoveries on the Club of Rome about *Limits to Growth*. And Bateson said, you keep the heat up the way you're keeping it up and the fog gathers up, and pretty soon you have a cloud over the sky and you have the greenhouse effect and the earth will heat up and melt

the poles, and the poles will melt and drown the cities with 200 feet
of water. . . . He was just pointing out the natural consequences of
over-activity and thoughtless feedback.

Bateson's lecture left a lasting impression on Allen, but it offered its own
immediate rewards as well, at least in an indirect way. Bateson's predictions set
off in Ginsberg a series of meditations about nature and the natural beauty of
the planet, the major result being his "Wales Visitation," an often-anthologized
poem universally recognized as one of his finest. After the conference, Allen
had gone to Wales, where he planned to spend a restful weekend with publisher
Tom Maschler at his retreat in the Black Mountains. Along the way, they
stopped to tour the ruins of Tintern Abbey, the sight of which put Allen in an
even more contemplative mood.

Wales's Llanthony Valley was beautiful, and on Saturday, July 29, Allen
took some LSD and sat cross-legged on a grassy hillside to contemplate the
natural wonder surrounding him. For all his talk about keeping LSD legal, this
was the first acid he had taken since his visit to Ferlinghetti's Big Sur cabin in
late 1965. Allen's fear of arrest in the States, along with his fear of having a
bad trip, had kept him from using the psychedelic drug with any frequency, but
the Big Sur trip had shown him the splendor of nature without any bad effects.
In the Wales countryside, there was little danger of his confronting narcotics
agents. Allen sat quietly for hours, observing everything around him. As a
result of the consideration he had been giving the ecology since the Dialectics
of Liberation conference, he looked at the minute particulars around him as a
part of a much vaster scheme. The earth—the entire universe—became a huge
breathing organism of which he, the mountains, the grass, the birds, and the
flowers were just a tiny part. The feeling was not unlike the sensation he had
experienced nearly twenty years earlier when he had watched the sun setting
on the building cornices in Harlem and realized that he was living in the tiniest
fragment of eternity. Taking up his pen, he wrote an exact description of what
he was seeing:

> Thru the thick wall'd window on the vale browed
>   white fog afloat
>   Trees moving in rivers of wind
>   The clouds arise
>   as on a wave, gigantic eddy lifting mist
>   above teeming ferns exquisitely swayed
>   by one gentle motion vast as the long green crag
>   glimpsed thru mullioned glass in valley raine. . . .

Such details, Allen noted later, were "the human things that everybody has
seen in nature" but that people seldom stopped to recognize and appreciate. The
LSD "clarified my mind and left it open to get that giant, vast consciousness," he
explained.

> Specifically, the one thing I noticed and tried to describe was the ocean
> of heaven. The atmosphere is like an ocean, and at the bottom of that

ocean of air are all sorts of rivulets [and] breezes, and those rivulets, like at the bottom of a fish tank, move all the trees, move the people around, the air, the beards, the grass. . . . So that it's like one giant being breathing—one giant being that we're all part of. . . .

If one was to compare Ginsberg's eyes to the lens of a movie camera, the lens movement in "Wales Visitation" collapses from the huge wide-angle shot to the most extreme microscopic close-up, as if a camera positioned above the earth continued to zoom in until it captured the tiniest detail and then moved back out again. For the long shot:

A solid mass of heaven, mist infused, ebbs thru vale,
   a wavelet of Immensity, lapping gigantic through Llanthony Valley,
the length of all England, valley upon valley under Heaven's
   ocean. . . .

While, for the close-up:

   . . . of the satanic thistle that raises its horned symmetry
      flowering above sister grass-daisies' pink tiny
         bloomlets angelic as lightbulbs. . . .

Ginsberg was able to fine-tune this effect in his revision of the original draft, but even as he was in the process of writing, his mind altered by LSD, he was conscious of the fact that, rather than try to describe his state of mind—as he had done in his earlier drug poems—he was describing what he was actually seeing. He told interviewer Paul Portugés:

In "Wales Visitation" I guess what I had come to was a realization that me making noise as poetry was no different from the wind making noise in the branches. It was just as natural. It was a *very important point.* The fact that these were thoughts flowing through the mind is as much of a natural object as is the Milky Way floating over the Isle of Skye. So, for the first time, I didn't have to feel guilt or psychological conflict about writing while I was high. Also, for the first time I was able to externalize my attention instead of dwelling on the inner images and symbols and keeping my eyes closed.

Like Ginsberg's other major works, "Wales Visitation" was a happy accident, the result of a number of influences colliding at the point of composition. The fact that he was away from his home base and seeing something for the first time, the consumption of LSD, the Bateson lecture—these and other factors prepared the poet for the writing. Most important, the poem was spontaneous—totally natural and unforced. As his body of published and unpublished work would show, Ginsberg's poetry would tend to fall short of his expectations whenever he consciously sought to create a major work; he would become entangled in words and images, trapped in a web of his own intention. When he was at his best—and there is no doubt that "Wales Visitation" represents

Ginsberg at his best—he trusted his mind and let it lead him wherever it would, the result being the poetry of pure thought, as alive as an instant, as artful as a step through the doors of perception and a walk down the halls of eternity itself.

3

Louis and Edith Ginsberg arrived in London and Allen proceeded to show them the sights of London, Paris, Rome, and Venice—all in a whirlwind tour that could have been the envy of many a travel guide. It was a tender time for the three of them. At seventy-two, Louis had not seen the Europe that Allen had visited at half his age, and though Louis had always received a vicarious thrill from his son's travels and success, he had hoped to see the Continent himself. For nearly a month, Allen played the dutiful son and host, guiding his father and stepmother on their tour, the only sour note coming on the evening of September 4, after Allen had left Louis and Edith behind and was out with friends, listening to a poetry reading on Rome's Spanish Steps. The police arrived and Allen was taken into custody for questioning, apparently because he was part of the undesirable hippie element. Allen was livid, but he escaped the incident without being charged. (The item *did* make the papers, however— no doubt adding to the Ginsberg "wild man" image.) Allen and Louis grew very close during their tour of Europe, Louis later writing Allen and saying that he was "touched, as was Edith, by your devotion and love for us. . . . You were wonderful all around, and I love you more than ever."

After his parents had departed for the States, Allen stayed for a while in Milan with Fernanda Pivano and her husband, Ettore Sottsass, Allen and Fernanda working on translations of Allen's poetry. Pivano knew Ezra Pound and Olga Rudge, his longtime companion, and she was able to arrange for Allen to meet them for lunch at their home in Sant Ambrogio. Their encounter was an improvement over Allen's introduction to Pound in Spoleto, but Pound was still not speaking very much. At eighty-one, he was old and frail and plagued by a form of deep melancholia that left him, quite literally, speechless. Before lunch, the group sat under a tree and sipped wine. Allen had brought along his harmonium and he chanted the Prajnaparamita Sutra and Hare Krishna mantra for Pound. Olga Rudge served pasta for lunch, and while they ate, Allen asked Pound whether he had ever met Céline. He had not, Rudge answered for Pound, and from there Allen went on to recall his and Burroughs's earlier visit with Céline. He told Pound that he had asked Céline to list the French prose writers he liked best. Céline had responded with three names: C. F. Ramuz, Henri Barbusse, and Paul Morand. Allen could not remember the book of Morand's that Céline had enjoyed, and Rudge, trying to encourage Pound to enter the conversation, asked, "Ezra, what was the name of that book by Morand you liked so much? You didn't like what he did later."

Pound looked up from his plate of pasta. "*Ouvert à la Nuit,*" he replied, then returned to his meal. He did not speak again for the rest of the day.

The encounter was by no means a failure, regardless of Pound's silence, and several weeks later Allen was invited to visit him again, this time in Venice, where Pound and Rudge spent their winters. Allen looked forward to another meeting with great anticipation. Ever since his anti-Semitic radio broadcasts during World War II and subsequent incarceration in a mental institution, Pound had fallen out of favor with a large percentage of the poetry establishment, but Ginsberg found him far too great an influence on modern poetry to be dismissed for his politics, no matter how wrongheaded they had been. Pound's use of the ideogram—the juxtaposition or free association of images—had been very influential on Allen's own work, and Pound's attention to the tone and pitch of vowels had brought back the sense of natural music in poetry, influencing Ginsberg, Dylan, and a host of others. Allen saw Pound not only as an important member in poetry's lineage over the centuries but also as a guru, someone who still might have something to teach.

In Venice, Allen took a room at the Pensione Cici, knowing that Pound often ate in its dining room. Hoping to meet Pound and Rudge after one of their luncheons there, he hung around the hotel lobby. His efforts were rewarded on October 21 when he saw them leaving the dining room. Allen reintroduced himself and they sat for a while and had coffee and made arrangements to get together for lunch the next day at Pound's home. Allen should have no trouble finding their house, Olga Rudge suggested; if he did, he should ask someone for directions. "Oftentimes Venetians will walk half a mile to show you a tiny alley," she said.

Pound, who had said nothing during the hour they were together, broke into the conversation. "Forty years since I've seen anybody do that," he said.

"Do what, Ezra?" Olga asked.

"Take the trouble to walk you along to show you the way," Pound responded before falling silent again.

Allen had no difficulty finding their home the next day. He had brought along records by the Beatles, Dylan, and Donovan. After a quiet meal, during which Allen sipped wine and conversed with Olga Rudge and another guest, Pound listening in silence, Allen casually lit a joint and smoked it without saying anything about what he was doing. Slightly high, he then went with the others to the third floor of the house, where he put on the records. He played the Beatles' "Yellow Submarine" and "Eleanor Rigby"—Pound smiling slightly at the line "No one was saved"—and Dylan's "Sad-Eyed Lady of the Lowlands," "Absolutely Sweet Marie," and "Gates of Eden"; he put on Donovan's "Sunshine Superman," as well. Pound had an ivory-handled cane, and on occasion he would tap it lightly on the floor in beat with the music, but he did not comment on it. Every so often, Allen repeated song lyrics for Pound's benefit, and at one point he asked Pound, "Is this all too much electric noise?" Pound sat impassively, smiling at the music. (Olga Rudge later assured Allen that had he been offended or bored by the music, Pound would have left the room immediately.) When he had finished playing the music, Allen ended the afternoon by chanting a selection of mantras.

He saw Pound and Rudge on several other occasions during his stay in Venice, sometimes by design, sometimes by coincidence. He had heard that Pound would address specific questions about his poetry—particularly queries concerning the earlier works—so he prepared himself for that eventuality by rereading Pound's *Cantos* and familiarizing himself with the places mentioned in those poems. He remained determined to have a literary discussion with the master.

The opportunity presented itself on October 28, when Pound agreed to see him again. On that day, Allen, critic Michael Reck, and English poet/critic Peter Russell, along with Reck's young son, sat in the dining room of the Pensione Cici, awaiting Pound's arrival. Outside, an Italian film crew set up to film a television documentary about the poet. After a while, Pound and Olga Rudge appeared at the door and, seeing the group waiting for them, walked over to the table, Pound taking a seat at Allen's right and across the table from Reck. Olga Rudge told the group Pound had spent the morning at work. He now had enough new poetry for another book of cantos, she said. This was quite a revelation, since Pound had not produced much new work in recent years. A new volume of his poetry would be welcomed as a literary event by those who still followed his career. Pound, however, was not about to discuss his new work and he remained silent during their luncheon, despite the group's efforts to draw him into their conversation.

After lunch, Allen put his research to work. He told Pound that he had been wandering around Venice, looking for the places mentioned in *The Pisan Cantos*, but had been unable to locate some of the places. "I found the 'Place of Carpaccio's skulls,' " he said, quoting Pound, "but where's the place where, 'in the font to the right as you enter/are all the gold domes of San Marco'?" For all his efforts, Allen told Pound, he had been unable to find a font with such a reflection.

"Yes, when the font was filled," Pound replied, looking up at Allen. "Now they've changed it. It used to be like that."

"I walked half a mile yesterday, looking for the spot in Dei Greci, in San Giorgio," Allen continued. "I finally looked in San Marco."

"It used to be like that," said Pound. "The center was filled with water, and the reflection had the domes."

Encouraged by Pound's responses, Allen asked about other references in Pound's works, and Pound, though hardly expansive in his responses, answered each of Allen's questions. Allen went on to say that he had been greatly influenced by the concrete detail in the works of Pound and Williams, by such specific details as Pound's phrase "tin flash in the sun dazzle."

"I've been trying to find language equivalent for that light on water," Allen explained, leafing through his notebook until he found a particular passage. "Yesterday, I arrived at this: 'Legend on Vaporetto/sun yellow in white haze, Salute's/silver light, crooked-mirrored on the glassy surface.' " For emphasis, Allen repeated the phrase "light, crooked-mirrored on the glassy surface" and smiled. "You approve of that?" he asked.

Pound smiled and looked Allen directly in the eye. "That's good," he said.

Allen had spoken to Pound of his Blake visions and of the early difficulty he had experienced in attempting to translate visionary perception to poetry. He had concluded that the only way to do it was by sketching the concrete details observed during the state of heightened awareness. This concentration on externals had been shown to him in Williams's dictum, "No ideas but in things," as well as in much of Pound's writing. "The phrasing of your poems had a very concrete value to me as reference points for my own perception," he said. "Am I making sense to you?"

"Yes," said Pound. He paused for a moment and then mumbled, "But my own work does not make sense."

Both Ginsberg and Reck protested, assuring Pound that his poetry made sense to them, but Pound rejected their praise. He characterized his work as "a lot of double-talk," noting that Basil Bunting had told him that in the *Cantos* there was "too little presentation and too much reference."

Allen spoke of his meeting with Bunting in England in 1965. At the time, Bunting had encouraged Allen to read Pound's work as an example of the "economy in presentation of sensory phenomenon, via language."

Reck added that Pound's work was "often shockingly direct," that a reader could identify with his words even if he had not experienced what Pound was writing about.

Pound offered no immediate response. He sat in silence, rubbing his hands together. Finally, he said, "At seventy I realized that instead of being a lunatic, I was a moron."

When Ginsberg and Reck contested that assessment, Pound, obviously expressing the feelings of deep depression and defeat he had experienced over the last decade, dismissed their disagreement by calling his work "a mess." His writing, he said, was "stupidity and ignorance all the way through."

Reck countered that Pound possessed the greatest gift that a poet could possess—an *ear* for poetry—and that his ear had influenced a large number of people, perhaps most prominently Ernest Hemingway, who had influenced a great number of people himself. With such an ear, it was difficult to write a bad line of poetry.

"It's hard for me to write at *all*," Pound replied, smiling slightly.

Allen interjected with an assessment of Pound offered by William Carlos Williams. "We were talking about prosody," Allen said. "I'd asked him to explain your prosody to me—in general, something turned approximation of quantitative. Anyway, Williams said, 'Pound has a mystical ear.' Did he ever tell you that?"

"No," Pound answered, "he never said that to me." Pound, pleased by Williams's remarks, looked away and smiled—"almost curious and childlike," as Ginsberg later recalled.

"Well, I'm repeating it to you now, seven years later, the judgment of that tender-eyed doctor," Allen said. Changing topics, he asked Pound when he might journey next to the United States. People were interested in his poetry; there would be no problem lining up readings, especially in San Francisco, or in Buffalo, where he was taught in a special class at the state university.

"Too late," Pound declared.

"Too late for what, for us or for your voice?" Allen laughed. It was never too late, he said, especially for someone of such influence. The more he read of Pound's work, the more he was convinced that it was the best of its time.

"Your economics are *right*," Allen insisted. "We see it more and more in Vietnam. You showed us who's making profit out of war. And the *humour*—using the word in the ancient sense, as a state of mind—the irritations against

Taoists, Buddhists and Jews fit into this place as a part of the *Cantos*—despite your intentions—as the theatre, the record, of the flow of consciousness. The Paradise is in the desire, not the imperfection of accomplishment. It was the intention of Desire we all respond to—*Bhakti*—the paradise is in the magnanimity of the *desire* to manifest coherent perceptions in language."

"The intention was bad," Pound remarked. "That's the trouble. Anything I've done has been an accident. Any good has been spoiled by my intentions—the preoccupation with irrelevant and stupid things." He hesitated for a moment, then added, speaking slowly and emphatically, "But the worst mistake I made was the stupid suburban prejudice of anti-Semitism. All along, that spoiled everything."

"It's lovely to hear you say that," Allen said, reassuring Pound, by quoting the *I Ching*, that there was "no harm." Pound's confession was astonishing, first because he must have known that Ginsberg was Jewish and second because there was little doubt that his words would be repeated. Until that moment, Pound had never shown public remorse for the statements he had uttered on the radio during World War II. Allen's enormous tolerance had allowed him to accept the imperfections in others, no matter how glaring, and now, even in light of Pound's admission, he was prepared to accept the imperfections of Pound's mind as a part of his art.

"Anyone with any sense can see it as a humour, in that sense part of the drama," he told Pound. "You manifest the process of thoughts—make a model of your consciousness—and anti-Semitism is your fuck-up, like not liking Buddhists, but it's part of the model as it proceeds, and the great accomplishment was to make a working model of your mind. I mean, nobody cares if it's Ezra Pound's mind. It is a mind, like all our minds, and that's never been done before. So you made a working model all along, with all the dramatic imperfections and fuck-ups. Anyone with sense can always see the crazy part and see the perfect clear lucid perception-language-ground."

Allen said it was important that Pound continue to work, that he record the last scenes in the drama of his mind; he still had much to say. "After all," Allen added, "now you have nothing to lose. You *are* working, aren't you?" When Pound did not reply, Allen plowed on. "What I came here for, all this time, was to give you my blessing. Despite your disillusion, unless you *want* to be a Messiah, then you'll have to be a Buddhist." The irony of the statement brought a smile from Pound. "But I'm a Buddhist Jew whose perceptions have been strengthened by the series of practical exact language models which are scattered throughout the *Cantos* like stepping stones—ground for *me* to occupy and walk on—so that, despite your intentions, the practical effect has been to clarify my perceptions. Anyway, now, do you accept my blessing?"

Pound opened his mouth as if to say something, hesitated, and then answered, "I do."

It was almost four o'clock, and the film crew had repaired to Pound's house for another session. Pound was tired. Allen and the others walked slowly to Pound's pensione, taking a route along a small canal lined with an iron rail. When they reached Pound's doorway, Allen took Pound gently by the shoulders and looked him in the eye.

"I have told you what I came here to tell you," he said. "I also came here for your blessing. And now, may I have it, sir?"

"Yes," Pound said, nodding, "for whatever it's worth."

Allen talked with Olga Rudge while the others bid their farewells. Earlier in the day, Rudge had spoken to Allen of the difficulties Pound encountered when he was approached by outsiders, so many of whom bothered him with questions about his writing. Many simply wanted to know whether he was still working. "Of course, it's different with someone like yourself," she had confided to Allen, noting that Ginsberg was a fellow professional.

Now, standing in the doorway, she encouraged Allen to be persistent, to try to see Pound again.

"If you wait and have patience," she said, "he needs to talk. He thinks all his work is so bad, whereas when he reads it into tape you can tell he reads with enthusiasm—some parts. Other parts, of course, he dislikes. But that's natural, after years, to be self-critical. Anyone would. . . ."

Pound, clearly moved by the events of the day, turned to Allen and took his hand. "I should have been able to do better," he said.

Allen kissed him lightly on the right cheek. "It was perfect," he said. "I haven't properly yet sung Hare Krishna to you, either. I'll be around a few days more, anyway. Maybe . . ." He paused, then added, "See you."

Pound watched them leave, waving to the group as it walked down the alleyway away from his home.

4

The opportunity to discuss poetry with one of the great artists of modern times—especially with a recluse like Pound—was not an occurrence one took lightly. Both Ginsberg and Reck took detailed notes of their conversation with Pound and both eventually published excellent accounts of the afternoon encounter.

It was Allen's good fortune to be able to continue his discussion with Pound the very next evening. Allen was at the Salute boat station, talking with friends and waiting for the vaporetto, when Ezra Pound and Olga Rudge appeared. They were on their way to Carmini Church, where a friend of theirs was helping to celebrate a local priest's five-year anniversary by singing a selection of Vivaldi. Seeing this as another opportunity to spend time with Pound, Allen asked whether he could accompany them. Rudge immediately agreed.

Allen sat on the bench behind them on the vaporetto. Leaning forward to speak in their ears, Allen talked of Julius Orlovsky, describing him as a Manichaean who refused to speak for fourteen years because he believed that all the evil in the universe was issued from his mouth and body. "Are you a Manichaean, Ezra?" Olga Rudge asked, laughing. Pound did not reply.

At the church, Allen sat in the pew behind them. He took out his notebook and wrote a sketch of Pound:

> . . . old man sat before me
>   brown canvas shoes, one heel raised alert,
>   hat and cane in hand

Smooth woodslab resting
   under a fold in his coatback—
white cheek beard dyed red by
   velvet light,
black not entirely faded from
   back of his skull,
fringed with grey hair,
   candle gleam through white web.

Pound and Rudge moved closer to the front when their friend began to sing. They stood quietly in the left aisle until she had finished, and then, without waiting for the concert to end, walked out of the church, Allen following. After walking in silence for a while, Allen initiated another discussion about Pound's work.

"I've been thinking about the problem you raised yesterday," Allen began, referring to Pound's calling his *Cantos* a mess and speaking of his inability to finish them. Perhaps, Allen suggested, the problem was one of perspective. "If they made a static crystalline ideological structure, it would be unresolvable, now. But it is an open-ended work—that is, epic, 'including history,' of movement of your mind and record of focused perceptions, existing in time and changing in time. Anything you write now will refer back to the beginnings and alter all that went before—like turning a Venetian blind. . . . In short, what I'm saying is *anything* you do now is OK and will be proper, appropriate, as means of altering preceding thought-flow by hindsight. Am I making sense?"

"It's all tags and patches," Pound said of the work.

Allen could not accept such a simple dismissal. He had been reading the *Cantos* all month, he said, and he had always found the different works to be related and, ultimately, unified. In Allen's opinion, Pound's inability or reluctance to finish his life's work had to be a personal rather than a literary problem. "Is your problem one of physical depression that keeps you from recording and registering these final perceptions—whatever you are now?" he asked Pound.

"The depression's more mental than physical," Pound replied.

Allen spoke more of the importance of the *Cantos*, trying to convince Pound that for all their strange turns, the poems were solid work. He had just begun reading Dickens's *Bleak House*, he mentioned, and it was full of hyperbole. It was the detail—the sense that the reader was seeing exactly what the writer was seeing—that mattered. Allen had also recently read Frank Norris's *The Pit* and had been impressed by the author's description of the din of the wheat trading on the stock exchange floor.

They arrived at the pensione and Olga Rudge built a fire while Ginsberg and Pound continued their discussion. Pound was again withdrawn, unwilling to discuss his work. Undaunted, Allen switched to a discussion of the effects Pound's poetry had had on a generation of younger poets—poets who, like Allen, were half Pound's age. "Do you know the enormous influence you've had?" Allen asked.

"I'd be surprised if there was any," Pound responded doubtfully, but Allen thought he looked as if he was interested in hearing more on the topic.

Allen read a few poems by Robert Creeley, whom Pound knew of, and then he talked briefly about Charles Olson and John Wieners. Pound was not familiar with Allen's work, but that did not bother Ginsberg. "Well, oddly, it might please you," he said of his own work. "But do you understand the influence your writing has been as a model for a whole generation of poets?"

"It would be ingenious to see any influence," Pound argued.

Allen spoke of Williams, Zukofsky, and Bunting, admitting that he had been initially influenced by Williams, more so than by Pound. Williams, Pound replied, had been in touch with human feelings. Allen felt his influence was more than that. Williams, like Pound, Hart Crane, and Shelley, was part of a literary lineage.

Olga Rudge returned with cups of Ovaltine and a copy of *Canto CX*. "Has Mr. Ginsberg seen this?" she asked Pound. Allen had not and he asked whether he could borrow it, assuring them that he would return it. Rudge told Allen he could keep the copy and then asked Pound to inscribe it for him.

Pound paused for a long time. "Oh, he doesn't *want* it," he finally said.

"Well, yes, sure I do," Allen responded. "If you want to check your perceptions, I absolutely do."

Pound inscribed the volume: "Alan Ginsberg—dall'autore—Oct 29, 1967. Ezra Pound."

The next day was Pound's eighty-second birthday. Allen lunched with Pound, Rudge, and an Italian poet and his girlfriend. The discussion was for the most part about nonliterary matters—drugs, the recent death of Ché Guevara, and the U.S. electronic spy network. When they were leaving, Olga Rudge invited Allen to return and sing to Pound that evening. Allen turned up at ten, wearing a special shirt given to him by Paul McCartney and carrying his harmonium. He found Pound sitting by the fire. He chanted the Prajnaparamita Sutra in Sino-Tibetan and English, then chanted the Hare Krishna mantra. After a pause for birthday cake and champagne, Allen decided to try some of his own work on Pound. He read a selection of his auto poesy, but when Pound failed to respond to the work or to Allen's mention that its composition had been influenced by Pound, he quickly put his work aside and concluded the evening with another mantra.

Pound had retreated back into himself and barely spoke to Allen again, either on his birthday or during subsequent encounters. The door had again been closed. Nearly two decades later, in remembering his conversations with Pound, Ginsberg was kind in his assessment of the poet's mental state at the time of their meeting: "I'd been told that he wasn't in his right mind and that his silence was some strange schizophrenic behavior. He was right on whenever he opened his mouth, his words meant something and were laconic and exact and precise." Of Pound's harsh criticism of his life's work and doubts that he was as influential as Allen claimed him to be, Ginsberg was equally charitable. "He was being straightforward actually," he said. "I had a sense of rue in him and at the same time a little humor, as if he were not defeated, but just simply trying to be sensible."

Pound and Rudge were departing for Padua to avoid the rain and floods of early November, and Allen recognized that it was time for his own return to the United States. He had been overseas for four months. He needed to see

Peter, who had been in some trouble since his departure, and he had an upcoming tour of poetry readings. There was also the matter of assembling a new collection of poems for City Lights. Unfortunately, a return to the United States also meant another confrontation with the news of war.

5

If anyone suffered as the result of Allen's fame, it was Peter Orlovsky. Peter's mental state was fragile to begin with, burdened with (and, consequently, depressed by) the responsibilities of looking after his brothers Julius and Lafcadio, and dealing with a complex sexuality that found him maintaining regular relationships with women while he continued to be Allen's lover. In addition, he handled many of Allen's practical affairs, such as entertaining the continual flow of visitors to the apartment, fielding uncountable telephone calls, and keeping Allen's schedule straight. It was a demanding full-time job that was bound to have an adverse effect on their relationship. While Allen forged ahead, living life to the hilt and having his ego gratified by his followers, literary enthusiasts, and the media, Peter's ego was in essence absorbed by Ginsberg's. Peter was both a vital person in Allen's life and another cog in the Ginsberg cottage industry.

To make matters worse, Peter was occasionally made to feel unwelcome or inferior by some of the people associating with Allen. The two appeared to be so entirely different that it was difficult for some people to see what Allen saw in Peter. By the mid-sixties, Allen was a larger-than-life figure; the name Ginsberg brought instant association in the minds of the counterculture and establishment alike. For all his complaints to the contrary, this was as he would have had it; he had always aspired to be famous and influential—it was an integral part of his ego structure. Conversely, Peter had little desire to be a public figure. He was quiet and shy by nature and, one suspects, wrote poetry only because he was encouraged to do so by Allen and some of his friends. To place it in another context, it is probably fair to say that Allen was the type of person who might have run for public office, while Peter might have been perfectly happy mailing campaign flyers.

Still, the demands placed upon Allen became the demands placed upon Peter. As he would admit later, Allen was often far too busy to notice or consider the effects that his public life had on this very private, sensitive individual. When they had exchanged vows in Foster's Cafeteria in 1955, they had in effect exchanged nuptual promises. Despite their separations, quarrels, and misunderstandings, they were together for better or worse—and to Peter, as Allen became more and more public property, the demands made it seem like the latter.

Too often, Peter's answer to these excessive demands was a dependence upon drugs. When he was around, Allen could monitor Peter's use of drugs and keep him on a fairly even keel, but when he was gone—which was more now than ever—Peter fell into heavy, virtually unchecked drug use, his main downfall being Methedrine. On speed, Peter was unpredictable. One day, he would go into a cleaning frenzy that found him scrubbing the sidewalk with a toothbrush;

the next, he might have hallucinations that left him in no better shape than his brothers. While in Europe, Allen heard of a couple of bad incidents involving Peter, one finding Peter hallucinating that the window moldings in the apartment were either smoldering, electrified, or bugged; he reacted by stripping them from the windows. He was taken to Bellevue for observation. Fortunately, Allen was able to rely on Eugene to oversee the legal issues involved.

For years, Allen had tried to discourage Peter from using Methedrine or heroin, and in light of Peter's troubles over the summer of 1967, Allen continued to campaign against the drug use. Methedrine, he pointed out to Peter, had been behind some of the madness they had both witnessed and endured on the Lower East Side; it brought out qualities in Peter that frightened him. Allen worried that Peter might go on a binge and burn all their manuscripts or, worse, hurt himself. "There's now so much chaos and craziness on all sides that I wish we two could just be calm and not swept into violence," he told Peter. "I say, fix up the house, fix windows fast, quit all needles and all meth, clean up and come over here to England."

To Allen's great relief, Peter was off speed by the time he returned to the United States. However, the conditions that drove Peter to Methedrine prevailed, and Allen and Peter would face Peter's drug problems in years to come.

6

While in Europe, Allen had tried to stay as informed as possible about the Vietnam War, and through his poetry he became involved in the largest antiwar demonstration to date—the October march on the Pentagon. The demonstration attracted tens of thousands of people, including Norman Mailer, whose account of the march, *Armies of the Night*, won the Pulitzer Prize and National Book Award, and poet Robert Lowell, whom Allen had met earlier in the year. One of the highlights of the march was an October 26 exorcism of the Pentagon, delivered by Ed Sanders, Tuli Kupferberg, and a host of protesters. The text for the exorcism, originally entitled "No Taxation Without Representation," was supplied by Ginsberg:

> Who represents my body in Pentagon? Who spends
> my spirit's billions for war manufacture? Who
> levies the majority to exult unwilling in Bomb
> Roar? *Brainwash! Mind-fear!* Governer's language!
> *Military-Industrial-Complex!* President's language! . . .

Soon enough, Allen was taking active part in demonstrations. He had barely arrived back in the States when he was involved in a large demonstration in New York. On December 5, an estimated 2,500 protesters staged an antiwar, antidraft demonstration in front of the Whitehall draft board offices. Although the rally was orderly, 264 people were arrested, including Ginsberg and nationally renowned pediatrician Dr. Benjamin Spock. Allen was charged with disorderly conduct and given a court date for January 1968.

One of Allen's main priorities after his return was the selection of poems for *Planet News*. It had been six years since the publication of his last collection of new poems and he had a wealth of material to choose from, including those poems composed in his journals while he was traveling in the Middle and Far East. He had six uncollected major works—"TV Baby," "The Change," "Kral Majales," "Who Be Kind To," "Wichita Vortex Sutra," and "Wales Visitation"—that had already been printed in poetry publications, as well as a large number of new poems—including the auto poesy and "Iron Horse"—that could be revised and prepared for publication. In assembling the volume, the issue was more what to leave out than what to include. Allen was faced with some difficult decisions. There was no question, for example, that "Wichita Vortex Sutra" belonged in his long "Poem of These States" sequence, but there was no telling when he would be finished with that ambitious project. "Wichita Vortex Sutra" was already being hailed as a magnum opus, and that, along with his wish to publish his own statement on the war in book form, made its inclusion in *Planet News* almost obligatory. He pondered his selections and worked on minor revisions for much of the rest of the year.

By the beginning of 1968, the war in Vietnam had taken a decisive turn for the worse. The Tet Offensive, launched by the North Vietnamese, had put to rest any hope of a quick military victory for the United States. The death toll rose at an alarming rate. President Johnson's popularity was falling to an all-time low and it appeared likely that he would receive a serious challenge from someone in his own party—certainly Eugene McCarthy, and perhaps Robert Kennedy—in the upcoming presidential primaries. The evening television news broadcast graphic footage of the fighting, driving an even deeper wedge between those who supported the government position and those who opposed it. With the new year, Allen saw little reason for optimism, as he noted in his journal:

> "The business of America is business"
> & "The Medium is the Message"
> The biggest single business in America
> is Defense via the Department of Defense.
> The "business of America is business"
> So "the Medium is the Message."
> Regimented by those 2 aphorisms
> Doom lurks in the above statistic
> Defense is the biggest industry.

Such notebook doodlings, though far from usable in a literary sense, were symbolic of the confusion the nation felt as it tried to sort through what seemed to be an unresolvable conflict. Even the courts were lax in their judgment of civil-disobedience cases. When Allen stood before a judge on January 9, he was given an unconditional discharge on his guilty plea of disorderly conduct. Five days later, he was in the news again—along with Norman Mailer, Susan Sontag, and Robert Lowell—this time for appearing at a rally at Town Hall in support of Dr. Benjamin Spock and other war protesters and draft registers. At the rally, 560 people, including Ginsberg, signed a scroll pledging "to counsel, aid, and abet any young man who wished to refuse the draft." In his interviews,

Allen was telling reporters that he would be willing to go to jail for his stance against the war.

Allen's readings now served several purposes. First and foremost was the poetry itself. With a new book in the works, he used his readings as a means of testing his new poetry for audience response. (A joint reading with his father on January 17, typical of his readings at the time, featured a large number of poems that would be collected in *Planet News*, including "Wales Visitation," "Who Will Take Over the Universe?" "Café in Warsaw," "Seabattle of Salamis Took Place off Parama," "Galilee Shore," and "Last Night in Calcutta.") The readings also afforded him the opportunity to climb upon what was now a well-worn and well-traveled soapbox, from which he offered opinions on the war in Southeast Asia; the developing police state in America; the avant-garde's on-again, off-again problems with New York's licensing bureaucracy; and LeRoi Jones, who, according to Allen, had been framed by police in Newark and whose conviction of gun possession during the city's riots had landed him a stretch in prison. (The court decision was later reversed.) Due to Allen's wide-ranging and outspoken political views, the question-and-answer sessions following his readings were often as interesting as the poetry itself.

In late January, he finally got to meet Maharishi Mahesh Yogi, the Indian spiritual leader who, thanks to an endorsement by the Beatles, was developing a substantial cult following in the United States. A great proponent of meditation, the Maharishi was fond of putting forth simple—and very quotable—statements about virtually any world issue imaginable. Allen strongly disagreed with the Maharishi's anti-LSD stance and especially with his apparent apathy about the Vietnam War. Although he tried to remain respectful while he had his audience with the Maharishi in his flower-filled room at the Plaza Hotel, he could not just sit at his feet and hang on his every word, as did so many of his disciples. For nearly a half hour, Allen challenged him on his views about the war and LSD—to no avail. He agreed with the Maharishi on his views about the importance of daily meditation, but he found his political opinions "definitely dim-witted and a bit out of place." Allen was not alone in his position of questioning what would have otherwise been an agreeable figure: Later in the year, John Lennon, disenchanted with the Maharishi, would write "Sexy Sadie," his scalding dismissal of the leader who, in Lennon's words, "made a fool of everyone."

7

Allen had lined up an exhaustive touring schedule for the first part of the year, and in early February he gave readings at Colgate, Cortland State College, and the University of Pennsylvania on successive evenings. He had no sooner returned to New York, ready to take a few days off before setting off for another two weeks of readings, than he received an early-morning telephone call from Denver.

"Have you heard the news from the West Coast?" asked an unfamiliar voice.

"No," Allen answered, suddenly fearful that he was going to hear another account of a friend's arrest. "I've been away all week."

"Have you heard from the West?" his caller repeated.

"I have been *away*," Allen said, growing irritated.

"Neal Cassady died in Mexico."

Peter Orlovsky, listening in on the other line, gasped.

Allen was then filled in on the details of Cassady's final days. Not surprisingly, his death became as legendary as was much of his life.

On February 2, Neal had taken a train to Mexico, stopping off in Celaya, a town not far from Mexico City. Leaving his bags at the train depot, he took a taxi to San Miguel de Allende, where he intended to stay with Janice Brown, a twenty-two-year-old friend and lover. The next day, Neal told J.B. (as she was known) that he had to return to Celaya for his bags. According to Neal's plan, he would walk from J.B.'s house to the San Miguel train depot—a two-and-a-half-mile hike—and from there he would follow the railroad tracks to Celaya. That was a fifteen-mile trek, but Neal, optimistic as always, was not concerned. He would count the railroad ties between the two towns, he told J.B. Since Neal's feet had been bothering him, J.B. did not take him too seriously.

Neal was at the San Miguel station by midafternoon. There, true to form, he became involved in a Mexican wedding party. He stayed for a while, drinking pulque and downing Seconals. Even though Cassady was aware of the hazards of mixing alcohol and drugs, he nevertheless set out for Celaya, undaunted by the long walk, wearing only a T-shirt and jeans. He apparently lost consciousness beside the tracks about a mile and a half from the San Miguel station, for Indians found him lying there on the morning of February 4. He was rushed to a nearby hospital, but it had rained the night before and the rain, combined with the frigid mountain air, had taken their toll. Neal died of exposure, four days from his forty-second birthday. According to legend, the last thing he said was, "Sixty-four thousand nine hundred and twenty-eight"—a reference to his promise to count the railroad ties. He had died as he had lived, in transit, moving toward a destination that, to all but the existentialist himself, would seem vague and possibly ill-advised.

Although he was saddened by the news of Neal's death, Allen was not entirely surprised. Cassady's final years, while buoyed somewhat by his association with Ken Kesey and the Merry Pranksters, had been difficult, as if a lifetime of rushing about had finally caught up with him. A year earlier while in Mexico, Neal had written Allen two cryptic notes that hinted of his desperation. Despite his boast of "big plans" for the future, Cassady begged Ginsberg to "save" him, though he was not specific from what. Most likely, he was weary and did not even know himself what he meant. Allen, like Carolyn Cassady, was partially relieved by Neal's death. "His happy Spirit in air, released from body," he wrote in his journal, hinting at the illusory nature of existence and the eternal nature of the human spirit.

"I'll be glad to get out of the burden myself—it's a dream," Allen continued, jotting down his immediate reaction.

> His solid sense—monumentally of person and physique and energy and love—that he touched me sexually of all living—spread Dharma thru America—the buildings outside Maya to my concerns compared to his

continuous presence—the thought of his vanishment casts unreality on the lit world remaining behind. . . .

Cassady's death had its own symbolic qualities. To Allen and Jack Kerouac, Neal had been the adventuresome, western-tending spirit—the kind of spirit that was disappearing in the conflict between American youth and authority figures. That Cassady would be vanquished while trying to fulfill a crazy promise—that he died on the move, in one last gesture that encompassed both a sense of aimlessness and a sense of purpose—was true to the enigma of his character; it was also indicative of a free spirit that could be silenced only by death.

Ironically, one of the next poetry readings on Allen's schedule was in Appleton, Wisconsin—hometown and final resting place of Joseph McCarthy, symbol of a repressive attitude that Cassady and the Beat Generation had rebelled against the most. During his appearance at Lawrence University, Allen dedicated his reading of "America" to the dead Republican senator. But he did not stop with this gesture. He visited McCarthy's grave and, along with Ed Sanders and a group of Lawrence students, conducted a ceremony intended to exorcise the illusion and suffering from McCarthy's spirit. The rite was conducted in a number of languages—including English, Latin, Greek, and Hebrew—with Allen chanting the Prajnaparamita Sutra as part of the hour-long proceedings. Once made public, the group's actions provoked outrage, suspicion, and confusion. Conservative news commentator Paul Harvey made the exorcism an item on his syndicated radio broadcast, while newspaper editorialists had a field day stating their opinions, calling the exorcism "a leading example of American moral rot" and "the ultimate in revolting," among other things. For his part, Allen wisely chose to let his involvement in this bit of political theater pass without further commentary.

His work on *Planet News* continued. He had sent City Lights a manuscript; in late February, Lawrence Ferlinghetti delivered his verdict. The book, he stated to Allen, was "beautiful," with a "great goofy tender world overview" that justified its title. He was particularly impressed with "Wales Visitation," which he said was "one of the greatest you have ever written," narrated in a style that he likened to "the English Romantic poets strained thru the Lake Country into Wales & you." The book itself, Ferlinghetti said, was virtually complete, requiring only a few minor adjustments. Allen had arranged the poems in chronological order of composition, which seemed fine to Ferlinghetti except that it meant leading off the collection with "Who Will Take Over the Universe?"—a poem he felt made the volume difficult to get into. Allen, however, offered his own solution: Set the first and last poems in the volume ("Who Will Take Over the Universe?" and "Pentagon Exorcism," respectively) in italic type, setting them off from the rest of the poems and yet giving the book a cyclical feeling. Ferlinghetti readily agreed. Allen's publisher also expressed some concern about the overlap of the poems in *Planet News* with those in *TV Baby Poems*, a small volume of Ginsberg poems recently published in England but being distributed in the United States. Allen dismissed the repetition as being insignificant, however. Neither the British volume nor a pamphlet of several Ginsberg poems being issued in the United States (*Scrap*

Leaves) contained the impressive grouping of major works of which *Planet News* could boast. By mid-March, poet and editor were in basic agreement about the book's contents, and the manuscript was shipped to Villiers for typesetting.

8

Without a doubt, 1968 was one of the most turbulent years in U.S. history, virtually without parallel in its violence and political unrest. In March, Lyndon Johnson announced that he would neither seek nor accept reelection, setting off a free-for-all in the presidential primaries. On April 4, Martin Luther King, Jr., was assassinated in Memphis, precipitating a series of riots that left some of the nation's largest urban areas in flames. Large demonstrations against the Vietnam War were becoming almost daily occurrences, especially on college campuses. In mid-March, students at Columbia boycotted classes in favor of attending lectures and antiwar protests staged at the university; on April 23, they went one step further, seizing the dean's office and, in effect, turning the campus into a battle zone.

Allen was both frightened and sickened by the violence that would reach its nadir on June 6, with the assassination of Robert Kennedy. Indeed, it seemed as if Whitman's prophecy about America's fall was commencing before his eyes. He could easily endorse—even encourage—rebellion against the masters of war, but not at the price of further bloodshed. "Shit, Violence, bullets in the brain Unavailing," he wrote in his journal. "We're in it too deep to pull out."

Since it was an election year, the national focus, along with a nation's hopes, turned to the presidential races. With Johnson out of the running, anything seemed possible. His vice president, Hubert Humphrey, was seeking the presidency, but he had recently backed the U.S. position in Vietnam and, for all his liberal achievements of the past, he seemed to offer little more than a continuation of the Johnson policy. Eugene McCarthy, who was basing his campaign on an antiwar stance, appealed to the country's youth but seemed too radical and idealistic to older voters. Robert Kennedy had a broader-based appeal and appeared to be gaining in popularity.

With an extremely close race in the making and special-interest groups jockeying for each candidate's attention, the Democratic National Convention, scheduled for August in Chicago, offered great potential for a mass demonstration. National interest would be high and media coverage extensive. Abbie Hoffman, by now well established as one of the country's foremost antiwar protesters and recognized for his political theatrics, approached Allen with the idea of staging a Festival of Life, similar to San Francisco's Human Be-In, in Chicago during the week of the Democratic National Convention. The festival, Hoffman told Ginsberg, was designed to be upbeat—a display of an alternative to the kind of life endorsed by the people at the convention. As Ginsberg recalled of his conversation with Hoffman:

> He said that politics had become theatre and magic; that it was the manipulation of imagery through mass media that was confusing and hypnotizing the people in the United States and making them accept

a war which they did not really believe in; that people were involved in a life style which was intolerable to the younger folks, which involved brutality and police violence as well as a larger violence in Vietnam, and that [we] might be able to get together in Chicago and invite teachers to present different ideas of what is wrong with the planet, what we can do to solve the pollution crisis, what we can do to solve the Vietnam War, to present different ideas for making the society more sacred and less commercial, less materialistic, what we could do to uplevel or improve the whole tone of the trap we all felt ourselves in as the population grew and as politics became more and more violent and chaotic.

Hoffman's proposal had been well conceived. For teachers, he suggested William Burroughs, Charles Olson, and Buckminster Fuller, among others; he had already contacted John Sinclair and the rock group MC 5 and Ed Sanders of the Fugs, as well as folksingers Phil Ochs and Arlo Guthrie. He hoped that Allen might use his influence to persuade Bob Dylan and the Beatles to perform. He assured Allen the event was intended to extend "the feeling of humanity and compassion" present at the be-in. They would even create their own political party—the Youth International Party (whose members would be known as Yippies)—to show the seriousness of their intended alternative lifestyle.

The festival idea appealed to Allen, but he did not immediately pledge his involvement. He worried about the logistics of setting up such a festival—would the government or Chicago city officials permit such a large demonstration?—and, even more, he feared the potential of violence that a mass rally of this nature might invite. He was well aware of his position as a youth leader and hesitated to connect his name to any event that might provoke violence. He had known Abbie Hoffman only since late 1967 and so he wanted to consult with the festival's other main organizer, Jerry Rubin, before he committed his name and time to the project.

Allen's association with Rubin dated back to their participation in the Berkeley war protest marches in 1965. From his involvement in the be-in in San Francisco, Rubin had proven his savvy in organizing large and yet peaceful gatherings. Allen contacted him shortly after his discussion with Hoffman. Rubin reassured Allen that he and Hoffman were working at organizing a nonviolent festival rather than a hostile, confrontational demonstration. As if to convince Ginsberg further, he asked that he contact a yogi or swami who could teach breathing exercises that might calm the masses. Rubin would soon be traveling to Chicago to apply for all the necessary permits, and if all went well, he would secure a permit allowing the thousands of youths to camp in the city's public parks. Finally convinced that the festival would be peaceful, Allen agreed to help in whatever way he could, given his limited time and hectic schedule.

On March 17, he participated in a press conference formally announcing the Festival of Life. Also present were Abbie Hoffman, Jerry Rubin, Phil Ochs, Arlo Guthrie, and a small group of others. In his statement, Allen told the media assembled at the Hotel Americana that the Festival of Life would be a commitment to the future of the planet, a statement declaring a new planetary consciousness. When he had finished addressing the press, Allen sang the Hare Krishna mantra for ten minutes, accompanying himself on harmonium, while television cameras rolled. The festival, for all it promised or threatened, was now a reality.

9

Allen's counsel and opinions were solicited by a large number of people during the three- or four-year period in which he enjoyed his greatest visibility as a media figure—often from unexpected or high-placed sources or from those who might be inclined to disagree with him. On one occasion, Robert Kennedy arranged a meeting with Ginsberg at his office. Although it was not widely known, Kennedy was a devoted poetry enthusiast. He had met Yevtushenko and Voznesenky; like Ginsberg, he determined that he preferred the latter Russian's poetry. He knew Robert Lowell well. The Ginsberg-Kennedy meeting was cordial, with Kennedy listening to Allen's theories about the persecution of drug addicts by the Bureau of Narcotics and of the link between the drug suppliers and the Mafia. Allen asked Kennedy whether he had ever smoked marijuana and Kennedy told him he had not. Not surprisingly, Kennedy was more interested in talking about politics. He wondered whether there was any possibility for an alliance between the hippies and the political militants, as well as between the Flower Power advocates and the influential Black Power groups. Like Allen, Kennedy feared for the future, which, he told Allen, was likely to get worse before it improved. Just before he left, Allen produced his harmonium and chanted the Hare Krishna mantra for a couple of minutes.

"Now what's supposed to happen?" Kennedy asked when Allen had finished.

Allen offered a brief explanation, saying that the Hare Krishna mantra was a magic chant to Vishnu, the preservation god of Hinduism; the mantra was an appeal for the preservation of the planet.

"You ought to sing it to the guy up the street," Kennedy quipped, making a gesture indicating the White House. "He needs it more than I do."

On the other end of the political spectrum, there was syndicated columnist and talk-show host William F. Buckley, who invited Allen to be a guest on his television program, "Firing Line." Allen taped his appearance on May 7. The discussion was spirited, more of a debate than the customary talk-show fare. Buckley, one of the country's best-known conservatives, challenged Allen on his views about drugs and the war and even ventured into an exchange about contemporary poetics, but Allen was up to the task. He remained calm and presented himself well, and even Buckley, who one imagines was not inclined to purchase or read Ginsberg poetry, was impressed when Allen gave a moving reading of "Wales Visitation." As it turned out, Allen's appearance was a much better representation of the evolution of the Beat Generation's ideals than the showing Jack Kerouac would make on the same program a few months later. Allen was indisputably a leader in the new generation, even if he was old enough to have fathered it.

By this point, Allen did not know what to make of Jack Kerouac. Jack, a staunch conservative sympathetic to Buckley's politics, had dismissed Allen a couple of years earlier when he began to act as a public spokesman for antiwar protesters. Although Kerouac was by no means a hawk to Ginsberg's dove, he was nevertheless offended by Allen's apparent lack of patriotism. He had remarried in November 1966. He and his new wife, the former Stella Sampas—sister of one of Jack's boyhood friends—lived in Lowell, Massachusetts. There, Stella attended to Jack's mother, now partially paralyzed from a stroke, while Jack was in the process of drinking himself to death. Kerouac made it clear that his old friends were not welcome in his new home, where even incoming telephone calls were discouraged. Allen would send Jack a note from time to time, encouraging him to visit or take a vacation in San Francisco, but Jack was unresponsive. When Ted Berrigan and Aram Saroyan came around to interview him for *The Paris Review*, Jack made several unkind remarks about Allen, of which he was unrepentant. "So be it," he told Allen in one of his rare letters, adding, "you're lucky Joe McCarthy's family didn't sue you for trompling around the family grave."

As always, Allen endured the abuse. A great portion of Jack's tirades could be written off to the cumulative effects of alcoholism, while another portion was just a matter of Jack's lifelong practice of playing "dirty dozens" with his friends—of insulting and testing them to see how attached they were to their egos. Allen loved Jack and knew that Jack still had tender feelings for him, despite some of the evidence to the contrary. To Allen, Kerouac was a "drunken ghost," a sad, almost illusory presence who bore little resemblance to the Kerouac he had known in his youth.

That Kerouac was nearing the end was also apparent in his writing. His latest novel, *Vanity of Duluoz*, did not stand among his strongest works. The book backtracked over much of the ground covered in *The Town and the City*, retracing Kerouac's youthful years and days at Columbia (including the previously off-limits Carr-Kammerer episode). This time around, however, much of the old Kerouac enthusiasm was absent, replaced by an almost glum acceptance of the past. When the lust for life *was* present, it was tempered by the knowledge one has in middle age when looking back on the past. In essence, Kerouac had traveled full circle, with what would prove to be the last book published in his lifetime standing as a middle-aged mirror image of his first. Although Allen would adjust his assessment of the book over the years, when he had more time to rethink the latent humor and religious zeal present in it, he initially judged the novel to be "atrocious visions of deaths and souls and thought." In this critique he was not alone. A number of reviewers referred to the book's negative tone. *The New York Times*, calling the book's episodes "a succession of feuds," wrote it off as "a garrulous monologue of a man talking a blue streak because he is afraid no one is going to listen." The *Christian Science Monitor* published a more charitable review, but it, too, noted Kerouac's apparent disillusionment in his latest novel and paid him a backhanded compliment by noting that, while the book was "shamelessly obvious," "Kerouac's ultimate charm is that he doesn't mind if he makes a fool of himself."

For Allen and others, Kerouac's descent into his own drunken gloom was painful to watch, but Allen remained fiercely loyal, defending Kerouac from his detractors, constantly pointing out his past contributions to literature.

Just how heavily all this weighed on Ginsberg's mind is apparent in two poems written in early May. The second, eventually entitled "A Prophecy," finds him contemplating his own death and place in history. He opens by encouraging future poets to "chant from skull to heart to ass/as long as language lasts"—a reference, no doubt, to a brief journal notation in which he writes that "poetry is the best that language can do." Again, Ginsberg is acting in the role of witness/prophet, realizing that the future hinges on what he is seeing today, and that his role is to witness history and leave a record as an artifact. His legacy, he states in "A Prophecy," is to leave "not my language/but a voice/chanting in patterns"—a voice which, like the voice in Ezra Pound's *Cantos*, represents the vision (however flawed), life, and spirit of one living soul, one witness of time. Nothing else, Ginsberg hints, really matters.

This is certainly consistent with his Buddhist-influenced thinking to this point, as well as with his musings at India's burning ghats and his poem "The Change." That he chose to express it in May 1968 is significant, not only because his mind was on Kerouac and Cassady but because the momentous events of the year were making history uncertain. In trying to exhort the poets of the future, he appears to be encouraging himself in the present.

The other significant poem, "Please Master," written directly before "A Prophecy," seems to bear this out. Shortly after Neal Cassady's death, Ginsberg wrote "Elegy for Neal Cassady," a lovely, wistful remembrance of his former lover's spirit:

> Tender Spirit, thank you for touching me with tender hands
> When you were young, in a beautiful body,
>   Such a pure touch it was Hope beyond Maya-meat,
>   What you are now,
>   Impersonal, tender—
> you showed me your muscle/warmth/over twenty years ago
> when I lay trembling at your breast. . . .

That poem, similar to Whitman's discreet remembrance of an affair in "Song of Myself" ("I mind how once we lay such a transparent summer morning/How you settled your head athwart my hips and gently turn'd over upon me . . ."), is greatly contrasted in "Please Master," a poem written in the present tense and much more direct, a work moving from the spirit to raw physicality:

> Please master can I touch your cheek
> please master can I kneel at your feet
> please master can I loosen your blue pants
> please master can I gaze at your golden haired belly
> please master can I gently take down your shorts
> please master can I have your thighs bare to my eyes . . .

At the time of its publication, "Please Master" was by far the most graphic depiction of homoeroticism ever published by an American poet. In it, Ginsberg unflinchingly guides the reader through the moments of disrobing and foreplay, through oral and, finally, anal sex, the poem skirting the margins of pornography without ever losing its tenderness. For heterosexual readers, the quasiviolent actions associated with anal sex might seem disconcerting—perhaps undignified, given the poet's reputation—but Ginsberg is anything but concerned about appeasing the straight community. Neal Cassady's death had given him pause to reflect upon the nature of his sexuality, and "Please Master" was an accurate detailing of the aspects of tenderness and sadism present in the Cassady/Ginsberg love affair. In its depiction of the physical love between two men, "Please Master" is an elegy in its own right, as powerful and moving as the earlier "Elegy for Neal Cassady."

However, because it does not address Cassady directly, the poem assumes another dimension. In the two decades that had passed since the beginning of Ginsberg's affair with Cassady, Ginsberg had stood in the front ranks of prominent Americans advocating gay liberation, and while some inroads had been cut in the national consciousness, progress was slow in arriving. "Please Master" is further assurance from Ginsberg that homoeroticism is not only acceptable but also to be celebrated. It is not as much a list poem, even with its fixed base ("Please master . . .") and litany of sexual actions, as it is a mantra, a poem that if chanted properly can make homosexual love as real as Hindu mantras make the deities they summon. As unlikely as it might initially appear, "Please Master" can be read as a prayer, offered not in silence or hushed whispers but spoken—or even shouted—in joy, in hope, in indisputable faith.

10

Allen flew to Chicago on August 24 to participate in whatever lay ahead at the Democratic National Convention the following week. The signs were not good. Not only had Chicago mayor Richard Daley refused to grant the needed permits for the staging of the Festival of Life but he had reacted to the prospects of thousands of youths arriving by turning Chicago into an armed camp. Police were working twelve-hour shifts, over 5,000 National Guardsmen had been mobilized and an additional 7,500 troops had been airlifted in from Texas. As he flew to Chicago, Allen brooded about the upcoming week's prospects. The preceding months had been among the most violent in recent years and he had no reason to believe that the days ahead would be a break from the trend.

Allen's summer had been typically eventful, finding him logging thousands of miles in his pattern of almost nonstop travel. There were the usual journeys to poetry readings, an excursion to the West Coast, and, as the date of the convention approached, a couple of trips to Chicago, where Allen met with Abbie Hoffman, Tom Hayden, Rennie Davis, and others to make plans for the convention week. In July, he accompanied his family for a brief vacation in Mexico—a respite that got off to a bad start when he was told he could not enter the country unless he shaved his beard; Mexico, Allen wrote Lucien Carr, appeared to have adopted a policy against admitting those whom it deemed to be "existentialists" unless they had prior approval from immigration officials. Fortunately, Allen had Eugene along to help him work through the legalities.

Literary projects demanded his attention, as well. Besides the customary prepublication chores associated with the preparation of a City Lights collection, Allen kept himself busy with a number of other works published in 1968. In Toronto, the House of Anansi Press was issuing *Airplane Dreams*, a forty-eight-page miscellany of journal notations, prose, and poetry. In England, the Fulcrum Press was releasing an annotated edition of *Angkor Wat*, while in the United States, City Lights published a limited-edition pamphlet of "TV Baby," complete with Ginsberg notes. Allen could have used an agent to handle the outpouring of requests for new poetry and reprint rights, but he continued to rely on Lawrence Ferlinghetti, who did an admirable job taking care of his literary affairs.

Allen needed a place to retreat and so Committee on Poetry, his nonprofit organization, purchased a ninety-acre farm near Cherry Valley, a tiny upstate New York community about an hour and a half's drive from Albany. Surrounded by woods and with a creek running through the property, the farm had an idyllic charm, even if it was in relative disrepair and needed a lot of work. Ideally, putting up fences, chopping wood, and tending a garden were endeavors to offset the demands and impositions of life in the big city, and Allen regarded the farm as a private refuge from accumulating daily pressures. He also viewed it as the kind of place that might help Peter stay away from the hazards of Methedrine, or as a pastoral setting needed by poet friends seeking a place of solitude for the accomplishment of their work.

On August 12, while making his way cross-country, Allen had stopped in Chicago at Abbie Hoffman's request. Hoffman had been unable to secure permits for the Festival of Life and he hoped Allen might be able to persuade city officials to grant eleventh-hour permissions for the gathering. Allen had no more luck than had Hoffman. He and Abbie then discussed the situation as it stood, with all its promises of violence, and tried to come up with a solution. Canceling the festival would not necessarily avert a confrontation with Daley's forces, they concluded, since thousands of young people were likely to travel to Chicago in any event.

"He asked me if I was going to come and I said yes," Ginsberg said later, remembering their conversation. "I felt obligated to come since from the very beginning I had put my name forward as one of the people cooperating with the Yippies and therefore I had a responsibility to go there even if it was going to be dangerous, because other young people were coming in my name, or coming because I said I was coming, so that I felt obligated by duty to go there and make sure it was as peaceful as possible."

Allen was genuinely concerned for his safety when he arrived for the convention less than two weeks later. As luck would have it, Bill Burroughs had flown in from England, arriving in Chicago the same day as Allen—Burroughs visiting Chicago for the first time in over a quarter century, this time to cover the convention, along with Terry Southern and Jean Genet, for *Esquire* magazine. Norman Mailer was also in town, reporting the convention for *Harper's*. Allen had press credentials of his own, though he was not reporting the convention for anyone. Upon his arrival in Chicago, Burroughs surveyed the scene and, like Allen, was apprehensive.

On the afternoon of their arrival, Allen met with Abbie Hoffman, Jerry Rubin, Ed Sanders, Paul Krassner, and a group of others who had helped plan the festival. Across the street in Lincoln Park, an 11,085-acre stretch of land, thousands of youths had already begun to gather. Allen and the group, sensing trouble for that evening, discussed what should be done if the police tried to uphold the eleven-o'clock curfew and close the park as they had said they would. Although he felt that the youths had every right to stay in Lincoln Park, Hoffman felt that the park was not worth fighting for, that the festival organizers had a responsibility to do everything in their power to discourage a violent clash with the police. Rubin doubted that it would come to that.

They all found out soon enough what would happen. At ten-thirty that evening, Allen was walking through the park with Ed Sanders. Several thousand young people had gathered there, grouped mostly around bonfires lighted in garbage cans. Suddenly, without any warning, there was a brilliant burst of lights in the center of the park and a phalanx of police moved in, kicking over the bonfires and driving the youths from the park. "They are not supposed to be in here until eleven," a surprised Ginsberg said to Sanders. Concerned about what was taking place, Allen began chanting "Om . . . Om . . . Om" as he and Sanders started to work their way out of the park. They walked slowly, trying to avoid inciting further police attention by rushing about. They picked up fifteen to twenty others along the way, everyone humming "Om," Allen and Ed walking in the center of the line. They walked without incident to the Lincoln Park Hotel. Once again, Allen's chanting had kept him and the people around him from panicking, and they had been delivered from what might have been a nasty situation. Unfortunately, the incident in the park only hinted at what would occur in days to come.

11

As Norman Mailer pointed out in *Miami and the Siege of Chicago*, his account of the presidential conventions of 1968, the Democratic National Convention was not the main event taking place in Chicago during the week of August 24 to 29; it was instead a part of a much larger historical setting. "The event," wrote Mailer, "was a convention which took place during a continuing five-day battle in the streets and parks of Chicago between some of the minions of the high established, and some of the nihilistic of the young."

Mailer's statement, although rather basic in light of the events taking place throughout the week, was reasonably accurate. The convention itself offered no surprises. After the death of Robert Kennedy on June 6, the Hubert Humphrey campaign gained impetus until it was all but certain that he would gain the nomination as the Democratic party's candidate in the November presidential election. The Democrats still needed to solidify the party platform, which meant hearing from various interest groups, the most complex and demanding being the representatives of black interests and the opponents of the Vietnam War. The assassination of Martin Luther King, Jr.—and subsequent rioting in such locations as Memphis, Harlem, Brooklyn, Washington, D.C., Chicago, Detroit, Boston, and Newark—demanded some kind of resolution to a civil rights movement that had been stalled by violence. The conflict in Vietnam, now the costliest war in U.S. history, demanded equal resolve. The Democrats, it seemed, were willing to address both issues but ill-prepared to deal with either.

In such difficult, frustrating times, the tensions were felt not only on the floor of the convention hall but in the streets themselves, where a gigantic battle of will—nothing short of a territorial imperative—was taking place. Mayor Richard Daley, the most visible of Mailer's "minions of the high established," was determined to maintain control of his city, regardless of the measures employed in doing so; just how far he would go to keep the upper hand was apparent in his "shoot to kill" directive issued at the time of the earlier racial upheaval in Chicago. The Yippies were equally determined to pursue their own agenda, though they were divided on how that might be accomplished. As Allen would later learn with great displeasure, there was a sizable faction— including Jerry Rubin—that had come to Chicago looking for a violent confrontation. As time would show, the events surrounding the Chicago convention comprised a type of turf war unprecedented in U.S. history.

On Sunday, August 25, Allen and antiwar activist David Dellinger spent a portion of their morning meeting with a city hall official at the Hilton Hotel. By this point, Allen had all but abandoned hope of securing permits for any kind of legal assembly in the city parks or for permission for the youths to camp in the parks, yet he recognized that people were going to gather regardless of the legalities involved. If this was the case, the festival leaders needed some way to speak to the crowd and calm it in the event of a confrontation with the police. Allen asked that the city at least grant them a permit for a public-address system to be used in the park. A city official who had witnessed and been impressed by Allen's chanting the evening before thought it was a good idea and told Allen he would look into the request.

That afternoon, Allen was back in Lincoln Park, listening to a performance by John Sinclair and MC 5. When they had finished their set, Allen asked whether he could chant at the microphone for a while. Some of the people in the park—"some of the Maoists . . . acting insulting and revolutionary in their ideological prophetic style," as Allen would describe them later—were worked up by the political rhetoric and music, and Allen hoped that a few minutes' chanting would relax the crowd. He was introduced and he chanted the Hare Krishna mantra for fifteen minutes, accompanying himself on harmonium. When he had completed his chanting, he sang William Blake's "The Grey Monk," a poem he had set to music a short time before leaving for Chicago. The nine-stanza poem expressed Ginsberg's hope for nonviolent change:

> But vain the sword and vain the Bow,
> They never can work War's overthrow.
> The Hermit's prayer and the Widow's tear
> Alone can free the World from fear.
>
> For a tear is an Intellectual Thing,
> And a sigh is the Sword of an Angel King,
> And the bitter groan of the Martyr's woe
> Is an arrow from the Almightie's Bow.

Allen remained in the park after he had finished and the rock music started up again. All of a sudden—as unpredictably as the night before—there was a rush of police moving through the center of the park toward the PA system. Allen felt, as he would describe it, a wave of adrenaline pass over him as he watched the masses of police making their way through the crowd. The panic frightened him and to settle himself he sat cross-legged in the full lotus position and began to chant "Om" on a small grassy hill. A group formed around him and joined him in the chanting. Before long, other groups were gathering in the area and, encouraged by their participation, Allen continued to chant. What had begun as a brief period of chanting, intended as a way of creating a calmer state for twenty minutes or so, stretched out for *seven hours*. For Allen, the chanting became easier when he received a note from an Indian in the crowd. "Will you please stop playing with the mantra," the note read, "and do it seriously by pronouncing the 'M' in OM properly for at least five minutes? See how it develops." Allen did so and was amazed by the way it regulated his breathing and gave him a vibrating, tingling feeling. It was like the trancelike states he had read about, an altering of his consciousness that left him with an ecstatic feeling. He remarked:

> It felt like grace. It felt harmoniously right that some psychophysical rarity should be happening on that political occasion as dusk fell on Lincoln Park and the Hancock Building lit up on the horizon. If there'd been panic and police clubs I don't think I would have minded the damage. Clubbing would have seemed a curiously impertinent intrusion from skeleton phantoms—unreal compared with the natural omnipresent electric universe I was in. . . . The fear of death was gone. . . . I was in a revolutionary mass of electricity. I was in a dimension of feeling other than the normal one of save-your-own-skin. I was so amazed and grateful that I don't think I would have minded any experiment, including death. This was the most interesting thing that happened, for me, in Chicago.

The convention began the next day. Such conventions were by tradition festive occasions, colorful and self-congratulatory, full of optimism as the two major parties sought unity for the election fight ahead. However, an air of oppression hung over this particular gathering. The serious business at hand was accompanied by an aura of violence in the streets, in the hotel lobbies, at the meals attended by politicians, delegates, and press corps, in the conferences and speeches. For all of Daley's efforts to isolate the convention attendees from the scenes taking place away from the hall, the realities were impossible to avoid. The press had witnessed and reported the weekend occurrences in the park, and even as the convention opened, the normally festive environment was clouded with feelings of dread. At best, those in attendance were insulated from the events on the street, not much different from a jury sequestered from reality, from glimpses of the outside world— and even then, only in the initial goings-on.

On Monday evening, the real battles began. The scene in Lincoln Park was similar to what it had been over the weekend, with youths gathered everywhere. A barricade about thirty-five yards long, made up of picnic tables and trash cans, had been set up. As the park curfew approached, Allen walked through the park with Burroughs and Genet, fearful of what he saw. At the barricade, a group of youths were beating on trash cans and taunting the nearby collective of police. It seemed to Allen as if the "fearsome noise" he was hearing was an invitation for trouble and he immediately began to chant "Om." Others joined in and for a quarter of an hour the chanting continued until, as Allen recalled, it reached "a great unison crescendo." A police squad car suddenly appeared from behind the group, rolling into the midst of the crowd and smashing the barricade. Screaming people scattered in all directions. Some youths, armed with bottles, rocks, or pieces of bathroom tile, resisted the onslaught of advancing police, while others fled for their safety. Nearby, there was the sound of breaking glass, along with cries of "Walk! Walk! For Chrissakes don't run!" Allen began to chant again and as he, Burroughs, and Genet made their way out of the park, they watched an unbeliev-able occurrence: A band of police ran out of the wooded section of the park and began to beat the news photographers. The police had removed their badges, nameplates, and unit patches, rendering them unidentifiable, and they swung their clubs at anyone in their way, making a special point of beating the television crews. In all, seventeen newsmen—including a photographer from the *Washington Post*, a reporter and photographer from *Life*, three reporters and a photographer from *Newsweek*, and cameramen from all three major television networks—were ferociously beaten and had to be taken to Henrotin Hospital for treatment. "The counterrevolution had begun," wrote Norman Mailer of the incident. "It was as if the police had declared that the newspapers no longer represented the true feelings of the people. The true feelings of the people, said the policemen's clubs, were with the police."

Fearful as it was, the violence was only beginning. The next day, August 27, was Lyndon Johnson's birthday. Allen spent the morning and much of the afternoon conducting mantra-chanting sessions. That evening, accompanied by Burroughs, Genet, Terry Southern, *Esquire* editor John Berendt, and Grove Press editor Richard Seaver, he attended an "un-birthday party" thrown for Johnson at the Coliseum. Allen was hoarse from all his chanting in recent days and could barely speak, so he had Ed Sanders read a prepared statement while he sat on the stage in a Buddhist meditation posture. After the ceremony, the group repaired to Lincoln Park, where a ceremony was taking place in the middle of the park. A gathering of priests, ministers, and rabbis, appalled by the violence that had taken place there on preceding evenings, had erected a ten-foot black cross and were leading several hundred people in such songs as "We Shall Overcome" and "Onward Christian Soldiers." Allen's group took a position on a nearby hill and watched. The police had drawn a line about a hundred yards away, and when the park curfew arrived, spotlights flooded the crowd. Holding the cross aloft, the clergy moved toward the light and positioned themselves between the police and the youths. Suddenly, after a short, quiet standoff, the police launched tear-gas canisters at the cross, the gas filling the air, shrouding the cross, and moving over the crowd. Stunned, Allen turned to Bill Burroughs. "They have gassed the cross of Christ," he said.

Allen took Burroughs's and Genet's hands and the group walked slowly from the scene. The clergy retreated with their cross. Police fired tear gas into the crowd and hysterical youths ran in all directions. Street-cleaning trucks, specially equipped with tear gas, moved in from the streets and sprayed the retreating youths, now caught between the trucks and the line of advancing police, who were swinging clubs at the stragglers. Infuriated youths threw rocks, bottles, bricks, tear-gas canisters, and chunks of concrete at the police and trucks. In the streets, patrol cars were surrounded by angry youths and destroyed. Kids, roaming in packs down the streets, broke storefront windows and set fires in trash cans. Police fired their guns in the air. Hundreds of people were beaten and arrested.

The battle relocated to Grant Park, where thousands of youths had regrouped after being driven from Lincoln Park. With no other place to stay, the young people had no choice but to take a stand in Grant Park. Frightened but defiant, they sang "This Land Is Your Land" and "We Shall Overcome" and chanted political slogans—all within hearing distance of the Hilton Hotel, where convention delegates were lodged. At one point, the police launched tear gas into the crowd, but the wind was blowing away from the park and much of the gas entered the air-conditioning ducts of the Hilton, giving its guests a hint of what was taking place in the far less comfortable environment outside. Youths congregated in the street outside the giant hotel, some shouting messages to the delegates inside. "We have the votes, you have the guns." "Dump the Hump." "If you are with us, if you are sympathetic to us, blink your lights, blink your lights." The crowd erupted when lights blinked throughout the hotel. The kids, now facing National Guard reinforcements dressed in full battle gear, may have lost the skirmish for Lincoln Park but they were gaining in a much larger battle—for the sympathy of the convention delegates.

That much was apparent on the floor of the convention hall, where tensions and frustrations were brought to the forefront during the August 28 debates about the party's Vietnam platform. By now, it was obvious that the Democrats were a party divided, that greatly differing proposals for the Vietnam solution made party unity an impossibility. Eugene McCarthy, the antiwar candidate, might have been losing ground in recent months but he still represented a sizable percentage of voters unwilling to accept the Johnson—and now Humphrey—policies. As the debates heated up on the convention floor, pro-McCarthy and antiwar demonstrations were staged by the delegates themselves.

That afternoon, the National Mobilization Committee, led by David Dellinger, held a meeting at the band shell in Grant Park. The events of the past evenings had left many people frightened, but Dellinger and others still hoped to stage a mass rally and march, even in the face of what was now an enormous police presence. The idea was met with some resistance. Such a march, said opponents, would be a matter of the demonstrators walking into a death trap.

Allen arrived at the band shell with Burroughs, Genet, and Southern. Getting into the park had been difficult. Police had blocked all entrances and overpasses leading there and the group had been turned away every time it tried to enter. Allen and the others continued to walk around the perimeter of the park until they found a way in that involved climbing over a bunch of wooden trestles that had been set up as a barricade. They found the stage and were asked to speak to the crowd. Allen had no voice left. At the microphone, he tried to chant but was able only to croak an "Om" at the crowd gathered for the meeting. In his raspy voice, he urged the masses of youths to chant to ease their fears and anxieties.

It was an afternoon of speeches and political rhetoric. "You are doing something workable about an unworkable system," William Burroughs told the crowd when it was his turn at the microphone. Dick Gregory, Norman Mailer, and Jean Genet, among many others, delivered messages. Phil Ochs gave a short concert that included a blistering version of his antiwar song "I Ain't Marchin' Anymore." Oddly enough, however, for all the talk of revolution in the air and the enormous assembly gathered in the park, watched over by the very symbols of authority the youths were rebelling against, there were few youth-police confrontations.

The march itself was a disaster. David Dellinger had hoped to lead the proposed march to the Amphitheatre, where the convention was being held, but the police and National Guard had effectively sealed off the park. Thousands of people had found their way in—or had been in the park since the evening before—but they were now completely surrounded and were unable to get out. Dellinger approached Allen and asked that he join him at the front ranks leading the march. Allen rounded up Bill Burroughs, Jean Genet, Terry Southern, Richard Seaver, and photographer Michael Cooper and the group linked arms and assembled behind Dellinger, who was carrying a bullhorn and leading the march. "This is a peaceful march," Dellinger called out to the crowd. "All those who want to participate in a peaceful march, please join our line. All who are not peaceful, please go away and don't join our line."

The huge mass of people began to move forward. When the march reached the edge of the park, the demonstrators found themselves face-to-face with a barricade of jeeps and with National Guardsmen armed with machine guns. Dellinger argued with several city officials at the scene, insisting that the marchers had a constitutional right to a peaceful assembly, but he was informed that they would not be allowed to leave the park. Both sides—the police and the youths—were tense. Dellinger turned to Allen and requested that he lead the crowd in a mantra. Allen was handed a portable microphone and he started to croak "Om Sri Maitreya." People chanted along with him. Sensing a long wait ahead, the marchers in front sat cross-legged on the ground. After a while, Allen's voice failed completely and the chanting ceased. Forty-five minutes passed with no sign of a change in the police position. Dellinger finally announced that the march was over but that it had been victorious because the government had denied the demonstrators their right to assemble for redress of grievances.

The problem with the impasse, Allen discovered, was that there was no place for the crowd—now estimated at ten thousand—to go. The park exits were blocked, as were the bridges leading into the city. Skirmishes broke out as youths tried to force their way across bridges, the police firing canisters of tear gas at the advancing ranks of young people. Allen walked around the park, temporarily separated from his group, until he came upon Bill Burroughs, who had been teargassed and was wandering about with a handkerchief held to his face. Allen and Bill kept moving north in the park until they discovered an unattended bridge and were able to leave without further incident.

Others were not nearly as lucky. The confrontations with the police continued, now with a greater sense of urgency, since the tear gas was choking and blinding the people in the park. A large group managed to break through the guard at one bridge. Thousands of people poured out of the park and ran toward Michigan Avenue, the police in pursuit. On Michigan Avenue, the main street of Chicago's downtown business district, the youths ran into a city-permitted march staged by Reverend Ralph Abernathy's Poor People's Campaign. The youths fell in line behind Abernathy, the marchers, and the covered wagons and mules in the parade, the police unable to take any action for the time being. Meanwhile, thousands more escaped the park and joined the march or ran through the streets.

The group proceeded toward the Hilton Hotel a few blocks away. They had nearly reached their destination when the police took action. They allowed Abernathy and his immediate group through at the Balbo and Michigan intersection and then sealed it off from the rest of the youths, who suddenly found themselves surrounded by police. The police moved in from all sides, compressing the masses tighter and tighter together, offering no escape, unleashing their fury in a storm of tear gas, mace, and flailing clubs. "They attacked like a chain saw cutting into wood, the teeth of the saw the edge of their clubs," Norman Mailer wrote of the violence. "They attacked like a scythe through grass, lines of twenty and thirty policemen striking out in an arc, their clubs beating, demonstrators fleeing. Seen from overhead . . . it was like a wind blowing dust, or the edge of waves riding foam on the shore."

In the incredible carnage that followed—later referred to as a "police riot"— the police beat anyone in their path. Long-haired youths, elderly people, newsmen and photographers, innocent bystanders, medical personnel, shoppers, and tourists—all were victimized at random by the policemen's blows. Masses of fleeing people were pushed together, falling atop each other, others being crushed against walls and storefront windows. A large number of bystanders were pushed through the plate-glass windows of the Hilton's restaurant, the Haymarket Inn, only to be pursued through the broken glass by police who beat them further. News cameras captured the riot as demonstrators repeatedly chanted, "The whole world's watching! The whole world's watching!" Bloody beaten bodies filled television screens across the United States, the images bearing eerie similarity to some of the footage seen daily from another war— the one the youths were protesting. The war had come home.

12

Allen Ginsberg's participation in the events in Chicago during the week of the Democratic National Convention was reflective of the successes and shortcomings of his prophetic role in the 1960s. With commendable courage he had positioned himself among the front ranks, a participant as well as a witness to tumultuous history in the making. Over two decades earlier, he had written: "It occurs to me that I am America," and while the statement was an obvious exaggeration—he was a *part* of America, no more or less authentic in the long run than a worker in Wichita—he was one of the country's foremost witnesses, as emblematic in the fight against the Vietnam War as James Baldwin was in the civil rights movement. Allen had seen his message of brotherly love embraced and rejected, just as his chants in the parks of Chicago had been both effective and ineffective. Yet, as he insisted, even if the message was not embraced by all, the effort was worthwhile.

For all practical purposes, the Democratic National Convention ended on the night of August 28. There were other skirmishes between the demonstrators and the police and other attempted marches and demonstrations, but they were fewer in number and seemed almost anticlimactic in the aftermath of the battles in the street on Wednesday afternoon and evening. George McGovern, a long-shot candidate who, like McCarthy, was running on a peace platform, declared that he was sickened by the "bloodbath" he had seen on the television news, adding that he had seen nothing of its kind since the movies he had seen of Nazi Germany. Such sentiments were far from unusual. In fact, the violence received a curious footnote during Connecticut senator Abraham Ribicoff's nominating speech for McGovern. After noting the violence and turmoil that had competed for America's attention during the convention, Ribicoff proclaimed the country in need of a sense of unity, led by a charismatic leader similar to John F. Kennedy or Robert F. Kennedy. McGovern, Ribicoff continued, was just such a man. "And with George McGovern as President of the United States," Ribicoff said, "we wouldn't have those Gestapo tactics in the streets of Chicago. With George McGovern we wouldn't have a National Guard." Mayor Richard Daley, seated at the front of the hall, had heard enough. He leapt to his feet and, shaking a fist at the senator, mouthed obscenities and anti-Semitic slurs, oblivious to the television cameras recording his actions for a national audience. Ribicoff stared him down. "How hard it is to accept the truth," he said.

Allen had a moment of his own in the convention hall. On Thursday evening, the night after the violence in the streets near the Hilton Hotel, a delegate from Wisconsin suggested that the convention be adjourned for a couple of weeks due to the violence that now seemed to be out of control. A priest in attendance then rose to lead the delegates in prayer, which to Allen seemed as if the reality of the violence was being ignored and a blessing pronounced upon those who had created the system that encouraged it. He jumped to his feet and, in a voice loud enough to counter the priest and be heard throughout the convention hall, he shouted "Om" for nearly five minutes. To Allen, the interruption was intended to be a form of exorcism—an exercise to dispel hypocrisy. While he later conceded that it was possible that most of the people in the hall might have thought his actions to be ill-advised, perhaps even crazy, he was not about to apologize for them. The exorcism, he claimed, was "white magic theater," designed to break up the hypnotic aspects of the priest's prayers.

None of the rhetoric or theatrics ultimately mattered. When the final delegate votes were tallied, Hubert Humphrey had nearly three times as many votes as Eugene McCarthy, his nearest competitor. Humphrey chose Senator Edmund Muskie of Maine as his running mate, completing a Democratic ticket that would lose by a narrow margin in November, beginning a backlash against political and social liberalism that would continue, virtually unopposed, for more than two decades.

As far as Allen was concerned, there was not likely to be a winner, regardless of how the election went. "Who wants to be President of the Garden of Eden?" he wrote in his journal, signing off a poem he had written about the Grant

Park riot. He had witnessed the fall of America, the flip side of 1967's Summer of Love. It mattered not whether Humphrey or Nixon won the general election: Either way, the war in Vietnam would continue. For one week, the city of Chicago had become a microcosm of America's sociopolitical system, symbolic of the frustrations and violence that had racked the nation since the beginning of the year. "The whole convention," Ginsberg concluded, "was an exercise in black magic and mass hallucination—just as the Vietnam War has been."

The politics on the convention floor were, in Ginsberg's opinion, a "shoddy sleight-of-hand shell game [that] was meant to make voters think they were getting a choice, while actually phantom manipulators were nominating a candidate who continued to apologize for a war the voters wanted to reject." Ginsberg's view of the violence outside the convention hall was equally pessimistic. He and others had hoped for a Flower Power revolution, a peaceful changing of the guard, but they had instead encountered the old revolutionary standard, as traditional in America as its own Revolution, in which the upper hand would eventually be gained through violence. Guns did indeed speak louder than voters. Violence was not the tool Allen would take up for his revolution, however. "I'm willing to die for freedom," he told *Playboy* interviewer Paul Carroll, "but I'm not willing to kill for it."

Could the violence of the convention have been avoided? Given the benefit of hindsight, it seems unlikely. There were too many players on both sides—provocateurs and reactionaries, Yippies and police—who, though being perhaps a minority, guided the events into the bloodshed so characteristic of 1968. A showdown, some would say, was inevitable. When Daniel Walker submitted his report of the violence to the National Commission on the Causes and Prevention of Violence, his study concluded that an unspecified number of police had lost control of themselves under extraordinary and provocative circumstances, and while Walker believed their actions might have been understandable to an extent, they could in no way be condoned:

> In principle at least, most Americans acknowledge the right to dissent. And, in principle at least, most dissenters acknowledge the right of a city to protect its citizens and its property. But what happens when these undeniable rights are brought—deliberately by some—into conflict?
>
> Convention week in Chicago is what happens, and the challenge it brings is plain: to keep *peaceful assembly* from becoming a contradiction of terms.

The debate would continue long after the convention, as if the country could not rest until it found someone—or some group—to blame for one of its most shameful episodes, as if the demons could not be expelled until one could actually understand the stunning image of tear gas enveloping a cross, the symbol and marker, standing against the night.

Book Three

TEACHER

My teacher was William Blake—my life work Poesy,
transmitting that spontaneous awareness to Mankind.
—Allen Ginsberg, "Who"

Top: Resting at the Cherry Valley farm, Woodstock weekend, 1969. *Photo by Elsa Dorfman. Above left*: John Clellon Holmes, AG, and Gregory Corso at Jack Kerouac's funeral, Lowell, Massachusetts, 1969: "I threw a kissed handful of damp earth/down on the stone lid/& sighed." *Photo by Ann Charters. Above right*: In meditation, 1970. *Photo by Elsa Dorfman.*

Top: Gary Snyder, honored in Kerouac's *The Dharma Bums,* longtime Ginsberg friend, teacher, and occasional traveling companion, in Sweden, 1972. *Photo by Ann Charters. Middle:* Although they were frequently in disagreement over poetry and politics, Allen and Louis Ginsberg remained very close throughout their lives; their joint poetry readings were popular attractions in the late sixties and early seventies. *Photo by Elsa Dorfman. Bottom:* Louis Ginsberg, 1976: "Old Poet, Poetry's final subject glimmers months ahead." *Photo by Allen Ginsberg.*

Right: Blocking the railroad tracks leading to the Rockwell Corporation's nuclear trigger facility near Rocky Flats, Colorado, June 1978, the day after writing "Plutonian Ode": "I dare your Reality, I challenge your very being!/publish your cause and effect!" *Steve Groer, courtesy Rocky Mountain News. Below left:* With controversial Buddhist "wild wisdom" teacher, Chögyam Trungpa, Rinpoche, in the spring of 1985: "Sometimes my guru seems a Hell King, sometimes familiar eyed father, lonely mother, hard working..." *Courtesy Allen Ginsberg. Below right:* Lawrence Ferlinghetti, poet, painter, and founder of City Lights Books, 1981. *Photo by Frank Falduto.*

Above: AG, William Burroughs, and Gregory Corso, 1982: "We were never nightmare hooligans but seekers of the blond nose for Truth." *Photo by Shawn Falduto. Right:* Steven Taylor (center) provided musical accompaniment during many of Peter and Allen's readings in the early 1980s. *Photo by Elsa Dorfman. Below:* Twenty-fifth anniversary reading of "Howl" at Columbia University, 1981: "Holy the supernatural extra brilliant intelligent kindness of the soul!" *Photo by Ann Charters.*

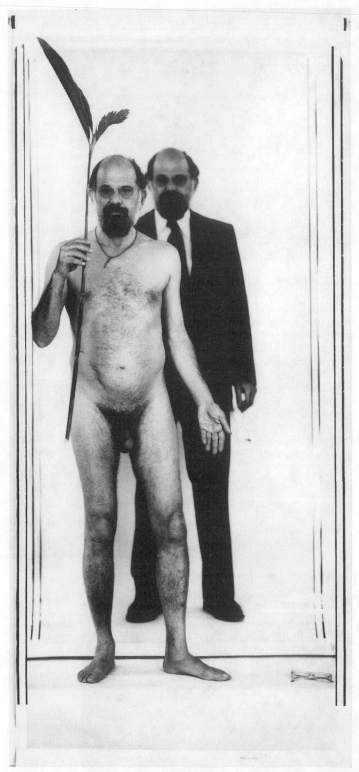

Hideous Human Angel: "We're not our skin of grime, we're not our dread bleak dusty imageless locomotive, we're all golden sunflowers inside, blessed by our own seed & hairy naked accomplishment bodies growing into mad black formal sunflowers in the sunset..." *Photo by Elsa Dorfman.*

21
Memory Gardens

Well, while I'm here I'll
do the work—
and what's the Work?
To ease the pain of living. . . .

1

Planet News, issued in the fall of 1968, was another splendid collection of poems. The volume was Ginsberg's largest to date and in many respects his most thematically unified. Whereas earlier collections had focused on flashes of epiphany or on the poet's mind in certain periods of his personal or artistic development, there was a sense of *movement* in *Planet News*, a feeling that the reader was following the prophet-wanderer on his quest. With its presentation of both the important and the mundane—garnered from journal entries, dreams, travel observations, drug-inspired babble, and spontaneously composed poetry—the book was an honest representation of the poet's ongoing changes. "*Planet News* is a likable, ecumenical series by the ace reporter for the *Daily Planet*," declared reviewer Herbert Leibowitz. "Part Superman, part Clark Kent, and part Buddhist Jew, [Ginsberg] works in the city or trips through galaxies, opening the portals to 'What Is.' . . ."

By and large, reviews of the work were favorable. By late 1968, Ginsberg was far too visible and influential a figure to be ignored. Even those critics who disliked his work could no longer dismiss him easily by focusing on such externals as his physical appearance or public image; nor could one fire glib statements, like silver bullets, at his work. In the past, Ginsberg had been taken to task for being excessively personal in his poetry, and while this criticism appeared in more than a few reviews of *Planet News*, reviewers were now giving this sense of excessiveness a second look.

There were still enough disapproving reviews to keep Allen humble. "Ginsberg stands at the end of a long line of American poets who have striven to embrace and comprehend everything in sight, but his poetry lacks the compensations of his predecessors," wrote Alan Brownjohn in *The New States-*

man. The reviewer further suggested that Ginsberg be more selective in what he chose to write about, that he "forget the mysticism and the egocentric sexuality" and concentrate on the finely detailed writing present in his clearer, objective writing.

Conversely, Paul Zweig found Ginsberg's excessiveness to be both charming and effective. "Ginsberg has made 'too much' the affair of his life," Zweig wrote in his review of *Planet News*. "Like Whitman, Blake, Traherne, [and] Rabelais, he has enacted what it means to say: 'I am the greatest lover in the Universe.' It is the mystery of seeing, and not judging, of understanding, and not discriminating." By being "selectively reckless," Zweig stated, Ginsberg was opening up "the marvel of endless possibility" rather than falling into the predictable.

For his part, Allen was both pleased with the book and relieved that it had finally come out. He had been so busy over the last year or so that just organizing the collection and seeing it through publication had been a chore.

After the Chicago convention, Allen retreated to the Cherry Valley farm, where he would spend the rest of the year. The events in Chicago had left him psychologically drained, and the old farm with its organic garden, need for repair, and lack of electricity seemed like a refuge. As soon as he arrived, Allen prepared a meditation room and altar in the farmhouse attic, complete with souvenirs and gifts he had picked up on his travels and other objects that made him feel restful. On the wall, he tacked a poster of four-armed Vishnu, a medal of the Sacred Heart (intentionally arranged so it dangled near a statue of Buddha), and a print of a Fra Angelico painting. On his shelves, he placed a variety of religious objects, as well as incense, rose-scented candles, the skeleton of a cactus he had found in New Mexico, an imitation Tibetan Tantric prayer bell, a red wooden fish, a shell fossil he had found on the farm, and statues. A bookshelf contained numerous religious texts from Eastern and Western faiths.

Allen decided to fix up the farm and spend his winter there, which meant installing a furnace and preparing the place for the rugged upstate New York winters. When he had purchased the farm, Allen had hired Gordon Ball, a young filmmaker, to work as the farm's full-time manager. In Allen's absence, Ball and Peter Orlovsky had done a commendable job making repairs and farming a two-acre section of land. They had grown tomatoes, cucumbers, beets, squash, and beans, all of which were preserved after the harvest. The farmstead had a cow and several goats for milk and an orchard of apple trees that supplied them with ample fruit for juice and table use. The demanding physical labor was especially appealing to Peter, who was again off drugs and in good shape, content to be mending fences, repairing the barn, insulating the house, and stacking cordwood for the winter. Herbert Huncke, visiting Cherry Valley to work on a book, was also around to help. During the daytime, Allen would busy himself with chores around the farm or sit near a small stand of maple trees and work on his writing projects; at night, he would work by lamplight inside the house or, on occasion, stand outside and look at the stars, trying to teach himself the constellations. It was a peaceful life, to which he made a large commitment when he took out a loan to pay off the money owed on the farm. "First time I've ever been living beyond my instant means," he said of the loan to Philip Whalen, though he added that it was "lovely, finally, to have the deed . . . signed and delivered and paid for."

He had a new project that took up much of his time that fall. The Beatles had formed Apple, their own record company, and one of their major objectives was to issue recordings by new or unusual artists who might otherwise be neglected or turned away by profit-conscious major labels. Paul McCartney was interested in releasing a series of spoken-word recordings, and through Barry Miles, a friend who had occasionally put Ginsberg up when he was in London, McCartney contacted Allen about contributing an album's worth of work.

Delighted by the prospect, Allen proposed three ideas to Miles. Ever since he had spoken to Phil Spector in Hollywood, he had hoped to make a recording of mantras. To Ginsberg, this seemed like an ideal project for Apple. Such a recording, he told Miles, could be a modest undertaking, with Allen accompanying himself on harmonium and dubbing in his own vocal harmonies, or it could be rather extravagant, bolstered by professional musicians and walls of sound that would give a selection such as the Hare Krishna mantra "a rock dimension" suitable for jukebox play.

Another suggestion was a recording of his poetry readings. Allen had already released two such albums, but he hoped to rerecord "Howl," as well as put on tape many of his newer, unrecorded works. He had hundreds of hours of uncataloged tapes of his poetry readings and auto poesy, some of them quite good, but he lacked the time and ambition to sort through them. Doing so would take months, and he was not at all eager to retrace his steps if that meant putting aside or failing to begin new work. The ideal solution, he mentioned to Miles, would be to find someone who could listen to the tapes, catalog them, and edit the best recordings onto a master tape.

Allen's third idea was the one that appealed to him the most. When he had set Blake's "The Grey Monk" to music, he had been uncertain how it would be received, but it had gone over well when he sang it in Chicago's Lincoln Park; Allen now hoped to make musical notations for all of Blake's *Songs of Innocence* and *Songs of Experience*. In his time, Blake had sung these poems, but there were no musical notations extant. Allen believed that through careful listening to the words in the poems, he might be able to duplicate Blake's original melodies, and throughout the autumn of 1968 he devoted many hours to doing just that. He purchased an old secondhand pump organ and began the slow, tedious process of working each syllable of Blake's poems into a musical note. He had little formal musical training, so the process was difficult, but he was helped along in early November when Lee Crabtree, a one-time member of the Fugs, visited the farm and taught him how to transcribe music.

Allen had always envied the Beatles, the Rolling Stones, and Bob Dylan their musical ability, and he had long believed rock 'n' roll to be a significant way to bring the immediacy and poignancy of contemporary poetry to large audiences. Ironically, his initial problem as a songwriter was not an inability to write melody; instead, it was a lack of faith in his own capacity to write lyrics. The Blake poems provided him the lyrics—and the confidence. On one occasion that fall, he drove to Woodstock, where he spent an afternoon improvising and singing "The Grey Monk" and the Hare Krishna mantra with members of The Band in their "Big Pink" studio, and he was encouraged by the way the session turned out.

This relatively peaceful season, however, was painfully interrupted on November 29, when Allen was involved in an automobile accident that left him with a broken hip and four cracked ribs. Lawrence Ferlinghetti was on the East Coast and had stopped by the farm for a visit. Allen had just seen him off at Albany County Airport when Peter, driving in heavy rain, missed a stop sign and collided with another car, Ginsberg receiving the brunt of the accident. It was the first time in his forty-two years that Allen had broken a bone, and he was almost morbidly fascinated by the experience, even if it did mean a three-week stay in the hospital and having to use crutches for months to come. The injuries were very painful and his mind was numb from the Demerol he was given to ease the pain, but even so, he was able to convert his misfortune into a basis for political commentary. When novelist William Kennedy, then a reporter for the *Albany Times-Union*, arrived to interview him in the hospital, Allen downplayed the extent of his injuries. They were just one man's pain, he said—nothing in comparison to the widescale suffering brought on by the bombs, napalm, and inhumanity that the United States was delivering to Southeast Asia. "What happens to all people in Vietnam?" Allen asked his interviewer. "We're mass producing this pain for them."

2

Allen did not have the luxury of being able to sit back and recuperate. There was too much work to do. He had now set enough of Blake's poetry to music for an album, and he wanted to begin recording as soon as possible. Miscellaneous writing projects, including the editing of his *Indian Journals* for publication, awaited his attention. And, if all this was not enough, he had scheduled a grueling four-month reading schedule—his most extensive yet—beginning in February.

His first reading was before two thousand people at the University of Miami on February 4, the huge crowd indicative of Allen's enormous popularity; he was now drawing the kind of attendance usually reserved for rock concerts. Two days later, in South Bend, Indiana, he was at Notre Dame, where he was one of several keynote speakers at the university-sponsored Pornography and Censorship conference. This, too, proved to be an ego-boosting experience. Not only had he been asked by the Jesuit-run institution to speak on censorship—a topic close to his heart for so many years—but for two days he was treated as an honored member of the literary establishment, to the extent of having his poetry discussed in an open forum, with Allen participating.

For all his claims to the contrary, Allen clearly cared about the way he was perceived by the academics. He savored every sign of acceptance. Such acceptance signified his success in breaking into the hallowed halls on his own terms, which was important if his work was going to survive him. Somehow his poetry had to be presented to new readers long after he was gone, and the most logical way was through educational institutions. Such concern was not entirely selfish: If his work survived, there was a good chance that of his friends might, as well.

This attitude created extra work. As he had noted when talking to Miles about his tape archives, working on his past affected the amount of time he had to devote to the present or future. Much of this extra work was self-imposed. He was now in the habit of correcting or editing many of the pieces written about him—in transcript, if he was fortunate enough to see one prior to publication, or by amending the published text stored in his files, if he was not. He regarded his interviews in particular as serious literary statements, and even if he was quoted accurately, he appreciated the opportunity to edit, clarify, expand upon, or, on rare occasion, change his remarks. When Paul Carroll, his poet friend from the *Big Table* days, interviewed him for *Playboy*, Allen requested the favor of previewing the final edited text, and while he was less than satisfied with the initial draft provided by Carroll, he was able to work out a text that he found acceptable.

The interview, published in the April 1969 issue of *Playboy*, was important to Allen. Not only was it by far his lengthiest published interview but it was also reaching an enormous audience. In the interview, he spoke extensively about drugs, human sexuality, politics, the Vietnam War, the evolution of the Beat Generation into the hippies, and the Chicago convention. As he had been in his 1966 interview with *The Paris Review*, Allen was in good form, even if he did slide occasionally into hyperbole. He was well aware of the audience he was addressing and he showed a flair for tailoring his remarks to the magazine's basically young, well-educated, heterosexual male readership.

Allen's reading tour of late winter/early spring 1969, although demanding, was a large success. In New York, he performed selections of his Blake songs for the first time at the New School, and then a few days later, he was a panel member at a drug seminar at the State University of New York at Buffalo. On March 13, he was onstage in Vancouver, sharing the billing with folksinger Phil Ochs. He appeared with Swami Bhaktivedanta at Ohio State. With his travels taking him by plane and automobile to all parts of the United States, Allen was able to resume work on his poems about America. As he flew from Albany to Baltimore, he directed one poem to Edgar Allan Poe.

> Poe! D'jya prophesy this Smogland, this Inferno,
> Didya Dream Baltimore'd Be Seen From Heaven
> by Man Poet's eyes Astounded in the Fire Haze,
>   carbon Gas aghast!
> Poe! D'jya know yr prophecies' RED DEATH
> would pour thru Philly's sky like Sulfurous Dreams?
> Walled into Amontillado's Basement! Man
>   kind led weeping drunk into the Bomb
>   Shelter by Mad Secretaries of Defense!

On his way to a reading at Washington State University, he dictated "Northwest Passage," a poem that represented his best auto poesy in nine months. The tour seemed to invigorate him. After months in Cherry Valley, living in virtual seclusion and working on his music, he was back in front of large audiences, listening to opinions and exchanging ideas. It was the kind of interaction that spurred his creativity. By the time he returned to Cherry Valley, he had nine new poems that he liked enough to save for his next collection.

The tour, however, exacted its toll. In early April, Allen spent a week in bed with an illness brought on by exhaustion. An attack of Bell's palsy, a nervous disorder, left the left side of his face partially paralyzed. Then, on April 30, while visiting the University of Arizona, he was punched in the mouth by a reporter after the two had spent some time in a heated exchange about homosexuality. Allen, who had already deemed the frantic pace of the reading tour "a burden," briefly considered retiring from the touring scene altogether. His ideal, he admitted, would be to live on the farm and write poetry and music—or, at the very least, move at a slower pace than in recent years.

As soon as he had returned to the farm and settled in, Allen began work on recording the Blake songs. Miles had flown in from England to oversee the album's production. The choice was a good one. Miles was knowledgeable about the music business, and from his association with the Beatles, he knew a great deal about the intricacies of piecing together an album of disparate songs that somehow managed to stay cohesive as an overall unit. To Allen, this was very important since he was only a rudimentary musician at best—but one who had an idea of what he wanted for each song nevertheless. "Allen knew the 'feel' he was after," Miles recalled. "It was the sound vibration of the voice of the ancient Blake he had once heard in audio-vision years before." In recording the music, Miles noted, he and Allen always aspired to capturing the "feeling and interpretation rather than technical perfection."

They worked on the album throughout that June and July, recording nineteen songs in all. Such musicians as Don Cherry, Elvin Jones, Jon Scholle, Herman Wright, and Julius Watkins were brought in as sidemen. The eleven selected works from Blake's *Songs of Innocence* included "The Little Black Boy," "The Chimney Sweeper," "The Little Boy Lost," and "The Little Boy Found"; from the *Songs of Experience* were two poems Allen had heard during his 1948 Blake visions ("The Sick Rose," "Ah! Sunflower!"), as well as the classic "Nurse's Song" and "The Human Abstract." Rounding out the collection, although not part of the original *Songs of Innocence* and *Songs of Experience*, was "The Grey Monk," the song that had initiated Ginsberg's quest. In their original form, the poems had been sung by Blake without accompaniment when he visited friends; in recording them, Allen tried to maintain their lyrical power while making them musically interesting.

"The purpose of putting them to music," explained Ginsberg, "was to articu-late the significance of each holy and magic syllable of his poems, as if each syllable had intention. These are perfect verses, with no noise lost of extra accents for nothing. I tried to hear meanings of each line spoken intentionally and interestedly, and follow natural voice tones up and down according to different emphases and emotions vocalized as in daily intimate speech: I drew the latent tunes, up or down, out of talk-tones suggested by each syllable spoken with normal feeling."

The result was an album of loving tribute, noteworthy for its simple melodies and subtle arrangements. At best, Ginsberg's voice had average range and timbre, but what he lacked in natural vocal ability, he compensated for with enthusiasm. Both Ginsberg and Miles were wise enough to avoid trying to make Ginsberg something he was not—that is, a rock 'n' roll star—and there is never a doubt when one listens to the album that the real star of the work is Blake himself. Two centuries after their composition, Blake's works were as poignant as ever, and hearing Ginsberg place them in the context of contemporary music was a delight to a number of the album's reviewers. "It's a beautiful record, which makes me happy every time I hear it," a writer for *The New Yorker* exclaimed after the album had been issued in 1970. Unfortunately, there were not enough buyers sharing the same enthusiasm. The recording would enjoy only meager sales and would be out of print before the second projected volume of Blake songs was ever released.

3

On July 20, 1969, the first astronauts stepped foot on the surface of the moon. To those who believed in a space race, a victor had been proclaimed: The United States had beaten the Russians to the prize! As if to prove the point, an American flag, unfurled and fixed stiffly in place in the windless atmosphere of the moon, was planted and saluted.

Allen followed the event with a mixture of fascination and disgust. At a time when one-quarter of the world's population was not permitted to watch the moon landing by decree of their rulers, when over a million and a half people had starved in the famine in Biafra, when the environment of the planet Earth was threatened by pollution and overpopulation, the moon landing had an ironic quality. After making a shambles out of their own planet, humans were now reaching out to virgin territory. In the little more than a decade since the launching of *Sputnik*, tremendous upheaval had taken place in the United States and around the world, and while Allen was thrilled by the thought of a man standing on the moon (just as he had been initially excited by *Sputnik*'s signifying human exploration of space), his thoughts were tempered by his concerns about the future of the world. "I didn't think we'd see this Night," he wrote, adding a warning of his own: "Plant the flag and you're doomed!"

Even though he spent most of the summer in Cherry Valley, he was anything but removed from worry. He was especially bothered by a series of money woes. The farm was proving to be expensive to run. In addition, he had spent a large sum of money on making the Blake album, and he owed nearly fifteen hundred dollars in back taxes, which he refused to pay as long as the money was allocated to financing the war. The financial problems depressed him; he worried about a confrontation with the IRS. "Ultimately, I wake in morn afraid of violent dispersal of my possessions, music books mss. and household," he wrote in his journal.

Adding to his frustration were the delays in the publication of *Indian Journals*, a book for which he had great hopes. The journals Allen had kept while he was in India were far from being mere diary entries or travel writing. They represented no less than a fascinating study of important personal and artistic development. Of *Indian Journals*, Allen confessed that he felt "more eager about this [as] an object than I have about a book for years." He had carefully selected and edited the text, gathered photographs from his archive, and overseen the book in every aspect of its production. Originally to be issued by a small publishing house, *Indian Journals* was stalled when Allen's publisher ran into money problems. Lawrence Ferlinghetti offered to put it out as a City Lights edition, an offer Allen readily accepted, but its preparation took longer than Allen would have liked, leaving him anxious and irritable. "I am sick seeing a

New Yorker biographical book on me advertised," he groused in reference to Jane Kramer's *Allen Ginsberg in America*, "[while] my own real prose [is] stuck all this year, useless and inert."

A measure of his sour mood could undoubtedly be attributed to matters out of his control. He regularly received calls from or about friends and acquaintances who had been arrested or who were being harassed by the police or government. Some of the problems were very serious. Eight of the organizers of different events during the Chicago convention—Abbie Hoffman, Jerry Rubin, Tom Hayden, Bobby Seale, David Dellinger, Rennie Davis, Lee Weiner, and John Froines—had been charged with conspiracy to incite riots and were scheduled for trial in Chicago later in the year. Other friends were broke and urgently needed money. These distractions, added to Allen's own problems, were bothersome enough to result in a series of cranky journal entries revealing of his mood at the time:

> I wake mornings breathing shallow, birds warbling in foggy light, my mind racing with eyes open or eyes closed trying to return to unconsciousness to escape fear—of body pain, of fatigue, of horses eating fences rotting squash leaves lost in green weedstalks—weeds round my life—I talk about God and don't see Him—talk about love and fear Peter—my belly tense, mind racing to revolutionary doom of planet—morning after morning nervous breakdown a cheerless self with my desk accumulating energetic papers, money worry above all, pestered by dollar needs first time in 42 years on planet money's gotten under my skin and into my consciousness like bedbugs that wouldn't let me sleep in the city.

Despite his ill humor, he carried on, devoting his energy to work around the farm and his writing projects. Beside the occasional poem of his own, he was editing and writing an introduction to a volume of his father's selected poems. Allen's excellent analysis was rivaled only by his open affection for the man who had been so influential in his own early interest in poetry. "Confronting my father's poems at the end of his life," Allen wrote,

> I weep at his meekness and his reason, at his wise entrance into his own mortality and his silent recognition of that pitiful Immensity he records of his own life's Time, his father's life time, & the same Mercy his art accords to my own person his son.
>
> I won't quarrel with his forms here anymore: by faithful love he's made them his own, and by many years practice arrived at sufficient condensation of idea, freedom of fancy, phrase modernity, depth of death-vision, & clarity of particular contemporary attention to transform the old "lyric" form from an inverted fantasy to the deepest actualization of his peaceful mortal voice.

Writing the introduction required some panache, for it would have been too easy at this stage of his life for Allen to come off sounding either sentimental or patronizing. To prepare himself for the task, he read and took copious notes on his father's poetry, treating the individual poems as if they were the works of a contemporary rather than the writings of a relative. Taking this approach gave the essay a sweet irony. For years, Louis had been carefully reading and offering criticism of Allen's poetry, judging the poems on their own merits despite not being fond of his son's style and subject matter at times. Now, with the roles reversed, Allen afforded Louis the same courtesy.

In addition to his preoccupation with the war and the forthcoming conspiracy trial in Chicago (for which he was asked to be a witness for the defense), Allen found himself returning once again to the front lines in what now seemed like a never-ending censorship battle. This time, it was a newspaper, the *New York Review of Sex and Politics*, that was under fire. In the twentieth century, Allen noted in a statement that he prepared in defense of the paper, sex *was* politics. In the Iron Curtain countries he had visited, Allen wrote, "strict puritanism of public imagery" was the rule, and the suppression of any kind of public expression of sexuality was a means by which authoritarian bureaucracies maintained control over the people. In the United States, such oppression was not only unconstitutional but, in Allen's view, immoral, antisocial, and unnatural. "As we have gone to the moon," he argued, "it is imperative that we go to our own bodies and into our own hearts and minds and sex to find out who we are. We will not find out who we are if exchange of public information as to our sexual identity, such as it is, is suppressed."

Applying the recent moon landing to a now very familiar theme was a new approach for Allen and he used this angle a short time later when he was asked to issue a statement for a peace rally in Houston. This time, he addressed the astronauts directly, imploring them to heed their concern for Mother Earth: "Houston in its space age Lunacy has to confront its personal Magic War in Vietnam as well as its psychedelic Moon Trip. . . . Armstrong Aldrin Collins in the Name of Mamma open your mouths like Patriot Paine like Ecologist Thoreau and call your nation to stop her Unnatural War!"

With the arrival of the autumn season, Allen and the others at the farm began to prepare for the winter. They put up crops and added insulation to the barn. Allen's mood had not improved and he and Peter argued frequently, which only added to his depression. "If Peter and I can't get along," he brooded, "how can Jews and Arabs? How can any war end?" To his dismay, answers were not within immediate reach.

4

Allen was scheduled to kick off his fall reading schedule at Yale on October 22. Gregory Corso was back in the country and had come out to the farm. The two were to give a joint reading at the Ivy League school, with Allen to present antiwar poems and a lecture on "The Politics of Love." Ginsberg, who had endorsed an October 15 moratorium in which students and faculty across the country left their classes and spent a day ringing doorbells and discussing the Vietnam War with neighbors, and who intended to participate in an October 23 teach-in at Columbia, was gearing up for another extended barrage against the war.

The focus of the tour—at its beginning at least—changed abruptly when, on the evening of October 21, the phone rang and Al Aronowitz delivered news that was as inevitable as it was tragic: Jack Kerouac had died at the age of forty-seven in St. Petersburg, Florida.

By all accounts, Kerouac's final days were sad and lonely, marked by heavy drinking and a lethargic inability to write anything of substance. The last time Allen had seen him—a year earlier at the taping for Kerouac's appearance on William F. Buckley's "Firing Line" television show—Jack had been hopelessly drunk and combative, and it was apparent to Allen, as it was to those who knew Kerouac well, that Jack was in the process of succumbing to his alcoholism. He offered only hints of the Kerouac Allen had known for nearly twenty-five years.

For those who revered the Duluoz legend and the zesty lives of Sal Paradise and Ray Smith, Kerouac's decline had been shocking. Ann Charters, author of the first Kerouac biography, recalled her initial meeting with the author in August 1966, when she had visited Kerouac with the intention of compiling a bibliography of his works:

> Nothing any interviewer had ever described prepared me for the sad figure in the doorway. He was always stocky, about five foot eight, but his muscular frame was soft under the rumpled T-shirt, his face puffy and petulant. He was only forty-four years old, but if anything he looked like the battered, lost father of the young Jack in all the dustjacket photographs. It was one o'clock, he was just getting up, just beginning to think about drinking his breakfast.

Similar accounts abounded. Kerouac himself seemed to realize the end was near. He had sold a large volume of his correspondence and archival materials to university libraries. His new home in St. Petersburg had been more of a retirement setup for his mother and wife than a new headquarters for future creative activity. He had seen both the joy and the suffering in life, and as his years went on and he felt himself trapped in some of life's sadness, he had resigned himself to it—had even written poignantly about it. "What he had done," Ginsberg offered as an explanation, "was try to follow the sad-comic view of things to the bottom of his own nature and transcribe it in its own onrushing spontaneous flow, and leave it there for later, for others."

The creative well, as it turned out, was not completely dry, even if Jack did appear to be trying to replace its water with wine. He might have lost the great self-discipline that had marked his early writing life, as well as much of the creative spark, but he continued to work. Not long before his death, he published "After Me, The Deluge," a poignant essay decrying the division in America between youths and elders. In the essay, he made clear his feelings that despite all the press accounts proclaiming him to be the father of the Beat and hippie generations, he was no more comfortable with the slogans of the youths than the cynicism of their elders. He was caught in the middle, able to identify with no party line, a libertarian to the bitter end: "I think I'll drop out—Great American tradition—Dan'l Boone, U.S. Grant, Mark Twain—I think I'll go to sleep and suddenly in my deepest inadequacy nightmares wake up haunted and see everyone in the world as unconsolable orphans yelling and screaming on every side to make arrangements for making a living yet all bespattered and gloomed-up in the nightsoul of poor body and soul all present and accounted for as some kind of sneakish, crafty gift, and all so *lonered*."

It was not important for Jack that he see such prophecy reach fruition; he had known it was true all along. Buddhist teachings had told him so, and he was leaving behind a substantial body of work to continue the teaching. There was an official reason given for Kerouac's death—cirrhosis of the liver, causing the rupture of a vein in the esophagus—but, like Neal, he had died when his body could no longer support his spirit. "He didn't live much longer than Neal" was one of Ginsberg's first observations after hearing of Jack's death.

Allen fulfilled his reading commitment to Yale the day he learned of Kerouac's death, although he devoted most of the evening to a remembrance and tribute to Jack. On the stage was a twelve-by-four-foot banner that read: IN MEMORIUM: JACK KEROUAC, 1922–1969 and, on the line below, NEAL CASSADY, 1927–1968. The audience was solemn, respectful. Allen and Peter opened the evening by chanting the Diamond Sutra, Kerouac's favorite Buddhist prayer, and when they had finished, they were greeted by a smattering of applause. "You don't have to applaud a prayer," Allen quietly admonished the audience.

He continued the memorial by reading selections of *Mexico City Blues*, choosing passages that seemed especially characteristic of Jack's spirit. He repeated the final lines of the "211th Chorus" three times for emphasis:

> *Poor!* I wish I was free
> of that slaving meat wheel
> and safe in heaven dead.

John Clellon Holmes, on hand for the reading, felt that Allen was trying to make a specific point by emphasizing the lines: "See, there's your politics, that's your art, that's your reality, *that* was life to him."

Allen went on to read the "242nd Chorus"—the final lines in the book—which closed with one of Kerouac's strongest (and most hopeful) statements:

> Stop the murder and suicide!
> All's well!
> I am the Guard.

Allen then read from his own work for nearly an hour and after a short intermission sang a number of his Blake songs, "smiling with the healing euphoria of songs," perhaps recalling a time over two decades earlier when they had all been in their youth, looking toward incomprehensible eternity. Kerouac and Blake had been joined in death, but they were as alive as their works being read and sung in the auditorium.

When he had completed the reading, Allen addressed questions from the audience. Not surprisingly, the focus was on Kerouac. To the students at Yale, it seemed inconceivable that Jack's life had taken such a different course from Allen's. What did *Allen* think of Kerouac's death? What were *his* feelings about Jack's drifting off into conservatism and alcoholism? Was Kerouac important? Why should they care about him?

"Well," Allen said after taking a long pause to consider a response, "he was the first one to make a new crack in the consciousness." From that fissure, he continued, came everything—from the drugs and rock 'n' roll to the idea of "doing your own thing" to the concept of creating a New Jerusalem—that had been associated with the Beat Generation and, later, the hippies. "He introduced that crack of consciousness all by himself, and broke upon a fantastic solidity in America as solid as the Empire State Building—that turned out not to be solid at all." Kerouac had followed his own unique view of the world to every limit, including his own decline, and he was generous enough to share it with his readers. For Kerouac, much of life was emptiness and illusion. "So he drank himself to death," Allen concluded, "which is only another way of living, of handling the pain and foolishness that it's all a dream, a great baffling silly emptiness, after all."

Despite being less than kind to Kerouac in his final years, the press echoed many of Ginsberg's observations in the flood of obituaries and analytical essays that followed his death. *The New York Times* mentioned "the upheaval in values that 'On the Road' helped signal"; Ward Just, writing for the *Washington Post*, also commented on Kerouac's influence on changing values, writing that "in retrospect, he seems to me to have been the first to sense the disintegration, to spot the seams tearing and coming apart in America." The *Christian Science Monitor* predicted that "the figure of Jack Kerouac will assert itself—much as the novelist, once a football fullback, tried to thrust himself into life or onto the literary scene or into the company of neighborhood bar mates in his hometown of Lowell, Mass., always hoping to break into the open into a vision of an expansive America and the he-man mystical culture."

After the Yale reading, the group retired to John Clellon Holmes's house in nearby Old Saybrook, where they spent the evening drinking and reminiscing. The next day, Holmes drove Allen, Peter, and Gregory to Lowell. The morning was bone-chillingly cold. As they drove along the Connecticut highway and into Massachusetts, Allen pulled out his harmonium and he and Peter sang some of the Blake songs. Soon enough, they were in Kerouac's hometown. Lowell, Holmes pointed out, was the kind of town that only a sensitive soul like Kerouac could have lionized. Not yet rejuvenated, Lowell was falling apart—a town full of boarded-up factories and run-down unpainted buildings. One needed to possess Jack's prodigious memory and imagination to recall the spark of childhood from which flared the warm recollections of snowball fights and steamy homecooked meals and first-love kisses on cold autumn nights. If life was a dream, as Kerouac had so often insisted, the author had created his own dream in this battered old factory town.

They located the tavern owned by Kerouac's brother-in-law, Nick Sampas, and they made themselves at home. The bartender recognized Allen from an earlier visit with Jack, and he told Allen that Sampas was at the airport picking up his sister, Jack's widow. Although the group looked like the kind of people the conservative working-class people of Lowell had grown to despise, Allen and his friends were made to feel welcome. When Stella Kerouac finally arrived, she was initially accusatory ("All of you here! *Why* didn't you come to Florida when he needed you?"), but only for a moment. "He loved you all," she said. "He never stopped talking about you."

The Sampas family, as congenial as Jack had portrayed them to be, were generous hosts, taking care of the group's every need. That evening, they feasted on a huge meal of steaks, lobster, shrimp, and homemade breads, washed down by bottles of retsina. Allen discovered the Sampases were a tight-knit family, not unlike the Martin family of Kerouac's *The Town and the City*, and whatever differences they may have had between one another were put aside as they came together and supported one another in a time of grief.

While they were eating, Allen and his friends realized that they had done nothing about ordering flowers for the funeral home. It was important to Allen that there be a symbol from Jack's friends and the literary community. Gregory sketched a design of a large red heart resting on a lotus, complete with spikes of fire and thorns. Allen suggested a ribbon saying HOLD THE HEART running across the arrangement, and Holmes countered with the suggestion that they use an idea at the end of *Mexico City Blues*: "Guard the Heart." Unfortunately, it was too late in the day for the florist to arrange such an elaborate design and they had to settle for a red heart of roses, the quotation, and ribbons with the individuals' names: Allen, Peter, Gregory, John, and, because they were close friends, Bill, Lucien, and Robert (Creeley).

After dinner, Nick Sampas led a small procession of cars to the funeral home, a Victorian-style structure with pale green walls and high ceilings. Allen, Peter, and the others made their way through the crowded room, filled mostly with people from Lowell but also youths dressed in hippie garb who seemed to Holmes as if they were lost. When they reached the casket, Allen reached out and touched Jack's forehead. "Touch him," he urged the others. "There's really nothing inside."

"The first glimpse I had of Kerouac lying in his coffin," Ginsberg wrote several years later, "was of a large meat doll in a state of empty meditation. Consciousness was no longer located in his head or body, but had escaped as if by some humorous and deliberate trick into the room, into trees, into America."

Indeed, the figure in the casket was not the familiar Kerouac. In his pale yellow shirt, red bow tie, and houndstooth sport coat, Jack looked more like the Thomas Wolfe–like writer seen on the dust jacket of *The Town and the City*. A rosary had been woven around his fingers—a last testament to his difficult but lifelong devotion to Catholicism. To Allen, Jack "looked like his father had become from earlier dream decades."

The funeral was held the following morning at St. Jean Baptiste Church, where Jack had served as an altar boy in his youth. Allen was a pallbearer. Robert Creeley had come in from Syracuse for the occasion; other out-of-towners included Sterling Lord (Kerouac's agent), writer Jimmy Breslin, and Ann and Sam Charters. A large number of reporters and photographers were also present. During the solemn requiem high mass, Reverend Armand Morissette, a friend of Jack's for over twenty years, offered words of comfort to the two hundred people in attendance, warmly remembering Jack and referring to the honesty in his work. "Our hope and prayer is that Jack has now found complete liberation," he said.

The service moved along quickly and before long they were at the cemetery, standing around Kerouac's open grave. October had been Jack's favorite month, and the day of his burial was a typically cool and breezy New England autumn day. Father Morissette read a few prayers, completing the service, and Allen and his friends plucked roses from a wreath and placed them on the casket. As it was being lowered, Allen was asked to throw down the first handful of dirt. The others followed his example.

Nearby, a young reporter talked with Sterling Lord. Like so many others, the reporter could not understand Kerouac's conservatism and right-wing politics in the later years of his life. "I mean, we can't relate to all that American shit," he told Lord.

Overhearing the conversation, John Clellon Holmes broke in. "Don't understand him too easily," he said.

5

After the funeral, Allen began his fall reading tour, which, despite his earlier protests about cutting back on the grueling schedule, was as busy as ever. While in Canada, he called John Lennon, who was staging a Bed-In for Peace, and who had included his name in "Give Peace A Chance," his new antiwar anthem. A few days later, in Montreal, a customs official siezed Allen's valise containing his clothing and a springboard binder of poems, journal, and other papers, all because the official was not certain if an underground newspaper in the valise was pornographic. Although the papers were returned, the seizure represented to Allen just another example of a global state of paranoid politics turning the world into a police state.

Kerouac's death continued to haunt Allen and he found himself thinking about days gone by, happier times. There was no escaping reality, however. The people he loved were dying. Even sleep could not shield him from his troubles. In one dream shortly after Jack's funeral, he saw "Kerouac's white stocky body naked under bedsprings wounded dead warm—the shrouded stranger." A few days later, he dreamed that he was sitting at a luncheonette counter with his mother, who, "looking cute spit curled 1930's," carried on a sweet, cheerful conversation. Allen told Naomi that he remembered her soul. "Pray for me, momma," he implored her.

The memories were not always disturbing. While in Lowell, Allen had begun a long elegiac poem to Kerouac, on which he continued to work, off and on, for a week. Entitled "Memory Gardens," the poem, recognizing that Jack "threw up his hands/& wrote the Universe dont exist/& died to prove it," had an ethereal quality, mixing memory and current reality, recalling a happier past in juxtaposition to the sad, violent present. Interspersed throughout the poem were quick photographic flashes of a youthful Kerouac—sitting on the subway, Allen peeking out at Jack through a hole he had cut in a newspaper; hurrying about Manhattan on unknown errands; stepping off subway cars. Ginsberg used color ("yellow leaves," "gold over Mannahatta's spires," "Black misted canyons," "Blue-tinted Columbia sign," "White mist," "sun set red over Hudson horizon," etc.) to make his memory more vivid, standing in contrast to the flatly described scenes of the present-day world, as if Kerouac, wherever he might be, and certainly in memory, was in a better position than those he left behind. After a brief description of Kerouac's funeral, Allen closed the poem in a manner that all but conceded this feeling. He, Allen, was still on earth, dedicated to his work—which he said was to ease the pain of those still living. "Everything else," he concluded, was "drunken dumbshow."

Allen had one other bit of his past to address, which he did in early December when he returned to Chicago to testify at what was now known as the Chicago Conspiracy Trial. By the time he entered the courtroom as a witness for the defense, the trial was a shambles, a perverse circus representative of the absolute worst the American judicial system had to offer. Judge Julius Hoffman, a diminutive seventy-four-year-old jurist who had contributed heavily to the Republican party in the past, had refused Bobby Seale the right to represent himself in lieu of his own attorney (who was ill and hospitalized at the time). When Seale protested this denial of rights, Hoffman ordered him gagged and chained to his chair. Hoffman would eventually declare a mistrial, eliminating Seale and reducing the defendants, initially known as the Chicago Eight, to seven. Courtroom theatrics and angry denouncements of the judge, by both the defendants and their attorneys, were commonplace, resulting in contempt-of-court sentences unprecedented in American legal history. In many respects, what occurred in the courtroom was a vivid reflection of what had transpired in the streets of Chicago during the Democratic National Convention: The defendants, who had little in common other than the fact that they represented key rebellious groups, were determined to take on the system, and the system—this time in the judicial rather than the executive branch—was ready to fight back, to maintain superiority. "From reading some of the editorials," one journalist commented, "you might be forced to conclude that the eight had cleverly tricked the United States Government into indicting them so they could lay waste to the Federal Courts."

If anything, Allen's turn at the witness stand was symbolic of the total chaos and lack of communication in the courtroom. From the time he walked up the aisle of the courtroom and offered Judge Hoffman a Hindu gesture of greeting to the time he ended his testimony by reciting portions of "Howl," Allen was subjected to continuous interruptions by the judge and prosecuting attorneys and scorn from those who could not and would not attempt to understand why he was in the parks, why he had used mantra chanting as a means of settling the crowd, and why as a poet he could be a viable force in political or social change. Allen's cross-examination by prosecutor Thomas Foran was especially offensive, focusing on Allen's homosexuality to such a degree that journalist Nicholas von Hoffman termed his line of questioning "a refined form of fag baiting."

Allen's testimony began innocently enough, with Ginsberg explaining his roles as a teacher and poet. He then cited his studies in India and Japan, trying to show the scholarship behind his interests in mantra chanting. He patiently and deliberately spelled the names of the different swamis and yogis he had studied under, leading to an interesting exchange when he attempted to describe the act of mantra chanting.

FORAN: Oh, your Honor, I object. I think we have gone far enough now to have established—

HOFFMAN: I think I have a vague idea of the witness' profession. It is vague.

FORAN: I might indicate also that he is an excellent speller.

HOFFMAN: I sustain the objection, but I notice that he has said first he was a poet, and I will give him credit for all the other things, too, whatever they are.

If such an exchange had been dialogue in a work of fiction written by Joseph Heller or Kurt Vonnegut, it might have been considered dark humor. As it was, spoken in the context of a legal proceeding in which the judge had felt compelled over the course of the trial to cite others for contempt of court, the exchange was both pathetic and frightening, indicative of the way the witness would be treated throughout his testimony.

It became even more ludicrous when Allen tried to demonstrate the Hare Krishna mantra for the court. Foran laughed openly, provoking a strong objection from defense attorney William Kunstler, who pointed out that the mantra was serious and religious. "I don't understand it," countered Judge Hoffman, who had made no attempt to hide his disdain for Kunstler throughout the trial. "The language of the United States District Court is English," he reminded the attorney, mentioning that Allen could have an interpreter if he so desired, even if Hoffman had no idea what Allen's mantra chanting had to do with the trial. Leonard Weinglass, the other defense attorney, then handed Allen his harmonium and asked him to examine and identify it. Allen looked at it and played a C chord, eliciting another objection from the prosecution.

"Your Honor, that is enough," said Foran. "I object to it, your Honor. I think it's outrageous for counsel to—"

"You asked him to examine it and instead of that he played a tune on it," Hoffman interjected, admonishing Weinglass and sustaining the objection.

"I mean," Foran went on, "counsel is so clearly talking about things that have no materiality to this case, and it is improper, your Honor."

"It adds spirituality to the case, sir," Allen interjected.

"Will you remain quiet, sir?" Hoffman scolded Allen.

And so it went. For the remainder of Allen's testimony on his first day on the stand, the tone from the judge and prosecuting attorney was contentious. Allen tried to hold his temper, but by the end of the session he was clearly frustrated by the interruptions.

The next day, December 12, began smoothly, with Allen talking about the original planning for the Festival of Life. He spoke about his fears of violence and of the attempts to obtain permits for the parks during convention week. There was the usual peppering of objections by the prosecution, but the defense managed to maneuver around attempts to block Allen's testimony. Allen went on to talk about his arrival in Chicago and of the events leading up to the first skirmish with the police in Lincoln Park. He had taken notes of these events and was therefore able to provide descriptive accounts of them. However, he ran into trouble when he tried to outline his actions during the time the police were moving through the park:

GINSBERG: I started to chant, O-O-M-M-M-M-M-M, O-O-M-M-M-M-M-M.

FORAN: All right, we have had a demonstration.

HOFFMAN: All right.

WEINGLASS: If the court please, there has been much testimony by the Government's witnesses as to this Om technique which was used in the park. Are we only going to hear whether there were stones or people throwing things, or shouting things, or using obscenities? Why do we draw the line here? Why can't we also hear what is being said in the area of calming the crowd?

FORAN: I have no objection to two Om's that we have had. However, I just didn't want it to go on all morning.

HOFFMAN: The two, however you characterize what the witness did, may remain of record, and he may not continue in the same vein.

WEINGLASS: Did you finish your answer?

GINSBERG: I am afraid I will be contempt if I continue to Om.

Allen testified for the rest of the day, describing for the court the way he had chanted for seven hours in the park, the violence he had seen over the week of the convention, the attempted march by David Dellinger and subsequent tear-gassing by the police. Over the course of many hours' testimony, Allen had proven himself to be an authoritative witness, capable of recreating events with great detail. The prosecution seemed to recognize this. During cross-examination, after asking him numerous questions to clarify earlier statements, Foran abruptly changed his line of questioning to focus on Allen's opinions about drugs and sex. It was a poorly disguised attempt to tarnish Allen's credibility, but the ploy may have backfired when upon request Allen recited from memory a substantial portion of "Howl." How the ten women and two men on the jury reacted to the poem is anyone's guess, but it is unlikely that they missed the poignancy of its "Moloch" section, placed within the context of the events in Chicago during the week of the convention. While Allen recited the lines, Judge Hoffman put a hand to his face, barely able to listen to the presentation.

Like his earlier appearance before the Senate subcommittee, Allen's testimony in Chicago was of little consequence to the trial itself. Five of the seven defendants—Rubin, Hoffman, Hayden, Davis, and Dellinger—were found guilty of the charges of crossing state lines to incite riots. The verdict would eventually be reversed in a court of appeals, but there was little doubt that for the time being the verdict cast a chilling shadow over any plans for large rallies or assemblies of dissenting political nature in the immediate future.

6

Allen had no sooner escaped the legal quagmire in Chicago than he found himself entangled in still another proceeding, this time in Miami. He had scheduled a couple of readings with his father in that city, and the first, in Miami's Temple Israel on December 21, was delivered without incident. The next evening's reading, however, was an entirely different affair. Promoted as the "Last Happening of the Sixties," the reading was staged at the Miami Marine Stadium. Allen had heard of a young writer who had been convicted of using profanity in the *Daily Planet*, an underground Miami newspaper, and Ginsberg decided to donate his reading fee to the writer's legal costs of appeal.

The reading was a fiasco. Officials refused to permit Louis to read because he had not been a part of the original bill, and a city ordinance required approval of performances in public arenas prior to scheduled events. Then, Allen, who had been approved, was cut off. Ironically, his problems began as he was reciting "Kral Majales," his poem about the police state in Czechoslovakia, when the stadium manager announced the reading was over. Allen continued to read. The manager ordered the sound turned off and the stadium lights turned on full. Allen ignored these actions as well. Finally, the manager played music over the stadium's sound system, drowning out Ginsberg. Allen walked from the stage to a standing ovation. Asked why he had gone to such lengths to cut the reading short, the stadium manager said he had been offended by Ginsberg's use of profanity. "It was not for one word but for lots of words," he explained—although, as it turned out, it was the assistant city manager, not the stadium manager, who had made the decision to terminate the reading.

In all likelihood, such a flap would not have been raised if Miami had not still been stinging from the notoriety it received from a recent Doors concert, during which Jim Morrison, the band's lead singer, had been arrested for exposing himself to his audience. The subsequent publicity, legal snafus, embarrassment, controversy, and debate created quite a commotion in a community generally regarded to be fairly open-minded toward the arts. Allen's reading caught the tail wind of the controversy, and once again the city was involved in a debate over what was and was not permissible in public performance.

"The city's performance gives Miami a black eye in the performing arts," declared an editorialist for the *Miami News*. Writing for the *Miami Herald*, columnist A. L. Lieber underscored the standpoint: "I find the entire episode most regrettable and believe it will stand as a blot on the liberal reputation of our city." These opinions, however, were countered by equally impassioned sentiments expressed by others working for the same papers. Outraged *Miami News* columnist Jack Roberts, in a strongly worded piece, compared Ginsberg to Jim Morrison and conjured up the old argument that Allen was using profanity simply to attract attention and make money. "Let's face it," he wrote, "Ginsberg is just another guy with a gimmick. . . . If he doesn't come up with a little mind-bending . . . and phrases you can't print in a family paper, [he] wouldn't be making those fees."

Allen chose to address the issue in court. Two days after the aborted reading, Allen's attorney announced that a suit would be filed in the U.S. District Court on behalf of Allen, his father, and the sponsors of the reading. The suit would request that the court order the city to reschedule the reading, with the new reading being free of charge. In addition, the suit demanded that the performance be free from any annoying, harassing, or oppressive actions by city officials and that the city be required to provide security for the event. Perhaps most important, the suit demanded a Miami ordinance (requiring the city manager's approval and a police background check of those appearing in city facilities) be struck down as unconstitutional. After years of battling oppressive ordinances aimed at New York coffeehouses, Allen was finally taking his show on the road. On New Year's Eve, he achieved his victory: Citing the First Amendment as the backbone of his decision, the district court judge ruled that Allen's rights had indeed been violated. The judge issued an injunction requiring the city to allow the free reading.

The new reading was billed as the "First Intellectual Happening of the 70's." Louis Ginsberg was unable to attend, so Allen devoted a portion of the evening to the reading of a selection of his father's poetry. The event received an abundance of media attention, not all of it favorable, but it was of little consequence to Allen. He had begun a new decade with an important moral victory.

22
First Blues

I tried singing Mantras   I
      tried singing out William Blake
Tried mantra chanting   Ah
      tried tuning up old holy Blake
Now I'll sing Him the blues if   Good
      God gives me a break. . . .

1

The dawning of a new decade found Allen in the enviable position of having achieved virtually everything a poet could have aspired to. He was easily America's best-known poet, even if the merits of his work were still being debated in literary circles and on college campuses across the country. His poetry had been widely translated and distributed throughout the world. His political influence, particularly with America's youth, could not be overlooked. His readings and speaking engagements now commanded fees of about a thousand dollars an appearance—a handsome amount for a poetry reading at the time and certainly enough to satisfy Allen's modest living expenses, with money to spare for his Committee on Poetry.

Despite the success, he was far from satisfied. His rather nomadic lifestyle left him feeling unsettled at times, as if he had "no home, no place to die," as he put it. There were occasions, although rare, when he would regret not having children. He worried about reaching middle age, complaining about everything from the paunch gathering at his waistline to minor illnesses, all of which convinced him that he was reaching the inevitable path to physical decline.

He was greatly troubled by the events of the world. The idealism of the 1960s had faded. If there had ever been a promise of Camelot, it had been long forgotten, replaced by the cynicism of the Nixon administration. Vice President Spiro Agnew, never judged guilty of possessing great intellectual prowess, may have typified the pervading attitude when he sneered at intellectuals, activists, war protesters, liberals, and anyone else in disagreement with the official position, using strings of hyperbolic invective to disguise the fact that the current administration had no better idea of how to solve the country's problems than had the preceding one. In Vietnam, the death toll continued to rise. By the beginning of 1970, over thirty thousand Americans had perished in a war to which there was no end in sight.

Allen remained one of the war's most visible and outspoken critics. He hated paying federal income taxes, knowing as he did that a large percentage of the money collected was being sunk in the war effort. For nearly two years, he had resisted the payment of such taxes in any way that he could imagine, often at the expense of confrontations with the Internal Revenue Service. However, he judged these actions to be inadequate. If there was to be any hope of making an impact through this form of protest, it had to be approached on a much larger scale.

With this in mind, Allen joined Dr. Benjamin Spock, singers Joan Baez and Pete Seeger, and journalist Kenneth Love in the formation of War Tax Resistance, an organization devoted to aiding and counseling those who wished to protest the war by refusing to pay taxes. In a statement to the press, the organization noted that "the right to conscientious objection to war belongs to all people, not just those of draft age," that taxpayers had the right to refuse service by withholding those taxes that would be applied to the war. Such actions, said Ginsberg at a press conference announcing the formation of the group, would help "short-circuit the nerve system of our electronic bureaucracy." Allen announced that he had written the secretary of the treasury to explain his reasons for refusing to pay taxes: "I am willing to pay your tax assessment by donating what money I will have to any tax-exempt program acceptable to your department which will benefit money-poor Americans or protect natural resources wasted as a consequence of war preparations." (Unimpressed with the proposal, the IRS seized the money Allen had in his bank account—all twenty dollars of it—to use toward the payment of his back taxes.)

Allen was at a loss over what to do about the violence that continued to dominate so many newscasts and newspaper headlines. Besides the Vietnam War and the violence in the country's urban areas, all but taken for granted by the media, there were the ageless tensions in the Middle East, the instability of Third World nations, and, closer to home, the racial turmoil that threatened to erupt into violence as militant blacks, angry about what they perceived to be shortcomings in the civil rights movement, urged their communities to take another approach. Allen and Louis Ginsberg argued about these issues in their correspondence, Allen still accusing Louis of being shortsighted when he let his patriotism or Jewish heritage cloud his vision of national or world events.

"As I would not see myself as Black if I were black," he wrote, "I don't see myself as a Jew and I am a Jew, and so don't identify with Nation of Jews any more than I would of Nation of America or Russia. Down with all nations, they are enemies of mankind! And nationalism is a disease. . . . I don't have a solution except not to take sides that involve bloodying anyone's ass or any kind of political violence. If, however, everyone insists on being violently right, then we will have to suffer it through and die violently at various idiots' hands—Jewish idiots, Arab idiots, American idiots, Maoist idiots, liberal idiots, reactionary idiots. All the same violence and it's always proved wrong."

This was the message Allen took on his March-April reading tour. The week of March 15 to 21 had been designated as National Anti-Draft Week, and

Allen, appearing at five universities during this period, made his feelings about the war and the draft well known. At Iowa State University, he participated in a brief demonstration protesting the appearance of army recruiters on campus, Allen setting an example of peaceful protest by presenting the recruiters not angry, confrontational rhetoric but peace beads. He was more vocal at Trinity University in San Antonio, where he held a press conference to speak out against the war.

April 22 was the first nationally celebrated Earth Day, and Allen was in Philadelphia for the occasion. Inspired by Wisconsin senator Gaylord Nelson and California senator Paul McCloskey, Jr., Earth Day was intended to be a means of raising public consciousness about important ecological issues. The United States Congress closed for the day, enabling senators and representatives to attend rallies in their home states or in selected locations throughout the country. In Philadelphia, thousands of people, including Ginsberg and former vice presidential candidate Edmund Muskie, marched for three miles from the city's art museum to an assembly in a park. Calling the gathering an "educational picnic," Allen delivered a less than optimistic message: "I would say that if the current polluting trend continues, it will take only fifteen years for this erosion of the environment to become irreversible." The world had the science and technology necessary to control the disaster, he said, but he was not certain that would happen.

2

Allen concluded his tour at the end of April and was back in Cherry Valley when he heard the news of the National Guard's shooting and killing of four students at Kent State University on May 4. The apparently ceaseless violence shocked him. Flower Power, once so hopeful as a peaceful means of protest and affirmation, was gone, replaced by vocal and radical leadership that seemed determined to confront violence with more violence. Innocents fell and the fight for control continued. Writing to Philip Whalen in Kyoto, Japan, Allen tried to describe the violent temperament of a country that seemed to be plummeting in a deadly tailspin. "I don't know what's happening," he admitted. "The perturbation in U.S. has moved everyone liberal a bit left to revolution of one peaceful kind or another warlike. So many people gassed and beat up and jailed it's like they're manufacturing violent radicals by the milliard. . . . I think U.S. headed for some kind of awful climax."

A number of his poems written during this period expressed his concern. "Catastrophe," an unpublished notebook poem written in mid-June, summarized his state of alarm:

> All day I read my Karma, I studied cardboard pages
> and Indian signs—
> Till I fell asleep and dreamed of myself & my nation
> in catastrophe,
> my home deserted my person in jail my state
> trapped in electric traffic court

all my loves ended, Peter abandoned, Gregory rejected,
                    Jack in the Grave,
Earth a planet lone in Heaven, man drifting away
                    on a ship
falling asleep dying.

Perhaps most disturbing to Allen was the role that so many official govern-
ment-supported agencies played in the disruption. In a meeting with former
Attorney General Ramsey Clark, he learned of J. Edgar Hoover's smear campaign against Martin Luther King, Jr.; he also learned that drug dealing by
narcotics agents could be traced back twenty-five years. Other Ginsberg investigations revealed a trail of an alarming number of lies, dirty tricks, cover-ups,
and misinformation campaigns connected to the control and distribution of
narcotics in the United States. Allen had suspected such malfeasance for a long
time—some of his suspicions dating back to his conversations with Burroughs
in the 1940s—but he now carried out his own research into these issues with
a newfound vigor. It was no secret that drug convictions were being used as a
means of silencing radical opponents of government policies. John Sinclair,
the publisher/poet and radical dissident, had been handed a heavy sentence for
offering two marijuana joints to an agent who had infiltrated his commune. He
had been denied bail while his appeal was pending and was sent instead to a
northern Michigan prison, where he was away from easy or direct contact with
his family, friends, or attorney. That he had been termed a "menace" by the
sentencing judge bore a striking familiarity to the words another judge had used
against Neal Cassady when sentencing him to a long prison term for a similar
offense over a decade earlier. Allen was incensed.

The case against Timothy Leary hinted of an even greater—and sometimes
very creative—effort of suppression. In May 1969, Leary's original Laredo
conviction had been overturned by the Supreme Court, the court ruling that
the law under which he had been arrested was unconstitutional. Undaunted,
federal officials refiled charges, this time accusing Leary of illegally transporting
marijuana when he had driven to the customs checkpoint. The maximum
sentence for that offense was a twenty-year prison term and a ten-thousand-
dollar fine. In addition, Leary faced charges elsewhere, all on minor pot offenses.
As his attorney pointed out, it was unlikely that Leary would win in the lower
courts, which meant that he could be financially broken in trying to appeal his
case and could conceivably be held in jail for up to two years during the
appellate process. Narcotics agents and federal officials were going to silence
Leary, one way or another.

Sinclair and Leary were but two examples. The more Allen delved into it,
the more he became convinced that drugs—both their distribution and the
laws concerning them—were at the base of an enormous control system that
was denying people their human and constitutional rights. He was equally
convinced that these efforts—especially those taken against outspoken radicals—might be behind much of the turbulence in recent years. Allen already
had a ponderous file on the history of drug laws and their enforcement in the
United States, but he realized this was only the beginning of the task ahead.

He now had to draw a stronger connection between what he already knew and what he was presently learning.

3

This is not to say that Ginsberg totally supported the widespread, wholesale use of all types of drugs. He recognized the harm that could come from the use of certain drugs, and throughout his life as a public figure, he drew a careful distinction between the use of hard drugs and soft drugs, between the use of such addictive drugs as heroin and amphetamines and such nonaddictive drugs as marijuana and LSD. To his critics, this might have seemed like a confusing, perhaps even hypocritical posture, since Allen admitted openly that he had experimented with all types of drugs, soft and hard, and since he had been so tolerant of those around him who used addictive and harmful drugs. In fact, a close look at Ginsberg's use of and attitudes toward drugs indicates that he was very consistent over the years. He never did use drugs to the extent that his detractors believed he did, and there is no question that he took an almost scientific approach to his experimentation with drugs that he knew to be addictive. His views toward junkies, Methedrine addicts, and other users were consistent as well: He did not make any moral judgment on their activities—to the point of being tolerant of those who committed petty crimes to support their habits—but he also considered those people to be individuals consumed by a type of illness that required patience and medical treatment rather than harassment or prosecution by the law.

For an example of how he took a pragmatic approach to these views, one had to look no further than the Cherry Valley farm and his relationship with Peter Orlovsky. Over the years, Allen had been intimately aware of Peter's off-and-on problems with drugs and was rigid in his rule that there be no drugs or alcohol used by those living on the farm. It had been purchased with the intention of being used as a means of keeping Peter away from the heavy drug culture so prevalent around their Greenwich Village apartment, and since the farm received a large number of visitors, some of whom were known to abuse alcohol and drugs, Allen had no choice but to impose the rule. This created tensions between Allen and Peter and among Allen and some of his guests, especially when Peter would hide drugs around the farm or when friends would use drugs or alcohol on the sly.

Allen spent the summer of 1970 on the farm, sharing the living quarters with Peter and his girlfriend, Denise, Julius Orlovsky, Gordon Ball, Ray and Bonnie Bremser and their three-year-old daughter, and a host of visitors who included Gregory Corso, Robert Creeley, Carl Solomon, Herbert Huncke, Ann Charters, French translators Claude Pelieu and Mary Beach, and others. Barry Miles, a visitor since March, worked on the organization and cataloging of Allen's extensive archive of taped readings and conversations. Like most inhabitants of communes at the time, the group at the Cherry Valley farm shared chores and expenses. It faced its share of disagreements, hurt feelings, shouting matches, and confrontations between individuals. Allen was horrified to learn that Peter had sold his correspondence from Allen, Kerouac, and others, only to use the thousands of dollars from the sale on drugs. When Gregory Corso arrived in July, the already-volatile situation grew worse, with Gregory badgering Peter much the way Burroughs had mocked him in Tangier and arguing with Allen about his policy of no drugs or booze. Allen recorded accounts of the turmoil in his journal: "Gregory here, one day drinking by roadside with Ray—beercans found on the pond, and their smiling faces turned snarling and screaming at each other at dusk—Peter drunk also screaming in garage. Second day, all calm and a wave of happiness passed through tranquil grassy-yard— yesterday more vodka'd swearing and threats of death."

There was much work to be done. Beside taking care of the ménage of livestock that included a horse, two cows, ten ducks, thirty chickens, a pig, and half a dozen dogs and cats, the garden needed tending and the farm required work. The meadow needed fencing, the roof of the barn patching, and rabbit hutches and a pigpen had to be built. Dirt insulation had to be placed around the house's foundation to keep the crops stored in the cellar from freezing during the winter. Allen was never without something to do. In addition to working around the farm and on new poetry, he assisted with the French translation of *Planet News*, helped Ann Charters with work on her Kerouac biography, worked on new songs of Blake poetry, kept up his correspondence, and continued the compilation of his drug file. The days passed quickly.

Indian Journals had finally been issued, to generally good reviews. The *San Francisco Chronicle*, calling Allen the guru Americans had been searching to find, was impressed with the history of the poet's growth depicted in the book: "Ginsberg's slow growth towards reverent and peaceful maturity is like a sunflower slipping up amongst a terrible devil's postpile of petrified monsters, always facing the sun." Louis Ginsberg, reviewing his son's book for a small poetry magazine, called *Indian Journals* "a veritable Niagara of grotesque details and cosmic broodings"; he concluded his comments by comparing Allen and Blake's sunflower in a short poem of his own:

Ah, Allen, you, too, like Blake's sunflower are half-way with Time,
    Ah, Allen, you too, seek for that sweet golden clime where
Your sunflower wishes to go. Peace be with you, Allen Ginsberg.

Not all reviewers were impressed with Allen's interest in Eastern religion and mysticism. Poet Reed Whittemore, writing for *The New Republic*, offered a dissenting opinion representative of the many critics who were skeptical of what Whittemore called "the sudden easy Easternness that descended on the American sensibility in the sixties." After exposing and tearing down the System in "Howl," Whittemore wrote, Ginsberg was seeking a way to rehabilitate it, and his interest in the East provided him with an alternative vision. To the reviewer, this was a quick fix, "the kind of cheaply acquired religious experience—hop the plane, get the drugs—that has come to take hold of so many so fast in the last few years." In the critic's estimation, too many of Allen's descriptions of India were too brief or incomplete to be useful, while the details of the events leading to his personal change, though offered in the proper spirit, were misleading to youths who approached a guru "like a new exotic flavor at Howard Johnson's."

Such cynicism, expressed by other Ginsberg detractors, symbolized a significant misunderstanding of Allen's long-held interest in Eastern religion, philosophy, and art. If anything, he was moving closer to establishing the meditation practice that he would undertake for the rest of his life. That autumn, after making a brief reading trip to Puerto Rico, Bermuda, and the Virgin Islands, he returned to New York City, where he met Swami Muktananda, who helped him begin a daily hour-long meditation practice. A short time before that, he had met Tibetan Buddhist guru Chögyam Trungpa in a chance encounter on the street in Manhattan. Trungpa's assistant recognized Allen, and the poet and Buddhist teacher exchanged addresses, beginning a very important friendship.

Allen's autumn reading tour was more limited than usual, keeping him in the eastern part of the country, particularly in New York State. By all indications, it was a busy but relatively peaceful time. While in the Caribbean, Allen had lost a large binder containing five years' worth of texts of his published poems and interviews, so he again found himself backtracking, recollecting works from his past. As always, keeping up with his correspondence was time-consuming, as was his continuation of the drug file, a portion of which he was now calling "Documents on Police Bureaucracy's Conspiracy Against Human Rights of Opiate Addicts and Constitutional Rights of Medical Profession Causing Mass Breakdown of Urban Law and Order." In addition, he was editing Neal Cassady's *The First Third*, which City Lights intended to publish, and trying to find a record company to issue his second volume of Blake songs.

"All more than I can complete, but only dabble into," he wrote of the work load in his journal, noting that his full schedule was keeping him from other activities. "My own last week's dreams at night faded unwrit, entire farm to supervise, the Fall day and red autumnal woods' bluesky to dwell in (while I sit and work in upstairs room addicted to paper careers)—I really should go to India and contemplate my nervous system."

4

In recent years, one of Allen's pet projects had been the assembly of a collection of his best recordings of spoken poetry—a "live album," to use rock 'n' roll recording terminology. Allen was satisfied with his poems in their written form, but he also realized that his readings brought forth the subtle humor and natural speech tones occasionally lost on the printed page. He had scores of tapes in his archive, including the recordings he had made at Neal Cassady's house in 1954, his early San Francisco readings, the memorable Albert Hall performance, and countless others. In most cases, the recording technique had been less than adequate and a number of tapes were marred by muffled noise from the audience, primitive recording conditions, or the use of poor tape. Barry Miles had done the yeoman's share of sorting through the tapes; at the beginning of 1971, he and Allen holed up in a room at the Chelsea Hotel, working from afternoon until the wee hours of the morning, auditing the tapes and trying to find the best available version of each recorded poem.

In mid-January, Allen flew to Michigan to testify on behalf of John Sinclair, who had been charged with conspiracy in connection to a September 1968 bombing of an Ann Arbor CIA office. Allen believed that the charges against Sinclair, founder of the radical White Panthers, had been based more on an official desire to put Sinclair behind bars than on any solid evidence linking him to the bombing. Significantly, he had not been charged with setting off the bomb.

While in Michigan, Allen read at several fund-raisers for the Sinclair defense. The legal proceeding itself had all the earmarks of the Chicago Conspiracy Trial, complete with William Kunstler acting as the defense attorney and the constant interruptions by the prosecuting attorney, who questioned Allen's authority to act as a spokesman for those under the age of twenty-nine, as the defense claimed he was. Ginsberg's opinions, the prosecutor charged, were nothing but "the fantasies of a middle-aged man who can't admit his youth is gone." Allen persisted in his testimony. "There is generally a mockery of the idealism and fear of young people," he said, pointing out that he had lectured at several hundred colleges and universities over the last decade and had observed the feelings of the country's young people. These people were scorned because they believed that with the way things were going, they would be unable to live in a peaceful world by the turn of the century. "This apocalyptic sense of the end of the planet is treated as a joke," said Allen.

Thus began what would prove to be one of Ginsberg's most active years of political, social, legal, and literary debate. His studies of the abuse of drug-law enforcement, coupled with his belief that the United States had become a police state, had left him obsessed with all issues concerning human rights. He began a new study that delved into the suppression of underground newspapers and magazines; collected clippings dealing with First Amendment cases; and broadened his file on issues pertaining to ecology. On occasion, he grew concerned that these diverse interests were cutting into the time needed for his literary endeavors, but rather than brood about it, as he had under similar circumstances in 1966, he seemed to find a reserve of energy that enabled him to accommodate his multitudinous interests.

Back in New York, he became embroiled in a new controversy, this one largely of his own making. Allen, along with Richard Howard, Carolyn Kizer, Thorpe Menn, and W. D. Snodgrass, had been asked to judge the poetry entries nominated for the National Book Award. The field of finalists was strong, with books by Gregory Corso, Richard Hugo, W. S. Merwin, Gary Snyder, Philip Whalen, and Mona Van Duyn competing. Quite naturally, Allen felt strongly about the merits of the books by his friends, particularly Gregory Corso's *Elegiac Feelings American* and Philip Whalen's *Severance Pay*, both considered today to be among the best of their respective authors' work. His predisposition to these two books, however, went far beyond personal or literary friendship. In his capacity as a judge, he was finally in the position to correct what he considered to be the wrongs of the past—when Ezra Pound, William Carlos Williams, and other innovative poets were passed over by awards committees that honored traditional rather than strikingly original work. Allen was determined to correct what he judged to be a historical mistake.

From the beginning, he correctly suspected that the other panel members would favor poets other than those he had chosen. Irritated by their criteria for judgment, Allen wrote them a seven-page single-spaced letter in which he tried to explain his position. There was nothing wrong with the other poets, he wrote, except that in his opinion they lacked "historic overwhelming genius," and there was nothing right with his nominees except for their possession of that genius. He used a comparison of Gregory Corso, his choice, and Mona Van Duyn, the panel's preference, as an example of what he meant. "So what are you proposing," he challenged the panel, "that Mona Van Duyn has a better EAR than Gregory Corso, a greater juxtapositional economy, a more fertile sense of invention, a greater grasp of history, a greater involvement of person with poetics, a superior shrewdness in phrasing, a loftier metaphysics, even a more practical hand? Are you all mad? Have you no sense of modesty or proportion to your dreadful ambition to reduce all poetic judgments to domesticated mediocrity? There is nothing wrong with Van Duyn's book except that it is not the work of Genius, and there is nothing right about Corso's book except that it is the work of Genius."

Allen's pointed opinions went back a long way. He was all too familiar with the attacks launched by academics over the years, not only against his work, but also against Kerouac, Corso, McClure, and others. As a judge, he had a forum—if not the deciding vote—and he was not about to let the opportunity to present his view slip by.

The acrimony, however, was not limited to private discussion. When Van Duyn's book, *To See, To Take*, was announced as the winner, Allen publicly disassociated himself from the panel and registered a dissenting opinion. "The jurors' opinion was ignominious, insensitive and mediocre," he told the press, "and I felt that I had to disassociate my name from that choice." Van Duyn, for her part, was far more gracious in her comments about the controversy. Comparing her work with Allen's, she stated, "I notice the obscenities but write about the heart and the lovers. He notices the heart but writes about the obscenities. Both are there and both are valid."

Allen was still not finished. Rather than simply let the controversy die, as he might have been well advised to do, he stoked its fires by submitting his original letter to the judges to *The New York Times* for publication. The newspaper asked Richard Howard to write a rebuttal. The two articles appeared in the paper on April 4. Rankled by Allen's attitude, Howard complained that he bandied about the term *genius* in a cavalier fashion, applying it to the modern, open form while denying it to those who worked in a more traditional style. Ginsberg's group of experimentalists, Howard wrote, was a closed group to which no new names were added, and worse yet, he resented the rather smug, anti-intellectual attitude that he felt was coming from its ranks. "You make out that if it's bad enough, it's got to be good," Howard scolded Ginsberg, "and that indeed is the parting between us."

The exchange was a mixed blessing. Ginsberg and Howard were contemporaries, both well respected in the poetry community, and their debate brought forth important and valid points about existing tensions and differences between two schools of poetry. For a refreshing change, the argument stayed focused on the literary merits of the respective groups' poetry rather than on a condemnation of lifestyles or political ideologies, and there was little doubting the sincerity of the two poets, even if they did display limited vision in their passionate arguments. Unfortunately, this "battle of the anthologies" would continue for a long time, each side struggling for limited review space in newspapers and magazines, grant money, positions with universities, and, ultimately, the upper hand in respect. At times, the battle would be petty and childish, neither side willing to admit that there was more than enough room for all types of poetry in the world of literature.

Ginsberg hated the bickering, but he engaged in some of the fighting to achieve a higher purpose. As he was quick to point out, he was generally well treated by the established poetry community—he would win the National Book Award and be admitted to the American Academy and Institute of Arts and Letters, as well as being awarded his share of grant money over the years—but he was concerned about the reputations of other poets who were not as fortunate. If he did not use his position to crusade on their behalf, they would not receive the attention he felt they deserved.

5

Allen had made tentative plans to join Lawrence Ferlinghetti on a reading tour of Australia in late spring, so his customary spring reading tour of college campuses in the United States was abbreviated. Nevertheless, it was one of his best. His lectures—many taped and eventually published in *Allen Verbatim*—were wide-ranging, many decisively political in tone, addressing the Vietnam War, his drug findings, the ecology, and police-state politics.

The tour commenced on March 4, with Allen and his father giving a joint reading at the Corcoran Gallery in Washington, D.C. At a reception before the reading, Allen met CIA director Richard Helms, and Allen wasted no time in presenting his findings about CIA involvement in drug-smuggling operations in Southeast Asia. Allen's research indicated that a CIA-run air base at Long Cheng was being used as a depot in the shipment of opiates to Saigon. Helms flatly denied Ginsberg's charge and the two set up a wager: If Allen was incorrect, he would give Helms his bronze *dorje*; if Helms was incorrect, he would have to spend an hour a day for the rest of his life in meditation. (Subsequent hearings in the Senate would indicate Ginsberg to be the winner.) Later, at the reading, Allen made a point of reciting "Pentagon Exorcism" to the dignitaries in attendance.

Allen stayed in the area for nearly two weeks, appearing at Georgetown, the University of Maryland, American University, and George Washington University. On March 11, he took part in the Counter Culture Conference on Peace and Justice at the College of William and Mary in Williamsburg, Virginia. His recent days in and around the nation's capital had done little to allay his fears about the future prospects for the United States, and his message to the conference was pessimistic. "Materialism in America has gotten so thick with poisons and so top heavy that capitalism is collapsing under its own weight in sociological crises," he stated. "The madness of our beer-can-television-conspicuous-consumption hypnosis becomes as visible as the dung-colored clouds that hang over the great cities, while gigantic war murder in Indo-China, on top of our our Ahab-like harpooning of Mother Nature, goes on. And we have a planetary crisis only soluble by the compassion of the long-haired, tender-bodied young, aided by those older politicians who realize that once and for all War History is bankrupt."

He did not relish his role as a sort of prophet of doom, but the events of recent years had led him to conclude that in a power struggle, the younger generation, even amassed, did not necessarily affect the power for change. He was reminded of this when he visited Kent State University in April, a month before the first anniversary of the National Guard's killing of four students. He stayed on campus for several days, delivering a series of splendid lectures on twentieth-century poetics, Jack Kerouac, and the Vietnam War. He read with Robert Duncan and Gary Snyder—both in the area on reading tours of their own. The passing of a year's time had not erased the anger, shock, and depression that followed the four students' deaths, and Allen, Gary, and Robert put their heads together in an effort to plan and stage a memorial service that featured prayer, mantra chanting, poetry, and a puppet-theater reenactment of the event. The vigil was conducted without a hitch.

The longer the tour went on, the more convinced Allen became that he would not be able to make the trip to Australia with Ferlinghetti. There was simply too much work to do. In addition to the completion of his sixteen hours of taped poems, he hoped to begin the compilation of *The Fall of America*, his projected volume of poems for City Lights. Assembling the new book would require a lot of work, including the integration of his written poetry and auto poesy into a large, thematically unified volume. As his tour worked westward, stopping briefly in Cleveland before moving on to Wisconsin, Minnesota, and then Wyoming, Allen began to focus more on these projects. The trip to Australia would have to wait.

6

He decided to spend the summer on the West Coast. Before traveling to Berkeley, where he intended to live on a local commune, Allen spent a week with Gary Snyder in his new home in the Sierras. In Japan, Snyder's hospitality and friendship had proved to be restful after Allen's long stay in India, and now in California, he found Snyder's latest retreat equally peaceful. He meditated, discussed mantras and yoga posture with Snyder, and in general unwound from the hectic pace of his reading schedule.

He was in the Bay Area by the first week of May. Shortly after his arrival, he heard that Chögyam Trungpa was going to be staying in Berkeley for a while, and he made an appointment to visit him.

The Venerable Chögyam Trungpa, Rinpoche was as eccentric a religious leader as one was likely to find. Born in 1939 in Geja, a small village in eastern Tibet, Trungpa was quite literally a child of destiny. When he was thirteen months old, he was deemed to be the reincarnation of the tenth Trungpa Tulku and therefore destined to a position of spiritual leadership. In 1959, he fled the country in the wake of the suppressive Red Chinese reformist policies that included the virtual abolition of Tibetan Buddhism. He spent some time in India where, in a strange turn of fate, he happened to meet Ginsberg and Orlovsky when they were in the country, though Allen would only remember the occasion many years later when he was shown a photograph of the occasion. Trungpa eventually moved to England, where he studied at Oxford and established a Tibetan Buddhist monastery in Scotland, the first of its kind in the Western world. However, strict monastic life was not for Trungpa, who preferred an active, "wild wisdom" Buddhist practice. After a 1969 automobile accident left him permanently paralyzed on his left side, he shed the traditional monastic robes and took on Western ways that not only seemed less hypocritical if he intended to stay in the West, but which also afforded him the chance to cultivate his tastes in alcohol, sports cars, and beautiful women. Less than a year after his accident, he married Diana Phybus, an aristocratic follower, and they moved to the United States.

He founded the Tail of the Tiger—the first Tibetan Buddhist meditation center in the United States—in Vermont a short time after his arrival, and from there he proceeded to buy land in eight other states. His outrageous style appealed to his American followers, who had less difficulty accepting his drinking, reported womanizing, and chronic tardiness at lectures and meditation sessions than his former collegues and disciples in Scotland; if anything, his pushing the margins made him more charming to his following.

On the night of their 1971 meeting in California, Allen found Trungpa in such an intoxicated state that he had fallen on the hotel balcony and had to be assisted to his room by two of his students. Trungpa had a lecture scheduled for later in the evening and a concerned Ginsberg asked Trungpa whether he might be drinking too much. Trungpa was not at all concerned. He and Allen repaired to the hotel restaurant, where Trungpa continued to drink heavily. The two discussed their travel schedules, Allen complaining that he was fatigued by his latest tour.

"Oh, that's because you don't like your poetry," Trungpa replied.

"What do you mean?" Allen asked, irritated by what appeared to be a glib response. "What do you know about poetry?"

Trungpa explained that in reading his old texts, Allen was growing bored with his own work. "Why don't you make up your own poems on the spot, right up onstage?" he asked. "Why use a piece of paper? Don't you trust your own mind?" All of his own poems were improvised, he told Allen, as were the poems of Milarepa, who had been a great poet.

Allen was intrigued. The advice reminded him of his discussions with Kerouac about spontaneous composition and of the evenings he and Jack had spent under the Brooklyn Bridge, making up poems and shouting them into the night. Even Trungpa's heavy drinking reminded him of Kerouac: Somehow, no matter how much Jack drank, there always seemed to be a kernel of wisdom in what he said. The conversation with Trungpa was similar. "It reminded me of Kerouac's genius for being drunk and inspired," Ginsberg recalled, "being an old Li Po zen master—mad, looney, truth-teller, soothsaying . . . priest."

Fully aware of the fate Kerouac suffered as a result of his alcoholism, Allen again asked Trungpa why he drank so much. Trungpa explained he hoped to determine the illumination of American drunkenness. In the United States, he said, alcohol was the main drug, and he wanted to use his acquired knowledge of drunkenness as a source of wisdom, as a means of using the energy of pain. This, too, reminded Allen of Kerouac.

Trungpa then presented Allen with a challenge of his own. "Why don't you take off your beard?" he asked. "I want to see your face. You're attached to your beard, aren't you?"

Allen denied it, and to prove his point, he left the restaurant and walked to the hotel pharmacy, where he purchased a pair of scissors. From there, he went into the men's room and trimmed his beard to a much shorter length.

Trungpa was unimpressed. "You didn't shave off your beard," he chided Allen. "All you did was cut off a couple of inches."

It was time for Trungpa to go to his lecture. He wanted to remain in the restaurant and have another Bloody Mary while Allen shaved off the rest of his beard, but Allen insisted that he would not be party to Trungpa's late arrival. At the lecture hall, Allen shaved off his beard while Trungpa prepared to go onstage. As he shaved, Allen looked in the mirror and realized that for the first time in years, he was free of his own image, of the look that made him the easily identifiable countercultural icon of the sixties. He could walk about incognito and it was a liberating sensation. When he saw Allen, Trungpa expressed his own delight. "He took off his mask!" he cried. "Now improvise a poem!"

Allen's initial effort at completely improvised poetry onstage was weak and full of forced rhymes. Nevertheless, he was impressed that in the span of a couple of hours Trungpa had persuaded him to alter his appearance and consider another way of composing poetry.

The next evening, Allen gave a benefit reading for a meditation center run by Tarthang Tulku, a Tibetan teacher of the N'yingma sect. Taking Trungpa's advice to heart, Allen walked onstage without prepared texts. He had brought his harmonium with him and he chanted a selection of mantras for over an hour. He immediately followed this with a twenty-minute improvisation on the theme "How sweet it is to be born here in America."

"It was both a lamentation and a celebration," said Ginsberg of the improvisation, describing it as a "sort of sweet and sour about living in the *deva loka*, or heaven world—one of the many possible worlds to be born into." Using only two chords on his harmonium, Ginsberg launched into his improvisation, celebrating the many advantages of living in America and lamenting the way "breathing gasoline and consuming 60 percent of the world's raw materials and causing wars and destruction in every direction" was ruining the world. The poem was far from polished, Ginsberg admitted, but like his auto poesy, it came much closer to representing pure thought than the carefully designed poetry he wrote on paper. The trick now was to find a way to be less self-conscious during the improvisation itself—to trust his mind, as Trungpa had suggested.

Trungpa's teachings, Allen decided, were worth exploring further.

7

Allen's time in San Francisco and Berkeley was exceptionally productive. He completed his tapes of his collected vocalized poetry, which had now been expanded to include twenty-five years' worth of work. In addition, he worked on another phonograph album's worth of Blake songs, as well as the taping of a modest collection of mantras. In writing extensive notes for his vocalized poems, Allen had been using the texts of all his 1946 to 1971 poems, including those written in recent months, and since he had them gathered and at his disposal, he arranged them into a "Collected Poems" manuscript, which he hoped to market sometime in the near future.

Two other works were already being prepared for publication: *Iron Horse*, Allen's long poem written on his 1966 cross-country train/bus journey, and *The Gates of Wrath*, a collection of his early rhymed poems. Like "Wichita Vortex Sutra," "Iron Horse" belonged in Allen's long "These States" sequence, but both poems by the merits of their length were impossible to include in the *Fall of America* manuscript, which was presently two hundred pages long. Allen had already broken the sequence when he included "Wichita Vortex Sutra" in *Planet News*, so when a Toronto publisher offered to issue "Iron Horse" as a single-poem booklet, he was less inclined to worry about interrupting the sequence's continuity. The two poems, he decided, would be put in their rightful place when he eventually published his collected poems in one volume.

The publication of *The Gates of Wrath* was an unexpectedly happy event. In the early fifties, Allen had entrusted his only complete manuscript of the book to a friend who offered to market it to a London publisher. The typescript had been subsequently lost, and since Allen did not have copies of many of the poems in the book, he had given up on ever seeing it published in its entirety. Incredibly enough, the manuscript eventually found its way into the hands of Bob Dylan, who returned it to Allen in 1968.

Although they are historically significant, the poems in *The Gates of Wrath*, composed between 1947 and 1954, pale in comparison to Ginsberg's later achievements. Most read like a young man's imitations of classical forms—which, in fact, they are. In his interviews over the years, Ginsberg stressed the imperfection of the poems, and his preface to the book—his 1949 letter of introduction to William Carlos Williams—underscores the notion that even then he recognized he was not writing the kind of poetry that he wanted to write. The period of composition for many of the poems in *Gates of Wrath* coincides with that of the poems in *Empty Mirror*, and by comparing the two greatly differing styles of the two books, one can see the struggle Ginsberg went through to develop his voice. The works in *Empty Mirror*, of course, are "accidental" poems—prose lines that were taken from journals and broken into poetry lines in an effort to please Williams. The works in *Gates of Wrath*, on the other hand, find the poet working painstakingly in rhyme and meter schemes, the works displaying technical mastery but very little of the poet's own signature.

Ironically, Bob Dylan, once influenced by Allen's open-form "Beat" poetry, was impressed enough with some of the rhymed lyrics that he encouraged Allen to write more poems of this nature. Ginsberg did. After experimenting with songwriting on the first Blake album, he had dabbled with the writing of song lyrics in his notebooks, though none of his efforts pleased him enough to prompt the creation of melodies for the lyrics. Trungpa's instructions to improvise had loosened him up somewhat, but he still lacked the confidence to push this type of writing any further. Both Dylan and Trungpa would play noteworthy roles in changing that attitude in the future.

For all the time that Allen devoted to his various book and recording projects over the summer of 1971, he never lost sight of what he considered to be his most important project—the compilation of the poems for *The Fall of America*. He had great hopes for the volume. In many ways, it was the realization of everything he had wanted his poetry to accomplish. The individual poems were as immediate and accessible as newspaper reports, yet when read in their proper chronological order, they caught the spirit of a country in turmoil, seen through the eyes of the witness prophet. Throughout the summer, Allen carefully arranged the contents of his most ambitious collection.

One of the high points of the season occurred on June 30, when he was finally able to find a way to set "The Tyger," perhaps Blake's best-known poem, to music. Allen had wanted the song to be special, and setting the words to music had eluded him for some time. The natural rhythm of the poem suggested a heartbeat, and he used this to create a rhythmic tune that when performed sounded as if it was coming from the chest cavity itself. Oddly enough, Allen decided against including it on his second Blake album, though he was thrilled finally to have it completed, as he noted in his journal:

> Thanks for this gift, Wm. Blake,
> my debt is paid,
> now I am free of thee and thy visions;
> It ends in thy heartbeat.

8

Throughout the summer, Allen faced the inevitable distractions, irritations, annoying interruptions, and serious political issues demanding his attention. In Switzerland, Timothy Leary was being held by the government while the United States prepared its extradition case. Meanwhile, in San Francisco, a group of twenty-five writers—including Allen, Anaïs Nin, Lawrence Ferlinghetti, Ken Kesey, Michael McClure, Laura Huxley, and Kenneth Rexroth—put together an eight-page petition requesting the Swiss government to grant Leary political asylum. According to the writers, Leary was a "literary refugee persecuted for his thoughts and writings" in the United States. The main issue, the group argued, was not Leary's criminality, based solely upon his conviction for the possession of a tiny amount of marijuana; rather, the issue was the extraordinary measure being taken by the United States to remove Leary from his sphere of influence. "At stake in the case," said the writers, "is Dr. Leary's freedom to manifest his thoughts in the form of poems, psychological commentaries, dialogues, and essays of a literary nature." The group delivered the signed document to the Swiss consulate in San Francisco and sent copies to the State and Justice departments in Washington, D.C.

Equally serious was a case developing in Brazil. Members of the Living Theatre, including founders Julian Beck and Judith Malina, had been jailed in the South American country, supposedly for marijuana possession—a charge that both Beck and Malina flatly denied. In some instances, confessions from members of the multinational theater group had been extorted by authorities through beatings and torture. Ginsberg, who had known Beck and Malina for over two decades, was certain that the group had been framed, that Brazilian authorities, trained by the CIA, were trying to silence the troupe because of their political beliefs and the controversial nature of their plays. Beck and Malina had been considered subversive when they lived in the United States— they had been arrested in the mid-1950s for protesting compulsory air-raid drills and had experienced numerous run-ins with authorities in the early days of the theater, when they worked out of New York—and in 1963, after enduring years of harassment, they took their company permanently on the road.

From his firsthand experiences, Allen was familiar with the feeling of being considered a subversive in a foreign country and he knew all too well the frustration of dealing with another country's legal system. In fact, only a few days before he heard of the Living Theatre's plight, he learned that he himself was in trouble overseas. For four years, the Italian courts had been debating his arrest for reading "Who Be Kind To" at the 1967 Spoleto poetry festival. In March 1968, a lower court had ruled that the reading did not constitute a crime, but an appeals court had recently overturned that decision and demanded that he stand trial for obscenity.

In comparison to what was happening to the Living Theatre in Brazil, the actions against Ginsberg in Italy were a mere annoyance. Working with a group calling itself the Bay Area Prose Poets Phalanx, Allen plotted a strategy to free Beck, Malina, and the others. Petitions were drawn up, a letter-writing campaign to Brazilian and American officials begun. With characteristic skepticism of the official version of the story, Allen drew up his own account of what had happened, based upon what he heard from Steve Ben Israel, a Living Theatre member who had avoided arrest and escaped Brazil. Press releases of the account were distributed to the news media.

Rallies and demonstrations were organized, benefit readings scheduled. People picketed the Brazilian Consulate in San Francisco. On July 30, a group of demonstrators, including Ginsberg, assembled outside a Brazilian Airlines sales office. In an interview with the press covering the demonstration, Allen explained U.S. involvement in the training of the Brazilian police and demanded the government take an active role in securing the release of the Living Theatre members. "America has the bureaucratic responsibility to stop these Frankenstein police from messing around with American citizens," Allen declared.

As far removed as he was from Switzerland, Italy, and Brazil, Allen was nevertheless capable of addressing from San Francisco the issues of Timothy Leary's political asylum, his own obscenity case, and the Living Theatre bust. One concern, however, demanded his presence as a witness. In India, floods and famine had caused unbelievable grief and human misery in the eastern section of the country. Allen had read reports of an estimated 7 million people who had been left homeless and were presently living in refugee camps, and he had spoken to a number of people about his wish to visit the country. One day in early August, he received a round-trip ticket to India from an unknown benefactor. He immediately made plans to go there in September.

Nothing prepared him for what he saw. On his flight to India, he felt a twinge of nostalgia for the time, less than a decade earlier, when he had visited the country with Peter. On his first night in Calcutta, he wandered around the city streets, eating an inexpensive meal of lentil soup and ordering a custom-built harmonium from an instrument shop; later in the evening, he visited the Nimtallah Ghat. He spent the next couple of days reacquainting himself with the country, touring Calcutta and meeting with poet friends. He visited a nearby refugee camp holding an estimated 25,000 people, and while he did take note of the shortages of food and medical services in the camp, he still had no idea of the extent of the suffering in the country. By all indications, the early portion of his trip was not all that different from other travels, which usually found him sightseeing and looking for souvenirs upon his arrival.

He witnessed the full horror soon enough and was deeply moved by what he saw. In refugee camps, masses of children waited in breadlines that could not begin to fulfill the demands for food. Wasted, starving people, overcome by malnutrition, dysentery, or disease, lay motionless and dying in makeshift hospitals. There was nowhere near enough medicine to go around, and officials feared that the lack of sanitary facilities would lead to a cholora epidemic. Countless people lined Jessore Road, the main road between Bangladesh and Calcutta. The burning ghats, flooded by the rains, would be needed as never before.

Ginsberg's lengthy lyric poem "September on Jessore Road" described the terrible scene:

> Wet processions   Families walk
> Stunted boys   big heads dont talk
> Look bony skulls   & silent round eyes
> Starving black angels in human disguise
>
> Mother squats weeping & points to her sons
> Standing thin legged   like elderly nuns
> small bodied   hands to their mouths in prayer
> Five months small food   since they settled there

Allen was both saddened and infuriated by the lack of response in the United States to the crisis. The wealthiest nation in the world seemed to be more concerned about investing its money and efforts into the killing of Southeast Asians than in saving the lives of those in such desperate need:

> Where are the helicopters of U.S. AID?
> Smuggling dope in Bangkok's green shade.
> Where is America's Air Force of Light?
> Bombing North Laos all day and all night?
>
> Where are the President's Armies of Gold?
> Billionaire Navies   merciful Bold?
> Bringing us medicine   food and relief?
> Napalming North Vietnam   and causing more grief?

The lyrics, though imperfect, were heartfelt and bold, heavily influenced by Bob Dylan's early protest songs, which at their best—in such songs as "Blowin' in the Wind" and "A Hard Rain's A-Gonna Fall"—asked questions that sounded more like demands. "September on Jessore Road" was intended to be sung—it was copyrighted by Poetry Music—and it would eventually be published with accompanying musical notation.

9

Allen spent much of the fall of 1971 working on different recording projects. Upon his return from India, he stopped briefly in San Francisco, where he signed a recording contract with Fantasy Records, the company scheduled to issue his second Blake album and a boxed set of his spoken poetry. Excited by the prospects of seeing these projects reach fruition, he threw himself into such production aspects as the albums' packaging and design, their liner notes, and the scheduling of musicians and singers for overdub work.

Back in Cherry Valley at the beginning of October, Allen began to prepare for his autumn reading tour. Just before he was scheduled to begin the tour, he received a number of telephone calls and telegrams from Yoko Ono, who invited him to join her and John Lennon for the opening of their sculpture show at the Everson Museum of Art in Syracuse. The opening coincided with Lennon's birthday on October 9, and when Allen arrived at the couple's hotel suite, he found John and Yoko surrounded by a group of friends, including record producer Phil Spector, editor Paul Krassner, Ringo Starr, drummer Jim Keltner, and artist/guitarist Klaus Voorman. The past year or so had been difficult for Lennon. The Beatles had broken up in one of the messiest, most difficult disillusions in recorded music history; John and Yoko had been facing constant criticism and derision from the press for their avant-garde art and political stands; John had released an album of angry songs reflective of his recent primal-scream therapy under Dr. Arthur Janov; and John and Yoko had been involved in a fierce custody battle over Yoko's daughter from a previous marriage.

Lennon's thirty-first birthday was a festive occasion. The day before, he had released *Imagine*, an album featuring some of his best music since his association with the Beatles; its utopian title song was quite possibly his most beautiful song ever. Lennon was in high spirits for his party. Gifts and well-wishing telegrams were strewn on the floor of his hotel room and a huge birthday cake was brought in. Lennon sat on the bed and talked nonstop while Ringo spun stories about the Beatles in another part of the room. Underground filmmaker Jonas Mekas filmed the scene.

When he arrived, Allen took a seat on the floor and made a small ceremony of arranging his harmonium, finger cymbals, Tibetan bell, and incense around him. From there, sitting in a half-lotus position, he began to chant the Padma Sambhava mantra. Lennon jumped up from the bed. "Wait a minute," he told Allen, "let me go get my guitar." A makeshift band was formed. Ringo fashioned a drum out of an overturned wastebasket and borrowed Allen's finger cymbals; Klaus Voorman and Phil Spector picked up guitars. Then, with Allen leading, the group improvised music to a number of mantras. Allen played a slowed-down version of Blake's "Nurse's Song." After about an hour, the group ran through a selection of Lennon and Beatles songs, including "Give Peace a Chance" and "Yellow Submarine," and from there they held a long jam session in which they improvised blues. In all, they played for six hours, turning Lennon's hotel suite, as Allen wrote, into "a tiny Madison Square Garden."

"What was interesting to me," Ginsberg explained later, "was I found I could improvise blues adequately enough to be counted in the circle of musicians, and lead them all in my own Indic specialties without strain."

Later that day, he accompanied John and Yoko to the art showing. This, too, turned out to be a memorable experience. Sitting in a limousine with Lennon and Phil Spector, Allen suddenly found himself surrounded by a throng of screaming teenagers pressing in around the car. The incident was both frightening and exhilarating, reminding him of the scenes he had seen in the Beatles' movies.

Allen was very pleased with the events of the day. In the past, his encounters with Lennon had been rather formal and not entirely relaxed. He had been an outsider, a poet and political activist in the midst of musicians. He felt more comfortable around Lennon now. "I think probably relations with Lennon and others [will be] easier in the future," he wrote. "This [was] the first time we really got together on art vibration." "

One musician Allen was already in sync with was Bob Dylan, who remained an enormous influence in Allen's development as a songwriter. Ten days before meeting with Lennon in Syracuse, Allen and Peter had given a reading at the Loeb Center at New York University. It was a large success, with Allen and Peter reading poetry, singing Blake, and chanting mantras. At one point, Allen engaged in an hour-long improvisation on the theme "Why write poetry down on paper when you have to cut down trees to make poetry books?"—the improvised poem a continuation of the discipline Trungpa had suggested a few months earlier.

Unknown to Allen, Bob Dylan and David Amram, Ginsberg's musician friend from the *Pull My Daisy* days, had slipped into the hall and were standing unrecognized in the back. Dylan had been very impressed with the improvisation and he told Allen as much in a telephone call later that evening. "Can you always improvise like that?" he asked. Allen explained that he had been improvising poems for nearly twenty-five years, dating back to the days when he and Kerouac had made up poems on their walks together. Dylan had always wanted that feeling of spontaneity in his recorded music and he had gone to some lengths to assume a rough-edged, made-up-on-the-spot feeling on his albums. Ginsberg had taken it a step further. By improvising his poetry onstage, he was, in essence, working without a net.

Dylan and Amram joined Ginsberg at his apartment later that same evening. Amram brought along his French horn, Dylan borrowed a Guild guitar from Peter's girlfriend, and they joined Allen in a jam session that ran well into the night. Allen played harmonium and improvised lyrics. He proved to be a quick study. After Dylan taught him several new chord changes on the harmonium, he found that he could play and improvise in a standard twelve-bar blues structure. With practice, the music began to sound good.

Allen was scheduled to fly to Puerto Rico for a series of readings in late

November. He was going with Lucien Carr and he hoped to make the trip a combination of business and vacation. He used this scenario as the basis for his first improvised blues with Dylan:

> I'm going down to Puerto Rico
> I'm going down on the midnite plane
> I'm going down on the Vomit Express
> I'm going down with my suitcase pain
>
> You can take an ancient vacation
> Fly over Florida's blue end
> Rise out of this madhouse nation
> I'm going down with my oldest tender friend. . . .

He improvised numerous verses and a chorus. The group worked on Latin rhythms and after a while the song gained a reasonably polished sound. Dylan was pleased. "Why don't we go to the studio and do this?" he suggested.

The first recording session commenced on November 9 in New York's Record Plant. Dylan had brought along folksinger Happy Traum, his Woodstock neighbor, for the occasion, and Allen had enlisted the help of David Amram, John Sholle, and others. Poets Andrei Voznesensky, Anne Waldman, and Gregory Corso were also on hand to offer moral support. A basic recording format was established: Allen would write lyrics on the spot, the musicians would run through the song in a brief practice session, with Dylan acting as an arranger, and then the song would be taped. The first session produced a good version of "Going Down to Puerto Rico," as well as several recorded mantras, some rough instrumental blues jamming, and a ten-minute version of Blake's "Nurse's Song."

Allen depended upon Dylan a great deal for advice. Although he had been the one to inspire the sessions with his improvisational poetry, he was still a little constricted in the recording studio. For one thing, studio time was expensive and he wanted to get as much as possible for his limited resources. In addition, he was very conscious of the words he was writing. It was one matter to improvise poetry in a setting in which a poor choice of words would not come back to haunt you, entirely another to improvise lyrics that would be issued on a recording for the public. "How far can I go?" he asked Dylan, referring to the topics and lyrics of his music. "You can go as far as you want," Dylan replied.

The initial session, then, represented Allen's testing of the waters. He stayed with familiar material and became comfortable with improvising in the environment of the recording studio.

The second session, held on November 17, was much more productive. The day before, Allen had appeared with a small musical group on an educational television station. With Dylan playing guitar as an anonymous sideman, Allen had improvised a song about the CIA's drug trafficking in Southeast Asia (a variation of which was later recorded as "CIA Dope Calypso"), and it had gone well enough to leave Allen feeling confident when he entered the studio the next day. As before, there was the recording of some mantras, as well as what

Allen called "a whole lot of ragged pieces of improvisation," but the day saw the composition of three works of note. The first, "Going to San Diego," was an eight-verse up-tempo blues calling for everyone to go to San Diego and help defeat Richard Nixon at the 1972 Republican National Convention. Composed entirely in the studio, the song was the most polished-sounding of Ginsberg's early recorded blues. "Many Loves," commemorating Allen's love for Neal Cassady, Jack Kerouac, and Peter Orlovsky, was a song fragment that he worked on but never completed. The third song, "Jimmy Berman (Gay Lib Rag)," was a happy accident. As the assembled musicians waited for the engineer to set up, Allen overheard Dylan and Traum talking about a young Times Square hustler known as Jimmy Newsboy. "Whozat Jimmy Berman?" Allen started, and from there the group began an improvisation. Luckily, the engineer had turned on the tape and the song was recorded in one take. Allen was thrilled. "What happy madness," he wrote of the scene.

The musicians also recorded two versions of "September on Jessore Road," which Dylan proclaimed to be the best poem he had seen in years. Allen had worked on the writing of the ballad both days in the studio and had hoped to record it with Dylan, but neither version—an acoustic ballad or the Indian-style blues—turned out to be usable. The failure was Allen's biggest disappointment of the sessions.

Although Ginsberg's venture into singing and songwriting would be greeted by a strongly mixed response from friends, critics, and poetry enthusiasts, he was by no means being whimsical in his explorations into music. His interest in blues forms dated back to his youth, when he would walk by a Baptist church on River Street in Paterson and listen to the spirituals being sung, and to the days when he and Kerouac would listen to Bessie Smith, Ma Rainey, and Billie Holiday. In addition, he believed that blues, in their use of American idiom and natural speech rhythms, were powerful contemporary lyric forms. "Traditionally, the popular songs of the day are some of the most beautiful lyrics preserved in anthologies," he said later. "Any anthology of twentieth-century United States literature should include specimens of black blues, rock 'n' roll, and popular song. If it doesn't, there may be an element of racism in the exclusion."

Ginsberg believed in the viability of the minstrel tradition, and when asked, he would admit that one of his ambitions was "to write a poem or song with words that are so inevitable that people will be able to use it all the time—like Dylan or Blake." His most vocal critics did not take issue with this; instead, they focused on his technical abilities. His singing voice was average, as he himself was quick to admit, and he had very little skill as a musician. Why then, asked his detractors, would he become so involved in something he was so marginally skilled at accomplishing, when he had already proven his mastery of another form?

This was a legitimate question, of course, but it failed to take into account Ginsberg's need to expand his own artistic horizons and reach his audience in the most effective way possible. Young people who had never heard of Blake or Williams could quote Dylan, the Beatles, and the Rolling Stones at length; people who would never read poetry would enjoy it if it were wrapped in song.

It didn't matter much to Allen what the critics thought. He and Dylan joked about his becoming an aging rock star, and while that would never happen, his enthusiasm for recording music would not dim, either. He would record music and sing at his readings for many years to come.

10

The sixties might have been dead, as critics of the left wing were fond of pointing out, but music and political commentary were still a powerful mix. On November 1, George Harrison had assembled an impressive group of musician friends, including Ringo Starr, Eric Clapton, Leon Russell, and—perhaps most surprising—Bob Dylan, for a benefit concert for the Bangladesh refugees. Phil Ochs, though embittered by the swing of conservativism accompanying the election of Richard Nixon, continued to write some of the most blistering political commentary set to music. John Lennon was in the process of completing *Some Time in New York City*, an album that commented on such topics and figures as sexism, the recent riot at Attica, feminist and radical activist leader Angela Davis, and the imprisonment of John Sinclair.

Sinclair remained a symbol of radicalism repressed by the government. At a time when marijuana law enforcement was loosening and pot was smoked openly and with little fear at rock concerts, it seemed inconceivable that Sinclair had already served two and a half years for a minor marijuana conviction and had repeatedly been denied bond during the appeal process. A mass rally was planned to protest the injustice. The all-star cast of speakers and performers included Jerry Rubin, David Dellinger, Bobby Seale, Rennie Davis, Ed Sanders, and Phil Ochs. Allen made a commitment to appear, as did Stevie Wonder and Bob Seger. The headliners, however, could not have been more unexpected: John Lennon and Yoko Ono announced their intention to appear, marking Lennon's first post-Beatles performance in the United States.

The rally was held on December 10 at the University of Michigan's Crisler Arena in Ann Arbor, and in its own way it was as revolutionary as the 1967 San Francisco Human Be-In or the music festival in Woodstock in 1969. The fifteen thousand in attendance were treated to nearly eight hours of speeches, music, poetry, and political rhetoric that proved, if there had ever been a doubt, that the counterculture was still capable of banding together and taking on the establishment in a large and peaceful demonstration.

Allen opened the event with a half hour of mantra chanting and the improvisation of a song about John Sinclair. He was performing before one of his largest audiences ever and he was thrilled to participate in an event that combined art and politics. A host of others followed: Phil Ochs sang his latest anthem, "Here's to the State of Richard Nixon," and Jerry Rubin proclaimed the rally to be just the first in a series intended to unseat the President in 1972. Perhaps the most moving moment of the evening occurred when John Sinclair addressed the crowd, including his wife and young daughter, via telephone hookup played over the arena's public-address system.

John and Yoko took the stage to thunderous applause at 3:00 A.M. If anyone wondered where Lennon's music was taking him, he quickly answered the question with a rousing version of "John Sinclair," a song he had written for his forthcoming album. The song, along with other protest works performed, put a fitting closing to an evening that was part rock concert, part political convention. To Allen, the rally represented "the great breakthrough that everybody had been waiting for," the kind of festival that had once been planned for Chicago, a unity of social, political, and artistic concerns.

There was no doubting the immediate effect of the rally: Fifty-five hours after John and Yoko ended their set, John Sinclair was released from prison. In a year of political frustrations, it was for Allen a sign of hope for the months ahead.

23
The Lion of Dharma

Some breath breathes silent over green snow mountains. . . .

1

Over the years, Allen had worked sporadically on a dramatic adaptation of "Kaddish," but lack of time and funding prohibited the project's reaching fruition. His vision for the play, largely influenced by his friendship and work on the production with Robert Frank, was ambitious. Allen felt a flat narrative of the events portrayed in the poem would not necessarily provide a viewer with a sense of the fragmented state of Naomi's mind—there would be a lot of shouting and screaming, but what was *behind* these actions?—so Ginsberg and Frank had worked on visual effects to accompany the action. In the film version, these effects would be edited into the main narrative; in the play, they would be projected onto screens at the back of the stage. The projections contained scenes that were alternately imaginary and real, giving the viewer a clearer indication of the extent of Naomi's mental illness.

The play finally made its way to the stage early in 1972. Directed by Robert Kalfin, *Kaddish* ran for nearly a month at the Chelsea Theater Center in Brooklyn. Not surprisingly, those in attendance had strong reactions to the play's powerful emotional content, and even those reviewers who did not care for it were mindful in their reviews to separate the emotional impact of the play from its technical imperfections. "My respect for Naomi Ginsberg's suffering is not enough to obscure for me the flatness, the narrowness, the beside-the-point-ness of this production," wrote a critic for *The New York Times*, who felt that the poem lost much of its impact in the translation.

This was a minority opinion. If anything, critics were amazed that Ginsberg had been able to transfer the great personal pain and confusion, expressed so masterfully in the poem, onto the stage. In his review for *Newsweek*, Jack Kroll offered high praise of the play, writing that "the Chelsea Theater Center of

Brooklyn has produced an extraordinary adaptation of this work, and in doing so has created one of the most moving American plays—and one of the most brilliant theatrical productions—of our time." Al Aronowitz, writing for the *New York Post*, called the play an "overwhelming" experience.

Strangely enough, one of the most even commentaries on *Kaddish* was provided by Louis Ginsberg, who for obvious reasons had a greater interest and more at stake in the production than a typical theatergoer who could be more objective in his or her judgment. "They used some of my own words and re-enacted incidents that I went through," said Louis to an interviewer. "While it was sad, it was very effective. It wasn't as tearful as I feared. You could say that my curiosity held at bay my feeling of sorrow at the re-enactment of the unhappy times that I experienced years ago with the sickness of my wife."

Allen was in New York for the play's opening performance, but he was in San Francisco by the time the reviews started to appear. He had little time to enjoy the positive reception or dispute the negative comments. He and Lawrence Ferlinghetti were finally getting around to taking the Australian tour they had planned for the previous year, but before he left, Allen had commitments to honor in the States. He needed to finalize preproduction work on *The Fall of America* and appear at several engagements on a brief reading schedule.

One of his appearances was at a Buddhist seminar with Chögyam Trungpa and Gary Snyder. The reunion convinced him that he needed to make an even greater commitment to his Buddhist studies. In addition, Trungpa had more advice for him. He was not enthusiastic about Allen's lengthy mantra chanting at his readings. The mantras, he told Allen, were setting up audience expectations that Allen could not fulfill by reciting poetry. Improvised poetry, he suggested, might be more effective. To the relief of those who preferred to hear poetry at the readings, Allen agreed to eliminate mantras from his performances.

2

Australia proved to be just the kind of working holiday that Allen needed. He, Ferlinghetti, and the publisher's eight-year-old son, Lorenzo, departed in late February, stopping for brief stays in Hawaii and the Fiji Islands before going on to Australia. Allen quickly swung into the spirit of tourism. He stayed in deluxe accommodations and spent days exploring Fiji, riding about in native buses, swimming in the coral reefs, and buying assorted souvenirs. He drank kava and was delighted by a performance of fire walkers.

Allen, Ferlinghetti, and Andrei Voznesensky were the featured readers at the Adelaide Festival of the Arts, the poets reading on separate nights. The festival, the largest of its kind in Australia, attracted huge crowds, and before long the poets were being asked to read in a number of other, smaller venues. At an appearance in the Adelaide town hall, Allen met two English-speaking aborigines who taught him several ancient native songs and danced onstage with him. For Allen, it was a restful time. "Big happy concerts, singing Jessore Road, improvising dirty blues, reading old poems, singing and dancing with Aborigines," he wrote of the readings to Lucien Carr.

The more Allen listened to native Australian music, the more he grew to love it. Written into the songs was the history of the continent dating back some twenty thousand years, and he felt these songs deserved more attention than they were getting from the country's poetry community. "It's a great tragedy that Aboriginal artists and poets are being ignored nationally," he told a Sydney reporter. "The Australian Aborigines carry in their heads one of the great epic traditions still alive on the planet. It's a tradition that is going to die in the next twenty or thirty years unless a distinct effort is made by the Government and the people of Australia to make it possible for the song men to pass their knowledge on."

Such sentiments were neither idle chatter nor an attempt to gain publicity in the Australian newspapers. Allen was genuinely concerned about the disappearance of certain types of cultural poetry. In the United States, Native American and black poetry and lyrics were in danger of extinction, and the disappearance of such poetry meant the loss of an important cultural inheritance. In Allen's opinion, aboriginal poetry represented "more efforts, more complicated syntax, more improvisation, [and] more ecological history" than he had seen in any body of literature in the world. It was a form of poetry that had to be preserved.

After their appearance in Adelaide, Allen and the group visited Melbourne and Sydney, where they had numerous scheduled readings. A disquieting incident occurred during an appearance at the Melbourne town hall, where a faction of Hungarian refugees turned out to protest Voznesensky's inclusion on the bill. The demonstration was nonviolent and short-lived, ending when people in the audience tore up the protesters' placards, but Voznesensky was shaken by the experience.

The members of the group went their separate ways in mid-March, freeing Allen to do some exploring on his own. His main interest was a pilgrimage to Ayers Rock in central Australia. Nearly five miles in length and over a thousand feet high, Ayers Rock was the world's largest monolith. It was also a sacred place to the aborigines, who had carved petroglyphs into the natural monument's sandstone surface in ancient times. Allen climbed to the top of the rock and meditated, looking out over the great expanse of desert below. A recent rainfall had renewed the life cycle in the otherwise barren region, prompting another Ginsbergian reflection on the transitory nature of the universe. Allen took out his tape recorder and dictated a poem, then wrote a few descriptive postcards to family and friends. "Great empty blue sky, ozone transparency laid over brush on red desert sand," he wrote. "Rare rain here a month ago—so lots of desert greens dotted below. Jack was right about emptiness."

Kerouac had been dead for almost two and a half years, but Allen thought about him often. Jack had been a model in so many ways, from influencing Allen's writing style to patiently guiding him in his early studies of Buddhism. Now, sitting at the top of Ayers Rock, Allen felt a twinge of melancholy when he remembered the youthful Kerouac, who had once said that you can't fall off a mountain, and the elder Kerouac, who had seemed hell-bent to fall off the mountain of life. His spirit was alive but he, too, was part of the emptiness. "Sorrowful Jack," wrote Allen in his journal, "fly over the desert to Central Australia and stand on a great big stone."

3

To a large extent, Chögyam Trungpa became Kerouac's replacement in Gins-berg's life. Allen saw a number of Kerouac's characteristics in Trungpa. Jack had antagonized and challenged Allen over the years, whether he was arguing poetics or playing "dirty dozens," and Trungpa had the same habit. He could anger Ginsberg with what appeared to be a casual or insensitive remark, and only later after some brooding and reflection could Allen see the intention and wisdom behind the remark. Allen had gone so far as to compare Kerouac and Trungpa when he met Trungpa at the hotel in San Francisco in 1971, when he had admonished Trungpa for drinking so heavily. Trungpa would hear none of it, however. By projecting Kerouac's image on him, Trungpa insisted, Allen was only displaying his own anxieties and creating more confusion in his mind. The comment had given Ginsberg pause.

Contrary to one popular misconception, Allen was not engaged in an active search for a teacher at the time he met Trungpa. He had more or less suspended his formal search for a guru after his trip to India, at the time of the "change." He was, however, all too happy to listen to strong advice. He had kept his mind open throughout the sixties and had received helpful instruction from time to time. As far as he knew on the occasion of their initial meeting in San Francisco, Allen could expect no more from Trungpa than the insights from another spiritual leader.

When Allen had first met Kerouac, he'd fallen instantly in love with him, even though he realized that Jack was not homosexual and that any love between them would be on a different level than he might have hoped for. The situation was similar with Trungpa. As Allen later admitted, "The reason I wound up with Trungpa was because I loved him. I fell in love with him. At first I thought it was my compassion to him, or his to me, but I wasn't sure which it was after a while. It was the excitement of seeing someone you love from city to city, and meeting and looking in his eyes, exchanging bashfulness. The relationship changed as time went on, [but] that was the original depth."

The teacher/student relationship developed quickly. Trungpa suggested that Allen adopt another mantra for his meditation and he had initially offered advice about how he could improve the ones he was already chanting. Allen had brought a harmonium to their earlier San Francisco meeting and Trungpa had stopped Allen while he was chanting the Guru Om mantra by placing his hand on the keyboard, bringing the music to a halt. "Remember," he told Allen, "the silence is just as important as the sound." This made sense to Allen. The mantra he had been playing for Trungpa was one of his favorites because he received a tingling sensation when he sang it in front of the audience. After a while, the high he received from the chanting had become as important to him as the mantra itself. By creating the pauses suggested by Trungpa, he was keeping his ego and any personal agenda in check.

Trungpa was especially effective at puncturing Allen's ego and in challenging his conceptions. From all his scholarship and experience, Allen had grown to trust his own intuition and judgment on numerous political and social topics.

He was also accustomed to having others defer to his opinions, as if his judgments were the voice of authority. Trungpa was different. Like William Burroughs, Lucien Carr, and Jack Kerouac during the years of Ginsberg's youth,
Trungpa challenged Allen at every turn. On one occasion, when overhearing
Allen expounding about politics, Trungpa remarked that he should never
consider running for President or he might wind up in *vajra* hell—the inescapable prison of his own making. Once again, he had given Allen occasion to
consider his ego and ambition.

"The relationship with him was altering my idea of myself," Ginsberg remembered of his early association with Trungpa. "I got more and more involved in
the inquisitiveness as to what further he had to offer and more and more in
love with him. He seemed more like a good teacher and a jolly fellow and a
deep soul or deep non-soul or whatever. I began to respect him as I respected
Kerouac or Burroughs or any close friend, but seeing also that he had this
fantastic classical background of Himalayan wisdom. Since I'd always dug Himalayan wisdom as a beatnik, I felt I'd better follow up."

Allen took a formal step in that direction in May, a short time after his
return to the United States from his trip to Australia. Included in the second
leg of his spring reading tour was a series of readings in Colorado. He, Gary
Snyder, and Robert Bly read at a May 6 benefit for Vajradkatu, Trungpa's
Buddhist group. During the reading, Trungpa was at his disruptive best,
angering Bly by appearing drunk onstage and banging on a gong as the poets
were trying to read, but Allen was nonplussed. "Your drunken behavior—is it
just you, or is this a traditional manner, or what?" he asked Trungpa. Replied
Trungpa, "I come from a long line of eccentric Buddhists."

Allen decided to take formal Buddhist refuge vows. The ceremony was held
in the Dharmadhatu meditation center in Boulder. Seated in the lotus position
onstage with Trungpa, Allen repeated three times the formal vows to take
refuge in Buddha, in Buddhist teachings, and in the Buddhist community. He
then took formal bodhisattva vows: "Sentient beings are numberless. I vow to
liberate them all. Obstacles are inexhaustible. I vow to cut through them. The
gates of the Dharma are countless. I vow to enter every gate. The Buddha Path
is endless. I vow to follow through."

At the ceremony, Trungpa bestowed upon Ginsberg a new Buddhist name,
which was both complimentary of Allen's quest in the past and rather daunting
for the responsibility it would demand of him in the future. Allen was named
Lion of Dharma.

4

Two decades after it had been written, the entire text of *Visions of Cody* was
finally being published, and Allen was asked to write its introduction. He
approached the task as if it was a sacred mission. Despite his initial misgivings
about Kerouac's novel, Allen had become one of its biggest boosters over the
years. In Allen's eyes, it was a masterwork, perhaps Kerouac's greatest novel.
Jack had always believed in the book but had not lived to see it published—
and, in all likelihood, savaged by the critics—and Allen was determined to see

that it would not be misunderstood now that it was finally reaching readers. He gave the book a slow, thorough reading, filling page after page of his journal with intricate line-by-line notes. These notes, published in 1974 as *The Visions of the Great Rememberer*, provided the basis for his introductory essay.

The essay was an unabashed tribute to Kerouac and Cassady, author and subject—the two great loves of his life. Since he was staying in Denver when he began to take his notes, Allen was at the origin of the book in a sense. He felt nostalgic. He remembered the summer of 1947, when he lived on Grant Street, worked at May Company, and had his ill-destined affair with Cassady. "Reading this book, some chapters are like excavating a tomb," he wrote in his journal on May 24. The exquisite details of Jack's prose, the transcription of Neal's stream-of-consciousness dialogue while he was high on marijuana, the flashes of incident and character, now a quarter century past—all haunted Allen as he reread the book:

> So I survived Neal and Jack—what for, all my temerity? The empty paradise? A great mirror in plastic Hilton? An ache in the left side of the breast, sweet love buried that might be tears? When'll I realize Neal's dearness again? Jack's prophetic tender eyelashes viewing mortal Colfax? Even fulfill the noble role of scribe and detail the memories? Ah, but Jack did that decades ago, forever.

Perhaps, but it was Ginsberg's duty to introduce Jack's youthful celebration of the spirit of the American West even on the eve of the publication of *The Fall of America*, his own account of a country's plummet from grace. The longer he read, the more Allen realized that Kerouac had captured a time of innocence, for both the youths and their country—a time before success had driven them all to their respective fates. Neal playing football, Jack hanging out at a diner, the long and frenetic conversations about everything and about nothing—what youth could have been more American? In writing his novel, Ginsberg said of Kerouac, Jack was "trying desperately to be a great rememberer redeeming life from darkness"; he was trying to save his youth—and his country's innocence—from what it had become.

Just what the country had become continued to loom as a large question in Ginsberg's mind. The United States faced another presidential election and, as in the two preceding ones in 1964 and 1968, the Vietnam War dominated much of the political rhetoric. According to the opinion polls, George McGovern, the Democratic party's front-runner who was campaigning on a platform to end the war, trailed incumbent Richard Nixon by a wide margin. Allen found this unacceptable. From all indications, another four years of Nixon would mean another four years of war.

Allen became obsessed with trying to find a way to prevent this from happening. He began a new notebook devoted entirely to the collection of statistics and information about the weaponry, casualties, and war strategies of Vietnam. He converted his interviews with the press into bitter harangues against the war. His poetry readings became antiwar statements. He was a featured speaker at a number of antiwar rallies and demonstrations.

The issue seemed clear enough to him: Public-opinion polls clearly indicated that the majority of Americans opposed the war, yet the government not only refused to bring an immediate end to the bloodshed but refused to talk to the majority leadership—not only that, the government was turning its forces against the voices of dissent. It was not a common occurrence for demonstrators, including Allen, to be tear-gassed and arrested at rallies protesting the war.

Allen decided to take his complaint to the White House itself. He called the White House and demanded to speak to Henry Kissinger, Nixon's secretary of state and top war adviser. Amazingly enough, after a short time Kissinger came on the line. Allen told him that it was important to establish an avenue of communication between top government leadership and those who opposed the war. He then proposed that Kissinger meet with some of these leaders. Kissinger neither rejected nor opposed the idea. Encouraged by their conversation, Allen tried to set up a meeting between Kissinger and David Dellinger. Unfortunately, what might have been an important dialogue never progressed beyond the planning stages.

Both political conventions were being held in Miami. This time, with Nixon enjoying a lopsided lead in the race, peace advocates decided to devote the great percentage of their activities to the Republican National Convention. Republican party officials worried about the prospects for a repeat performance of the violent confrontations in Chicago in 1968—for good reason. Different factions of political dissidents had announced their intentions to be on hand to demonstrate at the convention site. For the Republicans, this was not welcome news, though party leadership had been working overtime to keep the protest movement in check. From the beginning of its term in office, the Nixon administration, led by Vice President Spiro Agnew, had waged its own war against the now-fragmentary Left. The same was true of the Federal Bureau of Investigation. FBI director J. Edgar Hoover had died on May 2, but his influence and policies continued to be felt. One of Hoover's favorite ploys against dissidents involved his operatives infiltrating different leftist organizations and subverting their efforts by acting as agents provocateurs at rallies and demonstrations. Such actions led to the discrediting of the groups in the public eye and, in many cases, arrests of key figures.

The convention week featured a number of marches and sit-ins, complete with street theater and the usual lineup of impassioned political speeches. David Dellinger led a small group of protesters in a month-long hunger fast in protest of the war. In one demonstration, an elephant, symbolizing the Republican party logo, pulled a black coffin down the street to the convention hall, while in another, a float with a huge papier-mâché heroin spike, symbolic of the CIA-endorsed drug trafficking in Southeast Asia, was deposited at the gates of the hall. Overall, however, the week was relatively peaceful—but not without incident.

As documents released through the Freedom of Information Act would prove, the FBI had successfully infiltrated high-visibility groups, including the Vietnam Vets Against the War, and those agents were able to sabotage a number of demonstrations with their inflammatory rhetoric and disruptive—and even violent—behavior. Allen witnessed this at a peace march he had helped to organize. He and a group of about two hundred marchers were moving down the street, chanting mantras, when they were joined by a group of Vietnam vets that immediately began to disrupt the march by stopping cars, knocking over garbage cans, and shouting at traffic and pedestrians. The police arrived immediately and announced the march was over, that anyone not leaving would be arrested and charged with disturbing the peace. Allen and the group, protesting the denial of their right to a peaceful assembly, sat down in the street. Using tear gas and brandishing their nightsticks, the police moved in. Allen, Peter, poet John Giorno, and Jeff Nightbyrd, a leader of the Youth International Party, along with scores of others, were arrested and loaded into police wagons. Television cameras recorded the action, but this time it looked as if the protesters had initiated the confrontation. "A few police-infiltrated peace protesters spoiled the scene for many more sane anti-war folk," commented Ginsberg, who spent three days in a Miami jail cell before he was released from police custody. The war in Vietnam and the aggressive measures taken against those who opposed it both seemed to Allen to be "science-fiction style, dehumanized, remote control mass violence."

Nixon would go on to win the election by a landslide. However, within two years of this victory, after the events surrounding the Watergate break-in and its aftermath were revealed to the public, the country would learn just how far members of the administration would go to assure the defeat of their opponents.

5

After the convention, Allen returned to New York, where he spent time with his family and handled his ever-increasing number of business affairs. He appeared onstage during John Lennon's August 30 concert at Madison Square Garden, leading the full house in a rousing version of "Give Peace a Chance." From there, he was off to Cherry Valley for a month of relaxation before he began his autumn reading tour.

On September 25, Allen gave Gay Sunshine, a San Francisco–based cultural and literary publication, one of his most important interviews. By this point, Allen had become one of the country's best-known, most outspoken gay figures, but he had yet to issue a lengthy, detailed statement that specifically addressed his own experience and feelings. He had answered countless questions about his homosexuality in the past, but none of the published interviews focused exclusively on this critical aspect of his life. The Gay Sunshine interview changed all that.

Interviewer Allen Young, a longtime gay rights activist, skillfully directed Ginsberg through a sequence of questions that dealt with his relationships with Neal Cassady, Jack Kerouac, and William Burroughs. They discussed the development of Allen's sexuality, from his frightened, confused days at Columbia to his self-acceptance at age forty-six. Allen spoke of the Whitmanesque principle of love between men as it had evolved over the past century. He offered an in-depth account of his and Peter Orlovsky's relationship, which had undergone such immense changes over the years. The interview, eventually published as a small book, was both confessional and inspirational; few interviews before or since have featured such a well-known figure speaking with such honesty about his or her sexuality.

Ginsberg, of course, had been soundly criticized over the years for being so frank about his sexuality with the press and in his poetry. To his harshest critics, his remarks seemed undignified, impertinent, silly, overstated, or beside the point. Indeed, his remarks were all of these things at times. Ginsberg staked no claim to being a perpetual font of wisdom. He could be an ignu, a genius, and all things in between. Standards for literary criticism demanded that a serious artist present only the best and most polished work, but this standard flew in the face of what Ginsberg hoped to achieve in honest, spontaneous poetry. Ezra Pound had fashioned a career out of the raw materials of his life and mind, and Ginsberg was committed to this practice.

He did not relish the idea of exposing his private weaknesses to the public, however. Throughout his years as a public figure, Allen wrote scores of journal notations bemoaning what he considered to be his personal weaknesses and doubts. He felt a strong obligation to provide an exemplary life to those who might perceive him to be a leader, and he experienced a strong sense of failure when he did not or could not fulfill such an obligation. Despite his standing as an internationally respected figure, he could still be plagued by uncertainty. For example, a month after taking his Buddhist vows, Allen entered one particularly revealing dream notation in his journal:

> Wandering up & down side street of life looking for my
> old room—upstairs a big door, I have two keys, I put one in
> the wrong door & the key bends like dough (like the Hilton
> Denver key)—I look at the set of two keys they have Lion
> images at the center of the key and that's
> exactly
> where
> the key breaks, the Lion
> turns to putty—O Lion of Dharma (!)

Later that same year, in "To Marpa & Chogyam," a journal poem dedicated to two of his Buddhist models, Allen again expressed the doubt that bothered him:

> What good is peace in my heart
> If other hearts burst with pain?
> What good my silent meditation
> If bombs scream down on Vietnam?
> I have no ecstasy in my head,
> filled with pictures of button bombs,
> I sigh "Sa" remembering my full belly
> while napalm flashes in New York Times. . . .

Neither of these entries was ever revised or published, although Allen did issue numerous poems expressing doubt, pain, confusion, anger, and disappointment. If anything, he was accused of publishing too many of this type of poem, some critics incorrectly assuming that he published everything and anything he wrote. (In fact, Ginsberg's published writings represent perhaps 1 percent of his written work.) He was indeed selective about what he chose to publish, but the selection process rarely focused on his personal feelings of embarrassment; instead, the focus was on the quality of work and, on occasion, the need to protect others from embarrassment.

6

On January 21, 1973, while walking on the path outside the Cherry Valley farmhouse, Allen slipped on a patch of ice and broke his right leg. The experience had an almost surreal quality to it, as if Allen were outside his body and watching the accident occur to someone else. Lying on the ground near a snowbank, he sighed the mantra that Trungpa had assigned to him. His situation seemed very clear. So this could be a broken bone, he thought, remembering the car crash a few years earlier. On that occasion, while recovering from his injuries in the hospital, Allen had considered his own mortality in the context of his physical pain, concluding that the human spirit was, in a sense, imprisoned in a "body stump," an eternal flame housed in a package that was both mortal and weak. This time around, he would arrive at a similar conclusion, reasoning that "the body itself [is] a farce, that is, a play that ends, [a] cruel joke of pain for me and many unless we realize in time and experience [the] dimensions of silent space outside our brain formed meat houses."

Despite the physical pain and inconvenience of having to wear a full leg cast for another indefinite period of time, Allen tried to stay realistic, if not upbeat, about this latest setback. It was not easy. At the best of times, he tended to fret about what he perceived to be his physical decline—a head cold could send him on a long meditation about his mortality—and the pain associated with the injury, along with the dizzying effects of the medication he was given to relieve his suffering, left him frustrated and depressed. His journal entries included long analytical monologues about the nature of his physical and mental well-being, a moving prayer ("Help me bear my pain and others'. . . . Tell me what to do Lord O Lord tell me what I am Help me please. . . ."), and a clever blues lyric ("Broken Bones Blues"). His most clearheaded assessment came as a result of another challenge from Chögyam Trungpa, who asked him, "What would you do if you lost it?" This prompted a soliloquy about what Allen would be giving up if he was to die at that moment.

The broken leg may have given him occasion to reflect upon his humbler, mortal side, but Allen had reason to be pleased with the reception he and his literary endeavors were enjoying. In February, he and Kurt Vonnegut became the two most recently elected members to the National Institute of Arts and Letters. "Ecologue," his long poem about his life at Cherry Valley, had been published in *American Review 16* to extraordinary response. Newspaper and magazine requests for new poems exceeded the number of works he had to supply.

In addition, very encouraging reviews of *The Fall of America* were reaching the newstands, the large majority of critics praising the collection as a masterwork. Where Allen's early works had found him probing his mind, searching for his identity and sense of purpose, all within the context of an apathetic, perhaps even cruel world, the newer works were more confident and mature, tempered by experience and accumulated wisdom. Ginsberg had been America's most visible poet during the 1960s, but because his individual poems were for the most part printed in small, widely dispersed, and difficult-to-obtain publications, readers were generally deprived of the mosaiclike effect and continuity of thought in the body of work issued over the last five years of the decade. *The Fall of America* was enormous, both in terms of its physical size and ambition, and reviewers took notice.

"Ginsberg has become a geographer, and his one inexhaustible subject is the earth and what it looks like," wrote a reviewer for *The New York Times*. By traversing the continent and recording the details of what he saw, the reviewer intimated, Ginsberg had successfully portrayed the complexity and vast expansiveness of a country falling beneath the weight of its sins: "Ginsberg's avalanche of details is like the rain of dust and lava that preserved Pompeii—here lies America, in literally thousands of its emanations, recorded in minute particularity."

"Allen Ginsberg has taken the job of literary historian of the 1960s," mentioned another reviewer, who appreciated Ginsberg's gathering of his words from every source imaginable, including the newspapers, radio, and even graffiti scribbled on bathroom walls. "It is a language of the 70s with a message for the 70s," this critic wrote, "a poetry that confronts everyone of us today. And it is a poetry that we must confront."

As befitting the examination of a masterwork created by a longtime literary practitioner, many reviewers attempted to summarize Ginsberg's career and place him in historical perspective. "*The Fall of America*," wrote one critic, "confirms Ginsberg's status as the true successor to Whitman." "Ginsberg is by now an authentic institution," wrote another. Still another called Ginsberg "the undisputed effusive sidewalk bard of America." These and other reviews were clipped from their sources by Allen and stored in a massive file that would eventually be labeled "Faded Yellow Press Clippings" and housed in a deposit at Columbia University.

Allen's spring reading tour accommodated the usual assortment of college readings, poetry workshops, lectures, and benefit appearances. Watergate was the main topic of interest that spring and news of the scandal seemed to grow more perplexing by the day. Allen was outraged but by no means shocked. If anything, the scandal made his political ravings of the sixties and early seventies seem far less paranoid and more prophetic. "It's like a woolen sweater," Allen wrote of Watergate to Louis. "Unravel one thread and the whole cloth finally comes apart. If the thread keeps unraveling the whole fabric of 'mass hallucination' public imagery will fall—and what *should* be seen is that all of Vietnam, all the 'brainwash' imagery that Romney complained about in 1968, was also a giant Watergate-type conspiracy. . . . But the illegality of the war has yet to be publicized."

Ginsberg's other major concern at the time was the continuing struggle of Timothy Leary. Time, misfortune, and a massive government effort (involving the State Department, FBI, and CIA, among others) had finally caught up with Leary, who had been captured in Kabul, returned to the States, and placed in solitary confinement in lieu of $5 million bail. What had originally started out as an arrest for possession of a minuscule amount of marijuana had expanded into an international event.

That Leary had been arrested at a time when the events surrounding the Watergate break-in were being revealed was of no surprise to Allen. "Leary," he said, "is one of the victims of the Watergate mentality, in terms of setting up phony conspiracy charges against other people." The marijuana conviction, he argued, was beside the point. "In fact, he is being punished because he is a charismatic and persuasive speaker for a controversial cause."

Nor did Allen miss the irony in the revelation that G. Gordon Liddy, one of the leaders in the raid at Millbrook, New York, in the sixties, was now one of the principal figures in the Watergate investigation. The government's paranoia knew no bounds, and it would go to extremes to put its needless fears to rest. "Watergate gives me something to get up for in the morning," Allen said sarcastically. "Nixon is performing a great service: the complete de-mystification of the police state. He's doing a great job and we ought to keep him."

Allen's reading tour brought him back to the West Coast, and while he was in San Francisco, enjoying the acclaim he was receiving for *The Fall of America*, he did all he could to help with Leary's defense. He wrote letters to newspaper editors and visited their offices, making certain that all were informed of the facts in the case. He wrote a poem, "Mock Sestina: The Conspiracy Against Dr. Tim Leary," which was printed and circulated as a flier. On May 31, he participated, along with Michael McClure and others, in a benefit reading at the Telegraph Hill Neighborhood House, the proceeds to be applied to the Leary Defense Fund.

These efforts, while perhaps commendable, did not achieve an early release for Leary. They did, however, keep Allen's name in print—which was not always an entirely optimal situation. At the Canadian customs station, as he was entering the country for a benefit reading for Vancouver's Tibetan Buddhist Center, Allen was detained for a short time by an immigration official who was interested in some of his issued statements about drugs, particularly the opinions offered in the *Playboy* interview and his 1966 testimony before the Senate subcommittee. As Allen knew all too well, any history of drug conviction could be used as an excuse to keep a person from entering a country.

No one was learning this lesson—and with as much press coverage—as John Lennon and Yoko Ono. Their performance at the John Sinclair rally had angered government officials determined to keep Sinclair behind bars; almost immediately following the benefit, an all-out effort to deport Lennon was put into motion. Since Lennon was in America legally and had broken none of its laws, the best his enemies could do was reach back to an old pot conviction in England and use that as grounds for his deportation. Joined by a number of influential friends, Ginsberg included, Lennon fought back fiercely. Not surprisingly, Allen took the high road in his defense of Lennon and Ono. Boldly comparing them to such artists as Blake, Brecht, and Shakespeare, he argued that John and Yoko were great figures facing persecution at the cost of their art. "If Lennon/Ono disappear tomorrow to heaven," Allen wrote, "they'd take an immortal laurel crown (traditional poetic gift to the muses) to the pearly gates, great work finished."

This was only the opening volley. The battle to keep Lennon in the United States would continue for years.

7

Almost six years had passed since Allen's last extensive tour of Europe, so he was quick to accept invitations to attend poetry conferences in London and Rotterdam during the summer of 1973. He looked forward to spending time with Bill Burroughs, who was still living in London and whom he had seen only sporadically in recent years. Allen had already arranged a busy fall schedule that included a reading tour and three-month Buddhist retreat, and with all this facing him in the future, he decided to spend the summer overseas as a sort of working holiday.

London proved to be quite different from the city Allen had visited in 1967. Prices were high and housing scarce. The days of "Swinging London," as well as the idea of traveling on the cheap, were long gone. Allen stayed in a room without a bathroom in a fleabag hotel on his first night in London, but he was no longer excited about the prospects of exchanging creature comforts for grand experience. "You were lucky to be here in '67," he complained in a letter to Louis and Edith. "There was lots of money and lots of spirit and fine clothes. The economic depression has hit and there's less obvious spirit, poetry readings are duller and more formal, clothes are less showy, there's less of a center and less spirit—people more mature but no community poetic vivacity." Londoners treated him well, he noted, but he wondered what might have happened if he was now just starting out and trying to travel the way he had in his younger days.

Burroughs, too, had grown weary of life in London. Living off the income from his books was difficult, and to stay afloat he had sold a portion of his archives to a Swiss investor who intended to create a library of manuscripts and literary memorabilia. Depressed by the city, Burroughs began to formulate plans to escape, perhaps to somewhere in southern Ireland or Costa Rica, or in another country where the cost of living might be less expensive. At fifty-nine, Burroughs needed a place to relax in what—for all he knew—could be his final years. The United States was not totally out of the question, even if it had been nearly a quarter of a century since he had lived there. Allen had heard of a new course, taught by well-known, respected authors and offered at City College in New York, and he suggested to Burroughs that he might consider teaching it. Bill did not oppose the idea.

Allen made the most of his time in London, although with a cast on his leg and using crutches, he was less mobile than he had been on previous trips. With his "uniform" of bib overalls and T-shirt, the latter printed up with the bomb statistics from the Vietnam War, he must have looked like a bit of a throwback to a recently passed era. There was never a shortage of readings to give or places to visit, and before long he realized that he was again falling behind in his writing and correspondence. He also realized on the occasion of his forty-seventh birthday that he did not have the years ahead of him to accomplish everything on his constantly expanding list of ambitions.

After a brief trip to the Netherlands, where he participated in the Rotterdam poetry conference, Allen returned briefly to London to work with Fernanda Pivano on the Italian translation of *Indian Journals*, and from there he began to work his way north through the English countryside toward Scotland. In Cambridge, he stopped at a museum that housed a number of Blake manuscripts, including many of the songs. In Newcastle, he gave a reading at the Mining Institute.

With its rolling green meadows and beautiful oceanside, Scotland was a wonderful respite from recent activities. Allen toured Glasgow and Edinburgh, the country's two largest cities, but his greatest pleasure was derived from seeing the rural countryside, where sheep dotted the meadows like a scene out of *National Geographic* or off a picture postcard. On a train ride to the Inner Hebrides, he read the works of Robert Burns to a young Scottish poet traveling with him. He enjoyed an evening of simple pleasure sleeping in a tin shed on Iona Island. In general, he found Scotland to be a "lovely place," a pastoral setting similar to what he had seen in Wales in 1967. Unfortunately, very little writing survives from this period of travel.

Allen was back in the States by early September. He returned to Cherry Valley, where he helped harvest and preserve the summer's crops, and set his affairs in order before setting out on his extended and eagerly anticipated Buddhist retreat. While he had been out of the country, Abbie Hoffman had been arrested for trying to sell cocaine to an undercover agent, and though there was very little that he could do on Hoffman's behalf, Allen tried to fashion a letter of support. Then he was on the move again, heading west by the time the New England maple leaves were beginning to display their autumn colors.

8

Chögyam Trungpa had founded a Vajrayana seminary in Teton Village near Jackson Hole, Wyoming, and from mid-September until mid-December 1973 he sponsored a combination retreat and seminar designed to take advanced students through the three *yanas* of Buddhism. Trungpa, who had written some poetry of his own, had asked Allen to act as his poetry guru in exchange for his acting as Ginsberg's meditation guru—a proposal Allen readily accepted— and he persuaded Allen to attend the seminary that fall as a poetry teacher.

Allen was delighted by the prospects. "That'll be the first time I hit heavy yoga practice, sitting immobile 10–12 hours a day, 10 days at a time, mixed with teaching and technique discussion," he wrote his father in anticipation of the retreat. "I don't know too many poets except Gary Snyder and Phil [Whalen] and Diane Di Prima who have that experience. It'll be useful."

The experience—or at least the beginning of it—turned out to be similar to Jack Kerouac's youthful experience as a fire lookout in the Pacific Northwest. Theoretically, sitting alone and silent with one's thoughts promised to be a valuable experience, but when one was accustomed to an active life marked by a lot of motion and conversation, the isolation of meditation could be challeng- ing. Allen began his initial two-week sitting shortly before dawn on September

17. "Sun pink on Teton mountain tips—green pine heights flattered by rosy light," he wrote in his journal, excited by the prospects of the time ahead of him.

Sitting for hours at a time was more of a task than Allen had anticipated. He noticed every physical discomfort, all his aches and twinges, particularly in his back and in the leg that had been broken earlier that year. Silently repeating the mantra that Trungpa had given him, Allen tried to focus his attention elsewhere, but his thoughts were equally disconcerting. Politics, erotic fantasies, the events of his life—all thoughts seemed to hinder the meditation process. Allen struggled his way through: "By force of will, almost, [I] held fast, back straight, trying to plow through Time and Despair and Reflection and Angers and magic loves' nearly meaningless fantasies—put the real meaning in the warm heart!—and breathe there till empty and light. So saw the day through, holding fast to balance, spine stiff, belly pressed down for deepest breath, mind beating in hopeless resentment at being stuck loveless in dying body—trying to get out of that mind into free breath—into the atmosphere, into transparent crystal ball."

As the days went by, the long periods of meditation became less difficult. When Allen complained to Trungpa about some of the problems he was experiencing with his meditation, his teacher suggested that he focus on his breath as he was exhaling, to concentrate on its leaving the nostrils and dissolving into space. This discipline, know as *Samatha* meditation, differed from Allen's customary method of meditation, but Trungpa assured him that in paying attention to his breath and the space outside his body, he would be directing his concentration away from internal distraction and discomfort. "Annihilate body thought, pay attention or identify . . . the outbreath and let that measure the universe," Allen wrote as a reminder to himself in his journal. This practice, he noted happily, was easier and better than the one he had been using.

Allen wrote a prodigious amount of prose and poetry during his stay in Teton Village, most of it dealing with meditation technique and the thoughts that occurred while he sat on a pillow for those many hours and focused on his escaping breath. From this period of writing came "Mind Breaths," a lengthy poem that would eventually serve as the title poem of his next City Lights collection. In retrospect, "Mind Breaths" appears to be the penultimate statement of Ginsberg's lifelong pursuit of his different levels of consciousness. In discussing *Samatha* meditation with Ginsberg, Trungpa had suggested that this type of meditation was a two-step process. First, in concentrating on each individual breath, a person was creating a sense of awareness—of mindfulness—that in essence was more directed to the observation of the nature and character of thought than to its form. The second step was the awareness of the precise detail in each breath/thought.

In a sense, Ginsberg's experimentation with different drugs, particularly psychedelics, was a pursuit of this type of consciousness. He had been successful to limited degrees, but the form of the thought—the awareness of the thought as a product of the drug—had hindered his attention to detail. He was too preoccupied with the physical effects of the drugs to fully appreciate the effects they were having on his mental state. Meditation offered another alternative. Since breathing itself was natural, and because meditation was drug-free and offered no chemical alterations to the nervous system, the mind was in a sense freer to make its own natural explorations. In its discipline of repeatedly touching a thought and letting it go, *Samatha* meditation made room for interesting thought juxtaposition, not unlike Burroughs's cut-ups or haiku or even Ginsberg's earlier experiments with juxtaposition in "Howl" and other early poems. This form of meditation also accommodated Ginsberg's long-standing interest in long breath-length lines.

Meditation could also be used for building or layering thoughts. Trungpa told Ginsberg to compare it to the opening of a telescope: One breath (or thought) led to another, with each adding to the image. In "Mind Breaths," Ginsberg attempted to capture this sensation. He begins the poem by describing the thoughts he had while concentrating on the area immediately in front of him, and from there he "telescopes" outward, until his breath/thought is reaching all corners of the world:

> my breath through nostril floated out to the moth of evening
>   beating into window'd illumination
> breathed outward over aspen, twigs trembling September's
>   top yellow leaves twilit at mountain foot
> breathed over the mountain, over snowpowdered crags ringed
>   under slow-breathed cloud-mass white spumes
> windy across Tetons to Idaho, grey ranges under blue space
>   swept
> with delicate snow flurries, breaths Westward . . .

With each thought, Ginsberg's breath became more expansive, a part of the wind moving across the planet. The detail, however, remained absolutely specific, as much as the detail observed and spoken onto the tapes of his auto poesy. In the past, while talking about his quest to reach hidden areas of consciousness, he had spoken of the need to see with the eye in his mind, and in meditation he appeared to have found his vision.

"Mind Breaths" was by necessity a re-creation: It would have been impossible for Ginsberg to meditate properly and write at the same time. The poem, therefore, became a reenactment of his mental activity, not unlike the way he kept his journal at his bedside and re-created his dreams immediately upon awakening. Not that the method of composition mattered: In meditation, as in sleep, the mind was given room to pursue its own path, unencumbered by a consciousness of immediate surrounding. The poem, or dream notation, became an artifact of discovery.

9

Throughout his stay at Teton Village, Allen had to go out of his way to keep up with world affairs. Newspapers were not kept on the premises and group discussions rarely addressed current events. He made a point of picking up a newspaper whenever he could, and from his readings he learned of events that startled, angered, and saddened him.

Word was out about the CIA-assisted overthrow of Salvador Allende's government in Chile and of its bloody aftermath. In 1970, Allende made history by becoming the first Marxist-Leninist candidate elected in a non-Communist country in the western hemisphere. His socialist policies were met with great opposition, both within his country and abroad, the United States being an open and vocal opponent. On September 11, 1973, military forces aided by the CIA stormed the presidential palace, killed Allende, and seized control of the government. A military junta was established. A large number of artists, including poets, painters, and musicians, were subsequently tortured, murdered, or driven from the country.

Allen was understandably concerned. He had friends in Chile, dating back to his initial visit there in 1960. There was little doubt that the new government would judge them to be subversive. Adding to his concern was a report about the recent death of Pablo Neruda. The Chilean poet had died of natural causes—cancer—but the military government forbid a public funeral. Saddened by the news, Allen wrote a long journal poem in Neruda's memory:

> . . . Your poetry long as Chile your
> epics, verses, sonnets,
> line by line lie empty
> Your revolution your new
> Marxist peoples Government
> like poetry floating out of your mouth
> like breath out of one corpulent man
> empty as death the
> year 1973, empty as South
> America
> empty as Andes, Empty as Life
> empty as Pablo Neruda.

The events in Chile distracted him, disrupting his meditation. The U.S. role in the coup upset him no end and he swore that he would personally find a way to have Kissinger imprisoned if any harm came to Nicanor Parra and his other friends in the country.

There was more bad news. W. H. Auden had passed away. When Allen received the news of his death, he spent a tearful afternoon remembering his numerous encounters with the poet. He had first met Auden in 1946, while still a student at Columbia; he had taken a subway ride with Auden, down the length of Manhattan, just so he would have more time to talk to him. He had visited Auden's Cornelia Street apartment, which so impressed him with its modern entrance arch. Later, after Auden moved to a loft on Twenty-first Street, Allen had shown him a manuscript of *Empty Mirror* and listened to his suggestions. Then there had been the argument on Ischia Island in 1957, and their subsequent conciliatory meeting a few years later in London. In the late sixties, Allen had met with him and offered to sing his Blake songs, but Auden declined, saying, "Oh, no, I get too embarrassed when people sing to me alone. That's for the concert hall." Finally, only a few months ago, they had enjoyed a pleasant get-together in England. They had read together and afterward, at Allen's request, Auden had explained Welsh verse forms. Now he was gone. There would be much sadness in the poetry world, on both sides of the Atlantic. In Teton Village, Allen sat "in meditation silent, Ah'ing his wrinkled soul." He asked Trungpa to pray for Auden, as well.

Needing money to finance operations at the Cherry Valley farm and for the construction of a dwelling on a piece of land he had recently purchased near Gary Snyder's property in the California Sierras, Allen broke off his meditation retreat and embarked on another reading tour, this one beginning in Baltimore and working its way through upstate New York. His time at Teton Village had influenced him greatly, which was apparent in his meetings with the press. When asked—as he invariably was—about the connection between the Beat Generation and hippie movement, Allen answered that "emptiness" had been the goal of the Beat Generation. "The experience of loss of illusions and appreciation of unclogged space," he said, was the direction he, Kerouac, and the others had taken. "It is desirable in the sense that it's there and it's natural. It means a simple life with more sittings, more meditation." He had hoped the Beats and hippies would be the country's salvation, he confessed, but now it was apparent to him that these groups had only aggravated America's "big neurotic trip" evident in its foreign policy and the Vietnam War. "The left went wrong," said Allen, "because its gestures and actions out of anxiety and hatred totally confused an already confused situation."

Allen had been thinking along this line for two decades, but he had never vocalized it quite as bluntly, in such direct connection with the two groups with which he was so often associated. For all their rebellion, very few of the principal members of the Beat Generation were politically active, and even the hippies, eventually known for their activism, evolved more from their pursuit of an alternative lifestyle than from a purely political agenda. At the core of their philosophy was a spirituality that Judge Julius Hoffman had found so difficult to comprehend during Allen's testimony at the Chicago Conspiracy Trial.

During the passing years, confrontations with the authorities had eroded the good intentions. What Allen had learned from his experience with the college professor in India, implemented in his meeting with the Hell's Angels and participation in the Human Be-In, had been difficult to pass on during a turbulent decade of angry civil-rights and antiwar rhetoric. To top it off, he was disheartened to learn that some of the people he trusted and worked with had been seeking violent disruption all along.

Meditation afforded him the opportunity to return to the self. It also presented him with the contemplative time to consider his life. He could be his own harshest critic, especially when writing in his journal and emptying his mind of its troubles: "The Beat Generation was a mistake, my personality and person and beard and teaching a mistake, my acid a mistake my grass a mistake my clinging to Blake a mistake my poetry a mistake my loves a mistake my self a burden a weight an ache a samsaric load of heavy guts and strained muscles," he wrote. Meditation returned himself to his own mind, his breathing discipline giving him what he called "a few minutes of peaceful resignation."

10

Chögyam Trungpa planned to open a learning facility that would unite Eastern and Western thought, providing an education that combined "provocative intellectual environment and personal journey beyond concept." At first, the school, located in Boulder, Colorado, and known as The Naropa Institute, would offer a series of summer seminars by a distinguished faculty of teachers. If the seminars were well accepted and the school was able to receive accreditation, Naropa would become a year-round college.

Trungpa asked Allen whether he would be willing to participate in a poetics seminar. As Trungpa conceived it, the course would last the summer and be taught by a number of poets, each working a week or weekend in an intensive learning environment. For their efforts, the poets would be given round-trip airfare to Colorado, room and board, and a small honorarium.

Allen approved of the seminar, although he thought it should be called *spiritual* poetics in keeping with the school's goal of uniting the intellectual and the spiritual. They immediately began planning the course. Allen recommended Gary Snyder, Philip Whalen, Anne Waldman, Michael McClure, and Diane Di Prima as potential teachers. All had distinguished themselves as poets and all had great interest in Eastern or Buddhist thought. Waldman had run the St. Mark's Poetry Project in New York and was therefore aware of the organizational aspects of such an enterprise.

From such a modest origin sprang a new career that Allen would pursue from that point on. Like his father before him, he was going to teach.

24
Ego Confessions

Art's not empty if it shows its own emptiness
Poetry useful leaves its own skeleton hanging in air
like Buddha, Shakespeare & Rimbaud. . . .

1

Allen continued to worry about the staunch dogmatism expressed by angry and vocal political activists. With a renewal of fighting between the Arabs and Israelis in the aftermath of the Yom Kippur War, Allen found himself renewing the debate with his father about their Jewish heritage. Louis argued that the Israelis, geographically surrounded by enemies, would perish if they failed to stand up and fight. "It's a question of winning the war," he told Allen, "or another Auschwitz." Allen disagreed with this line of thinking. If the Jewish people accepted such an interpretation of the situation in the Middle East, he told Louis, Israel would be left with no alternative means of finding a peaceful resolution to the war. "It's a case of double bind, both sides absolutely decided on a fixed closed interpretation, of the same situation, each side with a mirror-image horrific interpretation, victory or death," he wrote, pointedly adding that "there should be room left for withdrawal and compromise of reevaluation of phenomenon on both sides. Space is what's needed: 'a new world is only a new mind.' . . . It is perhaps too late to believe otherwise, but both sides have been exacting a self-fulfilling prophecy."

Alarmed by the fighting, Allen decided to write another exorcism poem—this one to expel the "Mid-east battlegods." If there were no gods in the way, he reasoned, anything—any kind of solution—might be permitted. "Jaweh and Allah Battle," a lengthy poem written on January 13, 1974, became Allen's statement of displeasure with the war in the Middle East:

> Both Gods Terrible! Awful Jaweh Allah!
> Both hook-nosed gods, circumcised.

Jaweh Allah which unreal?
Which stronger Illusion?
Which stronger Army?
Which gives most frightening command?
What God maintain egohood in Eden? Which be Nameless?
Which enter Abyss of Light?

The poem, published in the *Los Angeles Times*, is similar in approach to a number of unpublished poems that Ginsberg had written during his college debating days, when he presented point/counterpoint in the context of verse. On this occasion, however, Ginsberg dismissed both point and counterpoint as being unacceptable, damning both sides for rejecting a peaceful, logical solution for all their chest-thumping religious posturing. In holy wars, people would sacrifice the earth in exchange for uncertain heaven.

As one might expect, reaction to the poem was strongly mixed. One letter to the *Los Angeles Times* editor described the poem as an "atrocity . . . hypocritical garbage," while another praised Ginsberg as "a master of relevant social commentary." One angry reader called the poem "balderdash and gobbledegook given respectability," and another wrote that "for those who are willing to go beyond AP and UPI news reports, and deeper than a U.N. debate, 'Jaweh and Allah' has provided us with that opportunity."

Allen could hardly miss the irony of such passionate commentary. In condemning the polarization of the Arab nations and Israel in the Middle East and dismissing the two seemingly incompatible gods, Allen had set up a forum by which the polarization could be made explicitly clear, the debate in the newspapers only serving to prove his point.

2

The highlight of Allen's spring reading tour was a seminar held in Grand Forks, North Dakota. Billed as "City Lights in North Dakota," the seminar was a reunion of seven poets who two decades earlier had been the heart of the San Francisco Poetry Renaissance. Allen, Peter, Michael McClure, Gary Snyder, Lawrence Ferlinghetti, Gregory Corso, and Kenneth Rexroth gathered together for the first time since those San Francisco days, read their poetry and participated in "open mike" discussions with students at the University of North Dakota. The poets' main message was unchanged—by now standard fare: Humans had polluted the earth and divided its people through wars and greed, and unless strong measures were employed to reverse the course of modern history, the planet's existence was in jeopardy. Noting that all the poets held strong political opinions, Allen attempted to explain the connection between their early literary and political ambitions:

> The function of poetry, as we saw it then, I think individually, was a kind of prophetic thing: we were registering our natural insights for the rest of the folk outside who had not yet broken through to understand that the American forms that we were living in were just limited

little local movie forms, that there was a vaster universe outside, that America was not going to last forever, in fact it was just coming on the edge of a big wakening of the fact of death, of long range death for the "American Century" that was advertised in the 40s and 50s, and that we have to find another way of life for ourselves personally, and as poets maybe even try and prophesy another way of life for America.

The evolution of the counterculture, from Beats to hippies, had sprung from these ideals. The counterculture had failed, said Rexroth, because its members did not recognize the strength of the forces it was battling. "The Beats and the flower children didn't realize that social balance was a question of power," he declared. "They didn't have anybody who was willing to deal with power."

Allen, on the other hand, was not prepared to concede total defeat even if he did agree with Rexroth in principle. These groups, he argued, had made their impact felt. Said Ginsberg: "The insights we had into war, sexual and racial discrimination and the prophecy of a police state are all available to the middle class now. The insights we're getting from Watergate came from 1964–1968."

And before: That much was evident when Allen read "Howl" on the final evening of the conference. After nearly twenty years in the public light, the poem still carried great impact.

That spring, Allen received fabulous, if not long-overdue, news when *The Fall of America* was awarded the National Book Award for poetry. Ginsberg's name was added to an especially impressive list of that year's winners, which included Adrienne Rich, Isaac Bashevis Singer, and, for his controversial, apocalyptic novel, *Gravity's Rainbow*, Thomas Pynchon. Allen was out of town when the awards ceremony commenced on April 18, but he was not about to pass up the opportunity to deliver a message to distinguished collegues and, by extension, the literary world. He prepared a statement that was read by Peter Orlovsky. That his book had won the prize was further proof of its prophetic nature, Ginsberg wrote, launching into an attack of what he called "an aggressive hypocrisy that has damaged the very planet's chance of survival":

> The materialist brutality we have forced on ourselves & world is irrevocably visible in dictatorships our government has established thru South and Central America, including deliberate wreckage of Chilean democracy. From Greece to Persia we have established police states, and throughout Indochina wreaked criminal mass murder on millions, subsidized opium dealing, destroyed land itself, imposed military tyranny both openly & secretly in Cambodia, Vietnam, & Thailand.

If the message seemed familiar to those who had followed Ginsberg's career, it was nevertheless one of his most vitriolic statements to date—especially when set, as it was, in the context of what were customarily speeches of acceptance and gratitude. Peter, wearing a handmade T-shirt citing the casualty figures of the Vietnam War, read the statement with the force with which Allen intended it. He continued to read Allen's words despite some audience disapproval. "We have all contributed to this debacle with our oppression and self-righteousness, including myself. There is no longer any hope of the Salvation of America proclaimed by Jack Kerouac and others of our Beat Generation, aware and howling, weeping and singing Kaddish for the nation decades ago, 'rejected yet confessing out the soul.' All we have to work from now is the vast empty quiet space of our own consciousness. AH! AH! AH!"

Regardless of how unhappy he was with U.S. government leaders or pessimistic about the country's future, Allen never totally closed himself off from the system. He thrived in playing the role of ageless gadfly. In Washington, D.C., where he gave an April 29 reading with Ishmael Reed at the Library of Congress, Allen derided the police-state tactics in the United States and suggested that he might be subjected to "jail, torture, death, and other romantic hideousness" for speaking out against the country's leadership. He further stated that he would like to gather a million people around the White House for a massive meditation session that would make government officials aware of meditation in such a way as to prompt "an examination of their own aggressions." For all he had been through in the past decade, he was losing none of his sense of political theater.

He was, however, equally determined to find self-sufficiency in a form that was independent of government, society, and the dictates of modern living. Gary Snyder had built a home in the California Sierras about twenty miles from Nevada City and Allen had subsequently purchased a tract of land across a meadow from him. When his spring reading tour came to an end, he, Peter, and Denise set out for this area, where they intended to build a West Coast retreat for themselves and other poets. The exhausting work tested Allen's skill and endurance. He was not naturally dexterous with tools and he knew virtually nothing about the process of building a house. In addition, the land, a site for gold mines in the 1800s, was now overrun with oak trees and ponderosa pine. Paths had to be cut through the brush to make enough room for a truck to deliver lumber, rocks, and supplies. There was no electricity, so all work was done by hand.

Fortunately, Allen had plenty of help. Gary Snyder was on hand to assist with the labor and offer expertise, as were a number of long-haired Buddhist carpenters who seemed to thrive on the work. Peter Orlovsky, always handy at the Cherry Valley farm, was especially useful in helping to create its California counterpart. Working naked for long hours, he shouldered an immense work load. "Peter labors all day long, digging and skinning trees, and has astonished everyone here with his endurance and solidity," Allen wrote. "The local woodsman carpenter Buddhist hippies never saw anyone so fanatically working as Orlovsky. I don't think the place would get done if he weren't around to open the earth and move rocks."

Allen received on-the-job training. He learned how to use axes, hammers, drawknives, and drills; he was taught how to mix concrete with the gravel they found in nearby abandoned mines. At night, after a hard day's labor, he slept under the stars in a nearby circle of ponderosa pine. He described the work in a July 10 letter/poem to his father:

> Hard work for me potbellied city-lax,
> Pushing wheelbarrows empty up hill, shoveling red dirt
> into a sieve, shaking out fine Mexican-red dust,

lifting iron spoons full of clay into flat-bed jeep,
mixing gravel from old gold mines with measures
    of grey concrete
with red clay dust, to color kitchen floor, then
watering hardened concrete with hose so it won't crack
And logs, draw knives strip bark, chisels
    smooth and branch-boles
tumbling round posts over lock over on a bed of two
    pine laid parallel,
helping dig foot deep holes for porch stone foundation
all work done in a month—then unseasonable rain—
days under apartment—high ponderosa's dripping water
onto lean-to roofed with black and white plastic rolls,
sleepingbags muddy wet at dawn, squirrels scampering
    away from our apples,
deer at Gary Snyder's pond-edge in garden. . . .

Allen was pleased by his ability to handle the work and watch a foundation and then the beginnings of the three-room cabin appear. However, building such a place was not accomplished without considerable expense, and though he had set aside money for construction of the building, he soon found himself running out of financial resources and having to consider the sale of more of his papers to Columbia University to keep the project afloat.

3

Allen's work on the house was interrupted for a couple of weeks in late July and early August when he traveled to Boulder to give readings and conduct workshops at Naropa. The school was faring well, boasting two thousand students at its last session. Trungpa hoped to encourage the formation of a Buddhist poetry center in Boulder, and shortly before Allen was to leave Naropa and return to California, he asked Ginsberg and several others, including Anne Waldman, to help him found a poetics school at Naropa. Allen favored the proposal, but his initial impulse was to avoid becoming too personally involved. He was not certain that the appeal of organizing the school was not to his ego rather than to his teaching instincts, and he was already bogged down by a busy schedule as it was. Allen was living in an apartment with Anne Waldman during his stay in Colorado and he consulted with her about Trungpa's idea.

Waldman was similarly reluctant to become so heavily involved. In talking about his visions for the poetics school, Trungpa had spoken of it as "a hundred-year project," meaning that its continued development would be generations in the making, outlasting all of the school's founders. Waldman, who had been working for the St. Mark's Poetry Project in New York since 1966, did not relish the thought of becoming an integral part of another ambitious, large-scale production. Nevertheless, she and Allen researched the possibilities for such a school. They talked to avant-garde musician John Cage about his involvement in the Black Mountain school in the fifties and with Jackson

MacLow and several others who were in Boulder that summer. All approved of Trungpa's proposal. Before long, lists were being drawn up and plans made.

The poetics school's name—Jack Kerouac School of Disembodied Poetics—came about in a rather playful way. In discussing the nature of the school, Ginsberg and Waldman had conceived of unusual, informal names for the school's different chairs, such as the Emily Dickinson Chair of Silent Scribbling and the Frank O'Hara Chair of Deep Gossip. For the name of the school itself, Waldman preferred Gertrude Stein School, but Allen felt that Jack Kerouac, with the spirit of spontaneous composition present in his landmark work *Mexico City Blues*, better represented what Trungpa had in mind for the school. Waldman initially suggested Jack Kerouac School of Poetics and then amended it to Jack Kerouac School of Disembodied Poetics, *disembodied* being a humorous reference to Kerouac's not being around to guide the school. As Allen later noted, neither he nor the others truly recognized how serious the school would turn out to be. The naming of the school after Kerouac was both a tribute and an irony.

"It seemed attractive and honorable and charming," recalled Ginsberg, "to found an academy in the name of Jack Kerouac, who died shunned by Academy, and to join the American tradition of awkward, first thought, eager, stumbling, blissful desire for some innocent utterance that would open the gates of Heaven, which was Kerouac's version of beatific for Beat, to the more ancient practiced tradition of spontaneous utterance historically echoed from Milarepa to Trungpa."

Never one to labor halfheartedly on a project to which he was committed, Allen applied himself to working with the others on the intricacies of the school's curriculum. The program was designed to afford students the opportunity to work very closely with teachers on all aspects of poetry writing. Beside classes, there would be weekly readings and apprenticeship programs in which students would work on transcribing teachers' journals and notes, the latter to show how raw materials were developed into publishable poetry. As codirector (with Waldman) of the school, Allen would be adding still another home base of operations to the list that already included New York City and Cherry Valley. "I'll probably spend more time in Boulder and around Rocky Mountains in far future, running a poetry school from distance and in residence a few months of the year," he wrote Louis of his plans. As he saw it, he would spend his summers in Boulder, participating in its annual seminars, and the rest of his time elsewhere.

His association with Anne Waldman led to the publication of another book. By summer 1974, Allen had compiled a large sheaf of blues lyrics, some fully developed and many fragmentary, which he felt were of strong enough character to publish. These works, he realized, were not a part of the poetry canon he had been assembling over the years at City Lights, but he wanted to see them in print in any event. If nothing else, *First Book of Blues* (later changed to *First Blues*) represented an honest, if imperfect, look at his spontaneous song composition. He turned a manuscript of the lyrics and lead sheets over to Waldman's Full Court Press for 1975 publication.

There were other writing projects, as well. *The Visions of the Great Rememberer*, Ginsberg's notes on Kerouac's *Visions of Cody*, was published in 1974, as was *Allen Verbatim*, an anthology of his 1971 to 1972 lectures and interviews recorded and edited by Gordon Ball. In addition, City Lights was issuing the American edition of *Iron Horse*, and Grey Fox Press was reprinting in small book form Allen's 1972 interview with *Gay Sunshine*. In the wake of the National Book Award, the Ginsberg name was as much in demand as ever, and while he could have easily obtained a lucrative contract with a large publishing house, Allen remained loyal to the small presses that continued to publish some of the most daring and innovative work on the market.

4

Allen resumed work on his cabin as soon as he had completed his obligations in Colorado. For the next six weeks, he lived in the woods and watched the cabin, little more than a frame when he had departed for Boulder, as it was transformed into living quarters. Insulation and plumbing were installed, a porch and sun deck finished. Allen purchased an old wood stove for the kitchen, and by the end of September he was helping with the hanging of doors and windows. "It's so beautiful that I hope you'll be able to come out here next spring and stay a while," Allen wrote his father in a letter as descriptive as a tourist brochure. For all the years he had lived in large cities, caught up in the frantic pace of daily living, Allen was clearly in his element in the rustic California Sierras, surrounded by green pine and red-tinged brush and mossy boulders that reminded him of the Forest of Arden.

Nevertheless, the cabin could serve only as a place for temporary retreat, for Ginsberg's main duties were still connected to the life of a public figure. By early October, he was back in San Francisco, taking part in the October 7 Dharma Festival, which included readings by Michael McClure, Robert Duncan, Anne Waldman, David Meltzer, and Joanne Kyger. Much of the talk that fall was about the resignation of Richard Nixon and the immediate future of the country under the leadership of Gerald Ford. Although he was happy to see Nixon out of office, Allen was skeptical of the prospects for any significant improvement under the new administration. Ford, Allen noted, had been Nixon's vice president and a supporter of the war in Vietnam, and Nelson Rockefeller, Ford's new vice president, was as much a part of the Nixon mindset as anyone. "I don't think much has been gained at all," Allen said of the change. "It's the states themselves and the people that are guilty, not just Nixon, because they elected him knowingly and accept Ford knowingly. There's been no reversal of basic energy and military destructiveness."

Allen spent several weeks in the Bay Area, giving readings, visiting friends, and frequenting the area's night spots. One evening, while sitting with Anne Waldman in a San Francisco nightclub, he pulled out his notebook and began a poem of startling candor:

> I want to be known as the most brilliant man in America
> Introduced to Gyalwa Karmapa heir of the Whispered
>   Transmission Crazy Wisdom Practice Lineage
> as the secret young wise man who visited him and winked
>   anonymously decade ago in Gangtok
> Prepared the way for Dharma in America without mentioning
>   Dharma . . .

Even as he wrote, Allen was uncomfortable with the obvious egotism of the poem, which seemed so hypocritical, so "politically unwise" that he declined to show his scribblings to Waldman once he asked to see what he was writing. His Buddhist refuge vows centered on the breakdown of the ego, but "Ego Confession," as he eventually entitled the poem, is the kind of bold proclamation that anyone but the most egotistical artist would have had the good sense to keep to himself. On the other hand, Allen was excited by the risk he was taking, not unlike the way he was excited by the chances he took when writing "Howl." The poem is naked thought, unadorned and embarrassing.

It is also honest, however. In making such a confession public, Ginsberg was offering himself up for ridicule and scorn, thereby puncturing his ego in the process of exposing it. It was an interesting experiment. Almost everyone had secret fantasies about being someone they were not, of being famous or wealthy or influential or loved by millions. The poem, then, represents an archetypal fantasy that, coming from a famous person, has a humorous quality.

It also put Ginsberg in touch with his own egotism—an important-enough exercise in itself. Ever since the days of his youth, he had aspired to be famous and respected, and much of his adult life had found him battling to keep his ego under control. Obviously, this was a healthy undertaking, but ego denial had its own damaging side effects, especially for a person who spent a good portion of his life trying to come to terms with his own self-image. In this light, "Ego Confession" provides one image lost in Ginsberg's *Empty Mirror* period. He had always been aware of his intelligence—and, in later years, influence— but it was crucial that he place his ambitions in the context of that intelligence and influence. "Ego Confession" became that exercise.

Allen's return to New York was greeted by a harrowing experience. On November 2, only a few days after his return, he was mugged by several youths who accosted him as he walked down the sidewalk near his apartment. In recent years, the Lower East Side had deteriorated into an urban war zone, complete with abandoned or burned-out buildings and menacing groups of youths gathered on the streets at all times of day and night. Drug use was rampant and neighborhood apartments were frequently broken into by addicts hoping to find something they could pawn for drug money. Fortunately for Allen, thieves and robbers did not realize the value of the books, papers, and manuscripts stored in his apartment, and on those occasions when his place was broken into, these invaluable texts were overlooked.

The mugging happened at dusk. Although it was early November, the weather was warm and humid, and Allen was lost in his thoughts as he walked along the glass-littered pavement of East Tenth Street. He had with him his shoulder bag containing his journal, address book, calendar, and other papers. All along his route, he saw young people, most of them products of impoverished black and Hispanic neighborhood families, huddled on the stoops or leaning against old rusty automobiles. Suddenly, a youth rushed up from behind him and applied a stranglehold to his neck while another tripped him. Terrified of what might happen next, he began to chant "OM AH HŪM" to calm himself and his attackers, the chant a Trikaya mantra of body, speech, and mind. As he was dragged into an abandoned, burned-out storefront, Allen removed his glasses and placed them on a step. He was taken to the building's basement, where a third youth was waiting.

"Where's the money?" they demanded, not content with the seventy dollars they found in his wallet.

"OM AH HŪM," Allen answered. "There isn't any."

Allen continued to chant while the youths rifled through his wallet and searched him further for money.

"Shut up or we'll murder you," they told him. The chanting, Allen later noted, "didn't stop 'em enough." One youth checked Allen's socks for hidden money and another stripped him of his wristwatch. Then, as suddenly as they had appeared, they were gone, leaving Allen on a dirty floor covered with old newspapers, cardboard, and dead cockroaches, his "shoulder bag with 10,000 dollars full of poetry" left behind on the basement floor.

The incident gave Allen occasion to look at his neighborhood in a new light. It occurred to him that he had lived in his apartment building for a decade but did not know anyone living more than a half a block away. People all around him lived in fear, in squalid conditions that stood in stark contrast to the peaceful environment of his places in Cherry Valley or the California Sierras.

Allen recorded the details of the mugging in a poem that he sold to *The New York Times* for five hundred dollars—a substantial increase over the money he had lost in the mugging. The poem, "Mugging," was eventually published in *Mind Breaths*, its placement immediately following "Ego Confession" providing an ironic juxtaposition that readers could not miss.

5

The passing of time and Ginsberg's elevation to high stature in the poetry community did not guarantee his work an open audience. All across the United States, his poetry continued to generate controversy, debate, hostility, and, in some cases, censorship. Such negative reaction was not limited to Ginsberg poetry collections or public appearances; on many occasions, it was aimed at textbooks in which his poems were reprinted. Allen took special interest in these cases. By denying students the opportunity to read works that were already recognized for their literary excellence, educators were depriving young minds of the chance to experience one element of American culture. Allen could not abide this and he occasionally found himself in dispute with would-be censors throughout the country.

One widely publicized censorship battle took place in Kanawha County, West Virginia, near the end of 1974. The controversy began when the county's board of education ruled that a large selection of controversial textbooks—over three hundred in all—could be used or made available in the public schools. In Charleston, protesters, claiming the books to be antireligious and anti-American, organized demonstrations and marches. People refused to permit their children to attend classes and wildcat strikes were held in coal mines, the area's main industry. Schools were firebombed, school buses fired upon by snipers. Angry rhetoric bordered on the hysterical: "I would rather see my daughter in the funeral home, in God's hands," said one minister, "than in five years have my daughter stab me in the back because of the books." "They will have to lock up everybody in Kanawha County before we stop this battle," vowed a housewife who refused to allow her two daughters to attend classes.

The texts in question contained works by Ginsberg, Ferlinghetti, Eldridge Cleaver, LeRoi Jones, Malcolm X, Jean-Paul Sartre, and many others. Much of the "objectionable" material addressed issues of racial or ethnic origin—as required by West Virginia law—but opponents felt the material was immoral and being forced upon their children. Religious groups from other states promised to send busloads of protesters to West Virginia to join the battle and offer moral support.

When notified of the controversy, Allen took an understated approach.

"I'm flattered," he told reporters. "I was of the opinion that nobody cared about poetry anymore. It says a lot for the penetrating power of the poems that they draw such a violent reaction."

Allen proposed that those who judged his work to be sacrilegious or anti-Christian were not reading his poetry closely enough, and he supplied his address to anyone who wished to communicate with him on the matter. Using characteristic patience and tact, he expressed sympathy for the protesters working in the mines. The open-form poetry in the textbooks, he allowed, might appear to these workers to be the product of poets living an easy, soft existence. Had the students in the area, he wondered, read Appalachian literature and folklore? "I'd be willing for them to forego reading 'Howl' if they could read literature of their own region and appreciate the music of the area they live in," Allen said, pointing out the intensity of the protest would, in all likelihood, drive the students to read the forbidden poets on their own.

It was difficult to criticize Ginsberg's approach to the controversy. In taking a calm, reasonable stance in addressing the issue, he became the voice of rationality, a strong contrast to the senseless, irrational acts of violence served up by those who claimed to be acting on God's behalf. To those who found it objectionable, "Howl" might have seemed like the expression of outrage by a poet who, like the other best minds of his generation, was about to be destroyed by madness, but when Allen defended his work the way he did, he appeared to be more sane than those who wished to suppress his work or lock him up.

6

Allen had originally set aside the first month of the new year for a meditation retreat, but his schedule would not permit it. He needed to prepare introductory essays for *First Blues* and *The Chicago Trial Testimony*, the latter an unedited transcript of his testimony in the Chicago Conspiracy Trial slated to be published by City Lights. In addition, he was working with translators on the French editions of *Kaddish* and *Indian Journals*; reading David Dellinger's book for the purpose of writing a promotional blurb; beginning the editing of his 1965 Cuba and Czechoslovakia journals; and preparing a statement on behalf of Timothy Leary, who was still ensnared in a web of legal difficulties. He did manage to see Chögyam Trungpa and attend a series of his tantra lectures while he was in New York, but the month-long retreat was out of the question.

Complicating matters was an infection of the gums that was serious enough to prompt a brief jaunt to Washington, D.C., to see a specialist. True to form, Allen worried obsessively about the procedure, which involved the removal of two teeth and the cutting and scraping of his gums. "My own skeleton being taken apart and changed 'forever,' " he noted in his journal, into which he wrote long and graphic descriptions of the procedure, as if to test his own squeamishness. To make matters worse, immediately after the periodontal work, Allen was bedridden for three days with the flu, touching off another period of rumination about his lost youth.

If he needed someone or some event to kick him out of the doldrums, he found it in late January while listening to Bob Dylan's new recording, *Blood on the Tracks*. After completing an enormously successful comeback tour with The Band in 1974, Dylan had returned to the recording studio and laid down tracks for what was without question his best album in years. Allen was awed by what he heard. Dylan's lyrics and vocal phrasing were in top form, as fresh and gripping and courageous as any of the Dylan songs Ginsberg had heard. Allen was particularly impressed with "Idiot Wind," Dylan's excoriating attack on hypocrisy and mindless stupidity. "His genius intuition's become scientific art," Allen gushed in a lengthy journal entry that examined the song line by line. Dylan had beaten Ginsberg at his own game: He had found a way to introduce elements of meditation into his music. This was what Allen hoped to accomplish in his poetry, and he had to congratulate Dylan for showing him a practical way of doing it. "What an unexpected victory for Dylan and the generations whose consciousness he carries forward into common sense," he wrote. "I want to see the words written out on the page, in stanzas, divided by pauses and breaths, into dependent droop'd symmetries."

Another old friend of enormous influence in early 1975 was Bill Burroughs, who had returned to the United States the preceding autumn to begin the teaching job that Allen had lined up for him. Burroughs had given a limited number of readings that fall and decided that he enjoyed them. His routines, delivered in his dry, sardonic tone, held enormous appeal for college students who were just discovering his works and found it difficult to believe that the author of such wicked satire was this tall, aging, frail-looking gentleman dressed in Brooks Brothers suits. The incongruity made the routines all the more hilarious. Eager to perform with Burroughs, Allen arranged for a number of joint appearances in the Chicago area for March 9–14, and he was delighted by the way they turned out. "First time we ever read together, after all these decades, oddly," Allen commented of the readings in a letter to Philip Whalen. "What a gas pleasure—with a fine sound-system at Northwestern he sounded like the voice of God, nuanced with a dozen separate characters."

On April 17, Allen and Burroughs, along with Gregory Corso and Peter Orlovsky, made a group appearance at Columbia University's McMillin Theatre. Advertised as "Another Night at Columbia" in reference to Diana Trilling's essay about the 1959 Ginsberg/Orlovsky/Corso reading, the evening was for the benefit of Naropa Institute. An audience of twelve hundred, including members of Allen's family, listened as he read what he described as "the best poems I've written since I was here last," including "Kral Majales," "Wales Visitation," a portion of "Wichita Vortex Sutra," "Please Master," "On Neal's Ashes," and, representing his most recent work, "Ego Confession." The festive atmosphere resounded like a Beat Generation reunion.

Two days later, Allen was in Florida to take part in the symposium "Energy and Consciousness." With Gary Snyder and Michael McClure in attendance during the week-long series of lectures, readings, and informal gatherings, there was a similar sense of reunion for Allen, although with such authorities as nuclear physicist Henry Gomburg and environmentalist Howard T. Odum on hand, he received as much information as he provided. From there, he was off to Montreal for another symposium, this one on the counterculture. In his lecture, an abbreviated history lesson, Allen offered the background of the counterculture as it evolved from the friendships established in the 1940s at Columbia University, through the Beat Generation, to the Flower Power movement of the 1960s. He spoke of how the war in Vietnam and the energy crisis had necessitated the development of a countercultural movement, and he outlined how police and FBI infiltration of leftist groups had led to aggression and paranoia. In years to come, he would develop speeches of this nature into his "Literary History of the Beat Generation" college lectures.

Allen's hectic schedule began to catch up with him. For months he had been fighting off a series of physical maladies, including bad headaches, viral infections, and bronchitis, and by early May he was physically exhausted and feeling poorly. Another attack of Bell's palsy landed him in the hospital for a two-week stay. While doctors put him through a variety of tests and treated him with numerous medications, Allen brooded about his physical state. He was only a few weeks from his forty-ninth birthday and it was clear his body was starting to betray him. He read everything he could find about the nature of Bell's palsy, taking copious notes in his journal and worrying about what he discovered. For instance, the partial paralysis and loss of taste associated with the disease could be permanent. Depressed, Allen wrote a series of angry poems about his declining health and what he perceived to be the main illnesses of the nation, as if the two were somehow inextricably connected. Looking out his hospital window, he wrote a strong new poem that was in a way an extension of what he was trying to accomplish in "Mind Breaths," this newer poem set in the urban landscape:

> A gauzy dusk, thin haze like cigarette smoke
> ribboned past the silver plate fins of Chrysler Building
> tapering delicately needletopped, Empire State's
> taller antenna filmed milky lit amid blocks
> black and white apartmenting veil'd sky over Manhattan,
> offices new built dark colored in blueish heaven . . .

The use of external detail, seen and imagined by one trapped in a hospital bed, makes the universe seem all the larger. By mentioning the details of his illness later in the poem, Ginsberg effectively contrasts his temporal existence with the more eternal setting of the New York skyline. Over the years, he had written a number of poems from the vantage point of his own bed, but rarely with such success. As he was discovering, youthful ponderings of the questions of mortality and eternity seemed almost fatuous later in life when one's health was deteriorating and the questions were even more direct.

7

The summer session at Naropa featured such guest speakers, readers, and lecturers as William S. Burroughs, Gregory Corso, Diane Di Prima, Ed Sanders, Ted Berrigan, John Ashbery, Peter Orlovsky, and Philip Whalen. Ginsberg and Anne Waldman had worked diligently to organize the session and it paid off with a large attendance and weeks of lively discussion. Allen delivered a series of lectures on objectivist poets. He proved to be an excellent lecturer, well versed in twentieth-century poetry history and well prepared to provide concrete examples of the poets and topics he addressed. For all the criticism he directed toward academics over the decades, Allen was as comfortable in the classroom as Lionel Trilling, Mark Van Doren, or, more similar in teaching style, Raymond Weaver. Allen could be very demanding of his students but he was also known and highly regarded for his patience.

Throughout his stay in Boulder, Allen worked on the expansion and shaping of the poetics program. The visiting writers had plenty of suggestions of their own, all duly noted and considered by Ginsberg and Waldman. The school's unusual nature made the development of curriculum challenging. Guest lecturers for summer sessions were relatively easy to find, but securing a distinguished full-time faculty—Naropa's ultimate goal—was more difficult. Most of Allen's friends were as nomadic as he, and getting them to commit to even a year-long program took some convincing. Nevertheless, by the end of the summer Allen was able to leave Naropa with the knowledge that the school was heading in the right direction.

During that summer, Allen began a serious personal study of nuclear energy, an issue that would be of continuing interest in years to come. The Rockwell Corporation had a facility that built triggers for hydrogen bombs in nearby Rocky Flats. In August, along with poet W. S. Merwin and others, he toured the plant. Armed with his notebook and pen, he made voluminous notes on what he observed and what he heard from the plant's tour guide. He filled pages of his journal with information on how plutonium was used and reprocessed, how it was transported, the safety measures being used to prevent accidents and disaster, and its measures of efficiency when used to produce energy. The more he heard, the more questions he had; pat or evasive answers only raised his suspicions. By the time he had completed his tour of the facility, he vowed to conduct his own research into the topic.

Allen closed out the summer by spending several weeks at Trungpa's Rocky Mountain Dharma Center in Livermore, Colorado. He was given a small cabin in which to meditate and do his prostrations. It was a mixed blessing for him. The hours of solitude were restful, but there were times when he had difficulty harnessing his physical and mental energy. Meditation required a kind of inner discipline that he had yet to master.

25

Rolling Thunder Stones, Father Death Blues

Genius Death   your art is done
Lover Death your body's gone
Father Death   I'm coming home. . . .

1

Allen had been back in New York for only a short time when he received a telephone call from Bob Dylan, who offered a very compelling proposal: Would Allen like to join him as a performing member of his upcoming tour?

Dylan's tour figured to be unlike any in recent history. The success of *Blood on the Tracks*, combined with a sellout national tour in 1974, had restored Dylan to his rightful place near the top of the recording industry. One of the most prolific songwriters in the business, he had another album's worth of music to present to the public. "Hurricane," his latest offering for single release, was his most pointed protest song in years. Dylan was eager to hit the road again, but this time instead of playing large arenas, which he'd had no trouble packing on his previous tour, he wanted to play small theaters and halls, thus restoring the sense of intimacy between musician and audience that had been missing in his concerts since his early days of playing folk clubs in New York.

As it was, the idea for the tour had originated in the Greenwich Village clubs during the summer of 1975. Dylan had attended a number of concerts in these clubs and had on occasion joined such artists as Muddy Waters, Bobby Neuwirth, and Ramblin' Jack Elliott onstage. The usually reclusive Dylan discovered that he again enjoyed playing in these smaller venues, and he starting talking to others about the idea of assembling a troupe of musicians for a tour of New England. According to Dylan's plan, the group would be a sort of wandering minstrel show, moving from town to town and showing up unannounced to play for whoever would come to listen. Since any Dylan appearance was certain to attract a lot of attention and, therefore, a large crowd, the tour would have to be conducted in great secrecy. Not even the musicians would know where they would be playing next.

This was by no means a new concept. Major recording artists spoke often about their desire to escape the demands of their touring schedules. In 1967, the Beatles, influenced by Ken Kesey's Psychedelic Tour, had attempted in their Magical Mystery Tour to accomplish much of what Dylan was now proposing, though the Beatles were more interested in making a film than taking their show on the road. A few years later, Joe Cocker had taken a large entourage of musicians on the road in his Mad Dogs and Englishmen Tour, though most of his shows were played in larger halls. The Dylan tour would be a sort of combination of the two ideas.

Dylan called his entourage the Rolling Thunder Revue, and though his initial plans were small in scale, the tour soon developed into one of the most ambitious enterprises in music history. At first, Dylan planned to set out with a tour bus, a minimal number of musicians, a couple of additional spotlight performers (such as Joan Baez and Ramblin' Jack Elliott), and a small road crew. Guest performers would be added as they went along, depending upon who was available and willing to appear in the areas where they were playing. However, when rumor of the project began to make the rounds in music circles, Dylan was approached by a number of others eager to join the group. The list of singers expanded to include Bobby Neuwirth, ex–Byrds leader Roger McGuinn, and singer/actress Ronee Blakley; guitarists Mick Ronson and Steve Soles joined a core band consisting of bassist Rob Stoner, drummer Howie Wyeth, percussionist Luther Rix, violinist Scarlet Rivera, and nineteen-year-old wunderkind David Mansfield on mandolin, Dobro, and steel guitar. Each member of the group seemed to have suggestions about other worthy members to add to the group—Allen suggested Peter Orlovsky, Denise Mercedes, and Anne Waldman—and before long the Rolling Thunder Revue had taken on the size and dimension of a full-scale theater company.

To a great extent, it was just that. Dylan originally intended to make a concert film of the performances, but with the addition of so many talented people, he decided to go even further. Beside showing the musicians onstage, the movie would feature members of the entourage playing ficticious characters in improvisational skits. This meant adding film technicians and more equipment handlers to the entourage. People were hired to print handbills and make posters, handle living arrangements, and oversee security. Lou Kemp, a friend of Dylan's from his boyhood days in Minnesota, was appointed tour manager, and Jacques Levy, who had cowritten a number of Dylan's most recent songs, including "Hurricane," assisted with the stage direction. By the time the Rolling Thunder Revue was finally ready to take its act on the road, it had over seventy members—an enormous number by that day's standard.

With so many performers, the shows by nature were going to be long. Each singer would be given his or her turn onstage. The extravaganza would feature Dylan performing a selection of songs to be included on *Desire*, his forthcoming album, as well as an assortment of his standards. That alone would have been considered worth the price of admission, but with all the others performing in a carnival-like environment, the Rolling Thunder Revue had the potential of being America's most interesting musical spectacle in many years.

Allen would not have dreamed of refusing Dylan's invitation.

2

Even after talking with Dylan about the Rolling Thunder Revue, Allen was unclear about what his role would be. He had sung a few of his newer blues songs over the phone to Dylan, but the tour had already enlisted the talents of so many vocalists, it was unlikely that another singer would be welcome. In addition, the revue had its own writer: Dylan had appointed playwright Sam Shepard the position of official scriptwriter for the film scenes of the tour.

"What do you want of me?" Allen asked Dylan of his role in the tour. "What's your fantasy, your idea?"

Dylan remained elusive. "Well, it's up to you to decide," he said. "You're the King. Whatever you want to do, get it together. I'm presenting you. It's about time. This country has been asleep. It's time it woke up."

Dylan's remarks were anything but patronizing. His admiration of Ginsberg dated back to his youth and he was pleased with Allen's venture into spontaneous blues. ("Your songs have everything, they are understandable at every level," he told Allen a short time later at a party at his home.) Dylan was impressed with Allen's energy level, which seemed to be contagious. When he referred to Allen as the "King," he was offering a compliment, and when he asked him to join the tour, it was because he wanted others to enjoy Ginsberg's work as much as he had. "You haven't found your kingdom," he told Allen, "but you've always been the King."

Allen had ideas to spare. He figured that when he was onstage, he could read poetry, sing as a background vocalist, or chant a mantra. For the filming done away from the stage, his ideas were more unusual, if not downright eccentric. He and Dylan could sleep together, with a film crew capturing their waking conversation. They could recreate the landing of the *Mayflower*, with Pilgrims chanting "AH," Allen's Buddhist mantra, as they stepped off the ship and discovered themselves to be American. The film, Allen believed, should have a sense of thematic unity, but it was not important that it have a linear plot. There could be a meditation scene with Trungpa and Burroughs, a shot of Dylan teaching Allen how to play guitar; they could film a scene of Dylan and Allen talking about God, or Dylan and LeRoi Jones talking about blacks and whites working together. Allen could read from a Sacco and Vanzetti speech, or Dylan's wife, Sara, could appear in a scene as a mother goddess. The whole revue could pose naked by a swimming pool in a kind of family portrait. Anything was possible! The film, Allen decided, should address such serious topics as the ecology, capitalism, communism, God, poetry, meditation, and America, with the different cast members talking freely about their opinions concerning LSD, marijuana, and sexual liberation.

Ginsberg had strong reasons for these and other ideas. Dylan had always credited the Beats—and particularly Jack Kerouac—as being major influences on his poetry, just as Dylan was now regarded as a major influence on countless poets and songwriters of the sixties. The film, then, could act in many capacities—as the documentation of a tour, a biography of its leader, an entertainment focusing on the question of individual identity versus perceived identity, and a history of cultural lineage begun by the Beats and carried through by their progeny. The film could be as enigmatic as Dylan's music, with all of its emotional impact.

The film got off to a forgettable start. During the initial filming, cameramen were to shoot from an apartment balcony, catching Allen as he stood on Eighth Street and read his poetry, but the scene in the apartment was too chaotic for any kind of work. As Sam Shepard recalled in *Rolling Thunder Logbook*, his published memoir of the tour, the apartment seemed to be "exploding with crazies," with virtually everyone in the place high on marijuana or some other substance. Folksinger Phil Ochs huddled with Dylan and tried unsuccessfully to explain the story line of the film *Hard Times*. T-Bone Burnett, scheduled to appear in another scene to be shot later and costumed to look like a professional golfer (right down to the cap and golf bag), tried to line up putts on the apartment's Persian carpeting. Down in the street, Ginsberg kept shouting that he was ready to begin, but no one seemed to be paying any attention. "We haven't even left town yet," Shepard wrote in dismay.

The revue rehearsed for several days, and when their buses finally left New York for the open road on October 27, bound for Plymouth, Massachusetts, they were ready to play—literally and figuratively. The first scheduled performance was for October 30. With several days to spare, there was more time for rehearsal and spontaneous filming before the tour officially began, and Dylan decided to rehearse in front of a live audience. He chose the Seacrest, a hotel in the resort town of Falmouth, as the location for the show.

If they had tried, they could not have arranged a more unlikely scene. Late October was off-season for the resort, and the only people in the hotel beside the Dylan entourage were a couple hundred elderly Jewish women taking part in a mah-jongg tournament. One can only imagine their thoughts when late one evening a camera crew arrived in the hotel lounge with Dylan and his group, or when the hotel manager stood to announce in his best lounge-act, master-of-ceremonies style that the ladies were about to be treated to a special reading by "one of America's foremost poets, Mr. Allen Ginsberg." In his brown suit and neatly trimmed beard, sitting on a tall stool and leaning into the microphone on the podium, Allen looked respectable enough. He told his audience that he would be reading a poem entitled "Kaddish," a work dedicated to his mother, and the women offered encouraging smiles. Movie cameras caught their reactions as Allen worked his way through the poem, the women giggling in embarrassment on occasion, gasping in disgust on others, deeply moved at still other times. The atmosphere in the room was tense and emotional—"close to being volcanic," as Shepard described it—the women listening to this contemporary poet, somehow both reverent and irreverent, as he read a work based upon one of the most sacred Jewish prayers. When Allen completed his reading of the long poem, the people in the lounge rewarded him with a respectful burst of applause.

Joan Baez followed with an a cappella rendition of "Swing Low, Sweet Chariot," and David Mansfield continued the evening with a short recital on his violin. When Mansfield had finished, Dylan, who had been sitting off to the side of the room throughout the evening, walked onto the stage, took a seat at an old beat-up upright piano, and launched into a foot-stomping version of "Simple Twist of Fate." His band gathered around him and joined in, and before long, as Shepard wrote, "every molecule of air in the place [was] bursting":

> This is Dylan's true magic. Leave aside his lyrical genius for a second and just watch the transformation of energy which he carries. Only a few minutes ago the place was deathly thick with tension and embarrassment, and now he's blown the top right off it. He's infused the room with life-giving excitement. It's not the kind of energy that drives people off the deep end but the kind that brings courage and hope and above all brings life pounding into the foreground. If he can do it here, in the dead of winter, at an off-season seaside resort full of menopause, then it's no wonder he can rock the nation.

Allen, too, saw Dylan as a leader and guru, a person capable of affecting spiritual change in a nation preparing to celebrate its bicentennial. "Dylan somewhat in position of Trungpa," he wrote, "handling his peers very lightly and carefully and trying to pull it all together into something wholesome and 'American'—Alchemical Transformation."

Ginsberg was well aware of the lineage and tradition that were being further enhanced by the tour. A quarter of a century earlier, Jack Kerouac had sought to find the heart of America in his long scroll of *On the Road*; a century before that, Whitman had celebrated his country's spirit in *Leaves of Grass*. It was no accident that the Rolling Thunder Revue closed each of its performances with a sing-along version of Woody Guthrie's anthem "This Land Is Your Land." At a time when American businesses were scrambling to find ways to cash in on the country's two hundredth birthday, the Rolling Thunder Revue offered its own subtle statement.

3

To rediscover America, the traveling minstrel show returned to Plymouth, where it all began. On a replica of the *Mayflower*, Ramblin' Jack Elliott scaled the rigging until he reached the top of the mizzenmast, while Allen, standing on the ship's deck with Dylan, announced, "We have, once again, embarked on a voyage to reclaim America." At Plymouth Rock, the film crew tried to capture a scene in which Dylan, Elliott, Bobby Neuwirth, and Peter Orlovsky landed a dinghy on the beach and "discovered" Allen sitting on Plymouth Rock. Filming the scene proved to be problematic. The group on the dinghy, shivering from the cold, had to drag the boat to the beach to avoid being swept out to sea. Meanwhile, Allen found it impossible to get beyond the iron cage that protected the historic rock—little more than a tip of granite sticking out of the sand—from being vandalized. Tourists stared at Allen as he sat in the lotus position in front of the commemorative plaque, chanting and playing finger cymbals.

"We're landing on a clean place," Allen recorded in his journal. "Nothin' but gentle rednecks all around. Think we can get along with them? Think they'll like us if we sing and sigh AH?"

Later that evening, as they waited to go onstage for their rehearsal performance, Allen had a telling conversation with Dylan. He noted it in his journal:

GINSBERG: Well, how do you like your party?

DYLAN: It's *your* party, it's not mine.

GINSBERG: Well, is it giving you pleasure?

DYLAN: Pleasure? Pleasure? No, not at all. I wouldn't want that, would you? That's too dangerous. I do what I do without thinking of pleasure.

GINSBERG: When did you come to that state?

DYLAN: Couple years back. I mean, at one time I went out for a lot of pleasure—all I could get because, see, there was a lot of pain before that. But I found that the more pleasure I got, subtly there was as much pain, and I began to notice a correspondence, the same frame. I began to experiment and saw it was a balance. So now I do what I do without wanting pleasure . . . or pain. Everything in moderation.

GINSBERG: Remember what the Lama told me in '63: "If you see something horrible, don't cling to it. If you see anything beautiful, don't cling to it." What about love, then?

DYLAN: Well, it depends on whatcha mean [by] love. It has all kinds of meanings.

GINSBERG: Yeah. Okay, no problem. But what about other polarities? Do you believe in God?

DYLAN: God? you mean *God*? Yes, I do. I mean, I know because where I am I get the contact with—it's a certain vibration—in the midst of—you know, I've been up on the mountain, and—yes, I've been up on the mountain and I had a choice. Should I come down? So I came down. God said, "Okay, you've been up on the mountain, now you go down. You're on your own, free. Check in later, but now you're on your own. Other business to do, so check in sometime . . . later."

GINSBERG: I *used* to believe in God.

DYLAN: You don't now?

GINSBERG: No, I *used* to believe in God.

DYLAN: Well, I used to believe in God, too. Yes, I *used* to believe in God. If you believed in God now you'd write better poetry now. I mean, there's no question I didn't get any answers. He's too busy to answer—I understand that. Making elephants. Anyone who can make camels go through needles' eyes is too busy to answer my questions. I'm on my own.

GINSBERG: Did you study Kabala?

DYLAN: Well, yeah, but it's complicated, and not satisfactory.

GINSBERG: Any good teachers?

DYLAN: Yeah, lots of teachers, but . . .

GINSBERG: So, you said the other day you had your own practice. What is it?

DYLAN: Oh, I'm not going to give away any secrets, be sure. I'll cover for God, I'll alibi for God anytime. I'll cover for him. Sure, absolutely! You don't want me to give him away, do you?

GINSBERG: Well then, how do you get on the mountain? Or where does the road to the mountain begin?

DYLAN: Oh, I can't tell you that, but I can take you there. I promise I'll take you there! You wanna go?

GINSBERG: [singing quote from "Mr. Tambourine Man"] "I'll come following you. . . ."

At first glance, this fragment of conversation might seem insignificant, perhaps no more than a brief, almost glib exchange between two wordsmiths playing with ideas. Both Ginsberg and Dylan had used plenty of biblical allusion in their respective works, so their talking about God is of no surprise, and since both had been cast in (largely self-made) prophetic leadership roles, it is similarly unsurprising that Dylan would make remarks about going up the mountain. Neither Ginsberg nor Dylan, even in their most egotistical moments, would have been foolish enough to compare themselves openly to Moses, yet both were familiar with the weight of the tablets of truth that they were expected to deliver to their followers. Ginsberg had sought refuge in Buddhism, but Dylan, as evident in this conversation, was still searching. In telling Dylan that he no longer believed in God, Ginsberg was goading him for a response.

In saying that he had received no answers from God, that he was on his own, Dylan was echoing John Lennon, who only a few years earlier in his song "God" had proclaimed that he no longer believed in anything but himself, that he had to find the answer to life's questions from within, that religious and government leaders—the traditional figures of authority and direction—had proven themselves to be a disappointment. One had to discover the world through one's self. However, that self, particularly in the case of artists such as Dylan or Ginsberg, could be deceiving and mercurial. It could drive an artist to great work—or despair. It was best, then, not to take the self too seriously. During the Rolling Thunder tour, musicians occasionally turned up onstage in masks or disguises—Dylan often appeared with his face painted white—to alter, conceal, or distort identity, to playfully take on other roles. Cultural icons shed their skins and presented new identities to their disciples.

To Ginsberg, this symbolic forsaking of ego was enormously important. If the fifties and sixties had proved anything, it was that the world was constantly changing and that humans were bound to suffer in this existence. He had addressed the issue in "Gospel Noble Truths," a recent song devoted to the basic Buddhist truths of change, suffering, and egolessness—all mentioned in the song's first stanza:

> Born in this world
> You got to suffer
> Everything changes
> You got no soul

In an interview with Peter Chowka for *New Age Journal*, Ginsberg explained that the stanza represented "suffering, change/transiency, and *anatma* or no permanent essential identity, meaning, in a sense, non-theism, or non-self-ism. It's a description of the nature of things, by their very nature. It might knock out Krishna and Joya and God and some notions of Christ and some notions of Buddha. It may not necessarily knock out devotion or the quality of devotion, though."

Ginsberg saw a number of Buddhist qualities in Dylan, even if his friend was reluctant to grasp Buddhism formally. In their conversation, Dylan had spoken of the futility of pursuing pleasure, and of its relationship to pain. Kerouac had made similar observations twenty-five years earlier when he was beginning his studies of Buddhism. In addition, Dylan seemed to recognize the importance of not becoming too attached to one's self, of pursuing an egoless existence. When Chowka mentioned, in framing a question, that Ginsberg knew Dylan well, Allen made a special point of correcting him: "I don't know him because I don't think there is any him, I don't think he's got a self!"

To Ginsberg, his conversation with Dylan caught one of the main themes of the Rolling Thunder Revue tour. Dylan, who had at one time taken on all the weight—and benefit—of celebrity, was now more easygoing, much more willing to stand in the background and let others step into the spotlight. He could be a "player," even if he and everyone else around him knew that he was the star of the show.

A short time after their conversation, Allen wrote a song addressed to Dylan, which was rooted in their discussion:

Lay down	Lay down yr mountain	Lay down God
Lay down	Lay down your music	Love lay down
Lay down	Lay down yr hatred	Lay yrself down
Lay down	Lay down your nation	Lay your foot on the rock . . .

4

The Rolling Thunder Revue staged its first shows in Plymouth and North Dartmouth, Massachusetts, Allen's role limited to playing finger cymbals and singing in the chorus during the show's finale, "This Land Is Your Land." To his disappointment, his suggestion about leading the audience in mantra chanting was scratched from the performances, which already ran for more than three hours per show. However, his role in the film was more pronounced, finding him featured in a number of its key scenes. He was an integral part of the scenes depicting the tour itself and he was featured in many of the improvised skits. In one such scene, he played a wizard opposite Ramblin' Jack Elliott's cowboy; in another, he acted the role of an emperor opposite Dylan, who played an alchemist.

On November 2, the ensemble made its appearance in Lowell, Jack Kerouac's hometown. Both Ginsberg and Dylan had been anticipating this particular show. Upon his arrival in town, Allen went immediately to Nick's Lounge, owned by Kerouac's brothers-in-law, Nick and Tony Sampas. A Polaroid picture of Kerouac, taken a month before his death, still occupied a place on the bar's wall. Tony Sampas volunteered to drive Allen and Sam Shepard to Kerouac's grave. On the way to the cemetery, he pulled out a tape recorder and turned it on. "This thing was recorded at the bar," he explained. "I don't think anyone outside the family's heard it."

Suddenly, the station wagon was filled with the sound of Kerouac's voice, going on in a drunken stream-of-consciousness monologue, occasionally breaking into song. Allen listened to the tape and smiled. Even in his final days, when sobriety was rare, Jack had a better command of the sound, rhythm, and nuances of the American language than most of the country's poets, and despite media accounts portraying him to be an embittered, lost middle-aged man, Jack still showed signs of spirit and humor.

The next day, Allen, Peter, Shepard, and Dylan, along with film and sound crews, made a formal visitation to Kerouac's burial place. A small marble plaque, already settling in the earth, marked his place of rest: TI JEAN: JOHN L. KEROUAC, MARCH 12, 1922–OCT. 21, 1969, HE HONORED LIFE. All around, trees were bare, their leaves fallen and scattered about the cemetery, some coming to rest on Kerouac's gravestone, as if in memorial to Jack's favorite season. Allen remembered Jack by quoting several of Kerouac's favorite lines from Shakespeare: "How like a winter hath my absence been/ . . . What freezings have I felt, what dark days seen! What old December's bareness everywhere!" The film crew recorded the scene. Allen and Dylan sat cross-legged before the plaque, Allen reciting a few lines from Mexico City Blues. Dylan played a wordless tune on Allen's harmonium, then he and Allen improvised a slow twelve-bar blues, Dylan playing guitar as the two exchanged improvised stanzas about how Kerouac was now up in the clouds, looking down on these pilgrims as they made up a song in his memory. At one point, Dylan quit playing long enough to lift a leaf from the grass and place it in his breast pocket, Allen singing a cappella during the pause. As Allen would recall, it was one of the loveliest moments of the tour. The song, like the words characterizing Kerouac on his gravestone, honored a life now gone.

While in Lowell, they visited a number of other sites of Kerouac's childhood and writing, Allen delighted to be showing Dylan some of the origins of their mutual influence. They saw Jack's birthplace and the high school he attended, the public library and St. Jean Baptiste Church. They visited the Catholic Grotto, site of the Stations of the Cross scene in Doctor Sax. In another poignant moment, preserved by the film crew, Dylan stood beneath a large stone crucifix and, looking up at the figure on the cross, thought aloud, "What can you do for a guy like that?" What was it like, he wondered, to be up there?

Allen was taken by the scene. "There was this brilliant, funny situation of Dylan talking to Christ, addressing this life-size statue of Christ, and allowing himself to be photographed with Christ," he remembered. "It was like Dylan humorously playing with the dreadful potential of his own mythological imagery, unafraid and confronting it, trying to deal with it in a sensible way. That seemed to be characteristic of the tour: that Dylan was willing to shoulder the burden of the myth laid on him, or that he himself created, or the composite creation of himself and the nation, and use it as a workable situation."

The scene in the Lowell grotto underscored Dylan's discomfort with some of the myths associated with his name. "It used to be my life was very simple," he told Jim Jerome in one of his rare interviews during the tour. "It consisted of hanging around with a certain crowd and writing songs. . . . I tried to get rid of the burden of the Bob Dylan myth for a long time, because it is a burden. Just ask anybody who is considered a star. There are certain advantages and rewards to it, but you're thinking: 'Shit, man, I'm only me.' You know, that's who I am. We are all the same. No one is on any higher level than anybody else. We've all got it within us for whatever we want to grasp for."

Dylan's statement goes far in explaining the nature of the Ginsberg/Dylan friendship that so many Ginsberg detractors have had such a difficult time understanding. To his harshest critics, Ginsberg had no business standing onstage and singing his or anyone else's work. He was too old for that kind of behavior, said the cynics; he looked more like a Dylan groupie than a peer. There was no denying Ginsberg's influence on Dylan's poetry, but as far as these critics were concerned, there was something unfathomable about their relationship.

The problem here was one of preconception—of the media's inability to see beyond what was obvious on the surface. The Ginsberg/Dylan friendship extended beyond their mutual artistic influence. Dylan admired Ginsberg's ability to handle his celebrity. Over the years, Allen had undergone numerous personal and artistic changes in public, and he had been regarded as a cultural guru, but he had always been able to maintain his energy and sense of humanity.

Conversely, Ginsberg admired Dylan's ability to guard his privacy. Dylan had been a public figure for over a decade and had gone through nearly as many personal and artistic changes during that period as Allen had, but he was always able to keep a portion of his life for himself. Through his music, he had given a fragment of his life to the public, but not so much that he would pay Kerouac's dear price for celebrity.

From Lowell, the Rolling Thunder Revue moved on to Providence, Rhode Island, where Allen participated in an Indian sunrise ceremony. Ramblin' Jack Elliott had mentioned to Dylan that he had a friend, Chief Rolling Thunder, who was a Cherokee medicine man living on a reservation in Nevada. Intrigued by the name, Dylan had Chief Rolling Thunder, his wife, and an assistant flown to Rhode Island. Just before dawn on November 5, a small group of about twenty people, including Allen, Dylan, and Chief Rolling Thunder, gathered at an out-of-the-way location on Rhode Island Sound. The medicine man built a fire and asked the group to form a circle around it. Each person was given tobacco to throw into the fire. As the ceremony was performed, Chief Rolling Thunder spoke of the significance of the sunrise, how it stood for the renewal of spirit and as a symbol of the Great Spirit's generosity, and he invited the participants to say prayers.

Allen was to read a poem to conclude the ceremony. Accompanying himself with a set of Australian aboriginal song sticks, he improvised a poem:

> When Music was needed Music sounded
> When a Ceremony was needed a Teacher appeared
> When Students were needed Telephones rang.
> When Cars were needed Wheels rolled in
> When a Place was needed a Mansion appeared
> When a fire was needed Wood appeared . . .

It was this sort of gathering—a convening of spirits—that made the Rolling Thunder Revue so compelling to Allen. Rock tours were infamous for their excesses, for egos run amok in one-night stands hazed over by unfamiliar rooms, drugs, strange faces in packed concert halls, sex, and enough hero worship to turn anyone's head. While the Dylan tour saw its share of excessiveness—some of the drug use, especially of cocaine, bothered Allen—the overall feeling of community was an unexpected development that Allen truly cherished. The revue even had its own daily newsletter that was distributed among its members. Allen had not felt such a warm communal feeling in a long time, and it was apparent that others felt the same way. During the early stages of the tour, he told one reporter:

> This tour may not end as all others have. There is some desire among us to have a kind of permanent community and Dylan is stepping very, very slowly to find out if that can work. Recordings would be one way and there may be other ways. One must proceed slowly and soberly— unlike the Beatles when they tried to expand their sense of community. Remember John Lennon trying to put together that whole Apple enterprise as a sort of umbrella organization for all kinds of collective work? But he didn't have the right personnel and so it wasn't done soberly and practically enough. This would be. Keep watching. The thing is to keep the Rolling Thunder spirit alive.

Although this was all wishful thinking on Allen's part, typical of the poet who was forever attempting to bring people together and form a community, there was no denying that the prevailing goodwill made the tour phenomenal in the music industry. Guest musicians added a sense of serendipity to a tour that was already fueled by improvisation. As the Rolling Thunder Revue worked its way through New England, visiting such locales as Springfield, Massachusetts, Burlington, Vermont, Durham, New Hampshire, New Haven, Connecticut, and onward, the regular musicians were joined onstage by Joni Mitchell, Arlo Guthrie, Robbie Robertson, and a host of others, each guest adding his or her signature to a performance.

By mid-November, the group was in upstate New York, engaged in a series of concerts near Niagara Falls and Rochester. They visited the Tuscarora Indian Reservation, where Dylan, his friends, and a group of Native American musicians on the reservation gathered and traded songs in an impromptu songfest. Their hosts prepared a meal of corn soup, venison, and corn bread, and Allen was again asked to improvise a poem, which he modeled after a Zen prayer of thanksgiving:

> We give thanks for this food, deer meat & indian-corn soup
> Which is a product of the labor of your people
> And the suffering of other forms of life
> And which we promise to transform into friendly song and
>   dancing
> To all ten directions of the Earth.

Throughout the tour, Allen made numerous journal notations addressing the feeling of renewal that was almost palpable both onstage and off. So inspired was he by their spirit that he made a note to "rewrite Howl with positive redemption catalogue," the new version to open with "I saw the best minds of my generation turned on by music. . . ."

Dylan's new poems, Allen was convinced, were the songs of redemption, the Rolling Thunder Revue a combining of poetic muses—"dance, history, theater, poetics and music"—into a physical and spiritual celebration that encompassed the visions of all the American poets. To Allen, Dylan was an alchemist, taking American thought and speech and turning them into gold. "The tour has been a poetic vision," he wrote his father. "What is amazing about the theater is the enunciation of vowels and syllables in rhythmic progression by Dylan, who seems to me to be epitomizing all the American poets from Poe thru Vachel Lindsay thru the poetry-jazz experimenters of a decade ago. He's able to stand up and chant/recite/sing intricately regularly rhymed irregular-lined narrative poems to continuous drumbeats and instrumental background, making a combination of music and poetry, with emphasis on the words that maybe hasn't been performed as theater since the Greeks."

Allen expanded upon these thoughts in a lengthy essay written and used as liner notes for *Desire*, Dylan's next recording:

> Dylan's Redemption Songs! If he can do it we can do it, America can do it. "It's all right Ma I can make it." Yes! with tough gold metal compassion, he's giving away Gold again—but remember, good Anarchists, "To live outside the Law you must be honest." Drunken aggressive beer bottles'll never redeem anybody—But clear conscious song can, every syllable pronounced, every consonant sneered out with lips risen over teeth to pronounce them exactly to a T in microphone, snarled out NOT for bummer ego put-downs but instead for egoless enunciation of exact phrasings so everyone can hear intelligence— which is only your own heart Dear.

Ginsberg had once written that death was a letter that was never sent. Dylan and the Rolling Thunder Revue were delivering another letter, this one of hope, and while it was arriving a little later, it bore a message that the country, nearly two centuries old, needed almost desperately to hear.

5

On December 8, 1975, Dylan and company rolled into New York City for a sold-out Madison Square Garden concert billed as "The Night of the Hurricane," a benefit performance staged to raise money needed for Rubin "Hurricane" Carter's appeal of a murder conviction that Dylan believed was a miscarriage of justice. "Hurricane," Dylan's account of the Carter arrest and conviction, had been issued in November, and by the time the Rolling Thunder Revue gathered on the New York sports arena's stage, Carter's conviction had become a topic of debate from coast to coast.

Hurricane Carter had been a promising middleweight boxer who, many fight experts believed, had a fair chance of capturing the World Championship title. All that changed on June 17, 1966, when two black men entered a Paterson, New Jersey, tavern and murdered the bartender and two customers. Carter and a friend, John Artis, were seen later that night in a car that supposedly matched an eyewitness's description of the getaway vehicle. They were questioned but not formally charged. However, four months later, two small-time burglars told police that they had seen Carter and Artis running out of the bar at the time of the murder.

Carter and Artis maintained their innocence during their trial for the triple murder, to no avail; they were convicted and given life sentences. Carter, however, would not be silenced. He continued to insist that he had been framed. His claim gained credibility in 1974, when the two prosecution witnesses told a *New York Times* reporter and a New Jersey investigator that they had lied in their testimony in exchange for police assistance in their own criminal cases. Based on this new evidence, the case was appealed, but it had yet to be reviewed at the time of the concert in Madison Square Garden.

Dylan's song, no doubt, helped push things along. Carter had sent Dylan a copy of his autobiography, *The Sixteenth Round*. Moved by Carter's story, Dylan responded with some of his most biting lyrics in a decade. Carter, wrote Dylan, was "an innocent man in a living hell," framed by a wrongheaded, hypocritical system in which some of the worst criminals were those wearing suits and drinking martinis. Dylan was not alone in his defense of the boxer. Other celebrities spoke out on Carter's behalf and a trust fund was established to help with his appeal. On November 6, the New Jersey Supreme Court announced that it would review Carter's case "on an accelerated basis."

The night before the New York benefit concert, the Rolling Thunder Revue performed before two hundred inmates, including Carter, at the New Jersey State Prison in Clinton. Allen and the others had the opportunity to meet and talk with Carter backstage, where a group portrait, minus Dylan, was taken. Allen kicked off the show at the prison with a brief poetry reading. He was followed by Dylan and the Revue, who had Joni Mitchell and Roberta Flack on hand as guest singers.

The Night of the Hurricane was an enormous success, raising $100,000 for the Hurricane Trust Fund. Allen had secured tickets for his father and stepmother, and Louis and Edith Ginsberg's first rock concert was a marathon four-hour affair. Former heavyweight champion Muhammad Ali gave a short speech, joking that he was amazed that someone other than himself was capable of packing Madison Square Garden. "This Bob Dylan must be something," he said, to a rousing ovation. Noting the largely white audience, Ali grew serious. "Now I just want to say that it's a pleasure to see such a turnout here tonight, especially when it's for the cause of a black man in jail. 'Cause everyone knows that you got the complexion and the connections to get the protection."

It was vintage Ali, using humor, charisma, and theatrics to gain attention, then sneaking in poignant messages. When Ali finished speaking, Rubin Carter spoke to the audience by telephone, his voice sounding over the arena's speakers. Informing the assembly that he was speaking to them from the bowels of the penitentiary, Carter thanked everyone for coming together on his behalf.

Doing so, he told them, was truly a revolutionary act. "I thank you from my heart, I love you all madly," he said.

The event reminded Allen of a similar occasion a few years earlier, when he and John Lennon had traveled to Ann Arbor to give a performance for John Sinclair's benefit. Once again, rock 'n' roll proved itself to possess considerable political force. The show itself was a tour de force, full of sparkling moments: Dylan, face painted white, whirling and stomping across the stage, as energetic as he had ever been in concert; Joan Baez running onstage dressed in an outfit identical to Dylan's; strong performances by Joni Mitchell, Roberta Flack, and Richie Havens.

However, for all the money and publicity it raised, the concert did not produce immediate results comparable to the Sinclair benefit in Michigan. The Carter appeal would drag on for years.

6

Although the Rolling Thunder Revue would schedule an additional extended national tour to begin in January 1976, the Madison Square Garden concert marked the end of Allen's full-time involvement with the group. Several days after the New York show, Louis Ginsberg fell very ill and had to be hospitalized. Louis was now eighty years old, and though he had shown admirable stamina and cheer in recent years when reading poetry with Allen and doing some traveling of his own, his health had been declining. This latest setback was serious: Louis had spots on his lungs and a tumor of the pancreas.

Allen spent the rest of December and the following month in Paterson, assisting with his father's care. Weakened by illness, Louis was no longer able to take the walks he enjoyed, or even handle some of the simple tasks he'd taken for granted since childhood. He needed help in and out of the bathtub and his armchair, and he was often too tired to so much as take off his shoes and socks. Peter, with all his experience working in hospitals, was exceptionally helpful and tender to Louis during these hard times. "Don't ever get old," Louis told him, saddened and embarrassed by his inability to look after himself.

Age was not entirely the issue. It was apparent to Allen that his father was dying, that he was standing at the "Gates of Ages," instructing his family on the final human passage. Allen had spent much of his life preoccupied with the questions of aging and death, but his youth and good health had spared him their darkest fears. Others—friends and relatives—had passed away, but it took Louis's failing health to bring the issue to Allen on a most intimate basis. He was about to turn fifty; his youth was long gone. Now, seeing Louis "too tired to be heroic," his stomach swollen while the rest of him was gaunt and feeble, his skin hanging off his bones, Allen faced the brutal questions about mortality:

> Will that happen to me?
> Of course, it'll happen to thee.
>
> Will my arms whither away?
> Yes yr arm hair will turn grey. . . .

For the two poets, father and son, there were questions of life's purpose and meaning. What did life mean when it came to an end? Did a human being, body and soul, leave a mark? What, if anything, lay ahead? In his illness, Louis grew bleakly realistic, almost cynical. Allen read him poetry to cheer him, but when he read Wordsworth's "Intimations of Immortality," Louis scoffed at the lines "trailing clouds of glory do we come/from God, who is our home." They were beautiful lines, Louis allowed, but they were not true. There were no guarantees that there was a God waiting for him in eternity, Louis said, and he was not inclined to believe in him, even on his deathbed. To illustrate his point, he reached back to his youth for a story. When he had been a boy in Newark, he told Allen, his family had lived in a house that had a large backyard bordered by bushes and tall trees. It was very beautiful. Louis had always wondered what lay beyond those shrubs and trees, but he was not permitted to go past the yard. Later, when he was older, he walked around the block to see what was behind the lot. To his disappointment, he found only a glue factory. Somehow, this betrayal of expectation seemed to be an appropriate metaphor for what he was going through now.

The story was troublesome but true enough. Late one evening, Allen took a walk around the scenes of his own youth, only to be depressed by what he saw. "All downtown changed, ghostly and empty streeted," he wrote of the scene in his journal. New buildings and shopping malls had replaced the old stores he remembered from his boyhood days; city blocks had been torn down and rebuilt. His old house was gone, replaced by a shining new plaza. The whole area was a mass of concrete buildings and walkways. Time had changed everything.

In his journal, he wrote a long poem that expressed some of his feelings about his father's impending death and his own questions and fears of dying:

> . . . Will it be Terror?
> or the tender tear'd farewell
> Sweet silence all the future—
> the clang of the red bell?
>
> Peace, lightness, bodiless
> you'll go your way—
> I'll follow after Father—
> I sit by you today.
>
> O how sweet-seeming to look back
> on this living time
> bodies speaking, weeping
> before the dread clock chime.
>
> Hands clasping, aged and thin
> voices talk or groan
> in modern rooms, television
> till light fades, gone

from the body—tongue and eye
gleam and weep, moon
No more to see you question
calm, where your life has gone.

Beginning in late January, Allen left Louis in Peter's care for several weeks while he traveled to Brussels and Paris on business. Under normal circumstances, he would have looked forward to the trip, but in his present state of mind, everything seemed gloomy, changed for the worse. He wandered past the old familiar places, remembering the time he had lived in Paris almost two decades earlier, but the memories failed to bolster his spirits. The Hotel Git-le-Coeur had been remodeled, but Allen did not bother to go inside and take a look. Other places had closed down. He was still approached by male prostitutes, he told his father, trying to sound cheerful, so some things never changed. Still, as he noted in his journal, nothing in the city seemed real: "Paris is a mirage, poetry is a mirage, I am a mirage. That's the reason dawn is white and empty. We are all mirage. Eighteen years gone and nothing to show for it but memories of love, poetry books, Paris grey buildings, Guru dreams, subway tickets cancelled, cigaret hunger returned, a pain on toe, dollars from Washington, toothless survivors gay, young beards and girls with long wool scarves in Bistro windows."

Upon his return to the States, he tried to put his life back in order. Although Louis was terminally ill, it did not appear likely that he would die in the near future, and while he would have preferred to stay with his father, Allen had commitments to honor. He was beginning to compile poems to include in his next City Lights volume and he was overseeing the editing and publication of *Journals Early Fifties Early Sixties*, another book of journal entries. In addition, he had a limited reading schedule lined up, he hoped to join the Rolling Thunder Revue for at least a portion of its national tour, and he had to visit Naropa, presently embroiled in nasty gossip generated by a fall 1975 confrontation between Chögyam Trungpa and poet W. S. Merwin.

There was one other bit of unpleasant business that Allen would have preferred to avoid. *Go*, John Clellon Holmes's early novel about Ginsberg, Kerouac, and the early Beat Generation days, was being brought back into print, and Holmes had asked Allen to write a preface for the new edition. The original edition had been published before Allen had made his name or anyone knew of his poetry. At the time, he had judged the book to be hyperbolic, the work of a young novelist who had overwritten his subject in an effort to establish credentials as a serious literary prose stylist. Allen had been embarrassed by the way he was portrayed in the novel, although he conceded that this embarrassment might have been more a matter of his own difficult memories and self-perception than Holmes misrepresenting him. Still, upon rereading the book in 1976, Allen found his opinion of the work unchanged, and though he still considered Holmes a dear friend, he ultimately had to refuse to write the preface. It was just too difficult.

7

Allen arrived in Boulder the last week of March 1976 prepared to teach a short course on poet Charles Reznikoff. A recent mountain blizzard had buried the city in snow, and from the vantage point of the windows in his room at the Hotel Boulderado, he could look out over the Flatirons and see the wondrous sight of the pine trees on the mountains, covered and glistening with snow. He found it an ideal setting for work and meditation.

He enjoyed teaching the course on Reznikoff. He had always admired the Russian objectivist poet's work, and in preparing his lecture notes and examining Reznikoff's poems on a line-by-line basis, his appreciation grew even more. Like Williams, Reznikoff had touched upon the universal human experience in his works, and many of his poems reminded Allen of the stories he had heard about his own Russian ancestors. "I get more and more moved by his simplicity," Allen wrote Louis in early April. "The short life-stories he tells are just like Abe and Anna, Abe and Arthur, and your laundry horse stories, in detail. I must read you a dozen pages when I get back. I think you'll like it."

While in Boulder, Allen busied himself with the planning of Naropa's curriculum for the months ahead and with writing grant applications for the school, which was in dire need of funds. He spent a lot of time on the telephone with Timothy Leary, Leary's attorneys, and members of PEN—all in an effort to compose an official statement demanding Leary's release from a federal prison in San Diego. To his displeasure, the work load prohibited him from keeping up with the prostrations that were part of his meditation discipline.

As soon as he completed his teaching obligations, Allen was back on the road again, zigzagging across the country, dividing his time between caring for his father and giving poetry readings. He caught up with the Rolling Thunder Revue when it performed in Wichita in mid-May. Two weeks later, he appeared onstage at a tribute to Phil Ochs at New York's Felt Forum. Ochs, for over a decade one of the country's most diligent protest singers, had committed suicide earlier in the month. The tribute featured such prominent folksingers as Pete Seeger, Peter Yarrow, Ramblin' Jack Elliott, and some members of the Rolling Thunder Revue. Allen, wearing the same gold lamé suit that Ochs had worn at his 1970 Carnegie Hall concert, played finger cymbals onstage. Despite the stinging, acerbic lyrics of some of his best-known protest songs, Ochs had been a Wolfean romantic, similar to Kerouac, heartbroken by the direction the country had taken, and Allen was saddened by his death.

While in New York, Allen spent a couple days in the recording studio, working on new music. He had reason to be optimistic. He had been very well received while he toured with the Rolling Thunder Revue, and even more encouraging was the response that his book *First Blues* had received from critics. The reception had been generally favorable, with reviewers willing to accept his lyrics as another step in his career. The songs, wrote one critic in a glowing review of the book, were "some of the most enjoyable Ginsberg since his 'Howl' days. In the Fifties, we all chanted along with him. Now he encourages us to sing."

This time, Allen's producer was John Hammond, the esteemed producer who included Bob Dylan and later Bruce Springsteen among his many discoveries. Allen had visited Hammond at his CBS office and had given him tapes of the improvised blues from the Dylan sessions in 1971, his Blake music, and a copy of *First Blues*. Impressed with the music, Hammond offered to work with Allen, and their early June recording sessions yielded eight new songs, which, combined with the three finished songs from the earlier Dylan sessions, comprised enough material for an album. The musicians working on the new recordings included Arthur Russell and Jon Sholle, who had appeared with Ginsberg on the Blake albums; Steven Taylor, a young musician who had played guitar behind Allen's poetry at several readings; and David Mansfield from the Rolling Thunder Revue. Unfortunately for Allen, some of the songs, with their explicit sexual content, were considered offensive by CBS officials, who refused to issue the record. "You've got a good record in you, Ginsberg," one executive told Allen in confidence at a party, "but you're shaking your cock around too much on this one."

Another half-dozen years would pass before Hammond released the recording on his own private label. In the meantime, it would gather dust on the shelf with Allen's second Blake album and the tapes of his spoken poetry.

8

Allen was back in Colorado, participating in the summer session at Naropa, when he received anticipated but dreaded news in the early morning hours of July 8: Louis Ginsberg had died in his sleep. Allen immediately caught a flight to New York. As his plane passed over Lake Michigan, Allen took out his harmonium and composed a slow blues in his father's memory, the words and music arriving at once:

> Hey Father Death, I'm flying home
> Hey poor man, you're all alone
> Hey old daddy, I know where I'm going
>
> Father Death, Don't cry any more
> Mama's there, underneath the floor
> Brother Death, please mind the store. . . .

Louis was laid to rest in a family plot in a cemetery near the Newark airport. Even though his father's death was anything but unexpected, Allen had a difficult time coming to terms with it. Despite their water-and-oil relationship on political issues and decades of bickering about poetry, Allen and Louis had been exceptionally close, especially over the last fifteen or twenty years. One of Louis's favorite puns, guaranteed to produce groans from Allen and others each time he repeated it, was, "How's life? Depends on the liver." Louis had lived his life well, suffering through hardship as nobly and with as much good cheer as could have been expected of anyone, and in his poetry he left a legacy that Allen admired. He would grieve the loss for a long time.

26
Mind Breaths

Homage
to the Gurus, Guru om! Thanks to the teachers
who taught us to breathe,
to watch our minds revolve in emptiness,
to follow the rise & fall of thoughts,
Illusions big as empires flowering &
Vanishing on a breath!

1

It had been years since Allen suffered an extended period of gloom comparable to the dark mood that hung over him for the remainder of 1976 and most of the following year. He tended to avoid the self-pity characteristic of his younger days, but he was nevertheless nagged by periods of self-doubt, irritability, depression, and difficulty with his writing. To a great extent, his father's illness and death contributed to this mood, as did the country's celebration of its bicentennial, which, coinciding with a presidential election year, served as a reminder to Allen of the ways in which the American people and their leaders seemed to wave a lot of flags in lieu of their actually setting out to address and solve America's—and the world's—problems.

His greatest distraction, however, may have been his worry about Naropa. He and Anne Waldman had done an admirable job in establishing the poetics school and overseeing Naropa's summer programs, but just as the poetics school seemed to be about to establish itself as one of the more important writing programs in the nation, Naropa was wracked by a scandal that in the long run—from initial incident to public backlash to resolution—would take years to overcome. It would expose the poetry community at its utter worst and divide its members in a war of words and principles, aggravated by anger, resentment, petty bickering, and general feelings of hostility and ill will. For Ginsberg, it would be one of his strongest tests of diplomacy and loyalty.

Ironically, Allen was nowhere near Naropa when the initial incident took place, nor was he a visible or vocal figure in its immediate aftermath of events.

Poet W. S. Merwin had spent the previous summer (1975) at Naropa as an informal artist in residence. He had delivered a lecture on Dante, given a poetry reading while he was there, and in general become part of the expanding community of poets with ties to Naropa. When he learned of Chögyam Trungpa's three-month Buddhist seminar to be held at the end of the summer at the Eldorado Ski Lodge in Snowmass, Colorado, Merwin and his companion, poet Dana Naone, applied.

Trungpa had reservations about admitting them and, in fact, turned down their initial application. These seminars were intended for advanced students already familiar with Trungpa's teachings and meditation practice. As it was, only a limited number of students could attend the seminar and Trungpa was forced to turn down three out of four applicants. Not only did Merwin and Naone fail to meet Trungpa's qualifications for potential seminar attendants, but they had also applied too late for consideration for the fall session, at a point when the roster of students had already been filled. Merwin persisted in his requests to attend, and though he was not at all pleased about granting preferential treatment to unqualified students while he was rejecting other qualified candidates, Trungpa decided to let Merwin and Naone attend.

There was a potential for problems from the very beginning. "I don't know to what extent they knew what they were getting into," Ginsberg said of Merwin and Naone in a 1979 interview with Tom Clark, "and to what extent, if they knew, they understood it in their hearts. Or to what extent Trungpa knew what he was getting into. Whether his vanity was appealed to, to have them there—or their vanity was appealed to, to go there." The situation, Ginsberg further explained, was risky for all parties concerned. Trungpa risked rejection by a prominent and influential poet, while Merwin and Naone were entering a scenario in which psychological submission was a matter of course and practice. Neither Merwin nor Naone were Tibetan Buddhists, and since they had not attended Trungpa's classes in Vermont or Boulder, neither was prepared for the demands that Trungpa's "wild wisdom" practice could make.

Nor were they inclined to embrace some of Trungpa's teachings and practices once the seminar had begun. They participated in the seminar's activities, but otherwise tended to stay to themselves. Merwin, a pacifist, objected to some of the Buddhist chants to what Ginsberg described as "blood-drinking deities"— the horrific gods symbolic of human passion, aggression, and ignorance—and even though these chants were meant to act as a way of putting the students in touch with their own fears and weaknesses, Merwin could not, in principle, take part in them. He was greatly offended by such lines as "You enjoy drinking the hot blood of ego" and "As night falls, you cut the aorta of the perverters of the teachings," and he refused to chant these and similarly violent lines with the other students. In addition, he and Naone were not willing to enter into Vajrayana Buddhism—a requirement at the end of the second month of study for all who intended to continue—and they met with Trungpa and told him as much.

The opening of the Vajrayana study was to commence at the beginning of November, and to celebrate the opening of the session, Trungpa called for a Halloween party on the evening of October 31. Merwin and Naone attended an early portion of the festivities, but they had left before Trungpa, drunk and dressed in jeans and a lumberjack shirt, arrived at about 10:30. One of the teachings of Vajrayana was the abandonment of privacy, and Trungpa, noting that the beginning of the group's Vajrayana study coincided with Halloween, a traditional time of festive masking, decided that he would strip some of the students as a type of lesson, as a form of baring one's naked self. One of the older students, a woman, was the first to be stripped by Trungpa's guards. Trungpa then removed his own clothing and was paraded, borne on the shoulders of two students, throughout the hall—the teacher naked and unashamed before his students, a human symbol. After he was assisted back into his clothes, Trungpa ordered his guards to strip others in the room.

Noticing that Merwin and Dana Naone were not present at the party, Trungpa dispatched William McKeever, a student, to summon them to the room. There would be a lecture on Vajrayana, he said. Merwin and Naone returned to the doorway of the hall, but seeing what was going on, they decided against having anything to do with the party. Instead of participating in an event they disapproved of, they planned to leave the seminary for the evening and stay overnight in Aspen. Trungpa insisted upon their attendance and sent McKeever back to their room to get them and escort them to the party. Merwin refused. An ugly scene quickly developed. The telephone line to Merwin's room was cut and a number of people began to assemble in the hallway and on the balcony outside the room. It was now clear that Merwin and Dana Naone were trapped in their room and unable to leave as planned. Trungpa insisted that they be brought to the party, forcibly if that was the only way. People kicked at the door, trying to break it down. Fearing for his and Naone's safety, Merwin pushed a large chest of drawers against the door and turned off the lights in the room so they could not be seen by people looking in through the glass doors on the balcony.

The assault continued, the people on the balcony trying to break the glass doors, the crowd in the hallway splintering the wooden door to the room. Merwin grabbed a wine bottle and announced that he would hurt whoever came into the room. The door gave in and Merwin lashed out with the bottle, shattering it and cutting people as they entered the room. He reached for another bottle and broke it on his attackers, as well. Behind him, the group on the balcony beat at the glass door until it, too, gave in. Merwin rushed across the room and tried to fend off the people coming in through the broken glass, but he and Naone were surrounded. Naone shouted that someone should call the police, which only drew laughter from the guards and students in the room.

Merwin held the people at bay with broken bottles until he saw blood on the people he had cut. Giving in, he held out the bottles to his attackers and was immediately subdued, as was Naone, who managed to punch a guard before having her arms pinned behind her. As they were being led from the room, Naone again implored that someone call the police, but to no avail. She was insulted by one of the women in the hallway and a man threw wine in her face.

Trungpa was waiting for them in the hall. He told Merwin that he had heard the poet was making a lot of trouble. He was disappointed, he said, that Merwin and Naone had turned down his invitation to the party. Merwin countered that an invitation, by nature, gave a person the right to decline, but Trungpa was hearing none of that argument. *They* had been the ones who had asked to attend his seminar, he reminded them, and as far as he could see, the only real force used during the confrontation had been Merwin's use of the broken bottles.

As their discussion dragged on, Trungpa became more combative, insulting the two and tossing a glass of sake in Merwin's face. He was particularly upset that Dana Naone, a Hawaiian, did not seem to understand his position. She was, he mentioned, of Oriental heritage and should have been smart enough to see why he felt the way he did. "The Communists ripped off my country," he said in reference to the struggles in Tibet. "Only another Oriental can understand that." He also hinted that he was disappointed she would be seeing a white man.

"You're a Nazi," Dana said in response.

After a while, Trungpa asked Merwin and Naone to take off their clothes and join the festivities. When they refused, he taunted them. Finally, he advised them that he would have them stripped by force if they did not voluntarily remove their clothing. Once again, they refused. Trungpa ordered his guards to do the job. Naone tried to cling to Merwin, but the two were pulled apart. In the ensuing struggle, both tried to get to Trungpa but were blocked by guards, who pinned them to the floor and pulled off their clothes.

"I could see William struggling a few feet away from me," Naone remembered. "I fought and called to friends, men and women, whose faces I saw in the crowd, to call the police. No one did. Only one man, Bill King, broke through to where I was lying at Trungpa's feet, shouting 'Leave her alone' and 'Stop it.' Trungpa rose above me, from his chair, and knocked Bill King down with a punch, swearing at him and ordering that no one interfere. He was dragged away. . . . Richard Assally was stripping me, while others held me down. Trungpa began punching Assally in the head, urging him to do it faster. The rest of my clothes were torn off."

Defeated, the two rose to their feet and stood naked, huddled against each other, before Trungpa and the rest of the partiers. "See? It's not so bad, is it?" Trungpa said. By Trungpa's thinking, the disrobing was symbolic of the exposure of one's neuroses necessary to enter vajra teachings. The sacrifice of ego, even if it involved humiliation, was part of the process. Merwin and Naone, of course, held another view, though both met together with Trungpa the next day and, after much discussion, decided to stay on at the seminary for Trungpa's Vajrayana lectures.

2

In the immediate aftermath of the incident, no one, including Merwin and Naone, offered public comment about what had occurred at the party. By virtue of their initial request to attend the seminar and their subsequent decision to remain at the seminary after the party, Merwin and Naone were perceived to be voluntary, if at times reluctant, participants in Trungpa's brand of crazy wisdom, even if some people questioned the wisdom of his actions on that Halloween evening. Since Buddhism and Trungpa's seminars were of a religious nature, there was also the matter of the separation of church and state to consider—a perplexing issue since Naropa was affiliated, although more as a technicality than as an active association, with the University of Colorado. The confrontation was by no means forgotten, but it was regarded by many as the type of unfortunate incident that could be misinterpreted by those who did not understand Trungpa and his teachings and who were looking for a reason either to persecute the Rinpoche or shut down Naropa. Opponents in the debate lined up, but quietly.

The incident provided plenty of grist for the rumor mill and Allen heard secondhand accounts of it while he was still touring with the Rolling Thunder Revue. The implications and possible repercussions were obvious to him. He considered Merwin a friend and associate, an admirable pacifist in an aggressive world, but he had also accepted Trungpa as his spiritual teacher, a relationship that, in Buddhism, is not regarded lightly. As codirector of Naropa's poetics school, Allen was caught in an especially awkward position, even if he remained silent about the Snowmass affair. He was both a teacher and a student. If he continued to associate himself with Naropa, his actions would imply endorsement of Trungpa's behavior and perhaps jeopardize his credibility among poets. If he offered any public sympathy or support for Merwin, he would be indirectly challenging the principle that, as an inheritor of the Dharma, Trungpa was a lifetime teacher and that his actions were teachings, even when he made a mistake, because mistakes were to be learned from.

Further, there was the threat to the poetics school itself. Eastern thought and religion were not readily embraced in the United States—certainly not by those holding the proverbial purse strings and in a position to hand out urgently needed grant money—and the Snowmass affair could only stand to harm public perception of Buddhism, Naropa, and the relationship between the two. It was unlikely that officials would be willing to supply government-issued grants to an institution that had the tiniest hint of totalitarianism—or, worse, fascism—in its general program, and there was no question that outsiders could judge Trungpa's behavior this way. (In fact, the applied-for grants *were* rejected in the wake of the Snowmass affair, and one can speculate that the incident had a direct bearing on the rejections.)

Allen, by nature, did not trust secondhand accounts, so he was cautious about voicing any opinions regarding the confrontation until he had spoken directly to Merwin and Trungpa. He had seen Merwin in New York in late 1975 and heard his version of the story, and a short time later he had questioned Trungpa about what had taken place. Still, there were no conclusive answers.

Allen managed to remain loyal to Trungpa without having to take an immediate stand on the incident. For much of the last part of the year, he attended the Vajradhatu seminary in Land O'Lakes, Wisconsin, where he spent hours in meditation, trying in his solitude to sort through his thoughts. Trungpa had written a book of poems and asked Ginsberg to write its introduction—a request that Allen, as Trungpa's poetry teacher, was honored to accept. The resulting essay, however, was very weak in comparison to the introductions he had written for his father's selected poems and for Kerouac's *Visions of Cody*. The essay rambled on, lacking clear focus, even as Allen tried to trace and align Trungpa's spiritual and poetic lineage. There were flashes of verbal pyrotechnics—"On Mt. Ida the Muses look up astonished by this bolt of lightning thru blue cloudless sky"—but Ginsberg, ever the promoter, seemed to be reaching too far in trying to find a way to place Trungpa among the pantheon of great poets. It was one matter to admire Trungpa's work—and Ginsberg offered fine analysis of Trungpa's poems, as he had done earlier with his father's—but to mention him in the same breath as Rimbaud, Shelley, Yeats, Hart Crane, Williams, Eliot, and Kerouac, to mention some of the names dropped throughout the essay, was quite a stretch, especially when Allen admitted in his introduction that Trungpa was a novice at writing poetry. "This book," wrote Ginsberg, "is some evidence of a child Buddha taking first verbal steps age 35, in totally other language direction that he spoke age 10, talking side of mouth slang: redneck, hippie, chamber of commerce, good citizen, Oxfordian aesthete slang, like a dream Bodhisattva with thousand eyes & mouths talking turkey."

For all its flaws, the essay reflected another subtle yet significant shift of position and self-perception. The poet, at the mid-century point in his life, was not pleased about his advancing years and the prospects of physical decline, but he was finally growing comfortable with his role as an elder statesman. He enjoyed teaching and using his influence to promote the works of others. No longer the enfant terrible of the Beat Generation or hippie prophet of the 1960s, Allen was accepting his new role with grace. "At one time," he told an interviewer in early 1977, "people kept saying, 'You were identified with the Beat Generation. How come you're active in the '60s, how come you're still around in the '70s?' When you come to high art and poetry generally, there's a development through generations and times and decades. But people assume you do one thing, and that's the end of you. I don't think Beethoven had that problem. It has something to do with pop culture."

Allen had always been aware of the development of poetry over generations of time, and he never neglected to pay tribute to his literary forebears, but now, in his middle years, recognizing that he and some of his friends had become a part of the continuum, he was ready to pass on his knowledge and experience— as well as the knowledge and experience of his colleagues—to others.

In January of 1977, Allen and Jonathan Robbins, a young poet friend, rented an apartment near Johns Hopkins University in Baltimore, where they spent a month visiting Edgar Allan Poe's old haunts and reading poetry, Robbins reading Poe while Allen pored over the complete works of Blake. They visited Poe's tomb in the Westminster Churchyard and his redbrick house at 203 Amity Street. Robbins had a copy of Poe's works with him, and he read a poem aloud in each room of Poe's house. Inspired by Robbins's enthusiasm, Allen sat down on an old cedar chest and scribbled this rhymed homage to Poe:

Reading words aloud from books, till a century has passed
In his house his heirs carouse, till his woes are theirs at last:
So I saw a pale youth trembling, speaking rhymes Poe spoke before,
Till Poe's light rose on the living, and His fire gleamed on the
    floor—

The sitting room lost its cold gloom, I saw these generations burn

With the Beauty he abandoned; in new bodies they return:
To inspire future children 'spite his *Raven*'s "Nevermore"
I have writ this ancient riddle in Poe's house in Baltimore.

Allen's time in Baltimore took his mind off his worries. He argued poetics with Robbins, Allen assuming the role of the bard instructing a young upstart. From their friendship and discussions came "Contest of Bards," Allen's first epic-length poem in years. An oratory patterned after Blake, "Contest of Bards" tells the story of a young poet who visits an aging bard, only to tell him that the master's poetry was no longer interesting and would be replaced by his, the younger poet's, work. However, the elder poet has in his possession an eternal riddle, cut in stone, which the youth seeks to read and understand. It is the riddle of eternal beauty.

On February 23, Allen was pleased to give a joint poetry reading with Robert Lowell at St. Mark's Place in New York. Allen had known Lowell from the days of their mutual protests against the Vietnam War, but they had never read their work together. He recognized Lowell as being one of the most influential poets in the academic community, and he regarded their St. Mark's reading as a moral victory of sorts, a means of bridging the gap between the academics and the open-form poets. "What this means," he told one reporter, "is that people won't be able to attack me so easy anymore because I'm, in a sense, protected by his regard. If he's willing to read on the same platform with me and say I wrote a masterpiece ('Kaddish'), it means I can't be considered a barbarian jerk. Which is what I've been having to listen to year after year."

Allen's words had a ring of truth to them, but they were not entirely accurate. Although he would not have had to expend much time and energy to find critics who looked down on his poetry or lifestyle, he did not need an association with Robert Lowell to legitimize or protect him.

Ironically, if he had a viable concern in terms of damaging, negative criticism, it was more connected to the people generally considered to be in his own camp. The Trungpa-Merwin affair would not go away and Allen could no longer stay publicly neutral in his feelings about it. Faced with the prospects of losing desperately needed grant money in the future, Allen found himself engaged in damage control. Both Naropa and the Jack Kerouac School of Disembodied Poetics were grounded in Buddhism, he admitted, but the school was independent of Trungpa's Buddhist seminaries. Trungpa may have been director of Naropa and his seminaries, but the poetics school had autonomy in its curriculum.

This was true enough in theory and practice, although it hardly excused Allen from the controversy. His position had not changed over the months. As a poet and administrator at the poetics school, he had students, faculty, and other poets to consider; as a student of Trungpa's, he had to consider questions of loyalty to his teacher. In addition, Allen had devoted a lifetime to rebelling against authoritarianism in political principle, yet the spiritual principles of Buddhism were not necessarily libertarian by nature. Buddhism tended to be authoritarian, and some of Trungpa's most vocal detractors, including Robert Bly and Kenneth Rexroth, were calling him a fascist. Allen agonized over the situation, vacillating in his sympathy for Merwin and his loyalty to Trungpa. "Playing all sides of argument at once," he wrote in self-characterization in his journal, "[he] doesn't show his hand, wants to stay out of trouble."

Talk of the Snowmass confrontation was in the air throughout the summer of 1977, even while Allen was at Naropa teaching a course entitled "Literary History of the Beat Generation." Ed Sanders was at the school, moderating a course entitled "Investigative Poetics," and his students had voted to look into the Trungpa-Merwin confrontation as their group project. The Naropa administration could not have been pleased by this decision, but it had little choice but to permit it. Trungpa refused to be interviewed by students trying to recreate the events of that Halloween 1975 evening, but he encouraged others to speak openly and truthfully about what they had witnessed. The class's lengthy report, *The Party: A Chronological Perspective on a Confrontation at a Buddhist Seminary*, was an exhaustive, well-prepared study that adhered to the journalistic standard of objectivity in reporting, though it is likely that most readers—or at least those with little or no knowledge of Buddhist practices—would have agreed that Trungpa did not fare well by the time his actions had been documented by the reporters. Fortunately for Trungpa, Naropa, and others involved, the students elected not to publish the report—at least for the moment.

3

Allen spent late summer and early fall working on two new volumes of poetry. He finalized his work on *Mind Breaths*, his next collection for City Lights, and began assembling a smaller volume, *Poems All Over the Place, Mostly Seventies*, for Cherry Valley Editions, a small press run by poet Charles Plymell, a longtime Ginsberg acquaintance.

Mind Breaths, with its title poem and such works as "Thoughts Sitting Breathing" and "Gospel Nobel Truths," signified Ginsberg's growing involvement in Buddhism and meditation. There were still samplings ("Hadda Be Playing on the Jukebox," "Who Runs America?" "Yes and It's Hopeless") of the kind of political pronouncements typical of his two previous collections, and "Ego Confession," "Jaweh and Allah Battle," and "Contest of Bards" were three works certain to command readers' attention. The sequence "Rolling Thunder Stones" represented the poetry written while he toured with the Rolling Thunder Revue, and "Sad Dust Glories," a sequence written while he was building his cabin in the Sierras, was a worthy homage to Gary Snyder's work poems. In short, the volume was another grab-bag Ginsberg collection, finding Allen checking in with his readers and telling them where he had been over a six-year period.

In some respects, however, *Mind Breaths* was Ginsberg's most contemplative, introspective volume in a long time. "Don't Grow Old," the moving account of Louis Ginsberg's death and Allen's reaction to it, and "Drive All Blames Into One," an account of an embarrassing childhood incident, were excellent samplings of confessional poetry that effectively offset the bluster of "Ego Confession," while the lyrical works at the end of the collection ("I Lay Love on My Knee," "Love Replied") rank among the most tender love poems

Ginsberg had written since his eulogies to Neal Cassady. Such introspective works, along with the meditation poems, seen in the context of the entire volume, balanced the collection and gave readers a glimpse of the very human poet in moments of withdrawal from the more familiar prophetic voice.

Poems All Over the Place, in contrast, was never intended to be a major collection. Cherry Valley Editions was just starting up and needed funds to publish works by Ray Bremser, Herbert Huncke, Janine Pommy Vega, and others, and Allen compiled the collection as a means of raising money for the press. From a historical perspective, the most noteworthy work included in the volume was "The Names," the addendum to "Howl" written while Ginsberg was in Paris, and "Fragment: The Names," a continuation of the work written a few years later. From these poems, one can see how Allen had at one time hoped to extend "Howl" into his own version, perhaps, of "Song of Myself." Other poems in the volume, mostly recent works left out of *Mind Breaths*, included Ginsberg's reflections as he flew to the 1972 Republican National Convention, thoughts recollected from meditation sittings, and a small selection of journal entries.

That fall, Allen's second volume of published journal writings, *Journals Early Fifties Early Sixties*, was issued by Grove Press. For those familiar with Ginsberg's work, the published entries, edited by Gordon Ball, were both interesting and perplexing: Rather than offer the journals kept during his San Francisco days, when he was writing "Howl" and other breakthrough poems, or the entries recorded in Paris and New York, where he was writing "Kaddish" and related compositions, Ginsberg provided selections that depicted him as a poet on the cusp of a great personal epiphany. After opening the book with several entries recorded while he was living with his father and stepmother in Paterson in the early fifties, including recordings of his encounters with William Carlos Williams, Ginsberg takes his readers on his first extended period of travel—to Mexico. These entries make up a large percentage of the book, and one can easily see why. As a general rule, a writer's published journals are viewed as ephemera incidental to the "real" work, but Ginsberg's travel writings rank among some of his best work. His eye for significant detail, coupled with his endless curiosity, make him a natural reporter even if, in the case of the journals, the writings were originally intended for his eyes only. The entries from Mexico compare favorably with the ones published in *Indian Journals*, written nearly a decade later, at a time when Allen had made a name for himself and had matured enormously as an individual. In fact, the other noteworthy period covered in *Journals* is the time leading up to his travels in India and the Orient—the period he spent in New York just before leaving the country and his travels in the Mediterranean—and from these entries we see a poet still on a personal quest for discovery, disenchanted with the United States and looking to the East. The prophetic voice, absent in the early Mexican entries, has now been established, and he is prepared to use it as he travels to Greece, the ancient birthplace of democracy, and Israel, homeland of his Jewish ancestors.

Journals was published in a hardcover edition, marking it as only the third Ginsberg book issued in such a manner. (*Indian Journals* had been issued in a limited number of hardcovers and *Allen Verbatim* had been published in a standard cloth-bound edition.) For years, Allen had complained, with justification, that influential large-circulation newspapers and magazines ignored books that were issued by small presses or that were published as paperback originals, and the reception of *Journals* seems to bear this out. It easily became his most widely reviewed book to date.

The critical response included the usual mixture of opinion. Those who did not care for Ginsberg or his poetry were not inclined to care for his journals, exemplified perhaps by one reviewer who commented that "there seems to be little in Ginsberg beyond drugs and narcissism." Another critic, writing that "the Ginsberg of the journals has outlived his time," was unimpressed with *Journals*, saying that "all of Ginsberg's best work has already been published somewhere else; what we have here amounts to the laundry list of a distinctive but minor talent." Others dredged up the old criticism that he was simply writing to shock, or writing to earn a buck, as if he had had all that in mind over a quarter of a century earlier when, unknown and unpublished, he was writing the earliest of these private entries.

The majority of reviewers, however, found the book a fascinating and enlightening study, an intimate look at the development of poet and individual. "I was able to see the young man struggling to become an artist, and the developing artist as a man on almost every page," wrote Richard Elman, who offered his highest praise to the travel writings in the journals. Louis Simpson, writing for *The New York Times*, lauded the book as a valuable record of Ginsberg's "actual travels and . . . mental journeys," and he included in his review an astonishing confession: "There are some entertaining 'political ravings' in these 'Journals,' including insults to some people at Columbia who did not pay sufficient attention to his poems when they first came out. As I am one of these people, I am happy to have this opportunity to say that I was wrong— not merely wrong, obtuse."

The opinions expressed in Simpson's review could be read between the lines of many reviews. After two decades of trying to ignore or dismiss Ginsberg as a poet with a gimmick, critics were beginning to reassess their original positions. For most, the old arguments and complaints were no longer valid. From his body of poetry, supported by two volumes of published journals and other writings, it was obvious that from his earliest days as a poet, he had been a serious artist and not out simply to shock his readers in an effort to publish his work and make money. There were those who could not bring themselves to agree with Ginsberg's methods or enjoy his poetry, but they were not about to deny him his intentions.

4

Allen saw another goal realized in early October when the television version of "Kaddish" finally hit the airwaves. He had taken an active role in its production, not only in his position of screenwriter but also as the program's narrator. At the opening of the production, he is seen in his present-day Lower East Side apartment, and from there the film becomes a series of flashbacks, with Allen reading "Kaddish" and offering commentary on the action. In comparison to the stage version, the television medium, through the use of special effects, was more successful in portraying Naomi's hallucinations. The viewer sees the movies in Naomi's mind, even as she struggles to play her role in the tragic movie that was her life. For example, in the scene in which young Allen is taking his mother on the bus to the New Jersey rest home, Naomi imagines the *Hindenburg* crashing inside the bus. Through different types of camerawork, the film achieved its purpose of depicting the various levels of consciousness found in the poem. "To bring these separate elements together into a whole," explained Ginsberg, "we utilized every conceivable kind of videotape production technology, from the earliest Sony black-and-white mini cameras for a grainy home movie look, to the most sophisticated computerized TV editing system."

As always, autumn was an active time for Allen. In September, he had spent ten days in a hut in Colorado, meditating for eight hours a day. From there, he was off to the University of California at Santa Cruz, where he participated in "LSD: A Decade Later," a conference with Dr. Albert Hofmann (inventor of LSD), Ram Dass, Timothy Leary, and others. The psychedelic drug phenomenon, Ginsberg was pleased to report, had swung full circle. After more than a decade of misinformation, hysteria, and abuse, LSD was back in the laboratory, gaining the benefit of professional research. Curious about the relationship between LSD and meditation, Allen ingested several tiny LSD tablets—the first acid he had taken in years—on his flight to the West Coast. The effects of *Samatha* meditation and LSD on the mind, he noted, bore some similarity:

> High on LSD, the Buddhist practice seems singularly appropriate because the message of LSD, or "the lessons you learn" with LSD, seems to be that there is no reference point and the mind creates its own universe. There's no need to get attached to or "hung up" on any single creation. For if you do get hung up on any single LSD conception or projection, if you get hung up on any of *your* projections, then it becomes real and you'll suffer the consequences or the history of that projection. So the lesson of the LSD experience seems to be that no attachment is necessary, not even to LSD, just as a lesson of Buddhism seems to be no "attachment" is necessary, even to Buddha.

"My own conclusion, parallel to Dr. Hofmann's," Allen told the conference, "is that LSD is OK because it teaches one not to cling to anything, including LSD. 'I've always known this truth,' one thinks high. That ghost notion, dismissed for later recollection, emerges later as a guide-thought for most experimenters who, like myself, come to accept Ordinary Mind as a working basis for infrequent later acid trips, charming as they are."

Immediately following the LSD conference, Allen flew to Hawaii to act as a panelist in the Colloquium on the Cross-Cultural Encounter in Literature, sponsored by the East-West Center in Honolulu. The conference discussions were spirited, occasionally heated, with such participants as African playwright/poet Wole Soyinka, West Samoan poet/novelist Albert Wendt, Australian novelist Thomas Keneally, and Indian poet Nissim Ezekiel talking about the literature and cultures of their respective countries and debating how they fit into a world community. Allen was in his element. In his address, he spoke of what he called "some rarified points of convergence and differentiation between Eastern and Western minds in cultural and literary practice." As esoteric as that sounded, the address was actually a summary of Allen's search for a higher level of consciousness, which included his experiments with LSD and, more recently, meditation. His remarks drew a wide variation of responses, especially from those who did not understand or agree with his talk about Buddhism and meditation.

Back on the East Coast, Allen fulfilled several other reading commitments before settling in for the winter at Cherry Valley. His mood had improved somewhat while he was traveling around, giving readings and attending conferences, but now that he was more confined, sitting on the farm and answering the piled-up mail and constant ringing of the telephone, he began to worry again about Naropa. Anne Waldman called to inform him that the school had accumulated large debts and had very little money, which Allen attributed to a backlash to what he called the "Merwin-Trungpa ghost fight." The gossip about the confrontation was as bad as ever and Allen felt frozen by his own indecision as to what course of action he should take. "Here I am in my room," he wrote in his journal in late November, "trapped 'like smoke going down bamboo tube' between poesy and dharma, Merwin and Trungpa, in their ghost war. Hypocrite, I take rides with each. I haven't pursued my prostrations, I push and preach Dharma and poetry in public, I *can't* face Merwin, I get angry at my boyfriends and students, I'm a hairy loss."

5

Renaldo and Clara, Bob Dylan's film about the Rolling Thunder Revue tour, was released nationally in January 1978. Checking in at just under four hours in length, the film was by turns charming, tiresome, compelling, and abstruse; for many critics and viewers, it was far too long. Bob and Sara Dylan played the title characters, while, in keeping with the film's theme of distorting and changing identities, Ronnie Hawkins and Ronee Blakley played Bob and Sara Dylan. Allen was listed in the film's credits as playing "The Father."

In terms of achieving its goals, the film was a success. The individual vignettes had a playful air of spontaneity to them and the concert footage was excellent, effectively catching the spirit of the Rolling Thunder Revue and, more important, the enigma of Bob Dylan. When asked for his opinion of the film, a less than objective Ginsberg had nothing but praise for it. "It's a great work of art," he proclaimed. "It is beautifully structured, totally logical. . . . Not rational, but logical. It's about God, women, men and women, rock and roll, identity, Dylan, poets—the main theme is poets."

Unfortunately, most critics failed to agree with Allen's assessment and the film was attacked ruthlessly. To the majority, it was little more than a long home movie that was confusing, unstructured, and meaningless to anyone outside the Dylan circle. The movie, said noted film critic Judith Crist, was "an ego massage masquerading as a feature film." *The New York Times*, in its review, was more diplomatic, stating that *Renaldo and Clara* "holds the attention at least as effectively as it tries the patience."

For the most part, Allen was treated well by the critics—including those who disliked the movie. Reviewers seemed to agree that he added a sense of charm to the self-indulgence of the typical rock tour. "Allen Ginsberg seems incapable of being anything but a delight," noted a critic for *Rolling Stone*, concluding that "the scenes of Ginsberg reading *Kaddish* and singing Blake poems set to his own music are the best in the movie. I even liked him in a rather silly scene where he tells Dylan about all the famous artists' graves he's visited."

Added a critic for the *Denver Post*: "There is the delightful incongruity of an affable Ginsberg, taking his seat on the bandstand for a poetry reading in a nightclub to the tune of 'Everything's Coming Up Roses.' And there are his cheerful responses when an elderly Italian woman reads his palm. 'You have been married twice,' she says to Ginsberg, generally known as a homosexual. 'In a way,' he says, accommodatingly." To this reviewer, Allen was one of the few bright spots in an otherwise lengthy, dreary movie.

That winter, Allen conducted a study that confirmed many of his suspicions about the government's role in harassing individuals and disrupting dissident political groups during the sixties and seventies. Through the Freedom of Information Act, Allen was able to obtain a large file of documents kept on him by such government agencies as the FBI, CIA, Bureau of Narcotics, and the Drug Enforcement Administration. He was not at all surprised to learn that such documents existed—he had been aware of some of them as early as 1965—but he was appalled and angered by both the pettiness and extensiveness of the records used against him and his friends. The earliest file, begun by the DEA in 1961, was the result of a television appearance during which Allen had advocated the legalization of marijuana. The Bureau of Narcotics started a Ginsberg file shortly thereafter. The different government agencies were also interested in Allen's sexual behavior, which some officials believed to be threatening in some way or another, though no one was very specific as to how. As evidence of Ginsberg's perversity, the New York Regional Office of the DEA kept on file what it described as an "obscene" photograph of Allen and Peter posing in the nude—which, as it turned out, was the famous Richard Avedon photograph that had appeared on the cover of *Evergreen Review* and in a host of other books and publications.

Allen was upset by such files, but he regarded them as being far less threatening than some of the other documents he saw. By carefully examining the files kept throughout the sixties, he received a clear picture of the measures taken against political dissidents, civil rights leaders and antiwar activists, avant-garde artists, and underground publishers. Much of the civil unrest, Allen concluded, had been government-created. "I've had my head in Freedom Info documents and books," he wrote Philip Whalen in early 1978, "and decided the whole split between white and black . . . was all along an FBI plot, just like my mother said. God, you should see all the awful documents—forged letters . . . black murder plots, Hitlerean insult rhetoric . . . all cooked up by secretaries in offices on Royal typewriters."

On another occasion, Ginsberg wrote:

In sum, there *was* a vast bureaucratic conspiracy to brainwash the public left and right, separate the generations, project obnoxious images of youth, divide Black and White citizens, abort and blackmail mental social leadership of Black citizens, set Blacks on each other, provoke Whites to murderous confusion, confound honest media, infiltrate, prevaricate and spy on reformist multitudes, becloud understanding and community, and poison public consciousness. These generalizations are proved if one examines Xerox facsimiles of government intelligence documents, more extensive and detailed in paranoid system than most Seekers ever guessed.

For all their diligent file keeping, the agencies were selective about what they retained in their records. The CIA kept copies of the Ginsberg-Helms correspondence regarding their wager about the CIA drug trafficking in Southeast Asia, but very little else was filed on Ginsberg's long-standing accusations of government malfeasance in drug dealing and questionable enforcement of drug laws. Allen decided to do his own small part in rectifying the situation. Like Lenny Bruce, who toward the end of his life had read court transcripts of his obscenity trials onstage, Allen began reading and commenting on his FBI file in select public appearances, including a guest spot on the "Dick Cavett Show." These appearances may not have been able to change the course of history or repair the damage that had been done to individuals and groups over the years, but they did go a long way in proving that a lot of Allen's talk about the United States being a police state was, at least to a certain extent, justified.

6

Mind Breaths, Ginsberg's sixth contribution to the City Lights "Pocket Poets" series, hit the bookstores early in the year. Generally speaking, with the exception of "Contest of Bards," which detractors found awkward in form and too self-absorbed, reviewers welcomed the changes in the kinds of poems included in the volume. They appreciated the humor and candor in "Ego Confession" and were moved by "Don't Grow Old," which, though stylistically dissimilar to "Kaddish," was regarded as one of Ginsberg's most heartfelt poems in recent memory and a powerful tribute to a dead parent. Critics admired the direct, simple approach to many of Ginsberg's new poems. "The old visionary, in his persona," said one reviewer, "has been inching along into Good Grey Poethood for some time now, but here we have the poetic evidence, and no one will be disappointed."

Hayden Carruth, reviewing *Mind Breaths* for *The New York Times*, delivered some of the highest praise that Ginsberg had received in years. Carruth admitted that he had not cared for Ginsberg's poems of the 1960s, which he described as being "too full of random, unassimilated political rage," nor had he appreciated his blues lyrics, but he was pleased by the poems in *Mind Breaths*. Singling out "Ego Confession" for special mention, Carruth wrote that the poem, for all its self-mockery, and mockery of poetic form and silly human ambition, was ultimately "infused with passionate tenderness.

"I once referred to Ginsberg's books, as they are published by City Lights Books in their little, square formats, as 'mousetraps of love,' which is exactly what they are," Carruth continued. There was, he noted, "no need to speak of kinds, qualities, degrees, [or] the intellect's inevitable meanderings. The poems *exist*. Think of all the millions of things that might have gone otherwise, so that they might not exist. Our times are bleak enough, heaven knows, but at least we have this."

For all the talk of his getting older, or of meditation mellowing him, Allen was a long way from being a passive graybeard. The old fires, especially his senses of rebellion and moral outrage, burned as hot as ever, and these qualities continued to find their way into his poetry. Two recent poems, "Punk Rock Your My Big Crybaby," an homage to the new style of music with strong ties to the Beat Generation's spirit of rebellion, and "C'mon Jack," a pornographic ditty that read like a footnote to "Please Master," indicated that Ginsberg, even as he approached his fifty-second birthday, had as much in common with those thirty years younger as he had with his own generation. He was as comfortable improvising poetry onstage with musician Iggy Pop—which he did, in January—as he was when reading at a university.

He could still provoke the masses, as he proved on April 20, when he appeared as a guest on a morning television talk show in Boston. Allen had heard that Suffolk County's district attorney had ordered a crackdown on homosexuals hanging around Revere and the Boston Public Library, and he used his television appearance to talk about his own homosexuality and speak out against the district attorney. Angry callers lighted up the television station's switchboard before he had finished speaking. Not that the opposing viewpoints would have mattered. The harassment and arrests of homosexuals in Boston so infuriated Ginsberg that he scribbled down a short addendum to "Howl"—his first such addition in years—that addressed the issue:

> who were arrested for teenage porn ring headlines
> in Boston Globe when the octogenarian bachelor D.A.
> got hysterical screaming thru his iron mask at
> election time lusting lusting lusting for votes, for
> heterosexual ballotboxes' votes
> who arrested bus driving fairies & put them in an
> iron cage on Charles St., who yelled at little
> homeless boys & made them sing & dance in tears to
> please the plainclothes courts & fink on middleaged
> lonesome bearded men kneeling to worship kid Drousus
> in Revere. . . .

Allen's 1978 teaching schedule at Naropa included conducting a course on Blake that spring and a class on spontaneous poetics and meditation that summer. The Blake course, a line-by-line examination of *The Book of Urizen*, was an ambitious project that, like Allen's "Literary History of the Beat Generation," expanded into a full-blown study that would last for several terms. In the era of the neutron bomb, in which science had devised a weapon that killed people while leaving structures intact, Blake's prophetic books, including *The

Book of Urizen, The Marriage of Heaven and Hell, Milton, and *Jerusalem,* seemed to be especially apropos.

"Teaching *Urizen,* I began digging how relevant Blake's psychology is to modern times," Allen told interviewer Michael Ellsworth:

> His figure of *Urizen* is that of human reason gone mad—into extreme—destroying body of the earth, the emotions and the imagination in its aggressive grasp to control the Universe. That seems symbolic or equivalent to the exasperatingly rationalized Military-Industrial madness such as nuclear industry, which is the triumph of zany reason—the entire military psyche which attempts to protect its territory by creating weapons so monstrous that they'll destroy everybody's territory, including its own.

According to Blake, there had to be an absolute balance between Reason (Urizen), Emotion (Luvah), Imagination (Urthona), and Body (Tharmas) for the world to function properly. Domination by any of the four could bring about disastrous results. Allen was not interested in Blake's system solely for its commentary on the contemporary scientific relationship to modern weaponry. Just as threatening, in Allen's view, were the ways in which scientific reason had addressed modern day-to-day living. Foremost in Ginsberg's mind that spring was the development of nuclear energy and technology. His private study of the industry had led him to grim conclusions about its relationship to the ecology. Given his history of concern for the environment, his opposition to the nuclear industry was inevitable—as were, in all probability, the measures he took to oppose it.

27
Plutonian Ode

I enter your secret places with my mind, I speak with
your presence, I roar your Lion Roar with mortal
mouth. . . .

1

The summer 1978 sessions at Naropa featured another noteworthy roster of
guest lecturers, including Allen, Peter, Anne Waldman, Daniel Ellsberg, Timothy Leary, Amiri Baraka (LeRoi Jones), Diane Di Prima, Gregory Corso, William Burroughs, and Miguel Pinero. It was a busy time in and out of the
classroom. An Italian film crew took footage of many of the lectures and activities
for a two-hour television documentary. Poetry readings abounded. Gregory Corso,
in his constant role of devil's advocate, entertained and infuriated attendants with
his Puckish behavior. Late-night bull sessions found students and teachers
discussing political and literary issues, occasionally in spirited debate.

The topic of nuclear energy dominated many a discussion. Nearby Rocky
Flats had become the focus of the national antinuke movement when in late
April protesters began what would amount to a summer-long occupation of the
railroad line leading into the Rockwell Corporation's weapons plant. On May
27, in the largest antinuke display of its kind in the United States, fifteen
thousand protesters marched to the United Nations in New York, where Andrew Young, U.S. ambassador to the UN, was presented with almost twelve
tons of petitions demanding global nuclear disarmament and an end to nuclear
production. Religious groups joined forces with the growing number of antinuke
organizations throughout the United States, making the national antinuke
movement the most significant protest movement in the country since the
antiwar protests of the previous decade. In Colorado, Rocky Flats demonstrators
were arrested on a regular basis, only to be replaced on the railroad tracks by
other protesters continuing the vigil.

Allen, of course, studied the situation with great interest. He needed no
prodding or convincing to take an antinuclear stance, which was a logical

extension of his pro-ecology and antiwar positions of the past. In addition to the possible environmental hazards that it presented, the nuclear energy industry posed security considerations that could lead to the establishment of complex policing bureaucracies. Allen was concerned that the government would have to set up what he called "a monolithic Surveillance State" due to the nature of nuclear waste and the long-range half-life of plutonium, along with the potential for international terrorism stemming from the theft of radioactive materials. As a result of his conversation with people at Naropa and his private research into nuclear energy, Allen decided that he ought to take a stronger public stand on the issue.

He took his first step in that direction through his poetry. Shortly before one o'clock in the morning on Wednesday, June 12, Allen sat down at a Formica-topped table in the kitchen of his Boulder apartment and scribbled in his journal the opening lines of a new poem that addressed the issue of nuclear power:

> What new element hitherto 'ere unborn in Nature?
> Is there a new thing under the sun?

He worked all night, filling six notebook pages with the new poem. He included as much as he could about the properties of plutonium, playing that information off the mythology of Pluto, the ancient god of Hades and Lord of Wealth. According to mythology, Pluto kidnapped Persephone, goddess of plants and flowers, for his bride. Each spring, he would release her for a few months to her mother, Demeter, the goddess of fertility, but he would then reclaim her each fall and drag her to the netherworld, this mythology giving an explanation for the seasons on earth.

In writing "Plutonian Ode," as he entitled the poem, Allen drew a parallel between the mythological Pluto and the destructive power of the element that received its name from the god. The day before he began the poem, Allen had learned from Gregory Corso that the 24,000-year half-life of plutonium radioactivity was also equal to the time it took the solar system to make a revolution around the core of the galaxy. That revolution was known as a Platonic "Great Year." This seemed more than a coincidence to Allen, and he used the information as a source of inspiration while he was writing the poem.

In its published version, "Plutonian Ode" is divided into three parts. In the first section, Ginsberg addresses the element itself and exposes it as a monster poised to devour the universe. The hazards of plutonium had been held secret or downplayed, and in revealing its danger, the poet is, in effect, expressing his superiority:

> I dare your Reality, I challenge your very being! I
>   publish your cause and effect!
> I turn the wheel of Mind on your three hundred tons!
>   Your name enters mankind's ear! I embody your
>   ultimate powers!
> My oratory advances on your vaulted Mystery! This
>   breath dispels your braggart fears! I sing your
>   form at last. . . .

As in "America" and "Wichita Vortex Sutra," Ginsberg attempts to disarm the enemy by publicly proclaiming its folly. Once again, he uses the long line to establish momentum and emotion. Absent in "Plutonian Ode," however, is the humor that accentuated his scorn in the earlier works. In "Plutonian Ode," Ginsberg is a nuclear age Jeremiah, taking his lines by way of Whitman. This form is effective if the reader agrees with the poet's stance, but for those who do not, the oratory, sans humor and containing references that literally require footnotes, comes across like the rantings of a pariah who somehow believes he can overcome a powerful and perhaps stronger foe simply by shouting him down. Ginsberg appears to have recognized this, for in the third part of the poem, he calls on the poets and orators of the future to continue the battle.

From his earliest poems, one of Ginsberg's strongest suits as a poet was his ability to use stark contrast as a means of underscoring the important points of his works, and he does so in "Plutonian Ode" to dazzling effect. After the fierce oratory of the poem's first section, Ginsberg abruptly changes tone, moving from the proverbial mountaintop (or, to cynics, the soapbox) to the silent, dimly lighted early-morning solitude of his apartment's kitchen. It is the dawning of a new day, with its sense of renewal and promise, and Ginsberg pauses to describe the beauty of sunrise in the Rocky Mountains:

> Blue sky transparent rising empty deep & spacious to a
>   morning star high over the balcony
> above some autos sat with wheels to curb downhill
>   from Flatiron's jagged pine ridge,
> sunlit mountain meadows sloped to rust-red sandstone
>   cliffs above brick townhouse roofs
> as sparrows waked whistling through Marine Street's
>   summer green leafed trees. . . .

Such vivid use of detail is as effective as a painting or photograph: People who have never traveled west of the Mississippi can picture the scene as if they, along with Ginsberg, were looking out of his apartment window at the splendor of the Colorado foothills. After hearing of plutonium's threat in the poem's first section, one can now see what might be lost. In addition, the second section of "Plutonian Ode" presents a hopeful note. The sun rises and life goes on, despite efforts by science and technology that jeopardize the planet.

In the months following the poem's composition, Allen worked mightily to fashion "Plutonian Ode" into a masterwork. In his revision, he tightened syntax and tried to make the poem easier to read aloud. The work was troublesome. Although with its sixty-five long lines, it was of epic length, it still seemed mired in its own intent. Ginsberg had much more to say, and with much greater sense of urgency, than in such recently issued epics as "Contest of Bards" and "Mind Breaths." At many points in "Plutonian Ode," his references are oblique, and he faced the danger of having the message of one of his most ambitious poems overshadowed by images that didn't quite connect with readers. He tried to resolve the problem by the inclusion of extensive footnotes, but that may have been only the best, most pragmatic means of addressing an unsolvable dilemma in an imperfect poem. It is ironic that in the long run he may have achieved less than he might have had he been able to find a way to follow his own advice and keep the poem simple and objective.

But then, the antiplutonium message itself is neither simple nor objective, and in the final judgment, message becomes more important than form.

2

In one of those rare conjunctions in which history and art meet in a significant way, Allen was arrested for blocking the Rocky Flats railroad tracks less than twelve hours after he had finished writing "Plutonian Ode."

As he was writing the poem, he had no inclination that he would be part of a demonstration later that day. After completing the work, he had gone to bed, confident that he had written a worthy poem, only to be awakened a few hours later by a student calling to inform him that a train shipment of nuclear waste would be leaving Rocky Flats that afternoon. A couple of weeks earlier, students had invited Allen to block the next train's passage and he had indicated he was interested. This was his first opportunity.

Allen, Peter, and four young women went to the railroad line and found a spur in the tracks that was out of sight of Jefferson County sheriff's deputies patrolling the area. Allen pulled off his shoes and sat cross-legged on a rail. A member of the news media was present and Allen announced his intention. "I want to sit on the tracks and meditate on this problem," he said, "and bring mindfulness to the situation here at Rocky Flats, where 150,000 tons of plutonium have been fabricated. I am here as a representative of the American Academy and Institute of Arts and Letters. I am interested in bringing meditation to the peace process. The best way to witness peace is to practice it—by doing nothing but sitting on the railroad minding my own business."

Soon enough, the train made its way around the curve in the tracks. Seeing the protesters blocking the route, the engineer applied the brakes. Almost immediately, three sheriff's officers arrived and warned Allen and the others that they would be arrested if they did not move. By this point, there had been scores of demonstrators arrested and the routine was familiar to the railroad and law-enforcement officials. The process of confronting protesters was peaceful, almost cordial. Earlier that very same day, eight people had been arrested for refusing to allow a train to enter the Rocky Flats facility, although it was believed that no hazardous materials had been on the train at the time. Now, a few hours later, there was a similar confrontation, with similar results. Allen and the group were led from the tracks and charged with criminal trespass and obstruction of a passageway.

Allen appeared in court for his arraignment on June 16. Dressed neatly in a sport coat and tie, he entered a plea of not guilty. When asked to explain his plea, he responded by reading "Plutonian Ode" to the packed courtroom. He was ordered to appear at a pretrial hearing on August 1. As soon as the proceeding ended, Allen returned to the railroad tracks and joined a group of protesters who had erected a tepee to obstruct the path of the next train coming through. The actions, Allen conceded, were futile in the respect that they did not prohibit trains from entering or leaving the nuclear-weapons facility. Still, the protests were very effective in raising public consciousness about the nature of nuclear power and the organized protests against it.

During his summer teaching sessions, Allen delivered a series of lectures about poetics and meditation. He had recently reread *Desolation Angels* and he was using Kerouac's haiku, included throughout the first section of the novel, as examples of a new kind of "self-invented" spontaneous poetry that followed a classical tradition. Sitting in solitude at Desolation Peak, Kerouac had been in a contemplative state and had experienced occasional flashes of insight suitable for poetic expression. This same kind of insight, Allen explained to his class, could be accomplished through meditation.

Throughout the summer, he jotted down haikulike works of his own, and while they did not follow the classical Chinese haiku syllable measure, they did reflect the way in which thought juxtaposition, achieved through meditation, could result in poetry similar to haiku. For example, while sitting in a courtroom and waiting to address the judge, Allen illustrated the scene with a three-line poem:

> Waiting for the Judge, breathing silent
> Prisoners, witnesses, Police—
> the stenographer yawns into her palms.

Allen used a similar three-line stanza ("Old pond/a frog jumps in/Kerplunk!") as the refrain in a country and western tune that he described as "Zen Bluegrass raunch." The refrain, Allen later explained, modeled after a seventeenth-century haiku by Bashō ("The old pond:/a frog jumps in,—/The sound of water splashing"), was representative of pure spontaneous writing, of "the realization of phenomena on the instant, without thought." In a season filled with demonstrations, court appearances, lectures, continuing worries about the backlash from the Trungpa-Merwin altercation, and even a pointed memorial for the victims of Nagasaki on the anniversary of the dropping of the atomic bomb, "Old Pond" was a playful release.

The Nagasaki commemoration, held on August 9, led to Allen's second arrest of the summer. Allen, Daniel Ellsberg, and a large group of demonstrators had arranged day-long memorial services that included song, prayer, a trip to the Rocky Flats nuclear facility, and a dramatic "die-in" to commence at 11:02 A.M., the time the bomb had been dropped on Nagasaki thirty-three years earlier. During the die-in, all demonstrators were to fall motionless on the highway, where they would remain until either the end of the day or such time as they were arrested. Allen did not get to participate in the die-in. He and Ellsberg were taken into police custody earlier in the day, when they appeared on the west side of the nuclear facility. Both had been previously arrested for blocking the railroad tracks, and as part of the condition for their release on bond, they were ordered to stay away from the plant. After their arrest, they were cited for violating the terms of their bond and for third-degree trespassing. In all, seventy-nine protesters were arrested on August 9, bringing to over two hundred the total number of those arrested for demonstrating against the Rocky Flats plant. Despite the escalating number of arrests and an increasingly impatient and overloaded justice system having to accommodate them in court, the demonstrators promised to keep up their protesting. The battle was only beginning.

3

Another continuing battle—and one that affected Allen much more directly—was heating up. A year had passed since Ed Sanders's Investigative Poetics class had filed its report on the Trungpa-Merwin confrontation. True to his word, Sanders had not allowed the report to be published—not that there was any lack of interest in the group's findings. Photocopies of *The Party*, prepared with Sanders's approval, were circulated around Naropa and in national poetry circles, and Sanders was feeling pressure to publish the document. Lawrence Ferlinghetti had expressed interest in issuing it under the City Lights imprint, and the *Boulder Monthly* had approached Sanders for permission to reprint it in the magazine. Sanders hesitated to grant such permission, even after his class voted in early September to allow its publication. Sanders correctly assumed that there would be terrible fighting in the poetry community, with poets lining up for and against Trungpa and Naropa, if the report was to be widely distributed.

Allen remained loyal to Trungpa in what were becoming very difficult times. The attacks on Trungpa were no longer directed solely against his actions in the Snowmass incident; they were now being aimed at his Buddhist organization, as well. To his critics, Trungpa's heavy drinking was not exemplary behavior for any kind of religious leader, nor was his houseful of maids and servants or his chauffeur-driven Mercedes-Benz. The Vajra guard, his group of private bodyguards, had a paramilitary look to them that made some people uncomfortable. Rightfully or otherwise, the word *cult* slipped into conversations about Trungpa's Buddhist group.

Allen tried to avoid direct involvement in the controversy. He had the poetics school to look after and keep him busy; as for the mounting criticism against Trungpa, Allen was steadfast in his belief that the bulk of ill will was the result of a long-held misunderstanding of Buddhism, Trungpa, and Eastern thought. Virtually no religion was by nature a democratic institution and Buddhism was no exception. Indeed, Trungpa's "wild wisdom" might seem unorthodox—perhaps even bizarre—to those unfamiliar with it, but in Allen's mind, Trungpa may have been a little eccentric but was by no means threatening.

Still, he could not keep himself from worrying about Naropa's fate. True to form, Allen turned much of his anger and despair on himself in an examination of conscience that led him to conclude that for all the respect accorded him and all the good things written or said about him, he was a "Fake Saint," no different from anyone else, famous or unknown. He was guilty of ignoring the dictum of not clinging to the horrible and he was paying a mental price for it. During his autumn meditation retreat at his Bedrock Mortar Hermitage in the California Sierras, Allen tried to empty his mind of its preoccupations, but if one can judge by his journal entries from the period, filled with statistics about plutonium, FBI surveillance matters, and other political concerns, he was not entirely successful.

His worries about Naropa were compounded by the news coverage of the mass suicides of over nine hundred men, women, and children on November 18 at Reverend Jim Jones's Peoples Temple in Guyana. In the wake of such horror, with religious cults under thorough examination by the press and public alike, Ed Sanders was again faced with the dilemma of what to do with *The Party*. If he refused to publish the document, it would look as if Naropa had something to hide, regardless of the fact that the Merwin affair was one of the institution's worst-kept secrets; if he released the report, he would be opening up the school to brutal scrutiny and criticism, which, in the worst-case scenario, could lead to the closing of the poetics school. Besides, in the aftermath of the Jonestown massacre, it was unlikely that the other media would ignore the Naropa controversy. Troubled by the situation, Sanders called for another vote from his class. It voted decisively to publish.

Allen was aware of this, and his preoccupation with the problems at Naropa, along with various other concerns, had an effect on his poetry production, at least in terms of the volume of new work being written. It would not have been noticed by the public, however. "Plutonian Ode," published in a number of magazines and newspapers, was being heralded as a major new work. Allen had several new poems, including the beautiful " 'Don't Grow Old' " (the quotation marks distinguishing the new poem's title from the poem of the same title in *Mind Breaths*), that he was working on. *Poems All Over the Place*, the miscellany he had compiled for Cherry Valley Editions, and *Mostly Sitting Haiku*, a pamphlet-sized grouping of short meditative poems published by a small press in Paterson, were in the bookstores, although both were considered minor efforts and were generally ignored by reviewers. The demand for public appearances and interviews with the media was as imposing as ever. Allen spent much of the latter part of the autumn in New York, catching up with friends and relatives, addressing business concerns, and trying to manage as much relaxation as he could find before his scheduled return to Naropa early the next year.

He closed out 1978 with two significant appearances. William Burroughs, now recognized as one of the fathers of modern avant-garde literature, was being honored in a gala three-day series of readings, film presentations, lectures, concerts, and panel discussions called the Nova Convention. Allen was delighted for his old friend. In the twenty-five years since the publication of *Junky*, Burroughs had established himself as one of the great iconoclastic writers of the twentieth century. His wide-ranging, indisputable influence was in evidence during the November 30 to December 2 convention, with its attendant aging hippies, punk rockers, university professors, writers, avant-garde painters and musicians, performance artists, college students, and virtually every other kind of countercultural or bohemian individual imaginable. The performers honoring Burroughs represented a similar range. Brion Gysin, Burroughs's friend and collaborator, was in from Paris, and he was joined by Allen, Anne Waldman, Ed Sanders, Merce Cunningham, and John Cage in opening-night performances. Frank Zappa, standing in for Keith Richards of the Rolling Stones, who had originally been scheduled to appear but had been forced to cancel, performed on the second night, along with new-wave singer/songwriter Patti

Smith and composer Philip Glass. Performance artist Laurie Anderson and poet John Giorno, founder of New York's Dial-a-Poet series, were lauded by *The New York Times* as being "high points" of the wildly divergent performances of the convention. Not to be outdone, the guest of honor delivered a noteworthy reading of his own and joined in a panel discussion, "This Is the Space Age," with Timothy Leary and Robert Anton Wilson. Such a retrospect was rare for any writer, but it was especially noteworthy when it recognized the contributions of someone as controversial as Burroughs.

One month later, on New Year's Day, 1979, Allen participated in another event honoring an important part of his past when he, along with over a hundred other poets, musicians, dancers, and performers, engaged in a benefit for St. Mark's Church in the Bowery. This Episcopal church, home of the St. Mark's Poetry Project, had an illustrious history of supporting Greenwich Village poets, dating back to the 1920s and 1930s, at a time when Allen had attended Maxwell Bodenheim readings with his father. St. Mark's had been gutted by fire the preceding July, and an estimated $2.5 million was needed to restore it. He helped with the organization of the reading and saw to it that the news media was aware that another major cultural event was taking place in the Village. When it was his turn to read, he read "Plutonian Ode," which, months after its original composition, he continued to modify and expand.

4

On February 22, the National Arts Club awarded Allen its prestigious Gold Medal in recognition for his lifetime achievement in poetry. The awards dinner, held at the club's Gramercy Park South headquarters, was attended by a host of Allen's friends and family, including Peter Orlovsky, Edith Ginsberg, Eugene Brooks, Lucien Carr, Bob Rosenthal (Allen's new secretary), and Steven Taylor, who performed with Allen at the end of the ceremony. Poet Ted Berrigan acted as master of ceremonies for the event. Throughout the evening's speeches, people paid tribute to Ginsberg's unflinching courage in pursuing his vision, as a poet and individual, for decades.

"I think he's changed the role of the poet in America," said John Ashbery, noting that Ginsberg had been largely responsible for the movement of the poet from the printed page to the reading halls—a development decisively for the better. "Now everybody experiences poetry," Ashbery continued. "It's much closer to us now than it was twenty years ago, and I think that is due not only to his poetry but to his truly exemplary way of living."

Norman Mailer, characterizing himself as "the world's worst printed poet," called Allen a "splendid and heroic poet" who, by virtue of his own enigmatic example, had challenged the way Americans perceived themselves. William Burroughs also praised Allen's courage, mentioning that Ginsberg had at one time been considered disreputable and unacceptable because of his outspoken views on sex and drugs, when, in fact, he had been striving to create an important human awareness. Ginsberg was an original thinker, Burroughs said, and his Gold Medal was testament to a shift in opinion that now recognized his respectability. "This shift, whereby original thinkers are accepted, is very beneficial both to those who accept them and to the thinkers themselves," concluded Burroughs, who stated his belief that within a decade or so Allen would be a very deserving recipient of the Nobel Prize for Literature.

The most remarkable testimony to Allen's effect on the world came from an unexpected source. Although they had attained their own achievements within the literary ranks, speakers such as Burroughs, Mailer, and Berrigan possessed outlaw reputations of their own; they had devoted a large and visible portion of their public careers to challenging literary and social norms and, as a result, could have been expected to praise Ginsberg for doing the same. This, however, was not the case with Henry Geldzahler, New York's commissioner of cultural affairs, who not only lauded Ginsberg's courage but also used the banquet as an occasion to publicly declare his own homosexuality.

"Allen announced to the world that you can be homosexual and inclusive," Geldzahler said. "He is a poet whose truths are described so feelingly and tellingly that the particularities become universal. [He is] a poet of human sexuality. We all feel as we read Allen Ginsberg what Allen Ginsberg feels. It is easier and more palatable for me to be an American and to be a homosexual because Allen has stood and spoken out. His eloquence allows us to share his victory."

For Allen, the awards banquet was a shining moment in otherwise troubled times. The problems at Naropa bothered him as much as ever, to the point that he was now suffering from severe headaches and having nightmares about them. The February issue of Harper's magazine, on newsstands in January, had featured an account of the Snowmass incident written by Peter Marin, a former teacher at Naropa. In his article, Marin portrayed Chögyam Trungpa as a cult leader who demanded absolute obedience from his students and followers. Marin's use of the adjective cult was extremely distasteful to those presently at Naropa, but their protests drew very little sympathy. In Boulder, a Daily Camera editorial attempted to strike a balance between its praise for Naropa's contribution to the community and its concern about Trungpa's eccentricity, particularly his use of a limousine ("as wasteful as it is egotistical"), his guards ("They call up the spectre of the late Nazi Party chief George Lincoln Rockwell"), and his excessive drinking ("it contains false wisdom"). Buddhism was not necessarily a cult, the editorialist wrote, and the interactions of those individuals at Naropa with the community did not indicate the kind of behavior one expected from members of a cult, who preferred an isolated existence. However, some of Trungpa's actions could be interpreted as being egotistical at the very least or, at the worst, the workings of a cult leader. "To avoid being called a cult," the editor suggested, recognizing the objections of Trungpa's students, "it might help not to act like one."

The Boulder Monthly had been wanting to publish an article about Naropa and the Merwin incident for some time but had been unable to secure permission to reprint the Sanders document. Tom Clark, a writer for the magazine and a poet himself, had written a reconstruction of the event, using The Party as his main source but employing fictional devices to avoid violation of copyright laws, and the Boulder Monthly considered publishing Clark's piece in lieu of publishing excerpts of The Party. Sam Maddox, the magazine's editor, appealed to Sanders's journalistic instincts in his final attempt to gain permission to publish at least part of the report. The Trungpa-Merwin episode, he wrote Sanders, carried numerous implications, not only to Buddhists but to the American intellectual community as well, and the Snowmass incident was more than a simple case of a drunken party that had gotten out of hand. "The seminary violence," wrote Maddox, "forces us to face the issue of tyranny and abuse within the blind homage of the enlightenment movement."

Allen would have preferred to avoid involvement in the growing controversy, but it was no longer possible, given *Boulder Monthly*'s intention of publishing its own account of the affair. Bad press coverage was certain to have a negative impact on Naropa and the poetics school, especially if Trungpa was compared to Jim Jones or his Buddhist following to the people of Jonestown. Although he had not been present during the Trungpa-Merwin confrontation and would therefore be delivering a secondhand account of it, Allen agreed to be interviewed by Clark, whom he trusted from his *Paris Review* interview of 1965 and who he felt would be fair in his reportage.

In retrospect, one can admire Ginsberg's courage for entering a no-win situation with the hope of defending his teacher and Naropa against impossible odds, but the interview wound up being a disaster that, rather than clarifying public understanding of Trungpa, as Allen intended, served only to add Ginsberg to a nasty stew that would simmer for years to come. Part of the problem can be attributed to his answers to Clark's questions, in which he attempted to explain complex ideas and beliefs in the byte-sized answers demanded by magazine editors. A portion of the problem could be attributed to the way the interview was edited by Clark, who had very little use for Trungpa and was therefore inclined to be sharper in his editing of Ginsberg's compliments of Naropa's leader than of his own negative comments regarding Trungpa. Finally, some of the blame for the interview's disastrous results could be attributed to a misunderstanding between Ginsberg and Clark. Allen was accustomed to having the opportunity to edit his longer interviews, such as the one he had given Clark for *The Paris Review*, or the one he had granted *Playboy*, and he incorrectly assumed that he would be able to go over the one he was giving *Boulder Monthly* before it was published, even though he demanded no such promise from Clark—nor was he offered such an arrangement as a condition for the interview.

In any event, the interview was not the best move Allen could have made at the time. Like anyone interested in the Naropa situation, Clark wanted Allen's views on Trungpa, his student/relationship with Trungpa, the Merwin episode, and Trungpa's "wild wisdom" practices. Such inquiries, while reasonable and warranted, were bound to put an interviewee on the defensive, and though Allen was generally patient and agreeable in the answers he provided to Clark's questions, there were times during the interview session when he became openly testy, as if he felt caught up in an ambush interview conducted by a friend in the process of betraying him.

Early in the interview, Allen admitted that, for him, reading the *Harper's* account was comparable to reading about one's marriage problems in the papers. Staying with the marriage simile, he likened his relationship to Trungpa to a nuptial arrangement. That relationship, he said, was both private and delicate and he was uncomfortable discussing it in public. "You know, you're talking about my love life," he informed Clark. "It's really complicated . . . shot

through with strange emotions, and self questionings, and paranoia, and impulses."

Clark understood Allen's position, yet, as he reminded him, their discussion
had a larger cultural scope than just the Ginsberg-Trungpa relationship. Besides,
if Allen wanted to practice a kind of spiritual submission to his teacher, that
was his voluntary decision. But what about Merwin and Naone, who obviously
did not want to submit to Trungpa but were forced to do so against their stated
wishes?

This, of course, was the conundrum. For months, Allen had been trying to
solve this riddle himself, both in private and in discussions with others. From
his answers in the interview, it was obvious that he had yet to determine a way
of explaining it so it would satisfy both spiritual and humanist concerns. In the
context of Tibetan Buddhism and his way of practicing it, Trungpa was well
within his bounds to demand submission from those who chose to follow him.
He was not, after all, forcing anyone to attend his lectures and seminary, nor
were people forced to stay once they had begun to study under him. Even the
Merwin episode, in which force had been used, was difficult to interpret, since
Merwin and Naone entered the study voluntarily and stayed on after it was
over.

Still, the mass suicides at Jonestown—many of which had been forced at
gunpoint—raised difficult questions not only about submission to a spiritual
master but also of the culpability of those witnessing or encouraging the forced
submission of others. At the Snowmass ski resort, Clark mentioned, a large
group of people had, by their silence or encouragement of Trungpa, condoned
his actions, even when it involved the humiliation of two unwilling subjects,
when one was pleading for someone to call the police.

At this point, Allen lost his temper. Throughout the interview, in his careful
discussion of Trungpa and his re-creation of the events at the party, Allen had
tried to explain that as voluntary students Merwin and Naone were sacrificing
some of their privacy and free will to their spiritual teacher. That much was
understood by all attending the seminary. Allen had tried to show how church
and state were separate in the case of such Buddhist studies, and he had
explained that Trungpa's Halloween party was a tradition in which people were
"supposed to blow their top[s] and get rid of all constraints . . . in a tradition
that's conscious making." He had allowed that he felt partially responsible for
encouraging Merwin and others to become part of a situation that required such
submission, and he also admitted that he was not comfortable talking at length
about such a delicate issue. Clark's mention of Jonestown, along with his
misunderstanding—or unwillingness to accept—some of the Buddhist precepts,
finally set Ginsberg off.

"In the middle of that scene, to yell 'call the police'—do you realize how
vulgar that was?" Allen said. "The wisdom of the East was being unveiled, and
she's going 'call the police!' I mean, shit! Fuck that shit! Strip 'em naked, break
down the door! Anything—symbolically. I mentioned privacy before—the
entrance into Vajrayana is the abandonment of all privacy. And the entering
on the Bodhisattva path is totally—you're saying, 'I no longer have any privacy
ever again.' "

Of all the statements made by Ginsberg during the course of the interview, this one would be the most damaging. In all probability, it would have been stricken or modified had Allen had the opportunity to review the interview transcript prior to its publication. After months of worrying about what position to take in the dispute, after casting both critical and charitable judgment on Trungpa and Merwin individually—even going so far as to wonder, in what he confessed to be his growing paranoia about the incident, whether Trungpa was connected to the CIA and perhaps involved in a brainwashing scheme—Allen had, in one passionate moment, taken his public stand. He would regret a number of his remarks from the interview session, but regret and apology would not spare him the consequences of his statements. Despite his hope of clarifying, or maybe even defusing, the bad feelings toward Trungpa, he had, in fact, supplied more grist for the gossip mill. As a journalist, Clark undoubtedly realized that Allen had given him the kind of material that would all but assure a sellout of the issue of *Boulder Monthly* in which the interview appeared.

Rather than soften or back away from his stance, Allen spent the remainder of the interview session trying to explain how, in all the subsequent coverage and criticism of the Snowmass episode, it may have been Trungpa who had been wronged. He said Trungpa may have been guilty of indiscretion, but he had not been wrong in the way he had behaved. Further, Allen resented feeling as if he had to defend Trungpa from his attackers—especially from poets who, by tradition, used their artistic license to write whatever they wanted or behave in whatever fashion they so desired. At one time, not that long ago, these same poets who were now criticizing Trungpa as a religious dictator or cult leader were railing against the American leaders and system as if they were a poison; many had even looked to Eastern thought and religion for enlightenment.

"*I'm* supposed to be like the diplomat poet, defending poetry against those horrible alien gooks with their weird Himalayan practices," Allen raged, using the violence of American racist language to drive home his point of the country's distrust, in the wake of Vietnam, of anything Oriental. "And American culture! 'How dare you criticize American culture!' Everybody's been criticizing it for twenty years, prophesizing the doom of America, how rotten America is. . . . Democracy, nothing! They exploded the atom bomb without asking us. Everybody's defending American democracy. American democracy's this thing, this Oothoon. The last civilized refuge of the world—after twenty years of denouncing it as the *pits*! You know, so now it's the 1970's, everybody wants to go back and say, 'Oh, no, we've got it comfortable. Here are these people invading us with their mind control.' "

The great irony of the Ginsberg-Clark interview was that up until that point no one had held Allen accountable for any of the controversy associated with Trungpa or Naropa. His position as codirector of the Jack Kerouac School of Disembodied Poetics, along with his visibility as Trungpa's most famous student, had made people curious about his opinions regarding the furor, but his reputation was untarnished. That would change dramatically with the publication of the interview, when Allen would find himself in the middle of the fray, attacked by friends and associates who felt that he had betrayed the interests of poetry and individual freedom in his defense of Trungpa.

5

As fate would have it, Allen had to leave for New York, where he was to receive his Gold Medal from the National Arts Club, before he had the opportunity to work with Clark on the interview transcript. In the aftermath of the *Harper's* article, *Boulder Monthly* was eager to present its coverage of the controversy as soon as possible, and Clark, constrained by a tight deadline, could not promise Allen the opportunity to review the transcript before the magazine went to press. Allen had little choice but to trust Clark's judgment in editing the transcript, though he did ask him to show the revised, edited version to Anne Waldman in his absence.

By the time Allen returned to Boulder, the manuscript had been edited and prepared for publication. Waldman had not seen the final version of the interview, though a copy was delivered to Allen's door upon his return from New York. After reading the edited version of the conversation, Allen felt that certain revisions were necessary. He was embarrassed by his remarks concerning Merwin and other poets, bothered by inaccuracies in the transcript, and horrified about the prospects of facing the reaction his comments were certain to elicit. He immediately went to work on the manuscript, believing that he still might be able to make some last-minute changes and clarifications before the piece was published. He also hoped to convince Clark and the magazine's editors to refrain from publishing the interview and accompanying excerpt of the Sanders report until Merwin was advised of their plans.

It was not to be. When Allen returned his own edited version of the interview to the *Boulder Monthly* offices, he was greeted by the sight of boxes and boxes of the March 1979 issue of the magazine, with Trungpa on its cover, filling the *Boulder Monthly* offices. Since copies were already being circulated around Boulder, it was too late to halt publication or distribution of the magazine. Tom Clark and Ed Dorn were in the magazine's office when Allen visited, and both were subjected to an angry Ginsberg. During his tirade, he accused Clark of deliberately betraying his trust and trying to get him in trouble with his friends and with the poetry community in general. In editing the interview, Allen complained, Clark had left in his unflattering remarks about Merwin, Sanders, and others, while his complimentary statements, such as his praise for the way Merwin had handled the Snowmass affair, had been cut from the published version.

Neither Clark nor Dorn was especially impressed by Allen's display. Like many a public figure who had mouthed off during an interview only to regret his or her words afterward, Allen was not contesting the accuracy of his printed statements as much as he was voicing concern about the effects his words would have on the people he talked about. Allen admitted as much himself: "I stopped yelling at Tom when I realized it was fait-accompli irreversible, and that he thought he was doing it (aside from pressure from the magazine) as the rare bold action of an honest reporter, and that my yelling was only making the situation worse by solidifying my own and Tom's self-righteousness. I also breathed a sigh of relief, that I had hit bottom, and my own hypocrisies were unmasked to fellow poets and fellow Buddhists, and that was almost a service rather than a stumbling block."

The interview and excerpt were every bit as controversial as Allen feared they would be. The magazine was an almost instant sellout. Trungpa's followers scurried about town, trying to keep the magazine off the racks by purchasing several copies at a time. Others, such as Sanders and Dorn, saw that the magazine was distributed to interested parties throughout the United States. The story became one of the hottest topics of discussion in Boulder and interest was growing elsewhere.

Allen tried with only marginal success to smooth over hurt feelings and minimize any damage his remarks may have caused. Encumbered by embarrassment and shame, he wrote Merwin and Naone a lengthy letter of apology in which he explained the circumstances of the interview and how it came to be published without his text approval. He had hoped to deliver an interview that explained the controversy, he told them, but he had instead exacerbated it, and in the process he had offended a number of people, including Merwin and Naone. He hated the fact that he had said such negative things about Merwin's poetry in the interview, and he confessed as much to the poet: "Please accept my apologies for my objectionable remarks about your writing—ill considered even for private yatter among friends, some kind of vanity got into me there, which is not my whole mind, an irritable and nasty arrogance in me which I can't disown except to acknowledge it as bad character on my part and ask your forgiveness."

But this, by his own admission, was not his most offensive transgression. "My main shame," he continued in the same letter, "is in having discussed your situation in public (re: the Seminary conflict) when you've had the delicacy to leave the situation ripen on its own without aggression on your part. Of all people, I certainly owed you equal courtesy, and am humiliated to find my own vanity and meanness in print, a situation somewhat of my own making since I did sit down to talk with Tom Clark and Ed Dorn, and knew that Tom wanted the interview for his magazine."

Allen agonized over the effect the *Boulder Monthly* article would have—for good reason. Responses were quick in arriving. A series of articles and editorials—including a couple of pieces written by Clark using a pseudonym—appeared in newspapers and magazines, all critical of Trungpa and Naropa. Bob Callahan, publisher of Turtle Island Press, drew up and circulated a petition calling for poets and artists temporarily to suspend participation in the Jack Kerouac School of Disembodied Poetics until a formal explanation of the Merwin episode was offered by Naropa authorities, the Vajra guards were disbanded, all efforts to discourage the press and other parties investigating the incident were halted, and measures were taken to prevent the recurrence of such a fiasco in the future. In no time, he had received about forty signatures on his petition, with poets in the Bay Area evenly divided on the issue. Many of the poets, Callahan reported, agreed with the petition but refused to sign it out of respect for Ginsberg, whose name was now being mentioned in association with Trungpa and Naropa, even though it was generally believed that he was innocent of any wrongdoing in connection with the actual incident.

When they saw the petition, Gary Snyder and Michael McClure rose to Allen's defense. In separate telephone calls to Callahan, both poets expressed doubts about Trungpa's behavior, but neither was prepared to see the poetry community boycott the poetics school as a response to the incident. Doing so, they suggested, would be more injurious to Ginsberg than to Trungpa.

"Those wimps at Naropa are no threat to *you*," McClure told Callahan, adding that he had been trying for years to convince Allen privately to disassociate himself from the school. "Still," he said, "Allen believes in it, it's his family. You can't attack him for it. You're trying to ruin Allen Ginsberg. You can't do that!"

Snyder took a similar approach. After talking to McClure, who was presently calling people to dissuade them from signing the petition, Snyder tried to convince Callahan that his response to the incident was not "generous enough." Even though he had agreed in a previous conversation with Callahan that Trungpa's behavior at the party was out of line with regard to Buddhist behavior, he now admitted he would have no problem taking off his clothes in a similar situation. "It's a big joke to me," he said. "Just don't criticize Allen in public."

Callahan was surprised and disappointed by some of the responses to his petition. It seemed to him that the reasoning behind signing or not signing had little to do with the incident itself. "It was a case of party lines, party loyalty, of not losing gigs or giving up a station," he told Tom Clark in an interview. "Here were poets showing the kind of block mind militancy you'd never expect from them. . . . It became a poet's war—poets at war with one another. . . . Can't you say something's *wrong*, whatever side you're on?"

Allen still hoped that a revised version of his interview with Clark might be published elsewhere, but Clark was in no mood to cooperate. He, Dorn, and Sanders had been confronted—and even issued vague threats—by angry Trungpa supporters, and in the face of such reaction, Clark was as convinced as ever that Trungpa was a menace and his followers "pods" who had been brainwashed by his teachings. He seemed determined to do whatever he could to expose Trungpa as a kind of religious charlatan.

As the weeks wore on, Allen was drawn deeper and deeper into the controversy. No matter how vigorously he argued, or what approach he took in trying to defuse the controversy, he was ineffective. Like the narrator of Poe's "Descent into the Maelstrom," Allen was being pulled into the vortex of a maddening storm that would leave him physically and emotionally drained—and, ultimately, wiser for the experience.

6

Allen returned to the East Coast to fulfill several engagements before departing on a reading tour in Europe. He had recently shaved off his trademark beard, and his new appearance, along with his habit of wearing a sport coat and tie to his readings, gave him a professorial look that reporters, long accustomed to his bohemian look, found amusing. In light of more pressing concerns, the attention to his appearance seemed trivial, but after being questioned about it by a number of reporters, he offered a formal explanation. The change, Allen said, was an intentional one and had been suggested to him some time ago by Chögyam Trungpa.

"Why are you always wearing black shirts?" Trungpa had asked Allen.

"Well," Ginsberg had responded, "they're easier to wash, and I travel a lot." Besides, he'd said, wearing work clothes and dungarees seemed more democratic—something with which his audience would identify.

Trungpa had wondered whether this might be detracting from his poetry, whether people were paying more attention to Ginsberg as an image and cultural icon than they were paying to Ginsberg as a poet. "Why don't you try some white shirts and see how people treat you?" he'd suggested.

As an experiment, Allen had purchased a number of inexpensive white shirts at the Salvation Army. To his delight, he discovered that he liked the way they felt and that Trungpa had been correct in his prediction of audience reaction to his new look. "I noticed that people actually were less scared of me," he said, pointing out that there seemed to be less anxiety at his readings. Indeed, his audiences seemed to be paying more attention to what he was saying than before. He decided to make the change a permanent one.

On May 5, Allen was the honored guest performer in the second annual William Carlos Williams Poetry Festival held in Paterson. He used the occasion to read "Plutonian Ode" and meet with younger poets from the area, whom he encouraged to write in the Williams tradition. A couple weeks later, on May 20, he and Eugene recited their father's poems at a Louis Ginsberg memorial reading held at Ramapo College. Not surprisingly, Allen was moved by the event, by the way Louis's poems were still so highly regarded. "It seemed right, correct that his spirit lived on my lips and Gene's," Allen noted in his journal, happy that Louis had been on the mark when he had assured Allen that one's spirit lives on after death.

The readings left Allen feeling nostalgic. He remembered his own youth in New Jersey, how he had been inspired by his nighttime walks through Paterson and by the sight of the Passaic Falls. The times, he recalled, were not always easy. He had heard his share of anti-Semitic remarks, and he had endured the scorn of classmates who called him "Mr. Professor" because of his sensitive and studious nature. As he recalled in "Garden State," a poem written that spring, New Jersey had once been a beautiful state, filled with farms and green lawns and quiet wooded parks. Time had changed it—and not always for the better. New Jersey, perhaps symbolic of the rest of the United States and the world, had grown numb in the face of impending disaster:

> Now turn on your boob tube
> They explain away the Harrisburg
> hydrogen bubble, the Vietnam war,
> They haven't reported the end of Jersey's gardens,
>
> much less the end of the world. . . .

To Allen, it was almost intolerably sad. Maybe it was time for a return to some of the values of yesteryear, typified by families gathering for picnics or taking summer vacations in the countryside. "Let's get our stuff together," he exhorted his readers at the end of the poem. "Let's go back Sundays & sing old springtime music/on Greystone State Mental Hospital lawn."

Significantly, the last line of the poem, with its inherent reference to his mother, was not included in the original draft of the work. Without that specific reference, "Garden State" ended on a utopian note that was uncharacteristic of Ginsberg's memories of his childhood and that ignored the price, real and metaphorical, people had paid for the "progress" cited earlier in the poem. The revised ending kept the poem consistent with those messages delivered over the decades, never lost in moments of nostalgia, celebrity, or personal turmoil.

7

Allen's European reading tour included visits to Paris, Cambridge, London, Newcastle, Amsterdam, Rotterdam, and Rome—all in a whirlwind schedule that lasted less than a month. He traveled with Peter and Steven Taylor, Taylor now providing musical accompaniment at all of Allen's readings. Never one to take the stage without some kind of message to deliver, Allen spoke to his European audiences about the benefits of meditation and the harms of nuclear energy. Meditation, he told the huge crowds of young people coming to see him, was more ample than drugs as a best means of getting in touch with and raising one's consciousness.

Summer poetry festivals were still quite popular in Europe, and Allen enjoyed being a part of the warm collective spirit that accompanied these gatherings. However, at the three-day Roman Summer festival on the beach of Castelporzi-ano in nearby Ostia, Allen had to use his best skills at diplomacy, along with his experiences in organizing large gatherings, to avoid becoming caught up in an ugly, violent scene. The festival, which featured a large roster of interna-tional poets, was disrupted repeatedly from the beginning by political dissidents, street poets, and self-described anarchists who demanded equal time on the makeshift stage. During the first two days of the festival, several poets had been shouted down and were unable to finish their readings. In addition, dissidents had commandeered the microphones and refused to let other poets read. Some of the protesters had thrown sand-filled bottles and cans at the poets, adding an element of physical danger to the already-tense environment.

Allen was scheduled to read on the last evening of the festival as a part of an impressive gathering that included William Burroughs, Lawrence Ferlinghetti, Amiri Baraka, Gregory Corso, Ted Berrigan, Diane Di Prima, Anne Waldman, and Yevgeny Yevtushenko. Before the performance, Allen and a number of the poets met with festival organizers to plot strategy. A veteran of such planning sessions, Allen suggested that organizers and poets alike avoid any hint of a confrontational attitude, that they try to accommodate the disrupters without actually turning over the stage to them. Some of the dissidents had said they were anarchists in the Beat tradition. In taking over the stage during earlier readings, they had announced that as far as the people were concerned, soup was more important than poetry. Well, said Ginsberg, if that was the case, he was more than willing to contribute money for a big kettle of minestrone soup.

This, however, was still not enough. When the poets took the stage for their performances, the anarchists disrupted the reading by bringing the soup kettle onstage—an action that threatened to collapse the stage itself. Peter Orlovsky, in what Allen later described as "one of his greatest moments," commandeered the microphone and ordered the dissidents from the stage. The soup was returned to the audience and the reading went on. Yevtushenko and Baraka drew enthusiastic response to their works, as did Allen when he read "Plutonian Ode." By the time the performance ended at two in the morning, the poets had won over their audience, with only a handful of dissidents—whom Allen suspected of being CIA agents provocateurs—continuing to disrupt the performances.

After completing his schedule in Europe, Allen returned to Naropa, where he led his summer class through a line-by-line discussion of Blake's "Vala, or the Four Zoas." Buried beneath a mountain of paperwork, unanswered mail, constant concerns about Naropa, and readings and activities in Boulder and elsewhere, he had little time to write. It was just as well. As he complained to Philip Whalen, he was mired in a case of writer's block that had limited him in recent months to "a few short musings and continuing work on monolithic Plutonian Ode." He had written nothing noteworthy while he was in Europe— a rarity for Ginsberg, who usually came up with at least one gem while he was traveling—and he was unhappy with what he was presently writing in Boulder. He was heartened somewhat when Whalen, a good poet and exemplary Buddhist, wrote back to say that he had gone through a similar prolonged period of writer's block himself and had not written anything to his satisfaction in years.

Allen's creative problems had little to do with lack of ambition or ability. In his journals, he wrote many new poems, some fairly good and salvageable. One such poem, a sequel to "America," showed promise:

> America it's 25 years since I talked to you, (it's) time we had
>   another conversation
> America, (this time) you better listen, with both ears!
> Open your eyes! Straighten your back! breath through your nose
>   & pay attention—
> Don't worry you can always daydream watching television.
> It's time you learned how to meditate! Stop shouting about
>   mysticism!

As the poem progresses, Ginsberg throws all of his rage and despair into the work—all of his concern about the environment, his anger over two decades of politics that included the Vietnam War and government spying on its own citizens, the CIA's meddling in other countries' affairs, mass consumerism and *Time* magazine mentality, nuclear energy, and domestic violence. As in the earlier poem, he challenges America to respond to questions that read more like accusations:

> Who shot John Kennedy?
> Who overthrew Allende?
> Who tried to kill Castro?
> Who killed Malcolm X?
> Who ordered Kent State?
> Who destroyed Martin Luther King?

However, unlike the earlier work, where the questions remain unanswered and America is indicted by its own silence, Ginsberg now answers the questions himself. He is far too angry to let the country hide behind silence or cover-ups, which he feels it has been doing for so many years. Unfortunately, his answers weaken the poem, robbing it of the biting sarcasm and poignant moments of the original. Without humor, the poem becomes a litany of accusations. Ginsberg wants the country to meditate, but from the tone of the poem, the message is lost in his tirade.

The new version is not without its charm, and it probably could have been worked into something worthy of publication, but Ginsberg was too constricted by worries and distractions to give it further thought. In the earlier poem, he challenges America to straighten up and give him something to believe in; in the newer work, he is still posing the same challenge, but it is obvious that he has become skeptical about the eventuality of that happening.

The reason for his anger and lack of focus is not difficult to determine. The summer session at Naropa was especially difficult, with Allen and school officials trying to find a way to fight off what was now, in the attendant negative publicity connected with the Trungpa-Merwin episode, a serious image problem. In their staff meetings, the main thrust of discussion was, as Allen put it, "how to make the school less star trip and more grounded, teaching students to actually read and write." As Allen was learning, getting beyond the ill will generated by the Trungpa-Merwin episode was not going to be an easy accomplishment. The more he addressed the issue, the stronger the alliance against Trungpa seemed to become. Kenneth Rexroth, comparing Trungpa to Devadatta, an anti-Buddha and spokesman for illusion, wrote a scathing statement that concluded that "many believe Chögyam Trungpa has unquestionably done more harm to Buddhism in the United States than any man living" and proposed that he be deported. Rexroth, a Buddhist himself, also hinted that Trungpa might be connected to the CIA, though he wasn't specific as to how. Tom Clark, in an article questioning the fund-raising tactics at Naropa, continued his campaign against Trungpa and his school.

Allen was at a loss as to what to do. Initial talks with Clark and Dorn had gone poorly, and he did not trust his temper and judgment enough to continue the dialogue. He wrote in his journal:

> I'm paralyzed on the score. For years I've refrained from explaining or arguing petty criticism, or avoided criticizing bad poetic behavior in public, until smoked out by Tom Clark. I answered his curiosity [about] what I thought of Trungpa-Merwin dispute four years ago, and later felt bad I'd taken sides and talked in public about other people's private business. . . . As time's gone on the last two years, the conflict's crossed my mind every morning on waking, and I've had difficulty knowing whether I'm lying to myself to cover Trungpa's Hierarchical secrecy, or lying to Clark in not openly and continuously confronting him in his journalistic spitefulness and intrigue. . . . This inhibits my working altogether since I don't want to waste my poesy and readers' time on gossip and spite, or exhibit my own confusion [and] anger with [a] phalanx of irritable critics.

There was other work to do. Allen had two book projects that urgently required his attention. The first, *Composed on the Tongue*, a collection of interviews, lectures, and a lengthy series of journal entries on his 1967 encounters with Ezra Pound, had been sitting in proofs, awaiting his attention for nearly two years. Allen was scheduled to be in San Francisco in early September and he hoped to use some of his time in the city meeting with Don Allen, the book's editor, to work on finalizing it. The other project, *Straight Heart's Delight*, was a documentation of Allen's and Peter's twenty-five-year relationship. The ambitious book project included Allen's and Peter's love poems, an excerpt from Allen's interview in *Gay Sunshine*, erotic drawings of Allen and Peter by Robert LaVigne, and a large selection of the Ginsberg-Orlovsky correspondence. Allen hoped to see the book issued on the silver anniversary of their exchange of vows in San Francisco, but as of early August, with the publishing date less than a year away, he still had much work to do on it.

8

Even though at fifty-three Allen had reached an age and reputation that might have afforded him an easier, less hectic life, he gave no indication of slowing down. No one would have begrudged his cutting back his reading schedules and taking on a full-time teaching job. Or he could have easily slipped into a life of semiretirement, living in either of his two rustic homes, writing poetry, and playing the part of man of letters. This, however, was not his disposition. If anything, he was taking on more work. Besides teaching at Naropa and taking his customary spring and fall poetry reading tours, Allen worked at the task of organizing his past for future scholars. He had hundreds of journals, pocket notebooks, calendars, address books, poetry manuscripts, unsorted letters and news clippings, tapes of readings, interviews, lectures, and countless photographs—all in need of organization and filing. In his New York apartment, there were, quite literally, shopping bags full of unsorted materials awaiting his attention. He had moved most of his archival material to a deposit at Columbia University, but that, too, was uncataloged and in need of organization. Bob Rosenthal oversaw Allen's current schedules and office activities, and students at Naropa transcribed his journals into neat typescripts, but no one ever seemed to catch up. Allen's energetic past had left behind a mountain of documentation, all of which could be useful to scholars in the future, but by being so active day to day, Allen was replacing the completed archival work with new material.

After an autumn tour that included visits to British Columbia and the Pacific Northwest, a brief stop in San Francisco, and a number of poetry readings as he worked his way back to the East Coast, Allen embarked on his second visit to Europe that year—a trip that included stops in England, Italy, and Germany. In London, he oversaw the production of a 33⅓ rpm flexi-disc recording of "Plutonian Ode," which was inserted into a British literary magazine. At the beginning of December, he made several appearances in Italy for the benefit of the cultural arm of the country's Communist party, and from there he was off to Germany for a month-long series of readings. Sadly, very little new work came from such constant movement.

Back in the United States, there was more rough road ahead. Two books about the Merwin affair, Tom Clark's *The Great Naropa Poetry Wars* and Ed Sanders's class report, *The Party: A Chronological Perspective on a Confrontation at a Buddhist Seminary*, were issued within three months of each other, and once again Allen found himself spending an inordinate amount of time answering questions about the incident. Clark's book, which made no pretense of being objective, was especially problematic. Where Sanders had attempted to reconstruct the event with a minimum of reportorial intrusion or interpretation, Clark took on the role of interpretative historian. That he did not care for Trungpa and his followers was apparent from the onset of the book, and the work might have been dismissed by readers and critics had his charges been any less serious. As it was, Clark's disapproval of Trungpa went well beyond the Merwin episode. He was concerned about the blind allegiance to Trungpa, the reports that his guards were armed with M-16s or submachine guns, what he perceived to be cronyism in the way National Endowment for the Arts grants were awarded to Ginsberg and his friends, and the ongoing war between poets lining up for or against Trungpa. *The Great Naropa Poetry Wars*, which opened with a forty-three-page account of the Halloween party confrontation and its aftermath, was well documented, even if prejudiciously so. Included in its lengthy appendix were newspaper and magazine articles and editorials about the controversy, Clark's interview with Ginsberg, an interview with a former Trungpa disciple, the Callahan petition, and a fairly extensive collection of correspondence about the affair. Clark may have tipped his journalistic hand by including Kenneth Rexroth's condemnation of Trungpa as his book's back-cover copy, but there was no question that the book's documentation supported Clark's contention that something very wrong had taken place at Naropa.

Allen was infuriated by what he read and he immediately undertook a line-by-line study of the text, entering copious notes in his journal about what he felt were factual errors in the book. He questioned many of Clark's statements and wondered whether some were libelous or had invaded people's privacy. The irony of being in such a position did not escape him. In the past, he had made public statements that were not entirely accurate, even if he had issued them in good faith. Further, Allen had recently become involved in a detailed PEN investigation of government suppression of underground publications, which, as he well knew, were far from objective in their reportage. Pursuing any kind of legal action, even if there was a basis for it, would have been hypocritical, while taking a strong vocal stance was risky, since the controversy had already driven a wedge into the poetry community, and Allen did not need any further alienation from his colleagues. Still, with the future of Naropa and the poetics school conceivably at stake, he felt he had to take some kind of action.

He began by disproving the serious charge that the Vajra guard was a heavily armed private army, and from there he went on to examine every error or harmful allegation in the text. He was obsessed not only by what had already been published but by the possibility that Clark or Sanders had other evidence or had heard other rumors that had not been included in their respective reports. He talked to Sanders, Clark, and Dorn and spoke to some of the principal figures in the books. His notes expanded, becoming almost as lengthy as the reports themselves. Allen admitted that he was having difficulty distinguishing fact from innuendo, truth from lies, guilt from innocence. One day, he would wonder whether Clark had been guilty of bad intentions; the next day, he would question his own motivations and ego. He was driven by worry for months on end and his journal entries stood as records of his concern:

> Waking early mornings, sometimes still with ache not of love but of dread in my body, spine chilled with the fear of the damage I've wrought to the Dharma assembly of Boulder and Trungpa through my association with egos of Tom Clark, Sanders and myself—how our wrangling and distrust and misunderstandings have led to appearance of scandal in newspaper mind, accumulations of hatred and conflict between poets over my image. So it becomes a battle over my "reputation" or public confidence in projection of myself over 25 years on American mind screen, ripped apart by Clark's truths or lies, or the cumulative karma or effect of my own truths and lies. Or so it seems in the passing mornings. When I do meditation practice the anxiety disappears and the dilemma remains, though apparently harmless, till the next morning's dread awakening to the situation.

Similar writings can be found throughout Ginsberg's journals from the period. As angry or disappointed as he could become with Trungpa's critics and enemies, he could be even more judgmental when examining his own conscience. In seeking the truth at the heart of the so-called poetry wars, he was as tough on himself as anyone else, and while some of the questions that he asked himself were painful to pose, they demanded honest answers:

> I used to boast no identity! Now why am I stuck with the accusation of a fixed identity as Trungpa's sucker? Am I? If so, where else could I go in sincerity if I want meditation? And if I am so fixed on meditation as my destiny and reputation, why don't I meditate more? Is this all my vanity? Why am I torturing myself so? To maintain a public identity? Is this all the play of an obsessive identity that wants perpetuation through all these changes of public character, position, and explanation? Is it because I make my living on the stage, reading supposedly real poetry? Is my poetry not now empty of expressing any true preoccupations, feelings, information, knowledge, anxieties and lies and truths? Will writing this dilemma here help me to sleep better in the morning? Should I renounce Trungpa and retire to my farm? Should I renounce the argument and my public identity altogether and retire to hermitage to meditate 100% till I die into Tibetan Book of the Dead? Who am I? I don't know! Isn't that really good? Or have I lost my nerve? When did I ever think in terms of nerve anyway? Who cares about aggressive Nerve? Who wants Macho Nerve?

Given the benefit of hindsight, the great irony—not only to Ginsberg's agonizing self-examination but to the conflict between poets itself—is that neither Ginsberg, Clark, Ed Sanders, Ed Dorn, Anne Waldman, or any of the others who found themselves debating the issue in public or private was truly responsible or held accountable for the events that had begun the debate. Ginsberg, Clark, and the others had their own interests to protect, yet, for all their bickering, posturing, and public proclamations, their intentions were generally honorable. In their roles as journalists, Clark and Sanders sought to present the facts, no matter how unpleasant. Ginsberg, who had developed a distrust of journalists skeptical of the spiritual aura surrounding so many public events, was naturally defensive about Trungpa, Buddhism, and the poetics school, especially when they were attacked by those who did not understand—or care to know about—the spirituality that was so much a part of Naropa's founding in the first place. Both Ginsberg and Clark had important messages to deliver on a topic of genuine concern, but with the air filled with arrows of distrust, resentment, defensiveness, ill will, accusation, and innuendo, the messengers were wounded before they could clearly state their message.

The damage caused by the fighting, which went on for years, is inestimable, but there is no question that it was very real. Allen, for example, had gone to great lengths to announce and promote the abilities of such young poets as David Cope, Antler, Andy Clausen, Jeff Poniewaz, and others, but in the wake of the cronyism charges, one can only wonder whether Ginsberg's credibility had been damaged. If he had been accused of playing favorites by trying to use his name and position to help secure grant money for such established poets as Ted Berrigan, Anne Waldman, Diane Di Prima, Larry Fagin, Gregory Corso, and others, what could be said about his trying to further the careers of unknowns? And was the rejection of some of Allen's favored younger poets a matter of editors not caring for the work, or were the editors reacting to Allen himself?

Antler was a case in point. A Milwaukee poet with a great love for Whitman, Antler had known Allen since 1967. He had attended Naropa a decade later, when gossip about the Merwin affair was reaching its peak. He had shown Allen "Factory," his long sequence of interconnected poems about the time he had spent working in a can factory in Milwaukee, and Allen's response had been very encouraging. Allen felt the work was a powerful outcry against dehumanization at the hands of modern industry. One could see from Antler's long lines, cataloging, and oratorical voice that both Ginsberg and Whitman were major influences. When Antler had difficulty finding a publisher for "Factory," Allen interceded on his behalf, but to very little immediate success. The text, a fragment of a much longer work entitled *Last Words*, remained unpublished until Ferlinghetti released "Factory" as part of his "Pocket Poets" series.

This is not to say that Allen's involvement hindered the poem's chances of being published. Major publishing houses have always been reluctant to issue poetry books, and Antler was showing his work to the better-known houses. Still, if Allen had recommended a work of such obvious merit prior to the Naropa publicity, he *might* have been able to use his influence to push it through. This is speculation, of course, but there is little doubt that, in light of the negative publicity coming out of Naropa and Allen's continued support of Trungpa, a portion of the poetry community had lined up against Allen in a battle that reached beyond a small Buddhist community in Boulder.

9

By mid-1980, Allen had begun to compile another collection of poems for City Lights. His new volume would feature "Plutonian Ode," which Allen had revised to his satisfaction, along with other poems written between 1977 and 1980. The works written during that period were of decisively uneven quality, reflective of Allen's writer's block and inner turmoil, but he had worthy poems to consider for inclusion in the volume nevertheless. There were the now-familiar blues and rhymed lyrics, meditative musings, Blake imitations, and political statements. Most recently written works for consideration included a series of three-line poems written while he had participated in a Vajrayana study in May, as well as a sequence of erotic poems patterned after Sappho. Most of the journal poetry written during this time was, to Allen's thinking, unsatisfactory, and though he had far less to choose from now than in such previous volumes as *Planet News* and *The Fall of America*, he had nearly enough acceptable material to fill out a book.

At this point, he was spending as much time as possible in Boulder, teaching his basic poetics course, lending a hand with the school's fund-raising activities, and continuing his efforts to smooth over the poetry wars. As usual, he had fallen far behind in his Buddhist studies, and while he was not happy about it, he was finally beginning to reconcile such failings in his studies and meditation practices. He tried to find time to meditate every day and to stay current in his Vajra reading assignments, but he was not as free as others to devote the ideal amount of time to it.

Knowing that he would be spending the last three months of the year in Eastern Europe and Germany, Allen gave very few readings the first half of the year; instead, he tried to put his affairs in order. At the end of July, he flew to Rome, where he participated in another summer poetry festival with William Burroughs, Gregory Corso, Michael McClure, Anne Waldman, and a large group of other American and Italian poets—without the kind of incidents that had marred his previous appearance at the festival. Unfortunately, Allen had little time to relax or tour the sites of Rome and he flew back to the United States as soon as his involvement in the festival was finished. He was needed at Naropa. The summer session at the poetics school went as well as could be expected. Burroughs and Philip Whalen stayed in Boulder for a portion of the summer and their presence seemed to ease Allen's mind.

It was presidential election year and the country's interest in and support of conservative politics, typified by the speeches of Republican party candidate Ronald Reagan, prompted many discussions around Naropa. Fundamentalist Christians, united behind Jerry Falwell's Moral Majority, greatly influenced the development of the Republican party's political platform and that, along with the nation's continuing frustration with President Jimmy Carter's inability to free Americans held hostage in Iran, all but guaranteed a conservative swing in the U.S. political arena. Allen feared the worst. In the 1950s, while serving as president of the Screen Actors Guild, Reagan had been a part of the anti-Communist McCarthy mind-set, and Allen was not at all comfortable with the notion of his becoming the country's next President. He was hardly alone in this line of thinking. Throughout his tour of Eastern Europe that fall, particularly after the general election in November, Allen would hear grave concerns expressed by students and intellectuals in the Soviet Bloc countries, all fearful about the potential problems that a hard-line anti-Communist President might present.

Allen was concerned about such changes in American politics but was not surprised by them. He had seen such a pendulum swing before, and though he continued to be openly critical of this latest brand of conservatism at his readings and in his public statements, in private he seemed almost resigned to what appeared to be an inevitable change: "The Right Wing! They had to put up with us all these years, the crazed left, so now we gotta put up with them. They had to absorb our aggression and intellectual pride, now we'll have to absorb their success and competence and impermeability." In the same journal entry, however, he expressed fears that a new administration and the conservative attitudes he was seeing could lead to such negative results as "police state, bureaucracy, intimidation of populace, media brainwashing, suppression of imagination and dissent."

Allen's visit to Yugoslavia and Hungary fortified his long-standing attitude that it was a mind-set and not a particular political party or system that made such a mess of the world. Corruption and contempt for the masses existed in all forms of government; ideals shriveled and died on the vine. What endured was the mind-set, which almost inevitably led to disaster. In his hotel room in Dubrovnik, Allen composed a chant that ridiculed this folly, which he called "Birdbrain!":

> Birdbrain rules the World!
> Birdbrain is the ultimate product of Capitalism
> Birdbrain chief bureaucrat of Russia, yawning
> Birdbrain ran FBI 30 years appointed by F.D. Roosevelt
>   and never chased the Mafia!
> Birdbrain apportions wheat to be burned, keep prices up on
>   the world market!
> Birdbrain lends money to Developing Nation police-states
>   thru the World Bank!
> Birdbrain never gets laid on his own he depends on his
>   office to pimp for him
> Birdbrain offers brain transplants in Switzerland
> Birdbrain wakes up in the middle of night and arranges his
>   sheets
> I am Birdbrain! . . .

After years of futile attempts, Ginsberg had found his follow-up to "America." Like the poem written a quarter of a century earlier, "Birdbrain!" casts a jaded eye upon the political climate of the day. Both poems possess a wicked humor scornful of the events and information cited throughout the works. Both use their respective poem's title as their base words, and in both, Ginsberg sarcastically identifies himself with the object of his scorn ("It occurs to me that I am America"; "I am Birdbrain!"). In the newer poem, Ginsberg borrows a riff or two from the new-wave music that was gaining popularity among the rebellious youth at the time. In thumbing their noses at the neoconservative Establishment, they were not so different from the Beats rebelling against the Establishment of the 1950s.

"Capitol Air," another political poem written a short time later while Allen was in Germany, is less successful. Ginsberg held the vanity that the poem was, in his words, an "International new wave hit lyric," but in this instance, the raw, garage band feeling to the poem seems inappropriate or silly in some places. The fixed base in the beginning section ("I don't like . . .") adds a sense of angry humor to some verses:

> I don't like Communist Censorship of my books
> I don't like Marxists complaining about my looks
> I don't like Castro insulting members of my sex
> Leftists insisting we got the mystic Fix. . . .

In the more serious verses, however, the fixed base weakens the impact of what Ginsberg was trying to say:

> I don't like K.G.B. Gulag concentration camps
> I don't like the Maoists' Cambodian Death Dance
> 15 Million were killed by Stalin Secretary of Terror
> He has killed our old Red Revolution forever. . . .

"Capitol Air" has its bright and occasionally brilliant moments, but at twenty-four stanzas and lacking a chorus giving them a sense of unity, the song is too long and has too many flaws to reach the "hit" status Ginsberg hoped to achieve.

The song did supply Ginsberg with a closing to *Plutonian Ode*. In his big political books of the sixties (*Planet News*, *The Fall of America*), he had placed mantralike poems ("Pentagon Exorcism," "Hūm Bom!") near the end of the collections, giving the books a sense of momentum as they ended. In "Capitol Air," *Plutonian Ode* had a similar finale. Allen was closing out with a kick.

10

Allen's tour in late 1980 took him through parts of Yugoslavia, Hungary, Austria, Germany, and Switzerland. He was seeing most of these places for the first time and they seem to have inspired him. Although he no longer kept the intricately detailed travel journals characteristic of his younger days, he wrote a great deal while on the trip. He composed many new poems, kept up his dream journal, and entered a number of political musings and observations into his journal.

His readings were greeted with enthusiasm. Allen used the occasions to introduce his audiences to such poems as "Howl," "Kaddish," and "Plutonian Ode," as well as other notable works. He also spoke of Williams and Kerouac, encouraged his audiences to meditate, and sang such selections of Blake's poetry as "The Tyger" and "Nurse's Song." He, Peter, and Steven had ample time for sight-seeing, which gave an otherwise exhaustive tour a sense of adventure.

On December 10, while riding on a train in Germany, Allen was approached by a young art professor bearing the news that John Lennon had been murdered outside his New York apartment by a disturbed young fan. Badly shaken, Allen pondered the loss. "All evening long deep thoughts," he wrote in his journal, "how it will change the world, the loss of a generation's father, end of Beatles forever, the foreverness of such a great early death, like the loss of Beethoven before he wrote his last five symphonies. Will the Western world repent its bitterness?"

To Allen, the loss was inconsolable—as if, he thought, someone had stolen the smile from the *Mona Lisa*. The Ginsberg-Lennon friendship had grown over the years. It had been awkward at first, during the glory years of the Beatles, when Lennon was the focus of endless attention and adulation, but as the years went by and the two saw each other more often and under better circumstances, they became more comfortable together. Lennon initially connected Allen more with his political activism than with his poetry, though he knew from his conversations with Bob Dylan that Dylan held Ginsberg in high esteem and considered him a large influence. That, in Lennon's eyes, was recommendation enough. Then in 1976, not long before Louis Ginsberg's death, Lennon had surprised Allen by telling him he had been listening to a late-night radio program and had heard someone reciting a poem that he really admired. The reader sounded like Dylan but, as it turned out, it was Allen reading "Howl." Lennon was impressed. He had been aware of the work but had never heard it recited before.

Along with his belief that Lennon was a true artistic genius, Allen had always admired Lennon's humanity. "How like Christ, vulnerable, humane, defenseless," he said of Lennon in his journal. Now he was gone, leaving a "big emptiness and sadness to all," the youthful innocence of a song like "I Want to Hold Your Hand" silenced and lost, "in the grave forever."

In addition to the news about Lennon, Allen was also saddened to hear that Barbara Rubin—the filmmaker friend who had helped him with the purchase and establishment of the Cherry Valley farm—had died of a postnatal infection in France. In helping set up the farm, Rubin had believed she and Allen might eventually marry and settle down. A devout Hasidic Jew, she had also hoped to convert Ginsberg to Judaism. His resistance to these ideas had been determining factors in her decision to leave the farm. She later married and moved to southern France. In October, shortly after giving birth to her fifth child, she had developed the infection and died.

Allen remembered her fondly. For all their disagreements—and, toward the end of her time at Cherry Valley, actual fighting—she had been a good friend. Beside helping with the farm, she had been especially understanding of Peter and Julius Orlovsky's respective problems. Allen could still recall one particular occasion when she had protected Julius from Peter, who had taken amphetamines and, out of his mind on the drugs, was threatening his defenseless brother. Rubin had lived at Cherry Valley during a difficult time and had helped Allen through it.

11

The reading tour, like some of his other extended periods of fast-paced activity, exacted a toll on Allen. He, Peter, and Steven had returned to the States in mid-December, stopping briefly in Houston, where at a writer's convention Allen delivered a lecture on keeping a journal. They then headed back to New York. Utterly exhausted, Allen spent the first week of the new year in bed with the flu. In his sickbed, Allen caught up with the nation's news and fumed about what he felt was certain to be a new Cold War under the new Reagan administration. While running for the presidency, Reagan had preached about the country's need to take a stronger, tougher stance in its international politics, and he had used the American hostages in Iran as symbols of the Carter administration's ineffectiveness in foreign policy. Allen was skeptical of Reagan's message. By tradition, presidential candidates from both parties sought to unify voters by finding a national rallying point, and all the rhetoric about the hostages, as well as the talk of the danger the Russians posed in the Middle East and Eastern Europe by their presence in Afghanistan, seemed like so much election-year posturing to Allen. Still, there was no denying that the Reagan strategy had worked. Although voters stayed home in droves, indicating disfavor with both candidates, the public had voted overwhelming in Reagan's favor, indicating a willingness to accept his tough-guy stance. "The accumulated karma of cold wars, hundreds of billions of armaments, [and] the mass of mentality brought by billion-dollar Armageddon budgets," wrote Ginsberg in his journal, "is hardening into definite public doctrine of might's righteousness."

Allen settled in for a winter's work. His East Village apartment, though small and modest, had been recently repainted by Caleb Carr, Lucien's son, and Allen spent the early portion of January arranging its contents to his liking, the place becoming an impressionistic portrait of the artist and man. In his bedroom, he set up a small square-topped altar covered with red cloth, on which he placed a Thai statue of a smiling Buddha, mantra beads, his prostration counter, a box of Japanese temple incense, a Chinese ceramic boat vase that acted as an incense holder, a book on Tantric exercise, and his bell and *dorje*. Nearby stood a Catholic lectern, on which Allen placed the Vajradhara tanka that he had bought while he was in India. He had designed his bed—a flat foam-rubber mattress on a platform with an oversized headboard, covered with oversized white sheets and a yellow and red diamond-patterned wool blanket that he had picked up in Mexico. His father's old desk, piled high with manuscripts, unanswered mail, magazines, and manila envelopes stuffed with files on political and human-rights issues, stood at the foot of the bed. His typewriter, covered with a handpainted red cloth, occupied one corner of the desk.

Evidence of his meditation practice could be found everywhere. A framed calligraphy of Allen's mantra, "AH," painted by Chögyam Trungpa, hung on the wall opposite Allen's bed. Above the altar, he placed a plastic-framed illustration of the Kagyu lineage tree. For his prostrations, he had a three-by-six-foot sheet of shiny brown composition board; for meditation, he had a brightly colored round *zafu* cushion and a brown *zabutan* flat meditation mat.

Naturally, there were plenty of books. One entire wall of his room was lined from floor to ceiling with ones that represented all his interests, from such friends and contemporaries as Kerouac, Burroughs, and Corso to classics by Poe, Shelley, and Blake. Zen and Tibetan Buddhist texts lined several shelves. On a small nightstand at the right side of his bed, Allen kept whatever book he was reading at the time, along with pens, pencils, and his journal.

The particulars of his daily routine had been more or less established for decades. Since he preferred to stay awake late into the night—or, more accurately, early morning—often eating his dinner at a time when most people were getting ready to retire for the evening, Allen liked to sleep late. Upon rising, he would record his dreams or waking thoughts in his bedside journal and then he would meditate or do his prostrations if his schedule permitted. He would discuss his daily schedule with Bob Rosenthal, who worked in an office in the next room on most weekdays. Allen had little trouble filling his waking hours.

The duties of screening Allen's calls, arranging his day-to-day appointments, working on travel arrangements, seeing that bills were paid on time, warding off unneeded distractions, and, in general, freeing Allen to write, read, study, or play fell to Rosenthal. He managed all of this with great efficiency, matched only by his cheerful disposition. Without Rosenthal—and, later, other office personnel hired to assist him—Allen might have been crushed beneath the weight of his own activity, which had become as much an industry as it was a lifestyle.

People came and went at all hours. Visitors and friends checked in whenever they were in town or the neighborhood. Bill Morgan, a full-time bibliographer, was often on hand, working on the cataloging of Allen's journals, letters, and published essays, as well as news clippings, magazine articles and interviews, and the poetry publications in which Allen's work appeared. People needing information from his various files would stop by, and students working on master's theses or doctoral dissertations would be assisted in their work. Overnight guests were common.

At the beginning of 1981, Allen had two specific projects demanding his attention. He needed to finalize the manuscript for *Plutonian Ode and Other Poems*, which Ferlinghetti hoped to publish before the end of the year. Most of the selections for the book's contents had already been determined, but he continued to revise some of the poems, particularly "Capitol Air," right up until the time the manuscript was to be set in type.

The other project involved a book by William Burroughs. A selection of Burroughs's letters to Allen—written between 1953 and 1957, when Burroughs was fighting his drug addiction and writing *Naked Lunch* in Tangier—was being published by Anne Waldman and Ron Padgett's Full Court Press. Allen had been asked to read through the letters and write the introductory notes to the volume. He was both disappointed and relieved that the correspondence was one-sided, that Bill had not saved the letters Allen had written during that period. He was also disappointed that Burroughs had chosen to edit much of the material, particularly the references to his and Allen's sexual relationship. ("Alas! the most extravagant passages, abject letters of complete schlupp-longing, and prophetic curse at my ingratitude, have been censored by the author," Allen wrote in the introduction, adding that in taking out some of the material, Burroughs had removed "the red heart valentine center" from the book.) Still, Allen was happy with the collection and with the honesty that came through in the letters that were included. Burroughs's publishing the letters, he wrote, was "an act of benevolence" to all eventual readers. In rereading the letters for the first time in many years, Allen realized what they had represented at the time of their composition. "I didn't deserve it!" he wrote in his journal, "the richness of his gifts, big long bawdy letters, unintelligible delights!"

Most of Allen's new writings dealt with his increasing dissatisfaction with U.S. involvement in other countries' affairs, especially in Central America, which had become a major focus of the Reagan administration. He felt the United States was caught up in the old anti-Communist position it had taken thirty years ago; he could not fathom how the country, even given its anti-Communist stance, could support the right-wing Salvadoran government and its death squads while at the same time doing everything it could to discourage the leftist Sandinista government in Nicaragua. He was further dismayed by the media's quick acceptance of official explanations for the country's policies in Central America. The setup seemed too similar to the way the United States had become involved in Vietnam.

Allen's journal entries from this period contain numerous statements expressing his concern: "Woke disturbed by the realization in half-sleep that the consequences of this numbed monolithic government media U.S. blanket of stereotype on Central America would lead to increased bloodshed, terror tyranny, endless armed conflict—another decade of military horror in Central America as in 1960's Vietnam." Something had to be done to prevent the kind of U.S. intervention that had led to Vietnam, but Allen was at a loss as to what course of action should be taken. "What can I do as poet to cut through this horrific confusion?" he wondered.

Meditation, he was willing to concede, was not enough to have any bearing on keeping "a recurrent war nightmare happening right now [from] becoming history." At one time, he had believed that getting all people to meditate might help settle their minds and ease their fears and confusions, but this, he now realized, was so much idealistic thinking. "What help is Buddhist meditation to the isolated Salvadoran rebels?" he wrote. "How would it affect and temper U.S. military confusion, except for Bodhisattvas on both sides to withdraw and leave the terrorized and ignorant populations struggling with each other in lethal wars for decades?"

Allen kept up on the developments in Central America as they unfolded. He collected news clippings and had long discussions about the events in El Salvador and Nicaragua with friends and professional associates. During one of their late-night telephone conversations, William Burroughs, in his typically dry, flat manner, offered one explanation for the world's seemingly endless political quagmire.

"No problems can be solved," he told Allen. "As soon as they're problems they're insoluble. No problems can be solved, and all solutions lead to more problems."

Burroughs's words sounded familiar to Allen. "Who wrote that?" he asked Bill.

"I did," Burroughs said.

It was a fascinating idea, Allen had to admit, but he was not entirely committed to accepting such a cynical premise. He continued to write his private soliloquies and poems in his journal, forging ahead for answers as he always did, by searching relentlessly for the precisely correct question.

12

On February 29 and March 1, Allen recorded about a dozen new songs at the ZBS Studio in upstate New York, the sessions financed by a CAPS grant from the New York State Council on the Arts and by the NEA. Almost five years had passed since his recording sessions with John Hammond. During that time, Allen had sung selections of his music at virtually all of his poetry readings. Although he was no longer writing new songs with the frequency characteristic of his songwriting in the early and mid-seventies, he was enthusiastic about putting such songs as "Capitol Air" and "Old Pond," as well as Blake's "Tyger" and "My Pretty Rose Tree," on record. The farmhouse studio, located on the banks of the Hudson and surrounded by maple trees, was an ideal environment for work. Along with Peter Orlovsky and Steven Taylor, Allen had enlisted David Amram, Jon Sholle, and Arthur Russell to provide the musical accompaniment and background vocals for his songs. Of the music recorded during these sessions, seven songs—including one written by Peter and one by Steven—would be included on Allen's 1983 Hammond-released *First Blues* album.

Allen was certainly getting his mileage out of the title *First Blues*—to the point where he would eventually have to explain which production he was talking about whenever he mentioned it. He had used *First Blues* as the title for his book of ballads and blues lyrics published by Full Court Press in 1975 and he was also using it as a generic title for all the songs he had recorded with Dylan, Hammond, and, most recently, at ZBS. In addition, Folkways Records was releasing a *First Blues* of its own—a recording taped by Harry Smith in the mid-seventies, on which Allen sang a selection of his early songs and accompanied himself on Benares harmonium. The Folkways album, produced by Ann Charters, featured such songs as "New York Blues," "4AM Blues," and "Prayer Blues"—all unrecorded in other sessions but included as lyrics in the book. Allen himself admitted that it could get confusing.

From a technical standpoint, his skills as a singer and songwriter had not changed a great deal over the years. The artistic quality of his music and lyrics still varied from song to song. However, Ginsberg was a spirited performer and the songs added a charming dimension to his readings. He would never receive the recognition for his music he would have liked, but that did not inhibit his efforts in years to come.

Allen was still in the recording studio, working on some of the songs' overdubs, when he learned that Billy Burroughs had died in Florida as a result of cirrhosis of the liver. William Burroughs and Joan Vollmer's son had lived a hard, difficult life. He had wandered aimlessly for a good portion of his adult years, many of which were recorded in *Speed* and *Kentucky Ham*, autobiographical books not unlike the early works of his father. He had been addicted to morphine and amphetamines and had destroyed himself by alcohol abuse. He had not yet reached thirty when his health began to fail. He had received a liver transplant in 1976, but even that had not halted his drinking. Allen tried to help Billy by finding him a position as a teaching assistant at Naropa, but it had done little to prevent his demise. Billy was thirty-three years old at the time of his death.

When he returned to Boulder for his spring teaching session, Allen held a small memorial service for Billy and saw that his ashes were buried in the mountains. He also sorted through Billy's personal belongings, manuscripts, and papers, assuming the role of literary executor. There was a wealth of unpublished, salvageable material in his notebooks and Allen hired a Naropa student to type this material into a clean manuscript suitable for presentation to a publisher.

That spring, Allen taught another installment of his "Literary History of the Beat Generation" course. The lectures, which were very detailed in their account of the literary movement, were taped and stored, awaiting transcription sometime in the future. Once the series of lectures had been completed, they would comprise the most complete autobiographical statement Allen would deliver outside of his poetry and published journals. They would have made an interesting book, but Allen did not have the time to work on it himself.

In fact, it would have not have been too difficult for him to write several books tracing his artistic lineage. Beside his "Literary History of the Beat Generation" lectures, he had lectured extensively on Blake, Williams, Kerouac, and objectivist poets. These lectures alone would have made up a lengthy volume.

Or, if he had so chosen, Allen could have written an interesting book about the artworks that had inspired his poetry. When asked about those influences, he always had an impressive list to offer and he could speak authoritatively on a variety of painters, from Cézanne to Franz Kline. His knowledge of Blake's paintings was enough for a scholarly work.

He could also have written about the way different types of music had influenced his work. That heritage was also fairly specific, from the blues, gospel, and classical music he had heard as a child to the jazz he had listened to as a Columbia student and young adult, from the folk music and rock 'n' roll he enjoyed in the sixties and seventies to his most recent interest in new-wave music. All were powerful influences at one time or another. Like so many noteworthy artists, Allen possessed the ability to integrate a huge spectrum of influences into work that, given the benefit of his unique vision, both maintained the established form and yet changed it into something else.

To his credit, Allen always stayed open to new forms of expression, and in June he was able to link up with another element in this cultural/artistic heritage when he performed onstage with the Clash, the most highly acclaimed of the current new-wave groups. The association was purely accidental and spontaneous. After completing his teaching at Naropa, Allen returned to New York, where he planned to wrap up some business before setting out on an intensive two-month period of international travel. The Clash had a long-running engagement at Bonds, a Manhattan rock club, and Allen was eager to see them. He had been aware of their working class, antiestablishment music for some time and felt they added a legitimate voice of protest to a political climate that, like the political arena of the fifties, found the populace willing to follow leaders blindly wherever they went. Allen went to Bonds to see the Clash on June 10 and was ushered backstage to meet them.

"Well, Ginsberg, when are you gonna run for President?" lead singer Joe Strummer asked when Allen was introduced to the band.

"Never," Allen answered. "I'll wind up in Diamond Hell." The comment referred to a remark Trungpa had made years earlier at a party, when he admonished Allen for acting like a know-it-all when he discussed political matters. If Allen ever ran for President, Trungpa had told him, he would wind up in Vajra hell, the inescapable prison of his own ego.

Strummer thought it would be interesting if Ginsberg became a part of that evening's performance, so he asked him whether he had any poems he could read to the audience. He pointed out that there was some risk involved. Their audiences had the reputation of being vocal and disruptive; they could be intimidating or abusive to guest performers. "We had somebody get up to lecture about El Salvador, and they were throwing tomatoes," Strummer told Allen.

Allen was not about to be discouraged. He had performed onstage with Bob Dylan and John Lennon in the past, as well as appearing with such controversial social commentators as Phil Ochs and the Fugs. Although these artists had not been known for attracting rowdy followings, Allen was not intimidated by performing with the Clash. If anything, doing so was fulfilling part of a long-time ambition. "I always wanted to get up in front of 100,000 screaming kids and sing a song I wrote myself," he would later admit. "That's when politics becomes an extension of poetic fantasy."

There were not 100,000 in attendance at Bonds that evening—an estimate placed the crowd at about 3,000—and the audience's level of political commitment is probably a subject open to debate, but Allen felt he had just the song for them. "I got a poem that has chord changes," he told the Clash. "You want to try that?"

The song was "Capitol Air." After rehearsing it backstage for about ten minutes, Allen and the band went onstage and performed it, to enthusiastic response. Allen could not have been more pleased. He had succeeded in creating his new-wave hit.

13

The summer of 1981 found Allen racing around, completing work on the proofs of *Plutonian Ode*, traveling extensively, and moving his residence from New York to Boulder. Even at fifty-five, he maintained an incredible reserve of energy that was recognized—almost with awe—by people half his age. One Naropa student may have summarized it best when she informed a reporter that "writing about Allen is like running after a train you'll never catch." The statement could have been made at any point in Allen's life.

Plutonian Ode, dedicated to Lucien Carr, was Allen's final contribution to the City Lights "Pocket Poets" series. Allen had remained loyal to Ferlinghetti and to other small presses for a quarter of a century, but now that he was advancing in years he was beginning to think about setting up a financial nest egg for his old age. He was also interested in finding a large hardcover publishing house to handle the publication and wide-scale distribution of a volume of his collected works. He would realize both goals within two years, when he signed a lucrative six-book contract with Harper & Row, the first book to be *Collected Poems 1947–1980.*

Although not as strong as some of the earlier Ginsberg collections, *Plutonian Ode* was a reasonable enough effort. Allen included what he considered to be his major works from the period—"Plutonian Ode," "Birdbrain!" and "Capitol Air"—along with a number of poems that continued the line of meditation-influenced ones found in *Mind Breaths.* Since Ginsberg was interested as always in presenting a graph of his mind, he was more concerned about the honesty in his poems than their artistic perfection. He had long ago concluded that the creative mind operated on a peaks and valleys principle, and he had come to believe that history would determine which poems represented his high points as a poet.

In a way, *Plutonian Ode* stands as Ginsberg's most pessimistic book, even if at the end of the opening and closing poems he is exhorting his readers to take action to defeat the maladies of the world. In the past, Ginsberg had taken an angry stance against death, his lifelong obsession, but in *Plutonian Ode* his Buddhist beliefs overpower this stance. We're all heading toward that great emptiness, he seems to be saying, and at the rate we're going, it may be sooner than we'd like. In addition, there is the matter of all the imitations in the book. Not since the early poems published in *The Gates of Wrath* had Ginsberg been so devoted to practicing the forms of his literary predecessors. In *Plutonian Ode,* one hears the unmistakable voices of Sappho, Whitman, Neruda, and Blake, among others, and when considering the overall tone of the book, one might wonder: Are these poems homages to the poets or are they intimations that, in seeing such a bleak future Ginsberg was turning back, consciously or otherwise, to his past? Granted, in "Birdbrain!" and "Capitol Air," one hears the distinct sound of the new wave, but that kind of music has never been accused of being overly optimistic.

The critics picked up on some of this when the book was published. "Political despair has swept the field, and the underground naivete and optimism are gone," wrote a reviewer for *The Village Voice,* presenting the opinion that "perhaps society has reached a stage where our language can no longer cope with the mess we find ourselves in." A critic for the *Los Angeles Times* added, "Seemingly fatalistic—as if Doomsday has already come—Ginsberg howls on. Small pleasures become sweeter, sillier, lasting. Now, he warns in his poems, we wait in that moment between the Bomb's vision and its strength."

Allen's travels that summer and early fall included trips to Mexico City—where he participated in an international writer's conference with such notables as Andrei Voznesensky, Günter Grass, Jorge Luis Borges, and Octavio Paz—and to Toronto—where he saw another opening of the stage adaptation of "Kaddish." He also made what by now was beginning to seem like an annual pilgrimage to Italy and its poetry festival. This time, he was reunited with Julian Beck and Judith Malina, his old friends from the Living Theatre, and they enjoyed a brief period of sight-seeing in Italy before Ginsberg had to return to the States.

In October, Allen relocated to 2141 Bluff Street in Boulder, which he would use as his full-time headquarters throughout the early 1980s. Although by nature he was more suited to the urban landscape and artistic environment of New York than he was to the quiet college town set in the foothills of the Rockies, Allen believed that the move was necessary in order for him to take a more active role in guiding the poetics school at Naropa. The worst of the poetry wars was behind him, but there were still enough hard feelings and suspicion aimed toward Naropa to cause him concern about the school's future.

Besides, teaching had become one of his main priorities. Naropa was an ideal situation, since the school afforded him the freedom to travel on business, for poetry readings and conferences, or for pleasure. When asked, Allen would admit that an added attraction to the job was the presence of young students willing and even eager to sleep with him. For all the gray in his beard, there was still youth in his heart.

14

On November 14, 1981, Allen traveled to New York to give a reading at Columbia University's McMillin Theatre. He had been a part of two previous historic readings at the theater, but this one, featuring a twenty-fifth anniversary reading of "Howl," was even more greatly anticipated. A sellout crowd, including members of Allen's family, was in attendance when Allen stepped onstage.

In his introduction to *Howl and Other Poems,* William Carlos Williams had expressed concern for the young Ginsberg's future. The elder poet's worries had been justified at the time. The intensely gifted, angry, depressed, and confused Paterson youth he had met appeared to be headed toward self-destruction. He was experimenting with drugs, hanging out with junkies and geniuses, brooding about his homosexuality, and struggling to find his voice as a poet. He had been expelled from a prestigious university, arrested for his involvement in a burglary ring, and placed in a psychiatric institution—all before he had reached his twenty-third birthday. Williams recognized Ginsberg's genius, but in Allen's case, it seemed to be both a blessing and a curse. His survival would depend upon how he used his gifts.

Allen, of course, survived not only his youth but his long, trying adulthood, and in a way it is too bad that Williams was not around to see his bohemian protégé, once clad in a work shirt and dungarees at his readings, now dressed in a suit and tie, as he stood before a roaring crowd and accepted their appreciation for the man he had become. Williams would have seen a poet who had traveled the world on his visionary and humanistic quest, a man unafraid to show that he could be brilliant, silly, wrongheaded, tender, generous, petty, and magnanimous. He would have seen a poet, prophet, and teacher.

But then, the spirit of Williams as well as the spirits of Blake, Shelley, Whitman, Kerouac, and all the other souls who had spoken to Ginsberg over the ages were somehow represented in the rather slight, neatly groomed figure on the stage. This time, Kerouac was not around to pound on a wine jug and shout at the end of each line, but no one in the audience needed encouragement on this occasion. Moloch was a familiar figure who took on many forms, but he was still demanding sacrifices of the generations' children. He breathed the fire of plutonium, of warfare, of racism, of misguided nationalism that led to distrust and hatred.

After being introduced by Anne Waldman as the product of "postwar materialist paranoid doldrums," Allen took the stage, carrying the text of a poem that, as Gary Snyder once said of the Beat Generation itself, had moved the world a millionth of an inch. It was a poem that would continue to astonish and antagonize readers long after this particular poet's time.

Postscript

One of the great misconceptions about Allen Ginsberg in the eighties concerned the poet's literary output. Although it is true that Ginsberg was not as public a figure as he had been in the fifties and sixties, his published work was as prodigious as that at any time in his career. Besides *Plutonian Ode and Other Poems*, Ginsberg issued *White Shroud*, a new collection of poems; *Howl*, a lengthy annotated version of his time-honored poem; and, most significant of all, *Collected Poems 1947–1980*, the eagerly awaited volume gathering all of Ginsberg's works from the previous four decades. As always, Ginsberg continued to publish widely in literary magazines, and interviews with Ginsberg were featured in both large- and small-circulation publications in the United States and abroad.

For Allen, the publication of *Collected Poems* was the realization of a long-held goal. Talk of publishing a volume of collected poems had begun two decades earlier, both in the United States and overseas. Allen had delayed the publication of such a work, first because he maintained his loyalty to Lawrence Ferlinghetti, his longtime friend and publisher, and second because if he was to leave City Lights for another publisher, he needed to find the right establishment for the eventual volume of collected poems—one capable of printing and distributing the book on a scale much larger than the small presses with which he was accustomed to working. In this sense, Harper & Row (later HarperCollins) was an ideal publisher.

Ginsberg's move to the large publishing house was not made without some controversy. Critics accused him of abandoning the smaller presses, which, by tradition, kept quality poetry alive in the United States. This line of criticism seemed especially apparent in 1982, when Allen decided to hire the services of a literary agent. Andrew Wylie—a former writer known for his hard-nosed, controversial, and occasionally combative relationship with publishers—secured for Ginsberg a six-figure, six-book contract that called for a book of collected poems, a collection of new poems, and individual volumes of letters, essays, and journals. The advance, although modest in comparison to the huge amounts commanded by popular fiction writers of the day, gave Ginsberg detractors more fuel for criticism. He had, they contended, sold out.

In fact, the move was entirely pragmatic. Whether he was happy about it or not, Allen had become a kind of poetry industry, with works so widely published and anthologized that he could not possibly keep track of them. Ferlinghetti had shouldered this enormous burden over the years, but even so, a substantial volume of Allen's poetry had been published or reprinted without his being paid for it—or, sometimes, his even being aware of it being published. Allen needed someone to look after his literary affairs, to see that his work was organized and that he had sufficient income to carry him into his old age. At Ferlinghetti's suggestion, Allen began to look for a larger publisher. His earlier works, published as part of the Pocket Poets series, would continue to be reprinted by City Lights, but future books, including the massive volume of collected poems, would go to Harper & Row.

Officially released on February 2, 1985, *Collected Poems* gathered all the poems published by City Lights, as well as those works issued by other small presses. In addition, Allen included a few previously uncollected poems from his published journals. In preparing the volume, which he dedicated to his parents, Allen referred to journals and original manuscripts in an effort to arrange the poems in their correct chronological order. He went over each poem line by line, drawing up voluminous notes that explained his references to historical figures, places, and events, and to Buddhist and Hindu terms. From his photo archives, he selected appropriate photographs of his parents, Kerouac, Cassady, Orlovsky, Burroughs, and others to insert as illustrations in the notes section at the back of the book. Directories of titles and first lines, proper names, and even the books' original flap copies and dedications supplemented the poems and notes. The cover design featured the three-fish Buddha footprint designed by Harry Smith. The book, as Ginsberg admitted, formed a kind of autobiography.

A volume of this nature tends to invite career assessment and overview by critics, and Allen was not disappointed by their response. Reviews poured in, the huge majority favorable. Many reviewers agreed with Allen's admission that his poems were of variable quality—"Ginsberg may be the most uneven of great modern poets," wrote one critic—and many paused to point out what they considered to be the literary sins of Ginsberg's past. After citing such weaknesses, however, the critics offered high praise for the lifetime's achievement represented in *Collected Poems*.

In its review, the *Atlantic Monthly* judged Ginsberg's work by the yardstick standard set by another notable contemporary poet. "A good poet," Randall Jarrell once said, "is someone who manages in a lifetime of standing out in thunderstorms to be struck by lightning five or six times. A dozen or two dozen times and he is great."

"By this measure," wrote the *Atlantic* reviewer, "Allen Ginsberg is doing well, and he still hasn't come in out of the rain."

Other reviewers were equally generous with their praise, many comparing Ginsberg to Whitman, his obvious literary forebear. Others cited Ginsberg's fame and how he had used it to advance interest in modern poetry. He had, said critics, made a big difference. "For 30 years, Ginsberg has been the most famous poet in America, an embodiment of everything this country has hoped and feared a poet could be," noted a reviewer for *The Village Voice*.

Old foes, however, were impossible to appease. *Commentary*, the publication edited by longtime Ginsberg adversary Norman Podhoretz, attacked Ginsberg and his work in a lengthy review entitled "Allen Ginsberg Then and Now." The reviewer, the poetry editor for *New Criterion*, sneered at Ginsberg's contract with Harper & Row and all but accused him of abandoning the rather danger- ous, revolutionary ethic of City Lights. Ginsberg's life and work, the reviewer hinted, had been carefully designed to project a certain image and mythology, and the reviewer could barely disguise his anger, and perhaps even envy, when he wrote that "no living poet and very few dead ones have been treated so respectfully by a publisher as has Allen Ginsberg." Such respect, this critic labored mightily to prove in his review, was not merited: "One need not read between the lines of Allen Ginsberg's life and work to find sleaziness abounding."

Such sentiments were shared by other Ginsberg enemies, who took occasion to ridicule what they considered to be a change in his public position. *Time* magazine, in a full-page review entitled "Mainstreaming Allen Ginsberg," took a lowbrow approach. The magazine's reviewer seemed amazed that the onetime countercultural icon was now living in the world of respectability, dressing in sport coats, meditating, and signing lucrative publishing contracts. In addition, he was less than kind toward Ginsberg's poetry. "Howl," wrote the reviewer, was now "an unconvincing historical oddity," while the love poems "read like high parodies of rest-room scrawl." ("Kaddish," the critic allowed, was "a masterpiece of candor and emotional persuasion.") *Time*, however, saved its unkindest cut for the end of its review, where, in what may be the most insensitive remark ever directed toward Ginsberg in a review or profile, the critic tried to find a clever conclusion to his theory that Ginsberg was interested both in making money and leaving his mark as a poet: "One can see it in his eyes: one wide and innocent, gazing at eternity; the other narrowed and scrutinizing, looking for his market share." Ginsberg, whose face had been partially paralyzed from his bouts of Bell's palsy, was justifiably offended by the remark.

Still, he would survive the cheap shots, as he had in the past. In fact, many of the reviewers praised his ability to survive adversity as one of his most admirable traits. He has lived through two major twentieth-century social movements and their inevitable upheaval, and he has managed to stay relatively calm through the often-difficult life of the artist. His works, uneven as they are, document both his life and times. In the large picture, the controversy generated by some of his poetry seems minor. He can no longer be legitimately accused of acting out just to gain attention. "All in all," wrote Kerouac biogra- pher Gerald Nicosia in a review for the *Chicago Tribune*, "these 'Collected Poems' ring less with the shock of a weird, gay radical's self-exposure, and far more as the testament of a bold and uncompromising survivor."

Had he followed in Whitman's path and written reviews of his own work, Allen could not have stated it better himself.

There was, of course, some merit to the mention of Ginsberg's knack for using publicity in his best interests, even if the reasons for it were misunderstood or written off. Allen has never ceased to employ his remarkable skills in promotion and publicity, developed in the early fifties when he was working in market research and honed by the experience of decades into a sharp understanding of the relationship between the act of creation and the art of promoting it.

He has understood, perhaps as well as any of his contemporaries, the mechanizations and politics of the publishing industry, and he has been tireless in his efforts to see that the central figures and texts of the Beat Generation remain a part of the public awareness. For journalists, an interview with Ginsberg has invariably meant that sooner or later during the course of the conversation one would hear mention of Kerouac, Burroughs, Corso, Huncke, or others. Allen's "Literary History of the Beat Generation" lectures assured the spreading of the Beat message by at least a small but dedicated group of hard-core followers. Allen has been generous with his archives and personal involvement whenever a study or biography of a Beat Generation member was being prepared. He has never lost touch with the vision that brought the original members of the Beat Generation together. He has continued to promote that purpose, occasionally at the cost of slipping into mythologizing or revisionist history, but always with the honorable intention of seeing that the writers and texts maintain a place in literary history.

By the beginning of the 1980s, Allen was well established as a master at organizing fund-raisers and benefit readings, his participation in such events providing numerous beneficiaries—from Buddhist organizations to small presses—with urgently needed money. One particular event seemed to illustrate this. During the summer of 1982, Allen was able to combine his fund-raising abilities and his interests in furthering knowledge of the Beat Generation by organizing a huge conference that became one of the literary events of the year. "On the Road: The Jack Kerouac Conference," held in Boulder in late July and early August, was designed to raise money for Naropa while honoring Kerouac on the eve of the twenty-fifth anniversary of the publication of his breakthrough novel.

At first, Ginsberg envisioned the conference as a high-visibility media event featuring performances and tributes, rather than as a serious study of Kerouac and his books. The Burroughs "Nova Convention" had been a large success, and Allen figured that something along that line might work well for Kerouac. He spent nearly a year planning and developing the convention, but the more he worked on it, the more the conference evolved from a rather glitzy presentation into a more serious endeavor. There would be lectures and panel discussions on a wide variety of topics, from Kerouac's relationships with women to the origins of the Beat Generation, as well as poetry readings, writing classes, film showings, and memorabilia displays. The highlight of the conference would be a complete reading of *On the Road*, performed by Kerouac's contemporaries, some of whom had been central characters in the book itself.

Naropa was far too small to handle the festivities and the number of people expected to attend the conference, so the nearby University of Colorado campus hosted a large share of the activities. The list of speakers, panelists, and guest artists was impressive. Besides the original Beat Generation core group of Ginsberg, William Burroughs, Gregory Corso, Herbert Huncke, and John Clellon Holmes, others in attendance included Lawrence Ferlinghetti, Robert Creeley, Carl Solomon, Robert Frank, Michael and Joanna McClure, and Diane Di Prima. Carolyn Cassady, Joyce Johnson, and Edie Parker Kerouac—three of Jack's former lovers—were joined by Kerouac biographers Ann Charters, Gerald Nicosia, and Dennis McNally. Ken Kesey and Ken Babbs, central figures in the famous cross-country psychedelic bus journey of the sixties, were present, as were Timothy Leary, Abbie Hoffman, Paul Krassner, and other well-known figures from the counterculture that sprang from the Beat Generation's influence. An enormous gathering of members of the national and international news media was on hand, interviewing conferees and filming the lectures, writing reviews of the readings, and photographing nearly everyone in sight.

To Allen, who once envisioned a phalanx of poets and writers capable of breaking through the inertia of the early 1950s, the assembly was inspiring. In the past, friends had occasionally referred to him as "Mama Ginzy"—in humorous tribute to his ceaseless efforts to mother the Beat Generation members and their progeny—and throughout the conference Allen was in great form, overseeing the festivities, meeting with reporters, and offering opinions on what the Beat Generation meant in the grand scale of human events in the latter part of the twentieth century. Typically, he was not shy about praising the group's accomplishments; nor was he afraid at least to attempt to find the common thread of influence running through nearly three decades of literary history.

"The real legacy of Kerouac and the Beats is one of literary liberation," he told reporters, underscoring a point he had been making all along—that the Beats were, first and foremost, artists, not some kind of social fad. "And that literary liberation," he continued, "was the catalyst for Gay liberation, Black liberation, women's liberation, and now, hopefully, liberation from the threat of nuclear destruction."

The conference became the grandest of reunions—the last time these figures would all be able to assemble for a major event. As to be expected, considering those in attendance, the conference brought very little new information about Kerouac to the scholarly canon. It was not a time to debate Kerouac, and participants avoided in-depth discussion of Kerouac's failings, personal or literary, choosing instead to lionize him in a long-overdue tribute. Not that it mattered: Critical books and essays about Kerouac's works were being written, other biographies were in the works, and Kerouac was being studied on college campuses across the country. In the early eighties, when a new conservatism was dredging up old censorship issues and proposing changes that flew in the face of many of the Beat Generation's ideals, it was time to pause and celebrate the past while, at the same time, considering prospects for the future.

Allen produced numerous recordings over the decade, including a noteworthy two-song demo tape with Bob Dylan that was never formally released; the long-delayed Hammond recording of *First Blues*; a raucous rendition of "Birdbrain!"

recorded with the Gluons, a Denver new-wave band; and, finally, *The Lion for Real*, his first collection of spoken poems in over twenty years. The sum of these recordings, when added to the others issued by Ginsberg over the decades, make up an impressive body of work—certainly the most substantial offering of recorded works by any poet in history.

"Do the Meditation Rock," one of the two songs Allen recorded with Dylan, is an up-tempo work that offers instruction on how to practice the Samatha-Vipassana method of Buddhist meditation. The lyrics to the song could not be more basic:

> Follow your breath out   open your eyes
> and sit there steady   & sit there wise
> Follow your breath right   outta your nose
> follow it out   as far as it goes. . . .

Allen still held the belief that popular song was one of the most efficient ways to reach people who might otherwise be turned off by poetry. He further believed that, if given decent circulation, "Do the Meditation Rock," with its catchy melody and sing-along chorus ("Do the meditation/Do the meditation/Learn a little Patience and Generosity"), might reach a reasonably large audience and be useful in teaching it meditation practice.

Unfortunately, neither this song nor "Airplane Blues," the other number recorded with Dylan, was enthusiastically received by record company executives, who were more concerned with sales figures than recording one of the country's poet laureates. "Airplane Blues" is, in its own way, an extension of Ginsberg's auto poesy, finding him exploring familiar themes and contemplating the state of the earth while he was in transit. Like "Father Death Blues," the song was written as he sat on an airplane. The lyrics are smooth, unforced rhyme, ranking among Ginsberg's best blues lines to date:

> I'm alone in the sky
>
>   where there's nothing to lose
> The sun's not eternal
>
>   that's why there's the blues
> majestical jailhouse
>
>   Our joy's in the Cage
> Hearts full of hatred
>
>   will outlast my old age. . . .

Allen worked on a handful of new lyrics in the early 1980s, but he never went far beyond the writing stage. He would perform some of the new songs at his readings, but going through the process of making high-quality recordings, with no promise of ever seeing the records pressed and distributed, involved more work and expense than he could afford. As it was, he had an unissued album of Blake songs, along with the spoken poems he had recorded with Barry Miles, gathering dust in the vaults.

He had more success elsewhere. In January 1982, at the invitation of the Clash, Allen went to a New York recording studio to help with the lyrics to several of the band's new songs. When he walked into the studio, Joe Strummer handed him the lyrics of "Ghetto Defendant"—a new song for *Combat Rock*, the album the band was recording—and presented both a request and a challenge. "You're the greatest poet in America," Strummer told Ginsberg, "can you improve on these lyrics?"

Allen went right to work on them, as well as on the lyrics to other songs. In most cases, his revisions consisted of no more than sharpening or clarifying images, or making the poetry more rhythmically sound. For "Ghetto Defendant," however, there was more work involved. Strummer wanted additional lyrics and a vocal to represent the voice of God—something to run counterpoint to the song's main voice. Allen provided both. Singing in a deep voice, he recorded the lyrics as a background vocal to Strummer's lead vocal on "Ghetto Defendant." He was pleased by the way it turned out, and so was the band. That song, along with others that Allen helped improve, appeared on the album.

Whenever he was on tour and had the opportunity, Allen would enlist the help of local musicians for what had evolved into a complex stage presentation of poetry and song. Although some of his friends cringed at his singing at the readings and impatient members of his audiences were known to walk out during the music portion of his shows, Allen continued to feature such songs as "Capitol Air" and "Do the Meditation Rock," as well as a Blake song or two, in his performances. He enjoyed the raw, spontaneous sound of the new-wave bands, which were often more noteworthy for their enthusiasm than for their musical talent. By hiring such local favorites to back him onstage, Allen was also guaranteeing an audience for his music. He would rehearse the songs with band members, much the way he had run through his early blues songs with Dylan and others, and hope for the best. The results of these performances were spotty, to say the very least, but they were generally well received. The recording of "Birdbrain!"—released in the Rocky Mountain area but never widely distributed—was an offshoot of one of these performances.

Of all his musical productions, the 1983 release of *First Blues* was by far the most personally rewarding. Unable to convince Columbia Records to release the album, producer John Hammond formed his own record company, and he and Allen assembled a package that was worthy of all their previous efforts to get the music recorded, mixed, pressed, and released. The song selection included the best of the recordings Allen had made in his three major recording sessions between 1971 and 1981. Robert Frank contributed a photo collage for the album's center spread, as well as a superb cover photograph of Allen and Peter. Allen put together a newspaper-style insert that included lyrics of all songs, as well as each song's recording history. *First Blues* was effective not only for its music but as a symbol of the electronic age that had vaulted Ginsberg into the public eye.

The Lion for Real, issued in 1989, featured both the spoken word and music. On this recording Allen read selections of his work while backed by musicians offering their own interpretations of his poems. This form, of course, was not without precedent. In the 1950s and 1960s, Kenneth Rexroth, Kenneth Patchen, and Lawrence Ferlinghetti, among others, had recorded their poetry with a jazz backdrop. Allen was simply continuing and updating this tradition.

It was an ideal form. Few poets were Ginsberg's equal when it came to reading their work, so by reciting his poems rather than singing them, Allen was doing what he did best—all within the context of a musical form. Allen had consulted other poets and musicians about his musical ability, and, as he wrote in the liner notes to *The Lion for Real*, he deferred to their opinions on the best way to make the recording:

> I'd produced several albums of blues, & gave cassettes to Marianne Faithfull then teaching lyric at Naropa, late summer 1987—She returned them the next day, "Maybe you shouldn't sing." I had 30 years' experience reading poetry aloud, vocalizing idiomatic intonations. Michael Minzer & producer Hal Willner had the sense to curb rocknroll ambitions, set me up with literate composers, encourage us to match music & recitation. I owe them thanks for reminding me my proper powers. Lyricist and vocalist, I followed their directions, relieved to leave music to the honorable musicians.

Singer Marianne Faithfull, whom Allen had met through Mick Jagger in the mid-sixties, played a large role in setting the project in motion. When Hal Willner first contacted Allen about making a recording, he had been vague about what he wanted to do with the project; Allen, who had myriad experiences in making records that never saw the light of day, was not inclined to jump at the prospects of working on another project with no future promise. Willner, however, proved his skills when he produced Faithfull's album *Strange Weather*, and that, along with Faithfull's further encouragement while she and Ginsberg were teaching together at Naropa, convinced Allen that working on the project might develop into something worthwhile.

Choosing the poems to be recorded involved some effort. Willner and executive producer Les Michaels read through Ginsberg's complete works and made a list of the poems they felt might work best in their recording concept. Similarly, Allen went through his works and drew up his own list of approximately eighty poems. He read each poem on his list in a single marathon session in his apartment, and after listening to the tapes from that session, he and Willner winnowed the list of possibilities to a new group of about fifty poems. Willner then contacted a number of his favorite musicians and composers and told them of his plans for the project. He invited them to join Allen and him at the A&R Studios in New York, where Allen was going to do another recording of the poems.

The musicians came to the studio with suggestions of their own. Allen read these selections, along with the ones he and Willner had chosen, in a six-hour recording session—"an amazing night," as Willner remembered. The musicians then picked several poems they wanted to score.

The actual recording took a week, Allen working with a strong team of professional musicians who performed a wide variety of composer interpretations of Ginsberg poetry, from the eerie sound track to "The Shrouded Stranger" to a New Age rendition of the spacey, marijuana-influenced "Guru Om." The selections covered every phase of Allen's career, making the recording the most representative album that he had yet issued. High points included the title

poem; a long overdue recording of "To Aunt Rose," one of Ginsberg's loveliest
early works; the ominous "The Shrouded Stranger"; and a funny, upbeat,
and almost danceable rendition of "C'mon Jack," Allen's semipornographic,
sadomasochistic sex fantasy. Due to time limitations, longer works were not
recorded—an unfortunate turn of events, because "White Shroud," a new
poem based on a dream Ginsberg had had about his mother, merited such
attention.

Setting the longer works to music continued to be an ambition for Ginsberg,
but there never seemed to be enough time. He and Steven Taylor did manage
to team up on a version of "September on Jessore Road," Taylor composing an
arrangement for a string quartet; and composer Philip Glass wrote a musical
interpretation of "Wichita Vortex Sutra" that Glass included on one of his
albums and that he and Ginsberg would occasionally perform in the late eighties
and early nineties. Engaging in such projects, though, was no longer as important to Allen as it might have been a decade earlier. There were more
pressing projects to pursue.

In four decades of keeping journal records of his dreams, Allen's subconscious
thoughts and obsessions had changed very little. The 1980s found him with
the same kind of erotic dreams he'd had as a youth; he also had the same kind
of "room dreams," as well as dreams in which he was lost on unfamiliar streets
and could not find his destination. He would occasionally dream about Kerouac,
and he frequently dreamed about his family and friends—often as they had
appeared in the years of his youth. For all the dreams carefully noted and
detailed in his journals, very few were ever translated into publishable poetry.
However, two powerful dreams supplied Allen with the material for "White
Shroud" and "Black Shroud"—two of his best poems of the eighties. Both
involved his mother.

On October 5, 1983, Allen dreamed that he and David Dellinger were
walking around the Bronx, through some of the familiar neighborhoods of
Allen's youth. To his surprise, he encountered his grandmother—Louis's
mother—who was lying in her bed, eating and complaining in Yiddish about
being abandoned by her family in her old age. Happy and relieved to see Buba
alive, Allen decided to find an apartment in the neighborhood—a place that
would allow him to live a quiet life, visit his grandmother whenever he wished,
and enjoy this newfound sense of family. He roamed the streets of the Bronx,
looking for such a place, seeing buildings that reminded him of his youth or of
some of the places he had seen in his travels abroad. Suddenly, he came upon
a makeshift shelter nestled in an alleyway between two buildings. A tin roof
kept the shelter's occupant—an old white-haired bag lady—protected from the
rain and snow, and a nearby subway grating provided her with minimal heat.
The shelter was furnished with a mattress and wooden bed. All of the old
woman's possessions were piled around her. A fan and an electric stove were
situated by one of the nearby building's walls.

The old woman seemed vaguely familiar to Allen, though he could not
immediately identify her. She was partially paralyzed, and she muttered angrily
as she moved about the shelter. Allen was troubled by the sight of the woman,
neglected by passersby and surviving the winters on the street; he wondered

what he could do to help her. Then, in a flash of recognition, he was shocked by the realization that this sad old woman was his mother. She had aged a great deal since he had seen her last, but there was no denying that this was who she was. She recognized him, as well.

"What are you doing here?" Allen asked Naomi.

"I'm living alone," she answered. She then launched into a typical rambling Naomi monologue, full of the familiar complaints of Allen's youthful days. "You all abandoned me, I'm a great woman, I came here by myself, I don't care, what are you doing here?"

Allen told her. He had been searching for a new apartment, he said, but now that he had found her, he could move into her shelter and take care of her; he could write his books and cook for her and see that all her needs were met.

"Best of all," he continued, cautioning Naomi not to get angry with him for bringing her the news, "you realize your old enemy Grandma's still alive! She lives a couple blocks downhill, I just saw her, like you!"

Allen was overjoyed. He had been waiting for such a moment—for such peace of mind—for most of his adult life. A large burden had been lifted from his shoulders.

At that moment of reconciliation, Allen awakened from his dream. It was almost dawn and he was in his apartment in Boulder. He scribbled down the details of the dream as well as he could remember them. Those details became "White Shroud," one of the most important poems of his literary career.

In many ways, "White Shroud" is exemplary of everything Ginsberg hoped to accomplish in dream-derivative poetry. He had always been greatly impressed with Kerouac's *Book of Dreams*, the best entries of which contained exquisitely detailed accounts of real people acting out events filtered through subconscious fantasy. The dream was a place where the imagination could confront reality, unfettered by the baggage that the conscious being brought to each real-life encounter. "In Society," the first of Ginsberg's published dream notations, established the pattern that the poet would follow throughout his life. In that poem, Ginsberg confronts the attitudes toward homosexuality expressed by both society and a small circle of homosexuals whom he knew at Columbia in the mid-1940s. In a conscious state, Ginsberg was ambiguous about stating his feelings, but in his subconscious, he was free to speak his mind.

So it was with "White Shroud." One would think that in writing as powerful a poem as "Kaddish," Ginsberg might have exorcised the demons of his youth. Rarely had a poet put so much on the line in a single work. Still, as is obvious from "White Shroud" and a number of journal entries written throughout his life, Ginsberg had never fully come to terms with his relationship with his mother or with his feelings of culpability connected to the final years of her life. Even as he approached his sixth decade, he was plagued—at least in his sleep—by feelings of guilt and ambivalence.

Nowhere was this as clear as in "Black Shroud," a mirror poem—and also a dream poem—written a short time later. It, too, finds Ginsberg coming to terms with his past, but on this occasion, he is confronting a horror rather than finding a happy solution.

For over three decades, Allen had been haunted off and on by the fact that as a young man he had authorized his mother's lobotomy. At the time, the procedure was suggested as the correct, humane solution to Naomi Ginsberg's suffering, and Allen had signed the legal documents permitting it only after a soul-searching period that found him considering his own feelings about the nature of insanity and unconventional behavior. He had paid a price of his own for his youthful interests in people living at the margins, and at the time he authorized the lobotomy, he had yet to travel to San Francisco, meet Peter Orlovsky, and take the decisive direction demanded by his own time and circumstance. He was still trying to find a way to adapt to society, for it had been suggested that conformity to society's norms might lead to his own peace of mind. By permitting Naomi's lobotomy, Allen had hoped to put an end to the paranoid schizophrenic delusions that had tormented his mother for much of her adult life. By obliterating that part of her consciousness, he was removing the danger of Naomi's hurting herself and, to an extent, others—or so he believed.

It also meant that he was cutting out a part of who Naomi was, and that idea had haunted Allen, in his waking moments and in his dreams, over the ensuing years. Carl Solomon had once suggested that lobotomy was a painless form of suicide. If that obliteration of consciousness was a form of death, what was Allen's ordering the lobotomy of his mother? Was it murder? And what did it say about Allen, the obvious product of his mother's body and spirit? What did it suggest about his own mind?

The "Black Shroud" dream was undoubtedly prompted by its happier predecessor. Allen had worked on "White Shroud" for some time, and he had seen it published to as strong a response as any of his individual poems had received in years. In its own way, then, "Black Shroud" was a punishment and a reminder.

The dream was precluded by a mild case of food poisoning that Allen had suffered on a visit to China. He had eaten a greasy chicken sandwich on moldy bread, and later in the evening, as he knelt before the toilet and vomited, he was reminded of a similar scene in his youth, recalled in "Kaddish," when his mother had been in a similar position. Then, as he slept in his hotel room in Kunming, Allen dreamed that he was again in the bathroom with his mother. She was tortured by her mind, imagining that an electric current was running up her spine. Something had to be done. As in real life, doctors had advised Allen to take some kind of action to eliminate her agony, to prevent her from banging her head against the wall in her distress. Believing it necessary, Allen beheaded his mother and, in a scene right out of *Hamlet*, he meditated upon the severed head before him, pondering the "To Be or Not to Be" question in the context of Naomi's madness. She looked peaceful in death, but Allen could not help but wonder whether he had been mistaken in his action. Had he, in the name of humanity, committed an unspeakable crime? Was *he* the crazy one? Unable to answer his questions, he left the bathroom.

At that point, the dream repaired to a wedding party for one of Allen's cousins. All of his living relatives were there. Naomi's headless body had been discovered, but since she was considered insane by the family, no one spoke of her death as a murder. Tormented by guilt, Allen revealed himself to be her murderer by asking inappropriate questions that only the murderer could have asked. Just as the protagonist of "The Tell-Tale Heart" could not bear to live with his guilt after murdering a similar innocent, Allen found confession to be the only way to cleanse himself from guilt. After making his confession, he awoke and the dream dissolved.

"Black Shroud" is a work of considerable achievement, even if one is unaware of Ginsberg's background. Freudians, of course, would have a field day interpreting the significance of the mother-son relationship and speculating on the meaning of Allen's violent termination of Naomi's life. On another level, the poem speaks forcefully about the idea of one's taking irreversible action for the good of another. Given Ginsberg's antiauthoritarian political stances over the decades, this is no small commentary, even though in a poem of such great personal meaning, it is presented in a very subtle subtext. Finally, the poem goes far in explaining the poet's great tolerance for the unconventional. If "Howl" and "Kaddish" can be viewed as Ginsberg's masterworks on this theme, "Black Shroud" is an important footnote, a clear explanation of his anger over the oppression detailed in "Howl" or of the grief compounded by guilt in "Kaddish."

Allen's relationship with Peter Orlovsky, unorthodox as it was from the very beginning, took on a new and not particularly ideal direction in the 1980s. Over the years, the two had gone through stretches during which they were extremely close—as much so as partners in a traditional marriage—but they had also endured long periods when their relationship was totally dysfunctional, during which they could not tolerate being together and subsequently had to live apart. Their sexual relationship, fragile during the best of times, had been declining for years and was no longer a factor in their life together. As early as 1968, in his interview for *Playboy*, Allen had conceded an ending to his and Peter's sexual partnership. "Our relationship was a big long fantasy that finally got played out," he told interviewer Paul Carroll. "As a matter of fact, once we'd reached a dead end homosexually, our relationship became lighter and happier. Now it's between two equals who've had a revolution within themselves that freed them from each other; we look at each other now as if we're newborn angels who shared an old history in another life."

A few years later, while talking to Allen Young for *Gay Sunshine*, Allen expanded upon these thoughts. "Our relationship has lasted from 1954 on," he said. "The terms have changed tremendously. Peter's gone through a lot of changes, and we've separated for a year at a time. And always come back. We've gone through a lot of phases of sleeping with people together, doing orgies together, sleeping alone together. Now Peter sleeps with a girl. I very rarely sleep with him. But the origin of our relationship is a fond affection. I wouldn't want to go to heaven and leave Peter alone on earth; and he wouldn't leave me alone if I was sick in bed, dying, gray-haired, wormy, rheumatic. He'd have pity on me. We've maintained our relationship so long that at this point we could separate and it would be all right. I think the karma has resolved and worn out in a sense."

These comments were a general, if not idealistic, portrayal of the relationship. Allen was aware that, as public figures, he and Peter had become living symbols of homosexual marriage, and since living such a life in public was still a relatively new idea, Allen felt a certain responsibility to those who might try to emulate him. In reality, as his journal entries indicate, he suffered greatly during the difficult times with Peter, especially during their periods of separation. He regretted the failings of their sexual relationship and he blamed himself for many of their problems.

Indeed, much of the blame was well deserved. Allen's fame, along with his natural tendency to dominate Peter, had a great bearing on many of the falterings in their relationship. Peter, quite understandably, resented much of Allen's unsolicited advice, which, more often than Allen was even aware of, resembled orders a parent might issue a child. There was little question that Peter needed occasional direction or guidance, but Allen had a habit of smothering him—of criticizing him or commenting upon his private and public behavior until Peter acted out as a form of frustrated response.

This was especially apparent when Allen, Peter, and Steven Taylor made an extensive tour of Europe in late 1982 and early 1983. Their itinerary, one of the most hectic in years, involved stops in France, Italy, Holland, Denmark, Sweden, Norway, Finland, and Germany, with an appearance schedule that would have challenged the endurance of men half of Peter's or Allen's ages. In addition, special arrangements had to be made for the tour. According to the plan, Allen and Steven would set out for Paris in early December, perform the first leg of the tour without Peter, and then link up with him in Amsterdam after the holiday season. At that point, they would perform as a trio for the remainder of their European visit.

There were both pragmatic and spiritual reasons for the arrangements. Oleg Orlovsky, Peter's father, had died of cancer on November 12, and Peter needed time to mourn his death and look after his family's immediate needs. Peter and his father had grown very close during the long, difficult months of the elder Orlovsky's illness. Peter had spent a large amount of time with his infirm father, helping with his care and trying to make his final days as bearable as possible. After Oleg's death, Peter had to address the eventuality that he might have to take care of his family. His brothers, Julius and Lafcadio, were still incapacitated from permanent mental disorders, and his mother and his sister had suffered periodic psychological afflictions, as well. For Peter, who had all he could handle in keeping just his own life in order, the responsibility was enormous, if not overwhelming.

Just how heavily these family obligations influenced Peter's behavior during the European tour is a matter of speculation, but there is no question that he was a different, very troubled man when he joined Allen and Steven in Amsterdam. On the evening of December 29, at a joint poetry reading with Andrei Voznesensky, Peter gave a disturbing reading, during which he drank heavily, challenged his translator to accentuate what might have been judged as objectionable words in his work, and beat himself about the head while reading a poem. Fortunately, Allen was able to usher him offstage without further incident, but this was only the beginning of Peter's erratic behavior. Throughout the tour, there was great tension between Peter and Allen, with Peter cursing loudly to himself and arguing with Allen. On occasion, he would go into one of his cleaning modes, during which he would meticulously scrub everything in sight—a habit that alarmed the people who were hosting Allen, Peter, and

Steven in their home. Worried about Peter's welfare, Steven wondered on more than one occasion whether Peter might be better off by leaving the tour and returning to the States. Peter hit bottom one day when, in a blind rage, he smashed his glasses and banjo, and Allen feared that he might harm himself physically.

Somehow, Allen managed to calm Peter, and they were able to complete the tour. His concerns about Peter's well-being, however, were far from over. In the months to come, there would be times when Peter was lucid and self-sufficient, followed by periods during which he would drink too much and act irrationally, presenting the threat of violence to himself or those around him. There was one very serious episode in 1984 while Allen was away in China. After staying up and drinking sake for a couple of days, Peter turned up, naked and brandishing a machete, at Allen's apartment. As Allen learned later, Bob Rosenthal had tried unsuccessfully to calm Peter, who had taken up a pair of scissors and, after cutting off patches of his own hair, had stabbed himself in the arm. The police were called and Peter was taken to Bellevue.

Allen was not about to abandon him in such times of turmoil. He still took his vows with Peter seriously, and he was determined to help him through each crisis. He sought psychiatric counseling—on his own and with Peter—and he struggled to come to terms with the cause of Peter's drinking problem, the nature of their relationship, and the direction to take in the future. Acting upon the advice of their respective therapists, Allen and Peter lived apart for a year—Peter moving to Vermont to live in Chögyam Trungpa's old Buddhist retreat, Allen staying in New York. To understand better the nature of Peter's alcoholism, Allen traveled to Minneapolis, where he attended a seminar at the Hazelden Hospital, headquarters of Alcoholics Anonymous. At the hospital, he was urged to try to shed the guilt he placed upon himself for his inability to solve Peter's problems. He could not force Peter to quit drinking, he was told, and he should not feel as if he was the cause of the problem.

In fact, the root of the relationship's main problem might be traced back to the beginning of their time together, to their original perception of the nature and requirements of their "marriage." That Peter wept the first time he and Allen made love was a telling sign, emblematic of the nature of their future sexual relationship. Peter was—and always would be—primarily heterosexual, and from all indications, his lovemaking with Allen often amounted more to his fulfilling a sense of obligation than to his being a happy, willing participant. There were many times when Peter resented Allen's sexual demands, many times when Peter yearned for a conventional relationship with a woman. Both Allen and Peter were aware of this, much more so than either let on in public and perhaps more so than either were willing or prepared to address honestly in private.

Although love and tenderness existed between the two men, their relationship, in retrospect, appears to have been initially formed more out of individual, rather than mutual, needs. Peter needed someone to take care of him and to provide a sense of stability in his daily life. Allen, stinging from Neal Cassady's rejection and from the knowledge that love relationships with Jack Kerouac and William Burroughs were, for different reasons, impossible, needed someone who could accept his love and sexuality on his own terms. When they first met,

Allen and Peter were able to fulfill each other's needs, at least to a certain extent, but those needs became greater trials as time eroded their relationship. For Peter especially, the vows began to resemble the constraints of a trap. Arguably, drugs and alcohol offered him flight, even as they exacted their price on his mind—although, it should be noted, the rocky relationship was not the sole reason for his chemical abuse.

Peter's problems would continue off and on in the years ahead, and he would be institutionalized from time to time, fighting a continual battle against substance abuse and subsequent mental breakdowns. Allen resolved to give him as much moral and financial support as he could muster. In a way, Allen's life had swung full circle. In his youth, he had taken care of his mother, shouldering enormous responsibility that often caused him hardship and grief; now, a half century later, he was taking similar care of the person he had at one time listed as his "wife" in his entry to *Who's Who*. His relationship with Peter had not been perfect by any means, certainly no more so than his father's marriage to his mother, but Allen held fast to his vows, his shoulder forever to the wheel, his tolerance to the test, as if final love, in the instability of life, found its balance in small, daily victories.

It is possible that Allen Ginsberg is the most widely traveled literary figure in history. By the time he had reached his sixtieth birthday in 1986, he had visited virtually every state in the union and every continent in the world. He had explored the sites of history's great civilizations, examined their artifacts, and had become in many ways a walking history book. He never settled for simply touring and taking a few notes or photographs; his inquisitive nature compelled him to learn as much as he could about each place he visited. He seemed incapable of passing through a city without inquiring about its historical background, social structure, and current politics. He had to absorb as well as witness.

He traveled extensively throughout the eighties, although in his advancing years he no longer possessed the desire or the stamina to zigzag back and forth across the United States at the pace characteristic of his youth. Instead, he preferred to spread out his travels and spend a longer period of time at each location. His traditional quick-stop reading schedules were gradually replaced by writing seminars, workshops, and other teaching ventures. He still logged more travel miles per year than most of his contemporaries, but he made concessions to his age by setting up more sensible, less frantic travel arrangements.

He made numerous excursions abroad, where his popularity never seemed to diminish. Time had seen him evolve into a kind of literary and cultural ambassador, his world vision, free of ethnocentricity, appealing to people of all nationalities and ideologies. His sincerity was rarely questioned, regardless of how outspoken he was or how his opponents disagreed with him. The man who had been expelled from Czechoslovakia as a bad influence in 1965 was, twenty-five years later, brought back to the country at the invitation of its president and, once again, crowned King of May. Time really did heal all wounds.

Of all his travels abroad, two journeys were especially noteworthy for their cultural significance. The first, in 1982, was to Nicaragua. At the time, tension between the Reagan administration and Nicaragua's Sandinista-run government was at its worst, and the Central American country's leadership feared that the U.S. government might take aggressive action, including war, against the country. Allen's trip there was innocent enough. He had been invited to Nicaragua by Ernesto Cardenal, the country's minister of culture, to participate in an international poetry festival that included such luminaries as Roberto Sosa from Honduras, José Antonio Cedrón from Argentina, and Yevgeny Yevtushenko from the Soviet Union. Still, Allen had no sooner landed at the Managua airport than he began to fret about how his presence in the country might be interpreted by Nicaraguans and Americans alike. He did not want a repeat of the problems he had experienced in Cuba and Czechoslovakia in 1965, nor did he wish to be a pawn in a propagandistic war of words between the two nations. Allen explained these concerns in an audience with Daniel Ortega on the night of his arrival.

The Nicaraguan leader was similarly concerned. Any remarks critical of Nicaragua or such allies as China and the Soviet Union could be taken out of context and used as propaganda by the country's enemies, he said. Ginsberg, who feared that a new Cold War was being instigated by the Reagan administration, had to agree.

However, Allen was also concerned about the free-speech issue in Nicaragua. On several occasions prior to his visit, the Sandinistas had tried to shut down the publication of La Prensa, a newspaper that openly opposed the government. As far as Allen was concerned, this was unacceptable. A couple of years earlier, in 1980, as a member of PEN's Freedom to Write committee, he had assisted with the preparation of a lengthy report detailing and condemning the U.S. government's efforts to destroy its own underground press; not long afterward, he had voted with PEN to denounce the Sandinista government's suppression of La Prensa.

However, as he learned during his stay in Nicaragua, there was another plausible explanation for the government's stern treatment of the opposition press. In helping to overthrow the Allende government in Chile, the CIA had successfully infiltrated an antigovernment newspaper in that country and, in the time just before the coup, had used propaganda to turn Chile's people against their leader. The type of writing in La Prensa, both in content and editorial slant, was very similar to the material published in El Murcurio, the Chilean newspaper infiltrated by the CIA. Ginsberg, who needed very little reason to suspect the CIA of wrongdoing, soon deduced that in all likelihood the agency was working in concert with the opposition newspaper in Nicaragua to help overthrow the revolutionary government.

While in Nicaragua, Allen was continually surprised by the disparity between what the U.S. government said about Nicaragua and what he actually witnessed. Like most Third World countries, it suffered from poverty, illiteracy, and inadequate living conditions, among other social maladies, but from all that Allen could see, the Sandinista government had instituted changes that had greatly improved the country since the revolution. To Allen, U.S. involvement in Nicaraguan affairs bore a striking similarity to the way the United

States had interfered with Cuba after the Castro revolution. If this was the case, he reasoned, Nicaragua, like Cuba, would be driven to dependency on the Soviet Union. A totalitarian, militaristic state would be inevitable.

Although he had vowed to be on his best behavior during his stay in Nicaragua, Allen was not about to enter a hotbed of international political controversy without speaking his mind. Indeed, his purpose for being in the country in the first place was a poetry festival celebrating the centenary of Reubén Darío, the Nicaraguan poet who, in his time, had issued a proclamation of cultural independence. At his reading at the Teatro Nacional, Allen presented poems indicative of his own declaration of cultural independence. He read selections from "Howl," "America," "Elegy Che Guevara," and "Birdbrain!" which he contrasted with such personally reflective poems as " 'Don't Grow Old' " and "Father Death Blues." In addition, he spent a considerable amount of time discussing the issues of political and spiritual freedom with Yevtushenko and Cardenal. All three, though from entirely different cultures, were concerned about the drama being played out in Central America, conceivably at the price of a widening of the gulf between the United States and the Soviet Union.

With this in mind, Ginsberg, Yevtushenko, and Cardenal composed a manifesto, "Declaration of Three," an appeal to the world's writers to unite in an effort to seek "liberty for Nicaragua independent of ambitions by either Cold-War Superpower to dominate the Nicaraguan national scene." Despite their cultural differences, the three poets wrote, they were all part of the greatest superpower of all—the human spirit. "The human soul must be the Church of all—religious or non-theistic in all parts of the world," they declared, adding:

> We don't want to see Nicaragua become a puppet in anyone's hands.
> At this moment we are witnesses that here in Nicaragua, which suffered
> so much under tyranny, misery and ignorance, there is an intent on
> the part of the people to defend their economic and intellectual inde-
> pendence. Nicaragua is a big experimental workshop for new forms of
> get-together wherein art plays a primordial role. Many Nicaraguans—
> not only intellectuals, but also workers, farmers, the militia—write
> verse today, with hands tired of weapons. Let's give them the possibility
> to write poetry with ink and not blood.

The writing of the manifesto was well timed. The Reagan administration was focusing a great deal of its foreign-policy attention on affairs in Central America, but public-opinion polls indicated that Americans opposed military intervention in that part of the world. People suspected that another Vietnam might be in the making, and they were reluctant to support even an otherwise-popular President if he was dishing out rhetoric that smacked of the tired, old, familiar talk of domino theories and Cold War paranoia. The rhetoric from the two superpowers, the three poets suggested, was consciously designed to distort the truth about the revolution in Nicaragua. Rather than blindly accept such government proclamations, writers were encouraged to visit Nicaragua and see the real alternative that the revolution proposed. "The Damocles' sword of aggression now hangs in the air above these people," the poets wrote in conclusion to their declaration. "We trust that if the writers of the world get together, their pens will be mightier than any sword of Damocles."

Upon his return to the United States, Allen worked on a much longer statement criticizing U.S. meddling in the affairs of the Central American countries. Drafted under the auspices of the New York Chapter of PEN, the statement was a twenty-one-point exposé of American misdeeds in Central America, particularly in El Salvador. Also listed were what Ginsberg considered to be the atrocities perpetrated by the U.S.-backed Salvadoran government—including murder, torture, and repression of intellectuals, artists, and dissidents.

The list went on for five typed pages, Allen using his collected information and news clippings, as well as his recent experiences in Nicaragua, to document his accusations. After drawing up his list, he called on the U.S. public, media, and government to see that all U.S. armed forces were withdrawn from Central America; that government aid be withheld from any country using or tolerating death squads; and that the United States allow these Third World countries to pursue self-determination in government and cultural affairs. For those who wondered whether he was backing away from strong political stands in his advancing years, Allen's trip to Nicaragua and subsequent writings provided a definitive answer.

Ginsberg's other major trip in the 1980s was a long-anticipated journey to China. When the United States and China began to loosen their rigorous and long-standing restrictions on travel between the two countries, cultural exchange programs became possible. In 1982, the year he had traveled to Central America, Allen was part of a historic meeting between Chinese and American writers, organized by Norman Cousins and Robert Rees and held at the UCLA campus. The conference was successful, and China was amenable to hosting a similar gathering in Beijing. Allen, along with Gary Snyder (another UCLA participant), Toni Morrison, William Gass, Harrison Salisbury, William Least Heat Moon, Maxime Hong Kingston, and others flew to Beijing in October 1984.

Allen had always wanted to see China on his own, and the conference provided him with the opportunity to enter the country. The writers' stay was officially scheduled for two weeks—four days in conference, ten days touring the country—but Allen, by arranging to teach at the Beijing and Hebei universities, was able to extend his stay for nearly seven more weeks, which, to a curious tourist such as Ginsberg, was a cultural bonanza. Not only would he be permitted to tour a country virtually unseen by Americans since the beginning of the Cold War but he would also be able to teach the writings of Whitman, Williams, Kerouac, and a host of other open-form, modernist, or New American poets to the Chinese.

To his surprise, the Chinese were much more aware of American poets and writers than he had imagined. Chinese intellectuals were reading a wide variety of Americans presently being published in the country, including such contemporary novelists as Mailer, Cheever, Bellow, and Malamud. Many had read Kerouac and Whitman. To Allen's delight, "Howl" was a popular text among intellectuals, who could identify Ginsberg's condemnation of his country's cultural and social oppression with the oppression in their own country's past.

The conference, then, was an eye-opening experience: The Chinese turned out to be more familiar with—and open to publishing—American writers than the United States was of their counterparts in China.

The Chinese were also aware of the Beat Generation, though they perceived it in strongly political terms, as a literary rebellion against capitalism, censorship, government repression, and U.S. imperialism. "They don't understand all of it," Allen wrote in a UPI dispatch to the States, "but they got a whiff of liberation, of Bohemian openness and freedom of speech, and that fits in with their current phase of getting rid of the heavy bureaucracy that controls literature."

Always interested in government censorship or cultural oppression, Allen instigated his own study of the 1966 to 1976 Cultural Revolution in China, much of which was still in evidence at the time of his visit. Writing about the revolution—or even inquiring about it—required diplomacy, since people still feared government reprisal if they spoke too openly or critically of their leaders. The conference, for instance, was entitled "The Source of Inspiration"— "a tricky title," Allen admitted, "designed to dodge the doctrine of art as revolutionary propaganda and give the Chinese and American writers a chance to talk about the real reasons they write." The Americans, naturally enough, were interested in knowing how free the Chinese writers were to express their ideas, especially those that did not adhere to the party line.

The best conversations, Allen noted in his report, took place in private, one-on-one encounters, where people were confidant that they could speak freely without danger of being haunted by their words. Even so, the Americans tried to avoid asking questions that might put their hosts on the defensive or in an awkward position. The Cultural Revolution had been a time of tremendous upheaval, during which the Chinese had been virtually cut off from the outside world, and, Allen learned, the country's professionals and intellectuals had been subjected to persecution and humiliation by dogmatists. As he noted in his report, "Everybody had a story about the Cultural Revolution, about how they were sent to the country as a Red Guard, or how their parents were fired from their jobs as translators or physicists, or their mothers sent off to the countryside, or how they themselves were exiled to jobs cleaning latrines. Elderly physicians were forced to stand bowed over, wearing dunce caps, answering questions from a bowed position day and night." How the Chinese culture, one of the oldest and grandest in human history, had fallen to this depth remained a mystery to the people.

Allen could not inquire or learn enough about these events. Never bashful about asking questions concerning even the most private or personal matters, he directed many of his conversations to the topic of sexuality in China. William Burroughs had theorized many years earlier that one of the main strategies of control in totalitarian governments was the control of human sexuality, and from what Allen had determined in his extensive travels, this appeared to be true. It was no different in China. Some of the Chinese were fascinated by his erotic poetry and by the freedom he had to express his feelings, and while Allen discovered that these feelings were shared by his guests, he also learned they were very guarded in expressing them. They were too afraid of gossip or scandal. Allen could understand this, but he had difficulty with the way the Chinese so readily accepted these government-imposed conditions. Open homosexuality was out of the question, he was informed, and even premarital sexual relations were discouraged.

"What of poor unmarried men? What do they do for love?" Allen asked during one of his conversations.

"They must live pure lives," he was told.

"Why?" Allen continued.

"If their behavior was loose, they would be considered troublemakers."

"You're married and have a place, a job, et cetera," Allen replied, "so you can talk. But what right have you or anyone to tell those without wits or jobs or station to live loveless the rest of their lives? What kind of communism community is that? What kind of equality? It's barbaric exploitation. You expect to have these people dig your ditches and plant your rice and live without love?"

The man smiled at Allen's passionate argument. "I really agree," he said. "That's what I think, too."

From this and other discussions, Allen drew his own conclusions. "There seems to be a level of political discourse," he wrote in his journal, "a level of more frank discourse among intimates, and another private level of consciousness with entirely different secret views. What people really think, they only tell their wives, not even their children, 'cause children can't understand—not sophisticated enough—till they grow up. Then (you) can talk with your son."

Allen's tour of China, marred only by a three-week bout with the flu and bronchitis, was one of his most enjoyable trips abroad in years. With the delegation of American writers, he went to Xi'an, the burial place of Emperor Han, who in his final repose had been surrounded by full-scale clay replicas of his army dressed in full battle gear. They also traveled to Shanghai, where they saw the Temple of the Jade Buddha, and to Suzhou, where they visited the Cold Mountain temple.

Captivated by the country, Allen filled his journal with some of the most inspired poetry and prose that he had written in years. Since he was filing reports of his visit to UPI, he was paying close attention to the details of Chinese life, and these details supplied the grist for his best objective writing since his auto poesy of the 1960s:

> Students danced with wooden silvered swords, twisting on hard
>   packed muddy earth
> as I walked out Hebei University's concrete North Gate,
> across the road a blue capped man sold fried sweet dough-sticks,
>   brown as new boiled doughnuts,
> in the gray light of sky, past poplar tree trunks, white washed
>   cylinders topped
> with red band the height of a boy. . . .

Allen did the great bulk of his writing after the American writers had returned to the States, when he was off on his own, exploring not so much the sites that the Chinese government was eager to show tourists as the realities of daily life

in the country. Three decades had passed since his first solitary explorations of
Mexico, and in that time, Allen had lost none of his enthusiasm for discovery.
The Chinese, he was delighted to see, were equally interested in learning
about Americans. In his lectures at the universities, he introduced students to
Kerouac, Corso, Creeley, Orlovsky, and others; he passed out mimeographed
pages of their work. He read poems by Williams, sang his Blake songs, voiced
Kerouac haiku, and performed selections of his own work, including the homages to his parents, "Kaddish" and "Father Death Blues." He spoke of his
literary friendships and of the way literature had sprung from these associations.

Allen's lectures and thoughts about his past led to a series of dreams that, in
this country so far from his own, addressed characters and unresolved issues
from his past. He dreamed of Trungpa, Williams, Kerouac, Dylan, and his
parents. He had his nightmare about beheading his mother. His dream about
visiting Williams at his home led to the writing of "Written in My Dream by
W. C. Williams"—an unusual work in which the dream Williams advises Allen
on poetry composition. In the most compelling—and perhaps most telling—
of the dreams, Allen took Louis to a Chinese bath, where he hoped his father
would watch him in homosexual lovemaking. Upon awakening and trying to
write down the dream, Allen could not remember whether his father had
actually witnessed anything.

The trip to China, like so many of his previous ones, had a rejuvenating
effect, both on his mind and in terms of new poetry. Allen's travels had supplied
him with a lifetime's education, and he used that knowledge to further his
artistic endeavors. Each excursion seemed to remind him of the distance his
mind had traveled from the days when, as a boy in Paterson, he had cut out
news clippings and debated the politics of countries he had not visited and
people he had never seen. He had been, he conceded, so naïve then:

> I grew up in Paterson New Jersey and was
> just a virginal kid when I left
> forty years ago. Now I'm around the world,
> but I did go back to visit my stepmother.
> Then I was 16 years old, now I'm fifty eight—
> All the fears I had in those days . . .

As he noted later in the poem, the only constant was the earth itself. People
passed through, living and dying, but the planet endured. His Blake visions
had told him as much in 1948 and, in their own way, had set him on a path
of personal discovery of this truth.

Although he was one of the country's best-known disciples of Buddhism, Allen
was never satisfied with his own meditation practice. He made every effort to
remain faithful to his sittings, but he regretted the time and business demands
that prohibited him from the kind of practice that Chögyam Trungpa encouraged. On occasion, he longed for a lengthy hermit's retreat that would take
him away from the hyperactive life he led and closer to the solitude that seemed
so ideal, but such hopes, he realized, were anything but realistic.

In time, and through Allen's patient, persistent efforts, the effects of the poetry wars diminished. Hurt feelings were smoothed over, temporarily severed relationships and friendships mended. He did, however, see less of Trungpa, whose health had begun to fail. He spent nearly a year and a half in a semicoma, nearly dying on a couple of occasions, before finally succumbing to a heart attack on April 4, 1987. He was cremated in a full Tibetan Buddhist ceremony at Karme-Choling, his first Buddhist center in the United States, located near Barnet, Vermont. To Allen, Trungpa's passing served as another reminder not only of the transitory nature of human existence but also of the way the spirit endures, inspiring and guiding, long after the individual is gone.

Allen felt similarly about himself. A major biography was published in 1989, and scholarly papers proliferated. An annotated edition of "Howl," including the various drafts of the poem, line-by-line annotation of the work, biographical information about Carl Solomon, and a collection of related correspondence, was issued in 1988. A massive collection of journals, letters, essays, and unpublished poetry awaited publication. There was little doubt, even among Ginsberg detractors, that the poet would continue to influence and inspire in future decades.

Allen, however, was nowhere near ready to slow down and let his past achievements carry him through his old age. Even at a time when doctors were advising him to cut back on his activities, he was moving ahead—to the point of discovering almost accidentally a new career that would take up even more of his time.

In January 1985, an exhibition of Ginsberg photographs, entitled "Hideous Human Angels," was held at New York's Holly Solomon Gallery. The showing featured a number of the photographs Allen had taken of his friends over the years and it officially kicked off what amounted to a new career—the serious pursuit of photography as more than just a hobby or personal interest.

This pursuit might have been anticipated. Throughout his adult life, Allen has taken thousands of photographs of his friends and literary associates, of his travels, of anything that suited his fancy. He has photographs of enormous historical interest—from a youthful Kerouac being "analyzed" by Burroughs, to Neal Cassady standing under a theater marquee with Natalie Jackson; from Gregory Corso in the Beat Hotel in Paris, to Gary Snyder in the mountains in the Pacific Northwest. All of these figures had become famous in their own right, and Allen's documentation had already been invaluable to those writing biographies or critical studies on their lives and work. Ann Charters, the Kerouac biographer and Beat Generation scholar, had compiled many of the photographs in the collection *Scenes Along the Road*, published by Portents/Gotham Book Mart in 1970 and reissued years later by City Lights.

Allen had never perceived himself to be much of a photographer, at least in a professional sense. He had taken the pictures, he said, for much the same reason as he recorded his thoughts and observations in his journals:

> As artist companions, my contemporaries & friends in the early 1950's photos were involved in seeing each other as mythical or sacred in a sacred world; or not so much *mythical* as seeing each other as *real* in a really sacred world. My motive for taking these snapshots was to make celestial snapshots in a sacred world, recording certain moments in

eternity with a sense of sacramental presence. The sacramental quality comes from an awareness of the transitory nature of the world, and awareness that it's the one and only occasion when we'll be together. This is what makes it sacred, the awareness of mortality, which Keat's Romantic poetry articulates as well as Buddhist dharma teaching. The very word "sacramental" was one Jack Kerouac and I used as far back as 1945. Looking for a "New Vision" we saw each other as sacred characters or spiritual comrades as in Dostoevsky. . . .

Not surprisingly, Allen's photographs were disorganized, and he had no idea of the extent and value of the pictures, most of which were stored at his archives at Columbia University. For the most part, he had taken the pictures and forgotten about them. In many cases, he had not even bothered to make prints of the film, because he did not have the time, the money, or the inclination to do so. Whenever someone wished to use his photographs for books or magazine articles or newspaper pieces, he would refer the person to his Columbia deposit. Unfortunately, there was a price to Allen's generosity: Far too often, prints or negatives were damaged; worse yet, they disappeared and were not returned.

Cataloging the photographs became a large part of Allen's efforts to organize his archives in the 1980s. With people already working at making typescripts of his journals and cataloging his enormous collection of news clippings, tapes, and magazines containing his published works, it only followed that he would seek similar organization of his photographs—a daunting task, to say the least. Art curator Raymond Foye, archivist Jacqueline Gens, and others sorted through the archive, organizing the existing prints and making contact sheets from the negatives of the countless rolls of undeveloped film. What merged from this tedious process was a striking autobiography and history in pictures—a collection that visually supplemented nearly four decades of Allen's writings.

Allen examined the prints and contact sheets, selecting what he judged to be the best works for further processing. He then asked Brian Graham, Robert Frank's printer, to make prints of these selections, and he was pleased to discover that the photographs were of a high-enough quality to show at an exhibition. Response to the "Hideous Human Angels" showing was very favorable, as was reaction to subsequent shows throughout the United States. The best of the photos were published in *Allen Ginsberg Photographs*, an impressive portfolio issued in 1990 by Twelvetrees Press.

The value of Allen Ginsberg, poet and human being, appears to be increasing in the public eye year by year. For all his weaknesses and foibles—and he is far from perfect—Ginsberg has evolved into a sort of living symbol of kindness and generosity, an artist who has dared to make his own life a form of literature, open to judgment and interpretation but never failing in its basic human honesty. The work becomes a rough history lesson, told by a witness who notices an arc of time exploding in brilliant color like one of Kerouac's Roman candles.

To which Ginsberg, new visionary and dharma bum, honors with the mind breath *AH*.

NOTES

Unless otherwise noted, all books cited are first editions. For reader convenience, corresponding page numbers from *Collected Poems* are also cited whenever applicable. Allen Ginsberg's journals are stored in his Columbia deposit, Columbia University, New York.

Abbreviations

EB: Eugene Brooks
WSB: William S. Burroughs
NC: Neal Cassady
GC: Gregory Corso
LF: Lawrence Ferlinghetti
AG: Allen Ginsberg
LG: Louis Ginsberg
JCH: John Clellon Holmes
HH: Herbert Huncke
JK: Jack Kerouac
PO: Peter Orlovsky
WCW: William Carlos Williams

Book Abbreviations (and short list)

CP: *Collected Poems 1947–1980* (1985)
EM: *Empty Mirror* (1961)
FALL: *The Fall of America* (1972)
GW: *The Gates of Wrath* (1972)
HOWL: *Howl and Other Poems* (1956)
KADDISH: *Kaddish and Other Poems* (1961)
MB: *Mind Breaths* (1977)
PAOTP: *Poems All Over the Place* (1978)
PN: *Planet News* (1968)
PO: *Plutonian Ode* (1982)
RS: *Reality Sandwiches* (1963)

Preface

xiv. AG/LG reading: Evelyn Leopold, "A Homecoming for Allen," (Paterson) *Morning Call*, October 24, 1966; Walter Weglein, "The Poets Ginsberg Share Stage Here to SRO Audience," *Paterson News*, October 24, 1966; "Allen Ginsberg Hopes That City Will Go Back to Sleep," *Paterson News*, October 24, 1966; "Ginsberg's Life with Father Goes to Pot," *Daily News*, October 25, 1966; "Ginsberg Not Only Beard Wearer, Paterson Discovers," *Passaic Herald News*, October 26, 1966; Barton Sotnick, "Cops Do Ginsberg Double-Take," (Paterson) *Morning Call*, October 26, 1966; author interviews with AG, Edith Ginsberg.
xiv. "It was an intimate . . .": Weglein, *Paterson News*, October 24, 1966.
xv. "bring back a full flavor . . .": "*Daily News*, October 25, 1966.
xv. "if by silence . . .": ibid.

xv. "back to sleep": "Allen Ginsberg Hopes," *Paterson News*, October 24, 1966.
xv. "It seems like . . .": ibid.

1. Garden State: Youth in New Jersey

3. Epigraph: AG, "A Poem on America," *EM*, 40; *CP*, 64.
   Naomi and Louis Ginsberg: Much of the background information about Allen Ginsberg's parents, as well as information about AG's childhood, comes from author interviews with AG, Eugene Brooks (brother), Hannah and Leo Litzky (paternal aunt and her husband), and Edith Ginsberg (stepmother). AG's papers at his Columbia University deposit include youthful diaries, school papers and report cards, school yearbooks, and other ephemera. AG referred to his childhood in entries made in his journals throughout his life. These journals are stored in his Columbia deposit. The original handwritten draft of "Kaddish," which differs substantially from the published version, is housed at the Fales Library, New York University; this, subsequent drafts, and the final published version were consulted in gathering information for this chapter, as was AG's screenplay for *Kaddish*, cowritten with Robert Frank, presently stored at AG's Columbia deposit. *See also*, Barry Miles, *Ginsberg* (New York: Simon & Schuster, 1989), 11–35; John Tytell, *Naked Angels: The Lives and Literature of the Beat Generation* (New York: McGraw-Hill, 1976), 80–81; Elanore Lester, "Allen Ginsberg Remembers Mama," *The New York Times*, February 6, 1972.
6. LG at Rutgers: In an interview with the author, Hannah Litzky, Louis Ginsberg's sister, noted that Pinkus Ginsberg was less than pleased with his oldest son's lack of interest in the family business when he returned home from school. "He would come home from Rutgers for the weekend and sit in his room and write poetry," Litzky said of her brother. "At that time, my father had a little laundry business and needed help, and he used to get annoyed with Lou. But my mother would say in Yiddish, 'He's writing, leave him alone.'" Years later, in 1952, a remarkably similar episode occurred when Allen took peyote and was sitting in reflection in his backyard in Paterson. When Allen's stepmother, Edith, asked him to hang up a piece of laundry that had slipped off the line, Louis told her to leave Allen alone. "He's busy with himself just now," Louis said (AG, *Journals*, 10).
7. "I was afraid . . .": AG, "Garden State," *PO*, 63; *CP*, 718.
7. "It was part . . .": author interview with AG. *See also*, Louis Ginsberg, "My Son the Poet," *Chicago Sun-Times*, January 12, 1969.
7. "the king or prince . . .": author interview with AG.
8. "stitching of . . .": AG, "Kaddish," *KADDISH*, 24; *CP*, 219.
9. "very close": author interview with EB.
9. "the absolute dogmatism . . .": ibid.
9. "They lost all . . .": ibid.
9. "bourgeois poet": author interview with AG.
9. communist meetings: AG, *Gay Sunshine Interview*, 41–42. *See also*, AG, "America," *HOWL*, 33; *CP*, 147: "America when I was seven momma took me to Communist Cell meetings they sold us garbanzos a handful per ticket a ticket costs a nickel and the speeches were free everybody was angelic and sentimental about the workers it was all so sincere you have no idea what a good thing the party was in 1835 Scott Nearing was a grand old man a real mensch Mother Bloor the Silk-strikers' Ewig-Weibliche made me cry I once saw the Yiddish orator Israel Amter plain. Everybody must have been a spy."
10. "little kissing bug": AG, unpublished fragment from first draft of "Kaddish."
11. "She imagined that my mother . . .": author interview with Hannah Litzky.
11. "beautiful Garbo . . .": AG, "Kaddish," *KADDISH*, 30; *CP*, 223.
11. AG's Jewish background: author interviews with AG, EB, Edith Ginsberg, and Hannah and Leo Litzky; Robert A. Cohn, "Allen Ginsberg 'Howls' His Poems; Discusses His Jewishness in Exclusive Interview," *St. Louis Jewish Light*, December 1, 1982.
11. "Being communists and socialists . . .": Cohn, "Allen Ginsberg 'Howls' His Poems, *Jewish Light*.
13. "My mother thinks . . ."; "My mother is worse . . ."; and "I stayed home . . .": AG journal entries, June 19, 21, and 22, 1937, respectively.
13. "I stayed home from school . . .": AG journal entry, June 24, 1937.
13. "Once locked herself . . .": AG, "Kaddish," *KADDISH*, 22; *CP*, 218.
13. "shivering in their nightclothes . . .": LG, "My Son the Poet."
13. "I expect to use . . ." and "the world is now . . .": AG journal entry, March 14, 1938.
14. "The world is . . .": AG journal entry, March 28, 1938.
14. "fourth-hand stereotypes": author interview with AG.
15. "Don't be afraid . . .": AG, "Kaddish," *KADDISH*, 21; *CP*, 217.
15. "Was this the comfortless . . .": ibid.

15. "baser emotions" and "about seven": AG undated journal entry.
16. "And that's . . .": AG, " 'Native Son' Makes Good," *The Spectator*, Easter 1941; AG Columbia deposit.
16. "I'll be a genius . . ." and "I have a fair . . .": AG undated journal entry.
16. "Either I'm a genius . . .": AG undated journal entry.
16. "a kid writing . . ." and "certainly wouldn't credit . . .": author interview with AG.
16. "I want people to bow . . .": AG, "Transcription of Organ Music," *HOWL*, 27; *CP*, 141.
16. "I want to be known . . .": AG, "Ego Confession," *MB*, 46; *CP*, 623.
17. "so enthusiastic and joyous . . ." and "[I] still remember . . .": AG, "The School Day I Remember Most," *Instructor*, May 1979.
17. "like croaking up . . .": AG, "Kaddish," *KADDISH*, 22; *CP*, 218.
17. "Kunming Hotel . . .": AG, "Black Shroud," *White Shroud*, 69.
17. AG and Naomi: AG, "Kaddish," *KADDISH*, 13–19; *CP*, 212–14; AG, "Kaddish," first and subsequent unpublished drafts; AG and Robert Frank, unpublished filmscript *Kaddish*; author interview with AG.
18. "I've told you a hundred times . . .": AG, *Kaddish* filmscript. All other direct quotations from this passage, unless otherwise noted, from this filmscript.
18. "the mystical assassin . . .": AG, "Kaddish," *KADDISH*, 13; *CP*, 212.
18. AG/Naomi/Lakewood: Over the years, there has been some speculation as to why Allen did not physically restrain his mother when it became apparent that she was having a serious emotional episode. First, as has already been noted, Allen was small and slightly built and was not much bigger than his mother; this, along with Allen's gentle nature, probably kept him from using physical force in restraining her. Further, Naomi Ginsberg could be very persuasive, especially to a son who wanted almost desperately to believe in her mental well-being. Finally, there is the most obvious reason of all: Naomi was Allen's *mother*. Even though he was aware of her mental illness and had been witness to some of her more bizarre episodes, he ultimately cherished her as the person who had given him life. His love for her was unquestionable and no doubt it played a role in preventing him from taking another course of action at this time. In short, he was listening to his heart.
18. "gasmask against poison . . .": AG, "Kaddish," *KADDISH*, 13; *CP*, 212.
19. "hoping it would end . . .": ibid.
19. "Would she hide . . .": AG, "Kaddish," *KADDISH*, 15; *CP*, 213.
20. "safe in her coffin": ibid.
20. "No greater depression . . .": AG, unpublished fragment from first draft of "Kaddish."
21. "We are, or should be . . .": AG to *The New York Times*, May 28, 1942 (unpublished); AG Columbia deposit.
22. "smearing, red-baiting . . ." and "honest discussion . . .": AG to Gordon Canfield, October 24, 1942.
22. "philosopher of the class": AG Columbia deposit.
22. "a fiend of Beethoven . . ." and "indulges in . . .": ibid.

2. Columbia and New York

23. Epigraph: AG, "Ignu," *KADDISH*, 58; *CP*, 204.
23. Scholarship and stipend: David L. Cole to AG, June 26, 1943; William A. Hance to AG, May 1, 1943; AG Columbia deposit.
23. AG crush on fellow student: AG, *Gay Sunshine Interview*, 6. See also, "Kaddish," *KADDISH*, 16; *CP*, 214.
23. AG courses: Columbia University transcripts, AG Columbia deposit.
24. "There was no genuine . . .": Yves Le Pellec, "The New Consciousness," *Entretiens* 34 (1975), reprinted in AG, *Composed on the Tongue*, 69.
24. AG on Columbia professors: author interview with AG.
25. "the wish to shock . . .": Diana Trilling, "The Other Night at Columbia: A Report from the Academy," *Partisan Review* (Spring 1959); reprinted in Diana Trilling, *Claremont Essays* (New York: Harcourt, Brace, & World, 1959); and in Fred W. McDarrah, ed., *Kerouac and Friends: A Beat Generation Album* (New York: William Morrow, 1985), 144–45.
26. AG meets Lucien Carr: AG journal entries; AG, fragment from unpublished novel, *Where Was the World*, AG Columbia deposit; Barry Gifford and Lawrence Lee, *Jack's Book* (New York: St. Martin's Press, 1978), 34–35.
26. "a little oasis . . .": AG, fragment of unpublished AG/Lucien Carr conversation, AG Columbia deposit.
26. AG reaction to LC: AG, *Where Was the World*.

26. "youthful innocence" and "a daemonic fury . . .": ibid.
26. "You've never worked . . ."; "I was suddenly . . ."; and "I realized . . .": author interview with AG.
26. Lucien Carr bio: JK, *Vanity of Duluoz* (New York: Paragon Books, 1979), 36–37. Gifford and Lee, *Jack's Book*, 36–37.
27. "jejune": author interview with AG.
27. "Know these words . . .": AG undated journal entry.
27. AG reading list: AG undated journal entry.
27. AG/Lucien Carr conversation: AG undated journal entry.
28. "creative self-expression" and "The concomitant potential of . . .": AG undated journal entry.
28. "Everybody was very serious . . .": author interview with Norman Podhoretz.
29. David Kammerer: AG journal entries; JK, *Duluoz*, 202; JK, *The Town and the City* (New York: Harcourt, Brace, 1950), 367–70.
29. AG meets WSB: author interview with AG.
29. WSB bio: Ted Morgan, *Literary Outlaw: The Life and Times of William S. Burroughs* (New York: Henry Holt, 1988); John Tytell, *Naked Angels: The Lives and Literature of the Beat Generation* (New York: McGraw-Hill, 1976), 36–39; John Tytell, "An Interview with William S. Burroughs," in *The Beat Diary*, eds. Arthur and Kit Knight (California, PA: unspeakable visions of the individual, 1977), 35–49; reprinted in *Kerouac and the Beats*, eds. Arthur and Kit Knight (New York: Paragon House, 1988), 14–39.
32. "This image . . .": WSB, *Roosevelt After Inauguration* (San Francisco: City Lights Books, 1979), 7.
32. "I could see . . .": ibid., 9.
33. "New Vision": AG journal entries; author interview with AG; JK, *Duluoz*, 217–18; William Triplett, "Q&A: Allen Ginsberg," *City Paper*, June 22, 1984.
34. "free will depends . . ."; "ideals are inextricably rooted . . ."; and "ideals are an extension . . .": AG journal entries.
34. "hung up on words": author interview with AG.
34. AG meets JK: author interview with AG; JK, *Duluoz*, 217–18; Alfred Aronowitz, "The Beat Generation," *New York Post*, March 10, 1959; Gifford and Lee, *Jack's Book*, 34–35.
35. "was very handsome, very beautiful . . .": AG, *Gay Sunshine Interview*, 4.
35. "spindly Jewish kid . . .": JK, *Duluoz*, 217–18.
36. "I do that, too . . .": Gifford and Lee, *Jack's Book*, 35.
36. "I suddenly realized . . .": AG, *Allen Verbatim*, 103.
36. Kerouac bio: JK, *Duluoz*; *The Town and the City*; *Visions of Gerard* (New York: McGraw-Hill, 1976); Tytell, *Naked Angels*, 52–57; Gerald Nicosia, *Memory Babe: A Critical Biography of Jack Kerouac* (New York: Grove Press, 1983); Ann Charters, *Kerouac* (New York: Warner Books, 1973); Dennis McNally, *Desolate Angel: Jack Kerouac, the Beat Generation, and America* (New York: Random House, 1979); Tom Clark, *Jack Kerouac* (New York: Harcourt Brace Jovanovich, 1984).
36. "For the first four years . . .": JK, *Visions of Gerard*, 7–8.
38. "This was the most important . . .": JK, *Duluoz*, 95.
39. "I was just about the least . . .": ibid., 168.
39. "[I]t was that last . . .": ibid., 195.
39. "a mischievous little prick . . .": ibid., 201.
39. "sensibilities were affixed . . .": JK, untitled manuscript, AG Columbia deposit.
40. AG and JK visit WSB: author interview with AG; Le Pellec, "The New Consciousness," reprinted in AG, *Composed on the Tongue*, 81–82; Gifford and Lee, *Jack's Book*, 36; JK, *Duluoz*, 211.
40. "examine his soul . . .": Gifford and Lee, *Jack's Book*, 36.
40. "contact with . . ." and "a crucial time . . .": Le Pellec, "The New Consciousness," in *Composed*, 81.
40. "If he was really evil . . .": ibid.
40. WSB book list: AG Columbia deposit.
41. "Burroughs was primarily . . .": Le Pellec, "The New Consciousness, in *Composed*, 82.
41. "There was the nostalgia . . .": JK, *Duluoz*, 220.
41. Carr/Kammerer: AG journal entries; JK, *Duluoz*, 200–02, 219–23; *Town*, 392–94.
42. "Doesn't he look pale . . .": JK, *Duluoz*, 219.
42. Carr/Kerouac plans: JK, *Duluoz*, 220–21; Gifford and Lee, *Jack's Book*, 39–40.
43. "I want to unburden . . .": AG undated journal entry.
43. "Looking down on the street . . .": AG journal entry, August 3, 1944.
43. Death of David Kammerer: JK, *Duluoz*, 229–36; *Town*, 417–18; author interview with AG. Ginsberg addressed the death of David Kammerer in "Howl": "Who created great suicidal dramas on the apartment cliff-banks of the Hudson under the Wartime blue/floodlight of the moon & their heads shall be crowned with laurel in oblivion" (*HOWL*, 13; CP, 128).
43. "And now . . .": AG undated journal entry.
44. "indiscreet" and "art awaits on humanity . . .": AG undated journal entry.

44. "Oh, a lot . . ." and "You missed . . .": ibid.
44. "competent": ibid.
44. Carr chanting Baudelaire: JK, untitled manuscript, AG Columbia deposit.
44. "I just killed . . .": JK, *Duluoz*, 229.
44. "I'll get the hot seat": ibid., 230.
45. COLUMBIA STUDENT KILLS . . .: *The New York Times*, August 17, 1945.
45. *A Vision* and *A Season in Hell: New York Daily News*, August 25, 1945.
46. AG dream: AG journal entry, September 7, 1944.
46. "daring and miserable . . ."; "a short man . . ."; and "it was the beginning . . .": ibid.
46. "The credit's his . . .": AG undated journal entry.
47. "I have attempted . . .": AG undated journal entry.
47. "You seek identity . . .": JK to AG, undated, ca. 1944.

3. Junkies and Geniuses

48. Epigraph: AG, "Two Sonnets," *GW*, 3; *CP*, 5.
48. "bad influences": author interview with Seymour Lawrence.
48. "well-rounded": AG to EB, undated, ca. fall 1944.
48. "some neurotic . . .": ibid. Besides the list provided in his letter to Eugene, Allen made a separate list in his journal, labeling it "Characters."
48. AG and JK: AG, *Gay Sunshine Interview*, 3–8.
49. "as a slightly older . . .": ibid., 4.
49. "Jack, you know . . .": ibid.
49. "Very soon . . .": ibid., 6.
49. "college policy": N. M. McKnight to AG, November 13, 1944.
49. "lout"; "smutty"; and "The road to hell . . .": AG undated journal entries.
49. "much detail and significance . . .": AG to EB, undated, ca. fall 1944.
49. "The rose . . .": AG, "Song," *Columbia Jester Review* (November 1944).
50. "a menace to society": LG to AG, undated, ca. fall 1944.
50. "Your clever . . ." and "I tell you, Allen . . .": ibid.
50. "from the authoritarianism . . .": AG, *Gay Sunshine Interview*, 6.
50. Conference with McKnight: N. M. McKnight to LG, January 2, 1945.
51. "real poems . . .": AG undated journal entry. The first four titles listed were "He Who Walks Within the Womb," "I Have Been Unleashed," "This Stormy Foundation Bursts Upon the Air," and "Now in This Park, by This Lakeside." None of these poems was ever published, however, and Ginsberg never referred to them as anything more than early exercises.
51. "normal": Louis Ginsberg, "My Son the Poet," *Chicago Sun-Times*, January 12, 1969.
51. AG as young poet: AG journal entries; author interview with AG.
51. Allen Raynard as pen name: AG undated journal entry.
51. "in terms of art" and "the humankind materials of art": JK to AG, undated, ca. early 1945.
51. "The new vision . . .": AG undated journal entry.
52. "How shall I live?" ibid.
52. "somewhat bastardized . . .": AG undated journal entry.
52. Models for "The Last Voyage": author interview with AG.
52. "Alas, there is no Mystery . . ." and "But, oh, my friend . . .": AG, unpublished poetry manuscript, "The Last Voyage," AG Columbia deposit.
52. "a marijuana garden . . .": ibid.
52. "We are blinded . . .": ibid.
53. Naomi Ginsberg: AG, "Kaddish" unpublished manuscript; "Kaddish," *KADDISH*, 22–27; *CP*, 218–21; author interviews with EB, AG.
53. AG/JK in dormitory: Yves Le Pellec, "The New Consciousness," in AG, *Composed on the Tongue*, 72–74; author interview with AG.
54. "I recommend . . .": N. M. McKnight to AG, March 17, 1945.
54. "cannot be repeated . . ." and "whose presence . . .": N. M. McKnight to LG, March 17, 1945.
55. "Mr. Ginsberg, I hope you realize . . .": quoted in Le Pellec, "The New Consciousness," *Composed*, 74.
55. "the argument of the idealist . . .": AG journal entry, September 18, 1944.
56. AG/WSB: Le Pellec, "The New Consciousness," in *Composed*, 82–83.
56. Menial jobs: Ginsberg often complained about his inability to perform some of the most basic menial tasks (*see*, "How Come He Got Canned at the Ribbon Factory," *EM*, 45; *CP*, 60).
56. Ginsberg writings: AG journal entries.
57. "I hope to tutor . . ." and "only a pilgrimage . . .": AG to JK, August 1945.

57. "By god those effete degenerates . . .": AG to EB, September 3, 1945.
57. "The motivating sense . . .": ibid.
57. "behaved like a gentleman" and "rather crude," AG to JK, August 1945.
57. "I was surprised . . .": AG to JK, September 1945.
57. "amused or wounded" and "unexpected attacks . . .": AG to JK, September 4, 1945.
58. "moved" and "You shouldn't have been . . .": JK to AG, September 6, 1945.
58. AG illness: AG to EB, September 3, 1945; AG to JK, September 4, 1945; JK to AG, September 6, 1945; AG to Lionel Trilling, August 27, 1945.
58. "I found myself . . .": AG to JK, September 4, 1945.
58. "Even the militarists . . .": AG to EB, September 3, 1945.
59. Herbert Huncke bio: HH, *Guilty of Everything* (New York: Paragon House, 1990); *The Evening Sun Turned Crimson*; (Cherry Valley, NY: Cherry Valley Editions, 1980); *Huncke's Journal* (New York: Poet's Press, 1965); AG journal entries; AG unpublished manuscript, "Portrait of Huncke," AG Columbia deposit.
60. "I took one look . . .": HH, *Guilty*, 69.
60. "get a little taste . . .": ibid.
60. WSB on morphine: WSB, *Junky* (New York: Ace Books, 1953); HH, *Guilty*, 70–71. *See also*, Barry Gifford and Lawrence Lee, *Jack's Book* (New York: St. Martin's Press, 1978), 49–50.
60. "I gave Burroughs . . .": HH, *Guilty*, 70.
60. "[H]e was so methodical . . .": ibid., 71.
60. AG's early interest in drugs: AG journal entries.
61. "stanzas of gibberish": AG, "Howl," *HOWL*, 13; *CP*, 129.
61. JK and Hal Chase: Gerald Nicosia, *Memory Babe: A Critical Biography of Jack Kerouac* (New York: Grove Press, 1983), 145–52.
61. "Wolfeans" and "non-Wolfeans": AG, *Indian Journals*, 175; JK to AG, November 13, 1945.
62. "transparent waterfalls . . ." and "So I talked . . .": AG, *Indian Journals*, 175. Not surprisingly, it was Jack Kerouac who saw through some of the nonsensical elements of the discussion and attempted to mollify Allen. In a November 13, 1945, letter, Jack told Allen that "I've grown very fond of you again," explaining that he and other members of the group were guilty of posing in such a manner that he was frozen and limited by his own self-perception. There was danger in getting too caught up in the idea of self-perception, Jack mentioned, pointing to Allen as "the least shammish and confused" member of the group. "Thus," Kerouac concluded, "I've seen you flare out into a sudden glory before my eyes, and I like to tell you about it."
63. "I wish . . .": AG, "To Kerouac in the Hospital," in Arthur and Kit Knight, eds., *Beat Angels* (California, PA: unspeakable visions of the individual, 1982), 175.
63. "several satires, laments . . .": AG, manuscript and introduction of unpublished poem, "Death in Violence," AG Columbia deposit.
63. "considering the personality . . .": ibid.
63. "it is difficult . . .": ibid.
64. "a substitute for . . .": ibid.
64. "a literary white elephant" and "a parade of sentimentalities": ibid.
64. "faults in conception . . .": ibid.
64. "You've nothing to say . . .": ibid.
65. "There is something seductive . . .": AG journal entry, August 27, 1944.
65. "a year of evil decadence": JK, *Vanity of Duluoz* (New York: Paragon Books, 1979), 269.
65. Life at apartment: JK, *Duluoz*, 268–71; HH, *Guilty*, 73–75; Alfred Aronowitz, "The Beat Generation," *New York Post*, March 10, 1959.
66. Arrests: HH, *Guilty*, 82–84.

4. Book of Doldrums

67. Epigraph: AG, "The Green Automobile," *RS*, 11; *CP*, 83.
67. AG readmission to Columbia: AG journal entry, September 20, 1946; N. M. McKnight to AG, July 10, 1946; Hans Wassing to N. M. McKnight, July 31, 1946.
67. "psychologically pretty much . . .": Hans Wassing to N. M. McKnight, July 31, 1946. This letter, although signed by Wassing, was actually written by AG.
67. AG reading list: AG journal entries.
67. AG reviews *Paterson*: AG journal entries, September 3, 1946; September 14, 1946. AG, "Paterson: No. 1," *Passaic Valley Examiner*, September 14, 1946.
67. "juvenile and blatant" and "I should have known . . .": AG journal entry, September 14, 1946.
68. "No new poems . . .": AG journal entry, September 3, 1946.

68. "I don't do anything . . .": AG journal entry, September 20, 1946.
68. "haunted by sterility" and "I see my trouble . . .": ibid.
68. "find a job . . .": LG to AG, undated, ca. fall 1946.
68. LG worries: author interviews with AG, Leo and Hannah Litzky.
68. "Until I am a man . . .": AG undated journal entry.
70. NC/LuAnne Henderson: Barry Gifford and Lawrence Lee, *Jack's Book* (New York: St. Martin's Press, 1978), 98–104.
70. Neal Cassady bio: NC, *The First Third* (San Francisco: City Lights Books, 1971), 1–70; William Plummer, *The Holy Goof: A Biography of Neal Cassady* (Englewood Cliffs, NJ: Prentice-Hall, 1981), 3–27; JK, *Visions of Cody* (New York: McGraw-Hill, 1972), 48–56.
70. "the sole replica . . .": NC, *First Third*, 1.
72. "[I]t was simply . . .": ibid., 58.
72. "only while inside . . .": ibid.
72. "The virgin emotion . . .": ibid., 105.
73. "Neal was something . . .": Gifford and Lee, *Jack's Book*, 103.
73. "a terribly decadent intellectual": NC, *First Third*, 118.
73. "a young college Jew . . ." and "soul had dried up . . .": ibid., 119.
73. "a young Gene Autry . . .": JK, *On the Road* (New York: Signet Books, 1957), 6.
74. "He was only conning . . .": ibid., 8.
74. "a western kinsman . . .": ibid., 11.
74. "Two keen minds . . .": ibid., 8.
74. "Two piercing eyes . . .": ibid., 8.
74. "intelligent, sensitive jocks": author interview with AG.
74. "pathos and fatality": AG to NC, undated, ca. fall 1947.
75. "I began to tremble . . .": AG, "Many Loves," CP, 156.
75. "a sensitive little kid . . .": AG, *Gay Sunshine Interview*, vol. 1, ed. Winston Leyland (San Francisco: Gay Sunshine Press, 1978).
75. "Thus I met Neal . . .": AG, "Many Loves," CP, 157.
75. "Last night I dreamt . . .": AG, " 'Drive All Blames into One,' " MB, 88; CP, 661.
76. "Spank me . . .": AG, "C'mon Jack," PAOTP, 38; CP, 649.
76. "Please master . . .": AG, "Please Master," FALL, 86; CP, 495.
76. NC sexuality: Carolyn Cassady, *Off the Road* (New York: William Morrow, 1990), 19; Gina Berriault, "Interview with Carolyn Cassady," *Rolling Stone*, October 12, 1972; author interview with AG.
77. "spent a wild weekend . . ." and "washed up on the shore . . .": AG journal entry, January 21, 1947.
77. "Wanting dearly . . .": JK, *On the Road*, 9.
77. "I think he *does* . . .": AG journal entry, March 2, 1947.
77. NC departure: AG journal entry, March 5, 1947; JK, *On the Road*, 9; Cody, 343–44.
78. "the hornrimmed wild . . .": JK, Cody, 343.
78. "like a thirty-year-old . . .": JK, *On the Road*, 9.
78. "never been west . . .": JK, Cody, 344.
78. "No tears . . .": AG journal entry, March 5, 1947.
78. "sacramental": NC to AG, March 30, 1947; AG journal entries.
78. "I *really* don't . . .": NC to AG, March 30, 1947.
79. "psychological oneness": ibid.
79. "dirty, double crossing . . .": NC to AG, April 10, 1947.
79. "I need you now . . .": NC to AG, March 14, 1947.
79. "I know I'm bisexual . . ." and "there's a slimmer line . . .": NC to AG, March 10, 1947.
79. "sexual stasis again": AG journal entry, April 29, 1947.
79. "a wonderful girl" and "a sense of peace": NC to AG, undated, ca. spring 1947.
79. AG in Denver: AG journal entries; AG, *Vision of Great Rememberer*, 2–3; JK, *On the Road*, 33–50; Carolyn Cassady, *Off the Road*, 16–33; Gifford and Lee, *Jack's Book*, 115–119; Drew Becker, "Cassady Was 'Light of Mind' to Ginsberg," *Denver Post*, August 12, 1979.
80. "a bit too straight . . ." and "knows all about . . .": NC to AG, undated, ca. spring 1947.
80. "I was under the impression . . .": Carolyn Cassady, *Off the Road*, 18.
80. "climbed with Carolyn . . .": AG, *Visions of Great Rememberer*, 3.
80. "such terrible nights" and "Denver Doldrums": AG journal entry, July 28, 1947.
80. "much like a Greek statue . . .": Carolyn Cassady, *Off the Road*, 20.
81. "the unity of the poem . . .": AG undated journal entry.
81. "Two bricklayers . . .": AG, "The Bricklayer's Lunch Hour," EM, 41; CP, 4.
81. "just sort of like . . .": Paul Portugés, *The Visionary Poetics of Allen Ginsberg* (Boulder & London: Shambhala, 1971), 408.

82. "the mad ones . . .": JK, *On the Road*, 9.

82. "good looks and shy . . .": Carolyn Cassady, *Off the Road*, 28.

82. "the slightest doubt . . .": ibid., 29.

82. "It's too bad . . .": ibid.

83. AG/NC/WSB in Texas: AG journal entries; unpublished manuscript, "The Monster of Dakar," AG Columbia deposit; JK, *Cody*, 123–29; HH, *The Evening Sun Turned Crimson* (Cherry Valley, NY: Cherry Valley Editions, 1980), 116–18; HH, *Guilty of Everything* (New York: Paragon House, 1990), 92–93; Ted Morgan, *Literary Outlaw: The Life and Times of William S. Burroughs* (New York: Henry Holt, 1988), 144.

83. "a happy holiday . . .": AG journal entry, August 29, 1947.

83. "He accepted it all . . ." and "just a poor . . .": AG, unpublished manuscript, "The Monster of Dakar." *See also*: JK, *Cody*, 127. In a taped conversation between Kerouac and Cassady, Neal mentions the incident, calling their agreement "an understanding to understand." In his poem "The Green Automobile" (*RS*, 14; *CP*, 85), Ginsberg recalls the event in two stanzas:

> The windshield's full of tears,
> rain wets our naked breasts
> we kneel together in the shade
> amid the traffic of night in paradise
>
> and now renew the solitary vow
> we made each other take
> in Texas, once:
> I can't inscribe here. . . .

84. "very queer . . .": JK, *Cody*, 140.

84. "a lot of meanings . . .": HH, *Guilty*, 92.

84. "The sacramental honeymoon . . .": AG journal entry, September 1, 1947.

85. "I had imagined . . .": ibid.

85. AG/NC in Houston: AG to LG, September 3, 1947; JK, *Cody*, 141; Morgan, *Literary Outlaw*, 144–45.

85–86. "My motives for shipping out . . ." and "I am aware . . .": AG to LG, September 12, 1947. In an earlier letter to Louis (9/3/47), Allen also spoke of his need for analysis, citing his "irritation & ennui & 'floating' anxiety & constant self-lacerating introspection" as a reason for looking for a ship. "A 50 day isolation at sea may or may not be pleasant," he wrote, "but the prospect of at last settling this analysis deal—however painful the analysis will be—is . . . the only concrete plan I have in mind for the next year."

86. "onerous job": AG to LG, September 3, 1947.

86. "the same process . . .": AG, unpublished notes for "Dakar Doldrums," AG Columbia deposit.

86. AG in Dakar: AG journals; AG unpublished manuscript, "The Monster of Dakar"; AG to HH, undated, ca. September 1947.

86. AG reading list: AG journal entries.

87. "Sex is nowhere here": AG to HH, undated, ca. September 1947.

87. "Remember me well . . .": AG to NC, undated, ca. fall 1947.

87. "What must I do . . .": AG to NC, undated, ca. fall 1947.

87. "There was something . . .": AG to NC, undated, ca. fall 1947.

87. "I think my mind . . .": AG to JK, undated, ca. fall 1947.

87. "obnoxious" and "If you really want to know . . .": ibid.

88. Naomi Ginsberg: AG, "Black Shroud," *White Shroud*, 69–70; "Kaddish" (manuscript and published version); author interviews with AG, EB.

88. "Humans sitting on the grass . . .": AG, "Kaddish," *KADDISH*, 25–26; *CP*, 220.

88. "a beautiful soul": AG, "Kaddish," *KADDISH*, 26; *CP*, 221.

89. "the head of a spider network" and "a spy . . .": ibid.

89. "main psychic difficulty" and "the usual oedipal entanglement": AG to Wilhelm Reich, March 11, 1947.

89. "wild wisdom": author interview with AG.

89. "your dear, your son . . .": AG, unpublished fragment from "Kaddish" manuscript.

89. "the gamut . . .": AG, "Kaddish," *KADDISH*, 27; *CP*, 221.

89. "so naïve . . .": AG, "Kaddish," *KADDISH*, 26; *CP*, 222.

89. "looking in the mirror . . .": AG, "Kaddish," *KADDISH*, 28; *CP*, 222.

89. "Why did you do this?": ibid.

90. "Some electric current . . .": AG, "Black Shroud," *White Shroud*, 69.

5. The Gates of Wrath

91. Epigraph: AG, "The Lion for Real," *KADDISH*, 53; *CP*, 174.
91. Completion of *The Town and the City*: WSB to AG/JK, June 5, 1948.
91. "It is very great . . .": AG to NC, undated, ca. April 1948.
91. "How I wish . . .": Naomi Ginsberg to AG, April 21, 1948.
92. "I don't know how good . . .": AG to Lionel Trilling, June 1, 1948.
92. "My mind travels . . .": AG journal entry, June 2, 1948.
92. "This round world . . .": AG, unpublished poetry manuscript, "The Dark Corridor," in AG Columbia deposit.
92. "Beat me up . . .": AG to JK, April 15, 1948.
92. "exorcise Neal": LG to AG, July 11, 1948.
92. Fourth of July weekend: JCH, *Nothing More to Declare* (New York: E.P. Dutton, 1967), 47–52.
92. Holmes bio: Author interview with JCH; Arthur and Kit Knight, *Interior Geographies: An Interview with John Clellon Holmes* (Warren, OH: Literary Denim, 1981), 1–4; John Tytell, "An Interview with John Clellon Holmes," in *Kerouac and the Beats*, eds. Arthur and Kit Knight (New York: Paragon House, 1988), 148–74.
93. "brothers in spirit": author interview with JCH.
93. "By all rights . . .": JCH, *Nothing More to Declare*, 51.
93. AG at July 3 party: Herbert Gold, "From *My Last Two Thousand Years*," in *The Beat Vision*, eds. Arthur and Kit Knight (New York: Paragon House, 1987), 67–72.
94. "lost child, a wandering child . . .": AG journal entry, August 3, 1944.
94. "I wearied in an endless maze . . .": AG, "A Western Ballad," *GW*, 11; *CP*, 13.
94. Blake, Yeats, and St. John: Paul Portugés, "Visions of Ordinary Mind," in *Talking Poetics from Naropa Institute*, vol. 2, eds. Anne Waldman and Marilyn Webb (Boulder, CO: Shambhala Publications, 1978), 386. In "Howl," Ginsberg remembered his study of the mystics: "who studied Plotinus Poe St. John of the Cross telepathy and bop kabala because the cosmos instinctively vibrated at their feet in Kansas" (*HOWL*, 11; *CP*, 127).
94. "solitude and inattention . . .": AG, *Allen Verbatim*, 16.
94. "narrowing circles" and "had the ideas without . . .": AG to NC, undated, ca. August 1948.
94. "Oh pure idea . . .": AG, unpublished poetry manuscript, "The Dark Corridor."
94. Cézanne: Ginsberg's lengthy term paper on Cézanne is included in his manuscript deposit at Columbia University.
95. "Cosmic Vibrations . . .": AG to Lionel Trilling, June 1, 1948.
95. "Ah, Sunflower . . .": William Blake, "Ah Sunflower," *The Portable Blake*, ed. Alfred Kazin (New York: Viking Press, 1946), 110.
95. "Where the youth. . .": ibid.
95. Blake visions: author interview with AG; AG, *Indian Journals, Journals Early Fifties Early Sixties* ("Psalm IV," 126); AG, "The Lion for Real," *KADDISH*, 53–55 and *CP*, 174–175; AG, "Gnostic Consciousness," *Allen Verbatim*, 15–23; AG, unpublished prose manuscript, "The Fall," in AG Columbia deposit; AG, unpublished manuscript, "Portrait of Huncke," in AG Columbia deposit; AG to JCH, June 16, 1949 (reprinted as "An Early Exchange on Poetics," in *the unspeakable visions of the individual*, no. 10, eds. Arthur and Kit Knight (California, PA: unspeakable visions of the individual, 1980); Tom Clark, "The Art of Poetry: Allen Ginsberg," in *Writers at Work: The Paris Review Interviews*, fourth series, ed. George Plimpton (New York: Viking Press, 1976), 300–10; Portugés, "Visions of Ordinary Mind," in *Talking Poetics*, 381–414; Edward Lucie-Smith, *Mysteries in the Universe: notes on an interview with Allen Ginsberg* (London: Turret Books, 1965), 1–3. A fictionalized version of Ginsberg's Blake visions can be found in John Clellon Holmes's novel *Go* (New York: Charles Scribner's Sons, 1952), 80–90.
96. "an exalted state . . .": Clark, "The Art of Poetry," in *Writers at Work*, 307.
96. "I've seen God!": ibid.
96. "I immediately rushed . . .": ibid.
97. "a great tormented soul": ibid., 308.
97. Response to visions: AG, "The Lion for Real," *KADDISH*, 53–55 and *CP*, 174–75; WSB to AG, March 10, 1949; NC to AG, August 20, 1948; Portugés, "Visions of Ordinary Mind," in *Talking Poetics*, 392–93; JCH, *Go*, 108. In "The Lion for Real," Ginsberg details the different responses to his visions. In 1976, he told interviewer Paul Portugés: "There was nobody to talk to, that was the problem, there was absolutely nobody to talk to who was, like, sane or clear—more difficult than 'coming out of the closet.' The few people I talked to told me to see a psychiatrist, or just turned off, so I got very splenetic, angry and irritable, thinking that other people were resisting acknowledging what they themselves knew" (*Talking Poetics*, 397).
97. "you'll get there yet": Mark Van Doren to AG, August 3, 1948.

97. "you haven't written . . .": Mark Van Doren to AG, December 24, 1948.
97. "Language, language . . .": AG, unpublished poetry manuscript, "Holy Doldrums," in AG Columbia deposit.
97. Abstract, esoteric qualities of AG poetry: see AG discussion of early poetry in Portugés, "Visions of Ordinary Mind," *Talking Poetics*, 394.
98. "I was just trying . . .": Ekbert Fass, *Towards a New American Poetics* (Santa Barbara, CA: Black Sparrow Press, 1979), 269.
98. "mystical riddle": Portugés, "Visions of Ordinary Mind," in *Talking Poetics*, 383.
98. Symbolism: In later years, Ginsberg would cite two quotations as being especially influential in the development of his poetry. The first, Williams's "no ideas but in things," has been previously discussed. The second, "things are symbols of themselves," was offered by his Tibetan Buddhist teacher, Chögyam Trungpa, Rinpoche.
98. "giant octopus . . .": Portugés, "Visions of Ordinary Mind," in *Talking Poetics*, 397.
99. "to shut up & live . . .": AG, *Indian Journals*, 154.
99. "My time is worth . . .": AG to LG, undated, ca. 1948.
99. AG's search for job in publishing: Louise Nicholl to Robert Giroux, October 8, 1948; JK to AG, December 15, 1948.
99. "steady creative labor . . .": AG to NC, undated, ca. September 1948.
99. "naturalistic-symbolistic novel . . .": AG to LG, undated, ca. 1948.
99. "I won't rely . . .": ibid.
99. "Very well . . .": ibid.
100. Birth of Cathleen JoAnne Cassady; NC plans: NC to AG, September 7, 1948. *See also*: Carolyn Cassady, *Off the Road* (New York: William Morrow, 1990), 72–77.
100. "I must be my own angel . . .": AG to NC, undated, ca. September 1948.
100. "The clearest expression . . .": AG to NC, undated, ca. August 1948.
100. Holmes/Kerouac frustrations: author interview with JCH; JK to AG, July 26, 1949.
100. "vague, speculative doubts . . .": author interview with JCH.
100. JK's coining of term Beat Generation: JCH, *Nothing More to Declare*, 106–07; JK, "Origins of the Beat Generation," *Playboy*, June 1959; Alfred Aronowitz, "The Beat Generation," *New York Post*, March 10, 1959.
100. "peculiar quality . . .": and "in the street . . .": JCH, *Nothing More to Declare*, 106–07.
101. "I guess you might say . . .": ibid, 107.
101. Atom bomb and Beat Generation's philosophy: author interview with JCH. *See also*, John Tytell, *Naked Angels: The Lives and Literature of the Beat Generation* (New York: McGraw-Hill, 1976), 17. Tytell draws the original link between the Beat Generation philosophy and the Merton quote.
102. Neal Cassady visit: JK, *On the Road* (New York: Signet Books, 1957), 91–110; JK, *Visions of Cody* (New York: McGraw-Hill, 1972), 345–47; Barry Gifford and Lawrence Lee, *Jack's Book* (New York: St. Martin's Press, 1978), 122–31.
102. "fitful and abortive starts": author interview with JCH.
102. NC New York plans: JK to AG, December 15, 1948.
102. "the devil incarnate": Gifford and Lee, *Jack's Book*, 132.
103. "like a monk . . .": JK, *On the Road*, 93.
104. "a stranger for all intents . . .": JK, *Cody*, 346.
104. AG on Cassady presence: JK, *On the Road*, 107.
104. "Cody is the brother . . .": JK, *Cody*, 320.
104. "What is the meaning . . .": JK, *On the Road*, 99.
104. "I wound all the people . . .": NC to Carolyn Cassady, January 11, 1949.
105. "ran like Groucho Marx . . .": JK, *On the Road*, 104.
105. "inauthentic" and "Kirilov in reverse . . .": JCH, *Go*, 127.
105. WSB letters and telegrams: (telegrams) December 28, 1948, and January 10, 1949; (letters) January 10, 16, and 17, 1949. All were sent to AG.
105. "What kind of character . . .": WSB to AG, January 10, 1949.
105. "Ah, it's all right . . .": JK, *On the Road*, 104.
105. Chaplin/Marx: AG to JCH, June 16, 1949.
105. "Pull my daisy . . .": JK and AG, *GW*, 27; *CP*, 24.
106. "lifestyle as literature": author interview with JCH.
106. "the great experiencer . . .": AG, "The Great Rememberer," introduction to *Visions of Cody*, ix.
106. "Neal is, of course, the very soul . . .": WSB to AG, January 30, 1949.
106. NC as Whitman figure: AG, *Visions of the Great Rememberer*, 30.
106. Huncke story: Much of the material for this segment is taken from two unpublished AG manuscripts, "The Fall" and "Portrait of Huncke," both on deposit at Columbia University. A fictionalized account can be found in JCH, *Go*, 235–37.

107. "Don't bother . . .": JCH, *Go*, 236.
107. "who was in . . .": ibid., 237.
107. "Sure, I'm old . . .": AG, "Portrait of Huncke."
107. Burroughs's objections to Huncke: WSB to AG, August 23, 1948; March 26, April 13, and April 16, 1949.
107. "about $200 . . .": AG to NC, undated, ca. September 1948.
108. "now on Times Square . . .": ibid.
108. "who walked all night . . .": AG, "Howl," *HOWL*, 13; CP, 128.
108. "General intimidation . . .": AG to NC, May 1949.
108. "Herbert was beat . . .": ibid.
108. "I was overjoyed . . .": Jane Kramer, *Allen Ginsberg in America* (New York: Random House, 1969), 124.
109. "For a time . . .": HH, "Guilty of Everything," in *the unspeakable visions of the individual*, no. 10, 47.
109. "a sort of subdivision cousin . . .": Kramer, *Allen Ginsberg in America*, 125.
109. "really a remarkable . . .": ibid., 125.
109. Theft ring: AG, unpublished prose manuscript, "The Fall"; Kramer, *Allen Ginsberg in America*, 124–26; JCH, *Go*, 256–63.
109. AG's plans to visit Louisiana: WSB to AG, March 26, 1949.
109. WSB arrest: Joan Vollmer to AG, April 13, 1949.
109. JK's and Lucien Carr's concern: AG to NC, May 1949.
109. "If you really wanted . . .": AG, "The Fall."
110. "I had gone along . . .": ibid.
110. "die, go mad . . .": Portugés, "Visions of Ordinary Mind," in *Talking Poetics*, 401.
110. "Zero is appealing . . .": AG, "Bop Lyrics," GW, 24; CP, 42.
111. Car chase: AG, "The Fall"; Kramer, *Allen Ginsberg in America*, 125–27; JCH, Go, 278–80; "Wrong-Way Auto Tips Off Police to Narcotics-Ruled Burglary Gang," *New York World-Telegram*, April 23, 1949; "Wrong-Way Turn Clears Up Robbery," *The New York Times*, April 23, 1949.
111. "very distinct sensation . . .": Kramer, *Allen Ginsberg in America*, 126.
111. "naturalist" and "How do you get . . .": ibid., 127.
112. "My God, Herbert . . ." and "Why get hung up . . .": JCH, *Go*, 283, 285.
112. "One of the accused . . .": "Wrong-Way Turn," *The New York Times*, April 23, 1949.
112. "I was advertised . . .": Kramer, *Allen Ginsberg in America*, 127–28.
113. "A lot of us around here . . .": ibid., 128.
113. AG's feelings about escaping prison sentence: AG, "The Fall."
113. "saint of old . . .": ibid.
113. "it would be quite a miraculous . . .": AG to JCH, June 16, 1949.
113. AG job frustrations: AG to NC, May 20, 1949; author interview with AG.
113. AG's thoughts at Columbia Psychiatric Institute: Kramer, *Allen Ginsberg in America*, 129.
114. "I feel as if I am . . .": AG, untitled poem, EM, 9; CP, 71.
114. AG meeting Carl Solomon: author interviews with AG and Carl Solomon; AG, *Gay Sunshine Interview*, 20.
114. "Carl Solomon was living proof that the best minds . . .": AG, "Howl," *HOWL*, 9; CP, 126.
114. JK response to AG in Psychiatric Institute: JK to AG, June 10, 1949; JK to AG, July 5, 1949; JK to AG, July 26, 1949.
114. "It shows your interest . . .": JK to AG, July 5, 1949.
114. "always trying to justify . . .": JK to AG, June 10, 1949.
114. "Next year . . .": JK to AG, May 23, 1949.
115. "I only want . . .": JK to AG, June 10, 1949.
115. WSB response: WSB to JK, June 24, 1949, and September 26, 1949; WSB to AG, November 2, 1949, and December 24, 1949.
115. "rational": WSB to JK, September 26, 1949.
115. "Imagine being herded . . .": WSB to JK, June 24, 1949.
115. "Besides, I don't see . . .": ibid.
115. "I think the U.S. . . .": WSB to AG, December 24, 1949.
115. "You and I . . ." and "only with effort": NC to AG, undated, ca. May 1948.
115. "Letters between you and me . . .": AG to NC, May 20, 1949.
115. "that anyone who doesn't . . .": Joan Vollmer to AG, October 31, 1949.
115. Carl Solomon bio: author interview with Carl Solomon; Carl Solomon, "Report from the Asylum," reprinted in Solomon, *Mishaps Perhaps* (San Francisco: Beach Books, 1968), 36–46; John Tytell, "An Interview with Carl Solomon," in *The Beat Book*, eds. Arthur and Kit Knight (California, PA: unspeakable visions of the individual, 1974), 163–71; AG, *Gay Sunshine Interview*, 35–36.
116. "literary, erudite . . ." and "insufficiently deranged . . .": author interview with Carl Solomon.

116. "obviously the product . . .": ibid.
116. "the dopey daffodil" and "the poet as brute": Tytell, "An Interview with Carl Solomon," in *Beat Book*, 166.
116. "survival in a world . . .": author interview with Carl Solomon.
116. "tendency toward intellectual . . .": ibid.
116. "more concerned with technique . . .": ibid.
116. "L'affaire auto . . .": AG to JCH, June 16, 1949.
117. "There are no intellectuals . . .": author interview with Carl Solomon.
117. "I'm with you in Rockland . . .": AG, "Howl," *HOWL*, 20; *CP*, 133.
117. "empty and uninspired": AG to NC, May 1949.
117. AG and suicide: AG to NC, May 20, 1949.
117. "my obligation was . . .": Portugés, "Visions of Ordinary Mind," in *Talking Poetics*, 401.
117. "I am living in Eternity . . .": AG, "Metaphysics," *EM*, 17; *CP*, 33.

6. Empty Mirror

118. Epigraph: AG, "Psalm I," *EM*, 11; *CP*, 18.
118. "an average neurotic": author interview with AG.
119. "I wish I could meet . . .": AG to JK, January 21, 1950.
119. Edith and Louis Ginsberg: author interviews with Edith Ginsberg, AG.
119. "A look startled . . .": AG, " 'Don't Grow Old,' " *PO*, 50; *CP*, 710.
119. "So, take my advice . . .": LG to AG, undated, ca. spring 1948.
120. "I am beginning . . .": AG to JK, January 21, 1950.
120. "actually be crucified . . .": ibid.
120. "I was just writing . . .": author interview with AG.
121. "Today out of the window . . .": AG, "The Trembling of the Veil," *EM*, 15; *CP*, 14.
121. "Trembling of veil . . .": AG journal entry, June 6, 1949.
122. "I figured . . .": Paul Portugés, "Visions of Ordinary Mind," *Talking Poetics from Naropa Institute*, vol. 2, eds. Anne Waldman and Marilyn Webb (Boulder, CO: Shambhala Publications, 1978), 405–06.
123. "Dear Doctor . . .": AG to WCW, March 30, 1950. William Carlos Williams used this letter as part of *Paterson (Book Four)*. See, WCW, *Paterson* (New York: New Directions, 1963), 173–75.
123. "I envision for myself . . .": ibid.
123. "samples of my best writing": ibid.
123. "no ideas . . .": WCW, *Paterson*, 6.
123. "In this mode . . .": AG undated journal entry; author interview with AG.
124. "[t]o make a start . . .": WCW, *Paterson*, 3.
124. "the poet's business . . .": WCW, *The Autobiography* (New York: Random House, 1951) reprinted in *Paterson*, iii.
124. WCW bio: Paul Mariani, *William Carlos Williams: A New World Naked* (New York: McGraw-Hill, 1981); Reed Whittemore; *William Carlos Williams: Poet from Jersey* (Boston: Houghton Mifflin, 1975); Paul Christensen, "William Carlos Williams," *The Beats: Literary Bohemians in Postwar America* (Detroit: Gale Research Company, 1983), 583–590; John W. Gerber and Emily M. Wallace, "An Interview with William Carlos Williams," in *Interviews with William Carlos Williams*, ed. Linda Wagner (New York: New Directions, 1976), 3–26.
124. "so much depends . . .": WCW, "The Red Wheelbarrow," *Selected Poems* (New York: New Directions, 1985), 56.
124. "Why bother with English . . .": WCW, "The American Idiom," in *Interviews*, 100.
124. "He was trying . . .": Alison Colbert, "Conversations: A Talk with Allen Ginsberg," *Partisan Review*, vol. 38, no. 3 (1971).
125. NY scene: AG journal entries; author interviews with AG, JCH. See also, Jay Landesman, *Rebel Without Applause* (Sag Harbor, NY: Permanent Press, 1987).
126. "It is a truly great book . . .": AG to JK, undated, ca. February or March 1950.
126. "[I]f anybody gets nasty . . .": ibid.
126. "This may sound . . .": AG to JK, undated, ca. late March 1950.
127. "It still looks good": ibid. Solomon's essay, "Report from the Asylum—Afterthoughts of a Shock Patient," published under the pseudonym of Carl Goy, appeared in the same issue of *Neurotica* (Spring 1950).
127. "a new season . . .": AG to JK, June 8, 1950.
127. "I love Helen . . ." and "a beautiful, intelligent . . .": ibid.
128. "a great lover" and "camp, unnecessary . . .": ibid.
128. "The Shroudy Stranger of the Night": AG journal entries; author interview with AG. Ginsberg

also called the poem "Song of the Shrouded Stranger." It was eventually published in *Empty Mirror* as "The Shrouded Stranger"—one of two early Ginsberg poems with that title.

128. "a long poem . . .": AG undated journal entry.
128. "an old beat . . .": AG undated journal entry.
128. "a tour de force . . .": AG undated journal entry.
129. AG job at ribbon factory: AG to NC, October 31, 1950; AG, "How Come He Got Canned at the Ribbon Factory," *EM*, 45; *CP*, 60.
129. "It's a kind . . ." and "Truly the real world . . .": AG to NC, October 31, 1950.
129. "a god of all the knots": AG, "How Come He Got Canned at the Ribbon Factory," *EM*, 45; *CP*, 60.
129. "Obviously he wasn't . . .": ibid.
129. Cannastra death: AG journal entries; AG to NC, October 31, 1950; *New York Daily News*, October 13, 1950; *New York Herald Tribune*, October 13, 1950; *New York Daily Mirror*, October 13, 1950. A fictional account of Cannastra's death is included in JCH, *Go* (New York: Charles Scribner's Sons, 1952), 302–05.
130. "fell out of . . .": AG, "Howl," *HOWL*, 14; *CP*, 129.
130. "[t]he great question . . .": AG to NC, October 31, 1950.
131. "every tragedy . . .": ibid.
131. *shadow changes into bone*: AG, "Refrain," *GW*, 10; *CP*, 11.
131. JK/Joan Haverty wedding: AG to NC, November 18, 1950.
132. "without real sadness . . .": ibid.
132. "largeness of spirit" and "I don't know . . .": ibid.
132. "Joan Anderson" letter: author interview with AG; AG to NC, undated, ca. early 1951; NC to AG, March 17–20, 1951; AG to NC, May 7, 1951; NC to AG, May 10, 1951. Neal Cassady's "Joan Anderson" letter was lost and only a fragment exists today, published in Cassady's *The First Third* under the title "To Have Seen a Spectre."
132. "a key moment . . .": author interview with AG.
133. "a colossus risen . . .": AG to NC, undated, ca. early 1951.
133. "an almost pure . . ."; "clarity and grace and vigor"; and "salvation and joy . . .": ibid.
133. "Mainly, since it was . . .": ibid.
133. "Can do same anytime": NC to AG, May 10, 1951.
134. "All the crazy fallderall [*sic*] . . .": NC to AG, March 17, 1951.
134. "a horrible stinker . . .": ibid.
134. "The real reason . . .": ibid.
134. *On the Road*: author interviews with AG, JCH; AG to NC, May 7, 1951. Kerouac's published version of *On the Road* is the book written in 1951. He had also given that title to an early, never-completed version of *Visions of Cody*.
134. WSB: WSB to Lucien Carr, March 5, 1951; WSB to AG, undated, ca. March 1951; WSB to AG, March 5, 1951.
134. "I don't justify . . .": WSB to AG, March 5, 1951.
134. "I don't mean . . .": ibid.
135. AG reviews: AG Columbia deposit; George Dowden, *A Bibliography of Works by Allen Ginsberg: October 1943 to July 1, 1967* (San Francisco: City Lights Books, 1971). Ginsberg's review of *Question on a Kite* (January 21, 1951) and *Toward Daybreak* (February 25, 1951) appeared in the *New York Herald Tribune*. His reviews of George Barker's *The Dead Seagull* (July 23, 1951), Vilhelm Moberg's *The Emigrants*, and Paul Wellman's *The Iron Mistress* (July 30, 1951) appeared, without byline, in *Newsweek*.
135. "I sit at Cantwell's desk . . .": AG to JK, undated, ca. July 1951.
135. "lost contact . . .": JK to AG, July 15, 1951.
135. "to have lost . . .": AG to JK, undated, ca. mid-July 1951.
135. "socially useful": ibid.
135. "I remember that eight-hour session . . .": author interview with JCH.
136. "The writing is dewlike . . .": AG to NC, May 17, 1951.
136. AG in Mexico City: AG to NC, September 7, 1951. *See also*, Ted Morgan, *Literary Outlaw: The Life and Times of William S. Burroughs* (New York: Henry Holt, 1988), 191–93.
137. "How fast . . .": Morgan, *Literary Outlaw*, 192.
137. Death of Joan Vollmer: WSB, *Queer* (New York: Viking Press, 1985), xvii–xxiii; AG to NC, September 7, 1951; "Heir's Pistol Kills His Wife; He Denies Playing Wm. Tell," *New York Daily News*, September 8, 1951; Morgan, *Literary Outlaw*, 193–204.
137. "My imagination of the scene . . .": AG to NC, September 7, 1951.
137. "I did not put . . .": "Heir's Pistol," *New York Daily News*.
138. "I am forced . . .": WSB, *Queer*, xxii.
138. Phil White: AG to NC/JK, February 15, 1952. Immediate reaction to White's death was sympathetic. Ginsberg wrote that it was like "a tragic movie." Burroughs, writing Ginsberg on January

19, 1952, expressed surprise that White would have made such a deal with the police—"He was so uncompromising and puritanical about stool pigeons"—but claimed that he had not changed his favorable opinion about White. In time, Ginsberg, Burroughs, and Huncke would learn the details about another side of White that he had kept hidden from them: There had been occasions when, out of his mind on heroin and other drugs, White had fired his gun without provocation at bystanders, killing at least one man.

138. "Joan, gone southward . . .": AG undated journal entry.
139. "This is what . . ." and "Phil White . . .": AG undated journal entry; AG to NC, January 1952.
139. "Where he fell . . .": AG, "The Names," *CP*, 178.
140. "weird poems" and "a bunch of short . . .": AG to JK/NC, undated, ca. February 1952. The poems AG submitted, all published in *Empty Mirror*, were: "Metaphysics," "Long Live the Spiderweb," "The Night-apple," "A Poem on America," "A Dream," "Sunset," "The Trembling of the Veil," "A Meaningless Institution" (originally entitled "Dead Man's House"), "Nite Thoughts" (untitled in *Empty Mirror*), and "Fyodor."
140. "How many . . .": WCW to AG, February 27, 1952.
140. "Now you realize . . .": AG to JK/NC, undated, ca. February 1952.
140. "We'll have a huge . . .": ibid.
140. "the first American Novel": ibid.
140. Gregory Corso bio: James McKenzie, "I'm Poor Simple Human Bones: An Interview with Gregory Corso," in *The Beat Diary*, eds. Arthur and Kit Knight (California, PA: unspeakable visions of the individual, 1977), 4–24, reprinted in *The Beat Vision*, eds. Arthur and Kit Knight (New York: Paragon House, 1987), 151–84; *Riverside Interviews 3: Gregory Corso* (London: Pinnacle, 1983); Bruce Cook, *The Beat Generation* (New York: Charles Scribner's Sons, 1971), 133–49; Alfred Aronowitz, "The Beat Generation," *New York Post*, March 18, 1959.
141. "[M]y phantasies . . .": AG to JK/NC, undated, ca. early March 1952.
141. "Don't worry . . .": JK to AG, March 15, 1952.
141. " 'Go, Go, Go' . . .": JK to AG, undated, ca. late March, early April 1952.
141. "You see I am . . .": AG to JK, May 15, 1952.
142. "Little Allen": author interview with AG.
142. "is coming to personify . . .": WCW to Robert Lowell, March 11, 1952.
142. "a clean, rigorously . . .": WCW to Marianne Moore, May 24, 1952.
142. "Williams is . . .": AG to JK/NC, undated, ca. February 1952.
143. "The book would then . . .": WCW to AG, April 7, 1952.
143. AG and WCW friendship: AG journal entries; AG to JK, undated, ca. April 1952; AG to JK/NC, undated, ca. February 1952; AG to JK/NC, undated, ca. March 1952; AG to JK, May 15, 1952; JK to AG, undated, ca. March or April 1952; Mariani, *William Carlos Williams*, 702–03; author interview with AG. One cannot help but wonder how Louis Ginsberg felt about the influence Williams had on his son. After all, Louis Ginsberg was a well-known poet and teacher himself. In an interview with the author, Edith Ginsberg mentioned, "I believe that Louie always felt hurt that Allen considered Dr. Williams more his mentor than his father was. I never told Louie that, but I knew him well enough to know that he felt that Williams was sort of taking his place as a father figure."
143. "What's it all for?" and "Yes, I think . . .": AG to JK, undated, ca. April 1952.
143. "My life is over . . .": AG journal entry, March 12, 1952.
143. "A young man . . .": ibid.
144. "A Novel . . .": AG undated journal entry.
144. "I must abandon . . .": AG journal entry, June 30, 1952.

7. Reality Sandwiches

145. Epigraph: AG, "Siesta in Xbalba," *RS*, 36; *CP*, 108.
145. "Blow, baby, blow!" and "When you 'open . . .' ": JK to AG, March 15, 1952.
145. "The 'formal ode' . . .": JK to AG, March 12, 1952.
145. "[T]he value of yr. mind . . .": ibid.
145. "informal might be better": AG to JK, undated, ca. April 1952.
145. "naked thought": JK to AG, March 12, 1952.
146. "your specific understanding . . ."; "mental work, time . . ."; and "Wish I could . . .": ibid. Ginsberg eventually realized this wish in *Collected Poems*, where he placed the poems back to back. In their initial publication, "Ode to the Setting Sun" was collected in *Gates of Wrath* and "Sunset" was published in *Empty Mirror*.
146. Prose sketching: JK to AG, May 18, 1952; Barry Gifford and Lawrence Lee, *Jack's Book* (New York: St. Martin's Press, 1978), 159–60; author interview with AG.

146. "like a painter . . .": JK to AG, May 18, 1952.
146. "[Y]ou just have to purify . . ." and "I read it . . .": ibid.
147. "The language is great . . .": AG to JK, June 12, 1952.
147. "I don't see . . .": ibid.
147. "a holy mess" and "it's great allright . . .": AG to NC, July 3, 1952.
147. "I changed my mind . . .": Yves Le Pellec, "The New Consciousness," reprinted in AG, *Composed on the Tongue*, 79–80.
148. "Certainly these . . .": AG, introduction to WSB, *Junky* (New York: Penguin Books, 1977), vii.
148. "This agenting is getting . . .": AG to JK/WSB, June 12, 1952.
148. "In these days . . .": Shirley Neitlich (of Random House editorial department) to AG, September 8, 1952.
149. "This is to notify . . .": JK to AG, October 8, 1952.
149. "I realize that . . ." and "Is this the fate . . .": ibid.
149. "And you who I thought . . .": ibid.
149. "my little petushka . . .": JK to AG, November 8, 1952.
150. "Any attempts to label . . .": JCH, "This Is the Beat Generation," *The New York Times*, November 16, 1952; reprinted in JCH, *Nothing More to Declare* (New York: Dutton, 1967), 109–15.
150. "More than weariness . . .": ibid.
150. "out of curiosity . . .": ibid.
150. "hip without being . . .": JK, *The Subterraneans* (New York: Grove Press, 1958), 2.
151. JK in New York: AG to NC, undated, ca. January 1953.
151. AG visits Naomi: AG journal entries; AG, "Kaddish," unpublished manuscript; AG, "Kaddish," *KADDISH*, 30; CP, 223–24; AG and Robert Frank, *Kaddish* filmscript; Naomi Ginsberg to AG/EB, January 5, 1953.
151. "Are you Allen . . .": AG, unpublished fragment from first draft of "Kaddish."
151. "The horror . . .": AG, "Kaddish," *KADDISH*, 30; CP, 223.
151. "Naomi! Naomi! . . .": AG, unpublished fragment from first draft of "Kaddish."
151. "as if she were . . .": ibid.
151. "experts on . . .": AG to JK, February 20, 1953.
152. "strictly business": JK to AG, February 21, 1953.
152. "dissolute and beat": AG to NC, undated, ca. January 1953.
152. "Amazing how truly . . .": AG to NC, May 14, 1953.
153. "the sublimity and sophistication . . .": ibid.
153. "not interesting . . ." and "the various dynasties . . .": ibid.
153. "you begin to see . . .": ibid.
153. "Sakyamuni": *See* AG, "Sakyamuni Coming Out from the Mountain," *RS*, 9–10; CP, 90–91. Ginsberg sent a copy of the first draft of the poem in a May 14, 1953, letter to Neal Cassady, reprinted in AG/NC, *As Ever*, 142–43.
153. "he realized . . .": AG, "Sakyamuni," *RS*, 9; CP, 90.
153. "he knows nothing . . .": AG, "Sakyamuni," *RS*, 10; CP, 90–91.
154. "collapse of the imagination . . .": unpublished notes for AG's recorded poetry, AG Columbia deposit.
154. "I discover life . . .": AG to NC, June 23, 1953.
154. "The green auto . . .": AG undated journal entry.
155. "Denver! Denver! . . .": AG, "The Green Automobile," *RS*, 13; CP, 84.
155. "I would like to build . . .": AG undated journal entry.
155. "the unspeakable visions . . .": JK, "Belief and Technique of Modern Prose," in *Heaven & Other Poems* (Bolinas, CA: Grey Fox Press, 1977), 47.
155. "Something that you feel . . .": ibid., 46.
155. "bookmovie": ibid., 47.
156. WSB in South America: WSB/AG, *The Yage Letters. See also*, Ted Morgan, *Literary Outlaw: The Life and Times of William S. Burroughs* (New York: Henry Holt, 1988), 215–25.
156. "Yage may be . . .": WSB, *Junky*, 152.
156. "Larval beings . . .": WSB to AG, April 15, 1953; WSB/AG, *Yage Letters*, 30.
156. "Yage is space . . .": WSB to AG, July 10, 1953; WSB/AG, *Yage Letters*, 47.
157. "What I look for . . .": WSB, *Junky*, 152.
157. "he is very great . . .": AG to NC, September 4, 1953.
157. "I don't want . . .": author interview with AG.
158. "my art and soul's sake": AG to Neal and Carolyn Cassady, November 24, 1953.
158. "This is a rare . . .": ibid.
159. "Square Cartaret . . .": AG undated journal entry.
159. "Trip off . . .": AG, undated journal entry.
159. "dark like . . .": AG, undated journal entry.
159. "the drum set . . .": AG, undated journal entry.

159. "immense preoccupied . . .": ibid.
159. "a very great writer": AG to JK and Neal and Carolyn Cassady, undated, ca. early January 1954.
160. "a wise distinguished . . .": AG undated journal entry.
160. "kind of dreary . . .": AG to JK and Neal and Carolyn Cassady, undated, ca. early January 1954.
160. AG's Mexico trip: AG unpublished journals; AG, *Journals*, 29–72; AG, "Siesta in Xbalba," *RS*, 21–39 and *CP*, 97–110; AG to NC, November 14, 1953; AG to Neal and Carolyn Cassady, November 24, 1953; AG to NC, November 25, 1953; AG to JK and Neal and Carolyn Cassady, undated, ca. early January 1954; AG to JK and Neal and Carolyn Cassady, January 18, February 18, and April 4, 1954; NC to AG, April 23, 1954; AG to Neal and Carolyn Cassady, May 12, 1954; AG to JK, undated, ca. mid-June 1954; AG to Lucien Carr, January 18, February 18, March 31, April 1 (telegram and letter), and May 21, 1954.
161. "the clap of hands . . .": AG undated journal entry, published in AG, *Journals*, 30.
161. "really quite beautiful . . .": AG undated journal entry; published in AG, *Journals*, 38.
161. "more glory . . .": AG to JK and Neal and Carolyn Cassady, January 18, 1954.
161. "Worrying about my fate . . .": AG undated journal entry; published in AG, *Journals*, 41.
162. "Landscape, mountains & jungle . . .": AG to Lucien Carr, January 18, 1954.
162. "perhaps the person . . .": AG to JK and Neal and Carolyn Cassady, January 18, 1954.
163. "Time's slow wall . . .": AG, "Siesta in Xbalba," *RS*, 28; *CP*, 102.
163. "Yet these ruins . . .": AG, "Siesta in Xbalba," *RS*, 30; *CP*, 103–104.
164. "to whom . . .": AG undated journal entry.
164. "I walked in the forest . . .": AG, "Green Valentine Blues," *CP*, 95.
164. "A great discovery . . .": AG to Lucien Carr, February 18, 1954.
164. "a friendly womb . . .": ibid.
164. "I break out . . .": AG to JK and Neal and Carolyn Cassady, February 18, 1954.
164. "so brilliant . . .": AG to Lucien Carr, February 18, 1954.
165. "honored important guest": AG to JK and Neal and Carolyn Cassady, April 4, 1954. This letter is dated March 4, but from its contents it is clear that it was actually written a month later, most likely an oversight of the changing months on Ginsberg's part. All references to this letter will be listed by its correct date.
165. "like a colossal . . .": AG to Lucien Carr, April 1, 1954.
165. "repetitive melancholy variations . . .": ibid.
165. "the whole mountain . . .": ibid.
166. "Dozens of indians . . .": AG to JK and Neal and Carolyn Cassady, April 4, 1954.
166. "a great trip . . .": ibid.
167. "I found the men . . .": AG to Lucien Carr, April 1, 1954.
167. "Indians have great . . ." and "a mountain named . . .": AG to JK and Neal and Carolyn Cassady, April 4, 1954.
167. "do something brave . . .": ibid.
168. Concern about AG's whereabouts: WSB to NC, March 12, 1954; WSB to JK, April 22, 1954; NC to AG, April 23, 1954; WSB to LG, May 2, 1954; WSB to NC, May 2, 1954; WSB to JK, May 4, 1954; WSB to AG, May 11, 1954; AG to Neal and Carolyn Cassady, May 12, 1954; Mortimer Burroughs to AG, May 17, 1954; WSB to AG, May 22, 1954.
168. "You must remonstrate . . .": WSB to JK, April 22, 1954.
168. "Naturally I'm very worried . . .": NC to AG, April 23, 1954.
169. "Allen said . . .": WSB to JK, May 4, 1954.
169. "It looks very bad . . .": ibid.
169. "better than . . .": AG to Neal and Carolyn Cassady, May 12, 1954.
169. "I thought . . .": AG, "Siesta in Xbalba," *RS*, 32–33; *CP*, 105.
170. "Empty Mirror poems . . .": AG undated journal entry.
170. "He sure is lonely . . .": ibid.
170. AG journey home: AG unpublished journal entries; AG, *Journals*, 63–72; AG, "Siesta in Xbalba," *RS*, 33–39 and *CP*, 106–10; AG to Neal and Carolyn Cassady, May 12, 1954; AG to JK, undated, ca. mid-June 1954.
170. "lunar landscape": AG undated journal entry; published in AG, *Journals*, 63.
171. "the far away likeness . . .": AG, "Siesta in Xbalba," *RS*, 34; *CP*, 107.
171. "of eternity . . .": AG, "Siesta in Xbalba," *RS*, 36; *CP*, 108.
172. "trip to Frisco . . .": AG undated journal entry; published in AG, *Journals*, 66.

8. In Back of the Real

173. Epigraph: AG, "Song," *HOWL*, 39; *CP*, 111.
173. "I wound up . . .": AG to JK, undated, ca. mid-June 1954.

173. "a German geologist": AG, *Journals*, 62.
173. "my character . . .": AG journal entry, June 8, 1954; published in AG, *Journals*, 73.
174. "Must find energy . . .": ibid.
174. JK visits Cassadys: JK to AG, March 1954, two undated letters, ca. May 1954, and undated letter, ca. June 1954; Carolyn Cassady, *Off the Road* (New York: William Morrow, 1990), 234–40; William Plummer, *The Holy Goof: A Biography of Neal Cassady* (Englewood Cliffs, NJ: Prentice-Hall, 1981), 95–96.
174. Cassadys and Edgar Cayce: JK to AG, March 1954 and May 1954; Carolyn Cassady, *Off the Road*, 231–38; Plummer, *Holy Goof*, 98–101. Some of Cayce's followers claimed that after going into a state of trance they could see a person's past lives. Neal Cassady's past-life reading, recorded in Carolyn Cassady's *Off the Road* (373–76), was, if nothing else, an astonishing interpretation of some of Neal's present-life personality flaws. The medium detailed six of Cassady's former lives. In the first, he was a vengeful and deceptive Bedouin prince who was eventually stabbed to death by his son and placed on public display. In another life, he had been publicly castrated for rape; in another, he had been a Chinese opium addict. Perhaps most interesting was his life as an Assyrian charioteer, in which he had seen his son killed by the knife blades he had mounted on the wheels of his chariot. Neal and Carolyn Cassady had known each other in the past, but their relationship had ended in tragedy, with Carolyn drowning, at Neal's beckon, in a pool of sheep's blood. The past-life readings, with their details of Neal's many vices, had a powerful effect on both Neal and Carolyn. "Whether or not these tales were true, I hardly think any writer of fiction could have imagined lives of such extreme depravity," Carolyn wrote. "In some ways, I felt I knew these six men, and Neal himself felt a very deep emotional kinship, convinced of the readings' authenticity." (*Off the Road*, 375.)
174. "Billy Graham . . .": JK to AG, March 1954.
174. JK and Buddhism: JK to AG, March 1954 and undated letter, ca. May 1954; Alfred Aronowitz, "The Beat Generation," *New York Post*, March 19, 1959; Ted Berrigan, "The Art of Fiction: Jack Kerouac," in *Writers at Work: The Paris Review Interviews*, fourth series, ed. George Plimpton (New York: Viking Press, 1976), 378–82; Carolyn Cassady, *Off the Road*, 234–35.
175. *Some of the Dharma*: JK to AG, undated, ca. May 1954. Kerouac loaned Ginsberg the manuscript for this text, which has never been published.
175. "I know that now . . .": ibid.
175. "Don't you forget . . .": JK to AG, May 1954.
175. AG at Cassadys: AG unpublished journal entries; AG, *Journals*, 73–86. AG to JK, undated, ca. mid-June 1954; AG to LG, June 30, 1954; JK to AG, July 30, 1954; AG to JK, undated, ca. August 1954; JK to AG, August 23, 1954; AG to JK, September 7, 1954; Carolyn Cassady, *Off the Road*, 242–48.
176. "more considerate, aware . . ." and "He filled each day . . .": Carolyn Cassady, *Off the Road*, 243.
176. "The *chess*, maniacal . . .": AG to JK, September 7, 1954.
176. "cold and bitter": ibid.
176. "by resurrection . . ." and "greatest pleasure . . .": AG to JK, undated, ca. mid-June 1954.
176. "sinful": AG to JK, undated, ca. summer 1954.
177. "I have no . . .": AG to JK, September 7, 1954.
177. "Would be willing . . .": ibid.
177. "like some doctrine . . .": ibid.
177. "everyone was more interested . . .": Carolyn Cassady, *Off the Road*, 244.
177. "crackpot": AG to JK, September 7, 1954.
177. "I feel like . . .": AG journal entry, June 27, 1954; published in AG, *Journals*, 76.
178. "it takes me . . .": AG to LG, June 30, 1954.
178. "The weight . . .": AG, "Song," *HOWL*, 39; *CP*, 111.
178. "I always wanted . . .": AG, "Song," *HOWL*, 41; *CP*, 112.
178. "The warm bodies . . .": ibid.
179. "symbolic meat": AG, "On Burroughs' Work," *RS*, 40; *CP*, 114.
179. "A naked lunch . . .": ibid.
179. "corolla of yellowing . . .": AG, "In back of the real," *HOWL*, 44; *CP*, 113.
179. "This is the flower . . .": ibid.
179. "and a soiled . . .": ibid.
179. "corolla of bleary spikes . . .": AG, "Sunflower Sutra," *HOWL*, 28; *CP*, 138.
180. "artificial" and "I can sleep . . .": AG undated journal entry, published in AG, *Journals*, 76.
180. "Once again . . .": ibid., 75.
180. "felt no threat . . .": Carolyn Cassady, *Off the Road*, 245.
180. "I'll go into . . .": AG, "Love Poem on Theme by Whitman," *RS*, 41; *CP*, 115.
181. "all before the mind . . .": ibid.
181. "in a weird way . . .": AG to JK, September 7, 1954.
181. "I feel myself . . .": AG undated journal entry.

182. "The force of the shock . . .": Carolyn Cassady, *Off the Road*, 246.
182. "I went cold . . ." and "I felt evil . . .": AG to JK, September 7, 1954. Although it is not difficult to pass judgment in retrospect, one cannot help but wonder about what Ginsberg and the Cassadys expected to happen when Allen visited San Jose. Carolyn had been enthusiastic in her invitations to Allen, perhaps out of feelings of guilt connected with their earlier Denver fiasco. Ginsberg, on the other hand, had not hidden the fact that he was still spending a lot of time thinking about his and Neal's past; he had gone so far as to send the Cassadys a copy of "The Green Automobile," along with an explanation of its meaning. Finally, as Ginsberg noted in his journal, Neal was well aware of Allen's sexual attraction to him. It is difficult to imagine any of the three realistically expecting Allen to settle for a strictly platonic relationship with Neal during his stay or, considering Neal's sexual history, that Neal would maintain his distance and not encourage or accept Ginsberg's advances. Furthermore, the individual reactions to Allen's sexual encounter with Neal, although open and frank, were off center. That Neal would simply go blank and refuse to discuss the situation with Carolyn was irresponsible, regardless of whether it was characteristic, and for Ginsberg to express anger at Carolyn for her reaction, as he did in his letter to Jack Kerouac, was grossly insensitive and selfish. Given the circumstances—and the times—the fact that Carolyn would apologize to Allen, one of the offending parties in her husband's infidelity, or that she would hope that Neal would not be angry with her (which was one of her worries) is indicative of the unusual nature of the relationships between many of the men and women of the Beat Generation.
182. AG in San Francisco: AG journal entries, Le Pellec, "The New Consciousness," reprinted in AG, *Composed on the Tongue*, 86–87; AG, "Early Poetic Community," *Allen Verbatim*, 145–47; AG to JK, September 7 and November 9, 1954.
183. "a wild mind . . .": AG to JK, September 7, 1954.
183. "the coldest aspects . . .": Le Pellec, "The New Consciousness," in *Composed*, 87.
183. "perceptive" and "It had a tradition . . .": ibid., 86.
185. "They are nearer . . .": AG to JK, undated, ca. fall 1954.
185. "My effort in last . . .": ibid.
185. AG and WSB: WSB to JK, August 18, 1954; WSB to AG, August 18, 1954; WSB to JK, August 26, August 30, and September 3, 1954; WSB to AG, September 3, 1954; AG to JK, September 7, 1954; WSB to AG, October 10 and 13, 1954; JK to AG, October 26, 1954; AG to JK, undated, ca. fall 1954; AG to JK, November 22 and 26, 1954.
185. "hooked . . .": WSB to JK, April 22, 1954.
185. "the whole state . . .": ibid.
185. "a queer matter": AG to JK, November 22, 1954.
185. "I dig Bill . . ." and "would end . . .": ibid.
186. "cupidities and concupiscences . . .": JK to AG, October 10, 1954.
186. "I am not . . .": ibid.
186. NC: AG to JK, September 7, 1954; AG to JK, undated, ca. fall 1954; AG to JK, November 22 and 26, 1954.
186. "everytime you talk . . .": AG to JK, November 26, 1954.
186. "more prey to . . .": AG to JK, undated, ca. fall 1954.
187. AG and LaVigne: AG undated journal entries; AG, *Gay Sunshine Interview*, vol. 1, ed. Winston Leyland (San Francisco: Gay Sunshine Press, 1978), 20; *Straight Hearts' Delight*, 111–12; AG to JK, December 29, 1954.
187. "Oh, that's Peter" and "He's here . . .": AG, *Gay Sunshine Interview*, 20.

9. Howl

188. Epigraph: AG, "Howl," *HOWL*, 9, CP, 126.
188. Orlovsky bio: Ann Charters, "Peter Orlovsky," *Dictionary of Literary Biography: The Beats: Literary Bohemians in Postwar America* (Detroit: Gale Research Company, 1983), 433–35; Barry Gifford and Lawrence Lee, *Jack's Book* (New York: St. Martin's Press, 1978), 192; Leyland and Shively, "Winston Leyland and Charlie Shively Interview Peter Orlovsky," in *Gay Sunshine Interviews*, vol. 1, ed. Winston Leyland (San Francisco: Gay Sunshine Press, 1978), 240–50; James McKenzie, "An Interview with Allen Ginsberg," in *The Beat Journey*, eds. Arthur and Kit Knight (California, PA: unspeakable visions of the individual, 1978), 249; AG, "Peter Orlovsky" (biographical notes for the back cover copy for PO, *Clean Asshole Poems & Smiling Vegetable Songs* (San Francisco: City Lights Books, 1978).
188. "He didn't have . . .": Gifford and Lee, *Jack's Book*, 192.
189. "You're a big . . .": Charters, "Peter Orlovsky," in *Dictionary of Literary Biography*, 435.
189. "After a year . . .": Leyland and Shively, "Winston Leyland and Charlie Shively Interview Peter Orlovsky" in *Gay Sunshine Interviews*, 246.

189. "An army is . . .": AG, "Peter Orlovsky."
189. AG and PO: AG undated journal entries; AG, *Gay Sunshine Interview*, 20–25; AG to JK, December 29, 1954; AG to JK, January 12, 1955; JK to AG, January 18, 1955.
190. "a tired dog . . .": AG, *Gay Sunshine Interview*, 20.
190. "Real sweetness . . .": AG to JK, December 29, 1954.
190. AG trip to NY: Ginsberg wrote one poem, "Over Kansas," as the result of his journey to his brother's wedding, and while the poem itself is a minor work, it is significant because it was Ginsberg's first poem written in transit, while he was actually in a moving vehicle. In this way, it is an important precursor to the poems included in *Planet News*, *The Fall of America*, and other collections.
191. "big messy rooms . . .": AG to JK, December 29, 1954.
191. "Don't think I don't . . .": AG to JK, January 12, 1955.
191. "changed in California . . .": AG to JK, December 29, 1954.
191. AG/PO problems: AG journal entries; AG, *Gay Sunshine Interview*, 21–22; AG to JK, December 29, 1954; AG to JK, January 12, 1955; JK to AG, January 14, 1955.
191. "how much he was giving . . .": AG, *Gay Sunshine Interviews*, 21.
191. "dominating, sadism part . . .": ibid.
191. "For the first time . . .": AG journal entry, January 1, 1955.
191. "You're both a pain . . .": AG to JK, December 29, 1954.
192. "I'm happy, Kerouac . . .": AG, "Malest Cornifici Tuo Catullo," *RS*, 47; *CP*, 123.
192. "So why don't . . ." and "Oh, you're a nice . . .": AG, *Gay Sunshine Interview*, 22.
192. "It was the last . . .": Jane Kramer, *Allen Ginsberg in America* (New York: Random House, 1969), 42.
193. "two special talents . . .": AG journal entry, January 5, 1955.
193. "AG/PO vows: AG journal entries; AG, *Gay Sunshine Interview*, 23–25; author interview with AG.
193. "an exchange of souls . . .": AG journal entry, January 5, 1955.
193. "to stay with . . .": AG, *Gay Sunshine Interview*, 24.
193. "a limited version": ibid.
193. "neither of us . . .": ibid., 23.
193. "We held hands . . .": ibid., 24.
194. "my fine sweet Allen" and "a real saint": JK to AG, January 18, 1955.
194. "Peter O. sounds . . .": ibid.
194. "Being famous . . .": Gerald Nicosia, *Memory Babe: A Critical Biography of Jack Kerouac* (New York: Grove Press, 1983), 471.
194. "For your beginning studies . . .": JK to AG, undated, ca. May 1954.
194. AG, JK, and Buddhism: JK to AG, undated, ca. May 1954; JK to AG, May 1954 and August 26, 1954; AG to JK, undated, ca. fall 1954; JK to AG, undated, ca. December 1954; AG to JK, January 14, 1955; JK to AG, January 18, 1955; AG to JK, February 14, 1955.
195. "totally empty" and "I am presuming . . .": AG to JK, January 14, 1955.
195. "rational inanity": AG to JK, undated, ca. May 1954.
195. *Bill in Europe*: AG journal entries; published in AG, *Journals*, 34–35; AG to JK, undated, ca. May 1954; JK to AG, undated, ca. May 1954; AG to Neal and Carolyn Cassady, May 12, 1954; AG to JK, undated, ca. fall 1954; JK to AG, October 26, 1954; AG to JK, November 9, 1954.
195. "The last great . . .": AG to JK, undated, ca. May 1954.
195. "so sublime . . .": JK to AG, undated, ca. May 1954.
196. "cityCityCITY": see LeRoi Jones, ed. *The Moderns* (New York: Corinth Books, 1963), 250–65. Burroughs's early routines can be found in WSB, *Letters to Allen Ginsberg* (New York: Full Court Press, 1982); WSB, *Roosevelt After Inauguration* (San Francisco: City Lights Books, 1979); WSB, *Interzone* (New York: Viking Press, 1989); WSB, *Exterminator!* (New York: Viking Press, 1973); and WSB, *Naked Lunch* (New York: Grove Press, 1959).
196. "What'll happen . . .": AG to JK, April 22, 1955.
196. "Except for Neal . . .": ibid.
197. AG reading list: AG journal entries; AG to JK, March 13 and April 22, 1955.
197. "nowhere particular": AG to JK, April 22, 1955.
197. "hard to follow": AG to JK, March 13, 1955.
197. "an egocentric method" and "promotes slop": AG journal entry, March 31, 1955. Throughout his career, Ginsberg suffered through prolonged periods of writer's block, usually followed by great bursts of creative energy. His two most critically acclaimed works, "Howl" and "Kaddish," were written in the aftermath of writer's block. Despite the self-criticism in his journals, noted here and in numerous entries throughout his lifetime, the journal writing was an important discipline for Ginsberg, even if nothing usable resulted from a day's entry.
197. "Lately in revising . . .": ibid.
197. Cézanne: AG journal entries; AG, unpublished term paper on Cézanne, AG Columbia deposit;

AG, *Annotated Howl*, 130–31, 137–38; Tom Clark, "The Art of Poetry," reprinted in *Writers at Work: The Paris Review Interviews*, third series ed. George Plimpton (New York: Viking Press, 1967), 291–297; Paul Portugés, "Allen Ginsberg's Paul Cézanne and the Pater Omnipotens Aeterna Deus," *Contemporary Literature* (Summer 1980).

198. "leaning/forward . . ." and "I saw her rain-stained . . .": AG, "Dream Record: June 8, 1955," *RS*, 48–49; *CP*, 124.
198. "notebooks filled with Buddha" and "golden in the East": ibid.
198. "stilted & somewhat academic": AG, *Annotated Howl*, xii.
198. "completely successful": WSB to AG, August 1, 1955.
198. "In a way . . .": ibid.
199. "Money problems . . .": AG to JK, June 5, 1955.
199. "I'm not writing . . .": AG undated journal entry.
199. "harsh and bleak": AG journal entry, June 2, 1955.
199. "I am no closer . . .": AG journal entry, June 10, 1955.
199. "monstrous nightmare" and "on the verge . . .": AG to JK, June 5, 1955.
199. "trouble deaf heaven . . .": ibid.
200. "Greek or prosody": AG to JK, July 5, 1955.
200. "It's a Buddhist . . ." and "child's play": JK to AG, July 14, 1955.
200. "Please, Allen . . .": ibid.
200. "Denver is lonesome . . .": AG undated journal entry, ca. July 1955. The line eventually appeared in "Howl."
200. "What consciousness . . .": AG undated journal entry, ca. August 1955. The line eventually appeared in "Dream Record: June 8, 1955."
200. "How to say no . . .": AG undated journal entry, ca. August 1955. This line was revised and eventually appeared in "America."
200. "*I saw the best mind* . . .": AG undated journal entry, ca. August 1955.
200. "Howl" composition: AG, *Annotated Howl*, xii–xiii, AG, "Notes Written on Finally Recording Howl," reprinted in *The Poetics of the New American Poetry*, eds. Donald Allen and George F. Butterick (New York: Grove Press, 1973); Clark, "Art of Poetry," in *Writers at Work*, 284; Alfred Aronowitz, "Portrait of a Beat," *Nugget* (October 1960); Bill Adler, "Poet Allen Ginsberg Comes Full Circle," *New York Daily News*, November 13, 1981; author interview with AG.
200. "I sat idly . . .": AG, *Annotated Howl*, xii.
201. "I saw the best minds . . .": AG, "Howl," first draft, reprinted in facsimile in *Annotated Howl*, 12.
201. "who poverty and tatters . . .": ibid.
201. "a huge sad comedy . . .": AG, "Notes Written on Finally Recording 'Howl,' " in *The Poetics of the New American Poetry.*
201. "We don't need time . . .": AG, *Annotated Howl*, 134.
201. "who bit detectives . . .": AG, "Howl," first draft, *Annotated Howl*, 17.
201. "who passed through . . .": ibid., 13.
202. "Carl Solomon! . . .": ibid., 89.
203. "rearrange and rehook . . ." and "refine rhythm . . .": ibid., 11.
203. "I enclose first draft . . .": AG to JK, undated, ca. mid-August 1955.
204. "very powerful": JK to AG, September 19, 1955.
204. "lingual spontaneity": ibid.
204. "with a vision . . .": This and other phrases singled out by Kerouac are from the original draft of "Howl."
204. "the first pages . . .": AG to JK, August 25, 1955.
204. "I realize how right . . .": ibid.
204. "lovely": ibid.
204. "One booklet . . .": AG to JK, August 30, 1955.
204. "To my mind . . .": WSB to AG, October 21, 1955.
205. "walked in at 3AM . . .": AG to JK, August 16, 1955.
205. "like being married . . .": ibid.
205. Berkeley cottage: AG to JK, undated, ca. mid-August 1955. *See also*, AG, "A Strange New Cottage in Berkeley," *RS*, 53; *CP*, 135.
205. "perfect place . . .": AG to JK, undated, ca. mid-August 1955.
205. AG and peyote: see AG, *Journals*, 7; Portugés, *The Visionary Poetics of Allen Ginsberg* (Santa Barbara, CA: Ross-Erikson, 1978), 123.
205. "the robot skullface . . .": AG, "Notes Written on Finally Recording 'Howl,' " in *The Poetics of the New American Poetry*, 319.
206. "Uprising in the timeless . . .": AG journal entry, October 18, 1954.
206. "Part I deals . . .": AG to Richard Eberhart, June 18, 1956. This letter was published as a small

book, *To Eberhart from Ginsberg* (Lincoln, MA: Penmaen Press, 1976), and was reprinted in *Annotated Howl*.

206. "Howl Part II" composition: AG, *Annotated Howl*, 56–57; AG, "Notes Written on Finally Recording 'Howl,' " in *The Poetics of the New American Poetry*; Clark, "Art of Poetry," in *Writers at Work*, 313; author interview with AG.
206. "I wandered . . .": AG, "Notes Written on Finally Recording 'Howl,' " in *The Poetics of the New American Poetry*.
206. "Moloch! Molock! . . .": AG, "Howl," first draft, *Annotated Howl*, 58–59.
207. "really a new poetry": AG, "Notes Written on Finally Recording 'Howl' " in *The Poetics of the New American Poetry*.
207. "You have to . . .": author interview with AG.
208. "I realized . . .": Aronowitz, "Portrait of a Beat."
209. "There's too many . . .": AG to JK, undated, ca. summer 1954.
209. "Carl Solomon! . . .": AG, "Howl," *HOWL*, 19; CP, 132.
209. "I'm with you . . .": AG "Howl," *HOWL*, 20; CP, 133.
210. "Footnote to Howl": Although this poem has always been published as a separate one, it is a crucial part of the work, an affirmation of Ginsberg's intentions in "Howl," and should be read as part of the poem.
211. McClure bio: William King, "Michael McClure," in *The Beats: Literary Bohemians in Postwar America*, 382–400; David Meltzer, ed., *The San Francisco Poets* (New York: Ballantine Books, 1971), 243–76; David Kheridan, *Six San Francisco Poets* (Fresno, CA: Giligia Press, 1969), 108–29; Mick McAllister, "An Interview with Michael McClure," in *The Beat Journey*, 93–111.
212. Snyder bio: Dan McLeod, "Gary Snyder," in *The Beats: Literary Bohemians in Postwar America*, 486–500; Donald Allen, ed., *On Bread & Poetry* (Bolinas, CA: Grey Fox Press, 1977), 3–5, 65; James McKenzie, "Moving the World a Millionth of an Inch," in *The Beat Vision*, eds. Arthur and Kit Knight (New York: Paragon House, 1987), 1–27; Peter Barry Chowka, "The East West Interview," *East West Journal*, February 1978.
212. "Whalen, Snyder and I . . .": Meltzer, ed., *San Francisco Poets*, 203–204.
213. "Japhy lived in . . .": JK, *The Dharma Bums* (New York: Signet Books, 1958), 16–17.
213. Whalen bio: Paul Christensen, "Philip Whalen," in *The Beats: Literary Bohemians in Postwar America*, 554–72; Allen, *On Bread & Poetry*, 4; Anne Waldman, "Interview with Philip Whalen," in *Kerouac and the Beats*, eds. Arthur and Kit Knight (New York: Paragon House, 1988), 40–65.
214. "Six poets . . .": AG Columbia deposit.
214. "purely amateur . . .": AG and Gregory Corso, "The Literary Revolution in America," in *Annotated Howl*, 165.
214. Six Gallery reading: AG journal entries; JK, *Dharma Bums*, 13–15; Michael McClure, *Scratching the Beat Surface* (San Francisco: North Point Press, 1982), 11–34; Barry Silesky, *Ferlinghetti: The Artist in His Time* (New York: Warner Books, 1990), 64–65; Neeli Cherkovski, *Ferlinghetti: A Biography* (New York: Doubleday, 1979), 98–99; Gifford and Lee, *Jack's Book*, 194–202; Alfred Aronowitz, "The Beat Generation," *New York Post*, March 22, 1959; author interview with AG.
214. Rexroth speech: Silesky, *Ferlinghetti*, 65; McClure, *Scratching the Beat Surface*, 12.
214. "a young priest": JK, *Dharma Bums*, 11. In all likelihood, this was probably also a reference to Lamantia's recent conversion to Catholicism.
215. "beautiful prose poems . . .": Michael McClure, *Scratching the Beat Surface*, 12.
215. "In all our memories . . .": ibid.
216. "had no sense . . ." and "a curious kind . . .": Gary Snyder, *The Real Work* (New York: New Directions, 1980), 162.
216. "It succeeded . . .": ibid., 162–63.
216. "deep and resonant . . .": JK, *Dharma Bums*, 14.
216. "This poem . . .": Silesky, *Ferlinghetti*, 65.
216. "I greet you . . .": LF to AG, October 13, 1955. In a July 21, 1855, letter to Walt Whitman, Ralph Waldo Emerson wrote, "I greet you at the beginning of a great career, which yet must have had a long foreground somewhere, for such a start."

10. The San Francisco Poetry Renaissance

217. Epigraph: AG, " 'Back on Times Square, Dreaming of Times Square,' " *RS*, 71; CP, 188.
217. Interest in "Howl": Ginsberg's greatest regret in publishing "Howl" was the notoriety it brought Carl Solomon. "I hadn't realized all the consequences of the Word," Ginsberg wrote in *Annotated Howl*. "I'd thought the poem a gesture of wild solidarity, a message into the asylum, a sort of heart's trumpet call, but was mistaken in my diagnosis of his 'case' ('You're madder than I am')."

As Ginsberg pointed out, he was writing in "relative literary obscurity," confident that publication of his poem offered "no promise of celebrity to the author or Carl Solomon outside a small circle of witty understanding readers in sophisticated poetry circles of the Bay Area mid 1950s." When the poem reached its internationally acclaimed status, Ginsberg noted, "Mr. Solomon bore the burden uneasily, and later was sorely tried by the situation." In an interview with the author, Solomon was quite frank in his assessment of being the focus of Ginsberg's poem. He reacted to the poem, he said, "with the awareness that I was not famous—also a sense of having fucked up somehow, since the poem called me mad rather than sane. What is mad? What is sane? Do you mean clinical, legal, or just what? Maybe I was sane in 1956 and 'Howl' was a poem appreciated only by the mad?"

218. "Holy Peter . . .": AG, first draft of "Howl," *Annotated Howl*, 98–99.
218. "No, no, that's enough": author interview with AG.
218. "the straining . . .": AG journal entry, September 8, 1955.
218. "the presence . . .": AG, "Transcription of Organ Music," HOWL, 27; CP, 141.
218. "America I've given you . . .": AG undated journal entry, ca. fall 1955, published in AG, *Journals*, 91. *See also*, AG, "America," HOWL, 31–34; CP, 146–48.
219. "America I'm putting . . .": AG, "America," HOWL, 34; CP, 148.
219. "It occurs to me . . .": AG, "America," HOWL, 32; CP, 147.
219. "*America* is an unsystematic . . .": AG to Richard Eberhart, May 18, 1955, reprinted in AG, *To Eberhart from Ginsberg*, 34.
219. "a dead gray shadow . . .": AG, "Sunflower Sutra," HOWL, 28; CP, 138.
219. "We're not our skin . . .": AG, "Sunflower Sutra," HOWL, 30; CP, 139.
220. "leaves stuck out . . .": AG, "Sunflower Sutra," HOWL, 28–29; CP, 138.
221. "Burroughs is in Tangiers . . .": AG, "America," HOWL, 31; CP, 146.
221. Lawrence Ferlinghetti bio: Neeli Cherkovski, *Ferlinghetti: A Biography* (New York: Doubleday, 1979), 1–82; Barry Silesky, *Ferlinghetti: The Artist in His Time* (New York: Warner Books, 1990), 3–58; David Meltzer, *The San Francisco Poets* (New York: Ballantine Books, 1971), 154–58, 163–68.
223. "a fantastic, dramatic sight": LF to author.
223. "You'd see hands . . .": Cherkovsky, *Ferlinghetti*, 39–40.
224. "Look what I . . ." and "beat & clearest . . .": AG to WCW, December 9, 1955.
225. "expressive human feeling": ibid.
225. "The release of emotion . . .": ibid.
225. "You have something . . .": WCW to AG, March 17, 1956.
225. "a little pruning . . .": ibid.
225. "nutty experimentation" and "great dawn": WCW to Louis Zukofsky, April 1, 1956.
225. "There is no need . . .": LG to AG, January 29, 1956.
225. "Too many writers . . .": LG to AG, March 31, 1956.
225. "a wild, rhapsodic . . .": LG to AG, February 29, 1956.
226. Death of Natalie Jackson: AG journal entries; Carolyn Cassady, *Off the Road* (New York: William Morrow, 1990), 273–75; JK, *The Dharma Bums* (New York: Signet, 1959), 86–90.
226. "I tried to explain . . .": Carolyn Cassady, *Off the Road*, 271.
226. "we should have known . . .": JK, *Dharma Bums*, 88.
226. "this is my last night . . .": ibid., 89.
226. "sobered with grief": Carolyn Cassady, *Off the Road*, 274.
226. "hit the road . . .": JK, *Dharma Bums*, 90.
226. "In the car . . .": AG, undated journal entry, ca. December 1955; published in AG, *Journals*, 92.
226. Seattle trip: AG undated journal entries; AG to NC, February 7, 1956. *See also*, AG, "Afternoon Seattle" and "Tears," both collected in RS.
227. "a veritable London": AG, undated journal entry, ca. February 1956.
227. "Walking down backstreet . . .": AG journal entry, February 5, 1956.
227. SF orgiastic scene: In 1973, Ginsberg commented on the orgies in San Francisco during the 1955 to 1956 period: "Peter and I used to get into scenes in San Francisco with girls and boys together, very nice. He liked girls, and that situation would set up a nice vibration when other men would come in. Since Peter and I were already close and making it, that opened the door to anybody. He'd make out with girls and I'd make out with boys. Sometimes I'd make out with girls too. Or we'd make out with each other. We had a two year period in San Francisco where almost every party we went to we took off our clothes and wound up in bed with one or two people. We didn't try to start orgies; we just took off our clothes, wandered around the party, had a good time and didn't make a big scene out of it." (AG, *Gay Sunshine Interview*, 35.)
227. "The thing I do . . ." and "to get them . . .": AG to LG, undated, ca. March 1956.
227. "I practically take . . ." and "certainly get me . . .": ibid.
228. "the West Coast . . .": Richard Eberhart, "West Coast Rhythms," *The New York Times Book Review*, September 2, 1956.

228. "spiritual quality" and "a grasp . . .": AG, *To Eberhart from Ginsberg*, 8.
228. "I am almost ready . . .": AG to LG, undated, ca. March 1956.
228. "[H]e disturbed me . . .": WCW, introduction to *Howl and Other Poems*, 7; reprinted in *CP*, 811.
229. "The wonder of the thing . . .": ibid., 8; reprinted in *CP*, 811.
231. Snyder party: JK, *Dharma Bums*, 151–66.
231. "I can just see you . . .": ibid., 159.
231. "East'll meet West . . .": ibid., 160.
231. AG as yeoman storekeeper: AG to EB, May 18 and 26, 1956.
232. "Thanks for naming . . .": AG to EB, May 26, 1956.
232. Death of Naomi Ginsberg: EB to AG, June 9 (telegram) and 11, 1956; LG to AG, June 20, 1956; author interviews with AG, EB, and Hannah and Leo Litzky.
232. "bent my head . . .": AG, "Kaddish," *KADDISH*, 31; *CP*, 224.
232. "The main problem . . ." and "It's not necessary . . .": AG to EB, May 18, 1956.
232. "How is my . . .": Naomi Ginsberg to AG, undated.
232. "My childhood . . .": AG undated journal entry.
232. Naomi Ginsberg's funeral: EB to AG, June 11, 1956; LG to AG, June 20, 1956; author interviews with Hannah and Leo Litzky.
232. "it was the smallest . . .": EB to AG, June 11, 1956.
233. "The pathos and tragedy . . .": LG to AG, June 20, 1956.
233. AG Arctic trip: AG journal entries. AG to EB, May 18, 1956; AG to Mark Van Doren, May 19, 1956; AG to EB, July 10, 1956; AG to PO, undated, ca. July 1956.
233. "a long green . . ." and "shouting my poetry . . .": AG undated journal entry, ca. late June 1956.
233. *Howl* proofs: AG to LF, July 3, 1956; AG to EB, July 10, 1956; AG to LF, undated, ca. July 1956.
233. "The writing is . . .": AG to EB, July 10, 1956.
233. "stinks on ice": AG to LF, June 22, 1956.
234. "It seemed to me . . .": Naomi Ginsberg to AG, June 1956.
234. "I wish I were . . .": ibid.
234. "I have been thinking . . .": AG to EB, July 10, 1956.
234. "we're all beautiful . . .": AG, "Sunflower Sutra," *HOWL*, 30; *CP*, 139.
234. "I had a moment . . .": AG, "Transcription of Organ Music," *HOWL*, 26; *CP*, 140.
234. "think nothing . . .": AG, "Kaddish," *KADDISH*, 23; *CP*, 218.
235. Whitman epigraphs: list in AG Columbia deposit.
235. "His feelings were very real . . .": AG undated journal entry, ca. July 1956.
235. AG reading list: AG journal entries.
235. "Funny gaiety of Joke . . .": AG, fragment from untitled and unpublished poem from journals, July 1956.
236. "in remembrance . . .": AG undated journal entry, ca. late July 1956.
236. "Earlier years had brought . . .": AG undated journal entry, ca. June 1956.
236. "Jack's holiness . . ."; "I myself write . . ."; and "The poems I build . . .": AG undated journal entry, ca. July 1956.
236. "Siesta in Xbalba": AG journal entries, copy of mimeographed "Siesta" in AG Columbia deposit.
236. "unbalanced and egotistic" and "shallow when reading . . .": AG undated journal entry, ca. late July 1956 (probably July 29, 1956).
237. "embarrassed by half . . .": AG to LF, August 9, 1956.
237. "I'm not sure . . .": ibid.
238. "If you like the poems . . .": AG to Mark Van Doren, May 19, 1956.
238. List of complimentary or review copy recipients: list in AG Columbia deposit.
238. "imaginative and concrete details": LG to AG, October 13, 1956.
238. "terrific" and "flattered to find . . .": WCW to LF, September 16, 1956.
238. "It lets you say . . .": Mark Van Doren to AG, May 21, 1956.
238. "ringing in . . ." and "I am carefully . . .": Gary Snyder to AG, October 12, 1956.
238. "the beautiful gentleness" and "real tenderness . . .": JCH to AG, September 26, 1956.
238. "very impressive": Lucien Carr to AG, September 21, 1956.
238. "touched" and "a certain anonymity . . .": ibid.
238. "I hope you bear . . .": ibid.
239. "You got more room . . ." and "If he's yours . . .": Ezra Pound to WCW, undated, ca. June 1956.
239. "I'm afraid I have . . .": Lionel Trilling to AG, May 29, 1956.
239. "dull"; "They are not . . ."; and "doctrinal element": ibid.
239. "The most remarkable . . ." Richard Eberhart, "West Coast Rhythms," *The New York Times Book Review*, September 2, 1956. This article is reprinted in its entirety in AG, *To Eberhart from Ginsberg*, 41–45.
239. "a lyric poem . . .": ibid.
240. "new, vital group consciousness . . .": ibid.
240. "Agh! I'm sick . . .": AG to JK, undated, ca. September 1956.

240. "Edith keeps a copy . . .": LG to AG, September 13, 1956.
241. LA reading: Lawrence Lipton, *The Holy Barbarians* (New York: Julian Messner, 1959), 194–98; JK, *Desolation Angels* (New York: Paragon Books, 1979), 230; Paul Carroll, "Playboy Interview," *Playboy*, April 1969. This type of public confrontation with hostile forces would become Ginsberg's trademark. Though he had a quick temper and strong sense of moral outrage, Ginsberg was never a violent man. His interest in Buddhism, along with his natural curiosity about the roots of his anger, helped him convert his rage into firm, positive action on many occasions. Over a decade later, he employed this philosophy of aggressive gentleness in winning over a hostile group of the Oakland chapter of the Hell's Angels motorcycle club.
242. "images, metaphors, [and] magic": Lipton, *Holy Barbarians*, 197. All quotes, unless otherwise indicated, are from this source.
242. "Nakedness": Carroll, "Playboy Interview."
242. "Reading we gave . . .": AG to LF, October 31, 1956.
242. "What's with you? . . .": WSB to AG, December 20, 1956.
242. Mexico trip: JK, *Desolation Angels*, 230–54.
243. "whiney": ibid., 253.
244. AG meeting with WCW: journal entries; JK, *Desolation Angels*, 289–90.
244. "lotsa bastards . . .": AG, "Death News," *PN*, 48; *CP*, 297; JK, *Desolation Angels*, 290.
244. "The music was . . .": JCH, *Visitor: Jack Kerouac in Old Saybrook* (California, PA: unspeakable visions of the individual, 1981), unpaginated.

11. Europe! Europe!

249. Epigraph: AG, "Death to Van Gogh's Ear!" *Kaddish*, 63; *CP*, 168.
249. Burroughs: JK, *Desolation Angels* (New York: Paragon Books, 1979), 305–16; Ted Morgan, *Literary Outlaw: The Life and Times of William S. Burroughs* (New York: Henry Holt, 1988), 257–67.
249. "The sexual mores . . .": WSB to AG, October 29, 1956.
249. "I get an average . . ." and "a perfect gentleman . . .": WSB to AG, October 13, 1956.
249. "declaring a two-day . . .": WSB to AG, October 29, 1956.
249. "There is something special . . .": WSB to AG, October 13, 1956.
250. "tanned, muscular, and vigorous": JK, *Desolation Angels*, 305.
251. "shitting out . . .": ibid., 311.
251. "I am badly in need . . .": WSB to AG, February 14, 1957.
251. "When will Allen . . .": JK, *Desolation Angels*, 313.
251. "autocratic" and "only fall in love . . .": ibid.
252. AG in Casablanca: AG journal entries; AG to Lucien Carr, April 4, 1957.
252. "much like Mexico . . .": AG to Lucien Carr, April 4, 1957.
252. Customs seizure of *Howl*: ibid.
252. "[Allen] wanted to do . . .": JK, *Desolation Angels*, 318.
253. AG in Tangier: AG journal entries; JK, *Desolation Angels*, 317–22; AG to LF, April 3, 1957; AG to Lucien Carr, April 4, 1957; AG to NC, April 24, 1957; AG to LF, May 10, 1957; AG to JK, May 31, 1957; AG to Lucien Carr, undated, ca. late May 1957; JK to AG/WSB, June 1957; JK to AG, June 7, 1957; AG to LG, undated, ca. June 1957.
253. "unable to convey . . .": JK, *Desolation Angels*, 321.
253. Work on *Naked Lunch*: AG to Lucien Carr, undated, ca. May 1957; AG to JK, May 31, 1957.
254. "It was really Allen . . .": author interview with Richard Seaver.
254. *Howl* obscenity bust: AG to JK, May 31, 1957; AG to LF, undated, ca. June 1957; AG to EB, June 20, 1957.
255. "I guess this is . . .": AG to LF, undated, ca. June 1957.
255. "I guess [an] open showdown . . .": ibid.
255. "to give a big reading . . .": AG to EB, June 20, 1957.
255. "Don't recall I ever meet . . .": WSB to AG, December 20, 1956.
255. "very courteous and lively . . .": AG to Lucien Carr, undated, ca. May 1957.
255. "He's like Burroughs . . .": AG to JK, May 31, 1957.
256. "only a people . . .": AG to EB, June 20, 1957.
257. "It's a place . . .": ibid.
257. "the greatest painting . . .": ibid.
257. "I'd vaguely remembered . . .": ibid.
258. Reviews of *Howl*: M. L. Rosenthal, "Poet of the New Violence," *The Nation*, February 23, 1957; John Hollander, "Poetry Chronicle," *Partisan Review* (Spring 1957); James Dickey, "From Babel to Byzantium," *Sewanee Review* (Summer 1957); Kenneth Rexroth, "San Francisco Letter," *Evergreen Review* 2 (Summer 1957); Frederick Eckman; "Neither Tame nor Fleecy," *Poetry*

(September 1957); Norman Podhoretz, "A Howl of Protest from San Francisco," *The New Republic*, September 16, 1957; Michael Rumaker, "Allen Ginsberg's 'Howl,' " *Black Mountain Review* (Fall 1957); Donald Justice, "San Francisco and Palo Alto," *Western Review* (Spring 1958).

258. "a very short . . ." and "a real talent . . .": Hollander, "Poetry Chronicle."
258. "the skin of . . .": Dickey, "From Babel to Byzantium."
258. "a very shaggy book . . .": Eckman, "Neither Tame nor Fleecy."
258. "He has brought . . ." and "poetry of genuine . . .": Rosenthal, "Poet of the New Violence."
258. "if he keeps going . . .": Rexroth, "San Francisco Letter."
258. "Nothing goes to show . . .": ibid.
259. *Howl* trial: AG to LF, June 10, 1957; LF to AG, September 17 and 28, 1957; AG to JK, October 9 and 16, 1957; J. W. Ehrlich, *Howl of the Censor* (San Carlo, CA: Nourse, 1961); Neeli Cherkovski, *Ferlinghetti: A Biography* (New York: Doubleday, 1979), 103–13; Barry Silesky, *Ferlinghetti: The Artist in His Time* (New York: Warner Books, 1990), 71–79; Lawrence Ferlinghetti, "Horn on Howl," *Evergreen Review* no. 4 (1957); John G. Roberts, "Juvenile Police head raids bookshop in San Francisco," *National Guardian*, August 5, 1957; "Big Day for Bards at Bay," *Life*, September 1957; John G. Roberts, "West Coast censorship trial draws big audiences in support of poem," *National Guardian*, September 9, 1957; Norman Podhoretz, "A Howl of Protest from San Francisco," *The New Republic*, September 16, 1957; Francis O'Hara, " 'Howl' Ruled not Obscene; 2 Acquitted," *San Francisco Chronicle*, October 4, 1957; John G. Fuller, "Trade Winds: Ginsberg Trial," *The Saturday Review*, October 5, 1957; "Howl Decision Landmark of Law," *San Francisco Chronicle*, October 7, 1957; "New Test for Obscenity," *The Nation*, November 9, 1957; David Perlman, "How Captain Hanrahan Made 'Howl' a Best-Seller," *The Reporter*, December 12, 1957.
259. "I assume . . .": Court transcript of Howl trial, reprinted in Ehrlich, *Howl of the Censor*. All citations, unless otherwise noted, are from this source.
262. "eloquent witnesses, together . . .": LF, "Horn on Howl."
264. AG in Venice: AG journal entries; AG to LG, July 9, 1957; AG to EB, July 15, 1957; AG to LG, August 10 and September 1, 1957; AG to EB, September 6, 1957; AG to LG, September 14, 1957; AG/PO/GC to Neal and Carolyn Cassady December 3, 1957.
264. "Everywhere you walk . . .": AG to LG, July 9, 1957.
265. "From the front . . .": AG to EB, July 15, 1957.
265. AG in Florence, Rome, Assisi: AG journal entries; AG to LG, August 10, 1957; AG to EB, August 10, 1957.
265. "a very striking place" and "the spot where . . .": AG to LG, August 10, 1957.
265. "I never saw the church . . .": ibid.
266. "I got the impression . . .": AG to EB, August 10, 1957.
266. "zombies": ibid.
266. "a poor hellbent atheist": ibid.
266. "All in all, the Catholics . . .": ibid.
267. "Arrived in Venice . . .": AG to LG, August 10, 1957.
267. AG in Naples and Ischia: AG journal entries; AG to LG, September 1, 1957; AG to EB, September 6, 1957; AG to NC, undated, ca. September 1957.
267. "vie with each other . . .": AG to LG, September 1, 1957.
268. "a bunch of shits": ibid.
268. "All this gives me . . .": ibid.
268. "a major novel" and "the clearest . . .": Gilbert Millstein, "Books of the Times," *The New York Times*, September 5, 1957.
268. "I almost cried . . .": AG to JK, September 1957.
268. AG in Paris: AG journal entries; AG poetry manuscripts, Columbia deposit; AG to LG, undated, ca. September 1957; AG to LG, September 18, 1957; LF to AG, September 28, 1957; AG to LG, September 30, 1957; AG to JK, October 9 and 16, 1957; PO to JK, October 16, 1957; JK to AG, October 18, 1957; AG to JK, November 13, 1957; AG to LG, November 30, 1957; JK to AG, November 30, 1957; AG to Neal and Carolyn Cassady, December 3, 1957; AG to Lucien Carr, December 11, 1957; AG to Edith Ginsberg, December 13, 1957; AG to LG, undated, ca. January 1958; AG to JK, January 4, 1958; JK to AG, January 8, 1958; AG to JK, January 11, 1958; AG to LG, January 14, 1958; AG to PO, January 20, 1958; JK to AG, January 21, 1958; PO to AG, January 22, 1958; AG to EB, January 23, 1958; AG to PO, January 28, 1958; LF to AG, February 1, 1958; AG to LG, February 2, 1958; AG to PO, February 3, 1958; WSB to AG, February 10, 1958; LF to AG, February 14, 1958; AG to PO, February 15 and 24, 1958; AG to LG, March 2, 1958; LG to AG, March 5, 1958; PO to AG, March 10, 1958; AG to EB, March 12, 1958; AG to PO, March 16, 1958; LG to AG, March 19, 1958; PO to AG, March 20, 1958; AG to PO, April 1, 1958; LG to AG, April 3, 1958; JK to AG, April 8, 1958; LG to AG, April 18, 1958; PO to AG, April 22, 1958; LG to AG, April 23, 1958; LF to AG, May 8, 1958; PO

to AG, May 15, 1958; AG to LG, May 24, 1958; AG to Lucien Carr, May 30, 1958; AG to PO, May 30, 1958; AG to LG, June 4, 1958; AG to PO, June 8, 1958; LF to AG, June 13, 1958; AG to PO, June 15 and 21, 1958; PO to AG, June 24, 1958; AG to JK, June 26, 1958; AG to PO, July 16, 1958; WSB to AG, July 24, 1958; author interviews with AG.

269. "Paris is beautiful . . .": AG to LG, September 30, 1957.

270. "The days never . . .": AG to Lucien Carr, December 11, 1957.

270. *Merlin* magazine: author interview with Richard Seaver.

270. Maurice Giordias: Morgan, *Literary Outlaw*, 275–77; author interview with Richard Seaver.

270. "We thought we were . . .": author interview with Richard Seaver.

271. "the greatest greatest book . . .": AG to JK, November 13, 1957.

272. "Farewell with long black shoe . . .": AG, early draft of "Kaddish," reprinted in AG to JK, November 13, 1957.

272. "a terrible masterpiece": author interview with AG.

272. "with your eyes . . .": AG, early draft of "Kaddish."

272. "I write best . . .": AG to JK, November 13, 1957.

273. "I am impressed . . .": AG to LG, November 30, 1957.

273. "I'm writing big poem . . .": AG to JK, October 16, 1957.

273. "If America is not . . .": AG journal entry, November 3, 1957.

273. "People keep seeing . . .": AG to LG, November 30, 1957.

273. AG's interest in visiting Soviet Union: AG journal entries; AG to JK, November 13, 1957; AG to Lucien Carr, December 11, 1957.

274. "I cried . . .": AG to PO, January 20, 1958.

274. Changes in WSB: AG to PO, January 20, 1958; AG to EB, January 23, 1958; AG to PO, January 28, 1958.

274. "Rather than trying . . .": AG to PO, January 28, 1958.

275. "very intimate . . .": ibid.

275. "Normal conversation . . .": AG to LG, undated, ca. January 1958.

275. "No more poesy . . .": AG to JK, January 4, 1958.

276. "Beware of fame . . .": JK to AG, January 8, 1958.

276. "the best writer . . .": JK to AG, January 12, 1958.

276. "You ARE . . .": ibid.

276. "Why don't you . . .": ibid.

276. "I'd like to write . . .": AG to JK, January 4, 1958.

277. "Poet is priest": AG, "Death to Van Gogh's Ear!" *KADDISH*, 61; *CP*, 167.

277. "Man cannot long . . .": AG, "Death to Van Gogh's Ear!" *KADDISH*, 63; *CP*, 168.

277. "Money! Money! . . .": AG, "Death to Van Gogh's Ear!" *KADDISH*, 65; *CP*, 170.

277. "Be a star-screwer": AG, "Poem Rocket," *KADDISH*, 37; *CP*, 163.

277. "Now at last . . .": AG, "Poem Rocket," *KADDISH*, 38; *CP*, 164.

278. AG in England: AG to JK, January 11, 1958; AG to LG, January 14, 1958; AG to EB, January 23, 1958; AG to PO, January 28, 1958; AG to LG, February 2, 1958; AG to PO, February 3, 15, and 24, 1958.

278. "I cried . . .": AG to PO, February 3, 1958.

278. "O Blake! . . .": AG, unpublished and untitled poem, included in AG to PO, February 15, 1958.

279. "We haven't got centuries . . .": AG to LG, March 2, 1958.

280. "Where I disagree . . .": LG to AG, April 18, 1958.

280. "You *are* both . . .": LG to AG, March 19, 1958.

280. "speaking to England": AG to PO, February 15, 1958.

280. "I started . . .": ibid.

281. "a great dreamcloud . . .": AG to PO, February 24, 1958.

281. "a winged live seagull . . .": ibid.

282. "I came home . . .": first draft of "The Lion for Real." The published version appears in *KADDISH*, 53–55; *CP*, 174–75.

282. "Lion I have remembered . . .": ibid.

283. "I was ashamed . . .": AG to PO, April 1, 1958.

283. "Do you know . . .": AG to PO, May 30, 1958.

283. AG/GC in England: AG to PO, May 12, 1958; AG to LG, May 24, 1958; AG to PO, May 30, 1958; AG to Lucien Carr, May 30, 1958; Paul O'Neil, "The Only Rebellion Around," *Life*, November 30, 1958.

283. "a bunch of assholes": AG to PO, May 30, 1958.

284. "Are birds . . .": AG to PO, May 30, 1958.

284. French politics: AG to LG, May 24, 1958; AG to PO, May 30, 1958; AG to Lucien Carr, May 30, 1958; AG to LG, June 4, 1958; AG to JK, June 26, 1958.

284. "First great mob scene . . .": AG to Lucien Carr, May 30, 1958.

285. NC arrest: AG to JK, June 26, 1958; Carolyn Cassady to AG, July 20, 1958; Carolyn Cassady,

Off the Road (New York: William Morrow, 1990), 297–313; William Plummer, *The Holy Goof: A Biography of Neal Cassady* (Englewood Cliffs, NJ: Prentice-Hall, 1981), 106–07; Alfred Aronowitz, "The Beat Generation," *New York Post*, March 11, 1959.

285. "Is there anything . . .": AG to JK, June 26, 1958.
285. "crucified" and "evil laws": ibid.
286. John Huston: Morgan, *Literary Outlaw*, 285.
286. Duchamp et al.: AG to PO, June 15, 1958.
286. "in a way . . .": ibid.
286. Céline: Mark D. Schleifer, "Here to Save Us, but not Sure from What," *The Village Voice*, October 15, 1958.
287. Michaux: AG to PO, July 16, 1958; AG, "Henri Michaux," in *Henri Michaux*, ed. Raymond Bellour (Paris: Editions de L'Herne, 1966).

12. Kaddish

288. Epigraph: AG, "Kaddish," *KADDISH*, 30; *CP*, 223.
288. "know-nothing bohemians": Norman Podhoretz, "The Know-Nothing Bohemians," *Partisan Review* (Spring 1958).
289. "stupid, small minded . . .": WSB to AG, undated, ca. July 1958.
289. "a lost cause": ibid.
289. "an immoral lout": Gabrielle Kerouac to AG, July 13, 1958.
289. "dirty actions"; "own kind"; and "I warn you . . .": ibid.
290. "weak and cowardly": WSB to AG, July 24, 1958.
290. "He seems . . .": ibid.
290. AG in NY: AG to JK, August 20 and September 17, 1958.
290. PO: PO to AG, February 10, March 10 and 20, April 22, and May 17, 1958; AG to PO, June 21, 1958; PO to AG, June 24, 1958.
290. "There's so much pain . . .": PO to AG, July 5, 1958.
291. "Lafcadio & Julius . . .": AG, first draft of "Message," in AG and PO, *Straight Hearts Delight*, 168. The revised version appears in *KADDISH*, 45; *CP*, 183. In the revised version, AG writes: "& your brothers are crazy/I accept their drunk cases."
291. AG literary activities: LF to AG, August 29, 1958; AG to JK, September 10, 1958; LF to AG, September 12, 1958; AG to JK, September 17, 1958; LF to AG, September 25, 1958; AG to JK, October 29, 1958.
292. "I explained how poetry . . .": AG to JK, September 17, 1958.
292. "a big teaching . . ." and "great funny . . .": AG to JK, September 10, 1958.
292. "Don't let Madison Avenue . . .": AG to JK, October 29, 1958.
292. "a record . . .": AG, "The Dharma Bums," *The Village Voice*, November 12, 1958.
293. Reviews of *The Dharma Bums*: Charles Poore, "Books of the Times," *The New York Times*, October 2, 1958; David Bordoff, "Dem Bums Back," *New York Post*, October 5, 1958; Nancy Wilson Ross, "Beat—and Buddhist," *The New York Times Book Review*, October 5, 1958; "The Yabyum Kid," *Time*, October 6, 1958; "Moonstruck Bop-Beater," *Newsweek*, October 6, 1958; John K. Hutchens, "The Dharma Bums," October 10, 1958; Anthony West, untitled review, *The New Yorker*, November 1, 1958; AG, "The Dharma Bums," *The Village Voice*, November 12, 1958.
293. "The role of women . . .": Bordoff, "Dem Bums Back."
293. "hostile to civilization": Norman Podhoretz, "The Know-Nothing Bohemians."
293. "out of touch . . ."; "writing for . . ."; and "a piece of vanity": Mark D. Schleifer, "Here to Save Us, but not Sure from What," *The Village Voice*, October 15, 1958.
293. "a new kind . . .": Mike Wallace, "Mike Wallace Asks Jack Kerouac: What Is the Beat Generation," *New York Post*, January 21, 1958. The Q/A excerpt following is also from this article.
294. Brandeis forum: Alfred Aronowitz, "The Beat Generation," *New York Post*, March 16, 1959. Kerouac's essay, "The Origins of the Beat Generation," was eventually published (in an expanded and edited form) in *Playboy* magazine. Kerouac's performance can be heard on *The Jack Kerouac Collection*, Rhino Records (R–70939).
295. "Laughing Gas": AG journal entries; AG, "Laughing Gas," *KADDISH*, 66–82; *CP*, 189–99; AG to JK, September 17, 1958; AG to Mark Van Doren, September 28, 1958; AG to JK, undated, ca. November 1958; AG to JK, December 31, 1958; Paul Portugés, *The Visionary Poetics of Allen Ginsberg* (Santa Barbara, CA: Ross-Erikson, 1978), 125–26.
296. "It gives the appearance . . .": Portugés, *Visionary Poetics*, 126.
296. "I discovered . . .": AG to Mark Van Doren, September 28, 1958.
296. "Nothing to fear . . .": AG to JK, September 17, 1958.
296. "I have always felt . . .": AG to JK, undated, ca. November 1958.

296. "too symmetrical . . .": AG undated journal entry.
296. "Mind is shapely . . .": AG, *CP*, xx. In *Indian Journals*, Ginsberg expands upon the thought: "We think in blocks of sensation & images. IF THE POET'S MIND IS SHAPELY HIS ART WILL BE SHAPELY. That is, the page will have an original but rhythmic shape—inevitable thought to inevitable thought, lines dropping inevitably in place on the page, making a subtle infinitely varied rythmic SHAPE." (41)
297. "The red tin . . .": AG, "Laughing Gas," *KADDISH*, 66; *CP*, 189.
297. "The universe . . .": ibid.
297. *Chicago Review/Big Table*: AG to JK, November 17, 1958; LF to AG, December 1, 1958; Rochelle Dubnow, "Chancellor Tells Maroon Views on Review," *Chicago Maroon*, December 12, 1958; Jack Mabley, "Filthy Writing on the Midway," *Chicago Daily News*, October 25, 1958; Alfred Aronowitz, "The Beat Generation," *New York Post*, March 16, 1959.
298. "kids chalking . . .": Mabley, "Filthy Writing on the Midway."
298. "The trustees . . .": ibid.
298. "Want to come to Chicago . . .": AG to JK, November 17, 1958.
299. "the best Kerouac . . .": LF to AG, December 1, 1958.
299. Ferlinghetti/City Lights: LF to AG, October 2, 1958.
299. "Kaddish" composition: AG, "How *Kaddish* Happened," originally published as liner notes to the phonograph record *Kaddish*, Atlantic Verbum Series 4001, reprinted in *The Poetics of the New American Poetry*, eds. Donald Allen and Warren Tallman (New York: Grove Press, 1973), 344–47; AG, unpublished notes to "Kaddish," stored with "Kaddish" manuscripts at the Fales Library, New York University; author interview with AG. The precise date of the composition of "Kaddish" is unknown. It is not remarked on specifically in Ginsberg's journals and letters at the time of the poem's composition. In later notes, written in 1960 and stored with the manuscript, Ginsberg dates the writing as February 1959, though his letters and journal notes indicate that it was probably written earlier, most likely in mid-November 1958.
300. "no idea what Prophecy . . .": AG, "How *Kaddish* Happened," in *Poetics of New American Poetry*, 345.
300. "I realized . . .": ibid.
301. "Now, Naomi . . .": AG, first draft of "Kaddish."
302. "Blessed be Heaven . . .": ibid.
302. "I didn't look . . .": AG, "How *Kaddish* Happened," in *Poetics of New American Poetry*, 346.
302. "higher and wilder than Howl": AG to Carolyn Cassady, January 10, 1959.
303. Neal Cassady: Carolyn Cassady to AG, January 7, 1959; PO to Carolyn Cassady, January 10, 1959; AG to Carolyn Cassady, January 10, 1959; Carolyn Cassady, *Off the Road* (New York: William Morrow, 1990), 313–26; Alfred Aronowitz, "The Beat Generation," *New York Post*, March 11, 1959.
303. "one of the most desperate . . .": Carolyn Cassady to AG, January 7, 1959.
303. "consumed with remorse . . .": ibid.
304. "I assume anyway . . .": AG to Carolyn Cassady, January 10, 1959.
304. *Pull My Daisy*: AG, "Robert Frank to 1985–A Man" (unpublished), AG Columbia deposit; AG to Carolyn Cassady, January 10, 1959; PO to Carolyn Cassady, January 10, 1959; JK, *Pull My Daisy* (New York: Grove Press, 1961); "Endsville: Zen-Hur," *Time*, December 14, 1959.
305. "harder to act . . .": AG to Carolyn Cassady, January 10, 1959.
305. "brilliant": Peter Bogdanovich, "Movie Journal," *The Village Voice*, January 5, 1961.
305. "the least dreary . . ." and "the first pure-Beat . . .": *Time*, December 14, 1959.
305. *Big Table* reading: AG journal entries; William Leonard, "Beatniks Shock, Amuse 700–at $1.50 a Head," *Chicago Tribune*, January 30, 1959; Dan Tucker, "Square's Beat—Verse Up in Hair," *Chicago Daily News*, January 30, 1959; "Manners as Morals—Fried Shoes," *Time*, February 9, 1959; Alfred Aronowitz, "Portrait of a Beat," *Nugget* (October 1960).
306. "I'm Peter Orlovsky . . .": *Time*, "Manners as Morals—Fried Shoes."
306. Columbia reading: AG to LF, February 12, 1959; AG to LG, May 12, 1959; Diana Trilling, "The Other Night at Columbia," *Partisan Review* (Spring 1959).
307. "stuck in the nineteenth century" and "drawn toward 'respectability' ": Diana Trilling, "The Other Night."
307. "Is there a chance . . .": Alfred Aronowitz, "The Beat Generation," *New York Post*, March 9, 1959.
308. "thunderstruck": LF to AG, January 17, 1959.
308. "hugest dark genius . . ." ibid.
308. "Caw caw caw . . .": AG, first draft of "Kaddish." See final version (*KADDISH*, 36; *CP*, 227) for revised and final form.
308. "I like it . . .": LG to AG, May 14, 1959.
309. "embarrassing scenes . . .": AG, "How *Kaddish* Happened," in *Poetics of New American Poetry*, 345–46.

309. "The line about . . .": AG to LG, May 20, 1959. This letter is dated March, but it is obvious from the line of AG/LG correspondence that Allen made a mistake when dating his letter.
309. "It's the climax . . .": ibid.
309. "I'm wondering . . .": EB to AG, May 16, 1959.
309. " 'Caw caw and Lord Lord' . . ." and "The decision is yours . . .": LG to AG, May 24, 1959.

13. Magic Psalm

310. Epigraph: AG, "Magic Psalm," *KADDISH*, 93; CP, 255.
310. "We came to present . . .": AG undated journal entry.
311. San Quentin reading: AG to JK, May 12, 1959; JK to AG, May 19, 1959; Carolyn Cassady, *Off the Road* (New York: William Morrow, 1990), 332–33.
311. LSD: AG to JK, May 12, 1959; AG to LG, May 20, 1959; LG to AG, May 24, 1959; *see also*, AG, "Lysergic Acid," *KADDISH*, 86–91; CP, 231–34.
311. "It was astonishing . . .": AG to LG, May 20, 1959.
311. "It's a very safe . . .": ibid.
312. "*Observation impeded function* . . .": Paul Portugés, *The Visionary Poetics of Allen Ginsberg* (Santa Barbara, CA: Ross-Erikson, 1978), 121.
312. "This image or energy . . .": AG, "Lysergic Acid," *KADDISH*, 88; CP, 232.
313. "Hindu-type gods . . .": AG to LG, May 20, 1959.
313. "Gods danced . . .": AG, "Lysergic Acid," *KADDISH*, 90; CP, 234.
313. "America is schizophrenic . . .": AG, unpublished and untitled journal poem.
313. "Scientists open . . .": ibid.
313. "up there in the mind . . ." and "somehow slide . . .": AG undated journal entries, ca. May 1959.
314. "It's all too much . . .": JK to AG, May 19, 1959.
314. "I am mentally . . .": JK to AG, June 18, 1959.
314. "What's going on . . .": JK to AG, May 19, 1959.
314. "endless complications . . ." and "tearing me apart . . .": AG to JK, July 7, 1959.
314. "slow trip home": AG to JK, May 12, 1959.
314. "bitchy and all . . .": AG to LG, May 12, 1959.
315. "Recent history . . .": AG, "Poetry, Violence, and The Trembling Lambs," *San Francisco Chronicle*, July 26, 1959, reprinted in *The Poetics of New American Poetry*, eds. Donald Allen and Warren Tallman (New York: Grove Press, 1973), 331–33.
315. "Who shall prohibit . . .": ibid., *Poetics*, 331.
315. "To be a junky . . .": ibid., 332.
315. "Who takes up . . .": ibid., 333.
315. "have had the luck . . .": ibid., 331–32.
316. AG dream: AG undated journal entry. Ginsberg's dreams about his mother, many addressing his feelings of betraying or failing her, haunted him for nearly three decades after Naomi's death. Two of his best later poems, "White Shroud" and "Black Shroud," written in 1983 and 1984, respectively, and collected in his volume *White Shroud*, bring some of these dream feelings to resolution.
316. "You've already forgotten . . .": ibid. All quotations in this passage from this journal entry.
316. "I shivered . . ." and "He delivered . . .": AG journal entry, September 6, 1959; published in AG, *Journals*, 102.
317. "In my opinion . . .": AG, unpublished testimony used in initial court decision in the *Big Table* hearing, AG Columbia deposit.
317. "concerned with an illumination . . .": ibid.
317. "If the actual . . .": ibid.
318. "Please do your best . . .": WSB to AG, September 6, 1959.
318. "Don't you ever . . .": Gabrielle Kerouac to AG, September 6, 1959.
319. "cult of nothing new"; "cult of uselessness"; "one of the most unwholesome . . ."; and "Experiment is the order . . .": Joe Hyams, "Good-by to The Beatniks!" *New York Herald Tribune*, September 28, 1959.
319. "The bulk of Beat writers . . .": Paul O'Neill, "The Only Rebellion Around," *Life*, November 30, 1959.
319. "deadbeat": Hyams, "Good-by to Beatniks!"
320. "How can a whole . . .": AG to JK, October 6, 1959.
320. "mockery is . . .": ibid.
320. "Rent a Beatnik": Sidney Fields, "Like Do You Want to Rent a Beatnik?" *New York Mirror*, June 23, 1960; Joseph Morgenstern, "Beatniks for Rent," *New York Herald Tribune*, May 1, 1960; author interview with Fred McDarrah.

320. "And tho we've been . . .": AG, "Sunrise," notebook poem; published in AG, *Journals*, 124.
321. AG in Chile: AG journal entries; LF to AG, January 10, 1960; AG to PO, January 24, 1960; AG to PO, undated, ca. January 1960; AG to Lucien Carr, January 26, 1960; AG to PO, February 9, 1960; AG to LG, March 8, 1960; AG to PO, March 25, 1960.
321. "dirty animals": AG undated journal entry, ca. late January 1960.
322. "without real feeling": AG to PO, January 24, 1960.
322. "We were a big hit . . .": ibid.
322. "Have run into . . .": AG to Lucien Carr, January 26, 1960.
322. "getting familiar . . .": AG to PO, undated, ca. January 1960.
322. "The whole beat . . .": AG to PO, February 9, 1960.
323. AG in Bolivia: AG journal entries; AG to PO, April 4, 1960; AG to Lucien Carr, April 6, 1960; AG to PO, undated, ca. mid-April 1960.
323. "Anybody who can . . .": AG to PO, undated, ca. mid-April 1960.
323. "big hypocritical speeches": ibid.
323. "the most fantastic . . .": AG to LC, April 6, 1960.
324. "a mildly stimulating effect": ibid.
324. Situation in States: PO to AG, March 24, 1960; LF to AG, April 13, 1960; PO to AG, May 13, 1960; LF to AG, June 2, 1960.
325. AG in Peru: AG journal entries; AG to Lucien Carr, April 20, 1960; AG to PO, April 27, May 12, and May 26, 1960; AG to LG, June 2, 1960; AG to PO, June 3, 1960; AG to JK, June 6, 1960; AG to WSB, June 10, 1960; AG to PO, June 12, 1960; AG to Lucien Carr, June 21, 1960; WSB to AG, June 21, 1960.
325. "very picturesque": AG to Lucien Carr, June 20, 1960.
325. "The view all around . . .": AG to PO, June 26, 1960.
325. "fearful . . .": AG to PO, May 12, 1960.
325. "The half-mad . . .": AG journal entry, April 28, 1960.
326. "God is so beautiful . . .": AG journal entry, May 20, 1960.
326. "trap": WSB to AG, April 18, 1960.
326. "Make it, man": ibid.
327. "I drifted away . . .": AG to PO, May 26, 1960.
327. "Being 'world famous' . . .": AG to LG, June 2, 1960.
327. "the sense of old . . .": AG to PO, June 5, 1960.
327. Yage: AG journal entries; AG/WSB, *The Yage Letters*; AG, "Magic Psalm," KADDISH, 92–95 and CP, 255–56; AG to LG, June 2, 1960; AG to PO, June 3 and 5, 1960; AG to JK, June 6, 1960; AG to WSB, June 10, 1960; AG to PO, June 12, 1960; AG to LG, June 21, 1960.
328. "the Great Being": AG to WSB, June 10, 1960.
328. "the whole fucking Cosmos . . .": ibid.
329. "I saw them . . .": AG journal entry, June 9, 1960.
329. "I was all wrong . . .": ibid.
329. "I wrote . . .": AG to LG, June 21, 1960.
330. "born in Newark . . .": AG, "Magic Psalm," KADDISH, 94–95, CP, 256.
330. "Escape, but not . . .": AG, "The Reply," KADDISH, 97; CP, 257.
330. "It seemed that . . .": AG to LG, June 21, 1960.
331. "My poetry is now . . .": AG journal entry, June 10, 1960.
331. "I am Thy prophet . . .": AG, "Magic Psalm," KADDISH, 93; CP, 255.
331. "And the braggart . . .": AG journal entry, June 11, 1960.
332. "O Blake . . .": AG journal entry, June 12, 1960.
332. "Widen the area . . .": AG journal entry, June 14, 1960.
332. "barefooted and hairy . . .": AG journal entry, June 19, 1960.
332. "Some joke . . .": AG journal entry, June 21, 1960.
333. "The Beat Generation . . .": ibid.
333. "its Eternal presence . . .": AG journal entry, July 1, 1960.

14. TV Baby

334. Epigraph: AG, "Journal Night Thoughts," *PN*, 14; *CP*, 270.
334. Completion of "Kaddish": AG journal entries; AG, "How Kaddish Happened," reprinted in *The Poetics of the New American Poetry*, eds. Donald Allen and Warren Tallmer (New York: Grove Press, 1973); AG, unpublished notes to "Kaddish" manuscript; AG to LF, July 5 and September 16, 1960; AG to JK, September 19, 1960; LG to AG, September 19, 1960; LF to AG, September 20, 1960; AG to LF, October 3 and 5, 1960; LF to AG, October 14, 19, and 26, 1960.
334. "Defeat like that . . .": AG, "How Kaddish Happened," in *Poetics of New American Poetry*, 346.

334. "I sat down . . .": AG to JK, September 19, 1960.
335. "Let me know . . ." and "huge white-elephant": AG to LF, September 16, 1960.
335. "read your Kaddish . . ." and "a magnificent . . .": LG to AG, September 18, 1960.
335. "too obscene . . .": ibid.
335. "You'll invite . . .": LG to AG, September 19, 1960.
335. "God, I'm having trouble . . .": AG to JK, September 19, 1960.
336. "It's right . . .": LF to AG, October 14, 1960.
336. JK: JK, *Big Sur* (New York: Farrar, Straus and Cudahy, 1962); JK to AG, September 22, 1960;
     Carolyn Cassady, *Off the Road* (New York: William Morrow, 1990), 345–59.
338. "realized I AM . . .": AG to JK, September 19, 1960.
338. "What Logia Jesus . . .": JK to AG, September 22, 1960.
338. "hysterical mind control": AG to JK, September 19, 1960.
339. "What good are . . .": AG undated journal poem, "Politics on Opium"; published in AG, *Journals*,
     151.
339. "What's happening who's starving . . .": AG untitled journal poem, November 1, 1960; published
     in AG, *Journals*, 158–59.
340. "Both are phony . . ." and "You don't think . . .": AG to JK, undated, ca. October 1960.
340. "an abused prisoner . . .": AG undated journal entry; published in AG, *Journals*, 162.
340. "He has a hole . . .": AG journal entry, October 31, 1959; published in AG, *Journals*, 111.
341. "well intentioned . . .": Peter Manso, *Mailer* (New York: Simon & Schuster, 1986), 260.
341. "fighting with sick . . .": Norman Mailer, "Open Letter to Fidel Castro," in *The Presidential Papers*
     (New York: Berkeley Medallion, 1970), 70.
341. "like many another vain . . .": Norman Mailer, *Advertisements for Myself* (New York: Berkeley
     Medallion, 1966), 15.
341. Mailer campaign: Peter Manso, *Mailer*, 311–12; Hillary Mills, *Mailer* (New York: Empire Books,
     1982), 218–220.
341. Podhoretz: Manso, *Mailer*, 313–14; author interview with Norman Podhoretz.
341. "a conspiracy . . .": Norman Podhoretz, "Where Is the Beat Generation Going?," *Esquire*, Decem-
     ber 1958.
342. "To my eternal shame . . .": Manso, *Mailer*, 314.
342. "high horse": ibid.
343. AG/Timothy Leary: AG journal entries; AG to NC, December 4, 1960; Timothy Leary, *Flashbacks:
     An Autobiography* (Los Angeles: Jeremy P. Tarcher, 1983), 45–50; Jane Kramer, *Allen Ginsberg
     in America* (New York: Random House, 1969), 185–88; Timothy Leary, "In the Beginning, Leary
     Turned on Ginsberg and Saw That It Was Good," *Esquire*, July 1968; author interview with AG.
344. "a polite, scholarly . . .": Kramer, *Allen Ginsberg in America*, 187.
344. "shaping me up . . .": Leary, "In the Beginning . . ."; all quotations in this passage are from this
     Esquire article.
346. "All these . . .": AG journal poem, "Police," December 1960; published in AG, *Journals*, 168–69.
347. "radio, newspapers, television . . .": ibid.
347. "Everyone plugged in . . .": ibid.
348. "walking on water . . .": AG undated journal entry; published in AG, *Journals*, 183.
348. "Stop giving . . .": AG to NC, December 4, 1960.
348. "Light dies! . . .": AG journal poem, "Hurrah for the American Revolution!" published in AG,
     Journals, 164.
349. "Here I am . . .": AG, first draft of "Television Was a Baby Crawling Toward That Death
     Chamber," in AG Columbia deposit.
349. "TV Baby": The first draft of this poem was substantially longer and different from the final version
     published in *Planet News*. Although Ginsberg managed to maintain the original spirit of the
     poem, saving lines and phrases whenever he could, it went through numerous drafts between its
     original composition and publication. For its published ending, Ginsberg returned to his journals
     and pulled out a large fragment from the poem he entitled "Police." As he had done with
     "Kaddish," he cut lines from "TV Baby" into strips and repositioned them in the poem. In short,
     while the published version was basically the piece of spontaneous writing Ginsberg claimed it
     was, it was by no means an unedited version of the work composed on that February 1961
     evening.
349. New York Methedrine scene: HH, *Guilty of Everything* (New York: Paragon Books, 1990), 143–59.
350. "PLEASE DO NOT . . .": LF to AG, March 16, 1961. The "Kaddish" manuscript was purchased
     by Ted Wilentz, a friend of Ginsberg's who, in recalling the purchase, noted in a text stored with
     the manuscript: "Buying his KADDISH manuscript was for me not only an expression of support
     for the Living Theatre but also a symbol of my involvement and friendship with Ginsberg and
     the 'new American poets.' Although Allen was not nearly as famous as he has become, the
     manuscript was a valuable one simply in terms of money. That he donated it when he himself
     had very little money is typical of him. In the years since the auction, I have come to know him

much better than I did then and I can say from personal knowledge that he has often done similar things with his reward being the proverbial one for virtue." (September 29, 1967)

351. "Don't be paranoiac . . .": AG to JK, February 21, 1961.
351. "You are talking . . .": ibid.
351. "when I called . . .": AG journal entry, March 23, 1961; published in AG, *Journals*, 191.
352. "Who knows . . .": AG journal poem, "Scrap Leaves," March 1961; published in AG, *Journals*, 186–87.

15. Mediterranean Planet Waves

353. Epigraph: AG, "Galilee Shore," *PN*, 39; *CP*, 289.
353. WSB "cut-ups": WSB to AG, June 21, 1961; WSB with Daniel Odier, *The Job* (New York: Grove Press, 1972), 27–36; Conrad Knickerbocker, "The Art of Fiction: William S. Burroughs," in *Writers at Work: The Paris Review Interviews*, third series, ed. George Plimpton (New York: Viking Press, 1967), 141–74; Ted Morgan, *Literary Outlaw: The Life and Times of William S. Burroughs* (New York: Henry Holt, 1988), 321–26.
353. "a certain juxtaposition . . .": Knickerbocker, "The Art of Fiction," in *Writers*, 149.
354. "It is unfortunately . . .": ibid., 156–57.
354. "Don't think about it . . .": WSB to AG, June 21, 1961.
356. "a non-commital [sic] transcription . . .": AG, "Abstraction in Poetry," *Nomad/New York* (Autumn 1962).
356. "No I don't know . . .": AG undated journal poem, "Bay of Pigs"; published in AG, *Journals*, 200.
356. "WE ARE ALL . . .": ibid., 201.
356. "explosive": JK to AG, June 14, 1961.
356. "impact of . . .": ibid.
357. "I graduated college . . .": AG journal poem, "Funeral Vomit," May 27, 1961; published in AG, *Journals*, 206.
357. "scampering and skipping . . .": AG to JK, June 11, 1961.
358. "spoiled brat . . .": AG to Lucien Carr, June 28, 1961.
358. "poison juices . . .": PO, "Thank God . . . I Wasn't a Whore Boy," in *Straight Hearts Delight*, 105.
359. "I wept . . .": AG journal entry, July 9, 1961; published in AG, *Journals*, 214.
359. PO decision to leave and tensions in Tangier: AG journal entries; AG to PO, August 2 and 3, 1961; AG to LG, undated, ca. September 1961; AG to Howard Schulman, October 1961; AG to LF, undated, ca. October 1961.
359. "Burroughs seems to . . .": AG to LF, undated, ca. October 1961.
359. Leary in Tangier: AG journal entries; AG to PO, August 2 and 3, 1961; AG to Barney Rosset, August 4, 1961; Timothy Leary, *Flashbacks: An Autobiography* (Los Angeles: Jeremy P. Tarcher, 1983), 95–96.
359. "This can't be . . .": Leary, *Flashbacks*, 96.
359. "I'm not feeling . . .": ibid.
360. "still a sort . . .": AG to PO, August 2, 1961.
360. "I didn't want . . .": AG to PO, August 3, 1961.
360. "During the day . . .": ibid.
360. "merger of souls . . .": ibid.
360. "I was confused . . .": ibid.
361. *Kaddish*: LF to AG/GC, June 28, 1961. In retrospect, *Kaddish*'s slow start is an interesting literary phenomenon, given the fact that it was the follow-up to one of the most successful volumes of poetry in history, and given Ginsberg's stature as one of America's most visible poets. Beside the title poem, widely regarded as Ginsberg's masterwork, the volume featured another of his most frequently anthologized poems ("To Aunt Rose"). In time, sales of *Kaddish and Other Poems* would be second only to *Howl*, with the title poem becoming one of the most enduring and studied works of its time.
361. "by far . . ."; "psychotherapy"; and "True to form . . .": A. Alvarez, "The Herd Instinct," London *Observer*, May 14, 1961.
361. "Ginsberg had become . . .": Harvey Shapiro, "Exalted Lament," *Midstream* (August 1961).
361. "this Allen Ginsberg trap": AG to LG, undated, ca. September 1961.
362. "Lately words and language . . .": AG to LG, undated, ca. October 1961.
362. "Church spire . . .": AG journal entry, August 24, 1961; published in AG, *Journals*, 220.
362. AG in Greece: AG journal entries; AG to LG, undated, ca. early October 1961; AG to LF, undated, ca. October 1961; LF to AG, October 7, 1961; AG to Howard Schulman, October 1961; AG to PO, October 21, 1961; AG to LG, November 12, 1961.

362. Money woes: AG to GC, August 30, 1961; AG to Howard Schulman, October 1961; AG to PO, October 21, 1961.
362. "Censorship of language . . .": AG to Howard Schulman, October 1961. *See Also*, "Prose Contribution to Cuban Revolution," the Ginsberg essay extracted from this letter, reprinted in *The Poetics of the New American Poetry*, eds. Donald Allen and Warren Tallman (New York: Grove Press, 1973), 334–44.
363. "sense of Spenglerian history . . .": AG, "Prose Contribution to Cuban Revolution," in *Poetics*, 336.
363. "Poet-prophet friend . . .": ibid., 338.
363. "I met *someone* . . .": ibid., 340.
363. "All governments . . .": ibid., 343.
364. "I am getting . . .": AG to LG, undated, ca. October 1961.
364. "marble skeleton": AG journal entry, August 29, 1961; published in AG, *Journals*, 223.
364. "The light . . .": AG to LG, undated, ca. October 1961.
364. "The whole human race . . .": AG to LG, October 16, 1961.
365. "prodded on through . . .": AG undated journal entry; published in AG, *Journals*, 257.
365. AG in Israel: AG journal entries; AG to LG, November 2, 1961; AG to LG, undated, ca. November 1961; AG to LG, November 25, 1961; AG to LF, December 20, 1961; AG to LG, December 27, 1961; AG to JK, May 11, 1962.
365. "Perhaps in Israel . . .": LG to AG, July 7, 1961.
365. "Yes, I am a Jew . . ." and "Jews and Arabs . . .": interview with AG, *Jewish Post and Opinion*, December 8, 1961.
366. "All I'm saying . . .": AG to LG, undated, ca. November 1961.
366. "Owing to the entire . . .": AG undated journal entry.
366. "Fishermen-nets over . . .": AG, "Galilee Shore," *PN*, 39; *CP*, 289.
366. "like a ratty . . .": AG to JK, May 11, 1962.
367. "reading books . . .": AG journal entry, November 20, 1961; published in AG, *Journals*, 265.
367. "the greatest thing . . .": AG to LG, November 25, 1961.
367. AG meets Martin Buber: AG undated journal entry; AG to LG, November 25, 1961; AG to JK, May 11, 1962. *See also*, AG, "Galilee Shore," *PN*, 39; *CP*, 289.
367. "too much American . . .": AG to LG, November 25, 1961.
367. "I been talking . . .": AG undated journal entry; published in AG, *Journals*, 266.
367. "endless jabber . . ." and "like the Ancient . . .": ibid.
367. "The atombomb . . .": AG undated journal entry; published in AG, *Journals*, 269.

16. The Change: India and the Orient

368. Epigraph: AG, "The Change: Kyoto-Tokyo Express," *PN*, 58; *CP*, 326.
368. "Yet like a dream . . .": AG journal entry, January 7, 1962; published in AG, *Journals*, 288.
368. "Jomo Kenyatta . . .": AG to LG, January 21, 1962.
369. "So cold . . .": AG journal entry, February 11, 1962.
369. AG in India: AG journal entries; AG to JK, January 26, 1962; AG to LF, February 25, 1962; LF to AG, March 10, 1962; AG to LG, March 16 and 22, 1962; AG to GC, April 19, 1962; AG to LG/Edith Ginsberg, April 21, 1962; AG to Howard Schulman, April 22, 1962; AG to JK, May 11, 1962; AG to PO, June 6, 1962; LF to AG, July 1 and 17, 1962; AG to JK, July 29, 1962; AG to LG, August 5, 1962; JK to AG, August 28, 1962; AG to JK, September 9, 1962; AG to LG, September 25, 1962; AG to NC, October 8, 1962; AG to JK, October 11, 1962; AG to Howard Schulman, October 11, 1962; AG to Lucien Carr, October 24, 1962; AG to JK, November 4, 1962; LF to AG, November 15, 1962; AG to WCW, November 19, 1962; AG to LG, December 7, 1962; AG to Fernanda Pivano, January 24, 1963; LF to AG, February 17, 1963; AG to Fernanda Pivano, March 2, 1963; AG to Howard Schulman, March 16, 1963; AG to JK, May 8, 1963; AG to LG, June 14–22, 1963.
369. "I never saw a place . . .": AG to JK, May 11, 1962.
369. "India is really . . .": AG to LG, March 16, 1962.
370. "Everybody in India . . .": AG to JK, May 11, 1962.
370. "I was under . . .": WSB to AG, February 16, 1962.
371. "Don't talk to Burroughs . . .": Timothy Leary, *Flashbacks: An Autobiography* (Los Angeles: Jeremy P. Tarcher, 1983), 100.
371. "completely ill intentioned" and "utterly no interest . . .": WSB to AG, October 26, 1961.
371. "He saw me . . .": Leary, *Flashbacks*, 100.
371. "a real wrong number": WSB to AG, October 26, 1961. Burroughs was much more charitable in his later assessment of Leary's experiments and research. In his foreword to Leary's *Flashbacks*,

Burroughs wrote, "Despite my own initial disgruntled reaction to 'Dr. Tim' and his save-the-world antics (I was no less skeptical at the time of my dear friend Allen Ginsberg's similar aspirations), I have come to regard Timothy Leary as a true pioneer of human evolution. Never stinting to dare all in pursuit of his idealistic dream of universal psychedelic enlightenment, he has suffered enormously in its service."

371. Ferlinghetti/AG: LF to AG, February 22 and March 10, 1962.
372. "Great, because . . .": AG to JK, May 11, 1962.
372. "You must not give . . .": ibid.
372. "I write . . .": ibid.
372. "charlatan of mass-production . . .": ibid.
372. "The only guru . . .": ibid.
373. "The way I look . . .": AG to LG, March 16, 1962.
373. "They're just advertisement . . .": AG to JK, May 11, 1962.
374. "Self Conscious . . .": AG journal entry, March 25, 1962; published in AG, *Indian Journals*, 10–11.
375. "The great rock . . .": AG to JK, May 11, 1962.
376. "intercessor": Joyce Johnson, *Minor Characters* (New York: Washington Square Press, 1984), 81.
376. "Elise was a moment . . ." and "in Elise's life . . .": ibid., 82.
376. "All worlds . . .": AG to Howard Schulman, April 22, 1962.
376. AG readings: AG journal entries; AG to LG/Edith Ginsberg, April 21, 1962.
376. "came up with . . ." and "the greatest nation . . .": AG to Howard Schulman, April 22, 1962.
377. "chasing each other . . .": AG to JK, May 11, 1962.
377. "The subjective result . . .": ibid.
377. "A whole series . . .": Clark, "The Art of Poetry," in *Writers at Work*, 315.
377. "The psychic problem . . .": ibid, 315.
378. "Air Raid . . ."; "Electric chair . . ."; and "the H Bomb . . .": AG journal entry, April 1962; published in AG, *Indian Journals*, 22–23.
378. "We'll go naked . . .": AG to JK, May 11, 1962.
378. AG meets Dudjom Rinpoche: AG journal entries; author interview with AG.
378. "looking like a woman . . .": AG journal entry, June 3, 1962, published in AG, *Indian Journals*, 26.
379. "Don't get attached . . .": author interview with AG.
379. "He offered . . .": AG to JK, July 29, 1962.
379. "perfect": LF to AG, September 3, 1962.
379. *Reality Sandwiches*: LF to AG, July 1 and 17, 1962.
379. "like a rapidly running movie": LG to AG, August 13, 1962.
380. "I'm sorry . . .": AG to LG, August 5, 1962.
380. "I am amazed . . .": AG journal entry, July 28, 1962; published in AG, *Indian Journals*, 48.
380. "very romantic . . .": AG to NC, October 8, 1962.
380. "deeper images": AG journal entry, September 1962; published in AG, *Indian Journals*, 53.
380. "Time comes . . .": AG, "The Names," PAOTP, 11; CP, 176.
381. "We both think . . .": Carolyn Cassady to AG, October 31, 1962.
381. "The Names": Carolyn and Neal Cassady were not the only ones concerned about Allen's use of real people and events in his poetry. Lucien Carr, who in 1956 had requested that Allen withdraw his name from the dedication page of *Howl and Other Poems*, disapproved not only of Allen's using his name in his works but of his using those of others, as well. In an October 24, 1962, letter, Carr called Ginsberg to task for it: "Isn't it enough that the past is there, without your returning again and again and again to nuzzle, smell, wallow, guzzle and paint yourself blue with it? Are you gonna run around in a circle of ever decreasing circumference forever? . . . As far as it affects me, can't you word bandiers stick to your own ghosts and leave mine alone?"
381. Durga Puja holiday: AG journal entries; AG to NC, October 8, 1962, AG to JK, October 11, 1962.
381. "We went . . .": AG to JK, October 11, 1962.
381. "a strange . . .": ibid.
382. "There's nobody . . ." and "It shows . . .": ibid.
382. "My message is . . .": ibid.
383. "Revolt of machines . . .": AG journal entry, October 24, 1962; published in AG, *Indian Journals*, 74.
383. "The nuclear technology . . .": AG to LG, September 25, 1962.
383. "Bertrand Russell makes sense . . .": AG to JK, September 9, 1962.
383. "What do you think? . . .": AG to LG, September 25, 1962.
383. "If we're going . . .": AG to JK, September 9, 1962.
384. "Is it worth . . .": AG to LG, September 25, 1962.
385. "most stupendous motel . . .": AG to Lucien Carr, undated, ca. January 1963.

385. "survived, triumphed . . .": AG journal entry, December 31, 1962; published in AG, *Indian Journals*, 144.
385. "take Blake . . .": AG, dedication page of *Indian Journals*.
386. CID harassment: AG journal entries; AG to Fernanda Pivano, March 2, 1963; AG to Howard Schulman, March 16, 1963; AG to LG, April 8, 1963; AG to JK, May 8, 1963.
386. "You wouldn't have talked . . .": AG to JK, May 8, 1963.
386. "One conclusion . . .": ibid.
387. "Biggest thing . . .": AG to LG, April 8, 1963.
387. "It isn't enough . . .": AG journal entry, September 6, 1962; published in AG, *Indian Journals*, 52.
388. "Today on balcony . . .": AG, "Describe: The Rain on Dasawamedh," *PN*, 46; *CP*, 295.
389. "He isn't dead . . .": AG, "Death News," *PN*, 48; *CP*, 297.
389. "all personal relations . . .": AG journal entry, May 19, 1963; published in AG, *Indian Journals*, 209.
389. "All month . . .": ibid., 208.
390. "All the holymen . . .": AG to JK, May 8, 1963.
390. "The gesture or feeling . . .": Bruce Kawin radio interview with AG, October 1964.
390. AG in Bangkok: AG journal entries; AG to PO, May 31, 1963.
391. "This is a place . . .": AG to PO, May 31, 1963.
391. AG in Vietnam: AG journal entries; AG to PO, June 6, 1963; AG to LG, June 17, 1963.
391. "horrible mess . . ." and "a nervous stomach . . .": AG to LG, June 17, 1963.
391. "Travelling by jetplane . . .": ibid.
391. AG in Cambodia: AG journal entries; AG, "Angkor Wat," *CP*, 306–23; AG to PO, June 11, 1963; AG to LG, June 17, 1963.
391. "serpent arms": AG, "Angkor Wat," *CP*, 308.
391. "wire singings . . .": AG journal entry, June 7, 1963.
392. "Tint blue lights . . .": AG journal entry, June 11, 1963.
392. "huge dark misty . . .": ibid.
392. AG in Japan: AG journal entries; AG to PO, June 16, 1963; AG to LG, June 17, 1963; AG to PO, June 2 and July 9, 1963.
392. "Japan amazing . . .": AG to LG, June 17, 1963.
392. "Well, young man . . .": AG journal entry, July 2, 1963; other citations from this dream are taken from this entry.
393. "interesting subjective effects": AG to LG, June 17, 1963.
393. Yage letters: LF to AG, June 11 and 28, 1963.
393. "a kind of . . .": LF to AG, June 11, 1963.
393. "greatest living . . .": LF to AG, June 28, 1963.
393. "I suddenly didn't . . .": Clark, "The Art of Poetry," in *Writers at Work*, 316.
394. "I started weeping . . .": Lucie-Smith, *Mystery in the Universe*, 6–7.
394. "The Change": AG, "The Change: Kyoto-Tokyo Express," *PN*, 55–63; *CP*, 324–30; AG journal entries; Bruce Kawin radio interview, October 1964; Clark, "The Art of Poetry," in *Writers at Work*, 315–16; Paul Carroll, "Playboy Interview," *Playboy*, April 1969; Edward Lucie-Smith, *Mystery in the Universe* (London: Turret Books, 1965), 6–8.
394. "Shit! Intestines boiling . . .": AG, "The Change," *PN*, 56; *CP*, 325.
394. "seeking the Great Spirit . . .": AG, "The Change," *PN*, 59; *CP*, 327.
394. "confronting the horrific": Ekbert Faas, *Towards a New American Poetics* (Santa Barbara, CA: Black Sparrow Press, 1979), excerpted in *On the Poetry of Allen Ginsberg*, ed. Lewis Hyde (Ann Arbor: University of Michigan Press, 1984), 434–50.
394. "I am a mass . . .": AG, "The Change," *PN*, 59; *CP*, 327.
395. "I am that I am . . .": AG, "The Change," *PN*, 60; *CP*, 327–28.
395. "Come, sweet lonely Spirit . . .": AG, "The Change," *PN*, 61; *CP*, 328.
395. "renounce my power . . .": AG, "The Change," *PN*, 62; *CP*, 329.
395. "The change . . .": Bruce Kawin radio interview, October 1964.

17. Planet News

397. Epigraph: AG, "Today," *PN*, 80–81; *CP*, 347.
397. "Listen to Everybody . . .": AG journal poem, "Grand Chorale in Honor of Human Being."
397. "I worship Man . . .": AG, unpublished and untitled journal poem.
398. "long Naomi hair . . .": AG journal entry, Labor Day 1963.
398. AG in Vancouver: AG journal entries; AG to LG, August 16, 1963; AG to LF, August 19, 1963; AG to LC, Lucien Carr, August 19, 1963; author interview with AG.

398. "the *place* we are": author interview with AG.

398. "I am one . . .": ibid.

398. "It *seemed* to me . . .": Tom Clark, "The Art of Poetry: Allen Ginsberg," in *Writers at Work: The Paris Review Interviews, Fourth Series*, ed. George Plimpton (New York: Viking Press, 1976), 316.

398. "Wrapped up teaching . . .": AG to LG, August 16, 1963.

398. AG in SF: AG journal entries; AG to PO, August 17, 1963; AG to NC, undated, ca. August 1963; AG to JK, October 6, 1963; AG to PO, October 10, 1963; AG to LG, October 14, 1963; AG to PO, November 29, 1963.

398. "like huge nine year . . .": AG to PO, October 10, 1963.

399. "Cannot write . . .": AG undated journal entry, undated, ca. October 1963.

399. NC: AG to PO, October 10, 1963; Carolyn Cassady, *Off the Road* (New York: William Morrow, 1990), 376–78; William Plummer, *The Holy Goof: A Biography of Neal Cassady* (Englewood Cliffs, NJ: Prentice-Hall, 1981), 120–22.

399. "General feel . . .": AG to PO, October 10, 1963.

399. AG pickets Nhu: Eric Mottram, *Allen Ginsberg in the Sixties* (Seattle: Unicorn Bookshop, 1972), 15–16; "The Literary Lion," *San Francisco Chronicle*, October 24, 1963; photo, *San Francisco News Call Bulletin*, October 28, 1963.

399. "black magic" and "Name hypnosis . . .": from photo taken by John W. Doss, reprinted in George Dowden, *A Bibliography of Works by Allen Ginsberg* (San Francisco: City Lights, 1971).

400. "I heard otherwise . . .": Donald Stanley, "A Literary Confrontation," *San Francisco Examiner*, November 13, 1963.

400. JK: Jack Kerouac visited John Clellon Holmes in Old Saybrook, Connecticut, on several occasions in September 1963, supposedly because he wanted to purchase a house in the area. Kerouac, wrote Holmes in his journal entry of September 13, 1962, was "probably the most prodigious, indefatigable drinker I've ever known. His genius is exhausting, unique, volcanic, and is fed somehow by booze. . . . His strange amalgam of spurious ideas, verbal illumination, cornball politics, dead certain aesthetic feeling, huge relish for life, fatalistic physical strength—all that I knew so well once, has come back to me in a rush." Kerouac, Holmes realized, was nearing the endgame stage of his life: "Way deep down, I think, he wants to die, and no amount of self-abuse, disaster or sadness can expunge the feeling of loss & estrangement which has always scarred him, dogged him, driven him. . . . Poor Ti Jean. Off on one of those saddening Odysseys that must end in dreary, drunken tears at four in the morning. No real place for him. Such people leave a permanent mark on one's years," Holmes wrote in his journal on September 16, 1962. Holmes probably saw or heard from Kerouac as much as anyone in the final years of Kerouac's life, and when I asked him whether anything could have been done to save him, Holmes replied, "Short of wet-nursing or hog-tying him, I can't think of much. I could have visited him more, I could have written him cautionary letters. But a deep friend doesn't lecture his brother-soul. Jack's dissipations weren't for 'kicks'—they were an attempt to ameliorate his pain at sight of the world, and the helplessness to alleviate that suffering, that was basic to his nature. Jack's was mostly a tragic view of life, and he remained faithful to it. Could anyone, who knew and loved him, have told Nietzsche to straighten up and get sane? I saw Anne Sexton a few months before her suicide, and glimpsed a hectic mote in her eye, but she seemed mostly on balance. Then . . . Nothing could be done about Jack in those last years except try to amuse and distract him. We were living mostly a thousand miles apart, and I was finishing a book. I knew he wanted to die; I knew this desire wasn't trivial; I grieved about it because I loved him, but I respected him and his vision too much to try to interfere in his fate."

400. "It seems very late . . .": Robert Phelps, "Tender Kerouac: Spontaneity Is Not Enough," *New York Tribune*, September 8, 1962.

401. "the most lazy . . .": ibid.

401. "the frozen moment . . .": WSB, *Naked Lunch* (New York: Grove Press, 1959), xxxvii.

401. "shapeless panorama . . .": Richard Kluger, "Panorama of Perversity," *New York Tribune*, November 25, 1962.

401. "disgusting and . . .": Mary McCarthy, "Burroughs' 'Naked Lunch,' " *Encounter* (April 1963).

401. "a meeting ground . . .": Charles Poore, "Books of the Times," *The New York Times*, November 20, 1962.

401. " 'Reality Sandwiches' . . .": Carl Morse, "Reality Sandwiches," *Village Voice Books*, November 14, 1963.

401. "Ginsberg's music"; "instinctive"; and "inexplicable gift": A. R. Ammons, "Ginsberg's New Poems," *Poetry* (June 1964).

402. "tasty scribbles" and "no big pronouncements . . .": AG to JK, September 9, 1962.

402. "fear in my intestines": AG journal entry, November 23, 1963.

402. "singing Hare Krishna . . .": ibid.

402. "feeling alone": ibid.

402. "In other words . . .": AG, "Statement to Burning Bush," *Burning Bush II* (1963).

403. "The trouble with the Israelis . . .": ibid.
403. "It's time . . .": ibid.
403. "O New York . . .": AG, unpublished and untitled journal poem, November 30, 1963.
404. "He was gone . . .": author interview with Edith Ginsberg.
404. "This problem with Jack . . .": AG to JK, undated, ca. April 1964.
404. "You can't . . .": ibid.
404. "DON'T show . . .": ibid.
405. AG meets Bob Dylan: author interview with AG; Anthony Scaduto, *Dylan* (New York: Signet Books, 1974), 212; Robert Shelton, *No Direction Home: The Life and Music of Bob Dylan* (New York: William Morrow, 1986), 153–55.
406. "there are more . . ." and "highway leads . . .": John Gruen, "The New Bohemia," *New York Tribune*, November 29, 1964.
406. "It represents . . .": ibid.
406. *Kaddish* filmscript: AG journal entries; AG and Robert Frank, *Kaddish* filmscript (unpublished), AG Columbia deposit; AG to JK, February 26, 1964.
407. "piecemeal and weak": AG to JK, February 26, 1964.
407. Andy Warhol: Jean Stein, *Edie: An American Biography*, ed. George Plimpton (New York: Alfred A. Knopf, 1982).
408. "Vietnam Morality Play": AG undated journal entry.
408. Coffeehouse controversy: AG journal entries; author interview with AG; Stephanie Cervis Harrington, "City Puts Bomb Under Off-Beat Culture Scene," *The Village Voice*, March 26, 1964; Michael Smith, "Drizzle Does Not Dim Ardor of Arts Marchers," *The Village Voice*, April 30, 1964; "Arts Harrassment Details Sought," *The Village Voice*, May 14, 1964; Nat Freedland, "Allen Ginsberg and The Law," *New York Herald Tribune*, May 24, 1964.
409. "to protest . . .": Smith, "Drizzle Does Not," *Voice*.
410. "Is the mayor's office . . .": AG, "Letter to the Editor," (Wichita) *Beacon*, April 16, 1964.
410. "We the undersigned . . .": AG, "Arts, Educational Leaders Protest Use of New York Obscenity Law in Harassment of Controversial Social Satirist Lenny Bruce," June 13, 1964.
411. "Bruce [is] only part . . .": AG to JK, June 20, 1964.
411. "should explode . . .": AG, jacket blurb for Hubert Selby, Jr., *Last Exit to Brooklyn* (New York: Grove Press, 1965).
412. *Politics*: LF to AG, January 10, 1964.
412. "so gregarious" and "Be a nice boy . . .": LF to AG, April 2, 1964. Ferlinghetti's comment about Ginsberg's gregarious nature was apropos, both in the context of its mention and in a larger picture. Ginsberg, like Kerouac a few years earlier, was learning about the demands of fame. At times, he found it annoying and distracting. (See AG, "I Am the Victim of Telephone," written in June 1964, in AG, *PN*, 75; *CP*, 344.) In most cases, however, Allen enjoyed being in the vortex of the storm, his great energy and gregarious nature helping him avoid the psychological pitfalls that claimed Kerouac. Indeed, it was a matter of differing personalities.
412. "The individual soul . . .": AG, "Back to the Wall," (London) *Times Literary Suppliment*, August 6, 1964; all other citations in this section are from this essay.
413. "queer assortment . . .": "Birds, Beasts, and Bach," *Newsweek*, September 20, 1964.
413. Ken Kesey/NC: AG journal entries; AG, *Visions of the Great Rememberer*, 40–41; Bruce Cook, *The Beat Generation* (New York: Charles Scribner's Sons, 1971), 196–200.
414. "eaten away by talk . . .": AG undated journal entry.
414. "Kesey respectful . . .": AG, *Visions of the Great Rememberer*, 42.
415. "I should write . . .": AG journal entry, November 28, 1964.
416. "a magical invocation . . .": "Demonstration Held to Protest Laws Against Marijuana," *The New York Times*, December 28, 1964.
416. "I'm interested . . .": AG, "Chamberlain's Nakeds," published as part of an announcement flier for Wynn Chamberlain's February 2 to February 19, 1964, art showing at New York's Fischback Gallery.
416. "extraordinary talent" and "possibly . . .": *Naked Lunch* trial transcript, reprinted in part in WSB, *Naked Lunch*, vii–xxxvi; all citations from the trial are from this source.
417. "Don't hide the madness": AG, "On Burroughs' Work," *RS*, 40; *CP*, 114.

18. Kral Majales

418. Epigraph: AG, "Kral Majales," *PN*, 90–91; *CP*, 354.
418. "I was at last . . .": AG journal entry, January 15, 1965.
419. "I forgot how beautiful . . .": AG to Lucien Carr, January 17, 1965.
419. "I come flying . . .": AG journal entry, January 18, 1965.

419. AG in Cuba: AG journal entries; AG to LG, February 5, 1965; AG to PO, February 15, 1965; LG to AG, March 2, 1965; AG to LG, undated, ca. March 1965; AG to Lucien Carr, March 28, 1965; AG, *Gay Sunshine Interview*, 25–30; Edward Lucie-Smith, *Mystery in the Universe* (London: Turret Books, 1965), 7–8; Henry Allen, "Allen Ginsberg: Burning for the Ancient Heavenly Connection," *The Washington Post*, May 1, 1977.

419. "being treated . . .": AG journal entry, January 18, 1965.

420. "They've forgotten . . .": AG journal entry, January 20, 1965.

420. "Tell Castro": AG journal entry, 18 January 1965.

420. "That's his identification . . .": AG journal entry, January 20, 1965.

421. "Obviously I have . . .": ibid.

422. "I just shot . . .": AG, *Gay Sunshine Interview*, 26.

422. "We all know . . .": AG journal entry, January 21, 1965.

422. "ten times more natural . . .": ibid.

423. "A quasi police state . . .": AG to LG, February 5, 1965.

423. "both great and horrible . . .": AG to PO, February 4, 1965.

423. "Really sad . . .": AG undated journal entry, ca. late January 1965.

423. "The politics . . .": ibid.

424. "You must understand . . .": AG journal entry, January 30, 1965.

424. "little sketch-dramas . . .": ibid.

424. "Perhaps you don't understand . . .": AG undated journal entry, ca. late January 1965.

425. "like a woman . . .": AG, undated journal entry, ca. early February 1965.

425. "Orwellian dreamworld" and "like having . . .": AG journal entry, February 7, 1965.

425. "I hope . . .": AG journal entry, February 3, 1965.

426. "Yes, but we have . . .": ibid.

426. "They have no ideology . . .": AG, *Gay Sunshine Interview*, 27.

426. "The Beatles . . .": AG journal entry, February 3, 1965.

426. "All told . . .": AG to PO, February 15, 1965.

427. "They obviously do . . .": AG journal entry, February 4, 1965.

427. "If a big Dostoevsky . . .": AG undated journal entry, ca. early February 1965.

428. "For breaking the laws . . .": AG, *Gay Sunshine Interview*, 30, all quotations from this passage from this source.

428. "I didn't go round . . .": ibid.

429. "half Kafkian . . .": AG to LG, undated, ca. March 1965.

429. "In Cuba . . .": ibid.

429. Czechoslovakia: Walter D. Friedenberg, "Czechs Avid for Fun—Made in U.S.A," *New York World Telegram*, October 17, 1963; Paul Underwood, "Poets of Prague Challenge Party," *The New York Times*, October 20, 1963.

430. "I have enough money . . .": AG to LG, undated, ca. March 1965.

430. AG in Prague: AG journal entries; AG to LG, undated, ca. March 1965; AG to LG, March, 1965; AG to PO, March 1 and 12, 1965.

430. "19th century nostalgia . . .": AG to LG, March 1, 1965.

430. "I run around . . .": AG to LG, undated, ca. March 1965.

430. "It is too long . . .": AG, "Message," *KADDISH*, 45; *CP*, 183.

431. "I'm still alone . . .": AG, "Message II," *PN*, 82; *CP*, 348.

431. "I will be home . . .": AG, "Message."

431. "Salute beloved comrade . . .": AG, "Message II."

431. "My Slavic Soul . . .": AG, unpublished and untitled journal poem.

431. AG in Soviet Union: AG journal entries; AG to PO, March 17 and 27, 1965; AG to Lucien Carr, March 28, 1965; AG to LG, March 29 and April 10, 1965.

431. "First smell of Russia . . .": AG journal entry, March 19, 1965.

431. "Elanor and Max . . .": ibid.

431. "Mud roads . . .": ibid.

432. "Let me advise . . .": AG journal entry, March 20, 1965; all quotations from this conversation from this source.

432. "as if all . . .": ibid.

432. "I felt like . . .": ibid.

433. "After midnight . . .": AG, unpublished and untitled journal poem.

434. "the expression . . .": AG journal entry, March 21, 1965.

434. "The collective heart . . .": ibid.

435. "I saw . . .": AG journal entry, March 23, 1965, all other citations from this conversation from this source.

437. "an old veteran": AG journal entry, March 28, 1965.

438. AG in Poland: AG journal entries; AG to LG, April 10, 1965; AG to PO, May 4, 1965.

438. "O Polish spectres . . .": AG, "Café in Warsaw," *PN*, 85; *CP*, 350.

439. AG/Kral Majales: AG journal entries; AG to PO, May 4 and 10, 1965; LG to AG, May 14, 1965; AG to LG, May 21, 1965; AG to GC, June 12, 1969; "Czechs Oust Ginsberg, 'Village' Poet," *The New York Times*, May 17, 1965; "Like Split, Dig?," *New York Herald Tribune*, May 17, 1965; Jeff Endrst, "How a Beat Bard Was Beaten by the Reds as Undesirable" (Paterson) *Morning Call*, May 20, 1965; Edward Lucie-Smith, "The King of May," (London) *Sunday Times*, June 6, 1965; Dan Lewis, "Did Ginsberg Stir Czech Unrest?," (Paterson) *Morning Call*, August 6, 1968; E. Klingenberg, "Ginsberg's Czech Expulsion," *Censorship* (Summer 1965).
439. "Is it all right . . .": AG journal entry, May 5, 1965.
439. "Mr. Ginsberg . . .": ibid.
440. "I'll be the first . . .": ibid.
440. "Nobody expected . . .": AG to PO, May 4, 1965.
440. "like a big idiot politician": ibid.
441. "The one thing . . .": Lewis, "Did Ginsberg Stir," (Paterson) *Morning Call*.
441. "I couldn't figure . . .": AG to PO, May 10, 1965.
441. "We found . . .": ibid.
442. "We must inform you . . .": ibid.
442. "Due to many complaints . . .": ibid.
442. "have nothing . . ."; "proffer napalm . . ."; "And I am . . .": AG, first draft of "Kral Majales," written in journal, May 7, 1965. See final version in *PN*, 89–91; *CP*, 353–55.
443. "On May 7th . . .": Klingenberg, "Ginsberg's Czech Expulsion."
444. "Aren't you sacrificing . . .": EB to AG, May 20, 1965.
444. "Pacifism is a trap . . .": AG to Howard Schulman, August 24, 1966.
444. "What had happened . . .": AG to GC, June 12, 1969.
445. AG in England: AG journal entries; AG to PO, May 10, 1965; AG to LG, May 21, 1965; "Ginsberg Makes the World Scene," *The New York Times Magazine*, July 11, 1965; Lucie-Smith, *Mystery in the Universe*, 9.
445. AG/Dylan/Beatles: AG journal entries; AG to PO, May 10, 1965.
445. "Why don't you . . ." and "Have you ever . . .": AG undated journal entry.
446. "Travelling around . . .": AG to LG, May 21, 1965.
446. "Liverpool . . .": Lucie-Smith, *Mystery in the Universe*, 9.
446. "Be kind to your self . . .": AG, "Who Be Kind To," *PN*, 95; *CP*, 359.
446. "Be kind to your neighbor . . .": ibid.
447. "Tonite let's all . . .": AG, "Who Be Kind To," *PN*, 98–99; *CP*, 362.
447. Royal Albert Hall reading: AG journal entries; AG to (London) *Times*, June 19, 1965; Ken Smith, "Unshy Poets Meet Press," *London Daily Worker*, June 10, 1965; "Man, just dig these crazy couplets," *Daily Sketch*, June 12, 1965; "Poets, But You Wouldn't Know It," *Daily Express*, June 12, 1965; "Stirring Times," *Times Literary Supplement*, June 17, 1965; "Revolutions, flowers, and poetry," *Peace News*, June 18, 1965.
448. "a 'happening' . . .": AG to (London) *Times*, June 19, 1965.
448. MAN, JUST DIG . . .: (London) *Daily Sketch*, June 12, 1965.
448. POETS, BUT . . .: (London) *Daily Express*, June 12, 1965.
448. "I'm tired . . .": AG, unpublished and untitled journal poem.

19. Wichita Vortex Sutra

449. Epigraph: AG, "Wichita Vortex Sutra," *PN*, 126–26; *CP*, 406.
449. "These persons . . .": AG journal entry, June 29, 1965.
449. AG in Pacific Northwest: AG journal entries; AG to Barry Miles, August 18, 1965; AG to PO, September 9, 1965; AG to JK, October 1, 1965.
450. "I have nothing . . .": AG, unpublished and untitled journal poem.
450. "I am wrong . . .": AG journal entry, September 10, 1965.
451. "Very beautiful afternoon . . .": AG to LG, November 6, 1965.
451. "The day I took . . .": AG, testimony before Senate subcommittee, June 14, 1966.
452. AG and Hell's Angels: AG journal entries; AG, "How to Make a March/Spectacle," *Liberation* (January 1966); AG, "Coming to Terms with Hell's Angels," published in *The Sixties*, ed. Lynda R. Obst (New York: Rolling Stone Press, 1976), 160–162; AG to LG, November 6, 1965; AG to LG, November 19, 1965; AG to LG, November 29, 1965; "The Hell's Angels Debating Debut," *San Francisco Chronicle*, November 13, 1965; William O'Brien, "Hell's Angels Warn VDC Against Oakland March," *San Francisco Examiner*, November 13, 1965.
453. "It wasn't just . . .": AG, "Coming to Terms," in *Sixties*, 160.
453. "a spectacle . . ." and "would be heard . . .": AG, "How to Make a March/Spectacle," *Liberation*.
453. "The parade . . ." and "manifest or embody . . .": ibid.

454. "We wonder whether . . .": "Hell's Angels Debating Debut," *San Francisco Chronicle*.
454. "If there is any . . .": O'Brien, "Hell's Angels Warn," *San Francisco Examiner*.
454. "like some strange . . .": AG, "Coming to Terms," in *Sixties*, 161.
455. "simply a tone . . ." and "monosyllabic . . .": ibid.
455. "It brought . . .": ibid.
456. "a continuous barrage . . ." and "mass hypnosis": AG to LG, November 19, 1965.
456. "I was looking . . .": Dick Hallgren, "Portrait of the Artists as Old Men," *San Francisco Chronicle*, December 6, 1965.
458. "Under the bluffs . . .": AG, "Beginning of a Poem of These States," *FALL*, 1; *CP*, 369.
458. "Moon like . . .": AG, "Beginning of a . . . poem," *FALL*, 4; *CP*, 371.
458. AG in LA: AG journal entries; AG to Lucien Carr, January 28, 1966. *See also*, AG, "These States: Into L.A." (*FALL*, 9–13: *CP*, 376–79) and "A Methedrine Vision in Hollywood" (*PN*, 106–108; *CP*, 380–381).
459. "Spectacle of Afternoon . . .": AG, "Hiway Poesy: L.A.-Albuquerque-Texas-Wichita," *FALL*, 15; *CP*, 383.
459. AG in Kansas: AG journal entries; Robert Whereatt, "Poet Says City Trains, Then Stifles Its Talent" (Wichita) *Beacon*, February 6, 1966; Bart Everett, "Poet Blasts Mid-West Culture Lag," *Kansas City Star*, February 13, 1966; "Poet Allen Ginsberg Slated to Speak for Dialectica," (Wichita State) *Sunflower*, February 14, 1966; Kent Britt, "Police, Poets in Standoff," (Wichita) *Beacon*, February 17, 1966; Dan Garrity, "A Poet's Pilgrimage," (Wichita State) *Sunflower*, February 23, 1966. *See also*, AG, "Hiway Poesy: L.A.-Albuquerque-Texas-Wichita," "Chances 'R' " (*PN*, 109; *CP*, 393), and "Wichita Vortex Sutra."
459. "Onward to Wichita! . . .": AG, "Hiway Poesy L.A.-. . . ." *FALL*, 22; *CP*, 388.
460. "Kansas must love . . .": Garrity, "A Poet's Pilgrimage," *Sunflower*.
461. "O. Wilde . . ." and "more accurate . . .": AG to Lucien Carr, February 14, 1966.
461. "orange gas flares . . .": AG, "Wichita Vortex Sutra," *PN*, 110; *CP*, 394.
461. "Thy sins . . .": AG, "Wichita Vortex Sutra," *PN*, 111; *CP*, 395.
461. "No more fear . . .": AG, "Wichita Vortex Sutra," *PN*, 112; *CP*, 395.
462. "Put it on the . . .": AG, "Wichita Vortex Sutra," *PN*, 117; *CP*, 399.
462. "a short magic formula . . .": Paul Carroll, *The Poem in Its Skin* (Chicago: Big Table, 1969), reprinted in part in *On the Poetry of Allen Ginsberg*, ed. Lewis Hyde (Ann Arbor: University of Michigan Press, 1984).
462. "Black Magic language . . .": AG, "Wichita Vortex Sutra," *PN*, 119; *CP*, 401.
462. "I call all Powers . . .": AG, "Wichita Vortex Sutra," *PN*, 126; *CP*, 406.
463. "all ancient Seraphim . . .": AG, "Wichita Vortex Sutra," *PN*, 127; *CP*, 407.
463. "I lift my voice aloud . . .": ibid.
463. "As U.S. language chief . . .": AG, "News for Media: Ginsberg Prophesies End of Vietnam War," unpublished press release.
463. "So I wanted . . .": Michael Aldrich, *Improvised Poetics*, in AG, *Composed on the Tongue*, 46–47.
464. "Some of the . . .": AG, "Wichita Vortex Sutra," *PN*, 129; *CP*, 408–09.
465. "The war is over . . .": AG, "Wichita Vortex Sutra," *PN*, 132; *CP*, 411.
465. Tape transcription: Aldrich, in *Composed*, 28–30.
465. "That the rest . . .": AG, "Wichita Vortex Sutra," *PN*, 123–34; *CP*, 404.
466. "It's not the clicks . . .": Aldrich, in *Composed*, 29.
466. Leary drug bust: AG journal entries; Timothy Leary, *Flashbacks: An Autobiography* (Los Angeles: Jeremy P. Tarcher, 1983), 232–39.
467. AG, Smith, et al.: AG, "Who Are We?" (unpublished essay, in AG, Columbia deposit); "U.S. Plot to 'Set-Up' Ginsberg for Arrest Is Described to Jury," *The New York Times*, April 14, 1966; Jay Levin, "Jazzman Who Accused Feds Is Convicted," *New York Post*, April 15, 1966.
468. "the noose . . .": "U.S. Plot," *The New York Times*.
468. "Such crudity of judgment . . .": AG, "Who Are We?"
468. Millbrook raid: Leary, *Flashbacks*, 243–44. For another perspective, see G. Gordon Liddy, *Will* (New York: St. Martin's Press, 1979).
468. "obviously a high-grade . . .": Leary, *Flashbacks*, 244.
469. "poets and philosophers . . .": AG, "Committee on Poetry" news release, March 26, 1966.
469. Crackdown on the avant-garde: Sidney E. Zion, "Avant Garde Group Charges Harassment by City," *The New York Times*, April 19, 1966; Susan Kastner, "The Avant Garde Organizes to Fight City Hall," *New York Post*, April 19, 1966; Sidney E. Zion, "Lindsay Placates Coffeehouse Set," *The New York Times*, May 3, 1966.
469. "toned down": Zion, "Avant Garde Group," *The New York Times*.
469. "We want to meet . . .": Kastner, "The Avant Garde Organizes," *New York Post*.
470. "we can't compete . . .": LF to AG, March 22, 1966.
470. "stimulating and inspiring": LG to AG, May 31, 1966.
471. AG/Senate subcommittee: transcript of AG testimony before the Senate subcommittee, with

address and question/answer session, in AG Columbia deposit; "Ginsberg's LSD Lecture to Senators," *San Francisco Chronicle*, June 15, 1966; Jean M. White, "Senators Hear Ginsberg, Poet of Pot, but Indicate They Agree with Him Not," *Washington Post*, June 15, 1966; Don McNeill, "Ginsberg in Washington: Lobbying for Tenderness," *The Village Voice*, June 23, 1966. All quotations from this passage are from AG testimony transcript.

474. "Archy the Cockroach . . .": McNeill, "Ginsberg in Washington," *The Village Voice*.
475. "Some kind of psychedelic-colored expressionism": Jaqueline Pellaton, " 'Response' Panel Rambles Through Night of Effluvia", (NJ) *Sunday Times Advertiser*, April 24, 1966.
475. "It was a mardi gras . . .": Ralph J. Gleason, "An Old Joint That's Really Jumpin'," *San Francisco Chronicle*, July 20, 1966.
475. "Yes, I write . . .": AG to Barry Miles, August 5, 1966.
476. "Who's the enemy . . .": AG, "Iron Horse," *Iron Horse*, 49; *CP*, 454.
476. "Too late, too late . . .": AG, "Iron Horse," *Iron Horse*, 32; *CP*, 445.
476. "Better to meditate . . .": AG, "Iron Horse," *Iron Horse*, 33; *CP*, 446.
477. "set another whole . . .": AG to Roy, Cooperman, Leavitt, and Violi, December 3, 1966.
478. " 'Wichita Vortex Sutra' . . .": AG, "Some Metamorphoses of Personal Prosody," reprinted in *The Poetics of the New American Poetry*, eds. Donald Allen and Warren Tallman (New York: Grove Press, 1973), 348–49.

20. The Fall of America

479. Epigraph: AG, "A Vow," *FALL*, 46; *CP*, 460.
480. SF Be-In: AG, *Chicago Trial Testimony*, 3–11; Jane Kramer, *Allen Ginsberg in America* (New York: Random House, 1969), 3–37; Barry Silesky, *Ferlinghetti: The Artist in His Time* (New York: Warner Books, 1990), 149; Bruce Cook, "Scruffy Vagabonds Who Shook Up America," *National Observer*, December 9, 1968; Henry Brandon, "The New Left and the 'Hippies' Are Motivated," *Sunday Times*, January 29, 1967.
480. "the joyful, face-to-face . . .": taken from poster announcing the Human Be-In.
480. "gathering together . . .": AG, *Chicago Trial Testimony*, 4.
480. "turn onto the scene . . .": Silesky, *Ferlinghetti*, 149.
481. "We went to considerable lengths . . .": Cook, "Scruffy Vagabonds," *National Observer*.
481. "a combination guru . . ." and "a kind of ultimate . . .": Kramer, *Allen Ginsberg in America*, 9.
481. "Preaching and colonizing . . .": ibid., 10.
481. "Social and political criticism . . .": "Poet Ginsberg Plans to Rescue Poet Levy," *Cleveland Press*, April 12, 1967.
481. AG reading schedule: AG Columbia deposit.
482. Portland State debate: Hundly Goodhue, "Ginsberg Address Pending," *Vagabond* (April 1967); Larry Smith, "Ginsberg Vows Propriety," (Portland) *Oregonian*, May 19, 1967; "Nude Photo Upsets PSC" (Portland) *Oregonian*, May 29, 1967; AG to *Oregonian*, May 29, 1967 (published as "Poet Doesn't Object to Nude Photo," *Oregonian*, June 4, 1967).
482. "famous for taking . . ." and "propriety demands": Smith, "Ginsberg Vows Propriety, *Oregonian*.
482. "I am not . . .": AG to *Oregonian*, May 29, 1967.
482. "All gossip . . .": ibid. A May 28, 1967, editorial in the *Oregonian* appears to have been especially infuriating to Ginsberg and was probably the catalyst in his decision to write a long letter to the paper. The editorial condemned Ginsberg, his poetry, and the Portland State reading in the sort of lofty rhetoric Ginsberg had grown to despise: "What puzzles us about the Allen Ginsberg fuss at Portland State College is why students who must scratch for money to get an education are willing to spend it to support a weirdo who makes a good living by substituting depravity for talent." As Ginsberg pointed out in his letter to the paper, the money earned from his reading was given to starving artists through his Committee on Poetry. As for his Portland critics, he offered his own opinionated conclusion: "Reviewing the entire situation, I judge that there is a sickness of language and opinionation in Portland, a clear lack of basic information, a failed sense of humor, overwhelming anxiety for no reason—almost all official persons concerned seem subject to nineteenth century fainting spells, the official kind that our Eastern grandmothers complained of."
483. Spoleto: AG journal entries; LG to AG, July 13, 1967; AG to Lucien Carr, October 1, 1967; James Harris, "Beard, Beer, Moon: An Interview with Allen Ginsberg," *Alternative Feature Service*, September 10, 1971; "Allen Ginsberg Charged with Obscenity in Spoleto," *The New York Times*, July 10, 1967.
484. "sudden recall . . .": AG journal entry, July 9, 1967; all other citations regarding this incident are from this source.
484. "tempest in a teapot": LG to AG, July 13, 1967.

484. AG in England: AG journal entries.
485. "I stared . . .": AG journal entry, July 18, 1967.
485. "to demystify human violence . . .": George Dowden, A *Bibliography of Works by Allen Ginsberg*, (San Francisco: City Lights, 1991).
485. "ecological perspective" and "Bateson gave . . .": James McKenzie, "An Interview with Allen Ginsberg," in *The Beat Journey*, eds. Arthur and Kit Knight (California, PA: unspeakable visions of the individual, 1978), 13–14.
486. "Thru the thick wall'd window . . .": AG, first draft of "Wales Visitation" (originally entitled "Wales 1967"). Very few changes were made between the first and final drafts; the poem was published in *PN*, 139–42; *CP*, 480–82.
486. "the human things . . ."; "clarified my mind . . ."; and "Specifically, the one . . .": AG, "Firing Line" television interview with William F. Buckley, May 7, 1968, taken from transcript.
487. "A solid mass . . .": AG, "Wales Visitation" (final draft), *PN*, 140; *CP*, 480.
487. "of the satanic thistle . . .": ibid.
487. "In 'Wales Visitation' . . .": Paul Portugés, *The Visionary Poetics of Allen Ginsberg* (Santa Barbara, CA: Ross-Erikson, 1978), 122.
488. "touched . . .": LG to AG, September 12, 1967.
488. AG and Ezra Pound: AG journal entries; AG, "Encounters with Ezra Pound," in *Composed on the Tongue*, 1–17; Michael Reck, "A Conversation Between Ezra Pound and Allen Ginsberg," *Evergreen Review*; author interview with AG.
488. "Ezra, what was the name . . .": AG, "Encounters with Pound," *Composed*, 117; all other quotes from Ginsberg/Pound encounters are from this source unless otherwise indicated.
491. "a lot of double-talk": Reck, "Conversation Between Ezra Pound and Allen Ginsberg," *Evergreen Review*.
491. "often shockingly direct": ibid.
491. "At seventy . . .": ibid.
493. "old man . . .": AG, untitled journal poem, published in *Composed*, 12.
497. "There's now so much . . .": AG to PO, August 7, 1967.
497. "Who represents . . .": AG, "Pentagon Exorcism," *PN*, 143; *CP*, 483.
498. " 'The business of America . . .' ": AG, unpublished journal poem, January 1, 1968.
498. War protests: AG journal entries; Sally Kempton, "Viet Critics: They put Themselves on the Line," *The Village Voice*, January 18, 1968; "Rallying for Spock," *New York Post*, January 15, 1968; "Poet Allen Ginsberg Willing to Go to Jail for War Stand," *Paterson News*, January 18, 1968.
499. AG and Maharishi: Al Aronowitz, "The Yogi Dusts Off His Cosmic Truths," *New York Post*, January 22, 1968; Barry Miles, *Ginsberg* (New York: Simon & Schuster, 1989), 408–10.
499. "definitely dim-witted . . .": Miles, *Ginsberg*, 409.
499. "made a fool . . .": John Lennon/Paul McCartney, "Sexy Sadie" (© 1968, Northern Songs Ltd).
499. "Have you heard . . .": AG journal entry, February 10, 1968.
499. NC death: AG journal entries; Carolyn Cassady, *Off the Road* (New York: William Morrow, 1990), 415–18; William Plummer, *The Holy Goof: A Biography of Neal Cassady* (Englewood Cliffs, NJ: Prentice-Hall, 1981), 156–58.
500. "big plans" and "save": NC to AG, undated, ca. April 1967.
500. "His happy Spirit . . .": AG journal entry, February 10, 1968.
500. "I'll be glad . . .": ibid.
500. "His solid sense . . .": ibid.
501. McCarthy ceremony: AG journal entry, February 21, 1968; "Hippie Rite for Senator Isn't Grave," *Milwaukee Sentinel*, February 21, 1968; David F. Wagner, "Controversy Boils Over Ginsberg 'Exorcism' Rites" (Appleton) *Post-Crescent*, February 22, 1968; unsigned editorial, "Repulsive Action," *Milwaukee Journal*, February 22, 1968; unsigned editorial, "We Are Visited by a Poet" (Appleton) *Post-Crescent*, February 24, 1968. In retrospect, Ginsberg's actions were probably ill advised, regardless of his intentions, if for no other reason than they set a precedent he would have to address in the future. It was not uncommon for people to approach him with unusual requests that had strong political implications or repercussions—requests that he get involved in activities not unlike the McCarthy "exorcism." Although Ginsberg was never one to shy away from controversy, he was not out to create it for its own sake, either. As he grew older, he became more sensitive to becoming involved in events that might be misinterpreted or that could fuel or create political controversy. I witnessed one such incident in Milwaukee in the early 1980s, when a group of local students asked him to visit the grave of a young man who had died while in police custody. Private citizens had charged the police with brutality in the case, and there was a lot of tension connected to the issue at the time of Ginsberg's appearance in Milwaukee. Although Ginsberg listened to the students' accounts of the story and was generally sympathetic, he declined a visit to the cemetery.
501. "a leading example . . .": Wagner, "Controversy Boils Over," *Post-Crescent*.

501. "the ultimate . . .": unsigned editorial, "Repulsive Action," *Milwaukee Journal*.
501. "beautiful" and "great goofy tender . . .": LF to AG, February 2, 1968.
501. "one of the greatest . . ." and "the English . . .": LF to AG, March 3, 1968.
502. "Shit, Violence . . .": AG, "Chicago to Salt Lake by Air," *FALL*, 80; *CP*, 491.
502. "He said that politics . . .": AG, *Chicago Trial Testimony*, 6.
503. "the feeling of humanity . . .": ibid., 5.
504. AG and Robert Kennedy: Arthur M. Schlesinger, Jr., *Robert Kennedy and His Times* (New York: Ballantine Books, 1978), 880–81. All quotations from this meeting are from this source.
505. "So be it . . .": JK to AG, June 4, 1968.
505. "drunken ghost": AG undated journal entry.
505. "atrocious visions . . .": AG journal entry, May 5, 1968.
505. "a succession . . ." and "a garrulous monologue . . .": Thomas Lask, "Run to Nowhere," *The New York Times*, February 17, 1968.
505. "shamelessly obvious" and "Kerouac's ultimate charm . . .": Melvin Maddocks, "Hit the space bar and GO!," *Christian Science Monitor*, March 21, 1968.
506. "chant from skull . . .": AG, "A Prophecy," *FALL*, 87; *CP*, 496.
506. "poetry is the best . . .": AG journal entry, May 5, 1968.
506. "not my language . . .": AG, "A Prophecy," *FALL*, 87; *CP*, 496.
506. "Tender spirit . . .": AG, "Eulogy for Neal Cassady," *FALL*, 75–76; *CP*, 487–88.
506. "Please master . . .": AG, "Please Master," *FALL*, 84; *CP*, 494.
507. AG in Mexico: AG to Lucien Carr, July 17 and August 17, 1968.
508. "He asked me . . .": AG, *Chicago Trial Testimony*, 25.
508. Chicago convention: AG journal entries; AG, *Chicago Trial Testimony*; Norman Mailer, *Miami and the Siege of Chicago* (New York: New American Library, 1968); Mark L. Levine, George C. McNamee, and Daniel Greenberg, eds., *The Tales of Hoffman* (New York: Bantam Books, 1970); Paul Carroll, "Playboy Interview with Allen Ginsberg," *Playboy*, April 1969; author interview with AG; author interview with Richard Seaver. All citations, unless otherwise noted, are from *Chicago Trial Testimony*.
509. "The event . . .": Mailer, *Miami and the Siege*, 131.
510. "some of the Maoists . . .": Carroll, "Playboy Interview," *Playboy*.
510. "But vain the sword . . .": William Blake, "The Grey Monk," David V. Erdman, ed., *The Poetry and Prose of William Blake* (Garden City, NY: Doubleday, 1965), 481.
511. "Will you please . . .": Carroll, "Playboy Interview," *Playboy*.
511. "It felt like grace . . .": ibid.
512. "The counterrevolution . . .": Mailer, *Miami and the Siege*, 149.
515. "They attacked . . .": ibid., 169.
516. "Who wants to be . . .": AG, "Grant Park: August 28 1968," *FALL*, 101; *CP*, 507.
517. "The whole convention . . .": Carroll, "Playboy Interview," *Playboy*.
517. "shoddy sleight-of-hand shell game": ibid.
517. "In principle . . .": *Rights in Conflict* (a reprint of the Walker Report) (New York: Signet Books, 1968), xiv.

21. Memory Gardens

521. Epigraph: AG, "Memory Gardens," *FALL*, 135; *CP*, 534.
521. "Ginsberg stands . . .": Alan Brownjohn, "Fblup!," *New Statesman*, January 10, 1969.
522. "forget the mysticism . . .": ibid.
522. "Ginsberg has made . . .": Paul Zweig, "A Music of Angels," *The Nation*, March 10, 1969.
522. "selectively reckless" and "the marvel . . .": ibid.
522. "First time . . ." and "lovely, finally . . .": AG to Philip Whalen, October 30, 1968.
523. AG's music: AG journal entries; AG to Barry Miles, September 24, October 7, and November 17, 1968; author interview with AG.
523. "a rock dimension": AG to Barry Miles, October 7, 1968.
524. AG auto accident: AG journal entries; AG, "Car Crash," *FALL*, 102–05; *CP*, 508–10; " 'Guru' Ginsberg, Beat Poet, Injured in Albany Accident," (Albany) *Knickerbocker News*, November 30, 1968; "Allen Ginsberg Resting After Crash Injuries," (Paterson) *Morning Call*, December 2, 1968; Bill Kennedy, "Life, Death, a Bodystump—Ginsberg in Demerol," *Albany Times-Union*, December 5, 1968; Bill Kennedy, "Ginsberg's Albany Pain, Jordan Pain," *Albany Times-Union*, December 22, 1968.
524. "What happens . . .": Kennedy, "Ginsberg's Albany Pain," *Albany Times-Union*.
524. AG reading schedule: AG Columbia deposit.
525. "Poe! D'jya prophesy . . .": AG, "To Poe: Over the Planet, Air Albany-Baltimore," *FALL*, 110–11; *CP*, 514.

526. "a burden": AG to Barry Miles, April 11, 1969.
526. Blake album: AG journal entries; AG, liner notes for *William Blake's Songs of Innocence and of Experience Tuned by Allen Ginsberg* (MGM/Verve); AG to Barry Miles, April 11, 1969; Barry Miles to AG, May 22 and December 10, 1969; Michael Aldrich, "A Sigh Is a Sword," *The Spectrum*, May 1, 1970; author interview with AG.
526. "Allen knew . . .": Barry Miles to AG, December 10, 1969.
526. "feeling and interpretation . . .": ibid.
526. "The purpose . . .": AG, Blake album liner notes.
527. "It's a beautiful record . . .": Ellin Willis, *The New Yorker*, December 12, 1970.
527. "I didn't think . . ." and "Plant the flag . . .": AG, "In a Moonlit Hermit's Cabin," *FALL*, 128; *CP*, 527.
527. "Ultimately, I wake . . .": AG undated journal entry, ca. July 1969.
527. "more eager . . .": AG to Dave Haselwood, September 11, 1969.
527. "I am sick . . .": ibid.
528. "I wake mornings . . .": AG journal entry, August 15, 1969.
528. "Confronting my father's poems . . .": AG, "Confrontation with Louis Ginsberg's Poems," introduction to Louis Ginsberg, *Morning in Spring and Other Poems* (New York: William Morrow, 1970).
529. "Strict puritanism . . .": AG, unpublished draft of letter in defense of *New York Review of Sex and Politics*, in AG Columbia deposit.
529. "As we have gone . . .": ibid.
529. "Houston in its space age . . .": AG, "Proclamation for Houston Peace Rally," September 8, 1969, in AG Columbia deposit.
529. "If Peter and I . . .": AG journal entry, September 5, 1969.
529. Death of JK: AG journal entries; JCH, "Gone in October," *Playboy*, February 1973; Eric Ehrmann and Stephen Davis, "There Is Really Nothing Inside," *Rolling Stone*, November 29, 1969.
530. "Nothing any interviewer . . .": Ann Charters, *Kerouac* (New York: Warner Books, 1973), 351.
530. "What he had done . . .": JCH, "Gone in October," *Playboy*.
530. "I think I'll drop out . . .": JK, "After Me, The Deluge," *Newsday*, October 25, 1969.
531. "He didn't live . . .": AG undated journal entry.
531. "You don't have . . .": JCH, "Gone in October," *Playboy*.
531. "Poor! . . .": JK, "211th Chorus," in *Mexico City Blues* (New York: Grove Press, 1959), 211.
531. "See, there's your . . .": JCH, "Gone in October," *Playboy*.
531. "Stop the murder . . .": JK, "242nd Chorus," in *Mexico City Blues*, 244.
531. "smiling with the healing . . .": JCH, "Gone in October," *Playboy*.
531. "Well, he was . . .": ibid.
532. "He introduced . . .": "A Memorial for Kerouac by Ginsberg," *New York Post*, October 23, 1969.
532. "So he drank . . .": ibid.
532. "the upheaval in values . . .": Joseph Lelyveld, *The New York Times*, October 22, 1969.
532. "the figure of Jack Kerouac . . .": "Polarity finder," *Christian Science Monitor*, October 24, 1969.
532. "All of you . . .": JCH, "Gone in October," *Playboy*.
533. "Touch him . . .": ibid.
533. "the first glimpse . . .": AG to *Playboy*, May 1973.
533. "looked like his father . . .": AG to Carolyn Cassady, February 19, 1970.
533. "Our hope and prayer . . .": "Over 200 at Mass Honor Jack Kerouac," *The New York Times*, October 25, 1969.
534. "Don't understand . . .": JCH, "Gone in October," *Playboy*.
534. "Kerouac's white stocky body . . .": AG undated journal entry, ca. early November 1969.
534. "looking cute . . ." and "Pray for me . . .": AG journal entry, November 10, 1969.
534. "threw up his hands . . .": AG, "Memory Gardens," *FALL*, 132; *CP*, 531.
534. "Everything else . . .": AG, "Memory Gardens," *FALL*, 135; *CP*, 534.
535. Chicago Conspiracy Trial: AG journal entries; AG, *Chicago Trial Testimony*; Nicholas von Hoffman, "The Chicago Conspiracy Circus," *Playboy*, June 1970; "Chicago Trial Hears Om-inous Note," *Philadelphia Evening Bulletin*, December 13, 1969; "Guru and Judge," *The New York Times*, December 14, 1969; author interview with AG.
535. "From reading . . .": Von Hoffman, "Chicago Conspiracy Circus," *Playboy*.
535. "a refined form . . .": ibid.
535. "Oh, your Honor . . .": AG, *Chicago Trial Testimony*; all other citations from Ginsberg's testimony are from this source, which is a complete and unedited transcript of his testimony.
537. AG in Miami: "Loud, Profane Vie in Miami Stadium," *Denver Post*, December 23, 1969; Carolyn Jay Wright, "Ginsberg Will Ask U.S. to Order His Poetry Concert Rescheduled," *Miami News*, December 25, 1969; "Censorship by the Bay," *Miami News*, December 26, 1969; A. L. Lieber, "Ginsberg Affair Is a Blot," *Miami Herald*, December 27, 1969; Ian Glass, "Poet finally does his thing: %?&¼&," *Miami Herald*, January 3, 1970; David Nelson, "Ginsberg Reads, Lights Stay

On," *Miami Herald*, January 3, 1970; Jack Roberts, "Double Standard in Ginsberg Case," *Miami News*, January 5, 1970; John Keasler, "Ginsberg recital better than counting sheep," *Miami News*, January 5, 1970.

538. "It was not . . .": "Loud, Profane Vie in Miami Stadium," *Denver Post*.
538. "The city's performance . . .": "Censorship by the Bay," *Miami News*.
538. "I find the entire . . .": Lieber, "Ginsberg Affair Is a Blot," *Miami Herald*.
538. "Let's face it . . .": Roberts, "Double Standard in Ginsberg Case," *Miami News*.

22. First Blues

539. Epigraph: AG, "Macdougal Street Blues," *First Blues*, 19.
539. "no home . . .": AG journal entry, May 9, 1970.
540. AG/taxes: AG journal entries; Robert Wolf, "Withholding Taxes," *Manhattan Tribune*, February 14, 1970; Chris Williams, "Pacifist War on the IRS," *New York Post*, March 3, 1970; "Ginsberg Won't Pay for Vietnam," *Chinook*, March 26, 1970.
540. "the right to . . .": Wolf, "Withholding Taxes," *Manhattan Tribune*.
540. "short-circuit . . .": Williams, "Pacifist War on the IRS," *New York Post*.
540. "I am willing . . .": Wolf, "Withholding Taxes," *Manhattan Tribune*.
540. "As I would not see . . .": AG to LG, February 15, 1970.
541. "educational picnic" and "I would say . . .": "20,000 in Park for Earth Day," *Philadelphia Evening Bulletin*, April 23, 1970.
541. "I don't know . . .": AG to Philip Whalen, May 22, 1970.
541. "All day I read . . .": AG, "Catastrophe," unpublished journal poem, June 17, 1970.
543. Early drug research: AG journal entries; AG, "Continuation of Notes on Tim Leary's Public Career and Politics of Ecstasy" (unpublished); AG to LG, February 15, May 5, and May 27, 1970.
543. Summer at Cherry Valley: AG undated journal entries; AG to Barry Miles, February 2, 1970; AG to LF, July 13, 1970; AG to GC, August 14, 1970. *See also*, Barry Miles, *Ginsberg* (New York: Simon & Schuster, 1989), 431–35—the biographer's personal account of the time he spent at Cherry Valley during that period.
544. "Gregory here . . .": AG journal entry, July 13, 1970.
544. "Ginsberg's slow growth . . .": Jerry Kamstra, *San Francisco Chronicle*, July 5, 1970.
544. "a veritable Niagara . . ." and "Ah, Allen . . .": LG, untitled review of *Indian Journals*, *WIN*, September 17, 1970.
544. "the sudden easy . . .": Reed Whittemore, "From 'Howl' to OM," *The New Republic*, July 25, 1970.
544. "the kind of cheaply acquired . . ." and "like a new . . .": ibid.
545. AG meditation: AG journal entries; AG to Philip Whalen, December 21, 1970.
545. "All more than I can complete . . .": AG journal entry, November 7, 1970.
545. AG recorded poems: AG journal entries; author interview with AG. Miles's work on this project was not only commendable but bordered on the heroic. Not only had he found a way to work amid the tension at Cherry Valley during the summer of 1970 but that fall, while working on the tapes at Ginsberg's Greenwich Village apartment, he was held up at gunpoint, a harrowing experience that necessitated his move from the apartment to a hotel. The disarray of the archive made Miles's task a daunting one, and while Ginsberg did pay Miles for his work, there is little doubt that, given the number of hours involved and the difficulty of the task, Miles's work was mostly a labor of love. Unfortunately, the tapes—converted into a sixteen-album set—have not been issued, although there have been substantial inquiries about them over the years.
546. Sinclair trial: AG journal entries; AG to LG, January 18, 1971; Jeffrey Hadden, " 'Beat' poet testifies in CIA case," *Detroit News*, January 15, 1971; Lee Winfrey, "Defense Seeks 18-Year-Olds for White Panther Jury," *Detroit Free Press*, January 16, 1971; Agis Salpakas, "Detroit Radicals Face Bomb Trial," *The New York Times*, January 17, 1971.
546. "the fantasies . . .": Winfrey, "Defense Seeks," *Detroit Free Press*.
546. "There is generally . . .": Salpakas, "Detroit Radicals," *The New York Times*.
546. "This apocalyptic sense . . .": ibid.
546. AG and NBA: AG journal entries; AG to National Book Award judges, January 20, 1971 (reprinted as "Allen Ginsberg and Richard Howard, 1971 National Book Award Poetry Judges, Explain Themselves," *The New York Times*, April 4, 1971); William McPherson, "Mr. Bellow's 3rd Award," *The Washington Post*, March 3, 1971; George Gent, "Bellow Wins 3rd National Book Award," *The New York Times*, March 3, 1971; "Poetess Mona Van Duyn Rebuts Ginsberg's Attack on Her Award," *Paterson Evening News*, March 6, 1971.
547. "historic overwhelming genius": AG to NBA judges, January 20, 1971.
547. "So what are you proposing? . . .": ibid.

547. "The jurors' opinion . . .": McPherson, "Mr. Bellow's 3rd Award," *The Washington Post*.
547. "I notice . . .": "Poetess Mona Van Duyn Rebuts Ginsberg's Attack," *Paterson Evening News*.
547. "You make out . . .": "Allen Ginsberg and Richard Howard," *The New York Times*.
548. AG and Richard Helms: AG journal entries; Flora Lewis, "CIA and Drugs," syndicated *Los Angeles Times* column, May 6, 1971; Steve Levine, "All of Us Have a Stake in Allen Ginsberg's Bet," *Denver Post*, June 6, 1971.
548. "Materialism in America . . .": "Allen Ginsberg," *Action*, March 20, 1971.
549. AG at Kent State: AG journal entries; AG to LG, April 8 and 12, 1971.
550. "Oh, that's because . . .": author interview with AG, all other quotations, unless otherwise noted, from author conversations with Ginsberg.
550. "It reminded me . . .": James T. Harris, "Interview with Allen Ginsberg," *Alternative Feature Service*, September 10, 1971.
552. Completion of books: AG journal entries; AG to LG, August 19, 1971; AG to Lucien Carr, August 19, 1971. The various drafts, manuscripts, and notes for these books can be located in AG's Columbia deposit.
552. *The Gates of Wrath*: AG, "Hindsight," *GW*, 56; *CP*, 813.
553. "Thanks for this gift . . .": AG journal entry, June 30, 1971.
553. Leary in Switzerland: Donavan Bess, "Writers Petition Swiss to Give Asylum to Leary," *San Francisco Chronicle*, July 15, 1971. *See also*, Timothy Leary, *Flashbacks: An Autobiography* (Los Angeles: Jeremy P. Tarcher, 1983), 311–31.
554. Living Theatre: AG, "On Living Theatre Mass Imprisonment in Brazil" (undated press release); AG, "The Living Theatre" (press release, July 23, 1971); John L. Wasserman, "Living Theatre's Terrible Plight," *San Francisco Chronicle*, July 30, 1971; "Skits, March Staged for Jailed Group," *San Francisco Chronicle*, July 31, 1971; "Living Poorly," *Good Times*, August 6, 1971.
554. Spoleto: "Italy to Try Ginsberg—Obscenity," *San Francisco Examiner*, July 18, 1971; Albin Krebs, "Notes on People," *The New York Times*, July 20, 1971.
554. "America has the bureaucratic . . .": "Skits, March Staged," *San Francisco Chronicle*.
555. AG in India: AG journal entries; AG to LG, August 19, 1971; AG to Philip Whalen, August 31, 1971; AG to LG, September 14, 1971; AG to Lucien Carr, September 16, 1971; AG to Barry Miles, September 25, 1971; AG to LG, September 30, 1971.
555. "Wet processions . . .": AG, "September on Jessore Road," *FALL*, 184; *CP*, 571.
555. "Where are the helicopters . . .": AG, "September on Jessore Road," *FALL*, 186; *CP*, 573.
556. Fantasy contract: AG to Barry Miles, September 25, 1971. Unfortunately, neither of these recordings was released by Fantasy.
556. AG and John Lennon: AG journal entry, October 9, 1971; AG to Barry Miles, October 12, 1971.
556. "Wait a minute . . .": AG journal entry, October 9, 1971.
557. "a tiny . . .": AG to Barry Miles, October 12, 1971.
557. "What was interesting . . .": ibid.
557. "I think probably . . .": ibid.
557. AG and Bob Dylan: AG journal entries; AG, "Explanation of First Blues," *First Blues*, ii–iii; AG, "The Ginsberg Gallimaufry" (liner notes to *First Blues*, Hammond Records); AG to Barry Miles, November 19 and December 6, 1971; author interview with AG.
557. "Can you always . . .": author interview with AG.
558. "I'm going down . . .": AG, "Vomit Express," *First Blues*, 1. The title of this song was subsequently changed to "Going Down to Puerto Rico (Vomit Express)."
558. "Why don't we go . . .": author interview with AG.
558. "How far . . .": ibid.
559. "a whole lot . . .": AG to Barry Miles, December 6, 1971.
559. "What happy madness": ibid.
559. "Traditionally, the popular songs . . .": author interview with AG.
559. "to write a poem . . .": ibid.
560. Sinclair benefit: AG journal entries; AG to Barry Miles, December 6, 1971; Bill Gray, "15,000 at Ann Arbor rally to aid John Sinclair," *Detroit News*, December 11, 1971; Roy Reynolds, "15,000 Attend Sinclair Rally," *Ann Arbor News*, December 11, 1971. *See also*, John Wiener, *Come Together* (New York: Random House, 1984), 187–96.
561. "the great breakthrough . . .": Wiener, *Come Together*, 195.

23. The Lion of Dharma

562. Epigraph: AG, "On Neruda's Death," *MB*, 25; *CP*, 607.
562. *Kaddish* (play): AG journal entries; Israel Shanker, "The Life and Rhymes of Ginsberg the Elder," *The New York Times*, February 13, 1972; Julius Novick, "After 'Kaddish's' Poetry Goes, What Is

Left?," *The New York Times*, February 20, 1972; Jack Kroll, untitled review, *Newsweek*, February 21, 1972; "Allen Ginsberg Remembers Mama," *The New York Times*, February 20, 1972.

562. "My respect . . .": Novick, "After 'Kaddish's' Poetry Goes," *The New York Times*.
562. "the Chelsea Theater . . .": Kroll, *Newsweek* review.
563. "overwhelming": Alfred G. Aronowitz, "Pop Scene," *New York Post*, August 15, 1972.
563. "They used some . . .": Shanker, "The Life and Rhymes," *The New York Times*.
563. AG in Australia: AG journal entries; AG to LG, February 29 and March 7, 1972; AG to Lucien Carr, March 8, 1972; AG to LG, March 16, 1972; AG to Lucien Carr, March 17, 1972; AG to LG, March 24, 1972; AG to Lucien Carr, March 27, 1972; Michael Shmith, "Ginsberg turns to music," *Melbourne Herald*, March 18, 1972; Frances McLean, "Avant garde poet's plea for the Dreamtime," *Sydney Morning Herald*, March 20, 1972. *See also*, Neeli Cherkovski, *Ferlinghetti: A Biography* (New York: Doubleday, 1979), 197–98.
563. "Big happy concerts . . .": AG to Lucien Carr, March 17, 1972.
564. "It's a great tragedy . . .": McLean, "Avant garde poet's plea," *Sydney Morning Herald*.
564. "more efforts . . .": ibid.
564. "Great empty blue sky . . .": AG to Lucien Carr, March 27, 1972.
564. "Sorrowful Jack . . .": AG journal entry, March 24, 1972.
565. "The reason I wound up . . .": AG, unpublished lecture, taken from transcript, in AG Columbia deposit.
565. "Remember, the silence . . .": author interview with AG.
566. "The relationship . . .": AG, unpublished lecture.
566. "Your drunken behavior . . ." and "I come from . . .": Eliot Weinberger, "Dharma Demagogy," *The Nation*, April 19, 1980.
566. Buddhist vows: AG journal entries; author interview with AG.
567. "Reading this book . . .": AG, *The Visions of the Great Rememberer*, 18.
567. "So I survived . . .": ibid., 1.
567. "trying desperately . . .": AG, "The Great Rememberer," introduction to JK, *Visions of Cody* (New York: McGraw-Hill, 1972), viii.
568. AG and Henry Kissinger: AG undated journal entry; author interview with AG.
568. Miami convention: AG journal entries; AG, "Television Address 1972," unpublished, in AG Columbia deposit; AG, "Ah, Wake Up!" *Newsday*, August 27, 1972. *See also*, Norman Mailer, *St. George and the Godfather* (New York: New American Library, 1972).
569. "A few police-infiltrated . . .": AG, "Television Address 1972."
569. "science-fiction style . . .": ibid.
570. "Wandering up & down . . .": AG journal entry, June 4, 1972.
570. "What good is . . .": AG, "To Marpa & Chögyam," unpublished journal poem.
571. "body stump": Bill Kennedy, "Life, Death, a Bodystump—Ginsberg in Demerol," *Albany Times-Union*, December 5, 1968.
571. "the body itself . . .": AG journal entry, February 8, 1973.
571. "Help me . . .": AG journal entry, February 11, 1973.
571. "What would you do . . .": AG, "What Would You Do if You Lost It?," AG, *Allen Verbatim*, 237.
572. "Ginsberg has become . . .": Helen Vendler, untitled review of *The Fall of America*, *The New York Times*, April 15, 1973.
572. "Ginsberg's avalanche . . .": ibid.
572. "Allen Ginsberg has taken the job . . .": Ned Abramson, untitled review of *The Fall of America*, *Footnotes* (undated).
572. "*The Fall of America* confirms . . .": Lyman Andrews, "Tones of Voices," (London) *Sunday Times*, April 15, 1973.
572. "Ginsberg is by now . . .": untitled review of *The Fall of America*, *Choice*, June 1973.
572. "It's like . . .": AG to LG, May 9, 1973.
572. Leary: AG journal entries; AG, "Declaration of Independence for Dr. Timothy Leary"; AG, "Mock Sestina: The Conspiracy Against Dr. Tim Leary"; AG to *San Francisco Examiner*, June 1, 1973; Dexter Waugh, "Ginsberg Sings the Blues," *San Francisco Examiner*, June 4, 1973; Timothy Leary, *Flashbacks: An Autobiography* (Los Angeles: Jeremy P. Tarcher, 1983), 328–331.
573. "Leary is one . . .": Waugh, "Ginsberg Sings the Blues," *San Francisco Examiner*.
573. "In fact . . .": AG to *San Francisco Examiner*, June 1, 1973.
573. "Watergate gives me . . .": Waugh, "Ginsberg Sings the Blues," *San Francisco Examiner*.
573. "If Lennon/Ono disappear . . ." AG, "Lennon and Yoko's Poetic Tradition," *Changes* #86 (1973).
574. AG in Europe: AG journal entries; AG to LG, June 26, July 1, July 5, and August 8, 1973; AG to Lucien Carr, August 14, 1973; AG to Philip Whalen, August 14, 1973.
574. "You were lucky . . .": AG to LG, July 5, 1973.
575. "lovely place": AG to Philip Whalen, August 14, 1973.
575. Teton Village: AG journal entries; AG to LG, July 5, September 17, September 21, October 14, and December 1, 1973; AG to Philip Whalen, December 1, 1973.

575. "That'll be the first . . .": AG to LG, July 5, 1973.
576. "Sun pink . . .": AG journal entry, September 17, 1973.
576. "By force of will . . .": AG journal entry, September 21, 1973.
576. "Annihilate body thought . . .": AG journal entry, September 25, 1973.
577. "my breath through nostril . . .": AG, "Mind Breaths," MB, 27; CP, 609.
578. ". . . Your poetry long . . .": AG, undated and untitled journal poem.
578. "Oh, no, I get . . .": AG journal entry, September 30, 1973.
579. "in meditation silent . . .": ibid.
579. "emptiness": Randi Henderson, "Ginsberg wonders why it's worse," *Baltimore Sun*, October 19, 1973.
579. "The experience of loss . . .": ibid.
579. "big neurotic trip" and "The left went wrong . . .": ibid.
579. "The Beat Generation . . .": AG journal entry, September 28, 1973.

24. Ego Confessions

581. Epigraph: AG, "Manifesto," MB, 40; CP, 617.
581. "It's a question . . .": AG to LG, October 1, 1973.
581. "It's a case . . .": ibid.
581. "Mid-east battlegods": AG, back cover copy for *Mind Breaths*.
581. "Both Gods Terrible . . .": AG, "Jaweh and Allah Battle," MB, 36; CP, 614.
582. "atrocity . . ." and "a master . . .": Letters to the Editor, *Los Angeles Times*, April 17, 1974.
582. "balderdash . . ." and "for those . . .": ibid.
582. AG in North Dakota: Michael Vadnie, "7 'Beat' poets appear at 'City Lights in N.D,' " *Grand Forks Herald*, March 19, 1974; Stuart Smith, " 'Beat Generation' poets lash out against dehumanization," *Grand Forks Herald*, March 20, 1974; Stuart Smith, "Poets seek new world view in readings," *Grand Forks Herald*, March 21, 1974; Michael Vadnie, "Beat poet delights large crowd," *Grand Forks Herald*, March 22, 1974; Stuart Smith, "Rexroth recites variety of poems," *Grand Forks Herald*, March 22, 1974; Michael Vadnie and Stuart Smith, "Poet recalls movement at conference," *Grand Forks Herald*, March 22, 1974; Stuart Smith and Michael Vadnie, "Writers conference ends with reading of classic poem," *Grand Forks Herald*, March 24, 1974; Michael Vadnie and Stuart Smith, "Views on the writers conference," *Grand Forks Herald*, March 24, 1974; "U writers meet, awarded grants," *Grand Forks Herald*, March 27, 1974.
582. "The function of poetry . . .": unpublished transcript of open-mike session, "City Lights in North Dakota," in AG Columbia deposit.
583. "The Beats . . .": Smith and Vadnie, "Writers conference ends," *Grand Forks Herald*.
583. "The insights . . .": ibid.
583. "an aggressive hypocrisy . . .": AG, "Acceptance Speech for the National Book Award," delivered April 18, 1974.
583. "We have all contributed . . .": ibid.
584. "jail, torture, death . . .": William Gildea, "Voices of Freedom Protesting," *Washington Post*, April 30, 1974.
584. "an examination . . .": ibid.
584. AG building cabin: AG journal entries; AG to LG, June 1, June 13, July 10, July 22, August 13, and September 8, 1974; AG to GC, September 9, 1974; AG to LG, September 30, 1974. *See also,* AG, *Sad Dust Glories*.
584. "Peter labors . . .": AG to LG, June 13, 1974.
584. "Hard work . . .": AG to LG, July 10, 1974.
585. Poetics school at Naropa: AG journal entries; AG to LG, August 13, 1974; J.D. Friedman, "Disembodied Tribute to Jack Kerouac," *Drummer*, August 26, 1975; author interview with AG; author interview with Anne Waldman.
585. "a hundred-year project": author interview with Anne Waldman.
586. "It seemed attractive . . .": Friedman, "Disembodied Tribute," *Drummer*.
586. "I'll probably spend . . .": AG to LG, August 13, 1974.
587. "It's so beautiful . . .": AG to LG, September 8, 1974.
587. "I don't think . . .": ibid.
587. "I want to be known . . .": AG, "Ego Confession," MB, 46; CP, 623.
588. "politically unwise": Paul Portugés, *The Visionary Poetics of Allen Ginsberg* (Santa Barbara, CA: Ross-Erikson, 1978), 152.
589. "Where's the money? . . .": AG, "Mugging," MB, 51; CP, 626; all other citations from this episode are from this source.
589. Textbook controversy: David Jolliffe, "Poet Allen Ginsberg Comments on Textbook Protest,"

(Wheeling, WV) *News-Register*, November 10, 1974; Frank T. Csongos, "Protest Held on Textbooks," *News-Register*, November 10, 1974; W. Robert Weller, "Disputed Texts Present Updated Issues, Roles," *News-Register*, December 15, 1974.

590. "I would rather . . .": Csongos, "Protest Held," *News-Register*.
590. "They will have . . .": Weller, "Disputed Texts," *News-Register*.
590. "I'm flattered . . .": Jolliffe, "Poet Allen Ginsberg Comments," *News-Register*.
590. "I'd be willing . . .": ibid.
591. "My own skeleton . . .": AG journal entry, January 20, 1975.
591. "His genius intuition's . . .": AG journal entry, January 22, 1975.
591. "What an unexpected victory . . .": ibid.
591. "First time . . .": AG to Philip Whalen, March 15, 1975.
591. Columbia reading: Lewis Grossberger, "Return of 'Beatnik Dope Fiends,' " *New York Post*, April 18, 1975.
591. "the best poems . . .": ibid.
592. Florida and Montreal symposiums: AG journal entries.
592. "A gauzy dusk . . .": AG, first draft of "Hospital Window." *See also*, final version of poem in *MB*, 58; *CP*, 634.
593. AG in Colorado: AG journal entries.

25. Rolling Thunder Stones, Father Death Blues

594. Epigraph: AG, "Don't Grow Old" ("Father Death Blues") *MB*, 83; *CP*, 655.
595. Rolling Thunder tour: AG journal entries; AG to LG, October 27, 1975, November 4 and November 10, 1975; AG to Lucien Carr, November 10, 1975; AG to LG, November 18, 1975; Sam Shepard, *Rolling Thunder Logbook* (New York: Viking Press, 1977); Larry Sloman, *On the Road with Bob Dylan* (New York: Bantam, 1978); Robert Shelton, *No Direction Home: The Life and Music of Bob Dylan* (New York: William Morrow, 1986); Nat Hentoff, "The Pilgrims Have Landed on Kerouac's Grave," *Rolling Stone*, January 15, 1976; Jim Jerome, "Even Robert Zimmerman sometimes must have to stand naked," *New Musical Express*, January 31, 1976; Richard Corliss, "Rolling Thunder Reviewed," *New Times*, February 20, 1976; Michael McClure, "The Poet's Poet," *Rolling Stone*, March 14, 1976; Peter Chowka, "This is Allen Ginsberg?," *New Age Journal*, April 1976; Henry Allen, "A Terrible Masterpiece," *Washington Post*, May 1, 1977; author interview with AG.
596. "What do you want . . .": AG journal entry, October 29, 1975.
596. "Your songs . . .": ibid.
596. "You haven't found . . .": ibid.
596. Ideas for Rolling Thunder Revue: AG journal entries.
596. Dylan and Kerouac: Dylan always credited Kerouac and Ginsberg as being major influences when he was growing up in Minnesota. In the liner notes to *Biograph*, he talks about the period during which he discovered poetry: "There was always a lot of poems recited . . . T. S. Eliot, e. e. cummings. It was sort of like that and it kind of woke me up. . . . Suzie Rotolo, a girlfriend of mine in New York, later turned me on to all the French poets but for then it was Jack Kerouac, Ginsberg, Corso and Ferlinghetti—*Gasoline, Coney Island of the Mind*. . . . Oh, man it was wild—*I saw the best minds of my generation destroyed by madness* that said more to me than any of the stuff I'd been raised on. *On the Road*, Dean Moriarty, this made perfect sense to me."
597. "exploding with crazies": Shepard, *Logbook*, 16.
597. "We haven't even . . .": ibid.
597. "close to being volcanic": ibid., 28.
598. "every molecule . . .": ibid., 31–32.
598. "Dylan somewhat . . .": AG to Lucien Carr, November 10, 1975.
598. "We have . . .": Shelton, *No Direction Home*, 524.
598. "We're landing . . .": AG journal entry, October 29, 1975.
599. "Well, how do you . . .": ibid.
600. "Born in this world . . .": AG, "Gospel Noble Truths," *MB*, 71; *CP*, 641.
600. "suffering, change/transiency . . .": Chowka, "This is Allen Ginsberg?" *New Age Journal*.
601. "I don't know . . .": ibid.
601. "Lay down . . .": AG, "Rolling Thunder Stones," *MB*, 73; *CP*, 643.
602. "This thing . . ." Shepard, *Logbook*, 90.
602. "What can you do . . .": AG, undated journal entry.
602. "There was this brilliant . . .": Chowka, "This is Allen Ginsberg?" *New Age Journal*.
602. "It used to be . . .": Jerome, "Even Robert Zimmerman," *New Musical Express*.
603. "When Music was needed . . .": AG, "Rolling Thunder Stones," *MB*, 74; *CP*, 643.

604. "This tour may not . . .": Hentoff, "The Pilgrims Have Landed," *Rolling Stone.*
604. "We give thanks . . .": AG, "Rolling Thunder Stones," MB, 75; CP, 644.
605. "rewrite Howl . . ." and "I saw the best . . .": AG undated journal entry, ca. late November 1975.
605. "dance, history . . .": AG to LG, November 18, 1975.
605. "The tour has been . . .": ibid.
605. "Dylan's Redemption Songs! . . .": AG, liner notes for Bob Dylan's album *Desire.*
606. "an innocent man . . .": Bob Dylan, "Hurricane," Ram's Horn Music, 1975.
606. "on an accelerated basis": "Hurricane Carter's Bid for New Trial Gets Boost," *The New York Times,* November 7, 1975.
606. "This Bob Dylan . . ." and "Now I just want . . .": Shepard, *Logbook,* 171.
607. "I thank you . . .": Shelton, *No Direction Home,* 534.
607. LG illness: AG journal entries; AG, "Don't Grow Old," MB, 79; CP, 651; AG, " 'Don't Grow Old,' " PO, 50–53; CP, 710.
607. "Don't ever get old": AG, " 'Don't Grow Old,' " PO, 51; CP, 710.
607. "Gates of Ages": AG journal entry, January 7, 1976.
607. "too tired . . .": AG, " 'Don't Grow Old,' " MB, 79; CP, 651.
607. "Will that happen . . .": AG " 'Don't Grow Old,' " MB, 82; CP, 653.
608. "All downtown . . .": AG journal entry, March 1, 1976.
608. "Will it be Terror? . . .": AG, unpublished and untitled journal poem, February 29, 1976.
609. AG in Paris: AG journal entries; AG to LG, January 28 and February 1, 1976.
609. "Paris is a mirage . . .": AG journal entry, February 1, 1976.
610. "I get more and more . . .": AG to LG, April 4, 1976.
610. "some of the most enjoyable . . .": "Soho's/Hot Spots," *Soho Weekly News,* January 15, 1976.
611. AG in recording studio: AG, "The Ginsberg Gallimaufry" (liner notes from *First Blues,* Hammond version); author interview with AG.
611. "You've got . . .": author interview with AG.
611. "Hey father death . . .": AG, "Father Death Blues," MB, 83; CP, 655.

26. Mind Breaths

612. Epigraph: AG, "Thoughts on a Breath," PAOTP, 35; CP, 631.
612. Snowmass incident: AG journal entries; Tom Clark, *The Great Naropa Poetry Wars* (Santa Barbara, CA: Cadmus Books, 1980); Ed Sanders, *The Party: A Chronological Perspective on a Confrontation at a Buddhist Seminary* (Woodstock, NY: Poetry, Crime and Culture Press, 1977); author interviews with AG, Anne Waldman.
613. "I don't know . . .": Clark, *Poetry Wars,* 54.
613. "blood-drinking deities": ibid., 56.
615. "The Communists . . .": ibid; all citations in this passage, unless otherwise noted, are from this source.
616. "On Mt. Ida . . .": AG, introduction for Chögyam Trungpa, *First Thought, Best Thought* (Boulder, CO: Shambhala Publications, 1983).
617. "This book is . . .": ibid.
617. "At one time . . .": Lynne McTaggart, "Up from the underground," *New York Daily News,* March 6, 1977.
617. ". . . Reading words . . .": AG, "Hearing 'Lenore' Read Aloud at 203 Amity Street," MB, 90–91; CP, 664.
618. "What this means . . .": McTaggart, "Up from the underground," *New York Daily News.*
619. "Playing all sides . . .": AG journal entry, July 19, 1977.
621. "there seems to be . . .": Thomas R. DiGregori, "Ginsberg's Journals," *Houston Chronicle,* September 18, 1977.
621. "the Ginsberg of the journals . . .": L. J. Davis, "A Beat Idol Past His Prime," *Chicago Tribune,* September 18, 1977.
621. "I was able . . .": Richard Elman, "Beyond Self-Absorption," *The Nation,* November 12, 1977.
621. "actual travels . . ." and "There are . . .": Louis Simpson, untitled review of *Journals, The New York Times Book Review,* October 23, 1977.
622. "To bring these . . .": *Kaddish* television listing, *New York Daily News,* October 16, 1977.
622. "High on LSD . . .": AG, unpublished speech delivered at Colloquium on the Cross-Cultural Encounter in Literature, October 1977, in AG Columbia deposit.
622. "My own conclusion . . .": AG, unpublished address to LSD: A Decade Later conference, October 1977, in AG Columbia deposit.
622. AG in Hawaii: AG journal entries; AG, unpublished Colloquium speech; John Unterecker,

(Honolulu) *Star-Bulletin*, October 19, 1977; Cobey Black, "Ginsberg's Neck is Still Out," *Honolulu Advertiser*, October 19, 1977.

623. "some rarified points . . .": AG, unpublished Colloquium speech.
623. "Merwin-Trungpa ghost fight": AG journal entry, November 28, 1977.
623. "Here I am . . .": ibid.
623. *Renaldo and Clara*: AG journal entries; Janet Maslin, " 'Renaldo and Clara' Film by Bob Dylan," *The New York Times*, January 26, 1978; Judith Crist, "Mr. Dylan's 'Renaldo and Clara' is a tiring bore," *New York Post*, January 26, 1978; David McQuay, "Poet Allen Ginsberg Can't Sing, But His Music and Poems Ring," (Baltimore) *News-American*, February 17, 1978; Ellen Willis, "Notes on Cant," *Rolling Stone*, March 23, 1978; Arlynn Nellhaus, "Dylan Takes a Long Time to Lionize Dylan in Film," *Denver Post*, April 3, 1978. In what has to be the most exhaustive coverage of any film in single-issue coverage, *The Village Voice* published seven separate reviews of *Renaldo and Clara* in its January 30, 1978, issue.
623. "It's a great work . . .": McQuay, "Poet Allen Ginsberg," *News-American*.
623. "an ego massage . . .": Crist, "Mr. Dylan's 'Renaldo,' " *New York Post*.
624. "holds the attention . . .": Maslin, " 'Renaldo and Clara' Film," *The New York Times*.
624. "Allen Ginsberg seems . . .": Willis, "Notes on Cant," *Rolling Stone*.
624. "There is the delightful . . .": Nellhaus, "Dylan Takes a Long Time," *Denver Post*.
624. Government documents: AG journal entries; AG to Philip Whalen, February 24, 1978; Anita Hoffman, ed., "What Six Nice People Found in the Government's Drawers," *Oui*, February 1977; Jim Graham, "Poet Ginsberg on Blake, Helms, LSD & FBI," *Washington Square News*, May 10, 1978.
624. "I've had my head . . .": AG to Philip Whalen, February 24, 1978.
625. "In sum, there *was* . . .": AG, "Nuts to Plutonium!" *Co-Evolution Quarterly*, Fall 1978. Ginsberg added: "The notorious Black-White split of the sixties was a workable neurotic situation resolvable in the natural course of mutual action, but the intervention of the F.B.I.'s Counterintelligence Program, and the C.I.A.'s Operation Chaos, among other Army and Navy secret plots, escalated the difficulties, magnified them to crisis, and orchestrated original community difficulties to unworkable cacophony for awhile. The paranoia between Black and White activists is now somewhat dissipated. Same for other neurotic problems of aggression, passion and ignorance in the peace 'movement.' 'Kill the Pigs' was also an F.B.I. provocateur party line, as well as 'lily-white Honkey middleclass intellectuals.' "
625. "The old visionary . . .": Paul Berman, "Intimations of Mortality," *Parnassus: Poetry in Review* (Fall/Winter 1979).
625. "too full of random . . .": Hayden Carruth, "Chants, Oracles, Body-Rhythms," *The New York Times Book Review*, March 19, 1978.
625. "infused with . . ." and "I once referred . . .": ibid.
626. AG television appearance: "Viewers protest homosexual remarks," *Boston Globe*, April 21, 1978.
626. "who were arrested . . .": AG, unpublished poetry fragment, "Addenda to Howl—Fag Rag," manuscript in AG Columbia deposit.
627. "Teaching Urizen . . .": Michael Ellsworth, "Interview with Allen Ginsberg," *Plainspeak*, Spring 1979, citation from corrected and edited interview transcript. *See also*, AG, *Your Reason and Blake's System*—a sample of Ginsberg's 1978 *Urizen* lectures.

27. Plutonian Ode

628. Epigraph: AG, "Plutonian Ode," *PO*, 13; *CP*, 703.
628. Rocky Flats protests: AG journal entries; Stephen Foehr, "Rocky Flats is national focus for anti-nuclear movement," *Colorado Daily*, June 12, 1978; "Poet Allen Ginsberg is among 15 arrested near Rocky Flats plant," *Rocky Mountain News*, June 15, 1978; Stephen Foehr, "Rocky Flats protesters vow to re-establish trackside vigil," *Colorado Daily*, June 16, 1978; John Ashton, "Poet Ginsberg muses on deadly plutonium," *Rocky Mountain News*, June 16, 1978; Marilyn Webb, "Ginsberg Puts Poetry Up Against Plutonium," (Boulder) *Daily Camera*, June 17, 1978; Marice Doll, "Flats Demonstrators Vow to Carry On," *Denver Post*, August 10, 1978; author interview with AG.
629. "a monolithic Surveillance State": AG, "Nuts to Plutonium!," *Co-Evolution Quarterly*, Fall 1978.
629. "What new element . . .": AG, first draft of "Plutonian Ode," taken from journal entry, June 12, 1978. See final version in AG, "Plutonian Ode," *PO*, 13; *CP*, 702.
629. "I dare your Reality . . .": AG, "Plutonian Ode," *PO*, 14; *CP*, 703.
630. "Blue sky transparent . . .": AG, "Plutonian Ode," *PO*, 16; *CP*, 704.
631. "I want to sit . . .": Foehr, "Rocky Flats protestors vow," *Colorado Daily*.
632. "self-invented": AG, unpublished Naropa lecture, delivered at Naropa Institute on August 11, 1978, transcript in AG Columbia deposit.

632. "Waiting for the Judge . . .": AG, "Nagasaki Days," *PO*, 40; *CP*, 700.
632. "Old pond . . .": AG, "Old Pond," *PO*, 45; *CP*, 707.
632. "Zen Bluegrass raunch": AG, back cover copy for *PO*.
633. "Fake Saint": AG, "Blame the Thought, Cling to the Bummer," *PO*, 48; *CP*, 709.
634. Nova Convention: "Avant-Garde Unites Over Burroughs," *The New York Times*, December 1, 1978; Robert Palmer, "3-Day Nova Convention Ends at the Entermedia," *The New York Times*, December 4, 1978. *See also*, Ted Morgan, *Literary Outlaw: The Life and Times of William S. Burroughs* (New York: Henry Holt, 1988), 547–50.
635. "high points": Palmer, "3-Day Nova Convention," *The New York Times*.
635. St. Mark's reading: Jennifer Dunning, "Poets Read the New Year in at Entermedia Benefit," *The New York Times*, December 29, 1978.
635. Gold Medal award: "Gold Medal of Literature," *The New York Times Book Review*, February 18, 1979; unpublished transcript of "The National Arts Club Literary Award Dinner for Allen Ginsberg," prepared by Victor Bockris; transcript in AG Columbia deposit. All citations from Bockris transcript unless otherwise noted.
636. Naropa: AG journal entries; Tom Clark, *The Great Naropa Poetry Wars* (Santa Barbara, CA: Cadmus Books, 1980); Peter Marin, "Spiritual Obedience," *Harper's*, February 1979; unsigned editorial, "To Avoid the Name, Shed the Disguise," (Boulder) *Daily Camera*, January 20, 1979.
636. "as wasteful . . .": *Camera* editorial, "To Avoid the Name."
636. "They call up . . ." and "it contains. . .": ibid.
636. "To avoid . . .": ibid.
637. "The seminary violence . . .": Sam Maddox to Ed Sanders, December 19, 1978, reprinted in Clark, *Poetry Wars*.
637. "You know, you're talking . . .": Clark, *Poetry Wars*, 53.
638. "supposed to blow . . .": ibid., 58–59.
638. "In the middle . . .": ibid., 60.
639. "*I'm* supposed to be . . .": ibid., 65.
640. "I stopped yelling . . .": AG to W. S. Merwin and Dana Naone, March 10, 1979.
641. "Please accept . . .": ibid.
641. "My main shame . . .": ibid.
642. "Those wimps . . .": Clark, *Poetry Wars*, 39.
642. "generous enough" and "It's a big joke . . .": ibid.
642. "It was a case . . .": ibid.
642. "Why are you always . . .": George DeWan, "Visions of Ginsberg," *Newsday*, May 8, 1979; all other citations from this passage are from this source.
643. WCW festival: Thomas Lask, "Poetry Festival Hails Paterson's Laureate," *The New York Times*, May 4, 1979; Michael Redmond, "Ginsberg's new image doesn't soften anti-nuclear howl," *Star-Ledger*, May 6, 1979.
643. "It seemed right . . .": AG journal entry, May 20, 1979.
643. "Now turn on . . .": AG, "Garden State," *PO*, 63–64; *CP*, 719.
643. "Let's get . . .": ibid.
644. AG in Europe: AG journal entries; Henry Tanner, "Poets of the World Tame Rowdy Romans," *The New York Times*, July 5, 1979. *See also*, Barry Silesky, *Ferlinghetti: The Artist in His Time* (New York: Warner Books, 1990), 216–17.
645. "a few short musings . . .": AG to Philip Whalen, August 21, 1979.
645. "America it's 25 years . . .": AG, unpublished and untitled journal poem, ca. summer 1979.
645. "Who shot John Kennedy? . . .": ibid.
645. "America": It is not difficult to criticize a work that someone correctly chose not to publish, and my intention in looking at this particular poem is not to kick the proverbial dead horse. Ginsberg was aware of the poem's flaws and the decision not to work on them was, of course, his choice and his right. In discussing the poem, which I believe to be typical of the Ginsberg "failures" of the period, I am hoping to show how Ginsberg's personal problems prevented him from either beginning or completing good work. Ginsberg critics have been especially harsh in their judgment of his work—or lack of work—from this period, and while his lack of production might be easily written off to the mentioned writer's block, it is crucial to realize that he *was* writing poetry at this time. If anything, his refusal to publish what he considered to be inferior work, even in the face of the constant demand for his poetry, is testament not only to his own standards but also to his ability to work through, and survive, very trying times.
646. "how to make . . .": AG to Philip Whalen, August 21, 1979.
646. "many believe . . .": Kenneth Rexroth, back cover copy statement for Clark, *Poetry Wars*.
646. "I'm paralyzed . . .": AG journal entry, August 5, 1979.
647. AG European tour: AG journal entries.
649. "Waking early mornings . . .": AG journal entry, June 22, 1980.
649. "I used to boast . . .": ibid.

652. "The Right Wing! . . .": AG undated journal entry, ca. December 1980.
652. "police state, bureaucracy . . .": ibid.
652. "Birdbrain rules the World! . . .": AG, "Birdbrain!," *PO*, 92; *CP*, 738.
653. "International new wave . . .": AG, back cover copy for *PO*.
653. "I don't like Commuunist Censorship . . .": AG, "Capitol Air," *PO*, 103; *CP*, 743.
653. "I don't like K.G.B. . .": ibid.
654. "All evening long . . .": AG journal entry, December 10, 1980.
654. "How like Christ . . .": ibid.
654. Barbara Rubin: AG journal entries.
655. "The accumulated karma . . .": AG journal entry, January 9, 1981.
656. "Alas! the most extravagant . . .": AG, "Recollections of Burroughs Letters," in WSB, *Letters to Allen Ginsberg* (New York: Full Court Press, 1982), 8.
656. "the red heart . . .": ibid.
657. "an act of benevolence": ibid.
657. "I didn't deserve . . .": AG journal entry, February 4, 1981.
657. "Woke disturbed . . ." and "What can I do . . .": AG journal entry, February 13, 1981.
657. "a recurrent war nightmare . . .": ibid.
657. "What help . . .": ibid.
657. "No problems . . .": AG journal entry, January 27, 1981.
658. AG recording session: AG journal entries; AG, "The Ginsberg Gallimaufry" (liner notes to *First Blues*, Hammond version); author interview with AG.
658. Death of Billy Burroughs: Morgan, *Literary Outlaw*, 495–536.
659. AG/Clash: author interview with AG.
660. "Well, Ginsberg . . .": ibid; all other citations from this account are from my interviews with Ginsberg.
660. "I always wanted . . .": Jennifer Parmelee, "Ginsberg Going Strong as Punk Rocker," *Los Angeles Times*, November 26, 1981.
660. "writing about Allen . . .": ibid.
661. "Political despair . . .": Paul Berman, untitled review of *Plutonian Ode*, *The Village Voice*, March 23, 1982.
661. "Seemingly fatalistic . . .": Kenneth Funsten, "Ginsberg's poetic politics to challenge the nuclear doomsday," *Los Angeles Times*, May 30, 1982.
662. AG reading at Columbia: "Ginsberg to Read Howl Saturday at Columbia," *The New York Times*, November 11, 1981; John Stickney, "The Beatnik Goes On: Poet Allen Ginsberg Throws a 25th Birthday Party for Howl," *People*, November 30, 1981; William A. Henry III, "*Howl* Becomes a Hoot," *Time*, December 7, 1981.
663. "postwar materialist . . .": Henry, "*Howl* Becomes a Hoot," *Time*.

Postscript

665. "Ginsberg may be . . .": Ken Tucker, "Power of Babble," *The Village Voice*, January 29, 1985.
665. "A good poet . . .": James Atlas, "A Modern Whitman," *Atlantic Monthly*, December 1984.
665. "By this measure . . .": ibid.
666. "For 30 years . . .": Tucker, "Power of Babble," *The Village Voice*.
666. "no living poet . . .": Robert Richman, "Allen Ginsberg Then and Now," *Commentary*, July 1985.
666. "One need not . . .": ibid.
666. "an unconvincing . . ."; "read like . . ."; and "a masterpiece of candor . . .": R. Z. Shepard, "Mainstreaming Allen Ginsberg," *Time*, February 4, 1985.
666. "One can see it . . .": ibid.
667. "All in all . . .": Gerald Nicosia, "Ginsberg collection puts bold repertoire, career in perspective," *Chicago Tribune*, February, 10, 1985.
667. Kerouac conference: AG journal entries; AG, "Documents from the Jack Kerouac Conference," *Friction*, vol. 1, no. 2/3; William E. Schmidt, "Beat Generation Elders Meet to Praise Kerouac," *The New York Times*, July 30, 1982; Henry Allen, "25 Years Later," *Washington Post*, August 2, 1982; William Robertson, "On the Road Again," *Miami Herald*, October 24, 1982; author interviews with AG, JCH.
669. "Follow your breath . . .": AG, "Do the Meditation Rock," *White Shroud*, 21.
669. "Do the meditation . . .": ibid.
669. "I'm alone in the sky . . .": AG, "Airplane Blues," *White Shroud*, 18–19.
670. "You're the greatest poet . . .": author interview with AG.
671. "I'd produced . . .": AG, liner notes to *The Lion for Real* (Great Jones/Island Records, CGD6004, 1989).

671. "an amazing night": Hal Willner, liner notes to *The Lion for Real.*
673. "What are you doing here? . . .": AG, "White Shroud," *WHITE SHROUD,* 49.
673. "I'm living alone . . .": ibid.
675. "Our relationship was . . .": Paul Carroll, "Playboy Interview: Allen Ginsberg," *Playboy,* April 1969.
675. "Our relationship has lasted . . .": AG, *Gay Sunshine Interview,* 25.
676. European tour: AG journal entries; Barry Miles, *Ginsberg* (New York: Simon & Schuster, 1989), 504–7.
680. "liberty for Nicaragua . . .": AG, unpublished introductory statement to "Declaration of Three," written February 4, 1982, in New York.
680. "The human soul . . .": AG, Yevgeny Yevtushenko, and Ernesto Cardenal, "Declaration of Three," in AG Columbia deposit.
680. "The Damocles' sword . . .": ibid.
681. AG in China: AG journal entries; AG, "China Through a Poet's Eyes," *San Jose Mercury News* February 20, 1985; Miles, *Ginsberg,* 512–17; author interview with AG.
682. "They don't understand . . .": AG, "China Through a Poet's Eyes."
682. "a tricky title . . .": ibid.
682. "Everybody had a story . . .": ibid.
683. "What of poor . . .": AG journal entry, November 29, 1984. All other citations from this conversation are from this source.
683. "There seems to be . . .": ibid.
683. "Students danced . . .": AG, "One Morning I Took a Walk in China," *White Shroud,* 61.
684. "I grew up . . .": AG, "Reading Bai Juyi," *White Shroud,* 68.
685. "As artist companions . . .": AG, "A Commentary on Sacramental Companions," *Allen Ginsberg Photographs* (Altadena, CA: Twelvetrees Press, 1990).

SELECTED WORKS OF ALLEN GINSBERG

Books and Pamphlets

Airplane Dreams: Compositions from Journals. Toronto: Anansi, 1968; San Francisco: City Lights Books, 1969.

Allen Verbatim: Lectures on Poetry, Politics, Consciousness. Edited by Gordon Ball. New York: McGraw-Hill, 1974.

Angkor Wat. London: Fulcrum Press, 1968.

As Ever: The Collected Correspondence of Allen Ginsberg and Neal Cassady. With Neal Cassady. Edited by Barry Gifford. Berkeley: Creative Arts, 1977.

Bixby Canyon Ocean Path Word Breeze. New York: Gotham Book Mart, 1972.

Chicago Trial Testimony. San Francisco: City Lights Books, 1975.

Collected Poems: 1947–1980. New York: Harper & Row. 1985.

Composed on the Tongue: Literary Conversations 1967–1977. Edited by Donald Allen. Bolinas, CA: Grey Fox Press, 1980.

Empty Mirror: Early Poems. Introduction by William Carlos Williams. Corinth, NY: Totem, 1961.

The Fall of America: Poems of These States, 1965–1971. San Francisco: City Lights Books, 1972.

First Blues: Rags, Ballads & Harmonium Songs, 1971–74. New York: Full Court Press, 1975.

The Gates of Wrath: Rhymed Poems, 1948–52. Bolinas, CA: Grey Fox Press, 1972.

Gay Sunshine Interview. With Allen Young. Bolinas, CA: Grey Fox Press, 1974.

Howl and Other Poems. Introduction by William Carlos Williams. San Francisco: City Lights Books, 1956.

Howl: Original Draft Facsimile, Transcript & Variant Versions, Fully Annotated by Author, with Contemporaneous Correspondence, Account of First Public Reading, Legal Skirmishes, Precursor Texts & Bibliography. Edited by Barry Miles. New York: Harper & Row, 1986.

Improvised Poetics. Berkeley: Anonym Press, 1972.

Indian Journals. San Francisco: Dave Haselwood Books and City Lights Books, 1970.

Iron Horse. Toronto: The Coach House Press, 1972.

Journals: Early Fifties Early Sixties. Edited by Gordon Ball. New York: Grove Press, 1977.

Kaddish and Other Poems, 1958–1960. San Francisco: City Lights Books, 1961.

Mind Breaths: Poems 1972–1977. San Francisco: City Lights Books, 1977.

Mostly Sitting Haiku. Paterson, NJ: From Here Press, 1978.

Planet News, 1961–1967. San Francisco: City Lights Books, 1968.

Plutonian Ode: Poems 1977–1980. San Francisco: City Lights Books, 1982.

Poems All Over the Place, Mostly 70s. Cherry Valley, NY: Cherry Valley Editions, 1978.

Reality Sandwiches, 1953–60. San Francisco: City Lights Books, 1963.

Sad Dust Glories: Poems During Work Summer in Woods. Berkeley: Workingmans Press, 1975.

Scrap Leaves. Millbrook, NY: Poet's Press, 1968.

Straight Hearts' Delight: Love Poems and Selected Letters 1947–1980. With Peter Orlovsky. Edited by Winston Leyland. San Francisco: Gay Sunshine Press, 1980.

To Eberhart from Ginsberg. Lincoln, MA: Penmaen Press, 1976.

T.V. Baby Poems. London: Cape Goliard Press, 1967; New York: Grossman, 1968.

The Visions of the Great Rememberer. With letters by Neal Cassady and drawings by Basil King. Amherst, MA: Mulch Press, 1974.

White Shroud, Poems 1980–85. New York: Harper & Row. 1986.

The Yage Letters. With William S. Burroughs. San Francisco: City Lights Books, 1963.

Your Reason & Blake's System. Madras and New York: Hanuman Books, 1988.

Recordings

First Blues. Recorded and produced by John Hammond. John Hammond Records W2X 37673. New York, NY. 1982.

First Blues: Rags, Ballads and Harmonium Songs. Recorded by Harry Smith, produced by Ann Charters. Folkway Records FSS 37560. New York, NY. 1981.

Kaddish. Atlantic Verbum Series #4001. New York, NY. 1966.

Howl and Other Poems. Fantasy-Galaxy Records #7013. Berkeley, CA. 1959.

The Lion for Real. Great Jones/Island Records CCD6004. New York, NY. 1989.

Wm. Blake's Songs of Innocence & Experience Tuned by Allen Ginsberg. MGM/Verse CTS 3083. New York, NY. 1970.

Photographs

Allen Ginsberg Photographs. Altadena, CA: Twelvetrees Press, 1990.

Scenes Along the Road. With Ann Charters. New York: Portents/Gotham Book Mart, 1970.

SELECTED BIBLIOGRAPHY

Ahearn, Barry, ed. *Pound/Zukofsky: Selected Letters of Ezra Pound and Louis Zukofsky*. New York: New
 Directions, 1987.
Allen, Donald, ed. *The New American Poetry*. New York: Grove Press, 1960.
———, and George F. Butterick, eds. *The Postmoderns*. New York: Grove Press, 1982.
———, and Warren Tallman, eds. *The Poetics of the New American Poetry*. New York: Grove Press,
 1973.
Anson, Robert Sam. *Gone Crazy and Back Again: The Rise and Fall of the Rolling Stone Generation*. New
 York: Doubleday, 1981.
Anthony, Gene. *Summer of Love: A Photo-Documentary*. Berkeley: Celestial Arts, 1980.
Ardinger, Richard K. *An Annotated Bibliography of Works by John Clellon Holmes*. Pocatello: Idaho State
 University Press, 1979.
Bartlett, Lee, ed. *The Beats: Essays in Criticism*. Jefferson, NC: McFarland, 1981.
——— *Talking Poetry: Conversations in the Workshop with Contemporary Poets*. Albuquerque: University
 of New Mexico Press, 1987.
Beaulieu, Victor-Levy. *Jack Kerouac: A Chicken Essay*. Toronto: Coach House Press, 1979.
Bockris, Victor. *With William Burroughs: A Report from the Bunker*. New York: Seaver Books, 1981.
Burroughs, William S. *The Burroughs File*. San Francisco: City Lights Books, 1984.
——— *Exterminator!* New York: Viking Press, 1973.
——— *Interzone*. New York: Viking Press, 1989.
——— *The Job*. New York: Grove Press, 1972.
———. *Junky*. New York: Ace Books, 1953.
———. *Letters to Allen Ginsberg*. New York: Full Court Press, 1982.
———. *Naked Lunch*. New York: Grove Press, 1959.
———. *Queer*. New York: Viking Press, 1985.
———. *Roosevelt After Inauguration*. San Francisco: City Lights Books, 1979.
Cassady, Carolyn. *Heart Beat: My Life with Jack and Neal*. Berkeley: Creative Arts Books, 1976.
———. *Off the Road*. New York: William Morrow, 1990.
Cassady, Neal. *The First Third*. San Francisco: City Lights Books, 1971; revised, 1981.
Challis, Chris. *Quest for Kerouac*. London: Faber and Faber, 1984.
Charters, Ann. *Beats and Company*. New York: Doubleday, 1986.
———, ed. *The Beats: Literary Bohemians in Postwar America* (Parts 1 and 2). Ann Arbor: Gale Research,
 1983.
———. *A Bibliography of Work by Jack Kerouac*. New York: Phoenix Bookshop, 1967.
———. *Kerouac*. San Francisco: Straight Arrow Books, 1973.
———, ed. *The Portable Beat Reader*. New York: Viking, 1992.
Cherkovski, Neeli. *Ferlinghetti: A Biography*. New York: Doubleday, 1979.
———. *Whitman's Wild Children*. Lapis Press, 1988.
Clark, Tom. *The Great Naropa Poetry Wars*. Santa Barbara, CA: Cadmus Books, 1980.
———. *Jack Kerouac*. New York: Harcourt Brace Jovanovich, 1984.
Cohen, Michael, and Dennis Hale, eds. *The New Student Left*. Boston: Beacon Press, 1966.
Cook, Bruce. *The Beat Generation*. New York: Charles Scribner's Sons, 1971.
Corso, Gregory. *Elegiac Feelings American*. New York: New Directions, 1970.
———. *Gasoline*. San Francisco: City Lights Books, 1958.
———. *The Vestal Lady on Brattle*. Cambridge, MA: Richard Brukenfeld, 1955.
Davidson, Michael. *The San Francisco Renaissance: Poetics and Community at Mid-Century*. New York:
 Cambridge University Press, 1989.
Dellinger, Dave. *More Power Than We Know: The People's Movement Toward Democracy*. New York:
 Doubleday, 1975.
Dickstein, Morris. *Gates of Eden*. New York: Basic Books, 1977.
Di Prima, Diane. *Revolutionary Letters*. San Francisco: City Lights Books, 1971.

————, and LeRoi Jones, eds. *The Floating Bear: A Newsletter, 1–37.* La Jolla, CA: Lawrence McGilvery, 1973.

Dowden, George. *A Bibliography of Works by Allen Ginsberg: October 1943 to July 1, 1967.* San Francisco: City Lights Books, 1971.

Ehrlich, J. W. *Howl of the Censor.* San Carlo, CA: Nourse Publishing Co., 1961.

Faas, Ekbert. *Towards a New American Poetics.* Santa Barbara, CA: Black Sparrow Press, 1979.

Feldman, Gene, and Max Gartenberg, eds. *The Beat Generation and the Angry Young Men.* New York: Citadel, 1958.

Ferlinghetti, Lawrence. *Back Roads to Far Places.* New York: New Directions, 1971.

————. *A Coney Island of the Mind.* New York: New Directions, 1958.

————. *Her.* New York: New Directions, 1960.

————. *Landscapes of Living and Dying.* New York: New Directions, 1979.

————. *The Mexican Night.* New York: New Directions, 1970.

————. *Northwest Ecolog.* San Francisco: City Lights Books, 1978.

————. *Pictures of the Gone World.* San Francisco: City Lights Books, 1955.

————. *The Populist Manifestos.* San Francisco: Grey Fox Press, 1981.

————. *Routines.* New York: New Directions, 1964.

————. *The Secret Meaning of Things.* New York: New Directions, 1968.

————. *Starting from San Francisco.* New York: New Directions, 1967.

————. *Tyrannus Nix?* New York: New Directions, 1969.

————. *Unfair Arguments with Existence.* New York: New Directions, 1963.

————, and Nancy Peters. *Literary San Francisco.* New York: Harper & Row, 1980.

Free (Abbie Hoffman). *Revolution for the Hell of It.* New York: Dial Press, 1968.

Genet, Jean. *May Day Speech* (Introduction by Allen Ginsberg). San Francisco: City Lights Books, 1970.

Gifford, Barry. *Kerouac's Town.* Berkeley: Creative Arts Books, 1977.

————, and Lawrence Lee. *Jack's Book.* New York: St. Martin's Press, 1978.

Gitlin, Todd. *The Whole World Is Watching: Mass Media in the Making and Unmaking of the New Left.* Berkeley: University of California Press, 1980.

Goodman, Paul. *Growing Up Absurd.* New York: Random House, 1960.

Halper, Jon, ed. *Gary Snyder: Dimensions of a Life.* San Francisco: Sierra Club Books, 1991.

Holmes, John Clellon. *Get Home Free.* New York: E. P. Dutton, 1964.

————. *Go.* New York: Charles Scribner's Sons, 1952.

————. *Gone in October.* Hailey, ID: Limberlost Press, 1985.

————. *The Horn.* New York: Random House, 1958.

————. *Nothing More to Declare.* New York: E. P. Dutton, 1967.

————. *Visitor: Jack Kerouac in Old Saybrook.* California, PA: unspeakable visions of the individual, 1981.

Huncke, Herbert. *The Evening Sun Turned Crimson.* Cherry Valley, NY: Cherry Valley Editions, 1980.

————. *Guilty of Everything.* New York: Paragon House, 1990.

————. *Huncke's Journal.* New York: Poet's Press, 1965.

Hunt, Tim. *Kerouac's Crooked Road.* Hamden, CT: Archon Books, 1981.

Hyde, Lewis, ed. *On the Poetry of Allen Ginsberg.* Ann Arbor: University of Michigan Press, 1984.

Jarvis, Charles. *Visions of Kerouac.* Lowell, MA: Ithaca Press, 1973.

Johnson, Joyce. *Minor Characters.* Boston: Houghton Mifflin, 1983.

Jones, Hettie. *How I Became Hettie Jones.* New York: E. P. Dutton, 1990.

Jones, LeRoi, ed. *The Moderns.* New York: Corinth Books, 1963.

Kerouac, Jack. *Big Sur.* New York: Farrar, Straus and Cudahy, 1962.

————. *Book of Dreams.* San Francisco: City Lights Books, 1961.

————. *Dear Carolyn: Letters to Carolyn Cassady.* California, PA: unspeakable visions of the individual, 1983.

————. *Desolation Angels.* New York: Coward-McCann, 1965.

————. *The Dharma Bums.* New York: Viking Press, 1958.

————. *Dr. Sax.* New York: Grove Press, 1959.

————. *Heaven & Other Poems.* Bolinas, CA: Grey Fox Press, 1977.

————. *Lonesome Traveler.* New York: McGraw-Hill, 1960.

————. *Maggie Cassidy.* New York: Avon Books, 1959.

————. *Mexico City Blues.* New York: Grove Press, 1959.

————. *On the Road.* New York: Viking Press, 1957.

————. *Pic.* New York: Grove Press, 1971.

————. *Pull My Daisy.* New York: Grove Press, 1961.

————. *Satori in Paris.* New York: Grove Press, 1966.

————. *Scattered Poems.* San Francisco: City Lights Books, 1971.

————. *The Scripture of the Golden Eternity.* New York: Totem/Corinth Books, 1960.

————. *The Subterraneans.* New York: Grove Press, 1958.

————. *The Town and the City.* New York: Harcourt, Brace, 1950.

————. *Tristessa.* New York: Avon Books, 1960.

————. *Vanity of Duluoz.* New York: Coward-McCann, 1968.

————. *Visions of Cody.* New York: McGraw-Hill, 1972.

————. *Visions of Gerard.* New York: Farrar, Straus and Company, 1963.

————, Albert Saijo, and Lew Welch. *Trip Trap.* Bolinas, CA: Grey Fox Press, 1973.

Kerouac, Jan. *Baby Driver.* New York: St. Martin's Press, 1981.

Kesey, Ken. *Demon Box.* New York: Viking, 1986.

————. *The Further Inquiry.* New York: Viking, 1990.

————. *Kesey's Garage Sale.* New York: Viking, 1973.

Kheridan, David. *Six San Francisco Poets.* Fresno, CA: Giligia Press, 1969.

Knight, Arthur and Glee, eds. *The Beat Book.* California, PA: unspeakable visions of the individual, 1974.

Knight, Arthur and Kit, eds. *Beat Angels.* California: PA: unspeakable visions of the individual, 1982.

————, eds. *The Beat Diary.* California, PA: unspeakable visions of the individual, 1977.

————, eds. *The Beat Journey.* California, PA: unspeakable visions of the individual, 1978.

————, eds. *The Beat Road.* California, PA: unspeakable visions of the individual, 1984.

————, eds. *The Beat Vision.* New York: Paragon House, 1987.

————. *Interior Geographies: An Interview with John Clellon Holmes.* Warren, OH: Literary Denim, 1981.

————, eds. *Kerouac and the Beats.* New York: Paragon House, 1988.

————, eds. *the unspeakable visions of the individual,* no. 10. California, PA: unspeakable visions of the individual, 1980.

Kramer, Jane. *Allen Ginsberg in America.* New York: Random House, 1969.

Kraus, Michelle. *Allen Ginsberg: An Annotated Bibliography 1969–1977.* Metuchen, NJ: Scarecrow Press, 1980.

Krim, Seymour. *The Beats.* Greenwich, CT: Fawcett, 1960.

————. *Shake It for the World.* London: Allison & Busby, 1971.

————. *Views of a Nearsighted Cannoneer.* New York: E. P. Dutton, 1968.

————. *What's This Cat's Story?* New York: Paragon House, 1991.

Kunen, James Simon. *The Strawberry Statement.* New York: Random House, 1968.

Landesman, Jay. *Rebel Without Applause.* Sag Harbor, NY: Permanent Press, 1987.

Law, Lisa. *Flashing on the Sixties.* San Francisco: Chronicle Books, 1987.

Leamer, Laurence. *The Paper Revolutionaries: The Rise of the Underground Press.* New York: Simon & Schuster, 1972.

Leary, Timothy. *Flashbacks: An Autobiography.* Los Angeles: Jeremy P. Tarcher, 1983.

Leyland, Winston, ed. *Gay Sunshine Interviews.* Vol. 1. San Francisco: Gay Sunshine Press, 1978.

Lipset, Seymour Martin, and Philip G. Altbach, eds. *Students in Revolt.* Boston: Houghton-Mifflin, 1969.

————, and Sheldon S. Wolin, eds. *The Berkeley Student Revolt.* New York: Doubleday, 1965.

Lipton, Lawrence. *The Holy Barbarians.* New York: Julian Messner, 1959.

McBride, Dick. *Cometh With Clouds (Memory: Allen Ginsberg).* Cherry Valley, NY: Cherry Valley Editions, 1982.

McClure, Michael. *Scratching the Beat Surface.* San Francisco: North Point Press, 1982.

————. *Selected Poems.* New York: New Directions, 1986.

McDarrah, Fred, ed. *Kerouac & Friends: A Beat Generation Album.* New York: William Morrow, 1985.

McNally, Dennis. *Desolate Angel: Jack Kerouac, the Beat Generation, and America.* New York: Random House, 1979.

McNeill, Don. *Moving Through Here.* New York: Citadel Underground, 1990.

Mailer, Norman. *The Armies of the Night.* New York: New American Library, 1968.

————. *Miami and the Siege of Chicago.* New York: New American Library, 1968.

————. *The White Negro.* San Francisco: City Lights Books, 1958.

Manso, Peter. *Mailer.* New York: Simon & Schuster, 1986.

Meltzer, David, ed. *The San Francisco Poets.* New York: Ballantine Books, 1971.

Merrill, Thomas F. *Allen Ginsberg.* New York: Twayne, 1969.

Miles, Barry. *Ginsberg.* New York: Simon & Schuster, 1989.

Milewski, Robert J. *Jack Kerouac: An Annotated Bibliography of Secondary Sources, 1944–1979.* Metuchen, NJ: Scarecrow Press, 1981.

Montgomery, John. *Kerouac West Coast.* Palo Alto, CA: Fels & Firn Press, 1976.

Morgan, Ted. *Literary Outlaw: The Life and Times of William S. Burroughs.* New York: Henry Holt, 1988.

Morgan, Bill, and Bob Rosenthal, eds. *Best Minds: A Tribute to Allen Ginsberg.* New York: Lospecchio Press, 1986.

————, eds. *Kanreki: A Tribute to Allen Ginsberg.* New York: Lospecchio Press, 1986.

746 Selected Bibliography

Mottram, Eric. *Allen Ginsberg in the Sixties*. Seattle and Brighton, England: Unicorn Bookshop, 1972.

Nicosia, Gerald. *Memory Babe: A Critical Biography of Jack Kerouac*. New York: Grove Press, 1983.

Norse, Harold. *Beat Hotel*. San Diego: Atticus Press, 1983.

Obst, Lynda R., ed. *The Sixties*. New York: Rolling Stone Press, 1976.

Olson, Charles. *Letters for Origin, 1950–1956*. Edited by Albert Glover. New York: Viking Press, 1969.

Orlovsky, Peter. *Clean Asshole Poems & Smiling Vegetable Songs*. San Francisco: City Lights Books, 1978.

Ossman, David. *The Sullen Art*. New York: Corinth Books, 1963.

Packard, William, ed. *The Poet's Craft*. New York: Paragon House, 1987.

Parkinson, Thomas, ed. *A Casebook on the Beat*. New York: Thomas Y. Crowell Books, 1961.

Peck, Abe. *Uncovering the Sixties: Life and Times of the Underground*. New York: Pantheon Books, 1985.

Plimpton, George, ed. *Writers at Work: The Paris Review Interviews*. Third Series. New York: Viking Press, 1967.

———, ed. *Writers at Work: The Paris Review Interviews*. Fourth Series. New York: Viking Press, 1976.

Plummer, William. *The Holy Goof: A Biography of Neal Cassady*. Englewood Cliffs, NJ: Prentice-Hall, 1981.

Podhoretz, Norman. *Making It*. New York: Random House, 1967.

Portugés, Paul. *The Visionary Poetics of Allen Ginsberg*. Santa Barbara, CA: Ross-Erikson, 1978.

Rembar, Charles. *The End of Obscenity*. New York: Random House, 1968.

Rexroth, Kenneth. *World Outside the Window: The Selected Essays of Kenneth Rexroth*. New York: New Directions, 1987.

Rips, Geoffrey. *Unamerican Activities: The Campaign Against the Underground Press*. San Francisco: City Lights Books, 1981.

Rodman, Selden. *Tongues of Fallen Angels*. New York: New Directions, 1974.

Rosset, Barney, ed. *The Evergreen Review Reader, 1957–1961*. New York: Grove Press, 1979.

Roszak, Theodore. *The Making of a Counter Culture*. New York: Doubleday, 1969.

Rubin, Jerry. *Do It! Scenarios of the Revolution*. New York: Ballantine, 1970.

———. *Growing (Up) at 37*. New York: Warner Books, 1976.

Sanders, Ed. *Investigative Poetry*. San Francisco: City Lights Books, 1976.

———, ed. *The Party: A Chronological Perspective on a Confrontation at a Buddhist Seminary*. Woodstock, NY: Poetry, Crime and Culture Press, 1977.

———. *Tales of Beatnik Glory*. New York: Stonehill Press, 1975.

Saroyan, Aram. *Genesis Angels: The Saga of Lew Welch and the Beat Generation*. New York: William Morrow, 1979.

Scaduto, Anthony. *Dylan*. New York: Grosset & Dunlap, 1973.

Seaver, Richard, Terry Southern, and Alexander Trocchi, eds. *Writers in Revolt: An Anthology*. New York: Frederick Fell, 1963.

Shelton, Robert. *No Direction Home: The Life and Music of Bob Dylan*. New York: William Morrow, 1986.

Shepard, Sam. *Rolling Thunder Logbook*. New York: Viking Press, 1977.

Silesky, Barry. *Ferlinghetti: The Artist in His Time*. New York: Warner Books, 1990.

Simpson, Louis. *A Revolution in Taste*. New York: Macmillan, 1978.

Skolnick, Jerome H. *The Politics of Protest*. New York: Simon & Schuster, 1969.

Smith, Larry. *Lawrence Ferlinghetti, Poet at Large*. Carbondale: Southern Illinois University Press, 1983.

Snyder, Gary. *Myths & Texts*. New York: Totem Press/Corinth Books, 1960.

———. *Riprap & Cold Mountain Poems*. San Francisco: Four Seasons Foundation, 1965.

———. *Six Selections from Mountains and Rivers Without End Plus One*. Bolinas, CA: Four Seasons Foundation, 1970.

———. *Songs for Gaia*. Port Townsend, WA: Copper Canyon Press, 1979.

———. *Turtle Island*. New York: New Directions, 1974.

———, Lew Welch, and Philip Whalen. *On Bread & Poetry*. Bolinas, CA: Grey Fox Press, 1977.

Solomon, Carl. *Mishaps Perhaps*. San Francisco: Beach Books, 1966.

———. *More Mishaps*. San Francisco: Beach Books, 1968.

Solomon, David, ed. *The Marihuana Papers*. Indianapolis: Bobbs-Merrill, 1966.

Stein, Jean. *Edie: An American Biography*. Edited by George Plimpton. New York: Alfred A. Knopf, 1982.

Strickland, Bill, ed. *On Being a Writer*. Cincinnati: Writer's Digest Books, 1988.

Taylor, Derek. *It Was Twenty Years Ago Today*. New York: Fireside, 1987.

Trungpa, Chögyam. *First Thought Best Thought*. Boulder, CO: Shambhala Publications, 1983.

Tytell, John. *Naked Angels: The Lives and Literature of the Beat Generation*. New York: McGraw-Hill, 1976.

Vassal, Jacques. *Electric Children*. New York: Taplinger Publishing Co., 1976.

Viorst, Milton. *Fire in the Streets*. New York: Simon & Schuster, 1979.

Waldman, Anne, and Marilyn Webb, eds. *Talking Poetics from Naropa Institute*. Vols. 1 and 2. Boulder, CO: Shambhala Publications, 1978.

Weinreich, Regina. *The Spontaneous Poetics of Jack Kerouac.* Carbondale: Southern Illinois University Press, 1987.

White, Edward M., ed. *The Pop Culture Tradition.* New York: W. W. Norton, 1972.

Whitman, Walt, *An American Primer.* Edited by Horace Traubel. San Francisco: City Lights Books, 1970.

Williams, William Carlos. *Interviews with William Carlos Williams.* Edited by Linda Wagner. New York: New Directions, 1976.

———. *Paterson.* New York: New Directions, 1963.

———. *Selected Poems.* Edited by Charles Tomlinson. New York: New Directions, 1985.

———. *Something to Say: William Carlos Williams on Younger Poets.* Edited by James E. B. Breslin. New York: New Directions, 1985.

Witemeyer, High, ed. *William Carlos Williams and James Laughlin: Selected Letters.* New York: W. W. Norton, 1989.

Zinnser, William, ed. *Spiritual Quests.* Boston: Houghton Mifflin, 1988.

Index